ARCHAEOLOGICAL SURVEY IN THE LOWER MISSISSIPPI ALLUVIAL VALLEY, 1940–1947

CLASSICS IN SOUTHEASTERN ARCHAEOLOGY

Stephen Williams, Series Editor

James A. Ford casting a long shadow while waiting for his compatriots in Baton Rouge, Louisiana, 1939. (Museum of Natural Science, Louisiana State University)

ARCHAEOLOGICAL SURVEY IN THE LOWER MISSISSIPPI ALLUVIAL VALLEY, 1940–1947

PHILIP PHILLIPS, JAMES A. FORD, AND JAMES B. GRIFFIN

Edited and with an Introduction by STEPHEN WILLIAMS

THE UNIVERSITY OF ALABAMA PRESS
Tuscaloosa and London

Manufactured in the United States of America

Typeface: Janson Text

∞
The paper on which this book is printed meets the minimum requirements of American National Standard for Information Science–Permanence of Paper for Printed Library Materials, ANSI Z39.48-1984.

Library of Congress Cataloging-in-Publication Data

Phillips, Philip, 1900–
Archaeological survey in the Lower Mississippi Alluvial Valley, 1940–1947 / Philip Phillips, James A. Ford, and James B. Griffin ; edited and with an introduction by Stephen Williams.
p. cm. — (Classics in southeastern archaeology)
Originally published: Cambridge, Mass. : Peabody Museum, 1951, in series: Papers of the Peabody Museum of American Archaeology and Ethnology, Harvard University : v. 25.
Includes bibliographical references and index.
ISBN 0-8173-1104-1 (cloth : alk. paper) —
ISBN 0-8173-5022-5 (pbk. : alk. paper)
1. Indians of North America—Mississippi River Valley—Antiquities. 2. Indian pottery—Mississippi River Valley. 3. Mississippi River Valley—Antiquities. I. Ford, James Alfred, 1911–1968. II. Griffin, James Bennett, 1905– III. Title, IV. Series.

E378.M75.P45 2003
976.3'301—dc21 2003047325

British Library Cataloguing-in-Publication Data available

Publication of this work has been supported in part by donations from the following agencies, institutions, and individuals.

Mr. Albert H. Gordon
Peabody Museum of Archaeology and Ethnology, Harvard University
Dan Josselyn Memorial Fund

Front cover
Background: Map of the Baytown Site, Arkansas [LMS Site Files, drawn by Philip Phillips]
Left: Plane table mapping at the Menard Site, Arkansas, Spring 1841. [LMS site files, work done by Philip Phillips and Mott Davis]
Middle: Excavation unit and workers at the Rose Site, Arkansas, April, 1947. [LMS site files, photo by Philip Phillips]
Right: Mound A at the Edgefield site, Mississippi, Spring, 1940. [LMS site files, photo by Philip Phillips]

Back cover
LANDSAT 7 satellite image of LMS survey area. Georeferenced and composited by Bryan S. Haley, Center for Archaeological Research, University of Mississippi.

CONTENTS

ILLUSTRATIONS AND TABLES

FIGURES

TABLES

FOREWORD

I DID not undertake this project, the reprinting of this well-known volume, without trepidation. As series editor of the University of Alabama Press's Classics in Southeastern Archaeology, I was quite familiar with the "drill." But still, this was a volume written not by nineteenth-century notables such as Charles C. Jones or Clarence B. Moore but instead the work of three old friends with whom I had had many decades of personal interaction. Did the work qualify as a "classic?"

The volume indeed passes that test, but I hesitated for other reasons—not the least of which was finding funding for the publication of this rather large volume. But what are old friends for? Now reaching back in time, in an almost archaeological manner, I would like to acknowledge the continued support and thoughtfulness of a very old friend of Phil Phillips, Albert Hamilton Gordon. He was a member of the Harvard class of 1921 and knew Phillips in Buffalo, New York, just after they had both graduated from college. Gordon regularly went to Buffalo on business for his father's company. There in those early days he met both Phillips and his bride, Ruth, a number of times. They never forgot that early connection.

I first met Gordon in the fall of 1967, when he had just been made chairman of the Peabody Museum's visiting committee. He had also just become a member of Harvard's Board of Overseers, and the Peabody had just had its 100th anniversary. It was thus my task, as the newly appointed director of Harvard's Peabody Museum, to help Gordon understand the complexities and problems of that wonderful old anthropological treasure. He was an easy learner, and we became fast friends. I even taught some of his grandchildren and also, much later, worked with him on a maritime antiquity, the vessel *Snow Squall*.

Speaking of centenary-year anniversaries, some Harvard friends asked me to help celebrate Gordon's own 100th birthday in 2001 by handwriting a letter to be included in a small volume honoring that event. I am happy now to thank the Albert H. Gordon Foundation for its generous subvention for the reprinting of this important volume. Old friends don't forget.

It was a marvelous surprise that we could turn that fifty-some-year-old "Peabody Paper" into a great 2003 monograph, with even a readable CD of the whole volume. Deep and heartfelt thanks to all who made this volume possible.

Stephen Williams
August 28, 2002

PREFACE

THE Lower Mississippi Archaeological Survey was initiated in 1939 as a joint undertaking of three institutions: School of Geology, Louisiana State University; Museum of Anthropology, University of Michigan; and Peabody Museum, Harvard University.[1] The purpose of the Survey was to investigate the northern two-thirds of the alluvial valley of the Lower Mississippi River — roughly from the mouth of the Ohio to Vicksburg, Mississippi, an area long regarded as one of the principal blind spots in the archaeology of the Southeast. This is not altogether due to lack of work in the area, or to the character of such work, but rather to the fact that it had so far failed to reveal anything concerning the earlier pre-Mississippian cultures. The need for a comprehensive survey had been repeatedly voiced at Midwestern and Southeastern conferences and various suggestions made for carrying out such a project. It was Ford, whose reconstruction of prehistory in the southern part of the Lower Valley had reached the point of need for verification farther north, who finally translated these suggestions into action. In the fall of 1939 he approached the other two of the present writers with a tentative plan, for which he had already secured the enthusiastic support of Dr. Arthur R. Kelly, then chief archaeologist of the National Park Service. The proposed collaboration appeared to offer one very considerable advantage since it combined the experience of two men whose previous activities had been centered to the north and south of the area to be investigated (Griffin and Ford) with a third (Phillips) who had done some work within it. Problems would be approached from opposed points of view, amicably it was hoped, and the resulting solutions might be the stronger for it. Such at any rate was the theory, and on the whole it worked out very well. There are difficulties inherent in a joint operation of this kind. The compensations, we hope, will appear in the pages that follow.

The first field party, in the spring of 1940, consisted of the three writers and Fisher Motz, a graduate student in the Department of Anthropology at Harvard. A shorter expedition was made in the fall by Phillips and his wife. In the spring of 1941, Griffin and Phillips were accompanied by Mott Davis and Chester Chard, graduate students at Harvard, and Mrs. Chard. Plans for a similar spring season in 1942 were canceled upon the outbreak of the war. The authors soon found themselves engaged in other activities, and it was not until 1946 that it was possible to get back into the field and then only in a rather limited manner. Short field trips were made in the spring of that year and again in the spring of 1947 by Phillips and his wife. In the first of these they were ably assisted by Paul Gebhard, then a graduate student at Harvard. Thus the present report represents a total of seven months in the field, in four of which there were two separate parties in two cars. Of this time approximately two-thirds was spent in survey work, one-third in stratigraphic excavation.

It is hardly necessary to point out that this is a very small record of accomplishment in relation to the area contemplated in the original project. Less than half of that area was covered even in a preliminary way. The amount of test excavation, in proportion to surface collecting, we now feel to have been inadequate. Notwithstanding these shortcomings, we believe that the results, however fragmentary, warrant publication at this time.

Grateful acknowledgment is due the directors at that time of the three participating institutions: Mr. Donald Scott, Peabody Museum, Harvard University; Dr. Carl E. Guthe, Museum of Anthropology, University of Michigan; and Dr. Henry V. Howe, School of Geology, Louisiana State University. All three overcame their entirely reasonable misgivings in respect to complicated joint undertakings and gave their unstinted support and assistance. Thanks are also due Dr. Arthur R. Kelly, who

[1] In 1946, Ford joined the staff of the American Museum of Natural History, New York City, which institution then assumed co-sponsorship of the Lower Mississippi Archaeological Survey in place of the School of Geology, Louisiana State University.

secured for us not only the moral support of the National Park Service, but material assistance as well. Part of the funds for the University of Michigan's share of the work and publication was a grant from the Horace H. Rackham School of Graduate Studies. The President of the Mississippi River Commission, Corps of Engineers, U. S. Army, was most generous in furnishing maps and other indispensable publications of the Commission, and remarkably forebearing in respect to the little received from us in return. To him also and to Dr. Harold N. Fisk particular thanks are due for permission to quote freely from the latter's monumental report on the geology of the Alluvial Valley of the Lower Mississippi River, published by the Commission.[2]

To the sometimes puzzled, but always good-natured, planters we tender thanks *en bloc*. Of the several hundred owners and managers approached, very few failed to understand the general objects of the Survey, and almost none withheld their co-operation. We regret that the large number of such friendly persons makes it impossible to mention them individually.

It remains to speak of assistance freely given by local archaeologists and collectors, among whom it is a pleasure to record names. Professor S. C. Dellinger of the University of Arkansas put the University Museum's large collections at our disposal and furnished valuable information out of his extensive knowledge of the area. The late Professor Calvin S. Brown permitted us to photograph the fine collection of pottery at the University of Mississippi, Oxford, Mississippi. Dr. and Mrs. Hodges of Bismark, Arkansas, put their collection at our disposal, as did the Honorable Harry J. Lemley of Hope, Arkansas; Dr. James K. Hampson of Nodena, Arkansas; and Mr. Charles Clark of Clarksdale, Mississippi.

A great many people have assisted in the rather considerable drudgery that takes place in what is generally referred to as the "laboratory." In particular, we have to mention the admirable work of analysis and classification performed by Mrs. Mary Slusser in 1946–47 at the Peabody Museum, without which the publication of this work would have been still further delayed. The seriation analysis and the resultant graphs were prepared at the American Museum of Natural History in 1948. In this work able assistance was rendered by Mr. Gary Vesalius and Miss Charlotte Fitzpatrick.

The three authors must jointly assume responsibility for the preparation of this report and the conclusions — except where it is made clear that some one of the three does not concur in a majority opinion. When we began the work we did not expect that complete unanimity would be reached on all points, particularly in view of the fact that the analysis and writing had to be done at our respective institutions and the opportunities for discussion would be few. We shall not attempt to minimize such differences of opinion, for to us they have been one of the most stimulating aspects of the collaboration. As the discerning reader will perceive, they derive principally from the differing degrees of caution used by the three of us in drawing conclusions from the same data.

The fact that this report had to be prepared while the writers were widely separated made it necessary for each to take the responsibility for doing the work and writing the first draft of various sections. In some cases these sections stand substantially as originally written; in others they have been considerably amended by criticisms and suggestions of the other two authors. For purposes of fixing ultimate responsibility, the authorship of the various sections is as follows:

I. The Geographic Setting. Phillips.

II. The Archaeological Field Work. Phillips.

III. Pottery Typology and Classification. Section on typology originally written by Ford, revised by Phillips, with many suggestions by Griffin. The pottery classification represents a joint effort extending over several years. Pottery descriptions written by Griffin.

IV. Distribution of Some Mississippi Period Vessel Shapes and Features. Griffin.

V. Seriation Analysis of Pottery Collections. Ford.

VI. Stratigraphy. Phillips.

VII. Correlation of Pottery Sequence with Recent Drainage History. Phillips.

VIII. Analysis of Occupation Site Plans. Ford.

IX. Identification of Sites from Documentary Sources. Phillips.

X. Summary and Conclusions. Various sections written by all three authors and patched together in consultation.

Philip Phillips, James B. Griffin, and James A. Ford

[2] Fisk, 1944.

INTRODUCTION TO 2003 EDITION

Phillips, Ford, and Griffin's Lower Valley Survey

Stephen Williams

PREAMBLE

In writing the introduction for this reprinting of the Lower Mississippi valley classic by Phillips, Ford, and Griffin, I must make clear my own prejudices as well as my strengths and weaknesses in taking on this effort. I knew all three authors well over a period of many decades; I worked with and was taught by two of them (Griffin and Phillips) and spent quite a bit of time both in museums and touring with the other (Ford). All have now passed away. But they are not forgotten, as this newly reprinted volume surely demonstrates.

I have also presented public eulogies for and published pieces about Phillips and Griffin (Williams 1995, 1999; Williams and Brain 1970). I created a timeline and bibliography for a Ford obituary (Willey 1969) and aided a colleague in another volume on Ford (Brown 1978). In addition, I put together with the help of Bill Haag a Southeastern Archaeological Conference (SEAC) resolution to honor Ford in November 1967, before Ford's death (Williams and Haag 1968). I put together a lengthy collection—more than 200 pages—of much of Ford's writings, including his little-known 1938 master's thesis on ceramic analysis for the University of Michigan, Ann Arbor (Williams 1970). I cared a lot about them all.

Thus, I am hardly a person writing about these individuals of the Lower Mississippi survey (LMS) from an unbiased point of view. I have also provided similar materials on two others of what I like to call the "LMS gang": William G. Haag (Williams 2001, 2002) and Robert S. Neitzel (Williams 1986). Both of this latter cohort participated directly in LMS field activities, Haag at Jaketown, and Neitzel at Menard, Lake George, and Natchez. Now none of them survives to argue with me on this personal view of "who, what, when, and how" things happened. I will try to be fair and straightforward about how I know what went on in both the fieldwork and the writing that provided the archaeological results and the text of the volume that is being reprinted herein. However, I must also mention that I have not used all the available archival data: Phillips's field notebooks and those of some of his field assistants do exist in the LMS Archives at the Peabody Museum.

There have also been many discussions of this volume both as book reviews and citations in everything from textbooks to monographs. I have investigated the later sources only briefly. Haag wrote several early positive book reviews (1953a and 1953b), and I must confess that even I wrote one early in my career (Williams 1952). It was the first thing I ever had published, and it is not significant. Many years later, Robert Dunnell (1985:297–300) wrote a short piece specifically on the importance of this survey as a "landmark study." For the most recent careful review of this volume, see Mark A. Rees's "Mississippian Culture History: The Contribution of Phillips, Ford and Griffin" in *Historical Perspectives on Midsouth Archaeology* (M. A. Rolingson, ed. 2001. Arkansas Archaeological Survey Research Series, no. 58: 85–92).

I must further confess that I do not have, and never did have, a great interest in convoluted philosophical controversies. Thus, when Michael O'Brien and Lee Lyman (1998:181–231) discuss at length the volume that is being republished herein, I will take the easy way out and decline to enter into the controversy over what they suggest these three archaeologists thought, meant, or intimated. When one must use terms like "essentialists" in one's exegesis of this trio's actions and intents, I must beg off completely. So be it.

INTRODUCTION

The year was 1939 and the Great Depression was finally beginning to ease in America, partially because of the military buildup due to the war in Europe that was about to break out that autumn. While there is little good that can be said about the suffering caused by the stock-market crash on Wall Street and the following difficult depression years, one benefit accrued to the field of archaeology. A long somnolent period of modest action in the field of archaeology in the eastern United States (1900–1930) ended with a series of depression-relief programs in archaeological fieldwork that changed the face and facts of the archaeology of that region.

Of course, this eastern part of America had produced the first significant research on the ancient Indian monuments (the Moundbuilders) as early as the 1780s. Dozens of books and articles had been written on the subject of eastern North American archaeology by the 1880s, with workers including everyone from American presidents (Thomas Jefferson) to local antiquarians. Throughout the East these individuals gathered together in early local museums of science or major institutions such as the Smithsonian Institution in 1846 or the Peabody Museum at Harvard, founded in 1867 (Williams 1991:28–76).

However, it was about this time (1860s–1870s) that Americans, with the opening of the West following the gold rush of 1849, discovered the wonders of southwestern archaeology. This region began to gain in importance as a new field of research, with intriguing discoveries of Cliff Dweller ruins and wonderfully preserved baskets and burials unlike anything ever found in the East. The Southwest caught the attention of newly trained scholars at the Peabody, which was matriculating the first Ph.D.'s in archaeology. The archaeology of the eastern United States in the post–World War I period was carried out in a much less exciting manner and with attention still focused mainly, but not exclusively, on the Moundbuilders (Willey and Sabloff 1993:38–64; Williams 1994:9–14).

The need for employment in the eastern United States during the depression shifted focus away from the Southwest. Roosevelt's make-work projects (e.g., WPA, CWA) included roads, soil-conservation projects, and, in 1934, archaeological projects. Those later projects started with site surveys followed by excavations in many regions especially at new dam sites on many southeastern rivers such as the Tennessee.

These major WPA excavation programs were the underpinnings for a revolution in the archaeology of the eastern United States. Armies of workers attacked large sites and their deep deposits in a manner never before seen. Mounds were excavated, too, and manpower resources allowed the mounds to be sectioned for stratigraphy rather than being attacked only with a few modest pits and trenches.

Of course, the workers made mistakes; nevertheless, new data swamped the burgeoning field of eastern archaeology and seemed to make it a worthwhile field of academic research. There had also been a series of regional archaeological conferences that were organized by the anthropological wing of the National Research Council in 1929, 1932, and 1935 (O'Brien and Lyman 2001). Reacting to the torrent of new WPA data, a series of annual Southeastern Archaeological Conferences was launched to help bring order to the mass of new data. These SEAC meetings began in 1937 at Ann Arbor, Michigan. Griffin and Ford were the first leaders of that still long-running series of conferences (Williams 1960).

FORD, GRIFFIN, AND PHILLIPS: ARCHAEOLOGICAL BACKGROUND

For the first time in half a century, eastern archaeology was now active on a broad scale, and new scholars were being trained to tackle the questions raised by the data being brought to light by these relief programs. Among this group were the three authors of this volume. James A. Ford was the youngest (1911–1968), next was James B. Griffin (1905–1997), and finally the oldest, Philip Phillips (1900–1994). Despite some disparity in their ages, they started tackling archaeology as a field of research around the beginning of the 1930s. They all received strong academic training in the field as well, a background not common to many eastern archaeologists in the early twentieth century.

In the fall of 1939 the three met in Baton Rouge at Louisiana State University (LSU) to put together research plans to study the archaeology of the Lower Mississippi River, that region south of the Ohio River confluence. Ford and Griffin had known each other for some time, and Phillips and Griffin were well acquainted too. However, I cannot now cite an earlier meeting of Ford and Phillips, although the latter did thank Ford for unpublished data he used in his Harvard dissertation (Phillips 1939:ii).

It was Ford who first advanced the idea for an archaeological survey of part of the Lower Mississippi valley in that fall of 1939, first getting in contact with the National Park Service group that was doing archaeological work nearby. Then Ford gathered the other two, Griffin and Phillips, together in Baton Rouge. An unknown LSU photographer took three "mug shots" at that time. One can rightly ask what real experience prepared these men, all in their 30s, for such a large undertaking as a survey of part of the Lower Mississippi valley, which they believed ran from the mouth of the Ohio River to the Gulf of Mexico (see Figure 1).

Ford was by far the most experienced fieldworker, beginning at the age of 15 to work with Moreau Chambers on a survey of sites in Mississippi (Chambers 1976:26; Collins 1932; Ford 1936:1). Ford was born in Water Valley, Mississippi, but moved as a teenager to Clinton, Mississippi, with his mother and brother, David (Willey 1969). Chambers and Ford had gotten some excavation experience in Mississippi with Henry B. Collins of the Smithsonian. However, their earliest techniques seem to have been pretty much self-taught. Chambers had first met Collins on June 23, 1926, at the office of Dunbar Rowland, who was head of the Mississippi Department of Archives and History in Jackson (Chambers 1976:24). Chambers had made an appointment to show Rowland some artifacts that he had uncovered. Contrary to much-published documentation including some from Ford himself, the leader of this duo of young men (Chambers, 17, and Ford, 15) was Chambers, who had long been interested in archaeology and had also written school papers on the subject (Chambers 1976:11–44). However, one author, Pat Galloway (2000:25), has just recently written about Chambers's contribution as being "vastly underrated."

Thus Chambers and Ford really had gotten their hands dirty in excavations and surveys well before 1930. Chambers continued to work in archaeology in Mississippi until the beginning of World War II (Chambers 1976:332). Later Ford carried out, on his own, a number of test excavations at other sites in Mississippi and Louisiana, such as the Peck village (Ford 1933). He also was exposed to other regions and techniques through time spent both in Macon, Georgia, (1934) and in the Southwest (Ford 1935), learning archaeological methods there as well. Therefore by 1939 he had had considerable, good field experience across the United States with a number of trained archaeologists.

Ford's academic background at this time included a bachelor of arts from Louisiana State University (1936). He had been urged by friends to go to the University of Michigan for a graduate degree and did so in the fall of 1937, according to Griffin (1999:638). It was there Ford first met Griffin, founded a lifelong friendship, and earned a master's degree. He soon became deeply involved in WPA-sponsored excavations in Louisiana (1938), but these other activities did not keep him from proposing the Lower Mississippi survey to his two friends.

Contrary to popular belief, Griffin had more field experience by 1939 than most have thought. As I have detailed elsewhere (Williams 1999:453–455), Griffin had begun his contact with archaeological digs in the late 1920s, as had Ford. He was a graduate student at the University of Chicago in 1928, and the next year, he began a three-year period of summer excavations that culminated in him leading a dig in Pennsylvania in 1931 (Griffin 1991). He was, therefore, not just an armchair archaeologist, as he has often been characterized. He cared about sites, excavations, and provenience, and well into his 90s, Griffin still enjoyed visiting sites and inspecting the excavations of others.

In the spring of 1933, Griffin left the University of Chicago and went to the University of Michigan to begin a three-year graduate fellowship in American archaeology sponsored by Eli Lilly. He completed his doctoral dissertation in 1936 under the mentorship of Carl Guthe, a Harvard Ph.D. Its topic was the Norris Basin ceramics, excavated under the direction of Major Webb. These materials were in the University of Michigan's ceramic repository, headed by Guthe. Early in 1936 he began a study on the "Fort Ancient Aspect" of the Ohio valley. The research for this study took him to many venues including Harvard's Peabody Museum, where a large collection of these materials (e.g., the Madisonville site) was located (Griffin 1985:6). While there he met Philip Phillips, who was finishing his own doctoral dissertation on Mississippian ceramics from the Mississippi valley (Phillips 1939). This meeting blossomed into a close and lifelong friendship that ended only with Phil's death in 1994. By 1939, Griffin thus had had both considerable archaeological field experience and a lot of hands-on work with ceramics from all over the eastern United States.

The field experience that Phillips had had prior to 1939 is a bit more difficult to document. His own published statement is laconic at best: "with a third [Phillips] who had done *some* work within it [the lower valley]" (this volume, 5, emphasis added). I know of only one piece of real fieldwork that applies to Phillips's statement. This was some rather extensive archaeological research in the Ouachita River valley, just west of Hot Springs,

Figure I-1. James A. Ford, fall 1939. (Museum of Natural Science, Louisiana State University)

Figure I-2. James B. Griffin, fall 1939. (Museum of Natural Science, Louisiana State University)

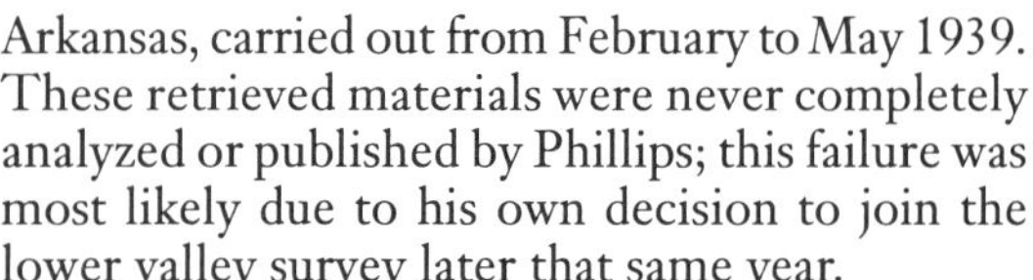

Arkansas, carried out from February to May 1939. These retrieved materials were never completely analyzed or published by Phillips; this failure was most likely due to his own decision to join the lower valley survey later that same year.

Many years later, in 1966, one of my own graduate students, Frank Schambach, did further research in the Ouachita valley region and wrote his dissertation on his own work and that of Phillips, as well as WPA excavations run by the University of Arkansas. This more recent Harvard project (1966–1970) had Phillips's complete support. This Harvard dissertation has now finally been published and therein Schambach (1998:2) indicates that Phillips recorded and collected from 59 sites and made important test excavations at several of them. Phillips was headquartered in Hot Springs, Arkansas. He and his wife, Ruth, and their three children lived in a hotel "apartment," where much of the "lab" work was carried out ("Saki" Phillips Sheldon, personal communication, 2002). Once reminiscing about this project, Phillips told me that one of his hired dig hands stole his lunch out in those boondocks—I wish I had taped his conversation then.

However, long before this Ouachita fieldwork, Phillips had also spent some months with Harvard-trained Frank H. H. Roberts Jr. (Ph.D., 1927) in 1934 at the Shiloh site in Tennessee. This was a government-run relief operation (CWA), and Phillips spent January through March at that site helping in that excavation (Phillips personal communication, n.d.; Chambers 1976:333–335). It was his first involvement with a professional dig. Paul Welch is currently (2002) carrying on research at the Shiloh site and has identified pictures of both Phillips and Chambers at work at the site (Welch personal communication, 2002).

Chambers described Phillips's arrival at Shiloh as follows: "I first met Phillips when he came down at his own expense, driving an old gas-thirsty Lincoln car, all the way from up in the Boston area down to Shiloh National Military, in the winter of '33–'34" (Chambers 1976:335). It is wonderful confirmation of a little-known part of Phillips's early exposure to field archaeology. I know there are some of Phillips's own photographs of this Shiloh experience, but I have not yet been able to recover them.

Finally, I can also report one other bit of south-

Figure I-3. Philip Phillips, fall 1939. (Museum of Natural Science, Louisiana State University)

eastern traveling by Phillips for added firsthand knowledge of research and specimens in the period prior to 1939. Thanks to research by John Walker we know that Phillips visited the Ocmulgee, Georgia, research operations in January of both 1936 and 1937. There in Macon, Georgia, he met Arthur Kelly and Gordon Willey for the first time and even visited Preston Holder's coastal excavations (Walker 1994:20, 23).

PHILLIPS, FORD, AND GRIFFIN: PERSONAL BACKGROUND

Before turning directly to the Lower Mississippi survey activities themselves, it is important to understand the personal backgrounds of these three archaeologists who were about to make eastern North American archaeological history with their broad survey of a major part of the Lower Mississippi valley. They were a mixed bag of characters, three vastly different individuals who separately decided to devote their lives to the field of American archaeology.

Phillips was born August 11, 1900, in Buffalo, New York. His mother had just returned from the Hawaiian Islands, where his father, a lawyer for the U.S. government, was working on the legal problems of the island's changeover to American territorial status. They wanted Phillips to be born in the United States. He was educated at private schools in Buffalo and went to Williams College, graduating in 1922. He had some military training while at college, but World War I was over before he could be taken into service. Upon graduation, Phillips married Ruth Schoellkopf, also from Buffalo, and then went to Harvard's School of Design for a graduate degree in architecture. As a young married couple, an exception for graduate school students at that time, they met a number of other students including a fellow architectural student, Singleton Moorehead. He was the son of Warren K. Moorehead, the archaeologist at the R. S. Peabody Foundation at Andover Academy, at whose home the Phillipses enjoyed occasional Sunday dinners.

More important to his study of archaeology, Phillips also met George Vaillant, a charismatic graduate student in Mesoamerican archaeology at Harvard, whom he got to know much better later on. With his architectural diploma in hand in 1927, Phillips then headed back to Buffalo, where he and Ruth built a fine home to Phillips's own design and entered practice in the field of domestic architecture. However, by the early thirties, seeing a slim economic future in that enterprise, he decided to turn to another field altogether: archaeology. He had had an interest in the history of the Buffalo region and indeed at one time or another briefly wrote about a nearby Indian burial site.

Phillips and Ruth returned to the Cambridge area in the fall of 1932 and remained there, or close by, for the rest of his long life. Phillips met Vaillant again and plunged into American archaeology as well as many other aspects of the broad field of anthropology. His first graduate mentor was Roland B. Dixon, one of the famous trio of Hooton, Tozzer, and Dixon, who created at Harvard one of the outstanding graduate programs in the field. In consultation with Dixon, Phillips had decided to work in North American archaeology, a field that his mentor had both taught and written about. However, Dixon died in 1934, and Alfred Tozzer became his mentor and later a good friend (Phillips 1955). Tozzer, a Middle American specialist, hoped to no avail that Phillips would change his mind and work in Tozzer's own field.

It was eastern North American archaeology, especially that of the Mississippi valley, that captured Phillips's interest. There is only a modicum of information concerning this choice, but it is specific: "To the late Professor R. B. Dixon I am indebted for the original impetus that led to its inception [the undertaking of his dissertation]" (Phillips 1939:i). Phillips then continues by thanking Professors Tozzer and Hooton for their guidance in the dissertation's continuation. Not terribly enlightening, but it is all we have.

At the time, the Peabody Museum had an expansive but little-noticed collection of ceramics from the Mississippi valley. Anyone reading the literature of North American archaeology in the 1930s would be impressed by the many mysteries of that region. Also, through Dixon, there was still a direct connection to Frederic W. Putnam. In the late nineteenth century, Putnam had seen to it that the Peabody's shelves were loaded with these Lower Mississippi vessels, especially those from southeastern Missouri and Arkansas, and the excavated collections from the Oliver site in Mississippi.

Apparently—and that is all one can honestly assert at this time—Phillips took his mentor's advice and plunged into the Mississippi valley collections that were readily accessible at the Peabody. As with all his later work, nothing was done in haste or without an amazing thoroughness. Indeed, there were a number of Mississippi valley pots at the Peabody, but so too were there Putnam-collected and -purchased Mississippian vessels at Putman's other "sometime" museum, the anthropological collections at the American Museum of Natural History (AMNH). Putnam served as curator there, too, in a period from 1894 to 1903. So, undaunted, Phillips traveled to AMNH and photographed its many Mississippian vessels during the late 1930s. The LMS Archives now holds more than 4,000 of Phillips's vessel photographs, though not all are from that New York museum, as Phillips lists four collections besides the Peabody.

Other things were going on in Phillips's academic life as well; besides Vaillant, he was also a friend of Clyde Kluckhohn, Douglas Oliver, and his mentor, Alfred Tozzer. Indeed, on December 7, 1941, Tozzer and Phillips were on a trip together in Mexico. Other close academic friends at Harvard were Carl Coon, A. V. "Alfie" Kidder Jr., and Hallam Movius.

Phillips was a private person, perhaps even a bit shy. He rarely went to professional meetings; however, he was greatly admired by his old archaeological friends Griffin, Haag, and Neitzel (Williams and Brain 1990). He had a wide range of concerns far from archaeology, including music, poetry, and literature; he studied Joyce's *Finnegans Wake* with great care. He was also widely traveled and was well versed in at least three foreign languages, German, French, and Spanish. This was the intellectual and personal background that Phillips brought to Baton Rouge when the team met in 1939. I have spent a bit more space on this view of Phillips, as both Griffin and Ford have quite lengthy and recently published biographical sketches (Williams 1991; Griffin 1991).

Griffin's own personal background is much better known as a result of some recent articles he and others have published (Williams 1999; Griffin 1991). He was born in Kansas in 1905, spent two years in Denver, Colorado, and then grew up in Oak Park, Illinois. Illinois was then his home and Chicago the place of his education until well into graduate school. While in graduate school in anthropology at the University of Chicago, Griffin, who earned his master's degree in 1930, was offered a special graduate fellowship at the University of Michigan. He accepted the offer in 1933. Griffin remained in Ann Arbor until 1984, when he moved to the National Museum of Natural History in Washington, D.C. He was a teacher par excellence; he studied the field of North American archaeology with great care and dedicatedly taught the subject until his retirement in 1976.

Such a description suggests a rather narrow and tightly focused individual; however, he enjoyed life with gusto and verve. His interests ranged from good food and fine wines to politics and history. He loved to drive cross-country at high speeds, and a roadside stop for a well-crafted maple-and-walnut ice cream cone gave him as much pleasure as a fine soufflé. Phillips's field notes indicate Griffin's similar enjoyment of doing survey work in the lower valley, especially the interesting encounters with the local populations. Griffin liked finding new ceramic data in the plowed fields of the Delta. He was no armchair archaeologist in those days (1939–1947); he did both quite a lot of surface surveying and oversaw the digging of a number of test pits as well.

Ford is the most written about of three, though he never wrote much about himself. He died at

57; both Phillips and Griffin lived into their 90s (Brown 1978; Griffin 1990). Ford has also recently been the focus of the Missouri duo of O'Brien and Lyman (1998, 1999). My own contact with him began early at the Southeastern Archaeological Conferences in the 1950s and lasted until his death in the spring of 1968, when Phillips and I had plane reservations to visit Ford's bedside in Florida. He died just before we left to see him. Phillips and I had also visited Ford in the field in Arkansas, and he had visited us at the Peabody Museum. I later made a return visit to AMNH to see the Marksville site collection that Ford was then working on. I traveled with him and Stu Neitzel several times across the country, returning from archaeological conferences, so our times together were quite informal. Naturally many of our conversations were about archaeology—Ford was not one for mere pleasantries—even most of his widely acclaimed jokes on colleagues were anthropological in nature as Griffin pointed out (1990:649); I can affirm that from my own experience with him. For yet another insightful view on Ford and his personality by someone who had worked closely with him for a number of years, I suggest a careful reading of Gordon Willey's foreword to O'Brien and Lyman's volume on Ford (O'Brien and Lyman 1998:vii–xiv).

Ford cared enormously about archaeology, especially that of the Lower Mississippi valley where he was born and raised. He had been working at the craft since age 15, when he started to work with his friend, Chambers, in Clinton, Mississippi. These teenagers became involved in local Mississippi archaeology for a number of years. They also worked some summers in the Arctic under the direction of Henry B. Collins. The trio, Collins, Chambers, and Ford, also undertook Christmas-holiday digs at the Deasonville site in 1929 and 1930 in Mississippi (Collins 1932; Chambers 1976:267–268; 295–296). Chambers had actual field training at the University of Chicago summer program in Fulton County, Illinois, in the summer of 1933. Later that same year and continuing into the next spring he worked with Frank H. H. Roberts at Shiloh, Tennessee, on a CWA project (Chambers 1976:278).

Chambers continued in Mississippi archaeology and history under the auspices of the Mississippi Department of Archives and History in a full-time capacity from the summer of 1934 until World War II (Chambers 1976:105). In the post-war period, following service in the navy (1942–1945), Chambers entered historical and archival work outside of Mississippi, which he continued for the rest of his professional career (Chambers 1976:106–110).

Ford on the other hand went to Mississippi College (1927–1930) in Clinton, Mississippi, where Chambers had also matriculated, and then he headed south to Louisiana for the last of his undergraduate education at LSU in 1934. The in-between years were significant as he pulled together the earlier Mississippi survey data and added some specific test excavations (Ford 1936). In contrast to Phillips, Ford was a regular attendant at Southeastern Archaeological Conferences throughout his life. He and Griffin put together the first conference in 1937 at Ann Arbor (Williams 1969). Ford's last SEAC meeting was at Avery Island, Louisiana, in 1966, when the then-unrecognized signs of cancer were troubling his ability to get around easily.

It was an interesting and diverse trio. Phillips was the oldest, a tall, quiet gentleman, who brought both Harvard graduate students and his wife into this field experience, but he had the least experience. Ford was even taller and much more self-assured about his experience for such an enterprise. Seemingly, he was the instigator of the operation. Yet Ford spent the least time involved in the field operations. Finally, there was Griffin, smaller and energetic but with well-deserved confidence in handling the results of the whole operation. Fate and history put Phillips in the position of ultimately running most of the field research and writing most of the final report. This structure was probably not at all what they had in mind that fall day in Baton Rouge in 1939 when they came together to plan this project. Unfortunately, I know of no documents that concern the details of that first meeting.

FIELDWORK OF THE SURVEY

The work of the survey in the field was confined to five field seasons. Each season seems to have encompassed at most two months in the valley. In retrospect this schedule seems like a rather small amount of time: the spring and fall of 1940, the spring of 1941, an interruption by World War II, then the springs of 1946 and 1947. (See Table 1.)

During the war, Phillips, the eldest of the trio, spent considerable time in the Pacific theater, with the rank of an army major, in a special-service operation run by his Harvard friend, the anthropologist Douglas Oliver. Phillips's mission, which took him to the islands of the western Pacific, was to find opportunities to provide foodstuffs for the armed forces in that region that did not have to be shipped in from great distances. It was not a great success, but Phillips did have some good tales to tell about it. Griffin spent the war years teaching special courses at the University of Michigan, a number of which were focused on economic and political geography in the university's military program (Williams 1999:455). Ford was taken into the army as "a senior design specialist for arctic and winter warfare" (Griffin 1999:643), and he went to the Arctic a number of times during the war to test those materials.

When everyone was back in the United States, the well-known trio split up the actual fieldwork. Ford, who by all measures was the most experienced in field archaeology, ended up with the least amount of time in the field—a single season in the spring of 1940 when all three of the group worked primarily in northeastern Arkansas, the northern-most part of the survey quadrants. Later, other important issues pulled at Ford. He was a well-known specialist in lower-valley archaeology but lacked a doctorate in the field. (He had earned a master's degree at Michigan in the academic year 1937–1938.) Ford left the survey to pursue his doctoral degree at Columbia University in the fall of 1940, and he did no more fieldwork on this lower-valley program. Instead, he went to Peru in 1946 for an important role in the Viru valley project; his report on that work was the basis for his doctoral dissertation.

Griffin worked with Phillips and Ford in that kickoff session during the spring of 1940. Much later, he wrote briefly about the experience with Ford (Griffin 1999:649). Griffin was also an important part of the second major season in the spring of 1941, with Phillips and two Harvard graduate students, when most of the test pitting was done. In the postwar period (1946–1947), Phillips was assisted again by some Harvard students and, especially, by his wife.

By far, Phillips directed the majority of the field explorations and excavations. He participated in two seasons with Ford, Griffin, or both, and three short seasons with his wife, one of those with a graduate student. Three other graduate students took part in two of the seasons. While it was not a large field crew, there was quite a number of locally hired crew members who did all of the actual test pit digging.

The area covered, the number of sites recorded, and the amount of data recovered is impressive (Figure 2 and Table 1). A total of 382 sites was recorded by the survey (pp. 47–58) (Phillips incorrectly gives the number as 385 [p. 41].) Of these, only 60 had been documented in the archaeological literature prior to their work. Twenty stratigraphic test pits were undertaken on 11 sites, and 17 were of sufficient value to be reported therein (p. 41). The amount of "hard" data included only the 346,099 potsherds that were later analyzed. A great number of plain body sherds were thrown away during the early fieldwork, as they were thought to be rather useless (p. 43). Much later, Phillips (1970:247) had some strong second thoughts on how the potsherds had been treated in this 1951 volume. Phillips, with Ford no longer looking over his shoulder, felt that he had thus handled these new collections from the Yazoo Basin and elsewhere in a much more coherent manner.

As the reader will soon find out, this monograph, with all its 457 pages, is of truly gigantic proportions. I will now consider the 10 major sections (or chapters) and their general import. The specific authors are not shown directly in the text, but are instead "listed" quite carefully at the very end of the preface on page vi herein. A number of readers seem to have missed this, so I have

Table I-1
Staffing of the Field Programs of the Lower Mississippi Survey, 1940–1947

Spring 1940	Fall 1940	Spring 1941	Spring 1946	Spring 1947
Philip Phillips	Philip Phillips	Philip Phillips	Philip Phillips	Philip Phillips
James A. Ford	Ruth Phillips	James B. Griffin	Ruth Phillips	Ruth Phillips
James B. Griffin		Mott Davis	Paul Gebhard	
Fisher Motz		Chester Chard and his wife		

added them in parenthesis in the sections below.

Section I: The Geographic Setting (Phillips)

Phillips starts his presentation with characteristic modesty and an apology for its length—little did he know that 50 years later there still would not be a more detailed discussion of this important topic. As archaeologists learn more about the impact and changes to this landscape, and to much of our nation, we are now showing much more concern for this topic. Phillips made good use of historic data and geological information as well. As Phillips well knew, there is a lot more to learn: "The student of prehistory in the Lower Mississippi Valley must in fact do more. He must attempt to reconstruct cultures that no longer exist in an environment that exists only in a profoundly modified state" (p. 36). So many years later the topic of "landscape archaeology" is still understudied in the lower valley. However, the late Roger T. Saucier of Vicksburg, Mississippi, an LMS friend of long standing, presented a masterful view of the geomorphology and Quaternary geology of the lower valley (Saucier 1994). There is also an excellent physiographic map of the survey area (Figure 1, this volume).

Section II: The Archaeological Field Work (Phillips)

This section briefly describes both the reasoning behind the survey and the program of operations, illustrated with two interesting maps of the project scope (Figures 2 and 4). The stated purpose was to discover the relationship between the earlier "Hopewell-Marksville affinity" and the later Middle Mississippian (p. 40). Of course, much more data than that were discovered.

The details of the field operations were specific, and there is even a list of "shortcomings"—not a common revelation in such monographs (p. 45). The section concludes with a listing of the 382 sites that were encountered by the program. Further details of the project's "hows and whys" are briefly covered in the preface (p. iv–v). The project's actual scope is quite amazing both in square miles and the number of sites and collections made; I do not know of any comparable survey in the southeastern United States until many decades later.

Phillips also drafted a rough map of the region, using dots to mark all of the sites visited, quadrangle by quadrangle. He color-coded the dots to show which sites had been visited season by season, but that map was not included in the published version (LMS Archives, Peabody Museum). However, thanks to great help from my LMS colleague, Vin Steponaitis—who does not suffer the color blindness of this author—we are able to separate out the four main survey seasons (1940–1946) and the sites located therein.

Thus we see that spring of 1940 covered mainly the sites on the west side of the Mississippi from northeastern Arkansas to just below the Arkansas River entrance. They visited only about ten sites in the Upper Yazoo Basin. In all, they located a relatively large number of sites that season, as this was the only time in which all three—Phillips, Ford, and Griffin—worked in the field together. The fall season of 1940 covered the Upper Yazoo intensively, mainly along the Mississippi, with considerable success. The spring season of 1941 continued the site survey in the Upper Yazoo—as far south as the 20 tier—with a large number of sites located, almost equaling the scale of the first season. The final season of surveying in the spring of 1946 collected a modest 24 sites.

The 1951 PFG volume does not sufficiently emphasize the fact that Phillips did most of the work that brought the project to full fruition. That's because Phillips, who helped get the volume published, genuinely lacked an ego. Table I-1 details the actual amount of time put in the field: Phillips, seven months; Griffin, four months; and Ford, two months.

There were also four field assistants during the various seasons, as indicated in Figure 1. All were Harvard graduate students whom Phillips brought down from Cambridge. They have received little notice in any of the later literature, and credit goes to one of my own field students, John Belmont, for pointing out this omission in an early draft of this paper. The only field assistant in the spring of 1940 was John Christian "Fisher" Motz (1909–1991), who had already done a fair amount of archaeological fieldwork. In 1935 Motz worked under the direction of Emil Haury at the Snaketown site in Arizona (Elliot 1995:142) and later a season at the Peabody southwestern excavation at Awatovi in Arizona. He completely dropped out of the field after World War II (Davis 2002).

The important third season in the spring of 1941 saw Phillips and Griffin assisted by two more Harvard graduate students, Mott Davis and Chester Chard. E. Mott Davis (1918–1998) later continued graduate training at Harvard and completed his doctorate in the field in 1954; his dissertation was on Paleoindian sites in the Great Plains. He had also been an undergraduate honors student in archaeology, graduating Magna Cum Laude from Harvard (1937–1940), and his senior honors thesis won a campus-wide prize. He went on to work primarily in the archaeology of the Great Plains and taught successfully for 32 years at the University of Texas, Austin. Davis later remembered, with great pleasure, his fieldwork with Phillips at the Menard site where they had camped out (Davis 2002).

Chester Chard, another Harvard College student, later completed his graduate training at the University of California, Berkeley. He was apparently one of Robert H. Lowie's last students. His dissertation focused on the Kamchadal tribe of eastern Siberia. After earning his doctorate at Berkeley, he taught, beginning in 1958, at the University of Wisconsin for his entire career. His interests rested mainly in the northern climes; he helped found *Arctic Anthropology*. He retired in 1974. Perhaps his lower-valley experience drove him to like cooler climes. He now resides comfortably in Vancouver, British Columbia.

In the only postwar session in 1946, another Harvard graduate student, Paul H. Gebhard, assisted Phillips. Gebhard had received his college education mainly at Harvard (class of 1940). He had also done some wide-ranging archaeological fieldwork in different areas, mainly in the West, prior to his arrival at Harvard. Even at Harvard he continued more fieldwork prior to his one season in the lower valley. His 1947 doctoral dissertation was on North American stone artifacts. He easily had the most prior field experience of any of the LMS graduate students, and Gebhard (2002) considered Phillips the best boss he ever had.

However, Gebhard soon took up the rather different field of anthropology, with a career at the University of Indiana where he joined the Alfred Kinsey project of sexual research. He had been encouraged by Clyde Kluckhohn in 1946 to have a look at this interesting new research project and decided to give it a try. After Kinsey's death in 1956, Gebhard continued to run the Kinsey Institute in this special area of anthropology. He is now a professor emeritus at that university (Gebhard 2002).

I might note that Phillips went back into the field in the Yazoo Basin, even as this report was going to press (1949–1951). In 1949 and 1950, he also had Harvard graduate students as assistants, E. N. Zeigler in 1949 and Warren Eames in 1950. In 1951, he was at Jaketown with Ford, again with Warren Eames. Later in 1954, he went again into the field for his last time with Robert Greengo, whose dissertation covered that year's work and another season as well (Phillips 1970:vii–viii).

Thus, the popular perception of Phillips as a solitary worker and even more as a theorist and ceramic typologist than a field person just does not fit the available data. He was instead a well-rounded archaeologist; he did both fieldwork and analysis.

Also listed in Table I-1 is Phillips's wife, Ruth. As a well-read woman of grace and charm, she was in some ways the least likely field companion imaginable. But as the table clearly shows, she was also Phillips's faithful companion in the field for three seasons. She later joined directly in the Jaketown excavations in 1951 as well, and she worked tirelessly in the LMS makeshift lab in Belzoni (Ford et al 1955:5).

Section III: Classification of the Pottery (cited as "Pottery Typology and Classification")

This section on typology was originally written by Ford and was revised by Phillips with many suggestions by Griffin. "The pottery classification represents a joint effort extending over several years. Pottery descriptions by Griffin" (p. vi).

This important section was the most problematic for the three authors. Ford had already been setting up pottery types for some years. Griffin had been instrumental, from his days at the University of Michigan ceramic repository, in creating types, too. By 1940, Phillips had handled a great number of whole vessels in his just-completed dissertation, and he had set up some ceramic wares with simple names used therein. As a joint-effort among the three, it wasn't a picnic.

The materials collected in the spring of 1940 were sorted in Baton Rouge by the trio as described herein. It was not an easy task, as these archaeologists carefully considered each sherd. This trio had three very different temperaments. Ford was forceful and quite adamant as to his own views. Griffin was more knowledgeable in a breadth of materials. Phillips was quiet but soon was familiar with all the sherds that they had collected.

Nonetheless the trio was able to make a preliminary sorting of the 1940 materials in Baton Rouge. They sorted the sherds by temper and decoration into 47 types and indicated that all these types were not "new" (p. 66). Ultimately Griffin and Phillips had the most direct command of the raw data; Griffin logged the type descriptions with Phillips's help. There is a short typewritten draft of the types in the LMS archives at the Peabody that has Griffin's easily recognizable handwriting penciling in corrections. Later on, all the "saved" sherds (many plain ware sherds were "tossed" without sorting in the first few seasons) were finally moved to the Peabody Museum, where Phillips, with the aid of Mary Slusher, did the rest of the analysis and counting. Thus, all the final sherd counts were his.

Although most readers will find the nearly 100 pages of pottery type descriptions rather laborious, Phillips was not without a sense of humor, and there is indeed a joke hidden in the description of one type. Long ago he told me about it but not where it was buried. Some years later, I found it on page 146, at the bottom of the first column: "three lugs (Ford, Phillips, and Griffin)." That discovery won me a beautiful leather-bound copy of this volume, which I still cherish. I also have Phillips's "working copy," which contains some minor text corrections.

The immense amount of labor that Phillips had put into the classification of the ceramics and their meaning was not soon forgotten. In his next great synthesis of lower-valley archaeology, the 1970 two-volume treatise focusing on the Lower Yazoo area, he also tackled a great number of sherds. This task reminded him of the LMS sherd-sorting experience two decades before. In these books, he makes it clear that he was disappointed with the treatment of the earlier sherds.

Phillips and his helper produced the sherd counts at the Peabody, and then Ford turned them into seriation charts at the American Museum of Natural History in New York. For Ford the counts were everything: "don't bother to look at the sherds again." Phillips, working in the late 1960s, felt much more comfortable to keep looking over the sherd data at hand, repeatedly if necessary: "The results [of the ceramic analysis] will, I hope come somewhat closer than did those in 1950 to reflecting cultural and chronological relationships in a world as real, if not as complex, as our own" (Phillips 1970:247). I think he was right.

Section IV: Distribution of Some Mississippi Period Vessel Shapes and Features (Griffin)

This chapter was primarily based on a 1930s survey of major eastern museums that Phillips created of more than 2,000 vessels from the survey area. Phillips actually photographed more than 4,000 vessels during this research project at a number of museums (listed on page 180). All the documentation resides in the LMS archives at the Harvard Peabody Museum.

Griffin's careful contribution discusses the major vessel shapes and their distribution and significance. The chapter is full of detailed analysis and comparisons that have been perhaps passed over by most readers. There is, for instance, an important and data-rich paragraph (pp. 177–179) on engraved pottery and the design distributions that bears rereading for evidence of Southern Cult connections across the Southeast. There is also a useful digression (pp. 173–177) on "Negative Painting in the Eastern United States" that has been cited more often. Tables 2 through 10 are also data rich for the inquiring researcher.

Section V: Seriation Analysis of Pottery Collections (Ford)

This chapter is Ford's gut-wrenching construction, and it was his greatest contribution to the project. Interestingly, O'Brien and Lyman (1998:194–197) have discussed this chapter, but they do not stress Ford's authorship of this segment, using the plurals "they" and "their" instead of "he" and "his." Most past readers have known for certain whose intellectual property the seriation charts were. As already noted, Ford actually did little of the fieldwork. It was also the most controversial part of the whole operation for the three scholars involved (see p. 219, paragraphs 1 and 2). There were serious and contentious arguments between them, some of which "bubble up" in the text. The section was just 17 pages in length, with a map of the area and the five seriation graphs set in. There exists a good picture of Ford's actual method of operation in creating these seriation tables; it is a piece of artwork executed by Ford himself showing the strips of paper held in place by numerous paper clips (Ford 1962).

However, before discussing the results of the seriation analysis, it must be made clear this chapter's necessity and the difficulty Phillips and Griffin had in accepting it. To put the debate in context, one must realize that there were no "absolute" dating methods available to eastern archaeology at this time. Carbon 14 dating, however, was just around the corner; Griffin would publish a number of such dates in 1952 in an appendix (Griffin 1952a:365–370). On the other hand, tree-ring dating in the American Southwest had, for many decades, given that area a great advantage in chronology (1920–1950).

The basic difference among Ford, Phillips, and Griffin was their views on the nature of cultural change. Ford was adamant: change took place slowly and with no sharp breaks in the continuity of cultures. The seriation charts were arranged to show that result over and over. Phillips and Griffin were not so sure. They felt there could be discontinuity that was obscured by mixing of deposits, and they thought that some of the stratigraphic data showed just that. Ford also strongly believed that there were not major gaps in the sequence. This was an argument that their data, unfortunately, could not yet solve, as we shall see in the Stratigraphy section.

This chapter starts out with the "basic assumptions" about the culture history of the area. First, (A) Ford felt that the sequence was based on an agricultural economy, that the region was well populated (as it is today), and that "these Indians did not wander" (p. 219). Second, (B) he assumed that most of the sites were occupied for "a short time in proportion to the entire chronology" (p. 219). But there were few single-component sites and finding them was "an unattainable goal" (p. 220). The third assumption (C) was that there was cultural continuity and no "abrupt cultural or population change" (p. 220). The fourth assumption (D) was that the ceramic types were "a more or less sensitive instrument for measuring culture change," but not all types were "equally well adapted for this purpose" (p. 220). The fifth assumption (E) was that pottery types had, as a logical derivative of the above, a "single-peak curve" when graphed through time (p. 220). Ford admits that these lovely curves were partly created by the way the types were defined (p. 221). I like to think of this situation in terms of a recreated scene at the site where the lucky archaeologist just so happens to get a sherd from the very first pot made of this type. Then later, very fortunately, he also gets a sherd from the last pot of this variety that was created too.

The sixth in Ford's list of assumptions (F) is self-created (not derived directly from real historic data) and shows up in Figure 15—his well-known seriation chart of "transportation types in Ohio" for the period of A.D. 1800 to 1940 (see his footnote 2, p. 221). Now Ford clearly indicates that this is a "rather far-fetched bit of imaginary analysis" (p. 222), but surely many recent authors have failed to let the innocent reader know that this is the case. Not too surprisingly this created graph shows exactly the kind of cultural change that Ford felt he regularly saw in the ceramic history.

The last of these assumptions (G) is simple: first, that the sampling of sites was adequate and, second, that pottery samples alone will cover all the sequence without any major time gaps. With regard to sample size, they considered 50 sherds adequate, although 100 or more was much better (these assumptions cover pages 219–223).

The facts are, as one looks at the data as we know them today, that many of these assumptions—though clearly needed at the time—are grossly oversimplified for the more complex culture histories that we can write today. In the 1950s, however, guesswork was often a part of eastern archaeological research. Far from being foolhardy or dumb, many of these assumptions were necessary for that time and locality.

Recently, there have been some continued attempts to use ceramic seriation, much in the manner of Ford. Perhaps those archaeologists have not lately read all of Ford's assumptions, or they would realize that many of them are untenable today. As I write this, I wonder how many of the volume's previous readers read the entirety of these paragraphs of assumptions. I confess I don't recall any such sustained effort on my own part.

It may be that discussing an analytical method of chronology is no longer viable in the twenty-first century. The major argument among the writers of this volume was about the nature of cultural change: was it a continuing flow (as Ford believed) or were there starts and stops that could be "seen" through the stratigraphic analysis of test-pit excavations (as Phillips and Griffin believed)? At the time, there were no "real" dates to append to these chronologies—they were all "guesstimates."

Section VI: Stratigraphy (Phillips)

Phillips took responsibility for this section, having personally directed most of the excavations. They amounted to some seventeen test pits ("cuts" in Phillips's terminology) at nine sites (p. 241) ranging from the Rose Mound in northeastern Arkansas to the Jaketown site in the Yazoo Delta (Table I-2). I must point out again that Phillips had the least experience in such work, but he was the one who carried out most of the excavations in this survey.

One of the interesting aspects of Phillips's stratigraphic work (including the Ouachita and the lower valley) is that it employed the metric system. His use of that measurement system in this region was preceded only by Charles Peabody and Warren K. Moorehead, who used it in their work at a cave in western Missouri at the turn of the century (Peabody and Moorehead 1904). Peabody had earlier used the English system when working for Frederic Putnam at the Oliver site, but by 1910 Peabody was using the metric system in all of his excavations in New England and in North Carolina (Peabody 1910).

The Chicago method for stratigraphy required using the English measurements of feet and inches, as had the Smithsonian. So, both Griffin, from his graduate years at Chicago, and Ford, from his experience with Henry Collins, were wedded to feet and inches. I had started out entirely with feet and inches in all my earlier field experience (Minnesota and Arizona) and in doing my research in southeastern Missouri, where I did my first test pits in 1950 for Griffin with English measurements. When I went to Harvard in 1954, I immediately changed to the metric system—thanks to Phillips—but I confess not to have thought hard about it at that time. Why meters for Phillips? I don't know. It wasn't the system Putnam had used in all his many Peabody excavations. I wish I had asked my old colleagues about this situation.

A chart (Table I-2) shows where Phillips, Ford, and Griffin concentrated test pits to sample the stratigraphic history of the survey region. Phillips and Griffin, who were aided by the aforementioned Harvard graduate students Davis and Chard, did most of this work, which was done in the spring of 1941. They completed a total of 17 test pits at 9 different sites. Six of the sites (Walls, Lake Cormorant, Oliver, Alligator, Jaketown, and Shell Bluff) were in the northern part of the Yazoo Basin in Mississippi. Two others (Menard and Massey) were across the Mississippi River in Arkansas, just north of the Arkansas River. The final site tested (1947) was the Rose Mound in northeastern Arkansas. They began a small number of other cuts on these same sites but they abandoned them for lack of substantial data.

The original text does not discuss those responsible for the actual digging of the test pits. It carefully names the supervisors of each excavation; indeed one could almost intuit that *they* were

Table I-2
Sites Excavated by Philip Phillips, James B. Griffin, Mott Davis, Chester Chard, and Paul Gebhard

Sites	Crew	Test Pits
	1941	
1. Walls (13P1)	Phillips, Griffin, Davis, Chard	2 cuts
2. Lake Cormorant (13P8)	Griffin and Chard	2 cuts
3. Oliver (16N6)	Phillips and Chard	3 cuts
4. Alligator (11N2)	Griffin and Davis	2 cuts
5. Menard (17K1)	Phillips and Davis	2 cuts
6. Massey (17L1)	Phillips and Davis	2 cuts
	1946	
7. Jaketown (20O1)	Phillips and Gebhard	2 cuts
8. Shell Bluff (19O2)	Phillips and Gebhard	1 cut
	1947	
9. Rose Mound (12N3)	Phillips	1 cut

the ones shoveling the dirt, but that is certainly not the case. The Lower Mississippi survey regularly used paid farmhands in all its major excavations. Phillips started that practice with his first 1939 excavations in the Ouachita valley. The text describes the methods quite clearly: "It was found that one shovel hand could keep two to four men busy at the screens, but constant supervision was required to maintain accuracy of level. With such a crew, two or three working days were sufficient for the completion of a cut" (p. 241). Phillips's carefully recorded photographs of his own work at the Rose Mound in April 1947 show these excavation techniques (Figure 75). The dig hands were sharecroppers, and they were always delighted for an opportunity to earn cash.

Phillips, Ford, and Griffin carefully selected these sites for stratigraphy hoping they would explain the cultural succession in the history of the lower valley. Although Phillips clearly recognizes the benefit of digging in cultural units based on stratigraphy, he clearly states that he felt the only way to dig these test pits was based on "metrical stratigraphy." From later analysis, when the pit was completed, then one could "see" the cultural stratigraphy. While Phillips's style of test-pit digging may seem counterintuitive, he provides justification on page 242 in the text. I cannot take the reader through all these excavations, but suffice it to say that they were carefully excavated. Phillips also restates the problem of slow change versus replacement at the end of the chapter (p. 292). He cries out for an absolute chronology "to scale the charts." Amazingly, he did know that such a thing was only a few years ahead, as he mentions carbon 14 dating (p. 306).

Section VII: Correlation of Archaeological Sequences with Recent Drainage History (Phillips)

Phillips also wrote this chapter, and it shows how clearly he recognized that every known dating method should be considered in answering the basic chronological problems of the region. It is a short chapter—only 12 pages long—but shows the importance of physiographic data from the old river channels. This was not the first use of Mississippi River channels for dating sites, as is noted herein (Kniffen 1936a). However, it kept alive these complex geomorphological questions, which are still very much a part of archaeological investigations in the lower valley today.

Section VIII: Analysis of Occupation Site Plans (Ford)

Ford wrote this chapter directly after his work in Peru's Viru valley in 1946, and it follows the settlement-pattern method. The basic fieldwork for this whole volume was not finished until 1947, so there was plenty of time for Ford to complete this chapter before it went to press. The chapter is hardly a "tour de force," but I must also confess I do not know if this chapter has ever been widely used.

It is a short presentation of only 35 pages, more than twenty of which are given over to either full-page maps or tables. The conclusions are tentative since this group of settlement data is weakened by the lack of good site dating, although I would argue that most of the sites are generally allocated to the approximately correct time period. Even this statement must be accepted with some care, as one can also point out that most of the sites were multicomponent, covering a considerable time range. Perhaps the most useful part of the chapter (pp. 340–343) is the listing of the distinctive "St. Francis–type" sites, presented for the first time here (Figure 63).

Unfortunately, it is impossible from information in the text to assign a name to the artist who created the site maps used in this chapter. Although not widely known, both Ford and Phillips were rather good artists. Ford, as a student at LSU, drew many of the illustrations for his own publications and for the volume of his former professor, Fred Kniffen (1936b), *Louisiana House Types*. Phillips's own work in architecture brought out this artistic talent too; he did some lovely pencil sketches of structures in Europe (LMS Archive, Peabody Museum). Almost all the early LMS site records have careful maps drawn by Phillips (see Figure 3, this volume). In many cases (as in Phillips 1970:577, Figures 250–251), the actually published site maps were but cleaned-up versions of his drawings. My guess is that Phillips created the maps, but I could be wrong.

Section IX: Identification of Sites from Documentary Sources (Phillips)

Phillips, again, wrote this chapter, and it is an impressive, major contribution. Phillips, however, was not convinced of its grandeur (p. 347). He apologized for the limited coverage of the ethnography of the valley; fifty years later, though, we still realize how difficult that subject is. The historical discussion of the Spanish and French documents shows Phillips's mastery of that literature. Rereading it, I wondered how many of the current DeSoto scholars have read his take on that explorer. I am happy to report that Frank Schambach (personal communication, 2002) relates much recent use of this section and confirmation of Phillips's Arkansas views on the DeSoto trips. Also, Patricia K. Galloway, writing as recently as 1996, has lauded this chapter by Phillips as "the first coherent expression of the new attitude" toward "elucidating the ethnic genealogies of the historic tribes" (Galloway n.d.:226).

Another well-known scholar on this topic was, of course, the Smithsonian Institution's John R. Swanton. Swanton was trained at Harvard, and I know that Phillips felt that he might be helpful. However, when Phillips (prior to 1950) personally saw Swanton in Washington, D.C., and discussed Swanton's well-known 1939 DeSoto report, Swanton was very short with him and did not support Phillips's ideas at all. Knowing that, one can understand why Phillips (e.g., p. 367) was comfortable voicing opinions contradictory to Swanton's views. Regardless of how much we know now about "late times in the valley"—and it is quite a lot (Mainfort 2001; Williams 2001)—readers of this volume should look over Phillips's long last paragraph in this chapter (pp. 420–421). There are causalities suggested therein that readers would find both interesting and enlightening.

Section X: Summary and Conclusions (Phillips, Ford, and Griffin)

Calling this chapter data laden would be a great understatement. Indeed, in that respect, one can only compare it with Griffin's 1946 solo publication, "Cultural Change and Continuity in Eastern North American Archaeology," for comparable thoroughness. Where else can one find such detailed references to sherds, artifacts, and site data? Pottery types are treated like old friends, turning up where they are most needed for important linkages. In this section, Griffin and Phillips rehash their argument with Ford about the meaning of "mixed" pottery collections and their concern for typology growth: could "type-varieties" be far away? They also bring up carbon 14 dating again (p. 428) as a possible solution to "absolute dating."

Griffin stated that this section of the volume was written when "we finally got together in Phillips's apartment in Cambridge, Massachusetts, for a week in late August 1949 and wrote the concluding chapter" (Griffin 1999:644). Despite the recognized differences between the joint authors that I have already discussed, Griffin indicated that "there was no decline in mutual respect" (1999:645).

The Summary by Periods is the meat of the text; herein the alphabetical periods A–G actually receive names for the first time in the volume. They range from the "Pre-ceramic period" (before G) to "Late Mississippian Period (B–A)." As quaint as this terminology may seem today, it is somewhat surprising to find it used only in the last chapter. Throughout the remainder of the volume, the reader has been only helped by time designations such as "G–H," with no further help in translation. The power of Ford's ceramic seriation was allowed to "manage" the chronology in that manner from the start of the monograph to its end.

Surely some of that angst comes out especially in this last chapter, where finally Griffin can use cultural words such as "Archaic" (p. 421–431) and even "Woodland pottery" (p. 432). One of the extraordinary things represented in this chapter is the lack of knowledge about the Poverty Point Mounds. The culture is discussed (p. 429–431) but nowhere in the site plan section (p. 310–311) is there a suggestion that there could be preceramic mounds. I, too, lived through that period of ignorance about Archaic cultures, before Clovis and Dalton points revealed Paleoindian data for the lower valley. That must seem quite quaint to all the younger readers of this volume, but Ed Scully, my Michigan colleague, and I saw both of these projectile points in southeastern Missouri collections in 1950–1951, just prior to the publication of this work. Ford would start his own Dalton project not too much later in 1961–1962.

After the lengthy discussion of the sequence of cultures in the Lower Mississippi valley (p. 429–451), they write about some much shorter topics. The first concerns the "Origin of Mississippi Culture in the Survey Area" (p. 451–454), where they assert that the Mississippian culture was not begun in the lower valley. A similar conclusion was recently affirmed at a Mid-South Conference held in Memphis in June 2001, with 100 percent agreement among the attendants (McNutt and

Williams 2002). Some of their other opinions, such as their ideas about the impact of other cultures from outside the lower valley, might be met with more skepticism (pp. 452–454). But, like all of this volume, these suggestions must be judged on the data available at that time.

Their next major topic was Chronological Alignments, Cultural and Calendrical. Table 17, on estimates of chronology, shows a lengthening of the ceramic sequence from Tchefuncte to Natchez, from a first estimate of 500 years to their own view of nearly 2,000 years. Even that timeline was much too short, of course. Carbon 14 dating is again mentioned, and the authors of this section (probably mainly Phillips) say with some humor that "We stand before the threat of the atom in the form of C14 dating. This may be our last opportunity for old-fashioned uncontrolled guessing" (p. 455).

The last segment of this large volume is entitled The Pattern of Eastern Prehistory (p. 455–457). Phillips, Ford, and Griffin certainly weren't afraid to tackle large and important topics. Indeed, one of the reasons for reprinting this volume is so that young scholars can read the perspectives of some of the "elders" of southeastern archaeology and learn how they approached the field's major questions. In these last pages, they deal with a pair of cultural climaxes. They compare and contrast Hopewell and Mississippian cultures as they then knew them. Unfortunately, they put much too much weight on external impact from Mesoamerica for these developments, as we have learned in the past 50 years.

With the aid of a much longer temporal sequence than any of them could have then imagined at the time, both Phillips and Griffin soon retreated from such foreign cultural contacts. Ford, however, heartily believed in the idea of distant contacts for the next decade and a half, and he wrote a tale of such foreign impact just before he died. In the 1960s, I received a strong letter from Ford urging me, in an almost evangelical tone, to join the gang of seekers for such distant ties. I demurred. Each of us finds a different way to deal with the past, I guess.

However, there is one final bit of "housecleaning" to complete before I end this review of the Lower Mississippi valley survey volume, which has to do with the "missing chapter" left out of your copy. Ford wrote it, and presumably it was to have been placed right before or after his Section VIII on Settlement Patterns. The title was Measurements of Some Prehistoric Design Developments in the Southeastern States. For a recent commentary on this piece of writing, see *James A. Ford and the Growth of Americanist Archaeology* by O'Brien and Lyman (1998:215–231). Although these authors assert that they know why this chapter was left out of the lower-valley survey volume (p. 251), I suggest that neither Ford's statements that "it needed some re-working" nor that "Griffin objected to it in both detail and principle" (Ford 1952:313) hardly gives the situation a fair hearing.

The facts are that both Phillips and Griffin felt uncomfortable with the chapter as it was presented to them. In personal conversations with me, they called it "through the Southeast with inkpot and slide rule." I do not think that an original copy of the Ford manuscript exists now. However, from my discussions with Phillips and Griffin, I can say with some confidence that both of them felt that the chapter went far beyond the available data by presenting detailed design connections over a broad expanse of space and time. They felt it fallible, and they did not want to be associated with such a chapter (see Griffin, quoted in Brown 1978:19, as cited in Belmont and Williams 1981:19). Ford therefore published the chapter as a separate monograph (Ford 1952).

John S. Belmont and I wrote another commentary on this same volume wherein we characterized it as a "bold attempt to cross-correlate Southeastern ceramic complexes" (1981:19). Although I never discussed this specific piece of writing with Ford, I do know how willingly he accepted a specific hypothesis and vigorously held onto it despite in-the-ground data to the contrary (Ford 1969).

For example, I was riding across country in the 1960s with Ford and told him about the recent fieldwork of the LMS in northeastern Louisiana, specifically, the Upper Tensas region. We had worked at a site that Ford personally knew well. There we had found in good stratigraphic position what I said was "early Coles Creek," something we had been seeking for a long time. Ford never saw the sherds but turned to me and said positively: "No, you haven't, Steve; early Coles Creek is to be found out in east Texas." That was the end of that discussion.

This volume, as printed, contains a data-rich encyclopedia of lower-valley archaeology that still deserves more mining. Though many decades old, the information of sites, excavations, pottery types, and comparative analysis—not to mention bibliographic data "in extenso"—make it a good read, worthy of the reader's careful attention.

Indeed this large tome has been an important source for many scholars throughout this half century. A quick survey of more than a dozen volumes on southeastern archaeology indicated its citation in ten of those volumes, including Judith A. Bense's (1994:33) interesting summary of that area and numerous references in the more recent collection by Shannon Tushingham, Jane Hill, and Charles McNutt (2002). It has also been cited in volumes of broader coverage of American archaeological history such as James A. Fitting's edited volume (1973:142) and Gordon R. Willey and Jeremy A. Sabloff's *A History of American Archaeology* (1993:185). Thus, one must conclude that it remains a classic piece of research of high value.

CODA

I think that the Lower Mississippi valley survey was a transcendental event for all three of the participants, and some of these feelings are captured in these pictures of Phillips, Ford, and Griffin. I don't ever recall talking to Ford directly about this project, but Griffin remembered clearly all his life the many events in the Yazoo Delta and elsewhere, including meeting some extraordinary southern women. One of Phillips's most memorable times was when he and Griffin drove to Oxford, Mississippi, and spent an afternoon with Calvin Brown, the only other twentieth-century archaeologist who had written extensively on the Yazoo Delta (Brown 1926). In the Peabody reprint of Brown's volume, Phillips mentions that event briefly (1973:xix).

Phillips and Ford continued their collaboration after 1951 with their Jaketown excavations, and Griffin maintained his interest in the lower valley, contrary to O'Brien and Lyman, who seem to think that the latter "drifted off to the north" (1998:204). Around the same time, 1950–1952, Griffin placed Ed Scully and myself in southeastern Missouri with the intent to extend their lower-valley survey north of the region that they had covered in this volume. In 1953, Phillips and Griffin also monetarily supported my own work on the Hampson Collection in northeastern Arkansas. The Powers Phase project (Price 1973; Price and Griffin 1979) and Griffin's continued

Figure I-4. Ford plowing a long furrow in northeastern Arkansas, spring 1940. (LMS Archives, Peabody Museum)

Figure I-5. Griffin resting in the late afternoon at the Vernon Paul site in northeastern Arkansas, April 1, 1940. (LMS Archives, Peabody Museum)

Figure I-6. Phillips, some years later in his study in Bolton, Massachusetts. Phillips took all the field pictures so he appears in none of them. (LMS Archives, Peabody Museum)

encouragement of his students in the Southeast are ample evidence that he did not simply "drift off to the north." Phillips and Griffin remained close friends, intellectually and personally, all their long lives.

As a result of the lower-valley survey, there was a special kind of relationship among these three men. Ford was never one to write about people often, but both Phillips, in an obituary for Ford, and Griffin, in a biographical chapter on Ford, wrote specifically about Ford in the setting of the lower valley. Phillips compared Ford to an undaunted lower valley "Faulkner-like" character (Phillips 1968), and Griffin related how he learned from Ford how to approach a sharecropper's home (Griffin 1999:649). They all certainly cared about each other.

For more than 50 years, I have frequently visited the Lower Mississippi valley from Cape Girardeau, Missouri, to the Gulf of Mexico, and I empathize with their strong feelings for this wondrous piece of American landscape. Its archaeology, history, landscape, and inhabitants, both past and present, make it a special place indeed. Today, a half century after its publication, Phillips, Ford and Griffin's field survey of this region still stands as an extraordinary attempt to steer Lower Mississippi valley archaeology in a new direction. This volume is a monument to that effort and its ultimate success.

Acknowledgments. I am grateful for the wisdom and help provided by James Stoltman, Charles McNutt, and Lewis Larson, who did me the great service of reading this manuscript for the University of Alabama Press and commenting on it in great detail. I am in their debt for their careful review and their numerous and helpful suggestions. I have considered their advice with great interest and accepted *almost* all of it.

They were not alone in helping me refine the text of this introduction. First, I must thank Greg Finnegan of the Tozzer Library for his wonderful long-distance help on sources and citations; in this last decade he has continually been a great and careful friendly scholar of wonderful bibliographic information who always goes the extra mile. Also, my old friend and colleague Hester Davis of the Arkansas Archeological Survey has provided me with essential biographical data on some of the LMS graduate student workers, including her late brother Mott Davis and the enigmatic Fisher Motz and the proper citation for Phillips's rarely cited obit on Ford.

Also, as has been my intellectual policy since leaving the sheltered province of the Peabody Museum, I have called on a large number of my archaeological friends for helpful comments on this introduction as well. Those who responded with careful, and often lengthy, thoughts on this manuscript include John S. Belmont, David

Browman, Jeff Mitchem, Marvin Jeter, Frank Schambach, Pat Galloway, Sayre Sheldon, Greg Finnegan, and Ian Brown. I am most grateful for all their suggestions and corrections. I have been greatly aided by them. Thank you all. I am especially thankful to Virgil R. "Duke" Beasley for unselfishly allowing the Press to use his original edition of this volume for the facsimile reprint.

Some of the helpful manuscript readers for the press have suggested that I have written more on Phillips than the other two authors. I confess that such a statement is true, as I have stated in the text. I have done so purposely, since both Ford and Griffin, who have received the larger amount of lineage in the archaeological literature, are much better known to most readers. (For Ford, see Brown 1978; Griffin 1999; O'Brien and Lyman 1998, 1999. For Griffin, see Williams 1976, 1999; and two Festschrifts, Cleland 1976, 1977.) Phillips, on the other hand, has received much less attention. There are only two short obituaries (Willey 1995; Williams 1995), and a small Peabody-published LMS volume (Williams and Brain 1970), plus a birthday present (Williams 1990).

REFERENCES

Atwell, K. A., and M. D. Conner (editors)
1991 *The Kuhlman Mound Group and Woodland Mortuary Behavior.* Kampsville Archaeological Center Research Series No. 9. Center for American Archaeology, Kampsville, Illinois.

Belmont, J. S., and S. Williams
1981 Painted Pottery Horizons in the Southern Mississippi Valley. In Traces of Prehistory: Papers in Honor of William G. Haag. Geoscience and Man 22, edited by F. H. West and R. W. Neuman, pp. 19–42. Geoscience Publications, Department of Geography and Anthropology, Louisiana State University, Baton Rouge.

Bense, J. A.
1994 *Archaeology of the Southeastern United States.* Academic Press, San Diego.

Brose, D. S., C. W. Cowan, and R. C. Mainfort, Jr. (editors)
2001 *Societies in Eclipse: Archaeology of the Eastern Woodlands Indians,* A.D. *1400–1700.* Smithsonian Institution Press, Washington, D.C.

Brown, C. S.
1973 *Archaeology of Mississippi.* Reprinted in *Antiquities of the New World,* vol. 16, AMS Press for the Peabody Museum, Cambridge, Massachusetts. Originally published 1926, Mississippi Geological Survey.

Brown, I. W.
1978 "James Alfred Ford: The Man and His Works." Southeastern Archaeological Conference, Special Publication No. 4.

Chambers, M. B. C.
1976 An Interview with Moreau Browne Congleton Chambers, June 8–14, 1976. Manuscript on file, courtesy of Mississippi Department of Archives and History, Jackson.

Cleland, C. E. (editor)
1976 *Culture Change and Continuity: Essays in Honor of James Bennett Griffin.* Academic Press, New York.
1977 *For the Director: Research Essays in Honor of James B. Griffin.* Anthropological Papers 61. Museum of Anthropology, University of Michigan, Ann Arbor.

Collins, H. B.
1932 Excavations at a Prehistoric Indian Village Site in Mississippi. *United States National Museum, Proceedings* 79(32):1–22.

Davis, H.
2002 Biographic data on Mott Davis and Fisher Motz. Personal communication and obituaries, June 16, 2002.

Dunnell, R.
1985 Archaeological Survey in the Lower Mississippi Alluvial Valley, 1940–1947: A Landmark Study in American Archaeology. American Antiquity 50:297–300

Elliot, M.
1995 *Great Excavations: Tales of Early Southwestern Archaeology, 1888–1939.* School of American Research Press, Santa Fe, New Mexico.

Fitting, J. E. (editor)
1973 *The Development of North American Archaeology.* Doubleday Press, New York.

Ford, J. A.
1936 Analysis of Indian Site Collections from Louisiana and Mississippi. Anthropological Study No. 2. Department of Conservation, Louisiana Geological Survey.
1952 Measurements of Some Prehistoric Design Developments in the Southeastern States. Anthropological Papers 44, No. 3. American Museum of Natural History.
1962 A Quantitative Method for Deriving Cultural Chronology. Pan-American Union, Technical Manual No. 1. Washington, D.C.

1969 A Comparison of Formative Cultures in the Americas: Diffusion or the Psychic Unity of Man? *Smithsonian Contributions to Anthropology* 11. Smithsonian Institution, Washington, D.C.

Ford, J. A., P. Phillips, and W. G. Haag

1955 The Jaketown Site in West-Central Mississippi. Anthropological Papers 45, no.1. American Museum of Natural History.

Galloway, P. K.

2000 Archaeology from the Archives: the Chambers Excavations at Lyons Bluff, 1934–35. *Mississippi Archaeology*, 35(1):23–90.

n.d. "Historic Tribes in Contact with Europeans." In unedited version of the State Historical Context Document for 1997, 1998, 1999, coordinated by R. J. Cawthorn, pp. 225–238. Mississippi Department of Archives and History, Jackson.

Gebhard, P.

2002 Letter to Stephen Williams, July 13.

Griffin, J. B. (editor)

1952 *Archeology of Eastern United States.* University of Chicago Press, Chicago.

Griffin, J. B.

1952a Appendix: Radiocarbon Dates for the Eastern United States." In *Archeology of Eastern United States, edited by J. B. Griffin*, pp. 365–370. University of Chicago Press, Chicago.

1985 An Individual's Participation in American Archaeology, 1928–1985. *Annual Review of Anthropology*, 14:1–23.

1991 Appendix 3: The Parker Heights Mound at Quincy, Illinois. In *The Kuhlman Mound Group and Woodland Mortuary Behavior.* Kampsville Archaeological Center Research Series No. 9, edited by K. A. Atwell and M. D. Conner, pp. 276–291. Center for American Archaeology, Kampsville, Illinois.

1999 James Alfred Ford. In *Encyclopedia of Archaeology: The Great Archaeologists*, vol. 2, edited by T. Murray, pp. 635–651. ABC-CLIO, Santa Barbara, California.

Haag, W. G.

1953a Review of *Archaeological Survey in the Lower Mississippi Alluvial Valley, 1940–1947*, by P. Phillips, J. A. Ford, and J. B. Griffin. American Anthropologist 55:118–119.

1953b Review of *Archaeological Survey in the Lower Mississippi Alluvial Valley, 1940–1947*, by P. Phillips, J. A. Ford, and J. B. Griffin. American Antiquity 18:275–277.

Hally, D. J. (editor)

1994 *Ocmulgee Archaeology: 1936–1986.* University of Georgia Press, Athens.

Kniffen, F. B.

1936a A Preliminary Report of the Mounds and Middens of Plaquemines and St. Bernard Parishes, Lower Mississippi River Delta. Geological Bulletin 8:407–422. Louisiana Department of Conservation.

1936b Louisiana House Types. *Annals of the Association of American Geographers* 36(4):179–193.

Mainfort, R. C., Jr.

2001 The Late Prehistoric and Protohistoric Periods in the Central Mississippi Valley. In *Societies in Eclipse: Archaeology of the Eastern Woodlands Indians, A.D. 1400–1700 A.D.*, edited by D. S. Brose, C. W. Cowan, and R. C. Mainfort, pp. 173–189. Smithsonian Institution Press, Washington, D.C.

McNutt, C., and S. Williams (editors)

2002 The Origins of Mississippian Culture. Proceedings of Mid-South Conference, June 2–4, 2001, Memphis, Tennessee.

Murray, T. (editor)

1999 *Encyclopedia of Archaeology: The Great Archaeologists.* 2 vols. ABC-CLIO, Santa Barbara, California.

O'Brien, M. J., and R. L. Lyman

1998 *James A. Ford and the Growth of Americanist Archaeology.* University of Missouri Press, Columbia.

O'Brien, M. J., and R. L. Lyman (editors)

1999 *Measuring the Flow of Time: The Works of James A. Ford, 1935–41.* University of Alabama Press, Tuscaloosa.

2001 *Setting the Agenda for American Archaeology: The National Research Council Archaeological Conferences: 1929, 1932, and 1935.* Classics in Southeastern Archaeology, S. Williams, general editor. University of Alabama Press, Tuscaloosa.

Peabody, C.

1904 Exploration of Mounds, Coahoma County, Mississippi. Peabody Museum Papers vol. 3, no. 2. Harvard University.

1910 The Explorations of Mounds in North Carolina. *American Anthropologist* 12(3):425–433.

Peabody, C., and W. K. Moorehead

1904 The Exploration of Jacobs Cavern. Bulletin No. 1. Department of Archaeology, Phillips Academy.

Phillips, P.

1939 Introduction to the Archaeology of the Mississippi Valley. Ph.D. dissertation, Department of Archaeology, Harvard University, Cambridge.

1955 Alfred Marsten Tozzer (1877–1954). *American Antiquity* 21(1):72–80.

1968 Obituary of James A. Ford. *Teocentli* 72 (October):3.

1970 Archaeological Survey in the Lower Yazoo Basin: 1949–1955. 2 vols. Peabody Museum Papers, Harvard University.

1973 Introduction to *Archaeology of Mississippi*. Reprinted in *Antiquities of the New World*, vol. 16, by C. S. Brown, pp. xvii–xx. AMS Press for the Peabody Museum, Cambridge, Massachusetts.

Price, J. E.

1973 Settlement Planning and Artifact Distribution on the Snodgrass Site and their Sociopolitical Implications in the Powers Phase in Southeast Missouri. Ph.D dissertation, Department of Anthropology, University of Michigan, Ann Arbor.

Price, J. E., and J. B. Griffin

1979 The Snodgrass Site of the Powers Phase of Southeast Missouri. Anthropological Papers No. 66. University of Michigan, Ann Arbor Museum of Anthropology.

Saucier, R. T.

1994 *Geomorphology and Quaternary Geologic History of the Lower Mississippi Valley*. 2 vols. U.S. Army Engineer Waterways Experiment Station, Vicksburg, Mississippi.

Schambach, F. F.

1998 Pre-Caddoan Cultures in the Trans-Mississippi South. Research Series 53, Arkansas Archeological Survey.

Tushingham, S., J. Hill, and C. H. McNutt (editors)

2002 *Histories of Southeastern Archaeology*. University of Alabama Press, Tuscaloosa.

Walker, J. W.

1994 A Brief History of Ocmulgee Archaeology: 1936–1986. In *Ocmulgee Archaeology: 1936–1986*, by D. J. Hally, pp. 15–35. University of Georgia Press, Athens.

West, F. H., and R. W. Neuman (editors)

1981 *Traces of Prehistory: Papers in Honor of William G. Haag*. Geoscience and Man 22. Geoscience Publications, Department of Geography and Anthropology, Louisiana State University, Baton Rouge.

Willey, G. R.

1969 James Alfred Ford, 1911–1968. *American Antiquity* 34:62–71.

1995 Philip Phillips Obituary. *Symbols* (spring):26, Peabody Museum, Harvard University, Cambridge.

1999 Foreword. In *Measuring the Flow of Time: The Works of James A. Ford, 1935–41*, edited by M. J. O'Brien and R. L. Lyman, pp. vii–xvi. University of Alabama Press, Tuscaloosa.

Willey, G. R., and J. A. Sabloff

1993 *A History of American Archaeology*. 3rd ed. W. H. Freeman, New York.

Williams, S.

1952 Review of *Archaeological Survey in the Lower Mississippi Alluvial Valley, 1940–1947*, by P. Phillips, J. A. Ford, and J. B. Griffin. Archaeology 5(2):124.

1960 A Brief History of the Southeastern Archaeological Conference. *Southeastern Archaeological Conference Newsletter* 7(1):2–4.

1970 The Long Furrow: A Collection of the Writings of James A. Ford. Manuscript on file at the Peabody Museum, Harvard University, Cambridge.

1986 "Some Reflections on the Long, Happy and Eventful Life of Robert Stuart Neitzel" *Southeastern Archaeological Conference Bulletin* 24:7–9.

1990 For Phil at Ninety. Handwritten document.

1991 *Fantastic Archaeology: The Wild Side of North American Prehistory*. University of Pennsylvania Press, Philadelphia.

1994 The Ocmulgee Investigations in Historical Perspective. In *Ocmulgee Archaeology: 1936–1986*, by D. J. Hally, pp. 8–14. University of Georgia Press, Athens.

1995 Philip Phillips Obituary. *Anthropology News* (February).

1999 James B. Griffin. In *Encyclopedia of Archaeology: The Great Archaeologists*, by T. Murray, vol. 1, pp. 451–459. ABC-CLIO, Santa Barbara, California.

2001a William G. Haag. *Anthropology News* (February):26–27.

2001b The Vacant Quarter and the Yazoo Delta. In *Societies in Eclipse: Archaeology of the Eastern Woodlands Indians, A.D. 1400–1700*, edited by D. S. Brose, C. W. Cowan, and R. C. Mainfort, pp. 191–203. Smithsonian Institution Press, Washington, D.C.

2002 The Life and Times of William G. Haag. Keynote address at Haag Symposium, March 7–9, 2002, Louisiana State University, Baton Rouge.

Williams, S., and J. P. Brain

1971 Philip Phillips: Lower Mississippi Survey

(1940–1970). Privately printed. Peabody Museum, Harvard University, Cambridge.

Williams, S., and W. G. Haag
1968 A Resolution to Honor James A. Ford: November 11, 1967. *Southeastern Archaeological Conference Bulletin* 8:1.

ARCHAEOLOGICAL SURVEY IN THE LOWER MISSISSIPPI ALLUVIAL VALLEY, 1940–1947

CONTENTS

CONTENTS

LIST OF TABLES

LIST OF LINE-CUT FIGURES

LIST OF COLLOTYPE FIGURES

ERRATA

The foldouts (figures 1, 2, 17–21, 72, and table 16) have been relocated for production purposes; therefore page numbers in contents refer to original placement.

P. 46, line 13: "the name name" should read "the same name."
P. 167: Table 4 references should read "p. 196."
P. 188: first state listed should be "Missouri" not "Arkansas."
P. 145, n. 61: "ideal" should read "entire."

Added notes
P. 93: In reference to the statement, "In some sites, such as Snyders in Calhoun County, Illinois, and Creve Coeur, north of St. Louis, Missouri, there is actually a higher proportion of zoned stamp pottery in the village debris than at any of the sites in the Survey Area or farther south in the Lower Valley," Phillips noted that, "We didn't have the Manny site when this statement was made."

P. 113: In reference to the statement, "These four types represent one of the clearest possible evidences of continuity over a period that practically covers the entire span of pottery-making in the area," Phillips noted that, "Maybe so but it is not present in Marksville and Issaquena."

Section I
THE GEOGRAPHIC SETTING

THE GEOGRAPHIC SETTING

INTRODUCTION

LEST this section be thought disproportionate to the size and importance of the report that follows, it may be well to explain that it is intended to serve as introductory to future reports as well. However, this only partly accounts for so much space being given here to geographical matters. There has developed in the writers, during the course of this investigation, a strong sense of the geography of the area. By this is not implied a return to the environmentalism of an earlier period, but rather a recognition of the special character of this particular region. Without going into the theoretical aspects of the interaction of culture and environment, which doubtless apply more or less equally in any part of the world, it may be pointed out that in the Lower Mississippi the importance of such a relationship is so obvious as to be inescapable. The first time you come down out of the "hills" onto the level flood plain you are conscious of having left one world and entered another. As time goes on, you feel it rather more than less. If nature enters so emphatically into the culture today, when man is supposed to have achieved some degree of technological independence, it is a reasonable assumption that it was at least equally important in the time of "natural" man. Thus the Region, rather than any theoretical preconception, has forced attention upon its natural conditions, and the result is to be found in the pages that follow.

These represent an effort to bring together materials for a prehistoric geography of the Lower Mississippi Valley. Obviously, these can include only features of natural origin. The far more interesting part of such a geography, dealing with those features added by man — in this case aboriginal man — can only be written when we know something more about his culture, which is the aim of archaeology. However, if the materials for the time being are those of physical geography, the point of view is emphatically that of cultural geography. Emphasis is upon the character and distribution of features in respect to their possible utilization by primitive man, rather than upon origins and processes. If some features appear to be grossly over-emphasized, while others are correspondingly slighted, it is because in our opinion they contribute or fail to contribute to our understanding of the region in terms of the archaeological record.

THE SURVEY AREA

The Lower Mississippi Survey was originally planned to cover the Mississippi Valley from the mouth of the Ohio south to the vicinity of Vicksburg, Mississippi, there to make contact with work already done by Collins, Ford, and their associates in southern Mississippi and Louisiana. This large area, about 350 miles long, was loosely thought of by the writers — and sometimes referred to in print — as the "Central Mississippi Valley." "Central" was judged preferable to "middle" on account of the cultural implications of the latter term. "Lower" was avoided because it had become associated in archaeological literature with the extreme southern portion of the valley only. Geographically, this was indefensible. Most geographers agree on a two-fold division of the Mississippi River into an upper and lower division, though not without some disagreement as to where the line is drawn between them, whether at the mouth of the Ohio or that of the Missouri. Occasionally, a three-fold division is made but without consistent definition of the middle portion. Thus, according to Williams,

> From a physiographic point of view, the river flows through a valley representing three types of formation. From its source to Minneapolis, the river flows through a shallow or "young" valley . . . through alternate lakes and marshes and over many rapids and falls until it plunges over St. Anthony into the gorge below.

Below Minneapolis is found the second part, which extends down the river 888 miles of its course to Cairo, Illinois. For this part of its length the river flows in a gorge varying from one to six and a half miles in width and with bluffs rising from 100 to 650 feet above the river. . . .

Below Cairo the valley is a level flood plain, 50–100 miles wide, with much of this area below water level of the river at high stages. . . .[1]

This appears to be a logical division and one that might in future prove useful for archaeological purposes. On the other hand, Elliott, expressing what we may assume to be the position of the Mississippi River Commission, divides the river quite differently:

From the standpoints of topography and physical geography, the basin of the Lower Mississippi River is considered as extending southward from the mouth of the Missouri. . . . The "lower river" is, however, popularly understood to extend from the head of the Alluvial Valley at Cape Girardeau to the Gulf of Mexico. . . . The reach between the mouth of the Missouri and Cairo is frequently spoken of as the "middle river." In this volume the term "upper river" will generally refer to that portion of the river above Cape Girardeau, while the term "lower river" will refer to the channel below that point. The term "middle river" will refer generally to that portion of the river between the mouth of the Missouri and the mouth of the Ohio.[2]

Such disagreements are of no present concern, for it is clear that, any way we look at it, our interest is centered in the Lower Mississippi Valley, and that to go on using the term "middle" or a substitute, "central," as an areal designation can only lead to further confusion. The concept "Middle Mississippi" is pretty firmly entrenched in the archaeological literature, but it should lessen rather than increase its ambiguity to insist upon a strictly cultural significance and dissociate it from any specific geographical sense.[3]

We cannot presume to settle the question as to where the geographical division between Upper and Lower Mississippi should come, nor is it necessary. For our purposes, a more precise term is available, Mississippi Alluvial Valley. This strictly physiographic area coincides almost exactly (except on the south) with the area of interest of the present survey. It would be correct, therefore, to designate the scene of our activities as the Alluvial Valley of the Lower Mississippi River. For the sake of brevity this area will be most often referred to herein simply as the Survey Area. By this is meant the area we intend to cover. The area actually covered to date is but a small and somewhat ragged portion thereof. In attempting to put before the reader a brief description of the geographic conditions, however, the entire Survey Area will be considered for the reasons already stated.

PHYSIOGRAPHY

THE ALLUVIAL VALLEY

It is not claimed at this point that our Survey Area represents a cultural or archaeological area, whatever those terms may mean. It is, however, a well-marked physiographic area of so pronounced a character that it would indeed be strange if it had not significantly affected the cultures developed upon it. In describing these physiographic characteristics, emphasis will be laid upon features that might be presumed to have affected aboriginal occupants and the archaeological record they left behind them. For a thorough geologic and physiographic treatment, the reader is referred to Fisk's monumental report already cited from which most of the following material has been taken.[4]

[1] Williams, 1928, p. 10.

[2] Elliott, 1932, vol. I, p. 28.

[3] In the present report, we are using "Mississippi" as a period designation and substituting the term "Mississippian culture" for the older "Middle Mississippi culture."

[4] Fisk, 1944. The authors are extremely grateful to Dr. Harold N. Fisk and the President of the Mississippi River Commission for permission to quote freely from this work, without which the physiographic section of this report could hardly have been written.

For a summary account, see Fenneman, 1938, also freely used in this section.

By way of definition, the Alluvial Valley is considered here as including the present flood plain of the Mississippi River, also those of its tributaries insofar as they merge and can be included in a generalized boundary, and certain dissected alluvial plains not completely covered by flood waters. These older alluvial plains, remnants of the Mississippi flood plain when it stood at a higher level, are set off from the present flood plain by low escarpments frayed by minor stream valleys. The stream valleys are subject to backwater flooding, but the general level of the older alluvium is above high-water mark. The land is almost as flat as that of the flood plain, but the drainage, the soils, and vegetation are markedly different, as we shall see. These older alluvial plains comprise between one-half and one-third of the Survey Area, mainly in the portions not yet investigated.[5] The difference between these older alluvial lands and the present flood plain, only a few feet in terms of elevation, is striking enough in terms of environment. The cultural significance of this fact will be discussed in a later section.

Flood-Plain Topography

At present we are most interested in the flood plain, since most of the Survey work so far completed lies in that portion of the valley. Characteristic of an aggrading stream is the fact that its flood plain slopes away from, instead of toward, the stream. The higher land along the river is called the "natural levee," the low land or "backswamp" lies away from the river. Tributary streams, inhibited by the natural levees, follow parallel courses for long distances before uniting with the main river. Their headwaters sometimes approach within a few feet of its banks, so that rain falling on the backslope of the levee may travel hundreds of miles before reaching the river again. The St. Francis, Sunflower, and Yazoo are rivers of this type. The Arkansas and White manage to reach the Mississippi more directly by means of tortuous channels higher than the surrounding plain. The Arkansas in its lower portion is in turn paralleled by streams of the Yazoo type. For example Bayou Bartholomew, which almost touches the Arkansas at Pine Bluff, parallels both it and the Mississippi for several hundred miles, finally reaching the latter by way of the Ouachita and Red rivers. These peculiarities of drainage can hardly fail to have had important effects on the distribution of peoples and cultures in the area.

Local topography is almost entirely the result of the characteristics and behavior of the Mississippi River and its major tributaries, present and past. Some knowledge of the mechanics underlying this behavior is therefore necessary to an understanding of present conditions. A flood-plain stream, working in alluvium of relatively uniform materials and therefore free to shift its location and adjust its shape, tends to establish a consistent "S"-shaped meander pattern. It is not necessary to go into the complex mechanics that bring about this result, which can be summed up in the word *oscillation*.[6] The size and shape of the meanders are the resultant of a large number of mechanical forces, and represent a sort of equilibrium of those forces. Relatively stable, so far as size and shape are concerned, meanders are decidely unstable with respect to position, but the exact nature of their behavior in this regard does not seem to have been agreed upon by the experts to the satisfaction of all concerned. The textbook theory is that meanders of flood-plain streams are in a steady and continuous process of migration downstream. The explanation is that greater velocity on the outside of bends enables the stream to excavate bank materials which are redeposited farther downstream on the outside of bends, on the same side. The theoretical result is that the entire meander pattern shifts downstream without essential change of shape, to which phenomenon the designation "meander sweep" is commonly applied. According to this view, lateral extension of bends resulting in eventual cutting-off and the formation of oxbow lakes is an irregularity, a "deformity," as Matthes terms it,[7] rather than a normal characteristic

[5] "The floodplain has a total area of about 35,000 square miles, including the 13,000 square miles of near sea level deltaic plain. . . . The dissected alluvial plains . . . cover nearly 15,000 square miles in the northern and central parts of the alluvial valley. . . ." Fisk, 1944, p. 5.

[6] Matthes, 1941.

[7] Matthes, 1941, p. 632.

of the process. If this were true of the Lower Mississippi, we might find ourselves with very little archaeology to work on. Sites on the river's banks would have very little chance of survival before the inexorable sweep of the meanders, and the archaeological material would have to be sought at the bottom of the Gulf of Mexico.

Fortunately, according to Louisiana geologists, the Lower Mississippi does not conform to the textbook theory. While not denying altogether the downstream migration of meanders, these experts tend to stress lateral movement as more characteristic, and one gathers that the termination of such lateral movement by a cut-off is regarded by them as a normal completion of the process.

Thus Russell:

> . . . Downstream migration, or sweeping, however, is probably a much more limited process than is ordinarily believed. It seems to take place only until a cut-off is formed, at which time an individual meander loses its identity and some entirely new meander likely develops.[8]

And Chawner, after some rather technical information on lateral migration, and the process of caving on which it depends, goes on to state:

> From a study of superimposed surveys of the Mississippi River, it can be seen that as a rule any single meander moves down valley only a short distance, considerably less than its width, before a cut-off takes place which leaves that particular meander as an oxbow lake. In fact, the upper limb of the meander may move upstream. The process might best be described as a slow increase in the radius of the meander curve which proceeds until the lower curve of one meander meets the upper curve of the meander next below. *The result is always the same.* [Italics ours.] Before migration either up or down valley has proceeded to more than a fraction of the width of the meander, the cut-off occurs, an ox-bow lake is formed, and the river has straightened its course. The straightening effect, however, is not permanent, for a new bend soon develops. Frequently new meanders develop in the same place as the old cut-off. Any idea of continuous down valley migration of meanders in the Alluvial Valley of the Mississippi seems unsupported by the facts.[9]

Fisk in reference to one of the smaller flood-plain tributaries of the Lower Mississippi describes the process in approximately the same terms:

> Meander shifting appears to be a fairly rapid and very regular process. A meander develops through more active cutting on the outside of a channel irregularity. As the meander grows, more active erosion on two adjacent outside curves gradually closes the neck of the loop. The opposing parts of the channel wear through the neck and unite, forming a straight stretch referred to as a cut-off and leaving an isolated remnant channel, which is known as an ox-bow lake if water filled.[10]

These oxbow lakes, which gradually fill to become swamps and cypress brakes, are the most attractive and characteristic features of the landscape today. They are doubly cherished by the archaeologist as affording favorable conditions for the preservation of sites as well as a possible means of dating them.[11]

It is important to note that the shifting of meanders, whether downstream, lateral, or both, is confined within a zone of definite width called a *meander belt.* It is thought that the relation between the size of a stream and the width of its meander belt is a fairly constant one, in the approximate ratio of 1 to 18. The present Mississippi meander belt conforms closely to this estimate.[12] The term *meander belt* will be found constantly recurring in these pages, but its exact nature and importance will not be appreciated without further discussion of the complex mechanics of flood-plain aggradation.

Another characteristic of flood-plain streams, of the greatest importance from the cultural standpoint, is their propensity to build *natural levees.* Such streams generally have wide variation in *stage* (i.e., height of water) and periodically overflow their banks — or did, before the construction of artificial levees. When water leaves the channel, there is an immediate reduction in velocity and consequent ability to carry its load, a large part of which is dropped at once. Sorting also takes place, the coarser sediments being deposited nearest the bank, the finer sediments being carried to a greater

[8] Russell, 1936, p. 122.
[9] Chawner, 1936, pp. 23–24.
[10] Fisk, 1938, p. 31.

[11] See Section VII, pp. 299–300.
[12] Chawner, 1936, p. 20, citing Jefferson, 1902.

distance. Thus, in general, both the quantity and character of levee deposits varies according to the distance from the parent stream. Deposits are thickest in the immediate vicinity of the stream bank, particularly on the outside of bends,[13] whence they slope back imperceptibly to the common flood-plain level. The resulting asymmetrical ridge-like formation is known as a *natural levee.* Height and width vary, of course, with the size of the stream, its velocity, and load. Natural levees of the Mississippi, for example, vary from 10 to 15 feet in height in the northern part of the Alluvial Valley, to 25 feet or more in the latitude of Baton Rouge, Louisiana. Width varies from ¾ to approximately 3 miles. Smaller tributary streams have levees of the same general shape, but of proportionately smaller size. Distributary streams have levees equal in height to those of the main channels from which they discharge, but of less width and consequently steeper backslope.[14] Under special conditions, however, smaller streams may have levees disproportionate to their size. Deer Creek, a small stream in the Yazoo Basin, is a famous example.[15]

Levee crests tend to attain uniform heights in adjustment to flood levels, but "absolute perfection is by no means realized, and some variation is to be noted almost anywhere." [16] The various causes of irregularities need not concern us here, but there is an important effect. If the levee crests were uniformly level, at high stages they would be overflowed at the same time — theoretically nothing would remain above water. Actually, while they may be awash for considerable distances, they are rarely if ever topped at all points.

Long-continued occupation by a stream of its *meander belt,* with all the shifts of position inherent in the processes of meander formation and cutting-off, results in a general coalescence and superposition of natural levees to form a continuous alluvial ridge, generally also referred to as a natural levee, but in reality a further stage in the aggradational process, more properly called a *meander-belt ridge.* The term "ridge" must be taken in a relative sense. Actually, its general elevation is only a few feet higher than the surrounding flood plain. A "ridge" 15 feet high and 15 miles wide is not a very conspicuous feature on the landscape, but its importance in this watery area is out of all proportion to its glamor.[17] Not only does it provide the highest and driest habitation sites, but also the lightest, best-drained, and most workable soil — the latter of particular interest to primitive agriculturists. It is only comparatively recently, and by means of heavy mechanical equipment, that the fertile but heavy clay soils of the backswamp areas have been brought under cultivation. We shall have a good deal more to say about this point in the section devoted to soil types. The advantages of natural-levee lands from every point of view are so patent that it is no occasion for surprise that archaeological sites in the flood plain are almost invariably located upon them.

In general flood-plain topography can be described as an alternation of meander-belt ridges and low-lying backswamp areas. The present Mississippi meander belt swings across the valley in wide arcs, blocking off large flood-plain areas, such as the St. Francis, Yazoo, and Tensas basins. Upon the flat surface of these basins, segments of older abandoned Mississippi (and Ohio) meander belts

> . . . can be traced . . . to the points where they diverge from the present meander belt. . . . Meander loops, natural levees, and other features characteristic

[13] The greater velocity on the outside of bends enables this part of the stream to carry a heavier and coarser load. Deceleration, on contact with the slower moving backwater, is likewise greater, causing a larger share of the increased load to be dropped. Thus, theoretically, "The most widespread and thickest natural levee deposits occur on the outside of bends" (Fisk, 1944, p. 18). It is necessary to point out, however, that the accuracy of the statement depends on the stage of meander-cutting. Russell is able to make a directly contrary statement on the width of levees, which is apparently no less true: "The tendency for meandering streams to shift laterally toward outer banks is ordinarily expressed in the narrow natural levees of those banks. The inner bank, on the other hand, acquires a residual natural spoil of width in proportion to the amount of shift and so has a wide natural levee" (Russell, 1936, p. 26).

[14] Russell, 1936, p. 75; Fisk, 1944, p. 19.

[15] See p. 17.

[16] Russell, 1936, p. 78.

[17] Alluvial ridges of abandoned Mississippi meander belts are from 10 to 20 miles wide and rise to elevations of 10 to 20 feet! Meander-belt ridges of tributary streams are smaller. Those of the Arkansas and Red rivers are the most extensive, maintaining widths of 3 to 5 and 1 to 3 miles, respectively. Fisk, 1944, p. 21.

of the parent stream are distinguishable along the abandoned courses, but the formerly wide channels are now largely filled with sediments and are followed by small streams. . . . Minor streams . . . follow the position of abandoned Mississippi River channels for long distances; other old courses are followed by a series of small streams each of which leaves the abandoned channel after following it for a few miles. The natural levees of older courses are partially buried under flood-basin alluvium and are somewhat narrower than levees along active streams, but their elevation and slope are similar.[18]

Between meander-belt ridges lie irregular flood-basin areas, locally known as "backswamp," subject to backwater flooding.

Floodbasin topography differs from that of other portions of the floodplain mainly in that original erosional and depositional irregularities have been subdued or buried by floodwater sediments. . . . Drainage patterns inherited from the original topography are preserved in the swamp networks which are utilized both for distribution and withdrawal of floodwaters.[19]

This all adds up to a very interesting, not to say peculiar, environment, one which might be assumed to have fostered, aboriginally, an amphibious type of culture. Even today, it is a very common sight to see a skiff tied up in the front yard. The dominant note in the landscape is muddy water. Along the courses of present and former meander belts are scores of oxbow lakes in various stages of degeneration into swamp — in this country almost every group of trees conceals a body of water — which, with their connecting waterways into the backswamp, spread a labyrinthine pattern of "lakes," "old rivers," "bayous," "bogues," "sloughs," "brakes," etc., across the almost level plain. These frequently intersect in such a way as to convert large areas into "islands." Probably no other section of the United States has so many bridges per mile of highway. Ask the first passerby where he lives and the answer, two to one, will be "across the bayou." With all this mileage of natural drainage channels, however, the land is poorly drained. Development of a protective levee system, first "completed" in 1880, gave some security against flood waters and made possible the drainage of backswamp areas. This has changed the picture somewhat, but there are large areas where conditions little different from those that greeted the first white settlers are still to be seen. One of the most fascinating things about the "Delta"[20] is that, traveling on a paved highway at 60 miles per hour, one has in a very few minutes a recapitulation of pioneer history, as the various stages in the transition from untouched wilderness to large-scale mechanized farming flash by.

SUBDIVISIONS OF THE ALLUVIAL VALLEY

The foregoing observations, applying generally to the Survey Area, and particularly to the flood-plain portions thereof, are intended to give a general impression of the country. Insofar as this treatment gives an impression of uniformity, it is misleading. Differences of elevation imperceptible to the eye may be profoundly significant, even under present conditions of relative security from high water. How much more so they may have been in prehistoric times is hardly necessary to point out. From the ecological and cultural standpoint, a difference of elevation here of 10 feet, let us say, may have more far-reaching effects than differences of 1000 feet in a mountainous country. It must, therefore, be emphasized again that the valley surface is not a continuous plain. Besides the large areas of older dissected alluvial plains already referred to, there are smaller remnants of older land surfaces, that are not only of interest on their own account, but also serve as natural boundaries for important physiographic subdivisions. These in turn may be further divided by abandoned meander-belt ridges so little elevated above the surrounding lowland that one would be hard put to find them on the ground, but which delimit subdivisions that appear in many cases to be archaeologically significant. This is by way of justification for the necessarily complex and detailed treatment that follows. The reader, who is not interested in the Lower Mississippi Valley in a specialized sense, will do well to

[18] Fisk, 1944, p. 5.

[19] Fisk, 1944, p. 21.

[20] The term "Delta" is commonly used locally to denote the Yazoo Basin and contiguous portions of other flood-plain areas in Arkansas. The actual delta of the Mississippi is called the "Lower Delta."

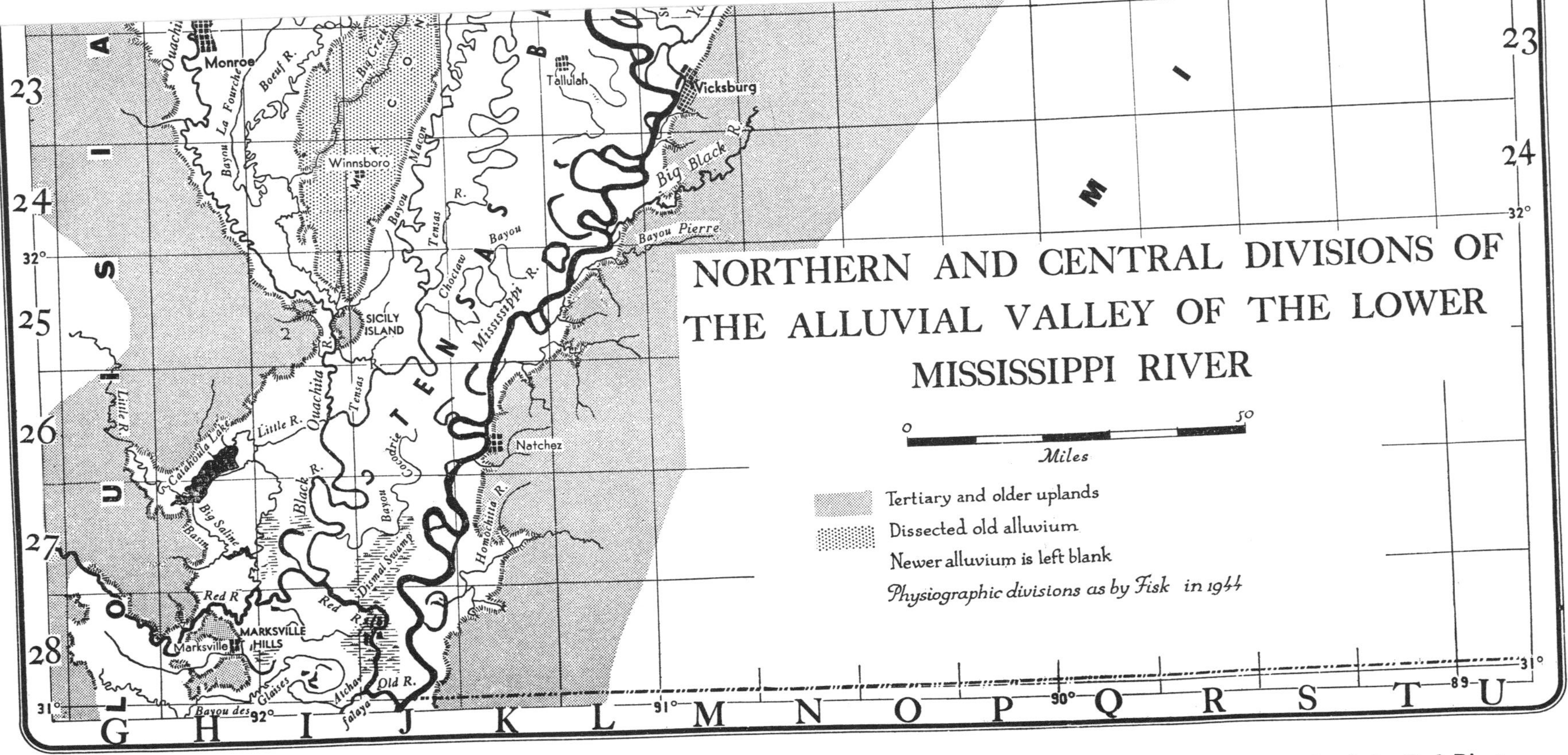

Fig. 1. Physiographic subdivisions of the Alluvial Valley of the Lower Mississippi River from Cape Girardeau, Missouri, to the mouth of the Red River. (After Fisk, 1944.)

skip these pages. As far as practicable, all subdivisions and other physiographic features mentioned in the text are shown on the accompanying map, figure 1. The classification followed is that of Fisk, with slight modifications and shifts of emphasis where warranted by archaeological considerations, and the subdivisions are described almost wholly in his own words. Wherever quoted passages are unacknowledged in footnotes, they may be taken as his. It would have been easier to simply refer the reader to Fisk's monograph, but the book is likely to be unavailable to many persons interested in Mississippi Valley archaeology. There is also, we hope, additional value in the remarks interpolated by ourselves.

Fisk's three-fold grouping of the Alluvial Valley into *northern*, *central*, and *southern* divisions is followed here. With the southern division, which consists of the deltaic plain, we have no further concern, since it lies entirely outside the limits of the Survey Area. These are arbitrary divisions in the sense that they are not physiographic entities, but rather groups of physiographic entities.

> The northern division, separated by Crowleys Ridge into the Western and Eastern lowlands, includes all of the valley north of a line drawn along the Mississippi River from Memphis, Tenn., to Helena, Ark., thence to the mouth of the Arkansas River and north along the eastern margin of Grand Prairie Ridge to the valley wall. The central division includes all of the valley south of the above described line and north of a line drawn from the mouth of the Red River westward along Bayou Des Glaises to the Marksville Hills. The southern division consists of the deltaic plains.[21]

What we are referring to in this report as the Survey Area corresponds approximately to the first two of these divisions, northern and central.

THE NORTHERN DIVISION

Crowley's Ridge

The northern division of the Alluvial Valley is divided axially by Crowley's Ridge. This is a long narrow belt of upland, arcuate in shape, touching the Mississippi at both ends, at Commerce, Missouri, in the north, and at Helena, Arkansas, in the south, a distance of some 200 miles. Its average width is about 3 miles in the southern half, where it stands about 100–50 feet above the plain, and about 12 miles in the northern half where it is considerably higher. Its upper surface, capped with Pleistocene deposits,

> . . . is generally in the form of a rolling plain sloping gently westward. All the creeks flowing upon it have broad flood plains, with high land only in the form of narrow ridges on the main and secondary divides. On the main divide the valleys are deep and narrow and the surface maturely dissected. The eastern side of Crowley's Ridge is a definite and steep bluff throughout; the western edge is not so definite, only a part of its course being marked by bluffs.[22]

Crowley's Ridge is a discontinuous feature, being interrupted by several important gaps. The Bell City–Oran Gap, the most northerly and widest, lies between Bell City and Oran, Missouri. It is 10 miles wide, but is interrupted by four small upland remnants of the ridge. This gap was occupied by the Whitewater River until recent canalization and diversion of that stream into the Mississippi near Cape Girardeau.

The Castor River Gap owes its name to the fact that the Castor River

> . . . before its canalization, flowed through a gap in Crowleys Ridge to join Little River near New Madrid, Mo. The valley of the Castor River through Crowleys Ridge is about 10 miles long and varies in width from ¾ of a mile to 1 mile . . . at its eastern end. The gap, unlike the Bell City-Oran Gap, is not bordered by abrupt escarpments.[23]

The St. Francis Gap, occupied by the present St. Francis River,

> . . . is located where the ridge is low and narrow. The gap is approximately one mile long and a little more than 1,000 ft. wide in its narrowest portion . . . . like the Castor River, [it] is the valley of a beheaded west-flowing stream through which the river was diverted into the Eastern Lowland.[24]

The Marianna Gap is occupied by an 8-mile-broad re-entrant of the Eastern Lowland. The L'Anguille River enters the flood plain just west of the gap through which it flows to join the St. Francis River.

[21] Fisk, 1944, p. 22.
[22] Bowman, 1911, p. 528.
[23] Fisk, 1944, p. 22.
[24] Fisk, 1944, p. 22.

Crowley's Ridge bisects the northern division of the Alluvial Valley, the resulting subdivisions being known as the Eastern and Western Lowlands, respectively. For a long period, ending about 3000 years ago, according to Fisk's chronology, the Ridge was an important divide, the Mississippi flowing on the west, the Ohio on the east, their junction being located far below, in the vicinity of Vicksburg.

To some extent Crowley's Ridge appears to have been a cultural divide as well, but this very likely has to do with the fact that the Eastern Lowland is largely composed of floodplain surfaces, whereas the Western Lowland is almost entirely composed of older dissected alluvial plains. The real cultural divide appears to be between recent and older alluvium; Crowley's Ridge only happens to accent that division. Apart from its importance or lack of importance as a divide, however, Crowley's Ridge should be interesting in its own right. As a considerable area of sharply contrasting landscape, entirely surrounded by alluvial lowlands, it might offer important sidelights on questions having to do with the relations of culture and environment. We use the conditional, because the Survey has so far covered only a very small portion of the Ridge. The very meager results of that limited exploration seem to indicate a radically different type of occupation from that of the surrounding lowland, but this is a point on which generalization would be unwise without further investigation.

The Western Lowland

This designation refers to the area lying between Crowley's Ridge and the western valley wall (Ozark Escarpment) as far as Searcy, Arkansas, from which point the western boundary follows the eastern edge of Grand Prairie Ridge down to the Arkansas River. The Arkansas and Mississippi rivers from the south and southeastern boundaries, respectively.

> The Western Lowland includes extensive remnants of the . . . Mississippi River, and the floodplain of the White River and its tributaries. The lowland is connected with the Eastern Lowland by a number of gaps through Crowleys Ridge [described above]. It joins the floodplain of the upper Mississippi River near Cape Girardeau, Mo., and is joined by the floodplains of a number of smaller streams along the western valley wall.
>
> The Western Lowland averages less than 5 miles in width between Cape Girardeau and Wappapello, Mo., where it abruptly widens to 20 miles. Near Jonesboro, Ark., it again widens and maintains a width of slightly over 30 miles to its southern margin.
>
> The narrow portion of the Western Lowland which extends for 50 miles between Cape Girardeau and Wappapello, Mo., is termed the Advance Lowland. It is 3 miles wide at Cape Girardeau and reaches its greatest width of approximately 8 miles near Advance, Mo., where Hickory Ridge and other small upland remnants set off the narrow 15-mile long Drum Lowland to the north. West of Drum Lowland the Advance Lowland maintains a width of about 4 miles to Wappapello, where it narrows to a width of 2 miles. . . .
>
> The southern end of the Advance Lowland was blocked by the alluvial fan of the St. Francis River and the resulting lowland is known as Mingo Swamp.[25]

In general, the topography of the Western Lowland is the result of a succession of huge alluvial fans of the Mississippi River, formed during the long period when the river flowed west of Crowley's Ridge. Seven terraces can be traced representing as many stages in the river's history. The surface of each terrace is marked by traces of braided channels and natural levees of the Mississippi and smaller tributaries which were active in constructing this fan. In addition, each of the present tributary streams, entering the Western Lowland, the Whitewater, Castor, St. Francis, Black, White, and Little Red rivers, has developed its own alluvial fan subsequent to the shift of the Mississippi to the Eastern Lowland.[26]

The dissected portion of the Mississippi alluvial fan terminates abruptly at the Big Creek Escarpment which

> . . . extends as a broad arc for 50 miles northeastward from the southern end of Grand Prairie Ridge to West Helena, Ark., where it stops at the foot of Crowleys Ridge. . . . The escarpment has an average height of about 30 ft. and reaches a maximum height of 60 ft. near West Helena. It is named after Big Creek, a tributary of the White River, which flows at its base for several miles.[27]

[25] Fisk, 1944, pp. 22–23.

[26] Fisk, 1944, pp. 23–24.

[27] Fisk, 1944, p. 23.

The Big Creek Escarpment is interesting geologically because of evidence of its having been produced by faulting. Such questions need not detain us here. We are not so much interested in the cause of natural features as their possible effects on human culture. The escarpment is important to us as a definite boundary between older and recent alluvium and their differing ecological possibilities.

The dissected alluvial plains just described account for about two-thirds of the area of the Western Lowland. The remaining third is made up of flood plains of the White and Black rivers and their principal tributaries, the Cache River, Bayou de View, Big Creek, and L'Anguille River. Flood plains of the Black and White rivers make a continuous lowland area extending the entire length of the Western Lowland south of the Advance Lowland. Except for certain narrow portions it varies from about 4 to 8 miles in width and is set off from the older alluvial surface by escarpments averaging less than 15 feet in height. At its southern end the White River Lowland merges with the present Mississippi flood plain in the area that lies between the Big Creek Escarpment and the Arkansas and Mississippi rivers. This is the only portion of the Mississippi flood plain within the borders of the Western Lowland as defined.[28] Fisk does not give this subdivision any name, specifically, but for our purposes it may be convenient to refer to it as the Lower White River Basin. Except for its southeastern border formed by the present Mississippi meander belt, it is an extremely low and watery district signally adapted to the purposes for which a large part of it is now used, as a floodwater reservoir and refuge for migratory waterfowl.

Topography of the Western Lowland

The surface of the Western Lowland, excluding the flood plains of its principal streams, lies about 15 to 30 feet higher than that of the Mississippi River flood plain, from which it is set off by definite escarpments. Stream valleys incised within it are shallow but are subject to backwater flooding. The level upland surfaces are entirely out of reach of flood waters.

Braided streams of old Mississippi alluvial fans, and fans of marginal tributaries, such as the White River, are the dominant agents in the construction of this plain, as evidenced by the lenticular character of the local drainage pattern. The parallelism of the principal streams with elements of braided stream topography on the adjacent surfaces shows that each stream follows the position of an abandoned main channel of the braided Mississippi River.[29]

The resulting topography presents an interesting contrast to that of the flood-plain areas. Whereas in the latter, the only high land is along the streams, here it is between them. In the flood plain, man was obliged to seek the river banks to keep his feet dry, here he might have to avoid them for the same reason. Such a contrast could hardly fail to be reflected in his culture.

The Eastern Lowland

This area comprises the Mississippi meander belt north of Helena, Arkansas, the St. Francis Basin, and extensive remnants of the alluvial fan of the Ohio River, dating from the time when Crowley's Ridge formed the divide between that stream and the Mississippi. It has a width of 40 to 50 miles in the northern portion, narrowing considerably at its southern terminus. The general surface of the Eastern Lowland, mainly composed of young flood plain, is lower than that of the Western Lowland, which is almost entirely an older alluvial surface, and the escarpments are higher, forming a series of straight bluffs, but slightly modified by scallops of major streams. The western boundary is formed by Crowley's Ridge, through which it connects with the Western Lowland by means of the four gaps already described. It connects with the Upper Mississippi Alluvial Valley by Thebes Gap, through which the present Mississippi flows, and with the Ohio Alluvial Valley by the Metropolis Lowland, followed by the present Ohio River, and the Cache Lowland, through which the Ohio previously flowed.[30]

Though, as already stated, most of the surface of the Eastern Lowland is made up of active flood plain, there is a fairly considerable

[28] Fisk, 1944, p. 24.
[29] Fisk, 1944, p. 23.
[30] Fisk, 1944, pp. 24–25.

area of older alluvium, the Malden Plain. There are also several smaller remnants of the same older alluvial surface, which together with abandoned meander-belt ridges serve to divide the flood plain into separate lowlands. One of these remnants in the north, Sikeston Ridge, separates the Cairo Lowland from the Morehouse Lowland to the west. Sikeston Ridge is a very interesting feature archaeologically, as the scene of some of the first extensive archaeological investigations in the Mississippi Valley.[31] This is a long, low "sand" ridge extending southward for a distance of 35 miles from the Commerce Hills to New Madrid. Its average width is between 2 and 3 miles and at its northern end it rises almost 40 feet above the flood plain, but slopes gradually to nearly flood-plain level at New Madrid in the south. Its level surface is marked by scars of braided channels showing it to be a remnant of an old Ohio River alluvial fan. Small isolated remnants of this same surface are found in the Cairo Lowland to the east.[32]

The Cairo Lowland is a basin bounded on the west by Sikeston Ridge and on the north and east by the valley walls. It includes that portion of the Mississippi meander belt between Commerce and New Madrid, Mo. It also includes eroded remnants of the Ohio alluvial fan in the area near Charleston, Mo., and braided Mississippi channels near the eastern edge of Sikeston Ridge. The northern end of the Cairo Lowland south and west of Commerce, Mo., is characterized by highly irregular erosional and depositional topography developed where the Mississippi River has cut across and reworked alluvial deposits of the Ohio fan. Where sands occur at the surface they form irregular hummocks which in many ways resemble sand dunes.[33]

The Morehouse Lowland . . . lies between two remnants of the Ohio alluvial fan, the Malden Plain to the west and Sikeston Ridge to the east. To the north the Morehouse Lowland connects with the upper end of the Western Lowland by the Bell City-Oran Gap; to the south it is continuous with the Little River Lowland with which it merges in the latitude of New Madrid, Mo. The Morehouse Lowland is slightly more than 30 miles long and increases from 10 miles in width at its northern end to almost 20 miles at its southern end.

The drainage pattern of the Morehouse Lowland . . . is determined by an anastomosing network of old Mississippi River braided channels. Smaller streams, such as the Castor River and Little River (named Whitewater on old maps), flow in these old braided courses and have modified the original channels.[34]

The Little River Lowland, 20 miles wide and 80 miles long, forms the central part of the St. Francis Basin and is the southward continuation of the Morehouse Lowland. It is bounded on the west by the Malden Plain, on the east by the Mississippi River, and on the south by the abandoned St. Francis segment of the Mississippi River meander belt. The topography of this lowland differs from that of the Morehouse Lowland mainly in that scars of braided Mississippi courses have been largely destroyed by erosion or burial. Before canalization of the region, drainage in the northern part of the Eastern Lowland was collected by the Pemiscot Bayou-Left Hand Chute of the Little River system which joins the St. Francis River at Marked Tree, Ark.

The Little River Lowland is obliquely crossed at its southern end by the meander belt ridges of the Pemiscot Bayou-Left Hand Chute of Little River and of their older counterpart, Tyronza River. Meander loops within these ridges were formed by a stream larger than any draining the region today, but they are smaller than those of the Mississippi or Ohio rivers.[35]

The southern boundary of the Little River Lowland, the "St. Francis segment of the Mississippi meander belt," requires a word of explanation. This refers to the period when the Mississippi swung in an 80-mile arc from the vicinity of Richardsons, Tennessee, to Helena, Arkansas, leaving a meander belt, the southern part of which is now occupied by the St. Francis River. The portion of this meander belt that obliquely crosses the lowland from the Mississippi to the St. Francis rivers is the boundary referred to.

Significant for archaeology is the fact that the meander belt of the Pemiscot Bayou–Left Hand Chute of Little River and its older counterpart, Tyronza River, which cross the southern part of the Little River Lowland obliquely in a northeast-southwest direction, were formed by a stream larger than any draining the region today. The resulting natural levees are larger, providing more favorable habitation sites than would be indicated by the present size of those streams.

The Lower St. Francis Basin . . . is the southernmost part of the Eastern Lowland. It includes that portion of the present meander belt of the Mississippi

[31] Swallow, 1858, 1875; Conant, 1879; Croswell, 1878; Potter, 1880, and Evers, 1880.

[32] Fisk, 1944, pp. 25–26.

[33] Fisk, 1944, p. 25.

[34] Fisk, 1944, p. 26.

[35] Fisk, 1944, p. 26.

River south of Richardsons, Tenn., [to Helena, Arkansas] . . . the abandoned St. Francis segment of the Mississippi River meander belt, and the area between the two meander belts.[36]

The resulting basin is a leaf-shaped area, about 80 miles long and 30 miles wide at its widest point. The term *basin* is somewhat misleading, suggesting a disproportionate amount of back-swamp area. Actually, the area is unusually well provided with natural levees, since it includes two long segments of Mississippi meander-belt ridge, present and past. These are only 20 miles apart in the middle of the basin and at the ends they coalesce. In addition, there is within the area a stream of more importance archaeologically than its size would appear to warrant, Fifteen Mile Bayou. This is the largest of several streams occupying a former diversion channel of the Mississippi, truncating the older St. Francis segment. Natural levees of this old channel are only slightly smaller than those of the present Mississippi. It is no wonder, therefore, that the Lower St. Francis Basin has long been known as one of the richest archaeological areas in the Mississippi Valley.

The Malden Plain, a portion of the abandoned alluvial fan of the Ohio River, lying between Crowley's Ridge and the Morehouse–Little River Lowland belt, is the only considerable area of older alluvium in the Eastern Lowland.

The plain is separated from the neighboring lowland by a 15 to 20 ft. escarpment at the north. The slope of the plain, however, is greater than that of the lowlands, and the escarpment loses in height southward where the alluvial fan surface merges with the floodplain in the vicinity of Marked Tree, Ark.

Braided stream patterns of the Ohio alluvial fan are well preserved on the Malden Plain which is largely undissected. Only a few streams are incised below the general surface level. The St. Francis River follows an abandoned main channel of the braided Ohio system across the plain and has but slightly modified original channel features. . . . Fans of small streams draining eastward from Crowleys Ridge coalesce to form an alluvial apron overlapping the western margin of the Malden Plain.[37]

At the southern end of the Malden Plain are the famous "sunk lands" of the St. Francis, a considerable area of swamp on both sides of the river, commonly thought to be the result of down-faulting and blocked drainage at the time of the New Madrid earthquake.

Subdivisions of the Eastern Lowland so far described lie west of the Mississippi River. East of the river, on the Tennessee side, are several minor features, also considered as part of the Eastern Lowland, that warrant brief mention.

Tiptonville Dome . . . is an uplifted area which lies opposite the southern end of Sikeston Ridge but it is not a continuation of that feature. It is separated from the adjacent Reelfoot Lake Basin on the east by a fault escarpment along which earth movement has taken place during the construction of the alluvial plain surface. Maximum uplift of the Tiptonville Dome amounts to at least 15 ft. . . . and the Reelfoot Lake Basin is downfaulted by at least 25 ft.; hence the total displacement is as much as 40 feet. . . .

Displacement along the fault has been very recent and probably slight movement occurred as recently as 1812, the time of the New Madrid earthquake.[38]

The small basin herein designated the Obion-Forked Deer Basin lies between the Mississippi River meander belt and the eastern valley wall. Besides the floodplains of the Obion and Forked Deer rivers, it contains two small remnants of the Ohio alluvial fan. The remnant on the north lies between Obion River and Running Reelfoot Bayou, the other is between Rock Slough and Forked Deer River.[39]

THE CENTRAL DIVISION

The principal elements of the central division [of the alluvial valley] are the floodplain of the Mississippi River and the great alluvial fan of the Arkansas River. The floodplain is separated by the present river into the Yazoo Basin on the east and the Tensas Basin on the west. The Tensas Basin is further divided into an upper and lower portion by the constriction in the valley between Sicily Island, La., and Natchez, Miss.

The Arkansas fan includes Grand Prairie Ridge to the north, the Arkansas Lowland between Grand Prairie Ridge and the Arkansas River, the Boeuf Basin, and parts of Macon Ridge to the south. Sicily Island, an upland remnant, lies at its southern tip. The fan is separated from the Mississippi River floodplain by the eastern escarpment of Macon Ridge, which extends from Sicily Island northward to Eudora, Ark. North of Eudora, the edge of the Arkansas alluvial fan corresponds to the western edge of the Mississippi meander belt as far as the mouth of the Arkansas River.

The eastern bluffs of the central division are similar to those of the northern division and rise 100 to 150 ft.

[36] Fisk, 1944, p. 26.

[37] Fisk, 1944, p. 26.

[38] Fisk, 1944, p. 25. For an extremely interesting account of the effects of the earthquake in this region, see Fuller, 1912.

[39] Fisk, 1944, p. 25.

above the floodplain. . . . There is no continuous alluvial apron along the foot of the bluffs, but many small streams entering from the east have low alluvial fans. . . .

The western escarpment of the valley in the central division is generally far less precipitous than the eastern one. Much of the area rimming the west side of the valley is a low Pleistocene terrace which rises slightly more than 40 ft. above the floodplain level. The only higher bluffs are found north of Pine Bluff, Ark., and near Sicily Island, La.[40]

Fisk's treatment of this central division is rather more detailed than that of the northern division, undoubtedly warranted by a more complex aggradational history. The question as to how far we are obliged to follow for purposes of archaeology is not an easy one. This is a preliminary report. Even for those portions of the Survey Area most thoroughly covered, we are in no position to assay the ultimate possibilities of correlating archaeologic and physiographic factors, either spatial or chronological. From what we can see at this stage, however, it appears that it can be set down as a working principle that any physiographic factor or set of factors of sufficient importance to delimit a physiographic area, however small, probably had sufficient effect upon the occupation of that area to be reflected in its archaeology. Therefore, we shall follow Fisk to the end merely attempting to abbreviate and simplify wherever possible.

The Yazoo Basin

The Yazoo Basin, or "Delta" as its inhabitants like to call it,

. . . extends for 200 miles from Memphis to Vicksburg; it is 60 miles wide opposite Arkansas City, Ark., from which point it narrows to north and south. The Yazoo Basin is divided into smaller basins by a number of low meander belt ridges. These ridges are from east to west, the abandoned Yazoo meander belt of the Mississippi and Ohio rivers, the abandoned Sunflower meander belt of the Mississippi River, and the Deer Creek meander belt. The basin between the Yazoo and the Sunflower meander belts is drained by the Quiver River, that between the Sunflower meander belt and Deer Creek by Bogue Phalia, and that west of Deer Creek by Steele Bayou. The Tallahatchie Basin lies between the Yazoo meander belt and the eastern valley wall. It is drained by the Tallahatchie River and Tippo Bayou.[41]

The Yazoo meander belt is a complex group of minor ridges and basins . . . has been occupied in successive periods by the combined Mississippi-Ohio River which left large scars between Tutwiler and Tchula, Miss.; by the full flow of the Ohio River as shown by smaller scars between Memphis and Tutwiler; and by only part of the Ohio River flow as indicated by smaller scars between Coahoma and Vicksburg, Miss. The flow of eastern marginal streams, such as the Coldwater, Tallahatchie, and Yalobusha rivers, has modified these older scars.[42]

The Quiver River Lowland

. . . between the Yazoo and Sunflower meander belts is mainly a backswamp area. The only features that interrupt the nearly level backswamp surface are the narrow meander belts now occupied by a minor floodplain stream known as Quiver River. This meander belt is a southwest continuation of the South Lake meander belt.[43]

The natural levees of this old channel, partly buried by more recent flood-plain sediments, are not high enough to afford favorable locations for habitation, so it is not surprising that our search for sites in this area was completely unsuccessful.

The Sunflower meander-belt ridge

. . . bisects the Yazoo Basin and extends as a 10-mile wide low ridge for 120 miles south from the Mississippi River near Helena to its junction with the Yazoo meander belt near the eastern valley wall near Yazoo City, Miss. This meander belt . . . is comparable in size and complexity to that of the present Mississippi River. The height of the ridge decreases southward and in the southern part of the Yazoo Basin it lies close to backswamp level.

The Sunflower meander belt takes its name from the Sunflower River, the largest stream in the area today. The Sunflower, however, nowhere follows the last channel position of the Mississippi River for more than 20 miles, and it occupies only 42 of the 315 miles of abandoned Mississippi River channel mapped in this area. The rest of the channel is followed by over 60 other streams of various sizes.[44]

The Bogue Phalia Basin takes its name from the principal stream between the Sunflower

[40] Fisk, 1944, pp. 26–27.
[41] Fisk, 1944, p. 27.
[42] Fisk, 1944, p. 27.
[43] Fisk, 1944, p. 27.
[44] Fisk, 1944, p. 27.

meander belt and Deer Creek. *Bogue*, we are told, is a Choctaw word for stream, is in fact the same word as *bayou.*

This stream drains the area which has a network of channels determined by the braided topography of part of the old Mississippi alluvial fan. . . . Bogue Phalia is a true floodplain stream and follows a succession of topographic lows related to older stream courses.[45]

This appears to be one of the few streams in the Yazoo Basin that is not occupying older and more important channels, consequently lacks the large natural levees favorable for human occupation.

Deer Creek is unique in the Mississippi Valley. It has angular bends and a deep, narrow channel, but its natural levees are almost as wide and high as those of the Mississippi River. This is attributed to the fact that it ". . . was a long-lived crevasse stream or distributary which carried Mississippi floodwaters long enough to build up its own meander belt."[46] This explains why Deer Creek appears to have an archaeological importance entirely disproportionate to its size today.

The Tensas Basin

This is an extensive lowland area

. . . lying west of the Mississippi River between the latitude of Eudora, Ark., and the mouth of Old River, near Angola, La. It lies east of Macon Ridge and east of the Western uplands between Sicily Island and Marksville, La. It is north of the alluvial ridge which marks the northern limit of the deltaic plain. The Tensas Basin varies in width between 25 and 45 miles from the latitude of Vicksburg to its southern boundary. . . .

The part of the lowland lying south of the constriction between Natchez and Sicily Island is termed the lower Tensas Basin. This widest part of the basin is periodically flooded by backwater from the Red and Mississippi Rivers. The upper Tensas Basin is less completely flooded."[47]

The upper Tensas Basin is drained by the Tensas River and its principal tributary, Bayou Macon. The former occupied an old meander belt of Mississippi origin, of a period, however, when the river was smaller than at present. The natural levees rise only 5 to 10 feet above the adjacent backswamps. Bayou Macon follows an abandoned Arkansas River meander belt along the eastern foot of Macon Ridge.

The low alluvial ridge averages 3 miles in width and holds meander loops slightly larger than those found normally in Arkansas River meander belts. It is possible that during their formation the Arkansas River flow was augmented by that of the White River.[48]

The eastern portion of the Upper Tensas Basin is drained by a ". . . plexus of bayous, some of which follow abandoned Mississippi channels, . . ."[49]

The lower Tensas Basin west of Black River is drained by a complicated network of streams which follow abandoned meandering channels of the Arkansas River and old braided channels of the Mississippi River. This network is connected with the Red River by Saline Bayou. East of Black River another network drains into Bayou Cocodrie which follows abandoned meander channels of the Mississippi River. The lowland south of Red River, called the upper Atchafalaya Basin, is drained by a swamp network which flows into Bayou Natchitoches and the Red River.[50]

The principal features of the Tensas Basin are the low meander belt ridges which separate the lowland into a series of basins. The Walnut Bayou meander belt ridge separates the Catahoula Lake Basin from the Dismal Swamp Lowland in the lower Tensas Basin. The swamps of the upper Tensas Basin are crossed by the upper Tensas and Bayou Macon meander belt ridges which delimit minor unnamed lowlands. The low Cocodrie meander belt ridge lies at the north end of the Dismal Swamp Lowland between the Walnut Bayou meander belt and the meander belt of the present Mississippi River.[51]

Of the aforesaid meander-belt ridges, that which takes its name from Walnut Bayou, a small stream occupying the last channel position at its northern end, is the most important from an archaeological point of view.

It extends for over 100 miles in Louisiana from Tallulah to near the mouth of Red River. . . . The general continuity of the last channel position of the Mississippi is traceable except near St. Joseph, La.,

[45] Fisk, 1944, p. 27.
[46] Fisk, 1944, p. 27.
[47] Fisk, 1944, p. 28.
[48] Fisk, 1944, p. 29.
[49] Fisk, 1944, p. 28.
[50] Fisk, 1944, p. 28.
[51] Fisk, 1944, p. 28.

where it is cut out by the present Mississippi River meander belt. At the southern end of the Walnut Bayou meander belt the Mississippi channel was occupied and much modified by the Black, Tensas, Red, and Atchafalaya rivers. The lower portion of the Mississippi channel, now occupied by Bayou Des Glaises, is the southern boundary of the central division.[52]

The Cocodrie meander belt of the same order of magnitude, but of earlier origin, has lower natural levees. This illustrates an important point to which perhaps attention should have been called before. In the course of flood-plain aggradation existing meander-belt ridges are slowly buried by accumulating deposits. In the case of the Cocodrie meander belt this process has reached a point when only the crests of the natural levees rise above swamp level.

The Dismal Swamp Lowland, between Walnut Bayou and the present Mississippi River,

. . . is crossed by the present course of the lower Red River below the mouth of Black River and by traces of an unnamed pre-Cocodrie meander belt. Neither the Red River levees nor those of the older Mississippi meander belt rise appreciably above swamp levels. A series of shallow lakes of very irregular outline fill parts of the lowland.[53]

The ephemeral lake that gives its name to Catahoula Lake Basin is an extremely interesting feature.

During high water, the lake is about 12 miles long and 3 to 4 miles wide; at low water, it largely dries up and its bottom is pastured. . . .

The only important perennial tributary of Catahoula Lake is Little River which drains much of central Louisiana east of Red River and has built an extensive delta into the lake. . . .

Saline Bayou and French Fork of Little River also connect with Catahoula Lake. The direction of flow in these two streams depends upon the relative stage of the lake, and of the Red and Black rivers. When the rivers are high, the lake fills; when they are low, the flow is reversed, and they drain the lake basin. French Fork of Little River has a fairly straight channel with wide natural levees and a plexus of distributory channels. The levees gradually decrease in height from the Ouachita River toward Catahoula Lake, . . .[54]

[52] Fisk, 1944, p. 28.

[53] Fisk, 1944, p. 28.

In sum, the Tensas Basin does not appear to have been as favorable a region as the St. Francis and Yazoo basins already described, although statements of this kind must be made with a great deal of caution. Generally speaking, meander-belt ridges are low because they are formed, either at an early period and subsequently partially buried, or by streams smaller than the present Mississippi. On the other hand, and equally important for archaeology, is the situation of the meander belt now followed by Bayou Macon, lying for much of its course at the immediate foot of Macon Ridge. This would appear to be a fortunate combination for human occupation, affording elevated locations for villages with fertile levee lands near by for cultivation. This, and the higher meander-belt ridges, mainly in the upper portion of the Tensas Basin, could have supported a considerable though perhaps somewhat amphibious population.

The Arkansas Alluvial Fan

The third major subdivision of the central division of the Alluvial Valley comprises

. . . a belt of Arkansas River sediments, 20 to 40 miles wide, extending in a great arc for over 200 miles along the western valley wall between Little Rock, Ark., and Sicily Island. The entire surface of the fan is covered with a network of abandoned Arkansas River courses, both meander belts and braided channels, which radiate away from the apex of the fan at Little Rock. These old drainage lines are reflected in the existing drainage and topography of the area. The fan properly includes the flood basin of the Arkansas River south of Little Rock and floodplain of minor streams which merge with the Mississippi River floodplain. The dissected alluvial plains, Grand Prairie Ridge and Macon Ridge, are older and higher parts of the fan.[55]

Of special interest from our point of view is the former, Grand Prairie Ridge. As a considerable body of higher and sharply contrasting terrain thrusting between the White River Lowland and the Arkansas River Lowland, it offers an excellent opportunity to observe the relations of environment and culture — if we knew somewhat more about the culture.

[54] Fisk, 1944, p. 29.

[55] Fisk, 1944, p. 29.

> The ridge starts at the valley wall northeast of Little Rock, Ark., and trends southeast for 72 miles to the Arkansas River at Arkansas Post, Ark. It averages 15 miles in width but narrows toward the southern end. Its northern edge . . . is an escarpment which has been scalloped by the Little Red and White rivers and rises from 20 to 30 ft. above the floodplain of these streams. A western escarpment separates Grand Prairie Ridge from the Arkansas River Lowland. It is both lower and less clearly defined than the eastern escarpment along the White River Lowland.[56]

The surface of Grand Prairie Ridge is remarkably flat and the topsoil is underlain by an impervious clay, a combination of features eminently suited to the cultivation of rice. As a result, the ridge is one of the outstanding agricultural districts of the South today. Originally, it supported a tall-grass prairie vegetation in sharp contrast to the heavily wooded lowlands on either side.

The Arkansas River Lowland

> . . . is bounded on the north by the Grand Prairie Ridge and on the south by the Arkansas River. It reaches a maximum width of 20 miles and extends from Little Rock to Arkansas Post, a distance of 72 miles. A series of nearly parallel meander belt ridges radiate from the mouth of the narrow upland valley at Little Rock . . . to cross the lowland. Each of the abandoned meander belts has been slightly obscured by subsequent activities of minor streams.[57]

The resulting topography, in its alternation of low ridge and backswamp, is very similar to that of the larger flood basins of the Mississippi, but on a smaller scale commensurate with that of the Arkansas River.

The boundary between the Arkansas River Lowland and the Boeuf Basin to the south is not well defined. The latter includes the area south of the Arkansas River from Pine Bluff, Arkansas, to the Mississippi River. Its eastern boundary follows the Mississippi from the mouth of the Arkansas to the northern end of Macon Ridge, thence south along the western edge of the ridge to Sicily Island. The western boundary is the valley wall and the Bastrop Hills. The surface of the Boeuf Basin is generally similar to that of the Arkansas River Lowland, the principal features being abandoned Arkansas River meander belts now occupied by smaller streams. The most recently abandoned one, now occupied in part by Bayou Bartholomew, can be traced over 100 miles along the western margin of the basin.

Macon Ridge, which forms the divide between the Boeuf Basin and the Tensas Basin, is a portion of the older Arkansas alluvial fan corresponding to Grand Prairie Ridge, except that upon it are small irregular "islands" of a still older surface.

> It extends from Eudora, Ark., 100 miles south to the town of Sicily Island [Louisiana] and reaches a width of approximately 25 miles near the latitude of Winnsboro, La. Its eastern margin is fairly straight and abrupt, and rises 20 ft. above the neighboring Tensas Basin. . . . Its western margin is poorly defined and merges with the Boeuf Lowland.[58]

The favorable situation of the eastern margin of Macon Ridge from the point of view of aboriginal settlement has already been commented on in connection with Bayou Macon which flows at its foot. It is not surprising to find that it was well occupied in prehistoric times, as evidenced by the archaeological studies of Lemley, Dickinson, and others. Our own Survey has not yet reached this portion of the valley.

The Bastrop Hills which form part of the western boundary of the Boeuf Basin are

> . . . located near the western valley wall from which they are separated by the gap occupied by Bayou Bartholomew and the Ouachita River. The abrupt eastern escarpment of the Bastrop Hills rises as much as 70 ft. above the neighboring floodplain. The hills are 17 miles in length and a little over 5 miles wide at their widest part. They slope westward toward Bayou Bartholomew and the Ouachita River, and most of the streams head near the eastern escarpment and flow west.[59]

Sicily Island, which has appeared in the foregoing pages as a useful landmark, is an isolated outlier of the western uplands, now entirely surrounded by the flood plains of the Ouachita and Tensas rivers. Nearly circular, about 5 miles in diameter, the "island" rises some 200 feet at its highest point above the plain.

[56] Fisk, 1944, p. 30.
[57] Fisk, 1944, p. 30.
[58] Fisk, 1944, pp. 30–31.
[59] Fisk, 1944, p. 30.

SUMMARY OF PHYSIOGRAPHY

The subdivisions described in the foregoing pages, in painful but unavoidable detail, may be grouped into three categories: flood-plain areas, dissected alluvial plains, and upland remnants. Flood-plain areas in turn may be divided into two groups depending on whether they were laid down by the Mississippi and/or Ohio rivers, or by other less important streams. In a different sense, they may also be divided according to elevation, into levee lands, bottom, and backswamp. Dissected alluvial plains may likewise be divided according to derivation, either from older Mississippi-Ohio fans or from the Arkansas River fan. The resulting classification may be tabulated as follows:

- I. Flood-plain Areas
  - A. Mississippi-Ohio Derivation
    - Advance Lowland
    - Cairo Lowland
    - Morehouse Lowland
    - Little River Lowland
    - Lower St. Francis Basin
    - Reelfoot Lake Basin
    - Obion-Forked Deer Basin
    - Yazoo Basin
    - Tensas Basin
  - B. Other than Mississippi-Ohio Derivation
    - White-Black River Lowland
    - Arkansas River Lowland
    - Boeuf Basin
- II. Dissected Alluvial Plains
  - A. Mississippi-Ohio Derivation
    - Western Lowland (excluding White-Black River Basin and minor flood plains)
    - Sikeston Ridge
    - Malden Plain
  - B. Arkansas River Derivation
    - Grand Prairie Ridge
    - Macon Ridge
- III. Upland Remnants
  - Commerce Hills
  - Crowley's Ridge
  - "Islands" on Macon Ridge
  - Bastrop Hills
  - Sicily Island

This grouping will prove extremely useful in dealing with other geographic elements, particularly soils and vegetation, in the sections that follow.

CLIMATE

The climate of the Mississippi Alluvial Valley may be dealt with very briefly. Though undoubtedly the most basic element in man's environment, it is determinant for regional subdivisions of the first magnitude only. The climate of a relatively small area such as we are concerned with here is not set off, in an over-all sense, from that of the surrounding regions. Nevertheless, there are some peculiarities of climate in the Lower Mississippi Valley that warrant consideration.

To innocent laymen like ourselves without any technical competence whatever, the best classification of climate would appear to be one that takes into account several elements, such as Köppen's, which is based on temperature, precipitation, and seasonal change. Unfortunately, no detailed classification of North American climate based on Köppen's system is yet available.[60] So far as his classification has been carried, our area is a small part of a very large subdivision covering practically the entire eastern United States, whose climate with mild winters and with mean temperature of the warmest month above 22 degrees centigrade.[61]

A more recent outgrowth of the Köppen system is the classification of Thornthwaite.[62] This "differs from Köppen's classification in that it makes use of two new climatic concepts, precipitation effectiveness and temperature efficiency." [63] On Thornthwaite's climatic map our area falls within a zone that closely corresponds to Köppen's Cfa zone, but is slightly smaller, the climate of which is designated by the symbol BB'r, translated as

[60] Kroeber, 1939, p. 13. Although this statement was made some time ago, we are told that it is still true. Recent modifications of the original Köppen classification for North America have shifted boundaries between subdivisions, but have not attempted to break them down into greater detail.

[61] Klages, 1942, p. 310.

[62] Thornthwaite, 1931, 1933. Summarized in Klages, 1942, pp. 314–21.

[63] Thornthwaite, 1933, p. 433.

follows: "temperate rain forest with abundance of precipitation at all seasons."

These classifications, assuming their validity, are of use in characterizing the climate of the Lower Mississippi Valley only in a very general sense, as part of a much larger southeastern area. We may pass, therefore, to climatic studies of more limited scope.

Temperature

Merriam's classification of "life zones," designed as a classification of the organic environment, is based primarily on temperature, "not mean annual isotherms, but cumulative heat, as determinative of physiological activity in plants and reproductive activity in animals. They run, therefore, generally from east to west, with marked swings and convolutions where altitude or other temperature factors are involved." [64] The major portion of our area, from Vicksburg north, falls into Merriam's *Austroriparian* zone, which in fact makes a considerable extension up the Mississippi as though purposely to include it. As a thrust of warmer climate into the colder *Carolinian* zone, the Survey Area therefore enjoys a favorable climatic situation relative to the contiguous upland areas on either side. The southern part of the area, from Vicksburg south, falls within a similar northward extension of the *Lower Austral* zone.[65]

In general, this tendency of isothermal lines to swing northward in the region of the Mississippi River is borne out by the more complex temperature studies of Livingston and Shreve. Their system is based on the length of the average frostless season. According to their map, the northern part of the Survey Area, down to the Arkansas-Louisiana line, falls within a *medium* zone, i.e., one having from 180 to 240 consecutive days frostless season per year. The line separating this medium zone from the *warm* zone makes a very considerable upward extension in the region of the Mississippi, or perhaps it would be more accurate to say that it makes a downward extension on either side. In any case, a large part of our area is *warm*, i.e., has 240 to 300 days frostless season. More significantly perhaps, within the *medium* zone, the 200-day line makes a very narrow loop up the river from about the latitude of the Arkansas River to Memphis. This would seem to indicate that the Mississippi itself has an ameliorating effect on temperature, at least as expressed in the length of the growing season. Whether or not this is actually the case, it is significant from our point of view that the major portion of the Survey Area is either *warm* or on the warm side of *medium* with an appreciably longer growing season than obtains on the uplands on either side of the valley.[66]

On the other hand, in terms of absolute minimal temperature, the area is far from warm. Here the river seems to have a contrary effect. Isotherms dip down instead of up. A tongue of *cool* zone, i.e., one having minimal temperatures ranging from −22 to −40 degrees Fahrenheit, comes down the Mississippi as far as the Missouri-Arkansas line. From there down to the Arkansas-Louisiana line minimal temperatures fall into the *medium* category, −22 to 4 degrees, and from there on into the *warm* zone, 4 to 14 degrees. Thus, most of the area suffers under occasional temperatures comparable to Massachusetts, and a small part has the honor to be in the same minimal temperature zone as northern Maine.[67] In short, notwithstanding its genial climate, measured by the length of frostless seasons, the area can be extremely cold on occasion, a source of considerable surprise to the visiting Yankee with preconceived notions about the "sunny South." It is hardly necessary to add, however, that from the standpoint of human culture, it is the long growing season, not the occasional "norther," that is of paramount importance. The fact that the Alluvial Valley is more highly favored in this regard, than the contiguous uplands on either side, may be not without cultural significance.

Moisture Conditions

Of equal importance with temperature, but harder to ascertain, are moisture conditions. Studies in this field seem to have progressed

[64] Kroeber, 1939, p. 13.

[65] Merriam, 1898. Map reproduced in Livingston and Shreve, 1921, pl. 73.

[66] Livingston and Shreve, 1921, pl. 34.

[67] Livingston and Shreve, 1921, pl. 41.

only so far as a recognition of the enormous difficulties of generalization, owing to the multiple factors involved. Precipitation data present only a small part of the total picture of moisture conditions, into which enter such additional considerations as rainfall intensity and evaporation. However, they will have to be sufficient for our purposes here.

In respect to total annual rainfall the Survey Area enjoys a favorable situation. Up to about the latitude of Memphis it falls within the 50- to 60-inch zone, which makes a very pronounced northward extension whose boundaries closely correspond to those of the Alluvial Valley.[68] More significant than total annual rainfall, especially for primitive agriculturists, is its seasonal distribution. A better scheme for our purposes, therefore, is that of Livingston and Shreve, based on normal daily precipitation for the period of the average frostless season.[69] On their map the Survey Area falls within the semi-humid zone, with values of 100 to 140 (in thousandths of an inch of rain per day). All but the extreme northern portion, however, lies within the more humid portion of that zone with values greater than 120. This represents a very favorable rainfall situation, especially for the cultivation of maize, which requires a good deal of summer rain, but it is a situation that is shared by practically the entire Southeast and by considerable portions of the Middle West as well. It cannot be adduced as an additional item in favor of this particular area in contrast to surrounding areas, except to the west and southwest. Going in this direction from the Mississippi Valley, isohedral lines representing successive reductions in rainfall are crossed in quick succession.

Sunshine

For a culture largely dependent on maize, sunshine is an important climatic factor. According to Livingston and Shreve, there was, at the time of writing, no really satisfactory method of measuring sunshine, nor were available records complete enough for satisfactory generalization. Their chart, based on U. S. Weather Bureau records, gives values in terms of hours of sunshine within the period of average frostless season.[70] If it can be trusted, which the authors would admit is rather doubtful, this chart shows a rather interesting picture. The isohelic lines run generally from west to east until the Mississippi is crossed whereupon they drop sharply to the south. Whereas in terms of rainfall, the Mississippi Alluvial Valley has an advantage over the neighboring areas to the west; in terms of sunshine, it appears to have an advantage over neighboring areas to the east. With due reservations it can, therefore, be stated that the Alluvial Valley appears to be more favorably situated from the point of view of *both* sunshine and rainfall than the contiguous areas on either side.

Storms

A climatic description of the Lower Mississippi Valley would not be complete without a word about storms. The region is famous for the frequency and violence of its thunderstorms. Readers of Mark Twain will recall the superb description of a Mississippi thunderstorm in "Huckleberry Finn." Oddly enough, such storms can also be considered as a climatic asset. "The suddenness with which they form, and the heavy precipitation while they endure, allow for a combination of a large amount of rainfall with a high percentage of possible sunshine — a very favorable condition for plant growth." [71] Unfortunately, the same cannot be said for tornadoes, or "twisters," as they are commonly called. These are perhaps the most violent and destructive of all storms anywhere, and they are a speciality of the Lower Mississippi Valley. "Wind velocities may reach five hundred miles per hour for short periods of time, but fortunately the area of devastation is usually less than a mile wide, and the force of the storm is generally dissipated after it has travelled a score or so of miles." [72] Considering the thin distribution of aboriginal settlements, it does not seem likely that tornadoes, however intense their psychic effects, could have appreciably affected the culture of the area in a material sense.

[68] Gannett, 1909. Map reproduced in Livingston and Shreve, 1921, pl. 52.

[69] Livingston and Shreve, 1921, pl. 46.

[70] Livingston and Shreve, 1921, p. 69.

[71] Klimm, Starkey, and Hall, 1940, p. 90.

[72] Klimm, Starkey, and Hall, 1940, p. 89.

Summary of Climate

Our brief examination of the climatic conditions of the Survey Area failed, not unexpectedly, to bring out any facts of striking significance. The area is too small to be differentiated climatically from the South as a whole. It does, however, appear to enjoy some advantages over the contiguous areas on either side. Isoclimatic lines, whether of temperature, rainfall, or sunshine, are generally deflected in the immediate vicinity of the Mississippi River, suggesting that the river, or the shape of its valley, has some effect on climate, usually on the favorable side. In particular, one very interesting possibility was noted. The Mississippi Alluvial Valley appears to be the area, *par excellence*, in the South, in which a long growing season is marked by abundance of *both* rain and sunshine. The fact that this is an ideal condition for the growth of plants, particularly maize, is sufficiently obvious.

SOILS

The soils of the Alluvial Valley of the Mississippi River have been in the main transported from elsewhere and may, therefore, be discussed largely in terms of derivation. This enables the use of the outline of physiographic subdivisions given on page 20 as a framework, which brings out some very satisfactory correlations. The classification and nomenclature of soil types used here is that of Marbut.[73] Particular reliance has been placed on the soil map prepared by this author. It is well to mention that the map is admittedly weak in the Lower Mississippi region, being based largely on general information rather than accurate soil surveys.

Soils Derived from Recent Mississippi-Ohio Alluvium

Soils brought down by the Mississippi or Ohio rivers, or the two in combination, as was the case during the greater part of the recent history of the Alluvial Valley, differ from those of other streams crossing the coastal plain mainly through their darker color resulting from derivation from the great central plains and prairies, whose soils are rich in organic material. These are the dominant soils of the Alluvial Valley, covering the greatest area and making it one of the favored agricultural sections of the country. The principal soil types are the Sharkey and Sarpy series. The first contains a high percentage of clay, is found chiefly in the bottoms and backswamp areas, and bears a hard reputation locally as "buckshot." Sharkey soils are fertile but difficult to work — a factor of decreasing significance with the rapid mechanization of farming in the area — and must be drained to make them produce well. Sarpy soils are the young natural-levee soils of relatively coarse sandy loam, underlain by still coarser material, usually sand. Natural-levee soils of older abandoned meander belts, which have developed a soil profile, are designated as Yazoo soils of the Sarpy series. Sarpy soils are well-drained, light in texture, easily worked, and extremely productive. It is no accident that the early white settlements in the Alluvial Valley were confined to areas bearing soils of this type. It is, however, remarkable that after more than a century of intensive exploitation, these soils still support the richest agricultural communities in the region.[74]

Soils of the Sharkey and Sarpy series cover most of the area of all flood-plain subdivisions of Mississippi or Ohio derivation. The only exception to this statement is that along the margins of certain flood-plain areas, facing the valley wall, are considerable areas covered by Waverly soils (to be described presently) brought down from the uplands by smaller streams. The most considerable areas of this

[73] Marbut, 1935. See key, showing relative reliability of the various sections of this map.

[74] See Colby, 1921, pp. 269–70. The soils of the Yazoo Basin are "popularly spoken of as of two kinds — the light loam soils near the streams, and the heavy clay or 'buckshot' soils of the lower lands between the water courses. The first drain well, the latter very poorly. All the older settlements in the Delta were upon the higher land along the streams, both because of convenience of transportation and immunity from overflow, as well as because this soil was more satisfactory to cultivate and more certain of crop."

sort lie along the eastern margin of the Yazoo Basin. Distribution, as between the two types, on Marbut's map shows up very much in favor of the Sharkey series. Small patches of Sarpy soils are laid down along the present Mississippi meander belt; otherwise, the flood-plain areas are shown as entirely covered by Sharkey soils. Undoubtedly, a detailed map at sufficient scale to show conditions along older meander-belt ridges would give a great deal more space to Sarpy soils. A guess, based on recollected casual observations, is that somewhere in the neighborhood of a third of the total flood-plain area in the subdivisions we are considering is covered by soils of the Sarpy type.

Soils Derived from Recent Alluvium of Non-Mississippi-Ohio Origin

Under this heading we shall consider three series of soil types: Waverly, Miller, and Portland.

Waverly soils are light-colored with a surface horizon that is almost white, except for a thin dark layer at the immediate surface. They have been developed under imperfect drainage on alluvial plains of smaller streams flowing down from the Ozark Plateau on the west and from the North Central Hills of Mississippi on the east. The inferiority of this type of soil to those derived from Mississippi-Ohio alluvium is to be expected considering their different origins. Waverly soils cover the White-Black River Lowlands and all other minor stream valleys in the Western Lowland. East of the Mississippi they are to be found, as already stated, along the eastern edge of the Yazoo Basin, principally that portion drained by the Tallahatchie River.

Miller and Portland soils derive from alluvial deposits of the Arkansas River and thus contain material brought down from the red beds of Kansas, Oklahoma, and northwest Texas. The Miller series, the more recent of the two, occurs significantly only at the southeast end of the Arkansas Lowland. The major portion of the Arkansas Lowland, and practically all the Boeuf Basin, are covered with Portland soils, an older type of the same derivation, in which the reddish surface color to the depth of about one foot has given place to the normal soil color of the region. According to Marbut, Miller and Portland soils, when not too fully leached, are highly productive but heavy and difficult to work. It is hardly necessary to repeat that the last is a factor of paramount importance to the primitive agriculturist.

Soils Derived from Older Alluvial Fans

The soils described up to this point have been young immature soils, most of which have not yet developed a soil profile. It is to be expected, therefore, that they clearly reflect their origins. When it comes to the older alluvial soils, it is no longer possible, apparently, to differentiate them on the basis of derivation.[75] Marbut shows the same soil types on surfaces that represent both Mississippi-Ohio and Arkansas fans. Under this heading, therefore, we are considering soils of all older alluvial surfaces without regard for origin.

The soils in this category comprise the Crowley and Olivier series. They are found only west of the Mississippi River. Crowley soils are silty, yellow soils, underlain by tough plastic clay, which breaks into hard angular lumps when dry but swells when wet to become practically impervious to water. This type of soil, entirely different from the younger alluvial soils described above, originally supported a tall-grass prairie vegetation. Today it fosters an important rice-growing industry, made possible by the fact that the clay subsoil permits artificial flooding without undue waste of water. It would be very surprising if the contrast, represented today by the difference between rice and cotton farming, were not reflected in the aboriginal culture of the region. Crowley soils cover most of Grand Prairie Ridge, all of the dissected portions of the Western Lowland, and the western half of the Malden Plain, i.e., between the St. Francis River and Crowley's Ridge.

[75] See Finch and Trewartha, 1936, p. 540. ". . . when mature soils are present, they show significant similarities of profile over large areas, even when they are derived from widely different parent materials. Moreover, even the soils of incompletely or imperfectly developed profiles in a region commonly have qualities that indicate a developmental progress in the direction of the regional type."

Olivier soils are not described in the text of Marbut's report. One gathers that they are related in type to the Crowley series, since the two are frequently associated together within the same physiographic subdivisions. Olivier soils are indicated on Marbut's map on the eastern half of the Malden Plain, along the margins of Crowley's Ridge, Macon Ridge, and the Bastrop Hills. This distribution cuts across physiographic boundaries to a greater extent than does that of the Crowley series, since it includes, in addition to remnants of Mississippi-Ohio and Arkansas River fans, remnants of still older surfaces represented by Crowley's Ridge and the Bastrop Hills.

Soils Derived from Loess

Fortunately for us, it is unnecessary to go into the complex problem of the origin of the Lower Mississippi Valley loess deposits. For present purposes it is sufficient that these controversial deposits, long regarded by geologists as true loess of eolian origin, do exhibit many of the characteristics associated with such deposits in other parts of the world.[76] The most striking of these is the capacity for standing in very steep faces, which results in a very striking topography of deep gorges with almost perpendicular walls. The principal deposits of loess, or what passes here for loess, are on the uplands bordering the Alluvial Valley, particularly on the east, where they form a continuous band about 5 to 15 miles in width, called the Bluff Hills. Within the Alluvial Valley the only considerable deposits are on Crowley's Ridge.

Soils derived from loess comprise the Memphis series. These are silty, calcareous, nonsandy soils, differing markedly from all the soils so far considered. They are easily worked and very fertile, but the rough topography affords insufficient level land for extensive farming.

Soils and Culture

It may be worth while at this point to refer briefly to the possibilities of correlation between culture distributions and soil types. One such possibility lies in the fact that, for primitive farmers, the young levee soils of the Sarpy series would appear to be far superior to all other soils of the region. In any period subsequent to the introduction of maize and the development of an advanced agricultural economy, these soils must have been a controlling factor in the distribution of settlements. We have repeatedly emphasized the desirability of levee lands from the standpoint of security from floods, but their light workable soils were probably even more compelling. If getting away from high water were the over-riding consideration, the older and higher alluvial lands in the western part of the valley would have been preferred for settlement, which is not borne out by the archaeological record. The reason is probably to be found in the heavy clay soils (Crowley) of these "upland" regions. This is no more than a casual sample of the fascinating problems that await the time when the results of detailed archaeological and soil surveys are available to the student of culture.

VEGETATION

Vegetation comes closer than any other single geographic element to summing up the environment of a region from the standpoint of culture. "It largely expresses climate; it tends heavily to determine the fauna; and it enters directly into subsistence, besides at

[76] Fisk (1944, p. 63) summarizes the question in the following terms: "The loess of the lower Mississippi Valley has attracted much attention, and many ideas have been advanced concerning its origin. . . . Recent work has shown that the thicknesses assigned to the loess deposits by earlier workers were often greatly overestimated; actually the loess in the Mississippi Valley region is a superficial mantle less than 50 feet thick in most places.

"Loess along the alluvial valley wall exhibits characteristics associated with loess in many places throughout the world. It has a sharp limitation in grain size, a tendency to split along vertical joints and to stand with steep faces, and a calcareous content large enough to cause effervescence with acid; it is marked by the presence of land-snail shells.

"Many geologists consider loess an eolian deposit, but Russell has recently demonstrated [1944] that in the alluvial valley region it is a soil developed from calcareous back-swamp deposits of the Pleistocene terraces through loessification, a process involving weathering and colluvial movement."

times affecting travel and transport." [77] It is, unfortunately, the most difficult of all geographic elements to summarize, even for a relatively small area. Long lists of genera and species quickly bring about a condition in which we are unable to see the forest for the trees. Vegetation maps, on the other hand, usually constructed on a continental scale, are necessarily generalized and over-simplified. Moreover, they are based on varying principles of classification and often fail to agree. Notwithstanding these drawbacks, they offer to the non-botanist the most practicable approach to the subject. Four of the most authoritative vegetation maps have recently been brought together by Kroeber, reprinted at the same scale on transparent paper, and furnished with a concordance key by means of which they may be readily compared.[78]

Harshberger's map is insufficiently detailed for our purposes. The Alluvial Valley is not differentiated from the surrounding coastal plain with its "pine-barren strand vegetation," hardly descriptive of a region in which a pine tree is something of a curiosity. Shelford gives the northern portion of the Alluvial Valley to the great central "temperate deciduous forest" but shows a narrow tongue of "cypress swamp, tree swamp" coming up the Mississippi to the mouth of the Arkansas River. Livingston and Shreve's arrangement differs only slightly from that of Shelford, in that the tongue designated "swamps and marshes" is not quite so narrow and takes in considerably more of the southern portion of the Yazoo Basin. Shantz and Zon, on the other hand, extend the swamp forest area, which they designate as "cypress-tupelogum, river bottom forest," farther up the river, taking in all the flood-plain portions of the Alluvial Valley. In complete ignorance of the botanical questions involved, it seems to the writers that this last arrangement comes closest to the facts. The present flood-plain vegetation, at any rate, seems all of one piece. Perhaps this is due to the fact that in the remnants of the original forest-cover that we see today, water-tolerant species are conspicuous. The swamp timber has been the last to go.

It may be well to keep in mind, however, the possibility of a minor shift in vegetation, corresponding to the boundary laid down by Shelford and by Livingston and Shreve, i.e., at the latitude of the mouth of the Arkansas River. In early descriptions of the Lower Mississippi country, the Arkansas River is frequently mentioned in this connection. For example, it is often stated by descending travelers that Spanish moss was first seen in the vicinity of Cypress Bend, a short distance below the mouth of the Arkansas.[79] Timothy Flint, the pioneer geographer of the Mississippi Valley, puts the northern limit of Spanish moss and the palmetto a little farther down the river at latitude 33 degrees.[80] It is also stated by reputable travelers that cypress was first encountered below the Arkansas River, which very likely accounts for the name "Cypress Bend." [81] This is obviously contrary to the facts of distribution, but may be explained as due to the circumstances that, in the limited view of the descending river traveler, not much cypress was to be seen until the extensive swamps on the west side of the river below Arkansas were revealed in all their gloomy vastness. This is confirmed by an interesting passage in the travel account of one, Christian Schultz, who made the Mississippi voyage in 1807–08.

> It [Arkansas River] likewise seems to be a dividing line between the upper and lower climates; as the alligator is seldom seen higher up than this river, and at no time numerous. The Arkansas is also a kind of boundary line to the growth of the cypress; for although above this you occasionally meet with it, yet below it soon becomes the principal tree of the forests.[82]

It is tempting to pursue this interesting point further, but we must get back to the subject at hand. At any rate, one feels that it cannot

[77] Kroeber, 1939, p. 206.

[78] Kroeber, 1939, pp. 14–19, maps 2–5. The maps are derived from the following sources: Harshberger, 1911; Livingston and Shreve, 1921; Shantz and Zon, 1924; Shelford, 1926.

[79] James, 1905, p. 129; Nuttall, 1905, p. 296; Richardson, 1940, p. 29.

[80] Flint, 1828, vol. I, pp. 85, 91. Nuttall (1905, p. 299) states that the palmetto "commences about Warrington," an old town not far below Vicksburg, Mississippi, but it appears from our casual observation that Flint was more nearly correct.

[81] Collot, 1924, vol. I, p. 43.

[82] Schultz, 1810, vol. II, p. 123.

be without significance that, whereas early descriptive accounts are at variance concerning the country above the Arkansas River, they are practically unanimous in giving the country below it, particularly on the west side, a bad name. Some do not hesitate to predict that this horrid wilderness of mosquito-infested swamps can never become the abode of civilized man. So, while following Shantz and Zon in regard to the entire Alluvial Valley, at least the flood-plain portions thereof, as an area in which swamp flora supplied the dominant note, we should not lose sight of the possibility that such dominance was more complete below the Arkansas River than above it. It is a possibility of great interest owing to the fact that the Arkansas River seems to mark a cultural boundary as well, as we shall attempt to show in a later section.

Returning to the vegetation map of Shantz and Zon, this is the only one of the four that makes any attempt to distinguish between vegetation of the recent flood plain and the older alluvial plains and upland remnants. The scale — we are referring now to the original publication — is too small to permit exact correlation between vegetation and physiographic areas. However, the correspondence is sufficiently close to make it seem advisable to discuss vegetation within the framework provided in the physiographic section and already used in the discussion of soils. In so doing, we shall attempt to make up the deficiency of detail, unavoidable in a classification of continental scope, by reference to studies of a more local nature to be found in various national and state agricultural and forestry reports.

Vegetation of Areas of Recent Alluvium

There does not seem to be any possibility, at this stage, of distinguishing between the vegetation on recent alluvial surfaces of different origins. Differences there must be, of course, because the soils are different, but our information is insufficiently detailed for such fine correlations. We shall attempt to describe the vegetation of the various flood-plain areas as though it were all the same.

As already stated, the vegetation of the entire flood plain is designated by Shantz and Zon as "cypress-tupelogum, river bottom forests." A brief description in the accompanying text qualifies this over-simplification somewhat. We find that flood-plain forest communities vary in two significant ways: (1) from north to south, as a result of climatic factors; and (2) from river to backswamp, as a result of minute changes in elevation.

The first kind of change is difficult to generalize. According to Shantz and Zon, bottomland forests near the Gulf Coast "are characterized by the presence of cypress, red gum, tupelo, yellow oak, overcup oak, and cow oak, and farther north by cottonwood, silver maple, white elm, river birch, sycamore, boxelder, and ash."[83] This is not very helpful since they fail to indicate what is meant by "farther north." Comparison of lists furnished by three different authorities writing on alluvial forest conditions of Louisiana, Mississippi (Yazoo Basin, specifically), and western Tennessee, respectively, gives a slightly more satisfactory idea of the sort of changes that take place from south to north.

Louisiana[84]	Mississippi[85] (Yazoo Basin)	West Tennessee[86]
Cypress	Red gum	Red gum
Tupelo gum	Tupelo gum	Oak
White oaks	Red oak	Ash
Swamp oaks	White oak	Cottonwood
Red gum	Overcup oak	Hickory
Ash	Elm	Cypress
Elm	Cypress	Elm
Hackberry	Ash	Sycamore
Hickory	Pecan	Soft maple
Black gum	Hickory	Tupelo gum
	Cottonwood	Beech
	Maple	
	Birch	

Assuming these lists to be in approximate order of frequency of occurrence, which is not altogether certain, a few tentative observations may be made. Going from south to north, cypress and tupelo gum, the dominant swamp varieties, evidently lose importance while the oaks and hickories gain correspondingly. Cot-

[83] Shantz and Zon, 1924, p. 14.

[84] Foster, 1912, p. 14.

[85] Dunston, 1910, pp. 30–33.

[86] Hall, 1910, p. 30.

tonwood, sycamore, maple, and beech likewise appear to be more important in the north.

Variation in flood-plain vegetation incident to local changes in elevation is possibly more significant and certainly more easily described. In general, there are three different situations in all parts of the flood plain, the ridges, the bottoms, and the swamps. To which might be added a fourth, the flats, i.e., the sand bars, islands, and points along the main courses of the Mississippi and other major tributaries.

1) The ridges, or "cane ridges," as they are sometimes called in the earlier literature, include present and former natural levees, remnants of braided topography, and any other bits of higher ground on the flood plain, of whatever origin. The ridges are only inundated by the highest floods and therefore support a vegetation in which swamp varieties are not conspicuous. In such situations, the latter give way to "oaks, red gum, ash, red maple, honey locust, hackberry and a few less important hardwoods." [87] In certain areas, hickory,[88] and in the north, beech,[89] can be added to the list. These ridges were formerly referred to as "cane ridges" because of the dense undergrowth of cane which was one of the conspicuous features of the landscape before white settlement. The importance of cane in aboriginal and pioneer white economy, and the causes of its disappearance will be discussed in a later section.

2) The bottoms, "hardwood bottoms," "glades," or "sloughs," as they are variously called, are those extensive areas of flood plain intermediate between the natural levees and the backswamp, which were, before the construction of artificial levees, flooded annually for a period of several weeks to several months. These bottoms were the home of a mixed cypress and hardwood forest. The lower portions of their slightly undulating surfaces were occupied by pure, or nearly pure, stands of cypress, the higher portions by cypress and various associates; red maple, water oak, red oak, ash, honey locust, hackberry, red gum, tupelo gum, white oak, overcup oak, elm, pecan, hickory, cottonwood, and birch.[90] This forest was characteristically dense, with a heavy canopy of leaves overhead and little undergrowth. This is undoubtedly the kind of forest that was in the minds of travelers when they spoke of the ease of penetrating the wilderness — in dry weather of course; in times of flood it would be under 6 or 8 feet of water.

3) The deep swamps that lie farthest away from the streams, called "backswamps," are generally under water throughout the growing season, and their characteristic forest growth is made up principally of cypress and tupelo gum. In these swamps, and in the partly filled oxbow lakes, pure stands of cypress, or "brakes," as they are called, frequently occur. Pure, or nearly pure, cypress forests of commercial importance occur, or did occur, only in the southern part of the Alluvial Valley, pre-eminentaly in the broad deep swamp area below Baton Rouge, Louisiana.

4) The flats support a dense and almost unbelievably rapid growth of cottonwoods and willows.

In terms of culture, the chief interest centers naturally on the vegetation of the natural levees. These are the only portions of the flood plain that were habitable. It is unlikely that the Indians made extensive use of the bottom and swamp forest vegetation. Further study should be directed toward an understanding of the vegetation of the natural levees in detail, but this lies outside the scope of the present report.

Vegetation of Older Alluvial Plains

It will be recalled that the subdivisions designated as older alluvial plains lie entirely west of the Mississippi River and mostly north of the Arkansas River. According to Schantz and Zon, these are about equally divided between river bottom forest and prairie grassland vegetation. A glance at figure 1 will make this perfectly clear. The Western Lowland, the largest area of older alluvium, is drained by moderately large north-south flowing streams, each of which has a considerable flood plain of its own. The tall-grass prairies occupied the higher land between them, and were — one has to use the past tense, because the prairies have been altered beyond recognition by farming — long and narrow in consequence. The total area must have been considerable, but since it was divided into so many separated areas, it may be doubted whether the effect

[87] Mattoon, 1915, p. 21.

[88] Foster, 1912, p. 14; Shantz and Zon, 1924, p. 14.

[89] Hall, 1910, p. 30.

[90] Dunston, 1910, p. 32; Mattoon, 1915, p. 48.

on culture was very considerable. The exception to this statement, however, was Grand Prairie Ridge, which takes its name from a prairie some 70 miles in length, by 15 to 20 miles in width, an area large enough to be interesting from the cultural standpoint.

Unfortunately, however interesting they may be to us, these prairies are too small in comparison with the great central prairies of Illinois and the trans-Mississippi region, to have received much notice from students of prairie vegetation. There is a voluminous literature on prairies, chiefly centering on the problem of origins, but a cursory reading of some of the more promising titles failed to produce even a mention of the prairies in our area.[91] Separated as they are by a great belt of oak-hickory and oak-pine forest from the central prairies, and surrounded by river-bottom forests, it seems likely that their vegetation would show a special character, differing from that of the great prairies so often described. Early accounts supply less information than one would expect, because most travelers had already seen and described the great prairies, or because they traveled by water and saw very little of them anyway. We are, therefore, unable to furnish a detailed description of the vegetation of these prairies, and will merely point out instead a few of the things that make them interesting to the student of culture.

In the first place, prairie lands in this area were not favorable for agriculture. The characteristics of the soil (Crowley series) have already been described. However suitable it may be for the production of rice under modern methods of farming, it was entirely unsuited to primitive agriculture. Add to the heaviness of the soil, the toughness of the tall-grass sod, and primitive farming becomes virtually impossible. This was still true in the early period of white settlement. Timothy Flint gives a very interesting account of the Grand Prairie Ridge in the early nineteenth century, in which, after commenting on the heavy gray clay "indented on the surface, with innumerable little cones raised by the craw-fish, a circumstance which is well known to indicate a cold and wet soil," [91a] he adds:

> The lands, that will yield crops without manure, lie at the points of the bends of the prairies, where the soil is uniformly much richer than the average quality of the prairie. But as these prairies are always skirted on their edges with young cane, affording winter range, as the summer range for cattle is inexhaustible; as these open plains are more swept by the winds, and are more free from mosquitoes, and healthier than the bottoms; all the planters, who prefer raising cattle to cotton, are settled on the edges of the prairies.[92]

The inference seems to be that out on the prairies themselves, at this time, there were no farmers at all.

The second point is a corollary of the first. If the prairies forbade agriculture, did they offer the possibility of a hunting type of economy instead? The *a priori* answer would almost certainly be in the negative, because these prairies were not large enough, were it not for that very interesting episode in the De Soto expedition, in which a small reconnoitering party sent out from Pacaha, on the west bank of the Mississippi, encountered on a treeless plain a small band of people living in portable shelters, with all the earmarks of a pre-horse prairie-hunting type of life.[93] This can only have been Grand Prairie Ridge or one of the smaller prairies of the Western Lowland or the Malden Plain, unless *all* guesses as to the probable location of Pacaha are wrong. For this reason alone the archaeology of these prairie districts should be investigated with particular care. So far as the present Survey is concerned, we have no more than felt around the southern edges of Grand Prairie Ridge with purely negative results. About all we can say now is that the late agricultural temple mound-building type of culture of the flood plain seems not to have penetrated very far into that area, but as yet no evidences of a hunting pattern of culture can be adduced.

The only other sizable older alluvial plain, Macon Ridge, is shown by Shantz and Zon as part of the great oak-pine forest that swings around inside the coastal plain from the piedmont of Virginia to eastern Oklahoma and Texas. "West of the Mississippi River this

[91] See bibliography in Shimek, 1911.

[91a] Flint, 1826, p. 255.

[92] Flint, 1826, pp. 255–56.

[93] See p. 358.

forest is made up of shortleaf pine, oaks, and hickories, particularly yellow oak and bitternut and pignut hickories; on the dry ridges post and blackjack oaks; in the fresher soils white and red oaks, big-bud or mockernut hickory, and red gum." [94]

Vegetation of the Upland Remnants

Of these only Crowley's Ridge is large enough to show on the vegetation maps. According to Shantz and Zon, it is divided between prairie grassland and oak-hickory forest.

> The oaks and the hickories, together with some ash, black walnut, elm, and box elder, are the species which push farthest into the prairie region. Hickory is particularly predominant in the lower Mississippi Valley.[95]

The oak-hickory areas are mainly located on the western flank of the ridge, along the edge of the Western Lowland.

Concluding Remarks on Vegetation

The foregoing brief and wholly inadequate summary gives an idea of the chief vegetal characteristics of the region and its important subdivisions. The principal difficulty still remains, however; how to translate such information into terms that will contribute to our understanding of the culture. More explicitly, how can we extract from it the answers to such questions as the following: What was the degree of penetrability of those forests in their original state; was it such as to make them barriers to communication? What about the ease or difficulty of clearing them for agricultural purposes? What was their effect on the supply of game and the means of taking it? Until we know the answers to such questions as these, we can claim little understanding of the area as a human habitat. A host of minor problems range themselves under the heading of vegetation. The nature and distribution of cane may be taken as an example. The subject has many cultural angles. Besides the more obvious uses that come to mind, such as material for arrows, spears, fish-poles, mats, and other articles of household furniture, and as wattles in house construction, cane seems to have been an important element in the food supply as well. Young shoots were boiled and eaten much as we eat asparagus. The seeds were ground and made into a kind of bread. Most significant is the fact that cane flourished on the higher land of the natural levees and on the richest soil. According to Timothy Flint, the ground was never better for maize than when cleared of cane.[96] Thus, the best corn land was at the same time the land most easily cleared, since cane could be removed by simply running fire through it. Game could be taken in the process, canebrakes being the favorite resort of some of the larger animals, notably bears and panthers. After the fires had cooled the new green shoots quickly sprang up to be gathered and eaten. On the debit side, perhaps, is the fact that the higher land, suitable for land travel and communication, was precisely that most likely to be blocked by impenetrable stands of this plant. After white settlement, the young cane proved excellent fodder for cattle and pigs, firing became a regular practice, and the canebrakes disappeared. It would be difficult now, if not impossible, to find out very much about its former distribution, but the subject might repay investigation.

The question of wild-food resources is an important one. Even a slight familiarity with the ethnographic literature leads to a suspicion that dependence on agriculture in this particular area may not have been as great as is generally supposed, even in the latest periods. A superficial review of a few outstanding documentary sources brings out the following list: persimmons, dried, pounded, and made into a kind of bread; pond lily, both seeds and tubers eaten; cane, seeds and young shoots; wild rice; wild potato (?); pawpaw; mulberry; Osage orange; Chickasaw plum; grapes; all sorts of berries; nuts, of which the most important was the pecan, as a source of oil. This list is by no means complete. Reconstruction of the economic botany of extinct cultures is a manifest impossibility, yet something of the sort must be attempted before we can begin to understand them.

[94] Shantz and Zon, 1924, p. 14.

[95] Shantz and Zon, 1924, p. 14.

[96] Flint, 1828, vol. I, p. 80.

Further laboring of this point is unnecessary. It should be clear that what we have done in this section on vegetation is merely to furnish a sort of background which is entirely meaningless until put into relationship with the culture, which, from where we archaeologists sit, occupies the foreground. That, however, requires a type of study for which the present writers have neither the time nor the competence.

FAUNA

We have perhaps made a mistake in appearing to aim at completeness in describing the geographical conditions of the Mississippi Alluvial Valley, for when it comes to the important subject of fauna, we find ourselves with very little to say. A mere catalogue of species, if such were available[97] — concluding with the inevitable comment that the area was a "veritable hunters' paradise" — would tell us nothing without the more significant information as to how and to what extent these gifts of nature were utilized by man. Perhaps even more than vegetation the subject of fauna is involved with culture. For example, it appears that the older alluvial plains with their large expanses of open prairie offered greater opportunity for buffalo hunting than obtained in the densely wooded flood-plain areas, but we have as yet no evidence that such opportunities were utilized. In the early eighteenth century, the French depended on these areas for supplying meat to garrisons and settlements on the lower river, and it appears that the friendly Quapaw were the principal hunters in this trade. From this we are tempted to infer that the Quapaw were always more interested in hunting, or let us say less fully dependent on agriculture, than the tribes farther down the river. But this is an assumption requiring proof that only archaeology can give.

So far, in this area, archaeology has furnished practically no information on this or any other question having to do with the utilization of fauna. The older practice of presenting a list of species represented in the food bones excavated on a site, without quantification, is practically useless to the student of culture. The very small numbers of identifiable bone specimens found in our own stratigraphic excavations do not even warrant description. A considerable body of interesting but entirely disarticulated facts can be dug out of the ethnographic literature but we have not yet found time to make the effort.

One or two general observations, however, may be warranted at this time as interesting subjects for further inquiry. In discussing vegetation, we referred to the possibility that the region about the mouth of the Arkansas River was a kind of frontier for the distribution of certain plants. Nothing but the vaguest sort of evidence could be adduced for this, mostly derived from the accounts of early naturalists and travelers. Similar inferences might be drawn from their comments on fauna. For instance, it is frequently said that below the Arkansas the beaver was rarely found, and above it, the alligator, never. It may be that the Arkansas River figures prominently in such observations because it is the most conspicuous topographical feature for a long stretch of the Mississippi Valley, from the foot of Crowley's Ridge to the bluffs of Vicksburg. In any case, such questions as these ought to be run to earth. If the present faint indications of a cultural shift in this same general area stand up under further investigation, the possibilities of a correlative ecological shift might become very interesting indeed.

Another problem under the heading of fauna is the distribution and utilization of edible shellfish in the area. We may say at once that the apparent extent of both is disappointing. Although occasional small lenses of shell appear in middens throughout the area so far investigated, only on the Yazoo River have we encountered anything that could properly be described as shell middens, and these of a size and thickness greatly inferior to the well-

[97] A partial list can be put together by combining local information by several authorities arranged by states in Shelford, 1926, pp. 454–66.

known shell heaps on the Tennessee River. There is a small commercial shellfishing industry (for "pearl" buttons) on the St. Francis today, but little evidence of their utilization here in prehistoric times. The characteristic deep sluggish streams of the Alluvial Valley no doubt are generally unfavorable to shellfish, but there is likewise a possibility that the local Indians were not overly fond of eating them. Whatever the cause, the paucity of shell middens has been distinctly unfavorable to archaeology. It is undoubtedly one of the reasons why we have as yet so little information on the pre-pottery cultures of the area.

The discerning reader will have noticed that in the paragraphs above we have glossed over a total ignorance of faunal conditions in the area by calling attention to one or two questions which, but for that ignorance, might not even be asked. However, if such an exposure has served to emphasize again the indivisibility of cultural and geographic problems, it will not have been a complete waste of time.

FLOOD CONDITIONS

Perhaps as important as any of the geographic elements already discussed, at least for the flood-plain portions of the Survey Area, is the question of floods. This brings us to the heart of a long-standing and sometimes acrimonious debate. Are the floods in the Lower Mississippi Valley the work of man or nature? It is a question of terrifying complexity. The two extreme points of view run somewhat as follows: (1) Nature's beautiful equilibrium has been destroyed by deforestation and levee-building, the first by increasing the run-off and the river's load, the second by confining the river and preventing it from depositing its load over the flood plain, forcing it instead to build up its bed. According to this view, the higher the levees are built, the higher becomes the river's bed, and the higher and more destructive the ensuing floods. (2) There is no such beautiful equilibrium of nature, and never has been. Deforestation is a negligible factor, since, though forests do check ordinary run-off, floods are the products of extraordinary conditions; and the increased burden of silt, far from being a danger, enables the river to scour its channel deeper, and the levees assist by increasing its velocity. This is obviously no question for the innocent layman, who is himself promptly overwhelmed by a flood of arguments and statistics. His only recourse is to turn back to early historical accounts predating both deforestation and levee-building. These do not appear to support the beautiful equilibrium theory. From De Soto narratives of the mid-sixteenth century on down to the travel accounts of the early nineteenth century, we find accounts of floods seemingly only less destructive than those of recent times because there was less to destroy. Thus Elvas, in some ways the most reliable of the De Soto chroniclers, on the flood at Aminoya, in 1543: [98]

> In March, more than a month having passed since rain fell, the river became so enlarged that it reached Nilco, nine leagues off; and the Indians said that on the opposite side it also extended an equal distance over the country.
>
> The ground whereon the town stood was higher, and where the going was best the water reached to the stirrups. Rafts were made of trees on which were placed many boughs, whereon the horses stood; and in the houses were like arrangements; yet, even this not proving sufficient, the people ascended into the lofts; and when they went out of the houses it was in canoes, or, if on horseback, they went in places where the earth was highest.
>
> Such was our situation for two months, in which time the river did not fall, and no work could be done.

Garcilaso's account of the same flood adds some interesting details showing what measures were taken by the Indians to protect their property, which in turn shows that floods were of common occurrence.

> It began about the tenth of March, of the year 1543. It gradually filled all its bed, and immediately after it impetuously spread itself over its border, then through the country, which was immediately inundated, be-

[98] Buckingham Smith, translation in Bourne, 1904, vol. I, p. 189.

cause there were neither mountains nor hills. And the day of Palm Sunday, which was that year the 18th of March . . . the waters violently entered through the gates of Aminoia, so that, two days after that, they could not go through the streets except in boats. This overflow did not appear in all its extent until the twentieth of April. Then they had the pleasure to see that which but lately was a vast country, had become, nearly all at once a vast sea; for the water covered more than twenty leagues of adjacent lands, where were seen only a few of the highest trees. . . . Because of the inundations . . . the Indians . . . place themselves, as much as possible, upon eminences, and build their houses in this manner. They erect in the form of a square, enough large posts in the shape of pillars, upon which they place many beams which take the place of floors. Then they make the house which they surround with galleries, where they lay up their provisions and furniture. Thus they protect themselves from the inundations, which probably occur on account of the rains and snows of the preceding year.[99]

The overflow lasted forty days. Strange coincidence! Similar descriptions are to be found in the accounts of almost all early travelers who happened to be in the Lower Mississippi Valley at the right time of year. The important thing to remember is that the floods were annual. Every year the bottom lands were covered; only the crests of the natural levees remained out of water. Taken in this sense, the word "flood" loses its meaning. Inundation is a milder and more appropriate word, suggesting benefits as well as injury. "Flood" should be reserved for occasions when the natural levees were also topped. Such there must have been, because that is how the natural levees were formed, but how often and how long-continued, and how high the stage above the levee crests, are questions to which we have no answers. But even if we had, we would still be unable to gauge their effect on culture. We seem to be in the same fix again. Until you know precisely where and how people lived at any given time, you cannot say very much about the effects of floods upon them. If we had complete flood-stage records in the Lower Mississippi Valley from the year A.D. 1, we would still be ignorant of aboriginal flood conditions, because man and his culture *are part of those conditions.*

It appears, then, that the emphasis in the first part of this discussion has been put in the wrong place. Whatever the state of nature's equilibrium, beautiful or otherwise, it is the state of equilibrium between man and nature that counts. We can assume that primitive man accepted the inevitability of annual inundations, and of occasional floods as well, and adjusted his more complaisant culture to them. It is characteristic of modern man that he has chosen to fight the river instead. We know as little about the success or failure of one solution as the other.

SUMMARY AND DISCUSSION OF GEOGRAPHIC SETTING

In the foregoing pages we have attempted to describe some of the geographic conditions of the northern and central divisions of the Mississippi Alluvial Valley, in terms of Fisk's detailed physiographic classification of that area. What might seem an unconscionable amount of detail was justified by the working principle that any physiographic factors sufficient to delimit a physiographic subdivision, no matter how small, might also be expected to have a sufficient effect on culture to be reflected in the archaeological record. A thorough testing of this principle is something for the future, when we have more complete and satisfactory archaeological data. In the meantime, it seemed wiser to maintain the discussion of culture-environmental problems on a coarser geographic scale and a higher level of generalization. Fortunately to this end, it was found possible to show that physiography, soils, and vegetation combined in a very satisfactory way to differentiate three types of area within the Alluvial Valley. These are, in reverse order of importance to the present study: (1) upland remnants, (2) older alluvial plains, and (3) the present flood plain.

[99] Shipp translation, 1881, pp. 457–58.

1) The few scattered areas of maturely dissected surface designated by Fisk as upland remnants are of insufficient extent in an overall archaeological sense, but are not by any means to be overlooked entirely. As isolated outliers of sharply contrasting landscape corresponding to that of the older land surfaces on either side of the valley, they can hardly fail to offer interesting sidelights on local culture-environmental problems in the area. In a limited sense, perhaps, they can be used as "controls" in such investigations. Their possible importance does not stop here, however. By reason of their greater geological age, these are the areas that should be most thoroughly searched for evidence of the earliest cultures in the valley. So far as the present writers are aware, no efforts have been made to this end.

2) Dissected alluvial plains, designated here as "older" in relation to the extreme geological youth of the present flood plains, account for a significant portion of the total land area of the Alluvial Valley, and are likewise important culturally. They lie at an elevation only slightly higher than the flood plains, to which, however, they exhibit a remarkable contrast in every respect. As remnants of older alluvial fans of the Mississippi and its major tributaries, their topography displays the lenticular character of the braided streams responsible for the up-building of those fans. Present streams for the most part follow main channels of the old braided systems. Perhaps most important from the standpoint of human occupation is the fact that these streams, lightly entrenched in the otherwise level surface, are subject both to freshet and backwater flooding. Their natural levees, for various reasons which need not be detailed here, are less developed than those of flood-plain streams of corresponding size, and in any case cannot offer the same advantages as natural levees in the flood plain. Such advantages depend on a wide-bottom and back-swamp area to act as collecting basin for the flood waters that top the levees. Natural levees of an entrenched stream, lacking such collecting basins, are consequently of negligible importance from the point of view of security in times of high water. The soils of these stream bottoms, moreover, deriving for the most part from the relatively infertile Ozark uplands, are distinctly inferior to those of the Mississippi-Ohio flood plain. In short, in the case of the older alluvial plains, there are not the same incentives for the concentration of settlements in the immediate vicinity of the streams. From the standpoint of high water, the higher inter-stream areas would be preferable, but their heavy clay soils and tough prairie-grass sod make them even less favorable for primitive agriculture. The practicable solution for an agricultural people was to locate along the bluffs and cultivate the bottoms, and this they seem to have done. Note that this is not necessarily a less favorable situation than that of their neighbors in the flood plain, but it is essentially a different one and was bound to lead to significant cultural differences. It might be that the risks of bottom-land agriculture and the poorer soils were compensated by a more abundant supply of game in the prairies. It would be a reasonable inference that the culture was less agricultural and sedentary. In terms of current archaeological concepts, it seems to be an environment unfavorable to the spread of the strongly agricultural "Temple Mound" or "Mississippi" type of culture. This undoubtedly goes a long way to explain the paucity of sites manifesting this culture in the areas under consideration. By the same token, these would be the areas in which one might expect to find traces of occupation more nearly approximating to the hunting stage of culture. It would not be unreasonable to look for a persistence of archaic forms in these older alluvial plains. There are interesting suggestions of this in the ethnographic literature. The famous hunting tribe, encountered by one of De Soto's exploratory parties is a case in point. Repeated references in the later French period to the Quapaw as hunters — not an idle term, considering the fact that for long periods they supplied the garrisons of Natchez and even New Orleans with meat — may also be cited. Even the French *habitants* at Arkansas Post, and later the Americans in the same region, are constantly reproached by their more progressive compatriots for following a hunting rather than a farming way of life. It is easy to overrate such examples, often specious, of continuity from one culture to another but in this case there may be something in it.

3) The third, and most important type of area from our particular standpoint, that of the active flood plains of the Mississippi and its major tributaries, is more difficult to generalize about. Its apparent uniformity is wholly deceptive. Its landscape, even today, is one of extraordinary contrasts by reason of minute differences in elevation. It is a land in which the thought of high water could never have been long absent from the aboriginal mind, a land hazardous but rewarding. This type of area has the greatest archaeological importance, because it reveals the most conspicuous and extensive remains.

We have spoken of contrasts within the flood-plain areas. The principal one of course is between levee lands and bottoms or backswamp areas, a contrast marked by striking differences in soils and vegetation. The advantages of levee lands for primitive occupation have been thoroughly exposed. What is not so clear are the differences between one set of levee lands and another, or, in physiographic terms, between one meander-belt ridge and another. In the aggradational process, older meander-belt ridges are being slowly buried under accumulating flood-plain deposits, which not only decreases their height relative to the general surface, but cuts down their width as well. It may be stated as a working principle, therefore, that, all other things being equal, the most recent levee lands, at any given time, are the most desirable for human occupation. The question is, at what point does an older abandoned meander-belt ridge begin to be less desirable, and how long does it take? At what point do the differences become appreciable in terms of culture? Correlation of archaeological and aggradational data will perhaps yield an answer to this important question. At this juncture it is merely adduced as an example of the difficulty of generalizing about the flood plain. A further difficulty is that we know so little about flood conditions in aboriginal times, and in particular about the cultural adaptations that were found to counter them. About all we can say with assurance is that levee lands provided the most favorable, in fact the only possible, habitat for primitive agriculturists in flood-plain portions of the Alluvial Valley, and the younger the levees the better. It is no accident that the large sites of the Late Mississippian-type culture are almost invariably located on natural levees of comparatively recent formation.

But what about the flood plain as a human habitat as compared with the older alluvial plains or the adjacent uplands and upland remnants? Theoretically, the conclusion is inescapable that for a late type of culture with relatively high dependence on agriculture, the flood plain had most to offer, and certainly archaeology supports such a conclusion. The advantages of fertile levee soils, and especially their workability, seems to have been sufficient to off-set the difficulties and dangers of periodic floods. Favorability for earlier types of culture, not so dependent on agriculture or without it altogether, is by no means so clear. Even a theoretical answer is impossible without a great deal more information on wild-food resources. The practical answer waits on archaeology. It must be admitted that present data on early cultures in the Alluvial Valley is almost nonexistent, but this is always the case in an area containing conspicuous later remains. In the flood plain, there is an additional reason: early sites are hard to find because they have been buried by recent sedimentation.

A general characteristic of flood-plain topography warrants re-emphasis at this time. The parallelism of streams and resulting linearity of physiographic features and subdivisions is bound to be reflected in the shape of culture distributions. A great deal has been made of the importance of rivers as avenues of communication and the consequent tendency for cultures to spread along them. Here there are perhaps more compelling reasons for that type of spread. People who have adjusted their existence, particularly their farming, to a certain meander-belt ridge can find similar conditions only by moving farther along the ridge or by crossing a backswamp area to another ridge. Only stringent necessity would be likely to force them to the second alternative. In applying methodological devices involving time-space concepts in this area, therefore, direction is likely to be more important than distance.

Toward a Concept of Environment. Up to this point, we have been concerned principally with the physical conditions of our area, as a sort of background or stage, more or less apart from the peoples and cultures that played their parts upon it. The term "geographic setting" was used advisedly in place of "environment," which in the present writers' view has a more comprehensive meaning. Environment, in this sense, does not come within the scope of an introduction to an archaeological report. If we had the necessary data, we would not be doing the archaeology. We have, of course, by no means exhausted the more limited approach comprehended in the term geographic setting. There is plainly a great deal more to be learned about the geographic elements described above, not to mention important elements that were not even considered. In the course of these inquiries, however, we have learned something about environment in the wider sense. It seems that every time you attempt to push your investigation of a geographic factor to the point of real understanding, you are brought up short by ignorance of associated cultural factors. The question of aboriginal flood conditions is a typical example. Here, we found it meaningless to speculate on the effects of floods upon man without knowing something of the nature and extent of his adjustments to them. To our surprise, it appeared that floods are as much a cultural as a natural phenomenon.

The environmentalist view, if we interpret it correctly, is that culture can only be understood in terms of environment. It seems no less true that environment can only be understood in terms of culture. The concept of environment as a background, therefore, is inept, unless we have in mind the sort of background that one sees in a well-constructed museum diorama, in which a three-dimensional model is projected upon a two-dimensional background so cleverly that the eye cannot distinguish where one leaves off and the other begins. In short, it appears that culture and environment must be comprehended simultaneously, if either is to be understood in all its bearings.

The student of prehistory in the Lower Mississippi Valley must in fact do more. He must attempt to reconstruct cultures that no longer exist in an environment that exists only in a profoundly modified state. This is no simple undertaking, and we therefore make no excuses for having merely sketched out some of the lines in which such a study might be expected to follow.

Section II

THE ARCHAEOLOGICAL FIELD WORK

THE ARCHAEOLOGICAL FIELD WORK

INTRODUCTION

The Problem

THERE is general agreement among students of Southeastern archaeology that the climax of the late prehistoric cultures is the archaeological facies long recognized under the designation "Middle Mississippi." At a comparatively late date — A.D. 1400–1500 is probably not too late for its peak of development — this culture type was firmly established over an immense area. The large prehistoric settlements represented by the remains at Cahokia, Moundville, Etowah, and Macon, not to mention some of the less-known but equally impressive sites described in the present work, are thought to have been occupied about this time, or even later. By 1939, when the present Survey was first discussed, an immense amount of data on Middle Mississippi had accumulated, but the problem of its origins and development appeared to be as far from resolution as ever. There was a general impression, shared by many students of Southeastern culture, that this was because the "central" Mississippi Valley, the assumed center of distribution of the culture, had not been sufficiently investigated. It was primarily to make good this lack that the present Survey was undertaken.

The existing status of archaeological studies in what we have defined elsewhere as the Survey Area was such as to make it a very attractive field for research. Except for the University of Chicago's work at Kincaid and other sites in southern Illinois, the investigations sponsored by the St. Louis Academy of Science in southeastern Missouri, and excavations by the University of Tennessee at the Shelby Site (12-P-2), in the vicinity of Memphis, Tennessee, none of which had been published, the area had been largely untouched by modern methods of investigation.

To understand this apparent neglect, it is necessary to review briefly some of the earlier work in the area. From the earliest beginnings of what used to be called "Mound Archaeology" it received its full share of attention. Private collectors were busy as early as the seventies and the Peabody Museums of Harvard and Yale, the Davenport Academy of Sciences, and the Bureau of American Ethnology of the Smithsonian Institution soon followed. The long series of investigations of the latter culminated in the publication of Thomas' monumental report of 1894[1] and Holmes' monograph on the pottery in 1903,[2] both of which gave a great deal of space to the archaeology of the area. Thomas' problem may be summed up in the question: "Were the Mound-builders Indians?" Consequently, the Bureau's investigators, under his direction, gave particular emphasis to mounds, enclosures, and other features of a constructional nature. Their reports provide invaluable data on such features, many of which have since disappeared, and all of which have been altered almost beyond recognition, but in questions involving the analysis of culture materials, particularly pottery, they contributed very little. Holmes' great treatise went far to make up the deficiency, and it is to this remarkable pioneer effort that we owe the term, "Middle Mississippi." It is important to remember that as used by Holmes, it was a broad typological concept applied to pottery alone. So far as our particular area is concerned, it has remained just that. The large-scale excavations and comparative studies necessary to convert that concept into a culture context have not been started. The later investigations of Peabody,[3] Moore,[4] Brown,[5] Lemley,[6] Dickinson, and Dellinger,[7] had, except for the last three named, been concerned almost entirely with burials and their asso-

[1] Thomas, 1894.

[2] Holmes, 1903.

[3] Peabody, 1904.

[4] Moore, 1908a, 1908b, 1908c, 1909, 1910, 1911, 1913.

[5] Brown, 1926.

[6] Lemley and Dickinson, 1937.

[7] Dellinger and Dickinson, 1940; Dickinson and Dellinger, 1940.

ciated artifacts. A mass of material, chiefly ceramic, was saved from the commercial pot-hunter, whose activities in this area have been unremitting, and is now moldering on museum shelves. Not unnaturally, the misconception arose that the field has been fully exploited through all this effort, professional and otherwise. Nothing could be farther from the truth. It so happens that in the Lower Mississippi Valley profusion of burial offerings is a late development characteristic of the Mississippian cultures, but not of the earlier cultures that preceded them. In planning the Survey, we had to accept the melancholy conclusion that accumulated materials were mostly late and therefore of little use in solving the questions we were interested in, but we could take heart from the circumstance that few of the earlier sites in the area had been disturbed. Pot-hunters had shied away from them in disgust, and professional archaeologists often followed their example. The problem, therefore, was not primarily that of securing with better methods more material of the sort already obtained, but of securing material that had not been obtained at all. We have been accused of coming in as outsiders and "skimming the cream" off the archaeology of the region. The metaphor is imprecise. The cream, in the sense of the topmost layer, had long ago been skimmed and safely removed to the collectors' shelves. It was the less attractive but far more important material that lay underneath that we were after.

This brings us again to what we may call the main Survey problem. We have spoken of the desirability of investigating Middle Mississippi on what was assumed to be its home ground in the hope that some light might be thrown upon its antecedents. These, it could be assumed, lay in a period dominated elsewhere by cultures of Hopewell-Marksville affinity. Originally recognized as a specialized development in the Ohio Valley, by 1939 the fundamental nature and wide distribution of this earlier culture type was beginning to be appreciated. Its known limits had been so widened as to include almost the entire Southeast, using the term in its broadest sense, and as a result, the Survey Area appeared as central rather than peripheral to the distribution. Marksville-type pottery had been reported by Lemley and Dickinson from sites on Bayou Macon in southwestern Arkansas [8] and by Ford from sites in the lower part of the Yazoo Basin.[9] In the northern part of the Survey Area, however, north of the Arkansas River, no signs of this culture had as yet been found. We had every reason to expect them, and may anticipate here by stating that they appeared on the first sites investigated in the spring of 1940. Thus, on the first day in the field, the Survey problem shifted from the general one of putting a floor under Middle Mississippi to the more specific one of the relationship between Middle Mississippi and an earlier Hopewellian culture, to which we gave the provisional name of Baytown, and it has remained there ever since.

THE SURVEY PROGRAM

Scope of Project and Accomplishment to Date

With a slight foreknowledge of the abundance of sites in the Mississippi Alluvial Valley, the writers approached the project in the winter of 1939–40 with a long-range point of view, which needless to say did not take into account the imminence of a second world war. The plan, insofar as it was formulated, envisaged three stages of work: (1) preliminary site survey and analysis of surface collections; (2) stratigraphic tests on a large number of sites; (3) small-scale excavations on key sites, selected on the basis of the results of (1) and (2). The extent of accomplishment may be seen by comparing the site map, figure 2, with the physiographic map, figure 1. In terms of the Mississippi River Commission grid, we have so far covered with unequal thoroughness 49 out of 171 quadrangles included within the area we have somewhat brashly designated as the Survey Area.

[8] Lemley and Dickinson, 1937.

[9] Ford, 1936.

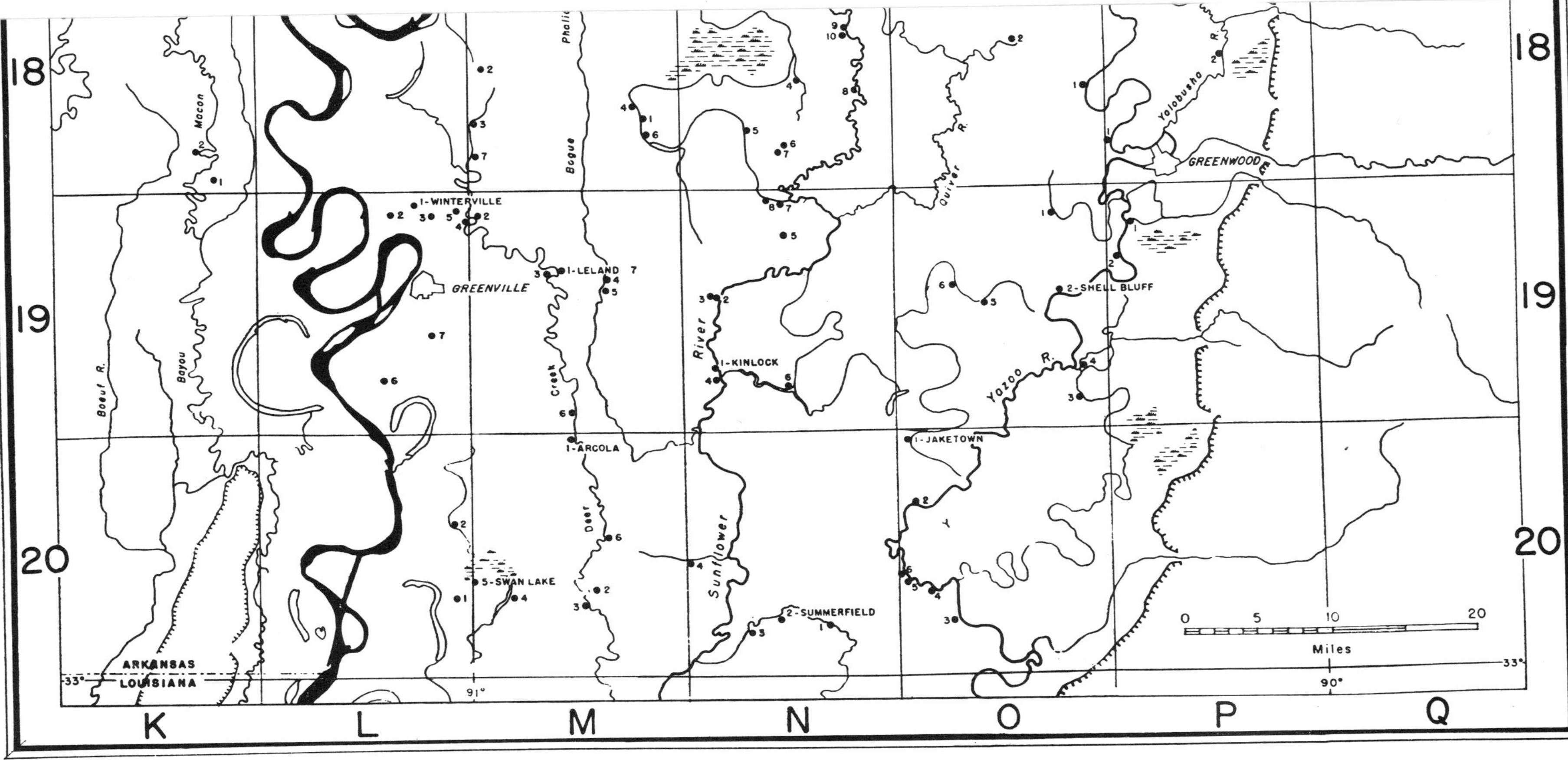

Fig. 2. Location of sites catalogued by the Lower Mississippi Survey to date.

In so doing we have catalogued 385 sites, the majority of which have not been heretofore referred to in print. Twenty stratigraphic tests have been carried out on 11 sites, 18 of which were sufficiently successful to warrant description in this report. Stage 3, that of site excavation, remains in the status of hopeful planning for a non-foreseeable future.

Survey Methods

It should be thoroughly understood that a complete archaeological survey, of the sort now in progress in many states, was never contemplated. Our catalogue of sites makes no pretense of completeness. The object was merely an adequate sampling of sites, sufficient to provide a safe coverage of the area and to insure against the omission of any significant cultural manifestation. This looks well on paper but is actually difficult to carry into practice. Deliberate avoidance of sites, particularly large and fruitful ones, requires a scientific rigor which the writers cannot claim to possess. It is inevitable, therefore, that our sample is weighted somewhat on the side of larger and more conspicuous sites. It must also be pointed out that this crude sampling method of reconnaissance, combined with certain conditions of the archaeology itself, notably the paucity of stone "workshop" sites and shell heaps, is unfavorable to the finding of early pre-ceramic manifestations, though we know from stratigraphic excavations that such existed in the area.

The general procedure in the first season (spring, 1940) was to establish headquarters in a town affording reasonable accommodation and work out from there within practicable limits, using both cars for reconnaissance, with the idea of getting a large sampling of sites and as much surface pottery as possible for purposes of preliminary classification. Temptations to get busy with shovels were ruthlessly suppressed. In subsequent trips, where two vehicles were available, as in the spring of 1941 and 1946, one was fitted up for excavation while the other carried on the Survey. It was, however, at all times a strictly motorized reconnaissance. Only rarely were attempts made to run down reported sites that could not be reached by car, or at least by jeep, and these were almost invariably unsuccessful. We made an effort to traverse all public roads and as many private roads as were passable, and thus managed to view from a reasonable distance practically all the cultivated land, which, in the flood-plain sections is practically equivalent to all the land that would have been suitable for Indian occupation and a great deal more besides. The term "reasonable distance" perhaps requires some explanation. In the cultivated portions of the flood plain a site with mounds or midden accumulations, however small, is generally visible from a considerable distance. This is the way the great majority of sites were located. A large number, of course, were found on information picked up along the roadside at the cost of innumerable coca-colas and some indigestion. If there are mounds in the neighborhood, everybody knows about them; in fact, almost everybody has dug into them. The presence of pottery and stone fragments, even where no mounds are present, is likewise a matter of common observation in this stoneless land. Other sites, and this applies to fairly large mound groups, were found by studying contours on the excellent Mississippi River Commission maps, and a few sites are actually designated as "Indian Mounds" on these maps. Our indebtedness to interested local students of archaeology has already been gratefully acknowledged. Information from published sources was used whenever possible but was often found to be insufficiently specific as to location.

The basis of cataloguing is the grid system used by the Mississippi River Commission in mapping the area. Their quadrangle sheets, comparable to those of the U. S. Coast and Geodetic Survey, cover 15 minutes of latitude and longitude (about 14 by 17 miles) at the scale of 1:62,500. They are numbered in tiers from north to south and lettered in ranges from west to east (see map, fig. 1). Each quadrangle is accordingly designated by a number and a letter. Site 12–N–3, for example, is the third site which was encountered in quadrangle 12-N. Finds have been catalogued in the same way with an additional term designating the particular location on the site from which the collection was taken. Fortunately, the entire area contemplated in the Survey has been mapped by the Commission, so it will be possible to follow this system throughout.

In the field each car was equipped with a bound volume of quadrangle sheets which was constantly in use. The route of the car was followed on the map in colored pencil and points at which information was sought or obtained were likewise indicated. This enabled us to judge the significance of negative evidence. Information obtained was noted on the map margins for future verification. Sites, when found, were laid down directly on the sheets, which can be done with considerable accuracy. At the same time a printed site index card was filled out, giving, along with other pertinent information, the site location in terms of quarter section, section, and township. As a further check, a descriptive location was given with reference to local landmarks. Mapping of sites was held to a minimum. For most sites a sketch map with estimated distances was deemed sufficient. This was drawn on the back of the site card which was furnished with a grid for that purpose. Large sites, particularly mound groups, where assemblage becomes an important factor, were mapped with plane table, and alidade. An example of a completed site card is shown in figure 3.

LOWER MISSISSIPPI VALLEY ARCHAEOLOGICAL SURVEY
SITE INDEX CARD "A"

SITE NO. 17-M-2 QUAD. Pace COUNTY Bolivar STATE Miss.
SITE NAME Blanchard COMPLEX M. Miss.
TYPE OF SITE Mound group, possibly village of St. Francis type
SITE LOC SE¼ NW¼ S. 11 T. 24-N R. 7-W
E bank Bogue Phalia at intersection of small bayou 3 mi. E of Gunnison
INFORMANT J. A. (Red) Wherry ADDRESS Waxhaw, Miss.
REMARKS
OWNER Harris – + ++ ADDRESS Gunnison, Miss.
OWNER'S REP. – + ++ ADDRESS
TENANT – + ++ ADDRESS
PREV OWNER Mrs. A. R. Blanchard
PREV EXCAV
COLLECTOR Phillips DATE 11/26/40 ADD. REC. Plane table map
DESCRIPTION OF SITE: First impression was that it was a site of the St. Francis type, particularly the southern end, which shows one very definite corner. Impression stregthened by the elevated surface of the site, which is everywhere a good three feet or more above the surrounding level, and by the character of the soil, rich dark midden to a considerable depth. Also seemed to be pure M. Miss. which is pretty rare in this part of the country. Plane table map was a disappointment from this point of view. Northern end of site (northeastern rather) is in tall cotton, difficult to see where the

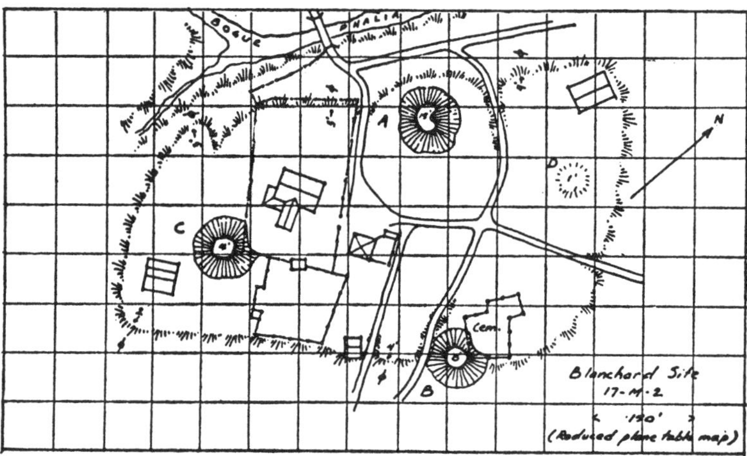

FIG. 3. Sample of completed field card with sketch map on reverse.

Surface Collections

In the initial stage of the Survey — and for all practical purposes we are still in that stage — it was our view that the sole object of surface collecting was to get adequate samples of associated material. The emphasis was therefore on the collection rather than on the site. The difficult question as to what exactly constitutes a site was deliberately avoided. We followed convenience rather than principle. In general, any area showing more or less continuous indications of occupation was regarded as a site, regardless of the extent or number of mounds involved. This is at variance with the approved methods used in some current State Surveys, in which village site and mounds, however closely related, are catalogued as separate units. In our case, this would have resulted in many times the number of sites and great increase of paper work without any corresponding return. The looser, more economical method was, in our opinion, entirely consistent with the purposes of the Survey. However, with an increase of emphasis on the problem of correlating archaeology with abandoned river-channel position,[10] the site as such takes on a greater importance, and we shall undoubtedly be obliged in the future to modify our care-free methods in the direction of closer definition of site and local topographical relationships.

In respect to actual collections, we have been somewhat more particular. Separate collections were made on different areas of a site wherever there was the slightest indication that they might differ in content. If, at the time of sorting, they were found to be the same, within the normal limits of variability, they were thrown together again to make a larger count for the site. No ideal canon for surface-collecting methods was formulated, much less followed. The system of picking up every sherd within a specified area is a counsel of perfection. On many sites it would be a physical impossibility. Generally speaking, our only concern was to get as large a sample as possible and a reasonably honest one. The last is not as easy as it sounds. On sites where sherds are thick enough to be shoveled into sacks, it is difficult not to favor decorated and rim sherds. The only sure way to eliminate this difficulty is to hire local people to pick sherds up at so much per sack. You sometimes get brickbats and other extraneous material, but the sample is an honest one.

Size of Collections

The size of surface collections varied enormously from site to site, but not appreciably from one part of the Survey Area to another. We have, from the standpoint of gross quantification, a fairly consistent coverage of that part of the area surveyed. This may be readily seen in figure 4. It is not necessary, therefore, to qualify interpretations on account of inadequacy or unevenness of sample.

[10] See Section VII.

Records

All records are kept on 5- by 8-inch cards. In addition to the site cards referred to above, a second card shows the pottery count, or counts, by types. Photographs and information from other sources are pasted on additional cards to the number required. A set of quadrangle sheets and record cards is on file at each of the participating institutions where it will be available to any interested student.

Excavation Methods

The simple procedures followed in making stratigraphic tests are described in detail in Section VI.

Disposition of Material

The first season's collections were trucked down to Louisiana State University at Baton Rouge, for "processing" — to use the jargon then in vogue to describe the simple operations of washing and cataloguing — by the laboratory staff of the Louisiana State Archaeological Survey, a WPA project that was going on at the time. At the end of the field season the three authors spent a week in Baton Rouge setting up a preliminary pottery classification. Material from subsequent field trips was shipped to Michigan or Harvard, depending on who made the collections. Further vicissitudes of the tremendous mass of ceramic material are described in Section V.

As time went on and our provisional classification became more firmly established in our minds, it was possible to sort sherds in the field, counting and throwing away body sherds of the common types. This was done by tying them up in sacks and quietly dropping them into the deepest stream available. This practice was followed in the 1946 and 1947 field seasons. We are not now convinced that this is an altogether sound procedure, except in the case of the very large collections of which sufficient rim sherds are saved to act as a control in case of future changes in the classification. For example, we have only re-

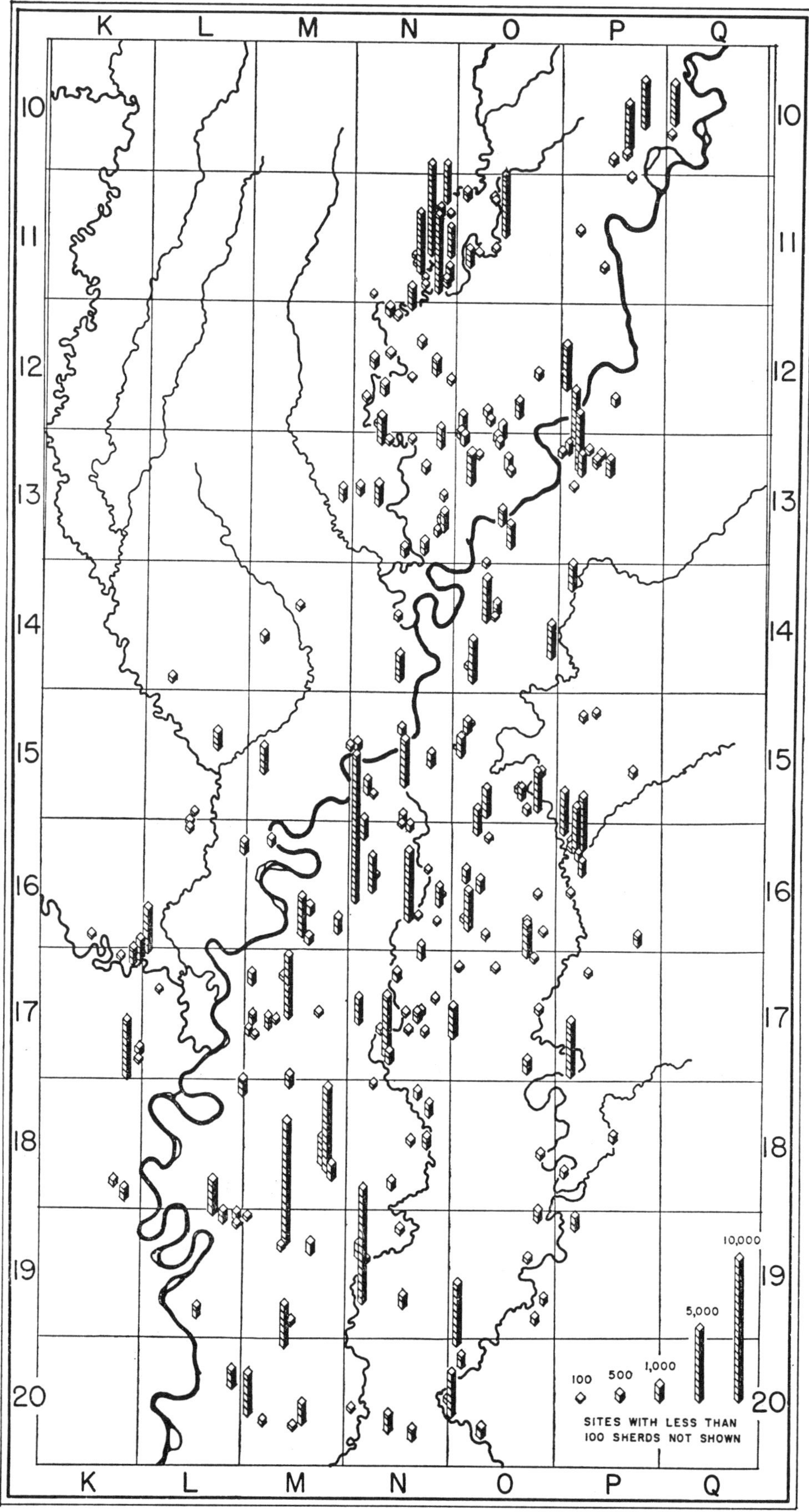

Fig. 4. Gross quantity distribution of surface sherd collections.

cently (1947) begun to distinguish what appears to be an early variant of Neeley's Ferry Plain, which might make it desirable some time to re-sort all plain shell-tempered pottery, at which time it will be embarrassing to think of all those sherds resting on the river-bottoms.

Photographs of Vessels

For several years prior to the inception of the Survey, Phillips had been assembling photographic data on "Middle Mississippi" pottery from the collections of various individuals and museums. During the course of the Survey, this project was continued jointly by the three participators with the result that we have at our disposal a collection of over 5000 photographs of vessels, mostly of known provenience. This material has been useful in defining and illustrating some of the later types.

Non-ceramic Materials

In this report the word "collection" may be read "potsherds." Generations of small boys and collectors have seen to it that very few stone artifacts are left on the sites. Local cultures are, understandably, poor in stone anyhow. A few specimens were picked up on some sites, to which we were occasionally able to add artifacts presented by generous owners. Stratigraphic excavations yielded a few more. The result is what would be a fairly large body of material if it came from one site, but under the circumstances, it is insufficient, in our opinion, to enter profitably into the discussion at this preliminary stage. This sounds like the familiar excuse of the ceramist for neglecting other categories of material, but at present we do not feel apologetic about it. It will undoubtedly be possible to correlate stone and pottery types as the work proceeds, and as we get back into the earlier periods stone, and other materials, are certain to become increasingly important.

Shortcomings

We have already spoken of the need for improving our field procedures in respect to the relationship of sites to the local topography, which is the result of a new orientation of interest unforeseen at the time the field work was done and therefore unavoidable. Another shortcoming, however, remains to be mentioned, that might have been avoided if we had given more consideration to the method of analysis to which the collections were going to be subjected. This matter is covered at length in Section V. Briefly, it amounts to this. We never sufficiently took into account the important distinction between site and pottery collection. The seriation method described and demonstrated in Section V is a method of dating pottery collections, not sites. The assumption implicit in the large seriation graphs is that the vertical position of each collection represents a theoretical average of the time span of that collection. The strip graph, in other words, has to be handled as though it represented an instant in time, whereas it really represents a variable slice of that commodity. Now obviously, the closer the collection comes to being in actuality what it is represented to be in theory, the greater the validity of the results. In other words, collections intended for use in seriation should be as "pure" as possible. Our mistake was that, thinking in terms of the dating of sites rather than collections, we more or less unconsciously strove to get collections representative of the site as a whole. The result is that several of the collections covered so long a span of time as to be useless for seriation purposes.[11]

In using this method in the future, the concept of site should be temporarily laid aside, while the collecting proceeds. The definition of site and the collection of pottery samples should be treated as distinct operations. More attention should be paid to small shallow sites indicating short periods of occupation. On large sites, a great deal more care should be taken to segregate collections. So far as possible separate collections should be made from each mound and house site. Deep sites should be tested stratigraphically if possible. These are, of course, counsels of perfection, and do not imply that everything we have done so far has been wrong. They are of general interest, only insofar as they evidence the need for constant checking of field procedures in relation to the archaeological problem.

[11] See Section V, p. 227.

TABULATION OF SITES

A complete list of sites catalogued by the Survey is given in table 1 (pp. 47–58), and their locations are shown on figure 2. The tabulation requires explanation on one or two points.

The naming of sites is sometimes a difficult business. So far as possible we have attempted to avoid giving new names to old sites, particularly when the older names have appeared in print. However, in cases of uncertain identification, it has been thought preferable to have two names attached to the same site rather than two sites to the name name. Other difficulties have arisen in cases where two or more contiguous sites, whose identity we thought it advisable to keep separate, have been known in the past under a single name. These explanations are offered in defense of some liberties taken with established nomenclature.

In order to make the descriptions brief enough for tabular presentation, certain adjectives have been arbitrarily standardized as follows:

"Large," as applied to conical mounds, indicates a height in excess of 3 meters, regardless of diameter; as applied to rectangular platform mounds, a height in excess of 3 meters and a maximum dimension in excess of 30 meters. "Small" indicates size less than those given. In cases where no adjective is used, it is either because the size of the mound was indeterminate or not stated in the field notes.

As applied to village sites, "large" indicates a size of more than 5 acres, or a maximum dimension of more than 200 meters, depending on the terms of measurement used in the notes. "Small," again, indicates sizes below these figures.

The term "St. Francis-type site" is explained at length in Section VIII (pp. 329 ff).

Except in a few cases where there can be no question about it, the number of mounds on a site is not given, this being so variable a figure, depending on the observers' idea of what constitutes a mound, the condition of the site, time of year, etc., that it can only lead to confusion of identification and lack of confidence in our Survey data.

The letters given under the heading "Range" will be intelligible only after the perusal of Section V in which the chronological seriation of surface collections is explained and the results given. It is emphasized there that these dates apply to pottery collections and only date the sites in a very rough average fashion. They are only included here to give a ready reference in respect to the relative position of the site in what is still a very arbitrary and provisional time scale. Blanks in this column indicate insufficient pottery collections for seriation purposes or other difficulties of a technical nature.

TABLE 1: LIST OF SITES CATALOGUED BY THE SURVEY.

SITE NO.	NAME	COUNTY	STATE	LOCATION	DESCRIPTION	RANGE
10–P–1	Carson Lake	Mississippi	Arkansas	NE¼SW¼ S5 T11N R10E	Large village site	C–B
10–P–2	Bell Place [12]	"	"	NW¼SE¼ S34 T11N R9E	Cemetery	B–A
10–P–3	Nettle Ridge	"	"	SW¼NE¼ S4 T10N R9E	Large village site	E–A
10–P–4	Notgrass Place	"	"	NW¼NW¼ S35 T11N R9E	Large village site	C–B
10–Q–1	Upper Nodena [13]	"	"	NW¼SW¼ S1 T11N R11E	Large village site and cemetery with mounds	B–A
10–Q–2	Sherman Mound [14]	"	"	SE¼SW¼ S24 T12N R10E	Village site with large platform mound	. . .
10–Q–3	Turnage [15]	"	"	NW¼SW¼ S13 T11N R10E	Village site with small mound	E–A
11–N–1	Parkin [16]	Cross	"	NW¼NW¼ S34 T8N R5E	Large St. Francis type site with large platform mound	B–A
11–N–2	Rogers Place	"	"	NE¼SW¼ S26 T8N R5E	Small conical mounds	E–D
11–N–3	Roberts	"	"	NE¼NE¼ S26 T8N R5E	Small mounds	E–D
11–N–4	Neeley's Ferry [17]	"	"	SE¼SE¼ S3 T8N R5E	Large St. Francis type site with large platform mounds	B–A
11–N–5	White Place	"	"	SW¼SE¼ S3 T8N R5E	Small conical mound	. . .
11–N–6	Block	"	"	SE¼SE¼ S29 T8N R5E	St. Francis type site with large platform mound and plaza arrangement	D–C
11–N–7	Harold	"	"	NE¼NE¼ S32 T8N R5E	Village site with small mounds	. . .
11–N–8	Williams	"	"	SE¼NW¼ S17 T8N R5E	Village site with mounds	D–C
11–N–9	Vernon Paul [18]	"	"	NE¼NE¼ S11 T8N R5E	Large St. Francis type site with large platform mounds and plaza arrangement	B–A
11–N–10	Cross County Club	"	"	NW¼SW¼ S4 T7N R4E	Village site with small mound	D–C
11–N–11	Delta	"	"	SE¼SW¼ S17 T8N R5E	Large conical and small mounds	D–C
11–N–12	Turnbow Place [19]	"	"	NW¼NE¼ S2 T9N R5E	Large platform mounds and plaza arrangement	C–B
11–N–13	Williamson	"	"	SW¼NE¼ S20 T8N R5E	St. Francis type site with platform mounds in plaza arrangement	C–B
11–N–14	Twist Plantation No. 1	"	"	SW¼NE¼ S22 T9N R5E	Small village site without mounds	. . .
11–N–15	Fortune Mound [20]	"	"	SW¼SE¼ S10 T9N R5E	Small St. Francis type site	B–A
11–N–16	Twist Group	"	"	S14 T9N R5E	Small conical mounds	C–B
11–O–1	Pittman	Poinsett	"	SW¼SW¼ S21 T10N R6E	Small conical mounds	. . .
11–O–2	Webster Cemetery	"	"	SE¼SE¼ S18 T10N R7E	Small conical mound	. . .
11–O–3	Emrich Place (East Cemetery)	"	"	NW¼NE¼ S20 T10N R7E	Two small mounds	. . .
11–O–4	Cummings Place [21]	"	"	SE¼SW¼ S29 T10N R6E	Village site with small mounds	B–A
11–O–5	Emory	Crittenden	"	SE¼NE¼ S2 T9N R6E	Small conical mound	D–C
11–O–6	Pinkston	Poinsett	"	SE¼SE¼ S35 T10N R6E	Small village site with small conical mound	E–D
11–O–7	Lewis Place	Crittenden	"	NE¼NW¼ S16 T8N R6E	Village site with small mounds	D–C
11–O–8	Richard Bridge	"	"	NE¼NW¼ S10 T8N R6E	Small St. Francis type site with small mound	C–B

[12] Dellinger and Dickinson, 1940, pp. 139–41.
[13] Dellinger and Dickinson, 1940, pp. 141–42.
[14] Thomas, 1894, p. 223.
[15] This may be Moore's "Stoffle Place" (1911, pp. 474–76).
[16] Moore, 1910, pp. 303–05.
[17] Moore, 1910, pp. 309–17.
[18] Probably Moore's "Jones and Borum Places" (1910, pp. 307–09).
[19] Moore, 1910, pp. 324–25.
[20] Moore, 1910, p. 324.
[21] Moore, 1910, pp. 326–29.

TABLE 1: LIST OF SITES CATALOGUED BY THE SURVEY (*continued*).

SITE NO.	NAME	COUNTY	STATE	LOCATION	DESCRIPTION	RANGE
11-O-9	Gilliland	Crittenden	Arkansas	NW¼NW¼ S31 T9N R7E	Small village site with small mounds	D–C
11-O-10	Barton Ranch [22]	"	"	NE¼NW¼ S30 T9N R7E	Large St. Francis type site without mounds	C–B
11-O-11	Prosperity	"	"	NW¼NW¼ S6 T8N R7E	Village site with small mound	D–C
11-O-12	Black Oak Church	"	"	NE¼NE¼ S10 T8N R6E	Village site with small mound	. . .
11-P-1	Shawnee Village	Mississippi	"	SE¼SW¼ S10 T10N R9E	Village site with small mounds	C–B
11-P-2	Bradley [23]	Crittenden	"	SW¼SE¼ S17 T8N R9E	Village site with platform mounds	C–B
11-P-3	Golightly Place	"	"	NW¼SW¼ S26 T9N R8E	Village site with rectangular platform mound	C–A
11-P-4	Pacific	"	"	NW¼SE¼ S23 T9N R8E	Small mounds	. . .
11-P-5	Lambethville Cemetery	"	"	NW¼SE¼ S30 T9N R9E	Small mounds	. . .
12-N-2	Manly [24]	St. Francis	"	NE¼NW¼ S18 T5N R4E	Village site	B–A
12-N-3	Rose Mound [25]	Cross	"	NW¼NW¼ S18 T7N R5E	Large St. Francis type site	C–A
12-N-4	Big Eddy [26]	St. Francis	"	NE¼SW¼ S20 T6N R4E	St. Francis type site with small mounds	B–A
12-N-5	Welshans Place	Cross	"	NE¼SW¼ S15 T7N R4E	Village site with large platform mound and small mounds	C–B
12-N-6	Westmorland	"	"	SE¼SW¼ S23 T7N R4E	Small conical mounds	E–D
12-N-7	Lansing	"	"	SE¼NE¼ S5 T6N R5E	Small mounds	D–C
12-N-8	Beckles	"	"	NE¼SW¼ S33 T7N R5E	Small mound	. . .
12-N-9	Burns	St. Francis	"	SW¼SW¼ S30 T6N R5E	Small mound	F–E
12-N-10	DeRossett's Place	"	"	NW¼SE¼ S4 T5N R4E	Village site with large conical mound	F–E
12-N-11	Johnson	"	"	NW¼NW¼ S9 T5N R4E	Small conical mound	. . .
12-N-12	Widener Cemetery	"	"	SW¼SW¼ S21 T5N R4E	Village site with small mound	D–B
12-N-13	Parks	"	"	NW¼SW¼ S22 T6N R5E	Village site with small mounds	F–C
12-N-14	Crow Creek [27]	"	"	NW¼NW¼ S2385 T5N R3E	Village site with small mounds	. . .
12-N-15	Swan Place	"	"	NE¼NE¼ S16 T6N R4E	Small conical mound	F–E
12-N-16	Dent	"	"	SW¼SE¼ S25 T6N R5E	Village site with small mounds	E–D
12-O-1	Turner Place	"	"	NE¼NE¼ S36 T6N R7E	Small mound	C–B
12-O-2	Pouncey	"	"	SE¼NW¼ S28 T5N R7E	Large village site with large platform mounds and small mounds in plaza arrangement	E–B
12-O-3	Thompson Lake	"	"	NE¼NE¼ S35 T5N R6E	Village site with large and small platform mounds	E–D
12-O-4	Davis Place	"	"	NE¼SW¼ S26 T5N R6E	Village site with large and small mounds	E–D
12-O-5	Cramor Place	"	"	SW¼SE¼ S32 T5N R6E	St. Francis type site	C–B
12-O-6	Brackenseed Place [28]	"	"	NE¼SW¼ S17 T5N R8E	Village site with large rectangular platform mound and small mounds	B–A
12-P-1	Mound Place [29]	Crittenden	"	NE¼SW¼ S4 T5N R8E	Village site with large platform mounds	B–A
12-P-2	Shelby	Shelby	Tennessee	½ mi. above original state line in West Loop T5N R9W	Village site with large square platform mound and small mounds in plaza arrangement	B–A

[22] Dellinger and Dickinson, 1940, pp. 135–36.

[23] Moore, 1911, pp. 427–46; Thomas, 1894, pp. 226–27.

[24] Probably Moore's "Bonner Place" (1910, p. 269).

[25] Moore, 1910, pp. 276–303.

[26] Moore, 1910, pp. 269–76.

[27] Thomas, 1894, pp. 227–28.

[28] May be same as Moore's "Rhodes Site" (1911, pp. 413–26).

[29] Moore, 1911, p. 427.

TABLE 1: LIST OF SITES CATALOGUED BY THE SURVEY (*continued*).

SITE NO.	NAME	COUNTY	STATE	LOCATION	DESCRIPTION	RANGE
12–P–3	Mound City	Crittenden	Arkansas	SE¼SW¼ S27 T7N R9E	Village site with small mounds	. . .
13–M–1	Hughes	Lee	"	SW¼SW¼ S10 T3N R3E	Large village site with large and small mounds	E–D
13–N–1	Sudan Cemetery	"	"	NE¼NE¼ S34 T3N R4E	Village site with small mounds	. . .
13–N–2	Alligator Bayou	"	"	NE¼NE¼ S32 T3N R5E	Village site with small mound	D–C
13–N–3	Mound Cemetery	"	"	SW¼NW¼ S14 T3N R5E	Village site with large rectangular platform mound and small mound	. . .
13–N–4	Kent Place[30]	"	"	NW¼NW¼ S1 T2N R5E	Large village site with large platform mound and small mound	D–A
13–N–5	Davis	"	"	SE¼SE¼ S14 T3N R5E	Village site with mound	C–B
13–N–6	Jerusalem Church	"	"	SE¼NW¼ S36 T3N R5E	Village site with small mound	C–B
13–N–7	Clay Hill	"	"	SE¼SE¼ S12 T3N R3E	Large village site with small mounds	B–A
13–N–8	Findley	"	"	SE¼NW¼ S36 T3N R5E	Small village site	D–C
13–N–9	Red Oak	"	"	SE¼NW¼ S18 T2N R5E	Small village site	. . .
13–N–10	Taylor Mound	"	"	NE¼NE¼ S1 T2N R5E	Village site with small mound	. . .
13–N–11	Grant Place	"	"	SW¼SE¼ S19 T2N R5E	Village site	D–B
13–N–12	Murdock Place[31] (Walnut Bend)	"	"	NW¼SW¼ S1 T2N R5E	Large village site with large rectangular platform mound and small mounds	D–C
13–N–13	Rawlinson	St. Francis	"	NW¼SE¼ S28 T4N R5E	Village site with mounds	D–C
13–N–14	Conner Place	Lee	"	NW¼NE¼ S21 T3N R4E	Village site	D–C
13–N–15	Nickel	St. Francis	"	SE¼SW¼ S11 T4N R5E	Large village site with large rectangular platform mound and small mounds	D–B
13–N–16	Starkley	Lee	"	NE¼NW¼ S21 T2N R5E	Village site with large mound	C–B
13–N–17	Greer[32]	"	"	NE¼NW¼ S27 T2N R4E	Village site with large rectangular platform mound	D–B
13–N–18	Lakeside	St. Francis	"	N½NE¼ S7 T4N R5E	Village site with large and small mounds	C–B
13–N–19	Riverside	"	"	SE¼NW¼ S10 T4N R4E	Small mound	D–C
13–N–20	Hargrave	"	"	SW¼NE¼ S10 T4N R4E	Small mound	. . .
13–N–21	Castile Landing[33]	"	"	NE¼NE¼ S9 T4N R4E	St. Francis type site	B–A
13–O–1	Barrett	Lee	"	SW¼NW¼ S3 T3N R6E	Large village site with large rectangular platform mound and small mounds	D–B
13–O–2	Green River Plantation	Crittenden	"	SW¼NW¼ S8 T4N R7E	Village site with large rectangular mound and small mounds	D–C
13–O–3	Huber	St. Francis	"	SE¼SE¼ S15 T4N R6E	Village site with mound	D–C
13–O–4	Nickey Mound	Crittenden	"	SW¼NW¼ S8 T4N R7E	Village site with large mound	C–B
13–O–5	Belle Meade	"	"	NE¼SE¼ S30 T4N R7E	Large St. Francis type site with large platform mounds and small mounds in plaza arrangement	B–A
13–O–6	New Bethel	St. Francis	"	NW¼NE¼ S8 T4N R6E	Village site with large platform mound	C–B
13–O–7	Beck	Crittenden	"	NW¼NW¼ S32 T4N R7E	Village site with mounds in plaza arrangement	B–A
13–O–8	Stoddard	St. Francis	"	SW¼NW¼ S9 T4N R6E	Village site with small conical mounds	D–C

[30] Moore, 1911, pp. 406–10.

[31] Moore, 1911, pp. 406–10 (either this site or 13-N-4 or both were excavated by Moore as "Kent Place").

[32] Thomas, 1894, p. 231.

[33] Moore, 1910, pp. 266–68.

TABLE 1: LIST OF SITES CATALOGUED BY THE SURVEY (*continued*).

SITE NO.	NAME	COUNTY	STATE	LOCATION	DESCRIPTION	RANGE
13-O-9	Collins	Crittenden	Arkansas	NW¼NE¼ S6 T4N R7E	Village site with small conical mounds	D–C
13-O-10	Hollywood[34]	Tunica	Mississippi	SE¼SW¼ S33 T3S R11W	Large village site with large rectangular platform mound and small mounds in plaza arrangement	B–A
13-O-11	Commerce[35]	"	"	SW¼SE¼ S17 T3S R11W	Large rectangular platform mound and small mounds	C–B
13-O-12	Indian Creek	"	"	NE¼SW¼ S34 T3S R7E	Large village site	C–B
13-O-13	Crystal Spring Md.	"	"	SE¼SW¼ S26 T3S R11W	Small mound	. . .
13-O-14	Sledge (Royal)	"	"	NW¼SE¼ S3 T4S R11W	Village site with small mound	. . .
13-P-1	Walls[36]	De Soto	"	SW¼NE¼ S24 T1S R10W	Village site and cemetery with mounds	B–A
13-P-2	Edgefield Mounds	"	"	SE¼SW¼ S13, NE¼SE¼ S14 T1S R10W	Two large conical mounds	. . .
13-P-3	Turkey Ridge	"	"	NE¼SE¼ S8 T2S R9W	Large village site	G–F
13-P-4	Dogwood Ridge	"	"	SE¼NE¼ S4 T2S R9W	Village site and cemetery	F–A
13-P-5	Shannon	"	"	SE¼SW¼ S24 T2S R10W	Village site with small mound	D–B
13-P-6	Cheatham[37]	"	"	NE¼SW¼ S29 T1S R9W	Village site with large rectangular platform mound	B–A
13-P-7	Norfolk	"	"	SE¼SW¼ S35 T1S R10W	Village site	B–A
13-P-8	Lake Cormorant	"	"	SW¼SW¼ S7 T2S R9W	Village site with small mound	F–A
13-P-9	Withers	"	"	SW¼NW¼ S18 T2S R9W	Two small mounds	G–D
13-P-10	Irby	"	"	NW¼NE¼ S16 T2S R9W	Large village site with small mound	F–A
13-P-11	Woodlyn	"	"	NW¼NW¼ S36 T1S R9W	Large village site with small mound	B–A
14-L-1	Webster's Camp	Monroe	Arkansas	SE¼NE¼ S23 T2S R2W	Large village site with large and small mounds	. . .
14-M-1	Turner	Phillips	"	NE¼NE¼ S3 T1S R2E	Small village site with small mound	. . .
14-M-2	Bonner	Lee	"	SW¼NE¼ S34 T1N R2E	Village site	D–C
14-M-3	Broom	Phillips	"	NE¼NE¼ S26 T1S R1E	Large village site with mounds	E–D
14-N-1	Moore	"	"	SE¼SE¼ S1 T1S R4E	Large village site with small mound	C–B
14-N-2	Steagall	"	"	SE¼SW¼ S6 T1S R5E	Village site	. . .
14-N-3	McCoullough Mound	Lee	"	SW¼SE¼ S25 T2N R3E	Large conical mound	. . .
14-N-4	Bowie Village	Phillips	"	SE part of irregular sec. (unnumbered) T2S R4E	Large village site	F–E
14-N-5	Coolidge Mound	"	"	N. Center irreg. sec. (unnumbered) T2S R4E	Small conical mound	. . .
14-N-6	Helena Crossing	"	"	NW part irreg. sec. S491 T2S R5E	Large village site with large conical mounds	. . .
14-O-1	Evansville[38]	Tunica	Mississippi	NW¼NW¼ S20 T5S R11W	Village site with large rectangular platform mound and small mounds	E–C
14-O-2	Owens	"	"	NW¼SE¼ S25 T5S R12W	Village site with large and small mounds	F–D
14-O-3	Beaverdam[39]	"	"	SE¼SE¼ S19 T5S R11W	Large village site with large and small mounds	C–B
14-O-4	Perry[40]	"	"	SW¼NW¼ S18 T4S R11W	Large village site with large platform mound and small mounds	B–A

[34] This almost certainly is Brown's "Bowdre Mounds" (1926, pp. 120–22). Barton, 1927, pp. 85–86, calls it the "DeBe Voise Mound."

[35] Moore, 1911, pp. 411–13.

[36] Brown, 1926, pp. 122–23 (Brown includes the "Edgefield Mounds" [13-P-2] in the "Walls Site").

[37] Brown, 1926, p. 122.

[38] Brown, 1926, p. 117.

[39] "Mound on Beaver Lake." Brown, 1926, p. 117.

[40] Moore, 1911, p. 411.

TABLE 1: LIST OF SITES CATALOGUED BY THE SURVEY (*continued*).

SITE NO.	NAME	COUNTY	STATE	LOCATION	DESCRIPTION	RANGE
14-O-5	McKinney Bayou	Tunica	Mississippi	NW¼SW¼ S23 T4S R12W	Village site	. . .
14-O-6	Johnson Cemetery [41]	"	"	NW¼NE¼ S16 T4S R11W	Village site with large mound	B–A
14-O-7	Oakwood Cemetery	"	"	SW¼SE¼ S31 T4S R11W	Small village site with small mound	G–F
14-O-8	Dundee [42]	"	"	NW¼NW¼ S34 T6S R12W	Large village site with large and small mounds	D–C
14-O-9	Norflett	"	"	NE¼SE¼ S17 T6S R12W	Small conical mound	. . .
14-O-10	West Mounds	"	"	NE¼SW¼ S21 T6S R12W	Large village site with large platform mounds and small mounds	C–B
14-O-11	Kendall Mound	"	"	NW¼NW¼ S22 T4S R10W	Village site with small mound	. . .
14-O-12	Jepson	"	"	SE¼NW¼ S28 T4S R10W	Village site with small mound	. . .
14-O-13	Canon	"	"	SE¼SE¼ S17 T6S R10W	Large village site with large mound	E–D
14-P-1	McKane	"	"	NE¼SE¼ S35 T4S R10W	Village site with small mounds	E–D
14-P-2	Prichard	"	"	SE¼SE¼ S27 T4S R10W	Large village site and cemetery	D–C
15-L-1	Butler Mound	Arkansas	Arkansas	SW¼SE¼ S17 T5S R1W	Village site with small mounds	C–B
15-L-2	Baytown	Monroe	"	SE¼SW¼ S2345 T3S R1W	Large village site with large rectangular platform mound and small mounds in plaza arrangement	D–C
15-L-3	Hall	Phillips	"	NW¼NW¼ S32 T2S R1E	Large rectangular platform mound	. . .
15-M-1	Tinsley Mound	"	"	NE¼NE¼ S24 T4S R1E	Village site with small mounds	E–B
15-M-2	Elaine	"	"	NE¼SE¼ S36 T4S R2E	Small conical mound	. . .
15-M-3	Elaine Consolidated School Mound	"	"	SE¼NW¼ S36 T4S R2E	Small conical mound	. . .
15-M-4	Crow	"	"	NW¼NW¼ S1 T5S R2E	Small conical mound	. . .
15-M-5	Vogel Mounds	"	"	NW¼SE¼ S35 T3S R1E	Small mounds	. . .
15-N-1	Fitzhugh	"	"	NE¼NW¼ S8 T3S R5E	Village site with small mounds	C–A
15-N-2	Ellis	"	"	NE¼SW¼ S19 T3S R5E	Village site with small mound	D–A
15-N-3	Old Town [43]	"	"	NE¼SW¼ S36 T3S R3E	Village site	B–A
15-N-4	Buie	"	"	SW¼SW¼ S36 T3S R3E	Village site	D–B
15-N-5	Parchman Place [44]	Coahoma	Mississippi	SW¼NW¼ S30 T29N R3W	Large village site with large and small platform mounds and small mounds in plaza arrangement	B–A
15-N-6	Montgomery [45]	"	"	SE¼SW¼ S14 T28N R5W	Village site with large rectangular platform mound and small mound	D–A
15-N-7	Stovall	"	"	NE¼NE¼ S23 T28N R5W	Large double conical mound	F–A
15-N-8	Carson Group	"	"	NE¼NW¼ S24 T28N R5W	Village site with large platform mound, large double conical mound and small mound	. . .
15-N-9	Vaught Mound	"	"	NE¼SE¼ S7 T29N R3W	Large platform mound	. . .
15-N-10	Dickerson [46]	"	"	NW¼SE¼ S9 T28N R4W	Large village site with conical mound and small mounds	F–E
15-O-1	Salomon [47]	"	"	NE¼NE¼ S22 T29N R3W	Large village site with large rectangular platform mounds and small mounds in plaza arrangement	E–B

[41] Brown, 1926, p. 119. Probably one of the mounds described by Barton, 1927, p. 85.

[42] Probably same as "Mounds of Dundee" in Brown, 1926, p. 116.

[43] Thomas, 1894, pp. 234–35 and fig. 142.

[44] May be Brown's "Roselle Place" (1926, p. 107).

[45] Montgomery (15-N-6), Stovall (15-N-7), and Carson (15-N-8) were described by Thomas as one site, "The Carson Mounds" (1894, pp. 253–54, pls. XI–XIII).

[46] There is a possibility that this site is not the same as the Dickerson Site of Thomas (1894, pp. 255–56).

[47] This is almost certainly the site referred to by Brown as "two and a half miles northeast of Coahoma (1926, p. 106).

TABLE 1: LIST OF SITES CATALOGUED BY THE SURVEY (*continued*).

SITE NO.	NAME	COUNTY	STATE	LOCATION	DESCRIPTION	RANGE
15-O-2	Barbee	Tunica	Mississippi	NE¼SW¼ S36 T30N R12W	Village site with small conical mounds	F-E
15-O-3	Maddox	"	"	SE¼SW¼ S27 T30N R12W	Village site	. . .
15-O-4	Lula	"	"	NE¼NE¼ S22 T30N R12W	Large village site with large and small mound	. . .
15-O-5	Moon	Coahoma	"	NW¼NW¼ S1 T29N R3W	Large village site	E-D
15-O-6	Posey Mound	Quitman	"	NW¼NE¼ S4 T28N R1W	Large village site with large rectangular platform mound and small mounds	F-D
15-O-7	Prowell	Coahoma	"	SE¼SW¼ S28N R2W	Large village site with small mounds	F-E
15-O-8	Gates	"	"	SW¼NW¼ S27 T28N R2W	Village site with small mounds	. . .
15-O-9	Hull Brake	"	"	NE¼SW¼ S15 T29N R3W	Village site	. . .
15-O-10	Wilford	"	"	NW¼NE¼ S15 T29N R3W	Village site with small rectangular platform mound and small mound	C-B
15-O-11	Morrison	Quitman	"	NW¼SW¼ S27 T28N R1W	Two small mounds	D-C
15-O-12	D'Orr	"	"	SE¼NE¼ S29 T28N R1W	Village site with small mound	F-E
15-O-13	Allison	Tunica	"	SE¼NW¼ S32 T7S R10W	Village site with rectangular platform mound and small mounds	E-A
15-O-14	Youngblood	Quitman	"	NE¼NW¼ S23 T8S R11W	Village site with small conical mounds	. . .
15-O-15	Whiting	"	"	NW¼NW¼ S12 T28N R11W	Village site with small mounds	E-C
15-O-16	Tidwell	"	"	SW¼NW¼ S12 T28N R11W	Small mound in village site	F-E
15-O-17	Miller Place	"	"	NE¼NW¼ S25 T28N R11W	Two small mounds	. . .
15-O-18	Ware	"	"	SW¼NE¼ S30 T28N R1W	Village site with small mounds	F-E
15-P-1	Thomas	Panola	"	NW¼SE¼ S8 T9S R8W	Small mound	F-E
15-P-2	Taylor	Quitman	"	SW¼SW¼ S27 T7S R10W	Small conical mound	. . .
15-P-3	Indian Creek	Panola	"	SW¼NW¼ S27 T7S R9W	Village site with large platform mound	F-E
15-P-4	Corn Lake	"	"	SW¼SW¼ S5 T8S R9W	Village site with mounds	D-B
16-K-1	Jones Place [48]	Arkansas	Arkansas	SW part of irreg. sec. S2350 T8S R3W	Village site with small mounds	B-A
16-K-2	Mill Bayou Prairie Mound	"	"	NE¼NE¼ S28 T6S R4W	Village site with small mound	. . .
16-K-3	McGahhey	"	"	N. Cen. irreg. Sec. S2361 T8S R2W	Small conical mounds	. . .
16-L-1	Bitely Place	"	"	SW¼SW¼ S15 T7S R2W	Rectangular platform mound	. . .
16-L-2	Essex	"	"	SW¼SW¼ T7S R2W	Rectangular platform mound	. . .
16-L-3	Stovall Mounds	"	"	SW¼NE¼ S20 T5S R1W	Village site with small mounds	F-B
16-L-4	Brandenburg Place A	"	"	SW¼NE¼ S20 T5S R1W	Village site with small mounds	C-B
16-L-5	Brandenburg Place B	"	"	SE¼NW¼ S20 T5S R1W	Village site with small mounds	C-B
16-L-6	Dupree	Phillips	"	NE¼SW¼ S10 T6S R1E	Large village site with large rectangular platform mound and small mounds in plaza arrangement	C-B
16-M-1	Avenue [49]	"	"	NE¼SE¼ S6 T6S R2E	Village site with small mounds	B-A
16-M-2	Tomanelli	Bolivar	Mississippi	SE¼NE¼ S5 T25N R6W	Village site with large conical mound and small mounds	C-B
16-M-3	Yates	"	"	NW¼ & NE¼ of NW¼ S24 T25N R5W	Large village site with large mound and small mounds	F-C

[48] Probably "Old River Landing," Moore, 1908a, pp. 511-23.

[49] Moore, 1911, pp. 401-05.

TABLE 1: LIST OF SITES CATALOGUED BY THE SURVEY (*continued*).

SITE NO.	NAME	COUNTY	STATE	LOCATION	DESCRIPTION	RANGE
16–M–4	Macedonia	Bolivar	Mississippi	NW¼SW¼ S27 T25N R5W	Small mound	. . .
16–M–5	Mount Olive	"	"	NW¼NE¼ S29 T25N R6W	Village site with small mounds	C–B
16–M–6	Stokes Bayou	"	"	SW¼NW¼ S20 T25N R6W	Large village site with platform mound and small mounds in plaza arrangement	C–B
16–M–7	Brook Bayou	"	"	NE¼NW¼ S33 T25N R6W	Large mound	. . .
16–N–1	Acree Place	Coahoma	"	SE¼SE¼ S22 T26N R5W	Village site with small mounds	F–E
16–N–2	Alligator Mounds[50]	Bolivar	"	NW¼NE¼ S32 T26N R5W	Village site with large rectangular platform mounds and small mounds in plaza arrangement	F–B
16–N–3	Ellis	Coahoma	"	SE¼ S1 T26N R4W	Village site with large and small mounds	F–E
16–N–4	Rufus Davis[51]	"	"	NE¼NE¼ S5 T27N R4W	Village site with large rectangular platform mound and small mound	F–D
16–N–5	Little Sunflower	"	"	NE¼SW¼ S5 T27N R4W	Small mound	D–C
16–N–6	Oliver[52]	"	"	NW¼NW¼ S10 T25N R4W	Village site with mounds	F–C
16–N–7	Bramlett[53]	"	"	SE¼SW¼ S11 T26N R5W	Village site with small mounds	E–B
16–N–8	Peter's Rock	"	"	SW¼NW¼ S5 T26N R5W	Large conical mound	. . .
16–N–9	Mattson	"	"	NE¼NW¼ S28 T26N R3W	Village site with large mound	B–A
16–N–10	Myer	"	"	NW¼NE¼ S32 T26N R3W	Village site with large rectangular platform mound	B–A
16–N–11	Hopson Bayou	"	"	NE¼NE¼ S7 T25N R3W	Village site with small mound	F–E
16–N–12	Black Bayou	"	"	NE¼NE¼ S27 T27N R5W	Village site with small mounds	. . .
16–N–13	Sherard	"	"	SW¼SW¼ S15 T27N R5W	Small conical mound	. . .
16–N–14	Harris Bayou	"	"	NE¼NW¼ S22 T27N R5W	Large village site with small conical mound	F–E
16–N–15	Dogwood Bayou	"	"	SW¼NW¼ S26 T27N R5W	Village site with small mound	. . .
16–N–16	Baugh	"	"	SE¼SW¼ S21 T27N R5W	Small mound	. . .
16–N–17	Howden Lake	Bolivar	"	SE¼NE¼ S9 T25N R5W	Village site with small mound	. . .
16–N–18	Bobo	Coahoma	"	NE¼SW¼ S26 T27N R4W	Small mound	. . .
16–N–19	Crawford Lake	"	"	SE¼SW¼ S2 T25N R4W	Village site with small mound	C–B
16–N–20	Aderholt[54]	"	"	SE¼SW¼ S9 T27N R4W	Village site with small mounds	F–E
16–N–21	Morning Star	"	"	SE¼SE¼ S10 T27N R4W	Small mound	. . .
16–N–22	Clark	"	"	SW¼SW¼ S26 T27N R4W	Small mound	. . .
16–N–23	Hopkins	"	"	NW¼NW¼ S36 T27N R4W	Small mound	. . .
16–N–24	Durham	"	"	SW¼SE¼ S6 T26N R3W	Small mound	. . .
16–N–25	Doadey	"	"	NE¼NW¼ S5 T26N R3W	Small mounds	. . .
16–O–1	Dunn	Quitman	"	NW¼NE¼ S14 T27N R3W	Village site with large platform mound and small mounds	F–B
16–O–2	Spendthrift	Coahoma	"	NW¼NW¼ S13 T26N R3W	Village site with large mound	E–B
16–O–3	Everett	Tallahatchie	"	SE¼NW¼ S15 T25N R2W	Two small mounds	F–E
16–O–4	Opossum Bayou	Quitman	"	SW¼NW¼ S33 T27N R1W	Small conical mound	. . .
16–O–5	Yager	"	"	NW¼SW¼ S33 T27N R1W	Small conical mound	. . .
16–O–6	Garmon	"	"	SE¼SW¼ S16 T27N R2W	Village site with rectangular platform mound	G–F
16–O–7	Henderson	"	"	SW¼NW¼ S5 T26N R2W	Village site with small mounds	G–F
16–O–8	Norman	"	"	NW¼NE¼ S19 T26N R2W	Small mounds	G–F

[50] Brown, 1926, p. 94.
[51] Brown, 1926, p. 106.
[52] Peabody, 1904; Brown, 1926, pp. 101–06.
[53] Possibly the "three small mounds west of Bobo," in Brown, 1926, p. 106.
[54] Probably the site, "three miles northwest of Clarksdale," listed in Brown, 1926, p. 106.

TABLE 1: LIST OF SITES CATALOGUED BY THE SURVEY (*continued*).

SITE NO.	NAME	COUNTY	STATE	LOCATION	DESCRIPTION	RANGE
16-O-9	Little Texas	Quitman	Mississippi	SW¼SW¼ S18 T26N R2W	Village site with small mounds	. . .
16-O-10	Vance	Tallahatchie	"	NW¼SE¼ S1 T25N R2W	Small mound	. . .
16-O-11	Oxbow Bend	Quitman	"	SE¼SE¼ S7 T27N R2W	Village site with small mound	E-D
16-O-12	Oliverfried	"	"	NW¼SW¼ S34 T27N R1W	Small mound	. . .
16-O-13	Denton	"	"	NE¼SW¼ S5 T26N R1W	Village site with large and small mound	. . .
16-O-14	Stover	Tallahatchie	"	SE¼SE¼ S10 T25N R1W	Village site with small mound	G-F
16-O-15	Garner	Coahoma	"	SW¼NW¼ S1 T26N R3W	Village site with small mounds	G-C
16-O-16	Flower	"	"	NW¼SE¼ S1 T25N R3W	Village site with small mound	F-E
16-O-17	Longstreet	Quitman	"	SE¼NE¼ S20 T26N R1W	Village site with large mound	. . .
16-P-1	Charleston [55]	Tallahatchie	"	NW¼SW¼ S26 T25N R2E	Village site with large conical and small mounds	D-C
16-P-2	Shady Grove	Quitman	"	SW¼NE¼ S27 T27N R1W	Large village site with large rectangular platform mound and small mound	E-B
16-P-3	Twin Lakes	"	"	SW¼NE¼ S32 T27N R1E	Village site with small mounds	G-F
16-P-4	White	"	"	SE¼NW¼ S32 T27N R1E	Village site with small mounds	F-B
16-P-5	Crosslyn	Panola	"	NW¼NW¼ S29 T27N R1E	Small mound	E-B
16-P-6	Cox	Quitman	"	SW¼NW¼ S29 T27N R1E	Village site with small mounds	E-B
16-P-7	Mitchell	"	"	SW¼NW¼ S5 T26N R1E	Village site with small mounds	E-B
16-P-8	Blue Lake	"	"	SW¼SE¼ S8 T26N R1E	Village site with small mounds	F-C
16-P-9	Carmichael	"	"	SE¼SE¼ S20 T26N R1W	Small mound	G-F
17-K-1	Menard Mound [56]	Arkansas	Arkansas	S Cor. irreg. S2303 T8S R2W	Village site with large and small mounds in plaza arrangement	D-A
17-K-2	Thiele Hill	"	"	E part irreg. S2422 T8S R2W	Village site with small mound	. . .
17-K-3	Wallace	"	"	SE¼ irreg. S2351 T85 R2W	Village site	B-A
17-K-4	Almond Farm	"	"	SE part irreg. S2369 T8S R2W	Village site	. . .
17-K-5	Cooks Mound	Desha	"	SE¼SW¼ S1 T11S R2W	Large rectangular platform mound	D-B
17-K-6	Bond	"	"	NE¼NW¼ S1 T11N R2W	Village site with small conical mound	F-E
17-K-7	Alma Brown [57]	"	"	SW¼SW¼ S11, NW¼NW¼ S14 T11S R2W	Large village site with large and small mounds	F-A
17-L-1	Massey Place	Arkansas	"	SW¼ irreg. S2425 T8S R2W	Large village site with small mounds	F-B
17-L-2	Ellerton Mound	"	"	SW¼ irreg. S2425 T8S R2W	Small conical mound	. . .
17-L-3	Poor Place	"	"	Irreg. S17 T8S R2W	Village site with small mounds	D-C
17-L-4	Wynn [58]	Desha	"	SW¼SW¼ S18 T9S R2W	Large rectangular platform mound and small conical mound	D-C
17-L-5	Waxhaw	Bolivar	Mississippi	N part irreg. S21 T24N R8W	Large and small rectangular platform mounds and small conical mound	. . .
17-M-1	Bear Ridge	"	"	NE¼SE¼ S23 T24N R8W	Large village site with large and small mounds	E-B
17-M-2	Blanchard	"	"	SE¼NW¼ S11 T24N R7W	St. Francis type site with large and small mounds in plaza arrangement	B-A
17-M-3	Perthshire	"	"	NW part irreg. S3 T24N R7W	Small conical mounds	. . .

[55] Brown, 1926, p. 95.

[56] Thomas, 1894, pp. 229-31; Moore, 1908a, pp. 486-509.

[57] Lemley and Dickinson, 1937, pp. 37-39.

[58] Thomas, 1894, p. 239. Thomas spells it, "Wyenn."

TABLE 1: LIST OF SITES CATALOGUED BY THE SURVEY (*continued*).

SITE NO.	NAME	COUNTY	STATE	LOCATION	DESCRIPTION	RANGE
17-M-4	Christmas	Bolivar	Mississippi	NW¼SE¼ S35 T22N R8W	Small conical mound	. . .
17-M-5	Walton	"	"	SW¼SW¼ S5 T22N R7W	Small mound	. . .
17-M-6	Mound City	"	"	SW¼SW¼ S3 T22N R7W	Large village site with rectangular platform mounds and small mounds	. . .
17-M-7	Moore	"	"	NE¼SW¼ S4 T22N R7W	Village site with small rectangular platform mound	. . .
17-M-8	Bob Williams	"	"	SW¼NW¼ S15 T23N R6W	Small mound	. . .
17-M-9	Spinks	"	"	SW¼ & NW¼ of SW¼ S29 T23N R6W	Small mounds	. . .
17-M-10	Reynolds	"	"	NW¼NW¼ S14 T23N R7W	Village site	E-C
17-M-11	Bush	"	"	SE¼SW¼ S3 T23N R7W	Large village site with large platform mound and small mounds	C-B
17-M-12	O'Donnell	"	"	NW¼SE¼ S9 T23N R7W	Village site with small platform mound	E-B
17-M-13	Boles Lake	"	"	NW¼NW¼ S18 T23N R7W	Village site with small mound	G-F
17-M-14	Boykin Bayou	"	"	NW¼NW¼ S7 T23N R7W	Village site with small conical mound	E-D
17-M-15	Dattel	"	"	NW¼NW¼ S8 T23N R7W	Small conical mound	. . .
17-M-16	MacGowan	"	"	SE¼SE¼ S12 T23N R8W	Village site with small mound	D-C
17-M-17	Nelson	"	"	SW¼NE¼ S14 T23N R8W	Village site with small platform mound	F-E
17-M-18	Roosevelt	"	"	NE¼SE¼ S5 T23N R6W	Small mounds	D-C
17-M-19	Firtell	"	"	NE¼NE¼ S31 T24N R6W	Small mound	. . .
17-M-20	Shelby	"	"	NW¼SE¼ S16 T24N R6W	Small mound	. . .
17-M-21	Laban Bayou	"	"	SW¼NW¼ S13 T23N R8W	Small mound	. . .
17-N-1	Merigold	"	"	NE¼SW¼ S10 T23N R5W	Large village site with large and small mounds in plaza arrangement	C-B
17-N-2	Walford	Sunflower	"	SE¼SW¼ S7 T22N R4W	Large village site with large and small mounds	C-B
17-N-3	Debow	"	"	NW¼SW¼ S1 T24N R4W	Large village site with small mounds	G-C
17-N-4	Penitentiary	"	"	SW¼SW¼ S32 T24N R3W	Village site with small mound	C-B
17-N-5	May	"	"	NE¼SE¼ S17 T24N R4W	Village site with small mounds	E-D
17-N-6	Sid Dodd	"	"	SE¼NW¼ S22 T24N R4W	Village site with small mounds	. . .
17-N-7	Baltzer	"	"	NW¼NW¼ S2 T24N R4W	Village site with small mound	. . .
17-N-8	Boyer	"	"	SW¼SW¼ S22 T23N R4W	Village site with small mound	F-E
17-N-9	Vance, L.L.	"	"	NE¼NE¼ S35 T25N R4W	Village site with small mound	B-A
17-N-10	Nora Smith	"	"	NW¼SE¼ S23 T23N R4W	Small mound	. . .
17-N-11	Dockery	"	"	NE¼SW¼ S14 T23N R4W	Village site with small mounds	C-B
17-N-12	Long Lake	"	"	NE¼NE¼ S14 T23N R4W	Village site with small mounds	C-B
17-N-13	Burnet	"	"	NE¼SE¼ S14 T23N R4W	Small mound	. . .
17-N-14	Kimball	"	"	SW¼SW¼ S10 T23N R4W	Village site	D-C
17-N-15	Cook	Bolivar	"	SW¼SE¼ S13 T23N R5W	Village site with small mounds	D-C
17-N-16	Wilnot	"	"	SW¼SW¼ S24 T23N R5W	Village site with small mounds	G-F
17-N-17	John Dickson	"	"	SW¼SW¼ S25 T23N R5W	Small mound	. . .
17-N-18	Joe Smith	"	"	SW¼NE¼ & NW¼SE¼ S36 T23N R5W	Village site with small mounds	F-E
17-N-19	Parker	"	"	SW¼NE¼ S1 T22N R5W	Small conical mound	. . .
17-N-20	Newton Bayou	Sunflower	"	SE¼NE¼ S28 T23N R4W	Small mound	. . .
17-N-21	Loosangle	"	"	SE¼SE¼ S28 & SW¼SW¼ S27 T23N R4W	Village site with mounds	. . .

TABLE 1: LIST OF SITES CATALOGUED BY THE SURVEY (*continued*).

SITE NO.	NAME	COUNTY	STATE	LOCATION	DESCRIPTION	RANGE
17-O-1	Buford [59]	Tallahatchie	Mississippi	SE¼SW¼ S36 T25N R2W	Village site with large rectangular platform mound and small conical mounds	D-C
17-O-2	James	"	"	SW¼NE¼ S11 T24N R2W	Conical mound	...
17-O-3	Petty	"	"	SE¼SW¼ & SW¼SE¼ S12 T24N R2W	Village site with large mounds	...
17-O-4	Flaut	"	"	SE¼SE¼ S33 T24N R1W	Village site with large and small mound	...
17-O-5	King Mound Group	"	"	SE¼NE¼ S34 T24N R1W	Village site with large platform mound and small mounds	F-E
17-O-6	Jernberg	"	"	SE¼NE¼ S21 T24N R2W	Village site with small mounds	D-C
17-O-7	Jacobs	Le Flore	"	SE¼SE¼ S8 T22N R1W	Large conical mound	...
17-O-8	Falls	"	"	NE¼NW¼ S17 T22N R1W	Village site with large mound	E-D
17-O-9	Powell Bayou	Sunflower	"	SW¼SE¼ S27 T23N R3W	Village site with large rectangular platform mound and small mounds	C-B
17-O-10	Sage	Tallahatchie	"	SW¼NW¼ S28 T23N R2W	Small mound	...
17-O-11	Cassidy Bayou	"	"	NE¼SE¼ S5 T24N R1W	Large village site with small mound	F-E
17-O-12	Rome	Sunflower	"	NW¼NW¼ S14 T24N R3W	Village site with small mounds	E-B
17-P-1	Tippo Bayou	Tallahatchie	"	SW¼SW¼ S11 T24N R1E	Village site with small mound	C-B
17-P-2	Cason [60]	Le Flore	"	SW¼NW¼ S20 & NE¼SE¼ S19 T22N R1E	Large village site with large rectangular platform mound and small mounds	E-B
18-K-1	Hogg Lake [61]	Chicot	Arkansas	NE¼NE¼ S4 T14S R2W	Village site with small rectangular platform mound and small mounds	F-C
18-K-2	Westlake [62]	Desha	"	NE¼NE¼ S29 T13S R2W	Village site with small mounds	F-E
18-L-1	Neblett Landing [63]	Bolivar	"	NW¼NW¼ S16 T22N R8W	Village site with large and small rectangular platform mounds	D-B
18-M-1	Porter Bayou	"	Mississippi	SW¼SW¼ S14 T20N R6W	Large village site with large and small mounds	F-E
18-M-2	Noble	"	"	SE¼NE¼ S30 T21N R8W	Small mound	...
18-M-3	Stringtown	"	"	NE¼NE¼ S23 T30N R8W	Small mound	...
18-M-4	Lipe	"	"	NW¼NE¼ S15 T20N R6W	Large village site with small mounds	D-B
18-M-5	Brooks	"	"	NW¼NW¼ S24 T22N R7W	Large mound	E-D
18-M-6	Choctaw	"	"	NE¼NW¼ S26 T20N R6W	Village site with large mound	E-D
18-M-7	Priscilla	"	"	SE¼NE¼ S35 T20N R8W	Village site with small mounds	F-E
18-N-1	Marlow	Sunflower	"	NW part irreg. S2 T21N R4W	Small rectangular mound	C-B
18-N-2	Marlow Cemetery	"	"	N part irreg. S2 T21N R4W	Village site with small conical mound	D-C
18-N-3	Cooper	Bolivar	"	NW¼NW¼ S25 T22N R5W	Village site with small mound	F-E
18-N-4	Steiner	Sunflower	"	SE¼NE¼ S4 T20N R4W	Village site with small mound	C-B
18-N-5	Moorhead Bayou	"	"	SE¼NW¼ S25 T20N R5W	Small mound	...
18-N-6	Anderson	"	"	SE¼SE¼ S29 T20N R4W	Small mound	...
18-N-7	Boyer	"	"	SE¼NW¼ S32 T20N R4W	Village site with small mounds	C-B
18-N-8	MacGregor	"	"	SE¼NE¼ S18 T20N R3W	Small shell midden	D-C
18-N-9	Eastland	"	"	SW¼NW¼ S30 T21N R3W	Shell midden	D-C

[59] Brown, 1926, p. 95.
[60] Brown, 1926, p. 95.
[61] Lemley and Dickinson, 1937, p. 18.
[62] Lemley and Dickinson, 1937, pp. 32-33.
[63] Moore, 1911, pp. 391-400; Brown, 1926, pp. 90-93.

TABLE 1: LIST OF SITES CATALOGUED BY THE SURVEY (*Continued*).

SITE NO.	NAME	COUNTY	STATE	LOCATION	DESCRIPTION	RANGE
18–N–10	Gillfield	Sunflower	Mississippi	NE¼NW¼ S24 T21N R4W	Small conical mound	. . .
18–O–1	Barry	Le Flore	"	SE¼NW¼ S14 T20N R1W	Shell midden	E–D
18–O–2	Garrard	"	"	NW¼NE¼ S36 T21N R2W	Village site with large and small mound	. . .
18–P–1	Lester Way		"	SE¼NE¼ S1 T19N R1W	Village site with small mound	E–D
18–P–2	Whaley	"	"	NW¼NE¼ S5 T20N R2E	Village site with small mounds	D–C
19–L–1	Winterville (Blum)[64]	Washington	"	NE¼NE¼ S19 T19N R8W	Village site with large rectangular platform mounds and small mounds in plaza arrangement	D–B
19–L–2	Bachelor Bend	"	"	SE part irreg. S16 T19N R9W	Village site with small mounds	. . .
19–L–3	Ely	"	"	NW¼SE¼ S20 T19N R8W	Village site with small mound	D–C
19–L–4	Deer Creek	"	"	SW¼NW¼ S26 T19N R8W	Village site with small mounds	C–B
19–L–5	Ireland	"	"	SE¼NW¼ S22 T19N R8W	Large village site	E–D
19–L–6	Refuge	"	"	Cen. irreg. S24 T17N R1E	Village site with large rectangular platform mound and small mounds	B–A
19–L–7	Ash Bayou	"	"	SW¼NE¼ S10 T17N R8W	Small mound	. . .
19–M–1	Leland (Avondale)[65]	"	"	SW¼SE¼ S11 T18N R7W	Village site with large rectangular platform mounds and small mounds	C–B
19–M–2	Sheldon	"	"	SW¼SW¼ S24 T19N R8W	Village site with small mound	C–B
19–M–3	Stoneville	"	"	NW¼NE¼ S15 T18N R7W	Village site with small mounds	B–A
19–M–4	Dunleith[66]	"	"	NW¼SE¼ S17 T18N R6W	Village site with rectangular platform mounds and small mounds in plaza arrangement	. . .
19–M–5	Hollyknowe	"	"	SW¼NW¼ S20 T18N R6W	Village site with small mound	D–C
19–M–6	Arcola High School	"	"	SE¼SW¼ S36 T17N R7W	Village site with small mounds	D–B
19–M–7	Polk	"	"	SE¼SE¼ S9 T18N R6W	Village site with small mound	D–C
19–N–1	Kinlock	Sunflower	"	SE¼SE¼ S15 T17N R5W	Village site with mounds	F–A
19–N–2	Shields	"	"	SE¼SW¼ S22 T18N R5W	Village site with small mounds—shell middens	F–E
19–N–3	Bay Lake	"	"	SE¼SE¼ S21 T18N R5W	Large village site with small mounds	C–B
19–N–4	Danzler	"	"	NE¼SE¼ S21 T17N R5W	Small conical mound and small mound	. . .
19–N–5	Failing	"	"	NE¼SE¼ S32 T19N R4W	Large village site with small mounds	C–B
19–N–6	Lake Dawson	"	"	NE¼NE¼ S29 T17N R3W	Village site with large and small mounds	D–B
19–N–7	Mitchell	"	"	SW¼NE¼ S20 T19N R4W	Village site with small rectangular platform mound	D–C
19–N–8	Horve Hope	"	"	NW¼NW¼ S19 T19N R4W	Small mound	. . .
19–O–1	McLean	Le Flore	"	SW¼NW¼ S33 T19N R1W	Village site with large and small mound	D–B
19–O–2	Shell Bluff	"	"	SE¼SW¼ S28 T18N R1W	Large shell midden with mounds	E–C
19–O–3	Fleming	Holmes	"	SE¼NE¼ S3 T16N R1W	Large shell midden	D–C
19–O–4	Archer	"	"	NW¼NW¼ S26 T17N R1W	Shell midden	E–D
19–O–5	Old Dominion	Le Flore	"	SW¼NE¼ S34 T18N R2W	Small conical mound	. . .

[64] Moore, 1908c, pp. 594–600; Brown, 1926, pp. 83–88.

[65] The "Avondale Mounds" of Thomas, 1894, pp. 259–60; Brown, 1926, pp. 81–82.

[66] Brown, 1926, p. 82.

TABLE 1: LIST OF SITES CATALOGUED BY THE SURVEY (*Continued*).

SITE NO.	NAME	COUNTY	STATE	LOCATION	DESCRIPTION	RANGE
19-O-6	Robinson Deadening	Le Flore	Mississippi	SE¼NW¼ S29 T18N R2W	Small rectangular mound	. . .
19-P-1	Palusha Creek	"	"	NE¼SW¼ S32 T19 R1E	Village site	E-D
19-P-2	Roebuck	"	"	NW¼NE¼ S18 T18N R1E	Village site with large and small mound	. . .
20-L-2	Silver Lake	Washington	"	SW¼SE¼ S9 T15N R8W	Village site with small mounds	F-E
20-M-1	Arcola [67]	"	"	SW¼SW¼ S12 T16N R7W	Village site with large and small mounds in plaza arrangement	B-A
20-M-2	Deer Creek	Sharkey	"	SW¼NE¼ S6 T14N R6W	Village site with large and small mounds in plaza arrangement	B-A
20-M-3	Panther Burn [68]	"	"	NE¼SE¼ S12 T14N R7W	Small mound	C-B
20-M-4	Lessiedell	Washington	"	NE¼SE¼ S6 T14N R8W	Large and small mounds in plaza arrangement	D-C
20-M-5	Swan Lake	"	"	SW¼SW¼ S35 T15 R8W	Large and small mounds in plaza arrangement	E-C
20-M-6	Clower	"	"	NW¼SE¼ S17 T15N R6W	Large mound	. . .
20-N-1	Midnight [69]	Humphreys	"	NW¼SE¼ S14 T14N R4W	Two small mounds	D-C
20-N-2	Summerfield	"	"	NE¼SE¼ S18 T14N R4W	Village site with large platform mound and small mounds	D-C
20-N-3	Straight Bayou	Sharkey	"	SW¼NW¼ S24 T14N R5W	Small mound	. . .
20-N-4	Kongo	Washington	"	SE¼NW¼ S30 T15N R5W	Large and small mounds	. . .
20-O-1	Jaketown [70]	Humphreys	"	SW¼NW¼ S15 T16N R3W	Large village site with large and small mounds	G-B
20-O-2	Belzoni [71]	"	"	SE¼NW¼ S2 T15N R3W	Village site with large and small mound	D-C
20-O-3	Lamkin	"	"	NW¼SW¼ S17 T14N R2W	Village site with large platform mound and small mound	D-B
20-O-4	Atchafalaya Bayou [72]	"	"	SE¼NW¼ S1 T14N R3W	Two small mounds	. . .
20-O-5	Silver City [73]	"	"	SW¼SE¼ S34 T15N R3W	Village site with large and small mound	C-B
20-O-6	Golson	"	"	SE¼NW¼ S34 T15N R3W	Shell midden	E-D

[67] Brown, 1926, pp. 80-81.
[68] Brown, 1926, p. 80.
[69] Brown, 1926, p. 64.
[70] Mounds on Wasp Lake. Brown, 1926, p. 66.
[71] Moore, 1908b, p. 579. Moore spells it, "Belzona," which is the way it is pronounced.
[72] May be Moore's "Holly Landing" (1908b, p. 579).
[73] Moore, 1908b, p. 579.

Section III

CLASSIFICATION OF THE POTTERY

CLASSIFICATION OF THE POTTERY

TYPOLOGY

SINCE practically everything in this report depends on the mass of potsherds collected at the expense of so much bending of backs, it becomes necessary to describe with candor the methods employed in their classification. Archaeology has not reached that stage of development in which there is only one correct way to do things, and, it is hoped, never will. What follows, therefore, is in no way intended as a treatise on the proper way to classify pottery, but merely a description of what was done by us and why — especially why. To say that the choice of methods of classification is governed by the nature of the material to be classified is a truism. But it is no less governed by the predilections and general attitudes of the classifier, and particularly by the ends which the classifier has in view. The extent to which classification may be a creative activity is perhaps not sufficiently recognized. Before embarking on a description of the actual methods of classification employed in the present study, we must therefore furnish a brief statement of our position in regard to the subject of cultural typology in general and pottery typology in particular.

The Concept of Type

In the study of archaeological materials there are, among others, two basically divergent interests: (1) interest in objects as expressions of the ideas and behavior of the people who made and used them; and (2) interest in objects as fossils for the determination of time and space relations. It cannot be maintained, of course, that these two interests are mutually exclusive, but it is an important fact that one's approach to problems of classification will depend very largely on which of them is being served. The first interest we may call, following Taylor,[1] cultural, as opposed to the second which is empirical, in the sense that the classifier is interested chiefly in what he hopes to get out of it. He is content to work with fragmentary materials such as potsherds — in fact, prefers them because of their susceptibility to statistical treatment — since he is concerned primarily with the distribution of "cultures" in time and space, and only secondarily with the cultures so revealed. The resulting apparent indifference to "culture-context" has been characterized by Taylor as little short of criminal, and there is no question that studies rigorously conducted along these lines make unconscionably dull reading. Nevertheless, the most casual glance at the history of archaeology in any part of the world where it has progressed beyond the stage of antiquarianism will show their utility. Indeed, one might go further in suggesting that at certain stages in the development of archaeological knowledge they are indispensable. Until a certain amount of order has been achieved in respect to time-space relations on a regional scale, it may be questioned whether satisfactory cultural inferences can be drawn from any archaeological materials. We are in such an early stage of development in the Lower Mississippi Valley. The classification which is to be described in the following pages, is, in consequence, the outcome of a frankly, if not fanatically, empirical attitude toward the material.

It has become practically mandatory in putting typological studies into print to declare at the outset that classification is regarded therein purely as a "tool," fashioned to suit the material in hand and the kind of information one hopes to get out of it. Unfortunately, the phenomenon of inter-changeability of ends and means is not confined to political science. Also, there is magic in names. Once let a hatful of miserable fragments of fourth-rate pottery be dignified by a "Name," and there will follow inevitably the tendency for the name to become an entity, particularly in the mind of him who gives it. Go a step further and publish a description and the type embarks on

[1] Taylor, 1948, p. 114.

an independent existence of its own. At that point the classification ceases to be a "tool," and the archaeologist becomes one. This fate we shall endeavor, probably not successfully, to avoid in the pages to follow.

The "tool" that best seems to fit the present undertaking is the system of classification formally introduced into Southeastern archaeology at the Field Conference held at Birmingham, Alabama, in 1938. It is adopted here, not because of a belief in the necessity for a single standardized pottery classification in the Southeast — a classification with a capital C — but because it was the outgrowth of work on material similar to ours by students with the same general point of view as our own. This system is essentially the binomial classification of the Southwest, without any phylogenetic implications, and with important modifications arising from differences in the pottery to be classified. So far as we are aware, the underlying concepts and assumptions of this classification system, as applied to the Southeast, have not been explicitly stated, although the methodology has been described by Krieger.[2] As interpreted by the present writers, they run somewhat as follows:

It is first of all assumed that, after the introduction of pottery-making into the Southeast, a gradual shift of all ceramic features took place.[3] Techniques of manufacture, surface finish, shape, and decoration constantly, but slowly, changed. Such changes were no doubt partly the result of new ideas from outside the area — whatever mechanisms were responsible for the introduction of pottery-making in the first place may have brought increments to the original stock of ideas from time to time — but in the main, changes are assumed to have been internal, resulting from play on the potentialities of current forms and styles. Revolutionary inventions, in the popular sense of the word, probably occurred rarely if at all. In general, therefore, pottery styles at any given time and place may be assumed to have derived from those that went before; if not in that particular spot, then in another region with which there was contact.

Each community that had reached a certain level of sophistication in pottery-making will be found to have been maintaining side by side several different vessel styles. These are normally closely related, particularly in the matter of construction, paste, and surface finish, and seem to mark vessels made for different purposes or vessel ideas derived from different sources. If any one of these particular styles is examined at a single place and a single point in time, it will be seen that, while each vessel varies in minor detail, such variations tend to cluster about a norm. This norm represents the consensus of community opinion as to the correct features for this particular kind of vessel. Variations from the norm reflect the individual potter's interpretation of the prevailing styles, and the degree of variation tolerated is also culturally controlled. With the convenient hindsight of the archaeologist, we can divide such variations into two classes: those which were not followed by the rest of the community, and those that were. The latter are, of course, significant as the means by which ceramic development was accomplished.

In areas where the distribution of population was relatively stable, as seems to have been the case in most of the Southeast for long periods, ceramic development was general and in a crude sense surprisingly uniform. There was always a tendency, however, for particularly vigorous centers to impress their ideas on less enterprising neighbors. When a cross section of a large area is viewed at a given point in time, popularity centers will be seen for certain styles. Between these centers, styles vary and trend toward those of other centers in rough proportion to the distances involved, subject of course to ethnic distributions and geographic factors.

Thus, we have in mind the concept of a continuously evolving regional pottery tradition, showing a more or less parallel development in and around a number of centers, each of which employs a number of distinct but related styles, each style in turn being in process of change both areally and temporally.

[2] Krieger, 1944.

[3] The word "introduction" is used here in its widest possible sense. It is not intended to imply the assumption that there was only one introduction of pottery into the Southeast, or even to rule out the possibility of independent invention. We can produce as good an evolutionary series from stone pots to Arkansas head vases as has been done anywhere else.

With this remarkably unstable material, we set out to fashion a key to the prehistory of the region. Faced with this three-dimensional flow, which seldom if ever exhibits "natural" segregation, and being obliged to reduce it to some sort of manageable form, we arbitrarily cut it into units. Such *created units of the ceramic continuum* are called *pottery types.*

The importance of this concept of type in the present study justifies a certain amount of repetition. It can be illustrated in a crude

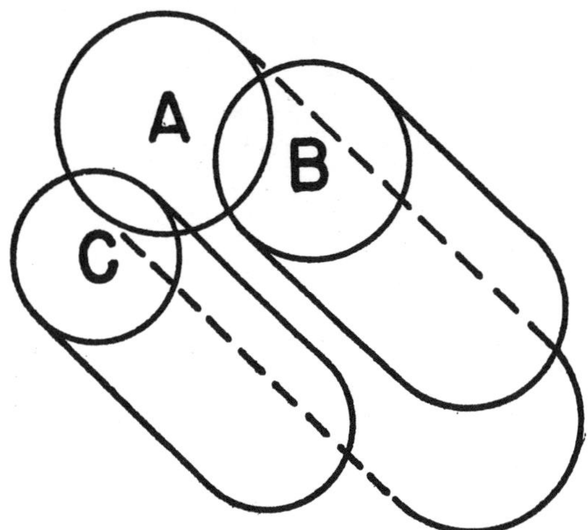

Fig. 5. Diagrammatic representation of the concept of pottery type.

diagrammatic form (fig. 5). Let the letter *A* represent a type and the circle around it, in purely abstract fashion, its limit of variability. That is to say, if an individual specimen does not fall within the range of variation represented by the circle, it does not conform to the type. We have already seen that variation and geographical range are closely related, so our circle represents, albeit crudely, the geographical range of the type as well. The circle thus describes the type two-dimensionally. To this, a third dimension, time, may be added by which our figure becomes a cylinder. The length of the cylinder represents the range of variability resulting from changes taking place in time. Several closely related and overlapping types — the most carefully defined types always overlap — can therefore be represented as above.

The length of the cylinders is shown as unequal because of the inevitable variation in persistence of the peculiarities we have used to define the types. Actually, of course, these cylinders are a tremendous over-simplification. If it were possible to show it diagrammatically, they would be irregular in shape, expanding, contracting, branching, and coming together, so that no two horizontal cross sections would be the same. The figure is a hopelessly crude approximation to the facts, but it serves to illustrate the point of interest here, to wit, the arbitrariness of the whole typological procedure. The drawing of the circles is arbitrary and highly subjective — no two classifiers will draw precisely the same circle — the cutting-off of the cylinders is equally so. It is scarcely necessary to draw attention to the additional difficulty of determining whether a given variation is the result of spatial or temporal factors. If this is anything like a true picture of what a pottery type is, can anyone seriously ask whether it corresponds to a "natural" or cultural reality?

Whether, among the primitive communities of the Mississippi Alluvial Valley, groups or classes of pottery were recognized, and whether such entities, if we may speak of them as such, were conceptualized in terms anything like those with which we define a pottery type, are intriguing and by no means unimportant questions. We need not go into them here, however, because by reason of the very nature of the material to be classified the possibility that our and their conception of a given type might coincide is so remote as to be negligible. These are questions that can scarcely arise in the initial stages of a comprehensive pottery survey. Before leaving the subject, however, let us make it clear that, although the empirical typology here described — "working" typology as Krieger perhaps would call it — cannot be expected to show any strong relationship to cultural "reality," it does not follow that such relationship is precluded now and forever. To a certain extent, the characters we select as criteria for type definition, however dictated by expediency, not to say necessity, are bound to correspond to characters that might have served to distinguish one sort of pottery from another in the minds of the people who made and used it. We should, of course, make every possible effort to increase this correspondence. In course of time, with increased information in respect to vessel shapes and over-all patterns of design — let us not forget that we are classifying vessels, though we have for most types only sherds to do it with — our types will be redefined in ever closer approximation to cultural "realities." In short, an eventual synthesis is possible between the seemingly antithetical attitudes loosely characterized above as "empirical" and "cultural," in which the product of classification, the pottery type, will finally achieve cultural meaning. The limits of the variability of the type will then no longer be wholly arbitrary decisions of the classifier, as is now the case, but will bear some correspondence to ethnographic distributions in time and space. On this hopeful note, let us conclude this brief introduction to the problems that beset those who set out to measure and relate, by means of wretched bits of fired clay, cultural phenomena of which there are as yet no other records.

The Concepts of "Pottery Complex" and "Series"

As already remarked, in cultures of the level reached by the pottery-making Indians of the Southeast, a given site, or level in a site, will show several discrete pottery types, each of which may have a separate history. It is convenient to refer to such a group of types as a "complex." This pottery complex in a given situation is usually described in terms of percentages of the several component types and, where so described, gives a very useful measure for comparison with other cultural situations. A further step is sometimes made in which all or several of the component types of a complex are given the same site designation and the group referred to as a "series." Thus, the types Alexander Incised, Alexander Pinched, and Alexander Dentate Stamped are members, along with O'Neal Plain and Smithsonia Zoned Stamped, of the well-known "Alexander Series" in northern Alabama. However tempting from the standpoint of simplicity, we are not using the device in the present work. As Krieger has pointed out, such linkage of types is a further step in the typological process.[4] Furthermore, when it becomes clear that related types have the same distribution in time and space, it may be preferable to lump them together as a single type whereupon the concept of "series" becomes superfluous. Until such a time, their separate identities have to be maintained, and it is perhaps less confusing in the long run to keep the names distinct as well. It is hardly necessary to add that, in our view, neither "complex" nor "series" are classificatory terms in the sense that they represent an order, more inclusive than type, in a taxonomic system. The fact that they do tend to acquire such a meaning is an additional reason, in our view, for avoiding their use, except in a context that leaves no room for ambiguity. When, therefore, in the following pages, we find it convenient to speak of a pottery complex it will be understood to refer only to a given archaeological situation, and the term "series" will be, so far as possible, avoided.[4a]

The Binomial System of Type Nomenclature

The above-described methodological freedom, however, does not by any means eliminate any of the difficulties or responsibilities of the classifier. As already pointed out, the norm of style, which we measure by means of pottery types, shifts both areally and chronologically in a manner so gradual that we are hard put to say at what point in either dimension one type leaves off and another begins. But this is not all. The separate characters of paste, surface, form, and decoration change also in time and space, and not all at the same rate. Each separate character has its own history and each history will provide a more or less sensitive register for the history of the culture as a whole. Now it would be unreasonable to hold that one character is unfailingly more important than another, or to insist that all pottery be classified on the basis of uniformly selected characters. It does, however, lessen the initial confusion to select

[4] Krieger, 1944, fig. 25.

[4a] Ford objects to this usage of the term "series" on the grounds of poor English. "1. A number of things or events standing or succeeding in order, and connected by a like relation; sequence; order; counsel; a succession of things; as, a *series* of calamities or triumphs." (Webster's New International Dictionary.)

the most sensitive — and at the same time most recognizable — characters as guides or "constants" in the process of classification. In Southeastern pottery generally, these are features of surface treatment and decoration, and thus it has come about that what may for convenience be called the Southeastern classification employs a binomial system of nomenclature in which the second term or "constant" is descriptive of surface treatment or decoration, as in Mulberry Creek *Cord-marked* or Indian Bay *Stamped*.

It may be asked why characters of shape are not regarded as equally sensitive and equally suggestive of culture change. The answer is found in our original point of departure and its paramount interest in sherds rather than vessels, and more objectively, perhaps, in the fact that except in the very latest periods the Southeastern potters had not reached an advanced stage of refinement in vessel form. Features of shape, particularly rim and lip modifications, have sometimes proved useful in sorting the present material, but it has not been found expedient to use them as constants in classification. All types set up by the Survey, therefore, are defined in the present work according to the Southeastern procedure.

By so doing, we shall have lessened but by no means removed the main typological difficulty. Type "A" let us suppose has been defined on the basis of what appears to be the "norm" at what appears to be a "center." We may as well admit that these "centers" are often only such because they first attracted our attention, or because of our ignorance of the intervening spaces. As we go away from that center in space — the same thing happens in time, but we may leave that unpleasant fact aside for the moment — the characters that we have selected as determinants for the type gradually shift, the all-too familiar phenomenon of "creep," until at some point we can stretch our original type definition no further and have to consider whether material "X" more closely resembles Type "B," already established at another center, or whether it is not sufficiently like either "A" or "B" and must be given an independent status as Type "C." These wretched hair-line decisions beset the classifier at every step. The only helpful principle the writers have been able to find is one of the sheerest empiricism — ability to sort. Rigorous application of this principle results in some rather startling distributions. For example, we were unable to distinguish certain clay-tempered, cord-marked sherds found in our area from the type Mulberry Creek Cord-marked, originally set up in the Pickwick Basin on the Tennessee River several hundred miles away. Candor compels the admission that we could not sort it from what was then called Deasonville Cord-marked in southern Mississippi and Louisiana either. If Mulberry Creek Cord-marked and Deasonville Cord-marked could be separated, as implied in the fact that they were set up as distinct types, our material obviously could not be both, so an arbitrary decision had to be made. We first encountered the pottery in the northern part of the Survey Area where it more closely approximates Mulberry Creek Cord-marked. If we had encountered it first in the south, we undoubtedly would have been struck by its resemblance to Deasonville Cord-marked. Our solution was to call it Mulberry Creek and quietly liquidate Deasonville. From this sort of dilemma there is no escape, but its effects can be minimized by more knowledge of the pottery and sharper definition of types.

It may be surmised from the above that much depends on the sort of constants by which types are defined. The "creep" of types in time or space is by no means uniform. A generalized surface treatment like cord-marking, for example, will extend farther without sortable change than a type based on a specialized scheme of decoration; a plain undecorated type may go farther than either. So far as possible, an attempt should be made to reduce these inequalities by careful choice and definition of constants. On the other hand, bearing in mind that classification is only a means to an end, the classifier will choose the sort of constants that he thinks are likely to turn out to be culturally and historically significant. Finally, let it not be overlooked in the glow of these fine thoughts that in the initial stages of classification one seizes upon *any* feature that will serve to distinguish one group of sherds from another.

Having, so to speak, walked around the pottery type as understood here, and examined some of the more obvious aspects of its anatomy, we may conclude by admitting that the practical necessities of the situation have virtually destroyed it as a concept in any *a priori* sense. We are left with — and this is as much of a definition as will be found in the present work — a named abstraction, representing a combination of selected characters, susceptible of recognition from sherds alone. An artificial, albeit useful, creation of the classifier, the pottery type has at this stage of being little, if any, correspondent cultural "reality," present or past. Exigencies of language require us to think and talk about pottery types as though they had some sort of independent existence. "This sherd *is* Baytown Plain." Upon sufficient repetition of this statement, the concept Baytown Plain takes on a massive solidity. The time comes when we are ready to fight for dear old Baytown. What we have to try to remember is that the statement really means something like this: "This sherd sufficiently resembles material which *for the time being* we have elected to call Baytown Plain." Frequent repetition of this and similar exorcisms we have found to be extremely salutary during the classificatory activities described below.

Methods of Sorting

The 1940 season's material, consisting of surface collections only, from 149 sites, mainly in the Lower Arkansas River Lowland and St. Francis River Basin, was shipped to Baton Rouge for cataloguing, and there sorted by the writers at the conclusion of the field season. This preliminary sorting was done in the time-honored way, that is, by piling the whole mass of sherds into one terrifying heap, and sorting them as many ways as possible. The experience in other Southeastern areas prompted the use of tempering differences as a primary breakdown,[5] and the result was that we ended up with 47 types loosely grouped into three temper groups: shell, clay, and sand. Fiber-tempering did not occur in the first season's collections. The "constants" selected were in the categories of surface finish and decoration. Under the latter, technique of decoration was relied on more than design, as is necessary when sorting surface material, on account of the small size of the sherds. It should be pointed out that these 47 types were not all "new." Eight of them had been previously named and described in the Lower Mississippi Valley, and two were among the types set up in the Pickwick Basin in northern Alabama. After sorting, the material was broken up into the original site collections, counted, and tabulated. Some preliminary graphic analysis, of the sort described in a later section, was carried on by Ford, so that in going back into the field in the following spring, we had a fair idea of the probable chronological relationships of our provisional types, which was a great help, particularly in the selection of sites for stratigraphic testing.

The second and third season's material, mainly from the Yazoo Basin, was handled differently. Site collections and stratigraphic material were kept intact. By this time, we felt we had a classification and that it was therefore unnecessary to throw all the pottery together, as was done the previous year. Now, this raises a question pertinent to the discussion of typological theory just completed. There is no question that, had we sorted this Yazoo Basin material afresh, forgetting as far as possible, our existing typology, we would have come out with a classification quite different from that presented here. Not that the list of types would have differed so much, but the types themselves would have been differently defined. The norms in the Yazoo Basin are not the same as in the St. Francis Basin. Throughout all our description and discussion of types, we are constantly being reminded of the "set" that was given to our typology by the fact that it was largely determined by the first season's work. In spite of all efforts, our type definitions in many cases really apply to the St. Francis Basin pottery. We have not been able to rid our minds entirely of the notion that corresponding type material in the Yazoo Basin is deviant if not atypical. Another interesting result is that we tend to see a culture divide or "frontier" about the latitude of

[5] So far as we are aware, the first use of tempering differences as a primary ceramic breakdown in the Southeast was in Griffin's study of the pottery of the Wheeler Basin in Webb, 1939.

the mouth of the Arkansas River, because it is here that the type definitions set up in the St. Francis begin to reach their limit of applicability; the types begin to lose their outlines. The fact is very neatly expressed in the increased percentages in the "unclassified" column of site tabulations south of this point. We have to be on guard against such appearances. Getting back to the point at issue, it seems now in retrospect that it would have been worth the extra effort to have piled all three season's collections together, and all subsequent material for that matter, and made a final grand sorting. However, our present purpose is to describe what we did, not what might have been done.

Sorting and analysis of the 1941 collection was interrupted by the war. When the work was resumed in 1946 the situation was as follows: The 1940 collections had been broken up. Approximately a third of the material was still in Baton Rouge. The remainder had been sorted at least once by one or more of the present writers, but it was felt that a new sorting by one of us was required not to eliminate the personal equation, which cannot be done, but to standardize the errors resulting therefrom, and accordingly all the material, to which was subsequently added the collections of 1946 and 1947, was assembled at the Peabody Museum. This was another opportunity to throw it together, but it was sorted by sites as before. In the process, a number of changes were made in the previous classification, several new types being set up to take care of the material in the southern part of the Yazoo Basin. At the same time a number of earlier types were abandoned. As each site collection was sorted, the types were segregated in small boxes and filed away by sites in cupboards where they were readily available for further study. Body sherds of the more common types were counted and put away in dead storage, and the counts entered in a dead-storage file. The material was thus in excellent shape for final analysis. This was done type by type in the following manner. All the rims and bases (in types that have bases) — or in the case of the numerically smaller types, all the sherds — were spread out on long tables in geographical order from north to south. Data sheets listing the occurrence by site of all measurable and observable features were prepared. Direct observation, backed up by these data sheets gave an excellent idea of the nature and extent of the variations of the type in its geographical range. "Centers" for the type, and for particular features within the type, were readily apparent. The gradual shift of the type away from these centers was clearly seen again and again. In some cases, this shift became so great as to require an arbitrary decision — thus far and no farther — and the creation of a new type. While the material was in this convenient form, quantitative distribution maps were made, which proved to be very useful in further delimiting the types.

At this point, it may be well to make another confession. What Hooton used to call the "fierce typologist" does not compromise with space or time. If two things look alike, he puts them together regardless. So, in theory, do we. But it sometimes happens otherwise in practice. When confronted with one of the innumerable hair-line decisions one has to make in sorting, it may be that the mere location of the site from which the sherd comes, or its chronological position, if it comes from an excavation, is sufficient to throw it one way or another. We have not scrupled to use such adventitious aids to sorting from time to time.

With the material still spread out on the tables and the data sheets as a control, a preliminary type description was written on the spot. Now to write a close description of a type represented by collections from several hundred sites covering a range of 200 to 300 miles, to say nothing of a considerable stretch of time, is not easy. There is an irresistible tendency to orient your description around what seems to be the "central" material of the type, and to describe the variations in terms of this assumed "center." It is hardly necessary to point out again that a center may be nothing more than the place where one happened to get the most material. It is also very apt to coincide with the place where one first set up the type. Pottery descriptions have always to be read with this in mind. Ours are only exceptional in that we admit it.

The last act before putting away one type and getting out another was to select a number of specimens for the type collection, and these were also inventoried by site in a card-index file. A further distillation from these was made for the photographs in this report.

Upon completion of the analysis, there remained a considerable residue of unclassified material. This was also spread out on the tables and sorted carefully for possible new types. Actually, none were found, which was reassuring in a way, as an indication that our classification was sufficiently thorough, for the present at least. Several tentative types were set up, and these are described in this section under the heading "Provisional Types." It was felt that these would no doubt attain the status of types with more material, so they are useful in pointing to areas for further investigation.

There remained only the final unexciting task of counting and tabulating on printed site inventory sheets to which were added the counts from the dead-storage and type-collection files. Totals and percentages were then calculated, and we were finally in a position to begin to get some returns on our investment.

GROUPING OF POTTERY TYPES

In order to understand the arrangement of the ensuing type descriptions, as well as the frequent reference to period embodied in them, it becomes necessary to outline briefly the tentative chronological scheme that derived from analyses that have not yet been described. These resulted in a framework of seven horizons designated by the letters A to G.[6] Horizon A is arbitrarily fixed at approximately A.D. 1650. Horizon G is the unknown date of the earliest pottery so far encountered in the area. The six time divisions marked off by these seven letters will be simply referred to hereinafter as "B–A," "C–B," and so on. For greater convenience, and because names give a satisfying if illusory sense of reality, these lettered divisions are grouped into three "major" divisions, Tchula, Baytown, and Mississippi, and these correspond to what is generally understood by "period" in archaeological writings. That is to say, while predominantly chronological, they do have typological implications as well. This point is discussed at greater length on pages 239ff. Tchula, the earliest pottery period, corresponds to G–F on the time scale; Baytown, the long middle period runs from F–C; Mississippi, from C–A.

Type descriptions are grouped under these three period headings, but such grouping is not to be taken too literally. It will be sufficiently evident, in the sections describing the analysis upon which these periods are based, that the life span of many types is not contained within a single period. Types have therefore been assigned to the period in which they appear to have reached their maximum use, an assignment not always easy to make, owing to the fact that the maximum is not necessarily reached at the same time in all parts of the Survey Area. With these reservations, the types to be described are listed as follows:

Tchula Period

Bluff Creek Punctated
Tchefuncte Plain
Jaketown Simple Stamped
Tammany Pinched
Tchefuncte Stamped
Lake Borgne Incised
Cormorant Cord-impressed
Withers Fabric-impressed
Twin Lakes Punctated
Crowder Punctated

Baytown Period

Baytown Plain
Mulberry Creek Cord-marked
Wheeler Check Stamped
Indian Bay Stamped
Evansville Punctated
Marksville Stamped
Marksville Incised
Churupa Punctated
Coles Creek Incised
Oxbow Incised
Mazique Incised
Chevalier Stamped
French Fork Incised
Woodville Red Filmed
Larto Red Filmed

[6] The term horizon is herein understood to mean an "instant" in time, with no duration involved.

Mississippi Period

Neeley's Ferry Plain
Parkin Punctated
Barton Incised
Ranch Incised
Vernon Paul Appliqué
Fortune Noded
Bell Plain
Kent Incised
Rhodes Incised
Walls Engraved
Hull Engraved
Old Town Red
Carson Red on Buff
Nodena Red and White
Avenue Polychrome
Hollywood White Filmed
Wallace Incised
Owens Punctated
Leland Incised
Arcola Incised

PROVISIONAL TYPES AND UNCLASSIFIED MATERIAL

In a preliminary pottery survey, such as the present, it is neither practicable nor desirable to classify all the material collected. As already noted, in addition to the types listed above, we set up a number of categories under the heading of tentative or provisional types. Strictly speaking, according to the concept of typology professed above, these are no less "types" than those already listed. In most cases, it is merely that we have as yet insufficient material for satisfactory type definition. In some cases, however, types have been relegated to provisional status because, upon analysis, they failed to show significant differences in time-space distribution from closely related types in full status and, therefore, could be thought of as variants of those types. In this connection, we sometimes gave way to strictly practical considerations, dropping types of this genre simply in order to provide more space on the already crowded seriation charts. Whatever the reason for denying them full status at this time, it is obviously undesirable to let these types drop out of sight. Some of them will undoubtedly turn out to be important, notwithstanding their poor definition, for the leads they furnish to relationships outside the area. Finally, and this is the over-riding consideration, failure to describe these types would result in a simplistic and incomplete picture of the pottery situation in the Survey Area.

For the abovesaid reasons we are presenting descriptions, as complete as we can make them, of the following provisional types:

Baytown Period

Thomas Plain
Blue Lake Cord-marked
Twin Lakes Fabric-impressed
Bowie Plain
Yates Net-impressed

Mississippi Period

Manly Punctated
Mound Place Incised
Blanchard Incised
Oliver Incised
Stokes Bayou Incised

POTTERY TYPE DESCRIPTIONS

BLUFF CREEK PUNCTATED

(Fig. 76, *a–f*)

Type as described in ref. (b), except as noted below.

Paste and Surface. Tempering and paste texture are as described by Haag with one notable exception, a sherd tempered with bits of fine cord about .5 mm. in diameter. Molds of these cords appearing on the surface suggest cord-marking, but they show clearly in the paste as well. Some interpreters might regard this as the beginning of cord-marked pottery in the eastern United States.

Color.[7] Surface color is more uniformly gray or buff than described in ref. (b) — the tendency toward mottling is not observed in the present sample — and lighter in shade. Most frequently occurring color is Light Pinkish Cinnamon (15′ ′*d*), with darker variations on the gray side and lighter variations in

[7] Color determination in this and subsequent type descriptions is according to Ridgway, 1912.

the direction of white. Several sherds fall between Pale Pinkish Buff (17' 'f) and white.

Thickness. Average thickness of paste is 10.5 mm., with a range of 8 to 13 mm.

Decoration. Most examples are punctated with a blunt instrument, producing a relatively shallow round depression about 2–4 mm. in diameter. Punctations are not as close-spaced as examples figured in ref. (b). They seem to extend over the entire vessel surface, even onto the bottom, judging from one of the two basal sherds in the collection. Several sherds suggest an arrangement of punctations in two parallel rows forming some sort of rude pattern. One sherd shows rectangular punctation with an effect closely approximating that of check-stamping. If the fiber-tempering were not clearly apparent, the sherd would be classified as Wheeler Check Stamped.

Form. Evidence is insufficient to say whether vessel shape corresponds to the large cup specified in ref. (b). The one rim available, however, suggests this form. Two basal sherds indicate a thick (15 mm.), flattened bottom.

Distribution. At present confined to six widely scattered sites in the Survey Area (Withers, 13–P–9; Yager, 16–O–5; Norman, 16–O–8; Garner, 16–O–15; Wilnot, 17–N–16; and Jaketown, 20–O–1). Only at Norman and Jaketown is the type represented by more than one sherd.

Chronological Position. General associations of the type, both within and without the Survey Area, led us to assume that it was among the earliest pottery types in the area. However, in its only stratigraphic appearance, in Jaketown Cut A, it occurred in Levels 10 and 11 and was absent in Levels 12 to 15 which contained the Tchula Period types (see fig. 44). It is possible, therefore, that our assumption of an extremely early date is incorrect.

It is curious that this is the only fiber-tempered type so far found in the Survey Area. Here, as in central Georgia and southeastern Alabama, fiber-tempered pottery is a minority type, associated with an early pottery complex. This influence into the Survey Area seems to have been derived from northwest Alabama.

Bibliography. (a) Griffin, 1939; (b) Haag, 1939a, pp. 4–5; (c) Haag, 1942a.

TCHEFUNCTE PLAIN

(Fig. 76, g, *h*)

Type as described in ref. (a), except as noted below.

Paste. *Method of Manufacture.* Not clearly discernible, but a few sherds suggest the coil technique.

Tempering. In some sherds there is little or no tempering material visible while others have small clay particles similar to Baytown Plain. Some sherds have a slightly sandy texture, but the carbonized vegetal material mentioned in ref. (a) is not present.

Texture. The paste is fine textured but is contorted and in some cases presents a laminated appearance.

Hardness. 2–2.5 [8] Some of the specimens are poorly fired and are quite friable. This latter characteristic is not as pronounced, however, as in the type material in Louisiana.

Color. Light buff to grayish brown on the surfaces with the core somewhat darker. Most frequently occurring color is Sayal Brown (15' 'i), with lighter variations in the range of Cinnamon (15' '), Pinkish Cinnamon (15' '*b*), and Vinaceous Cinnamon (13' '*b*); darker variations in the range of Snuff Brown (15' '*k*) and Verona Brown (13' '*k*). Grayer colors, less frequent, in the neighborhood of Wood Brown (17' ' ') to Olive Brown (17' ' '*k*).

Thickness. Average thickness of paste, 6.2 mm., with range of 4 to 8 mm.

Surface Finish. The surfaces have been compacted by surface smoothing, particularly on the exterior.

Form. The evidence for shape is not satisfactory. Presumably, bowls and small jars. Evidence of flat bases with four legs as described in ref. (a) is not present in the small sample available.

[8] These figures are given for what they are worth. It has been the writers' experience that hardness tests by means of the Moh scale are unreliable because of insufficient standardization in methods of making them, and of no great utility in the differentiation of pottery types anyhow.

Discussion. The identification of this type was not made until the excavations at Jaketown produced decorative types of the Tchefuncte complex. It is likely that some of the sites placed in the G–F time period also had specimens of this type and that these were typed as Baytown Plain. It can be regarded as a southern and early expression of the clay-tempered plain ware which is dominant in the Lower Mississippi Valley from the earliest appearance of pottery to the shell-tempered dominance of the Mississippi Period.

Relationships Outside Survey Area. The considerable variability shown by Tchefuncte Plain, as found in the original Tchefuncte sites, is not present in the Survey collection perhaps because of the limited number of specimens. Tchefuncte Plain specimens from the type sites in the Ceramic Repository suggest a connection with St. Johns Plain on the basis of shape, surface finish, and construction.

Chronological Position. In the Tchula Period (G–F).

Bibliography. (a) Ford and Quimby, 1945, pp. 52–54, fig. 16.

JAKETOWN SIMPLE STAMPED

(Fig. 76, *i–k*)

Type not previously described.

Paste and Surface. Similar to Tchefuncte Plain, as described herein.

Decoration. Exterior covered with more or less parallel but haphazardly applied lines or grooves, which appear to be the result of malleating the suface with a paddle, the sharp edge of which produces the marks in question. Such malleation apparently covered the entire vessel surface.

Form. Insufficient material for shape criteria.

Discussion. Type has the same restricted southerly distribution within the Survey Area as other Tchefuncte-like types. It has not been reported from Tchefuncte sites in Louisiana. The nearest comparable type is Pickwick Simple Stamped, a fiber-tempered and presumably earlier type from the Pickwick Basin of the Tennessee River in northern Alabama (Griffin, 1939, called it "parallel incised lines"; Haag, 1939a; Haag, 1942a). This latter, in turn, may have a connection with Mossy Oak Simple Stamped of Georgia. Another analogue is found in the treatment of certain Fayette Thick sherds in southwestern Indiana from late Archaic or early Woodland sites. A possible prototype may be seen in the tooled surfaces of the pre-pottery steatite vessels widespread from the eastern Appalachians as far west as Poverty Point, Louisiana (Webb, 1944), and the sandstone vessels of a similar archaic horizon in northern Alabama.

Chronological Position. In the Tchula Period (G–F).

TAMMANY PINCHED

(Fig. 76, *l–q*)

Type as described in ref. (a), except as noted below.

Paste and Surface. Similar to Tchefuncte Plain, as described herein.

Decoration. As described in ref. (a).

Form. Very little can be said in respect to details of shape. Only two rims are available in the Survey collections, of which one indicates a slightly incurved bowl or beaker form; the other, a thickened rim, is embellished with bosses of the type associated with the Alexander Series in the Pickwick Basin, made by punching from the inside not quite through the full thickness of the wall and then filling and smoothing off the interior surface. This feature was not included in the original description of Tammany Pinched in ref. (a), but occurred in various Alexander Series types found in association with it on Tchefuncte sites.

Discussion. Compare remarks on Tchefuncte Stamped. A similar effort has been made to keep this type reasonably pure, with the result that its occurrence is limited at present to three sites along the eastern margin of the Survey Area, Norman (16–O–8), Aderholt (16–N–20), and Jaketown (20–O–1). Its presumed derivative, Evansville Punctated, has a more general and northerly distribution within the Survey Area, and the apparent center for the later shell-tempered type, Parkin Punctated, is found still farther to the north. The distributions of these three types, which are perhaps merely arbitrary divisions of a continuum, invite the inference that this particular technique of pottery decoration was slowly moving up the Mississippi Valley. A little caution must be observed, however, in view of the fact that the technique is early in the Tennessee Valley, as exemplified in the type, Alexander Pinched. A further cautionary factor is seen in the relationship of Tammany Pinched and Bluff Creek Punctated in the Survey Area. One or two sherds from the Norman Site (16–O–8), classified as Tammany Pinched because of the Tchefuncte-like paste, closely resemble Bluff Creek Punctated in decoration. In this connection, it is significant that the original definition of Bluff Creek Punctated includes semi-lunar impressions or "nail-marks." A similar decorative technique is found on Fayette Thick, an early Adena type. The rim bosses are part of the Baumer ceramic complex and are widespread in the northern Woodland area.

Chronological Position. In the Tchula Period (G–F).

Bibliography. (a) Ford and Quimby, 1945, pp. 58–59, fig. 20, *a–g*; for the comparable Alexander Series type called Alexander Pinched, see Griffin, 1939, pp. 136–39; Haag, 1939a, p. 7; Haag, 1942a, p. 515.

TCHEFUNCTE STAMPED

(Fig. 76, *r–u*)

Type as described in ref. (a), except as noted below.

Paste and Surface Finish. Similar to Tchefuncte Plain, as described herein.

Form. Little or no evidence. Probably small jars.

Discussion. Care has been taken to classify as Tchefuncte Stamped only such material as conforms closely to the type description. The line between it and its cognate, Indian Bay Stamped, is very hard to draw (cf. fig. 76, *r* with fig. 80, *k* and *l*). Borderline cases have been thrown in with Indian Bay. The result is a very small showing of Tchefuncte Stamped confined to a limited range of distribution, as follows:

SITE	SHERDS
16–O–8, Norman	1
18–M–1, Porter Bayou	7
20–O–1, Jaketown	8

Relationships Outside Survey Area. See comments under this head, for the type Indian Bay Stamped.

Chronological Position. In the Tchula Period (G–F).

Bibliography. (a) Ford and Quimby, 1945, pp. 56–57, pl. 2.

LAKE BORGNE INCISED

(Fig. 76, *v–c′*)

Type as described in ref. (a), except as noted below.

Paste and Surface. Similar to Tchefuncte Plain, as described herein, except that a number of sherds otherwise typical show more than "small amounts of fine sand."

Decoration. As defined in ref. (a), with one or two additional features not covered by that description. Decoration was not always made with the "blunt" instrument described. A hollow reed or cane was frequently employed resulting in semi-lunar punctations. In one example (fig. 76, *c′*), a very small reed is used vertically, giving a fine linear punctation of quite different effect. The pattern, however, is typical. One rim from the lower level of Cut A on the Jaketown Site (fig. 80, *b′*) carries a row of bosses similar to those found in several types of the Alexander Series, except that the interior holes have not been plugged.

Form. The only rim of sufficient size for shape determination indicates a simple straight-sided bowl or beaker with unthickened rim and bosses described above.

Discussion. Distribution of the type, like that of other Tchefuncte and Tchefuncte-like types, is limited to a few sites in the southern and eastern part of the Survey Area. Of these, the northernmost sites, Garner (16–O–15) and Twin Lakes (16–P–3), have shown only somewhat uncertain examples. In particular, examples from the Twin Lake Site are on a very sandy paste, and the decoration seems to be confined to the rim in a style similar to that of Twin Lakes Punctated with which it is probably associated. These rims are vaguely reminiscent of the "Hopewellian" cross-hatched rim. What might be called "good" Lake Borgne Incised is practically confined so far to the Jaketown Site (20–O–1). Lake Borgne designs are similar to those on Orange Incised, a fiber-tempered type of eastern Florida, and to designs on Alexander Incised in northern Alabama.

Chronological Position. In the Tchula Period (G–F).

Bibliography. (a) Ford and Quimby, 1945, pp. 61–62, pl. 4.

CORMORANT CORD-IMPRESSED

(FIG. 77, *a–l*)

Type not previously described.

Paste. Similar to Baytown Plain with addition of variable amounts of sand, making in some cases an extremely sandy textured paste. In almost all specimens, particles of clay are clearly present; only a minority would qualify as sand-tempered, in the usual sense of the term. Color of majority of sherds corresponds to that described for Baytown Plain, but the sandier textured sherds tend to run on the one hand to darker grays and on the other to red (Terra Cotta, 7′ ′). On these red sherds the clay-tempering shows up as light buff in sharp contrast to the red paste, giving a characteristic mottled effect. There is no evidence as yet, however, that the difference is typologically significant.

Decoration. Treatment consists of impressing short lengths of twisted cord into the soft clay in such a manner as to produce simple rectilinear patterns. So far as can be seen from the small sample available, decoration is confined to the rim and lip area. Designs consist of sets of short vertical or oblique lines, chevrons, cross-hatchings, horizontal lines extending around the rim, or on the lip, and combinations of these simple motives. Occasionally, such cord-impressed decoration is combined with horizontal rows of small punctations reminiscent of the type Crowder Punctated.

Form. Commonest shape seems to be a simple straight-sided or outflaring bowl. One rim sherd indicates a jar or bowl with rather sharply recurved rim.

Rims tend to be thickened, exteriorly, interiorly, or both. Exterior thickening is often by means of a rim fold which is used as a field for decoration.

Discussion. The type is heavily concentrated in quadrangle 13-P (39 sherds out of 46). The one sherd found north of this point on the Turnage Site (10–Q–3) is a very characteristic example, but all sherds found south of 13-P are somewhat questionable, showing merely one or two horizontal impressions on rim or lip on a typical Baytown Plain paste.

The type is related to Twin Lakes Punctated in the sense that both seem to be after the same effect but arrive at it by different means. In view of their distributions — Twin Lakes Punctated being confined to quadrangles 16–O and 16–P — it is probable that the difference is areal rather than chronological.

Relationships Outside Survey Area. This decoration is found on Baumer sites in southern Illinois on a clay or limestone paste, and in the Guntersville Basin, in a type called Sauty Cord-impressed, on sand-tempered paste. The latter type was also found in the Wheeler Basin Ct^{o}17 site (Griffin, 1939, pp. 139–40) and at Ct^{o}27 and Lu^{v}65 (Haag, 1942a, p. 525). One was also found at Lu^{o}59 where it was noted by Griffin in 1937. Clay-tempered, cord-impressed decoration is found in Lu^{o}25, Lu^{o}59, and Lu^{o}92 in the Pickwick Basin (Haag, 1942a, p. 526). In the Pickwick Basin, this type is Gunters Cord-impressed. In north-central Mississippi, at site Nc^{o} 4, it is associated as a rim decoration with pottery types running from Wheeler Dentate Stamp, Alexander Incised, and Saltillo Fabric-impressed to Hopewell Zoned Stamp (Jennings, 1941, pl. 9, *f*).

Chronological Position. Cormorant Cord-impressed may be slightly earlier than the cord-impressed types in Alabama on either sand or clay temper, but it is likely that it is somewhat later than Baumer. It is in the Tchula to early Baytown Period in the Survey Area (G–E).

WITHERS FABRIC-IMPRESSED

(FIG. 80, *a–d*)

Type not previously described.

Paste. Same as Baytown Plain with somewhat greater tendency toward sandy texture in certain portions of the Survey Area, where the typological border line between this type and the provisional type, Twin Lakes Fabric-impressed, is very hard to draw. On one or two sites, notably Norman (16–O–8), there

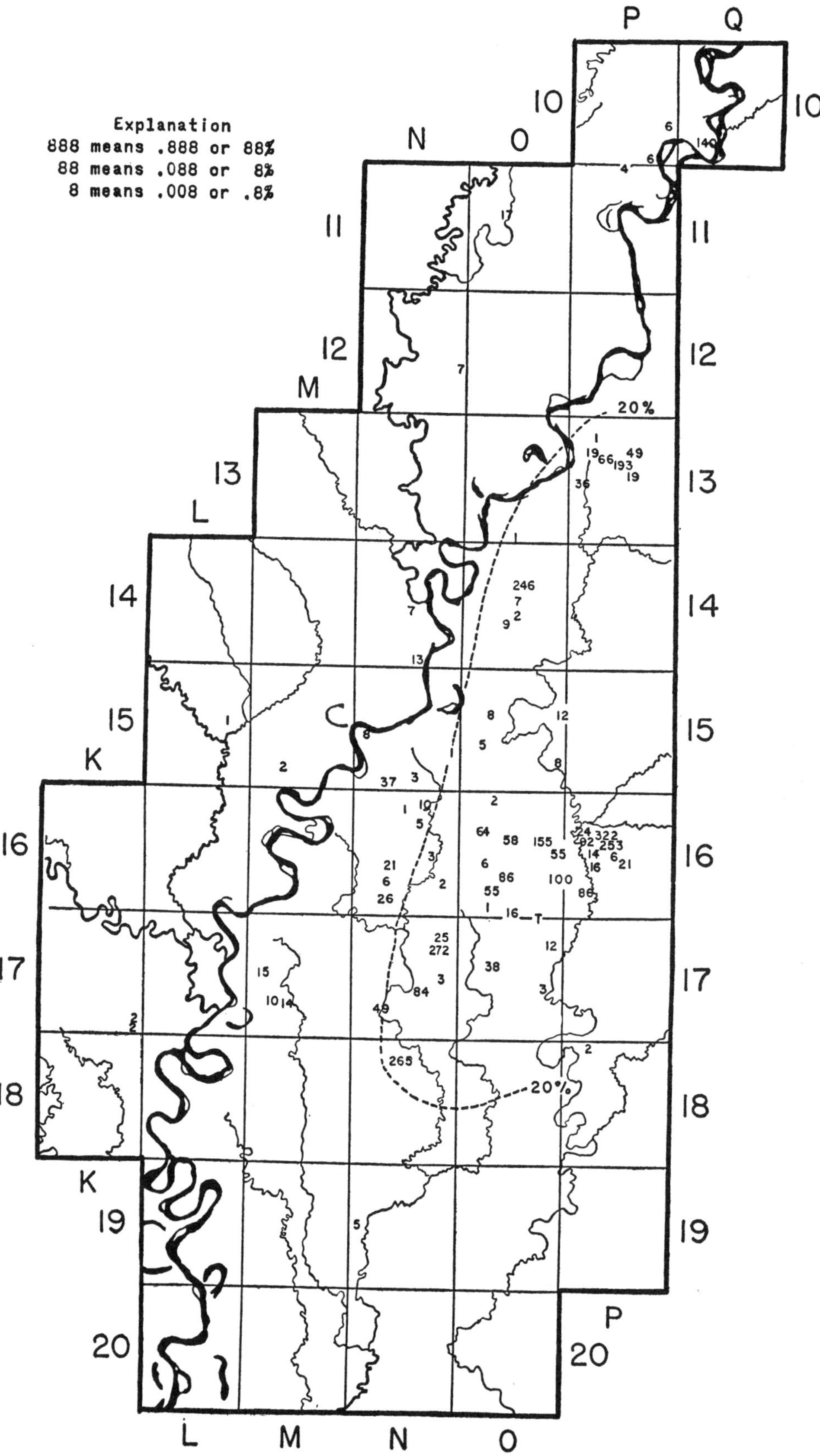

Fig. 6. Percentage frequency distribution of the type Withers Fabric-impressed. For explanation of this and figures 7–13, see pp. 223–24.

is a similar approximation to the Tchefuncte type of paste.

Surface Finish and Decoration. Fabric impressions of textile-wrapped paddle as an all-over treatment, covering the vessel from lip to base. Impressions are carelessly applied and often partly obliterated by subsequent smoothing, so that it usually is impossible to distinguish the sort of textiles involved. In a few cases, a coarse open-twined weave can be made out.

Form. *Vessel Shape.* Very few shape criteria available. Sherds of this type are generally small and badly weathered. The few rims large enough for estimating vessel shape are about evenly divided between simple curved-sided bowls, occasionally slightly incurved, with oral diameters running from 26 to 40 cm., and beakers or jars with slightly recurved rims and somewhat smaller diameters, 16 to 30 cm. No estimate of depths for either class of vessels is possible. Thickness (all shapes) averages 7.7 mm. (range, 5 to 10 mm.; 1 basal sherd, 15 mm.).

Rim. Majority of rims are vertical and unmodified. Rim folds occur on 8% of the rims, but with one exception are confined to sites in the 13–P quadrangle. Average depth of fold is 2.3 cm. One rim carries a double fold. In all but one doubtful case, textile impressions are carried up onto the rim folds.

Lip. Round or slightly flattened, rarely square. Considerable number of lips particularly in the southern portion of the Survey Area are thinned or pointed. Majority of lips are smooth, i.e., fabric impressions are not carried up onto the lip area. Notching and nicking of lips are present but rare (5%).

Base. Almost total lack of basal recognizable sherds (one in entire collection) indicates that bottoms are round and not markedly thicker than ordinary body sherds.

Appendages. None.

Distribution. The general easterly distribution of this type is clearly seen in the accompanying map, figure 6. It is significant perhaps that the southerly distribution of Withers Fabric-impressed in the Survey Area ends rather abruptly about the latitude of the mouth of the Arkansas River. Mulberry Creek Cord-marked (see fig. 7) continues on southward with diminishing importance to the limit of the Survey Area, and a good deal farther. If we are correct in assigning to Withers Fabric a slightly earlier time position, these facts of distribution indicate clearly a north to south movement of the two closely related types. There are a number of details of distribution of interest and possible significance. First, the tendency for occurrences to pile up in the eastern part of the Yazoo Basin specifically at two points, one near the point where the Coldwater River comes down out of the "hills," two where the Tallahatchie and Yocona do the same. It is in these same areas that the closely related type Twin Lakes Fabric-impressed is concentrated. It may be a little far-fetched, but the occasional occurrences of Withers Fabric-impressed up in quadrangles 10–P and 10–Q are near the mouth of the Hatchie. The headwaters of all these streams lie in the old "Chickasaw" country, the center for Saltillo Fabric-impressed, not far from the Pickwick and Wheeler basins of the Tennessee River, where the comparable limestone-tempered type, Long Branch Fabric-marked, is at home.

A further detail of interest is the lack of Withers Fabric-impressed in the St. Francis region, a circumstance that lends further weight to the abovesaid supposition that the type was brought in from the east. If it had moved down the Mississippi, it is hardly conceivable that it would not have found its way into the near-by St. Francis.

Relationships Outside Survey Area. The distribution of Twin Lakes Fabric-impressed is given elsewhere (see p. 144). It should be noted that on the whole fabric-impressed ware tempered with sand is on the eastern margin, while the clay and other larger forms of granular temper are to the north. Clay-tempered, fabric-impressed sherds are found in southeast Missouri, but the exact time position is unknown. Fabric-impressed pottery with various types of grit tempering is found on an early level in a large part of the central-eastern United States. Its distribution has been given in a number of publications (Griffin, 1938, pp. 263–66; 1939, pp. 161–65; 1941, pp. 222–23; 1945; Griffin and Morgan, 1941, pp. 18, 47–48).

Chronological Position. The type begins and has its peak in the Tchula Period (G–F) and runs in small percentages well into the succeeding Baytown Period.

TWIN LAKES PUNCTATED

(Fig. 77, *m–r*)

Type not previously described.

Paste and Surface. Intermediate between Baytown Plain and Thomas Plain, i.e., clay-tempered with a sandy texture. Paste of some sherds would be indistinguishable from that of Baytown Plain. One or two sherds are sandy enough to qualify as sand-tempered. Usually, on a reddish fired pottery.

Decoration. Short wedge-shaped lines produced by jabbing with a sharp implement held at an oblique angle to the body wall. Punctations run about .5 to 1.0 cm. in length and 1 to 2 mm. in depth.

Design. The most typical scheme seems to be strictly a simple rim treatment with two or more rows of oblique punctates arranged herringbone fashion just below the lip.

Form. A simple curved-sided bowl about 20 cm. in diameter is the only vessel shape indicated by the scanty evidence. Rims are either unmodified and slightly pointed or (in a few cases) folded, in which case the folded surface carries the decoration.

Discussion. A minority type so far found on only two sites Norman (16–O–8) and Twin Lakes (16–P–3). Probably merely an occasional method of decorating rims of Baytown Plain or Thomas Plain, which two types meet and mingle in this particular portion of the Survey Area. Resemblance to, and possible relationship with, Cormorant Cord-impressed is discused under that type (see p. 73). It is also on occasion difficult to sort from the type Crowder Punctated which is probably nothing more than an alternative method of decorating rims in this Baytown-Thomas borderland.

Relationships Outside the Survey Area. Twin Lakes Punctated is related to the type in north-central Alabama in the Guntersville Basin called Alexander Pinched. Similar decorative techniques were used in the Savannah area in the Deptford Period, in northern Florida, and southern Alabama.

Chronological Position. In the Tchula to early Baytown periods in the Survey Area, time G–E.

CROWDER PUNCTATED

(Fig. 77, *v–z*)

Type not previously described.

Paste and Surface. Same as Twin Lakes Punctated.

Decoration. Small round punctations made with a blunt-ended implement. Most common arrangement in two parallel rows about 1 cm. apart around the rim just below the lip. In several examples, these punctations are carried down onto the body, but there is insufficient evidence to show the pattern.

Form. Simple curved-sided bowls and jars or beakers with slightly incurved or recurved rims are indicated. Rims are unmodified, tend to be slightly pointed with some interior beveling. Lips are round or slightly pointed.

Discussion. Like Twin Lakes Punctated this appears to be merely a type of rim treatment of purely local significance. In its typical form, it is concentrated in quadrangles 16–N, 16–O, and 16–P. Close relationships with Twin Lakes Punctated is indicated on both typological and distributional grounds.

Relationships Outside Survey Area. Is related in style to sherds in the Guntersville Basin called Columbus Punctated.

Chronological Position. In the Tchula and early Baytown periods, time G–E.

BAYTOWN PLAIN

(Fig. 78)

This is the fundamental clay-tempered type for the entire Survey Area and is therefore described in considerable detail. Analysis was based on a sample of 7171 rims and 617 basal sherds.

Paste. *Method of Manufacture.* Coiled. Pronounced tendency to fracture on coil lines.

Tempering. Predominantly clay, with particles varying in color and in size from minute to over 5 mm. in diameter. Sherd-tempering occasional. A minor amount of sand often occurs with the clay, possibly as an accidental inclusion in the pottery clay. Carbonized particles are frequent. Shell is sometimes found in what otherwise is typical clay-tempered paste, probably also unintentionally included. Occasionally, such fragments are dense and angular in shape suggesting limestone or fossil shell. However, in all cases where some material other than clay is found (except possibly sherd-tempering) clay appears to be the dominant tempering material. This is basic to the definition of Baytown Plain. For example, when the amount of sand is greater than the amount of clay, the sherd has been arbitrarily classified as Thomas Plain. Sherd-tempering, which may have a regional significance, is unfortunately difficult to distinguish megascopically from clay, except when surface portions of the ground-up sherds happen to be visible. It is impossible, therefore, to say whether it is used merely in addition to clay or as an alternative material.

Texture. Sherds when broken have a tendency to chip rather than crumble and give a jagged, irregular break. The irregularity of the break is further emphasized by the nature of the tempering inclusions which, as described, are often large and angular, varying greatly in size. Much of the Baytown Plain paste has a coarse, lumpy, and contorted appearance, depending on the nature of the tempering material.

Hardness. Surface hardness in a random sample of 50 sherds averaged 2.9 with a range of 2 to 4.5.

Color. Surface color is predominantly warm gray or drab. Average color would fall somewhere near Wood Brown (17''') or its lighter shade Avellaneous (17' ' '*b*). Darker shades tend toward drabs and grays rather than browns, Drab (17' ' ' ') and its darker shades Hair Brown (17' ' ' '*i*) and Chaetura Drab (17''' '*k*) or Mouse Gray (15' ' ' ' ') and its darker shades Deep Mouse Gray (15' ' ' ' '*i*). and Dark Mouse Gray (15' ' ' ' '*k*). Lighter shades are more variable, tending on the one hand toward grays, Smoke Gray (21' ' ' '*d*), Pale Smoke Gray (21''''f), Light Oliver Gray (23' ' ' ' '*d*), and Pale Olive Gray (23' ' ' '*f*), but more commonly toward buffs and pinks, Pinkish Buff (17' '*d*), Pale Pinkish Buff (17''f), Pinkish Cinnamon (15' '*b*), and Light Pinkish Cinnamon (15' '*d*). A very small percentage of sherds, probably as a result of overfiring, could be called red, Orange Cinnamon (13''), Vinaceous Cinnamon (13' '*b*), and Vinaceous Tawny (11'').

Surface color penetrates to a depth of from less than 1 mm. to several mm., the greater depth usually being on the exterior. Differences in core color are often not apparent, but if discernible they range from black, through gray and buff.

Thickness. Average thickness of paste based on 760 sherds chosen throughout the collections is 7.6 mm. with a range of 4 to 13 mm. In the northern part of the Survey Area (Tiers 10 to 14),[9] the ware runs slightly thicker than in the middle and southern parts, averaging 8.1 mm. In the middle (Tiers 15 to 16), the average is 7.6 mm. whereas in the south (Tiers 17 to 20), it is only 7.1 mm.

Surface Finish. Though there is considerable variation in surface finish, the large majority of sherds have a characteristic chalky feel and are normally well smoothed both on the interior and exterior, sometimes on one or the other side only. From this average type there are extremes; on the one hand, very highly smoothed and polished, compacted surfaces which in a few instances are even slightly lustrous; on the other hand, there are some sherds which are very rough, completely unpolished, often sandy feeling, and often with tempering particles protruding from the surface. A few sherds appear partially vitrified.

Surfaces which are highly polished appear to have been evened with some smooth hard object, the marks of which are visible, when the paste was at least leather hard. There are sherds, however, which show that the fingers were used while the clay was still plastic for the minute striations are clearly visible, the surface is quite undulating, and tiny tempering particles protrude from the surface, all of which are characteristic of finger-finishing.

Form. *Vessel Shape.* Information on vessel shapes is confined to what can be inferred from the larger rims and basal sherds. Three hundred sixty-one were large enough for

[9] The word "tier" as used herein refers to the Mississippi River Commission grid. See map, figure 1.

shape analysis, and it is on this adequate sample that the following observations are based.

Simple bowls are definitely in the majority, making up 43.8% of the sample. Of these, probably the most common is a bowl with curved sides and unmodified rim. Less common, though occurring with regularity, is a slightly more outflared bowl. The former probably had round bottoms while the latter may well have been flat bottomed, for in one instance sherds of such a bowl could be definitely joined with a portion of a flat base.

Bowls with incurved sides are next in point of frequency, composing 29.5% of the sherds. These range from extremely incurved, the "seed bowl" type of the Southwest, to those which are only moderately incurved.

Jar forms are slightly less common than incurved bowls, comprising 26.7% of the sample. The most common jar shape has a well-defined recurved rim and "vague" rounded shoulder. The bodies are presumably globular, though they possibly had a flat, or flattened base. Somewhat less frequent is a more sharply profiled jar form with a short recurved rim. A few straight rim sherds indicate a barrel or beaker shape.

Size. Oral diameter indicated by all measurable rims, irrespective of shape, is 36.8 cm., with a range of 10 to 96 cm. Average for the northern tiers, 10 to 14, runs slightly higher than for the middle and southern, 38.6 cm. against 35.2 cm., and 35.4 cm., respectively. This is apparently due to the larger size of vessels from the St. Francis River sites, which average 41.6 cm. as compared with 33.0 cm. on the Mississippi in the same tiers, and this in turn is partly due to the extreme size (96 cm.) of a few St. Francis rims that could hardly have come from anything but salt pans of the shallow, round-bottom bowl type.

Rim. In respect to form, the characteristic Baytown rim is simple and unmodified with a plain rounded or slightly flattened lip. A few rims in the collection are modified by thickening, usually on the interior adjacent to the lip which is often beveled or flattened. Occasionally, rims are thickened on both sides resulting in a T-shaped cross section. Such thickened rims, however, are too infrequent to be regarded as within the normal range of the type, but rather suggest possible types or variants not yet recognized by our classification.

The great majority of rims (85.5% of the present sample) are without decoration or elaboration of any kind. Of the remaining 14.5% (or 1039 rims) which, with a certain amount of latitude, we will call "decorated" rims, 7.8% involved the exterior or interior rim area or both; 6.7% involve the lip only.

With respect to the former, elaboration of the rim, the principal types of treatment are as follows:

1) Rim Folds: The usual method of finishing off rims in Baytown Plain — as well as other clay-tempered types in this area — seems to have been as follows: On conclusion of the thinning process, presumably by paddling, the upper edge of the wall was turned outward (rarely inward) and smoothed down onto the body wall. Usually, the joint of the folded portion to the body wall was obliterated. On the other hand, it was possible by trimming the edge and folding it carefully to produce a simple but satisfactory decorative effect. This is called a rim fold. Unfortunately, there are a great many intermediate cases in which it is impossible to say whether the final effect is the result of carlessness or design.

In the present classification, therefore, rim folds are required to have a reasonably uniform width and enough definition of the lower border to rule out the possibility of having been produced unintentionally. In a very few instances, after completion of the rim fold, the upper edge was turned again making a secondary fold, a fold upon a fold. The lower edge of a fold may merge with the rim or be demarcated either by sharply trimming off the clay of the fold or by undercutting.

Rim folds, both interior and exterior, may be round, square, rectangular, and in a few instances almost triangular, in cross section, and they may project for several millimeters or lie quite flat against the rim, often tapering up to a thin, pinched, round, or square lip, the latter being most characteristic for Baytown Plain.

Depth of rim folds varies widely. A random sample of 20 folded rims gave an average of 2.25 cm.; range, 1.5 to 3.2 cm.

Rim folds may be decorated in a number of ways, the most common being variations of nicking, notching, pinching, and punctation. Elaboration of the fold may be at the upper edge of the fold, the lower edge, often both, or on the face.

2) Single Incised Line on Rim: Single horizontal lines are incised on rim exteriors, frequently on interiors, often on both, at variable distances below the lip, but usually not more than 2 cm. The average width of incision is from 1 to 1.5 mm., but some are as wide as 4 mm. The depth averages about 1 mm., but some are 2 to 2.5 mm. deep.

Punctations are found in or beneath the line very rarely.

Incised rims occur with increasing frequency going from north to south in the Survey Area, in the north comprising only 8.4% of rim decorations as compared to 34.4% for the south (see discussion of "Baytown Plain with Coles Creek characteristics," p. 81).

3) Notched and Pinched Rims and Rim Strips: This classification covers a variety of decorative treatments which includes nicking, notching, pinching, etc., the general effect of which is to produce a row of closely spaced indentations around the upper portion of the rim. Most commonly, this treatment is applied to that part of the rim immediately adjacent to the lip and often slightly overlapping the lip (when restricted to the lip surface alone, it is considered lip decoration and is discussed below).

The terms nicking and notching refer to gaps or indentations along the rim edge or lip which are made with a relatively small, hard object as a twig, fingernail, or shell edge, which compacts the clay beneath the pressure and leaves very little "burr." In Baytown Plain, these may be long and narrow cuts, short and wide, deep or shallow, straight or diagonal, or any combination thereof. As used here, the term "nicking" refers to a shallow, rudimentary treatment, while "notching" describes deep, definite cuts.

Pinching denotes an impression made usually with a lateral motion of a finger and nail or some hard instrument which rolls or lumps up the clay ahead of the thrust producing a characteristic appearance of alternating nodes and hollows, sometimes creating such an essentially nodal effect that it is difficult to distinguish between this treatment and one of pinched-up or luted-on nodes.

A very similar effect is also achieved by applying an additional strip of clay which is then usually pinched in the same manner, but sometimes nicked or notched.

In the matter of decoration by nicking, notching, and pinching of rims, there seems to be a definite distributional pattern. In the north, these combined features account for 33.5% of all rim decoration (38.7% if rim strips, so decorated, are included, which never occur in the middle and southern tiers), only 6.9% in the middle tiers, and 13.2% in the southern tiers.

4) Punctation: Punctation is also used as a technique of decorating Baytown Plain ware, and though in the main similar to the above-described techniques, it is restricted to the rim surface, never interfering with the lip to produce the ragged appearance so characteristic for those already discussed. Punctations are often several centimeters below the lip and in some instances seem to mark the junction of rim and shoulder area in the case of jars. Some punctation, however, is only a few millimeters below the lip, and in one instance there are two parallel rows circling the inside of the rim. Punctations may be circular, as if done with a reed or straw, or may have an irregular outline, often done with a fingernail. They may be shallow or deep, and neatly or haphazardly applied, usually with an essentially vertical pressure, but in a few instances with a lateral motion producing a slight burr.

Punctation is a relatively infrequent mode of decoration, but it occurs sporadically throughout the collections. The punctation that occurs far down on the rim wall (regarded at one time as a possible type and tentatively designated Cypress Punctated) has a more southerly distribution, being concentrated especially in the vicinity of Tier 16, making up 42.6% of decorated rims, as compared with 7.2% in the north and 2.4% in the south.

5) Nodes: A single row of closely spaced nodes immediately adjoining the rim edge is another method of decoration, but is used very infrequently, and its use is concentrated in Tiers 10 to 14.

Perforated Rims. In several sherds throughout the collections, holes are drilled in the rim from 1 to 4 cm. below the lip, probably to serve as a means of suspension rather than as decoration. It is evident that these holes were drilled after firing, not punched when wet, for one sherd in the collection has a hole partly drilled through from either side but failing to make a perforation, and several others indicate that drilling was done from both sides, meeting in the middle. Perforations may also indicate attempts to repair broken pottery by "crack lacing."

Rims showing gourd features. There are several rim sherds in the Baytown Plain collections which are clearly imitative of a sectioned gourd as it would appear if divided vertically through the center, each half then comprising one bowl. The halved stem depression is shown with a greater or lesser degree of naturalism so that the rim exterior is depressed and interior raised. Sometimes, it is merely a rudimentary finger print on the exterior, often with a clearly modeled node on the interior. In one instance, it is done with considerable realism and the hard "stem" center very well modeled.

Unfortunately, our examples are limited to less than a dozen, but the distribution of them is interesting for none occur above Tier 17.

Lip. Only 6.7% of the Baytown Plain lips are elaborated with decoration. Of the large residue of plain lips, the two leading forms are round and square, comprising 47.5% and 30.6%, respectively. Of less numerical importance are interior or (more often) exterior beveled lips and thinned or "pinched" lips. A very few lips are rolled or protruded toward the exterior. The rolled or protruded lips are largely associated with jars, as are also the exterior beveled lips, the latter also being common for inslanted rims. Interior beveled lips are usually confined to bowls with outslanting rims.

With respect to decorated lips, there are two primary treatments, the most usual being some variation of nicking, notching, or pinching, a little less than two-thirds of the decorated lips being so treated. Next in order of frequency is that of incising one or more lines around the lip. There are only a very few sporadic occurrences of punctations in the lip.

Decorating the lip by incisions is usually confined to a single, relatively wide (1 to 3 mm.), deep (averaging ca. 1 to 1.5 mm.), and well-defined line, applied in most cases to a flat lip, sometimes to an interior beveled lip, and in a very few instances to a lip with a slight exterior roll or protrusion. When lips are incised with several lines, which is frequent, the rim is often thickened immediately adjacent to the lip so that a larger area is formed for the application of the lines. More flat surface is achieved for the application of multiple incisions, also, by sharply beveling the interior wall so that the incisions are actually one below the other.

Base. The number of flat or flattened basal sherds in the collections is only 7.5% of the number of rims, which indicates that the great majority of vessels had round or only slightly flattened bottoms.

The flat bases are either round, square, or square with rounded corners. Corners are occasionally extruded to form flanges or incipient feet.

In respect to the distribution of flat bases, there are more square than round bases in the northern tiers (10 to 14), 24.4% square as against 14.2% round. In the middle and southern tiers, the numerical relationship is just the reverse. In Tiers 15 to 16, there are 11% square bases as against 22% round; and in Tiers 17 to 20, there are 9.2% square as against 19.2% round. There are only a few bases with extruded corners, and these seem largely confined to the northern tiers (12 to 15) with only one appearing below Tier 15.

Appendages. Appendages of any sort are of infrequent occurrence in Baytown Plain. Not a single identifiable handle has appeared in the collections, and only a few fragments of effigy features, possibly generalized zoomorphic heads of insufficient character to warrant description.

Lugs occur with a little more frequency, however. These are for the most part quite flat and ear-like, projecting upward and outward from the rim edge, and their shape may be half-oval or triangular. If we may infer from kindred types in the Lower Valley such as Coles Creek Plain, these lugs are normally four in number, giving the vessel a quadrangular appearance.

A very few lugs consist of a horizontal flange extending from the rim with a rounded or triangular edge similar to those described for Neeley's Ferry Plain, but without the latter's massiveness.

Lugs occur so infrequently that it is difficult to generalize about their distribution. The few small triangular lugs, horizontal flanges, and effigy features are distributed throughout the Survey Area without any significant pattern.

Discussion. In its incipient stages typology will inevitably err in two contrary directions: some types being over-specialized, others, over-generalized. Baytown Plain is an outstanding example of the latter tendency. Being a plain type, this is practically inevitable. Future excavation, bringing additions to our scanty information on factors of shape, will undoubtedly result in breaking the type down into more meaningful categories. Because of its generalized nature it is useless to talk of a "center" or "centers" for the type. It is found in great abundance throughout the Survey Area. Its distribution in time is almost equally diffuse. It is the basic plain ware in this area for the Tchula and Baytown periods. Small wonder, then, that the type gets us into classificatory difficulties. For example, we find sherds that are practically indistinguishable from Marksville Stamped and we classify them as such. The plain ware associated with them ought logically to be called Marksville Plain. We call it Baytown Plain. Why? Because we cannot sort that plain ware from the plain ware associated with equally authentic Coles Creek types, or from plain ware associated with types that have no Lower Valley associations at all. The resolution of this and kindred anomalies are problems for future typologists with more satisfactory material at their disposal. For the present, we may simply state them as candidly as possible and pass on.

Baytown Plain with Coles Creek Characteristics. Particularly embarrassing are the relationships of Baytown Plain with Coles Creek Incised and Coles Creek Plain. A certain amount of material was found, mainly in the southern part of the Survey Area, that showed what might be called incipient Coles Creek characteristics, i.e., a single incised line about the rim (Coles Creek Incised has by definition two or more such lines), one or more lines on a flat horizontal lip (occasionally an interior beveled lip), or both. This material could be classified as Coles Creek Plain: the published definition allows for such simple embellishments. This would involve us, however, in a serious difficulty. Having brought Coles Creek Plain into the picture, we would be obliged to classify the plain rims and body sherds associated with the material described above as Coles Creek Plain also. But this material cannot be sorted at present from typical Baytown Plain occurring in collections without any Coles Creek associations, incipient or otherwise. Rather than have two plain types, which in the majority of cases cannot be sorted, it seems preferable to exclude Coles Creek Plain from the scene altogether. For purposes of discussion, we shall adopt the formula "Baytown Plain with Coles Creek characteristics," which the reader may interpret as Coles Creek Plain if he so desires. After all, it matters not very much what we call these things, provided it is clear enough what we are talking about.

Relationships Outside Survey Area. Baytown Plain is equivalent to Lower Valley plain ware from Tchefuncte Plain to Addis Plain of the Plaquemine Period. McKelvey Plain, its counterpart in northern Alabama, is apparently limited to a period corresponding to our middle to late Baytown. A small number of McKelvey Plain sherds are recorded from the Tennessee Valley area (Kneberg and Lewis, 1947) from the West Cuba Landing Site, classified as part of the Eva Focus. As a generalization, it would seem that plain-surfaced clay, limestone, or other types of granular-tempered pottery were not particularly popular in western Tennessee and Kentucky or in the Lower Ohio Valley during the period corresponding to the Tchula and early Baytown of the Survey Area. The Baumer Focus of the Lower Ohio Valley has a small amount of plain ware which is limestone tempered. Throughout the Tennessee Valley from eastern Tennessee to Paducah, it is the early limestone plain types associated with early fabric- and cord-marked that correspond to the early Baytown in the Survey Area.

In southeast Missouri, a comparable type was tentatively called Matthews Plain (Adams and Walker, 1942). This is in all respects equivalent to Baytown Plain, except that the known time depth in this area is not equal to that obtained farther south.

To the west, a comparable plain pottery is found in various rock shelters in northwestern Arkansas associated with Hopewellian types together with some suggestion of its continuation into the late Baytown Period. The eastern Oklahoma area has not undergone sufficient investigation of pre-Spiro cultures, but the pottery of the Fourche Maline complex is comparable in appearance and in its predominance over malleated types to Baytown. Spiro Plain is analogous to late Baytown. In northwestern Louisiana, Smithport Plain and Belcher Plain are regional representatives on a late Baytown level.

Chronological Position. Baytown Plain is the basic, clay-tempered plain ware of the Survey Area from the beginning of the Tchula to the end of the Baytown Period (time G–C). East of the River, during the long Baytown Period, the proportion of Baytown Plain fluctuated with the rise and fall of various malleated body surfaces, such as fabric-impressing, cord-marking, and check-stamping; west of the River, it dominated numerically throughout the entire span of its use.

MULBERRY CREEK CORD-MARKED

(Fig. 79)

Type as described in ref. (a), except as noted below. This description also includes the now-defunct Deasonville Cord-marked.

Paste. Same as Baytown Plain. As in that type, in some districts paste contains a minor amount of fine sand, presumably not intentionally included, thus approximating the provisional type Blue Lake Cord-marked. Paste differs from that described in ref. (a), in that grit or gravel particles are not usually present.

Surface Finish. Paddled with cord-wrapped implement from lip to base and frequently upon base as well. There is one instance, a shallow bowl, in which cord-marking occurs on the interior as well as the exterior. Most typical cord-marking shows impressions of twisted cords of unidentified material ("twisted grass fibers," mentioned in Haag, 1939a, not indicated here), ranging in size from .5 to 4 mm. in diameter, with average falling somewhere near 1 mm. Cords are usually close-spaced, averaging, 2.9 cords per centimeter, for the entire collection (range, 1 to 8 cm.). One of the surprising things is the extent of variation in this particular from site to site, even in sherds from the same site. In general, there is a correlation between cord-size and cord-spacing; consequently, figures for the latter give a fairly satisfactory index of the former. Averages of site collections show a consistent increase in cord-spacing from north to south, the highest average figure (the closest-spaced) being 4.4 cords per centimeter on the Nettle Ridge Site (10–P–3), compared with .9 cords per centimeter on the Shields Site (19–N–2). This indicates a definite increase in the size of cords used toward the south, but not quite to the extent suggested by the figures, owing to the fact that collections in the south frequently show wide spacing of moderate-sized cords, thus producing an effect quite distinct from the more typical material from the northern and central tiers. It is possible that further study will result in subdivision of the type in favor of this wide-spaced southern variety.[10]

Quite apart from the question of spacing, there seems to be a coarse type of cord-marking that may have some chronological significance. Cords are large and close-spaced and, although they are twisted, the twisting is not particularly in evidence, resulting in a sort of "soft" look that is distinctive but difficult to describe. This type of cord-making occurs here and there, but on certain early sites it is the characteristic type.

Direction of cord impressions on rims is as follows in order of frequency of occurrence: normal to lip, right oblique, two directions (criss-crossed), left oblique, parallel to lip. In most cases, sherds classified as oblique are not far off the perpendicular, particularly in the case of left oblique markings, so it is apparent that perpendicular or nearly perpendicular marking is dominant and typical. The small

[10] This is not Deasonville Cord-marked, which in respect to spacing of cords closely resembles typical Mulberry Creek.

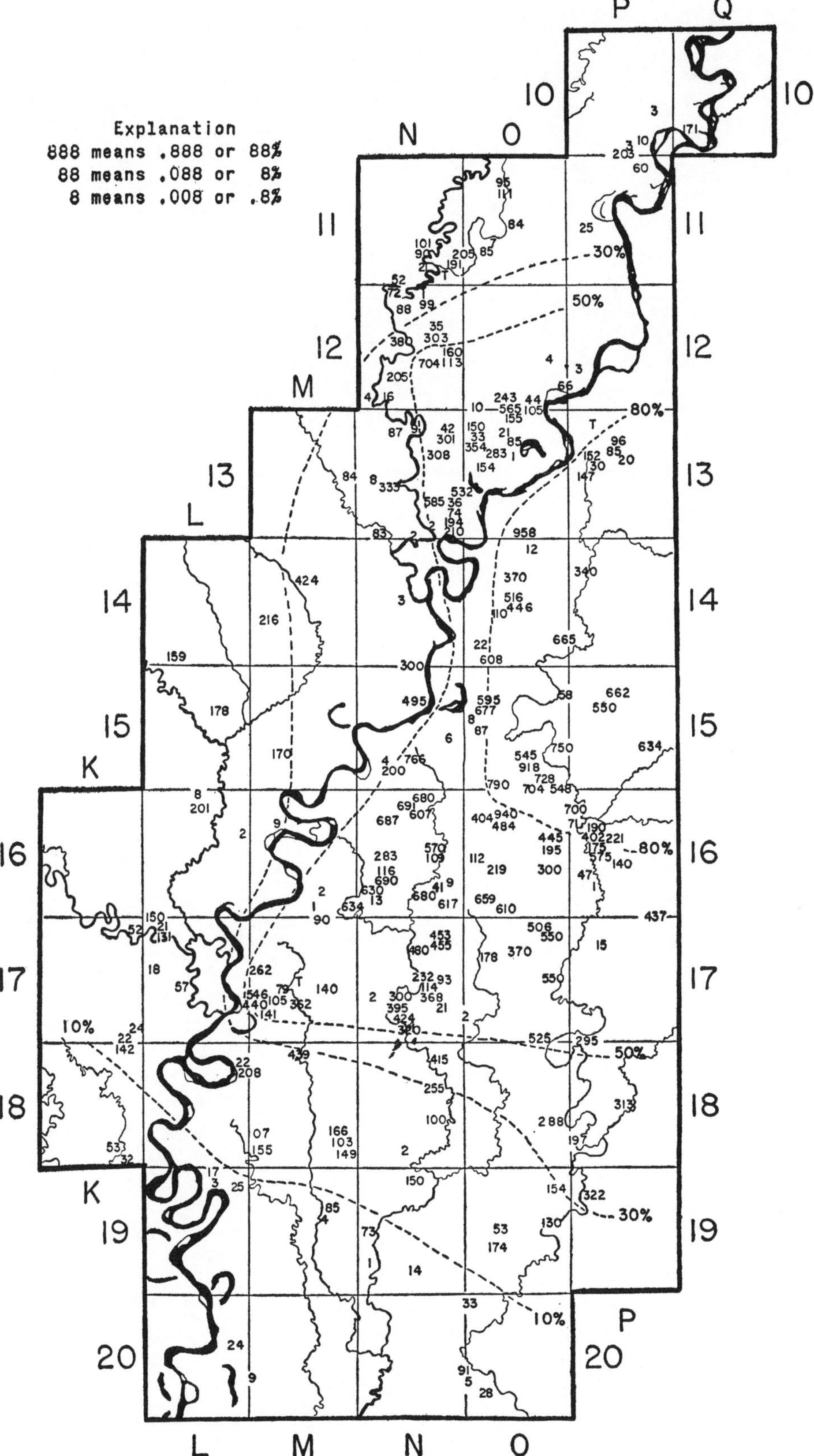

Fig. 7. Percentage frequency distribution of the type Mulberry Creek Cord-marked.

percentage of definitely left oblique marking (less than 10%) may have something to do with left-handedness.

Cord-marking can hardly be considered as decoration, but rather an all-over effect inherent in a technological process, with a possibly purely mechanical significance. It is interesting in this connection that when a rim strip was added, or produced by folding (see below), it was usually subsequent to paddling, as may be seen in detached fragments of strip which show cord impressions in reverse. The possibility that cord-marking was sometimes used decoratively cannot be ruled out, however, particularly in the wide-spaced variety referred to above. A few sherds show, at least, a very careful application of the paddle (fig. 79, *c*, *s*), but no consistent patterns are observable.

In some site collections, there is a marked tendency toward obliteration of cord-marking by smoothing, making sorting difficult. This is a further indication that cord-marking was not decorative in purpose — why take trouble to cord-mark vessels if you intend to smooth later? In a few cases, however, there is evident a decorative intention in the smoothing. There are occasioned examples in which cord-marking has been left on the rim area to form a band contrasting with the smoothed body surface. A few examples with incising over the cord-marking are in the type collection.

Decoration. With the doubtful exceptions noted above, decoration is confined to various simple kinds of rim and lip treatment which will be discussed below.

Form. *Vessel Shape.* The following discussion is based on an analysis of 4618 rims and 196 bases from 218 sites in the Survey Area. This seemingly adequate sample permits us to say a good deal about rims and their modifications, but surprisingly little about vessel shapes. Three general categories of shape are apparent: (1) jars with recurved rim and rounded shoulder; (2) deep, vertical, or slightly incurved-sided vessels, which might be called bowls, or beakers, depending on their depth which is almost invariably an unknown factor; and (3) bowls. Over-all distribution between these three shapes can be stated only approximately. Because these shapes intergrade into one another and because of the prevailing large vessel sizes in all three, only unusually large rims are susceptible of classification. This reduced the sample to 476 rims, distributed as follows: jars, 13.9%; deep bowl or beaker, 33.8%; bowls, 52.2%.

These figures are apt to be misleading. Owing to the fact that it requires an extra-large sherd to identify a jar, it is probable that the figure for jars is too low. There is no question, however, that bowls are the most common shapes, and this is particularly true in the southern part of the area, where jars are remarkably scarce indeed.

1) Jars: The commonest jar shape has a globular or sub-globular body, a rounded shoulder, slightly flared rim, and round, flattened, or flat base. Diameters at the mouth, about the same as the maximum diameter at the shoulder, average approximately 30 cm. (range, 15 to 40 cm.). Precise information on depth is lacking, but there are some indications that it is about equal to the diameter. Two variants of this basic jar shape are occasionally observed. In the first, the recurve of the rim is not complete, resulting in a slightly restricted orifice. In the other, there is a pronounced recurved and short flaring rim. All possible intergradation between these three typical shapes are present. In view of the small number of recognizable basal sherds (see below), it may be assumed that the great majority of jars have rounded or only slightly flattened bases, sherds of which would be indistinguishable from ordinary body sherds except by their greater thickness. Evidence of conical or conoidal bases is entirely absent.

2) Deep Bowls or Beakers: This category of shapes is difficult to define on the basis of rims alone. These are of two types — vertical and incurving. The first apparently belongs to a shape not unlike that of an old-fashioned derby hat, minus the rim, with diameters in the neighborhood of 35 cm. The second appears to pertain to a barrel-shaped beaker, or in extreme cases, something not unlike a seed jar. Oral diameters, naturally, are smaller, averaging about 25 cm. This shape is fairly common, particularly in the southern part of the area and is probably related to the Marksville-Troyville-Coles Creek shapes in the lower Valley. If so, it is more than likely that many

of the flat bases in the collections, both round and square, belong to this type of vessel. Often, these rims are indistinguishable, except for surface finish and decoration, from rims of such Coles Creek associates as Mazique Incised and Chevalier Stamped.

3) Bowls: Commonest bowl shape in all parts of the Survey Area is a simple curved-sided bowl, the kind of shape that would be obtained by slicing off a shallow section of a sphere. This regular shape is frequently modified by a slightly outflaring rim. Bowls with straight, flaring sides, which imply a flat or flattened base, are present but rare. Bowl diameters of 150 large rims from all parts of the Survey Area average 39.5 cm. (range, 16 to 55 cm.), with no significant areal difference noted. A considerable number of these rims are large enough to warrant guesses as to depths, which range from one-half to one-fourth — the most common being one-third — of the diameter. Shallower vessels, properly called dishes, are very rare.

Rim. Cord-marking is normally carried up onto the rim area and frequently onto the lip as well. It appears that the standard practice was to finish off the vessel by turning the rim edge outward after paddling. This turned edge was either smoothed onto the exterior rim wall, making a smooth and slightly rolled lip, or was lightly paddled, resulting in a cord-marked, flat, and slightly expanded lip, often slightly inclined outward. Relationships of these two types of lips will be discussed below.

A few exceptions to the rule must be noted. Occasionally, a smooth uncord-marked band was left on the rim — or subsequently smoothed. This occurs only in the central portion of the area, Tiers 13 to 18, and with frequency only in Tiers 16 to 17, which account for more than half of the observed occurrences. Another exception is the smooth rim fold, which will be dealt with below.

Cord-marking aside, the great majority of rims are otherwise unmodified and undecorated. Only 16.8% show any form of elaboration, the three principal sorts being as follows: rims folds, 10.1%; nicked and notched. 4.7%; pinched, 1.5%. Other types of elaboration, such as the use of incised lines, punctations, scallops, crimping (piecrust fashion), etc., show negligible percentages.

1) Rim Folds: These are a logical outcome of the method of finishing off the rim described above (see description of Baytown Plain, p. 78). They are most commonly cord-marked (85% of the total), with the cord impressions usually vertical to the lip. Very commonly, the paddle was handled in such a manner as to produce a concave outer surface. Lips of rims with cord-marked rim folds are usually smooth, but are occasionally cord-marked also. The distribution of plain and cord-marked folds shows a remarkably consistent trend from one end of the area to the other as follows:

TIER	TOTAL FOLDS	PER CENT CORD-MARKED
10	0	—
11	4	100
12	2	100
13	52	96
14	26	77
15	75	98
16	129	75
17	34	56
18	7	57
19	8	50
20	0	—

Interior rim folds, as in Baytown Plain, are rare and principally confined to the southern part of the area.

Depth of rim folds is considerably less than the figure given for Baytown Plain: 276 rims gave an average depth of 1.75 cm. (range, 1.0 to 3.4 cm. Note: in most cases folds less than 1.0 cm. were regarded as merely extreme cases of lip turning and consequently not counted). A slight but possibly nonsignificant decrease in the depth of folds was noted in the southern tiers, possibly correlated with the increase of smooth folds in the same area.

Rim folds are by no means confined to jar forms. They are frequently found on large simple curve-sided bowls of relatively shallow depth.

2) Nicked and Notched Rims: Attempts to differentiate between nicking and notching have not been very successful (see description of Baytown Plain, p. 79). The fact is, a great variety of treatment is included under those headings, the only difference being that, in general, nicking is shallow and confined to the lip area, usually the external portion. Notch-

ing is deeper, involving more than the lip area. Both nicking and notching occur throughout the area sporadically with insufficient frequency to indicate any significant trends. One type of notching, however, already noted for Baytown Plain (see p. 79), in which a small stick or other implement is laid across the lip and impressed deeply in the clay, making a sort of crenelated rim, does occur in strength on certain sites otherwise known to be early (Bowie, 14–N–4 and Porter Bayou, 18–M–1). This type of notching may also show areal significance through a tendency to pile up in the central and southern portions of the area.

3) Pinched Rims: Pinching as described for Baytown Plain (p. 79) is fairly common in Mulberry Creek Cord-marked throughout the Survey Area without showing any pronounced areal trends. Indented or pinched rim strips, which occur in Baytown Plain in the site collections from the northern part of the area, do not seem to occur in Mulberry Creek Cord-marked, though short rim folds are sometimes pinched in a manner that produces practically the same result. Also similar in effect is the practice of applying a line of nodes on the rim which are subsequently pinched, resulting in a sort of exaggeration of the normal pinched rim. This appliqué type of pinching, however, is very rare.

It may be of interest to note that pinching occurs not only on the extreme upper portion of the rim, as a termination to the cord-marking, but also lower down as a line marking the juncture of the rim and body wall, or the point of greatest constriction in jars with constricted necks, in which case it overlies the cord-marking. This appears to be a specialty of certain sites in the central portion of the area where at one time we contemplated giving it type status.

A few rims have been characterized as punctated, but the practice is significantly different from the pinching described above.

A single incised line on the rim is occasionally seen giving an effect somewhat similar to a rim fold. There are also cases in which the lower edge of rim folds are accentuated by an incised line. Neither occurs with sufficient frequency to suggest any trends.

A type of rim treatment designated here as "crimped" shows up occasionally. In this treatment, indentations are made alternately on the inside and outside edges of the lip, producing a wavy effect. This seems to be confined to a single site so far (Everett, 16–O–3); may therefore be no more than an individual variation.

Two examples of the scalloped rim appeared in one site collection (Nelson, 17–M–17), a matter of considerable interest as the treatment is very similar to one that is very characteristic in the later type, Bell Plain.

Lip. Majority of lips are round or oval. As already suggested, flattening is usually, though not always, the result of paddling; consequently, the relationship is adequately expressed by figures on the distribution of smooth to cord-marked lips, as given below:

TIER	SMOOTH	CORD-MARKED	TOTAL	PER CENT CORD-MARKED
10	—	2	2	100
11	6	30	36	83.3
12	22	22	44	50
13	151	71	222	32
14	348	82	430	19
15	425	205	630	32.5
16	1157	224	1381	16
17	587	52	639	8.1
18	184	15	199	7.5
19	38	7	45	15.5
20	18	—	18	—

The trend is seen to be very definitely in the direction of reduction in flattened cord-marked lips toward the south. That there is also a chronological factor is suggested by the fact that in the central area, where both treatments are common, there is a wide variety in respective frequencies from site to site. It may be assumed that in general cord-marked lips represent the older practice.

Direction of cord impressions is most frequently across the lip at right angles to it or nearly so. Quite often, however, the paddle is held in such a manner that impressions are parallel to the lip, which usually is wide enough to receive only one or two cord impressions, with a resulting effect recalled in the incised lines on lips of Baytown Plain (see discussion of "Baytown Plain with Coles Creek characteristics," p. 81).

Pinched (pointed) lips occur as a scattered minority feature without apparent significance.

Base. The number of recognizable basal sherds is so small as to indicate that the vast majority of bases were rounded or only slightly flattened. Flat bases are, however, a consistent minority in this type. They are identical to those described for Baytown Plain. Of 187 flat basal sherds that emerged from the general sorting, 28 were circular, 59 square or squarish with rounded corners and convex sides, and the balance indeterminate as to shape. No significant trends in distribution of flat bases, whether round or square, were observed.

Appendages. None.

Discussion. Distribution of Mulberry Creek Cord-marked (fig. 7) shows two significant features: (1) concentration of the type east of the Mississippi, and (2) a piling up of frequencies in the center of the area.

1) The extent to which the River seems to have been a delimiting factor in the distribution of cord-marking is extremely interesting. It may actually prove to have been more marked than appears on the present map, when we have straightened out the relationships of archaeology and recent drainage history. There is a possibility — but we cannot go into it here — that many of the sites showing large percentages of Mulberry Creek in the Lower St. Francis Basin were on the east side of the Mississippi at the time of occupation.

2) From the standpoint of distributions north and south, the concentration of high frequencies in the center, particularly in Tiers 16 and 17, and well east of the River, can be interpreted in one of two ways: either this was the "center" for the type, or it moved into this part of the area from the east, by way of the Coldwater, Little Tallahatchie, and Yocona rivers. A parallel distribution of the earlier type, Withers Fabric-impressed has already been discussed (see p. 75).

In any case, it can be said with a certain degree of assurance that cord-marking did not come down the river from the north, and it certainly fades out rapidly to the south.

Relationships Outside the Survey Area. Similar in most characteristics to specimens of the same type in northern Alabama. It should be noted, however, that in northern Alabama clay-tempering does not appear as a dominant ware until what would correspond to middle and late Baytown. It is recommended that the names Deasonville Cord-marked be abandoned in the area to the south, Korando Cord-marked in southeast Missouri, and Harmons Creek Cord-marked in central-west Tennessee, where these two latter types are clay tempered. These types are sufficiently covered by the definition of Mulberry Creek Cord-marked in reference (a) and the description here.

Chronological Position. Begins in the Tchula Period (G–F) but reaches its peak in early to middle Baytown, dies out in late Baytown.

Bibliography. (a) Haag, 1939a, p. 17. The references given for Withers Fabric-impressed (p. 75) also contain discussion of the general distribution and significance of cord-marked pottery.

WHEELER CHECK STAMPED

(Fig. 80, *f–j*)

Type as described in ref. (a), except as noted below.

Paste. Same as Baytown Plain. Generally similar to that described in ref. (a), except that grit particles are not present.

Surface Finish and Decoration. Entire surface stamped with checker or grid die, as described in ref. (a), but size of individual checks runs somewhat larger, commonest size being about 4 by 6 mm. Stamping is usually applied at right angles to the lip but this is rarely exact, and in many cases the direction of the pattern is sharply oblique. In general, stamping is carelessly applied, resulting in a haphazard effect to which is added a consistent tendency to subsequent smoothing which all but obliterates the impressions. Withers Fabric-impressed displays the same tendency. The two types of decoration when partly obliterated are difficult to distinguish. When almost completely obliterated, they are difficult to sort from Baytown Plain.

Form. *Vessel Shape.* Few criteria available. Rims large enough to suggest shape are about equally divided between those indicating a simple curved-sided bowl with vertical or outflaring rim and those indicating a deeper straight-sided vessel with vertical, slightly incurved or recurved rims. The latter would qualify as jar rims, but we have no information on the depth of such vessels. Sizes of both bowls and jars run pretty large from 26 to 50 cm. oral diameter. Thickness averages 8.3 cm., comparable to that of Baytown Plain in the northern part of the Survey Area. The few recognizable basal sherds indicate that all vessel types had thick (1.5 to 2 cm.), round, or at most slightly flattened bottoms. There is no sign of the flat, square bases that sometimes occur in Baytown Plain and Mulberry Creek Cord-marked.

Rim. The great majority of rims are unmodified. Exterior rim folds, occurring on 6% of the 182 rims comprising the sample, average 1.9 cm. in depth (range, .9 to 2.5 cm.). They are always stamped along with the body surface. There is no evidence of stamping having been applied previous to the folding of the rim, as is occasionally seen in Mulberry Creek Cord-marked. No examples of rim demarcation by single incised line as described in ref. (a), and only one rim shows the pinching described therein as common. One rim shows a band of cord-marking applied vertically to lip extending a short distance onto the body which is check stamped in the normal way.

Lip. Lips are either round, slightly flattened, or square, in about equal proportions. Flattened or square lips show marks of stamping, which is undoubtedly what made them flat. The latter quite often show an exterior bevel. Exteriorly rolled lips are fairly common (about 10%), a practice which, when carried a little farther, results in the rim folds described above. There was only one example of nicking or notching on the lip.

Discussion. A few differences from the type as originally described in the Pickwick Basin have been noted, but none seem to be particularly significant. Practical differentiation in sorting would be difficult if not impossible. Retention of the name Wheeler Check Stamped is therefore in order. The type is remarkably homogeneous and has a surprisingly narrow distribution in the Survey Area. Comparison with the distribution of the type Mulberry Creek Cord-marked is interesting. Its failure to occur in the area where that type is most in evidence suggests that it may have been an alternative treatment with a somewhat specialized history, possibly at a slightly different and presumably later time period.

Relationship Outside Survey Area. This is clearly a western marginal area for the appearance of check-stamping. Judging from the distribution of the type in the Survey Area, it most likely came in from northern Alabama. In the New Orleans area, check-stamping moved in from the eastern Gulf Coast. This western movement along the coast seems to have been at about the time of its maximum appearance in the Memphis area. Check-stamping centered in the southern Appalachian area and in the north half of Florida. In these regions it begins very early and continues at some sites up to the Historic Period. West of the Mississippi and south of the Missouri, check-stamping is of little importance. It is very rarely found north of Virginia and Kentucky or in the Ohio Valley. In the latter area it is sparsely found during the early and middle Woodland (Adena and Hopewell) periods.

There are two prominent centers of check-stamping in the north. One of these is in the Upper St. Lawrence area during the Iroquoian development. The other is in the Upper Missouri Valley during late prehistoric times.

Chronological Position. The type reached its maximum in the middle to late Baytown Period (D–C) in the Memphis area. There were, however, scattered occurrences possibly as early as time F–E.

Bibliography. (a) Haag, 1939a, p. 16.

INDIAN BAY STAMPED

(Fig. 80, *k–p*)

Type not previously described.

Paste and Surface Finish. Generally similar to Baytown Plain. On certain sites, notably Porter Bayou (18–M–1), paste is poorly wedged, slightly sandy in texture, approximating the Tchefuncte type of paste. At this end of its range, typologically speaking, it is very difficult to sort from Tchefuncte Stamped. At the other end, and this seems to be true particularly in the north, the paste and surface is precisely that of Baytown Plain and associated types.

Decoration. *Treatment.* A similar range in decorative technique is observable. Essentially a plain rocker-stamping, made with an implement averaging 2 cm. in length (range, 1 to 4 cm.), rarely dentate. In the Tchefuncte-like paste there is a tendency to accent the ends of each zigzag, characteristic of Tchefuncte Stamped, whereas on the purely Baytown paste the execution is smoother and less deeply impressed approximating the style in northern Hopewellian examples.

Design. Very little can be said about design-layout of this type. It appears to be an over-all body treatment with rocker-stamping forming parallel bands. Generally, these bands are close-spaced but a minority of sherds show a considerable smooth area between them. Some rims show a smooth undecorated band while in others the decoration is carried right up to the lip. Two rims are incised, one with a series of oblique lines, the other showing a cross-hatched arrangement suggesting a crude approximation to the characteristic Hopewellian rim.

Form. Practically no information is available on vessel shapes. The most probable form is a jar or beaker with vertical or slightly outflaring rim. The sole basal sherd in the collection indicates a thick flat base of characteristic Baytown type, but is not sufficiently large to determine whether it is round or square.

Discussion. The type is cognate to Tchefuncte Stamped from which it may have derived. In its earlier stages it resembles this type so closely that sorting is a completely arbitrary proceeding. In its later stages it approximates to the type Chevalier Stamped.

Relationships Outside Area. These are somewhat difficult to find. To the south, Tchefuncte Stamped is very crudely done and in many examples does not look like a rocker-stamp at all. Within Tchefuncte Stamped there could be arranged the developmental steps from linear punctate to rocker-stamping or these steps could be said to represent the degeneration of rocker-stamping by pottery-makers accustomed to linear punctate decoration. In Marksville there is some over-all rocker-stamping, but it is usually confined in zones outlined by incised lines.

Relatives of Indian Bay Stamped are not at present available from southwestern Louisiana or the Texas Gulf Coast. However, a similar type of rocker-stamping has been found in the valley of Mexico and in the state of Tabasco. At the Tlatilco Site, on the west side of Mexico City, the plain rocker-stamp has appeared on effigy vessels of a peccary and a duck as well as on a flat-base cylindrical bowl with a black polished exterior. (Personal communication from Miguel Covarrubias.) On the bowls the stamp is sometimes confined to zones by incised lines. An associated type might be likened to Marksville Incised but most of the pottery from this Mexican site resembles other local Archaic wares. This is the only Archaic site in the valley of Mexico with rocker-stamping. At the site of La Venta in Tabasco the rocker-stamp has recently been recognized (Drucker, 1947, p. 3) and appears to be a very minor type in the time period around A.D. 200 to 600. In northern Honduras a zoned rocker-stamp is one of the designs on Ulua Bichrome from one of the earliest ceramic levels (Strong, Kidder, and Paul, 1938, pl. 9, *e*). It is also an element of the early Chavín-Cupisnique Period in Peru, dated about 400 B.C.

To the east the plain rocker-stamp as an over-all body design appears in the northwest Florida coast area, seemingly skipping Mississippi and Alabama. At the Yent Mound, Franklin County, Florida, one tetrapodal vessel with a sandy micaceous paste was found with 16 vertical rows of plain rocker-stamping. The technique is something like that in Tchefuncte Stamped. Other examples of plain rocker-stamping are employed in zones and will be discussed under Marksville Stamped.

In the area south of the Ohio, east of the Mississippi and north of the Tennessee, there is very little evidence of plain rocker-stamping similar to Indian Bay Stamped; likewise in most of the area south of the Missouri and west of the Survey Area. In the Renner Site of the Kansas City Focus of Hopewellian, however, this type of body decoration is unusually common, running up to 30% of the body sherds (Wedel, 1943). In many examples here this technique of body treatment is accompanied by a Hopewellian cross-hatched rim.

In the area of Illinois Hopewell the plain

rocker-stamp is a minority body treatment which belongs in the middle to late Hopewell occupation. It is also a minor element in the Trempeleau Focus of western Wisconsin. It is not known to occur in other complexes in the northern Mississippi Valley or in the area of the Ohio Valley except in Ohio Hopewell where it is rare. It does not occur in Adena at all.

In New York it appears in the Vinette 2 complex. In New England and eastern Canada it is represented in the shell heaps of Massachusetts and Maine and related inland sites.

Chronological Position. In the Survey Area, Indian Bay Stamped begins in the Tchula Period (G–F) and lasts until late Baytown (D–C). It is most common in early and middle Baytown (F–D).

EVANSVILLE PUNCTATED

(Fig. 80, *g–a'*)

Type not previously described.

Paste and Surface Finish. Same as Baytown Plain.

Decoration. Punctations made with fingernail or other implement. These are generally oval, semi-lunar, or occasionally hemi-conical in shape. Most frequently, the punctations are made at an oblique angle to the body wall with a resulting tendency to push back some of the clay onto the surface. This "burr" is sometimes carefully exploited for decorative purposes. Punctations are commonly arranged in horizontal rows. Several rims in the collection show an arrangement of three such rows starting immediately beneath the lip. Occasionally, punctations are carefully aligned vertically so that the "burr" forms continuous ridges running at right angles to the rows. Further emphasis on the ridged effect is obtained by "pinching." In spite of the fact that the latter seems to involve a basically different mechanical treatment, it is difficult in sorting to differentiate the two techniques. The term "punctation" as used here will therefore be understood to include pinching as well.

Design. Very little evidence of design is at hand, beyond the three horizontal rows of punctations mentioned above, and occasional examples of vertical or diagonal pinched bands. Otherwise, the type seems to be an over-all body treatment as we know to have been the case in the analogous shell-tempered type, Parkin Punctated.

Form. The only shape indicated with surety by the few rims available is a jar or beaker with slightly recurved rim. It is very probable, however, that bowl forms are also included. No basal features or appendages are present in the collections.

Distribution. No significance in distribution is apparent. A total of 103 sherds classified as Evansville Punctated are distributed among no less than 45 sites, more or less scattered over the entire Survey Area except that there are no occurrences north of Tier 13.

Relationships Within Survey Area. The type is closely related to Alexander Pinched and Tammany Pinched, from one of which it probably derives. Such differences as are observable are purely factors of paste: as decorative techniques the three types are precisely similar. Evansville Punctated was in turn succeeded by Parkin Punctated which likewise shows little if any change in treatment. The series Tammany-Evansville-Parkin offers one of the clearest possible evidences of general ceramic continuity in the Survey Area over a long period of time.

Relationships Outside Survey Area. The nearest relative to the south is La Salle Punctated which is apparently a marginal expression of Carrabelle Punctated of the Florida Gulf Coast. In these types the punctates are usually restricted to the upper body. Punctates of various types appear on Coles Creek sites but are rare.

In the Southeast generally, the use of body punctates or pinched decoration is not common. The same statement can be made in regard to the Ohio Valley and the Northeast.

In eastern Texas, punctates are used as a rim decoration on Pedro Punctated, a minor type of the Alto Focus. This resembles some of the Carrabelle specimens. Body punctates are found on such types of the Alto Focus as Weches Fingernail-impressed and Duren Neck Banded and are very common. In northwestern Louisiana the type Smithport Incised-Punctate is on a somewhat later level. The "Caddo" area has a considerable use of punctates over a time period equivalent to the late Baytown and Mississippi periods in the Survey Area.

In the Illinois Valley Hopewell, there is considerable use of punctates in the southern part of that region. In this complex the punctates are usually arranged in horizontal rows on the body of the vessel.

Chronological Position. The type occurs in minor quantities throughout the entire Baytown Period (F–C).

MARKSVILLE STAMPED

(Fig. 81, *a–p*)

Type as described in ref. (a), (b), and (c), except as noted below.

Paste and Surface Finish. Similar to Baytown Plain, but thinner (average 6.5 mm.) and has a smoother finish. In other words, comparable to the better examples of Baytown Plain.

Decoration. *Treatment.* As described in ref. (c, pp. 72–73). "Deep wide lines, U-shaped in cross section, are used to outline the designs. Figures are always depicted by smoothed bands, and the backgrounds are roughened by rocking a fine dentated stamp as it is moved sideways. The designs are so arranged that smoothed and roughened bands alternate." Lines average 3.5 mm. in width (range, 2 to 5 mm.), by about 1 mm. in depth. Generally speaking, designs are curvilinear but material is too fragmentary to specify further. There are no examples in which the characteristic Hopewellian bird figure can be identified.

Form. *Rim.* The 17 rims available for study show considerable variation. Eight are thickened, 3 interiorly and 5 exteriorly; 3 are cambered in characteristic Marksville fashion. One of these bears the characteristic fine cross-hatching underlined by a row of hemi-conical punctations (see ref. c, fig. 41, *b*).

Lip. Ovate or flattened ovate with frequent interior beveling.

Vessel Shape. Only three rims are of sufficient size to reconstruct the vessel shape, two of which indicate a simple flaring-sided bowl, about 30 cm. in diameter, the other a small bowl or beaker, with incurved rim about 20 cm. in diameter.

Base. No information.

Appendages. None present.

Relationships Within Survey Area. There is little question that the specimens collected by the Survey were manufactured close to the sites where they were found, and were not an intrusive minority resulting from trade or some other agency, for they show the same paste characteristics as the Baytown Plain associated with them. For example, the one sherd from the Bowie Site (14–N–4) is identical in paste to the "Bowie" variant of Baytown. The examples from the Jaketown Site (20–O–1) likewise show specific characteristics of the Baytown Plain on the site.

As is clearly evident on the distribution map, figure 8, the type is almost confined to the southern half of the Survey Area. Only 4 sherds (out of a total of 147) were picked up north of Tier 15 and none north of Tier 13. A similar distribution in the case of Coles Creek Incised and Baytown Plain with Coles Creek characteristics led to the assumption that we were on the northern periphery of the distribution of these types. In this case, however, in view of the known relationships of Marksville Stamped with comparable Hopewellian types in the Ohio Valley, Illinois, and farther west, we should be somewhat wary in making a similar generalization. It seems more likely in the case of Marksville Stamped that the failure of the type to show up in the northern part of the Survey Area is the result of our failure to locate a sufficient number of early sites.

Relationships Outside Survey Area. In northeastern Louisiana and adjacent parts of Mississippi it has been possible to recognize two zoned rocker-stamped types, Marksville Stamped and a later Troyville Stamped. Though closely related, these types are differentiated by features of paste, rim treatment, design, and the kind of rocker-stamping employed. We are as yet unable to make an equivalent differentiation in the Survey Area, since all but one of the small total of 147 zoned rocker-stamped sherds in the collections more closely resembled Marksville than Troyville Stamped.

Sherds of this type have been found to the west in east Texas surface collections and

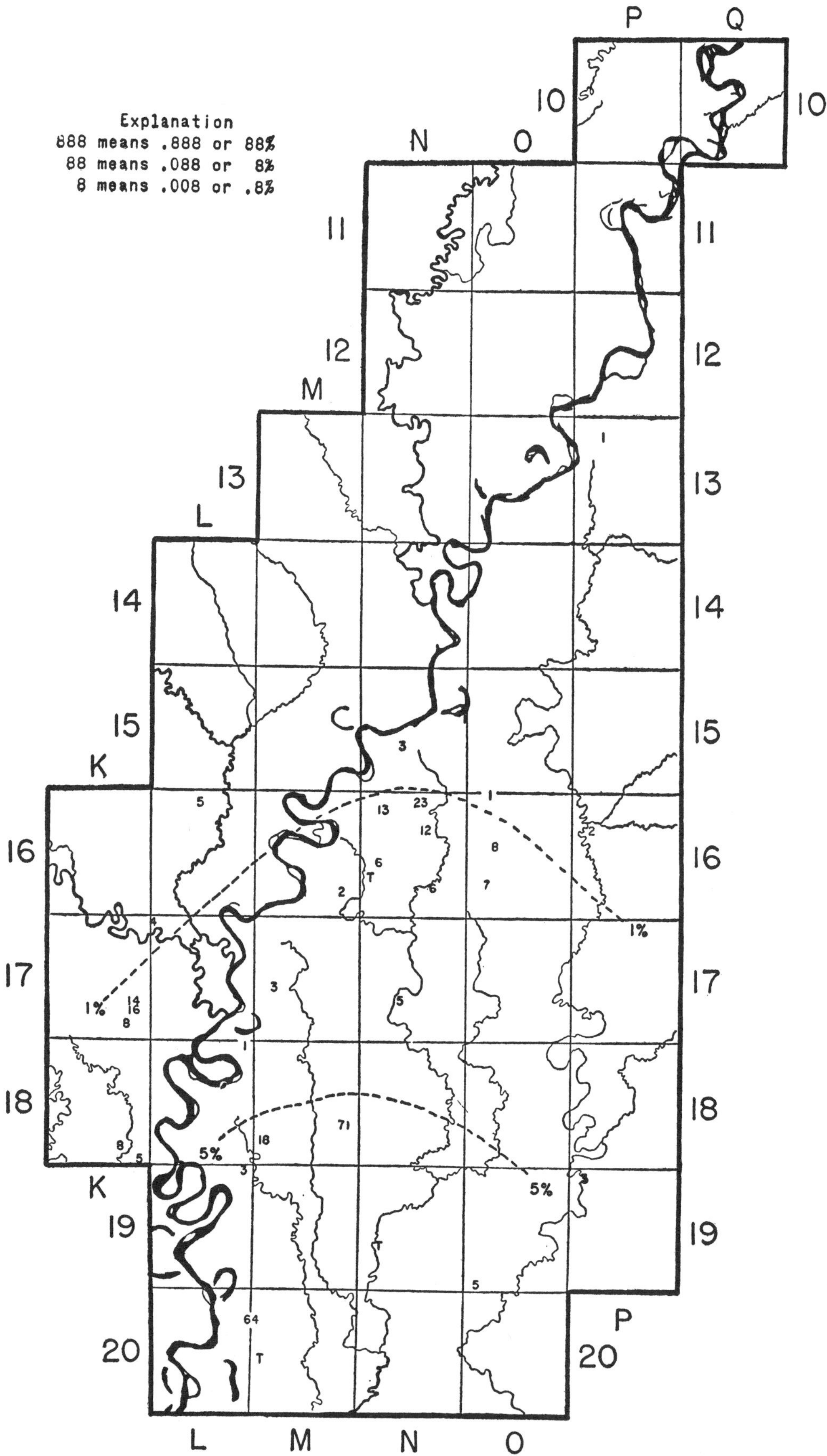

FIG. 8. Percentage frequency distribution of the type Marksville Stamped.

have been recovered from the Davis Mound, the type site of the Alto Focus. This is the nearest point in the United States to the stylistically related Mesoamerican examples, which, except for the Honduras specimens illustrated by Strong (Strong, Kidder, and Paul, 1938, pl. 9, *e*), are not as similar to the Hopewellian Zoned style as are specimens from the Chavín Period in Peru (Tello, 1943, pp. 135–60, pl. XV).

Zoned stamping also has an eastward distribution along the Gulf Coast where, in northwest Florida, it enters into the Santa Rosa–Swift Creek complex at a time approximately equivalent to early Baytown (Willey and Woodbury, 1942. C. B. Moore illustrates a vessel of this type from Alligator Bayou (Moore, 1902, fig. 34), and Griffin has examined similar material from northwest Florida in the Heye Museum.

Directly east of the Survey Area in eastern Mississippi, zoned rocker-stamping on a sandy paste has been picked up on sites in Oktibbeha and Lauderdale counties (U. S. N. M. collections). These sites in the drainage of the Tombigbee are evidently connected with such sites as Choctaw Bluff in Clarke County, Alabama (U. S. N. M. Cat. No. 836120). This site has tetrapodal vessels, Crooks Stamped, a check stamp, a crescent dentate stamp, a relative of Twin Lakes Punctated, Bluff Creek Punctated, Marksville Incised, and a linear punctate type. According to Wimberly of the Alabama Museum of Natural History, there are several similar sites from lower Clarke County.

In central and northern Alabama, Tennessee, Georgia, the Carolinas, and most of Kentucky, pottery of the Hopewell Zoned style is conspicuous by its absence. The few scattered specimens which have so far been reported may best be explained as trade specimens.

In Arkansas west of the Survey region Marksville Stamped has been recognized in the Ozark area as part of an early pottery complex. This material still awaits an adequate presentation to place it in its full cultural context and correct time position. Eastern Kansas and Oklahoma have a small representation of a zoned stamp type. These specimens usually have a plain dentate stamp, thus resembling the Illinois Valley Hopewell pottery more than the Lower Mississippi Valley Marksville.

The northern Mississippi and Illinois Valley Hopewell sites have a considerable representation of pottery of the Hopewell Zoned Stamp tradition. In this region the tempering materials are largely of finely crushed granite rock, or limestone. Some rare examples, as among the other local types, have clay temper. There are a number of misconceptions about this zoned Hopewell style in the north which have their roots in the nineteenth century. The first of these is that this style was used only as a mortuary offering. This belief was fostered because of the finds of Squier and Davis and various other archaeological publications reporting mound explorations, where, naturally, the best specimens were illustrated, not the associated cord-marked and plain specimens. A corollary misconception is that this zoned stamp pottery does not occur in the village sites. This was also the result of inadequate knowledge, for earlier archaeologists paid little attention to the analysis of village-site pottery or of the pottery within the mound fill gathered from a dwelling area. It is clear, however, from more recent excavations and studies, that the Hopewell Zoned Stamped style is well represented in Hopewellian sites of the Illinois and northern Mississippi Valley areas. Furthermore, the percentage relationship here is approximately the same as that in the Lower Mississippi Valley. In some sites, such as Snyders in Calhoun County, Illinois, and Creve Coeur, north of St. Louis, Missouri, there is actually a higher proportion of zoned stamp pottery in the village débris than at any of the sites in the Survey Area or farther south in the Lower Valley.

In southwestern Indiana, Hopewell Zoned Stamped is found associated with Swift Creek Complicated Stamped pottery. In the southern Ohio area the Tremper Site, which Webb has suggested is early Ohio Hopewell, is not known to have any Hopewell Zoned Stamped types. The most nearly representative collection is from the Turner Site where the proportion of decorated to utility ware is approximately the same as in the Marksville sites.

The chronological position of the zoned stamp decoration is not too well known in the north, particularly in Ohio. In the Illinois Valley area, a proposed sequence within Hopewellian would place the Hopewell Zoned Stamp pottery in the middle Hopewell Period, with its descendant Baehr Zoned Stamp in late Hopewell. The early Hopewell Period as represented by most of the Havana Mound 6 collection and the lower half of the Snyders Site does not have this distinctive pottery, but many other Hopewell characteristics are well developed.

Chronological Position. Time F–D, with maximum occurrence in the early Baytown Period (F–E).

Bibliography. (a) Setzler, 1933; (b) Ford, 1936, pp. 222–23, Type 31: $\frac{23}{101/102}$. (This early type description covers both Marksville and Troyville Stamped.) (c) Ford and Willey, 1940, pp. 65–74, figs. 28–33; (d) Griffin, 1941, pp. 192–93.

MARKSVILLE INCISED

(Fig. 81, *s–z*)

Type as described in ref. (a), (b), (c), (d), and (e), except as noted below.

Paste and Surface Finish. Same as Marksville Stamped.

Decoration. *Treatment.* Incision with thick blunt instrument producing a broad, generally shallow line with a smooth basin-like cross section. Lines vary in depth. The maximum is about 2 mm., but most of them are considerably less. The average width of the line is 3.7 mm., with a range of 2 to 5 mm.

Design. There is a slight majority of curvilinear elements over straight ones. Our series is inadequate, and the small sherds give little indication with respect to all-over design, but there are indications of scrolls, concentric circles, and in one example at least there is part of the characteristic Hopewell bird design.

The straight-line motifs seem to be line-filled triangles, meanders, and in a very few instances cross-hatched elements.

Only two examples of punctations terminating incised lines, described as rare for Marksville Incised but common for Yokena Incised, appear in collections from the Survey Area.

Almost all rim sherds have a rim fold from 2 to 3 cm. wide and the decoration begins immediately below.

Form. *Vessel Shape.* Simple bowls with incurved walls are indicated. A very few straight and flaring-walled bowls also occur. Average thickness is 5.7 cm., with a range of 4 to 8 cm.

Rim. The most common rim is that of the incurved bowl, with a definite camber and usually an exterior fold which may extend as much as 3 cm. down vessel exterior, but is usually less, about 2 cm. A straight rim also occurs with a smaller fold, tending to be rectangular in cross section.

Lip. Lips may be pointed, flattened in the plane of the rim, rounded, or beveled to the interior.

Base. No information in the collections.

Appendages. None present.

Discussion. The broad-line incised decoration of the general Hopewellian-Marksville horizon in the Mississippi Valley was first described by Setzler in 1933, ref. (a), and by Ford in 1935 and 1936, refs. (b and c). These rather tentative definitions were later refined as a result of stratigraphic excavations, and by 1939 it was apparent that two divisions could usefully be made in this material near the mouth of Red River. These were defined as an earlier Marksville Incised (ref. c, p. 78) and a later Yokena Incised (ref. d, pp. 7–8). The first was confined to the Marksville Period in that area and the second marked the Troyville Period.

In the present study we have not been able to maintain the distinction that has been made farther south. Perhaps this will be possible later on when larger amounts of material are available from excavations. Consequently, Marksville Incised, as applied to the Survey Area, is not identical with the original type descriptions in that it may include features which, with further information, would be referrable to Yokena Incised.

Relationships Within Survey Area. A parent type is absent in the Survey Area, and lineal descendants are also difficult if not impossible to find. Marksville Incised is one of the markers of the early Baytown Period. It is found on more sites (34) and in greater numbers (197 sherds) than Marksville Stamped.

Relationships Outside Survey Area. The closest relative is Marksville Incised in the southern Louisiana area which should logically be an outgrowth of the incised types in the Tchefuncte Period such as Tchefuncte, Lake Borgne, and Alexander Incised. It is also possible that it may have derived from its companion Marksville Stamped.

The related type in northwest Florida has recently been named Basin Bayou Incised by Willey. As was seen in the comparative statement on Marksville Stamped, the Hopewell marker types are absent in northern Alabama, Tennessee, Georgia, and Kentucky in a Hopewell context. Montgomery Incised in Kentucky and the closely related specimens in southeastern Indiana and Ohio are on an earlier time level. Their style of incising resembles that of the Hopewell Period more closely than does Tchefuncte Incised while the designs hark back to Orange Incised.

In the Illinois Valley area, incising is found on the earliest cord-marked pottery and has a period of development from Black Sand through the Morton Focus before the Hopewell Period begins. Within Illinois Hopewell the zoned incising at Havana Mound 6 appears to precede the appearance of Hopewell incising on the more classic shapes resembling Marksville Incised.

Chronological Position. Approximate contemporaneity with Marksville Stamped is indicated in time F–D, with maximum occurrence in the early Baytown Period (F–E).

Bibliography. (a) Setzler, 1933; (b) Ford, 1935, pp. 11–12 (type 12a); (c) Ford, 1936, pp. 223–24 (types 45; 23; 6 and 51; 23); (d) Ford and Willey, 1940, p. 78; (e) Haag, 1939c, pp. 7–8.

CHURUPA PUNCTATED

(Fig. 81, *a′*, *b′*)

Type as described in ref. (e) and (f), except as noted below.

Paste and Surface Finish. Same as Baytown Plain.

Decoration. Bands or zones of hemiconical punctations framed by wide incised lines as described in references. Sample is insufficient for generalizations about placement and design, but all examples appear to fall within the published definitions. A number of sherds showing only groups of hemiconical punctations have been classified as Churupa Punctated on the theory that they are fragments out of punctated zones whose framing lines do not happen to appear. There is, of course, a possibility that these sherds represent a variant of the type in which there are no framing lines.

Form. The rims (two) present in the collection are incurved and apparently pertain to simple curved-sided bowls or small pots of the general Marksville Period type. One of them shows evidence of thickening by means of an interior fold.

Discussion. The type is very rare in the Survey collections, being represented by 13 sherds, all from sites in the southern half of the area. It seems safe to interpret the situation as an extreme marginal distribution — possibly one in which there was an element of trade — of a type whose center lay to the south. French Fork Incised shows precisely the same thin southerly distribution.

Relationships Outside Survey Area. Churupa Punctated was originally described for the area of Louisiana near the mouth of Red River where the type is also rare. There it has a frequency of less than 1% and in time is confined to the Troyville Period.[11] It is peculiar that there is no comparable type found in similar proportions in the Marksville Period in that area in view of the fact that close resemblances to this decoration are found in the Tchefuncte Period type Orleans Punctated (ref. f, pp. 62–63). See figure 77, *a′–d′*. Resemblance may also be seen to the linear punctated types in Stallings Island and early zoned punctated decorations on the northwest coast of Florida (Santa Rosa Punctated), suggesting that the sequence of Orleans-Churupa is a faint reflection of a ceramic development that has a popularity center to the east along the Gulf Coast from Mobile to Tampa.

[11] In ref. (e), the date of the type is given as "middle and late Marksville Period." Since that publication, the temporal position of the type has been more clearly delimited and also the Troyville Period has been set up between the former Marksville and Coles Creek periods. The type has a time range in what is now defined as the Troyville Period as stated by Ford and Willey in ref. (f), p. 77.

Probable descendants of Churupa are found in the Lower Mississippi area but in even smaller percentages, so small that the type — or types — have not been formally named. However, the decoration idea of line-zoned punctations lasted to comparatively late times both in the "Caddo" area and in the region near the mouth of the Yazoo River. (Moore, 1909, figs. 61, 68; Ford, 1936, figs. 21, *i*, 23, *g*.) The later phase of this history is suggested by Ford in ref. (b, fig. 46). Another possible descendant found in the Survey Area is the type Owens Punctated (see p. 136).

In northern Hopewell a zoned punctate is a part of the Morton Focus of the Illinois Valley (Cole and Deuel, 1937, figs. 1, 5, 6, and 7), in a context which is clearly pre-Hopewellian but which carries many of the decorative techniques and designs which, with subsequent modifications, form a part of Illinois Hopewell. The excavations at Havana Mound 6 produced ceramic styles regarded as showing clear evidence of derivation from Morton Focus. These vessels are also unmistakably Hopewellian, but the site lacks the fine limestone-tempered ware considered "classic" Hopewell. At this site a zone punctate appears as well as zoned cord-wrapped stick. (Griffin and Morgan, 1941, pl. 11, *2*; pl. 16, *1* and *2*; pl. 18, *5*).

Evidence from Ohio Hopewell is inadequate, but zoned punctate specimens were found at Turner (Willoughby, 1922, pl. 24, *m*) and Seip (Shetrone and Greenman, 1931, fig. 52, *i*).

Chronological Position. Early to middle Baytown (F–D). There is a possibility that the type appeared earlier in the Survey Area than the Troyville Period assignment farther south.

Bibliography. (a) Ford, 1935, type 14d, pl. 2; (b) Ford 1936, figs. 32, *i*; 40, *t*, *x*; 43, *h*, *i*; 44, *d*, *e*, *v*; (c) Walker, 1936, pl. 14, *b*, *g*; (d) Dickinson and Lemley, 1939, pl. 37, *b*, *d*, *e*; (e) Haag, 1939c, p. 2; (f) Ford and Willey, 1940, p. 77.

COLES CREEK INCISED

(Fig. 82, *a–e*)

Type as described in references cited, except as noted below.

Paste and Surface Finish. Same as Baytown Plain but slightly thinner (average, 6.9 mm.) and has a smoother finish.

Decoration. *Treatment.* In general, the same overhanging line, characteristic of Coles Creek farther south occurs, but as in the type there we have variations including relatively narrow incisions made with a thin, pointed implement and relatively wide, smooth lines which do not overhang.

Design. As in the type description, the lines are placed parallel and horizontal to the rim, spaced usually less than .5 cm., but in some instances as high as 1.5 to 2 cm. apart. They usually begin just below the lip, but often there is an undecorated portion of rim before the incising begins. As a departure from typical Coles Creek Incised, only once do we find punctations beneath the incised zone.

Form. *Vessel Shape.* Very little information. Vertical-walled bowl or beaker indicated. Occasional incurved rims suggest barrel-shaped beaker.

Rim. As in the typical Coles Creek Incised, vertical rims are most common. In our collections, incurved and inslanted rims are second in order of frequency, and there are only a few with outcurved or outslanted walls. Exterior rim folds are common, usually small and rounded, occasionally triangular in section.

Lip. Lips are usually flattened, sometimes tend to be rounded in cross section or a flattened oval. Thin lips often occur where the rim wall tapers off toward the lip. On a few examples there is an interior beveling, and one has a notched lip.

Base. None in the collections.

Appendages. None in the collections.

Discussion. Coles Creek Incised is not an abundant type in the Survey Area, and the majority of examples are found in the southern Yazoo Basin sub-area. It is evident that, with respect to this type, our area is marginal to regions farther south. As with Mazique Incised, most of the specimens here called Coles Creek are so identified only by reason of considerable latitude in typing.

Although this simple decoration has superficial resemblance to Tick Island Incised in eastern Florida, to Tchefuncte Incised in southern Louisiana, and certain designs in the

Alexander Series, there does not now seem to be any direct connecting links between these manifestations and the later horizon in which Coles Creek Incised is found.

Relationships Outside Survey Area. In the eastern Gulf Coast, Moore has illustrated specimens similar to Coles Creek Incised from northern Florida (Moore, 1902, fig. 78; 1903a, fig. 65), and there are a number of specimens probably from Cedar Keys in the Ceramic Repository for the eastern United States. Surfside Incised in the Glades area of Florida is a related style. At Kolomoki, a late Swift Creek-Weeden Island site in southwest Georgia, Fairbanks reports "overhanging incised sherds were provisionally assigned to the Weeden Island complex" (Fairbanks, 1946, p. 259).

At present, the best opinion is that this design in the eastern Louisiana area and in the lower part of the Survey Area was imported from the west and helps to mark the beginning of the Coles Creek Period. In east Texas the types Hickory Fine Engraved and Davis Incised of the Alto Focus must be related. Krieger is of the opinion that this early Alto Focus ceramic complex is related to the Miraflores horizon in highland Guatemala (Newell and Krieger, 1949, p. 227). Ford suggests this decoration may ultimately be derived from the trait of neck-banding as practised in the Southwest which also appears at the Davis Site. Other possible ancestors might be found in the Huasteca area (Du Solier, Krieger, and Griffin, 1947, p. 27 and pl. 2, *h* and *i*; Ekholm, 1944, fig. 9, *x*, Zaquil Black Incised).

In the Southwest, attention might be called to storage jars from the Taos Valley in northern New Mexico that have multiple parallel incised lines on the upper body. On one of these there is a wide band of roughly horizontal punctates placed between an upper and lower zone of incised lines (Jeançon, 1929, pl. 12). The use of such multiple parallel horizontal lines on the upper body of jars is also found on vessels in the Mill Creek culture of northwestern Iowa. In this case, the type is without apparent progenitors or descendants. At Taos it may have derived from neck banding.

In northern Chihuahua, multiple parallel lines are found on the shoulder of jars either on plain surfaces (Hewett, 1908, pl. XIV, *a*, B–10), or on polychrome specimens (Sayles, 1936, fig. 15 and pl. 2). This style of decoration is regarded as having been derived from Mimbres Corrugated.

To the north of the Survey Area at Cahokia a similar engraved-incised decoration is found but its chronological position and ceramic associations are not clear. In view of other connections between Cahokia and the "Caddo" area, which largely bypassed eastern Louisiana, this style of decoration may also be early here.

Chronological Position. Most of the chronological graphs show a somewhat spotty temporal position for the type in the Baytown Period. In the Yazoo sub-area, where the greatest number of examples occur, it shows a popularity peak in the late Baytown Period D–C).

Bibliography. (a) Setzler, 1933, pl. 6, *D*; (b) Ford, 1935, pl. 3, Type 5a; (c) Ford, 1936, many illustrations; (d) Walker, 1936, pls. 11, *a* and *f*; 15, *b*; (e) Haag, 1939c, pp. 11–12.

OXBOW INCISED

(FIG. 82, *n-p*)

Type not previously described.

Paste and Surface Finish. Same as Baytown Plain.

Decoration. *Treatment.* Narrow incision with pointed implement, making sharp clean lines on a moist clay surface. Average width of line is considerably less than 1 mm., and there are many examples in which linework approximates that of "engraving."

Design. In contrast to the relatively careful, closer-spaced, fine-line treatment of Mazique Incised (fig. 82, *f–m*) is the excessively haphazard layout of decoration in Oxbow, so carelessly executed in the main that it is impossible to say very much about design as such. A few of the better sherds show that groups of line-filled triangles and more commonly simple cross-hatching, comparable to those of the later type Barton Incised, were planned, but in the majority of cases nothing better is achieved than the sort of scratching that mother applies to the soles of Junior's new shoes.

Decoration is on the upper portion of rim or shoulder. It usually starts with a line or row of punctations a short distance below the lip.

Form. *Vessel Shape.* The very small amount of information available indicates a jar or beaker with vertical or slightly recurved rim. There is a frequent tendency for lips to be beveled interiorly which accentuates the effect of recurve and in one or two cases results in a sharp outflaring rim making a sharp angle with the shoulder.

Rim. Mainly unmodified. A small percentage of rims have exterior smoothed folds about 1 cm. wide.

Lip. Lips tend to be pointed as result of interior beveling referred to above.

Base. No information.

Appendages. None present in the collection.

Distribution. The type is found throughout the Survey Area, with a tendency to pile up in Tiers 15 to 17 of quadrangles (see Discussion of relationship of Oxbow to Mazique Incised in description of the latter type, p. 99).

Discussion. A considerable percentage of sherds of this type would be classified as Barton Incised if they were shell-tempered. It is possible that Oxbow is ancestral to the later type. If so, the difference in distribution becomes a matter of interest, since the "center" for Oxbow Incised is considerably farther south than that of Barton Incised. Relationship to Harrison Bayou Incised is also suggested, except that the horizontal row of punctates below the lip is not mentioned in the brief description of Harrison Bayou Incised (Ford and Willey, 1940, p. 50). Instead an upper horizontal delimiting line is illustrated by Ford and Willey (1940, fig. 15). These same considerations apply as well or better to Mazique Incised.

In the seriation and stratigraphic analysis, this type was combined with Mazique, as "Oxbow-Mazique Incised," in the belief that it included merely the carelessly executed examples of that type. In most cases there appeared to be no significant differences in temporal distribution of the two kinds of material. However, in stratigraphic cuts on the Jaketown Site (see p. 276) Oxbow-type material appeared (without Mazique) in the lower-middle levels, indicating the possibility of an earlier date than that assigned to Mazique, and the consequent advisability of returning to the original separation of the two types pending further information.

MAZIQUE INCISED

(Fig. 82, *f–m*)

Type as described in ref. (a), except as noted below.

Paste. Same as Baytown Plain.

Decoration. *Treatment.* Close-spaced lines incised with blunt-ended tool on fairly "dry" surface showing little "burr." In a few cases it looks as though a multiple-pointed implement has been used, giving a "brushed" or "combed" effect. The attempt to differentiate typologically between simple incision and "brushing" was not successful. A type, provisionally set up under the name "Salomon Brushed," was subsequently abandoned and the material thrown into Mazique.

Incised lines average about 2 mm. in width (range, 1 to 3 mm.) and less than 1 mm. in depth. Sharper lines, i.e., deeper in relation to width, occur occasionally. Spacing of lines averages 3.5 per cm.; range, 2 to 6 lines per cm.

Punctation, generally in the form of a single row of jabs on the rim, occasionally occurs in combination with this type of incision and there is one example in which this line of punctates seems to have been made with a dentate stamp (Oliver, 16–N–6).

Design. Decoration is entirely rectilinear consisting mainly of juxtaposed fields, generally but not always triangular, of close-spaced parallel lines, the over-all effect being obtained by change in direction of the lines from one field to another. Occasionally, these fields of parallel lines are outlined by a single line, but more often they simply abut against the outside line of the adjacent set. The surface is thereby broken up into a system of triangular or trapezoidal spaces lightly contrasted by the change in the direction of the lines. An occasional variant is an arrangement of vertical bands hatched in herringbone fashion.

Form. *Vessel Shape.* Sherds do not afford much information on vessel shape. At least two shapes seem to be indicated: (1) jar or beaker with short slightly recurved rim, and (2) barrel-shaped beaker with slightly incurved rim.

Rim. Rims are often plain for a short distance below the lip, the resulting horizontal smoothed area being terminated by a horizontal line or a row of punctations below which begins the incised decoration that defines the type. Several rims, however, show the aforesaid decoration beginning immediately below the lip.

Small rounded exterior folds occur occasionally. These are smoothed and the incised decoration begins below this horizontal zone. Large rectangular folds do not occur in the collections.

Lip. Lips are round or flattened, rarely square. The broad flat lip produced by exterior thickening does not seem to occur, and there are no incised lines or punctations on the lip.

Base. The very little evidence available indicates flat or flattened bottoms and in one case at least it seems to have been square (Oliver, 16–N–6).

Decoration in Relation to Shape. In the case of barrel-shaped beakers, the decorated field extends far down onto the body, in one case as far as the flat base. For the other shape (jar with recurved rim), there is no information.

Distribution, Variation and Relationships Within Survey Area. Material classified under this heading was originally set up as a new type called Alligator Incised but was subsequently combined with Mazique. The description above applies to its characteristics in the Survey Area only. Distribution of this type in the Survey Area is distinctly southerly. Going from north to south, the type first appears sporadically in Tier 13. A few more examples appear in Tier 14, while increasing amounts appear in Tier 15. From Tiers 16 to 20 the type is scattered about more or less uniformly, but with the largest sherd count definitely falling in Tier 20. The Alligator Site (16–N–2), where the type was first set up, turned out to be on the northern periphery of its distribution.

Relationship with Oxbow Incised. Both of these types were based on insufficient material. There is unquestionably a close relationship between them and, as we have already explained (p. 98), in the seriation and stratigraphic analyses they were combined. That the separation is not entirely the result of arbitrary selection of criteria, however, is evidenced by differences in distribution. For example, taking the line between Tiers 16 and 17 as a demarcation, 33.5% of the total amount of Mazique Incised was found to the north, and 66.5% to the south of that line. Comparable figures for Oxbow Incised are 59% and 41%. In addition to this significant difference in over-all distribution, there are interesting differences in detail. Within the same quadrangle, sites may vary widely in the relative frequency of the two types. This suggests that differences may be in part chronological, an indication supported by stratigraphy on the Jaketown Site (p. 276). In any case, added to the fairly consistent typological differentiation, they appear to be sufficient to warrant continued separation of the two types until additional information has been obtained.

Relationships Outside Survey Area. Although we provisionally considered this as a distinct type, there were many resemblances to Mazique Incised which caused us to label this type Mazique in the Survey Area. The designs of alternating line-filled triangles with steeply inclined lines, the panels of opposing oblique lines separated from one another by a single vertical line, and parallel vertical incisions are all characteristic of Mazique. The termination of lines by deep triangular punctations, occurring often in Mazique Incised, does not, however, appear in the Survey Area. The distribution of the design seems to be essentially the same as that for Mazique Incised in the Lower Valley, with the decoration beginning beneath the lip or beneath an undecorated zone of varying width and sometimes coming well down onto the body.

In technique, however, there seems to be considerable divergence, for in southern Mississippi and Louisiana Mazique the lines usually overhang, while this feature occurs rarely in the Survey Area. There is less regularity in the application of lines in our collections, some almost giving the appearance of a brushed technique and diverging markedly from the precise technique of Mazique Incised as originally defined in ref. (a). These variations more nearly correspond to Manchac Incised of the Plaquemine Period (Quimby, 1942, p. 267).

In general, the vessel form corresponds to that of Mazique Incised, but in the Survey

Area the lip folds described for Mazique Incised are rare, and there are no triangular ears.

In sum, what we originally described as a separate type is a northern expression of Mazique Incised which in some respects shows considerable divergence from its southern relative.

In northern Alabama the clay-tempered complex has little evidence of a close relative to either Mazique or Oxbow Incised. At the McKelvey Mound (Site Hn°1), a few rims have a horizontal zone delimited by an upper and lower incised line, within which are groups of three oblique lines alternating in direction with plain triangular areas between. There do not seem to be any close relatives in western Tennessee, Kentucky, or southeastern Missouri. A possible affiliate in the "Caddo" area is Dunkin Incised, an Alto Focus type (Newell and Krieger, 1949, figs. 41–42), and there are other later related types in the east Texas area. Another relative to the east can be found in one of the motives of Carrabelle Incised (Moore, 1918, fig. 2).

Chronological Position. Since this type was combined with Oxbow Incised for purposes of analysis, the chronological position indicated by the graphs may be misleading. Oxbow-Mazique in combination runs from F to C, in other words throughout the Baytown Period, but it is probable that what we are here calling Mazique had its greatest popularity in the later part of that period (D–C).

Bibliography. (a) Ford and Willey, in Haag, 1939c, pp. 8–9.

CHEVALIER STAMPED

(Fig. 82, *q, r*)

Type as described in references cited, except as noted below.

Paste and Surface Finish. As described in references (a) and (e), except that "some sand" and "carbonized vegetable material" are not apparent. Paste is similar to that of Baytown Plain.

Decoration. As described in references cited.

Form. Insufficient material.

Distribution. Very scattered occurrences in the extreme southern part of the Survey Area, indicating an extreme marginal situation (Tiers 18 to 20).

Chronological Position. The statement of Ford and Willey that Chevalier Stamped reached its peak of popularity about the mouth of the Red River in the Troyville Period is now regarded as erroneous; it is now assigned to the Coles Creek complex. So far as the Survey Area is concerned, the very limited information available appears to indicate a middle to late Baytown position for the type.

Bibliography. (a) Setzler, 1933, pl. 6, *D;* (b) Ford, 1935, p. 16 and Type 13b on pls. III and IV; (c) Walker, 1936, p. 42, pl. 12, *g*; it was not found at the Great Mound; (d) Ford, 1936, p. 187, figs. 34, *m* and *o*; 38, *b*, 39, *e*, 40, *g*; (e) Ford and Willey, in Haag, 1939d, pp. 4–5.

FRENCH FORK INCISED

(Fig. 82, *s–w*)

Type as described in references cited, except as noted below.

Paste and Surface Finish. As described, except that "small particles of carbonized matter" are not present in the paste, which is similar to that of Baytown Plain.

Decoration. Only a few of the wide variety of decorative treatments described in the references cited appear in the present small collection. These are in order of frequency: zones of small close-spaced punctations enclosed by incised lines; zones of incised hatchure enclosed by punctate-incised lines; parallel punctate incised lines on rim and/or lip; incised lines interrupted by or terminating in large shallow punctations.

Form. Insufficient material for generalizations.

Distribution Within Survey Area. Like other "classic" Coles Creek types, French Fork Incised has a very thin and scattered distribution, generally confined to the southern half of the Survey Area indicative of a marginal situation.

Relationships Outside Survey Area. French Fork Incised was originally set up as a type of the Coles Creek complex in Louisiana as a result of excavation at the Peck Village Site ref. (a) and work with surface collections ref. (b). After stratigraphic excavations made near the mouth of the Red River revealed the details of ceramic succession, the

Troyville Period was inserted into the chronology between the Marksville and Coles Creek periods. French Fork Incised lasted through the time covered by what are at present called the Troyville and Coles Creek periods, and its maximum of 3% in the Red River mouth region falls on the line which has been drawn between the two periods (Willey, 1945, p. 242).

Some elements of the type may have evolved from the earlier Marksville Period decorations in the Lower Mississippi Valley, as suggested by Ford and Willey in their type description ref. (d). The practice common to both of forming designs by smoothed areas contrasting with roughened backgrounds is suggestive of relationship. In addition, there are indications that even earlier techniques have contributed to these decorations. The punctated lines suggest the linear punctate decoration of Stallings Punctate (Griffin, 1943a, pl. 11, and Claflin, 1931, pls. 12, 13, 17–20) and Tchefuncte Incised of the Louisiana Gulf Coast (Ford and Quimby, 1945). In the latter type there is a merging with Orange Incised of the Florida designs and technique (Griffin, 1945, p. 222).

It seems that the occurrence of French Fork in the Lower Mississippi Valley should be viewed as being on or near the western periphery of a development which had a popularity center along the northwest coast of Florida where this decoration class has been designated Weeden Island Punctated and Weeden Island Incised (Willey and Woodbury, 1942, pp. 242–43 and Willey, 1945, pp. 242–46). It is here that the basic ideas for this related group of types probably evolved. There is very little repetition of design elements in Weeden Island Incised, but repetition is a feature of French Fork and the similar types found in southwestern Arkansas, eastern Oklahoma, and northeastern Texas. These have recently been named Crockett Curvilinear Incised and Keota Curvilinear Incised (Krieger, 1946, pp. 227–28 and fig. 19). Material of this general group has been reported from sites excavated by Harrington (Harrington, 1920), from Gahagan (Webb and Dodd, 1939, pl. 26, *3*), the bottom level at the Crenshaw Site (Lemley, 1936, pl. 7), and at Spiro (Orr, 1946, fig. 3, *d*).

At least two sherds suggestive of Weeden Island-French Fork relationship have been found in the area around Monks Mound at the Cahokia site.

Chronological Position. Middle to late Baytown Period (E–C).

Bibliography. (a) Ford, 1935, pl. IV, Types 16–16d; (b) Ford, 1936, pp. 174–76, figs. 30, *o*, *p*, 35, sherds *a*, *b*, *e–g*, *l* on p. 197; vessel, fig. 37; (c) Walker, 1936, pl. 14, *e*, *f*, *h–j*; pl. 15, *c*, *e*, and *g* — note that Walker clearly identifies these as later than the Troyville Stamped and Yokena Incised sherds of the bottom of the Great Mound; (d) Ford and Willey, in Haag, 1939c, pp. 9–11.

WOODVILLE RED FILMED

(Fig. 83, *a–k*)

Type as described in ref. (b), except as noted below.

Paste and Surface Finish. In general, same as described in reference (b), except that filming is not restricted to vessel interiors. About one-half of our Survey material is slipped on both sides and a few sherds on the exterior only.

Decoration. Curvilinear and rectilinear incised patterns of undetermined design. Incised lines border red-slipped bands and areas sometimes in contrast with unslipped areas. A wide red-filled band outlined by an incised line below the lip seems fairly common. Small areas, usually triangular but occasionally circular, formed usually at the intersection of the larger incised lines, are filled with scattered punctations. Larger areas are sometimes filled by hatching of fine incised lines.

In general, the larger curvilinear patterns seem to occur on vessel interiors while line-filled areas are more likely to be on exteriors.

Form. Wide-mouthed bowls with straight or flaring rims seem to be the most common shape, but beakers and bowls with incurved rims (diameter ca. 20 to 22 cm.) also occur.

Rim. All direct and of even width with no thickening observed.

Lip. Square.

Base. None in collections, but see ref. (b).

Appendages. One rim appears to be that of a quadrated bowl, and a triangular ear extending up from the rim also occurs once.

Discussion. In general, our material follows the published description of Woodville Red Filmed, but with slight differences noted above. There seem to be obvious relationships with both Larto Red Filmed and French Fork Incised in the matter of design and treatment. A greater abundance of material would no doubt make these relationships clearer.

Distribution. The type occurs in very small percentages on a number of scattered sites in the southern part of the Survey Area only.

Relationship Outside Survey Area. At the mouth of the Red River area this type occupies a chronological position touching the end of Marksville in its earliest appearance and the beginning of Coles Creek in its latest. The popularity maximum of the type is quite small, only about .2%, and it lies a little earlier than the maximum of the related French Fork Incised. The type is related to Weeden Island Zoned Red of the northwest coast of Florida, and it has been suggested that the ancestral form for this idea of zoning red paint between incised lines is to be found in Marksville Red Filmed. (Ford and Willey, 1940, pp. 82–85.)

Chronological Position. In the Survey Area, Woodville is mainly in the middle Baytown Period (E–D), with a few scattered occurrences in sites of a later date.

Bibliography. (a) Setzler, 1933, pl. 6, *F*, note the association of types; (b) Haag, 1939c, pp. 6–7.

LARTO RED FILMED

(Fig. 83, *l–u*)

Type as described in ref. (a), except as noted below.

Paste. *Tempering.* Clay; same as Baytown Plain. On two sites (16–P–3, Twin Lakes and 16–P–8, Blue Lake) the sherds have a sandy texture, but the tempering itself is typical lumpy clay.

Color. The characteristic coloring of Larto Red Filmed is the result of an applied film or slip. The most common colors are warm, rich orange-reds and oranges. In terms of the Ridgway nomenclature the most frequently occurring color is Testaceous (9″) followed by Terra Cotta (7″). These are both an orange-red shade and are more common than the orange shades alone, among which the most commonly occurring colors are Vinaceous Cinnamon (13″*b*), Orange Cinnamon (13″), and Cinnamon (15″). Of quite frequent occurrence is a reddish-purplish-brown color whose closest analogy in the Ridgway scale seems to be Vinaceous Brown (15‴*i*). Other colors occurring are: Army Brown (13‴*i*), Cacao Brown (9″*i*), Mikado Brown (13″*i*), and Vinaceous Tawny (11″).

Cores are generally very dark, firing penetrating but little. A few sherds show deep penetration of surface color but only rarely does the surface color penetrate completely through the sherd.

Thickness. Average, 6.7 mm.; range 4.5 to 10 mm.

Surface Finish. Characteristically well-smoothed and finished both on the interior and exterior. Tool marks often visible.

Most of the ware is covered with a red slip which is usually applied to both interior and exterior, but occasionally only to one or the other.

Form. *Rim.* Only a little less than half (47.5%) of the 375 rims are modified. Modification consists primarily (28.9%) of thickening that part of the rim adjacent to the lip either inside, outside, or both. There are at least 20 different thickened rim profiles. Of these the most common is the application of a strip of clay, half round or oval in cross section, to the exterior wall of a simple outcurved bowl. Next, in order of frequency, is a thick, half circular strip applied to the interior of a bowl with incurving rim. This is always tapered off and smoothed into the body wall at the lower end and at the upper is thick and round. Slightly less frequent is thickening achieved by adding a thick strip of clay to the inner wall of a simple curved bowl, smoothing it at the lower end and rounding it up over the lip to give an almost completely round cross section at the lip, or something of a comma shape for the whole rim. Another frequently occurring rim is a gradual swelling up from the body wall on both sides of a simple outcurved bowl with a rounded or flattened lip.

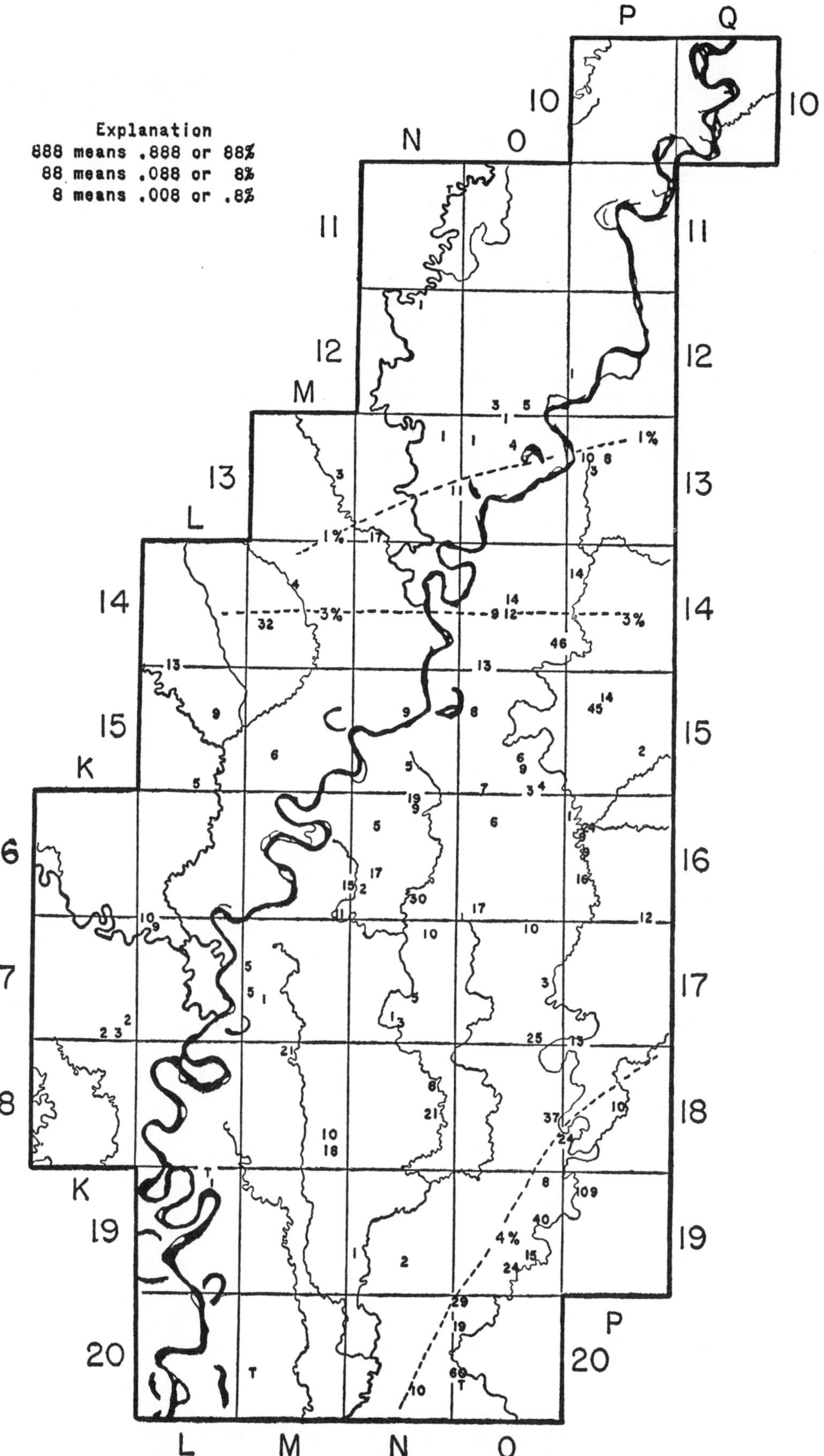

Fig. 9. Percentage frequency distribution of the type Larto Red Filmed.

In addition to thickening, there are a few occurrences of rim folds. Of 12 examples; 8 are on the exterior, 2 on the interior, and 1 vessel has a fold both inside and out.

Rims embellished with a single incised line are slightly more common — 19 occurrences in all distributed as follows: 2 rims incised both in and out; 6 rims incised on the outside; and 4 on the inside.

In addition to the simple incising, however, there are 4 occurrences of a single incised line underscoring a thickened rim and with deep angular punctations in it. Of these, 2 are on the interior and 2 on the exterior. Several other rims (10 in all) are punctated in a similar manner, but the incised line is lacking. Of these, 7 are on the interior and 3 on the exterior.

Flat lips, T-shaped lips, and beveled (both in and out) lips do occur; but the great majority are rounded as a result of the thickening described above.

Vessel Shape. The most characteristic shape, comprising 57.3% of the classifiable rims, is a simple curved bowl, with average diameter at the mouth of 31.5 cm. (range, 16 to 48 cm.)

About half as common is a bowl with incurved rim of the "seed bowl" type comprising 26.1% of the measurable rim sherds. The oral diameters naturally run considerably smaller, 27.6 cm. average (range, 12 to 48 cm.).

In addition to these primary forms, which make up almost 85% of the collections, there are several other recognizable forms which are listed here in the order of their frequency of occurrence:

1) Globular or sub-globular jar or deep, wide-mouthed bowl, with recurved rim. Small rim sherds precluded possibility of separating into two classifications.

2) Bowl or jar with flat, inslanting sides, almost always with a flat, rather uneven exterior rim fold.

3) Bowl, shallow or deep with flat outslanting sides.

4) Bowl, similar to the above, but with flaring sides.

5) Deep almost straight-sided bowl with only slight outward curve of body wall, and with upper rim portion sharply out-turned.

6) A very deep bowl, similar in shape to the above, but without the everted rim.

Base. Only 2 basal sherds are present in the collections from which it is inferred from this that bottoms are normally round.

Appendages. In view of the common occurrence of quadrated bowls described in ref. (a), it is surprising that ears and lugs are completely lacking in the Survey collections. There are no occurrences of lugs or handles of any kind.

Discussion. Like Baytown Plain, Larto is a generalized type that will undoubtedly have to be subdivided as we find out more about it. At present it includes all red-filmed ware that is on a clay-tempered paste; in other words, all plain red pottery that was made throughout the long Baytown Period and perhaps earlier. Its areal distribution is not quite so comprehensive (fig. 9). Although found in every part of the Survey Area, it is particularly concentrated along the eastern margins of the Yazoo Basin in the Yazoo-Tallahatchie-Coldwater drainage.

Relationships Outside Survey Area. Larto Red Filmed in the Survey Area corresponds closely to the type material from southern Mississippi and central and southern Louisiana described in ref. (a). It is also related to Weeden Island Red Filmed along the eastern Gulf Coast.

A possible prototype is Tchefuncte Red Filmed. The very rare appearance of red filming and "fugitive red" as early as the Tchefuncte Period might be used as an argument for the priority of the Lower Mississippi in the use of red filming. Of the possible outside sources the spread of red-slipped ware from Mexico into the Southwest to produce San Francisco Red Filmed of the Mogollon culture may also have had an eastern prong, but as yet this has not been identified in Texas or Oklahoma at a sufficiently early period. Another possibility is that the red-filmed development first appeared on the Florida northwest coast. It must be admitted that the origins of red filming in the Southeast are not well understood.

A major mystery is the apparent absence of red ware from the Louisiana area in the Marksville Period. Also notable is its absence in the northwestern Alabama area in any time period. Red filming does not spread very far inland from Weeden Island during the pre-Middle Mississippi levels of Alabama and Georgia. It appears in this region and eastern Tennessee in the Small Log Town House–Hiwassee Island–Macon Plateau Period, although the type Laws Red Filmed of the Guntersville Basin is apparently earlier, as it is found on limestone temper, thus forming a counterpart of Monks Mound Red.

In the Illinois Valley center of Hopewell, red filming or a counterpart of Marksville Red Filmed is rather rare, but is apparently more common than on Louisiana Marksville sites. The presence of red filming in either Adena or Ohio Hopewell has not been recognized. In the Cahokia area the limestone-tempered Monks Mound Red is regarded as a part of Old Village, the earliest Middle Mississippi complex. It is also found on late Woodland sites, some of which have large platform mounds. It is in this area that a possible shift from limestone- to shell-tempering can be postulated.

Chronological Position. Runs throughout the Baytown Period with its maximum occurrence in the middle (E–D).

Bibliography. (a) Haag, 1939d, p. 7.

NEELEY'S FERRY PLAIN

(Figs. 84; 93, *a–o*; 100, *a–g*, *i–m*; 101, *a–b*, *d–h*, *j–m*, *p–q*; 103, *a–b*, *d–k*; 104, *a–c*, *i–n*; 105, *d–e*, *i–o*; 106, *a–b*, *f–g*, *n*, *r*; 107, *e*, *g*; 108, *h*, *j*; 109, *a–b*; *d–f*, *h–i*; 113, *h*)

Type not previously described.

Paste. *Method of Manufacture.* Coiled.

Temper. Coarse shell, at times attaining a diameter of 5 to 7 mm., but usually running considerably smaller. There is a wide variation in the size of the particles, a single small sherd often showing considerable range.

Texture. Characteristic lamination of shell-tempered paste, often showing open spaces from poor wedging of clay. When tempering particles are especially large, the paste tends to look swirled and contorted.

Color. Surface color in general approaches that of the average or most frequently occurring color of Baytown Plain, Avellaneous (17'''*b*), but with a greater tendency toward gray and grayish buff, Vinaceous Buff (17'''*d*); Light Drab (17''''*b*); Drab Gray (17''''*d*); Light Mouse Gray (15'''''*b*). There are very few red or reddish extremes. Those that do occur are Pinkish Cinnamon (15''*b*) and Light Pinkish Cinnamon (15''*d*). Dark sherds run usually to Hair Brown (17''''*i*) and Mouse Gray (15''''') or Deep Mouse Gray (15'''''*i*) and are quite frequent in the Survey collections. Generally speaking, there is little difference between surface and core color, the firing having been quite uniform throughout. Red and reddish-colored sherds do, however, tend toward gray cores.

Thickness. Average, 7.7 mm.; range, 3.5 to 13 mm. Thickness runs slightly greater in the southern part of the Survey Area, 8.1 mm. as compared with 7.1 mm. and 7.2 mm. in the northern and central sections.

Hardness. 2.5 (range, 2 to 4).

Surface Finish. Smoothed on both exterior and interior, moderate polishing being very rare. Surface finish often assumes a rough appearance from the leaching out of the shell-tempering particles through weathering. Occasionally, however, even the original surfaces are quite rough with scoring of the tool marks clearly visible.

Form. *Vessel Shape.* Jars are the most common vessels in Neeley's Ferry Plain, and of these the most characteristic is a globular or sub-globular vessel with recurved rim and vague shoulder, hereinafter referred to as the "standard Mississippi jar form." This is the same jar which, when decorated, forms the basis for such types as Barton Incised, Parkin Punctated, etc. Typical examples may be seen in figure 93, *a*, *e*, *h–l*.

Next in importance are bowls in a wide variety of sizes and shapes, of which some are shown in figure 100, the commonest being a simple curved-sided bowl of shallow-to-medium depth with round or slightly flattened bottom. Such bowls frequently have a slightly recurved rim, making it difficult to distinguish between rim sherds from bowls and jars. Bowls with incurved rims are less common.

Bottles, which bulk large in collections of whole vessels from burials, are a good deal less in evidence in sherd collections. The commonest type is globular with vertical neck of low-to-medium height (fig. 104, *a–b*). Other less common bottle forms are shown in figures 103 and 104.

Shallow flat-bottomed dishes and plates are present but rare.

Such are the principal categories of shape that occur in sherd collections of Neeley's Ferry Plain, in approximate order of numerical importance. In addition, there is a vast number of specialized shapes, effigies and eccentric forms, some of which are discussed at length in Section IV of this report.

The 2792 rim sherds of Neeley's Ferry Plain analyzed for shape showed a preponderance of jars over bowls of almost three to one, 55.6% as against 20.8% (22.2% being indeterminate). The number of identifiable bottle rims was almost negligible, 38 (1.1%), but it is extremely interesting that these were almost all from sites in the northern part of the Survey Area. The sample was selected to give a fairly uniform geographical coverage which makes it significant that 34 of the 38 bottle rims were from sites north of Tier 14.

Size. Throughout the large sites in the northern quadrangles, an attempt was made to measure the size of bowls and jars separately, but the average diameters were so similar, 31.9 cm. and 30.8 cm., respectively, that this was given up in subsequent measuring. Five hundred and twenty sherds, selected at random throughout the collections, including bowls and jars, gave an average oral diameter of 31.9 cm., with a range of 6 cm. to 52 cm. Only slight areal differences from north to south are to be observed, the average for Tiers 10 to 14 being 31.2 cm.; Tiers 15, 16, 29.8 cm.; Tiers 17–20, 34.7 cm.

Rim. Although for the most part rims and lips of Neeley's Ferry Plain are undecorated, a little over 10% are elaborated with a variety of simple treatments similar to those described for Baytown Plain (see p. 80), which needs no further description here. These include nicking and notching, pinching, punctating, incising, application of nodes, rim strips, and plain folds, both interior and exterior. There are also two additional features in Neeley's Ferry Plain, however. One of these is the application of vertical ribs or strips of clay, plain and nicked, and the other a crimped rim edge. There are very few examples of the former and all are in the northern tiers (10 to 14). The latter rim decoration, having the appearance of a crimped piecrust, is found only below Tier 15.

A rim having rectangular scallops occurs rarely and sporadically throughout the collections, and seems to be closely related to a similar treatment in Bell Plain.

Nicking and notching of the rim is by far the most common decorative treatment, comprising about 42% of the decorated rims. Pinching, application of horizontal rim strips — sometimes plain, usually nicked or notched — and a single incised line are next in descending order of frequency, each making up less than 13% of the decorative treatments. Folds, nodes, crimping, and punctations are all considerably less frequent, each comprising less than 7% of the total decorated rims.

In the matter of areal distribution, nicking and notching are more important in the north, a little over 57% of all such treatment being in Tiers 10 to 14. Pinching is also largely confined to the same tiers (77.3% of all pinching), as is punctating and the use of nodes. Rim strips are almost exclusively confined to the northern tiers.

Incising, on the other hand, infrequent in the northern and middle tiers is concentrated in the south (90.0%), as are also folds (98.1%).

Perforated rims are of infrequent occurrence and are distributed throughout the Survey Area.

Lip. In form, Neeley's Ferry Plain lips may be round, flat, pinched, or beveled on the interior or exterior. Lips that are round or rounded in profile are most frequent, composing about 40.7% of all sampled rims, with flat or square lips slightly less frequent (32.8%). About 21.0 per cent of lips are beveled, but whereas in the north exterior and interior beveling are about equal in frequency, in the south exterior beveling is about twice as frequent as interior beveling. Thinned or pinched-out lips comprising about 4.2 per cent of the Neeley's Ferry collections are slightly more common in the south.

Base. There are very few recognizable basal sherds in the collection, and of these almost all are from the Williamson Site (11-N-13). Of these, all are rounded except one which is flat. It is inferred, therefore, that most of the vessels must have rounded or only slightly flattened bases.

Appendages. Lugs are of very frequent occurrence, and of these the most common is a horizontally projecting semi-circular lug. These usually project in the plane of the lip, but a few are bent quite sharply down making an acute angle at the juncture of lug and rim. They may also occasionally project upward. There is considerable range in size from massive lugs attaining a length of 16 cm., and a projection of 3.5 cm., to very small ones only 5 or 6 cm. long. They are often so small as to be little more than a rudimentary flange. In cross section these lugs may be either very thick (22 mm.) or quite thin. The lug contour varies from a true triangle to a half-round.

Lugs are occasionally bifurcated, but more often they are depressed or dimpled on the upper surface. These are sometimes just shallow depressions, as if from the pressure of a finger tip, or they may be strongly grooved. Quite a number of horizontal semi-circular lugs are decorated along the edge, the most usual method being by relatively shallow nicks or notches, or by deep indentations. Several have very fine punctations over the upper surface and a depressed ring. A few are vertically pierced, possibly for suspension.

Less common are lugs placed below the lip. These lugs are generally of even width and project only a few centimeters (average, 5 cm.) from the rim. Some are only a few centimeters long, but judging from whole deep bowls in other collections from the St. Francis areas, some of these probably encircled the vessel in a continuous band. A very few are decorated by incision on the upper surface. One sherd has two such strips, one above the other, each with slanting incisions on the upper surface. A few are also bifurcated.

By comparison with whole pots and photographs, it is clear that many of the lugs described relate to deep straight-sided bird and fish effigy bowls so characteristic of the Mississippi ceramic complex in this region. Bifurcated lugs are often bird or fish tails, notched semi-circular lugs probably relate to bird effigies, while lugs with parallel incised lines represent fish fins. One of the semi-circular projecting lugs with a node on the upper surface is clearly a fish head.

Lugs are definitely concentrated in the northern tiers (10 to 14) where there are about 15½ lugs per hundred rim sherds. In the middle tiers (15 to 16) the ratio is only about 7½, while in the southern tiers there are only about 2½ lugs per hundred.

Handles. Handles are of frequent occurrence throughout the collections, but less so than lugs. The most common type is a vertical strap handle with parallel sides. Though usually plain, the upper surface near the lip is occasionally embellished with paired vertical nodes (sometimes only one), more rarely with an additional pair adorning the lower end.

Decidedly less common are vertical strap handles with converging sides tapering downward toward the shoulder. About one-half of these are decorated with converging incised lines and occasionally 3 diverging ridges depend from the lower end reminiscent of the tail and legs of an animal effigy.

In a very few instances the strap handles are shortened and widened to give the appearance of a tube which may have parallel or converging sides, and may be plain or decorated with deeply incised parallel lines.

Strap handles usually give the appearance of massiveness, their maximum length being about 7 to 8 cm. and 1.5 cm. wide. Without exception, strap handles are confined to jar rims, and all appear to be attached by luting.

Less common to the collections from the Survey Area are loop handles. These are usually very small, completely unelaborated, and apparently also confined wholly to jar rims. It is clear that several of the loop handles in the collections were attached by riveting to the vessel wall.

A third type of handle occurring rarely in collections of Neeley's Ferry Plain is the arcaded handle (fig. 92, *n*) more commonly associated with Rhodes Incised and associated decorated shell-tempered types of the Memphis area. They are of a triangular shape with the wide base attached to the rim edge and depending therefrom, and may be flush with the rim wall or partially free standing. They usually form a continuous horizontal band about the rim.

Handles, like lugs, are concentrated in the north with 4.5 per hundred rim sherds. The ratio decreases progressively toward the south with 2.3 handles per hundred in Tiers 15 to 16 and 1.2 in Tiers 17 to 20. The ratio of strap handles to loop handles is much higher in the north than in the south.

Discussion. *Relationship of Baytown and Neeley's Ferry Plain.* An important question centers on the degree of continuity between these two basic plain wares as indicated by the typological evidence.

1) Over and above the morphological differences in common bowl and jar shapes, which are expectable, there are frequency differences that are perhaps more significant. In Baytown, for example, bowls greatly outnumber jars, while the reverse situation is true for Neeley's Ferry. Bottles, though not very common in Neeley's Ferry sherd collections, are not present at all in Baytown. Of the great number of effigy and specialized forms in Neeley's Ferry few, if any, can be shown to have crossed over from Baytown.

2) Difference in size: Average oral diameter for Baytown Plain is 36.4 cm., compared to 31.9 cm. for Neeley's Ferry. There is also a difference in distribution of size with larger vessels in the north for Baytown and the reverse for Neeley's Ferry. There is little difference in average thickness, but the same reversal with thickest paste in the north for Baytown and in the south for Neeley's Ferry.

3) Complete lack of handles in Baytown, whereas, in Neeley's Ferry there are 2.7 handles per hundred rim sherds.

4) Difference in appearance and frequency of lugs; e.g., triangular and projecting ear-like lugs in Baytown Plain and these infrequent, contrasting to large massive lugs of Neeley's Ferry and variety of types which together give about 8.5 lugs per every hundred rim sherds.

5) Difference in bases, with flat bases round or square, fairly common in Baytown and none at all in Neeley's Ferry.

6) About the same percentage of all rims is decorated in both Baytown Plain and Neeley's Ferry Plain (7.8% and 8.3%, respectively), but the marked differences in quantity of each particular method of decoration and its areal distribution must not be overlooked; e.g., in Baytown Plain, folds make up 41.9 per cent of all decorative treatment of rims, while in Neeley's Ferry Plain this drops to 6.5%. Incising follows a similar pattern comprising 21.1% of total rim decoration for Baytown Plain and only 12.3% for Neeley's Ferry Plain. In both types, however, there is a marked concentration of incising in the south, and folds in Neeley's Ferry Plain are definitely concentrated in the south with only slightly higher frequency in the south for Baytown Plain. Nicking and notching and pinching, on the other hand, comprise only 19.6% of the total decorative treatment of rims in Baytown Plain, and make up 54.7% in Neeley's Ferry Plain.

7) Lip form is quite similar to both types with rounded lips being more common than flat. Beveled lips, however, occur almost twice as often in Neeley's Ferry Plain (21.0% to 11.8% in Baytown), and pinched or thinned lips are more frequent in Baytown Plain (8.1% to 4.2%).

8) The difference in quantity of decoration of lips is quite marked. Only 1.8 per cent of lips are decorated in Neeley's Ferry Plain to 6.7% in Baytown Plain. Incised lips make up about one-third of lip decoration for Baytown Plain but only a little less than 9% for Neeley's Ferry. There is again some difference in distribution. In Baytown Plain there is no observable difference in areal distribution of the practice of nicking lips, occurring with almost equal frequency in the north and south. In Neeley's Ferry, however, three-quarters of all nicking and notching and two-thirds of all incising is concentrated in Tiers 17 to 20.

In short, it is clear that by Neeley's Ferry time, folds and the incised rims and lips of Coles Creek Incised and Baytown Plain are giving way to nicking, notching, and pinching. The popular incising of lip and rim of clay-tempered handleless bowls and beakers of Coles Creek Incised and Baytown Plain has given way before a more popular shell-tempered jar shape, equipped with handles and lugs, and bowls are now decorated more often with nicking, notching, and pinching techniques, with frequent addition of modeled effigy features, and only a lingering on of its predecessors is seen in the form of an occasional Baytown-like lug, a few thickened rims, and infrequent incising. The element of continuity is doubtless considerable, but the changes appear to be too great to have been brought about without influence from outside the area.

Possible Variants of Neeley's Ferry Plain. On account of difficulties inherent in sorting plain pottery, this type, like Baytown Plain, takes in too much territory. The possibility, with greater information, of breaking it down into variants or even separate types must always be kept in mind. For example, the plain ware associated with Wallace and Leland Incised falls within the range of Neeley's Ferry as defined, but is almost sortable. A similar separation was once considered between the St. Francis and Memphis sites. At the point where we can begin to recognize such variations, the type will begin to be more useful for culture determination. At present it can only be indicative of very broad chronological and areal relationships. This point should be insisted on so that it is clear to the reader that, for example, the presence of say 85% Neeley's Ferry Plain on two widely separated sites does not necessarily indicate an intimate cultural relationship between them.

Relationships Outside Survey Area. Throughout the distribution of the complex called by Holmes the Middle Mississippi Valley group or in terms of the Midwestern Taxonomic Method the Middle Mississippi Phase, the dominant pottery is usually shell-tempered plain so that Neeley's Ferry Plain is simply this pottery in the Survey Area and is generally related to all other Mississippi plain types by virtue of that fact. The closest connections on the basis of vessel shape are in the New Madrid Focus and the Cumberland Aspect with less connection indicated to Cahokia, Moundville, and the late lower Mississippi Valley types of the lower Red River area. Regional relationships have to be developed on the basis of shape and decoration features rather than by means of the common possession of plain shell-tempered pottery.[12]

The area in which shell was initially used as tempering material is still not definitely known. At present Cahokia seems to be the most logical candidate, as has been mentioned elsewhere. Possible transitions from the limestone-tempering of post-Hopewell Woodland pottery into the Old Village complex have been noted and one of the Old Village types, Monks Mound Red, maintains the limestone-tempering well into the Mississippi Period. The unpolished vessels of Powell Plain and the local St. Clair Plain are the regional relatives of Neeley's Ferry. From Cahokia, shell-tempered plain spread north into central Illinois, southern Wisconsin, and up the Missouri into the Kansas City area. From there, it spread north into eastern Nebraska and western Iowa and helped produce the eastern modification of Upper Republican which is called the Nebraska Aspect.

In the Plains from north-central Texas to central Kansas there is a shell-tempered plain type which is almost entirely confined to simple utilitarian jar and bowl shapes. In the Henrietta Focus of Texas this is called Nocona Plain and in Kansas it has been tentatively identified as Geneseo Plain of the Paint Creek culture. This is believed to be Wichita and is the farthest western area for shell-tempered pottery. Because of its geographical position and other connections to Mississippi cultures, it is assumed that these plain shell-tempered types are later than the comparable types along the Mississippi. It is now thought likely that Nocona and Geneseo were in existence by A.D. 1450.

The Oneota Aspect of the northern Mississippi and central Mississippi Valley has shell-tempered pottery as its basic ware which is best regarded as a development from the Old Village–Aztalan level in the area of its primary occurrence. The Fort Ancient pottery complex is also mainly shell-tempered, particularly in the southern foci. This spread up the Ohio of the essential features of the Mississippi ceramic complex took place initially on an Old Village level and was subsequently modified in the central Ohio Valley. In this area,

[12] For this reason, an attempt such as that of Krieger to connect Henrietta Focus pottery with that from sites in southern Indiana can be regarded as almost meaningless. Krieger, 1946, p. 159.

as in Oneota, many of the more complicated vessel forms, effigy features, and painted types did not make their appearance.

In eastern Tennessee and Georgia, the early Mississippi cultures have a plain surface pottery with Mississippi shapes, and this continues to be the common utilitarian form until the colonial period. In the Cumberland culture, shell-tempered plain is the abundant utilitarian type and the same is true of the northern and central Alabama areas.

Shell-tempered plain pottery made its appearance late in the southern part of the Survey Area and to the south in southwestern Mississippi and eastern Louisiana. In these areas the older clay-tempered tradition hung on, and at such sites as Anna and Emerald (née Seltzertown) clay-tempered types very close to Leland Incised and its associates continue in existence.

Chronological Position. According to the seriation charts, Neeley's Ferry Plain becomes an important factor in period D–C in the St. Francis, Memphis, Arkansas, and Lower Yazoo areas, but does not become dominant until C–B in these areas and is losing popularity in the Memphis area in time B–A. Our present opinion is that shell-tempering appeared first in the northern part of the Survey Area and gradually moved south. In its earliest appearance it did not have the elaborate effigy and decorative features which were to become so marked a part of the Mississippi culture.

Bibliography. New type, but illustrated in the older literature and extensively in this volume.

PARKIN PUNCTATED

(Figs. 85; 94)

Type not previously described.

Paste and Surface Finish. Same as Neeley's Ferry Plain.

Decoration. Punctation produced by variously shaped instruments, resulting in a wide variety of size, shape, and arrangement. The commonest characteristic, to which there are few exceptions, is that the instrument is jabbed obliquely into thc clay, producing a ridge or "burr" alongside the punctations of corresponding size and shape. Most frequently, the shape is oval or semi-lunar, often suggesting "nail-marking," by which term this type of treatment is sometimes described. However, there is a wide variety of shapes including round, square, triangular, U-shaped, etc., most of which could not have been produced by the unaided fingers. Punctations vary as widely in size and depth. An average would fall somewhere around .5 mm. in greatest diameter (extremes ranging from .1 mm. to 1 cm.) and about .2 mm. in depth.

In arrangement, punctations generally show little attention to design. Most often, they are simply scattered seemingly at random over the entire vessel surface, including the base, with all possible variety in spacing from practically contiguous to 2 or 3 cm. apart. Next in frequency, to no arrangement at all, is an arrangement in horizontal or vertical rows, occasionally a combination of both, suggesting something a little more decorative. Quite often, a single horizontal row or series of rows of punctations form a band about the rim or shoulder of the vessel. Less often, punctations are aligned vertically so that the "burr" forms a continuous ridge, an effect which is sometimes accentuated by "pinching," described below. When punctations are aligned both horizontally and vertically, as sometimes happens, a rather striking "corrugated" effect is obtained.

Alignment of punctations, in whatever direction, imperceptibly slides over into a type of decoration more accurately described as "linear-punctated" or even (as a further stage) "punctate-incised" (fig. 85, *m*, *r*). So far as our present information is concerned, however, it appears to be merely an extreme variant of the more fundamental punctated type and is therefore included in Parkin Punctated.[13]

Closely related typologically to the "linear-punctated" variant just described is the type of decoration properly described as "pinched." As the term implies, this is effected by convergent punctations from two directions or

[13] In the early stages of classification, the type "Castile Linear Punctated" was set up to take care of this variant. Sorting produced only a handful of sherds, however, and these occurred invariably in association with Parkin Punctated with no apparent significance from the standpoint of chronology or distribution, so the type was abandoned.

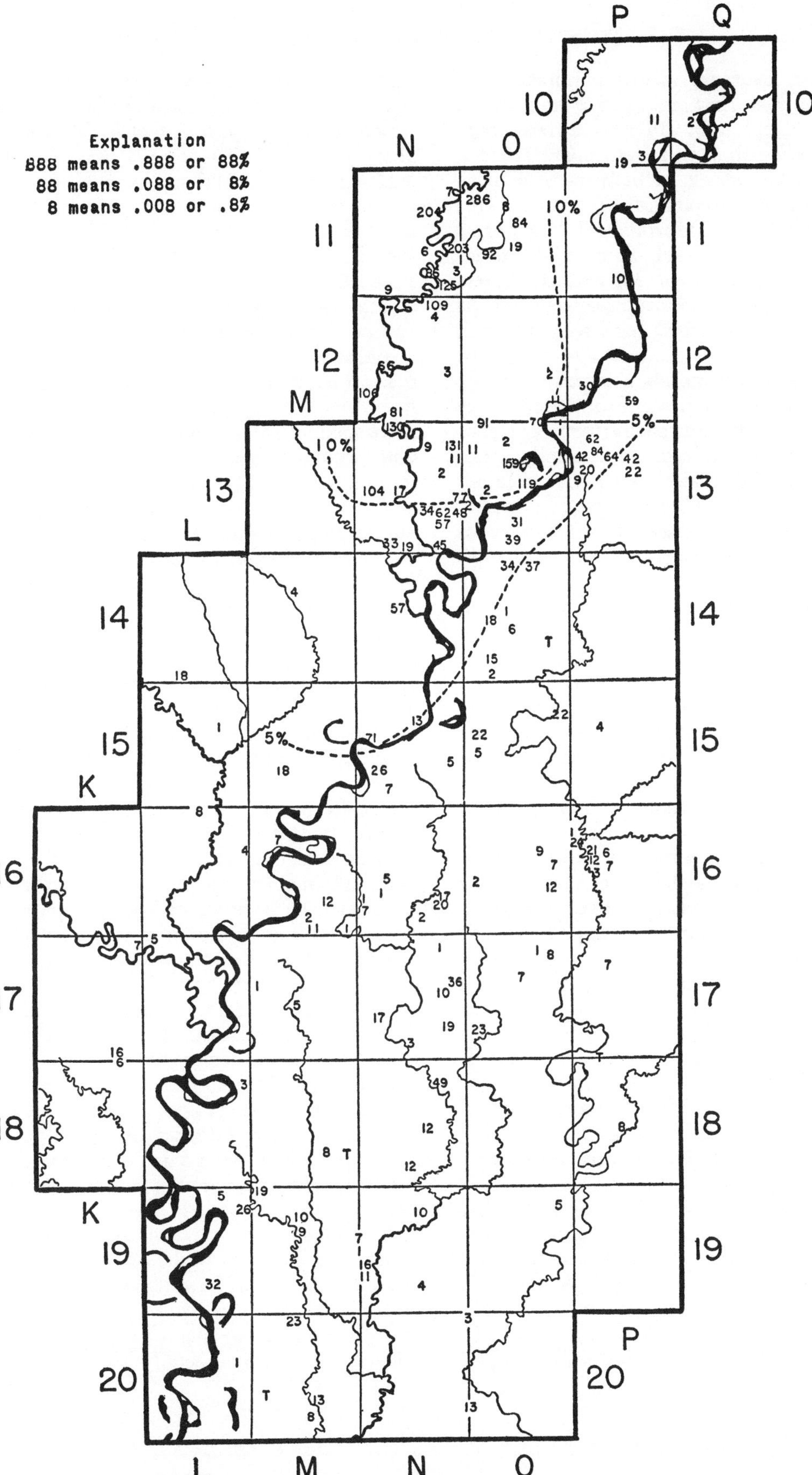

FIG. 10. Percentage frequency distribution of the type Parkin Punctated.

actual finger-pinching and the resultant ridges are often worked into linear patterns. The end result may look totally different from the typical punctation described herein, but the material shows every stage between, indicating that it is merely a technical elaboration of the fundamental type. A further development, in which all traces of pinching are removed by smoothing, results in something that is practically indistinguishable from the type Vernon Paul Appliqué, in which precisely the same ridged effect is obtained by smoothing applied strips of clay onto the vessel surface (see fig. 87, *j*, *k*).

The use of a hollow cane or reed as punctating instrument produces a variant type, not particularly common anywhere, but more apt to occur in the southern portion of the area. It seems advisable to treat this as a variant included in Parkin Punctated, at least until more material is obtained.

Placement of Decoration. Parkin Punctated is essentially a body decoration. Rims are either plain or of the type *Barton Incised*, often with the addition of a row of nodes separating the incised rim area from the punctated body. In collections from Walls (13-P-1) and related sites, rims are often of the arcaded type in which case the decorative handles making up the arcade are frequently covered with punctations as well. In the south there is a greater tendency for punctations to be carried up onto the rim area. This is clearly revealed by the fact that in certain southern sites the number of rims classified as Parkin Punctated are more numerous than in the north. This may be shown by comparative figures for selected quadrangles as follows:

QUADRANGLES	RIM	BODY	PER CENT RIMS
11-N	23	618	3.7
19-M	42	131	32.0

The rest of the area would show percentages intermediate between these two extremes.

Form. The type runs almost exclusively to jar forms, with globular or sub-globular bodies, round or slightly flattened bases, and recurved rims; in short, the standard Mississippi jar form already described as the dominant shape in Neeley's Ferry Plain. Considerable variation is present in the relative size of the rim area, which in some cases is very short. There is also a shape in which the rim flares sharply making a sharp angle with the body wall. No significance in distribution of these shape variants is observable. A small number of rims, not more than a half-dozen, seem to pertain to a simple curved-sided bowl of deep proportions, and there is one example that seems to indicate an incurved-sided bowl.

Size. Variations in size appear to be areally significant. In the St. Francis sub-area, oral diameters average about 30 cm. — maximum diameters would run slightly larger. In the Memphis sub-area, diameters average about 20 cm. Farther south, sizes range between these figures.

Thickness. Differences in size noted above are based on an insufficient number of measurable rims, but are very significantly borne out by differences in thickness. Averages for St. Francis sites range from 7.5 to 8.2 mm., for the Memphis sites, from 5.1 to 5.6 mm. These two groups could be sorted on the basis of thickness alone with an error of probably not more than 10%. It is interesting to note that border-line sites like Clay Hill (13-N-7) and Belle Meade (13-O-5) show intermediate values for thickness. Farther south, thickness varies somewhat but tends on the whole toward the thinner Memphis area material.

Rim. Rims are simple, usually vertical, and without further elaboration. The only notable exception is a type which seems to be a specialty of the Memphis sub-area, in which an interior bevel is combined with a sharp outthrust of the upper rim wall to produce a sort of flanged rim, which is frequently indented. This is the sort of treatment that is generally associated with the so-called arcaded rim, a speciality of this area.

Lip. Lips are about evenly divided between round and square, with a tendency toward more square lips in the north and more round lips in the south. Square lips occasionally show an outer bevel.

Base. Round or only slightly flattened. Considerably thicker than body wall. Recognizable basal sherds show thicknesses ranging from 9 to 18 mm., the heavier bases being associated with the thicker St. Francis ware.

Appendages. Of the total series of rims (215), 11% show appendages, of which the great majority are lugs. The dominant lug is the horizontal, semi-circular type, occasionally placed below the lip, but normally on the same plane with it. Bifurcated lugs occur occasionally. Lugs are almost entirely from the northern sites — there being only two examples south of the 15 Tier of quadrangles. Of the four handles present in the collections, one is a narrow strap, two are of the broad trianguloid strap type, and the fourth is a zoomorphic handle. The first three are from sites on the St. Francis, the last, a rather life-like lizard peering over the jar rim, is from the Silver City Site (20–O–5) on the Yazoo.

Distribution. Like Neeley's Ferry Plain, Parkin Punctated is pretty well represented throughout the Survey Area, but as is clearly evident in figure 10, shows a pronounced tendency to pile up in the northern part, particularly on the St. Francis River, where on a number of sites it runs considerably higher than 10% of the total sherd count.

Variations Within Survey Area. The only prominent variation as between the northern and southern parts of the area is the tendency already noted for punctation to be carried up onto the rims in the south. There is also a greater frequency of the pinched variant in the south. A more impressive division of the material is seen within the northern area itself, between the St. Francis and Memphis sub-areas. This has also been discussed above under the headings of size and thickness. What it amounts to is that this type is represented by significantly smaller, hence thinner, vessels in the Memphis group. There are other associated variations: in the Memphis material, punctations tend to be more closely spaced and the implement or fingernail is employed in a way that produces more of a "burr." There is also a tendency for punctations to be more regularly spaced, particularly in linear arrangements leading up to the pinched variant, which, as already mentioned, seems to be more important in the south. Memphis material also tends to run somewhat darker in color. Added to these rather basic differences, are such secondary, but no less significant factors, as the association with the characteristic decorative handles, arcaded rims, etc. In short, it would be possible to sort the St. Francis and Memphis groups of material — if that was all we had it might have been justifiable to set up two types. Unfortunately, throughout the balance of the area, i.e., middle and southern sections, the material tends to be intermediate, closer in general to the Memphis variant, but lacking the specific rim features just mentioned.

Relationships to Other Types in the Survey Area. Parkin Punctated is typologically related to Evansville Punctated, its clay-tempered counterpart, from which it apparently derived. A similar relationship may be postulated between Evansville and the still earlier types, Tammany and Alexander Pinched. These four types represent one of the clearest possible evidences of continuity over a period that practically covers the entire span of pottery-making in the area.

Relationships Outside Survey Area. To the east, in north-central Mississippi, specimens of Parkin Punctated are grouped in the late Chickasaw complex by Jennings, corresponding to the appearance there of Barton Incised (Jennings, 1941, pls. 4, *c* and 5, *b*). In contrast to many other Middle Mississippi pottery features, this type of punctated decoration does not occur in any important way in Alabama, Tennessee, or throughout the Southeast. One of the few comparable examples is a sherd illustrated by Moore from Durand's Bend in south-central Alabama which is believed to be the site of the Creek town of Talisi (Moore, 1899, fig. 12). In the Ohio Valley this style is rare to absent in the Mississippi Period cultures, and the same observation may be made with regard to the northern Mississippi Valley. Even in southeast Missouri immediately adjacent to the Survey Area, Parkin Punctated rapidly fades out of the ceramic complex.

In Calhoun County, Arkansas, at the Keller Place, Moore obtained a vessel with punctates similar to Parkin on the body of a small jar which has multiple parallel horizontal lines on the rim. This vessel was not illustrated by Moore, but he does illustrate other vessels suggesting affiliations with the northern part of the Survey Area (Moore, 1909, pp. 91–96). Other examples in southwestern Arkansas are not uncommon (Harrington, 1920). The University of Texas has presented the Ceramic Repository with samples of Weches Fingernail-impressed, a type of the Alto Focus that indicates that this decorative technique is not limited to the rim area but also is found on the body (Krieger, 1946, fig. 19). In the Sanders Focus a type called Monkstown Fingernail Punctated is also suggestive of Parkin Punctated (Krieger, 1946, pl. 29, *d–g*. Vessel *f* is probably closer to Canton Incised).

It is interesting to find stylistic relatives for this type in the Southwest. In central Utah, Gillin has classed as his Type IV A and C specimens which are strikingly similar to Parkin Punctated even including the loop handle (Gillin, 1941, pls. V–VIII). Even farther to the west, fingernail punctates (along with rim incising suggestive of some types of Barton Incised) is a feature of Promontory pottery from around Great Salt Lake (Steward, 1937, p. 46 and fig. 19, *a*, *n*, *p*). Specimens of this type were collected in the area as early as 1870 (Judd, 1926, p. 143 and pl. 37, *e*). This type has been called Great Salt Lake Gray and Punched by Steward who interprets it as an imitation of corrugated pottery on the northwestern margin of the Anasazi area (Steward, 1936, pp. 6–10, pl. 3, *a* and *c*). In southern Nevada a similar punctated pottery was attributed to the Paiute (Harrington, 1930, p. 24 and fig. 3,*d*). At Pecos there is a small representation of punctated pottery on the culinary pottery where it is called "Nail-marked and Tool-marked" (Kidder, 1936, fig. 263, pp. 319–20). At Swarts Ruin there are a minor number of examples of tool-marked pottery some of which suggest a connection to Pecos, if not to Parkin (Cosgrove, H. S. and C. B., 1932, pl. 95). Others from the Mimbres area are from Cameron Creek Village (Bradfield, 1931, pl. LXXXIII, *408* and *373*). Identical specimens are called Alma Punched by Haury (Haury, 1936) and along with incised and tooled pottery were indicated as non-Southwestern and perhaps of Eastern origin. He indicates they begin as early as the Georgetown Phase of Mogollon.

Attention has been called to the Weeden Island type, Carrabelle Punctated, in the section describing our Evansville Punctated type. In the same Florida area another named punctated type is called Tucker Ridge-Pinched (Willey, 1945, p. 240). This calls to mind our late lamented Pouncey Pinched which was set up to take care of this style of decoration but later abandoned because of difficulties in sorting.

Chronological Position. The type occurs in considerable strength throughout the Mississippi Period in all parts of the Survey Area, reaching its maximum in B–A, the latter half of the period.

BARTON INCISED

(Figs. 86; 87, *a–d*; 95)

Type not previously described.

Paste and Surface. Same as Neeley's Ferry Plain.

Decoration. *Treatment.* Incision by a pointed implement applied to a moist surface producing a line with a considerable amount of "burr." Lines vary considerably in width, from less than 0.5 to 3.0 mm. In general the character of the line varies considerably, but in most instances it is irregular and carelessly executed. Where lines should abut there is a tendency for them to cross.

Design. The designs are predominantly groups of parallel, oblique lines slanting downward from the lip to the beginning of the shoulder area and in some cases extending onto the shoulder area.

These groups of lines are arranged to form various designs, the commonest of which is based on a system of alternating line-filled triangles. Often, however, these alternating sets of lines extend laterally over a considerable distance forming trapezoidal rather than triangular fields. For convenience, however, both arrangements will hereinafter be referred to as "line-triangles."

Next in point of frequency is a simple cross-hatched arrangement. Of the specimens classifiable from point of view of design, almost 70% would fall into the line-triangle type, compared to about 23% for the cross-hatched. It should be noted, however, that there is a wide range in percentages from site to site. Line-filled triangles run as high as 90% on the Turnbow Site (11–N–12), and as low as 54% on the Williamson Site (11–N–13). The cross-hatched ranges from 40% on the Williamson Site to 7% on the Turnbow Site.

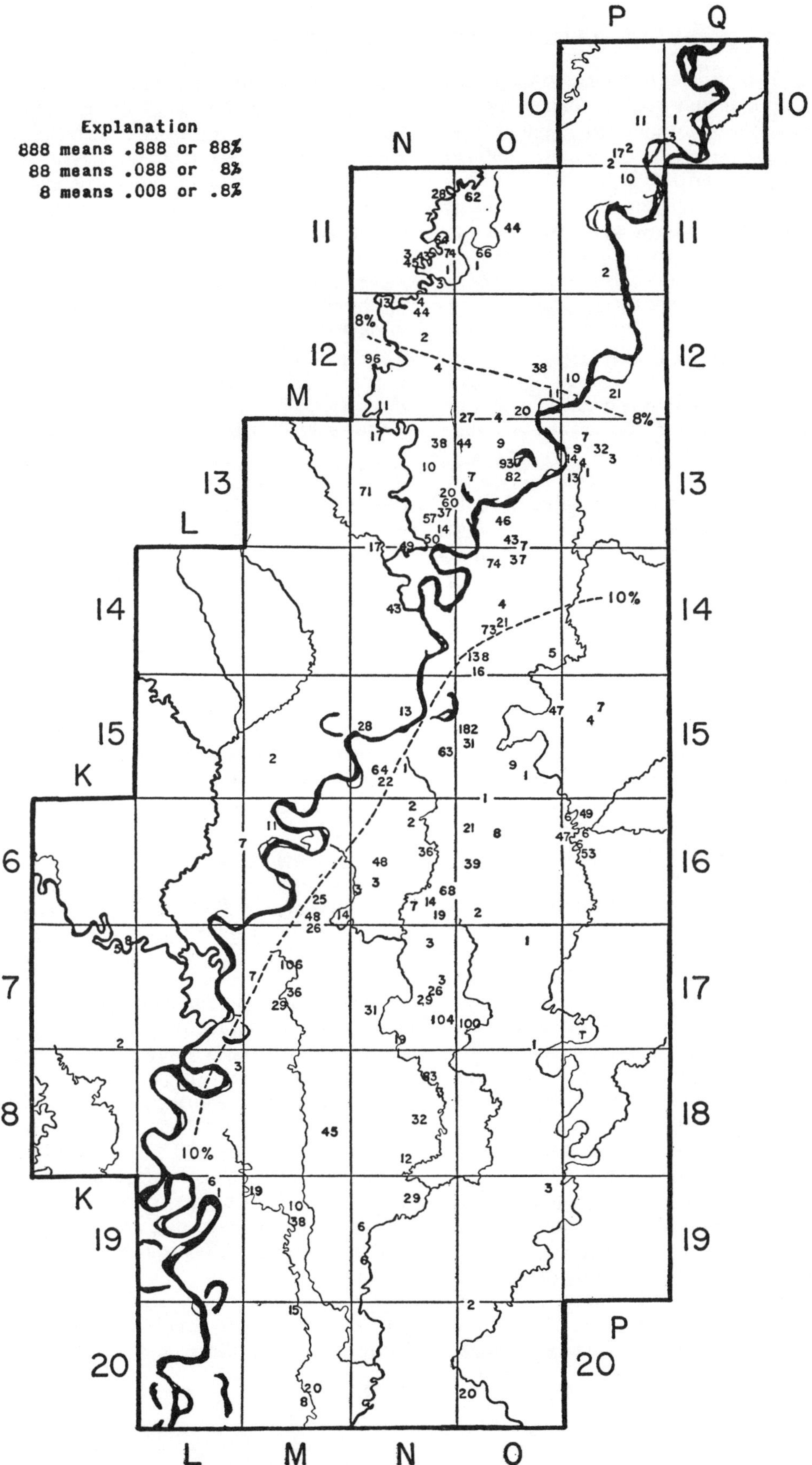

FIG. 11. Percentage frequency distribution of the type Barton Incised.

The remaining 7% of classifiable design occurrences is made up mainly of a chevron pattern, and there is one example in which oblique sets of lines alternate with blank spaces to form a checker-board.

There is more variation in the handling of these simple patterns than is indicated in the foregoing description. It appears to be not so much a matter of group variation from site to site, but of individual variations within site collections. This is related to the fact that decoration in general is carelessly and haphazardly executed.

The design field is frequently terminated at the junction of rim and shoulder by a single line (in no case more than one), a single row of punctations, or, less frequently, a row of small appliqué nodes. The first method is overwhelmingly in the majority in the St. Francis collections, is considerably less in evidence in the Memphis area, and progressively less so going south from there. Termination by punctation is distinctly a minority factor in both St. Francis and Memphis area collections, but becomes significant about the latitude of the mouth of the Arkansas River (Tiers 16 and 17). Farther south, however, and with surprising suddenness, it drops out almost entirely. Termination of the design field by a single row of nodes on the shoulder is definitely a St. Francis specialty. It occurs very rarely in the Memphis group and sites farther south and not at all in the 19 to 20 Tiers.

In addition to the above, Barton Incised occurs as a rim decoration in combination with several distinct types of body treatment. Sherds showing such combinations have been counted as Barton Incised on the principle that the rim decoration determines the type. For further particulars, see descriptions of Parkin Punctated, Fortune Noded, Ranch Incised, Kent Incised, Rhodes Incised.

Form. *Vessel Shape.* The dominant vessel shape is the large globular or sub-globular cooking jar with vague shoulder and recurving rim which we have called elsewhere the standard Mississippi jar. Bottoms are round or slightly flattened. Little information is available on details of shape, but there are indications that the diameter is slightly in excess of height. Small Barton Incised jars from the same sites where the Survey collections were made — commonly used as burial offerings — furnish the accompanying illustrations. We cannot be certain, however, that the sherds from larger jars that make up the Survey collections represent precisely the same type of vessel.

Size. Where large enough for measurement, sherds indicated an average rim diameter of 32 cm., with a range of 14 to 54 cm. Body diameters would doubtless slightly exceed these figures. Most averages come from the large St. Francis collections, but the few averages taken farther south show no significant divergences.

Thickness. Paste thickness averages 7.8 mm. in the St. Francis collections with a range of 5 to 13 mm. Memphis area material is significantly thinner, averaging 6.2 mm., with a range of 3 to 9 mm. Selected averages on collections farther south show a continuation of the thinner ware. It seems rather surprising that the thinner paste is not associated with significantly smaller vessel sizes. Possibly more information on the latter detail would be desirable.

Rim. By far the greatest number of rims descend from a plain, unelaborated lip in a gentle to strong recurve, blending with the body in a vague shoulder.

Lip. Lips are formed merely by trimming off with a straight smooth edge, and only a few sherds show labial modifications in the form of interior beveling (a Memphis subarea specialty) or extension by modeling. Occasionally, the outer lip is elaborated with punctations, notches, nicks, etc. This occurs in the northern sites, both St. Francis and Memphis, but drops out very fast to the south, becoming very rare south of Tier 15. Other labial modifications are produced by the use of lugs which are described below.

Base. Little may be said under this heading, since this is a rim type and there are no basal sherds. Such would fall into Neeley's Ferry Plain which type shows predominantly round or slightly flattened bottoms. Complete vessels from the same sites and area as the Survey collection all have round to slightly flattened bottoms.

Appendages. A relatively small percentage (about 10%) of sherds indicates the presence of lugs or handles. If we may judge from smaller examples of the type that occur as mortuary offerings, these may occur in the following combinations in approximate order of frequency: 2 lugs only, 2 handles, 4 handles, 4 lugs, and more rarely 2 lugs and 2 handles.

Lugs. These are decidedly more numerous than handles, and are about equally common wherever Barton Incised is found in the Survey Area. Most characteristic is the horizontally projecting type, made by drastically modifying the lip which appears to be first thickened at the desired spot and then pulled out into shape. They seem, in other words, to have been an integral part of the lip. No examples show fracture, indicating that the lugs were prefabricated and luted on. The upper surface is generally horizontal and in the plane of the lip. Lugs often extend horizontally as much as 3.5 cm. and in one instance (Rose, 12–N–3) as much as 5 cm. Shape varies from semi-circular to triangular, the latter, however, being confined to the St. Francis collections. Lugs are occasionally embellished with notches, and one of this type (Nickel, 13–N–15–B) has a vertical perforation presumably for suspension. Smaller semi-cylindrical lugs are occasionally placed below the lip area, but these appear only in the northern part of the Survey Area. In addition to the above, a somewhat different type of lug appears, generally less massive, with the upper surface sloping outward and downward from the lip. This occurs very rarely in the St. Francis collections, but is fairly common in sites farther south.

In general, though occurring in considerable frequency in all parts of the Survey Area, lugs seem much less obtrusive in the southern collections owing to the fact that they are very much smaller. In the most southerly collections they become little more than small nodal protuberances of no very definite shape.

Handles. The characteristic handle is a parallel-sided vertical strap handle, with the upper end attached to or just beneath the lip, and the lower end to the shoulder area at the base of the decorated zone. These are particularly large and common in the St. Francis collections, becoming smaller and less frequent toward the south. In some cases this reduction in size takes the form of narrowing, this approximating the loop type of handle. In others the handle is shorter vertically which makes for a relatively broad ribbon-like handle, giving the appearance of a horizontally applied half-tube.

Evidence so far available indicates that handles of all types were luted on, not "riveted."

The very small showing of handles in collections from the Memphis sub-area is no doubt related to the fact that the decorative handle (arcaded rim), so popular in that area, is seldom combined with Barton Incised (see descriptions of Kent Incised, Ranch Incised, Rhodes Incised, etc.).

Decoration in Relation to Shape. In the northern area the incised linear design covers the rim from lip to shoulder and in general is restricted to the rim, only occasionally, and this seemingly where we are dealing with relatively careless workmanship, slipping down over the shoulder to the body proper. In very few instances does the linear design begin at any distance below the lip, but this becomes increasingly popular as we go south, as does also the application of the design to the shoulder, accompanied with occasional shifts to the body proper.

Nodes and punctations, design features described elsewhere as Fortune Noded and Parkin Punctated, but often in combination with Barton Incised, are primarily applied as shoulder and body decoration, but also quite often are used to elaborate handles, lugs, and lips. Linear incisions are also applied to handles and sometimes to lugs, especially to the sloping undersides.

Distribution and Variations Within Survey Area. As may be seen in figure 11, Barton Incised is well distributed throughout the Survey Area except for the Lower Arkansas River region where its counterpart Wallace Incised to a large extent takes its place. Highest percentage frequencies are in the 17 Tier of quadrangles, but the largest samples come from the St. Francis River sites, and it is largely on the basis of this material that the type was first defined. The foregoing description, therefore, has special reference to this area. Typical sherds occur in all the Mississippi Period collections in the Survey Area, but with diminishing frequency as one goes south. About the latitude of Tier 19, the type begins to lose definition. Sherds have become thinner — an average thickness of 6.2 mm., compared with 7.8 mm. for the type "center" — but vessel sizes seem to remain about the same. The sherds give no evidence of changes in vessel shape, except for certain minor details in respect to handles and lugs. Decoration follows the same general pattern, line-filled triangles remaining the dominant arrangement, but the cross-hatching, always a fairly popular alternative arrangement in the north, becomes less frequent. Lines tend to be closer spaced, somewhat "drier" in execution, that is to say, less "burred," and are drawn at a steeper angle to the rim. In many cases the decorated field extends down onto the shoulder area and occasionally it starts well below the lip, leaving a portion of the rim undecorated. Termination of the design by a line at the base of the rim, so popular in the northern part of the Survey Area, becomes less frequent in the south. Termination by a single row of punctates, however, maintains — and even increases — its frequency. The combination of Barton Incised decoration on the rim with all-over punctation of the body (Parkin Punctated) almost disappears about the latitude of Tier 15 with only an occasional appearance farther south. Combination of Barton Incised rims with nodes either in a single row on the shoulder or all over the body (see Fortune Noded, p. 120) and fig. 87, *l, m*) also seems to be virtually limited to the northern sub-area.

In spite of all these minor changes, it is not possible to sort the southern material from typical Barton Incised. It is clear, however, that in this southern area the type is sliding over into something else that cannot be covered by the type definition. A few sherds appear in each collection in which the variant characteristics mentioned above are accentuated to the point where they are readily sorted from typical Barton Incised, which seems to warrant the establishment of another type. This is designated Arcola Incised and will be found described on page 140. It would be a reasonable guess that collections from sites farther to the south, beyond the limits of the area surveyed, will show an actual dominance of Arcola Incised. It must be freely admitted that in the southern ranges of the Survey Area, on important sites such as Leland, Arcola, Silver City, etc., the separation of Barton Incised and Arcola Incised is a very arbitrary proceeding. In consequence, in collections from these sites, the size of the category "Unclassified Shell-tempered Incised" is greatly increased by sherds that could have been thrown either way.

Relationships Outside Survey Area. Barton Incised with its relatively simple line-filled triangle design on the rim has a great many relatives. The stylistic connections to Mazique Incised are clear, but at least one of the authors (Griffin) is by no means certain that Mazique is the source of Barton.

In the northern Mississippi Valley a companion to Barton is not found in the Cahokia area, and the style is not often represented in the Spoon River Focus. At Aztalan a similar line-filled triangle is one of the rarer designs. In the Lower Ohio Valley, on the basis of present information, this design is not common, but does appear farther east in the central Ohio Valley in the Fort Ancient culture. The line-filled triangle is of course one of the hall-marks of developed Iroquois and also appears in Oneota. Its latest appearance in the Nebraska area is in the Lower Loup and Hill foci. This design is rare in typical Cumberland Aspect sites of the Nashville area. It is absent in the small log town-house sites, the Hiwassee Focus of southeastern Tennessee, and the Macon Plateau Focus of central Georgia. It is found in some strength on vessels called Dallas Decorated and in combination with punctates on Dallas Incised. It is rare to absent in northern Alabama along the Tennessee River and at Moundville. If it does appear it should be close to the historic horizon. It is found in small amounts around Montgomery where it has been attributed to Alibamo sites (*Arrow Points*, vol. 21, nos. 3 and 4, p. 33a). Jennings illustrates specimens of Barton Incised from various Chickasaw sites in north-central Mississippi (Jennings, 1941, pls. 4, *b-1* and 4, *c-1*).

In the "Caddo" area Dunkin Incised of the Alto Focus and Canton Incised of the Sanders Focus have interesting resemblances to Barton Incised, while at a later period the type Maydelle Incised of the Frankston Focus has strap handles as well as the design resemblance. At a fairly early level, similar incised designs are at Fourche Maline sites in eastern Oklahoma (Newkumet, 1940). On the late prehistoric to historic level in eastern Oklahoma, and the adjacent Arkansas and Missouri areas in the Neosho Focus (specimens sent to the Ceramic Repository for examination in 1940 by David A. Baerreis) and in "Osage" sites, there is found an incised shoulder decoration resembling Barton. These are also illustrated from the Top-layer culture of the Ozark Bluff shelters (Dellinger and Dickinson, 1942, pl. XXIV, *d*, *e*).

In the Pecos area this type of decoration, but on an entirely different vessel shape, has been called Potssuwi'i Incised by Mera (Mera, 1932). The latest description is by Kidder (Kidder, 1936, pp. 370–72). It is a late prehistoric type in the Pajarito Plateau and Chama area. It is described as one of the intrusive types in Kidder's report. Pecos is one of the few areas where an incised style similar to Barton Incised is found with a punctated style. Another is the Swarts ruin where an incised bowl (Cosgrove, H. S. and C. B., 1932, pl. 90, *j*) resembles the design but is not the shape of Potssuwi'i Incised, while other specimens (Cosgrove, H. S. and C. B., 1932, pl. 92, *e–g*) are on jars. Jar *e* is reminiscent of Oneota patterns.

Chronological Position. The information from the seriation graphs as to the time position of this type is an interesting example of this method of time measurement. Scattered occurrences preceding time D in several of the sub-areas are probably not significant. Like Parkin Punctated, with which it is normally associated, Barton Incised is found throughout the Mississippi Period (C–A), but its maximum of popularity seems to have been somewhat earlier than that of its companion type. This is borne out by stratigraphic evidence at Rose (12–N–3), Walls (13–P–1), Alligator (16–N–2), and Oliver (16–N–6).

RANCH INCISED

(Fig. 87, *e–i*)

Type not previously described.

Paste and Surface Finish. Same as Neeley's Ferry Plain.

Decoration. Decoration consists of groups of parallel, curved incised lines, rarely linear punctated, that intersect one another to give an imbricated design somewhat like the appearance of fish-scales. The number of lines in each design element varies from a minimum of 4 to a maximum of 17, but average from about 4 to 8. Width between the lines varies from 4 mm. to over 1.5 cm., and depth of incisions varies, but averages ca. 1.5 mm. and about the same for width.

Size of the complete elements also varies from very small ones measuring less than 2 cm. at the widest part to those measuring over 8 cm. at the widest part. The elements adjacent to the rim appear to depend therefrom as a festoon, and this festoon arrangement appears to continue over the entire body of the vessel.

Form. In the dozen rims available for analysis, only the standard jar form is represented.

Thickness. Average thickness is 6.8 mm., but the variation is marked, from 3 mm. to 12 mm. The material from sites in the Memphis sub-area is thinner than that from other portions of the Survey Area.

Base. No evidence.

Appendages. A semi-circular, horizontal lug projecting from the rim seems fairly common with 3 occurrences in 12 rims. These are relatively small, ca. 8 cm. long and projecting a little over 1 cm. One of the rims with this type of lug has also a small horizontal strip or knob lug at the shoulder.

Discussion. Ranch Incised is very thinly scattered throughout the Survey Area, with perhaps a slightly higher concentration in the 11–N quadrangle, the largest number of sherds coming from the 11–N–1 Parkin Site and 11–N–9 Vernon Paul Site. About 80% of this type is concentrated in the 11 to 13 Tiers. Designs similar to Ranch Incised are reported from Ouachita Parish, Louisiana (Moore, 1909, fig. 6) and from Franklin Parish in the same state (Moore, 1913, fig. 17 and 19). A very similar design is found on Hull Engraved. The design appears to be rare outside of the Survey Area.

Chronological Position. The great majority of sites with this type have been assigned to the late Mississippi Period (B–A). It appears to be a characteristic type for the late occupation in the St. Francis and Memphis sub-areas particularly.

VERNON PAUL APPLIQUÉ

(Figs. 87, *j, k*; 97, *a–c*)

Type not previously described.

Paste. Same as Neeley's Ferry Plain.

Decoration. Surface is worked into parallel ridges presumably by the addition of applied strips of clay smoothed into the vessel-body wall. When close-spaced the effect is similar to grooving or ridging, but the term appliqué seems more suitable. Most of the small sample of available body sherds of this type show a convergence of the ridges or grooves indicating a vertical placement on the vessel. Ridges are from .5 to 2 cm. apart and not more than 2 to 3 mm. high.

Form. Insufficient material for generalization. Body sherds similar in general configuration to sherds from standard Mississippi globular jar forms, but there is no evidence as to the type of rims that went with them. There are no identifiable basal sherds and no appendages. The whole vessels in our photograph collection do not show a consistent shape associated with appliqué treatment.

Discussion. Available material is plainly insufficient for adequate type description. However, as a highly characterized decorative treatment which does not fit into any other recognized type, there does not seem to be anything else to do with it, unless to ignore it altogether. There is a convergence between this type and a type of pinching with subsequent smoothing that has been included in Parkin Punctated, but the technical means employed are altogether different.

Distribution. Practically confined to the St. Francis sub-area, except two occurrences on sites farther south which have shown other St. Francis connections.

Relationships Outside Survey Area. Horizontal appliqué strips are of uncommon occurrence in southeast Missouri (Evers, 1880, pls. 3, *210*; 5, *473*) where this technique of decoration is found on bottles, sometimes as a snake effigy.

In the "Caddo" area this technique of decoration is more common than in the rest of the eastern United States. In the Titus Focus the type Harleton Appliqué (Krieger, 1946, fig. 18) has the technique but the design and form of the vessel are quite different. Somewhat more similar is Belcher Ridged from the Shreveport area, although here the resemblance is not specific enough to suggest a close connection (Webb and Dodd, 1941, pp. 101–02; Webb, 1948, pp. 113–14). It is doubtful if these ridges were produced by appliqué strips, but the effect produced is much the same.

Appliqué treatment of this style is not found in other Mississippi groups and is not at home in the southern Mississippi Valley.

Chronological Position. The sites where this type is found cluster around time B in the St. Francis sub-area. Farther south, there are several occurrences that suggest a somewhat earlier date. All that can be said with certainty is that Vernon Paul Appliqué is a Mississippi Period type.

FORTUNE NODED

(Figs. 87, *l, m*; 97, *j–q*)

Type not previously described.

Paste and Surface Finish. Same as Neeley's Ferry Plain.

Decoration. Application of small hemispherical or conical nodes in rows, groups, or as an all-over treatment of the vessel body. Nodes average about 1 cm. in diameter (range, .75 to 1.5 cm.), with an average projection of about .5 cm. (range, .2 to 1.0 cm.). Most commonly, nodes are luted onto the vessel surface resulting in a shape about like that of a conical mound. Occasionally, they are simply flattened onto the surface with a resulting shape more like that of a small thick pancake. There is not very much to say under the heading of design. A single horizontal row of nodes on the rim or shoulder area is perhaps the commonest treatment. This is very often combined with incised and punctated decoration (see descriptions of Barton Incised and Parkin Punctated, pp. 110, 114). Occasionally, small patches of nodes appear in the sherd collections, which may be purely a decorative factor, but may also be the basal nodes of conch-shell effigies, same as found in Neeley's Ferry Plain.

The sort of usage described so far would hardly warrant the establishment of a type, which only begins to make sense in cases where nodes are applied as an all-over treatment resulting in what has been termed in other areas a "nubbin" vessel. The difficulty, of course, is that most sherds only show one or two nodes, making it impossible to tell whether they are merely incidental or whether a "nubbin" type is really indicated. In the few examples that are unmistakably of the latter type, nodes are spaced from 1 to 2 cm. apart, generally scattered in hit-and-miss fashion, occasionally arranged in horizontal rows.

Form. Incidental nodes are found on both bowl and jar forms, more often on the latter. All-over treatment seems to be confined to the familiar standard Mississippi jar form. The nodes cover the entire vessel, except possibly the base, up to and including the shoulder area. Rims are plain.

Appendages. Only one strap handle in present sample, but it would seem likely that typical semi-circular lugs will also be found when more material is available. (Handles, particularly those of the decorative or "arcaded" type, frequently have nodal decoration, but these are usually adjuncts of other decorative types and have been classified accordingly.)

Discussion. Incidental nodes are widely distributed throughout the Survey Area, with most frequent occurrence, however, in the northern portion. Genuine, all-over nodal treatment worthy of the name Fortune Noded is practically confined to the northern sites with particular emphasis in the St. Francis sub-area.

Relationships Outside Survey Area. This style and technique of decoration is not only rare and of limited spread in the Survey Area, but the same conditions are true in the rest of the eastern United States. A search for comparable specimens to the south and north was quite unproductive. Vessels with over-all nodes do not seem to occur in the New Madrid Focus, the Monks Mound Aspect, the Cumberland area, or Moundville.

In the Tennessee Valley in northern Alabama, noded vessels were recovered by Moore (Moore, 1915, figs. 25, 32–34, 42) and in the same area during the excavations under the general direction of W. S. Webb (Webb, 1939, pl. 66, 89, *a*, 107, *b*; Webb and DeJarnette, 1942, pls. 61, *2*; 127, *2*; 261, *3*). Most of these, however, do not have nodes over most of the body surface, but the nodes are confined to one or more rows about the upper body. The type of noded decoration which appears in northern Alabama is found as far east as Fains Island, Jefferson County, Tennessee. (Specimens in the Ceramic Repository, Museum of Anthropology, University of Michigan.) In the Tennessee Valley of eastern Tennessee, nodes are found as decorative features on bowls in the Dallas and Mouse Creeks foci (Lewis and Kneberg, 1941, pp. 11 and 16; Lewis and Kneberg, 1946, p. 105, pl. 62, *c* and *h*). Noded vessels do not seem to be part of the complex around Nashville of the Cumberland aspect.

One noded vessel from the Illinois Valley was a part of a collection made by Dr. J. F. Snyder at the Crabtree Site in Brown County. This Middle Mississippi site also had two engraved spider-shell gorgets. The noded specimen is a cylindrical-neck water bottle with vertical rows of nodes on the globular body (Snyder, 1908, fig. 10).

There are two noded vessels from southwestern Arkansas that Moore obtained from the Haley and Foster places (Moore, 1912, pp. 556 and 603). At Haley the noded cup was associated with Haley Fine Engraved. The Foster Site is in the Belcher Focus. Other sites in the same area such as Washington and Ozan (Harrington, 1920, pls. XXIII, *b*; XXXIX, *b*; and fig. 16) have noded bowls. At the Spiro Site noded vessels are assigned to the post-Spiro Fort Coffee Focus (Orr, 1946, p. 243). At Belcher, near Shreveport, Louisiana, a noded cup similar to that from Haley was recovered, although it is not specifically mentioned in the publication on the site (Webb and Dodd, 1941). Examples were recently found at the Battle Mound. In east Texas noded vessels are found in both the Gibson and Fulton aspects. One from the Sanders Site is shell-tempered, and is evidently one of the unclassified vessels in Krieger's discussion of this site (Krieger, 1946, p. 188).

It may seem somewhat far afield to refer to the presence of noded vessels in the Southwest, but the results of this and other comparisons will not be without interest. As a technique of decoration, it is rare, but occurs more frequently in the southern part of the Southwest. One example was found at Alkali Ridge (Brew,

1946, p. 272 and fig. 99, *n*) where it is assigned to Pueblo I. It is somewhat more common in central Utah (Gillin, 1941, pls. VII, *b*, *43* and *51*; VIII, *34*). An earlier report gives additional evidence for this technique in the area (Judd, 1926, pl. 37, *b*).

In the Mimbres area a noded bowl was found at Swarts Ruin (Cosgrove, H. S. and C. B., 1932, pl. 88, *h*), and at Cameron Creek Village (Bradfield, 1931, pl. XCIII, *270*). In northern Chihuahua a noded vessel is illustrated by Kidder (Kidder, 1916, pl. 1, 7), but is included as a part of a "Redware" complex. This vessel also has an appliqué effigy snake.

Chronological Position. Confined generally to the Mississippi Period, but occurrences are too infrequent for closer dating.

BELL PLAIN

(Figs. 88; 100, *n–v*; 101, *c*, *i*; 102, *a*, *d–p*; 103, *c*, *l–p*; 104, *d*, *f–g*, *q–t*; 105, *a–c*, *f–h*, *p–s*; 106, *c*, *h–l*, *o–q*; 107, *a–c*, *f–k*; 108, *a–g*, *i*, *k*; 109, *k*; 113, *c*, *e*, *g*)

Paste. *Method of Manufacture.* Coiled, with pronounced tendency to break along the coil lines.

Tempering. Very fine shell particles; minute in size, never approaching even 1 mm.

Texture. Fine, soft, friable. Sherds when broken have a tendency to crumble, and the nature of the fracture is generally smooth and square.

Hardness. Average, 2.6 mm.; range, 2 to 3.5 mm.

Color. Surface color tends definitely toward the darker shades of gray. Mouse Gray (15'''''), according to the Ridgway nomenclature is the most common color, its darker shades of Deep Mouse Gray (15'''''*i*), Dark Mouse Gray (15'''''*k*) and Blackish Mouse Gray (15'''''*m*) occurring less frequently but in the order named. There are also a few Drab (17'''') sherds present. Sherds on the reddish side are fairly common, the most usual color being Vinaceous Cinnamon (13''*b*). Other reddish colors occurring with less frequency are Cinnamon (15''), Pinkish Cinnamon (15''*b*), Vinaceous Buff (17'''*d*), and Avellaneous (17'''*b*).

Mottling of the surface occurs, so that there may be several shades on a single sherd.

The core color of the gray sherds tends to be uniformly dark, almost black. Firing rarely penetrates over a millimeter in depth, and usually not that deep. On occasional sherds the surface color penetrates more deeply on the exterior than on the interior. Red sherds are usually well fired throughout so there is no recognizable difference between core and surface. In a few, however, surface color penetrates only a few millimeters leaving a thin, dark core.

Thickness. Average, 6.9 mm.; range, 4.5 to 10 mm.

Surface Finish. Bell Plain is characterized by well-smoothed surfaces, both interior and exterior. Many sherds are highly polished, "soapy" to the touch, and lustrous. Polishing marks are often visible, in the form of shallow groovings. A minority of sherds are rather rough and less carefully finished, but more often this is the effect of weathering.

Form. *Vessel Shape.* The most frequently occurring shape is the simple curved-sided bowl, which accounts for 31.2% of the rims large enough for shape determination (709). Bottles are next in order of frequency, 26.2% of the sample. The most characteristic Bell Plain bottle has a flattened globular or ellipsoidal body, with a low to medium high cylindrical neck terminating in a rim that has a pronounced exterior roll combined with an interior bevel. The engraved bottle in figure 110, *d*, gives a good idea of the shape. Next in importance is a bowl with flat or flattened bottom and flaring sides, 21.7% of the sample, figure 100, *l*, *o*, *v*. These are only the most common shapes. In addition there is a wide variety of specialized forms closely paralleling those in Neeley's Ferry Plain but usually carried out with greater skill and finer finish. Most of the better effigy forms described and illustrated in this report are on a Bell Plain base.

Rim. While the majority of Bell Plain rims are plain, about 28% of them are decorated by nicking, notching, pinching, incising, etc.

Nicking and notching is by far the most important treatment comprising about 43.8% of the total number of decorated rims. By and large the treatments are identical with those described for Neeley's Ferry Plain and Baytown Plain.

Next in order of frequency is the notched or pinched horizontal rim fillet comprising 32.2% of the decorated rims, a treatment that occurs in Neeley's Ferry Plain but is more characteristic of Bell. A typical example may be seen in figure 100, *1*.

Together these two techniques account for over three-quarters of the decorated rims, all other techniques being included in the remaining 25%. Of these less important decorative treatments, also described elsewhere, pinching is first (5.8%), followed by punctation (3.6%), a single incised line and application of nodes (each 2.4%). Two additional features are a scalloped rim and the so-called "Haynes Bluff" rim, each comprising 4.5% of the total rim decoration. The scalloped rim has an undulating appearance, and the scallop may be squarish or round in contour varying in size and number from a few deep, long ones, to many small ones closely spaced. The "Haynes Bluff" rim found here is one that flares out rather sharply adjacent to the lip, is thickened, and has a beveled interior. The bevel is usually either incised or terraced, and the lip, always rounded, is usually very deeply notched with long, right-slanting (occasionally left) grooves, giving somewhat the appearance of a large heavy rope laid around the rim edge (fig. 88, *g*). Sometimes the beveled rim is not incised or terraced, while the lip only is deeply notched, or vice versa.

Lip. Lips are often beveled in, and occasionally out, the former being a dominant feature in the Memphis sub-area. Flat and round lips occur with about the same frequency.

A very few vertical fillets or "ribs," as described for Neeley's Ferry Plain, occur in Tier 13.

Base. There are only 2.8 recognizable basal sherds per hundred rim sherds in the collections, and one-third of these are simply flattened bases, rounded up smoothly to the sides. We must conclude that the majority of the bases were of this simple, undifferentiated type and thus rarely to be separated from body sherds.

In addition, however, there are a few bases that are really flat, joining to the body wall in a sharp angle. Of the recognizable bases, next to the rounded ones mentioned above, these are the most common. Disk and annular or ring bases also occasionally occur, and there is one pedestal base of the Natchezan style.

A feature sometimes appearing in Bell Plain is the use of single encircling rows of punctations or nicks at the juncture of base and body wall.

Appendages. There are very few appendages of any kind in the collection of Bell Plain. A single loop handle came from the Cheatham Site (13–P–6), and there were only 19 lugs for almost 2000 rims. Of these, 17 were of the horizontally projecting semicircular variety, 11 of which were decorated with nicked edges, nodes, or incising. They probably came from rim effigy bowls.

Distribution, Variation and Relationships to Other Types in Survey Area. Percentage distribution of the type is shown in figure 12. There appear to be two centers of high frequency, a northern and a southern. The northern high frequencies are distributed along both sides of the Mississippi with Memphis as the approximate center. The southern center is on the east side only of the Mississippi in the vicinity of Deer Creek. Between the two, in Tiers 17 and 18, frequencies tend to be low, likewise on the St. Francis, notwithstanding its proximity to the northern center. The type is practically nonexistent on the west side of the River below the mouth of the St. Francis.

Features which distinguish the northern variation of Bell Plain (bottle shapes, decoration of nicked or notched lips, rim edges, and applied fillet) dwindle out markedly in Tier 16 to become almost completely lacking in Tiers 17 to 20. In these middle tiers the actual quantity of fine shell-tempered pottery also drops off markedly, and, repeating the pattern of the coarse shell-tempered Neeley's Ferry, picks up again in the 17 to 20 Tiers. In these tiers, Bell comes in for some rather radical changes.

Bowls, both simple and curved-sided and flared, are now definitely the primary form, and our diagnostic Bell bottle form is almost completely lacking. Hardly a rim fillet occurs, and the decorative nicking and notching is rare indeed. These are replaced by a massive rim, thickened either inside or out by additions of clay strips which may be well-

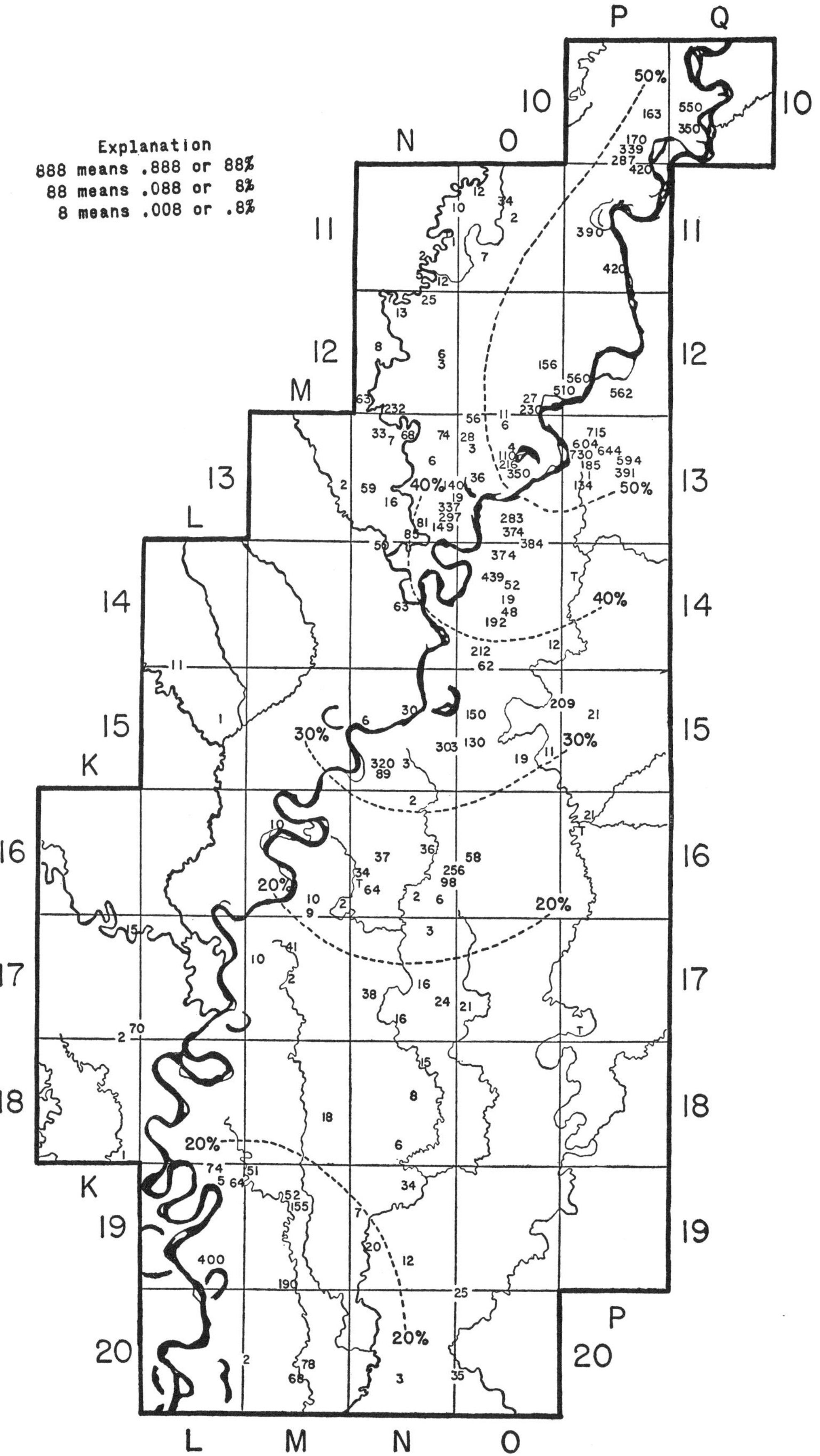

FIG. 12. Percentage frequency distribution of the type Bell Plain.

smoothed into the body wall or left standing relatively free.

Single, rather broad, encircling incised lines are now a dominant feature and may be applied to inside, outside, or to both.

Bell Plain from the south also runs slightly thinner, 6.5 mm., compared with 6.9 mm. in the north.

But even with these definite differences, it did not seem advisable at this time to call the southern variation of Bell Plain another type, as e.g., Leland Plain, for two reasons:

1) Certain features of the northern Bell Plain type do occur throughout as
   a) types of bases;
   b) the "composite silhouette" bowl with a simple curved body separated from its flared rim by a sharp beak;
   c) the scalloped rim; and
   d) especially the "Haynes Bluff" type of rim.

2) The sorting difficulties. Actually, most of the heavy thickened rims underscored by incising can be pretty easily pulled out and the occasional occurrence of incipient depending lines leads one to believe that many of them are nothing more or less than the extreme upper edge of a Leland Incised rim and that others are a "Leland Plain" type. But along with these and certainly without apparent paste differences are Bell rims of the "Haynes Bluff" variety and the "composite silhouette" bowls. In addition to these two generally sortable types, however, there are a large quantity of rims which cannot be put with one group or the other. In addition, an obvious problem here is that of trying to sort out the quantities of fragmentary body sherds which without identifying rims have no apparent features on which they can be sorted.

In the face of these many difficulties we decided to call all this material Bell Plain but to keep our description pure for the time being by describing only the Bell Plain in Tiers 10 through 16. As the description now stands, it obviously does not include the thickened rims, incised lines, and other southern features. As the Survey continues on farther south, it will undoubtedly be necessary to set up one or more additional types for this aberrant material.

Relationships Outside Survey Area. Bell Plain is related to polished or well-smoothed plain ware which carries most of the finer Mississippi culture pottery decoration, effigy features, and other vessels of better quality, all over the Southeast. In the Cahokia area Powell Plain is an early analogue, but of course the decoration and shape are much different. In the Illinois Valley few examples are found of this finer-grained, well-polished pottery (Cole and Deuel, 1937, p. 51; also studied by James B. Griffin). In southern Illinois a type comparable to Bell has not yet been described formally and the same holds true for the southwestern Indiana area. Farther up the Ohio in the Louisville area the polished ware seems to fade out and is not a part of the Fort Ancient ceramic complex farther to the east.

In the Cumberland area there is a fine-paste polished dark ware. It is the dominant type in collections because it was the most common type placed with the dead. Many of the best vessels illustrated from this area are of this type. Most of the jars are small. The bowls are flat-bottomed with outsloping sides or are hemispherical. The indented or beaded rim bowl so characteristic of the Cumberland, bowls with medallion heads (Thruston, 1897, pl. VIII, lower right), human effigy head bowls, or other effigy heads on the rim, rare bottles, shell and gourd effigies, human effigy figures, and the hooded bottle form are all found in collections from this area.

The eastern Tennessee region is most closely connected to the Cumberland, particularly on the Dallas and Mouse Creek level. In the earlier Hiwassee Island–Small Log level the fine-paste polished black ware is not at all common. In the Norris Basin the Cox Mound (Site 19) has examples of this type of relatively fine paste, smooth to polished surface, and black color. It also has other features of the bowls which link this site to a Cumberland ancestor (Griffin, 1938, p. 340).

In southwestern North Carolina a paste comparable to Bell has been described from the Peachtree Site as Ware B (Setzler and Jennings, 1941, p. 43–45). The authors of that report point out the occasional difficulty in separating some of the better-made Ware A specimens from Ware B but emphasize that Ware "B is uniformly well made." They also indicate that this type was more common in the early (Mississippi) occupation of the site (Setzler and Jennings, 1941, p. 50).[14] In central Georgia the fine polished black ware does not seem to make its appearance until well after the first introduction of the Mississippi complex at Macon Plateau and does not become important until the Lamar Period. There are examples of fine polished black pottery at Etowah and in the Lower Chattahoochee which appear to be most closely connected to Moundville Black Filmed.

The famous site of Moundville and its associated sites in northern Alabama have in this Black Filmed type a very close relative to Bell Plain. The Moundville type often appears to have a slip which is rarely the case with Bell Plain. The common Moundville bottle is the wide-mouth, short-neck form with globular body and plain flattened base or disk base and is very similar to the characteristic Bell Plain bottle described above. This, taken into account along with the practice of engraving and some highly specific designs in common, clearly indicates that the Moundville complex and what we have referred to as the Walls-Pecan Point complex in the Memphis sub-area had close cultural connections. Apparently from the Moundville center this polished black ware moved south and east along the Gulf Coast to appear sporadically in sites of the Fort Walton Period.

The Coles Creek ceramic complex around the mouth of the Red River also has a polished type. On the whole it seems to be somewhat earlier than the major appearance of Bell, and the majority of the forms are significantly different. It now appears possible that Coles Creek Polished Plain is derived from the Alto Focus of the Gibson Aspect of the "Caddo" area because of the introduction of the beaker or cylindrical jar, the low vertical-rimmed bowl, and the horizontal incised lines around the rim (called Coles Creek Incised in the Coles Creek area), which are characteristic of Hickory Fine Engraved, Dunkin Incised, and Davis Incised (Newell and Krieger, 1949, figs. 33, *A–E*; 42, *A B*, and *F*; 45). The corresponding plain type of the Alto Focus, Bowles Creek Plain, Krieger did not differentiate into proportions of polished and unpolished surfaces. In east Texas, on this early level at least, vessels with completely plain surfaces are not nearly as common as in the Lower Mississippi Valley. The bottle form with the straight insloping neck so typical of the Alto Focus did not move east into the Coles Creek area, whereas the carinated bowl form and cylindrical jar or beaker form did. This is also the situation in the Old Village complex of Cahokia where there are some indications that engraving and "Caddo"-type projectile points also arrived with influences from the "Caddo" area. These early similarities between Old Village and Alto do not seem to have moved up the Mississippi by way of the Coles Creek complex because of the absence of the connecting types between the mouth of the Red River and Cahokia. Furthermore, the vessel forms of Bell with the heavy emphasis on the bottle, with effigy associations, and the use of engraving on this paste, do not argue for derivation of Bell from Coles Creek Plain.

Chronological Position. Bell Plain appears first in the Memphis sub-area in the late Baytown between Period D–C, becomes a dominant type in the early Mississippi (C–B), and is more common than Neeley's Ferry Plain in the late Mississippi (B–A). This is in marked contrast to the St. Francis area where it never is numerically strong and is only noticeable in the last period and at sites with other connections to the Memphis area. In the Lower Yazoo area the combined Bell and Leland indicate a growing strength of polished or well-smoothed plain pottery in late C–B and B–A.

KENT INCISED

(Figs. 89, *a–d*; 96)

Type not previously described.

Paste and Surface Finish. Same as Neeley's Ferry Plain.

Decoration. Vertical incised lines extending from lower rim area to base, sometimes

[14] This does not mean the earliest Woodland occupation of the site which the authors seemed reluctant to recognize.

from lip. Character of line similar to that described for Barton Incised. Lines average about 1 cm. apart (range, 4 to 17 mm.) at point of greatest diameter, converge like meridians of longitude at base and (slightly) at neck. The only significant variation is a herringbone effect between widely spaced lines. This herringbone pattern may be continuous or may be in bands alternating with smooth areas.

Broken lines are sometimes used resulting in a punctate-incised variant which imperceptibly grades into a linear-punctate version and finally into pinching, included under Parkin Punctated.

Form. Most sherds identifiable as to form pertain to the standard Mississippi jars as described for Neeley's Ferry Plain, Barton Incised, etc. In this shape rims are either plain or of the type Barton Incised, with typical appendages, i.e., lugs and handles described in connection with that type. Rims from sites in the Memphis sub-area often show typical decorative (arcaded) handles distinctive of that group. A few rims indicate a simple curved- or straight-sided bowl (one incurved) with direct vertical rims, and in these the Kent style of decoration is carried up to the lip.

Distribution. Centers in the northern part of the Survey Area in St. Francis and Memphis sub-areas, particularly the latter. Occurrences sporadic and scattered south of Tier 13, where the type is represented by somewhat doubtful examples.

Relationships Outside Survey Area. Decoration on the body and particularly the lower body is not often found on Middle Mississippi jars. There are thick-walled vessels of jar shape from St. Louis to the mouth of the Ohio area with vertical incised lines, but there is no strong resemblance to Kent Incised. On Oneota jars a similar employment of vertical incised lines beginning at the base of the rim and running well down the body is not uncommon. In the Titus Focus of northeast Texas, Glenwood Incised is quite similar to Kent Incised.

Chronological Position. Mississippi Period (C–A), with maximum occurrence about time B.

RHODES INCISED

(FIGS. 89, *e–i*; 98)

Type not previously described.

Paste and Surface Finish. Usually the same as Neeley's Ferry Plain, but occasionally is found on Bell Plain paste.

Decoration. *Treatment.* Wide, deep, generally U-shaped curvilinear incisions, closely spaced. Incisions vary in width from ca. 2 to 3 mm. Spaces between the lines are sometimes narrower than the incisions themselves but are usually somewhat wider.

Design. Whorls and festoons cover the body and occasionally the rim. This design, as observed on whole pots, characteristically spirals from a nuclear swastika or triskele repeated four times on the vessel.

Form. Since this is primarily a body decoration, there are very few rim sherds that have been classified in the type. The few in the collections, however, indicate a small globular or sub-globular jar with a recurved rim, or with a short, straight collar. One sherd has an arcaded rim. Judging from examples in burial collections, this appears to be a common feature (see fig. 98, *f–m*). The Rhodes type of decoration also occurs on bowls and bottles on a Bell Plain type paste (fig. 98, *a–e*).

Discussion. This decorative style was used to define the type, even though it is found on both Neeley's Ferry and Bell paste, as well as a number of different forms. It is essentially a Memphis sub-area feature which centers in the usual quadrangles of 10–Q, 12–P, 13–N, O, and P, and extends on down into Tiers 16 and 17.

Relationships Outside Survey Area. Comparable types are not found to the north of the area nor to the east. The connections seem to be with Foster Trailed-Incised and Keno Trailed of the "Caddo" area. Other suggestive examples in southern Louisiana are at Sycamore Landing (Moore, 1909, fig. 118) and Saline Point (Moore, 1912, fig. 5).

Chronological Position. Primarily late Mississippi Period (B–A).

WALLS ENGRAVED

(FIGS. 89, *j–n*; 110, *a–m*; 111, *e–h*, *l*)

Type not previously described.

Paste and Surface Finish. Same as Bell Plain.

Decoration. *Treatment.* Fine-line engraving. Curvilinear bands of diamond-shaped cross-hatching contrasting with one or more plain bands. Width of cross-hatched bands varies from about 0.5 cm. to almost 3 cm., but most commonly is less than 1 cm.

Triangular areas of cross-hatching set off by plain areas are also common, and there is one occurrence of a wide (2 cm.) band of checker-board composed of contrasting plain and cross-hatched squares.

Design. This is a rather free style of decoration which makes generalization difficult. Commonest design appears to be a series of spirals made up of the cross-hatched bands described above, the outermost band being further embellished with cross-hatched triangels giving a "crested" effect (fig. 110, *a–d*, *f*, *h–j*). Less common, but present in collections of burial pottery, are some of the esoteric motives of the well-known "Southern Cult" (fig. 111, *e*, *g*, *h*, *l*) in a style very similar to that of Moundville. For further discussion, see Section IV under the heading "Various Exotic Designs" (p. 213).

Form. Rim sherds are almost nonexistent, since plain ones would have been classified as Bell Plain. The only rim in the collection of Walls Engraved is of the typical Bell Plain bottle neck. Two other lipless rims in the collection also indicate the bottle rim. Most known whole pots with this design and treatment are bottles. A bowl form is indicated, however, since one sherd was decorated inside and out.

Relationship to Hull Engraved. It is possible that the type crosses over into Hull Engraved, inasmuch as Moore, 1911, fig. 58, figures a bowl which combines both Hull and Walls. So far, however, our collections have failed to show the two associated.

Distribution. The type is definitely concentrated in the northern area, only 3 sherds from a total of 74 appearing south of Tier 14.

Relationships Outside Survey Area. The introduction of engraving into the eastern United States has been commented upon at some length in a recent publication on a site in San Luis Potosi, the Huasteca area of Mexico (Du Solier, Krieger, and Griffin, 1947, pp. 26–30). The interested specialists are referred to this article for opinions of Krieger and Griffin as of that date. Since that time Krieger has fastened his sights for the origin of Alto Focus engraving on the far-distant highlands of Guatemala and the remarkably localized early Miraflores Phase of that area (Newell and Krieger, 1949). Griffin, being somewhat more pedestrian at this point, would continue to look hopefully to the northern marginal zone of Mesoamerica.

Engraving is certainly well concentrated within the boundaries of the United States in what is called the "Caddo" area and has its presumed earliest appearance in that area. From there it spread into the Mississippi Valley. The northern limit of this technique was in the Cahokia–Peoria area where engraving is a part of the Trappist and Spoon River foci, particularly on bean pots and more rarely on plates. Recently, specimens from Cahokia have indicated the presence of engraving on a Powell Plain paste and some specimens have red paint rubbed into the lines. Others have excised areas made through the black exterior and these in turn have been filled with red paint (Moorehead, 1929, pl. XXI, *1*). Better specimens are now in the Ceramic Repository. In the area about the mouth of the Ohio, and particularly on the Kentucky side, there is a concentration of engraving on plate rims with a line-filled triangle, the most common design. This is not common in the Survey Area but reappears in the Red River area in a late period on a type called Anna Interior Engraved.

Engraving does not seem to have been included in the decoration techniques which spread west from Cahokia up the Missouri to the Steed-Kisker Focus or up the Mississippi to the Apple River Focus of the Dubuque area or the Rock River Focus of Aztalan. Engraving does not appear in the early Mississippi levels of eastern Tennessee or central Georgia. It is absent in the central Ohio Valley and in the Cumberland. It would thus seem that if Cahokia was a center for the dissemination of early Mississippi ceramic ideas, engraving (presumably from the "Caddo" area) had not yet been integrated in the decorative complex.

Except for a few inept examples, engraving is rare in the St. Francis sub-area. It appears to be concentrated in the Memphis sub-area in what we have sometimes called the "Walls-

Pecan Point" complex. Here, its resemblance to Moundville Filmed Engraved in vessel shape, technique, and design, is very close indeed. We can justifiably assume that Moundville is the center for this style of engraving and for the art concepts employed on the vessels found in the Survey Area.[15] From Moundville this technique, if not the actual vessels, was disseminated into the Tennessee Basin in northern Alabama, in the Chattahoochee Valley between Alabama and Georgia, and to Etowah and the Hollywood Mound near Augusta, Georgia. It also moved to the Gulf Coast and for some distance into Florida.

Chronological Position. Late Mississippi Period (B–A) in the Memphis sub-area which is the only part of the Survey Area that has so far yielded enough material for dating purposes.

HULL ENGRAVED

(Fig. 89, *p–s*)

Type not previously described.

Paste and Surface Finish. Same as Bell Plain, but with more sherds fired to buff, reddish buff, and red.

Decoration. Fine-line engraving on bowl interiors consisting of groups of parallel concentric arcs, abutting against other groups to form a fish-scale-like imbricated pattern, similar to that described for Ranch Incised. These lines always curve down from the rim edge in a festoon pattern, never arching upwards toward the rim.

The number of lines varies from 5 to 16 in each element, but 6 to 7 is the most common number. Space between the lines varies from 1 to 6 mm., but 2 to 3 mm. is most common. There is also variation in the size of the elements from about 1.5 cm. across to 6 cm. and over, but generally they are about 3 to 4 cm.

Form. *Vessel Shape.* Bowls of two types are represented by rim sherds: (1) a simple curved-sided bowl with slightly thickened rim and flat insloping lip. Average diameter, 29 cm.; range, 22 to 42 cm. (2) "Composite silhouette" bowl common to Bell Plain. This bowl has a simple curved body with a flared or recurved rim joining it at a sharp angle—often emphasized on the interior by a wide incised line.

Thickness. Average, 6.3 mm.; range, 5 to 8 mm.

Rim. One of the simple bowls has a "Haynes Bluff" rim with long incisions in the flange. Two other simple bowl rims also suggest a "Haynes Bluff" treatment in that they are insloped and have similar incisions on the slope.

Lip. Flat, rounded, and beveled lips represented in the dozen rims available for examination. One has light diagonal nicks on it.

Discussion. Hull Engraved is clearly closely related to Bell Plain both in characteristics of paste and surface finish. The design is identical with that described for Ranch Incised, but the latter is incised on a coarse Neeley's Ferry Plain paste while Hull is engraved on the fine paste of Bell Plain.

A close relationship is also indicated with Walls Engraved. Moore, 1911, fig. 58, figures a bowl interior with a triskele pattern of Walls Engraved cross-hatch combined with an interior decoration very like Hull Engraved, except that the arcs arch upward toward the rim instead of festooning from it. However, no sherds in our collections demonstrate their association on the same vessel, and Hull is primarily an interior decoration and Walls an exterior treatment.

Chronological Position. The seriation charts indicate that this type occurs in the Memphis sub-area throughout the Mississippi Period (C–A). It may be slightly earlier than its companion, Walls Engraved.

OLD TOWN RED

(Figs. 90, *a–f*; 100, *h*; 109, *c, g, j*; 113, *a–b, d*)

Type not previously described.

Paste and Surface Finish. Same as Neeley's Ferry or Bell Plain, except for color.

Color. Slipped ware, having the same color range as Larto Red Filmed.

[15] Ford and Phillips are not entirely in agreement with this statement. Deducing origins from comparative frequencies is an unsafe business. When a late site in the Memphis area has been excavated as thoroughly as Moundville, the position may look different.

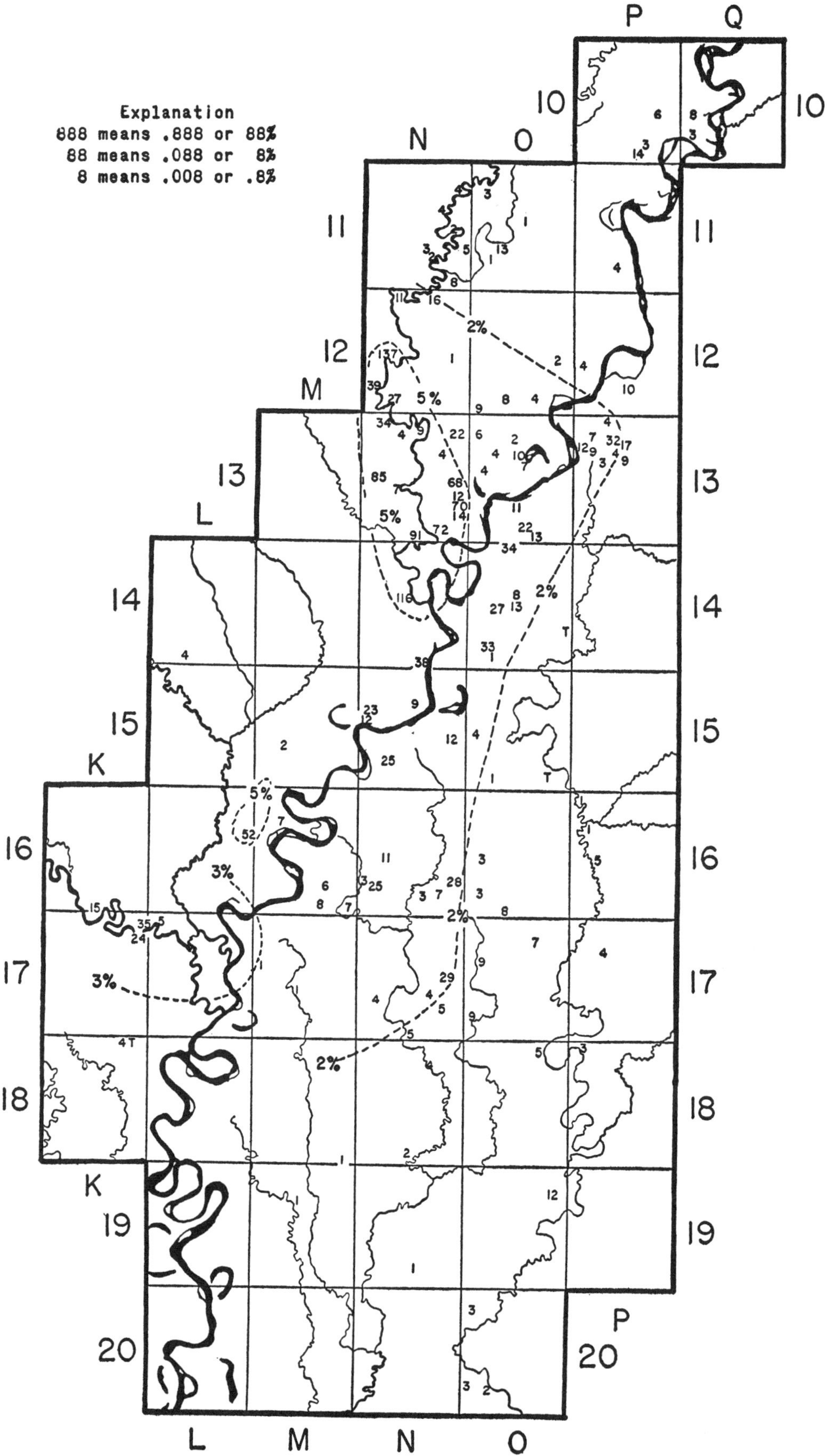

FIG. 13. Percentage frequency distribution of the type Old Town Red Filmed.

Decoration. Absent, except for simple rim treatments discussed below.

Form. *Vessel Shape.* A simple curved-sided bowl, shallow or deep, is the most commonly occurring form, but other characteristic forms are a "composite silhouette" bowl with curved body joining at an angle with a flared rim (average oral diameter, ca. 25.4 cm.; range, 20 to 38 cm.); and a tall, small-necked bottle with oral diameter often only 6 or 8 cm.

A bowl with flared rim also appears to be common, but most of the sherds so classified are probably only the flared upper rim of the "composite silhouette" bowl.

Other forms also occur, but infrequently. These are a deep bowl with gently recurved sides, a jar or beaker with inslanting sides, and a jar with recurved rim.

Vessels with fairly elaborate shapes are indicated by body sherds, but there is not enough material for reconstruction. Sherds from "teaspouts" also appear to be fairly numerous.

The above observations are based on sherd collections. We know from a vast number of vessels in collections taken from burials that practically every shape found in Neeley's Ferry or Bell Plain is also present in Old Town Red. The only exception is that red filming was almost never applied to jars.

Thickness. Average, 6.4 mm.; range, 4 to 10. This is significantly thinner than Neeley's Ferry, but only slightly thinner than Bell Plain.

Rim. Rims are for the most part direct and unelaborated by thickening. A little over 10%, however, are decorated by some form of nicking, notching, pinching, or punctating. Such treatment is usually applied to the rim edge in a right-slanting direction, only a few examples occurring below the edge.

A pinched rim fillet also occurs a few times in the northern quadrangles. It is identical with the treatment which is common to Bell Plain.

Lip. Lips are commonly flat, but may also be round, thinned, or beveled.

Base. Of the 7 bases occurring in the collections, 3 are simple flat bases, one joining the body at a slight angle, the other 2 blending quite smoothly. Three others have annular bases and a fourth, now broken, appears to have also had a supporting ring.

Appendages. Only one strap handle is present in the entire collection, but lugs are of fairly frequent occurrence and are similar to those described for Neeley's Ferry Plain.

Relationships Within Survey Area. The type as defined is the red-filmed counterpart of both plain shell-tempered types, i.e., it occurs on both the coarse paste of Neeley's Ferry and the fine paste of Bell Plain. Logically, there should be two divisions. We originally set it up that way, but they broke down under sorting difficulties, the reason being that Old Town Red even when directly associated with Neeley's Ferry is inclined to have a somewhat finer paste. Since the differentiation of Neeley's Ferry and Bell turned out to be culturally significant, it is to be hoped that some means will be found to distinguish their associated red and painted wares also. This may be possible when we have more information on shape.

Distribution. Percentage distribution of Old Town Red is shown in figure 13. Outstanding features are the general westerly distribution — most of the higher frequencies occurring west of the Mississippi — and the very poor showing of the type in the south. The heaviest concentration is on the St. Francis, but there is a secondary center of importance in the Lower Arkansas–White River region. The almost complete absence of Old Town Red in the large late Mississippi Period sites on Deer Creek (19–M, 20–M) is noteworthy. Comparison with the distribution of Larto Red (fig. 9) seems to indicate an inverse relationship between the two types. With the exception of the Deer Creek area mentioned above, which does not have either, Old Town is strong where Larto is weak and *vice versa.* What bearing, if any, this has on the question of continuity between the two types, which we have rather tended to assume, is not altogether clear.

Relationships Outside Survey Area. A red-slipped relative of Old Town Red is rare in the New Madrid Focus where it is most often found on effigies, and is almost completely absent from the Cumberland Aspect of Nashville. It is also rare in the early horizons of eastern Tennessee and Georgia but at least in eastern Tennessee is more common than in the Cumberland. It is conspicuously absent in the central Ohio Valley. At the Angel Site red-slipped pottery is not as common as negative painting but at least one owl effigy has been found (Black, 1944, p. 520), indicating a connection to the New Madrid area where this form is apparently more at home.

In the Cahokia area the type Monks Mound Red is a part of the jerry-built Old Village ceramic complex which spread as far north as Aztalan but does not seem to have moved west to the Kansas City area. At Cahokia red filming seems to have preceded the full-blown Old Village, for at the South Mound Group (Bushnell, 1922) in the fall of 1948, in company with Dr. P. F. Titterington of St. Louis, Griffin collected a limestone pottery complex which typologically seems to precede the Old Village level and represents a late stage of the Woodland roughly comparable to the Lewis Focus of southern Illinois and the McKelvey complex of northern Alabama.

Surface collections from Cahokia indicate that both in Old Village and in Trappist extensive use was made of red filming, as it appears not only on the more ornate and decorative types, but also on the common jars and even on salt pans.

In northern Alabama and at Moundville it is relatively rare and this is also true of the eastern margins of Middle Mississippi in the later manifestations. In the Lower Red River area, after Coles Creek, red filming is rarely found.

Chronological Position. According to the seriation graphs, the type begins to be popular shortly before time C and reaches its peak around time B or shortly after.

The strata cuts at Walls (13–P–1) suggest that it is relatively late there while the Lake Cormorant (13–P–8) excavations merely indicate its association with the other Middle Mississippi types. At Oliver (16–N–6) and Alligator (16–N–2) it seems to lag behind the earlier Middle Mississippi types such as Neeley's Ferry, Parkin Punctated, and Barton Incised. At Menard (17–K–1) it appears early but is late at Jaketown (20–O–1) and at Rose (12–N–3). It does not seem to be associated with the early Mississippi component on the latter site.

CARSON RED ON BUFF

(Figs. 90, *i*, *j*; 112, *c*, *f*, *o*)

Type not previously described.

Paste and Surface Finish. Same as Neeley's Ferry Plain with lighter buff shades predominating.

Decoration. *Treatment.* Broad bands of heavy slip-like paint, of the same material and consistency as the over-all filming in Old Town Red, applied directly on the unslipped buff surface.

Design. Commonest design elements are the spiral meander and swastika spiral (fig. 112, *c*, *f*), as already described for the types Rhodes Incised and Walls Engraved, and a simple arrangement of alternating vertical panels (fig. 112, *d*) related to the type Kent Incised. Other simple motives may be seen in figure 112, of which the stepped design (fig. 112, *a*, *b*) may be important for its possible Southwestern connections. Whatever the design, treatment is always broad and relatively crude. Mississippi potters had scarcely begun to exploit the possibilities of painting as a decorative medium.

Form. Shapes as described for Neeley's Ferry and Bell Plain with particular emphasis on bottles, which are frequently provided with basal features including disk, ring, annular, and tripod bases. Bowls are less often painted, mainly on the exterior, but in the case of shallow bowls sometimes on the interior, occasionally on both. Effigies and eccentric forms were often painted. Jars never.

Relationships Within Survey Area. The type is less common in both sherd and vessel collections than its companion, Nodena Red and White. It has a scattered distribution over the northern part of the Survey Area but is rare in the south. Nodena Red and White, on the other hand, is distributed over the entire area. These facts lend some support to the hypothesis that painting was moving down the Mississippi, and that red on buff was the earlier style.

However, both chronological and typological relationships of these painted wares remain to be worked out. Though we have given them separate type status, we have actually treated them (and Avenue Polychrome as well) as nonsignificant variants of a single type, which for purposes of seriation we have called Avenue Painted. This procedure was based somewhat on Phillips' analysis of whole vessels in his Ph.D. thesis, in which he found little difference in design and distribution between the two types. That such a conclusion was inadequate is now apparent.

Another inadequacy in our treatment of painted wares lies in our failure to differentiate the red on buff style of the Lower Arkansas sub-area, the so-called "intaglio" ware of Dellinger and Dickinson (1940, p. 134).

Relationships Outside Survey Area. The only other named red on buff pottery in the Southeast is Hiwassee Island Red on Buff of southeastern Tennessee, which was first illustrated by Moore (Moore, 1915, pl. VIII) and Harrington (Harrington, 1922, pl. LXII). The latter recognized that it preceded the complex he called Cherokee and which is now the Dallas Focus. The data presented on the excavations at Hiwassee Island (Lewis and Kneberg, 1946, pp. 90–94) strongly indicate that it is late within the Hiwassee Island component, although the authors do not seem to have reached this conclusion. This same pottery type has been found in the Guntersville Basin. It is extremely localized and as far as is known has no close relatives in style or shape elsewhere in the eastern United States.

As long as it is open season for cultural migratory movements or dispersions without evidence in intervening areas, which would put most bird flights to shame (Ford and Quimby, 1945, p. 95; Webb and Snow, 1945, p. 332; Newell and Krieger, 1949, pp. 231–32), Griffin would like to transport this type from the Tarascan area. In 1943 and again in 1946 he found the resemblance of a red on buff ware from the Chupicuaro area in the collections of the Museo Nacional in Mexico City to be most provocative. The shapes include a constricted mouth bowl with the rim area bearing a red painted band. There is strong use of cross-hatched and small triangular areas. Similar designs are also found to the north at La Quemada. In this same area there is a black polished ware that has shape, surface finish, handles, and a broad incised decoration that is suggestive of Ramey Incised and Powell Plain of the Old Village level at Cahokia. Unfortunately, Hiwassee Island Red on Buff does not occur at Cahokia nor are the Old Village types found in eastern Tennessee.

Outside of the Hiwassee Island Red on Buff in the eastern marches of Middle Mississippi distribution, there are no resident red on buff types in that area. Considering the extensive excavations carried on during the thirties in eastern Tennessee, central and east Georgia, and in northern Alabama the absence of red on buff and white painted pottery must be given considerable weight. Red and white vessels have been found at Moundville but are very rare and by their shape suggest a connection with the northern part of the Survey Area (Moore, 1905, fig. 15).

Painting, other than negative painting, is rare in the Cumberland and Lower Ohio. In southern Illinois there is some slight extension of painted types. In the Cahokia area and up the Illinois River, painting is very rare. In southeast Missouri direct painting sometimes is found on vessels which are also negative painted.

In the Mississippi Valley south of the Survey Area and west into the "Caddo" area painted vessels of Mississippi styles are very rare and such painting is not a part of the ceramic complex. A red and white painted vessel from the Medley Place is almost certainly an importation from southeast Missouri (Lemley and Dickinson, 1937, pl. 3, *3*. The vessel was incorrectly numbered *3* on the plates, see legend for *4*).

Thus, on a distributional basis, it can be argued that direct painting was a late development which did not accompany the early spread of Middle Mississippi ceramic ideas and did not have sufficient appeal to spread widely during the latter part of the Mississippi occupation of the northern Survey Area.

Chronological Position. Mississippi Period (C–A), with maximum probably falling well after time B.

NODENA RED AND WHITE

(Figs. 90, *h*, *k–m*; 103, *q–t*; 111, *a–d*, *i*, *k*; 112, *a–b*, *d–e*, *g–n*)

Type not previously described.

Paste and Surface Finish. Same as Carson Red on Buff.

Decoration. Same as Carson Red on Buff, with the addition of a heavy, white, slip-like paint applied to the buff areas. (See remarks above on Carson Red on Buff.) If there are significant differences in design between the two types, these remain to be worked out. The sherds indicated a greater use of the alternating vertical panel motive in Nodena, but this is not borne out by the study of whole vessels.

Form. Same as Carson Red on Buff, except that sherd collections showed a predominance of bowls over bottles. Thirteen out of the 20 rim sherds available indicated a fairly deep curved-sided bowl with an average diameter of 32.6 cm.

Discussion. See remarks under Carson Red on Buff. The more southerly distribution of Nodena and the apparent predominance of bowl forms in the sherds are possibly related facts since the bottle form in general is practically nonexistent in the southern part of the Survey Area. However, the sample is too small to permit any far-reaching conclusions.

AVENUE POLYCHROME

(Figs. 90, *n–p*; 113, *f*)

Type not previously described.

Paste and Surface Finish. Same as Nodena Red and White, with addition of a thin dark stain applied to portions usually left unslipped in that type.

Decoration. Primarily wide bands or zones of red and white separated by narrower bands of "black" mentioned above. Patterns seem to be largely encircling bands, but other simple geometric zoning is also indicated. Spiral, meander, and swastika spiral patterns are known from whole vessels.

Form. There are only 2 rim sherds and these appear to be from simple curved-sided bowls. Body sherds also indicate either a globular bowl form or bottle or jar body. Vessel photographs show same general range of shapes as Carson Red on Buff and Nodena Red and White.

Discussion. See comments on Carson Red on Buff and Nodena Red and White, particularly the latter. All these painted types are closely related, and it will take a great deal more information than we at present possess to differentiate them areally or chronologically.

HOLLYWOOD WHITE FILMED

(Fig. 90, *g*)

Type not previously described.

Paste. Same as Old Town Red and painted types already described.

Surface Finish. White slip, tending to cream or buff when thinly applied or worn. Only an occasional sherd has both sides slipped. Many sherds are probably simply from the white portions of Nodena Red and White and Avenue Polychrome. A few vessel photographs, however, show that an all-over white slip was sometimes used, particularly in the Lower Arkansas River area.

Form. A bowl form is indicated by the fact that several sherds are slipped on both sides. Several rim sherds from the Hollywood Site suggest a large (oral diameter, 34 cm.) flared-sided bowl with flat lip and rim. One sherd suggests a very small bottle neck.

Thickness. Average, 6.3 cm.; range, 4 to 10 cm. All of the sherds from the Hollywood Site (13–O–10) are very thick, ca. 10 cm., and have been subjected to subsequent firing or burning.

Base. One fragment from West (14–O–10) may possibly be a circular flat base.

Appendages. None, except for a single small node on the upper part of the bottle neck from Owens (14–O–2).

Discussion. This was set up merely as a tentative type to embrace white-slipped sherds — some of which undoubtedly belong to Nodena Red and White or Avenue Polychrome, but since we know that in some cases white paint was applied without any other color, it seems logical to give it type status, at least for the time being.

WALLACE INCISED

(Figs. 91, *a–d*; 97, *d–f*)

Type not previously described.

Paste and Surface Finish. Same as Neeley's Ferry Plain, except that the ware is thinner and colors run more to buffs and reddish buffs (Vinaceous Buff, 17′ ′ ′*d* and Vinaceous Cinnamon, 13′ ′*b*) than is usual in that type.

Decoration. *Treatment.* Incising with occasional brushing and punctation. Incision is by means of a broad, round, or flat-ended instrument that produces a characteristic shallow U-shaped line, considerably broader than is usual for incised types in the area. Lines average 4 mm. wide (range, 3 to 8 mm.) by about 1 mm. in depth. There is a characteristic tendency when two lines meet at an angle for them not to intersect, instead of which one of them is stopped by a slight extra pressure of the tool, making a very definite, often squarish, termination. Occasionally, brushing is employed apparently as a background to bring out the design by contrasting smooth and roughened areas. Apparently, the designs are so arranged that the simple figures depicted are brought out by the roughened areas (see Marksville Stamped and other early types where the reverse is the case). Rarely, punctations are used for the same purpose resulting in a style closely related to Owens Punctated.

Design. Both recti- and curvilinear patterns occur, the former usually on the rim area, the latter more often but not always, on the body. Most common design on the rim area consists of parallel rows of oblique lines forming line-filled triangles, as in Barton Incised. Another rectilinear arrangement consists of groups of oblique lines slanting from the lip with a plain area between. Principal curvilinear rim design consists of broad shallow concentric festoons, or its reverse, concentric arches.

Most, if not all, body sherds have curvilinear arrangements of concentric circular elements. Presumably, some of these body sherds are associated with rims having rectilinear designs described above, but there are no sherds including both areas so it cannot be stated with certainty. On the other hand, it is clear from the large percentage of rim sherds in the collections (38% of the total) that most vessels with decorated rims have plain bodies.

Form. Predominant shape appears to be a rather large deep bowl (or shallow jar) with rather pronounced flaring rim. The rim takes off from the body in a gentle recurve or quite often at a sharp angle making a definite break at the point of maximum constriction. This shape is quite distinct from the standard Mississippi jar so common in the area, in fact it is the shape as much as the character of the decoration that sets the type off from Barton Incised which from point of view of design alone it much resembles.

The deep bowl with punctated rim mentioned above is a rare shape and may be assignable to another type yet unrecognized.

Size. The few available rims large enough for measurement give average oral diameters of 35 cm. (range, 20 to 50 cm.), slightly larger than average for the "standard" jar of Barton Incised, etc.

Thickness. Average, 5.6 mm. (range, 4 to 7 mm.) which is significantly thinner than the dominant shell-tempered types in the area (cf. 7.7 mm. for Neeley's Ferry Plain, 6.2 to 7.8 mm. for Barton Incised, depending on locality).

Rim. Marked tendency for rims to break off along line of maximum constriction (i.e., base of rim area). From this point to lip averages 4.5 cm. Some rims are straight, but in most there is an exterior concavity accentuating the flare. Only rim elaboration noted is a series of shallow indentations on the outer lip edge giving a wavy piecrust effect. This occurs in 27% of rims, most of which, however, are from one site, Dupree (16–L–6).

Lip. There is a general tendency for rims to be slightly thinned at the lip edge. Lips are about evenly divided between round and flattened.

Appendages. None in collections.

Discussion. A rather well-characterized type (if definition is kept fairly strict) distinct from the dominant Mississippi types (in St. Francis and Memphis sub-areas particularly) in color, thickness, character of decoration, and shape.

Distribution. In preliminary sortings, a lot of material was classified as Wallace Incised on the possession of wide-incised lines alone. On bringing all these sherds together, it was apparent that the definitive characteristics of the type were present only on a half dozen sites in the Lower Arkansas–White River area, but on these sites the type occurred in significant strength, was in fact the dominant decorative type in four of them.

Quapaw Hypothesis. This very restricted distribution corresponding so closely with the territory occupied by the Quapaw in late times (end of seventeenth century) combined with the fact that trade material was found on or near the Menard Site (one of the 4 sites in question) encourages the hypothesis that Wallace Incised was made by the Quapaw Indians, a theory which will be discussed at length in another section.

When Wallace Incised was found the first week of the Survey in the Menard area, Griffin, who was familiar with Oneota pottery, was at once struck with the resemblance in technique to the incising found in some of the Orr Focus centers, at sites attributable to the Missouri Indians and to some of the Top Layer pottery from the Ozark Bluff shelters. The presence of small thumbnail flint scrapers on these same sites near Menard, also characteristic of Oneota, added to the feeling of relationship. A more vague connection could be seen to the incising of Fort Ancient vessels.

The characteristic medium wide, squarish incising typical of Wallace Incised has some interesting connections with styles both within and outside of the Survey Area. Some of the examples of Rhodes Incised have a somewhat similar technique, though the total effect and associated shapes and other features are quite different. Farther south in the Survey Area the technique of a provisional type, Stokes Bayou Incised, is not too dissimilar, and there is some overlap which caused initial confusion in sorting. It is also a common style of incising in the late Mississippi complex at Deasonville (Collins, 1932, pl. 5, *a–k*).

Within the area and complexes recognized as Caddoan, there are analogues to Wallace Incised in the types known as Foster Trailed Incised and Keno Trailed. Foster has some connection with the design found on the Survey Area Rhodes Incised and seems to belong to an earlier time period than does Keno Trailed which comes into the historic period.

Chronological Position. On the basis of the Survey strata cuts at Menard and Massey (see pp. 265–73), as well as the position indicated by the comparative statements above, Wallace Incised is clearly seen to be one of the latest decorated types in the Survey Area. This has led two of the authors (Phillips and Griffin) to feel that the terminal periods of the seriation chart for the Lower Arkansas sub-area are slightly out of line. On this chart (fig. 18) the maximum for Wallace Incised falls at about time B. Phillips and Griffin would expect it to fall well within the late Mississippi Period (B–A). This apparent discrepancy is discussed in a later section (p. 229).

OWENS PUNCTATED

(Fig. 97, *g–i*)

Type not previously described.

Paste and Surface Finish. Same as Neeley's Ferry; also a few very fine shell-tempered Bell Plain paste sherds.

Decoration. Fine incised lines both curved and straight, enclosing bands of fine, scattered punctations. In general, sherds are too fragmentary to recognize design, but curving bands of punctations outlined by incising and separated from each other by plain areas are common. A chevron design formed by alternating plain and punctated bands is also present.

Form. The very few rims included in this type belong to jars, probably the usual Mississippi variety, with average oral diameters of 25 cm. (range, 18 to 34 cm.) Most of the jars have the usual simple recurve but one (Silver City, 20–O–5) has a definite neck or collar joining at an angle with the body. A bowl form is perhaps also suggested.

Appendages. One small node-like triangular lug, flattened on top, and projecting on a line with the lip. The contour of the upper surface is outlined with incising.

Discussion. Sherds are small and fragmentary, and it is to be doubted whether we are actually dealing with a "type" or merely with a collection of sherds which share similar *observable* characteristics. Its irregular and scattered distribution makes one skeptical as also its occurrence on clay-tempered ware, and coarse and fine shell-tempered ware.

Relationships Outside Survey Area. This type has connections into the "Caddo" area and has been called Menard Punctate Banded by C. H. Webb, who points out that it is sometimes found with Natchitoches Engraved and Keno Trailed, two historic "Caddo" types (Webb, 1945, pp. 69 and 80). The predominance of this type in certain portions of the

Survey Area is perhaps a reflection of its connection to the historic "Caddo" type. A further indication of the lateness of Owens Punctated is its appearance at Keno (Moore, 1909, figs. 61, 68, 143). To the south and east of the Survey Area, related types are found on sites associated with the complex formerly called Tunica (Ford, 1936, figs. 21, *i*; 23, *g*). They were also included as a portion of the shell-tempered part of the "Deasonville complex" (Collins, 1932, pl. 6; Ford, 1936, fig. 30, *g*).

To the north of the Survey Area a zoned punctate decoration is found on Middle Mississippi pottery in the Lower Ohio Valley. This style is not described from the Cahokia area or farther north, nor does it appear in the middle Ohio Valley, in the Cumberland, northern Alabama, or eastern Tennessee.

A handful of clay-tempered sherds with similar decoration suggests the possibility of a local ancestry for the type. As a general statement, the type could be regarded as a descendant of the zoned punctates which go back as far as Churupa and Orleans Punctated.

Chronological Position. On the seriation graphs this type is scattered from C to A. At the Menard Site Cut A, it is definitely late (fig. 18). Our best guess at the moment, based on far too little information, is that Owens is a late Mississippi type on the same time level as Wallace Incised.

LELAND INCISED

(Figs. 91, *e–n*; 99, *i–k*, *m–n*)

Type not previously described.

Paste. *Temper.* Fine particles of shell, very little of which shows on the surface. Some sherds show fine particles of carbonized matter.

Texture. Fine and homogeneous. In some examples it is difficult to see any shell particles which makes the type difficult to sort from some of the finer clay-tempered types of the Coles Creek complex. In coarser examples, which are in a minority, the cross section appears laminated as in many moderately coarse to coarse shell-tempered types.

Color. Normally variable but is comparable to that of Bell Plain.

Surface Finish. Well smoothed and generally polished. Almost all of the examples show some trace of polishing, the finer ones showing a highly lustrous, generally black finish. Such examples are sometimes harder than the thumbnail, probably because of the more compact surface, but the majority of sherds fall within the normal range for shell-tempered pottery generally.

Decoration. *Treatment.* Generally speaking, the incised lines made with a rounded implement are of the type sometimes called "trailing," and the vessels were polished over the incisions. The lines range from 1 to 5 mm. wide, with the majority falling somewhere around 2 mm., and they are rarely more than 1 mm. deep — in other words, medium wide and shallow. Curvilinear lines tend to be broader and less deep in proportion to breadth than straight lines. Narrower lines tend to be less evenly made. Occasionally, pairs of lines are filled with fine engraved cross-hatching, similar to that of Walls Engraved but finer in scale.

Design. A considerable number of sherds show several parallel horizontal lines around the outer rim, only one of which is large enough to show further decoration lower down, and in this case the design is rectilinear. There seems to be a high probability that some bowls had no further decoration. Other rims have a beginning of curvilinear designs formed by single, paired, or groups of lines. These are usually found on sherds which have only one or no horizontal line on the rim below the lip.

The commonest design is a spiral meander, probably made up of four spirals. Small circles are sometimes used as nuclei for the spirals, and there are other incidental figures that seem to have been used to fill up space left vacant by the basic meander pattern. Only one sherd shows definite use of a rectilinear motive of nested triangles. Several sherds have festoons depending from the rim, but these were probably combined with the spiral meander pattern. A simple pattern is also present which possesses the elongated meanders characteristic of Fatherland Incised. In view of the close relationship to Natchezan types, it is important to ascertain the number of lines

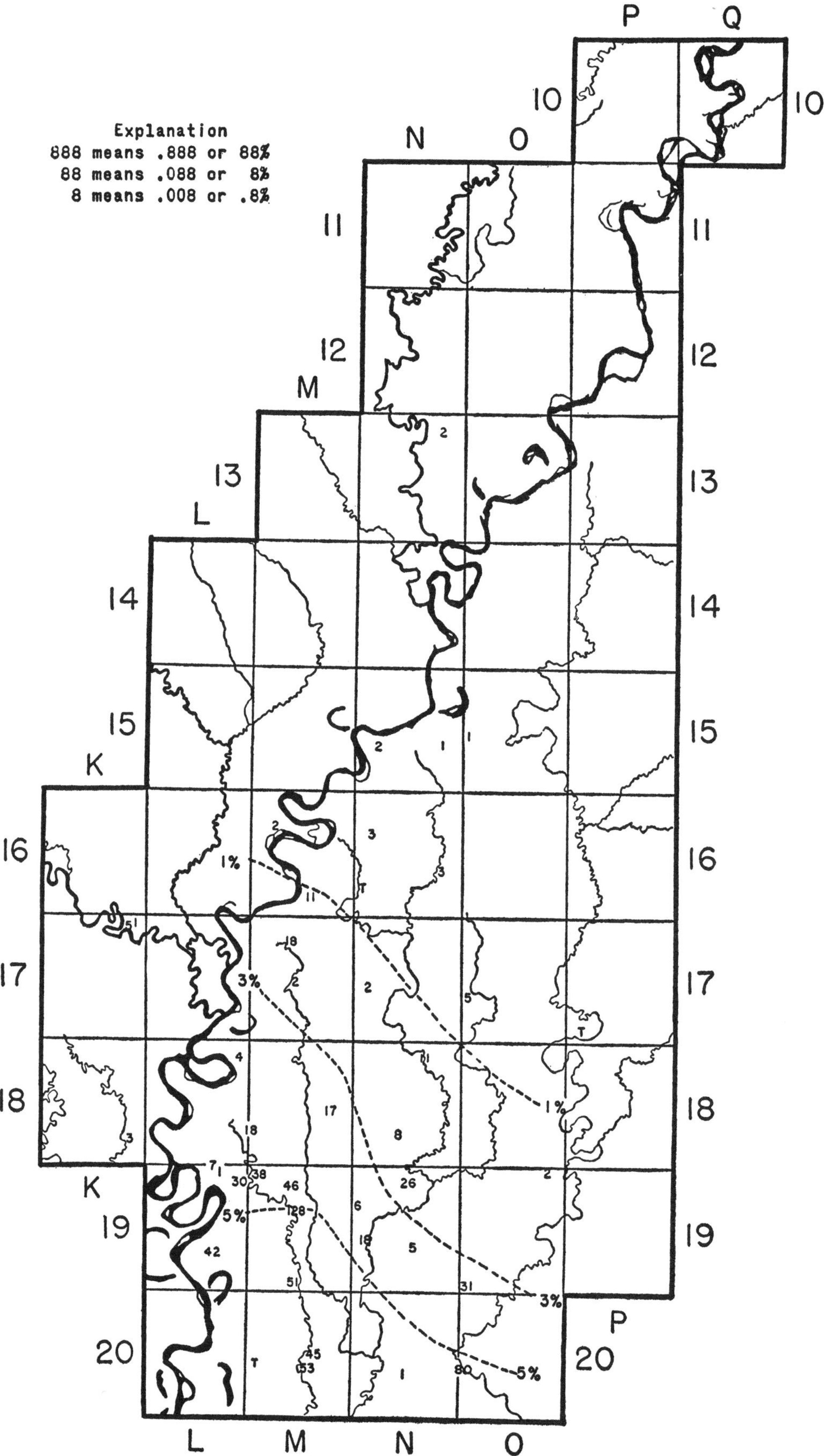

FIG. 14. Percentage frequency distribution of the type Leland Incised.

which make up the bands forming the design. In the examples where this could be determined the result is as follows:

1 line	8 examples
2 lines	19 examples
3 lines	14 examples

Form. *Rim.* The majority of rims are thickened more often exteriorly but occasionally on the interior, sometimes both. The thickened portion, which is about 1 to 2 cm. high, is generally defined by an incised line on the exterior, occasionally on the interior as well. Heretofore, rims with this line, or lines, but with no further decoration showing have been classified as Bell Plain. A few examples, in addition to the exterior line have a row of punctations just above it, on the exterior portion of the rolled or thickened upper rim section. This is so far localized at the Jaketown Site (20–O–1). Two examples, which have a line on the lip thus approximating the "Haynes Bluff" type rim, are from simple bowls with vertical or slightly incurved rims. Such incurving is occasionally rather abrupt giving the effect of a so-called cambered rim. The bowls range in size from 9 to 21 cm. in diameter with the average of 20 examples being 18.4 cm. The thickness is from 4 to 9 mm., with an average of 5.4 mm. Most of the bowls are round bottomed, but published examples indicate that a flat circular base is not uncommon.

Appendages. There are no lugs, handles, or effigy features connected with this type.

Distribution. The southerly distribution of Leland Incised in the Survey Area is clearly brought out by the percentage frequency map, figure 14. In working down the river from north to south, we have evidently just got into the northern periphery of its distribution. The "center" of the type is probably still farther south, in the general vicinity of the Lower Yazoo River. More than half the sites and about 90% of the specimens attributed to this type are from Tiers 19 and 20. Since most of our collecting has been on the east side of the river, our present concentration of the type is naturally in that area.

Discussion. The relationship with Fatherland, Natchez, and Bayogoula Incised is very close, particularly to the first two. The differences seem to be mainly in the rim and lip treatment and possibly in vessel shape, although our collections hardly allow a dogmatic statement on the point. In the original definition of Fatherland Incised, Ford expressly states that rims are "usually unthickened" (Ford, 1936, p. 55), and the cross sections to illustrate rim shapes have only one thickened rim. This is also true of one of the platform base jars from Fatherland Mound C. Quimby's brief description does not refer to the rim or lip treatment, but his illustrations do not have the thickened rim. This rim specialization is related to that found on pottery of Ford's former Tunica complex (Ford, 1936, fig. 20). There is the possibility that as the historic horizon is approached this specialization dropped out in favor of the simple rim.

The distribution of this Leland-Fatherland-Natchez design style suggests that prehistoric Natchez extended farther north. Quimby lists it from the Fatherland and Foster sites of Adams County, Mississippi, and the Ring and Glass sites of Warren County, Mississippi. To these may be added the Lewis Plantation of Adams County, Mississippi; Oak Bend Landing, Warren County, Mississippi; and Neblett Landing of Bolivar County, Mississippi.

Very similar vessels are also found in sites usually attributed to eastern Caddoan-speaking people such as Glendora, Ouachita Parish (Moore, 1909, figs. 58–60, 62, and 80), Keno (Moore, 1909, figs. 145, 153, 154, 156, and an additional vessel from the same site in Buffalo Museum), Ward (Moore, 1909, figs. 161 and 164), and Seven Pines Landing (Moore, 1909, fig. 173), all in Morehouse Parish, Louisiana. At Turkey Point Landing, Franklin Parish (Moore, 1913, fig. 16), and at Canebrake Mounds, Madison Parish (Moore, 1909, figs. 20 and 23), additional vessels related to Leland Incised were recovered.

Farther west a considerable degree of similarity of decorative style can be seen in the Titus Focus and to a diminished degree in the Frankston Focus. There is also a connection into the Belcher Focus or to a late descendant in the area, for Fatherland Incised has been found at the Battle Site (Webb, 1945, p. 68).

In the Lower Arkansas Valley at Menard Mound, Moore found a number of vessels that are either Leland or Fatherland (Moore,

1908a, figs. 7, 8, 10, 11, and 19). A good-sized sherd of Fatherland Incised has been found by the University of Chicago–Illinois State Museum excavations at Starved Rock–La Salle County, Illinois, which is surely a reflection of the early French trips into the Lower Valley which had Fort St. Louis as one of their bases.[16]

At Moundville the platform base appears with a decoration engraved on the characteristic Moundville filmed ware and has a general resemblance to Leland (Moore, 1907, fig. 15), while a simple bowl form (Moore, 1905, fig. 75) has a two-line swastika design also suggestive of connections to the type under discussion. Numerous vessels at Moundville have a decoration of multiple curving lines which resemble Bayogoula Incised or Chickachae Combed of the southern Mississippi–Louisiana area.

There are also design relationships along the Gulf Coast to the east in the Fort Walton Period at sites such as Point Washington (cf. Quimby, 1942, pl. 14, *4*, with Moore, 1901, figs. 80 and 81, also 87) and Chipola Cut-off (Moore, 1903b, fig. 117). These are perhaps some of the culminations of design and vessel-shape relationships between the Lower Mississippi Valley and the northwest coast of Florida which persisted over many years.

Ford is of the opinion that this group of late decorations derive from Marksville Incised through later types such as Yokena Incised and French Fork Incised.

Chronological Position. According to the seriation graphs, Leland Incised tends to cluster around time B, while the closely related types of Fatherland, Natchez, and Bayogoula Incised would be at time A (A.D. 1650) and later.

ARCOLA INCISED

(Fig. 91, *q–u*)

Tentative type.

Paste and Surface Finish. Same as Neeley's Ferry Plain, except that it is on the paste of the southern variant of Neeley's Ferry, which is somewhat thinner, and the surface is often well-smoothed before the decoration was applied.

Decoration. *Treatment.* Incising with some degree of variation. It is usually a medium wide to narrow V-shaped line, but sometimes is medium wide with a U-shaped cross section. The decoration is finer in scale, the lines are more closely spaced, and in the majority of cases more carefully executed than in Barton Incised.

Design. Predominantly rectilinear lines on the shoulder area forming line-filled triangles similar to Barton Incised. Horizontal lines sometimes encircle the base of the undecorated rim, setting it apart from the shoulder area which carries the decoration.

Form. *Lip.* Usually rounded and about the same thickness as the rim. Some lips are thickened slightly like the typical Fatherland lips.

Rim. Belong to jars and are slightly flaring to vertical. A typical rim is short and vertical with a strongly profiled shoulder. The rims are almost always plain.

Base. Usually rounded.

Discussion. An associate of Leland Incised and related to Stokes Bayou, Wallace, Blanchard, and Oliver. It is also related to Barton Incised but is a shoulder area and not a rim decoration. Crossed lines, which are common in Barton Incised in the St. Francis are very rare in Arcola. This is also closely related to Manchac Incised of the Plaquemine-Natchez sequence and should be the intermediate form between Barton and Manchac Incised.

Distribution. As defined at present it is entirely in the 19, 20, and 21 Tiers. Further work in this area and to the south will eventually call for a revision of this and the related types.

Chronological Position. Clusters around time position B on the seriation graphs.

PROVISIONAL TYPES

For reasons set forth on page 69, the types described in the following pages are being held in a provisional status pending further information and clarification of their relationships to types already described. It seems worthwhile to describe them briefly, since they have to some extent entered into the seriation and

[16] Courtesy of Dr. Kenneth G. Orr.

stratigraphic studies presented in this report, as follows:

Thomas Plain — included with Baytown Plain.
Blue Lake Cord-marked — included with Twin Lakes Cord-marked.
Twin Lakes Fabric-impressed — included with Withers Fabric-impressed.
Bowie Plain — included with Baytown Plain.
Yates Net-impressed — not included.
Manly Punctated — not included.
Mound Place Incised — treated as a type on the graphs, but subsequently relegated to provisional status.
Blanchard Incised — not included.
Oliver Incised — not included.
Stokes Bayou Incised — not included.

THOMAS PLAIN

Tentative type, not previously described.

Paste. *Method of Manufacturing.* Coil sherds observed.

Tempering. Sand, by definition, is the primary tempering material, having a considerable range in size of particles but in general falling within the medium-to-coarse range of 0.25 to 1.0 mm. in diameter as defined by Anna Shepard (1936, p. 444). In addition to this basic ingredient there are often inclusions, sometimes quite coarse and lumpy, of clay particles and tiny stones or gravel particles.

Texture. The texture of the paste is essentially soft and friable, crumbling beneath pliers when tested for fracture. The sand temper produces a granular paste which often tends to something of a porous appearance in cross section. Clay is in general well wedged and the tempering is more or less homogeneous in distribution.

Hardness. 2.5; range, 2 to 3.

Color. Lighter colors run to orange-buff or Cinnamon shades (Cinnamon, 15″; Pinkish Cinnamon, 15″*b*; Orange Cinnamon, 13″; Vinaceous Cinnamon, 13″*b*; and Light Vinaceous Cinnamon, 13″*d*). Occasional reddish-colored sherds also are to be seen as Testaceous (9″) and Vinaceous Tawny (11″).

Darker sherds fall in the Mouse Gray (15″‴) shades, in both its darker and lighter values. Very often the interior of the cinnamon-colored sherds are of the Mouse Gray shades, though this is by no means the rule.

Lighter sherds seem to be somewhat more common than the gray ones.

Cores may be light but are characteristically quite dark, firing often penetrating but slightly.

Surface Finish. Surfaces are generally even, but rarely smoothed and never burnished. Surface texture is generally quite rough and gritty to the touch. The most typical finish appears granular or slightly pitted as if the sand were not compacted into the surface or as if the clay itself weathered away from the tempering particles.

Form. *Vessel Shape.* On the basis of the very scanty information available to us, a simple open bowl with average diameter of 26 cm. (range, 24 to 34 cm.) is the most characteristic shape, making up about two-thirds of the measurable sherds. Other shapes occurring are (1) globular jars with recurved rim, average diameter, 21 cm. at the mouth; (2) jar or bowl with flat insloped walls and small mouth; (3) shallow bowl with recurved rim, average diameter at mouth, 20 cm.; and (4) small bowls with incurved sides and small mouth, average diameter, 12 cm.

Thickness. Average, 6.5 mm.; range, 4 to 10 mm.

Rim. Rims are generally simple and unelaborated. A few, however, are thickened by a strip of clay attached to inner or outer rim wall adjacent to the lip. These for the most part correspond to the rim treatments of Larto Red Filmed. One rim sherd of an open bowl or beaker has a slight groove on the exterior rim wall adjacent to the lip and is reminiscent of the single incised line so frequently encountered on some types from the Survey Area. A few rims of simple bowls are finished by turning down the ragged rim edge to the interior, or more frequently the exterior, of the body wall, achieving a very rough uneven fold or roll.

Lip. Rounded lips seem to be most common, but flat and pinched or pointed lips as well as insloped and outsloped lips occur. No lip decoration was observed.

Base. None present. A round or only slightly flattened base undifferentiated in general thickness or appearance is inferred.

Appendages. None.

Discussion. At best, Thomas Plain is a very unsatisfactory type composed of a miscellany of heterogeneous plain sherds which share in common the like element of sand-tempering.

Although such sherds are scattered throughout the Survey Area, they are for the most part fragmentary body sherds that do not admit of intelligible classification. Only in a few sites centered in the quadrangles 15–O, 15–P, 16–O, and 16–P are there enough rims to be relatively assured that we are actually dealing with a definable type, and it is on the basis of these that the present description is written.

Many sherds which would normally be classified as Baytown Plain are opened to question from the point of view of inclusions of sand, but if the typical dense, contorted Baytown paste with large clay-tempering fragments were observed along with sand, these sherds were considered to be Baytown. Thus it is sometimes a rather arbitrary procedure of sorting, and it is probable that some Baytown Plain sherds are misclassified as Thomas Plain and vice versa. Lacking further information, it seems proper to consider Thomas Plain as centered in the four quadrangles mentioned, but with a wider distribution indicated.

Relationship Within Survey Area. Thomas Plain seems to be closely related to Blue Lake Cord-marked. The differences between Blue Lake Cord-marked and Furrs and Tishomingo Cord-marked are very like the differences between Thomas Plain and Baldwin Plain and Tishomingo Plain. Also the sorting difficulties between Thomas Plain and Baytown Plain are closely paralleled by the difficulties of sorting Blue Lake from Mulberry Creek Cord-marked. The center of distribution of the type is the same as for Blue Lake Cord-marked.

Chronological Position. The type appears in the Tchula and early Baytown periods (G–E) in the eastern part of the Survey Area only.

Relationship Outside Survey Area. There are certain ill-defined relationships of Thomas Plain to Baldwin Plain and Tishomingo Plain as described by Jennings, 1941, for northeastern Mississippi, but relationships are not great enough to consider them at this stage as identical types. An observable difference between Thomas and Baldwin is the thickness of the paste, being 6.5 mm. in the former and 8 mm. in the latter. In Thomas Plain simple bowls are the most common form, but are not mentioned for Baldwin. No burnished sherds were observed for Thomas and no lines of punctation about the rims. Mica flakes do not seem to occur in the Thomas material. Color of Baldwin is warmer and redder than the buffs of Thomas.

The same differences in vessel form are to be noted with respect to Jennings' Tishomingo Plain. Thickness of the two types is also at variance with only 4.4 to 5.0 mm. recorded for the latter type.

BLUE LAKE CORD-MARKED

Tentative type, not previously described.

Paste. Same as Thomas Plain.

Surface Finish. Paddled with cord-wrapped implement from lip to base, leaving impressions of twisted cords of unidentified material, ranging in size from 1 to 3 mm. in diameter. Cords are normally close-spaced, averaging 2.9 cords per centimeter (range, 2 to 5 cm.).

Direction of cord impressions on rims is as follows in order of frequency: right oblique, normal, parallel; left oblique, two directions. Marked divergence is shown from Mulberry Creek Cord-marked in which the direction normal to rim was clearly dominant and parallel to rim, very rare.

Form. *Vessel Shape.* There is insufficient material (101 rims) for anything but the most tentative statements. The few rims large enough for shape determination show that the following shapes are present, in order of frequency: (1) Simple curved-sided bowl; (2) Deep bowl or beaker with straight or incurved rim, (3) Jar with globular or subglobular body and recurved rim. Sherds are not large enough for reliable estimates of size.

Thickness. Average, 6.1 mm.; range, 5 to 8 mm.

Rim. Cord-marking is normally carried up onto the rim to, and sometimes including, the lip. No exceptions to this rule were noted (cf. smooth band about rim in Mulberry Creek Cord-marked). Only a very small percentage of rims show any other sort of elaboration or decoration, as follows: nicked or notched rims, 5%; rim folds, 4%. Notching is of a type that consists of an irregularly spaced series of sharp cuts across the lip approximately at right angles to it. For rim folds, see description of Mulberry Creek Cord-marked. These are substantially the same, but appear to run somewhat smaller in size, average width being 1.5 cm. Three out of four rim folds are cord-marked.

Lip. Majority of lips are smooth, only about 20% showing traces of cord-markings. Smooth lips are normally round or only slightly flattened, though a few smooth flat lips were noted. Cord-marked lips are usually flat as might be expected. Thinning of the rim resulting in a pinched or pointed lip is a common tendency in both smooth and cord-marked lips.

Base. Absence of basal sherds indicates that most, if not all, vessels had round or only slightly flattened bases.

Appendages. None.

Discussion. Description is based primarily on material from a small number of sites on the eastern border of the Survey Area in the general vicinity of the point where the Tallahatchie River, and its confluent the Yocona, enter the Yazoo Basin (quadrangles 15–O, 15–P, 16–O, and 16–P, particularly the last). This is the only part of the area in which sand-tempering occurs as a consistent and important element in the pottery complex. There is perhaps a secondary center in quadrangle 13–P, not far from the point where the Coldwater enters the Basin. All three streams flow out of the hill section of northeastern Mississippi, the home of comparable sand-tempered types (see below). Apart from these two centers, in various scattered locations in the northern part of the area, sandy-textured sherds occur in small numbers usually as minority components of larger Mulberry Creek Cord-marked samples. It is impossible in many cases to judge whether it is the result of the use of pottery clay containing substantial amounts of sand. When one or two sherds of this nature occur in a large sample of ordinary Mulberry Creek Cord-marked with important characteristics *other than temper* corresponding exactly with that type, it would seem unreasonable not to classify them as Mulberry Creek. Such a course has been followed here with the result that material classified as Blue Lake Cord-marked has been reduced to a minimum. With more information and material, it is possible the distribution may be extended, particularly in the northern and eastern portions of the Survey Area.

Relationship Outside Survey Area. Blue Lake Cord-marked is closely related to the types Furrs Cord-marked and Tishomingo Cord-marked found by Jennings in northeastern Mississippi. However, it is not sufficiently covered by the published descriptions of these types (Jennings, 1941) nor does direct comparison with type series kindly furnished by Jennings indicate a sufficient identity. Between the two its affinities seem to lie more with Furrs than with Tishomingo. It is a coarser type than Tishomingo, significantly thicker, its impressions showing the use of heavier cords. Fossil shell or limestone-tempering (as additional to sand) seldom, if ever, occurs in Blue Lake Cord-marked. Whether volcanic tufa, found by petrographic analysis to be a further tempering addition in Tishomingo Cord-marked, is present in Blue Lake Cord-marked can only be determined by similar detailed analysis. The color of Blue Lake runs more to grays and buffs than to the "dull reds, browns, and tans" of Tishomingo. In the matter of shape, Blue Lake evidently shows greater variety, with simple curved-sided bowls with straight rims dominant in contrast to the dominant jar form and everted rim of Tishomingo.

Departures from the definition of Furrs Cord-marked are almost equally significant. Tempering of Blue Lake Cord-marked is less fine, clay particles are present in larger amounts, mica flecks are not present. Texture is not as fine and homogeneous. Color, again, is more in the range of grays and buffs than reds and browns. Blue Lake is significantly thinner than the 8-mm. average given for Furrs. In form, the same remarks given above in comparison with Tishomingo hold.

In short, while there is undoubtedly considerable overlap, and it might be difficult to sort what we are calling Blue Lake Cord-marked from either or both of Jennings' cord-marked types, it does not sufficiently resemble either for type identity. The reason, of course, is that Jennings' definitions are based on more abundant material, much of it excavated, and have had the advantage of Matson's expert analysis, with the result that he has been able to cut his divisions finer than we can hope to do at this stage of our investigation. It is necessary, therefore, to hold Blue Lake Cord-marked as a separate provisional type until more material is available. In general, sand-tempered, cord-marked pottery is common in sites of eastern Mississippi and western Alabama to within a short distance of the Gulf of Mexico. It is a companion to the fabric-impressed pottery of the same area but appears to have lasted longer. However, it does not have as wide a distribution to the east as fabric-impressed pottery.

Chronological Position. Appears in the Tchula and early Baytown periods (G–E) in the eastern part of the Survey Area only.

TWIN LAKES FABRIC-IMPRESSED

Tentative type, not previously described.

Paste. Same as Thomas Plain and Blue Lake Cord-marked.

Surface Finish. Fabric impressions of textile-wrapped paddle as all-over treatment from lip to base. Impressions are carelessly applied on soft clay surface so that it is usually impossible to make out what sort of textiles were involved and often difficult to make out any textile impressions at all. In the clearer examples a coarse-twined weave can be made out. Warps are about 5 to 8 mm. on centers, wefts average about 4.5 to the centimeter (range, 4 to 6 mm.). Sherds occasionally show deep indentation of warp lines indicating the use of heavy warps, but the superficial resemblance to impressions of coiled basketry is doubtless misleading.

Form. Insufficient sample for anything but the most tentative statements. Three shapes suggested by the few rim sherds large enough for determination are in order of frequency: (1) Bowl or jar with insloping wall, incurved or slightly recurved rim; (2) Simple curve-sided bowl; (3) Jar with recurved rim.

Rim. Rims are most commonly straight and unmodified, but there is a fairly common tendency to show poorly developed rim folds, generally small and with ill-defined lower edges, as though incidental to the process of manufacture rather than a deliberate effort at decoration. One rim shows crude oblique notching across the lip and another a row of small close-spaced punctations on the interior just below the lip.

Lip. Majority of lips are round, smooth, and slightly rolled toward the exterior producing a short roll or rim fold as described above. Next in point of frequency is a thinned or pointed lip. A few lips look as though they had been paddled with the same textile-wrapped instrument that produced the fabric impressions on the body, but in most cases the result is so crude as to be difficult to make out.

Base. No recognizable basal sherds in the collection.

Appendages. None observed.

Distribution. Same as for Thomas Plain and Blue Lake Cord-marked. Two sites, Twin Lakes (16–P–3) and Blue Lake (16–P–8) furnished the bulk of the material. But for one doubtful example from the Alma Brown Site, 17–K–7 the type seems to be absent from the western (trans-Mississippi) and southern portions of the Survey Area.

Relationship Within Survey Area. Twin Lakes Fabric-impressed is the sand-tempered counterpart of Withers Fabric-impressed. The two types are extremely similar, but for temper, and sorting is often arbitrary. Distribution of the two types is roughly similar, except that Withers covers a slightly wider area, and the important center for Withers is in the 13–P quadrangle, which is a secondary center for Twin Lakes Fabric-impressed. Nothing in typology or distribution suggests a chronological difference in favor of either type. The apparent explanation is that in certain districts sand was used for tempering as an alternative to clay in what otherwise is a typological continuum. If further information fails to reveal more significant differences, the two types ought to be amalgamated.

Relationships Outside Survey Area. The type is closely related to Jennings' Saltillo Fabric-impressed. It would have been desirable for the sake of simplicity to use that name for the material here described, but it does not sufficiently conform to Jennings' description (Jennings, 1941, p. 201). Our material is tempered with coarser sand, its texture less fine, compact, and homogeneous. Color runs more to grays and drabs than to the "warm reds, tans, and browns" (the two types can be readily sorted on color alone). Evidently, there is a greater variety of shapes in Twin Lakes, since Jennings makes no reference to bowls. The general character of the fabric impressions are also quite different, Twin Lakes being coarser, deeper, and more carelessly applied, an effect that may be due to paddling on a softer clay surface.

This sand-tempered, fabric-impressed surface is found south of Lee and Monroe counties, Mississippi, as recorded by Jennings. The U.S.N.M. has pottery from seven sites in Oktibbeha County in the area around Starksville which was collected by Lewis E. Long with sherds of the Wheeler and Alexander series as well as an early Woodland complex of plain, cord-marked, fabric-impressed, check stamp, and a few Hopewellian sherds. The next county south, Noxubee, has fabric-impressed, sand-tempered pottery (Griffin, 1939, p. 162). In Lauderdale County, Mississippi, in 1925, H. B. Collins excavated a small Hopewellian mound containing a sheet copper and silver conjoined tube ornament and flake knives identical in every respect with the flake knives from Flint Ridge in Ohio (Collins, 1926, p. 92). A preliminary study of the pottery from the site by Griffin shows a predominance of sand-tempered types and a minority of clay. Fabric-impressed, sand- and clay-tempered sherds are part of the group of malleated surfaced sherds.

In the Guntersville Basin of northern Alabama, Benson Fabric-marked is a very early sand-tempered type. It was found at only three sites in the Pickwick Basin, especially at Lu^{v}65. In west-central Tennessee most of the fabric-impressed pottery from Eva Focus sites is sand-tempered. In Georgia and adjacent areas this type has been called Dunlap Fabric-impressed.

Relationship to the type Long Branch Fabric-marked from northern Alabama is discussed under Withers Fabric-impressed.

Chronological Position. Appears in the Tchula and early Baytown periods (G–E) in the eastern part of the Survey Area.

BOWIE PLAIN

Type not previously described.

Paste. *Tempering.* The basic tempering material consists of clay particles, usually lumpy and of varying sizes, quite often showing up at the surface as irregular, light tan patches against the darker gray or red paste color. Very commonly quantities of sand occur along with the clay, giving the appearance of sand-tempering, and in some sherds at least there seems to be more sand than clay. Sand particles range from about medium to very coarse (0.25 to 1.0 mm.; some particles as large as 2 mm. observed).

Texture. Texture is generally dense and compact, with an irregular fracture and contorted appearance resulting from large tempering particles. Pockets as evidence for poor wedging are often observed. Those sherds without sand or only minor amounts of it are often smooth and "soapy" to the touch like Baytown Plain.

Hardness. Average, 2.7; range, 2.0 to 3.0.

Color. Surface colors tend primarily to warm oranges, especially Cinnamon (15″) in both its lighter and darker shades, with the duller buff shades as Avellaneous (17‴*b*) and Fawn Color (13‴) also occurring. Several sherds exhibit a striking pinkish shade (Japan Rose, 9″*b*).

Darker colors are less frequent and run to varying shades of Mouse Gray (15′′′′′).

A few sherds have light-colored cores, but firing penetration is usually almost negligible, and cores are primarily dark.

Thickness. Average, 6.4 cm.; range, 4.5 to 9 cm.

Surface Finish. Surfaces are never polished but in general are well smoothed on both exterior and interior. A few, however, have rather irregular undulating surfaces and occasional irregularities caused by protrusion of large tempering particles.

Form. *Vessel Shape.* The primary vessel shape is a curved-sided bowl comprising 83.5% of the measurable rims in the collections. About one-third of these are simple bowls with average diameter at the mouth of 28.6 cm. (range, 16 to 40 cm.). Most of the rest are elaborated by the addition of a rim fillet to the exterior wall and are considerably larger in oral diameter (35.2 cm. average; range, 26 to 38 cm.).

A very shallow bowl or plate is fairly common (ca. 10% of measurable rims). In appearance its rim is identical with the bowl above, but its average diameter is smaller by 8 cm.

Of the 210 rims in the sample, there are 6 rims of incurved bowls (average diameter, 28 cm.; range, 24 to 38 cm.) and 4 of jars with recurved rims (average diameter, 27 cm.; range, 20 to 34 cm.). A bowl with slightly flaring sides is also indicated by two small rims.

Rim. Rims of the simple curved-sided bowls are of relatively uniform thickness without modification of any sort. Their lips are usually flat, often insloped, occasionally rounded.

Rims of the larger, more numerous bowls are thickened by the addition of a clay fillet to the exterior (occasionally on the interior) wall adjacent to the lip. Several broken-off fillets present in the collections indicate these were a separate clay addition, not merely the edge of the vessel folded over. Usually, the strip is smoothed into the body wall in such a manner as to give the rim a triangular cross section. A few (12 out of 100) are not so merged with the body and retain the appearance of a flat, rectangular strip (sometimes triangular) encircling the rim edge. Strips range in width from 12 mm. to 3.5 cm. and project in some cases several millimeters from the vessel wall.

Rims of plates, or flat shallow bowls, are in appearance identical with the deeper version, except that all strips were smoothed into the rim wall. Lips of both plates and bowls are almost always flat or slightly insloped.

There are 6 bowl rims in the collection with a flat, thin, horizontal flange with a projection of from 1 to 2 cm.

In addition to thickening the only decorative treatment is infrequent nicking or notching. Only one of the simple bowl rims is nicked at the edge while two of the thickened rims are so treated. Of the latter, four have deeply notched "jagged" lips and one is slightly nicked. On two the lower edge of the applied fillet is nicked.

Base. None.

Appendages. There were 3 lugs in the collections (Ford, Phillips, and Griffin). One appears to be a semi-circular, horizontally projecting type; one is a miniature version of the same thing having the appearance of a tiny vertically flattened node; the third is similar except that it projects on both the interior and exterior, having an oval appearance when seen from above.

Discussion. The apparent center for the type is west of the Mississippi on the Bowie Site (14-N-4) from which come 197 of the 210 rims in the collection. The remaining 13 rims and 59 body sherds are in the following quadrangles: 13-P, 14-O, 15-O, 16-N, 16-O. The material from the 13-P quadrangle actually is in some respects quite different from the rest of the sherds classified as Bowie Plain, in that the color is generally redder.

Owing to the fact that practically all our information on this type comes from one site, Bowie, there is very little to say about its relationship within the Survey Area. It seems very likely that we have stumbled into the outer margin of a distribution that lies outside the Survey Area.

Chronological Position. Owing to the loss of figures on the number of plain body sherds, the Bowie Site was not seriated. The low percentage of cord-marking and the presence of Marksville Stamped and Marksville Incised, however, indicates a date in the early Baytown Period (F-E).

YATES NET-IMPRESSED

(FIG. 80, *e*)

Tentative type, not previously described.

Paste. Same as Baytown Plain. Clay lumps. Several fragments from the Oliver Site (16-N-6) have large inclusions which may be sherds. The fragments mentioned above are extremely lumpy and contorted, and paste tends to crumble and break apart from poor firing. The other 3 pieces of this type are dense and compact with a texture like Baytown Plain.

Hardness. Average, 2.5; range, 2.5 to 3.0.

Color. The poorly fired fragments are Blackish Mouse Gray (15''''' *m*) on the interior and Dark Mouse Gray (15''''' *k*) on the exterior. One sherd is Wood Brown (17'''), one Hair Brown (17'''' *i*), and one a Dark Gull Gray with a great deal of Avellaneous-colored clay-tempering apparent.

Thickness. Average, 7.6 mm.; range, 7 to 10 mm.

Surface Finish. Variation in finish but tends to be somewhat rough and undulating. Poorly fired fragments have something of a slight interior polish over a rather rough surface. One sherd has protruding tempering particles and tool marks are visible.

Decoration. Is made by impressing a net into the surface of the moist clay, resulting in an all-over diamond pattern with deep depressions at the intersection of the lines made by the knots. In the few sherds available the mesh is uniformly about 1 cm. square.

Design. Most of the impressed lines show the marks of the twisted cord. One sherd appears to have been completely but irregularly cord-marked all over before being impressed with the net.

Form. The two rims in the collection come apparently from simple curved-sided bowls (diameter, 30 to 34 cm.).

Discussion. Since there are only 9 sherds in this type, and 5 of these from the Oliver Site (Peabody collection), it is difficult to discuss them at this point. All are from quadrangles 16–M, 16–N, and 17–N.

Net-impressed sherds are very rare in this general area. Jennings (1941, p. 205) reports one from Lee County, Mississippi. The type has been described here because there are indications that it will have some significance in inter-areal comparisons. It appears to have come into the area from southern Alabama, probably from Clarke County where it is rather common.

MANLY PUNCTATED

(Fig. 87, *n–q*)

Tentative type, not previously described.

Paste and Surface Finish. Same as Neeley's Ferry Plain.

Decoration. Incised meander, usually a single line on upper shoulder area making an arcaded effect around the vessel. The triangular spaces between this line and the neck are filled with punctations. Sometimes one or several lines of punctations accompany the incised line.

Form. Only identifiable sherds pertain to standard Mississippi jar form. Typical strap handles represented in collection, but no lugs. Probability that horizontal semi-circular lugs are also typical.

Discussion. The type is represented by a mere handful of sherds from northern sites. In view of the similarities to known vessels from southeastern Missouri, western Kentucky, Tennessee, and northern Alabama, it was thought advisable to hold this as a type pending further information.

Chronological Position. Because of the small number of examples and limited distribution, this type was not placed on the seriation graphs. The sites where Manly Punctated is found fall into the Mississippi Period (C–A) with a tendency to cluster around time B.

MOUND PLACE INCISED

(Figs. 89, *t–w*; 102, *j–l*)

Tentative type, not previously described.

Paste and Surface Finish. Generally similar to Bell Plain. Some sherds have been included having a Neeley's Ferry type of paste, which is in fact the main reason why the type is tentative. It is perhaps nothing more than a simple decorative treatment, more often associated with a Bell type of ware, but not confined to it.

Decoration. Two or more parallel lines are placed horizontally on the exterior rim. Occasionally, these lines dip down on each side of the vessel in concentric festoons. Sometimes these festoons occur beneath semi-circular lugs. This is quite typical for rim effigy vessels, in which such lines are festooned beneath the head and the lug which represents the tail of the bird or animal concerned.

The technique of decoration varies from a moderately broad incision comparable to that of Barton Incised to fine engraving comparable to that of Walls or Hull Engraved.

Form. Simple curved-sided bowls with vertical or slightly incurved rims.

Discussion. A small sample, but the distribution is interesting. The finds are sporadic and in most cases are represented by one or two sherds per site. In the north, such occurrences are confined to the region west of the river, particularly in the Memphis sub-area sites — but there are no occurrences in Memphis area sites east of the river. A number of whole vessels in collections from the Walls Site (13–P–1), however, have this decoration.

Relationships Outside Survey Area. To the west, in the "Caddo" area, related types are found associated with effigy bowls in the Titus and Frankston foci. Some of these are very close to St. Francis forms, indicating a northeast to southwest movement. A similar development has not been found in the Southwest, or in Chihuahua where effigy bowls and jars are common.

To the north of the Survey Area, relatives of Mound Place Incised are found in southeast Missouri, western Kentucky, and southern Illinois. Similar decoration is found in the Cahokia area, both on the shallow bowl form which is associated with bird effigies (the human effigy head is almost never found) and also on the beanpot forms which became dominant in the Trappist Focus. It is apparently absent at Aztalan and is not a part of early Mississippi in the southern Appalachian and Piedmont area. This suggests it is not a part of early Mississippi in the areas surrounding the Survey Area to the north and east. It is not common in central Illinois. A strong representation is found in the Nashville area (Thruston, 1897, fig. 50, pl. 8), where the effigy heads are very similar to those of the Memphis area. It is apparently rare in northern Alabama but is fairly common at Moundville, which has many connections to the Walls-Pecan Point complex of the Survey Area. This style of decoration is not common in the Dallas or Mouse Creeks foci, but may be included in Dallas Incised as a part of the "miscellaneous and nondistinctive designs" (Lewis and Kneberg, 1946, p. 101, table 22). Its presence at the Walters and Cox sites in the Norris Basin (Webb, 1938, pp. 79 and 118) suggests that this is the case.

Mound Place Incised is analogous to Lamar Incised which dominates the southern Appalachian area, and it should be noted that Lamar is almost never associated with effigy heads. This strengthens the interpretation already advanced that relatives of Mound Place Incised along the northwest Florida coast (Moore, 1901, figs. 19, 37, 52, for example) represent a strong connection to the central Alabama area and to Moundville in particular.

Chronological Position. Sparsely represented in Survey collections but tends to cluster around time B.

BLANCHARD INCISED

(Figs. 91, *o*, *p*; 99, *p*)

Tentative type, not previously described.

Paste and Surface. Similar to Leland Incised, with possibly not as many examples of high polished surface.

Decoration. *Treatment.* Similar to Leland Incised, lines perhaps a little broader, but this is probably a result of the broader treatment of design.

Design. Only two sorts of design appear in the sample. Most common is a series of broad, shallow festoons depending from a horizontal line on the interior of the rim, just below the lip. In three examples these festoons are turned around vertically to the lip, making a sort of Greek E figure. Such is the limited repertory of the type so far as the present sample goes. With one or two doubtful exceptions these decorations are made up of single lines. A published example is from Neblett Landing (Moore, 1911, fig. 20).

Form. *Lip.* Lips rounded to squarish, one or two pretty definitely square.

Rim. Unthickened or slightly thickened interiorly, the effect somewhat emphasized by the interior line just below the lip which is almost standard equipment. These lines are about 1 cm. or less below the lip.

Body. Bowls with flaring sides, presumably shallow, or plates with a rather indefinite break between rim and bottom. Since the type is essentially an interior rim treatment, there are not enough body sherds to give information on the shape of the vessel as a whole.

Size. Ten rims selected at random gave an average of 26 cm. diameter, with range of 18 to 32 cm. This is significantly above the Leland average of 18.4 cm. Twenty sherds gave average thickness of 7.0 mm., range, 4 to 9 mm. This is considerably thicker than Leland, but it must be borne in mind that these are mostly rims and that these plate rims have a tendency to be thicker than the remainder of the vessel.

Discussion. This type is probably only a variant of Leland Incised. It belongs in a late prehistoric complex of shell-tempered types in the Lower Yazoo Basin which needs considerably more work both in the field and laboratory. It does not have a wide distribution or relationships outside the Survey Area.

Chronological Position. Late Mississippi Period (B–A).

OLIVER INCISED

Tentative type, not previously described.

Paste and Surface Finish. Same as Neeley's Ferry Plain.

Decoration. Incised lines of the same character described for Barton Incised, in a guilloche meander on rim, neck, or shoulder area employing two or more lines.

Form. Very little evidence. Apparently confined to standard Mississippi jar.

Discussion. The only justification for setting up even a tentative type is to keep material showing this design together, since the design itself is significant of wider connections. Distribution is very limited, being confined, with a single exception, to sites in the 16 and 17 Tiers of quadrangles.

Relationships Outside Survey Area. This design is best known in the Fort Ancient Aspect (Griffin, 1943b). It is also found in the Mississippi sites of the Lower Ohio Valley particularly at Angel and the Wickliffe Site ("Ancient Buried City"). In this area the design is usually rectilinear as it is in the Nashville region. It has been reported from the extensive excavations along the Tennessee River in northwest Alabama as one design on McKee Island Incised. It is also found on late sites around Montgomery, Alabama. In eastern Tennessee this design forms a part of Dallas Incised.

In southeastern Arkansas an excellent curvilinear guilloche was found with Burial 8 at Mound B on the Medley Site. (Lemley and Dickinson, 1937, pl. 2, *8*. The vessel is lettered 8 on the plate through an error; see legend fig. *6*). Another guilloche from even farther south was obtained by Moore at Seven Pines Landing in Morehouse Parish, Louisiana (Moore, 1909, fig. 172). At Ward Place, cemetery no. 1, Moore found a small, shell-tempered jar with flat base and short flaring rim which has a three-line guilloche. This is not illustrated or mentioned specifically in his report but was deposited in the Buffalo Museum of Natural Science.[17] From Keno Place, Moore recovered a small globular vessel with a short bottle neck bearing a punctate zone which has a crude three-line guilloche design on the body.[18]

Chronological Position. Mississippi Period, probably late (B–A).

STOKES BAYOU INCISED

Tentative type, not previously described.

Paste and Surface Finish. Same as Neeley's Ferry Plain, but somewhat thinner.

Decoration. Straight, broad incised lines both shallow and deep (sometimes deep enough to form ridges on the vessel interior), arranged primarily in line-filled triangles, but other geometric figures also occur. Width of lines vary but ca. 3 mm. is average. Spaces between the lines are slightly wider than the lines themselves. Lines usually stop just short of abutting a second line, and ends are square or rounded. Decoration is applied to both rims and body.

Form. A Mississippi jar form seems to be characteristic judging from the few rims available for examination. A bowl form is also suggested.

Base. Almost certainly a rounded base.

Appendages. One tubular handle may possibly belong to a jar with this type of decoration. The handle is covered with closely spaced irregular punctates and appears to be from a jar.

Discussion. This is a *very* tentative type, based on collection of Neeley's Ferry paste sherds in the "Unclassified" lot with two characteristics in comomn: (1) wide, smooth incisions; (2) straight lines. Probably is not a type at all, but something very closely akin to Wallace Incised on the one hand and Arcola on the other.

Chronological Position. Mississippi Period, probably late (B–A).

[17] Buffalo Museum of Natural Science, Cat. No. 3385 (Moore collection, vessel no. 25).

[18] Buffalo Museum of Natural Science, Cat. No. 2372 (Moore collection).

HANDLES

(Fig. 92)

General. A good deal has been said about handles in the course of the individual pottery descriptions just concluded, but owing to the fact that they occur with a number of plain and decorated types, it seems worth-while to summarize this information here. Handles are associated with the following types in the quantities shown:

Neeley's Ferry Plain	179 [19]
Barton Incised	38
Parkin Punctated	12
Kent Incised	3
Manly Punctated	2
Rhodes Incised	1
Stokes Bayou Incised	1
Arcola Incised	1
	237

Classification. Sorting of the 237 handles listed above, without regard for type, resulted in the following categories, used hereinafter as a tentative classification:

Loop	14
Intermediate	18
Strap	98
Tube	11
Decorative	55
Miscellaneous	7
Unclassified fragment	34
	237

Loop Handle (fig. 92, *a–d*). Loop handles are by definition round in cross section, but tend actually to be oval, being somewhat thinner back to front. Examples in which flattening is pronounced but not sufficient to result in a strap handle have been classified as "intermediate." Loop handles in the present collections are placed vertically, the upper end being either slightly above the normal plane of the lip which humps up slightly at the point of attachment, or in slightly less than half of the cases, a short distance below the lip. The difference may have something to do with the method of attachment. Several sherds show unmistakable evidence of riveting at the lower end, and it seems probable that where the upper end is below the lip, attachment is by riveting also. Where the attachment is higher than the lip, riveting would seem to be out of the question.

Size of loop handles averages 2.3 cm. in length top to bottom (range, 2.0 to 4.0 cm.) by 1.1 cm. diameter (range, .7 to 1.4 cm.). They bow outward sufficiently from the vessel wall to make a round or D-shaped loop, depending on the amount of constriction at the neck.

No decoration or elaboration of any kind occurs in the present sample. This seems also to be the case with the few whole vessels with loop handles from the Survey Area.

Intermediate. Handles listed above as intermediate are not essentially different from the loop handles just described, except for greater flattening and consequent approximation to the more common strap handle. It may be significant that none of them have their upper attachment below the lip, a feature which apparently is confined to the loop type. Also they run somewhat larger in size than loop handles.

Strap (fig. 92, *e–i*). Strap handles may be divided into two groups: one in which the sides are roughly parallel and one in which they converge (downward). The latter can hardly be called triangular as the convergence is seldom sufficiently pronounced. At the present time the distinction does not seem to be significant areally or chronologically. However, if arcaded rims turn out to be a late development, this triangularization may represent a step in that direction. This could correlate with the emphasis on strap handles with converging sides in the Madisonville Focus, especially at the Madisonville Site which comes up into the Historic Period.

Strap handles are frequently elaborated by the addition of nodes; either one, centrally placed at the top; two, laterally placed at the top (ears), or four, two top and two bottom. The second appears to be the most common treatment.

Strap handles offer a fairly large surface for decoration, but it is seldom utilized. There

[19] Includes fragments of handles, etc., on which decoration could not appear. Some of these handles are probably from other types.

are a few cases in which punctations on the body are carried up onto the handle, one or two handles embellished with a few vertical incised lines, and one with an appliqué head.

In regard to method of attachment, there is no direct evidence in the form of revealing fractures, but it would seem to be a safe inference that straps were first luted to the lip, upside-down, and then bent around to the required shape and luted onto the body wall.

Strap handles vary greatly in size, but in general are considerably larger than loop handles. Random sample of 20 handles gives average of 4.8 cm. long (range 2.5 to 7 cm.) by 2.8 cm. wide (range, 1.5 to 5 cm.).

Broad Strap or Tube (fig. 92, *r–v*). A markedly different type of handle. Strap handles described above, though varying greatly in size, maintain a consistent proportion of length to breadth of almost two to one. The handles considered here tend to reverse that proportion, being as broad or broader than long. The result is a very characteristic tubular sort of handle, very similar to those associated with the Fisher Focus and other Upper Mississippi cultures. It is not surprising, therefore, to find that they have a different distribution in the Survey Area from the dominant strap-handle type (see below).

Decorative (fig. 92, *j–o*). Handles considered under this term include such a wide variety of forms as to make definitions almost impossible. They are called "decorative" because in the majority of cases they seem to have lost any functional significance. With few exceptions, they fail to stand free of the vessel, but are simply applied flat against the body surface. There is also an increase in the number of handles which, together with the tendency toward triangular shape, results in an arcaded effect. In the latter case it looks as if the entire set of handles was cut out of one strip of clay and attached in one operation. In a number of cases this arcaded collar is merely simulated by incised lines. In other cases the "handles" have become no more than small vertical strips suggesting faintly by their shape the triangular handles from which they may have derived. It is tempting to interpret this whole development in terms of the process of conventionalization, with an originally functional handle becoming at first purely decorative and finally skeuomorphic and vestigial,[20] but it would be well to wait for some better evidence of relative chronology on this point.

Decorative or arcaded handles are usually embellished by punctation, incision, or the application of nodes. The former is the most common treatment.

Miscellaneous. Under this heading are several interesting types represented by only one or two specimens. One type, which may be southern, has a pronounced medial groove (fig. 92, *f*). Another, represented by a single example from the Neeley's Ferry Site (11–N–4), consists of two elements crossed diagonally one above the other. From one of the most southerly sites, Silver City (20–O–5) comes the zoomorphic handle shown in figure 92, *p*, reminiscent of Fort Ancient and other late Mississippi divisions (Griffin, 1943b, pp. 135–37, 201–05).

Distribution. The general over-all distribution of handles is interesting. The greatest frequency is in the St. Francis sub-area, the home of the strap handle in the Survey Area. Second in importance numerically is the Memphis sub-area in which the decorative type is concentrated. From here on south the occurrence of handles is sporadic, the greatest number in any one collection being six, from the Bush Site (17–M–11). Scarcity of handles in the central portion might be explained by the fact that we have fewer large shell-tempered collections, but in the south such is not the case. The fact that we have only 2 handles from the very large collection at the Leland Site (19–M–1) and one from the Arcola Site (20–M–1) is very significant. It is difficult to escape the conclusion that, in this part of the Mississippi Valley, the handle is a northern feature that has just about reached the southern limit of its distribution.

Detailed distribution by types offers some interesting suggestions. Loop and "intermediate" handles are perhaps too scattered for

[20] Holmes was probably the first to advance this theory.

any far-reaching conclusions, but it is very interesting to see that they have almost entirely avoided the sites of the late Walls-Pecan Point group in the Memphis sub-area, which seems to support the typological argument to the effect that decorative handles represent an elaboration of the strap handle. Thus we may set up a tentative sequence loop-strap-decorative as something to check in future excavations and comparisons.

The extent to which strap, decorative, and broad strap (or tube) handles occupy more or less mutually exclusive areas is very interesting and satisfactory. One may predict that these centers of distribution will coincide with later-period foci yet to be established, strap handles with the St. Francis, decorative with Walls-Pecan Point, broad strap with something we are just beginning to see in the 16 and 17 Tiers east of the River. The almost complete lack of handles of any sort in the south suggests too a significant negative characteristic for the Deer Creek center.

Relationships Outside the Survey Area. The presence of handles of the loop and strap type is one of the outstanding features of the Mississippi ceramic complex and its derived Upper Mississippi relatives. So far, there are no known antecedents for this handle complex not only within the Survey Area but in any other area which can be included within the eastern United States. These features then either sprang *de novo* in the area along with many other elements of Mississippi culture or the idea of handles along with some of these features was introduced from the outside. The closest area where handles form an essential part of the pottery and where they occur earlier than in the Mississippi Valley is the Southwest.

The two major areas where loop handles were utilized are the Old Village Aztalan region and the Small Log Town House–Hiwassee Island–Macon Plateau continuum in the southeast. In the eastern Tennessee–Georgia area the loop handles are rather elaborately specialized with knobs, nodes, protuberances. While the Mississippi culture in this eastern region does appear to have been introduced from an as yet unknown area to the west, the extreme loop-handle elaboration is probably a local development. The Old Village–Aztalan complex also does not seem to have any antecedents in its native area. Since as a ceramic unit it seems to be more refined and sophisticated than that of eastern Tennessee and Georgia, one might logically postulate the former as a development from the latter. This interpretation runs counter, however, to current opinion. In the Kincaid excavations the loop handles are known to be in the early shell-tempered levels where they are accompanied by a few specimens resembling Old Village types. A progressive shift from loop to strap handles has been demonstrated at certain of the Kincaid units. In the central Ohio Valley the presence of loop handles in Fort Ancient is associated with vessel shapes resembling Old Village jars and is interpreted as part of the early Mississippi influences which gradually made their way into the Fort Ancient area. The Steed-Kisker Focus, Nebraska, and Mill Creek Aspects are found on the Missouri River from Kansas City to Sioux Falls. Particularly in the former and in the latter there are some loop handles. These cultural divisions in the eastern plains are probably best interpreted as having been derived from the Old Village–Aztalan level of the northern Mississippi Valley.

On the other hand, strap handles throughout the eastern United States are found in the latest cultural units of each area and many of these units come up into the Historic Period. This is true in the Fort Ancient area, in the south Appalachians, in the Oneota Aspect, and in the eastern Plains. It is hardly likely then that the appearance of strap handles in the Survey Area is appreciably earlier than in the surrounding regions. The same kinds of handle decoration such as punctating and incising that are found in the Survey Area are also found in eastern Tennessee, and in the Oneota-Fisher complexes. They are quite rare in Fort Ancient.

The closest analogue to the decorative handles of the Walls-Pecan Point group is to be found in the Lower Loup Focus of Nebraska. This resemblance was noticed by Strong and Wedel and formed part of their reasons for suggesting a Mississippi Valley origin for the Pawnee. If there is any connection between these two developments, it has yet to be demonstrated by material from sites in the intervening area.

Handles do not seem to appear in the Alto and Gahagan foci of the Gibson Aspect of east Texas. They are present, however, in Haley and Spiro, and punctates are found on handles in the Sanders Focus of north Texas that are very close to the strap style. Other Sanders handles more nearly resemble the loop handle. As a generality, handles are not at all common in the "Caddo" area.

Along the northern and eastern Gulf Coast, handles do not appear until late Weeden Island or early Fort Walton as a clear Middle Mississippi introduction from the north.

In the Southwest single handles, either loop or strap, are in Basket Maker III on slender-necked bottles. Others are placed horizontally instead of vertically on the lower shoulder of large storage jars. In Pueblo I, handles appear rarely on plain and banded small jars. They are almost always one to a vessel. Handles are common on small pitcher forms. These same general forms continue the use of the single handle into Pueblo II and III as in the large storage jars with horizontal handles. In both, there seems to be a tendency for the loop to be completely replaced by the strap in Pueblo II and III. Handles are almost nonexistent in Hohokam. They do not seem to be present in the earliest or southern Mogollon but are noticeable and highly similar to Basket Maker III in the Forestdale variety of Alma Plain (Haury, 1941, p. 91). Two small handled ollas are described by Kidder (1931, p. 47) in the Pecos report. In the Casas Grandes area of northern Chihuahua two small loop handles are present on small jars of red and black polished surface as well as on polychrome vessels (Sayles, 1936, fig. 15).

Section IV

DISTRIBUTION OF SOME MISSISSIPPI PERIOD VESSEL SHAPES AND FEATURES

DISTRIBUTION OF SOME MISSISSIPPI PERIOD VESSEL SHAPES AND FEATURES

DURING the late 1930's, Phillips prepared a Ph.D. thesis called "An Introduction to the Archaeology of the Mississippi Valley," [1] in which he analyzed some 2000 whole vessels from the Survey Area. Some of his findings are incorporated into the following paragraphs. The division between the St. Francis and Mississippi River (Memphis sub-area) sites was apparent to him, but it was noted that certain sites on the St. Francis such as Rose (12–N–3) and Turkey Island in Cross County, Arkansas, were not typical of that area while others along the Mississippi River were not typical of the Memphis area grouping.

The whole vessels clearly reflected the predominance of Bell Plain over Neeley's Ferry Plain in the Memphis area, and there were very few cases where it was difficult to decide whether the specimen was Bell Plain or Neeley's Ferry Plain. The Memphis sub-area also had a much higher percentage of incised and engraved decoration placed on Bell Plain paste. On the other hand, the St. Francis sub-area had the largest percentage of red-filmed and other painted types.

JARS

Jar forms found with burials run to small sizes. These small jars have a slight excess of width over height (figs. 94–98). The average diameter of a series of representative specimens was found to be 14.2 cm., with a range of 10 to 20 cm. Most of the jars have either lugs or handles or both. Jars with two lugs or four lugs at the level of the lip are typical of the St. Francis. Jars with four lugs placed on the rim a few centimeters below the lip are present in both areas. Strap handles are much more common than loop handles, and handle combinations of two straps and two lugs easily make up the most common group.

The most common decoration technique on the jars is by punctation or incision. In the St. Francis area the rim decoration is usually incised, and this style produced the Barton Incised pottery type, while the great predominance of body punctating resulted in Parkin Punctated (figs. 94, 95). In the Memphis area incised decoration is more common on the body, and punctates are placed both on the body and on the rim. In general, the Memphis potters are more skillful and particularly with the spiral meander designs their products have a pleasing appearance. This has reference to the type Rhodes Incised (fig. 98). Phillips made a quantitative comparison of certain general characteristics of decorated jars on a sample of 69 vessels from the Memphis area and 71 from the St. Francis, as follows:

	MISSISSIPPI MEMPHIS	ST. FRANCIS	TOTAL
Incision on rim	2	20	22
Incision on body	30	10	40
Punctation on rim	15	3	18
Punctation on body	6	15	21
Punctation on both	—	4	4

Examples of Fortune Noded (fig. 97, *j–q*) were also included in this study of whole vessels, and a number of appliqué features including one example of the "climbing lizard," (fig. 96, *g*) were noted.[1a] Lobate jars usually with four lobes, which are quite common in the Nashville area and in southeast Missouri, are very rare in the Survey Area. A special feature of the Memphis area is the multiple-handled jar in which the handles apparently passed completely from a utilitarian to a decorative feature. This trait has been discussed at some length in the pages devoted to handles (pp. 151–53).

[1] Phillips, 1939.

[1a] See Griffin, 1943b, pp. 135–37; 201–05, for a discussion of this feature.

BOWLS

A study of bowl forms in the two areas with respect to size indicated little significant difference. In the St. Francis, one of the most common shapes is a deep straight-sided bowl which often has lugs (fig. 100, *b*) and also is often converted into a fish or bird effigy bowl. This shape illustrated in figure 109, *a*, *a'*, is very characteristic of the typical St. Francis sites. Plain lips are more common in the St. Francis on low, medium, or deep bowls, while in the Memphis area notched or incised lip edges are quite common (fig. 100, *n*, *o*, *q*). The notched rim strip placed on bowls just below the lip so common in the Nashville area, and to a somewhat less degree in southeast Missouri and western Kentucky, occurs more often in our Memphis area (fig. 100, *h* and *l*) than in the St. Francis. In both areas the low and medium-deep bowls have two to four lug handles which project horizontally from the lip, the four lug examples being more common. On the deep St. Francis-type bowls, however, two lugs are the rule.

Various unusual bowl shapes deserve special mention. Rectangular forms occur infrequently in the Survey Area,[2] as also, and probably in greater numbers, in southeast Missouri.[3] They have not been mentioned from the Cumberland Aspect. This shape is of course present in the Southwest. It apparently is more common in Hohokam and comes into Pueblo sites around the Great Pueblo Period and after.[4]

BOTTLES

There are a number of distinctive variations of the bottle form which have areal significance, and perhaps chronological as well, although that problem cannot at the present be presented with too much confidence. Phillips arranged some 620 photographs of bottles according to globular (fig. 103, *d*), subglobular (fig. 103, *m* and *p*), and carinated (fig. 103, *f* and *g*) body shape, and according to neck height. Thus, in the low-necked category are necks up to about 1/3 of the body height (fig. 103, *a*, *m*); medium, from 1/3 to 2/3 (fig. 103, *b*, *d*); high, 2/3 and over (fig. 103, *c*, *e*). The St. Francis has predominantly a globular bottle body with low and medium necks which are vertical and generally without modification (fig. 104, *a–d*). Tall neck bottles are present, however, and often have carinated bodies. The typical Memphis area bottle, in addition to a finer finish, often has a flattened ellipsoidal body, a sharper break between the neck and shoulder, and a higher neck (fig. 104, *f*, *g*). Bottles of this type normally have a beveled inner lip, which is also found on some of the decorated jar forms from this sub-area. The carinated bottle is a rare form in the Memphis sub-area. Carafe-neck bottles (fig. 103, *t*) are not common in either sub-area and when found are probably evidence of contact with the New Madrid and Cumberland areas.

Ring bases, and to a less extent annular bases,[5] are a fairly common feature of the bottle shapes in the northern part of the Survey Area (fig. 103) but are not exclusively associated with any particular bottle form. There is a marked tendency in the St. Francis for the ring and annular bases to be associated with a shoulder fillet (fig. 103, *d*, *f*, *l*). The higher annular bases of these bottles generally flare outward sharply and are often decorated with punctations, and in some instances with perforations (fig. 103, *f*, *i–l*, *o*). There are also perforated bases from the Memphis area. This type of base is quite limited in distribution to southeast Missouri, the Survey Area, and to a limited degree in the Lower Arkansas where it is found on bowls, seemingly in a

[2] Holmes, 1903, pl. VIII, *a*.

[3] Evers, 1880, pl. 17, *342*.

[4] Hough, 1903, pl. 9; Fewkes, 1914, fig. 18; Bradfield, 1931, pl. LXXXII, *264*; Woodward, 1931; Cosgrove, H. S. and C. B., 1932, pl. 88, *f*; Martin and Willis, 1940, pl. 42, *9*.

[5] The term "ring" refers to a low type of base made by luting on a single rope of clay. Annular bases are higher and presumably made by coiling or superimposing two or more rings of clay.

late context. It is quite rare in the Southwest but does occur in Chihuahua in the Casas Grandes area, although so infrequently even there that its presence has not been generally recognized.

Another feature of the bottle form is the disk base, which in the main is associated with the flattened and carinated bottle bodies rather than with the globular forms. It is somewhat more common in the Memphis area than in the St. Francis. There is also a marked tendency for the disk base to be notched along its outer border, and this is particularly common in the Memphis area (figs. 98, *a*; 103, *m*). Bottles decorated with four pushed-out protuberances around the shoulder or rare lobate forms are apparently confined to the St. Francis. Dimpled bottles (fig. 104, *g*), especially where they are associated with engraving (fig. 110, *a*), are so similar to Moundville specimens that this feature along with a great many others indicates that the Memphis area sites around time B were contemporary with and very closely connected to Moundville. The gadrooned bottle is almost entirely limited to the Memphis area [6] and is not found in the eastern United States outside of the Survey Area.

Bottles decorated with crude medallion heads are found in both the St. Francis [7] and Memphis areas. In the Memphis area particularly, bottle necks are sometimes shaped to represent small jars, usually of Parkin Punctated (fig. 104, *p*, *s*), but sometimes of Kent Incised (fig. 104, *o*). On other vessels the neck "vessel" simply carries the small strap handles. This feature might have been presented under the heading of compound vessels. It seems to be a Memphis specialization which penetrated into the St. Francis at some of the sites such as the Rose Mound. Another feature of Memphis area bottles is the appliqué collar design, which has been described as an eye, anus, or "ogee collar." [8] It is a common symbol asociated with the "Southern Cult" art forms, particularly at Moundville, but its use on vessels in this manner is apparently confined to the Memphis and St. Francis areas, particularly the former. It is almost invariably associated with flattened bottles.

RED AND PAINTED TYPES

In the study of vessel shapes in the red-slipped ware, now defined as Old Town Red, Phillips observed that the bottle was much more common than the bowl and that the finish and shape of the red-filmed specimens generally was very close to the better polished and finished plain wares. The percentage distribution of shapes in the two sub-areas was as follows:

Old Town Red Vessel Shapes

	Memphis		St. Francis		Unplaced		Totals	
	No.	Per cent	No.	Per cent	No.	Per cent	No.	Per cent
Bowls	4	21.1	20	26.3	10	37	34	27.1
Bottles	9	47.4	48	63.2	14	51.9	71	58.2
Effigies	6	31.6	2	2.6	1	3.3	9	7.4

Vessels of Old Town Red are illustrated in this volume (figs. 100, *h*; 107, *d*; 109, *c*, *g*, *g'*, *j*, *j'*; 113, *a*, *b*, and *d*). There are a number of colored illustrations in the literature.[9]

A study of the distribution of whole vessels of the two most common painted types, Carson Red on Buff and Nodena Red and White, again indicate a clear majority for the St. Francis area over the Memphis area. Typical examples of Carson Red on Buff are illustrated in color in the literature of the area.[10] A study of the shapes represented in these painted types indicates very clearly that bottles are even more important than in the Old Town Red division.

[6] Holmes, 1903, pl. XV, *b*.
[7] Moore, 1910, figs. 32, 33.

[8] Holmes, 1903, pl. XIII, *f*; Moore, 1911, pp. 458–59.
[9] Holmes, 1903, pl. XLII, *a*; Moore, 1910, pl. IX.
[10] Moore, 1910, pl. XII.

Numerical Distribution of Eastern Arkansas Painted Types

	Memphis		St. Francis		Unplaced		Totals	
	No.	Per cent	No.	Per cent	No.	Per cent	No.	Per cent
Carson Red on Buff	8	1.53	35	3.81	8	1.44	51	2.55
Nodena Red on White	12	2.3	26	2.84	13	2.32	51	2.55
Avenue Polychrome	—	—	1	.11	1	.18	2	.10
	20	3.83	62	6.76	22	3.94	104	5.20

Distribution of Shapes in Painted Wares

	Memphis		St. Francis		Unplaced		Totals	
	No.	Per cent	No.	Per cent	No.	Per cent	No.	Per cent
Bowls	—	—	8	13.1	—	—	8	7.1
Bottles	15	75	49	80.3	14	63.6	78	75.7
Effigies	5	25	3	4.9	7	31.8	15	14.6
Eccentric	—	—	1	1.6	1	4.5	2	1.9
	20		61		22		103	

Bowls are not commonly painted in red on buff or red and white except in some of the sites nearest the Arkansas, in the Lower Arkansas sub-area, and in the Sunflower sub-area opposite the mouth of the Arkansas River (fig. 113, *i–k*). It should be observed that this late use of red and white on bowls in the Lower Arkansas is the type of painting which was present on the original Deasonville site associated with a late complex of incised Middle Mississippi types. While occasionally a jar form received a red slip, there are no vessels of that shape that are included in the painted category.

The St. Francis sub-area not only seems to have a greater quantity of painted ware, but also shows a greater variety of designs. The two most common motifs in both sub-areas are the swastika spiral meander and a simple arrangement of alternating vertical panels. Fairly common is the step design which is often placed on the neck of bottles or on bowl interiors (figs. 103, *s*; 111, *k*; 112, *a*, *b*, *g*).[11] One of the vessels illustrated by Moore of Nodena Red and White from Turkey Island on the St. Francis has a swastika spiral which takes off from a white circular core.[12] This is suggestive of the decoration found on many Fatherland Incised specimens where the curvilinear lines are associated with an incised core. There have been a number of shoe-form pots found in northeast Arkansas with Nodena Red and White decoration (fig. 112, *j*, *l*). Another almost identical specimen is illustrated by Holmes in color.[13] The owl effigy is very rarely found in the Survey Area so that its appearance in Nodena Red and White is even more interesting (fig. 112, *k*). A number of Moundville designs also appear in the red and white painted vessels, such as the hand (fig. 111, *i* and *j*) and the design resembling the small copper gorgets often with a swastika design (fig. 112, *h*). It will be remembered that painted decoration is very rare at Moundville, so that there is little possibility of importation of vessels from one area to the other here but rather of common possession of a particular design.

EFFIGY FORMS

Rim Effigy Bowls

One of the most characteristic ceramic features of the Survey Area is the rim effigy bowl (figs. 101, 102). Some of them are so highly conventionalized that it is difficult if not impossible to determine what life form is represented. In a study of 155 vessels, 52 from the Memphis sub-area and 78 from the St.

[11] See also, Holmes, 1903, pls. XVI, *b*; XLI, *b*. Moore, 1910, pls. XII, XVII, XXVI, fig. 59. Moore, 1911, fig. 80.

[12] Moore, 1910, pl. XXII.

[13] Holmes, 1903, pl. XLII, *b*.

Francis, with the others of unspecified provenience, Phillips recorded the following proportionate representation.

	MEMPHIS	ST. FRANCIS	UNPLACED	TOTAL
Human	9	—	1	10
Animal	11	3	1	15
Bird	11	25	7	43
Serpent	18	11	3	32
Unidentifiable	—	30	7	37
Problematical	3	9	6	18
	52	78	25	155

The complete absence of human heads in the St. Francis, the small number of recognizable animals, and the large number of unidentifiable specimens is in marked contrast to the Memphis sub-area which is much closer in these features to the southeast Missouri and Cumberland areas. In the Memphis sub-area human effigy features are often quite well done (fig. 102, *j–p*) and, especially those with a "dunce-cap" head-dress (figs. 101, *o*; 102, *o*) exhibit marked similarity to the New Madrid Focus.

There is a type of human effigy most commonly found on bowls in the Cumberland Aspect in which both facial features and details of hair-dress and ornamentation are carefully delineated. This is also found in western Kentucky and southern Missouri. Such heads are often hollow and contain small clay pellets which rattle when the vessel is shaken. In the Memphis area comparable hollow effigy heads, sometimes with rattles are somewhat different stylistically and do not reveal the emphasis on the details of head-dress.

One very distinctive effigy type seems to have its center in the Memphis area. This is the serpent-cat effigy head which is characteristically placed on a long vertical neck and has a curled tail. This beast often has the "weeping" symbol delineated around the eye and has a swastika on the back of the head. While the classic examples are along the Mississippi Memphis area, there are a number of crude representations in the St. Francis area, usually at sites which have other evidences of contact and contemporaneity with the Walls-Pecan Point cultural facies of the Memphis area. It is not found in the southern part of the Survey Area, nor does it seem to have been accepted in the New Madrid, western Kentucky, Cahokia, Cumberland, or other Middle Mississippi centers to the north and east. This same creature is sometimes portrayed as a four-footed beast with a short-neck, wide-mouth bottle forming the body which has obvious analogies to the dog-bear effigy bottle with carafe neck of the Cumberland and associated areas. It also has features of the composite creature represented on the effigy pipes recovered from Moundville and Emerald-Seltzertown, but these lean more heavily on cat features while the pottery effigy heads appear to favor the serpent. In view of a number of similarities of the Walls-Pecan Point complex with Moundville, it is a little surprising that the serpent-cat effigy head has not been reported from that site.

The rim effigy bowl is one of the most constant features of the Middle Mississippi vessel complex, as it is found throughout the Southeast and is found in both the early levels and the late. As a ceramic concept it is widely distributed throughout the New World but it is so relatively simple that it could easily have been developed independently many times, once the idea of presenting life forms in clay became a part of the ceramic tradition. The area within the eastern United States where this idea is present reaches from Aztalan on the north, to the northeastern Fort Ancient sites, to the Georgian and Florida coastal areas on the southeast, to Nebraska and Mill Creek sites on the northwest, and to "Caddo" sites on the southwest. Their relative scarcity around the periphery of this distribution makes it clear that the center for this idea, irrespective of its origin, is the Middle Mississippi area as originally defined by Holmes. Apparently, it is not a part of the early Gibson Aspect sites but came into the "Caddo" area during late Gibson and Fulton periods.[14] On the northwest coast of Florida, a beautiful developmental picture can be arranged, from the Hopewell bird incised on

[14] Newell and Krieger, 1949, fig. 63 and description of vessel *H*.

vessels, to lightly raised bird heads, to Weeden Island effigy forms, and thence to Middle Mississippi. It was proposed thirty years ago that a wooden effigy bowl was the probable prototype.[15] In the Southwest, bird effigy forms are usually not placed as a simple head and tail on the rim of a bowl,[16] but the vessel is more jar-shaped with the effigy head protruding from the upper body of the vessel,[17] or the vessel is an effigy body rather than an effigy head and neck appendage.

It has been noted that the effigy heads on bowls of Monks Mound Red are usually small, ill-defined heads, which commonly face inward and with the eyes, mouth, and nose barely recognizable. This poor attempt at facial characterization and infacing effigies is also found on Bibb Plain of the Macon Plateau types in central Georgia and on Hiwassee Red Filmed and the Small Log Town House sites of eastern Tennessee. This type of head also is found on red-filmed pottery at Aztalan. At this site Barrett has reconstructed the vessel with the head facing outward [18] but, from the illustration [19] and from the drawing, it may be that it faces inward.[20] It is interesting that the one or two rim effigy heads in Baytown Plain found in the Survey collections are of this undifferentiated type.

Another example of a type of effigy head that should have areal and chronological significance is also found at Aztalan;[21] southeast Missouri,[22] and probably adjacent area in Kentucky. It is part of the Moundville complex.[23] None of this angular flattened block style of effigy was picked up by the Survey parties. It is almost certainly rare in the Survey Area and would seem to center in the New Madrid Focus.

The most widely spread rim effigy type is that of a duck form made of solid clay and shaped into a fair representation of a bird head. This general style probably has less areal and chronological importance for distinguishing local cultural units and cultural contacts than some of the other effigy styles. It is certainly the most common type in the St. Francis sub-area.

Effigy Vessels

Not to be confused with rim effigies, are vessels in which the entire vessel enters into the concept that is being represented. This usually, but not necessarily, involves modification of the original vessel shape.

Phillips' study of 189 effigy vessels from the Survey Area indicated very clearly that the Memphis potters made more different kinds of effigies, attached the same effigy concept to more varied vessel shapes, and turned out a much better product than their cousins on the St. Francis.

	EFFIGIES	MEMPHIS	ST. FRANCIS	UN-PLACED	TOTAL
1	Frog	16	10	4	30
1a	Conventionalized frog type	—	(7)	(1)	(8)
2	Snouted, (opossum)	4	1	6	11
3	Fish	18	30	22	70
4	Swan	3	—	—	3
5	(?) Animal	2	—	—	2
6	Bird	1	—	—	1
7	Spouted effigies	1	1	—	2
8	Gourd	1	—	2	3
9	Animal	3	2	1	6
10	Shell	4	2	2	8
11	Owl	1	—	—	1
12	"Blank-face"	1	3	1	5
13	"Lemon-squeezer"	3	3	1	7
14	Human	10	7	11	28
15	Foot	3	1	—	4
		71	67	51	189
		(392)*	(645)	(428)	(1465)

* Figures in parentheses give the total number of available vessels in the St. Francis and the Memphis areas of the Neeley's Ferry Plain or Bell Plain types which were likely to furnish effigy forms.

Next to the fish, the frog is the most common effigy form and was listed first because it more nearly approaches the standard Mississippi jar form without modification (fig. 108, *d–i*).

[15] Hooton, 1920, pl. 21, *e*.

[16] One of the best examples is in Cosgrove, H. S. and C. B., 1932, pl. 87, *c*.

[17] Martin and Willis, 1940, pl. 51, *4*.

[18] Barrett, 1933, pl. 97, *9*.

[19] Barrett, 1933, pl. 94, *5*.

[20] Barrett, 1933, fig. 138.

[21] Barrett, 1933, fig. 139 and pl. 97, *8*.

[22] Potter, 1880, pl. 15, *1*.

[23] Moore, 1905, fig. 51.

In some instances the strap handles are placed on the jar. Not only is this form common in the northern part of the Survey Area, but it is also one of the most widely distributed effigy forms in the eastern United States generally. It is not a part of the early Mississippi level in the Cahokia area or in eastern Tennessee and north-central Georgia, and in fact effigy vessels as distinct from rim effigy bowls are not part of the early Mississippi levels in those areas. It is also not reported in central Illinois from later Mississippi levels but will probably be found in that part of lower Illinois which is contiguous to southeast Missouri and the western Kentucky extension of the Cumberland culture. It may be found in southwestern Indiana at the Angel Site but does not occur much to the east of this point. It appears in the eastern Tennessee area at the time of the Dallas and Mouse Creeks foci. There are no known specimens from Georgia, but in Alabama the frog appears in Moundville and in the Montgomery area. Getting back to the Mississippi it may be said that in general, south of the mouth of the Arkansas, as the Mississippi shell-tempered complex moved south, effigy forms were not commonly accepted. One might suggest that a movement of people is not represented, or if so, it was after the emphasis on effigies had taken place.

The fish effigies were placed on a wider variety of forms, particularly in the Memphis area, as the following table indicates.

	MEMPHIS	ST. FRANCIS	UNPLACED	TOTALS
Shallow to medium bowls	3	14	8	25
Deep bowls	2	14	7	23
"Seed" bowl or jar	7	—	1	8
Bottle	6	—	6	12
Bottle (vertical type)	—	2	—	2
	—	—	—	—
	18	30	22	70

Some of the fish effigy forms are indeed excellent products of the primitive potters' art, and their perfection is reached in the Memphis area (fig. 109). The better specimens along the St. Francis appear to have reached there by trade.[24] Also in the St. Francis, in quite a few cases, the fish is pretty well conventionalized, and the deep bowl form so typical of the area did not lend itself too well to the production of a naturalistic fish effigy. In the Memphis area a constricted-mouth bowl ("seed jar"), the common bowl, jars, and bottles all had fish effigy features. The fish bottle has some striking similarities in the Mesoamerican area.

Swan effigies are confined to the Memphis area and recall somewhat the excellent stone bowl from Moundville.[25] Shell effigy forms resembling those of the southeast Missouri and Cumberland regions are found in both the St. Francis and Memphis sub-areas. The owl is much less common here than in southeast Missouri and this is also true of the hooded effigy bottle (fig. 107, *h–k*). One hooded form which Phillips called the "lemon-squeezer" is a conventionalized version of the pointed or "dunce cap" which is found in the Cumberland and southeast Missouri (fig. 107, *i*). On these forms all human attributes have been conventionalized out of existence. There are a number of foot forms in northeastern Arkansas (fig. 106, *t*),[26] but the shoe-form pot or "duck" pot which is fairly common in Middle America and the Southwest is found in southeast Missouri but is very rare in the Survey Area. A similar shape also appears in eastern Tennessee area and would now probably be included in the Dallas and Mouse Creek foci.

Human Effigy Figures

(Table 2, pp. 183–93)

One of the most characteristic forms of the Mississippi effigy complex is the human figure, which is usually associated with the bottle form, with shape modifications to suit local concepts. While the form is common in certain areas, it is by no means found in all regions of Mississippi culture and is definitely concentrated in the New Madrid, Memphis, and Cumberland areas. It is not reported from the Monks Mound Aspect, from the Ohio Valley east of the mouth of the Wabash, and does not occur in the early Mississippi sites in eastern Tennessee or central Georgia. It

[24] Moore, 1910, fig. 23.

[25] Cf. Moore, 1911, fig. 32, with Moore, 1907, figs. 76–79.

[26] Moore, 1911, fig. 35.

is relatively rare in Alabama and most of Mississippi and Louisiana. It is not a "Caddo" form.

In the New Madrid area considerable variety of form and treatment is accorded these human effigies. The most characteristic feature is a tendency for the body to appear bloated, or they might perhaps be described as pleasingly plump. In any event, the body and the lower limbs particularly are rounded and full.[27] There are a fair number of the effigies that are the upper part of vertical compound vessels and are placed upon either a globular bottle or upon a squared or rectangular vessel.[28] One of the specialized forms in the New Madrid area is that of the seated figure which is more compressed from front to back than the "normal" human effigy. It also has a vertical neck rising from the top of the head. These figures are most often male.[29] This type of orifice is the one favored in the Anasazi area on what Pepper called the "Pueblo Bonito" type. The arms are usually contiguous with the body, with the hands resting on the knees or placed on the chest or abdomen. Since most of these vessels are female, the breasts are commonly emphasized, and occasionally the genitalia also. The back is often curved and the backbone is represented by a vertical row of small knobs or sometimes by a single vertically extended flattened lug. On some rare examples the arms, scapulae, and clavicles, and even an attempt at ribs are portrayed, suggesting a skeletonized figure and presumably having some sort of mortuary significance.

A more significant feature is the frequent representation of these figures as hunchbacked both in the Mississippi and in the Southwest and Chihuahua. There are also certain decorations about the eye that occur in both regions.

The majority of the human effigies in the Survey Area are in the Memphis sub-area where they clearly indicate their close connection to the forms in the New Madrid section. Connections with death concepts are emphasized even more here, as on the notable vessel from the Rhodes Site, which has a vertical orifice.[30] There are also a number of the figures which have faces with obvious connections to the classic head vases which bears out the fact that the latter form is more at home in the Memphis sub-area than in the St. Francis.

Another relationship that might be indicated is to the stone human effigy figures of the Cumberland area, for various features of headdress, and the common portrayal of the protruding tongue, are found on both. The human effigy pipe from Moundville with a seated figure holding a Mississippi jar in her lap is certainly connected with these effigy vessels. This comparison may be extended to the excellent effigy pipe from Gahagan representing a male figure holding a typical Mississippi bi-conical elbow pipe in his lap.[31] Quite a few of the human effigy pipes of the Mississippi Period show these connections, on the one hand to the stone figures most characteristic of the Cumberland, and on the other hand to the human effigy figures of clay. It should again be emphasized that none of these are typical of the "Caddo" area.

Along the northwest coast of Florida there have been recovered a series of human effigies that belong to the Weeden Island period of that area. They are quite different from the Mississippi forms. They were found at the following sites:

Burnt Mill Creek	Moore, 1902, fig. 22
Burnt Mill Creek	Moore, 1902, figs. 32, 33
Davis Point	Moore, 1902, fig. 88
Hare Hammock	Moore, 1902, fig. 125
Mound A — Warrior River	Moore, 1902, fig. 321
Aspalaga	Moore, 1903b, fig. 150
Carney's Bluff	Moore, 1905, fig. 8
Davis Point	Moore, 1918, fig. 22
Lewis Place	Moore, 1918, fig. 38
Basin Bayou	Moore, 1901, figs. 49, 50

Most of these figures, because of the tightly compressed lips and plain eye surfaces, have a rather lugubrious appearance which suggests referring to them as the Aspalaga effigy.[32] These effigies have a vertical opening in the head or *mirabile dictu* have a hooded appear-

[28] Evers, 1880, pl. 24, *8*; Holmes, 1903, pl. XXXVI, *b*.
[28] Evers, 1880, pl. 24, *8*; Holmes, 1903, pl. XXVI, *b*.
[29] Moore, 1898, figs. 19 and 20.
[30] Moore, 1911, fig. 30.

[31] Moore, 1912, figs. 13–16.
[32] The effigy from this site has a curious resemblance to the late M. R. Gilmore.

ance, as on the Hare Hammock specimen, which is very close to the Casas Grandes hooded effigies. They are Weeden Island Plain and, although the identification is not certain, the locations from which the vessels came would appear to be Weeden Island I sites. The probable exception to this is the effigy from Carney's Bluff, Clarke County, Alabama, which has a different facial expression and is suggestive of some of the crude faces engraved on shell of the Spiro Focus.[33]

In table 2, giving the distribution of the effigy figures, there are a fair number of references to forms in the Anasazi area, some in the Hohokam, and quite a few in Chihuahua. Heretofore, suggestions of connection between the Mississippi effigy figures and the Southwest have been primarily concerned with the resemblance to the Chihuahua figures. If any readers of this report will take the trouble to examine the references cited for the Anasazi area, they will see a striking morphological resemblance in these Pueblo I to III forms to those from the New Madrid area, particularly in the variety with the vertical neck rising from the head. Naturally, the vessels are painted in black and white in the Anasazi culture and unpainted in southeast Missouri. By and large, the Hohokam effigies in the early period are not particularly suggestive of the rest of the Southwest or the Mississippi Valley, but the Los Muertos find is surely connected to the Chihuahua effigies.

It might be observed that these human effigy forms are more at home in the Mississippi than they appear to be in the Anasazi area, where they may be as early as Pueblo I, and certainly not later than Pueblo II and III.

That there are other connections of these effigy forms into Mesoamerica and northern South America we are fully aware, but in this publication our comparisons are for the moment sufficiently broad.

Head Vases
(Table 3, pp. 194–95)

The rare head vases from eastern Arkansas are quite exceptional pieces of Indian handicraft which have excited the interest and admiration of students for many years. In this publication there are given data on the distribution of these vases, and as the result of the extensive survey, and seriation of ceramic features, the relative time position is also made known. The head vases are always shell-tempered (where data are available on this point), and the red on buff or red and white painting usually applied to them indicates their association with the appearance and spread of these decorative techniques.[34] While this is a fairly limiting factor, as has been indicated in the descriptions of these painted types (pp. 132ff.), the distribution of head vases is even more restricted, being confined to the area north of the Arkansas River, south of the Missouri state line, and almost entirely in the area between the St. Francis and the Mississippi rivers. The work of this Survey has confirmed the recognition of the St. Francis and Memphis sub-areas as more or less distinct archaeological entities. The latter in the Mississippi Period (C–A) is dominated by the Walls-Pecan Point complex as distinct from the St. Francis with its special village layout and high proportion of Neeley's Ferry pottery. The head vases are found predominantly in the Walls-Pecan Point sites and in those sites in the St. Francis which have other indications of highly specific association with the Walls-Pecan Point complex, such as the Rose Site (12–N–3). It is also probable that the head vases are a relatively late development, not only because of their limited distribution but also because they are found in the Lower Arkansas in a form modified from the classic style. In this sub-area aboriginal materials were manufactured after they had disappeared in the St. Francis and Memphis regions.

The classic Pecan Point head vases (fig. 111) are excellent representations of the human head and face at a size somewhat smaller than that of a normal adult. The vessel opening is in the top of the head and varies in size from a wide mouth to a narrow aperture, which almost always has a low rim. The facial area is sometimes painted white and is

[33] Burnett, 1945, pl. XXXV.

[34] For illustrations of head vases in color, see Holmes, 1903, pl. XLIII.

well smoothed, while the rest of the head is covered with red. The ears have from three to six perforations, the eyes are closed, the lips are usually slightly open so that the teeth or tongue is partly visible. Most of the faces of the classic type have incised lines forming various designs which may represent tattooing or scarification. Whether these are clan symbols, markings for performances by special individuals in dances or ceremonies, is not known. Since very similar designs are found on different faces, they were evidently not individual decorations. Another fairly constant feature is the presence of a small knob projecting from the forehead at about the hairline and in the midline of the face, and this is usually perforated.

Some of the human heads on the human effigy water bottles carry a decoration like those on the head vases. One illustrated by Moore from Pecan Point and one from the Vernon Paul Place are particularly striking in this respect.[35] Another from the Walnut Site is illustrated in this volume (fig. 107, *c*). With this as a lead and the undoubtedly greater distribution of the human effigy water bottle with its strong emphasis on the representation of the human head, one might hypothesize that the head vase was a localized development out of the older more widespread form. Vaillant has called attention to the Mesoamerican distribution of the head vase which is concentrated in Costa Rica. He also refers to two heads from Ticoman, San Francisco Mazapan near Teotihuacan, "and others, particularly in the form of death's heads, occur scatteringly in the regions occupied by the Aztec and their cultural affiliates."[36] One of the best examples is from the Huasteca, but the time position of this specimen is not clear.[37] The absence of this form from the Southwest and even from the Casas Grandes area which offers so many parallels to the modeled pottery of the Mississippi afford no leads in this direction.

Variations on this classic type are numerous, some of which appear to reflect the varying skill of the potters rather than any fundamental change in concept or stylistic drift. While the usual orifice is wide with a short rim, the fine vessel from the Fortune Mound (11–N–15) has a noticeably high and narrow rim.[38] It is also distinctive because it is taller than it is wide. This head is also unusual in having a perforation through the forehead in the midline instead of the more common perforated knob. A somewhat similarly shaped rim is on a head vase from Pecan Point illustrated by Moore.[39] There are two other interesting features of this vase, in that the face is painted red, and the head is shown on a "neck" which very closely resembles the basal form of jars from Moundville and the Lower Arkansas and Natchezan areas.

Another feature of these heads is the extraordinary similarity between vessels from different sites. One from Bradley Place (11–P–2) in Crittenden County, in the Memphis Museum, is almost identical to one in the Chicago Natural History Museum from Cross County (cf. figs. 111, *b–b''* with *c–c''*). A third very similar specimen is in the Davenport Public Museum.

Usually, the St. Francis potters produced specimens which were not as well made or finished as those along the Mississippi, but some of the specimens from the Walls-Pecan Point sites along the Mississippi are also quite crude and some of those in the St. Francis sites are excellent. We are not yet able to say whether the Pecan Point type was produced in both areas or whether it was the product of a single group of potters and traded.

Along the Lower Arkansas most of the head vases are on the local bottle form with short "hour-glass" neck. The mouth is usually small and pouting and the facial expression is suggestive of a fish. This type has been referred to in table 3, giving the distribution of head vases, as the Conway type, and a characteristic example is illustrated by Holmes.[40] On this type the vessel form has a face applied to it rather than the head form being the vessel shape as in the Pecan Point type. Conway-

[35] Moore, 1911, fig. 70; Moore, 1910, pl. XX.
[36] Vaillant, 1932, p. 17, footnote 60.
[37] Strebel, 1889, vol. 2, pl. XXII, *11*.
[38] Moore, 1910, fig. 62; Douglas and D'Harnoncourt, 1941, p. 79.
[39] Moore, 1911, pl. XXXVI.
[40] Holmes, 1903, pl. XXIX, *a*.

type vessels seem to have dropped the symbolic designs of the classic type and taken on either a uniform red film or have a limited portion of the face covered with a white film. Closely related on the basis of general morphological characters is a form called here the Garland type in which the vessel is similar to the Conway and other late Lower Arkansas bottles. This is named after the county which produced another specimen illustrated by Holmes.[41] Another example with similar curvilinear trailed lines on an unpainted surface is in the Lemley collection and is also from Garland County.

A very distinctive type of head portrayal can be called the Charleston type because it is localized in the southeast Missouri area. Four bottles of this group have come from mounds near Charleston, in Mississippi County. The normal bottle body forms the head, and the face often shows considerable skill in modeling. The bottle necks are of the usual southeast Missouri carafe shape and rise directly out of the head. There are knobs, perforated or unperforated, on the forehead in the midline, above the ears, and at the back of the head. The eyes are usually rendered as though open, in contrast to the classic Pecan Point style, and the mouth is open. There is usually an annular base which is either vertical or flares outward slightly. The vessels are either of the plain, drab Mississippi ware (which in southeast Missouri is often clay-tempered) or are painted. At least one of these head vessels (No. 42 in table 3) is negative painted.[42]

The closest approach in the Southwest and Chihuahua to the head vases is a specimen from Casas Grandes illustrated by Lumholtz.[43] This is a polychrome vessel of red, white, and black. The human face is molded from the vessel wall. The eyes are almost closed. The mouth is open and indentations represent the teeth. The ears are not portrayed. This vessel and the one from the Huasteca have not been included in the list of the distribution of head vases.

[41] Holmes, 1903, pl. XXIX, *b*.

[42] Illustrations of these vessels may be seen in Evers, 1880, pl. 23, *1*, *2*.

[43] Lumholtz, 1902, vol. I, pl. V, *d*.

The Man-bowl or "Chacmool" Effigy
(Table 4, p. 169)

This somewhat bizarre form, in which the vessel forms the body of a reclining figure with the head protruding on one side and the feet on the other, is not illustrated in this publication, but its distribution is given in table 4. It is most common in the Cumberland, and the one example from Moundville is reminiscent of that area. There are some specimens from northeastern Arkansas, but their exact provenience is not known. The specimen from southwestern Indiana is from a site which is out of place in that area, for the ceramic complex is strongly suggestive of southeast Missouri and northeastern Arkansas. The specimens from southeastern Missouri are perhaps not exactly man-bowls since they are on the bottle form, but the similarity is so marked that they have been included under this heading.[44] Again, when looking for a similarity to the complex, modeled forms of a Mississippi culture, we find our closest analogy in specimens from northern Chihuahua. After some number of these connections one begins to wonder at the psychic unity of man which causes him (or her) to duplicate forms once the concept of modeling life forms has been evolved or introduced. A form very similar to those in the Cumberland and Survey Area was found in Salcaja, Guatemala.[45] It has been considered a South American trait which diffused into Mesoamerica and thus would have traveled the path of the stirrup spout and the human effigy vessel.[46]

Quadruped Effigies
(Table 4, p. 169)

Included in our illustrations (fig. 108, *j'*) is an effigy figure with teapot-spout tail and an incised facial area suggestive of the composite serpent-cat effigies. This is from the Beck Place (13–O–7), one of the late Mississippi sites in the Memphis sub-area. The effigy recalls very strongly one from Pecan Point with Rhodes Incised decoration but which is a quadruped jar.[47] Another quadruped from the Menard Site (17–K–1) with Leland Incised

[44] Evers, 1880, pl. 20, *1*.

[45] Vaillant, 1927, fig. 120.

[46] Thompson, 1936, pp. 16, 80, 107.

[47] Moore, 1911, fig. 68.

decoration on the body is illustrated by Moore.[48] On this vessel the effigy head is almost unrecognizable. From the Bell Site (10–P–2) the Lemley brothers (Cat. No. V-807) have obtained a small four-footed effigy with a "dog" head projecting from the middle of the body and a balancing short horizontal tail. It is a wide-mouth, short-neck bottle of Bell Plain paste. In the collection of Dr. P. F. Titterington (Cat. No. 1057), there is a Bell Plain wide-mouth, short-neck quadruped bottle with a serpent-cat head and curled tail. The body has two "dimples" on the side much as appears in the Walls-Pecan Point complex and at Moundville. This vessel is from Dunklin County, Missouri, 6 miles northeast of Hooversville. The Engelmann collection in the Peabody Museum, Harvard University (Cat. No. 48695), has a quadruped effigy from "Mound XV" in the New Madrid area. It is a carafe-neck bottle with a rather well-modeled "dog" head and curled tail. The surface finish is the well-polished dark gray of the better southeast Missouri pottery. The American Museum of Natural History has an unusual "dog" pot from near Charleston, Missouri, Mississippi County (Cat. No. 2319 [Terry]). It is an elliptical bowl with a rather large protruding modeled head and a curled tail. It is a mottled gray to buff, slightly polished, plain type. From Perry County, Missouri, there is a "dog" pot, with the carafe neck broken off, that appears to be of this same plain ware.[49] Probably from the New Madrid area is a four-legged, carafe-neck bottle with a serpent-cat head and curled tail. The vessel has a yellowish to buff color and has red and white designs on the body of small red and white disks with a three-line curvilinear meander connecting the disks which is somewhat unusual. It is suggestive of the typical designs found in the Leland-Fatherland-Natchez types to the south.[50]

A four-legged animal effigy vessel of Old Town Red is in the Memphis Public Museum. It is probably from Bradley Place (11–P–2). It is a bottle form with a reconstructed neck. The head has attributes of the serpent-cat effigy and the tail is reconstructed as a strap handle. It has button eyes, a protruding nose, and incised lines along the neck.

In the University of Arkansas there is an excellent Rhodes Incised bowl with four legs, tail, and a serpent-cat neck and head from the Beck Site (13–O–7). From Nodena (10–Q–1) the Alabama Museum of Natural History obtained an excellent Rhodes Incised wide-mouth bottle with serpent-cat head and weeping eye. It has a curled tail. Another Rhodes Incised wide-mouth bottle with four legs and the composite serpent-cat effigy features including the curled tail is in the Davenport Public Museum. It is almost certainly from eastern Arkansas along the Mississippi. In the Hampson collection at Nodena, Arkansas, there is a Nodena Red and White serpent-cat, four-legged, wide-mouth bottle from the Bishop Site (Mississippi County, Arkansas). The body design is a six-line swastika.

Another four-legged form usually has short slab-like feet on an elongated "duck"-pot body and a cylindrical neck protruding from the "head end" of the body. An Old Town Red example is in the Lemley collection (Cat. No. U-1624) from the Cummings Place (11–O–4). There is an excellent example in the collection of Dr. P. F. Titterington of this vessel style with Nodena Red and White decoration. It is from Marked Tree, Poinsett County, Arkansas, and is very close to the vessel from "Arkansas" illustrated by Holmes.[51]

The Tail-riding Effigy Bowl

This somewhat crude term refers to a highly specialized effigy feature which is fairly common in the St. Francis and Memphis sub-areas, and according to the available distributional evidence is more at home here than in any other known region. Without presenting the evidence for this position in any great detail, some substantiation will be afforded by referring to figure 101, *i*, *j*, *l*, *m*, *q*, and *q'*. These vessels from the Hazel Place near Marked Tree in Poinsett County, Arkansas; the Warner Place, Mississippi County; Vernon Paul, Cross County; if considered with a specimen from Nodena,[52] and Rhodes in

[48] Moore, 1908a, fig. 7.
[49] Evers, 1880, pl. 24, *3*.
[50] Evers, 1880, pl. 9, *1*.
[51] Holmes, 1903, pl. XLII, *b*.
[52] Thruston, 1897, fig. 53.

Mississippi County, will demonstate that this concept was completely familiar to the potters of both the St. Francis and Memphis regions.

South and west of the Survey Area very similar specimens have come from the Glendora Site in Louisiana; [53] from Watermelon Island, Hot Springs County, Arkansas; [54] Battle Place, Lafayette County, Arkansas; [55] and from the Frankston Focus of east Texas,[56] which belongs in the Fulton Aspect. Harrington also recovered a vessel with the tail-riding effigy from Site No. 4 near Hot Springs.[57]

This form serves to connect the later "Caddo" area sites with the northern part of the Survey Area as do quite a number of other traits. The effigy forms are in the main moving south and west from the Mississippi Valley to the "Caddo" area.

The Gourd Form

The New Madrid district of southeast Missouri is the center of Mississippi vessel forms in the shape of the bottle gourd. This is, of course, a natural form which would be easily copied in clay, and there are specimens in the Peabody Museum from Kentucky cave deposits of actual gourds with an aperture cut precisely like the opening in the clay effigies. Probably the earliest appearance of this form in the eastern United States is at the Brangenberg Site in Calhoun County, Illinois, a Hopewell mound group atop the bluffs on the west side of the Illinois River.[58] This particular specimen bears an incised design, another indication of its uniqueness. Specimens of the gourd effigy are found sparingly in the Survey Area,[59] particularly in the Memphis sub-area, but here they are usually combined with representation of the human head (fig. 107, *h–k*). They are usually of the type Bell Plain.

Outside of southeast Missouri the gourd bottle appears only rarely in the Cumberland region.[60] It does not occur in the "Caddo" area, southern Louisiana, or the Florida Gulf Coast.

This is another one of the Mississippi forms which has interesting analogies in the Southwest, particularly in the Anasazi area. Here they apparently first appear in Pueblo I and are particularly common in the La Plata area. It is said that they were not made frequently in Pueblo II and thereafter are very rare.[61]

ECCENTRIC FORMS AND SPECIALIZED FEATURES

Compound Vessels — Horizontal Style (Table 5, pp. 197–98)

Vessels of this class are illustrated in figure 106, *j–m*, and their distribution is given in table 5. It is believed that this vessel shape is somewhat more limited in its chronological and areal distribution than is the vertical compound form discussed below. In the Survey Area the vessels joined are normally two small wide-mouth jars with the bodies touching each other and an opening between, or a cylindrical rod joining them. There is often a second connecting rod or bar of clay in the rim area. These horizontal compound forms are most often found with Bell Plain paste and finish, although there is one Nodena Red and White example and one Kent Incised. They seem to be limited practically to the Memphis sub-area.

Only two similar vessels from the Southeast and one from Illinois have come to our attention. One of these is from the excavations of the University of Tennessee in Stewart County, Tennessee, while the other is from the Etowah excavations. The Illinois specimen is from the Crable Site, Fulton County, Illinois. In the Southwest this form seems to occur rather late and to be concentrated in the Casas Grandes area of northern Chihuahua. The Anasazi specimens are Pueblo II–III.

[53] Moore, 1909, fig. 79.
[54] Hodges collection, Cat. No. 307.
[55] Moore, 1912, fig. 65.
[56] Krieger, 1946, fig. 18.
[57] Harrington, 1920, pl. XXXI, *a*.
[58] Griffin and Morgan, 1941, pp. 39–44, pl. 45.
[59] Holmes, 1903, pl. XIX, *f* and *g*.
[60] Thruston, 1897, pl. V.
[61] Morris, 1939, pp. 163–64.

Vertical Compound Vessels

Another expression of shape virtuosity in the northern part of the Survey Area is the vertical compound vessel in which one shape is portrayed as resting upon or half inserted in or covering up the shape below (fig. 104, *k–o*, *t*). There are numerous variations, including jar on jar, bottle on jar, bottle on bowl, etc. This treatment is of course rather widespread and is found in the eastern United States in Hopewell times but reaches a peak in the Mississippi cultures and particularly in southeast Missouri and the Survey Area. It is also found in the "Caddo" area, but not as commonly as in the St. Francis, Memphis, and southeast Missouri. The negative-painted vessel with a high cylindrical-neck bottle placed upon a four-handled jar at the Sanders Site, Lamar County, Texas, is almost certainly from the New Madrid area, and would appear to be one of the items which was traded into the Sanders Site from the north and east.[62] Vertical compound forms are found in the Southwest and particularly in the Casas Grandes area of Chihuahua. This was one of the vessel shapes which Vaillant included as a form which possibly belonged to the "Q" complex.[63] It is not a very specific feature and might easily have been developed independently in more than one place.

Basket-handle Bowl
(Table 6, p. 199)

This form is quite rare in the Southeast and is known to occur in the Survey Area only in Poinsett County, Arkansas, although it has been found on a ware equivalent to Neeley's Ferry Plain in New Madrid County, Missouri.[64] The very close connection of the material in southeast Missouri to our collections is sufficient excuse for commenting on this form and its distribution (see table 6). It has also been found in eastern Tennessee at two sites; [65] also by the University of Tennessee excavations at the Dallas Site, type site of the Dallas Focus, and these three examples are the only ones known from the eastern United States. We have found but three examples in the literature of the Southwest, where the vessels date around A.D. 800 to 1000. There are two or perhaps three vessels from Chihuahua. A similar handle is associated with vertical spout jars in the Huasteca country.

Vessels with Tetrapod Feet

This is a rare trait on Mississippi pottery, but has been encountered in the Survey Area. One example with Bell Plain paste from the Beck Site (13–O–7) is illustrated in figure 105, *s*. In the Hampson collection at Wilson, Arkansas, there is a tetrapod bottle with a wide and medium-high neck. It is from the Twist Site (11–N–14), Cross County, Arkansas, and is either Neeley's Ferry or Bell Plain. The legs are cylindrical and come to a conical point. Another bottle form with the neck missing and with an angled shoulder is from Wapanoca, in Crittenden County, Arkansas, figure 105, *r*. In the Nashville area one tetrapod jar has been taken from a stone grave at Old Town, Williamson County, which seems to be a Middle to late Mississippi site.[66]

There is no indication that there is any direct connection between these tetrapods and those which begin in the Tchefuncte-Adena level and carry on into early Hopewellian times.

Tetrapods are also very rare in the Southwestern area.[67] They appear first in the Santa Cruz and Sacaton phases of Hohokam, with cylindrical legs attached to a low open-bowl form of Sacaton Red on Buff, dated around A.D. 900 to 1100. Another form has four somewhat conoidal feet with a sharply flaring rim on what is essentially a bowl form.[68]

Tripod Vessels
(Table 7, pp. 200–04)

These vessels are fairly common in the Survey Area (fig. 105, *e–g*) and lend themselves rather well to distributional examination (see table 7). They are of course a vessel feature which "is a very characteristic Middle American trait, almost universally distributed

[62] Krieger, 1946, p. 191. The bottle on a jar at Moundville also seems to be an interloper from the Survey Area. Moore, 1905, fig. 72.

[63] Vaillant, 1932.

[64] Collection of Dr. P. F. Titterington, Cat. No. 920.

[65] Holmes, 1884, p. 444.

[66] Jones, 1876, fig. 51.

[67] Sayles, 1936, fig. 16, *5*.

[68] Gladwin, et al., 1937, fig. 68, *e* and *f*.

in that region." (and) "Since the idea of the tripod is so foreign to North American ceramics as a whole, it looks therefore Central American in origin."[69] Unfortunately, there is little direct evidence as to the time period and route which might have carried the tripod idea into the Survey Area. Some concepts can, however, be formulated on the basis of the evidence available.

Tripods are primarily found in the St. Francis and Memphis sub-areas and a few in southeastern Missouri. They do not go much farther north up the Mississippi than the mouth of the Ohio in any significant number, and do not go up the Ohio. They do not appear in the Cumberland Aspect on plain shell-tempered pottery and are not part of the late Mississippi foci of the south Appalachian area. This can be taken to mean that they are not part of the Old Village–Macon Plateau complex of early Mississippi. They do not spread far from their area of concentration in the later Mississippi levels. The specimen from Moundville[70] looks very much like Neeley's Ferry Plain from the St. Francis, brought back by some redskin trader who had been selling good Moundville Engraved vessels in the swamps of northeastern Arkansas. There is a secondary center of tripods in the southwestern Arkansas "Caddo" area and the adjacent Texas region. They do not seem to be particularly common in Texas, and Krieger in his discussion of the tripartite Maxey Noded Red ware vessel from the Sanders Site refers only to the rather general occurrence of tripods in the central Mississippi Basin.[71] The Davis Site and other early sites of the Gibson Aspect do not have the tripod, so that the form appears only in late Gibson and the succeeding Fulton Period. One is reported from Spiro.

That the form is relatively late, no matter when it had its inception, is evidenced by its presence at the Greer Site in Jefferson County, Arkansas, at three sites of the Glendora Focus in eastern Louisiana, and at the Bradley Site (11–P–2) just west of Memphis and at the Oliver Site (16–N–6). Both of these latter sites had European materials in small amounts.

In the Survey Area the overwhelming majority of the tripods are found on bottles. They are especially typical of the St. Francis sites and are found less often in those of the Memphis sub-area. They are on Neeley's Ferry and Bell Plain, Old Town Red, Carson Red on Buff, Nodena Red and White, and Avenue Polychrome vessels. They are on short, wide-mouth bottles, cylindrical-neck bottles of varying neck height, and on carafe-neck bottles in the New Madrid area. The form of the tripod itself also varies. The most common has been called a bulbous leg in this report and looks something like the commercial mushroom. Others are conical, cylindrical, spherical, or ball-shaped, slab-shaped which is often stepped, and peniform. The bulbous type of tripod feet are usually hollow, opening into the vessel body. Occasionally, these become so swollen and the body of the vessel so reduced that the result is in effect a compound vessel of three compartments. More rarely these hollow feet are closed and provided with rattles.

This variability of type is confusing and makes it difficult to associate the tripods with their Middle American counterparts. They do not suggest Mexican Archaic forms. It might be noted, however, that the slab legs, including some with stepped design, do not appear in Middle America until the Mixteca-Nahua Period and are particularly characteristic of Aztec III–IV. They are limited to the St. Francis and Memphis sub-areas in the Mississippi Valley with the exception of one from the Greer Site on the Lower Arkansas.

In the Southwestern area tripods are very rare and only occur in the Hohokam on bowls beginning in the Sacaton Phase. They are also rare in Chihuahua. There is not much connection between the Mississippi Valley and the Southwest on the basis of tripod and tetrapod supports. It might be added that the Hohokam supports are not suggestive of Mesoamerican forms either early or late.

Stirrup-neck Bottles

(Table 8, pp. 205–06)

One of the most significant shapes in the Mississippi ceramic complex is the stirrup-neck bottle (fig. 106, *a–c*) because of its im-

[69] Vaillant, 1932, pp. 12–13.

[70] Moore, 1905, p. 240, fig. 172.

[71] Krieger, 1946, p. 216.

portance in suggesting cultural contacts over a wide area in the Americas. The accompanying table 8 gives the distribution of this form in the Mississippi Valley, the Southwest, and Mexico. Various authors have already called attention to the connection with the stirrup-neck bottles of Peru where the form is found as early as Chavín, now estimated to be at least as old as 400 B.C. It seems to have skipped the Central American and Maya area, appearing at Tlatilco in the Valley of Mexico at the earliest suggested date for that region, which would be somewhere around A.D. 1. Other occurrences in Mexico are concentrated in western Mexico in the Michoacan "Tarascan" region. In the Southwest the stirrup-neck bottle is found primarily in the eastern part of the Anasazi occupation and ranges in time from Basket Maker III to the late nineteenth century.

In the eastern United States this shape primarily occurs in the northern part of our Survey Area and, less commonly, in southeast Missouri. It is one of the forms which indicates close cultural connections between the above-mentioned sub-regions on the full Mississippi ceramic level. It has not been found in the southern part of the Lower Mississippi Valley or in the "Caddo" area. In the lower Southeast there is one occurrence at Chipola Cut-Off, a Fort Walton Period site on the northwest coast of Florida. Only rarely does it occur in the Mississippi or Ohio valleys to the north. This form cannot be dated accurately except that it falls around time line B. It does not seem to have been one of the early Mississippi forms, nor did it spread far once it appeared. While it may have been independently developed, it is at least as likely that it can be connected with the Southwestern examples, from there to western Mexico, and ultimately to Peru.

The Teapot Vessel

(Table 9, pp. 207–09)

This distinctive form has produced considerable comment as well as controversy. Its distribution is given in table 9, and several examples are illustrated in figure 113, *a–h*. Vessels of this shape were found in the Menard area during the Mound survey conducted under the direction of Cyrus Thomas. They were illustrated and briefly described by Holmes who pointed out their curious resemblance to the European teapot.[72] In his first discussion of *The Ancient Pottery of the Mississippi Valley*, Holmes said:

> The neck is low and wide, and the body is a compressed sphere. The spout is placed upon one side and a low knob upon the other. The absence of a handle for grasping indicates that the vessel was probably not intended for boiling water. These characters are uniform in all the specimens that have come to my notice.[73]

Holmes then attempted to derive the teapot form from animal effigies such as are common in the area. Moore's excavations provided considerable additional information. In the sites he dug along the Lower Arkansas he uncovered twenty-eight teapot vessels ranging in size from 4.9 cm. to 19.3 cm. in height. Since all but one of the sites he excavated contained a small amount of early European goods, and at Douglas in Lincoln County he unearthed a burial with teapot vessels and glass and brass beads in direct association, the time position of them is quite clear.[74] In addition, Moore was apparently the first to suggest a connection with the spouted vessels of the Panuco Valley in northeastern Mexico. He also recognized the geographical limits of the form in the eastern Arkansas and near-by regions.

Vaillant considered the teapot to be a closely related form to the Mesoamerican spouted vessel and stated that "The form wherein the spout acts as the tail of an animal reaches its maximum development in Vera Cruz. Modeled animal forms in the West Mississippi drainage parallel in area, spouted vessels."[75] In this we think that he was in error, for the modeled animal forms have a much wider distribution and are earlier in time than the teapots. Vaillant at the time was promoting the "Q" complex, a postulated early basic ceramic complex which spread widely over Mesoamerica and into the Southeast. The teapot was one of the traits of this

[72] Holmes, 1884, p. 482.
[73] Holmes, 1886, p. 403.
[74] Moore, 1908a, p. 525.
[75] Vaillant, 1932, p. 15.

complex. Phillips took the position that: "The teapot is a problem all by itself. Its extremely narrow distribution in the Middle Mississippi, coupled with demonstrable lateness in time would seem to argue strongly against derivation from an early horizon in Middle America."[76] Dickinson and Dellinger, in reporting on material from a site on the Lower Arkansas River, illustrated a teapot and maintained that this vessel and the others from the site represented the earthenware of the Quapaw.[77] Quimby included the "Red-Filmed" (Old Town Red) teapot as a Natchez form, for one was excavated from Fatherland Mound C, accompanied by trade materials. He referred to the presence of this form in historic "Caddo" sites in northern Louisiana and suggested that possibly this shape was the result of Indian copying of a French form, for Du Pratz tells of asking the Natchez to make copies of French earthenware. The same author also pointed out that vessels of this type have come from sites showing no evidence of contact so that it might predate European influence.[78] Obviously, however, all Indian sites of the early historic period did not receive European trade goods.

An examination of the distribution table of this form brings out some very interesting comparative information. First of all, there is the obvious fact of its predominance in the Lower Arkansas area, a short distance to the north in the Lower St. Francis, and up the Mississippi to Mississippi County, Arkansas. Its distribution extends south to northern Louisiana. In the Lower Arkansas the teapot is usually covered or partly covered with red paint; one example is Nodena Red and White and four are Avenue Polychrome. Some are plain shell temper, and the incising first illustrated by Holmes from near Menard is very close to Fatherland Incised. The vessels in the St. Francis and Memphis areas are largely plain with some red-filmed and red and white painting. There are more vessels of this type from sites of the Memphis sub-area than from the St. Francis, and in the latter area they are from sites with other indications of contact with their neighbors to the east.

On the basis of this information, the bald-headed author of this section of the report draws some rather interesting conclusions, to wit: that red-filmed, red and white, and polychrome pottery continued to be made up to approximately 1700; that the Walls-Pecan Point complex of the Memphis area, no matter when it "began," came up into the historic period and died a sudden death; that the late Mississippi complex at the Oliver Site comes up into the historic period and is contemporary with Natchezan.

In spite of a fondness on the part of the present authors for moving culture traits about with somewhat reckless abandon, the teapot shape does not seem to be one which has any connection with the Mesoamerican spouted-vessel forms. We are practically forced to admit an invention, for while the theory of its being a copy of a French form is a happy one, who knows whether Du Pratz stopped for tea?

NEGATIVE PAINTING IN THE EASTERN UNITED STATES

(Table 10, pp. 210–15)

Out of all the sherds picked up during the Survey, only one specimen from the Spendthrift Site (16–O–2) was negative painted. Consequently, this may seem not to be the place to present in any detail the distribution of this decorative technique. But since excellent examples of whole vessels have come from the Survey Area (fig. 111, *j*) and since it is associated with a number of contemporary and closely related groups and since this detailed record has never before been presented, it is included in this publication.

The paper by Willey and Phillips[79] and the more recent statement by Willey[80] has very clearly identified a number of negative-painted specimens in the Crystal River Focus

[76] Phillips, 1940, p. 363.
[77] Dickinson and Dellinger, 1940.
[78] Quimby, 1942, p. 263.
[79] Willey and Phillips, 1944.
[80] Willey, 1948.

of the Hopewellian Period along the Florida Gulf Coast. These examples both precede the Mississippi expression of negative painting and are quite different stylistically. At the moment, there does not seem to be any direct connection in ceramic negative painting between Crystal River and the Mississippi. Some time ago, Willoughby [81] observed that certain Hopewellian cloth fragments must have been decorated by the lost-color technique in the same way as the specimens from Etowah and from Spiro. Thus, the technique once introduced, presumably from South or Mesoamerica, by an as yet unknown route, could well have been preserved as a part of the textile industry, and undergone an independent development on pottery during the Mississippi Period.

In his Ph.D. thesis Phillips made a study and analysis of the available specimens of negative painting, recognizing two major centers in the southeast in the Mississippi Period. Much of the ensuing discussion is taken from his material, with modifications based on later information.

Nashville Negative Painted

Lewis and Kneberg have introduced the term Dallas Negative Painted into the literature on the basis of the few sherds and vessels they have illustrated. This was not, however, accompanied by any kind of a description of the type. Since it is fairly obvious that the entire Dallas Focus was derived pot, point, and pyramid, including the negative painting, from the Cumberland Valley in central Tennessee, it is felt that the designation "Nashville" recognizes the historic priority as well as the much greater concentration of this technique in central Tennessee.

Nashville Negative Painted may be divided into two groups, depending on whether or not a slip has been applied to the paste. The exact significance of this is not immediately apparent but does recognize a practical difference. The specimens in which there is no slip are distinctly in the minority. They have a thin, faded black pigment on a polished pinkish-buff surface. Designs, where they can be made out, are simple concentric circles or scalloped disks circumscribing a cross. Decoration on the effigies is precisely similar to that of effigies in white-slipped ware. Negative painting on a white slip, evidently the definitive decorated pottery for the Cumberland, was represented by some twenty whole vessels in the specimens studied by Phillips, and most of the examples in published sources belong in this group. It has the same fine, shell-tempered pinkish-buff paste as the unslipped group, over which a fine, polished white slip was applied. The slip showed a marked tendency to disappear carrying with it, of course, the decoration. Many examples look very much as though the slip had come off in washing the vessel. Added to this is the unfortunate tendency for the black stain to fade. Several writers refer to the fact that designs which can be made out plainly when the vessel is first taken from the ground quickly disappear upon exposure to the air. Further, in some cases, it appears that the black has turned white, probably as a result of misfiring. The upshot of all these adverse conditions is that in most cases very little can be made out of the original design. Sometimes it is necessary to dampen the surface merely to ascertain whether or not there was a design. This same tendency is also a characteristic of negative-painted vessels in South and Mesoamerica.

Jars are never decorated by negative painting nor is it found on the exterior of bowls. It was confined to bottles and related shapes which might be considered under the heading "closed" containers. This seems also to be the case with the majority of vessels decorated by negative painting in South and Mesoamerica and is in marked contrast to the Crystal River Negative-painted bowls. A few plates with decoration on the inner rim are found in the Cumberland area around Nashville, but the great center for this shape is apparently at the Angel Site in southwestern Indiana. The most common shape in the negative-painted ware of the Cumberland is the carafe-neck bottle, often with four lobes on the body separated by shallow vertical grooves. This bottle shape is normally with-

[81] Manuscript in possession of Henry Hamilton of Marshall, Missouri.

out basal features, although one example with tripod feet has been reported from central Tennessee and one from Etowah.[82] These two vessels are so similar that we are inclined to believe the Etowah specimen is either a trade piece or was made by a potter from central Tennessee. One of the most common designs is the sun symbol, with a cross portraying the four world quarters placed in the center, and with the rays of the sun forming a peripheral circle. Other examples without all the distinguishing characteristics have been listed in the accompanying table 10 as "modified sun symbols." [83] The tall necks are usually horizontally striped, sometimes solid black.

One of the most striking negative-painted forms is the so-called "dog" pot, the distribution of which is given in table 10, and these are amply illustrated in the literature. It seems likely that its center is in the Cumberland and that the specimens in eastern Tennessee and Georgia were either derived from there or inspired from that center. The ramifications of the "dog" pot extend beyond that of negative painting, for some of the specimens reveal a connection with the serpent-cat effigy concept which is widely distributed in the Southeast in Mississippi Period cultures. This mythological creature is represented not only in unpainted rim effigy bowls and quadruped vessels already discussed in this section, but appears on the effigy stone pipes from Moundville and related sites and has an intimate part in the socio-religious complex of the late Southeastern cultures.

Also apparently confined to the Cumberland area are negative-painted human effigies which have been reproduced by Thruston and Myer.[84] The decoration consists of oblique hatching in zones which suggested to Myer that it represented a rattlesnake motif. While this may be applicable to the specimen described by him, it is doubtful if all the painted human effigies have a rattlesnake motif. Myer's specimen was a thin, hollow, elongated form without an opening. Another form with a hooded neck has the shoulders broader than the waist and is hump-backed. Others are more similar to the normal human effigy figure with its somewhat blocky form.

Another effigy form associated with negative painting is the owl which is usually rendered as a tripod vessel with the tail acting as a third support. As a negative-painted form this seems to be confined to the Cumberland, although somewhat similar owl effigies are also found in southeast Missouri. These are of course elaborations of the hooded bottle or vice versa. There are a few examples of human effigy heads on the hooded bottle forms with negative painting on the bodies.

One of the most striking pieces is the specimen illustrated by Thruston,[85] with a hand and skull design in negative painting which has very closely related specimens at Moundville and from a site in northwestern Alabama which we may point out is on the way from the Cumberland to Moundville. Not only is negative painting uncommon at Moundville but painting of any kind is very rare at that site. Incised designs of the skull, hand, and eye are, however, much more common there, than at any other site or area in the southeast and are among the strongest connecting links to Mesoamerica.

It should be emphasized that negative painting seems to be the only form of painted decoration in the Cumberland area.[86] It is also significant that negative painting in the Cumberland is strongly associated with effigy forms which does not seem to be the case at the Angel Site or in southeast Missouri, the two other major Southeastern centers of this technique.

Angel Negative Painted

Whether this term will actually be used by Glenn A. Black in his description of the predominant painted ware at the Angel Site in southwestern Indiana is not known, but certainly there is present at that site a phenomenally large number of examples of negative painting on the inner rim of plates. There is considerable variation in the designs which include rectilinear and curvilinear patterns and the portrayal of various signs and symbols inti-

[82] Moorehead, 1932, fig. 33, *a*.

[83] Ford is dubious of these Fewksian deductions.

[84] Thruston, 1897, pl. IX; Myer, 1917, fig. 2 and pp. 98–99.

[85] Thruston, 1897, fig. 40.

[86] Red filming of vessels which is relatively rare in this area is arbitrarily not regarded as a form of painting.

mately associated with the "Southern Cult." Examples of Angel Negative Painted have been found at Kincaid where they should be associated with the closing days of that large Mississippi site in southern Illinois. The negative-painted plate illustrated by Thruston[87] from the Nashville area may be from Angel. Other negative-painted plate rims, such as those found along the Tennessee River in northern Alabama and even at the Peachtree Site, may have had their inspiration from southwestern Indiana.

Sikeston Negative Painted

In southeast Missouri, classification of painted wares is beset by difficulties. Unfortunately, the aboriginal artists did not realize that archaeologists would distinguish between negative painting and direct painting. This apparently did not confuse them but does us. One fact is certainly clear, and that is that the two were contemporaneous, for they appear on the same vessels. In the Cumberland area the potters were much more considerate except in one or two instances. On Sikeston Negative Painted there are numerous instances where negative painting is the only method displayed, and this is particularly true in vessels with a modified sun-symbol design. There are, however, a sufficient number of vessels in which both negative and direct painting are so combined as to make their separation difficult. Negative painting was apparently used as the primary method for blocking out the design which was subsequently filled in by direct painting. As a result of this, and the well-known tendency for the black stain used in negative painting to fade, it is frequently very difficult to detect any remaining traces of the negative-painted design.

In southeast Missouri none of the vessels have a white slip, and the stain was applied directly to a polished surface which ranges in color all the way from a light vinaceous buff to a dark red brown. Efforts to segregate types such as black on buff as opposed to black on red were entirely unsuccessful. Shapes and styles of decoration cut across any differences in color. Designs are simple and not particularly varied, the commonest motifs being concentric or radiating star-like figures of the sort usually referred to as "cosmic symbols." These are generally repeated four times and are sometimes connected by sets of horizontal lines. Horizontal lines alone make a simpler decorative scheme, possibly intended to show as a series of concentric circles when viewed from above. Shapes are almost entirely confined to carafe-neck bottles, though occasional human, animal, and fish effigies from this area are decorated by negative painting.[88]

From the above, it will be seen that, as in a fair number of other cultural traits, there is a strong New Madrid–Cumberland axis in negative painting. Two negative-painted "spouts" have been found in the "Caddo" area. The vessel from Haley Place was recognized by Moore, as well as others, to be connected from the standpoint of its origin with the southeast Missouri–Cumberland area, which would indicate that these centers were in full bloom at the time of the Haley Focus.[89] A similar attribution may be assigned to the negative-painted compound vertical vessel at the Sanders Site.[90] The present tendency on the part of some archaeologists to regard certain "Caddo" sites as significantly earlier than similar ceremonial representations in the major part of the Southeast will probably not find wide acceptance, and the presence of these negative-painted bottles is one of the strongest evidences against this viewpoint.

In considering the probable chronological position of negative painting, it is abundantly clear that it is not associated with early Mississippi cultural units such as Old Village, Aztalan, or the Small Log Town House–Hiwassee Island–Macon Plateau group. We also have no reason to think that it is part of the earlier Mississippi materials in the Survey Area. No matter when this technique first appeared, it is certainly associated most commonly with the full-blown manifestations of the "Southern Cult" and was contemporary with the major centers showing cult material in such sites as Moundville and Etowah. Its absence at Spiro is puzzling, for it is difficult to believe that the major ceremonial develop-

[87] Thruston, 1897, fig. 41.
[88] Evers, 1880, pl. 9, *1*, *4*.
[89] Moore, 1912.
[90] Krieger, 1946, p. 191.

ment at Spiro is significantly earlier than the centers in the east. It is also apparent that negative painting at Bull Creek in Georgia, at the Crable Site in Illinois, and at the Angel Site in Indiana are relatively late and their occupation probably came up well into the seventeenth century.

The areal distribution of this ceramic decoration is also interesting, for its marked absence in the "Caddo" area, except as occasional trade vessels, is not particularly encouraging for a land connection into eastern Mexico, although negative painting has been found as far north in Mexico as San Luis Potosi. There is also no likelihood of a connection via the Southwest or Chihuahua, because negative painting has not been reported in these areas.[90a] We are again left, as in so many other instances, with a prehistoric trait which has many connections with South and Meso-america but the way in which they were transmitted to the Southeast is still inexplicable.

VARIOUS EXOTIC DESIGNS

Among the pottery decorations that indicate inter-areal connections, there is a group which ties the Walls-Pecan Point sites of the Memphis area with Moundville and other centers where expressions of the "Southern Cult" have been recovered. Three vessels from the Rhodes Site in the University of Arkansas collection belong in this group. The first of these is a variant of Walls Engraved. It is a flattened-globular, wide-mouth bottle with a low ring base and well-polished surface. On the upper body there are four engraved hand designs with a simple cross or "X" design in the center. Two of the opposing hands depend from the base of the neck while the other two rise from the lower body. The second vessel from Rhodes is illustrated in this report (fig. 111, *i*) and is Nodena Red and White with an outline of a hand on the neck. The third vessel (fig. 111, *h*) is a variant of Walls Engraved. It has a slightly flattened globular body with a notched-edge disk base and a short, wide neck with a beveled inner rim. The engraved design is very close to the heart design found on a vessel at Moundville.[91] These two examples at Moundville and Rhodes are the only known examples of the "heart" in the Southeast. The Rhodes vessel is certainly not an import from Moundville, as all of its characteristics are of the local Walls-Pecan Point complex.

In the Lemley collection at Hope, Arkansas, there is a Walls Engraved wide-mouth, long cylindrical-neck bottle with a notched-edge disk base (Cat. No. V–317) from the L. W. Gosnell Place near Blytheville, Mississippi County, Arkansas. It has engraved on the body the hand and long-bone design. The fingers have cross lines representing the finger joints as on the Moundville hands. In the palm of the hand there is a cross design.

A third site in Mississippi County, Arkansas, Bell Place, has produced a Bell Plain wide-mouth bottle with the neck broken off, which has two small appliqué human effigy heads on opposite sides of the body at the greatest diameter. Equidistant between these two heads and on the same plane are two small crude appliqué four-fingered hands. This vessel is in the University of Arkansas collections. Also from Bell Place is a Nodena Red and White bottle (fig. 111, *k*) with low ring base and wide, high neck that has the hand and long-bone design. On this vessel it is associated with the step design.

A vessel from Pecan Point obtained by Moore is a Bell Plain, wide-mouth, medium-high neck bottle with a low ring base. "On two opposite sides, in relief, are modeled human faces, while on two other opposite sides, also in relief, human hands are represented. Between the hands and the faces are four long bones, in relief." [92] Moore refers to a vessel from Blytheville, Arkansas, in the Mitchell collection in St. Louis, "which bears in relief three hands, three faces, and seven long bones." [93]

In the Hampson collection at Wilson, Arkansas, there is a wide-mouth, short-neck bottle

[90a] This statement must be modified for Brew, 1946, fig. 101, *w*, unfortunately reports a fine example from southeastern Utah in a Pueblo I context. Perhaps this is another example of the priority of painted decoration in the Anasazi area. Two negative painted vessels from Chihuahua are reported by H. P. Mera (1945). The general conclusion that the Southwest played no part in the transmission of negative painting from nuclear America to the Southeast is still sound.

[91] Moore, 1905, fig. 147.

[92] Moore, 1911, pp. 459–60 and fig. 69.

[93] Moore, 1911, p. 460.

with a low vertical ring base from Bishop Site (Hampson Cat. No. 610). On the body there is an appliqué hand and long-bone design repeated four times around the vessel. Vessel No. 29 in the Hampson collection is from the Upper Nodena Site. It is a wide-mouth bottle with appliqué long bones and hands on the shoulder area. Across the river from Mississippi County, Arkansas, is Tipton County, Tennessee, and from the Richardson Landing Site, Dr. Hampson has acquired a wide-mouth, low-neck bottle with a disk base which has the appliqué hand and long-bone decoration. The vessel has Bell Plain paste and polish and an everted lip. It is Cat. No. 645 in the Hampson collection.

From St. Francis County, Arkansas, in the Chicago Natural History Museum (Cat. No. 50723), there is a Bell Plain wide-mouth, short-neck bottle with appliqué hands and long bones. It has a disk base with a diagonally notched edge.[94]

From the Twist Plantation near Togo, Cross County, Arkansas, the Lemley brothers acquired an engraved bottle with a hand and eye design (fig. 111, *l*).

The Walls Site (13–P–1) in De Soto County, Mississippi, has furnished a Bell Plain bottle with eight appliqué hands.[95] Four of these on the upper body point downward while on the lower body the hands point upward. Also from Walls is an engraved wide-mouth bottle with a swastika whorl design on the body. On the neck area there are two human heads in profile with an arrow-shaped figure protruding from the mouth. There are two hands with "eye" designs depending from the lip of the vessel placed between the heads, while below each hand there is a long-bone design.[96] Another bottle of the Walls-Pecan Point style of portrayal of the long bones and hand design in relief is from Hickman County, Kentucky. It may now be in the Museum of the American Indian.[97] It should also be noted that the hand design is represented in negative painting on the vessel from Barton Ranch (fig. 111, *j*).

Another decoration technique and design which closely links the northern part of the Survey Area with Moundville is the engraved conventionalized feathered or winged serpent which is common at the famous Alabama Site.[98] It is most common in the Walls-Pecan Point sites. One example from Beck Place (13–O–7) is illustrated in fig. 111, *g*. Other examples are on figure 112, and two more are from the Beck Site (13–O–7), two are from the Walls area (13–P–1), and one each from Rhodes, Nickel (13–N–15), Bradley (11–P–2), Pecan Point, Neeley's Ferry (11–N–4), and Rose Mound (12–N–3). Other known examples are from Bell Place (10–P–2) in the University of Arkansas collection and one from New Madrid County, Missouri, in the collection of Dr. P. F. Titterington. A bird conventionalized engraved design which is best known at Moundville has been found at Rhodes.[99] Most of these specimens certainly are local products, indicating participation in a socio-religious milieu common to the late Memphis area sites and Moundville. The engraved bottle with the flying serpent design from Beck Place (fig. 111, *g*) is very close in every feature to an engraved bottle from northeastern Arkansas described by Holmes.[100] These decorations are so similar to those from Moundville where they are more at home that it seems highly probable that these Arkansas serpents from Walls-Pecan Point sites were made by some one who learned to draw at the school on the banks of the Black Warrior, but the ware is typical of the local Walls Engraved type.

The only other area where these engraved short-necked bottles appear in any number is in northern Alabama in what has been called the Koger's Island complex. The vessels are found on Hobbs Island,[101] Seven Mile Island, the Perry Site, and Koger's Island. The vessel from Hobbs Island is only represented by one sherd which has a decoration suggestive of a sun design. There is a restoration of a feathered or flying-serpent vessel from the Seven Mile Island Site,[102] but it was found in the general digging and little information

[94] Martin, Quimby, and Collier, 1947, fig. 90.
[95] Brown, 1926, fig. 304.
[96] Brown, 1926, figs. 278–80.
[97] Young, 1910, p. 136.
[98] Moore, 1905; Moore, 1907.
[99] Moore, 1911, fig. 41.
[100] Holmes, 1903, p. 91.
[101] Webb, 1939, pl. 106, *b*, 7.
[102] Webb and DeJarnette, 1942, pl. 67, *1*.

is available on its associations. At the Perry Site a bottle with an engraved bird,[103] and one with dimples as the basis for a scroll[104] were excavated in association with plain shell-tempered jars with strap handles, notched rim fillet bowls, and wide-mouth, short-neck bottles. Koger's Island is very strongly connected to Moundville and has the dimpled engraved bottle.[105] This vessel has a disk base and very low neck. It was associated with a large sherd of a similar engraved bottle. Burial No. 6 at Koger's Island had an unusual amount of grave goods including a Moundville Engraved vessel with a winged-serpent design.[106] Other vessels associated with the same burial included a small jar with two raised rim sections and strap handles with a double row of nodes on the upper body and rim,[107] and a black-filmed, plain-surface, wide-mouth bottle.[108] Also with this burial were wooden disk ear ornaments formerly covered with sheet copper, 25 small shell beads, 16 triangular projectile points of small size, bone awls, and a Moundville-type stone disk with a notched edge. The hand design engraved on a vessel also was found at Koger's Island[109] where it alternated on the vessel with a serpent design. This finding of a Moundville disk in northern Alabama along with the filmed engraved pottery is interesting from the Survey Area standpoint for the Chickasawba Mound near Blytheville in Mississippi County, Arkansas, produced a similar notched circular "palette" which is 13.3 cm. in diameter. It has 18 notches present on the broken section and originally must have had 25 or 26. It was collected from the north slope of the mound by G. G. MacCurdy, and is now in the Peabody Museum at Yale University.[110] The only other site in the Survey Area from which a stone disk has been obtained is from the Almond Site (17–K–4). This is one of the better disks and has led to considerable speculation,[111] but no single explanation is as yet satisfactory. The listing of this disk in one of the publications[112] as "near Arkansas Post" is not quite accurate, and the location of Arkansas Post on the distribution map is definitely misleading. The Almond Site was not listed in the seriation charts because of an inadequate sherd collection almost entirely composed of Neeley's Ferry Plain except for two small "Caddo" engraved sherds.

One of the best examples of engraved pottery was taken from the Jolly Bay Site, Walton County, Florida, by Moore.[113] This wide-mouth, short-neck, flat-base bottle is in good Moundville style and is apparently to be associated with the Fort Walton Period. On one side of the body there is portrayed a bird head (eagle?) with the weeping eye design and conventionalized feathers. On the other side there is a human head wearing a hooked-beak bird mask with weeping eye design, and above the head and on each side are markings representing a serpent.

Two famous examples of engraving are from the Hollywood Mound on the Savannah River.[114] One is a bowl with engraved horned rattlesnakes with protruding forked tongues and speech symbol(?), and representations of human faces with weeping eye. The other cup has a single engraved serpent. The present writers interpret this site as beginning in the early Lamar Period.

One of the rarest examples of engraving from the far Southeast is from the Walker Mound, McIntosh County, Georgia, on the Georgia coast. Not only are these vessels engraved, but they also have excised areas to help bring out the design which is part of the Gibson Aspect technique in the "Caddo" area and is also found at Cahokia on some of the engraved-incised pottery from that site. One of the bowls has a highly conventionalized human skull associated with conventionalized feathers.[115] The latter may represent the

[103] Webb and DeJarnette, 1942, pl. 119.

[104] Webb and DeJarnette, 1942, pl. 122, *2*.

[105] Webb and DeJarnette, 1942, pls. 261, *1* and 267, *2*.

[106] Webb and DeJarnette, 1942, pp. 217–18, pls. 263, *2*, *b*; 268, *1*.

[107] Webb and DeJarnette, 1942, pl. 261, *3*, *b*.

[108] Webb and DeJarnette, 1942, pl. 262, *1*, *b*.

[109] Webb and DeJarnette, 1942, pls. 262, *2*; 268, *2*.

[110] We are indebted to Dr. John M. Goggin for supplying the data on this specimen. Cat. No. 5840.

[111] Stoddard, 1904; Moore, 1908a, p. 492; Moorehead, 1910, p. 452; Abell, 1946.

[112] Webb and DeJarnette, 1942, table 36 and fig. 94.

[113] Moore, 1901, p. 462.

[114] Thomas, 1894, p. 324; Holmes, 1903, pl. CXIX, p. 138.

[115] Moore, 1897, pl. XVI; Holmes, 1903, pls. CXIX, *b* and *c*, CXX, and pp. 138–39.

bird-serpent monster. The companion vessel is less elaborate and the design is not as easy to interpret but may represent a composite monster.[116] In any event, these vessels are in the coastal area associated with cremated "urn" burial and are here associated with a Lamar-like culture of the Irene Period.

SUMMARY

As a result of the foregoing distributional survey of various specific forms and features, combined with the comparative statements in the preceding classification section, we are entitled to make a number of interpretations regarding the make-up of the culture complex known as Mississippi.

The early Mississippi ceramic complex was a relatively simple assemblage with certain continuities in shape and decoration from the immediately preceding horizon in the area. These were augmented by some ceramic features from Mesoamerica diffused by way of eastern Texas. There is also a possibility of additions to the complex from the Southwest and from the northwest Florida Gulf Coast. Shell-tempering, a fundamental feature of the complex, seems to have evolved from a limestone-tempered pottery in the Cahokia region. This early Mississippi combination spread into the Southeast as far as central Georgia. There were other disseminations to the north and west.

The more complex and developed forms which later appeared in the Mississippi culture also have a complex background, pointing in many instances to Mesoamerica on the one hand and the Southwest on the other, but there is no evidence of a major single cohesive influence from either one of these directions. They seem to result from more than one contact over a considerable period of time. For example the gourd, shoe-form, and stirrup-mouth vessels may have come in relatively early while the human effigy forms, with strong connections in the Southwest and Chihuahua, were probably later. In the Southeast, at what may be called the climax of the Mississippi Period, a number of centers existed each with its own distinctive version of the common tradition. In addition, we have specific evidences of interchange between them of ideas and even vessels. So we can say with confidence that there was no single center for this Mississippi climax development.

An invasion of "Toltec" warriors from Mexico moving into the Mississippi Valley and there reproducing their Mesoamerican culture will hardly serve as explanation. A wholly autochthonous development is likewise an inadequate explanation. Nor is it possible to see a single center nor a single point in time in which the development of Mississippi culture took place, a center which, once found, would solve all outstanding problems of Southeastern archaeology in the late period. The common belief that Mississippi or Mississippi-like cultures on the margin of the Mississippi drainage system must have once existed in, or stemmed from, a nuclear culture in the geographical center of the basin, is not supported by the facts that have been so far adduced. We will return to this important question of the origins of Mississippi culture in a later section, after we have reviewed all the evidence at our disposal.

[116] Moore, 1897, pl. I, *2*; Holmes, 1903, pl. CXX and pp. 139–40.

TABLES 2–10

ABBREVIATIONS

Al.M.N.H.	Alabama Museum of Natural History
A.M.N.H.	American Museum of Natural History
C.A.M.	Cincinnati Art Museum
C.N.H.M.	Chicago Natural History Museum
D.P.M.	Davenport Public Museum
F.S.M.	Florida State Museum
M.A.I.	Museum of the American Indian (Heye Foundation)
M.A.U.M.	Museum of Anthropology, University of Michigan
M.D.A.H.	State of Mississippi Department of Archives and History
P.M.H.U.	Peabody Museum, Harvard University
R.O.M.A.	Royal Ontario Museum of Archaeology
R. S. Peabody Foundation	Phillips Academy, Andover, Mass.
S.M.L.A.	Southwest Museum, Los Angeles
St.L.A.S.	St. Louis Academy of Science
U.S.N.M.	United States National Museum
U.T.D.A.	University of Tennessee, Department of Anthropology

TABLE 2: DISTRIBUTION OF HUMAN EFFIGY FIGURES (see pp. 163–65)

	State	County	Site	Collection or Source	Type	Culture	Time	References
1.	Arkansas	Poinsett	Near Lepanto	Lemley V–398	Hooded male figure, plain shell	....	....	....
2.	"	Mississippi	Chickasawba	C.N.H.M. 7951	Hooded female water bottle — Bell Plain	....	....	C.N.H.M., Neg. 74881–2
3.	"	"	"	C.N.H.M. 7957	Hooded female effigy bottle — Bell Plain	....	....	U.M.M.A., Neg. 6001
4.	"	"	"	U. of Arkansas	Hooded female effigy bottle — Bell Plain	....	....	Phillips, Neg. 3421
5.	"	"	Gosnell Place	Lemley V–415	Hooded female effigy bottle — Bell Plain	....	....	....
6.	"	"	"	Lemley V–477	Human effigy bottle, vertical neck — Bell Plain	....	....	....
7.	"	"	"	Lemley V–480	Hooded effigy bottle — Old Town Red (?)	....	....	This vol. fig. 107, *d*
8.	"	"	Pecan Point	M.A.I.	Hooded female effigy bottle — Bell Plain	....	....	Moore, 1911, fig. 72
9.	"	"	"	M.A.I. (?)	Male effigy bottle, vertical neck — Bell Plain (?)	....	....	Moore, 1911, fig. 71
10.	"	"	"	M.A.I.	Hooded effigy bottle — Bell Plain (?)	....	....	Moore, 1911, fig. 73
11.	"	"	"	M.A.I. (?)	Bell Plain (?)	....	....	....
12.	"	"	"	Lemley V–823	Hooded female effigy bottle	....	....	....
13.	"	"	Nodgrass	Lemley V–27	Human effigy hooded female (?) — Bell Plain	....	....	....
14.	"	"	"	Lemley V–12	Low rim; neck-modeled human head projects above lip	....	....	....
15.	"	"	"	Lemley V–127	Hooded female effigy bottle — Bell Plain	....	....	....
16.	"	"	Bell	Lemley V–1602	Hooded human, facing humpback	....	....	....
17.	"	"	"	Lemley V–578	Hooded human bottle — Bell Plain (?)	....	....	....
18.	"	"	Near Bassett	Lemley V–399	Hooded human effigy bottle — Bell Plain (?)	....	....	....
19.	"	"	Nodena	Al.M.N.H. Nod. 494	Hooded human female bottle — Bell Plain (?)	....	....	Al.M.N.H., Neg. 1852
20.	"	"	"	Al.M.N.H. Nod. 76	Short-necked, wide-mouthed human effigy bottle; head modeled on neck	....	....	Al.M.N.H., Neg. 1812
21.	"	"	"	Hampson 20A	Hooded female figure — Bell Plain	....	....	....
22.	"	"	"	Hampson Nodena	Hooded female figure — Bell Plain	....	....	....
23.	"	"	"	U. of Arkansas U.N. 12a	Human effigy bottle design on face; Rhodes Incised design on back — Bell Plain	....	....	This vol. fig. 107, *a*, *a'*

	State	County	Site	Collection or Source	Type	Culture	Time	References
24.	Arkansas	Mississippi	Walnut	Al.M.N.H. Wal. 712	Hooded male figure with head vase face — Bell Plain	....	....	This vol. fig. 107, *c*
25.	"	"	"	Al. M.N.H. Wal. 12	Hooded effigy bottle — no limbs indicated; notched disk base	....	....	This vol. fig. 107, *b*
26.	"	"	½ mile east of Wilson	Hampson 505	Hooded human effigy	....	....	....
27.	"	"	"	Lemley V–401	Hooded human (?) effigy	....	....	....
28.	"	Crittenden	Rhodes	M.A.I. (?)	Vertical-necked human effigy bottle; well made — Bell Plain	....	....	Moore, 1911, fig. 30
29.	"	"	"	M.A.I. (?)	Vertical-neck; face on side; female effigy	....	....	Moore, 1911, fig. 29
30.	"	"	Bradley (11–P–2)	Lemley V–949	Hooded human effigy — Bell Plain	....	....	....
31.	"	"	"	Lemley V–947	Hooded human effigy — Bell Plain	....	....	....
32.	"	"	Bradley (?)	Memphis Pub. Mus. 1–A–40	Hooded female effigy — Bell Plain	....	....	Al.M.N.H., Neg. 1107
33.	"	"	"	Memphis Pub. Mus. 95	Human effigy — Bell Plain; orifice at top of head	....	....	Al.M.N.H., Neg. 1104
34.	"	"	Bradley	M.A.I. (?)	Hooded human effigy — Bell Plain	....	....	Moore, 1911, fig. 47
35.	"	"	Bradley 48	M.A.I. (?)	Hooded female effigy with hair-do	....	....	Moore, 1911, fig. 48
36.	"	"	Bradley	U. of Arkansas Br. 102a	Hooded human effigy — Nodena Red and White	....	....	Phillips, Neg. 3422
37.	"	"	"	U. of Arkansas Br. 61a	Human effigy, tall wide-necked bottle — Bell Plain (head projects from shoulder)	....	....	Phillips, Neg. 3438
38.	"	"	Bradley (?)	Memphis Pub. Mus. Mason Coll. 1–A–39	Hooded female bottle — Bell Plain	....	....	Phillips, Neg. 4213
39.	"	"	"	....	Hooded female effigy — Bell Plain	....	....	Phillips, Neg. 4242
40.	"	"	Beck Place (13–O–7)	U. of Arkansas	Hooded human effigy; no face — Bell Plain	....	....	Phillips, Neg. 3412
41.	"	"	"	U. of Arkansas	Female human figure on short-necked bottle; face modeled on upper-shoulder area — Bell Plain	....	....	Phillips, Neg. 3415
42.	"	" (?)	....	C.N.H.M. 50717	Hooded female effigy bottle — Bell Plain (?)	....	....	Martin, Quimby, & Collier, 1947, fig. 90, *right*
43.	"	Cross	....	C.N.H.M. 50716	Hooded female effigy, pear-shaped body — Bell Plain (?)	....	....	C.N.H.M., Neg. 74845–6
44.	"	"	....	C.N.H.M. 50817	Human effigy bottle	....	....	C.N.H.M., Neg. 74847–8
45.	"	"	....	C.N.H.M. 50719	Male effigy bottle; head in front; short, wide-mouthed bottle neck	....	....	C.N.H.M., Neg. 74847–8
46.	"	"	Conner	Lemley V–1595	Human effigy head set in front of vertical bottle neck — Nodena Red and White	....	....	....

47.	"	"	Rose Mound (12–N–3)	M.A.I. 17/4241	Hooded human effigy — Neeley's Ferry Plain	....	....	Phillips, Neg. 2384
48.	"	"	"	M.A.I. (?)	Standing human effigy — Neeley's Ferry Plain	....	....	Moore, 1910, fig. 22
49.	"	"	"	M.A.I. 17/1395	Human effigy bottle; orifice on shoulder of vessel	....	....	Moore, 1910, fig. 27
50.	"	"	Parkin	Lemley V–475	Human effigy bottle, face on side of bottle neck — Neeley's Ferry Plain	....	....	This vol. fig. 107, *e*
51.	"	"	Neeley's Ferry	M.A.I. (?)	Hooded human effigy — Neeley's Ferry Plain	....	....	Moore, 1910, fig. 38
51a.	"	"	Vernon Paul	....	Old Town Red male effigy with head-vase face	....	....	Moore, 1910, pl. 20
52.	"	"	Turkey Island	M.A.I. 17/4748	Hooded human effigy — Bell Plain (?)	....	....	Moore, 1910, fig. 46
52a.	"	"	"	....	Small hooded effigy in a Parkin Punctated jar	....	....	Moore, 1910, fig. 46
53.	"	Crittenden	Earle	U. of Arkansas	Human effigy; medallion face projects from wide-mouthed neck — Bell Plain (?)	....	....	This vol. fig. 107, *g*, *g'*
54.	"	"	"	U. of Arkansas	Human effigy; face on side at wide-mouthed bottle neck — Bell Plain (?)	....	....	Phillips, Neg. 3440
55.	"	Lee	Kent Place (13–N–4)	Formerly in W. P. Murdock Coll.	Human effigy bottle	....	....	Murdock print
56.	"	"	Harness	Lemley V–174	Hooded human effigy bottle	....	....	....
57.	"	St. Francis	Bonner	M.A.I. (?)	Sealed human figure; orifice at back of head, tongue protrudes (suggests stone effigy figures)	....	....	Moore, 1910, fig. 5
58.	"	Yell	Carden Bottoms	Gray LaDassor	Male human effigy figure — Carson Red on Buff	....	....	Titterington print
59.	"	Arkansas	....	C.N.H.M. 111221	Hooded female effigy bottle	....	....	C.N.H.M., Neg. 74847–8
59a.	"	"	Near Menard	M.A.I. (?)	Unusual effigy with large swollen legs — Bell Plain	....	....	Moore, 1908a, pp. 504–05
60.	"	....	Point Remove Creek	U. of Arkansas	Human effigy; neck rises from top of head; face scarified — Bell Plain (?)	....	....	Phillips, Neg. 3514
61.	"	....	R.L.	U. of Arkansas R.L. 13a	Hooded human effigy figure — Bell Plain	....	....	Phillips, Neg. 3417
62.	"	....	....	D.P.M.	Hooded human effigy figure — Old Town Red	....	....	Phillips, Neg. 667
63.	"	....	....	D.P.M.	Hooded human effigy — Neeley's Ferry	....	....	Phillips, Neg. 668
64.	"	....	....	D.P.M.	Hooded human effigy — Bell Plain (?)	....	....	Phillips, Neg. 669; Holmes, 1903, p. 96

	State	County	Site	Collection or Source	Type	Culture	Time	References
65.	Arkansas	....	....	D.P.M.	Hooded human effigy — Bell Plain	....	....	Phillips, Neg. 670
66.	"	....	....	D.P.M.	Human effigy figure, head missing — Bell Plain	....	....	Phillips, Neg. 671
67.	"	....	....	D.P.M. 9302	Hooded effigy bottle; painted cross design on body — Bell Plain	....	....	Phillips, Neg. 672
68.	"	....	....	D.P.M. 7742	Human effigy bottle; head missing — Bell Plain	....	....	Phillips, Neg. 689
69.	Missouri	Stoddard	Richwood	M.A.I. (?)	Human effigy figure; vertical neck rising from head	....	....	Moore, 1898, figs. 19, 20
70.	"	....	....	P.M.H.U. 81729	Hooded human effigy figure — Bell Plain (?)	....	....	Phillips, Neg. 937
71.	"	Mississippi	Near Charleston	U.S.N.M. 65556	Human effigy figure; most of body missing; seated on squared vessel	....	....	Holmes, 1884, fig. 174
72.	"	"	"	U.S.N.M. 65603	Hooded effigy figure, seated on globular bottle body	....	....	Holmes, 1884, fig. 175
73.	"	"	"	U.S.N.M. 65604	Hooded human effigy	....	....	Holmes, 1884, fig. 176
74.	"	"	"	U.S.N.M. 65605	Hooded human effigy	....	....	Holmes, 1884, fig. 176
75.	"	"	"	U.S.N.M. 65606	Hooded human effigy	....	....	Holmes, 1884, fig. 176
76.	"	"	"	U.S.N.M. 65607	Hooded human effigy	....	....	Holmes, 1884, fig. 176
77.	"	"	"	U.S.N.M. 65611	Hooded human effigy	....	....	Holmes, 1884, fig. 176
78.	"	"	"	U.S.N.M. 65612	Hooded human effigy	....	....	Holmes, 1884, fig. 176
79.	"	"	"	A.M.N.H. 2307 (Terry Coll.)	Human effigy figure	....	....	Phillips, Neg. 234
80.	"	"	"	A.M.N.H. (Terry Coll.)	Hooded human effigy, seated on bottle body	....	....	Phillips, Neg. 244
81.	"	"	"	A.M.N.H. 2290 (Terry Coll.)	Human effigy figure on bottle body	....	....	Phillips, Neg. 245
82.	"	"	"	A.M.N.H. 2233 (Terry Coll.)	Hooded human effigy	....	....	Phillips, Neg. 246
83.	"	"	"	A.M.N.H. 2104 (Terry Coll.)	Hooded human effigy	....	....	Phillips, Neg. 252
84.	"	"	"	A.M.N.H. 2182 (Terry Coll.)	Human effigy figure, seated on square vessel	....	....	Phillips, Neg. 254
85.	"	"	"	A.M.N.H. 2328 (Terry Coll.)	Hooded human effigy, seated on bottle body — Old Town Red	....	....	Phillips, Neg. 257
86.	"	"	"	A.M.N.H. 2181 (Terry Coll.)	Hooded human effigy vessel	....	....	Phillips, Neg. 258
87.	"	"	"	A.M.N.H. 2214 (Terry Coll.)	Hooded human effigy figure	....	....	Phillips, Neg. 259

88.	"	"	'	A.M.N.H. 2184 (Terry Coll.)	Hooded human effigy on bottle body	....	....	Phillips, Neg. 260
89.	"	"	"	A.M.N.H. 2185	Human effigy, vertical neck; red-slipped negative-painted; black diagonal stripes	....	....	Phillips, Neg. 265
90.	"	"	"	A.M.N.H. 2180	Hooded human effigy figure	....	....	Phillips, Neg. 266
91.	"	"	"	A.N.M.H. 2212 (Terry Coll.)	Hooded female effigy figure	....	....	Phillips, Neg. 267
92.	"	"	"	A.N.M.H. 2348 (Terry Coll.)	Hooded human effigy figure	....	....	Phillips, Neg. 268
93.	"	"	"	A.M.N.H. 2349 (Terry Coll.)	Hooded human effigy figure	....	....	Phillips, Neg. 269
94.	"	"	"	A.M.N.H. 2183 (Terry Coll.)	Human effigy figure, orifice at back of head	....	....	Phillips, Neg. 270
95.	"	"	"	A.M.N.H. 2211 (Terry Coll.)	Hooded effigy figure	....	....	Phillips, Neg. 271
96.	"	"	"	A.M.N.H. 2325 (Terry Coll.)	Human effigy with orifice at back of head; red-filmed	....	....	Phillips, Neg. 272
97.	"	"	"	A.M.N.H. 2248 (Terry Coll.)	Hooded human effigy figure	....	....	Phillips, Neg. 278
98.	"	"	"	A.M.N.H. 2410 (Terry Coll.)	Hooded human effigy; red-filmed	....	....	Phillips, Neg. 279
99.	"	New Madrid	....	Mo. Hist. Soc. 928	Hooded human effigy vessel	....	....	Titterington print
100.	"	"	....	M.A.I. 16/6015	Human effigy figure; long bottle neck rising from top of head	....	....	An accidental resemblance to Moore, 1898, figs. 19, 20
101.	"	"	....	M.A.I. 16/6016	Hooded female effigy, carrying child on back	....	....	Phillips, Neg. 2320
102.	"	"	Lewis Prairie Big Mound	P.M.H.U. 7776	Hooded human effigy on bottle body	....	....	Phillips, Neg. 1915
103.	"	"	....	P.M.H.U. 7775	Hooded human effigy on bottle body	....	....	Phillips, Neg. 1934
104.	"	Southeast	....	P.M.H.U. 11213	Human effigy figure, head broken off	....	....	Phillips, Neg. 940
105.	"	"	....	P.M.H.U. 11211	Hooded human effigy	....	....	Phillips, Neg. 1926
106.	"	....	Diehlstat	P.M.H.U. 64093	Hooded human effigy	....	....	Phillips, Neg. 1936
107.	"	....	"	P.M.H.U. 64091	Hooded human effigy	....	....	Phillips, Neg. 1940
108.	"	Southeast	Potter & Engelman, Mound 15	P.M.H.U. 48686	Hooded human effigy figure with face toward back of figure	....	....	Phillips, Neg. 938
109.	"	"	"	P.M.H.U. 48690	Hooded human hermaphrodite	....	....	Phillips, Neg. 1923
110.	"	"	"	P.M.H.U. 48687	Hooded human effigy figure	....	....	Phillips, Neg. 1928

	State	County	Site	Collection or Source	Type	Culture	Time	References
111.	Arkansas	Southeast	"	P.M.H.U. 48688	Hooded human effigy figure	....	....	Phillips, Neg. 1933
112.	"	"	"	P.M.H.U. 48689	Hooded human effigy; female	....	....	Phillips, Neg. 1938
113.	"	"	"	P.M.H.U. 48691	Hooded human effigy, sitting on square vessel	....	....	Phillips, Neg. 1941
114.	"	"	....	P.M.H.U. 11694	Hooded human effigy	....	....	Phillips, Neg. 954
115.	"	"	....	P.M.H.U. 11693	Hooded human effigy	....	....	Phillips, Neg. 1927
116.	"	"	....	P.M.H.U. 11695	Hooded human effigy	....	....	Phillips, Neg. 1931
117.	"	"	....	P.M.H.U. 12362	Hooded human effigy	....	....	Phillips, Neg. 1932
118.	"	Mississippi	....	P.M.H.U. 14284	Hooded human effigy	....	....	Phillips, Neg. 1937
119.	"	Southeast	Wolf Island	P.M.H.U. 14997	Hooded human effigy	....	....	Phillips, Neg. 1925
120.	"	"	"	P.M.H.U. 14996	Hooded human effigy	....	....	Phillips, Neg. 1935
121.	"	Dunklin	"	Titterington Coll.	Hooded human effigy; well-modeled face resembling no. 28	....	....	Titterington print
122.	Illinois	Union	....	C.N.H.M. 55611	Hooded human effigy	....	....	C.N.H.M., Neg. 74545–6
123.	"	"	....	C.N.H.M. 55534	Small hooded female effigy	....	....	C.N.H.M., Neg. 74898–9
124.	"	"	....	C.N.H.M. 55609	Human effigy with neck rising vertically from head	....	....	C.N.H.M., Neg. 74898–9
125.	Indiana	Posey	Mouth of the Wabash	Indiana Hist. Soc.	Hooded female effigy	....	....	Lilly, 1937, p. 237
126.	"	....	....	U.S.N.M. 45583	Hooded female effigy shaping a jar	....	....	Holmes, 1903, pl. XXVIII
127.	Kentucky	Fulton	....	M.A.I. (?)	Hooded human effigy — Bell Plain	....	....	Young, 1910
128.	"	Trigg	Duncan	....	Hooded human effigy	....	....	Funkhouser — Webb, 1931, fig. 45
129.	Tennessee	Lauderdale	Hales Point	....	Human effigy; face modeled on side of wide-mouthed bottle neck	....	....	Moore, 1916, fig. 25
130.	"	Dyer	Neeley	....	Human effigy vessel	....	....	Moore, 1916, p. 500
131.	"	Tipton	....	Memphis Pub. Mus.	Hooded human effigy	....	....	Phillips, Neg. 4338
132.	"	Cumberland area	....	P.M.H.U. 14044	Hooded human effigy	....	....	Phillips, Neg. 2778
133.	"	"	....	P.M.H.U. 13999	Solid human effigy	....	....	Phillips, Neg. 2990
134.	"	Sumner	Rutherford	P.M.H.U. 17300	Solid human figurine	....	....	Phillips, Neg. 2850
135.	"	"	Lovell	P.M.H.U. 18487	Hollow human effigy; pellets inside	....	....	Phillips, Neg. 2887
136.	"	Williamson	Old Town	P.M.H.U. 15993	Human effigy bottle	....	....	Phillips, Neg. 2820
137.	"	"	Fewkes	U.S.N.M. 317473	Hooded human effigy bottle	....	....	Myer, 1928, pl. 132, *c*
138.	"	"	Brentwood-Gordon	....	Hooded human effigy	....	....	Jones, 1876, p. 41
139.	"	"	Boiling Springs	....	Human effigy figure, head missing	....	....	Jones, 1876, p. 132; fig. 71, *b*

140.	"	Davidson	Gale	....	Hooded human effigy	....	....	Jones, 1876, p. 41
141.	"	"	"Sacrificial Mound"	....	Hooded human effigy	....	....	Jones, 1876, p. 44
142.	"	"	Byser	Vanderbilt U. (?)	Hooded human effigy	....	....	Thruston, 1890, pp. 99–100, fig. 22
143.	"	"	Noel	"	Hooded effigy bottle	....	....	Thruston, 1890, p. 99
144.	"	"	Near Nashville	Vanderbilt U. (?) (Thruston Coll.) Sitting Bull	Hooded male effigy figure	....	....	Thruston, 1890, p. 100, fig. 23
145.	"	"	"	Vanderbilt U. (?) (Thruston Coll.) Mrs. Sitting Bull	Hooded female effigy figure	....	....	Thruston, 1890, pp. 100–01
146.	"	"	"	Tenn. Hist. Soc. (?)	Solid human figurine	....	....	Thruston, 1890, p. 102, and pl. 3, *upper left*
147.	"	"	Noel Cemetery	Vanderbilt U. (?)	Hooded human effigy bottle	....	....	Thruston, 1890, p. 102, pl. 3
148.	"	"	"	"	Hooded human effigy bottle	....	....	Thruston, 1890, p. 102, pl. 3
149.	"	"	"	"	Hooded human effigy bottle	....	....	Thruston, 1890, p. 102, pl. 3
150.	"	"	"	"	Hooded human effigy bottle	....	....	Thruston, 1890, p. 102, pl. 3
151.	"	"	"	"	Hooded human effigy bottle	....	....	Thruston, 1890, p. 102, pl. 3
152.	"	"	Near Nashville	"	Human effigy figure	....	....	Thruston, 1890, p. 98, *frontis.*
153.	"	"	"	"	Human effigy figure	....	....	Thruston, 1890, p. 98, *frontis.*
154.	"	"	"	"	Human effigy figure	....	....	Thruston, 1890, p. 98, *frontis.*
155.	"	"	"	"	Human effigy figure	....	....	Thruston, 1890, p. 98, *frontis.*
156.	"	Giles	Near Pulaski	....	Hooded female effigy	....	....	Jones, 1876, p. 108; fig. 61
157.	"	"	"	....	Hooded effigy figure	....	....	Jones, 1876, p. 108; fig. 61
158.	"	"Middle"	....	....	Hooded human effigy with painted cross in circle on shoulder	....	....	Jones, 1876, p. 77
159.	"	Cumberland Valley	....	....	Human effigy figure	....	....	Jones, 1876, p. 133; fig. 72
160.	"	Sequatchie Valley	....	....	Clay effigy figure	....	....	Thruston, 1890, p. 110
161.	"	....	Dallas	U. of Tennessee	Hooded human effigy bottle	Dallas Focus	....	Personal communication — Lewis & Kneberg
162.	Alabama	Hale	Moundville	Al.M.N.H. N.E. 82	Hooded human effigy bottle	....	....	Jones & DeJarnette, 1936, pl. 2, *e*
163.	"	Elmore	Mouth of Chubahatchee	Burke Coll.	Hooded human effigy with incised on back	....	....	*Arrow Points*, 1931, p. 2
164.	"	"	Mouth of Coosa	H. H. Paulin Coll.	Hooded human effigy	....	....	*Arrow Points*, 1931, p. 2
165.	"	Lowndes	Mouth of Pintlala Creek	E. M. Graves Coll.	Hooded human effigy, with burial urn	....	....	*Arrow Points*, 1931, p. 2

	State	County	Site	Collection or Source	Type	Culture	Time	References
166.	Florida	....	....	F. S. M. Coll. 45255	Human effigy figure — Middle Mississippi type	....	....	J. M. Goggin print
167.	"	....	....	C.N.H.M.	Zoned punctate human effigy bottle	Ft. Walton (?)	....	Martin, Quimby, & Collier, 1947, fig. 90, *center*
168.	Louisiana	Ouchita	Glendora	M.A.I. (?)	Human effigy figure; face modeled on side of wide-mouthed bottle neck	Glendora Focus	....	Moore, 1909, fig. 78
169.	Oklahoma	Wagoner	Norman	U. of Oklahoma	Hooded human effigy bottle — Neeley's Ferry (?)	Spiro Focus	....	Bauxar, 1940
170.	Colorado	....	Mesa Verde (?)	Ralph Altman Coll.	Human effigy figure, vertical neck rising from head — Black on White	Pueblo III (?)	1100–1300	Brainerd, 1949b, p. 121
171.	New Mexico (?)	....	....	....	Female effigy figure — Black on White; vertical mouth rises out of head	Pueblo I	900–1100	Brainerd, 1949b
172.	New Mexico	Chaco Canyon	Pueblo Penasca Blanca	P.M.H.U. (?)	Human effigy bottle; vertical neck projecting from head — Black on White	Chaco	1200–1300	Pepper, 1906, p. 331, fig. 13, *a*
173.	"	....	Pueblo Bonito, Room 105	A.M.N.H.	Black on white, human effigy figure	Pueblo II–III	1000–1300	Pepper, 1906, fig. 13, *b*
174.	"	....	Pueblo Bonito, Room 170	A.M.N.H.	Black on White, human effigy figure	"	"	Pepper, 1906, fig. 13, *c*
175.	"	....	Pueblo Bonito, Rooms 38, 48	A.M.N.H.	Chaco Black on White female with vertical neck rising from head; face bears tattoo marks	"	"	Pepper, 1906, pl. XXVIII
176.	"	....	Chaco Canyon	P.M.H.U.	Human effigy bottle — Black on White; vertical neck rising from head	"	"	Pepper, 1906, pl. XXIX
177.	"	San Juan	Aztec Kiva II	U. of Colorado (?)	Human effigy hunchback figurine	"	"	Brainerd, 1949b, pp. 122–23
178.	"	"	Aztec	....	Human effigy figure — Black on White; vertical neck rising from head	Pueblo III	....	Morris, 1919, fig. 56
179.	"	"	¼ mile south of Aztec	....	Human effigy figurine	Pueblo II–III	1000–1300	Brainerd, 1949b, p. 123
180.	"	....	Hawikuh	....	Human effigy figure — Casas Grandes style	Pueblo IV	1300–1540	Brainerd, 1949b, pp. 123–24
181.	New Mexico (?)	....	....	A.M.N.H. (?)	Human effigy figure — Casas Grades style	....	....	Brainerd, 1949b, p. 123
182.	New Mexico	Socorro Region	....	....	....	....	....	Pepper, 1906, p. 333

183.	Colorado	West of Cortez	....	....	Human effigy figure	....	....	Brainerd, 1949b, p. 123
184.	Utah (?)	Southeast (?)	....	Fruitland, N.M.	Human effigy figure	....	....	Brainerd, 1949b, p. 123
185.	Arizona	Graham	....	....	Female effigy figure — Cases Grandes style	....	....	Fewkes, 1898, pp. 165–70
186.	"	Near San Jose	....	....	Dumbbell-shaped red ware human effigy in relief	....	....	Fewkes, 1904, fig. 122
187.	"	....	Snaketown	....	Sweetwater Red on Gray; appliqué on side of small bottle	Pioneer	....	Haury, 1937, pl. CLXXIV
188.	"	....	"	....	Crude effigy on Sacatan Red	Sendentary	900–1000	Haury, 1937, pl. CLXXXVI
189.	"	....	"	....	Gila Plain — appliqué limbs on side of vessel	Sweet-water Phase	500	Haury, 1937, pl. CLXXXIX
190.	"	....	Roosevelt:6:3	Gila Pueblo	Salado Red ware human effigy — Casas Grandes style	....	....	Gladwin, W. & H. S., 1930, pl. VIII
191.	"	....	Sacaton:6:7	"	Santa Cruz Red on Buff	Sendentary Hoho-kam	....	Gladwin, W. & H. S., 1933, pl. V, *a*
192.	"	Salt River Valley	Los Muertos	P.M.H.U.	Casas Grandes Red on Buff	Classic Period	....	Haury, 1945, fig. 29
193.	"	....	Village near Sacaton	P.M.H.U.	Casas Grandes Red on Buff broken head segment	Classic Period	....	Haury, 1945, fig. 29
194.	"	....	Fort Defiance 12:4	....	Puerco Black on White, Chaco-style figure	Pueblo II–III	1000–1300	Gladwin, W. &. H. S., 1931, p. 24
195.	Mexico	Chihuahua	Casas Grandes area	....	Hooded effigy — Polychrome; only face portrayed	....	....	Hewett, 1908, pl. XIV, *19*; also, Kidder, 1916, pls. 2, 3
196.	"	"	"	....	Hooded effigy — Polychrome; only face portrayed	....	....	Hewett, 1908, pl. XIV, *20*; also, Kidder, 1916, pls. 2, 3
197.	"	"	"	....	Hooded effigy — Polychrome; only face portrayed	....	....	Hewett, 1908, pl. XIV, *21*; also, Kidder, 1916, pls. 2, 3
198.	"	"	"	....	Hooded effigy — Polychrome; only face portrayed	....	....	Hewett, 1908, pl. XIV, *41*; also, Kidder, 1916, pls. 2, 3
199.	"	"	"	....	Hooded effigy — Polychrome; only face portrayed	....	....	Hewett, 1908, pl. XIV, *42*; also, Kidder, 1916, pls. 2, 3
200.	"	"	"	....	Hooded effigy — Polychrome; only face portrayed	....	....	Hewett, 1908, pl. XIV, *44*; also Kidder, 1916, pls. 2, 3
201.	"	"	"	....	Hooded effigy — Polychrome; only face portrayed	....	....	Hewett, 1908, pl. XIV, *45*; also, Kidder, 1916, pls. 2, 3

	State	County	Site	Collection or Source*	Type	Culture	Time	References
202.	Mexico	Chihuahua	"	....	Polychrome hooded effigy figure; limbs in relief	....	....	Hewett, 1908, pl. XIV, *25*; also Kidder, 1916, pl. 3
203.	"	"	"	....	Polychrome hooded effigy figure; limbs in relief	....	....	Hewett, 1908, pl. XIV, *26*; also Kidder, 1916, pl. 3
204.	"	"	"	....	Polychrome hooded effigy figure; limbs in relief	....	....	Hewett, 1908, pl. XIV, *27*; also Kidder, 1916, pl. 3
205.	"	"	"	....	Polychrome hooded effigy figure; limbs in relief	....	....	Hewett, 1908, pl. XIV, *29*; also Kidder, 1916, pl. 3
206.	"	"	"	....	Polychrome hooded effigy figure; seated on side wall of jar	....	....	Hewett, 1908, pl. XIV, *23*; also Kidder, 1916, pl. 3, *2*
207.	"	"	"	....	Polychrome human effigy, compound-hooded male and female	....	....	Hewett, 1908, pl. XIV, *22*; also Kidder, 1916, pl. 3
208.	"	"	"	....	Polychrome human effigy, compound-hooded male and female	....	....	Hewett, 1908, pl. XIV, *24*; also Kidder, 1916, pl. 3
209.	"	"	"	....	Polychrome human effigy, compound-hooded male and female	....	....	Hewett, 1908, pl. XIV, *28*; also Kidder, 1916, pl. 3
210.	"	"	"	....	Polychrome human effigy, compound-hooded male and female	....	....	Hewett, 1908, pl. XIV, *30*; also Kidder, 1916, pl. 3
211.	"	"	"	Gila Pueblo	Babicora Polychrome hooded male effigy bottle; limbs in relief	....	....	Sayles, 1936, pl. 4, *b*
212.	"	"	"	"	Ramos Polychrome hooded effigy bottle; limbs in relief; hands holding bowl	....	....	Sayles, 1936, pl. 12, *c*
213.	"	"	"	"	Villa Ahumada Polychrome; limbs in relief; hooded effigy figure	....	....	Sayles, 1936, fig. 16
214.	"	"	"	"	Playas Red or Ramos Black; limbs in relief	....	....	Sayles, 1936, fig. 16
215.	"	"	"	R.O.M.A.	Playas Red effigy with face delineated; of hooded type	....	....	R.O.M.A., Neg. 415
216.	"	"	"	"	Playas Red effigy with face delineated; of hooded type	....	....	R.O.M.A., Neg. 415
217.	"	"	"	"	Polychrome hooded human effigy; face painted on hooded portion	....	....	R.O.M.A., Neg. 419
218.	"	"	"	"	Polychrome hooded human effigy; face painted on hooded portion	....	....	R.O.M.A., Neg. 419
219.	"	"	"	"	Polychrome hooded human effigy; face painted on hooded portion	....	....	R.O.M.A., Neg. 419
220.	"	"	"	"	Polychrome hooded human effigy; face painted on hooded portion	....	....	R.O.M.A., Neg. 419

221.	"	"	"	"	Polychrome hooded human effigy; face painted on hooded portion	....	....	R.O.M.A., Neg. 419
222.	"	"	"	"	Polychrome hooded human effigy; face painted on hooded portion	....	....	R.O.M.A., Neg. 419
223.	"	"	"	"	Hooded polychrome effigy; limbs in relief	....	....	R.O.M.A., Neg. 419
224.	"	"	"	"	Hooded polychrome effigy; limbs in relief	....	....	R.O.M.A., Neg. 419
225.	"	"	"	El Paso Arch. Soc.	Polychrome effigy; face delineated on side of vertical-rim jar	....	....	Photo. from Mrs. G. E. Moore

TABLE 3: DISTRIBUTION OF HEAD VASES (see pp. 165–67).

	State	County	Site	Collection or Source	Type	Culture	Time	References
1.	Arkansas	Mississippi	Pecan Point	U.S.N.M.	Pecan Point	....	....	Holmes, 1903, pls. XXI, XLIII, *a*
2.	"	"	"	D.P.M. 7741	"	....	....	Holmes, 1903, pls. XXIX, *c*, XXX, XLII, *b*
3.	"	"	"	D.P.M.	"	....	....	Phillips, Neg. 726
4.	"	"	"	D.P.M.	"	....	....	Phillips, Neg. 763
5.	"	"	"	M.A.I. (?)	....	....	....	Moore, 1911, pl. 36
6.	"	"	"	U.S.N.M. (?)	....	....	....	Holmes, 1903, pl. XXXII, *a*
7.	"	"	"	"	....	....	....	Holmes, 1903, pl. XXXII, *b*
8.	"	"	"	"	....	....	....	Holmes, 1903, pl. XXXII, *c*
9.	"	"	"	"	....	....	....	Holmes, 1903, pl. XXXII, *d*
10.	"	"	....	St.L.A.S. Whelply	Pecan Point	....	....	Titterington; Moorehead, 1910, vol. II, figs. 682–83
11.	"	"	....	"	"	....	....	Titterington, print
12.	"	"	....	"	"	....	....	Titterington, print
13.	"	"	....	"	"	....	....	Titterington, print
14.	"	"	C. M. Bell	Lemley V–468	"	....	....	Titterington, print
15.	"	"	"	Lemley V–852	"	....	....	Titterington, print
16.	"	"	Mattock Place	U. of Arkansas	"	....	....	This vol. fig. 111, *d–d″*
17.	"	Crittenden	Bradley Place	"	"	....	....	This vol. fig. 111, *b–b″*
18.	"	"	"	Memphis Pub. Mus.; Mason Coll. 1114	"	....	....	This vol. fig. 111, *a*
19.	"	"	"	U. of Arkansas, Br. 42	"	....	....	Phillips, Neg. 3143
20.	"	Cross	"	C.N.H.M. 50292	"	....	....	This vol. fig. 111, *c–c″*
21.	"	"	....	C.N.H.M. 50275	"	....	....	M.A.U.M., Neg. 6009–10
22.	"	"	....	C.N.H.M. 50291	"	....	....	M.A.U.M., Neg. 6004–5
23.	"	"	Rose Mound	M.A.I. (?)	"	....	....	Moore, 1910, pl. XIV
24.	"	"	"	"	"	....	....	Moore, 1910, pl. XV
25.	"	"	Parkin	C.A.M.	"	....	....	Moore, 1911, p. 469
26.	"	"	"	Dr. Self	"	....	....	....
27.	"	"	Conner Place	Lemley V–1560	"	....	....	Titterington, print
28.	"	"	"	Lemley V–1662	"	....	....	Titterington, print
29.	"	Poinsett	Fortune	P.M.H.U. 21542	"	....	....	Douglas & D'Harnoncourt, 1941, p. 79

30.	"	Mississippi	Blytheville	U. of Arkansas, L.F.R. 1a	"	....	....	Vaillant, 1939, pl. 24
31.	"	....	....	....	"	....	....	Phillips, Neg. 3419
32.	"	....	Near Little Rock	U.S.N.M. (?)	Conway	....	....	Holmes, 1903, pl. XXIX, *b*
33.	"	....	"	"	Garland	....	....	Holmes, 1903, pl. XXIX, *a*
34.	"	Garland	....	Lemley V–2110	"	....	....	Titterington, print
35.	"	....	Fields Chapple	U. of Arkansas, P. 104	Conway	....	....	Phillips, Neg. 3517
36.	"	Conway	....	Lemley V–926	"	....	....	Titterington, print
37.	"	Yell	Howells	Lemley V–467	"	....	....	Titterington, print
38.	"	"	Wayne	Lemley V–919	"	....	....	Titterington, print
39.	Missouri	Mississippi	Near Charleston	A.M.N.H. 2304 (Terry Coll.)	Charleston	....	....	Phillips, Neg. 249
40.	"	"	"	A.M.N.H. 2305 (Terry Coll.)	"	....	....	Phillips, Neg. 247
41.	"	"	"	A.M.N.H. 2303 (Terry Coll.)	"	....	....	Phillips, Neg. 250
42.	"	"	"	A.M.N.H. 2306 (Terry Coll.)	"	....	....	Phillips, Neg. 238
43.	"	"	"	P.M.H.U. 7748	"	....	....	Phillips, Neg. 840
44.	"	New Madrid	Near New Madrid	Lemley V–1281	"	....	....	Titterington, print
45.	"	"	"	Lemley V–1280	"	....	....	Titterington, print
46.	Tennessee	....	Cany branch of Cumberland	....	Charleston (?) 3 faces forming a tripod; Negative painted; unique	....	....	Atwater, 1820, pp. 238–39
47.	Ohio	Hamilton	Madisonville	P.M.H.U. 79660	Unique	Madisonville Focus, Ft. Ancient	....	Griffin, 1943b, pl. LXIX, *4*
48.	Missouri	Southeast	New Madrid area	....	Charleston	....	....	Evers, 1880, pl. 23, *1*
49.	"	"	"	....	Charleston with red film and decoration about face	....	....	Evers, 1880, pl. 23, *2*

TABLE 4: DISTRIBUTION OF MAN-BOWL OR "CHACMOOL" EFFIGY (see p. 167).

	State	County	Site	Collection or Source	Type	Culture	Time	References
1.	Arkansas (?)	....	Carson Lake	U. of Arkansas	Neeley's Ferry (?)	....	....	Phillips, Neg. 3445
2.	Missouri (?)	....	....	A.M.N.H. 2101 (Terry Coll.)	....	....	....	Phillips, Neg. 296
3.	"	Mississippi	Near Charleston	A.M.N.H. 2295 (Terry Coll.)	Bell Plain bottle	....	....	Phillips, Neg. 251
4.	"	"	"	A.M.N.H. 2294 (Terry Coll.)	Bell Plain bottle	....	....	Phillips, Neg. 253
5.	"	"	"	A.M.N.H. 2296 (Terry Coll.)	Bell Plain square body	....	....	Phillips, Neg. 301
6.	"	....	....	Evers	Bell Plain (?) bottle	....	....	Holmes, 1903, pl. XXVII, *a*
7.	Arkansas	....	....	U.S.N.M. (?)	Neeley's Ferry or Bell Plain	....	....	Holmes, 1903, pl. XXVII, *b*
8.	"	....	....	"	Neeley's Ferry or Bell Plain	....	....	Holmes, 1903, pl. XXVII, *c*
9.	Alabama	Hale	Moundville	Al.M.N.H. NR 118	Shell-tempered plain	....	....	Al.M.N.H., Neg. 1265
10.	Tennessee	Davidson	Noel Cemetery	Vanderbilt U. (?)	Shell-tempered plain	....	....	Thruston, 1890, pl. VIII, p. 150
11.	"	"	5 miles west of Nashville	"	....	....	....	Thruston, 1890, fig. 59
12.	Tennessee (?)	....	....	....	....	....	....	Thruston, 1890, p. 151
13.	Missouri	....	....	U.S.N.M. (?)	....	....	....	Thruston, 1890, p. 151
14.	Mexico	Chihuahua	Casas Grande area	Gila Pueblo (?)	Ramos Polychrome	....	....	Sayles, 1936, pl. XII, *d*; fig. 16
15.	"	"	"	....	....	....	....	Carey, 1931, p. 343
16.	Indiana	Posey	Mouth of the Wabash	Indiana Hist. Soc.	Shell-tempered bowl	....	....	Moorehead, 1906, fig. 21
17.	Arkansas	Crittenden	Bradley Place (?)	Memphis Pub. Mus.; Mason Coll. 1–A–32	Bell	Walls	....	Phillips, Neg. 4220
18.	"	"	"	Memphis Pub. Mus.; Mason Coll. 1–A–33	Bell	Walls	....	Phillips, Neg. 4217
19.	"	"	"	Memphis Pub. Mus.; Mason Coll. 1–A–35	Bell; small double-bodied bottle stirrup neck	Walls	....	Phillips, Neg. 4208
20.	"	"	"	Memphis Pub. Mus.; Mason Coll. 1–A–36	Bell	Walls	....	Phillips, Neg. 4221

TABLE 5: DISTRIBUTION OF COMPOUND VESSELS — HORIZONTAL STYLE (see pp. 169–70).

1.	Arkansas	Mississippi	Nodena	Al.M.N.H. Nod. 555	2 small Bell Plain wide-mouthed bottles joined in body and by rod connecting upper rims	Walls	....	This vol. fig. 106, *j*
2.	"	"	"	Al.M.N.H. Nod. 675	2 Bell Plain fish effigy bottles; bodies joined and a horizontal strap handle	"	....	This vol. fig. 106, *k*
3.	"	"	Gosnell Place, near Blytheville	Lemley V–154	2 Bell Plain bottles connected by short rods at the body and by a horizontal strap handle at the upper rim	"	....	This vol. fig. 106, *l*
4.	"	"	"	Lemley V–341	2 small Nodena Red and White wide-mouthed bottles connected by body; bar handle connecting upper rim	"	....	This vol. fig. 112, *g*
5.	"	"	Chickasawba	C.N.H.M. 7940	2 small jars joined horizontally at shoulder level — Neeley's Ferry Plain	"	....	....
6.	"	"	Nodena	Hampson 195	2 small jars, arcaded handles — Neeley's Ferry Plain	"	....	Ford, Neg. 1639
7.	"	"	"	Hampson 198	2 small jars; joined horizontally; arched handles connecting adjoining lips — Neeley's Ferry Plain	"	....	Ford, Neg. 1642
8.	"	Crittenden	Bradley Place	M.P.M. (Mason Coll.) 1–A–44	2 small Kent Incised jars, joined horizontally	"	....	Phillips, Neg. 4209
9.	Mississippi	De Soto	Walls	U. of Mississippi 3489	2 Bell Plain short-neck, wide-mouthed bottles attached in body and just below lip	"	....	Brown, 1926, fig. 313
10.	Tennessee	Stewart	....	U. of Tennessee, print from Charles Nash	2 small plain jars attached in body; 2 small loop handles on each jar	....	....	....
11.	Georgia	....	Etowah Mound C	R. S. Peabody Foundation 61407	2 small plain shell-tempered jars; 4 raised points on each rim with nodes beneath	Etowah	....	....
12.	Colorado	....	Mesa Verde	U. of California	2 small Mesa Verde Black on White (?) jars with 2 connecting handles	Mesa Verde Pueblo III	....	Kelemen, 1943, pl. 104, *b*
13.	New Mexico (?)	....	Chaco area (?)	C.N.H.M. 111441	2 small narrow-neck bottles of Puerco Black on White joined at body and upper neck by connecting cylinder	Chacos Branch	....	Martin & Willis, 1940, pl. 72, 7
14.	Arizona	....	Kiet-Siel Canyon	U. of Arizona	2 Black on White seed jars joined by a strap and handle, one is Kana-a style and the other Black Mesa	....	....	Beals, Brainerd, & Smith, 1945, p. 165, footnote 120

	State	County	Site	Collection or Source	Type	Culture	Time	References
15.	Mexico	Chihuahua	Casas Grandes area	P.M.H.U.	El Paso Polychrome small jars whose sides are connected by a hollow bar and the rims by a solid curved handle	....	....	H.S. & C.B. Cosgrove, 1932, p. 93
16.	"	"	"	Gila Pueblo	2 small jars joined at body and by bar at lip level of Playa Red and Ramos Black	Babicora and Ramos Phases	....	Sayles, 1936, fig. 15
17.	"	"	"	"	Corralitos Polychrome Incised; 2 small jars joined at body and by bar at lip level	"	....	Sayles, 1936, p. 38
18.	"	"	"	R.O.M.A.	Corralitos Polychrome Incised; 2 small jars joined at body and by bar at lip level	"	....	R.O.M.A., Neg. 413
19.	"	"	"	R.O.M.A.	Corralitos Polychrome Incised; 2 small jars joined at body and by bar at lip level; one jar is broken away	"	....	R.O.M.A., Neg. 413
20.	"	"	"	R.O.M.A.	Playas Red(?); 2 small jars joined at lower body by a cylinder and at lip by bar	"	....	R.O.M.A., Neg. 415
21.	"	"	"	P.M.H.U.	Playas Red Incised; 2 small jars connected by rod at body, bar handle at lip carrying small rectangular bowl	....	....	Kidder, 1916, pl. 1, *1*
22.	"	"	....	....	Red or black ware. Two closely joined bottles with bar handles	....	....	Hewett, 1908, pl. XIV, *12*
23.	"	"	....	El Paso Arch. Society	2 small plain jars connected by rod at body and arched bar handle at the lip	....	....	Photo from Mrs. G. E. Moore
24.	"	"	San Diego	....	Playas Red Incised(?) 2 small jars connected by a hollow rod at body, bar handle at lip	....	....	Lumholtz, 1902, p. 92
25.	Arkansas	Crittenden	Beck (13–O–7)	U. of Arkansas, Beck 225	Two small narrow neck Bell Plain bottles connected at body and by hollow rod just below lip	....	....	Phillips, Neg. 3034

TABLE 6: DISTRIBUTION OF BASKET-HANDLE BOWL (see p. 170).

1.	Missouri	New Madrid	....	P. F. Titterington Coll.	Neeley's Ferry	New Madrid Focus	....	......
2.	Tennessee	Meigs	Dallas	U.T.D.A.	Mississippi Plain	Dallas Focus	....	....
3.	"	Sevier	McMahan	U.S.N.M.	....	Dallas (?)	....	Holmes, 1884
4.	Colorado	Ackmen	Lowry	C.N.H.M.	La Plata Black on Orange	Pueblo I	760	Martin, 1939
5.	Arizona	....	Rainbow Bridge	....	....	....	....	Beals, Brainerd, & Smith, 1945
6.	"	....	Snaketown	Gila Pueblo	Sacaton Red on Buff	Sedentary	1000	Gladwin, et al., 1937, pl. CXXXIX, *g*
7.	Mexico	Chihuahua	....	....	Red and Black	Babicora	....	Sayles, 1936
8.	"	"	....	R.O.M.A.	Red or Black	Babicora (?)	....	R.O.M.A., Neg. 413
9.	"	"	....	....	Red or Black	Babicora (?)	....	Hewett, 1908
10.	Arkansas	Poinsett	....	C.N.H.M. 50799	Neeley's Ferry Plain	Mississippi	....	....
11.	Arizona	....	Las Acequias	P.M.H.U.	Tonto Polychrome (?)	Classic	1350	Haury, 1945, pl. 77, *d*; p. 165

TABLE 7: DISTRIBUTION OF TRIPOD VESSELS (see pp. 170–71).

	State	County	Site	Collection or Source	Type	Culture	Time	References
1.	Arkansas	Cross	Vernon Paul (11-N-9)	....	Neeley's Ferry; melon leg	St. Francis	....	Moore, 1910, fig. 34; this vol. fig. 105, *e*
2.	"	Mississippi	Pecan Point	Lemley V-956	Bell Plain; bulbous tripod bottle	....	....	This vol. fig. 105, *f*
3.	"	"	George Looney Place	Lemley V-913	Bell Plain; ball-leg tripod bottle	....	....	This vol. fig. 105, *g*
4.	"	Cross	Halcomb	P.M.H.U. 21561	Bell Plain; bulbous-leg tripod bottle	....	....	This vol. fig. 105, *h*
5.	"	"	"	P.M.H.U. 21717	Neeley's Ferry; cylindrical tripod base bottle	....	....	This vol. fig. 105, *i*
6.	"	"	Neeley's Ferry	P.M.H.U. 21320	Neeley's Ferry; cylindrical tripod bottle	....	....	This vol. 105, *j*
7.	"	Mississippi	Bell Place	Lemley V-776	Neeley's Ferry; bulbous-leg tripod bottle	....	....	This vol. 105, *k*
8.	"	"	Pecan Point	Lemley V-535	Neeley's Ferry Plain(?); stepped slab-leg tripod bottle	....	....	This vol. fig. 105, *l*
9.	"	Cross	Neeley's Ferry	P.M.H.U. 21071	Neeley's Ferry Plain; bulbous tripod bottle	....	....	This vol. fig. 105, *m*
10.	"	"	"	M.A.I. 17/4208	Neeley's Ferry; short cylindrical tripod bottle	....	....	This vol. fig. 105, *n*
11.	"	"	"	P.M.H.U. 21302	Neeley's Ferry; narrow cylindrical tripod bottle	....	....	This vol. fig. 105, *o*
12.	"	Crittenden	Bradley Place	Lemley V-951	Bell Plain; stepped slab-leg tripod bottle	....	....	This vol. fig. 105, *p*
13.	"	"	"	Lemley V-950	Bell Plain; stepped slab-leg tripod bottle	....	....	This vol. fig. 105, *q*
14.	"	Cross	Halcomb	P.M.H.U. 21635	Nodena Red and White; stepped slab-leg tripod bottle	....	....	This vol. fig. 112, *a*
15.	"	"	Vernon Paul	Lemley V-1596	Nodena Red and White; stepped slab-leg tripod bottle	....	....	This vol. fig. 112, *b*
16.	"	"	"	C.N.H.M. 50467	Neeley's Ferry(?); bulbous-leg tripod bottle	....	....	C.N.H.M., Neg. 74904-5
17.	"	St. Francis	....	C.N.H.M. 50269	Neeley's Ferry Plain(?); wide cylindrical-leg tripod bottle	....	....	C.N.H.M., Neg. 74845-6
18.	"	Cross	....	C.N.H.M. 50442	Neeley's Ferry Plain(?); bulbous-leg tripod bottle	....	....	C.N.H.M., Neg. 74845-6
19.	"	Poinsett(?)	....	C.N.H.M. 50492	Neeley's Ferry Plain; bulbous-leg tripod bottle	....	....	....

20.	"	Cross	....	C.N.H.M. 50485	Neeley's Ferry(?); stepped slab-leg tripod bottle	....	....	C.N.H.M., Neg. 74877–78
21.	"	"	....	C.N.H.M. 50439	Neeley's Ferry Plain(?); short bulbous-leg tripod bottle	....	....	C.N.H.M., Neg. 74877–78
22.	"	....	....	C.N.H.M. 50627	Neeley's Ferry(?); stepped slab-leg tripod bottle	....	....	C.N.H.M., Neg. 74877–78
23.	"	Cross	Neeley's Ferry	P.M.H.U. 21083	Old Town Red; slab-leg tripod bottle	....	....	Phillips, Neg. 1338
24.	"	"	"	P.M.H.U. 21298	Old Town Red; large bulbous-leg tripod bottle	....	....	Phillips, Neg. 1755
25.	"	"	"	P.M.H.U. 21320	Neeley's Ferry(?); tripod bottle	....	....	Phillips, Neg. 1497
26.	"	"	"	P.M.H.U. 21028	Bell Plain; bulbous-leg tripod bottle	....	....	Phillips, Neg. 1350
27.	"	"	Halcomb	P.M.H.U. 21622	Nodena Red and White; short slab-leg tripod bottle	....	....	Phillips, Neg. 1131
28.	"	"	"	P.M.H.U. 21624	Old Town Red; ball-leg tripod bottle	....	....	Phillips, Neg. 1130
29.	"	"	Rose Mound	P.M.H.U. 22206	Bell Plain(?); large conical tripod bottle	....	....	Phillips, Neg. 1189
30.	"	"	Turkey Island	M.A.I. (?)	Neeley's Ferry; cylindrical tripod bottle	....	....	Moore, 1910, fig. 47
31.	"	"	"	M.A.I. 17/4550	Neeley's Ferry; bulbous-leg tripod bottle	....	....	Phillips, Neg. 1989
32.	"	"	Vernon Paul	Hampson 328	Neeley's Ferry Plain; short conical-leg tripod bottle	....	....	....
33.	"	"	Fuller Conner	Lemley V–1597	Old Town Red; stepped slab-leg tripod bottle	....	....	....
34.	"	"	Stanley Mounds	P.M.H.U. 20190	Neeley's Ferry; cylindrical tripod bottle	....	....	Phillips, Neg. 1516
35.	"	"	....	M.A.I. 12/6483	Neeley's Ferry Plain; stepped slab-leg tripod bottle	....	....	Phillips, Neg. 2448
36.	"	St. Francis	Big Eddy	M.A.I. 17/4327	Old Town Red; slab-leg tripod bottle	....	....	Phillips, Neg. 2102
37.	"	Crittenden	....	U. of Arkansas	Old Town Red; stepped slab-leg tripod bottle	....	....	Phillips, Neg. 3402
38.	"	Poinsett	Fortune Mound	P.M.H.U. 21509	Old Town Red; stepped slab-leg tripod bottle	....	....	Phillips, Neg. 1382
39.	"	"	Miller Place	M.A.I. 17/4302	Bell Plain; slab-leg tripod bottle	....	....	Phillips, Neg. 1990
40.	"	"	"	M.A.I. (?)	Nodena Red and White cylindrical tripod bottle	....	....	Moore, 1910, pl. 26
41.	"	"	Cummings	Hampson 426	Old Town Red; slab-leg tripod bottle	....	....	....
42.	"	"	"	Hampson 428	Neeley's Ferry Plain(?); slab-leg tripod bottle	....	....	....

	State	County	Site	Collection or Source	Type	Culture	Time	References
43.	Arkansas	Poinsett	"	Hampson 504	Old Town Red; stepped slab-leg tripod bottle	....	....	....
44.	"	Mississippi	C. M. Bell Place	Lemley V–813	Neeley's Ferry Plain; with short bulbous-leg tripod bottle	....	....	....
45.	"	"		Hampson 293	Nodena Red and White(?); stepped slab-leg tripod bottle	....	....	....
46.	"	"	Upper Nodena	Hampson 48	Carson Red on Buff; large human effigy pear-shaped tripod bottle	....	....	....
47.	"	"	"	Al. M.N.H. Nod. 722	Old Town Red(?); 3 large effigy heads form tripods	....	....	Al.M.N.H., Neg. 1881
48.	"	"	"	Al. M.N.M. Nod. 821	Nodena Red and White; bulbous-leg human effigy face on each foot support	....	....	Al.M.N.H., Neg. 1884
49.	Missouri	....	....	P.M.H.U. 48521	Bell Plain; small bulbous-leg tripod pot	....	....	Phillips, Neg. 2704
50.	"	....	....	P.M.H.U. 48522	Bell Plain; large pear-shaped supports with connecting bridge	....	....	Phillips, Neg. 2702
51.	"	....	....	P.M.H.U. 48523	Bell Plain; large pear-shaped supports with connecting bridge	....	....	Phillips, Neg. 2703
52.	Mississippi	De Soto	Walls	U. of Mississippi 3492	Avenue Polychrome; large tripods joined to single neck; connecting bridge	....	....	Brown, 1926, fig. 314
53.	"	"	"	U. of Mississippi 3491	Bell Plain; 3 small bottles joined to single neck	....	....	Phillips Neg. 4506
54.	"	Coahoma	Oliver	P.M.H.U.	Old Town Red; 3 bottles joined to single neck	....	....	Peabody, 1904, pl. XV
55.	Arkansas(?)	....	....	D.P.M. 6565	Bell Plain; 3 small cylindrical-leg tripod bottles	....	....	Phillips, Neg. 690
56.	"	....	....	D.P.M. 141	Old Town Red; 3 large mammiform supports	....	....	Phillips, Neg. 703
57.	Arkansas	....	....	D.P.M.	Neeley's Ferry Plain; stepped slab-leg tripod	....	....	Phillips, Neg. 705
58.	"	....	....	D.P.M. 8212	Bell Plain; bulbous-leg tripod bottle	....	....	Phillips, Neg. 706
59.	"	....	....	D.P.M. 4952	Neeley's Ferry Plain(?); large bulbous-leg tripod	....	....	Phillips, Neg. 707
60.	"	....	....	D.P.M. 7978	Neeley's Ferry Plain(?); small cylindrical-leg tripod	....	....	Phillips, Neg. 710
61.	"	....	....	D.P.M. 7979	Neeley's Ferry(?); short cylindrical-leg tripod	....	....	Phillips, Neg. 712

62.	"	....	....	D.P.M. 9269	Carson Red on Buff; small conical-leg tripod	....	....	Phillips, Neg. 766
63.	Missouri	Mississippi	Charleston	A.M.N.H. 2322 (Terry Coll.)	Old Town Red; large bulbous-leg tripod	....	....	Phillips, Neg. 292
64.	"	....	New Madrid area	P.M.H.U. 14296	Bell Plain; large bulbous-leg tripod	....	....	Phillips, Neg. 811
65.	"	....	New Madrid area	P.M.H.U. 48534	Bell Plain; stepped slab-leg tripod	....	....	Phillips, Neg. 799
66.	Arkansas	Clark	James Huff	Hodges 147	Polished Plain; large bulbous-leg tripod	....	....	Phillips, Neg. 3543
67.	"	Hot Springs	Watermelon Island	Hodges 402	Blakelytown Engraved; large bulbous-leg tripod	....	....	Phillips, Neg. 3544
68.	"	"	Fowler	Hodges 86	Blakelytown Engraved; large bulbous-leg tripod	....	....	Hodges, 1945, p. 107
69.	"	"	Upper Tisdale	Hodges 70	Belcher Engraved (?) large bulbous-leg tripod	....	....	Phillips, Neg. 3645
70.	Louisiana	Ouachita Parish	Glendora	M.A.I. (?)	Natchitoches Engraved peniform tripod	Glendora Focus	....	Moore, 1909, fig. 71
71.	"	Morehouse Parish	Sycamore Landing	M.A.I. (?)	Plain vessel; broken tripod support	Glendora Focus	....	Moore, 1909, p. 119, fig. 116
72.	"	"	Keno Place	M.A.I. (?)	Natchitoches Engraved peniform tripod	....	....	Moore, 1909, fig. 144
73.	Arkansas	Crittenden	Bradley Place	M.A.I. 17/4157	Bell Plain; tripod bottle	....	....	Moore, 1911, fig. 45
74.	"	"	Bradley Place (?)	Memphis Pub. Mus.; Mason Coll. 1–A–29	Bell Plain; bulbous-leg tripod bottle	Walls	....	Phillips, Neg. 4224
75.	"	"	"	Memphis Pub. Mus.; Mason Coll. 1–A–30	Bell Plain; ball-leg tripod bottle	....	....	Phillips, Neg. 4207
76.	Alabama	Hale	Moundville	M.A.I. (?)	Neeley's Ferry; cylindrical-leg tripod bottle	Moundville	....	Moore, 1905, fig. 172
77.	Arkansas	Yell	Carden Bottom	M.A.I. 12/6561	Zoned engraved pear-shaped tripod	....	....	Harrington, 1920, pl. LXXXVIII, *a*
78.	"	Hempstead	Ozan Site 1	M.A.I.	Ball tripod bottle	....	....	....
79.	"	Garland	Sumpter Place	Lemley V–1726	Blakelytown Engraved; bulbous-leg tripod bottle	....	....	....
80.	"	Hot Springs	J. E. Stanley Place	Lemley V–490	Blakelytown Engraved; bulbous-leg tripod bottle	....	....	....
81.	"	Jefferson	Greer	M.A.I. 17/4829	Zoned Engraved; slab-leg tripod bowl	....	....	Phillips, Neg. 2419
82.	Louisiana	Caddo Parish	Belcher	C. H. Webb Coll.	Belcher Engraved; conical tripod bottle	Belcher Focus	....	Webb & Dodd, 1941, pl. 16, *3*

	State	County	Site	Collection or Source	Type	Culture	Time	References
83.	Texas	Lamar	Sanders	U. of Texas	Maxey Noded Red ware	Sanders Focus (Gibson Aspect)	....	Krieger, 1946, pl. 29, *a*
84.	Georgia	Richmond	Hollywood	U.S.N.M.	3 small head vases forming tripod	....	....	Thomas, 1894, fig. 199
85.	Tennessee	Cany Branch Cumberland River	....	....	3 small head vases forming tripod	....	....	Atwater, 1820, pp. 238–39

TABLE 8: DISTRIBUTION OF STIRRUP-NECK BOTTLES IN THE MISSISSIPPI VALLEY (see pp. 171–72).

1.	Missouri	Stoddard	Evans Farm	Lemley V–1742	....	Mississippi	....	....
2.	"	Pemiscott	....	Titterington 923	Bell	"	....	....
3.	"	Phelps	Lost Ridge District	Titterington 1127	Bell	"	....	....
4.	"	....	....	....	Bell (?)	"	....	Evers, 1880, pl. 23, *4*
5.	Tennessee	Tipton	Richardson Landing	Hampson 696	Bell or Neeley's Ferry	"	....	....
6.	Arkansas	Mississippi	Pecan Point	Lemley V–691	....	"	....	This vol. fig. 106, *c*
7.	"	"	Pecan Point (?)	D.P.M. 7980	Bell Plain	"	....	Holmes, 1903, pl. XVIII, *f*
8.	"	"	"	D.P.M. 9300	Bell Plain	"	....	Phillips, Neg. 685
9.	"	"	Walnut	Al. M.N.H. Wal. 74	....	"	....	This vol. fig. 106, *d*
10.	"	"	Bell Place	Lemley V–563	....	"	....	This vol. fig. 106, *e*
11.	"	"	"	Hampson 509	Nodena Red and White (?)	"	....	....
12.	"	"	Upper Nodena	U. of Arkansas, U.N. 214a	....	"	....	This vol. fig. 106, *g*
13.	"	"	Nodena	A.M.N.H., Nod. 72	....	"	....	This vol. fig. 106, *a*
14.	"	"	Catching	Lemley V–651	Neeley's Ferry or Bell	"	....	....
15.	"	Crittenden	Bradley	Memphis Pub. Mus.	Bell	"	....	Al.M.N.H., Neg. 1110
16.	"	"	"	Memphis Pub. Mus.; Mason Coll. 1–A–34	....	"	....	This vol. fig. 106, *i*
17.	"	Poinsett	....	C.N.H.M. 21971	....	"	....	....
18.	"	"	....	M.A.I. 4/1591	Neeley's Ferry	"	....	Phillips, Neg. 2572
19.	"	"	Cummings	M.A.I. 17/4300	Nodena Red and White	"	....	Moore, 1910, pl. XXIV
20.	"	Cross	Neeley's Ferry	M.A.I. (?)	....	"	....	Moore, 1910, fig. 43; this vol. fig. 106, *b*
21.	"	"	Stanley	P.M.H.U. 20170	....	"	....	This vol. fig. 106, *f*
22.	"	"	Halcomb	P.M.H.U. 21714	Neeley's Ferry	"	....	Phillips, Neg. 1106
23.	"	"	Star Woods Place	Lemley V–1746	Neeley's Ferry	"	....	....
24.	"	"	....	P.M.H.U. 56991	Neeley's Ferry	"	....	Phillips, Neg. 1096
25.	"	St. Francis	....	C.N.H.M. 50728	....	"	....	....
26.	"	....	....	....	Old Town Red	"	....	Evers, 1880, pl. 18
27.	Arkansas (?)	....	....	P.M.H.U. 48760	Old Town Red	"	....	Phillips, Neg. 1420

	State	County	Site	Collection or Source	Type	Culture	Time	References
28.	Florida	Gulf	Chipola Cut-off	....	Fort Walton Incised	Fort Walton (?) Period	....	Moore, 1903a, fig. 127; Willey, 1949, p. 255
29.	New Mexico	Catron	Vanderbilt U.	C.N.H.M.	Red Mesa Black on White	Mogollon	900 A.D.	Martin & Rinaldo, 1947, fig. 129, *a*
30.	Colorado	....	La Plata	....	....	Anasazi	Basket Maker III	Morris, 1939, p. 149
31.	"	....	"	....	....	Anasazi	Pueblo I	Morris, 1939, p. 169
32.	New Mexico	Zuñi Reservation	Great Kivas	U.S.N.M.	Kiatuthlana Black and White (?)	Anasazi	Pueblo III	Roberts, 1932, p. 115
33.	"	....	Hawikuh	M.A.I.	....	Anasazi	....	Hodge, 1923, pl. 28, *c*
34.	Arizona	....	Chaves Pass	U.S.N.M.	....	Anasazi	....	Fewkes, 1904, pl. 36, *b*
35.	"	....	Old Walpi	C.N.H.M.	Sikyatki Polychrome	Anasazi	Pueblo IV	Martin & Willis, 1940, pl. 53, *3*
36.	New Mexico	Pajarito Plateau	....	P.M.H.U.	....	Anasazi	....	Kidder, 1915
37.	"	....	Pecos	Andover	Glaze II or III	Anasazi	....	Kidder, 1915
38.	"	....	"	....	Glaze V	Anasazi	....	Kidder, 1915
39.	"	....	Santa Clara	U.S.N.M.	....	....	1300–1700	Stevenson, 1883, fig. 706
40.	"	....	Laguna	U.S.N.M.	....	....	....	Stevenson, 1883, fig. 596
41.	"	....	Jemez	U.S.N.M.	Modern	....	Modern	Stevenson, 1883, fig. 676
42.	"	....	Puye	....	....	....	....	Brainerd, 1949a, p. 7
43.	"	....	Rito de los Frijoles	....	....	....	....	Brainerd, 1949a, p. 7
44.	Mexico	Lower California	....	S.M.L.A.	....	....	....	Brainerd, 1949a, p. 5
45.	"	Guerrero	Coyuca de Catalan	....	....	....	1400–1500 (?)	Lister, 1947, p. 71
46.	"	Michoacan	Tzingtzuntzan	....	....	....	....	Moedano, 1941, fig. 1, *14, 15*
47.	"	Vera Cruz	Isla de Sacrificios	....	....	Mazapan	950–1200	Mayer, 1846, p. 95
48.	"	D. F.	Tlatilco	Covarrubias	....	Formative	200 B.C. (?)	Covarrubias, 1943, pp. 43–44
49.	"	Michoacan	Chehuayo	Museo Regional de Michoacan	....	"Tarascan"	....	Toscano, Kirchoff & Rubin de la Borbolla, 1946, pl. 132
50.	"	"	Uruapan	....	....	....	....	Lumholtz, 1902, vol. 2, p. 334
51.	"	Jalisco	Tuxpan	....	....	....	....	Lumholtz, 1902, vol. 2, p. 334
52.	"	Guanajuato	Chupicuaro	....	....	....	....	Toscano, Kirchoff, & Rubin de la Borbolla, 1946, p. 18

TABLE 9: DISTRIBUTION OF TEAPOT VESSELS (see pp. 172–73).

1.	Arkansas	Arkansas	Menard	M.A.I. 17/3307	Old Town Red	....	....	This vol. fig. 113, *a*
2.	"	"	Near Menard	M.A.I. 17/4171	Old Town Red	....	....	This vol. fig. 113, *b*
3.	"	"	"	M.A.I. 17/4170	Old Town Red	....	....	Phillips, Neg. 2080
4.	"	"	"	M.A.I. 17/4168	Old Town Red	....	....	Phillips, Neg. 2082
5.	"	"	"	M.A.I. 17/4173	Old Town Red	....	....	Phillips, Neg. 2380
6.	"	"	"	M.A.I. 17/4176	Neeley's Ferry Plain	....	....	Phillips, Neg. 2365
7.	"	"	"	M.A.I. 17/4475	Neeley's Ferry Plain	....	....	Phillips, Neg. 2133
8.	"	"	"	M.A.I. 17/4172	Old Town Red	....	....	Phillips, Neg. 2096
9.	"	"	Menard	M.A.I. 17/4755	Old Town Red	....	....	Phillips, Neg. 2089
10.	"	"	"	M.A.I. 17/4587	Old Town Red	....	....	Phillips, Neg. 2087
11.	"	"	"	M.A.I. 17/4756	Old Town Red	....	....	Phillips, Neg. 2091
12.	"	"	"	M.A.I. 17/4757	Bell Plain	....	....	Phillips, Neg. 2117
13.	"	"	"	M.A.I. 17/4586	Bell Plain (?)	....	....	Phillips, Neg. 2383
14.	"	"	Near Menard	Hodges 463	Engraved (?)	....	....	Phillips, Neg. 3847
15.	"	"	"	U.S.N.M.	Neeley's Ferry (?)	....	....	Holmes, 1884, fig. 159
16.	"	"	"	U.S.N.M.	Neeley's Ferry	....	....	Holmes, 1884, fig. 160
17.	"	"	Old River Landing	M.A.I. 17/4771	Old Town Red	....	....	Phillips, Neg. 2381
18.	"	"	"	M.A.I. 17/4582	Bell Plain	....	....	Phillips, Neg. 2132
19.	"	"	"	M.A.I. 17/4190	Avenue Polychrome	....	....	This vol. fig. 113, *f*
20.	"	Pulaski	Mainard (?)	U. of Arkansas	Old Town Red (?)	....	....	Dickinson & Dellinger, 1940, pl. 19
21.	"	Faulkner	....	M.A.I. 14/1711	Old Town Red	....	....	Phillips, Neg. 2477
22.	Arkansas (?)	"	....	Courthouse, Little Rock	....	....	....	Moore, 1911, p. 470
23.	Arkansas	Miller	McClure	M.A.I. 17/4189	Old Town Red	....	....	....
24.	"	Phillips	North of Helena	M.A.I. 11/8299	Neeley's Ferry Plain	....	....	Phillips, Neg. 2584
25.	"	"	"	M.A.I. 11/8300	Neeley's Ferry Plain	....	....	Phillips, Neg. 2581
26.	"	"	Near Helena	Lemley V–1082	Bell Plain (?)	....	....	....
27.	"	"	Avenue	M.A.I. (?)	Nodena Red and White	....	....	Moore, 1911, fig. 25, pl. XXX
28.	"	Lee	Kent Place	M.A.I. 17/4291	Old Town Red	....	....	Moore, 1911, p. 410
29.	"	"	Kent	....	Old Town Red	....	....	Moore, 1911, p. 410
30.	"	"	Kent	....	Avenue Polychrome	....	....	Moore, 1911, p. 410

	State	County	Site	Collection or Source	Type	Culture	Time	References
31.	Arkansas	Lee	Kent	....	Bell Plain	....	....	Moore, 1911, p. 410
32.	"	Miller	McClure Place	M.A.I. 17/4189	Old Town Red	....	....	Phillips, Neg. 2088
33.	"	Jefferson	Greer	M.A.I. 17/4816	Old Town Red	....	....	Phillips, Neg. 2189
34.	"	Lincoln	Douglas	M.A.I. 17/4775	Old Town Red	....	....	Phillips, Neg. 2086
35.	"	"	"	M.A.I. 17/4776	Avenue Polychrome	....	....	Phillips, Neg. 2090
36.	"	"	"	M.A.I. 17/4174	Old Town Red	....	....	Phillips, Neg. 2093
37.	"	"	"	M.A.I. 17/4774	Neeley's Ferry	....	....	Phillips, Neg. 2382
38.	"	Lee	Forrest Place	....	....	....	....	Moore, 1910, p. 263
39.	"	St. Francis	....	C.N.H.M. 50446	Bell Plain	....	....	M.A.U.M., Neg. 6012
40.	"	"	Near Hughes	Lemley V-257	Bell Plain	....	....	....
41.	"	"	"	Lemley V-1085	Bell Plain	....	....	....
42.	"	Crittenden	Beck Place	U. of Arkansas	Bell Plain	....	....	This vol. fig. 113, *c*; Phillips, Neg. 3468
43.	"	"	"	U. of Arkansas Beck 249	Bell Plain	....	....	Phillips, Neg. 3026
44.	"	"	Bradley Place	U. of Arkansas Br. 49a	Bell Plain	....	....	Phillips, Neg. 3510
45.	"	Cross	....	C.N.H.M. 50446	Bell Plain (?)	....	....	....
46.	"	"	....	C.N.H.M. 50834	Bell Plain	....	....	M.A.U.M., Neg. 6011
47.	"	"	Rose Mound	M.A.I. 17-4234	Bell Plain	....	....	Moore, 1910, fig. 17
48.	"	"	"	M.A.I. (?)	Nodena Red and White	....	....	Moore, 1910, pl. XVIII
49.	"	Mississippi	C. M. Bell Place	Lemley V-1603	Bell Plain	....	....	....
50.	"	"	....	Lemley V-1266	Nodena Red and White	....	....	....
51.	"	....	Bishop	Hampson 606	Old Town Red	....	....	....
52.	"	....	....	D.P.M. 8209	Fatherland Incised	....	....	Holmes, 1903, pl. XVIII, *b*
53.	"	....	....	D.P.M.	Nodena Red and White	....	....	Phillips, Neg. 722
54.	"	....	....	D.P.M. 9284	Bell Plain (?)	....	....	Phillips, Neg. 723
55.	"	....	....	D.P.M. 9283	Bell Plain (?)	....	....	Phillips, Neg. 725
56.	Tennessee	Tipton	Richardson Landing	Hampson 643	Bell Plain (?)	....	....	....
57.	Mississippi	De Soto	Walls area	U. of Mississippi 3349	Bell Plain	....	....	Brown, 1926, fig. 284, *a*
58.	"	"	"	U. of Mississippi	Bell Plain	....	....	Brown, 1926, fig. 284, *b*
59.	"	"	"	U. of Mississippi	Bell Plain	....	....	Brown, 1926, fig. 284, *c*
60.	"	Coahoma	Oliver	....	Old Town Red	....	....	Brown, 1926, p. 303
61.	"	"	"	P.M.H.U.	....	....	....	Peabody, 1904, pl. XIV
62.	"	"	"	P.M.H.U.	....	....	....	Peabody, 1904, pl. XIV

63.	"	....	....	U.S.N.M. (?)	Old Town Red	....	....	Holmes, 1903, pl. XL, *b*
64.	"	Bolivar	Neblett Landing	M.A.I.	Bell Plain (?)	....	....	Moore, 1911, fig. 17; this vol. fig. 113, *g*
65.	"	Adams	Fatherland Mound	M.D.A.H.	Old Town Red	Natchezan Historic	....	Ford, 1936, fig. 9, *m*
66.	Louisiana	Ouachita Parish	Glendora	M.A.I. (?)	Fatherland Incised	Glendora Focus	....	Moore, 1909, p. 75
67.	"	Morehouse Parish	Keno	M.A.I. (?)	Old Town Red	Glendora Focus Historic	....	Moore, 1909, pp. 124, 131

TABLE 10: DISTRIBUTION OF NEGATIVE PAINTING IN THE EASTERN UNITED STATES (see pp. 173–77).

	State	County	Site	Collection or Source	Type	Culture	Time	References
1.	Georgia	Richmond	Hollywood	U.S.N.M. 135295	Carafe-neck bottle with sun design; grit and mica tempering; thick walls	Lamar	....	Thomas, 1894, fig. 200; Holmes, 1903, pl. CXVIII, *a*
2.	Tennessee	Williamson	DeGraffenreid	....	Hooded bottle with central cross and an outer ray sun circle; shell temper	Cumberland	....	Jones, 1880, fig. 26
3.	"	"	"	....	Sun design with 16 outer rays and 26 unpainted dots; shell temper	"	....	Jones, 1880, p. 62
4.	Georgia	Bartow	Etowah	Andover 61461 Ga.	Sun design with wide-mouthed bottle; grit and mica tempering; cross with ray and dot pattern; horizontal rows of dots on neck	Etowah	....	Ashley, 1932, fig. 33; *b*; Moorehead, 1932, p. 130
5.	"	"	"	....	Carafe-neck bottle sun design with central cross; 13 rays in natural buff color; grit and mica temper(?)	"	....	Ashley, 1932, fig. 33, *c*; Moorehead, 1932, p. 130
6.	"	"	"	Andover 61462 Ga.	Carafe-neck, ball-leg tripod with circular dark spot in center of circular band; alternate light and dark bands on tripods; shell temper	....	....	Ashley, 1932, fig. 33; *a*; Moorehead, 1932, p. 130
7.	Alabama	Madison	Hobbs Island (Ma°3)	Al.M.N.H.	Carafe-neck sun design bottle with cross center dots and sun rays; grit temper(?)	Kogers Island or "Pottery 3"	....	Webb, 1939, pl. 97, p. 87
8.	"	"	"	Al.M.N.H.	Wide-necked bottle; sun design with cross center rays in natural buff; shell temper	"	....	Webb, 1939, pl. 96, p. 87
9.	"	Jackson	Hardin (Ja^{v}27)	Al.M.N.H.	Carafe-neck bottle with 3 sun designs on body; center cross, sun rays in black; shell temper	"	....	Information from Marion Dunlevy
10.	"	"	Rudder (Ja°180) Burial 25	Al.M.N.H.	Carafe-neck bottle with 3 sun designs on body; center cross, rays in black projecting from buff dots; sandy grit temper; cross design on lower neck	"	....	Information from Marion Dunlevy
11.	Kentucky	Christian	Glover	U. of Kentucky(?)	Carafe-neck bottle with center cross; buff dots and black rays; has unusual design features; shell temper(?)	Cumberland	....	Webb & Funkhouser, 1929, pp. 24–28
12.	Tennessee	Meigs	Hiwassee Island	U. of Tennessee	Sherd with sun design with center cross and rays in black; probably fine shell	Dallas Focus		Lewis & Kneberg, 1946, p. 96, fig. 18

13.	"	"	"	U. of Tennessee	Carafe-neck bottle trilobate with 3 concentric circles around lobe and a dot at center; 4 horizontal lines around neck	"	....	Lewis & Kneberg, 1946, p. 96; pls. 58, *c* and 102
14.	Arkansas	Craighead	Monette region	M.A.I. 5/1082	Wide-necked bottle with low annular base; 3 sun rays on body with center cross, sun rays in black; shell temper(?)	....	....	Vaillant, 1939, pl. 28
15.	"	Miller	Haley	M.A.I.(?)	Carafe-neck bottle with sun design, center cross sun rays in black; dot design on bottle neck	....	....	Moore, 1912, pl. XXXVII
16.	Missouri(?)	....	....	P.M.H.U. 12925	Carafe(?)-neck bottle with rim fillet and handles; quadrilobate and 5 modified symbols, center cross and light rays; shell temper	New Madrid	....	Phillips, Neg. 2691
17.	"	....	....	P.M.H.U. 15013	Tall and cylindrical-neck bottle with rim fillet; modified "sun-planet" symbol	"	....	Phillips, Neg. 2675
18.	"	....	Potter & Engelman Mound	P.M.H.U. 48510	Bottle with symbol, center cross, sun rays in buff	"	....	Phillips, Neg. 979
19.	"	....	New Madrid area	P.M.H.U. 48705	Small carafe with neck broken; very modified sun symbol with dots and spiral center	"	....	Phillips, Neg. 2687; Evers, 1880, pl. 4, *47*
20.	Missouri	....	New Madrid area	P.M.H.U. 48710	Carafe(?)-neck; modified sun symbol with central cross on a buff 7-pointed "star" around the central cross	"	....	Phillips, Neg. 2680; Evers, 1880, pl. 4, *1*
21.	Missouri(?)	....	....	P.M.H.U.	Carafe-neck bottle; modified sun symbol with central black circle and ray design in natural buff	"	....	Phillips, Neg. 2678
22.	Missouri	....	Potter & Engelman Mound	P.M.H.U. 48736	Bottle with neck gone; modified sun design with central black circle and sun's rays in reddish surface color	"	....	Phillips, Neg. 786
23.	"	Mississippi	Near Charleston	A.M.N.H. 2321 (Terry Coll.)	Carafe-neck bottle; modified sun with center of black circle and sun's rays in reddish surface color	"	....	Phillips, Neg. 289
24.	"	"	"	A.M.N.H. 2310 (Terry Coll.)	Wide-necked bottle; modified sun symbol with central black circle, sun's rays in buff background; horizontal black band on neck	"	....	Phillips, Neg. 287

	State	County	Site	Collection or Source	Type	Culture	Time	References
25.	Missouri	Mississippi	"	A.M.N.H. 2097 (Terry Coll.)	Modified sun symbol, carafe-neck bottle	"	....	Phillips, Neg. 291
26.	Missouri (?)	"	"	D.P.M. 8026	Carafe- or narrow cylindrical-neck bottle with modified sun symbols, central black circle, sun's rays in light background	"	....	Phillips, Neg. 678
27.	Missouri	"	"	A.M.N.H. 2306 (Terry Coll.)	Charleston-type head bottle; horizontal stripes on neck of bottle and head; face has light spots in broad black band	"	....	Phillips, Neg. 238
28.	Missouri (?)	....	New Madrid area	P.M.H.U. 48713	Carafe (?)-neck with rim fillet; scroll design on body; neck bands	"	....	Phillips, Neg. 2679; Evers, 1880, pl. 3, *18*
29.	"	....	"	P.M.H.U. 15036	Wide-mouthed bottle with vertical bands covered with red film	"	....	Phillips, Neg. 2676
30.	Missouri	Mississippi	Near Charleston	A.M.N.H. 2323 (Terry Coll.)	Hooded bottle, animal effigy face; star design and dots in large dark circle; red added to design	"	....	Phillips, Neg. 229
31.	"	"	"	A.M.N.H.2309 (Terry Coll.)	Carafe (?)-neck bottle; concentric circle, separated by areas of horizontal stripes	"	....	Phillips, Neg. 281
32.	Missouri (?)	....	....	P.M.H.U. 48696	Carafe-neck bottle; oblique dark bands on body with dark spot in center of light circle; stripes on neck	"	....	Phillips, Neg. 2677; Evers, 1880, pl. 4, *12*
33.	Missouri	....	New Madrid area	P.M.H.U. 48708	Negative painting with red and white overlay; carafe (?)-neck; pendant triangle on lower body; scroll on shoulder area	....	....	Philips, Neg. 2686; Evers, 1880, pl. 1, *35*
34.	"	....	....	P.M.H.U. 12376	Carafe (?)-neck; body has modified sun symbol of central dot and two concentric dark circles; sawtooth upper edge	....	....	Phillips, Neg. 2681
35.	Illinois	Massac	Kincaid	U. of Chicago	Carafe-neck, sun symbol design repeated 4 times; sun's rays in light color	....	....	Courtesy U. of Chicago, Dep't. of Anthropology
36.	Tennessee	Sumner	Rutherford	P.M.H.U. 17269	Human effigy figure seated on bottle; oblique hatching in zones	Cumberland	....	Phillips, Neg. 2847
37.	"	Davidson	Gower	P.M.H.U. 18618	Hooded human hunchback effigy; oblique hatching in zones on back	"	....	Phillips, Neg. 2853

38.	"	Williamson	Old Town	P.M.H.U. 15999	Hooded human hunchback effigy; design almost gone	"	....	Phillips, Neg. 2800
39.	"	"	"	P.M.H.U. 15983	Hooded human effigy; design almost gone	"	....	Phillips, Neg. 2799
40.	"	"	"	P.M.H.U. 15870	Hooded human effigy; oblique hatching in large zones on body and head	"	....	Phillips, Neg. 2798
41.	"	"	"	P.M.H.U. 15898	Hooded human effigy; design almost gone	"	....	Phillips, Neg. 2797
42.	"	"	"	P.M.H.U. 15853	Hooded human effigy; slip preserved by design is lost	"	....	Phillips, Neg. 2796
43.	"	"	"	P.M.H.U. 16000	Human effigy; head missing; design almost gone	"	....	Phillips, Neg. 2794
44.	"	Davidson	Overton	P.M.H.U. 14138	Human effigy; hooded and hunchback; decoration gone but probably negative painted	"	....	Phillips, Neg. 2866
45.	"	Wilson	Lindsley-Lebanon	P.M.H.U. 12100	....	"	....	Phillips, Neg. 2739
46.	"	Davidson	Noel	Vanderbilt U. (?)	Human effigy figure; oblique hatching in large zones on body	"	....	Thruston, 1890, pl. IX
47.	"	"	"	Vanderbilt U. (?)	Human effigy figure; oblique hatching in large zones on body	"	....	Thruston, 1890, pl. IX
48.	"	Sumner	Castalian Springs	U.S.N.M.	Human effigy figure; oblique hatching in zone forming "rattlesnake" design	"	....	Myer, 1917, fig. 2; p. 99
49.	"	Montgomery	Allen	Vanderbilt U.	Carafe-neck ball-leg tripod; quadrilobate body with central dark dot in light circle on lobes; design repeated on each foot	"	....	Thruston, 1890, fig. 40 and pl. VIII, p. 150
50.	"	Davidson	Noel	Vanderbilt U.	Carafe-neck bottle; hand and possibly skull design; cross design in hand	"	....	Thruston, 1890, fig. 40, pp. 135–36
51.	Alabama	Hale	Moundville	M.A.I.	Carafe-neck bottle; skull-and-hand design	Moundville	....	Moore, 1907, fig. 20, p. 356
52.	"	Franklin	Near the Mississippi state line	D.P.M. 6653	Carafe-neck bottle; skull-and-hand design; pendant triangles on neck	....	....	Holmes, 1886, pp. 433–34; 1903, p. 106 is in error
53.	Tennessee	Davidson	Byser	Vanderbilt U. (?)	Hooded bottle with human head; quadrilobate body; dark dot in center of circular light area on each lobe	Cumberland	....	Thruston, 1890, fig. 40, pl. VIII, p. 150

	State	County	Site	Collection or Source	Type	Culture	Time	References
54.	Tennessee	....	Bannister	P.M.H.U. 18351	Hooded owl effigy tripod; vertical row of negative v's on chest; different design on back	"	....	Phillips, Neg. 2947
55.	"	Davidson	Noel	Vanderbilt U.(?)	Hooded owl effigy tripod; feathers portrayed in alternating areas of light and dark	"	....	Thruston, 1890, pl. III, p. 101
56.	"	"	"	Fisk University(?)	Hooded owl effigy tripod	"	....	Thruston, 1890, p. 101
57.	"	Monroe	Callaway	U.S.N.M.	Hooded owl effigy tripod; feather design on chest; wing markings on back are "of the strictly Mexican type"	Dallas	....	Thomas, 1894, p. 386; figs. 267–68; Holmes, 1903, pl. XXII, *c*
58.	"	....	Hixon	U. of Tennessee	Hooded owl tripod; drawing has light circles on chest and thighs; rest of design not visible	"	....	Courtesy U. of Tennessee, Dep't. of Anthropology
59.	Kentucky	Hickman	McLeod Bluff	U. of Kentucky	Vertical compound bottle on rounded base; part of neck missing, probably carafe; running scroll in light background against dark mass	....	....	From print of the U. of Kentucky
60.	Illinois	Massac	Kincaid	U. of Chicago	Plate rims of Angel Negative Painted	....	....	Courtesy U. of Chicago
61.	Indiana	Vanderburgh	Angel	Indiana Hist. Soc.	Plate rims of Angel Negative Painted	....	....	Courtesy G. A. Black
62.	Tennessee	Davidson	Noel	Vanderbilt U.(?)	Negative-painted plate of Angel Negative Painted style	....	....	Thruston, 1890, p. 136; fig. 41
63.	Alabama	Madison	Hobbs Island (Ma°4)	U. of Alabama	Negative-painted plate rim; Angel style(?)	....	....	Webb, 1939, pl. 105–a, *5*
64.	North Carolina	Cherokee	Peachtree	U.S.N.M.	Negative-painted(?) plate rim; exterior body is complicated stamped	....	....	Setzler & Jennings, 1941, pl. 39
65.	Ohio	Hamilton	Madisonville	P.M.H.U.	Small bowl with black circle on interior divided into 4 quarters with a dark dot in each quarter	Madisonville Focus; Fort Ancient Aspect	....	Hooton, 1920, pl. 24, *b*
66.	Alabama	Lauderdale	Seven Mile Island (Lu°21)	Al.M.N.H.	"Dog pot" with carafe neck and spotted design on body	Kogers Island or Pottery 3	....	Webb & DeJarnette, 1942, pl. 63–1, *1*, p. 53
67.	Tennessee	....	Hixon	U. of Tennessee	"Dog pot" with spiral elements on body and lower carafe neck	Dallas	....	Lewis & Kneberg, 1941, pl. V, *12*
68.	"	Davidson	Bosley Farm	Vanderbilt U.(?)	Carafe-neck "dog pot" with concentric circle design on body within a frame of horizontal alternate light and dark lines	Cumberland	....	Thruston, 1890, pl. IX, p. 152

69.	Georgia	White	Nacoochee	M.A.I.	Carafe-neck "dog pot" concentric circle design on lower body; scroll on upper body; 3 horizontal bands on lower neck; pendant triangles from lip	Lamar	....	Heye, Hodge, & Pepper, 1918
70.	"	....	Neisler	....	Painted effigy "dog pot"	"	....	Kelly, 1938, p. 51
71.	"	Muscogee	Bull Creek	Columbus, Ga.	Wide-mouthed medium-high-necked "dog pot" with scroll design on body and erect triangles on neck; red and white	"	....	Kelly, 1938, p. 51
72.	"	"	"	"	Almost a duplicate of the above vessel	"	....	Kelly, 1938, p. 51
73.	"	"	"	"	Wide-mouthed tall-necked "dog pot"; black and red decoration	"	....	....
74.	Tennessee	Wilson	Lindsley-Lebanon	P.M.H.U. 13998	Carafe-neck "dog pot"; design almost gone	....	....	Putnam, 1878, p. 359; fig. 55; Douglas & d'Harnoncourt, 1941, p. 76
75.	Illinois	Fulton	Dickson (F°34)	Dickson Mound, State Park	"Water bottle, design painted on neck and bottom as well as body, black and white" cylindrical neck, tall	Spoon River Focus	....	Cole & Deuel, 1937, p. 125; fig. 11, 7*c*
76.	"	"	Crable	"	Water bottle	"	....	Smith, 1951, pl. VII, *e*
77.	Kentucky	....	McCabe	U. of Kentucky	....	....	....	Willey & Phillips, 1944, p. 177
78.	Arkansas	Poinsett	Hazel Place	U. of Arkansas Haz. 217a	Wide-mouthed, short-necked bottle; appliqué heads on shoulder area	....	....	Phillips, Neg. 3442
79.	"	Crittenden	Barton Ranch (11–O–10)	U. of Arkansas Br. 14a	Wide-mouthed, short-necked bottle; 4 hands on body with red dot in palm outlined in red	....	....	This vol. fig. 111, *j*
80.	Mississippi	Coahoma	Spendthrift (16–O–2)	P.M.H.U.	....	....	....	....
81.	Alabama	Mobile Bay area	....	U.S.N.M.	Flaring rim bowl with white and red nested v's on inner rim; identified as negative painting by Willey & Phillips	....	....	Holmes, 1903, fig. 56; Willey & Phillips, 1944, p. 177
82.	Florida	Citrus	Crystal River	M.A.I. 17/3523	Bowl with T-shaped lip; large light dots and meander pattern; black and buff	Crystal River Focus of Hopewellian	....	Willey & Phillips, 1944, pl. XVI, *a*; Moore, 1903a, fig. 27

	State	County	Site	Collection or Source	Type	Culture	Time	References
83.	Florida	Citrus	"	M.A.I. 18/326	Bowl with rectilinear pattern of black and buff; superimposed pattern in direct painting in maroon-red	"	....	Willey & Phillips, 1944, pl. XVI, *b*; Moore, 1903a, fig .27
84.	"	"	"	M.A.I.	Scalloped rim jar; constricted neck, angular 4-line guilloche (?) design on shoulder area; red and black	"	....	Moore, 1903a, fig. 28
85.	"	Franklin	Green Point	R.S. Peabody Foundation 39147	Bowl with "T-shaped" lip; horseshoe design in black on buff body; lower body black	"	....	Willey, 1948, fig. 56; 1949, pl. XXIII, *a*
86.	"	Taylor	Warrior River	M.A.I.	Buff bowl with lines, triangles, and circles in black	....	....	Moore, 1902, p. 341
87.	Texas	Lamar	Sanders	U. of Texas	Cylindrical long-neck compound vertical bottle on jar with 4 strap handles; red triangles pendant from base of neck on shoulder	Lamar Focus, Gibson Aspect	1400	Krieger, 1946, pl. 28, *c*
88.	Illinois	Union	....	C.N.H.M. 55630	Bottle with neck missing, and flaring annular base; design is 4 dark circular areas on body in each of which is a light cross	....	....	C.N.H.M., Neg. 74898–9
89.	Tennessee	Wilson	Lindsley-Lebanon	P.M.H.U. 12036	Carafe-neck bottle; quadrilobate; design almost completely obliterated	Cumberland	....	....
90.	"	Davidson	Cain	P.M.H.U. 15240	....	"	....	....
91.	"	....	....	U. of Tennessee	Carafe-neck bottle with 4 appliqué effigy heads on shoulder	Dallas Focus	....	Courtesy U. of Tennessee, Dept. of Anthropology

Section V

SERIATION ANALYSIS OF POTTERY COLLECTIONS

SERIATION ANALYSIS OF POTTERY COLLECTIONS

Assumptions

NOW the 346,099 sherds from 383 sites, collected by the Lower Mississippi Survey and duly classified as described in Section III, could be stored away in cabinets and forgotten for the time being. The data was safely on paper and time would heal our wounded consciences and dim our suspicions that at several points our classification was less than perfect. During the winter of 1947 Phillips turned to the problems of physiography, and the identification of historic sites; Griffin began the description of pottery types; and Ford started work on analysis, assisted and checked at every point by his somewhat fearful colleagues.

The basic assumptions which served as a foundation for the analytical procedure need to be stated in some detail. They will help to explain the procedure followed and it is hoped will prevent the reader from accepting the conclusions in an any more "positive" sense than the writers intend. We consider these assumptions as a set of probabilities which lead to conclusions that are our best guesses. Not that we intend to apologize for this admission. This we think is the real method of science. We are trying to expose our limitations and are not setting out to *prove* anything beyond all doubt.

A. In the portion of the Mississippi Valley which was surveyed and for the greater part of the span of history which is being studied, the aboriginal people were presumably agriculturists. The population was rather numerous, as will be shown later, and was collected in small villages. For these reasons it seems reasonable to think that there was comparative stability of peoples. These Indians did not wander as did the historic Indians of the Plains and, from the archaeological evidence, there seems to have been little or none of the frantic shifting of tribes that marks the post-contact history of the Eastern Indians. We are assuming then until the evidence indicates the contrary that the people who carried the cultural traits we are studying were probably relatively stable geographically and that for the most part population changes were slow gradual ones.

B. While the prehistoric populations were comparatively stable in the larger geographic sense, this does not appear to have been true of the great majority of village sites. Some sites were inhabited throughout the time span which is being studied. Most, however, were occupied for a short time in proportion to the entire chronology. This assumption was based on archaeological experience in other parts of the Southeast and on a preliminary glance over the collections gathered in this Survey. The condition seems to be due to the limitations of the agricultural methods and equipment of the Indians. After a field had been cleared and used for crops for a few years, the grass and weeds probably moved in and took over. With the inefficient tools which the Southeastern Indians had, control of this vegetation very likely became so difficult after a few years that it was easier to ring and burn trees for a new field than it was to continue planting in the old one. In the course of a few decades, when all the desirable agricultural land in the vicinity of a village had been opened up to weeds in this fashion, the village would have to be moved to a new location.[1] This was the practice of the Southeastern tribes in the early Historic Period before they acquired plows, and such names as "Chickasaw Old Fields" and "Tuckabachee Old Fields" undoubtedly refer to such weed-grown abandoned land.

The securing of short time-span collections is essential if the method of seriating of surface collections is to be successfully applied. For this reason, careful attention was paid to the combinations of sherd material which were gathered from various parts of each village site. In the course of field work, where it was evident that one portion of a site yielded a different complex from that found on another part, two or more separate collections

[1] Linton, 1940, pp. 37–40.

were made. These were labeled "A," "B," etc., and were treated all through the course of analysis as though they came from different sites. A cross section of the ceramic styles in vogue at these different sites at one instant in time would have been the ideal material for seriation purposes, but that, of course, is an unattainable goal.

C. The third assumption has already been stated in the foregoing section on ceramic classification. Until the evidence suggests differently, we are assuming that in any large area cultural continuity in both time and space is to be expected as the normal state of affairs. A gradual change of feature with the passage of time and across the area, when it is viewed on any one time horizon, was our very idealized concept of the cultural history with which we are dealing. This does not mean that we did not anticipate the possibility of finding evidence of (1) the replacement of one population bearing a certain variety of culture by another population having entirely different customs; (2) the replacement of cultural features through acculturation from sources outside the region in which we are working; or (3) the specializing of cultural complexes in certain regions due to their being protected from the prevailing patterns of the area as a whole by such factors as geographical isolation, peculiarities of population distribution, linguistic barriers, or political groupings. These conditions were some of the things of which we expected to get hints from our study.

So we did not begin our analysis with any assumption that changes in ceramics, such as the shift from clay- to shell-tempering, necessarily indicate any abrupt cultural or population replacement. If the refuse deposits of the two time periods really should have a layer of clean white sand separating them after the classic model of stratigraphy, we wanted to be shown by the evidence.

D. Our fourth basic assumption has also been stated in the discussion of ceramic typology. We are assuming that each of our pottery types is a more or less sensitive instrument for measuring cultural change with the passage of time and distribution over space. We are a little complacent about this assumption and feel that we are on fairly certain grounds because we went to great pains to set up and adapt each type for exactly those purposes. Rearranging, merging, and splitting of type groups were guided by preliminary analysis and the resultant information about chronological relations.

However, as has been made clear in the type descriptions, all of the types are not equally well adapted for this purpose. Because of the practical difficulties of making distinctions, some of the types, especially the undecorated ones, include material that represents long spans of time and large amounts of area. In other examples we are aware that the original concepts have changed during the classifying so that the resultant categories are somewhat broader than would have been desired. Mazique Incised is an example of this latter kind of type weakness. Despite this, we feel that we are fairly aware of this factor and thus have it under reasonable control.

E. The next point to be considered is not a basic assumption but rather a logical derivative of the preceding discussions. It has to do with the relative popularity of types through time. If our pottery types are successful measuring units for a continuous stream of changing cultural ideas, it follows that when the relative popularity of these types is graphed through time, a more or less long, single-peak curve will usually result. Put in another way, a type will first appear in very small percentages, will gradually increase to its maximum popularity, and then, as it is replaced by its succeeding type, will gradually decrease and disappear.

This interesting phenomena can be illustrated by endless examples taken from any span of culture history. Consider the popularity curve of the "Charleston" dance fad in the United States. A specific political concept, a particular word, or any other carefully defined cultural type will show the same popularity curve that Spier found in the history of Zuñi pottery.[1a]

This is an interesting phenomenon but do not let us be misled. We have not discovered a natural law operating independently of our own humble efforts. This peculiar charac-

[1a] Spier, 1917.

teristic of type popularity distribution through time is something we have helped to bring about through our own conceptualization of the pottery types that manifest said behavior. How the curves come out is partly controlled by how the types are defined.

F. The sixth assumption is also a derivative of the foregoing discussions. If a complex of cultural materials representing a space-time continuum of culture history is classified in a consistent manner, the popularity curves of the various constituent types will form a pattern. Each portion of this pattern will be peculiar to a particular time and area. This concept may best be illustrated from contemporary culture. Lacking accurate data, as this sort of information is usually ignored by historians, let us manufacture some for purposes of illustration.[2] Let us say that in the State of Ohio in the year 1920, the following were the relative popularities of the indicated types of travel for distances over 5 miles:

	PER CENT
Walking	5
Riding horses	5
Horse and buggy	15
Gasoline-powered boats	5
Steamboats	5
Automobiles	20
Airplanes	2
Railways	43

Here is a ratio of popularity of transportation types which will never be exactly repeated in Ohio or anywhere else.

Now let us take a look at a supposed history of the relative popularity of transportation types in Ohio for a period extending sometime before and after 1920. This we have graphed in figure 15.[3] Not only is the pattern different for each ten-year interval, but the quantitative picture of this stretch of culture history is a unique thing. The pattern of the popularity peaks of the different transportation types have never been repeated. A similar graph for Texas would doubtless show larger popularity of horse-riding. There wouldn't have been any steamboat travel at all in Utah. Indiana would show the same type as Ohio but in differing quantities and temporal relations.

So long as we maintain our classifications strictly as they are, we may review any number of representative samples of Ohio transportation history, and the same frequency pattern will result. The only way in which the pattern might be changed would be to change the classification. This can be done in a number of different ways. Let us show a few:

1. Travel without vehicles
   Vehicles that travel on land
   Vehicles that travel on water
   Vehicles that travel in air
2. Man-powered travel
   Animal-powered travel
   Steam-powered travel
   Gasoline-powered travel
   Electric-powered travel
3. Travel 0–5 miles an hour
   Travel 5–10 miles on hour
   etc.

Note that in each case where the classification is rearranged, the quantitative-historical picture would be completely different. This is not to say that it would be any more true or false than the scheme which we have illustrated in figure 15. All of these classifications will measure time change in a cultural feature. The point of interest to the classifier is that the first scheme with the finer type divisions will do the job a little more accurately than the others. Still finer divisions which will do even better jobs will occur to the reader.

While this fanciful illustration is set up, let us go a little farther and show how the dating and seriation techniques that will be discussed later will work. Suppose that we

[2] Historical statistical data about manufacturing, trade, etc., will give this kind of information. However, it is easier to make up our illustration than to dig it out of the census

[3] Here we have used the type of diagram which will often reoccur in this study, so we might as well explain it now. The passage of time is always represented by proceeding from the bottom to the top of the figure. Each cultural type is assigned a vertical "axis," or imaginary line, which is indicated at both top and bottom of the figure. The relative popularity of the type is shown by the length of the horizontal bars that center on the type axis. This may be measured by means of the percentage scale given in the figure. Try it for the year 1920 and see if the graph agrees with the tabulation given above.

have a sample of the transportation habits of the Ohioans for an unknown date which showed the following percentages of popularity:

	PER CENT
Walking	5
Riding horses	12
Horse and buggy	28
Paddling and rowing boats	1
Steamboats	12
Automobiles	0
Airplanes	0
Railway	40

with frequency data on the transportation customs of Ohio for a number of years. We do not know the dates of these samples and have no idea as to their chronological sequence. We can't get a complete history out of this data but we can do something. By rearranging our samples, we can find the type frequency pattern and the relative order of the samples. We will not know the calendrical dates of the samples, the relative lengths of time occupied by the various sections of the chronology, or even which end of the chronology is the most recent in time, but we can develop the quan-

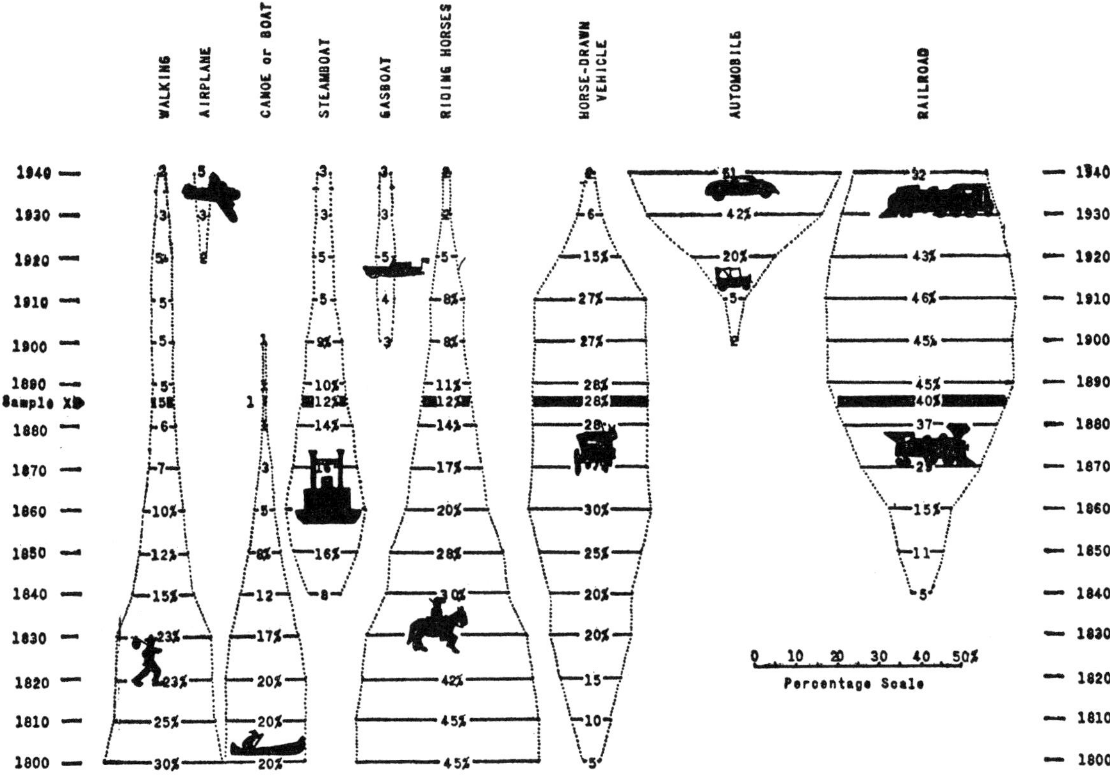

FIG. 15. Theoretical percentage frequency graph of transportation types in Ohio from A.D. 1800 to 1940.

When this information is graphed after the fashion used in figure 15, and the graph is placed on this chronology, it will be seen that the type frequencies of this sample, which we may as well call "X," will fit the chronology at only one point. As our figure shows, it dates about 1885.

Let us suppose again that we are faced with a situation in which we are merely provided titative-historical pattern. This, in effect, is the seriation technique we have used.

This rather far-fetched bit of imaginary analysis is only worth-while if it brings out the point that systematic classification of cultural data representing a particular range of time creates in each case a characteristic quantitative pattern. We had this in mind as our sherds from the Mississippi Valley area were classified, and the analytical procedure that will be described were the steps which were taken in search of these patterns.

G. Two more assumptions which we have made may be grouped together. We have assumed that our sampling of sites in each part of our Survey Area has been sufficiently thorough. We think that we have secured a sample of the pottery which was made during each stage of the chronologies which we will present so that no large time gaps remain unrepresented.

We are also guessing that a random sample of over fifty sherds is sufficient to indicate the proportionate type frequencies existing in the refuse from which the material was collected. A total of fifty is considered to be usable, but not particularly reliable. One hundred is much better and every sherd above one hundred is all to the good.[4] It will be noted that some of our collections are quite large.

The foregoing assumptions which we made at the start of the analytical work, and which we intended to act upon until the evidence indicated that they were wrong, may be summarized as follows:

A. The distribution of prehistoric populations of the Survey Area was relatively stable.

B. The majority of the village sites were probably inhabited for a short time as compared to the entire time with which we are dealing.

C. The culture of the area in the main probably changed gradually rather than by means of mass migration from other areas.

D. If propositions A and C were true, the pottery types which we had defined would each show a single-peak popularity curve when measured through time, but the duration of such peaks, and the resulting curves, would vary from one type to another.

E. If D is true, then all the pottery-type frequency curves would be different in each part of the area on each time horizon, and a distinct pattern will appear when each part of the area is viewed through time.

F. Our sampling technique has been successful in getting samples representing continuous segments of time in all parts of the area and also in securing enough material from the sites which we will treat to give a more or less reliable picture of the material available on the surface.

Analytical Procedure

The first step in our ceramic analysis was a simple and tedious one. On the sheets which recorded the classification of the material from each collection, the totals of these collections were run up on an adding machine, and the percentages of each type calculated by slide rule. The "Unclassified" sherds were included in these totals. This was done for all surface collections which contained more than fifty sherds, as well as for each level in the stratigraphic excavations.

Then a roll of graph paper marked with a centimeter-millimeter grid was secured. On a piece of this paper a "key" was prepared very carefully. This key indicated the position of the axis of each type from which bars showing the relative frequency of the types were to be drawn. The best spacing of the types along the key was something that had to be developed in the course of the analysis to prevent overlapping of the frequency bars. The arrangement was changed several times, and its final form is as given at the tops and bottoms of figures 17–21.

After the first key was worked out, the type frequency data for each collection was placed on a 5-centimeter-wide strip graph. This second step was also a routine mechanical matter and took some time to accomplish, particularly as this work several times pointed out defects in the positions of the types on the key. When the key was changed, all strip graphs made with the old key had to be discarded. Finally, however, all of the classification data was in this graphic form.

While this work was underway, the classification data was being analysed in another way by several student assistants[5] at the American Museum. This was a distributional study of type frequencies. For each type a sheet of tracing cloth was placed over a map showing all site locations. Then, the percentage frequency of the type at each site, say

[4] For a brief discussion of quantitative reliability of collections, see Ford, 1936, pp. 13–14.

[5] Miss Margaret Rose, Miss Eileen Boecklen, and Mr. Gary Vesalius.

Mulberry Creek Cord-marked for example, was recorded in its proper geographical position on the traced map. Now, if the above-discussed assumptions are correct, that the average village site was inhabited for a relatively short period (see assumption B, above), and that our Survey work has gathered a sample of the material from sites representing each time period in all parts of the area (F, above), then in each part of the Survey Area there should be sites which show Mulberry Creek Cord-marked near or at its popularity peak. Other sites, which cover time ranges before or after the maximum popularity of the type, will, of course, show their occurrence in smaller percentages. With all of this in mind, the completed distribution maps of Mulberry Creek Cord-marked were inspected with particular attention to maximum occurrences. It was seen that it would be possible to draw lines which would enclose maximums in descending order, after the fashion of contour lines (see figs. 6–14). If we wished to coin a new word and help our science to become more profound, we might call these "Iso-ceramic Lines" — but let's not.

These distributional studies made plain something which we knew already from classifying the material: there would be both quantitative and qualitative variation at all time periods in the different parts of the Survey Area. They also showed something else which we had suspected would be true. Regional specialization tended to increase with the passage of time so that late complexes from the northern and southern ends of our Survey were more unlike than were the early. This is a common phenomenon for cultures at this stage of development and seems to be owing to factors such as decreased population mobility due to an increased dependence on agriculture; the establishment of more stable centers, such as ceremonial mound groups and towns; and an increase in the cohesion of political groupings made possible and necessitated by the improved food supply and consequent population increase; to which was added the increased availability of cultural ideas which could be combined to form "new" varieties.

With this data in hand, it was decided that the practical way in which to treat the chronology of the Survey Area would be to divide it up into sub-areas based on the differences that could be observed in the material of the latest time horizons. A chronological column could then be worked out for each sub-area and comparisons between the areas could be made at the different time levels. We realized that the procedure which we were adopting was fully as arbitrary, and indeed was of the same kind of high-handed ruthlessness as were our decisions in regard to ceramic classification. We are again preparing to set up artificial boundaries, which this time are geographically defined, and draw the borderline cases back toward the selected concepts.

From the beginning, the Lower St. Francis River area in Arkansas looked like a "natural" for a "Focal Grouping." Here are a number of highly similar sites, already known in archaeological literature (Parkin, Rose Mound, etc.), that seemed to stand off by themselves. This happy condition was improved by the fact that Survey work was not extended very far up the St. Francis River above these sites, so we were ignorant of any gradual transition toward any different-appearing complex in that direction. All the arbitrary decisions which would trouble us lay to the south and east. Ignorance and a classical tradition; it couldn't be better. We immediately set up a Lower St. Francis area and accepted the sites in quadrangles 11–N and 12–N as appropriate for starting chronological analysis.

The second area also looked good. Its literary background is provided by Calvin Brown's description of the material from the Walls Site [6] near Memphis. The material from this and a number of closely related sites differed in a number of respects from the typical St. Francis area complex, as we have abundantly shown in Section IV. That this distinction proved to be partly due to difference in time does not lessen the initial lure of the situation. A *Memphis area* was definied and the sites included in quadrangles 13–O, 13–P, 14–O, and 14–P were taken as nuclear for starting the analysis.

We had a little more difficulty about the other three areas which were eventually set up. The literary background did not focus our attention so effectively, and we knew a

[6] Brown, 1926, pp. 288–319.

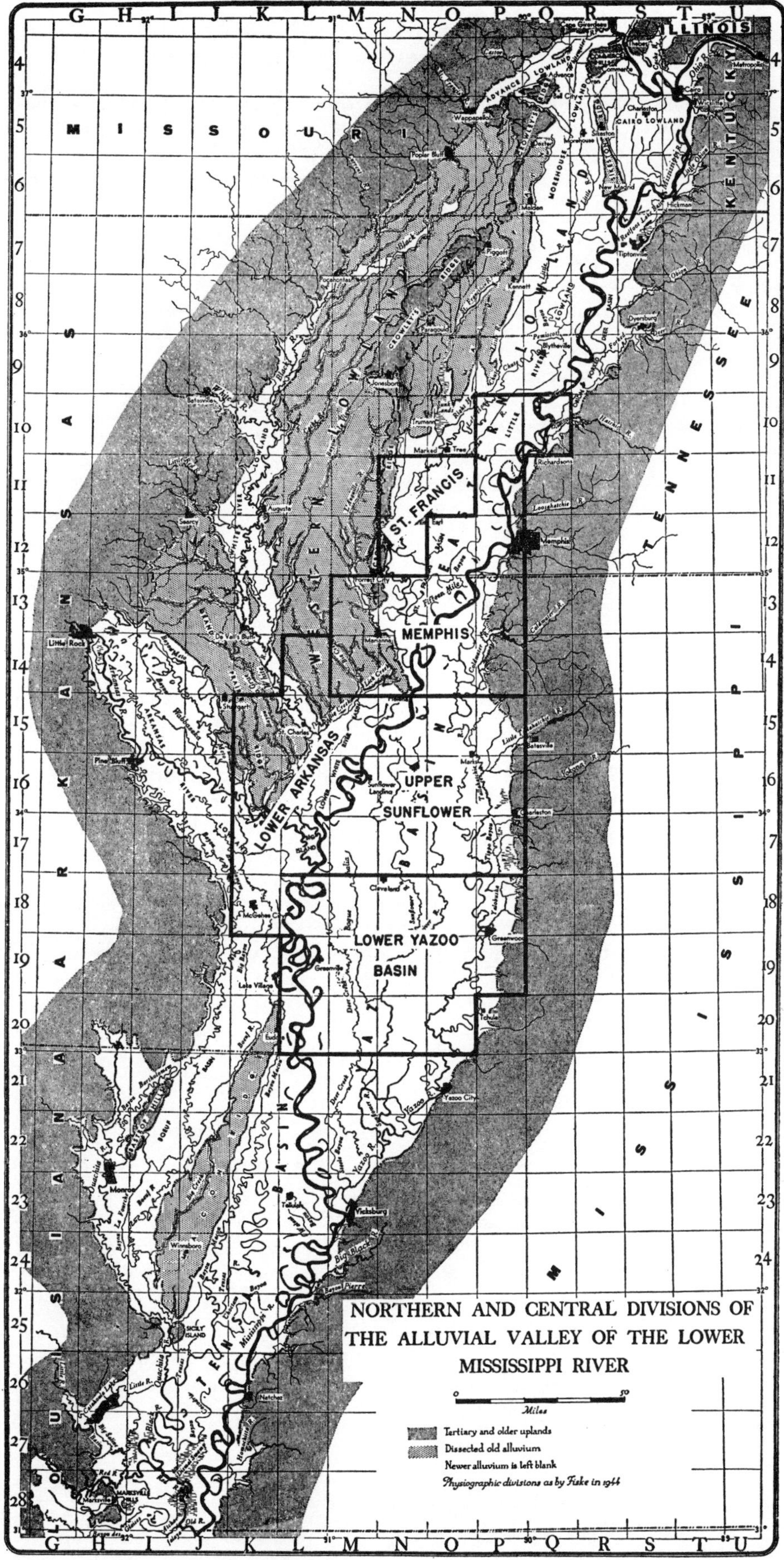

FIG. 16. Subdivision of Survey Area into analysis units for purposes of seriation.

little too much about "transitional" sites and material. After several false starts the following areas and beginning quadrangles were selected (fig. 16):

St. Francis Basin	11–N, 12–N
Memphis area	13–O, 13–P, 14–O, 14–P
Sunflower area	16–N, 16–O, 17–N, 17–O
Lower Yazoo Basin area .	19–M, 19–N, 20–M, 20–N
Lower Arkansas River area .	16–K, 16–L, 17–K, 17–L

It must be emphasized again that these areas have been set up solely for purposes of seriation and are therefore not to be confused with "foci" in the Midwestern taxonomic sense, or any other sort of cultural grouping.

It will be seen that the starting quadrangles for each area are geographically separated from the starting quadrangles of the other areas. This was intentional and was for the purpose of emphasizing the differences. The borderline cases were dealt with later as will be described.

By the time the study had reached this stage, we already had at hand considerable information as to the outlines of the ceramic chronologies in the region. One source of information was the sequences which had been worked out in the adjoining regions by Webb and his associates in northern Alabama;[7] Jennings along the Natchez Trace Parkway in north-central Mississippi;[8] Ford and his co-workers around the mouth of the Red River in Louisiana. A second very essential source of information were the stratigraphic excavations made by Phillips and Griffin, described in detail in a later section of this report. These revealed portions of the ceramic histories which could be used as partial backbone for the area chronologies. Our third source of information was the preliminary seriation analyses which we had made while classifying the site collections. So we had a rather good idea as to the relative time positions and distributions of many of the ceramic types. Despite this, the analytical procedures described here were followed out in detail, so far as possible, as though we had been completely innocent of such fore-knowledge.

Five sheets of heavy paper about 48 inches long and 20 inches wide were laid out on a large table side by side. The 20-inch width of these sheets corresponded to the length of the strip graphs which recorded the type frequencies of each collection. Each of these sheets was headed with the name of one of the seriation areas, and they were placed on the table in the geographical relation of the areas from north to south. Then all of the strip graphs that represented collections from sites included in the quadrangles that served as the nucleus, or starting point, were separated out and placed on the appropriate sheet. The strips were laid horizontally across the sheets and were held in place at the edges by paper clips. As they were arranged and rearranged, particular care was taken to see that the type axes coincided.

We were now ready to begin the search for the quantitative patterning of pottery types, which for reasons that have been discussed in the foregoing, should exist in the area chronologies. This work was started with site collections of the Lower Yazoo Basin area (see fig. 17). These were relatively easy to seriate as two stratigraphic excavations were available to serve as guides for part of the history. The deepest of these excavations, Jaketown (20–O–1) Cut A, had fourteen levels and seemed to cover the greatest range of time. Accordingly, the strip graphs representing these levels were arranged on the sheet in the order in which they had come from the ground and immediately showed the frequency patterning for the time covered by the cut. The strips representing the second strata excavation, Shell Bluff (19–O–2) Cut A, were next put in place. The graph of the top level of this cut was slid along the sheet of paper until a point was found at which all its type frequencies best fitted the corresponding frequencies of the Jaketown cut. It was clear that the second level at Shell Bluff was older than the top level, but we could not know how much older it was in relation to the picture given by the Jaketown cut. Consequently, the second-level graph was placed below the first and slid downward until the best fit was secured.

Vertical arrangement of the material in the ground gave some control over the collections from the stratigraphic pits, and we knew that the collections from the lower levels had to

[7] Webb and DeJarnette, 1942.

[8] Jennings, 1941.

be older than those from the upper. However, for the surface collections we had no such guide. All we had was our assumption that the majority of these surface collections represented relatively short spans of time (see B, above) and the logic which led us to think that a quantitative patterning must be there.

The surface-collection graphs were taken one at a time and compared to the beginning that had been made with the stratigraphic material. If they fitted somewhere along the time represented by the excavations, the graph was fastened down to the backing sheet with paper clips. If percentages of such late types as Neeley's Ferry Plain and Bell Plain were too large, and proportions of such older types as Baytown Plain, Larto Red Filmed, and Mulberry Creek Cord-marked were too small, the collection was obviously later and the graph was placed above the excavations. These surface-collection graphs were shifted about in vertical relation to one another until patterning was developed as is shown in the upper part of figure 17.

The data from the starting quadrangles of the other four seriation areas were dealt with in a similar fashion, figures 17–21. Where stratigraphic information was available, it was used as a guide. Where there was none, the surface-collection graphs were shifted about to develop the best patterning that could be secured. In this way the five chronological columns were developed side by side.

The next phase of the analysis was to assign the sites in the intervening quadrangles to one or another of the five areas which had been set up. All of the site-collection graphs for each of these remaining quadrangles were seriated and then compared to the five area graphs. For example, the chronological patterning of quadrangle 18–M looked more like the chronology begun for the Lower Yazoo area than any of the other sub-areas, so the collections from this quadrangle were fed into the Yazoo graph at the points where they fitted best.

Now, the area chronological graphs were virtually complete and good patterning of types could be seen. Apparently, our assumption that most of the surface collections represented relatively short lengths of time was correct. But while the majority did, some obviously did not. In a number of collections, early and late types were associated together in a fashion that showed either that the sites had been occupied for a long time, or there had been reoccupation. In order to clear up the patterning, the strips representing these collections were taken out. The numbers of these long time-span collections as compared to the shorter-lived sites that are used in the final graph are as follows:

AREA	NUMBER OF SHORT-TIME-SPAN SURFACE COLLS. USED IN FINISHED GRAPH	NUMBER OF LONG-TIME-SPAN COLLS. TAKEN OUT TO CLARIFY GRAPH
Lower Yazoo Basin	48	1
Lower Arkansas River	19	1
Sunflower	81	9
Memphis	66	7
St. Francis	37	0
	—	—
Colls. used in graphs	251	Discarded 18[9]

Although eighteen surface collections with respectable sherd totals have been eliminated from the graphs because of the special requirements of this kind of analysis, this does not mean that the effort devoted to these sites has been lost. It may be expected that these are places where rather long spans of history may be examined in stratigraphic relation, if there is any depth to the deposits. So far,

[9] The full list of site collections excluded from the seriation graphs is as follows:

	Sherd Total
Lower Yazoo	
20–O–1 (Jaketown)	4226
Lower Arkansas	
16–L–3 (Stovall)	218
Sunflower	
17–N–16 (Wilnot)	244
16–P–7 (Mitchell)	418
16–P–5 (Crosslyn)	127
16–P–1 (Charleston)	646
16–O–14 (Stover)	110
16–O–17 (Longstreet)	160
17–O–11 (Cassidy)	249
16–O–1 (Dunn)	94
16–P–6 (Cox)	144
Memphis	
10–P–3 (Nettle Ridge)	477
10–Q–3 (Turnage)	328
14–N–6 (Helena Crossing)	80
13–P–4 (Dogwood Ridge)	354
13–P–10 (Irby)	1381
11–P–3 (Golightly Place)	241

tests have been made in one of these sites, 20–O–1 (Jaketown), the results of which are discussed in the section on Stratigraphy (VI). It was quite evident why surface collections from this site were useless for seriation purposes; the occupation covered practically the full range of ceramic history in the area.

Handling of the Data from Stratigraphic Excavations

The incorporation of the data from the stratigraphic excavations into this analysis was done in a purely arbitrary fashion. Each level was treated as though it were a separate surface collection from a distinct site, except for the fact that care was taken to keep the levels in proper vertical order. The relation of stratigraphic levels to the soil profiles revealed by the walls of the excavations, which is discussed in detail in the next section of this report, was not worked out at the time this analysis was made, but had it been available would not have received consideration in this phase of the work. The seriation of the data in these five sub-areas was an attempt to discover the chronological patterning of the pottery types in each region and to reveal the consistency with which the types followed that pattern. In this handling of the data it was expected that such anomalies as the reoccupation of sites after they had been abandoned for any considerable length of time would be revealed by comparison with the evidence given by neighboring sites as to the chronological pattern of each sub-area.

There are some discrepancies between the interpretation given to the stratigraphic data in this section, written mainly by Ford, and the section on Stratigraphy which follows, written by Phillips. These disagreements are not basic differences as to the gross outlines of the chronology; there are no differences as to this. They have to do principally with the problem of whether the evidence indicates that there was a break in the deposition between the Baytown refuse characterized by clay-tempered pottery and the shell-tempered Mississippian deposits. In most cases this involves a question as to whether late Baytown (period D–C) or the early Mississippian Phase (period C–B) is missing in the stratigraphic sequence. With the evidence which we have at present it does not seem possible to resolve these discrepancies to everyone's satisfaction, so we will allow them to stand. However, they can be explained by the fact that Phillips' judgments have been based on detailed examination of the internal evidence supplied by each strata cut while the guesses of Ford have attempted to reconcile the evidence given by both surface and excavated collections.

Co-ordinating the Area Chronologies

We are now in possession of five quantitative graphs representing the ceramic history of the five selected areas. However, these are relative histories. There is no absolute chronological scale by which the appropriate amounts of vertical spacing, which represents time that should be given to the early, middle, or late portions of each can be measured. The best that can be done is to try to correlate them one with another. This was done in the following fashion. Six strings, spaced and running parallel, were stretched from end to end of the table on which the graphs lay. Then portions of the graphs were adjusted up or down until the same types showed comparable relative quantities under the appropriate string. Thus, the third string down from the top, which has become line C on the time scale used in the finished drawings (figs. 17–21), was made to mark the point in each graph where Baytown Plain and Neeley's Ferry Plain were about equal, Mulberry Creek Cord-marked had practically disappeared, Bell Plain was just getting a start, and Larto Red Filmed was almost gone. In each case this procedure was a compromise. If the upper portion of the Lower Arkansas graph had been slid downward until all the percentages of Bell Plain were equal to those in the Sunflower and Memphis areas along the C horizon line, then the Baytown-Neeley's Ferry relationship would have been all out of adjustment. All the type patterns were considered in this correlating process and the A to G time-scale arrangement given in the five final graphs is the end result of many compromises. So this scale is presented as a time framework for the chronologies. Time F in the Yazoo area, for

example, is supposed to be the same as F in the Lower St. Francis.

The necessity for compromises of this kind was not unexpected. As a matter of fact, they are an inherent part of this kind of cultural analysis. The groups of ideas to whose products have been tagged such names as Mazique Incised did not spring up simultaneously all over the area. They moved from one part to another, and that took time. For example, the ideas of red slipping on clay-tempered vessels (Larto Red Filmed) apparently was moving from south to north through the region, while cord-marking on clay-tempered pots (Mulberry Creek Cord-marked) was moving from northeast to south. Naturally, the former is earlier to the south and the latter to the north.

The student who is particularly interested in the history of this area, or of the procedure by which this balancing was done, may check it — if he has the time and patience — by placing the five area graphs (figs. 17–21) side by side and following across the relative time position of each type. This process has been a subjective weighing of the evidence provided by each type position and of course is always open to question. As a matter of fact, there has been considerable question as to certain aspects of this arrangement which should receive attention at this point. Griffin and Phillips are of the opinion that the late materials in the Arkansas area actually date somewhat later than they are represented in the graph of that area (fig. 18). They think that the pottery type Wallace Incised probably extends up to the time when the Quapaw were discovered by the French. This opinion is somewhat reinforced by the fact that the type is practically confined to the region in which the Quapaw were described and occurred in appreciable amount in the top levels of two cuts in the Menard Site (17–K–1), and on the surface of the near-by Wallace Site (17–K–3) which there is reason to believe may have been the site of the Quapaw village of Osotouy (Uzutiuhi), first visited by the French in 1686 (see p. 414). As additional evidence, Clarence B. Moore excavated burials in the fields near the Menard Site that were accompanied by European material. Admitting that the cemetery excavated by Moore almost certainly is of Quapaw origin, Ford has hesitated to raise the upper part of the Arkansas graph for several reasons. First, to do so would also bring the types which accompany Wallace Incised up to a later date where their proportions would not be consistent with those of the same types in the neighboring areas. Second, Moore's illustrated material does not show any examples of the types Wallace Incised. However, this does not mean that he may not have found such vessels. The third and most convincing point (to Ford) is the fact that Moore does illustrate three vessels of the type Fatherland Incised, the pottery which the Natchez tribe farther down the Mississippi were making about A.D. 1700.[10] In addition, he found "teapot vessels," another trait shared with the Natchez. Neither Fatherland Incised nor any of the late "Caddo" types with which it is normally associated appeared in the Survey collections from the Menard and near-by sites. While far from denying that this vicinity is the likely site of a historic Quapaw village from which Moore sampled the burials, it does not appear likely to Ford that the site collections and uppermost strata levels in our Arkansas area graph represent this historic occupation.[11]

Comparison of the area graphs will show that the late collections in the Memphis area have been allowed to come up to the most recent times. This was practically forced by the large percentage of Bell Plain found on the surfaces of the late sites in that area. In contrast the other areas show much smaller percentages of this type as a very late feature. It is possible, as discussed in the next section, that a part of this Bell Plain is pot-hunter refuse or is burial ware which has been ripped

[10] Moore, 1908a, figs. 8, 10, 19. Compare with Quimby, 1942.

[11] Griffin's reposte to this is simple. He thinks that the Yazoo and Sunflower columns also have their latest portions placed too early. More of the sites in those areas should fall after time B.

Phillips thinks that this is an instance where the assumption of continuous distribution of a pottery type has played us false. Bell Plain, which carried the weight of identification of the late time, seems to have a discontinuous distribution in space. Therefore, according to this view, the near lack of Bell Plain in the top portions of the Lower Arkansas graph is not chronologically significant.

from graves by cultivation. However, the trends in accompanying types: decrease of Barton Incised, increase of Parkin Punctated, and the appearance of Rhodes Incised and Vernon Paul Appliqué, suggests that there is a certain consistency to this situation that makes the increase of Bell a significant marker of the passage of time in this area — whatever may be the factors involved.

It is thought that probably none of these columns extend to the beginning of reliable historic documentation about A.D. 1700. This is consistent with the fact that the French explorers of that period indicate that the population of the Mississippi flood-plain area between the mouth of the Yazoo River, where villages of Yazoo and Tunica were found, and the northern limits to which our Survey has extended was very scanty indeed. About the mouth of the Arkansas River were found the Quapaw or Arkansea, and those are the only people who can be placed with any certainty. In the upper drainage of the Yazoo were the Tiou,[12] Chakchiuma,[13] and Ibitoupa.[14] Swanton estimates that the total of this Upper Yazoo population was less than 1000 people.[15]

This is far from enough people to account for the number of sites which we have dated as occupied during the later Mississippian period, and, in fact, is markedly in contrast to the population picture given by the De Soto narratives for the year 1542 as will be shown in a later section.

Clarence B. Moore found burials accompanied by glass beads and other European material at several sites through the area we have surveyed.[16] The pottery which he illustrates from the Rhodes and Bradley Places is clearly of late Memphis area types but, as Moore's report does not associate the illustrated materials with the burials that are described, it is impossible to state definitely that the European material was found with this complex. Even if it is associated with it, it should be noted that the possibilities for the aborigines acquiring glass beads probably go back somewhat before 1700 in this area, if not back to the period of De Soto's exploration in 1542.

There is some reason to expect that the ceramic complex which prevailed at least as far north as the Sunflower area in 1700 had a small percentage of incised pottery resembling in both decoration and shape the historic Natchez-type Fatherland Incised.[17] It has already been pointed out that Moore found a small proportion of this type associated with European material near the Menard Site. Charles Peabody's excavations in the Oliver Site in our Sunflower area produced at least one vessel of this type.[18] Again, the association with the European material which was found in some quantity cannot be determined from the report. However, the type did not appear in any of our late collections. Clearly, further search needs to be made for rare contact sites in the Survey Area with a view to determining the exact forms of the late ceramic complexes in the different parts of the region. Until this is done, it cannot be stated with certainty exactly when these columns end.

The finished area graphs are given as figures 17, 18, 19, 20, and 21. The collections are listed by site designations, 12–N–7, etc., down the left side of each graph. Collections which were made from restricted areas in certain sites are indicated as A, B, etc. (12–N–3A). The stratigraphic cuts made in certain sites are shown by staffs on the left side of the diagrams, and each level of such excavations is indicated with depth in centimeters. Each staff is shaded to aid in relating it to the corresponding type frequency bars given in the body of the charts.

The pottery types are represented by vertical "axes" which are labeled at both top and bottom of the diagrams. Equally spaced on either side of the appropriate axes are horizontal bars the length of which represents type percentages according to the scale given in the lower right-hand corner of the graph. It will be noted that only one-half of the full length of the frequency bars for the relatively

[12] Swanton, 1946, p. 194.
[13] Swanton, 1946, p. 105.
[14] Swanton, 1946, p. 140.
[15] Swanton, 1946, p. 107.
[16] See Moore, 1911, pp. 406, ff., Kent Place (our 13–N–4); pp. 413, ff., Rhodes Place; and pp. 427, ff., Bradley Place.
[17] Quimby, 1942, pp. 263–64.
[18] Peabody, 1904, pl. 14, line 4.

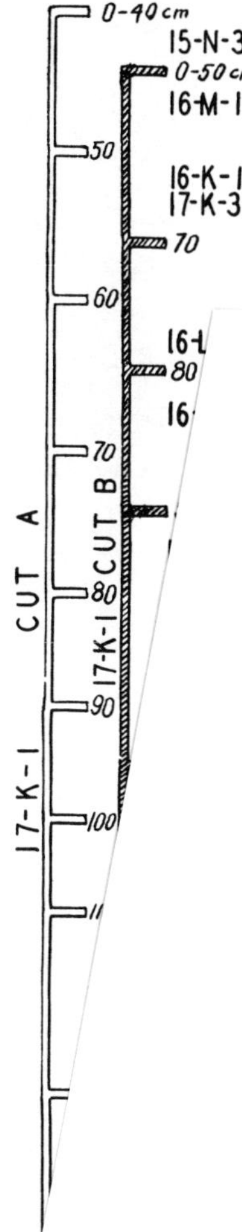
0-40 cm
15-N-3
0-50 cm
16-M-1
50
16-K-1
17-K-3
70
60
80
70
CUT A
CUT B
80
17-K-1
90
17-K-1
100

abundant types Neeley's Ferry Plain and Mulberry Creek Cord-marked has been shown. These types are arranged at the left and right-hand sides of the graphs, respectively, and this device has enabled us to decrease the over-all width of the illustrations.

On the right-hand side of each graph are listed the collection totals. These will indicate the amount of reliance that may be placed upon the samples. The time scale, A, B, C, etc., which relate the graphs to one another in the manner which has been described above, is on the right-hand side of each. These are the smallest time divisions which we have felt justified in making in the chronologies. The more comprehensive names which we are using Tchula, Baytown, and Mississippian are also given with the time range of each period indicated.

Explanations of complicated diagrams are tedious reading and frequently serve mainly to hide the essential simplicity of the scheme. The reader who is still confused at this point may be less so after comparing the following tabulation of types at Site 19–L–6 (Refuge) with the collection as graphed at the very top of the Lower Yazoo Basin area diagram (fig. 17).

19–L–6 (Refuge)

TYPE NAME	NO. SHERDS	PERCENTAGE
Neeley's Ferry Plain	304	.463 *
Baytown Plain	31	.047
Bell Plain	263	.400
Parkin Punctated	21	.032
Leland Incised	28	.043
Unclassified	9	.014 †

* Half of percentage shown in graph.
† Not graphed.

Discussion of the Seriation Technique

Such, then, was the analytical procedure followed in developing the area graphs, and some of the reasons why it was done so. The seriation of surface collections might have carried the full weight of the evidence for developing the chronological type patterning, but as some stratigraphic excavations were available in each area it did not have to. There is a tendency among some archaeologists to affect an attitude of suspicion and doubt in regard to the seriation technique, and it has often been asserted that the results of such "juggling" cannot be accepted unless supported by vertical stratigraphy. It seems likely that such an attitude may arise from one or both of two sources: either a misconception of the phenomena of cultural change and the part that typology plays in measuring that change, or a lack of understanding of the seriation technique. As a matter of fact, both seriation and the vertical stratigraphic technique have certain advantages and defects under different conditions and must be applied to chronological problems with a careful regard for their limitations.

The chief limitation of seriation is the fact that it must work with degrees of probability which are often quite difficult to measure or even estimate. Usually, the measure has to be the pragmatic one of the results obtained. In our area, for example, any one or all of the probabilities stated at the beginning of this section may not have been true. The population may not have been relatively stable. There might have been sudden and frequent movements of populations so that the cultural change in any one locality would have had little semblance of order. Had this been true, we might expect either that the development of a sequence by this means would have been impossible, or that cultural periods would have been developed which were clearly delimited, one from the other.

It is also possible that a majority of the villages might have been inhabited for very long periods of time. If this had been true, it would have been impossible to separate early and late pottery features by surface collecting and seriation techniques. There is, of course, a degree of this kind of error in all of the samples which we have handled, and this is probably the principal defect of the technique. None of the collections are the instant cross section of the ceramic content of the culture at each site which would be the ideal situation. The fact that each of the surface collections does represent a time span of a certain length must, in theory, result in a certain "fogging" of the quantitative history. For example, if we assume that we have done a perfect job of sampling and classifying and have placed one of our strip graphs so that its vertical position correctly represents the mean date of the site occupation, then it is plain that this graph will represent the early types which were fading or perhaps disappeared soon after the site was first occupied, too high in the chronological scale. Conversely, the late types which belong to the latter part of the occupation are also pulled back to the mean position and show as too early.

Again, the occasional reoccupation of sites after a lapse of time might be a disruptive factor. It is even possible that there might have been at some periods the general custom of utilizing older sites. This also would result in our securing a mixture of old and new cultural materials and would invalidate our assumption for continuous occupation. Had this happened in a majority of cases, the odds are very much against there having been any consistent pattern to the selection of the earlier sites which would be utilized. Only in the event that a region had been cleared of a previous population by conquest, and the conquerors had moved in and begun to utilize the settlements and fields of the people whom they replaced, could there be any probability of a consistent sequence of types. In such a case the seriation technique would reveal the cultural chronology, but interpretations as to cultural and population continuity might be led astray. It is very probable, however, that there would be "pure" deposits of the late phase of the earlier occupation, and the early phase of the later, which would illustrate the break in cultural continuity.

We can also be certain that none of the collections show type frequencies to the exact percentage that would be found if every sherd at a site had been gathered and classified. For these reasons, we would like to say again that success in this type of work demands numerous collections, and the imperfections of the technique are such that the majority of the indications must be taken as evidence. Two or three sherds of a type that seems to be quite late in a surface collection from a site that by all other indications is rather early do not worry the seriator at all. There are too many ways in which such a chance mixture could have occurred. He is more concerned by the fact that the overwhelming majority of the sherds of this type take a late position, and that the preponderance of the material from the site fits into the early ceramic pattern. Add to all this the uncertainties of classification which we have outlined in a foregoing section, and it is easy to see why we would like to stress the fact that success in this type of work demands a number of fairly sizable collections, and that only indications given by the majority of the situations must be accepted as evidence.

The Use of Stratigraphic Data in Seriation

The analysis of stratigraphic data as such will be discussed at length in the following section. Here we are concerned principally with the use of stratigraphic along with surface collections in the seriation technique and their limitations from this point of view.

Phillips and Griffin in the 1941, 1946, and 1947 field seasons made a total of seventeen stratigraphic excavations at nine different sites. All of these gave the anticipated results and showed evidence of change in type frequencies with the passage of time. Of these, fourteen were clear-cut enough to be incorporated in the area graphs and three could not be used for reasons that are explained below. This high degree of success in the effort to obtain this type of evidence was directly due to a careful selection of sites to excavate. Before beginning, each excavator had a fairly clear notion as to at least a part of the chronological patterning which the site would reveal.

The principal defect, from the point of view of seriation, in the information provided by stratigraphic excavations is a result of what might be termed migration, particularly upward migration of material in midden deposits. This is most pronounced in middens in which refuse and soil was accumulated very slowly. Apparently, the activities of the Indians who lived on such sites, the digging of post-holes and pits, and overturning the soil in other ways, has tended to bring old pottery and other refuse to higher levels in the growing deposit. This is particularly true of the later Mississippian horizons. Analysis of stratigraphic studies in such deposits make the older type appear to have lasted much longer than really was the case. This factor is doubtless always present in the analysis of all midden deposits. Usually, however, the distortion of the graphs is so small that it falls well within the limits of the variations that have to be allowed in this kind of analysis.

The control which we have over this accidental upward weighting of midden-deposit evidence is the comparison of such unusually slow-growing cuts with the results of other excavations in the same area. A still better check is the comparison of these cuts with seriated short time-span surface collections.

The most pronounced example of upward migration which we have encountered in this study are the two strata cuts that were made at Lake Cormorant (13–P–8). These are described on pages 249–52. The site is located in the Memphis area and the excavations revealed about 120 cm. of refuse deposit, the material from which, when analyzed, proved to represent the entire ceramic chronology for the area from time G to A. All of the types found in the area are well represented, for the collections from each level were substantial. The popularity peaks of the types form a pattern which is in perfect agreement with the seriation graph of the Memphis area as a whole as can be seen by comparing the stratigraphic and seriation graphs (figs. 25 and 27 with fig. 20). However, if we were to accept the evidence offered by the Lake Cormorant Site we would have to believe that the types Withers Fabric-impressed and Baytown Plain were still being made in time B to A. All the other sites collected from the Memphis area by both the surface and stratigraphic techniques show that this was not so. We conclude then that these older types in the Lake Cormorant Site have been brought up to the surface of the midden by overturning of the soil. For this reason, it has not been possible to incorporate the Lake Cormorant data in the Memphis area graph.

The second phenomenon found in strata-cut tests is that at times they misrepresent the history of the site being studied by completely skipping or being deficient in the material that represents certain spans of time. The reason for this is not difficult to find. While a village was occupied, the midden material accumulated at any one spot only so long as it was being actively deposited at that place. In the Southwest, where intentional dumps were utilized or in Peru where substantial buildings of stone and adobe were occupied uninterruptedly, there was little reason to change the locales of garbage disposal. However, in the eastern United States the houses were impermanent structures of wood, and from the excavation of numerous sites it is clear that considerable shifting of house locations was done in rebuilding. Thus, it may happen that one of our strata pits was put down at a spot where a house stood for the first third of the time the village lasted; was rather far from any dwellings during the second third; and was again near a house during the last third. A graph of the type frequencies will — if it is clear enough — show a definite shift in percentage frequencies at the level where deposition paused. The same thing will result if the pit chanced to pass through a house floor or a courtyard which was intentionally kept clean of débris.

The Question of Population and Cultural Continuity

One of the most interesting questions raised in the interpretation of the data which we have to present is whether there are indications of cultural and, by inference, population discontinuity between the Baytown and Mississippian periods. This has an important bearing on the matter of how and where did the Mississippian cultures develop, the major current mystery of Eastern archaeology. Did the Mississippian culture come into the Survey Area from outside, carried by a new population in such a way that there was a distinct break in the cultural sequence, or was there a period of gradual but possibly rapid cultural change at the beginning of this period when new cultural ideas (carried perhaps by some intruding people) came into the area and merged with the Baytown. We cannot pretend to settle this question, for our data are confined to ceramics. However, the ceramic histories and the villages that have been investigated give enough evidence to permit some discussion. This discussion centers about the more specific question of whether reoccupation has occurred on these sites where the shell-tempered Mississippian pottery complex is mixed with the clay-tempered Baytown ware. A glance at the five area graphs will show that there are a substantial number of such sites in each sub-area, most of them represented by surface collections and a few by stratigraphic excavations. Do all of these sites represent reoccupation?

There can be little doubt that reoccupation is represented by some of these collections. These sites where an early Baytown complex is mixed with shell-tempered pottery, such as 14-O-1 and 14-O-2 near the bottom of the Memphis area graph (fig. 20), seem to have a thin Mississippian occupation mixed with early Baytown, with material of the intervening periods missing. Some of the surface collections excluded from seriation may also be interpreted in this way. Also, there may be some examples of reoccupation where the time during which the site was unoccupied was so short that it is impossible to measure it in cultural terms. The real question is whether the *majority* of mixed sites represent reoccupation. If site reoccupation were the explanation for this mixture, it might be expected that late Mississippian material would be mixed with early Baytown pottery about as often as occupations of the early part of the Mississippian chanced to be placed over late Baytown refuse. The early Baytown sites are in just as favored geographical locations as the late, and there is little reason why these spots should have been avoided by the later invaders. In this event, little or no patterning would appear in either the attempts at seriation or in the strata excavations. However, there is also the possibility that the later people conquered the territory and settled down to use the cleared fields and villages of those whom they had displaced. The techniques applied here would not be able to clearly detect such an event. Even if this somewhat unlikely kind of population replacement had occurred, it is probable that there would be some early Mississippian villages which were established in new, unoccupied spots which would not have the late Baytown mixture, and conversely some of the conquered late Baytown villages which were not reoccupied, and thus did not show the early Mississippian mixture. There are several sites which may be interpreted in this way such as Collins (13-O-9), of the late Baytown in the Memphis area graph (fig. 20), but the number is small. The patterning revealed by the majority of the site collections indicates to one of the present writers at least (Ford) that there was essential continuity of the ceramic complex and, by inference, of the majority of the population.

Another and parallel approach to this question of continuity lies in an examination of the possibility of certain ceramic decorations which are found on clay-tempered pottery being directly ancestral to similar decorations on the shell-tempered wares. This will be treated elsewhere, and it is sufficient to say here that this evidence does not suggest that there has been a cultural break.

Relative Dating of Village Sites

The foregoing was the analytical procedure which was directed toward the development of the five area chronological columns (figs. 17-21). Now, we call attention to the fact that in the analysis process we have also provided relative dates for the collections studied. The vertical positions in which the collection graphs have been arranged in the five chronological columns show the relative mean dating of these collections. However, it must be emphasized that this is a *mean* or *average* date. As has been mentioned above, each of these collections represents refuse which was in the process of deposition for a shorter or longer period of time — 10, 25, 50, or 100 years, we do not know. There is no external evidence which can be used to resolve this uncertainty. We are aware that what has been done is to "flatten out" the cultural evidence which accumulated during the occupation span that each collection represents and treat the collection as though it were a cross section of the cultural content at one moment in time. If our analytical operations were perfect, we might expect that the time at which the collection best fitted in the chronology would be about the mid-point of the period through which the refuse was accumulating. This is the reason for the term "Mean Date" which will be applied to the graphed time position of the collections.

Frequently, there is in the collections some evidence on which a judgment of the relative time span represented may be based. The presence of types which are chronologically earlier or later than the mean date may indicate approximately how far the time span of a site extended from its mean date. This evidence has served as a basis for the judgments of the time spans of site collections listed under the heading "Range" in table 1. The majority of collections, it will be noted, are listed as falling within one of our lettered subdivisions. These are collections which show no evidence of any long period of occupation and which seem to be about as homogeneous in content as is the usual 10-centimeter level of a stratigraphic cut in this part of the Mississippi Valley.

The above discussion has reference, it will be noted, to the dating of collections. The question as to whether a collection completely and fully dates a site is another matter. There is always the possibility that either (1) only the top and latest refuse is on the surface of the site, or (2) earlier refuse is on the surface but at some point which was not investigated. There can be little doubt that we have made this error in the dating of some sites, but we suspect that the proportion will be quite small. The principal reason for thinking so is that refuse deposits that extend below the plow zone are not common. Numerically, there are more of these deposits than has generally been supposed in the Mississippi Valley, but the proportion of deep to superficial sites is undoubtedly small. The second reason is that this possibility was kept in mind during the course of the field work, and as far as possible all sites were examined to see if areal differentiation of material could be detected. In these cases localized collections were made. Thus, while we cannot say with complete confidence that site "X" is fully dated by its surface collection, we are fairly well satisfied that the great majority of the mean dates do not suffer from serious error of this kind.

An interesting comparison can be made between the graphed positions of surface collections from certain sites and the later stratigraphic excavations in these same sites. Although Ford insists that at the time these collections were being seriated he paid not the slightest attention to site designations but concentrated on type frequencies, the reader had best judge the appropriateness of each position for himself.

On the area graphs, we make the following comparisons:

19-O-2, general surface collection with 19-O-2 strata cut (fig. 17);

17-K-1, a general surface collection with the two strata cuts made on the site, A and B (fig. 18);

17-L-1B, a localized surface collection with strata Cut A, made in same part of the site (fig. 18);

17-L-1C, a localized surface collection with strata Cut B, made in the same part of the site (fig. 18);

16-N-2,[19] a general surface collection with the two strata Cuts A and B made in old and younger parts of the site (fig. 19);

16-N-2B, a localized surface collection with strata Cut B, made in the same part of the site (fig. 19);

16-N-6,[19] a general surface collection with the three strata cuts made in this site, A, B, and C (fig. 19).

The Walls Site (13-P-1) and the Rose Site (12-N-3) are the only cases where such collections fit in the graphs at the upper end of the time span indicated by excavations in the same sites (cf. figs. 20, 21). When the fact is recalled that the sites enumerated were selected for excavation partly on the basis of their showing a depth of midden deposit, and that these depths ranging from 75 to 240 cm. are exceptional rather than the rule on sites in this region, it can be seen that the chances are rather good that we have secured samples representing the full time range of most sites. The problem of buried strata can virtually be ignored so long as we are considering the *majority* situation.

However, this slight degree of doubt which

[19] Note that the graphs of these two surface collections show mixture of both early and late types, a condition that is clearly explained by the length of time represented in the deposits as shown by the stratigraphic excavations. Their lessened value for giving a clear seriation is obvious, and possibly they should have been excluded from the graphs as were the 18 long time-span surface collections described above. However, they are included here both to illustrate this effect and to point out the tendency of these surface collections to take a position intermediate of the time range of the site. The surface collection from site 20-O-1 (fig. 17), another long time-range site, would have illustrated the same condition, but was not included, as explained above.

must be admitted for the fullness of the site-dating shown by any particular surface collection has no bearing at all on the validity of the quantitative-chronological patterning which derives from the seriation of these collections. The probabilities are still in favor of each collection representing a continuous segment of time, whether this segment be only the latter portion of the length of time any one site has been occupied or not.

Section VI
STRATIGRAPHY

STRATIGRAPHY

INTRODUCTION

Seriation and Stratigraphy

BEFORE embarking on a detailed cut-by-cut analysis of the stratigraphic excavations conducted by the Lower Mississippi Archaeological Survey, it will be well to clarify further the relationship, from the standpoint of method, between seriation and stratigraphy as used in the present study. In a sense we have to regard them as independent methods of analysis. This is perhaps less a result of choice than necessity, owing to the circumstances that the seriation analysis was done in New York by Ford in 1947 and the stratigraphic analysis by Phillips in Cambridge in 1948, both assisted by long-range advice and criticism from Griffin in Ann Arbor. Ford made significant use of stratigraphic data in the seriation by interpolating strata with surface collections as explained on page 228 and shown in figures 17–21. Wherever practicable, the strip graphs representing individual levels in strata cuts were laid down first as a guide to the ordering of surface collections, so it might be more correct to say in such cases that the surface data were interpolated into a stratigraphic framework. The results in our opinion fully justified this unorthodox combination of two distinct kinds of data.

However, it might be pointed out that this is not stratigraphic analysis *per se* and cannot take its place entirely. It was done, in fact more or less has to be done, without regard for what may be called the ground context, i.e., without consideration for the sometimes complex relationships of pottery-type frequencies to special conditions on the site. It is the latter "tied-down" sort of interpretation that will be described in the present section. That the results will always tally with the broader patterning produced by the seriation technique is hardly to be expected, and in fact they do not. Instances of disagreement will be noted as we come to them, and a general discussion of their over-all significance will be given in the concluding remarks at the end of the section. It may be asked why we do not resolve — "hide" would be a better word — such disagreements by adjusting the discrepancies on the seriation charts. Such a procedure would carry the implication that stratigraphic analysis is a more "accurate" and sure method of dating than seriation, which is by no means certain. We must not lose sight of the fact that interpretation of a stratigraphic cut is accurate, assuming that it *is* accurate, for that cut only. In attempting to extend that interpretation to the site as a whole, or beyond, we have to make use of the same concepts of patterning upon which the seriation technique is based. No, we may as well admit that, in most cases of disagreement, we simply do not know which method has produced the correct interpretation and let both stand — for the present. Fortunately, the discrepancies are not serious. Given the conditions of physical separation under which the two analyses were carried out, and the not identical points of view of those who carried them out, the extent of agreement is a matter for self-congratulation.

The Chronological Framework

It cannot be too strongly emphasized that we have not yet reached the stage of having, or even requiring, a cultural typology in the Survey Area. In fact, we have not yet taken the first step toward such a typology, the determination of significant cultural units or "foci," if you prefer the term. The nomenclature used in this and all other sections of the present report is derived solely from the seriation analysis described in the preceding section. As may be readily seen by reference to any of the charts in that section, the scheme consists of six time divisions set off by the letters A to G, which are in turn grouped into three periods, Mississippi, Baytown, and Tchula. Thus we have two different ways of designating time position, by the use of letters or by the use of names. Both are subject to the ambiguity that attaches to most archaeological designations. They refer primarily to time but have cultural, or better say, since we are dealing with pottery alone, typological implications. As an example of such limited typological implication, it will be recalled that C on the seriation time scale, representing the division point between the Mississippi and Baytown periods, was arbitrarily fixed at the point where Baytown and Neeley's Ferry Plain were approximately equal in percentage frequency; in other words, at the mid-point of a theoretical transition from the use of clay- to shell-tempering in the area. It would be vain to assert, therefore, that the distinction between Baytown and Mississippi is wholly chronological and in no sense typological.

Such being the case, we have to guard against confusion between our period designations and typological concepts already in use. Fortunately, the archaeology of the earlier periods, Tchula and Baytown, has not been sufficiently dealt with in this area to have become seriously involved in concepts of culture type. That of the Mississippi Period, however, has long been identified with the generic concept "Middle Mississippi," which, in our understanding, is primarily a typological concept, not without chronological implications to be sure, but fundamentally a concept of culture type. As indicated above, our studies have not reached the stage of total (archaeological) culture analysis leading to the delineation of "cultures" or culture types. Furthermore, the pottery of the Mississippi Period in our area, while included within the general definition of Middle Mississippi pottery, does not appear to exhibit its full typo-chronological range. Except as faintly foreshadowed in one or two stratigraphic components to be described presently, we have not found anything typologicaly comparable to early Middle Mississippi pottery as exemplified elsewhere in Hiwassee, Old Village, and related foci. We have, therefore, deemed it advisable to substitute for Middle Mississippi the more general term Mississippi, carrying (we hope) a minimum of cultural and typological implication. This involves us in certain terminological difficulties, which must be made as explicit as possible. Like Middle Mississippi our Mississippi Period is also divided into two parts, early and late, C–B and B–A, but this is an arbitrary and strictly chronological division, as devoid of typological significance as can be, being based on differences in percentage frequencies rather than differences in constituent types. If, in the interest of clear expression, it becomes necessary to refer to the "early portion of the Mississippi Period" or simply "early Mississippi" it is not to be understood that this means that the local early Mississippi material dated between C and B is typologically correspondent to what has been referred to as early Middle Mississippi in other parts of the Southeast.[1] If this point has been made sufficiently clear, we should be able to proceed without undue misunderstanding and without raising the sort of questions with which we are not yet prepared to deal.

[1] Ford and Willey, 1941; Griffin, 1946, fig. 6.

Definitions: Stratification and Stratigraphy

As outlined in the introductory section of this report, the original over-all Survey program contemplated three successive stages of investigation: (1) preliminary site survey and analysis of surface collections; (2) stratigraphic testing; and (3) site excavation. To date, only a slight beginning has been made on stage (2). To what follows in this section, therefore, the word "preliminary" is more than usually applicable. The results, however, justify a rather detailed presentation, not only for their bearing on the immediate problems, but from the broader point of view of archaeological method in the Southeast.

The use of stratigraphic methods in the eastern United States has not yet developed to an extent comparable with their use in other areas of American archaeology. This is mainly due to an earlier impression on the part of Eastern archaeologists that the method was not applicable, owing to the paucity of deep deposits yielding long cultural sequences. It is also partly due, perhaps, to a misconception regarding the stratigraphic method. To many archaeologists, stratigraphy necessarily involves a situation in which materials can be segregated on the basis of distinct and separable soil zones. Such is fortunately not the case. It frequently happens, as we shall show, that a homogeneous deposit, without observable soil stratification, may be made to yield a stratigraphic record of the utmost value. Obviously, such an unstratified deposit will have to be excavated by arbitrary levels, to which method the term "metrical stratigraphy" has sometimes been applied in derogation,[2] as opposed to "natural stratigraphy" obtained by peeling stratified layers. If we were to regard "natural" stratigraphy as the only valid method, the discouraging outlook referred to above would be justified. On the other hand, unstratified or weakly stratified midden deposits of sufficient depth for excavation by "metrical" analysis are not rare. An example of successful exploitation of such deposits is to be seen in the excavations of Willey and Woodbury on the Gulf Coast of Florida in 1940.[3]

There is no need for injecting this terminology into the present discussion, since our stratigraphy — so far at least — is all of the metrical variety. The distinction, however, between "stratification," the description of the actual ground situation, and "stratigraphy," as applied to the chronological interpretation of the ground situation, whether by "natural" or "metrical" methods, is a useful one and will be maintained here. Under the heading "stratification," we shall refer to soil zones as revealed by trench profiles; under "stratigraphy," the analysis of the excavated material and interpretation of the results. The one is what you find, the other is what you do with it. The separation will serve to bring out the fact that it is possible to have stratigraphy without stratification and *vice versa.* In line with this distinction, the terms "stratum," "zone," "deposit," etc., will be hereinafter used to refer to the ground stratification, the term "level" being reserved for the arbitrarily excavated unit of "metrical" stratigraphy.

Methods of Excavation

The simple methods of stratigraphic testing used by the Lower Mississippi Archaeological Survey may be described very briefly. Village site deposits in the Alluvial Valley rarely exceed 1 to 2 meters in total depth. Ten centimeters was therefore chosen as a unit of depth, convenient for seriating, without presenting serious difficulties in excavating. The first cut (Walls A) was dug 3 meters square, but on finding that a sufficient yield of sherds could have been obtained from a smaller area, subsequent cuts were made only 2 meters square. Ideally, cuts should be dimensioned to get an adequate sherd sample per level from the smallest possible space, but we could never agree as to just what constituted an adequate sample, and therefore adhered to the convenient 2-meter square throughout. In only one instance (Rose A) was the yield per level below what we should have liked.

Field procedures were of the most elementary description. Cuts were laid out with a compass, corner stakes leveled with a carpenter's level lashed to a two-by-four and used as datum for all subsequent leveling. Plans at successive levels and profiles upon completion of cut were drawn to scale. Cuts were located by reference to a "permanent" bench mark, consisting of an iron pipe with brass cap stamped with symbols guaranteed to mystify all future visitors to the site. Cuts were designated by the site number and a capital letter A, B, C, etc., in the order made. Levels were numbered from top to bottom. Finds catalogued 16–N–6/A–9 would therefore read "Oliver Site (16–N–6), Cut A, Level 9."

Excavated material was put through ½-inch screens. It was found that one shovel hand could keep two to four men busy at the screens, but constant supervision was required to maintain accuracy of level. With such a crew, two or three working days were sufficient for the completion of a cut. As far as practicable, sherds were washed, catalogued, and sorted on the spot to avoid useless labor on unsatisfactory cuts.

In all, 17 cuts were made in 9 sites, not including several which were abandoned for one reason or another, usually lack of depth. These cuts varied from 50 to 240 cm. in depth, the average being 106 cm. or between

[2] In the Southwest. Information by J. O. Brew.

[3] Willey and Woodbury, 1942; Willey, 1949.

10 and 11 levels. Not one of the 17 failed to yield some stratigraphic information of value, several of them revealed pottery sequences covering almost the entire known span of pottery-making in the Lower Mississippi Valley. No other answer is needed for those who may still be skeptical about the practicability of stratigraphic studies in the Southeast.

Method of Analysis

The crucial operation in the interpretation of stratigraphic data is the correlation of pottery distributions with soil stratification, if the latter is present. In a homogeneous deposit without observable profiles you have to take the pottery distribution at face value so to speak, assuming that the changes or lack of changes from level to level mean just what they say. Where stratification has been recorded, however, an opportunity is given to evaluate such changes a little more realistically. It is hardly necessary to point out that the effect of local conditions and events, as revealed by the profiles, may be such as to materially affect the distribution of pottery in the ground. Thus, two distinct phases of interpretation are involved: (1) interpretation of profiles for what they may reveal of events on the site, or that particular portion of it; and (2) interpretation of pottery distributions in the light of such events. No attempt is made here to minimize the possibilities for error in such a complicated interplay of guesswork. Limitations of excavation technique guarantee that the chances of 100-per cent successful interpretation are nonexistent. One simply does the best one can with the available information.

Assuming for the moment that there is a complete record of the four profiles of a given cut, the specific mechanical difficulty is how to effect a graphic comparison of that record with the pottery picture. After considerable experimentation, we have found the most satisfactory method is to construct the pottery graph by the usual manner of seriating bar graphs for each level, in the same vertical scale as the profile drawing, and superimpose one upon the other. Unfortunately, it happens rarely that stratification is so congruent that the profile of one wall of the cut may be allowed to stand for the other three. One way around this difficulty is to construct an ideal profile by averaging the stratification of all four walls of the cut. This method is sometimes sufficient, but has to be used with caution, because it gives a misleading effect of conformity. In most cases we have found it more satisfactory to use an alternative method involving a composite profile drawing, a sort of palimpsest of all four profiles such as may be seen in figure 23. This, of course, has the opposite effect of exaggerating incongruities, but the resulting errors of interpretation are more likely to be on the side of safety.

Presentation

Although most of the interpretations presently to be described are based on the superposition of strata graphs on composite profile diagrams, as described above, it has not been thought necessary, in most cases, to expose the reader to the confusion inherent in that kind of presentation. The scheme adopted here represents a compromise between completeness and intelligibility. The diagram is in effect an idealized section of the cut, outlined in heavy lines, drawn to the scale indicated, with the pottery graph superimposed at the same vertical scale. The narrow rectangles above the top line represent the corner stakes, the tops of which are the data for all vertical measurements, which are in centimeters. The panel on the left shows the levels as excavated, with the total sherd count for each level in parentheses. The right-hand panel shows an idealized stratification obtained by averaging all four profiles as explained above. Soil zones, thus defined, and numbered in Roman numerals, are described textually in detail. As already stated, in a few cases where the interpretation hinges on ground conditions that are not sufficiently brought out by the idealized profile, extra figures showing composite profiles are run into the text. Without the use of color to differentiate the several zonal boundaries, these diagrams are hopelessly confusing but may serve at least to give the reader a general impression of the conditions involved in the particular question at issue.

Cuts are described in the order in which they were made, the only reason being that such an arrangement brings out the fact that we became more successful in locating deeper deposits as time went on.

Site Plans

We have not thought it necessary to present site plans showing the location of stratigraphic cuts except in a few cases where the relationship of deposits to local geographic or constructional features is involved in the interpretation. To any one desirous of obtaining such data, we will gladly furnish site maps and any other information that may be required.

WALLS SITE (13–P–1)

This site, long known as a rich village site and cemetery, produced most of the high-grade pottery of the Davies and Schubach collections described by Calvin Brown in his monograph on the archaeology of Mississippi.[4] The site is located near the south shore of Mud Lake in the extreme northwest corner of the state, about 5 miles northwest of Walls Station, De Soto County, Mississippi. Though less than half a mile from Mud Lake, which together with the larger Horn Lake occupies a former Mississippi channel of Stage 15, the site is actually on the bank of a still earlier channel of Stage 7, now occupied in part by an intermittent stream known locally as Alpika Bayou.[5] It is a large village site strung out along the south bank of the old Stage 7 channel for a distance of at least 300 meters with a maximum breadth of something over 100 meters. Directly on the former river bank not far from the western end of the site are the remains of a mound of uncertain type, much spread and reduced by cultivation to a height of approximately 1 meter. No other constructional features were observed on the site.

The two cuts put down on the Walls Site were to some extent experimental, a sort of marking time while negotiations were in progress for permission to dig on the more promising Lake Cormorant Site (13–P–8) near by. The entire personnel of the 1941 expedition, Griffin, Phillips, Davis, and Chard, took part in this excavation. Surface collections made the previous fall had given no promise of stratigraphy, but there were indications of reasonable depth and so it was judged a good site to practice on. These poor promises were considerably exceeded in the event, and the time spent here was by no means wasted. As a "normal" village site of the Mississippi Period in the Memphis area, it offers an excellent introduction to some of the more obvious difficulties of stratigraphic interpretation.

Cut A (Figure 22)

Our first cut was located near the southern (landward) edge of the site, about 60 meters due south of the center of the ruined mound described above. It was made 3 meters square, but we soon discovered that a 2-meter cut would have yielded sufficient sherd samples per 10 cm. level and with far less complicated stratification and disturbance to be reckoned with, and subsequently that was the standard dimension used.

Stratification was extremely complex, owing to the considerable house-building activity in this portion of the site; consequently, the idealized profile shown in the right-hand panel of figure 22 requires some explanation.

Zone I. −20 cm. to −35 cm. Plowed zone.

Zone II. −35 cm. to −48 cm. Compact dark gray-brown sandy loam, containing small fragments of charcoal and daub. This thin deposit was quite distinct from Zones I and III and was well marked on three profiles but pinched off on the fourth, and was therefore interpreted as a lens of local significance only, which seems to be borne out by the pottery stratigraphy as we shall see.

Zone III. −48 cm. to −110 cm. Similar to Zone II but less homogeneous and darker in color. Dense lenses of charcoal and concentrations of daub at

[4] Brown, 1926, pp. 288–319.

[5] This and subsequent references to Mississippi channel dating is derived from Fisk's reconstruction of the recent geological history of the Mississippi River (1944, pl. 22). For further particulars of his elaborate chronological scheme and its important bearings on archaeological dating, see Section VII, herein, pp. 295–306.

−80 cm. and −100 cm. gave evidence of at least two burned houses in the lower half of this zone. Post-holes were extremely numerous but no alignments could be worked out giving satisfactory evidence of individual house plans.[6]

The complexity of stratification and extent of disturbance from pits and post-holes, an impression of which is given in figure 23, are such that it would be vain to expect a clear-and Hull Engraved, and relatively low percentages of Neeley's Ferry Plain and its associates. This appears to be a significant indication of the priority of Neeley's Ferry over Bell, but there is a point involved which must not be overlooked. This site has been a famous resort of the pot-hunting confraternity and the plowed zone is undoubtedly heavily charged with pot-hunters' débris.

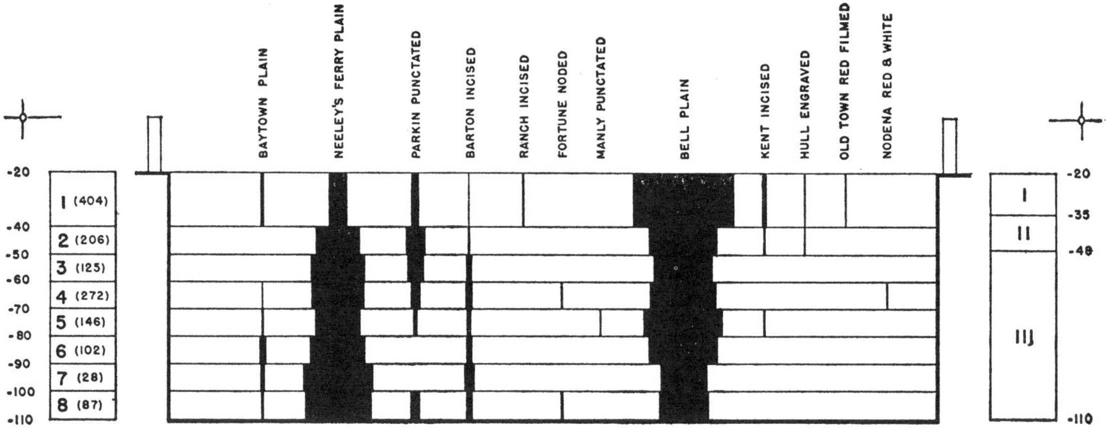

Fig. 22. Stratigraphic diagram, Cut A, Walls Site (13–P–1).

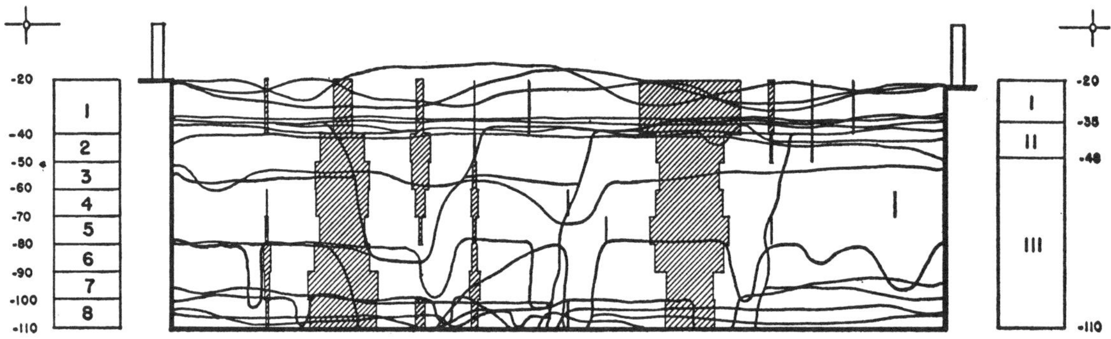

Fig. 23. Composite profile diagram, Cut A, Walls Site (13–P–1).

cut stratigraphic picture. The only sharp break in pottery distributions is between Levels 1 and 2. Level 1, which is mostly from the plowed zone, is marked by a relatively high percentage of Bell Plain and its associated decorated types, Ranch Incised, Kent Incised, Parenthetically, the small percentage of Baytown Plain in Level 1 was probably thrown up from the deeper levels by pot-hunters. Since mortuary pottery in this area is predominantly Bell Plain and its associated types, it becomes a question to what extent the

[6] Evidence indicated walls of light poles, 7 to 8 cm. in diameter; interior supporting posts 12 to 18 cm. in diameter (inferred); walls plastered with clay daub bearing impressions of whole canes and/or split-cane matting; thatched roofs of grass or rushes. Plan of houses not ascertained but some indication of circular shape.

dominance of these types in Level 1 is the result of such activity. Perhaps a good deal of it, but probably not all.[7] We have concluded, therefore, that this top-level situation does offer positive evidence that Bell Plain is on the increase in the latest period on this site.

Between Zones II and III and in Zone III, clear to the bottom, pottery changes are minor and gradual, as is to be expected in a cut showing such extremes of incongruity of stratification and so much disturbance incident to house-building activities. The heartening thing is that there are any observable changes at all. The lower half of Zone III, Levels 6 to 8, which has been referred to as the house-building phase in this cut, contained appreciably fewer sherds and showed a slightly different complex from that of Zone II and the upper half of Zone III, with more Baytown Plain, more Neeley's Ferry, less Parkin Punctated but more Barton Incised, less Bell Plain and none of its decorated associates. Percentage differences are minor to be sure, but, considering the "blurring" caused by disturbance, extremely significant. If we had had the good luck to come down upon the center of the house floor at −80 cm., instead of hitting one corner of it, so that the bottom three levels had been more or less sealed off, the shift in pottery percentages would undoubtedly have showed up in a very definite fashion.

A detail of some interest is the relationship of Parkin Punctated and Barton Incised. Their distribution here is almost certain proof that the latter ranged farther back in time than the former, as already indicated by seriation in this area, figure 20.

Our conclusion, therefore, is that this cut, in spite of expectations to the contrary, yielded valuable stratigraphic information on what is probably the latest prehistoric occupation of the area. (According to seriation results, figure 20, the time span covered by the cut corresponds to the last two-thirds of the Mississippi Period.) The lower levels are represented by burned remains of wattle-and-daub houses and a pottery complex in which Neeley's Ferry Plain is dominant and a minority of Baytown Plain is present. The upper levels contained no house remains and a pottery complex in which Bell Plain and its associated decorated types Ranch Incised, Kent Incised, and Hull Engraved are dominant. There is every reason to believe that the shift was a gradual one and that a single continuous occupation is represented. The net result is a satisfactory indication that on this site the complex dominated by Bell Plain is later than Neeley's Ferry Plain and its decorated companions, an important contribution to our understanding of the archaeology of the area.

From the standpoint of method, this cut demonstrates the fact that a very unpromising pottery stratigraphy may yield significant results when closely analyzed in conjunction with the ground stratification.

Cut B (Figure 24)

Cut B was put down on the northern edge of the site about 80 meters east of the center of the mound referred to above, choice of location being determined by the finding of several Baytown Plain sherds on the surface. This was taken as an indication that this part of the site was older than the southern portion where Cut A was already in progress, and so it proved to be.

The profiles in this cut were a great deal more congruent than those of Cut A and revealed the following stratification:

Zone I. −23 cm. to −36 cm. Plowed zone.

Zone II. −36 cm. to −58 cm. Compact brown sandy loam with few signs of disturbance. The small amount of daub indicated little if any building activity in this period, or a type of construction other than wattle-and-daub. Several moderately large pits extended from the bottom of this zone into Zone III.

Zone III. −58 cm. to −105 cm. Dark brown midden soil containing considerable daub. At −75 cm. a row of seven evenly spaced post-holes extended diagonally across the cut, but the level in which they

[7] It should be pointed out that pot-hunters' collections of mortuary pottery are always selected. The fact that Bell Plain and its associates dominate in such collections in this area may be partly due to the fact that they are high-grade types. It is not impossible that pot-hunters' leavings contain a higher percentage of Neeley's Ferry than of Bell Plain.

originated was not determined.[8] At −90 cm. a thin lens of sand, presumably sterile, showed up in the southeast quarter of the cut. Though a purely local feature, it warrants mention on account of the sharp break in pottery distributions at this level.

Burial. The lower portions of an extended burial obtruded into the cut at −65 cm., the top of Zone III. As we did not want to precipitate a new onset of pot-hunting on the site, we refrained from disturbing the rest of it, thereby depriving ourselves of one or several pots, which are usually placed near the head in burials of this culture. Insofar as this may be taken as a clue to the depth of burials in the famous old cemetery, it suggests that the burial activity, usually accompanied by Bell Plain and its associates, was subsequent to the house-building period represented by the burned houses in Cut A and faintly represented here by the post-hole alignment described above, at which time a dominance of Neeley's Ferry Plain and its associates is indicated. This is an independent confirmation of the priority of Neeley's Ferry over Bell Plain.[9]

The stratigraphy of Cut B is unmistakably clear, and backs up in very satisfactory fashion our interpretation of Cut A, where the evidence was not so forthright. There are two important differences, however. First is the possibility of a break in stratigraphy between Zones II and III. Note that Level 3, which shows an even mixture of Bell and Neeley's Ferry Plain straddles the line of separation between these zones and therefore has to be discounted. The more correct relationship between Zones II and III may be seen by comparing Level 2 with Level 4. This is hardly indicative of anything so drastic as a cultural discontinuity on the site, but it does greatly reinforce the conclusion that Bell Plain is becoming increasingly dominant over Neeley's Ferry in the latest period on this site. By the

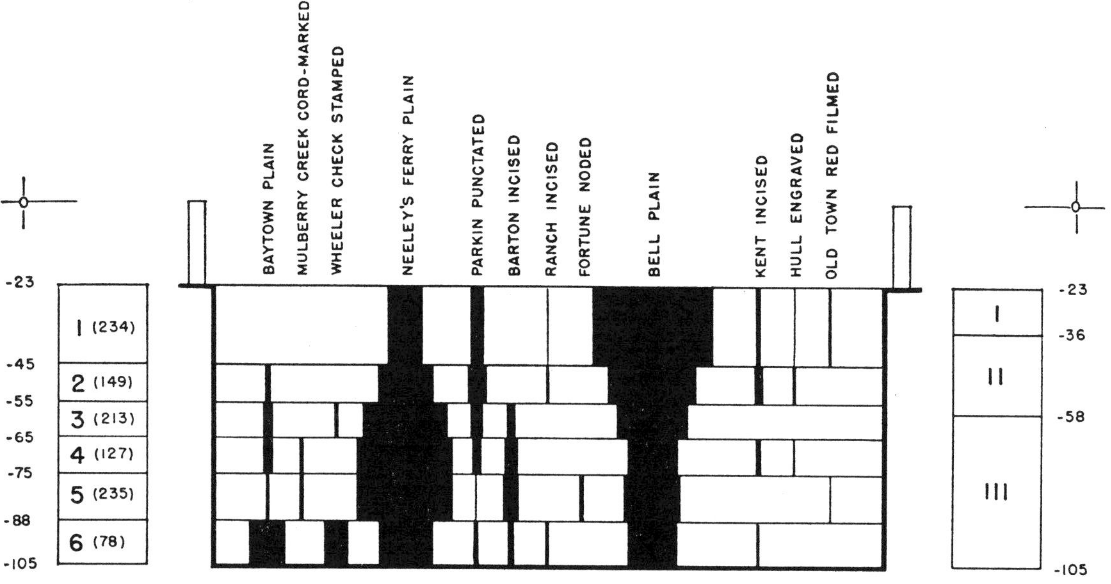

FIG. 24. Stratigraphic diagram, Cut B, Walls Site (13–P–1).

[8] A lacuna in field notes at this point indicates that some information is missing. A plan of this post-hole alignment must have been drawn. Not having it, we cannot say for certain that a rectangular house plan is indicated, though it can be inferred from the wording of the notes. The fact that the post-holes when first encountered at −75 cm. were filled with lighter soil than the surrounding midden suggests that they originated at a lower level.

[9] Brown (1926, p. 123) says that burials in this cemetery were generally from 1½ to 2 feet below the surface which checks very closely with the observations made above.

same token, the priority of Barton Incised over Parkin Punctated is here strongly confirmed. Whereas in Cut A Baytown Plain appeared as an unimportant minority unaccompanied by any other clay-tempered types, here in Zone III, particularly at the bottom, in Level 6, it shows up in considerable strength, accompanied by Mulberry Creek Cord-marked and Wheeler Check Stamped. If our seriation analysis is correct, the latter type is a reliable marker type for the late Baytown Period (fig. 20), so we must conclude that the beginning of the occupation represented in Cut B reaches back to, if not into, the Baytown Period. This raises the question as to the nature of the transition from Baytown to Mississippi in this area, which will be discussed in a moment. It is important to note here that the sharp rise in Baytown types from Level 5 to 6 is not accompanied by any sign of a break in stratification, although the lens of sand already discussed, which might be taken as an indication of a pause in refuse accumulation, occurred precisely at this level (−90 cm.).

Discussion of the Walls Site

Before analyzing the stratigraphy on this site, we regarded it as the type site for the cultural facies that has Bell Plain as its dominant pottery type. Incidentally, this is the complex that is responsible for most of the well-known effigy pottery of the St. Francis and Yazoo basins. In conversations among ourselves we have used the term Walls (or Alpika, name of the bayou on which the site is located) in the sense of focus, in anticipation of the time when enough is known about the non-pottery traits to permit a complete description of the archaeological culture. The analysis of these cuts raises some interesting questions in regard to the site and the propriety of using its name as a focal designation. If our interpretations are correct, the only evidence we found of a constructional nature pertains to an earlier Mississippi Period occupation in which Neeley's Ferry Plain is the dominant pottery type. The extent to which the refuse overlying this occupational level is referrable to the later "Walls culture" in which Bell Plain is the dominant type is difficult to estimate, because of the uncertain quantity of Bell Plain and its associates that may have derived from pot-hunting operations on the site. It would probably be too much to say that all, or even most, of these types were so derived; in other words, the site was probably more than just a burial site of the "Walls people." On the other hand, it is now clear that it cannot be regarded as a pure "Walls" site either, hence the designation Walls Focus should remain, for the time being, in a provisional status.

Leaving aside this premature question of focal designation, the important result of these cuts on the Walls Site is the clear indication that Neeley's Ferry Plain reached its maximum popularity at an earlier date than did Bell Plain. The net result is to give an effect of greater depth to the Mississippi Period in this area.

Cultural Continuity versus Cultural Stratification. The presence of clay-tempered types of the Baytown Period in the bottom levels of this site raises a problem that will come up repeatedly in this section of the report and will be discussed at length at its conclusion. This is perhaps not the best place to state the problem, because the evidence here is not very clear one way or the other, but without such a statement the possible significance of this particular clay-tempered pottery is apt to be overlooked. In the briefest possible terms the question amounts to this: Did the pottery of the period we call "Mississippi" develop locally out of the preceding Baytown Period complex in the Survey Area, or did it "come in" from somewhere else? In terms of stratigraphy, the question may be rephrased as follows: Does the superposition of Mississippi over Baytown pottery in a given situation evidence a continuity of occupation during a process of culture change, or does it indicate a reoccupation of the site by a new population bearing a different culture type? This is a statement of the extremes of the question. It is revealing no trade secrets to admit that the three authors are not in agreement as to how this question should be answered. Let us hasten to add that an answer could only be in the nature of a working hypothesis at this stage of investigation, but we cannot even agree on an hypothesis. However, our differences are of degree and emphasis and are not irreconcilable. Ford is inclined to favor the side of continuity as is clearly set forth in the sections of this report that he has prepared. He believes that most (not all) sites exhibiting such cases of Mississippi-Baytown superposition were continuously inhabited through a period of cultural change, represent in short a "transitional" phase in the cultural development of the area. Griffin, while not denying the role of internal development in the process, tends to look for the principal origins of Mississippi ceramics in sources outside the area, and in the main tends to regard the afore-said superposition of Mississippi over Baytown as evidence of cultural stratification in the ordinary acceptance of the term. Phillips, characteristically, cannot make up his mind.

The evidence here, on the Walls Site, slightly favors the continuity theory. There is not enough Baytown pottery in Cut A to be significant, but in the bottom levels of Cut B there is an appreciable amount of it that has to be accounted for. The sudden jump in Baytown percentages from Level 5 to Level 6 suggest a stratified situation, but there was nothing in the profiles or the field notes to indicate that such was the case. In short, if there was a distinct and separable pre-Mississippi occupation of the site, our excavations do not show it. If there was no pre-Mississippi occupation on the site, how did these clay-tempered sherds get there? According to the hypothesis of continuity, they simply represent a period in which a shell-tempered pottery complex still retained a substantial minority of clay-tempered types. The same group of people (not necessarily the same individuals) were making and using both. It must be admitted that the evidence of Cut B, so far as it goes, favors this type of solution, but it is hardly necessary to add that the evidence of one minute excavation is not sufficient basis for generalization about the site, to say nothing about the area as a whole. It would scarcely be worth mentioning at all except as a means of introducing a stratigraphic problem that was encountered on almost every site that was tested, and in every case presented the same difficulty of interpretation. Lothrop was right when he said that the evidences of stratigraphy do not always have the force and authority of Holy Writ. On the other hand, neither the small scale of our excavations nor the difficulty of interpreting their results excuses us from attempting to wring from them the last ounce of meaning. If we do not get some sort of answer to this question, it will not be for lack of trying.

LAKE CORMORANT SITE (13-P-8)

This site, also in De Soto County, 5 miles due south of the Walls Site, was high on our list for stratigraphic testing in the spring of 1941, owing to the fact that a surface collection made in the previous fall showed types that were already known as both early and late in the area. In particular this was one of the first collections made by the Survey in which pottery referrable to the Marksville culture appeared. It was, in short, the most promising site from the standpoint of chronological depth encountered up to that time. We were, therefore, extremely grateful to the owner, Mr. Tom Withers, for permission to excavate.

The site is located on the natural levee of an old Mississippi meander of Stage 4 in the angle formed by the junction of this meander and Lake Cormorant. It is bounded on the north by Dead Nigger Slough, which elegant title designates the stream that now occupies the western portion of the said meander, and on the east by Lake Cormorant. The western, and highest part of the site, is terminated by a cut of the Yazoo and Mississippi Valley Railroad, which has undoubtedly destroyed a considerable portion of it. At the extreme northeastern point of the site, in the angle formed by the two streams mentioned above, are the remains of a mound whose original size and shape have been rendered indeterminate by plowing, and the owner told of another, traces of which are no longer to be seen. The rest of the site has been cultivated down to a dead level, thickly covered with sherds and other cultural débris. The presence on the surface of human bone fragments and large potsherds of Mississippi types, and the absence of daub, suggested intrusive burials in an earlier occupation site, an indication which seems to have been partly confirmed by the excavations.

Two cuts were put down in this site by Griffin and Chester Chard.

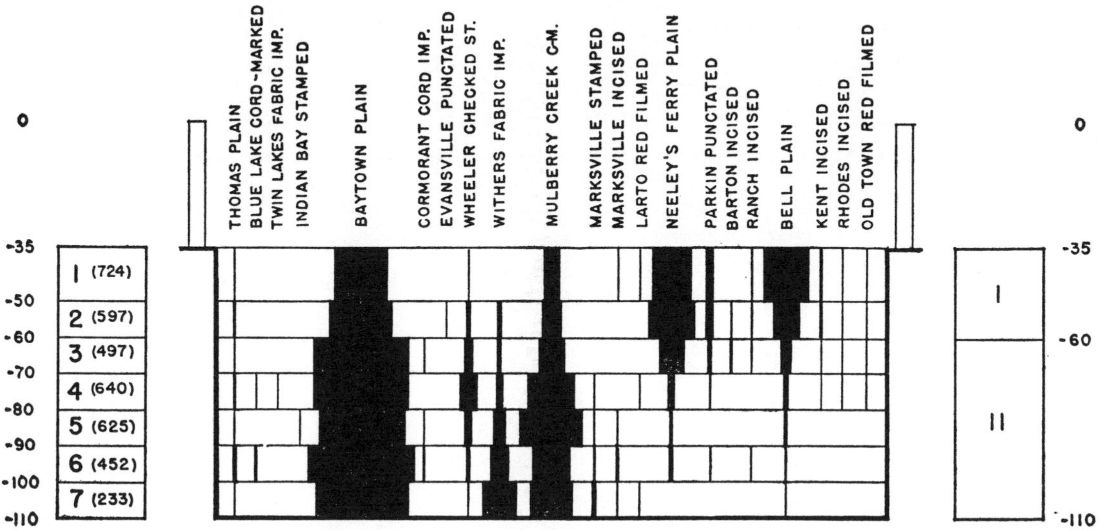

FIG. 25. Stratigraphic diagram, Cut A, Lake Cormorant Site (13–P–8).

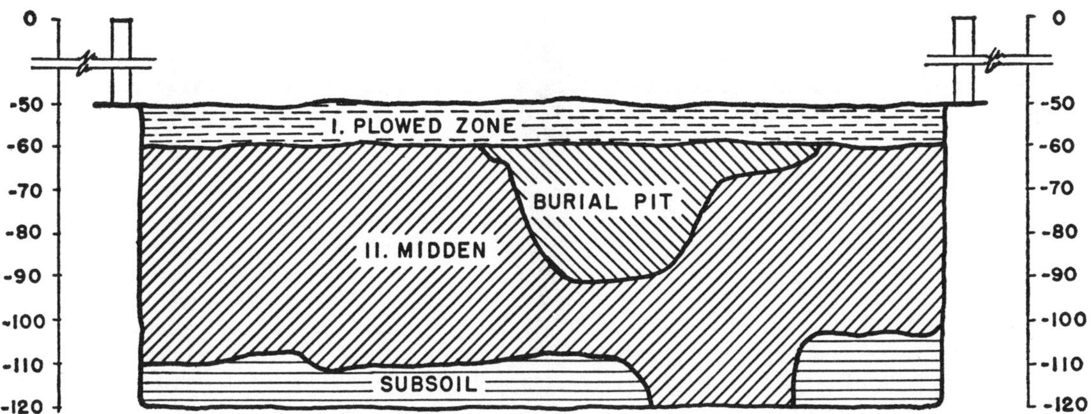

FIG. 26. Profile, South Wall, Cut A, Lake Cormorant Site (13–P–8).

Cut A (Figure 25)

The first cut was located in the northwestern corner of the site, 12 meters from the top edge of the railroad cut and a like distance from the edge of the bluff overlooking the old Stage 4 channel and Dead Nigger Slough. The simple stratification, or rather lack of stratification, complicated only by a series of pits, was as follows:

Zone I. −35 cm. to −60 cm. Cotton ridges and plowed zone.

Zone II. −60 cm. to −105 cm. Black midden soil containing lumps of burned earth but no daub. No horizontal lines of stratification were observed in this midden, but there were faint vertical or sloping lines on the profiles indicating a very irregular deposition of refuse, or pitting, or both. One definite burial pit containing disarticulated fragments of bone from at least three individuals was encountered immediately below the plowed zone and showed up clearly in the profile of the south wall (fig. 26). Another series of smaller pits extended from the bottom of the midden at −105 cm., down a short distance into the sterile sub-soil. An additional Level 8, dug to recover material from these pits, is not represented on the diagram, the small number of sherds so obtained (55) having no stratigraphic significance, since the points of origin of these pits could not be determined.

Notwithstanding the fair amount of disturbance described above, the stratigraphy of this cut is unusually clear and unequivocal. To begin with, it is to be noted that the only significant showing of Mississippi Period types was in the cotton ridges and plowed zone corresponding to Levels 1 and 2. Below Level 2, percentages of shell-tempered types diminished very rapidly. This appears to confirm the interpretation made on the basis of surface conditions alone that the occupation of the site by Mississippi Period people was very superficial. It is perhaps not impossible that it was used by them for burial purposes only. The amount of such pottery in and immediately below the plowed zone was not more than could be derived from the uprooting of graves by the plow which in fact is still going on. The group burial referred to above is a case in point. The outline of the grave was clearly traceable from the bottom of the plowed zone, indicating that the burial was intrusive into the earlier midden deposit of Zone II (fig. 26). According to the field notes, Mississippi Period sherds were "almost certainly localized" in this pit. This accounts for some, if not all, of the small amounts of Mississippi pottery that got down into the lower levels of the deposit, and practically eliminates any possibility of a "transition" from Baytown to Mississippi in this particular cut.

The chief importance of the cut, however, lies not in the relationship of shell- and clay-tempered types but in the inter-relationships within the clay-tempered group. Particularly helpful is the clear indication of the priority of Withers Fabric-impressed over Mulberry Creek Cord-marked and Wheeler Check Stamped in that order. As a result of this and Cut B on the same site, it was possible to use Withers Fabric-impressed as an early marker type in lining up the seriation of surface collections. As an additional detail, it might be noted that the Marksville types, in their first appearance in the archaeology of northern Mississippi, showed up in the lower levels just about where Ford, who was not present at the excavation, would have expected to see them.

Cut B (Figure 27)

Cut B was excavated concurrently with Cut A by Chester Chard under the general supervision of Griffin. It was located in the northeastern corner of the site immediately south of the ruined mound already mentioned. Basically, the ground conditions were the same as those of Cut A, except that there was even more disturbance in the unstratified midden in the form of large pits. Such pits, being filled with black soil identical with that of the midden are generally not detected until they impinge on the lighter-colored sub-soil, which for stratigraphic purposes is invariably too late. The idealized profile shown in figure 27 may be described as follows:

Zone I. −55 cm. to −75 cm. Cotton furrows and plowed zone.

Zone II. −75 cm. to −125 cm. Dark midden soil corresponding to Zone II in Cut A. The figure −125 cm. is a rough average of a very uneven bottom, rendered still more so by the intrusion into the underlying sub-soil of several large pits.

Zone III. −125 cm. to −145 cm. Excavation of arbitrary levels was continued on below the bottom of the midden to −145 cm., picking up considerable material from the pits that obtruded into the sub-soil. Beyond this point, two large pits which had not yet run out were troweled separately, one of them terminating at −165 cm., the other at −210 cm. Sherds from these pits were bagged separately, but on being sorted showed no significant differences. Since the pits were not excavated in 10-cm. levels below −145 cm., the stratigraphy cannot be shown below that level. Parenthetically, the manner of excavating these pits was a mistake. It was done on the theory that the relative ages of the several pits would be subsequently revealed by the profiles, which to a certain extent was the case, but nothing came of it because the material in the pits failed to show significant differences. In the meantime, the record of changes that might have taken place within the pits was lost. The lesson of this experience is that, if material from pits cannot be segregated and eliminated as the digging proceeds, it is better to dig them in arbitrary levels right to the bottom and incorporate the results in the general stratigraphic record.

With all this disturbance, it would not be reasonable to expect any clear stratigraphy in this cut. However, on comparison with Cut A, where disturbance of this kind was less in evidence, there is a surprising general correspondence and even some agreement in detail. The shell-tempered types occupy the same top-level position, except in one very interesting particular which will be noted presently. in the stratification at this point, and yet there must have been something of the sort. It cannot be attributed to the pits, assuming they originated that high up in the midden since their effect would be to minimize the break rather than to accentuate it.

The position of Indian Bay Stamped in this cut is interesting insofar as priority over Marksville Stamped is indicated. Evidently,

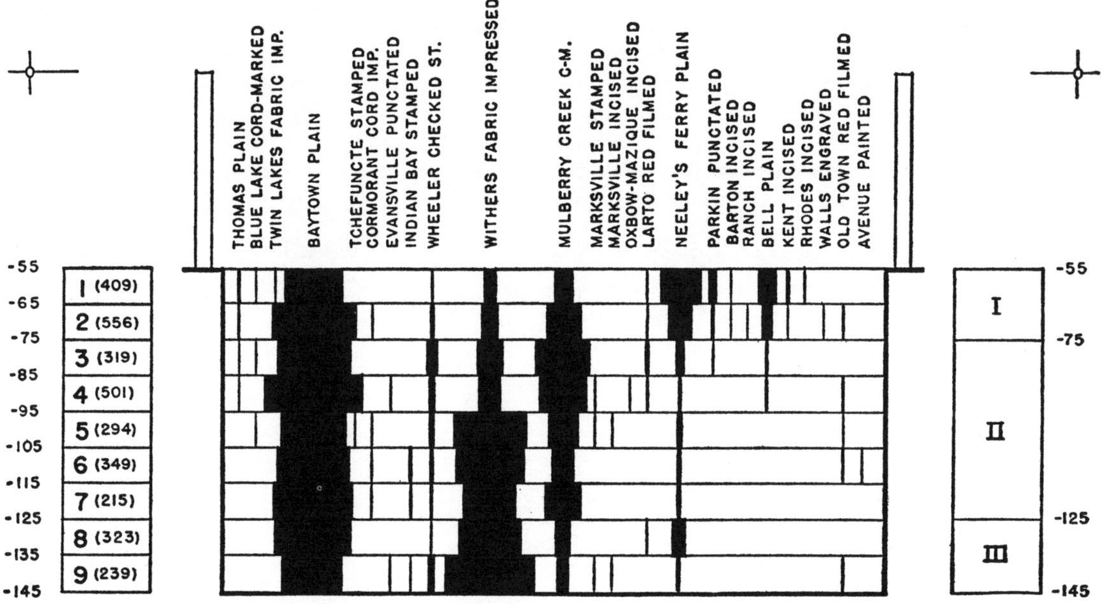

Fig. 27. Stratigraphic diagram, Cut B, Lake Cormorant Site (13–P–8).

The same relative positions of Wheeler Check Stamped, Mulberry Creek Cord-marked, and Withers Fabric-impressed are observed but with this very important difference, that in Levels 5 through 8 there is an actual dominance of Withers Fabric-impressed over Mulberry Creek Cord-marked. Evidently, this is an older, though only slightly deeper, portion of the site. Level 4 in this cut is approximately equivalent in pottery content to Level 7 in Cut A. In effect, Levels 5–8 could be transferred from this graph and slipped under the lowest level in the graph of Cut A without doing violence to the historical probabilities.

The sharp rise in strength of Withers Fabric-impressed from Levels 4 to 5 is impossible to account for. There is nothing in the field notes or profiles to indicate a break Indian Bay Stamped is an early type, perhaps either a local correspondent of Tchefuncte Stamped or a close derivative. This cut seems likewise to have established Cormorant Cord-impressed as an early type.

The most curious thing on this diagram, however, is the sudden appearance of Neeley's Ferry Plain in a significant percentage (8.35 per cent, or 27 sherds) in Level 8. Obviously, these sherds were in a pit, which originated at a higher level — for a comparable percentage, you have to go almost to the top — but if so, why did the type not occur in similar strength in the intervening levels? The sherds are considerably thinner than the usual run of Neeley's Ferry Plain as a whole. Similar material was found more abundantly in Cut A on the Rose Site (12–N–3) in 1947 under conditions that left no doubt that it is an earlier variant of the type. Its possible significance will be discussed in connection with that excavation.

Status of Sand-tempering on the Lake Cormorant Site

Another result of the excavations just described was to undermine the significance of sand-tempering in this portion of the Survey Area. At the time the material was first sorted in 1942, we had a stronger belief in what we used to call the "sand-tempered series" than we have today. The assumption was that it was earlier than the "clay-tempered series." This site offers a good test of that assumption. A few examples with enough sand in their composition to be sorted as Thomas Plain, Twin Lakes Fabric-impressed, and Blue Lake Cord-marked turned up in various levels of both cuts. Their distribution, according to Griffin's original 1942 sorting, is shown on the left side of figures 25 and 27. In Cut A, Thomas Plain shows a very slight tendency to increase with depth, but this is exactly reversed in Cut B. The two other sand-tempered types show no significant distribution whatever. The fact that there are fewer sandy-textured sherds in the early fabric-impressed ware is likewise damaging to the assumption. We must conclude, for this site at least, that the occasional presence of moderate amounts of sand in the pottery has no chronological, and presumably no cultural, significance. The writers are not yet in perfect agreement as to the applicability of this conclusion to the area as a whole.

Discussion of the Lake Cormorant Site

The two cuts on this site tell a consistent and, considering the extent of disturbance in both, remarkably satisfactory story. All indications point to a single long-continued occupation in the Baytown Period, followed by the use of the site in the Mississippi Period possibly for burial purposes only. The important contributions of the site are within the Baytown Period, itself. The lowest levels, found only in Cut B, evidently belong to a very early time in that period, when Withers Fabric-impressed was an important type. There is some evidence that Indian Bay Stamped and possibly Cormorant Cord-impressed belong to this same early period. The Marksville types seem to be somewhat later, about the time when Withers Fabric-impressed was giving way before Mulberry Creek Cord-marked. Still later, Wheeler Check Stamped becomes an important minority type, though it does not become dominant over Mulberry Creek. This check-stamped type we have tended to regard as a marker for the late Baytown Period in this area, taking the place for diagnostic purposes of Coles Creek Incised farther south. If these assumptions are correct, the time represented by this apparently homogeneous deposit is very long in terms of Lower Alluvial Valley sequences, from the early Marksville, or even late Tchefuncte, through the Coles Creek periods. We are obliged to conclude either (1) our interpretations are at fault or (2) it was a very slow accumulation indeed.[10] If it is a case of faulty interpretation, the fault is most likely to lie in our assumption that Wheeler Check Stamped is necessarily a late Baytown Period type. This assumption is largely based on the results of seriation in the Memphis area (see fig. 20), where the type appears to reach its maximum popularity in the earlier part of time D to C, tentatively designated as late Baytown. Unfortunately, we have at present no further opportunity to check this position stratigraphically, this and the Walls Site (13-P-1) being the only sites in which the type appeared in stratigraphic cuts. For the time being, therefore, we shall have to accept the rather surprising conclusion that on this site, in about 1 meter of refuse, the entire Baytown Period is represented. To Ford, however, this situation merely confirms his belief that under special conditions refuse may accumulate very slowly over long periods of time (see p. 233). The obvious thing to say at this point is that more time could be usefully employed in further excavations on the Lake Cormorant and related sites.

[10] See p. 233.

In respect to the question of continuity or discontinuity between Baytown and Mississippi Period occupations on the site, the evidence is equivocal. Owing to the fact that the Mississippi pottery was almost entirely in the cotton ridges and plowed zone, we have to assume a thorough mixture of late types and consequent "blurring" of the stratigraphic relationship of Neeley's Ferry and Bell Plain, which is our principal criterion for dating within the Mississippi Period in the Memphis area. The general dominance of Neeley's Ferry over Bell, however, indicates a fairly early position in that period, an indication that is reinforced by the presence in the lower levels of Cut B of a variant of Neeley's Ferry which may be typologically early. Thus no wide gap between Baytown and Mississippi is necessarily indicated on the typological side. On the stratigraphic side, however, the Mississippi Period occupation is so plainly superficial, notwithstanding the many factors favoring the migration of potsherds in these cuts, as to raise the question whether it can be called an occupation at all, a doubt which is greatly fortified by the lack of daub on the site.[11] That it was a burial site in the Mississippi Period, however, is attested by the burials with Mississippi pottery that are still being rooted out by the plow.

Our tentative conclusion, therefore, with all customary reservations attached, is that the Lake Cormorant Site was occupied continuously or intermittently throughout the long Baytown Period and reoccupied briefly and/or used for burial purposes in the Mississippi Period. Continuity between these two phases of the site's history, while not ruled out absolutely, is not indicated by our fragmentary stratigraphic record.

OLIVER SITE (16–N–6)

The Oliver Site was chosen for testing because the indications of cultural stratification obtained, though not entirely appreciated by Charles Peabody in extensive excavations on the site in 1901–02,[12] were confirmed by our surface collections. It was hoped that a small-scale excavation here might enable us to extract more meaningful results from Peabody's published data. This is in no sense a criticism of his work, which was of a high order, considering the time it was done. Such hopes were only partly fulfilled for reasons that will be sufficiently apparent. In respect to our own immediate purposes, however, the three cuts put down on this site by Phillips and Chard in 1941 were eminently satisfactory. Our thanks are due to the owner, Mr. F. C. Duleny, for permission to excavate.

The site, located on the east bank of the Sunflower River about 15 miles below Clarksdale, in Coahoma County, Mississippi, consists of a large but mutilated rectangular platform mound (Peabody's "Edwards Mound") and several smaller mounds of uncertain size and shape (fig. 28). This portion of the Sunflower River country has seen enormous change since Peabody's time, when it was as yet largely unreclaimed for agriculture. The site is a disheartening example of the ravages that can be wrought by cultivation in a comparatively short time. Peabody's description, therefore, gives a better idea of the original features of the site than we can give at the present time.

Cut A (Figure 29)

Cut A was put down close to Mound A (Peabody's "Edwards Mound"), 10 meters from the foot of the mound slope, on the southeast side (fig. 28). Two reasons prompted the choice: (1) the possibility of revealing the relationship of mound and village site, and (2) the hope of avoiding Peabody's extra-mound excavations, on the theory that he would not have been likely to push these so close to the mound already dug. It was to be expected that the upper levels of the cut would be affected by outwash from the mound, and such proved to be the case. Below

[11] We have come to regard the presence of daub (fragments of fired clay from burned wattle-and-daub houses) as *sine qua non* for an occupation of the Mississippi Period.

[12] Peabody, 1904.

the outwash zone, the cut presented unusually clear and undisturbed stratification:

Zone I. −45 cm. to −52 cm. Plowed zone.

Zone II. −52 cm. to −71 cm. Brown sandy loam, homogeneous and compact with little cultural material showing other than small bits of daub scattered throughout. Very little shell. This deposit was thought by the excavators to be largely composed of outwash from the mound.

Zone V. —119 cm. to —170 cm. Substantially same as Zone IV, though somewhat lighter in color, gradually fading out to the light olive-brown sandy sub-soil of the region. The separation between Zones IV and V was arbitrarily drawn, based entirely on a slight difference in color. For all practical purposes, these two zones may count as one.

The "critical level" in this cut, to borrow a term from Peabody, is the separation between

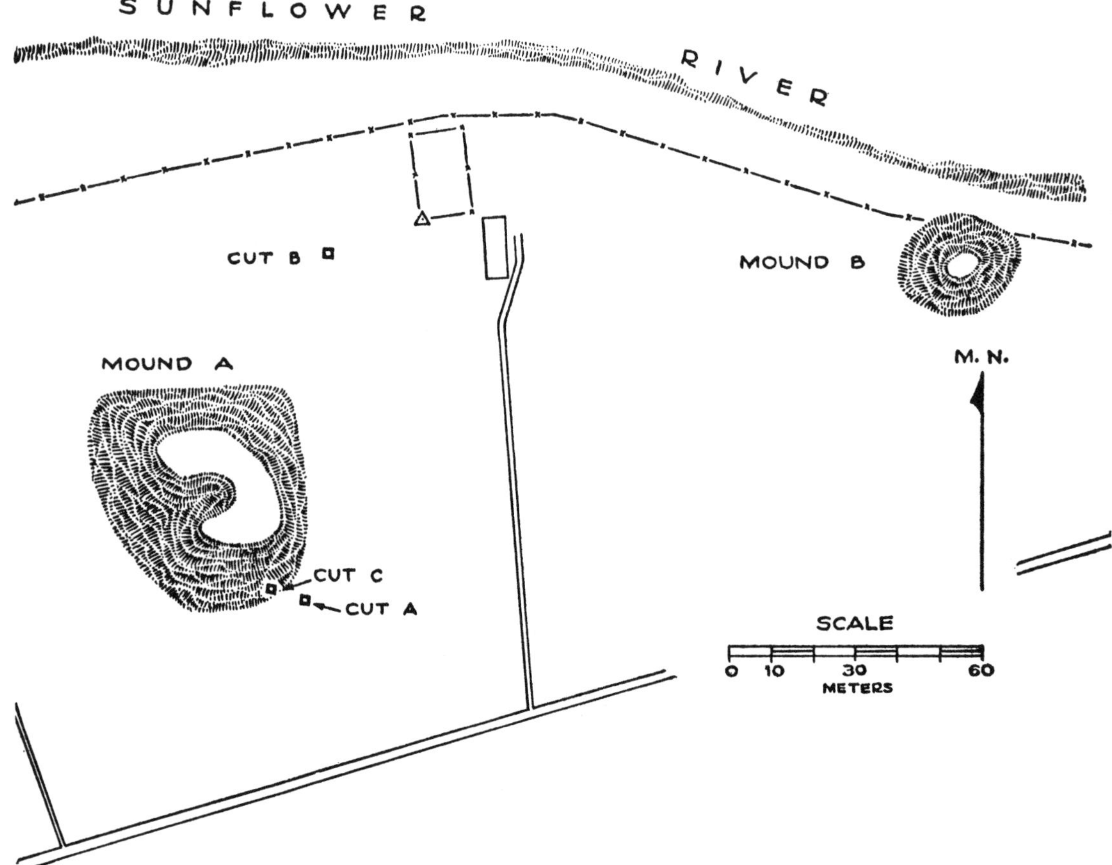

Fig. 28. Plan of Oliver Site (16–N–6).

Zone III. −71 cm. to ca. −96 cm. Loose dark midden soil with lenses of shell, ash, and charcoal, and fragments of daub scattered throughout. Both upper and lower limits of this deposit were unusually level and unaffected by pits and other disturbances as may be seen by the remarkably congruent lines of stratification in the four profiles (fig. 30).

Zone IV. Ca. −96 cm. to ca. −119 cm. Dark brown to black midden soil, more compact and homogeneous than Zone II. Scattered shell, but no lenses as in Zone III. No daub.

Zones III and IV. Above this line, in Zone III was what could almost be described as a shell midden, with fragments of daub scattered throughout, below it only scattered individual shells and almost no daub. This striking discontinuity of deposits is of prime importance in the interpretation of the stratigraphy as we shall see (fig. 30).

It is a pleasure, not often experienced, to describe such a clear-cut correlation between

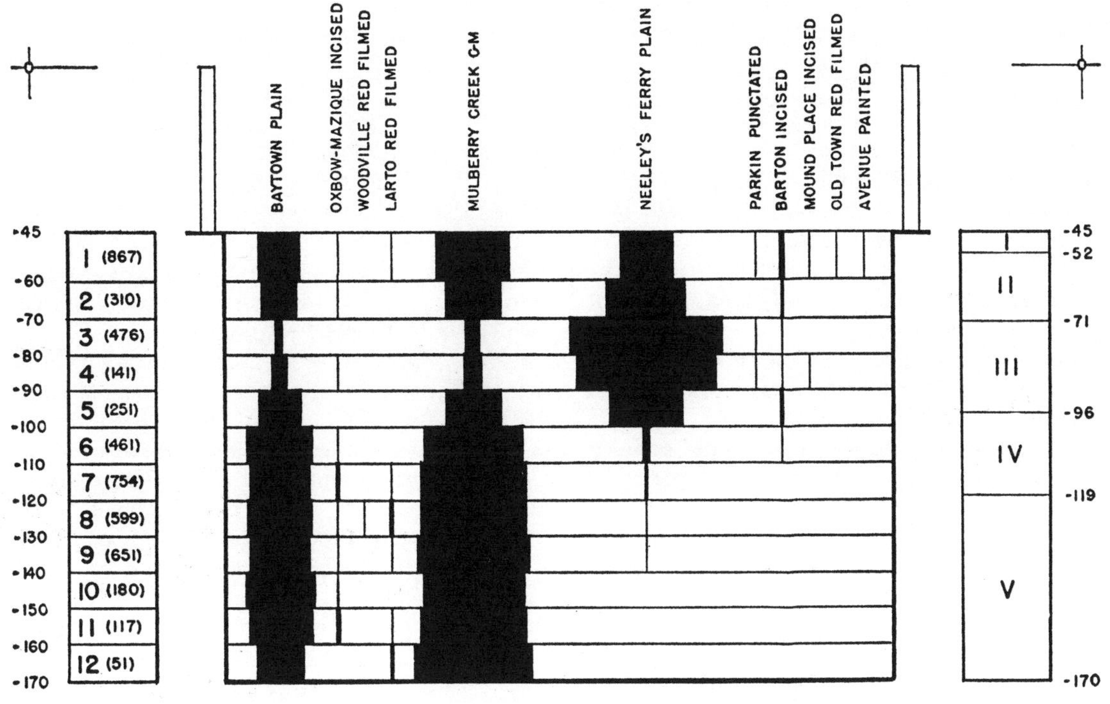

FIG. 29. Stratigraphic diagram, Cut A, Oliver Site (16–N–6).

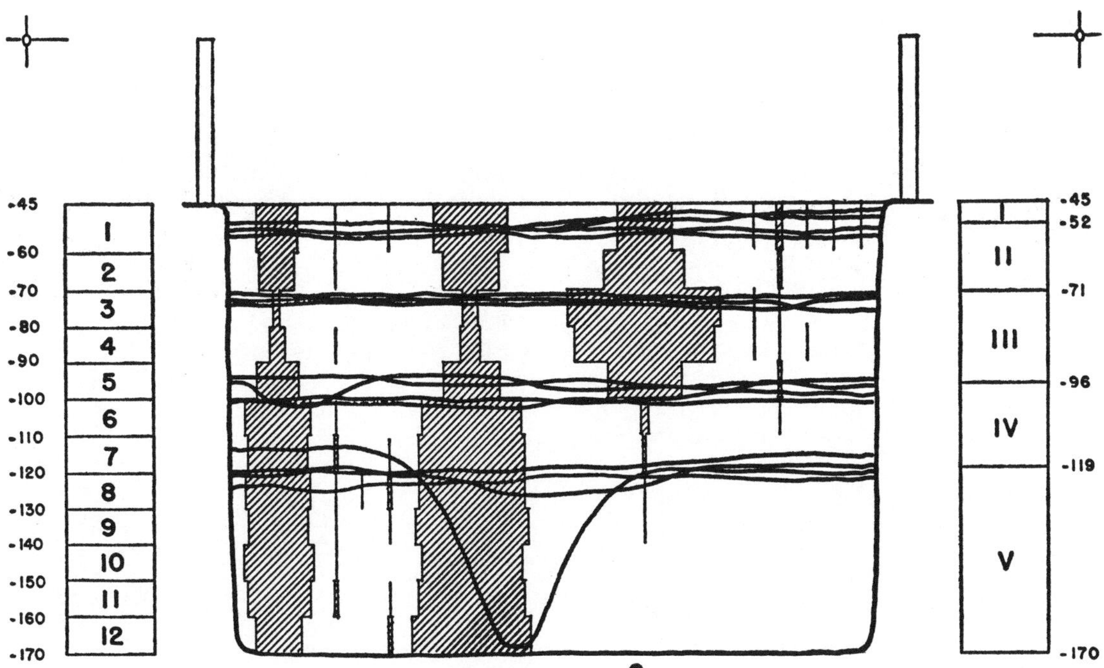

FIG. 30. Composite profile diagram, Cut A, Oliver Site (16–N–6).

pottery stratigraphy and ground stratification. Levels 1 and 2, corresponding closely to Zones I and II, representing the plowed and outwash zones, contain just that sort of mixture of pottery types we would expect. Levels 3 and 4, corresponding to the upper three-fourths of Zone III, indicate an almost pure Mississippi Period occupation. The small percentages of Baytown Plain and Mulberry Creek Cord-marked in these levels might be interpreted as the result of persistence of earlier types into a later period, but the amounts are not greater than could have resulted simply from minor disturbances and "normal" upward migration in the ground, and in view of the mound-building activity near by, the latter seems the most probable explanation. More substantial amounts of these types in Level 5 are attributable to the fact that this level straddles the critical plane of separation between Zones III and IV. This has the effect of furnishing a spurious transition on the pottery graph between the two zones in question. A truer approximation to actual conditions would be obtained by the omission of Level 5 and the direct comparison of Levels 4 and 6, which would show as sharp a "break" as you can hope to see in a stratigraphic column. From Level 6 on down we are in a pure Baytown horizon corresponding to Zones IV and V in the ground.

The Mississippi deposit is marked by a complete absence of Bell Plain. This can be interpreted in one of two ways: (1) an earlier pre-Bell Mississippi phase or (2) location of the site outside the range of distribution of Bell Plain. Comparison with the gross distribution map of the type (fig. 12) indicates that the latter is the correct explanation.

The Baytown deposit is fairly deep but remarkably stable, in sharp contrast to the situation on the Lake Cormorant Site. Lack of Withers Fabric-impressed and the other early types, on the one hand, rules out the early Baytown Period, while the large and constant percentage of Mulberry Creek Cord-marked, plus the lack of Wheeler Check Stamped and/or Coles Creek Incised, seems to rule out the late Baytown Period on the other. The occupation, therefore, appears to be bracketed within the middle Baytown Period. We must admit, however, that our late Baytown criteria in this area are not well established. Nothing has been said yet about the time position of Mazique Incised. The type reached its maximum in the Lower Alluvial Valley in the late Troyville Period but persisted well on into Coles Creek. This would appear to support our tentative dating of this deposit as middle Baytown, but we are not altogether happy about the type as represented here in the Survey Area. It is poorly defined and covers too wide a range, typologically speaking, to be a good period determinant.

The results of this cut are so satisfactory and of such potential significance as to warrant re-emphasis. It is impossible to escape the conclusion that we have here a stratified situation. A deposit of considerable depth but remarkable homogeneity containing remains of a middle Baytown occupation (corresponding approximately to period E–D in our provisional chronology) is overlain by a thinner but no less pure Mississippi occupation, which in turn is overlain by an outwash deposit from the big mound in which the two complexes are mixed, as might be expected if the mound contained earth scraped up from the earlier village site. There is every reason to believe that the Mississippi occupation corresponds to the period of construction and use of the mound. It is of course not impossible that other portions of the site might show a transition from one type of culture to the other, but the evidence of this cut, taken alone, would support the contrary hypothesis of discontinuous cultural stratification.

It is interesting to note that in seriating the data from this cut, without regard for ground stratification, Ford found it necessary to leave a wide gap corresponding to D–C (late Baytown) on the time scale between Levels 5 and 6 to make the patterning come out right (fig. 19). This is a very satisfactory confirmation of the essential soundness of the seriation method.

We have already referred to what may be called the basic stratigraphic problem in this area, the question whether Mississippi culture evolved out of Baytown in place or "came in" and supplanted it (see p. 233). In the cuts on the Walls Site (13–P–1) there was a faint indication, hardly to be called evidence, in favor of the hypothesis of cultural continuity.

On the Lake Cormorant Site (13–P–8) the evidence pointed rather weakly the other way. Here the indications are somewhat stronger. There can be no question, in this cut, that there is a break between Baytown and Mississippi Period deposits. However, it must be pointed out that, according to present interpretations, the Baytown pottery represented here is middle not late Baytown. This may well be a case, where the "transitional" phase, a postulation required by the continuity theory, is missing simply because the site, or this portion of it, was not being occupied at the time.

doubt on our interpretation of that deposit as mainly composed of outwash from the mound. However, we know from Peabody's report that there were other mounds on the site, which have since disappeared, so it is not unlikely that this cut was on or near one of these other mounds.

Zone III. −65 cm. to −110 cm. Same, slightly darker, and without daub. Clearly corresponds to Zones IV and V in Cut A, though not so thick. The separation between Zones II and III was not well marked but consisted in part of a burned floor. On checking its level with reference to a common datum, however, it was found to correspond precisely to the level of the well-marked separation between Levels III and IV in Cut A.

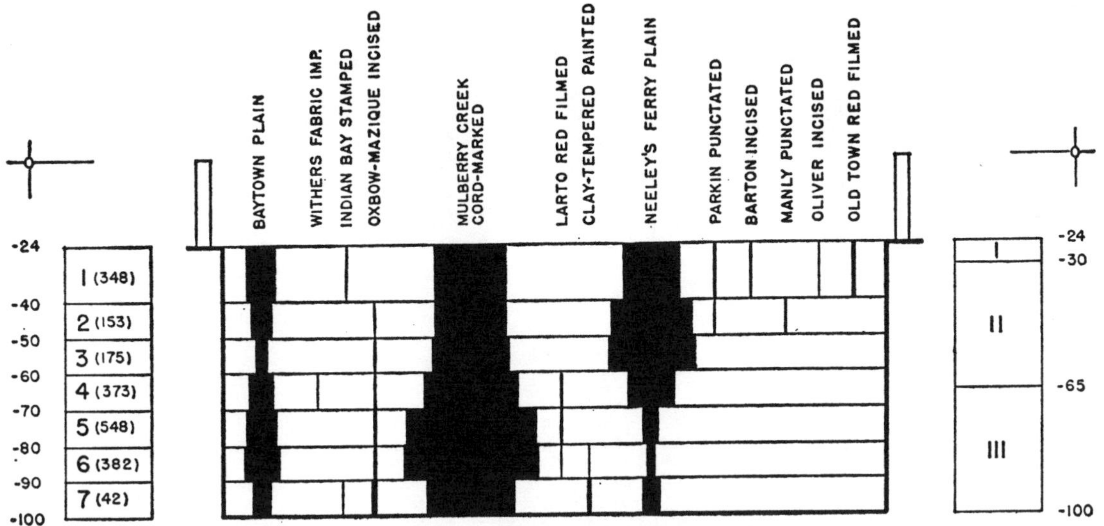

FIG. 31. Stratigraphic diagram, Cut B, Oliver Site (16–N–6).

Cut B (Figure 31)

While the excavation of Cut A was proceeding, Cut B was dug by Chester Chard on another portion of the site northeast of Mound A, beyond the reach of any possible outwash from the mound, figure 28. The location turned out to be a shallower portion of the site, only seven pottery-bearing levels being obtained, but the stratigraphy was quite satisfactory and generally confirmatory of the results obtained in Cut A. Stratification was simple and well defined, as follows:

Zone I. −24 cm. to −30 cm. Plowed zone.

Zone II. −30 cm. to −65 cm. Brown sandy loam with scattered lumps of daub. Appears to correspond in character to Zone II in Cut A, which throws some

The separation between the Mississippi and Baytown occupations is not as clear as in Cut A, but with a little "interpretation" the two cuts can be made to tell the same story. The difficulty is that there is no "pure" Mississippi refuse corresponding to Zone III in Cut A. Our Zone II here, which corresponds in position, has an even mixture of pottery types. The chances are that mound-building activity, as already suggested, is responsible for the mixture, but there is, of course, no way to prove it. Peabody's map is not sufficiently accurate for detailed comparison, but his Mound 1, which no longer exists, was very close to the location of this cut.[13]

[13] Peabody, 1904, pl. 7.

From the general standpoint of stratigraphic method, there is an interesting point here. If we had dug only Cut B and were therefore unaware of the existence of any pure Mississippi refuse on the site, the separation between Zones II and III, which was not particularly distinct anyhow, would doubtless be regarded as nonsignificant. In this case the pottery graph showing a partial and gradual replacement of Baytown by Mississippi types might logically be interpreted as representing a single late Baytown occupation about the time of the first appearance of Mississippi pottery in the area. In other words, this might be the "transitional" period which we found to be missing in Cut A. With the results of that cut fresh in mind, however, such an interpretation is impossible and we are able to recognize the true importance of the line separating Zones II and III, as the counterpart of the more definite and conspicuous "break" in Cut A to which it corresponded in absolute level. This shows how very careful one must be in making assumptions based on single small stratigraphic excavations.

A detail of importance in this cut is the appearance of Withers Fabric-impressed in the Baytown Period component, particularly in the bottom level. This type, which we know to be early from its position in the Lake Cormorant Site was not present in Cut A on this site nor in Cut C, as we shall see, a circumstance which indicates that this is perhaps an earlier part of the site. It also confirms our tentative dating of the Baytown component as middle rather than late Baytown.

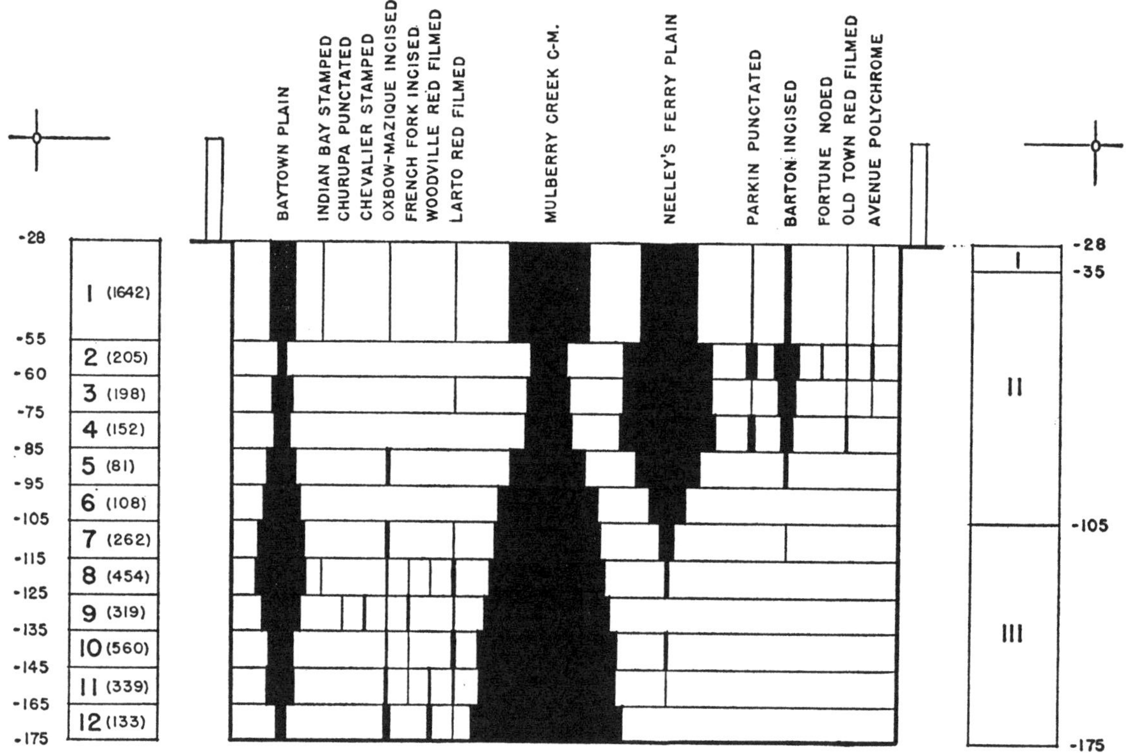

Fig. 32. Stratigraphic diagram, Cut C, Oliver Site (16-N-6).

Cut C (Figure 32)

Cut A failed in one of its objects, i.e., to give us any certain information about the relationship of mound and village site, so a third cut, Cut C, was put down 8 meters nearer the mound, in fact, on the lower edge of the mound slope. The stratification was as follows:

Zone I. −28 cm. to ca. −35 cm. (very uneven). Plowed zone.

Zone II. −35 cm. to −105 cm. Brown sandy loam, homogeneous and compact with small bits of daub scattered throughout. No shell. Lenses of ash toward the bottom overlay a burned "floor" separating this from Zone III below. The major portion of this deposit was certainly made up of thoroughly disturbed and re-deposited material resulting from long-continued cultivation and erosion of the mound, and therefore corresponds to Zone II in Cut A.

Zone III. −105 cm. to −175 cm. Dark brown midden soil containing some shell but no daub, corresponding to Zones III and IV in Cut A.

The "floor" separating Zones II and III corresponds morphologically to that separating Zones III and IV in Cut A, but shows more pronounced evidences of occupation in the form of burned areas and post-holes. It is, moreover, at a slightly higher level in the ground,[14] probably due to its position higher up the mound slope. It may be that at the time this surface was being lived upon, mound-building, inadvertent or deliberate, had already taken place, or that the occupiers were taking advantage of a natural rise. It is very interesting that this occupational surface corresponds very closely with Peabody's "critical level" in the mound. It cannot be correlated with mathematical precision, owing to the fact that his levels and ours are not tied into a common datum, but the two are at approximately the same depth relative to the ground surface.

Before embarking on an interpretation of the stratigraphy of this cut, there are one or two things about the diagram that require explanation. The strange look at the top is due to the side-hill location of the cut, which necessitated a deep first level in order to get a horizontal bottom. This is also the reason for the large sherd sample. Sixteen hundred and forty-one is the total sherd count in the top level, not the date — though it might not be far off at that. This deep level got considerably below the plowed zone, in the up-mound portion of the cut, but corresponds very closely with the first level in Cut A, nonetheless.

In general, the stratification of Cut C, as might be expected, lends itself to the same general interpretations as that of Cut A near by, but there are certain differences, particularly in Zone II that are not easily explained. For example, there is no "pure" Mississippi refuse comparable to that of Zone III in Cut A. The lack of anything corresponding to the separation between them might be attributable to the location of Cut C up on the mound slope where the accumulation of undisturbed refuse is hardly to be expected. Unfortunately for this simple explanation, the pottery does not agree. In Cut A the "pure" Mississippi deposit lay directly above the "critical level," which we are now able to characterize as a "floor," whereas in Cut C the levels occupying the same relative position (Levels 5 and 6) are heavily charged with Baytown types. There does not seem to be any satisfactory explanation of the disagreement, but it is almost certain that mound-building had something to do with it. Parenthetically, it may be pointed out that the ordinary difficulties of stratigraphic interpretation are enormously increased by mound-building activities involving the transfer of masses of soil from one part of a site to another, not to mention the subsequent erosion of mounds and consequent redistribtion of cultural material.

Below the "floor," Levels 7 through 12, we have in Zone III the same relatively pure and undisturbed Baytown deposit as in both Cuts A and B, the only difference being that, although not quite so thick, it seems to reach back into a slightly earlier period, as evidenced by the larger percentages of Mulberry Creek Cord-marked.

This cut is more important for its bearing on our general problem of stratigraphic interpretation, already alluded to several times under the heading of continuity versus stratification. A simple bar graph of pottery distribution in this cut without reference to ground conditions would present an ideal picture of the gradual replacement of one series of types by another. It would hardly require smoothing. Yet, in Cut A only 8 meters distant, we have the same two series sharply stratified, and, in fairness to the continuity hypothesis, have concluded that the sharp break is probably due to the fact that the late Baytown Period (where the transition must be if there was a transition) was missing on this site. Therefore, logically, the appearance of smooth transition in the pottery distribution of Cut C cannot be a reality because the transitional

[14] It should be pointed out that in the primitive excavation methods used, levels in each cut were taken from its own datum, and subsequently tied in to a "permanent" bench mark. Comparison of levels from one cut to another, therefore, requires additional data not shown on the diagrams.

material is not here. The only conclusion left is that disturbance, in this case probably redistribution of material as a result of mound-building and/or mound erosion, can and does produce a spurious gradation of type distributions that is apt to be misleading.

Correlation with Peabody's Excavations

It was hoped that our very limited excavations might be tied in with Peabody's work in such a way as to make some use of his far more abundant material. Unfortunately, owing to the manner of presentation of archaeological reports of the time, this cannot be done without a thorough reworking of his field notes which are available in the files of the Peabody Museum. It would probably be worth doing, for there is a good chance that what he called the "critical level" in the mound corresponds to the occupation surface or "floor" which separated the Baytown and Mississippi deposits in our excavations. There is a possibility, therefore, that his extended burials, generally without pottery, below this level, are associated with the Baytown component, while the "bundle" burials with pottery belong to the Mississippi Period.[15]

Conclusions on the Oliver Site

The evidence of the three cuts on this site, while raising all sorts of interesting questions in regard to stratigraphic interpretation generally, shows a satisfactory degree of internal consistency. The site is definitely stratified in the sense of having two distinct occupations or components with no evidence of transition between them. The earlier component appears to relate specifically to the middle Baytown Period, while the later component is in the Mississippi Period, but we are not yet able to place it definitely within that period. The absence of Bell Plain and its associates would indicate an early Mississippi position were it not for the fact that the site is in an area in which Bell Plain seldom appears. Arguing against an early Mississippi date is the fact that Peabody found turquoise and glass beads with burials in the upper level of the mound. These may, of course, have been intrusive burials dating from a still later Mississippi Period. We may as well admit that we do not yet have satisfactory criteria for dating within the Mississippi Period in the Sunflower area.

But whether early Mississippi or late, the superposition of this culture over one of the Baytown Period does not signify conclusively in the argument between the hypothesis of continuity and that of cultural stratification, because the transitional phase is missing anyhow. That elusive Baytown-Mississippi transition, if it took place, took place elsewhere. There are no traces of it so far discovered in the Oliver Site.

ALLIGATOR SITE (16–N–2)

The well-known Alligator Site is located in northwestern Bolivar County, Mississippi, on the southern bank of an old Mississippi meander of Stage 5, now occupied in part by Alligator Bayou, about 1 mile west of the point where the latter stream enters the said meander. It is on the property of Mr. J. N. Dunn to whom thanks are due for permission to excavate and many kindnesses to the excavators. The site consists of a typical Mississippi assemblage of large rectangular platform mounds and smaller "house" mounds arranged about a central plaza (see fig. 33). It was not typical, however, in that the extremely abundant pottery on the surface showed a heavy dominance of clay-tempered types. It was primarily on this account that the site was tested. It seemed a possibility that we might find here a Baytown Period occupation associated with rectangular mounds and plaza assemblage.

Cut A (Figure 34)

Two cuts were put down on the site in 1941 by Griffin, assisted by Mott Davis. The first was located on Mound D on the west side of the plaza, a low mound about 1 meter high, much spread by cultivation. This was one of the spots that yielded the highest percentages of clay-tempered types, yet there was every

[15] Peabody, 1904, pp. 51–52.

reason to believe that the mound was a house mound associated with the plaza complex. It was thought worth-while to put down a cut to prove or disprove this apparent association, though ordinarily a mound is not the best place to try for stratigraphic results.

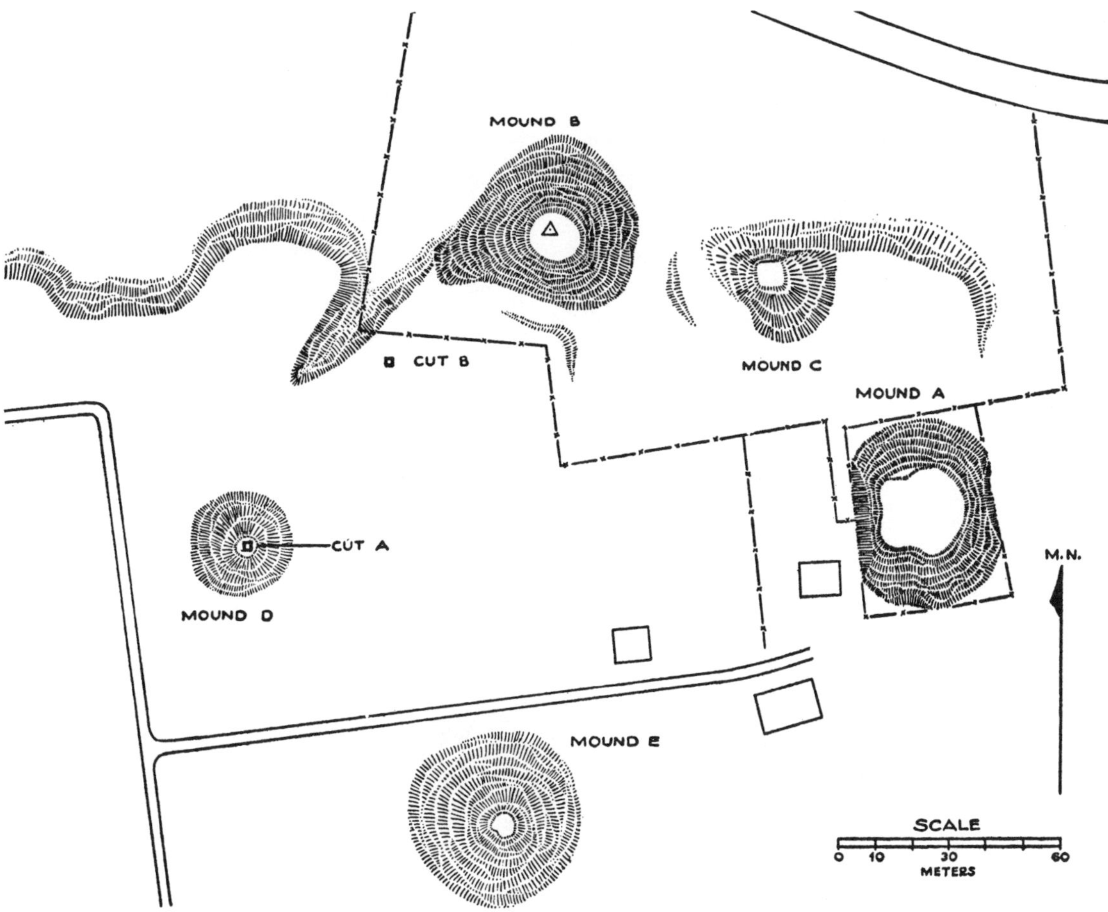

Fig. 33. Plan of Alligator Site (16–N–2).

The stratification was as follows:

Zone I. −30 cm. to −52 cm. Plowed zone.

Zone II. −52 cm. to −66 cm. This zone is arbitrarily dimensioned to include a thin layer of charred matted cane, several charred logs, and a quantity of charcoal and burned earth which, say the field notes, "may have been daub," in all probability the remains of a burned house, the ill-defined floor of which was at approximately −66 cm.

Zone III. −66 cm. to −105 cm. Fairly homogenous mottled brown soil with flecks of light earth and charcoal, the latter confined mainly to the upper portion. Post-holes were encountered in this level, but their point of origin was not ascertainable. The lower portion of this zone contained patches of clay, and the general composition of this portion of the zone is described as "clayey." A reasonable inference from this description is that this is transported "mound" soil, partly derived from village-site midden and partly composed of sterile clay. No other interpretation fits the description, though it must be admitted that this interpretation was not recorded at the time of excavation.

Zone IV. −105 cm. to −160 cm. Rich dark midden containing quantities of charcoal, ash, animal bones, etc.; in other words, typical village-site refuse. Evidences of pits and post-holes were encountered at all levels. The separation between Zones III and IV was far from level and not always distinct. A small patch of the lighter "clayey" soil of Zone III was still observable at −130 cm. If our interpretation of

Zone III as mound fill is correct, the mound must have been built over a very uneven village site.

At −138 cm. a wall trench containing post-holes appeared extending diagonally from southwest to northeast across the cut. The bottom of this trench was clearly defined at −160 cm., as shown below (fig. 35). Although the first appearance of this trench was recorded at −138 cm., it was subsequently established from a study of the profiles that the trench originated at approximately −100 cm., i.e., at the very top of Zone IV. Consequently, the structure represented by the wall trench cannot be said with certainty to belong either to the mound (Zone III) or to the older village site (Zone IV). It may have been the last construction of the earlier phase or the first construction of the later.

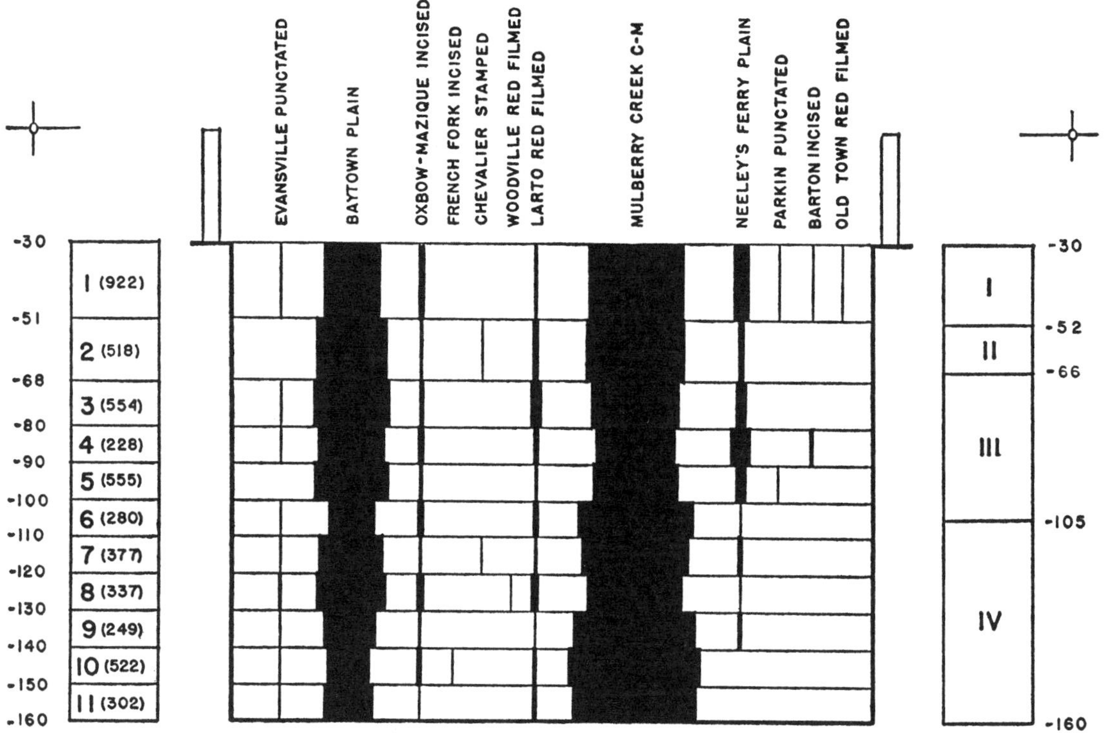

Fig. 34. Stratigraphic diagram, Cut A, Alligator Site (16–N–2).

At first glance the stratigraphic diagram (fig. 34) seems to confirm the general rule that mounds do not make good testing ground for stratigraphy. However, if our own interpretation of the stratification is correct, if Zone III is mound fill and Zone IV the village site from which most of that fill was taken, then a closer look at the diagram may be taken. Note that in the Neeley's Ferry column something happens between Levels 5 and 6, approximately coincident with the separation of Zones III and IV. The drop in frequency of Neeley's Ferry is more than the percentages indicate because it coincides with a sharp drop in total sherd count. The actual drop is from thirty-three Neeley's Ferry sherds in Level 5 to one sherd in Level 6. That it picks up slightly again in the next three levels is not surprising in view of the unevenness of the separation between Zones III and IV (it appears to dip down at one point as low as −130) and the numerous pits and post-holes recorded by the excavators.

Zone IV is quite evidently a deposit of the middle Baytown Period comparable to the earlier component on the Oliver Site (16–N–6). It seems only slightly less evident that Zones I through III are the result of mound-building activity in the Mississippi Period making use of soil so heavily impregnated with pottery from the Baytown village site as almost to submerge the pottery left by the people who made and used the mound. A possible alternative explanation is that the entire deposit represents a single long span covering the middle and late Baytown periods, and that the mound-building took place in the latter part of that span when shell-tempering was an element in the pottery complex. The difficulties of such an explanation, however, are almost insuperable. In the first place, the unvarying percentage relations of the various clay-tempered types do not indicate a long

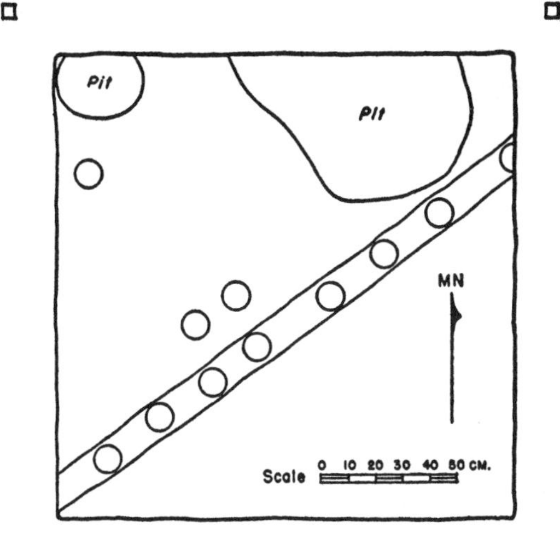

FIG. 35. Plan at -160 cm. showing wall trench and post-holes, Cut A, Alligator Site (16-N-2).

period, being characteristically those that obtained in the middle, but not the late, Baytown Period; in the second place, granting that we know very little as yet about Mississippi Period pottery in this part of the Survey Area, there is no reason to assume that this is early Mississippi material. In Cut B, where, as we shall see, it appears in the upper levels unmasked by earlier material included in mound fill, it shows as a fully developed Mississippi complex.

Finally, we have in the stratigraphic record, a break, small but significant, between the lower and upper levels of the cut. In short, the evidence here, so far as it goes, parallels the much clearer evidence at the Oliver Site, in support of an hypothesis of cultural stratification, a reoccupation of a middle Baytown village site in the Mississippi Period; and so far as the admittedly scanty evidence goes, it is to the later people that the construction of the mounds must be attributed. The lack of correspondence between the foregoing interpretation and the results of seriation (fig. 19) is rather marked, to say the least, but is not difficult to account for. If these data are handled at face value, so to speak, as they must be in the seriation technique, without regard for the special conditions inherent in the fact that the cut was made in a mound, they are bound to give an erroneous result. Specifically, they give a false appearance of continuity, because the "break" between Baytown and Mississippi is masked by the heavy percentages of Baytown types in the mound fill. If this cut had been analyzed stratigraphically first, it would not have been used in the seriation. It may be asked why we do not take it out now. The answer is that, in our opinion, it is more important to expose the limitations of a method, still in an experimental stage, than it is to present a smooth and possibly misleading appearance of accomplishment.

Cut B (Figure 36)

The second cut on this site was located about midway between Mounds B and D, where, in making surface collections, a heavy concentration of shell-tempered pottery was noted. In view of the predominance of clay-tempered pottery on other portions of the site, this appeared an excellent spot to try for stratigraphy. The results justified the expectation. This was one of those unusual cases, however, where a very marked stratification of pottery types was not accompanied by evidence of a correspondent stratification in the ground. The latter was of the simplest possible description.

Zone I. −32 cm. to −42 cm. Plowed zone.

Zone II. −42 cm. to −110 cm. Dark homogenous midden deposit with some shell shading off at −95 cm. in gradual transition to the yellow sandy clay sub-soil of the region. Several thin lenses of burned earth, ash, and charcoal at various depths, none of sufficient extent to justify division of the deposit. The most conspicuous of these was in the northeast corner of the cut at −62 cm. "It looks as if we had cut into the very corner of a house floor" (field notes). A few post-holes were encountered in upper levels of this zone, and a great many more, and pits as well, from −70 cm. on down. Some of these penetrated into the sub-soil. The small samples of pottery in Levels 7 and 8 were almost, if not entirely, derived from these post-holes and pits and therefore have no stratigraphic significance.

The interpretation of this cut is relatively easy. In spite of the lack of a clear-cut line of division in the ground, it is obvious that something revolutionary occurred between Levels 4 and 5. The actual break in pottery was probably even greater than appears on the diagram, because we have the evidence of the field notes that a large number of post-holes and pits of uncertain origin were struck in Levels 5 through 8, which must account for some, if not all, of the shell-tempered pottery in those levels. We have, therefore, an unusually clean break, an almost pure Mississippi Period deposit overlying a thin Baytown deposit without any sign of transition between them.

The lack of corresponding break in the ground is not so easily explained. If our interpretation of Cut A on this site and the three cuts on the Oliver Site is correct, the earlier component here is of middle Baytown date. Theoretically, a considerable lapse of time ought to separate it from the Mississippi component, regardless of whether it is early or late Mississippi, and this lapse of time ought to have been represented in some way on the profiles of this cut. However, we are going to see other cases, notably Cut A on the Jaketown Site (20–O–1), in which a very long stretch of time has been compressed into a short space (vertically speaking) of ground without any sign of soil stratification. We can only repeat that we have a great deal more to learn about the alleged "science" of stratigraphy.

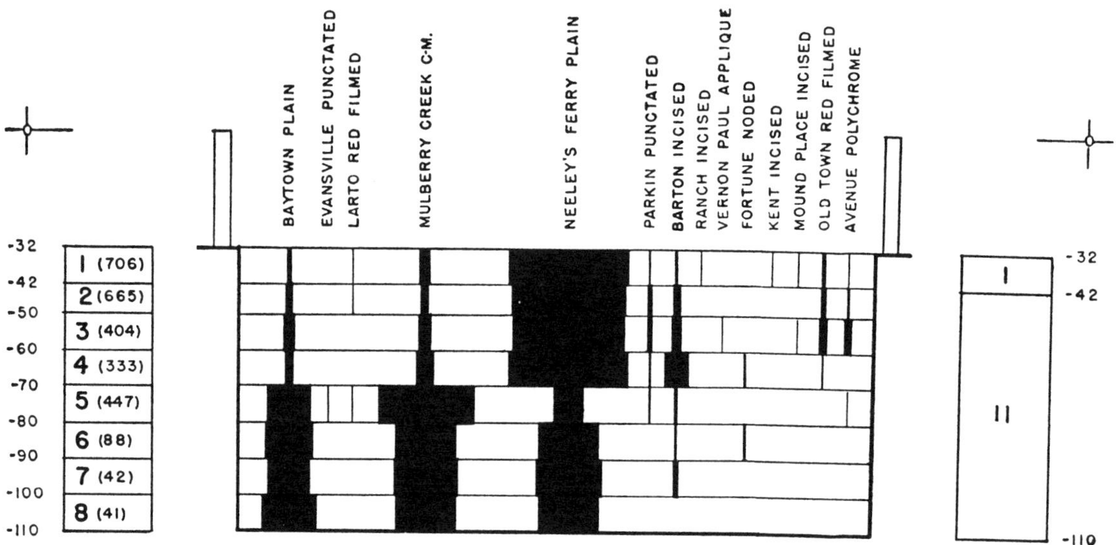

FIG. 36. Stratigraphic diagram, Cut B, Alligator Site (16–N–2).

Conclusions on the Alligator Site

The stratigraphy of the two cuts on this site appears to support one another pretty well. The cultural stratification, which in Cut A was obscured by the fact that the upper levels were composed of mound fill containing earlier material, was in Cut B clearly exposed. The net conclusion is so similar to that already given for the Oliver Site as to raise some misgivings on the part of the interpreters. Is it the archaeology or our reasoning that is getting into a rut? The only difference in the two sites is the possibility that the Baytown component at Oliver may have started earlier than at Alligator. This is based on the greater proportion of Mulberry Creek Cord-marked to Baytown Plain in the first-named site, and the absence of Withers Fabric-impressed and other early types in the second. The difference does not appear to be sufficient, however, to throw the "Alligator I" component into the late Baytown Period.

So far as the authorship of the mounds is concerned, the fact that there was a pure Mississippi component on the site makes it very unlikely that the Baytown people had anything to do with their construction. As in the case of the "Edwards Mound" on the Oliver Site, the heavy percentages of clay-tempered pottery in the fill of Mound D must be taken as evidence that the fill was scraped up from the earlier Baytown Period village site. It is a reasonable inference that the Baytown sherds picked up on the surface and immediate vicinity of the other mounds were of similar derivation.

Again, we have to report a lack of agreement between the results of seriation and stratigraphic analysis. Because of their heavy percentages of Neeley's Ferry Plain, Levels 6 and 7 in Cut B (Level 8 was for some reason omitted) were given a late Baytown position in the seriation (fig. 19). To have placed them lower down would have pulled their sizable Neeley's Ferry percentages out of accord with the general pattern. However, it can be shown that these large percentages are an exaggeration of the actual situation. First let it be noted that the Baytown deposit was very thin on this part of the site, being concentrated in Level 5 and thinning out rapidly in Levels 6 to 8. In Level 5, of a total sherd count of 447 there were 72 sherds of Neeley's Ferry Plain, or 16 per cent. In Level 6 there were 30 Neeley's Ferry sherds, but with a total count of only 88, the percentage jumped to 34 per cent. In Level 7 there were 16 Neeley's Ferry sherds, but with a total count of only 42, the Neeley's Ferry percentage increased again to 37 per cent. Now, if we are correct in postulating a sharp discontinuity in this cut, that is to say, a heavy Mississippi deposit overlying a thin Baytown deposit, and if the latter was penetrated to varying depths by pits and post-holes filled with Mississippi refuse, as the field notes indicate, the effect on percentage distribution from level to level would be just what we see here. The diminishing numbers of Mississippi sherds, in this case Neeley's Ferry Plain, would build up increasing percentages as the Baytown material thinned out. To go a step farther, for purposes of illustration, supposing some of the pits or post-holes penetrated clear through the Baytown deposit, you might have 100 per cent Mississippi pottery in the bottom level.

The purpose of this discussion of what may appear to be a minor discrepancy is to bring out the point that percentages have no inherent sanctity, nor can their validity be judged solely by the size of the sample. In ordinary circumstances, for example, the 88 sherds in Level 6 of this cut would be an adequate sample; under the actual conditions here it evidently is not.

We can only repeat that we have a great deal to learn about both seriation and stratigraphy before they can be regarded as "scientific" procedures.

Again, in regard to the question of cultural continuity versus stratification, we must point out that this site proves nothing one way or another owing to the fact that the late Baytown Period is not represented. What can be said, however, is that once more a mixture of clay- and shell-tempered pottery types, which in a surface collection would perhaps be interpreted as representing a single occupation at a "transitional" time when both clay- and shell-tempered types were in use, has turned out on close analysis to be more susceptible to an explanation based on two distinct occupations without any apparent transition between. As we have pointed out before, this does not prove that such a transition did not take place, merely that once more, in two small cuts, no conclusive evidence of it was obtained.

MENARD SITE (17–K–1)

Since the first published description by Thomas Nuttall in 1821, the Menard Site, or "Menard Mound," as it is generally called, has figured prominently as the key site of the Lower Arkansas River. It was dug extensively by Edward Palmer who referred briefly to the site in letters published by the Arkansas Historical Society [16] and later reported on it for

[16] Palmer, 1917, pp. 431–32, 445–47.

the Bureau of American Ethnology,[17] and more extensively by Clarence B. Moore, whose excavations described as "near the Menard Mound" included the adjacent Wallace Site (17–K–3) as well.[18] Recently, the site has received additional attention from the support given by the De Soto Expedition Commission to Colonel Fordyce's theory that Menard is the famous Quiguate, characterized by several chroniclers of that expedition as the "largest town in Florida." The correctness of this identification is discussed at length in a later section of this report (p. 382). In the same section (p. 414) is presented the evidence for identifying the near-by Wallace Site (17–K–3) with Uzutiuhi, the Quapaw village at which Tonti established his post in 1686. The site, therefore, is closely tied up with both the De Soto and Quapaw problems. Our surface collections of 1940 led us to believe that it had an earlier history as well, which, together with the fact that the big mound is conical, rather than pyramidal, determined the choice of the site for stratigraphic testing in 1941.

We are deeply grateful to the owner of the site, Dr. T. L. Hodges and Mrs. Hodges of Bismarck, Arkansas, both well-known students of archaeology, who not only afforded every encouragement to the work but assisted in it as well.

The Menard Site (fig. 37) is located at the extreme southern margin of Grand Prairie Ridge, at an elevation well above the reach of high water, yet close enough to the Arkansas River — which was in fact closer at the time of occupation than today — to afford the benefits of a riparian situation, the first location so favored above the river's mouth. That such natural advantages were not overlooked is attested by the fact that the edge of the Ridge extending northeastward from Menard along the banks of the present Menard Bayou is said to be practically a continuous village site for several miles. Much of this land is wooded so we were able to check the accuracy of this statement only at intermittent points with the result that we have catalogued as Menard (17–K–1), Wallace (17–K–3), Poor (17–L–3), Massey (17–L–1), and Ellerton (17–L–2) what may actually be only separate portions of a continuous area of occupation. With this in mind, the stratigraphic results on the Menard and Massey sites may be used to supplement one another by interpolation for the sake of the greater chronological depth thus afforded.

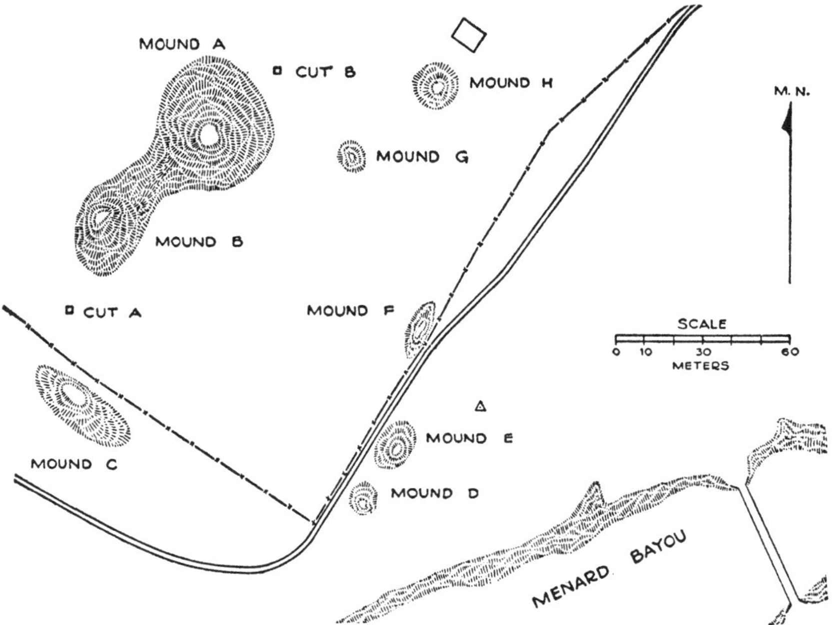

Fig. 37. Plan of Menard Site (17–K–1).

[17] Thomas, 1894, pp. 229–31.

[18] Moore, 1908a, pp. 486–509.

Cut A (Figure 38)

The principal features of the site are shown on the map. Cut A was put down by Phillips and Davis in 1941 in the area immediately south of Mound B. Stratification was as follows:

Zone I. −23 cm. to −66 cm. There was no plowed zone; apparently, this portion of the site had not been in cultivation for a long time, if ever. All but the extreme lower portion of Zone I consisted of brown clay loam mottled by small scattered fragments of daub and charcoal. This deposit was interpreted by the excavators as mainly the product of outwash from the mound. The separation between Zones I and II consisted of discontinuous areas of one or more hard burned floors overlaid by compact lenses of ash.

Zone II. −66 cm. to −107 cm. A variegated light brown midden deposit containing lumps of yellow and white clay of undetermined origin and some scattered shells. This zone was penetrated deeply by large pits and post-holes apparently originating at the occupation level which formed its upper boundary. The separation between this and Zone III, distinct and level on all four profiles, consisted in part of a patch of burned clay "probably a fireplace" and the first appearance of a new set of pits and post-holes.

Zone III. −107 cm. to −160 cm. A more homogenous midden than Zone II, dark brown in color and without the patches of light-colored clay mentioned above. Contained no daub and no shells. A considerable number of pits and post-holes showed up in this zone, most of which were clearly traceable to the zone above, so notwithstanding the clean break in stratification there was ample opportunity for Zone II pottery to find its way into Zone III and *vice versa.*

Though not very deep, this cut was a highly successful operation, susceptible to interpretation without too much difficulty. The three strata were marked off by two unusually level planes of separation as may be seen in the composite profile diagram (fig. 39), of which the upper one surely, and the lower one probably, can be characterized as habitation levels. The upper habitation level and the refuse upon it (Zone I) is pure Mississippi, the slight and downward decreasing minorities of Baytown Plain being interpreted as the result of outwash from the mound. The lower habitation level and its overlying refuse (Zone II) is also Mississippi, but with a difference. It contains more Baytown Plain and less of the Mississippi Period decorated types. If Zone I is late Mississippi, a question which hinges on the position of Wallace Incised, of which more anon, this may be early Mississippi; at any rate, it is earlier than Zone I. The big question as usual centers around the significant percentages of Baytown Plain in this zone, specifically in Levels 6, 7, and 8. These can be explained in one or two ways: (1) persistence of Baytown into the early Mississippi Period; (2) upward migration from Zone III. Figure 39 shows sufficient disturbance in the upper levels of Zone III to have brought up a considerable amount of the Baytown Plain in question. However, to show that something *could* happen is not equivalent to showing that it *did*. Therefore, we must recognize, as a possibility at least, that Zone II in its lower "undisturbed" two-thirds represents an early phase of the Mississippi Period in this area, characterized by the persistence of Baytown Plain in a dominant shell-tempered complex. It is when we try to define this complex that the weakness of the position becomes evident, since it has to be defined purely in negative terms, such as lack of Wallace Incised and Owens Punctated and low percentages of Parkin Punctated and Old Town Red. This is not a very satisfactory definition of the "early Mississippi Period" in this area, but it will have to stand for the present for want of anything better.

Despite appearances to the contrary, Zone III is interpreted as a "pure" Baytown deposit. The pits and post-holes intrusive into Zone III that showed up on the profiles (fig. 39), a good deal less than the actual number in the cut, are sufficient to account for the Mississippi pottery in that zone. Again, we have an example of the spurious transition in the pottery graph caused by irregularities and disturbances in the plane of separation. Nevertheless, though the break is sharper than appears stratigraphically, Zone III must be dated as late Baytown. There is no other way to account for the almost complete lack of Mulberry Creek Cord-marked. To be sure, the type at no time achieved great popularity in the Lower Arkansas River area (see fig. 7), but it is far more significant numerically in the cuts on the earlier Massey Site near by, as we shall see. A late Baytown date for Zone

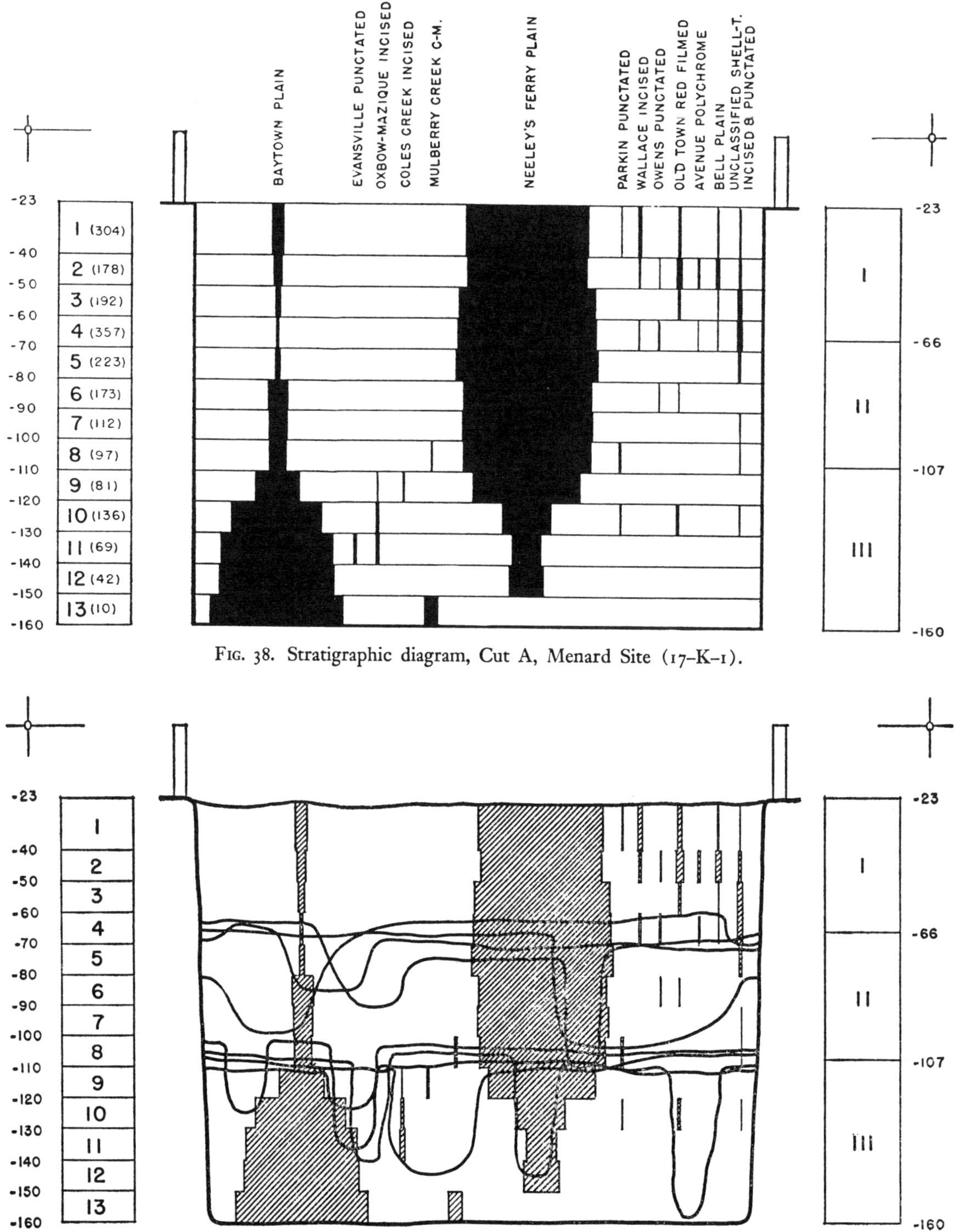

Fig. 38. Stratigraphic diagram, Cut A, Menard Site (17-K-1).

Fig. 39. Composite profile diagram, Cut A, Menard Site (17-K-1).

III is also borne out by the presence of Coles Creek Incised.

There remains only to speak of the position of Wallace Incised. In this cut it seems to be not only late, but very late, later than Parkin Punctated and Old Town Red, for example. This confirms a suspicion long entertained by two of the present writers — Ford demurring (see p. 229) — that Wallace Incised may be a Quapaw type. Suspicion is not proof, however; before we can positively identify Quapaw pottery, we must first identify a Quapaw site. This is attempted in Section IX.

We have, then, roughly equated the lowest levels of this cut with the late Baytown Period, the highest with the late, possibly very late, Mississippi Period. Our difficulty, as usual, is with what lies between. Obviously, it should be early Mississippi, and if it were, a case could be made for the persistence of Baytown Plain into the Mississippi Period. However, the early Mississippi represented here, if such it be, is ill-defined and, to account for the presence of Baytown Plain in it, accidental factors cannot be completely ruled out. The result is that in the dispute between cultural stratification and cultural continuity as between Baytown and Mississippi, this cut merely gives weak arguments to both sides, but settles nothing.

Agreement between this interpretation and that implied in the seriation of the Lower Arkansas River area (fig. 18) is reasonably close except at the top. For rather complex reasons which we cannot go into here, the seriation stops short about the middle of period B–A. If we were to trust this result absolutely, we should have to conclude that the Survey has not yet collected from sites representing the latest occupation of the area, i.e., the Quapaw. This assumption appears to be less tenable than at the time the seriation analysis was made, so it is probable that the interpretation advanced here is closer to the truth than that presented on the seriation graph. However, until we can have certainty on this point, it seems better to let both interpretations stand on their merits.

Cut B (Figure 40)

The second cut on the Menard Site, though a disappointment in respect to depth, was by no means barren of stratigraphic results, though it must be admitted that these do anything but clarify the problems raised in the interpretation of Cut A.

The deposit was a homogenous and relatively undisturbed midden about 70 cm. deep without any sign of stratification on the profiles, so we cannot speak of soil zones. Stratigraphically, Levels 1 to 5 correspond almost exactly with the same levels in Cut A, except that Wallace Incised and Owens Punctated make a stronger showing. It will also be noted that Wallace Incised reaches its maximum a little lower down in the cut which throws some doubt on our assumption that it is the latest pottery on the site and is therefore Quapaw. Level 6 corresponds closely to Level 9 on Cut A with significant percentages of Baytown Period types. This is interesting in view of the lack of stratification on the profiles, but the number of sherds involved (14) is extremely small, hardly enough to justify an argument in favor of the persistence of Baytown types into the Mississippi Period. If such a line were taken, however, it is interesting that the alleged persistence would be into a period that we have already characterized as late Mississippi on the evidence of Cut A. There is nothing in this cut corresponding to the "early Mississippi" of Zone II in Cut A.

In short, this shallow cut, it appears, must be interpreted in one of two ways: either (1) the whole deposit is early Mississippi with a little Baytown Period pottery showing on the bottom level only, in which case the "early Mississippi" we so painfully tried to define in Zone II of Cut A is meaningless, or (2) it is a stratified situation with late Mississippi refuse piled up on a portion of the site that had a few Baytown sherds lying upon it, such a situation as could hardly be expected to reveal itself on the profiles. The balance of probability seems to lie with the second alternative, but to state it as a conclusion would indicate more faith in some of our postulations than we in fact possess.

Discussion of the Menard Site

Our only certain conclusion on this important site is that we ought to go back and do some more work there, and on the Wallace Site next door. Passing over to conclusions of a more tentative nature, hardly to be distinguished from opinions, it appears that this is a culturally stratified site in the ordinary acceptance of the term, with a late Baytown culture overlain by a Mississippi culture which appears to represent the latest occupation of the site. In one of the cuts there was an ill-defined twilight zone between, hardly to be called a transitional phenomenon, though there is a possibility that earlier pottery types persisted into it. In the other cut there was no sign of such a zone, and the persistence of earlier types — if that is what it was — was directly into the full-blown Mississippi complex first mentioned. This lack of consistency between the two cuts throws wide open the question of the date of the Mississippi component on the site. This question which is closely tied up with the problem of Quapaw archaeology is too complex for discussion at this point. We can only conclude somewhat lamely by repeating that the seriation analysis in this area, which puts it mainly into period C–B, the earlier half of the Mississippi Period, is not supported by stratigraphic analysis and that if we have allowed it to stand, it is only for want of positive and clean-cut evidence to the contrary.

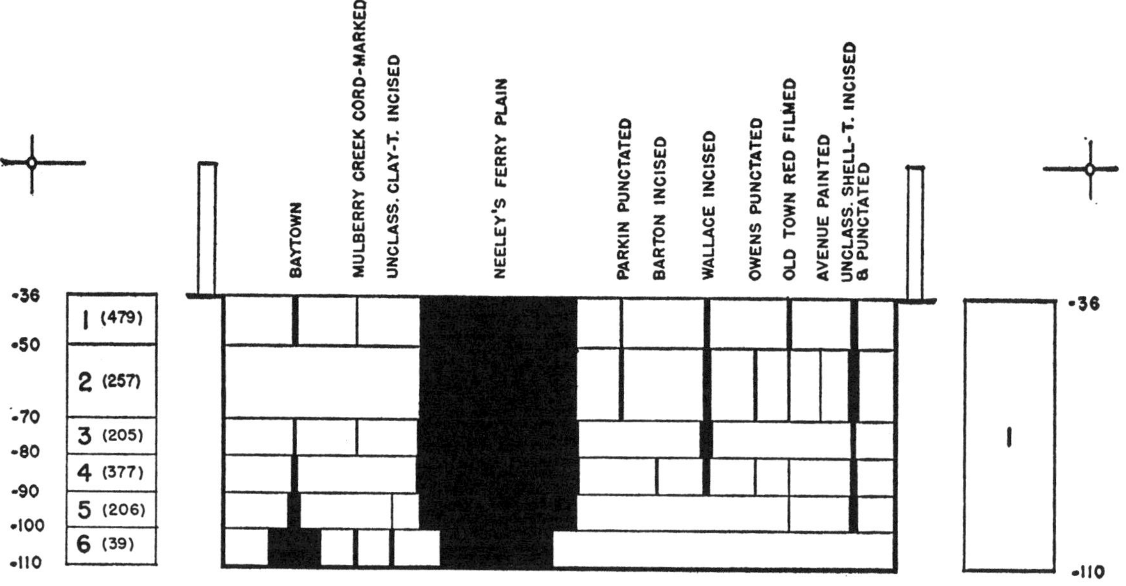

FIG. 40. Stratigraphic diagram, Cut B, Menard Site (17–K–1).

MASSEY SITE (17–L–1)

The Massey Site is located 1¼ miles northeast of the Menard Site on the north bank of a former Arkansas River channel now occupied by Menard Bayou. Between the two sites are other areas of occupation which have been catalogued as Wallace (17–K–3) and Poor (17–L–3), but as already stated, all may be parts of a continuous village site. The Massey Site was chosen for stratigraphic testing in preference to the others, because the surface collections obtained in 1940 showed materials that were both early and late. Parenthetically, this was the site on which we picked up Marksville Period types on the first day out in 1940, a minor historic occasion.

The two cuts put down on this site by Phillips and Davis in 1941, while individually shallow, complemented each other in such a way as to give a picture of considerable chronological depth.

Cut A (Figure 41)

The first cut was located in the central portion of the site where the surface pottery comprised an approximately equal mixture of Baytown and Mississippi types. Stratification was of the simplest possible description, as follows:

Zone I. −35 cm. to −42 cm. Plowed zone.

Zone II. −42 cm. to −100 cm. Rich dark homogenous midden resting on undisturbed yellow clay with a very sharp transition from one to the other. There was no apparent over-all stratification in this midden, but in the upper portion, at −50 cm., there was a small section of bedded ash in one corner of the cut. This and occasional bits of daub near the plow line, and a number of post-holes that appeared to have originated at the plow line, were the only evidences of a habitation level in the cut. If house remains are indicated by this scanty evidence, the house in question must have been very near the surface.

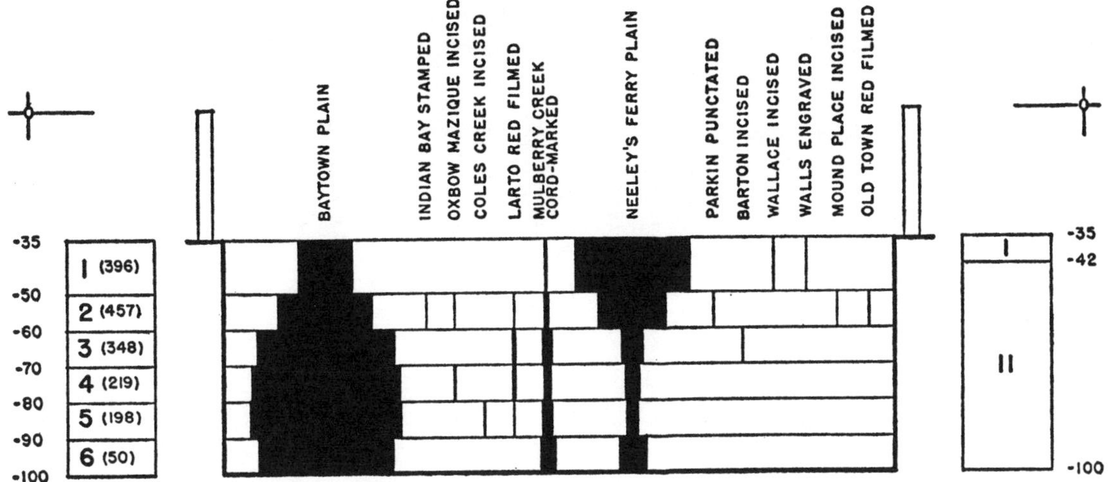

Fig. 41. Stratigraphic diagram, Cut A, Massey Site (17-L-1).

This is one of those cases in which an abrupt shift in pottery content is not accompanied by sufficient evidence of stratification in the ground to explain it. Interpretation is thereby made extremely difficult. Aside from the doubtful evidence of the partial house floor and post-holes, described above, we have only the pottery itself to go on. Notwithstanding the smooth "transition" presented by the graph, continuity of occupation in our opinion is not indicated. The Baytown pottery in the lower levels is not unlike that of Zone III of Cut A on the Menard Site, but appears to be earlier, as may be deduced from the presence of Indian Bay Stamped and Larto Red Filmed, both absent in the Menard cut, and the significant showing of Mulberry Creek Cord-marked, present only in the bottom level at Menard. The Mississippi pottery in the upper levels, on the other hand, is approximately equivalent to that of Levels 4 and 5 in the Menard cut, on the borderline between Zones I and II. In other words, in terms of the pottery distributions in that cut, and our interpretations thereof, there is a gap in this cut roughly equivalent to Zone II, in the Menard cut, or about a half meter of deposit. Our tentative conclusion, therefore, on the situation revealed by this first Massey Site cut, is that a thin Middle to late Mississippi Period occupation, represented by the remains of a house, took place directly upon a middle to late Baytown Period midden, and the spurious appearance of continuity in pottery type distribution is the result of the intrusion of Mississippi sherds into the Baytown midden via post-holes and other disturbances.

It must be emphasized, however, that this interpretation is partly based on a previous interpretation, which itself was declared to be tentative. We must, therefore, point out that an alternative explanation may be the correct one. It may be that what is seen here is an actual replacement of Baytown by Mississippi pottery types during the course of a continuous occupation. If so, the Baytown material must be later and the Mississippi material earlier than is postulated above, or it must be a case of a long time span compressed into less than a meter of deposit with consequent telescoping of type ranges. This raises the question as to what such a replacement might be expected to look like on a pottery graph, a question we prefer not to go into just yet. It can only be pointed out here that, assuming the interpretation of continuity to be the correct one in this case, either a very rapid shift in pottery types or a very slow accumulation of refuse is indicated with the upward movement of Baytown sherds.

Stratification was very simple and confirmatory of the designation "house mound" used above:

Zone I. −40 cm. to −48 cm. Plowed zone.

Zone II. −48 cm. to −69 cm. Rich dark brown midden resting on a hard-burned "floor" which was continuous throughout the area of the cut.

Zone III. −69 cm. to −105 cm. Continuation of the midden, as above, shading off to a reddish sterile clay at about −90 cm. Three small pits penetrated this sub-soil to a depth of −105 cm.

In regard to stratigraphy, there is little to add. No significant difference appears between

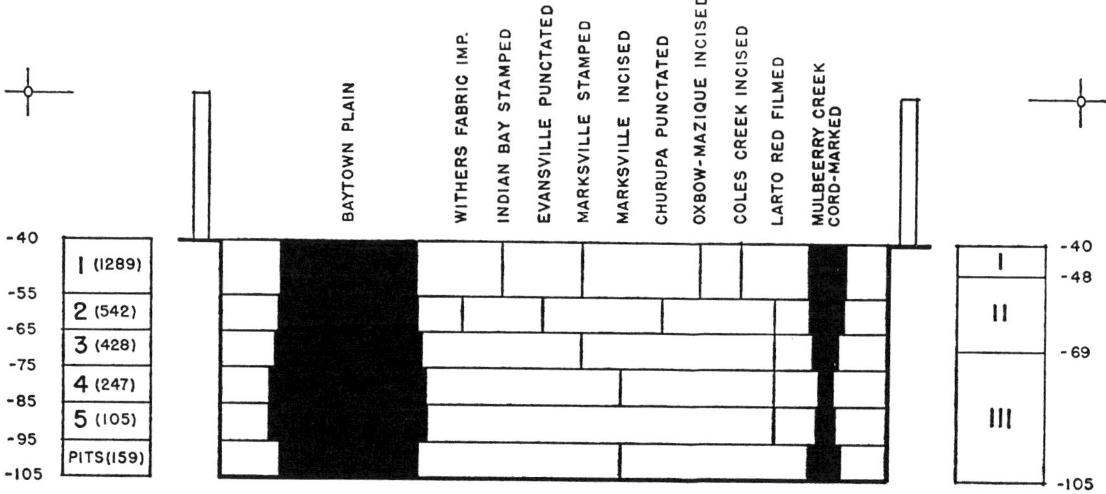

Fig. 42. Stratigraphic diagram, Cut B, Massey Site (17-L-1).

Cut B (Figure 42)

At the extreme southern end of the site, in the southeast corner of the Massey field, is a low elevation about 30 meters in diameter which had every appearance of a house mound, much spread by cultivation. The surface collection made upon this mound in 1940 was 100 per cent clay-tempered, so it was a natural place to look for evidence of the earlier history of the site, though there were no indications of any great depth of deposits. The results of Cut B, put down in the center of the mound, bore out the surface indications of shallow depth as well as the general rule that a mound is not the best place to look for stratigraphy. However, it is worth presenting briefly, as it adds another and earlier chapter to the record of the cut already described.

the midden above and below the well-marked floor at the bottom of Zone II. Types known to be early are present in all levels, and it is safe to conclude that the entire deposit represents a relatively short time interval in the early Baytown Period, which conclusion, we are happy to say, agrees with the results of seriation in this area (fig. 18).

Discussion of the Massey Site

There is apparently a gap of uncertain length between the end of the occupation represented by Cut B and the lowest level of Cut A, but aside from this, the two cuts taken together probably give a reasonably complete picture of the chronology of the site, with the main occupation extending through most of the Baytown Period, followed by a relatively thin and presumably brief occupation in the Mississippi Period. This evidence is not clear enough to permit use of the term "reoccupation," though the situation has been tentatively interpreted in that sense. The site as a whole is evidently considerably earlier than the Menard Site, where the proportions are reversed, a heavy and possibly long Mississippi occupation (again we hesitate to use the word "reoccupation"), following a relatively short occupation in the Baytown Period. Taking the two sites together, we get a sketchy outline of the local archaeology covering a considerable period of time on both sides of the thin and possibly imaginary line that separates the Baytown and Mississippi periods, but as yet no conclusive evidence as to what that line means in terms of cultural dynamics. It therefore goes without saying that these sites, together with the intervening Wallace and Poor sites — not forgetting the possible De Soto and Quapaw connections — would be an excellent place for further work on the important problem of Baytown-Mississippi relationships.

JAKETOWN SITE (20–O–1)

This site was located by Griffin late in the 1941 field season and immediately marked down for stratigraphic testing. The surface collection made at the time "had everything." However, it was not until 1946 that we were able to get back to do it. The two cuts put down by Phillips and Gebhard at this time more than fulfilled expectations, affording not only an almost complete recapitulation of ceramic history in the area, but also a quite unlooked-for glimpse of what may turn out to be a pre-pottery horizon.

The site is located about 3½ miles north of Belzoni, Humphries County, Mississippi, on the west bank of Wasp Lake, a former Ohio River channel. It consists of a characteristic Mississippi Period assemblage of rectangular platform mounds, the largest showing definite traces of a ramp, but it was clear from the surface indications alone that these mounds had been constructed upon a very much older village site with extensive midden accumulations (fig. 43).

Cut A (Figure 44)

Prior to locating stratigraphic cuts, the whole site was examined rather thoroughly and tested with a 3½-foot post-hole auger, which in most places failed to reach bottom. From the standpoint of early material, the most promising midden appeared to be that located in the southeastern portion of the site between the highway and Wasp Lake. Here an old pit about 3 feet deep, the result of digging out a stump, permitted a deeper sounding with the auger and, as it still failed to reach bottom, Cut A was put down as near this old pit as practicable. It proved to be an excellent location. The midden at this point was about 2 meters deep and unusually well furnished with potsherds in all but the lowest levels, where their absence was far more interesting than their presence would have been. Of soil stratification there was none. Below the plowed zone (Zone I) extended a uniform dark brown to black midden deposit containing scattered shells, fragments of bone and pottery (Zone II), which at about –185 cm. gave place gradually to the sterile olive-brown sub-soil of the region. The transition was complete at –215 cm., but another 10 cm. level was dug to make sure. Upon completion of the cut, the walls were carefully troweled and studied without the slighest result. Not only were there no observable lines of stratification but there were not even any local features worthy of recording. We have encountered a similar homogeneity in some of the midden deposits already described, but nowhere so deep nor so comprehensive in respect to pottery chronology.

In all, seventeen culture-bearing levels were excavated of which only the first fourteen contained sufficient pottery to be treated diagrammatically. As a matter of fact, the sherd total in Level 14 (23) would ordinarily be judged insufficient for graphic presentation, but this being the first time that Tchula Period types have shown up stratigraphically in a significant fashion, we cannot afford to be too particular in regard to their numerical strength. Levels 15 and 16 had only six and four sherds, respectively, but contained a large number of fragments of Poverty Point objects about which we shall have more to say presently. Level 17 contained a few fragments of Poverty Point objects and nothing else.

The stratigraphy speaks for itself, most of the types falling into their proper places as though under orders. In general, it is remarkably confirmatory of the results obtained by seriation in this area (fig. 17). The Tchula Period, represented for the first time stratigraphically, corresponds roughly to Levels 11 to 14; the bulk of the midden, Levels 4 to 10, is Baytown with early and middle periods well represented, and a somewhat doubtful showing of the late. The Mississippi Period is well represented in Levels 1 to 3. There is the

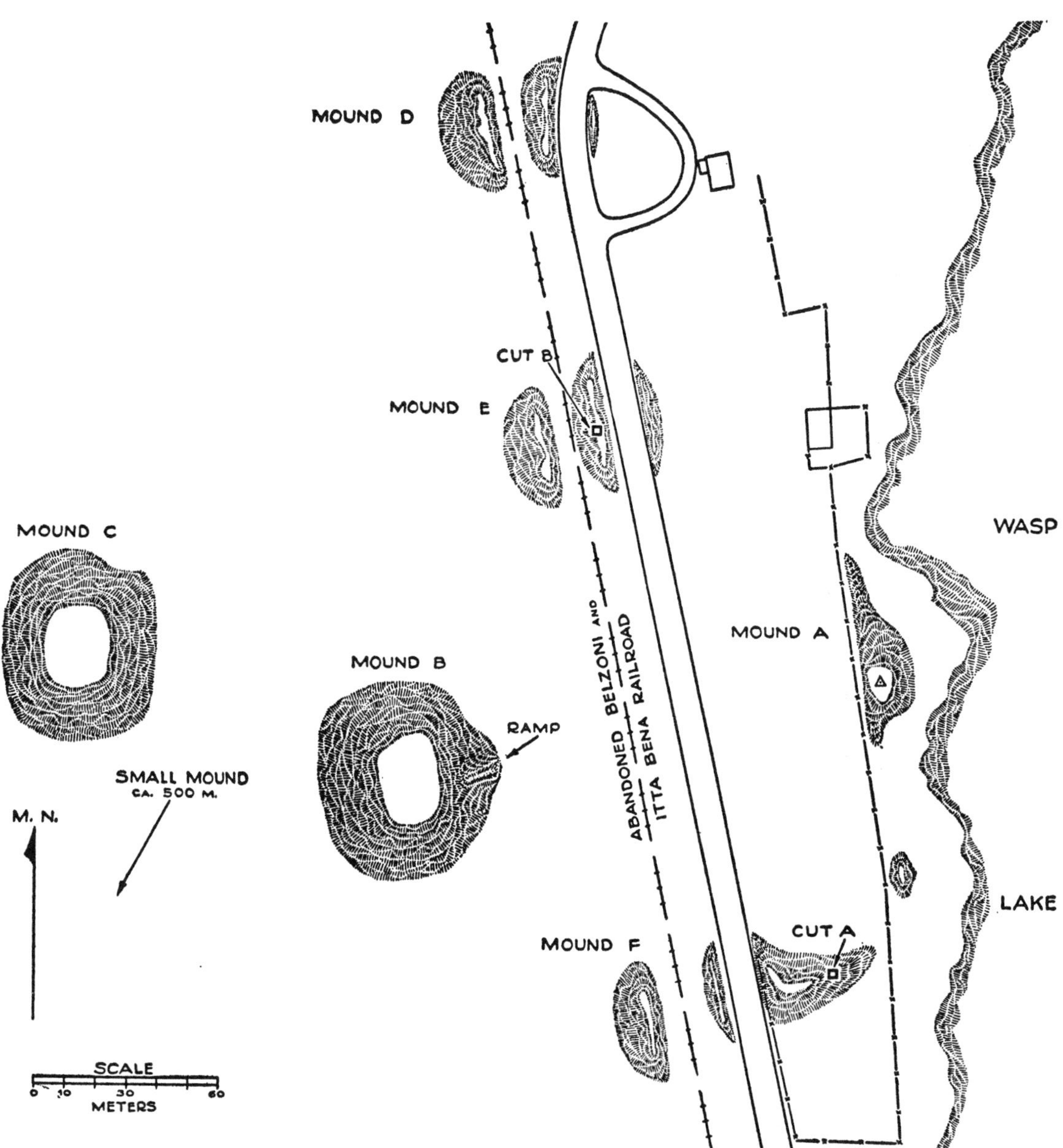

Fig. 43. Plan of Jaketown Site (20–O–1).

usual difficulty of interpreting the relationship of the Mississippi material to the underlying Baytown. It is, in fact, becoming increasingly apparent that the weakness of our whole chronological scheme lies in this late Baytown–early Mississippi transitional zone. In short, a rather definite break is indicated, though not confirmed by ground stratification, between what we are calling Tchula and the Baytown Period, which seems to indicate that we have been justified in setting the earlier period off by its own designation. That

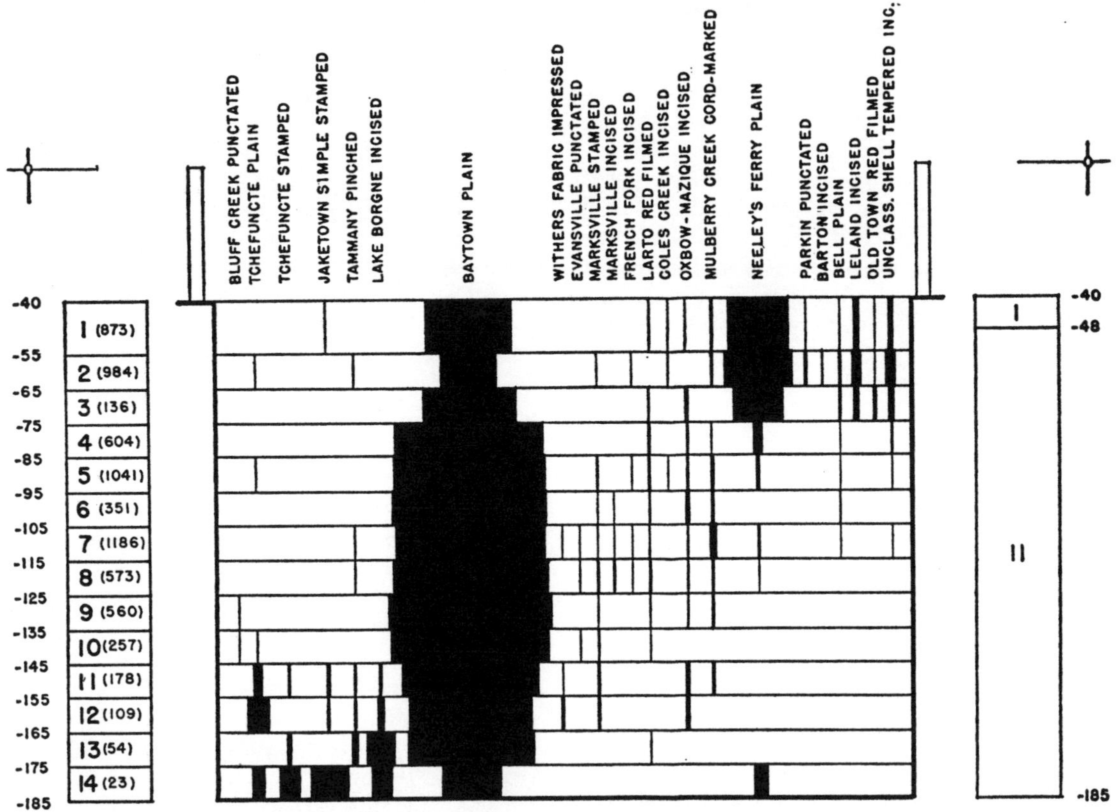

Fig. 44. Stratigraphic diagram, Cut A, Jaketown Site (20–O–1).

Before commenting further on the general interpretation of the cut, however, it may be worth-while to consider briefly certain distributions in detail. The depth here is sufficient to give some idea of the life span, if we may be permitted to use such an expression, of individual types. Beginning at the bottom, it is noteworthy that the early types, Tammany Pinched and Lake Borgne Incised are neatly concentrated into Levels 11 to 14, with surprisingly little indication of persistence on into later times. Their scattered appearance in ones and twos higher up in the midden is just what we have learned to expect and may be put down to sorting errors or mechanical causes about which it is idle to speculate. In Bluff Creek Punctated, our only fiber-tempered type, is not down in there with the early types is rather surprising. Possibly, the idea that fiber-tempering lies at or near the base of the pottery development in our area is a premature assumption. Withers Fabric-impressed is poorly represented in this cut, as in this area generally, but its vertical distribution backs up the early date we have already assigned to it in the areas further north where it is a more important type.

The specifically early Baytown Period types, Marksville Stamped and Marksville Incised, occupy their appropriate positions in the lower central part of the midden with some overlap into the lower levels, followed closely by French Fork Incised and Larto Red Filmed. The latter is never a good time-marker. Like Baytown Plain, it needs further subdivision when we have the necessary shape information. Nevertheless, its vertical distribution here may be significant, and if so we can tentatively state that it reached its maximum in the middle Baytown Period, a very close agreement with the results of seriation in this area. These types are followed by a weak showing of Coles Creek Incised, marker type for the late Baytown Period. All this agrees with Lower Valley sequences in a manner that is almost too good to be true. If Ford had built this midden with his own hands, he would not have done it differently.

The long vertical distribution of the material designated as Oxbow-Mazique Incised betrays the weakness of our classification in respect to this particular type. Its maximum, however, corresponds closely with that of Larto Red Filmed, strongly suggesting that here at least it relates chiefly to the middle Baytown Period.

The vertical distribution of Mulberry Creek Cord-marked is very interesting. It is possible to say pretty definitely that it was not here at all in the Tchula Period. Apparently, it comes in, in a small way, about the end of that period and rises to a modest peak about the beginning of the middle Baytown Period, going out again in the late Baytown. Its presence in Levels 1 and 2 need not trouble us. There was material from all periods on the surface of this midden and sufficient disturbance below the plowed zone (mentioned in the field notes) to have allowed it to get into Level 2 as well. Notwithstanding the small percentages involved, the distribution corresponds very well with the seriation in this and other areas.

Getting back to our basic difficulty, the interpretation of the Baytown-Mississippi relationship, there is not very much we can say about the particular situation revealed here. Having no soil stratification to serve as control for the pottery stratigraphy, we have to accept the latter at its face value, so to speak. It shows an abrupt replacement of Baytown by Mississippi types in Levels 1 to 3, masked somewhat by the heavy percentage of early types in Level 1, most of which can be attributed to redistribution. The break, if there is one, comes between Levels 3 and 4. Starting with Level 5, we have a pottery complex that does not look later than middle Baytown, leaving precious little space for late Baytown and early Mississippi. We are obliged to do one of three things: (1) postulate a discontinuity in the upper levels of this cut, for which there is no evidence in the ground; (2) assign Levels 1 to 3 to late Baytown, notwithstanding the heavy showing of late Mississippi Period types; or (3) admit that we still have a lot to learn about Baytown-Mississippi relationships in this, as well as some other areas. The first alternative is chosen here, the second was chosen in seriating (see fig. 20), and the third is self-evident.

Cut B (Figures 45 and 47)

There are three pairs of small mounds strung out along the highway that passes through the Jaketown Site. The easternmost of the middle pair, Mound E, is cut in half by the highway, the ditch face exposing a rich dark midden deposit under the mound. By making a small excavation in the bottom of the ditch and sinking an auger hole in the bottom of that, we were able to sound to a total depth of 2½ meters from the top of the mound. The dark midden soil ran out at about 2 meters, but a half meter farther down, along with what looked like sterile sub-soil, the auger brought up a fragment of a stone point. This indicated the possibility of an earlier occupation underneath the midden, and it was therefore decided to put a cut down from the surface of the mound, notwithstanding our experience of the general unfavorability of mounds for stratigraphic testing. We did not find out until Cut B was well along that these curiously regular pairs of mounds were partly of recent origin, the result of an ephemeral railroad, the Belzoni and Itta Bena, passing through three higher spots which probably were mounds. Not only were six mounds produced where there were but three before, but they received an increment in the form of the earth dug out of the railroad cut. This fact will have to be taken into account in discussing the stratification. If we had known about it in time, we would have dug somewhere else, but in spite of all the disturbances in the upper levels, the cut was distinctly worth-while as we shall see.

The stratification is best shown in figure 47.

Zone I. −19 cm. (on the uphill side) to −45 cm. An ill-defined zone of loose brown soil containing shell, charcoal, bone, and sherds, interpreted as the fill taken from the railroad cut, mentioned above. The uncertain bottom of this deposit was penetrated by pits and post-holes, possibly of recent origin (fence posts, etc.), possibly relating to an occupation level on the mound through which the railroad cut was made. These disturbances penetrated deeply into Zone II as shown in figure 47.

Zone II. −45 cm. to −120 cm. A lighter brown soil, more compact and containing less pottery, no shell or bone, and very little charcoal. This was interpreted by the excavator as mound fill, containing culture material from the older village site. The bottom of this zone was well defined and approximately level.

Zone III. −120 cm. to −175 cm. Rich dark brown to black midden containing shell, bone, charcoal, and many sherds, corresponding in all probability to Zone II in Cut A. The bottom of this zone was fairly level, except for post-holes and pits penetrating into the zone below.

Zone IV. −175 cm. to −215 cm. A compact, sterile layer composed of olive-brown clay silt, lighter in color than Zones I, II, and III. This sterile layer was penetrated by several small pits and a good many post-holes originating above in Zone III. The soil of this zone where undisturbed by these features was definitely sterile. A great deal of care was taken by the excavator to determine this point. On the other hand, nothing was said in the notes that would indicate in any way its origin, whether wind- or water-laid, etc.

Zone V. −215 cm. to −235 cm. A darker stratum of olive-brown clay silt, similar to that of Zone IV except in color, containing charcoal, some bone, very little shell, a great many Poverty Point fragments, and very few if any sherds. Both upper and lower boundaries of this zone were very indistinct, and

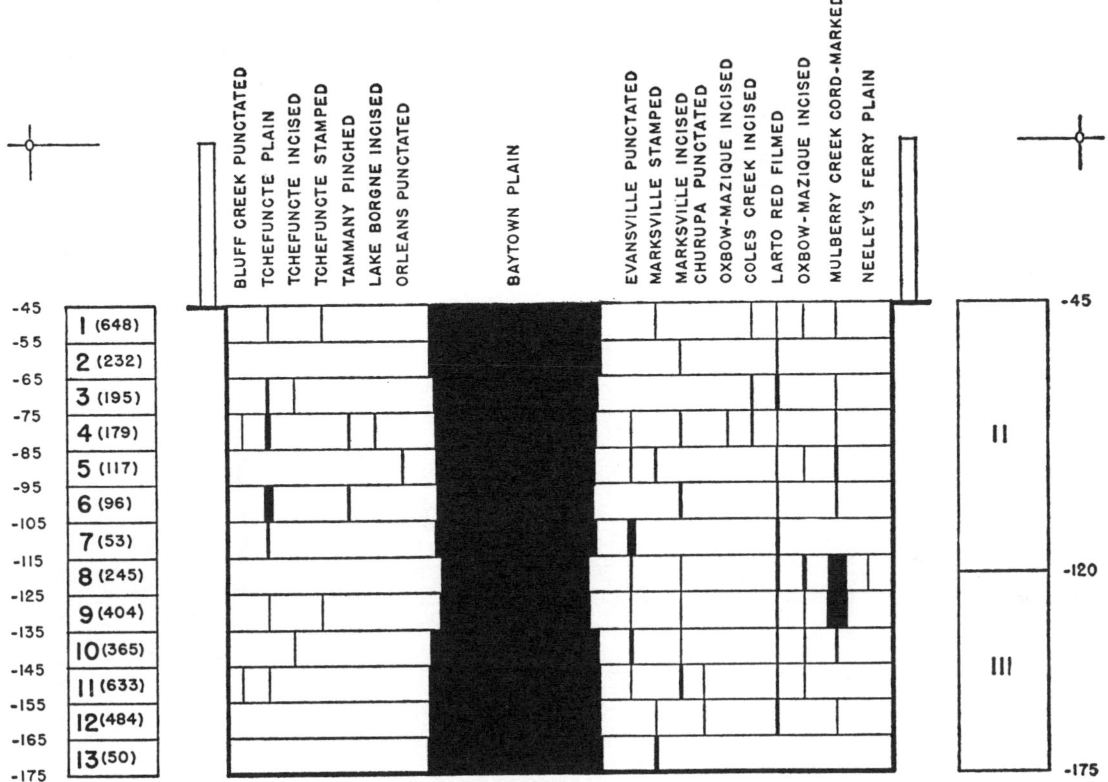

FIG. 45. Stratigraphic diagram, Cut B, Jaketown Site (20-O-1).

there were lenses of the lighter-colored soil within it.[19]

Zone VI. −235 cm. to −265 cm. Same as Zone IV, except for occasional flecks of charcoal and small fragments of Poverty Point objects.

The pottery stratigraphy shown in figure 45 may be described very briefly. The disturbed soil comprising Zone I was removed in leveling off, so the stratigraphic record begins at the top of Zone II. The stratigraphy in this zone, Levels 1 to 7, shows a complete scramble of Tchula and Baytown Period types, which is all the proof we require that this zone consists of mound fill scraped off a pre-existing village site, as the excavator believed at the time. Zone III corresponds closely in pottery content to the middle portion of Zone II in Cut A (Levels 7 to 10, approximately); in other words, early and early middle Baytown. Thus the mound fill contained earlier material than the village midden upon which it was built, resulting in a reversed stratigraphy which would be disconcerting if the reason for it were not apparent. There is a little stratigraphy within Zone III, but the only new feature is the possible priority of Marksville Stamped over Marksville Incised. Below Zone III, there was not enough pottery to show on the graph. In these lower zones the interest shifts to Poverty Point objects and their chronological relationship to the pottery on the site.

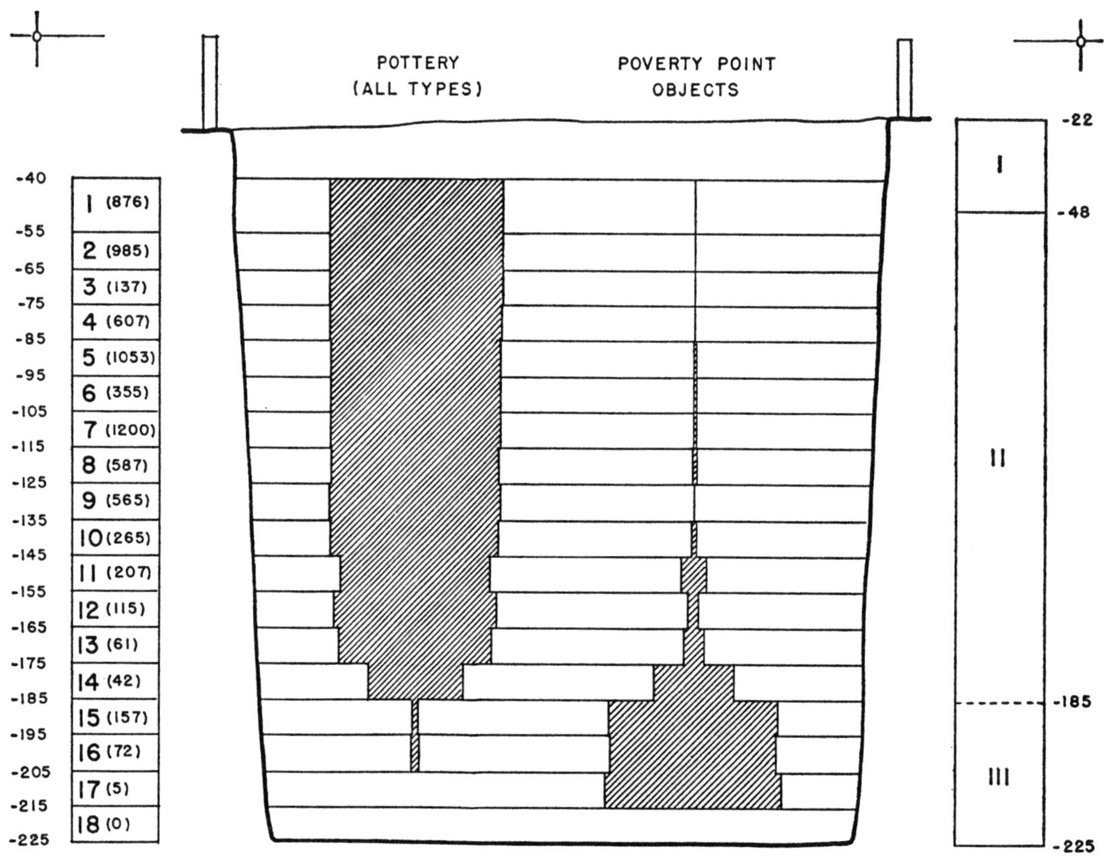

FIG. 46. Stratigraphic diagram showing vertical distribution of pottery and Poverty Point objects, Cut A, Jaketown Site (20–O–1).

[19] "There seems to be some admixture of lighter olive-drab soil and this whole stratum may actually consist of as many as three very thin dark habitation zones separated by equally thin olive-drab soil zones." Gebhard's field notes.

A Pre-Ceramic Horizon?

Figures 46 and 47 were drawn to show the vertical distribution of Poverty Point objects in the two Jaketown cuts in relation to pottery in general without regard to type. Totals by level, in the left-hand column include both sherds and fragments of Poverty Point objects. These curious and enigmatic artifacts have been described in many publications.[20] Here, it is sufficient to note that they occurred mainly in fragmentary condition and that the fragments are often indistinguishable from ordinary lumps of fired clay. In the present study only those pieces were counted that showed enough of the original surface of the object to leave no doubt as to their nature. Probably most of the clay fragments not counted were from Poverty Point objects as well, so the stratigraphic results shown here might have been even more telling. They are sufficiently striking as it is.

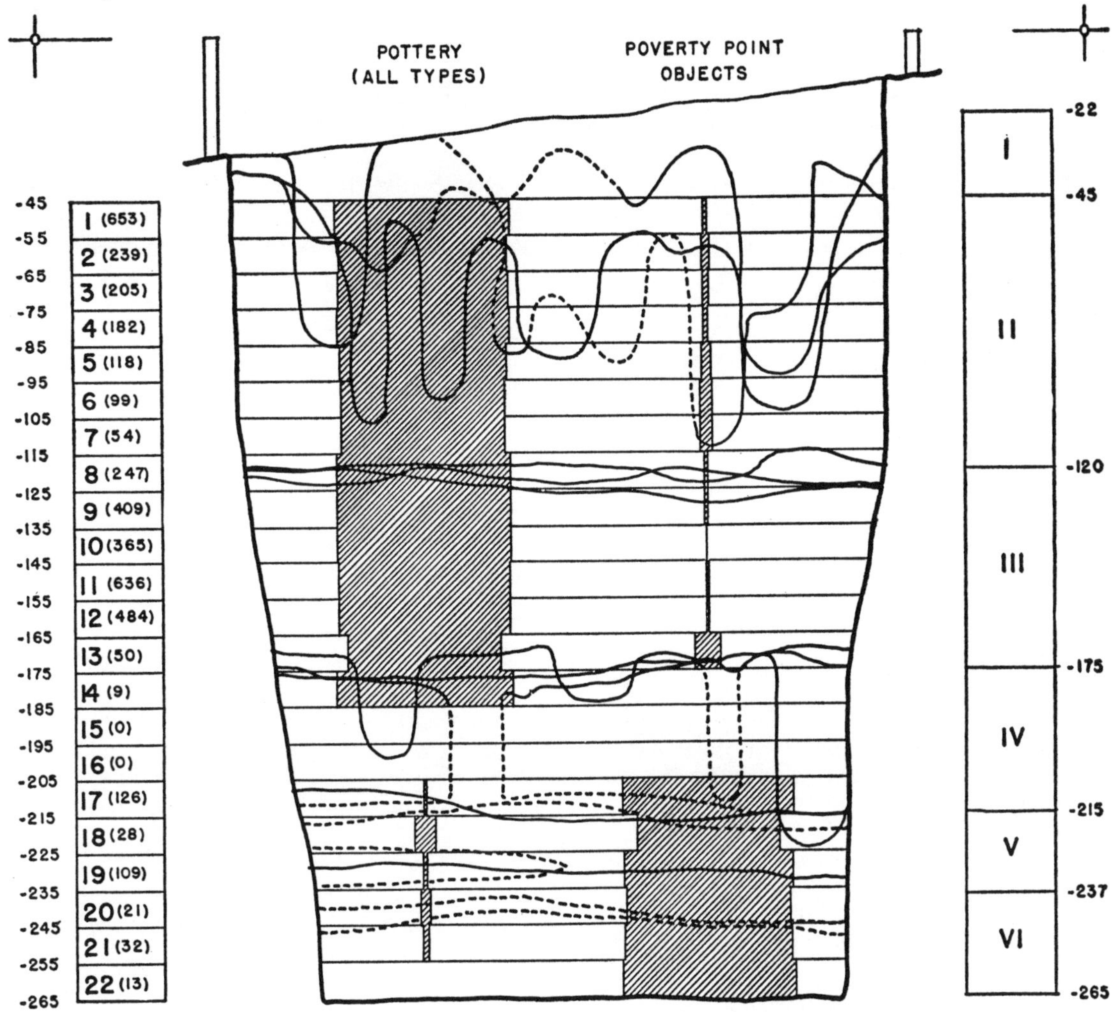

Fig. 47. Composite profile drawing showing vertical distribution of pottery and Poverty Point objects, Cut B, Jaketown Site (20–O–1).

In Cut A (fig. 46) is clearly exhibited the general priority of Poverty Point objects over pottery. This is nothing new. What we would

[20] Moore, 1913, pp. 72–74, pl. 2; Ford and Quimby, 1945, p. 31, pl. 1; Webb, 1944, pp. 386–94.

like to be able to establish is the hypothesis that the Poverty Point objects represent a pre-pottery, hence pre-Tchula, period on this site. There is better evidence in Cut B, but a strong case could have been made on the basis of Cut A alone. The only difficulty is that in this cut there was no apparent change in the character of the deposit coinciding with the abrupt shift from pottery to Poverty Point objects in the neighborhood of Level 14. The dotted line in the right-hand column at −185 cm. simply represents an arbitrary point which might be regarded as the bottom of the midden. The change in color from almost black midden soil to the olive-brown sub-soil began at −155 cm. and was complete at −225 cm. Minus 185 cm. is thus only a kind of average. The bulk of the Poverty Point objects in Levels 15 and 16 lay in soil, therefore, that scarcely differed from the sterile sub-soil. It gave no appearance whatever of being an occupation level distinct from the overlying midden. All of which makes it very difficult to imagine how they got there, a difficulty which is not lessened by the fact that we do not know what they are.

The situation in Cut B (fig. 47) is more interesting. Starting at the top, we have in Zone II a considerable number of Poverty Point fragments which bears out the conclusions already drawn from the appearance of the soil and the pottery evidence, that this zone is mound fill, containing material from the older portions of the site. Percentages of Poverty Point objects vis-a-vis pottery in Zone III correspond to those in the middle portion of Zone II in Cut A, so closely that we might almost be led to think we were practising an exast science. (Compare Cut B, Levels 8 to 13 with Cut A, Levels 5 to 11.) Zone IV was as barren of Poverty Point objects as of everything else, which makes Zone V extremely interesting. This zone gave evidence of being an occupation level, or a series of superimposed levels separated by thin lenses of sterile soil, probably water-laid. There is no question about its being distinct from Zone III, the main pottery-bearing deposit. It becomes important, therefore, to examine the pottery in Zone V and figure out if possible how it got there. To begin with, the amounts are very small, one sherd in Level 17, three in each of Levels 18 and 19, one in each of Levels 20 and 21. All but one of these nine sherds are Baytown Plain, the exception being a sherd of clearly recognizable Oxbow-Mazique Incised. The fact that there are no early (Tchula Period) types among this handful of sherds is significant. In Cut A, it will be remembered, the Poverty Point-bearing levels were immediately overlain by levels containing sizable percentages of Tchula Period types. The question then resolves itself into this: Is it possible to account for the presence of these nine sherds in Levels 17 to 21 otherwise than by assuming that they are contemporary with the Poverty Point objects in those levels? There are two such possibilities to be considered, both having to do with the mechanics of excavation.

When a 2-meter-square pit reaches a depth of 2 meters or thereabouts, it becomes difficult to throw the dirt out with a shovel. Gebhard resorted to the use of an ash can hauled up to the surface by means of a rope. In spite of all care, it was impossible to prevent the can from occasionally banging against the walls of the cut, which might have dislodged a few sherds.[21] The other means by which these sherds could have found their way into the Poverty Point levels is the more likely one. When Gebhard got down to the sterile soil of Zone IV, he encountered a number of post-holes and pits filled with the dark midden soil of Zone III. These he excavated individually, throwing the material away, and it is fortunate that he did so, otherwise we would not be able to say that Zone IV was sterile. Some of these pits, as may be seen in the profiles on figure 47, penetrated down into the darker strata of Zone V. Upon reaching dark soil again, it would have been difficult, if not impossible, to continue separate excavation of the pits, and there is no evidence in the notes

[21] In his notes on Level 16 in Cut A, Gebhard writes, "Poverty Point fragments still very common but sherds have become scarce. It is possible, that of these sherds, a few fell from above as in lifting out the heavy garbage can, it occasionally banged against the walls of the pit. Precautions against such a mixture of stratigraphy were taken, but one or two sherds may have escaped us."

that Gebhard did so below Level 16. Therefore, it is possible that sherds got into Zone V via the fill of these pits.

In sum, while we cannot say categorically that there is a pre-pottery or non-pottery horizon on the Jaketown Site, there is at least a very strong presumption that such is the case. If this be admitted, it follows as a strong probability that the Tchefuncte-like pottery complex of the Tchula Period is the earliest pottery in this part of the Alluvial Valley. It goes without saying that further excavations ought to be carried out on this extremely interesting and important site.

SHELL BLUFF SITE (19-O-2)

Shell Bluff is one of the few shell-heap sites found by the Survey, and for this reason was tested by Phillips and Gebhard in 1946. The site is located on the west bank of the Yazoo River about 7 miles due south of the town of Itta Bena, LeFlore County, Mississippi, on property belonging to Mr. W. G. Poindexter, to whom thanks are due for permission to excavate. It consists of a large shell midden with one or several mounds built upon it. The mound, or mounds — it is not clear whether we have to do here with three mounds or one mound with three summits — is irregular in shape and badly eroded, about 2½ meters high and of uncertain dimensions, and impossible to classify (fig. 48). The shell midden, of more immediate interest than the mound, extends along the river bank for about 225 meters. Its extent back from the river was not ascertainable, as the area is covered with turf and vegetation. Being located on an outside bend, bank-caving has exposed a vertical profile of the shell stratum over most of its length, out of which it was possible to pluck enough sherds to get a fair idea of the stratigraphy prior to excavation. Shell content, in the richest portion of the midden, estimated at 75 per cent of the total bulk, consisted mainly of whole shells of the genus Unio. There was some evidence, not altogether conclusive, that the thickest part of the midden had already been carried away by the river. In any case, its situation on an outside bend renders it very probable that the present is only a remnant of the original midden, and by the same token it can be inferred that the oldest part no longer exists.

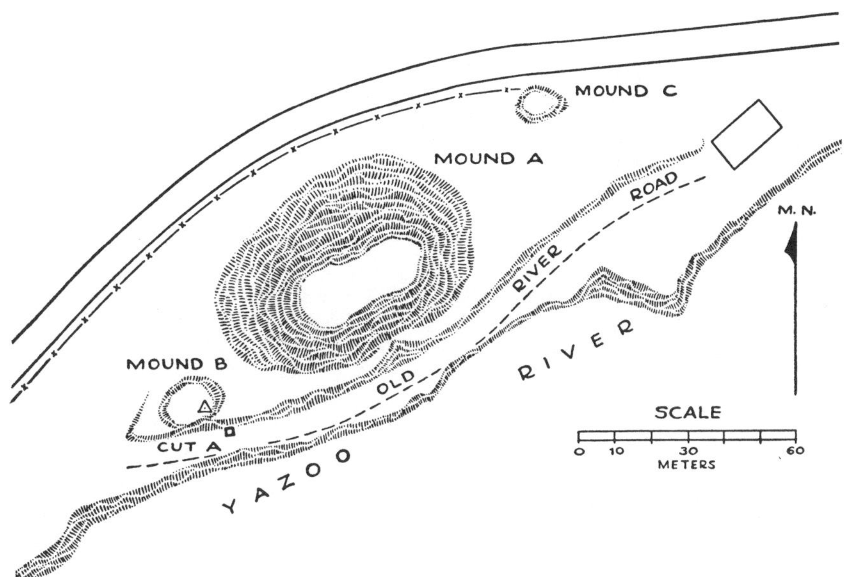

Fig. 48. Plan of Shell Bluff Site (19-O-2).

The greatest thickness of shells exposed in

the river bank, about 1 meter in depth, was a short distance down stream from the highest part of the mound, so it was decided to test here in the hope of finding, in addition to pottery stratigraphy, some evidence of the relationship of mound and midden. At this point an old roadway cuts into the mound forming a narrow shelf between it and the river bank. Cut A (fig. 49) was laid out on this old roadway with its north side a slight distance up the mound slope. By this means, it was possible to determine that the mound was built on top of the midden, the evidence for which will be discussed presently.

Stratification is difficult to describe, because that of the north profile, on the mound side, showed additional features not appearing in the cut as a whole.

Zone I. −25 cm. to −36 cm. Compact, light-colored clay soil, containing a small amount of finely broken shell but no charcoal and no bone. On the north side this zone was about 30 cm. thick, from which it tapered off to almost nothing on the south wall. Also on the mound side this zone was underlain with a thin compact stratum of water-laid clay about 10 cm. thick, which tapered off very rapidly and did not appear on the south profile at all. This condition was shown most clearly on the east wall profile (fig. 50).

Zone II. −36 cm. to −120 cm. Dark midden soil with an estimated 50 to 80 per cent shell content and large quantities of charcoal and bone. The upper surface of this midden sloped upward from north to south, indicating that the mound had been built on the landward slope of the original shell heap. The lower limit of the midden was at approximately −120 cm., though some additional material was recovered from pits extending down into the sub-soil, not shown in the diagram.

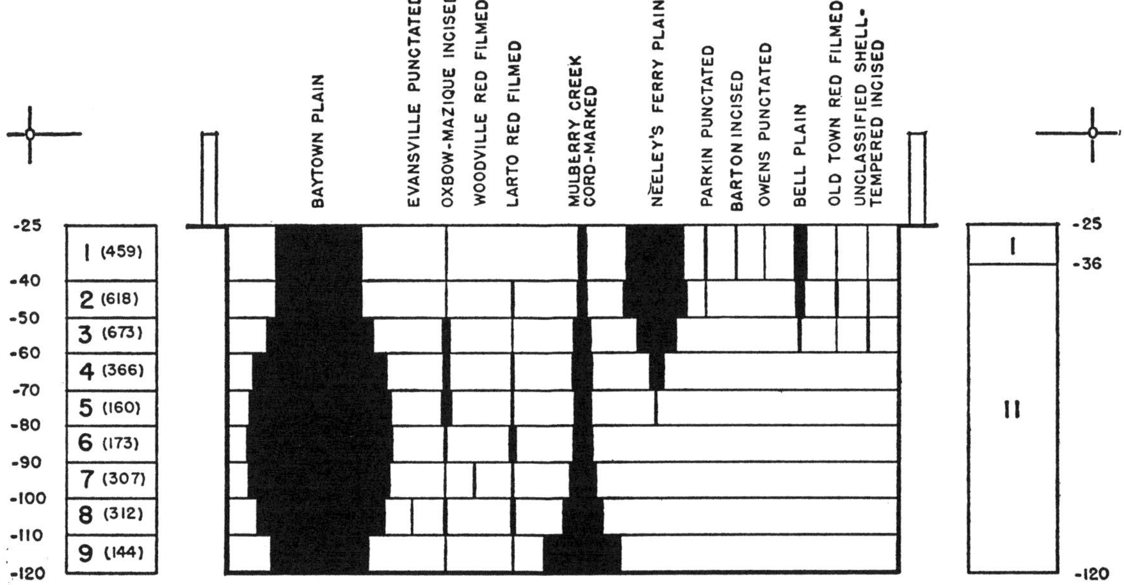

Fig. 49. Stratigraphic diagram, Cut A, Shell Bluff Site (19-O-2).

The stratigraphic interpretation of this cut appears to be relatively simple. The effect of the mound hard by is confined to Level 1. Below −40 cm. we are in a homogeneous shell midden with no observable break in stratification to correspond to the introduction and rise in shell-tempered percentages in the upper levels. This is the second clear instance (the first being the Massey Cut A) in which a pottery situation suggesting the replacement of a clay- by a shell-tempered complex is found, without any discontinuity in the ground stratification to correlate with it. The main bulk of the midden is middle to late Baytown. If there is continuity here, the shell-tempered complex must be early Mississippi. Offhand, it does not look it. Bell Plain, in some areas, has been used as a late Mississippi determinant. However, as repeatedly emphasized, this type gives the greatest difficulty in sorting outside the Memphis area where it was first set up, and this is a case in point. The sherds classified here as Bell Plain are indistinguishable from the type material in surface finish but are distinctly thinner. A random sample of twenty sherds from Levels 2 and 3 gave an average thickness of 4.5 mm., as compared with 6.9 mm. for the type material. Several of these sherds are from sharply profiled bowls, probably of the "cazuela" form, a shape which is rare or absent in typical Bell Plain of the Memphis area. Further indication that this polished plain ware is not the equivalent of Bell Plain is found in the lack of the usual decorated types associated with that type, and the substitution therefor of decorative types which we have not yet defined. In particular, there was in the same polished thin ware a delicately engraved rim sherd from a "cazuela"-type bowl quite distinct from anything so far encountered in the area (fig. 51).[22] It is clear, therefore, that we are outside the limits of competence of our present classification, so there is no occasion to regard the Bell Plain minority here as indicative of a late Mississippi Period. This being the case, the time span of the cut as a whole may be estimated as running from sometime in middle Baytown through late Baytown into the early Mississippi Period, without any significant "break" in continuity indicated. This agrees closely with the position given on the seriation chart for this area (fig. 20).

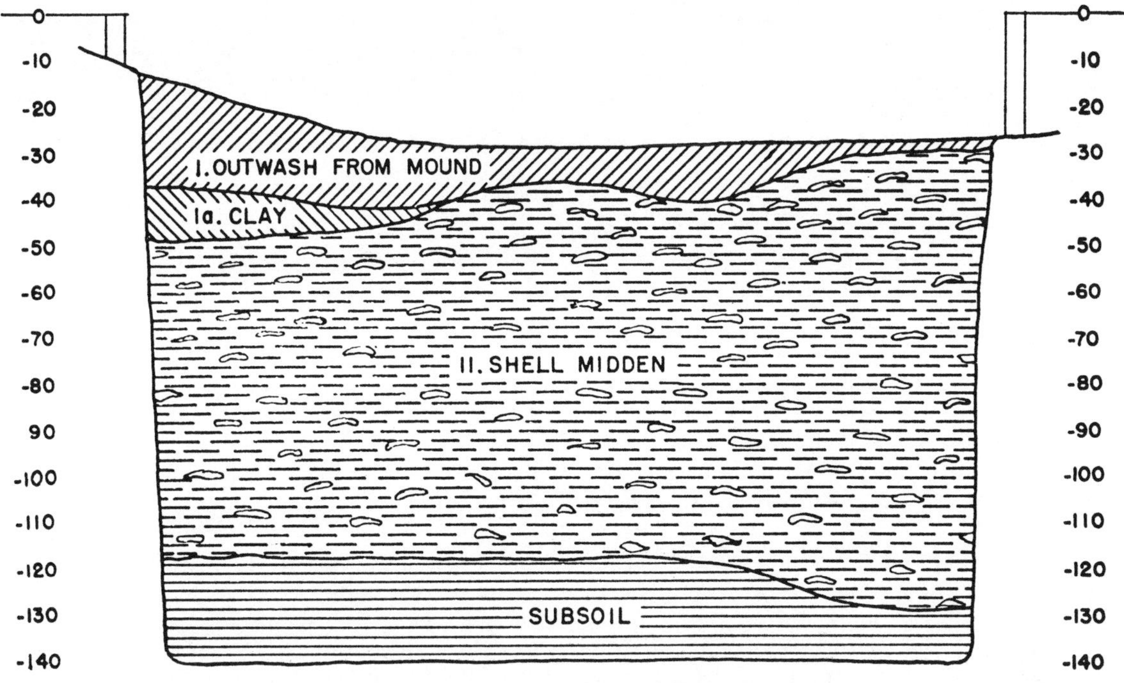

Fig. 50. Profile, East Wall, Cut A, Shell Bluff Site (19-O-2).

That the mound, or mounds, were built upon and subsequent to the shell midden is sufficiently clear from the diagram of the east wall profile (fig. 50). The fact that the pottery-type distribution in Level 1 which consisted mainly of mound fill and/or outwash differs scarcely at all from that of Level 2 (which was definitely in the midden) indicates either that there was no significant time

[22] The nearest approach to this sherd is the type Holly Fine Engraved, recently described by Krieger from the Davis Site in east Texas (Newell and Krieger, 1949).

interval between midden and mound or that the latter was constructed of soil taken from the upper levels only of the midden. This latter seems inherently improbable, so it is perhaps safe to say that midden and mound represent a single continuous occupation. This profile is also our best evidence that the midden was formerly of greater extent and thickness. The upper surface of the midden is highest on the river side from which it is evident that the mound was built on its landward slope. On the other hand, the bottom of the midden was lowest on the river side, indicating that it was formerly not only of greater extent but also deeper. This at least encourages the hope that we may yet find on the Yazoo River shell heaps comparable to those on the Tennessee.

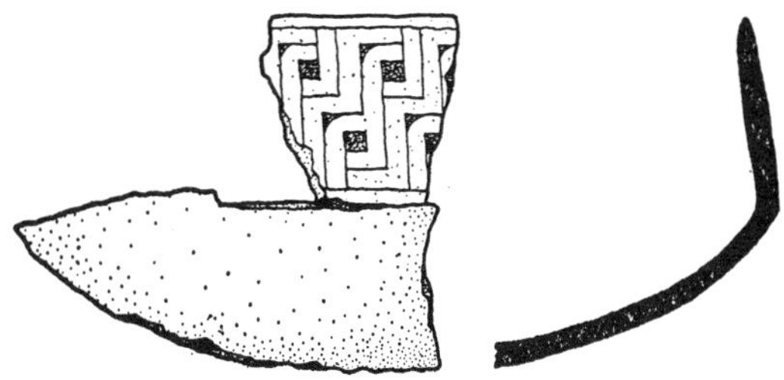

Fig. 51. Engraved sherd from Level 2, Cut A, Shell Bluff Site (19-O-2).

ROSE MOUND (12-N-3)

The Rose "mound," a famous resort of archaeologists and pot-hunters for many years, was tested as an afterthought by Phillips in the spring of 1947. Having in 1946 decided to publish this preliminary report, the writers felt that it would be excessively incomplete without at least one stratigraphic test in the St. Francis area. The Rose Site was chosen because it was the only large St. Francis-type site visited by the Survey in 1940 that showed a significant minority of clay-tempered types in the surface collection. A secondary reason for interest in this site is the fact that C. B. Moore, who made a rich haul of pottery from it during 1910, illustrates many vessels that would be more at home on the Mississippi in the Memphis area.[23] It was hoped that a stratigraphic test in this site might clarify the chronological relationships of these two subareas.

The site (fig. 52) is located about a half mile south of the St. Francis River (east bank), 4 miles southeast of Parkin, Cross County, Arkansas, on the Tipler Farm, to whose owner, Mr. A. J. Tipler, and manager, Mr. C. F. Stewart, we owe thanks for permission to dig and many kindnesses during our brief stay on the site.

About 300 meters south of the site lies a partly filled ox-bow lake representing, according to Fisk, a St. Francis channel of Stage 15,[24] but nearer at hand, on the west, is the remnant of what is probably a still older channel, now drained and difficult to locate exactly. It appears to have turned east and followed closely along the southern flank of the mound where it is now represented only by a shallow depression and a ditch. The northern boundary of the site is also flanked by what may have been a similar old channel. The eastern and western boundaries of the "mound" consist of broad ditches which look very much like artificial cuts, as though the inhabitants had cut through at these two points, the narrow tongue of higher land between two swales, one of which may have been an active channel at the time. Thus, in effect, the site occupies a sort of rectangular island surrounded on all four sides by depressions of slight depth which increase the mound-like effect the site gives when viewed from any direction (fig. 74, *c*). It is about 300 meters long by 150 meters wide at one end and 100 meters at the other, and the total height above the surrounding depressed areas is at present about 4 meters. There are at present no traces of mounds upon its flat summit, which has evidently been under cultivation for some time, but in Moore's time, there was a mound 4 feet high and 40 feet in diameter, described by

[23] Moore, 1910, pp. 276–303.

[24] Fisk, 1944, pl. 15, sheet 1.

him as conical (which is hardly likely), not far from its center.[25] The visual effect which has caused this site to be invariably referred to as a "mound" is not altogether a deception. It is in fact a huge refuse mound, so sharply defined either by its "island" situation or by a former stockade — of which no evidences are at present visible — as to present the appearance of a deliberate artificial construction, which, of course, it is not. Like other large St. Francis sites of the Mississippi Period, it is simply a result of the accumulation of house remains and refuse in a circumscribed space. The depth of this accumulation was estimated from surface indications alone at 2 meters, and this turned out to be approximately correct for the portion excavated.

We have referred to the possible "ditches" to the east and west. One cannot help recalling the descriptions of Pacaha visited by De Soto in 1541 quoted at length in a later section (pp. 356–57). Though we presume that site to have been on or near the Mississippi, the description fits the Rose Mound in a way that is almost uncanny.

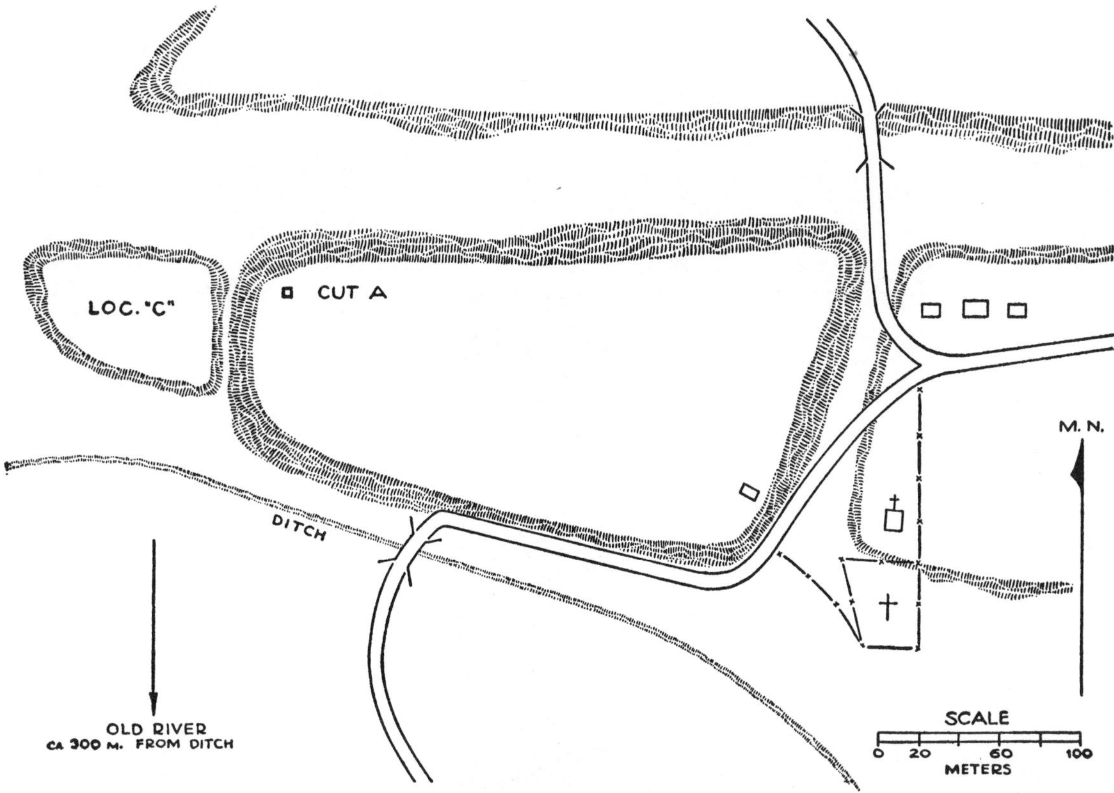

FIG. 52. Plan of Rose Mound (12–N–3).

Cut A (Figure 53)

The ditch on the west cuts off a smaller "island," designated as location "C" on the map (fig. 52), which also has village-site material upon it. The lower level of the surface and the large percentages of clay-tempered types show clearly that this is an older portion of the site and give a great deal of

[25] Moore, 1910, p. 277.

weight to the assumption that the ditch was artificial. This was the deciding factor in selecting a location for testing at the west end of the mound as near this ditch as was practicable. If, on getting down to a level comparable to that of location C we were to find a pottery situation similar to that on the surface at C, it could be assumed that the older village site was continuous and that the ditch was cut through at a subsequent time. This sounds like a large order for a 2-meter-square excavation, but it proved to be not inadequate for the purpose. The pottery in Zone IV of Cut A — to anticipate slightly — was identical in type distribution to the surface collection from location C and the absolute levels checked very closely, so there can be scarcely any doubt that the ditch cut through an older

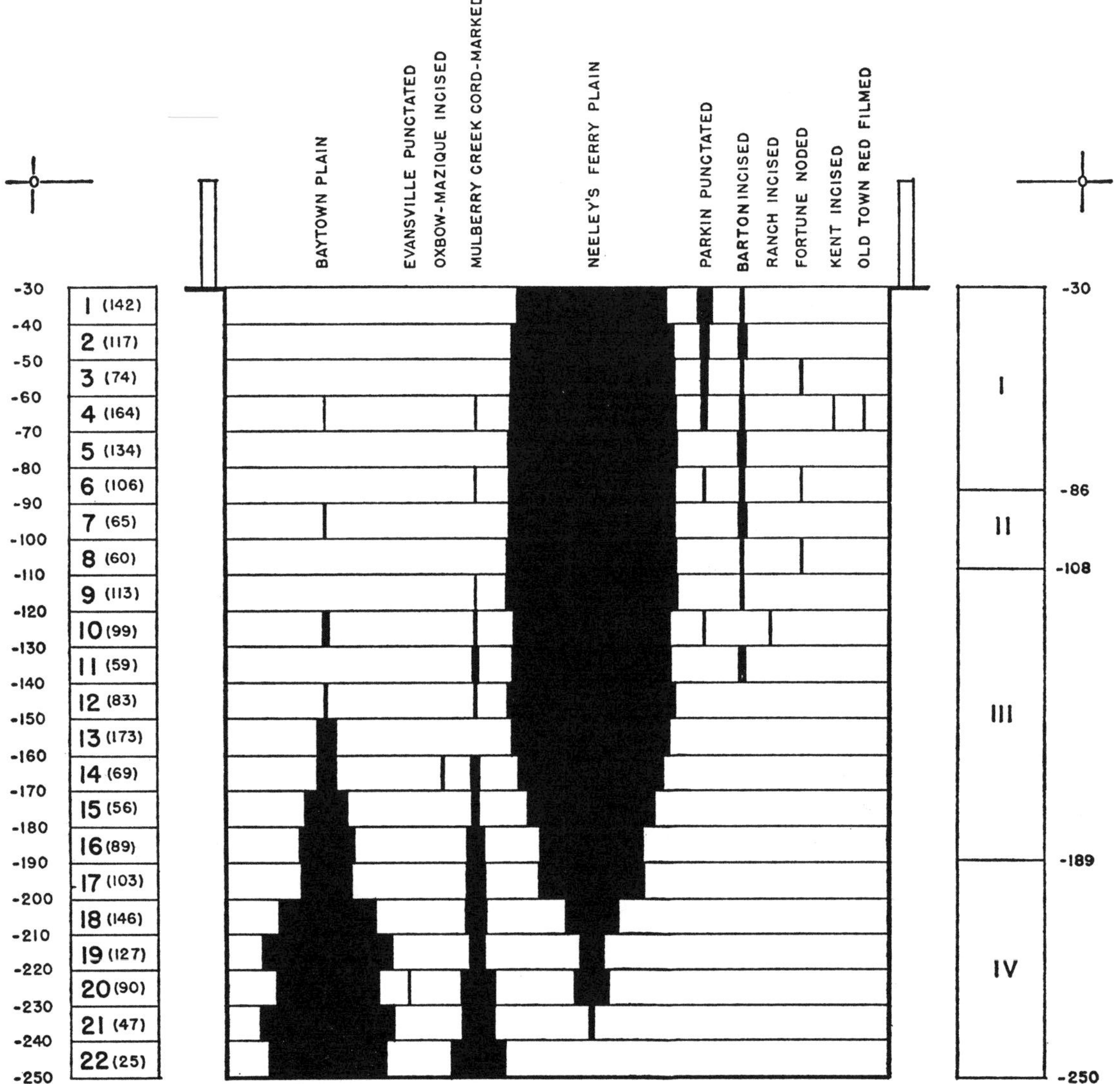

Fig. 53. Stratigraphic diagram, Cut A, Rose Mound (12-N-3).

village site and therefore was of artificial origin.

The stratification of this cut has a particularly important bearing on the interpretation of the pottery stratigraphy and will therefore be described in some detail.

Zone I. −30 cm. to −86 cm. Loose midden soil predominantly gray in color, containing scattered bits of charcoal but no concentrated lenses or beds of either ash or charcoal. Occasional bits of shell were present and a great deal of daub often in large chunks. Sherds not abundant. Except for the small portion of a grave containing an extended burial that obtruded into the cut at Level 5, filled with the same soil as the midden and therefore impossible to delineate, this zone was completely undisturbed so far as the excavator could determine. No post-holes or other features were observable. As the cotton furrows were removed before the start of excavation, the top of this zone at −30 corresponded approximately with the plow line.

Zone II. —86 cm. to —108 cm. Homogeneous olive-brown sand with dark vertical streaks interpreted as stains due to leaching from the darker midden above. Contained very little cultural material of any sort; in fact, the excavator thought he had reached sterile sub-soil at this point and was much disturbed thereby. There was no positive indication that this sand was water-laid, but it of course is quite possible since a thin layer of this description could be dumped in a single flood and hence fail to show any characteristic structure. That it was a lens, probably of merely local significance, is indicated by the fact that it pinched out in the northern part of the cut and failed to show on the north wall profile at all. This is also the reason why pottery counts, though sharply reduced in Levels 7 and 8, do not reflect the relatively sterility of this deposit.

Zone III. −108 cm. to −189 cm. Heterogeneous deposit of uneven texture and variegated color, ranging from gray to olive brown. Contained numerous lenses of sandy clay similar in color to Zone II but stickier in texture. Some of these had flat upper surfaces and showed traces of fire. According to the field notes, "these may have been floors, but if so, a poor sort of floor." There were numerous post-holes and other signs of local disturbance in this zone. It looked like a busy time at the Rose Site. At -130 cm. was an arcuate alignment of five post-holes, averaging 13 cm. in diameter, and spaced 36 cm. on centers, indicating a small circular structure with a diameter of approximately 3 meters. At -200 cm. a similar alignment showed up, but in this case it appeared to be straight. (It is hardly necessary to add that an alignment of five post-holes is not sufficient evidence for determining the shape of an entire structure.) Daub was present but not as abundant as in Zone I. The bottom of this zone sloped sharply from south to north and was rendered still more uneven by the intrusion of shallow post-holes into Zone IV below.

Zone IV. -189 cm. to -250 cm. Homogeneous dark brown sandy soil, gradually darker and more compact toward the bottom where it became a sort of "buckshot," finally changing to the light olive-brown sub-soil. Very little cultural material observed in the profiles, a few bits of burned clay (not daub), charcoal, and shell. Only features recorded in this zone were a thin lens of carbonized grass, possibly thatch, in Level 16, and one or two burned areas overlain with ash and charcoal. No post-holes were recorded and the absence of daub was specifically noted, so the evidence for house-building and house types was practically nil.

Interpretation of the pottery stratigraphy, though relatively simple and clear-cut, is extremely important for the general problem of Baytown-Mississippi relationships which has become the major theme of our stratigraphic comments. Zone I, comprising the superficial levels at the site, exhibits the full-blown St. Francis variety of the Mississippi complex which almost certainly represents the latest prehistoric occupation of this part of the St. Francis Basin. The comparatively sterile Zone II is probably of local significance only, as inferred from the field notes, since there is little or no perceptible change in pottery-type distributions from the lower levels of Zone I. The same may be said of the upper levels of Zone III, but the deposit as a whole offers a very interesting possibility. Although Levels 9 to 11 show little change from Zone II and the lower levels of Zone I, it is significant, that in the lower levels of Zone III, Levels 12 to 16, Neeley's Ferry Plain appears as the dominant type without any of its decorated associates. This might not be particularly significant, in view of the small sherd totals, were it not for the fact that we have to do here with a different sort of Neeley's Ferry Plain, thinner, smoother, and showing distinct differences in vessel shape. Thickness of twenty sherds from these levels averaged 5.3 mm., as compared with 7.7 mm. for the typical Neeley's Ferry Plain in Zone I. Rims, unfortunately few in number, are incurved indicating considerable restriction of the orifice, not a typical Neeley's Ferry characteristic. Lugs, where present, are small semi-circular affairs, and the one handle present in the collection is of the small loop variety (fig. 54). This is not only early Mississippi in the purely chronological sense in which we use the term, it is typologically early Mississippi, or early

"Middle Mississippi," as it is more often called, though only in a generalized way. Ironically enough, in the last strata test conducted by the Survey, we found our first evidence of this presumably earliest phase of Mississippi culture in our area. It has helped us somewhat in reinterpreting work previously done, as has been shown in the preceding discussion, but nowhere else has this Neeley's Ferry variant appeared either stratigraphically or on the surface in such clear-cut fashion. We shall be on the lookout for it in future, and if we find it in significant quantity, it is not unlikely that we shall have to modify our present tentative chronology and nomenclature of the Mississippi Period in the Survey Area.

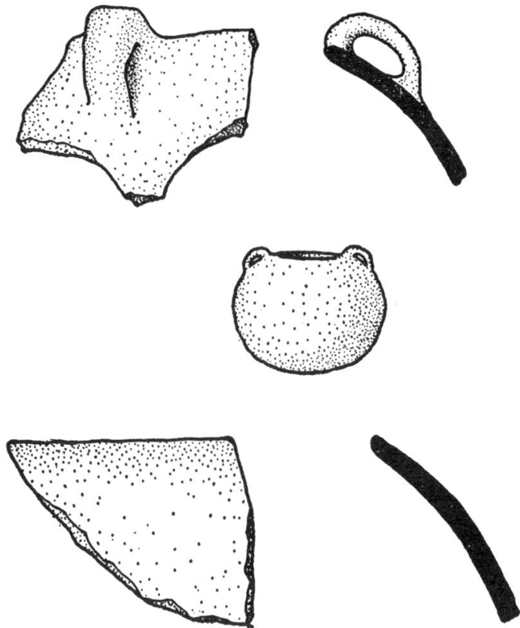

FIG. 54. Rim sherds of "thin" Neeley's Ferry Plain from Zone III, Cut A, Rose Mound (12-N-3).

The burials which have done so much to line museum shelves and collectors' pockets almost certainly belong to the later phases of this Mississippi Period occupation. In terms of the stratification of Cut A, Moore's statement concerning the depth of burials can be interpreted to read that most of them were in Zones I and II, and only a few as deep as the bottom of Zone III.[26] Allowing a reasonable depth for the grave pits, it would seem that practically all the burials originated in Zones I and II. It is doubtful, then, if any burials have been found belonging to the period of Zone III, which accounts for the lack of typologically early Mississippi vessels in Moore's and other collections of pottery from the Rose Mound. It also checks with the general dearth of early Mississippi burials in the whole area, the major reason for our lack of knowledge about the pottery of the period.

There is no apparent break between Zones I, II, and III. Pottery changes are gradual and generally indicative of cultural continuity throughout the fairly long period represented by this portion of the cut. Aside from the appearance of a possible early variant of Neeley's Ferry Plain already discussed, the only significant feature is the apparent priority of Barton Incised over Parkin Punctated, which backs up the results obtained by seriation in this area (fig. 21) in a very satisfactory fashion.

When it comes to the shift that takes place between Zones III and IV, it is an entirely different matter. This is the really important stratigraphic feature in the cut. The character of the two deposits was quite distinct, and the contrast in soil color was striking. The plane of separation, which registered clearly on all four profiles, dipped sharply from about −165 cm. on the south wall to −205 cm. on the north. This can be clearly seen on the composite profile diagram (fig. 55). The effect of this slope on the pottery stratigraphy is to introduce a spurious transition of a new and insidious kind. Levels 14 to 18 are involved in the transition. Due to the above-said slope, each of these levels cut into, and therefore included, material from both Zones III and IV but in varying proportions. Level 14 for example, included a lot of material from Zone III and only a little from Zone IV; while Level 18 included a little material from Zone III and a lot from Zone IV. The proportions shifted in the intervening levels in a regular

[26] Moore, 1910, p. 277. "Some of the burials lay just below the surface, though, as the mound has been under cultivation, originally they probably had been at a greater depth. A few other burials were so much as 5 feet below the present surface."

fashion, subject to the irregularities of the slope. The resulting pottery graph could not fail, therefore, to show a smooth transition in this portion of the cut. To judge correctly the stratigraphic relationship between Zones III and IV, these five levels would have to be eliminated from consideration. The resulting conclusion is that there was an abrupt shift from a pure Baytown to an equally pure Mississippi pottery complex in this cut. The small percentages of Baytown types above the critical plane can be attributed to upward migration and the small percentages of Mississippi types below it, to pits and post-holes intruding into the lower zone. The significance of this break is augmented by the fact that the pottery of Zone III is typologically early Mississippi. Zone IV pottery is pretty certainly late Baytown. The general dearth of decorated types in the Baytown Period in this area makes dating uncertain, but the few sherds present in this cut are of types that we consider to be middle to late Baytown, and the proportion of Mulberry Creek to Baytown is about what we have learned to expect for the late Baytown Period. Therefore, we have in this cut late Baytown followed by early Mississippi with a rather definite break between. This dating corresponds closely to the results of seriation in this area (fig. 21), except

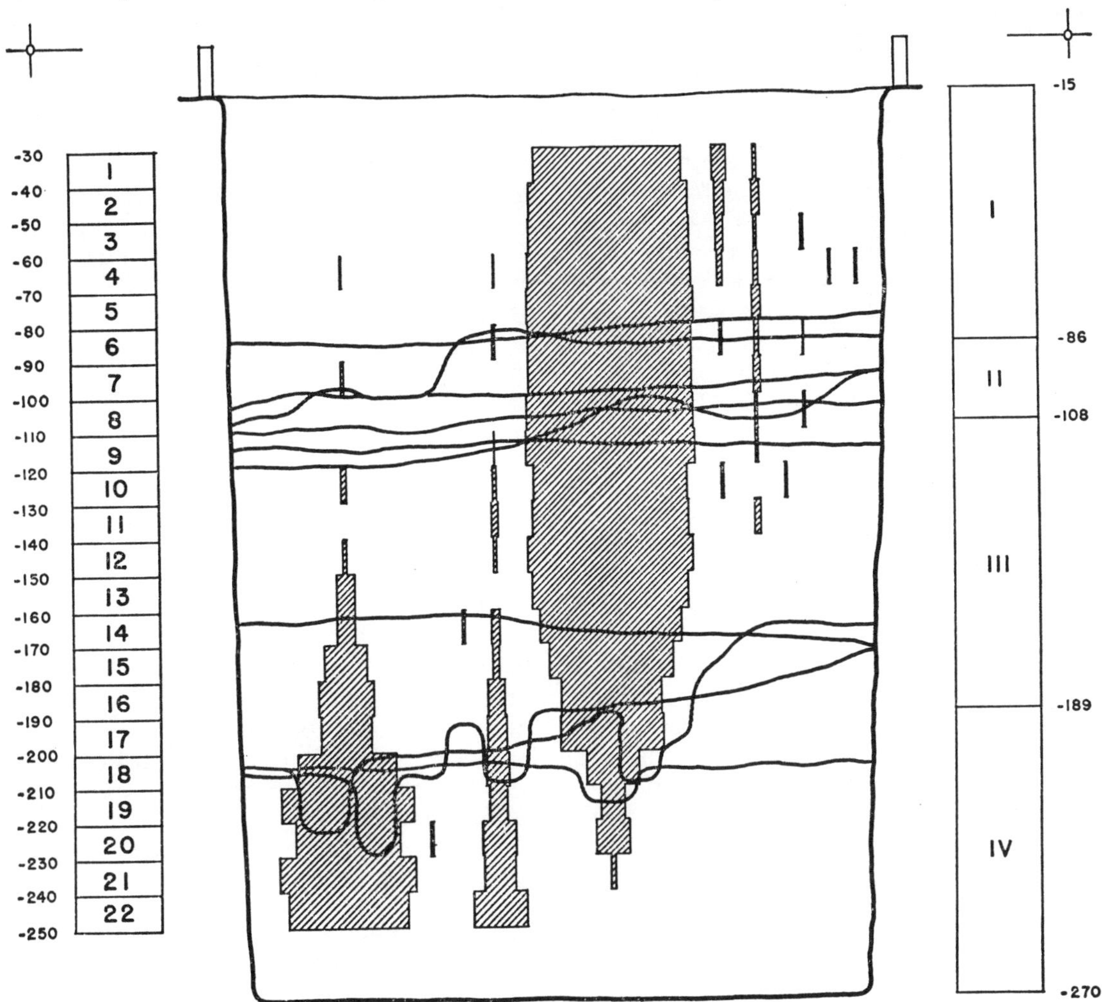

FIG. 55. Composite profile diagram, Cut A, Rose Mound (12-N-3).

that at the time the seriation was done, the significance of the differences between the pottery of Zones I and III was not appreciated, so that possibly not enough time was allowed for the Mississippi Period occupation as a whole. It would probably be more correct to bring the upper levels up into the B–A, or late Mississippi Period.

Conclusions on the Rose Site

To offer deductions in respect to what happened on a site of this magnitude from a tiny excavation on one end of it may be judged ridiculous if not impertinent. However, there are one or two things that can be said with a degree of confidence. A narrow point of land or "ridge" between two depressions, one of which was probably at the time an active channel of an unidentified river or a cut-off oxbow lake, was occupied in the late Baytown Period, perhaps earlier. Subsequently, the tip of this point was cut off by a ditch and probably at the same time a similar ditch was dug 300 meters to the east, making a virtual island, strikingly similar to the island stronghold of Pacaha described in the De Soto narratives. Upon this a large settlement which could almost be called a town, flourished for a period long enough to build up about a meter and a half of refuse. The ditches were almost certainly cut sometime early in the Mississippi Period, and it is a reasonable inference that the site was occupied continuously throughout a large part of that period.

The relationship of this long Mississippi Period occupation with the underlying late Baytown occupation represented in Zone IV is, as usual, the crucial issue. So far as evidence from 4 square meters can be considered valid for purposes of generalization, there was a discontinuity between these two periods of occupation on the site. Or let us put it this way: If the Rose Site was occupied continuously from the late Baytown into the Mississippi Period, the evidence will have to come from some other portion of the site.

There is a final point of optimistic tenor. The Rose Site is one over which many tears have been shed by archaeologists on account of the activities of several generations of indefatigable pot-hunters. Our small excavation was undoubtedly the first time the site was ever dug into by any one who was not looking for pots. If it accomplished nothing else, it proved that the important phases of the history of the site are still intact, safe in the deeper levels below the reach of sounding rod and casual shovel. Notwithstanding all the crimes that have been perpetrated here and the righteous, if slightly envious, indignation they have evoked, the Rose Mound would still repay excavation, in fact from the point of view of Mississippi culture beginnings, in the Survey Area it is the most promising site we have so far encountered. Until a better one is found, it will remain high up on our list for further investigation.

SUMMARY OF STRATIGRAPHY

The results, if such they may be called, of the small-scale excavations described above may be summarized under three headings: (1) the actual stratigraphic results; (2) the light they throw on the stratigraphic and, indirectly, on the seriation methods; (3) the Baytown-Mississippi problem.

(1) Stratigraphic Results

These were, in general, most encouraging. Out of a total of seventeen cuts, all but two gave positive stratigraphic results. In both cases the failure was due to the fact that the cuts had been put down into low mounds. In one of these (Alligator A) stratigraphy, as between mound and sub-mound, was indicated but was masked statistically by the large percentages of early types in the mound fill. The other (Massey B) was completely negative. Of the fifteen successful cuts, four gave information on relationships within the Mississippi Period (Walls A, B, Menard A, Rose A); six on relationships within the Baytown Period (Lake Cormorant A, B, Oliver B, C, Jaketown A, Shell Bluff A); all but one (Walls A) gave evidence of the relationship of the Baytown and Mississippi periods; one (Jaketown A) covered all three periods, Tchula, Baytown, and Mississippi; and two (Jaketown A and B) furnished a glimpse of a possible pre-pottery period underlying the Tchula. In relation to the time and expense involved, these excavations paid off extremely well.

Not only were they individually successful, but the story they tell is completely consistent, so far as it goes. In no case was there conflict or uncertainty so far as the position of individual types or complexes is concerned. They are always in the same — hence we can call it the right — order. The uncertainties are on a higher level of interpretation, but before considering these, it will be well to summarize the results of this study under the second heading outlined above.

(2) The Stratigraphic Method

First, let it be recalled that any remarks made here on the subject of method apply solely to "metrical" stratigraphy. Most if not all of our difficulties of interpretation might have been avoided if we had been able to "peel" stratified deposits instead of digging them in arbitrary horizontal levels. The first generalization, then, is that "metrical" stratigraphy is not good enough. On the other hand, it is, in most cases, the only practicable method. Of the seventeen cuts described here, only four (Oliver A, C, Menard A, and Rose A) were in deposits that might possibly have been peeled by means of the block. The others, among them some of the most successful cuts from the point of view of pottery stratigraphy, could only have been dug by arbitrary levels. We did not consider using the block technique, for reasons of economy, but will in the future be on the look-out for opportunities to do so. Comparison of results of the two methods applied side by side might be very revealing.

While on the subject of excavation technique, another detail we learned the hard way is that great care should be taken to eliminate material from pits and post-holes in the course of digging. We were deliberately careless in this regard on the theory that such material would not be in sufficient amount to upset the over-all statistical results. As a matter of fact, it rarely does so, but in questions having to do with continuity or discontinuity of deposits, in other words, the presence or absence of a "transitional" phase, out-of-place material in pits and post-holes may be important if not decisive. A great deal of tedious discusison in this section might have been avoided if we had not such material to account for.

Of first importance, on the side of interpretation, is a repetition of the warning, several times repeated in the foregoing pages, that interpretations based on one cut are valid for that cut only; insofar as they are extended to apply to the site as a whole, or a larger area, they lose their force in direct ratio to such extension. We have pointed out several instances in which the interpretation of an individual cut would have been very different but for additional information derived from other cuts on the same site. This leads to the recommendation that, except under special circumstances, more than one cut should be made on a site. This seems so obvious it may be wondered why we mention it. However, it is often overlooked. In our own private disagreements, the existence of which the careful reader may detect here and there, we have often found ourselves using what we *think* happened in 4 square meters of deposit as proof of cultural events on an extensive regional scale.

(3) The Baytown-Mississippi Problem

The most difficult problem raised by these excavations is the nature of the relationship between the Baytown and Mississippi complexes in the area. This problem was repeatedly brought into sharp focus in the course of the interpretations of the several pits. It could only be dimly perceived in the course of the seriation analysis, because that method assumes that the collections used represent continuous occupation. Collections that could be seen to be from stratified or reoccupied sites were not used in the analysis. Collections containing a mixture of Baytown with Mississippi types that were used were assumed to include a transitional phase between these two periods in a continuum and were placed on the graphs in that position. There are certain mechanical factors involved in this that must not be overlooked. Depending on the number of such mixed sites, the resulting pattern in each area was one of a gradual replacement of Baytown by Mississippi types. The precise shape of the individual type frequency patterns, i.e., the degree to which they show a sharp or gradual increase or diminution, is to a certain extent influenced by the mere number of these mixed collections, since space for them has to be found on the graph. In other words, the seriation technique, without more careful controls than we were able to bring to bear, tends to draw out the patterns vertically, with the result that changes and replacements tend to look more gradual than they are in fact. The net result is to reinforce the assumption of continuity upon which the method is based. The effect of stratigraphic diagramming is just the reverse, particularly in a refuse deposit of slow accumulation. Compare the generally abrupt pattern of the first appearance of Neeley's Ferry Plain on the stratigraphs with its slow, gradual increase on the seriation charts. There is no point in discussing which is right. Such terms are meaningless until you have absolute chronology by which to scale the charts. But the difference is important in terms of interpretation and general thinking. The slowly expanding figures on the seriation charts fortify the original assumption of gradual change in a cultural continuum. The rapidly expanding figures of the stratigraphic charts lead to an impression of abrupt cultural change, an impression not a little influenced by the fact that sites were *selected* for excavation on the expectation that they would show cultural change. In short, the results of both methods, as used here, are "rigged" to a certain extent in favor of one side or the other of this important question.

With this in mind, we may summarize the stratigraphic evidence on the Baytown-Mississippi question. Of the fifteen cuts, that showed superposition, one (Shell Bluff A) appeared to show positive evidence in favor of continuity; two more (Walls B, Menard B) favored, but weakly, the same interpretation; three (Oliver A, Alligator B, Rose A) showed definite evidences of discontinuity; and three more (Oliver B, C, Massey A) were interpreted that way with somewhat less assurance; the remaining six gave no indications on this particular issue one way or the other.

It is important to note that certain cuts that gave the clearest evidence of a discontinuity (Oliver A, Alligator B, Rose A) showed up as transitional on the seriation charts. The final conclusion is that, while the assumption of general continuity between Baytown and Mississippi periods in this area is not disproved, there is sufficient evidence on the other side to call it into question. If this is correct, it follows that more vigorous controls have to be introduced into the seriation method to eliminate the use as "transitional" of mixed collections that are actually the result of reoccupation. In the meantime, if we have succeeded in exposing some of the difficulties inherent in *both* seriation and stratigraphy, the foregoing pages will not have been written in vain.

Section VII

CORRELATION OF ARCHAEOLOGICAL SEQUENCES WITH RECENT DRAINAGE HISTORY

CORRELATION OF ARCHAEOLOGICAL SEQUENCES WITH RECENT DRAINAGE HISTORY

THE idea of using geological data for dating archaeological remains in the Lower Mississippi Valley is not new. Kniffen utilized this technique in a report on Indian sites in Plaquemines and St. Bernard parishes, Louisiana, published in 1936,[1] and Chawner discussed it at somewhat greater length in a geological study of Catahoula and Concordia parishes of the same year.[2] In his report on village-site collections from Louisiana and Mississippi, also published in 1936, Ford showed that he was well aware of the possibilities of geological dating with his discussion of Marksville Period sites on Brushy Bayou in Concordia Parish, Lousiana.[3] It was not until the publication of Fisk's monumental report on the recent geological history of the Lower Mississippi River,[4] however, particularly the magnificent series of maps showing the reconstructed channel positions of the present Mississippi meander belt,[5] that the above-said possibilities were put within reach of fulfillment. It is not reckless to predict that this pioneer work of Fisk and his associates will profoundly affect the direction of archaeological research in the Lower Mississippi Valley for a long time to come.

Before examining the possibilities of correlating our pottery chronology with Fisk's reconstruction of recent Lower Mississippi hydrography, it must be pointed out that, not having Fisk's report at the time of doing the field work, we were not as aware of the importance of relating our sites to the local drainage as we might have been. This tends to reduce the amount of usable data at our disposal and to a regrettable extent renders our conclusions uncertain. On the other hand, the fact that these collections represent a more or less random sample, chosen without any prevision of this particular use to which we are putting them, is perhaps in their favor.

FISK'S RECONSTRUCTION OF RECENT DRAINAGE HISTORY

The "recent" history of the Lower Mississippi River covers the time during which its late Wisconsin entrenched valley was filled and the present hydrographic system evolved. This period is divided by Fisk into two two epochs:

1) Early — a period of rising sea level.
2) Late — a period of standing sea level.

It is only with the late epoch that we are at present concerned. It is long enough to cover all the archaeology we know anything about with considerable time to spare.

The history of the late epoch, that of standing sea level, has been reconstructed from traces of stream activity exposed on the surface of the alluvial plain. The late stages are separated on the basis of such major changes as a shift in the position through which the stream enters the valley, an abandonment of a segment of a meander belt, or a shift in delta position. The drainage stages are designated by letters from A to J and by numbers from 1 to 20. The A_1 stage is the oldest of which traces are still preserved and stage 20 is the present drainage. Stages from A_1 through J are of unequal length and cover an interval of approximately 4,000 years; those from 1 to 20 are approximately equal in length and cover a period of 2,000 years. Separation of stages 1 to 20 is based on analogy to known migration of bends of the present river. Stages 17 to 20 correspond to mapped historic courses of 1765, 1820, 1880, and 1940. Stage 1 represents the time when the Mississippi and Ohio rivers first joined near Cairo, Ill. The designation of this and succeeding stages by numbers and the earlier stages by letters is largely a matter of convenience, used because it sets apart stages related to modern

[1] Kniffen, 1936, p. 417.
[2] Chawner, 1936, pp. 44-45.
[3] Ford, 1936, p. 238.
[4] Fisk, 1944.
[5] Fisk, 1944, pl. 22.

meander belts from those related to earlier stages of drainage evolution.[6]

The difference between lettered and numbered stages of the "late" period of standing sea level has a further meaning of great importance from our point of view. The end of the one and the beginning of the other marks the establishment of the present Mississippi meander belt and the end of the period of valley aggradation. Starting with Stage 1, the Mississippi is considered to be a poised stream having since shown no tendency to either aggrade or degrade its channel.[7] The importance of this fact will be discussed later. Here, we are interested solely in pointing out that there are two possible approaches to the correlation problem, each of which will require its own methods and may be expected to yield its own results.

CORRELATION IN THE PERIOD OF FLOOD-PLAIN AGGRADATION

The first possibility involves the correlation of archaeology with the older (and longer) lettered stages of the period of flood-plain aggradation. Since the period ended approximately 2000 years ago, according to Fisk's estimate, and we have as yet uncovered no archaeological horizons that can be safely considered to be that old, we cannot reasonably expect to find a direct correlation of archaeological sites with actual channels represented by these lettered stages. There is another possibility, however. As explained in the physiographic section of this report (Section I, p. 9), it is inherent in the process of flood-plain aggradation that the youngest drainage system is always the highest. The most recent meander belt has the highest natural levees. Abandoned meander-belt ridges are not only lower in absolute terms, but their natural levees, in process of being buried by more recent flood-plain deposits, are reduced in width in consequence. In theory, as this process continues, there comes a time when an older meander-belt ridge becomes less desirable as a place to live. Whether this is true in fact is for us to find out. If true, we might expect to find a tendency for sites on older meander belts to be earlier than sites on the present meander belt, not because they were contemporary with those older stream positions, but simply due to a slow drift of population to the younger and hence more desirable natural levees. A possible additional factor might be the superior fertility and workability of the younger levee soils. In this type of correlation, results will depend, not on the association of actual site locations with datable channel positions, but on broader statistical interpretations, for which our present sample is not adequate. However, as a tentative inquiry into the future possibilities of this sort of treatment, a trial comparison is here made of sites in the Yazoo Basin, quadrangle Tiers 14 through 20 (see fig. 2). The results are not astonishing, but do appear to offer some encouragement for the future. There does appear to be a significant difference in age between sites along the present Mississippi meander belt and sites along tributary streams occupying former Mississippi meander belts, though it can only be expressed in the crudest of terms. For example, we find that sites along the present Mississippi tend to run considerably later than sites along the Sunflower, which occupies in part a Mississippi meander belt of Stages D to J, and sites in the Yazoo-Tallahatchie drainage, representing a still earlier Mississippi meander belt of Stage A–C, are slightly earlier than those in the Sunflower group. The figures are presented in the chart shown on page 297.

Just how to interpret this data is not entirely clear. The smaller number of early sites on the present Mississippi meander belt is probably due to the fact that the continual shifting of the active channel has tended to destroy the earlier sites. But how account for the comparative paucity of late sites on the Sunflower and Yazoo-Tallahatchie rivers? According to the theory outlined above, it should be due to the fact that the natural levees of these older Mississippi meander belts are lower than the

[6] Fisk, 1944, p. 37.

[7] Fisk, 1944, p. 50.

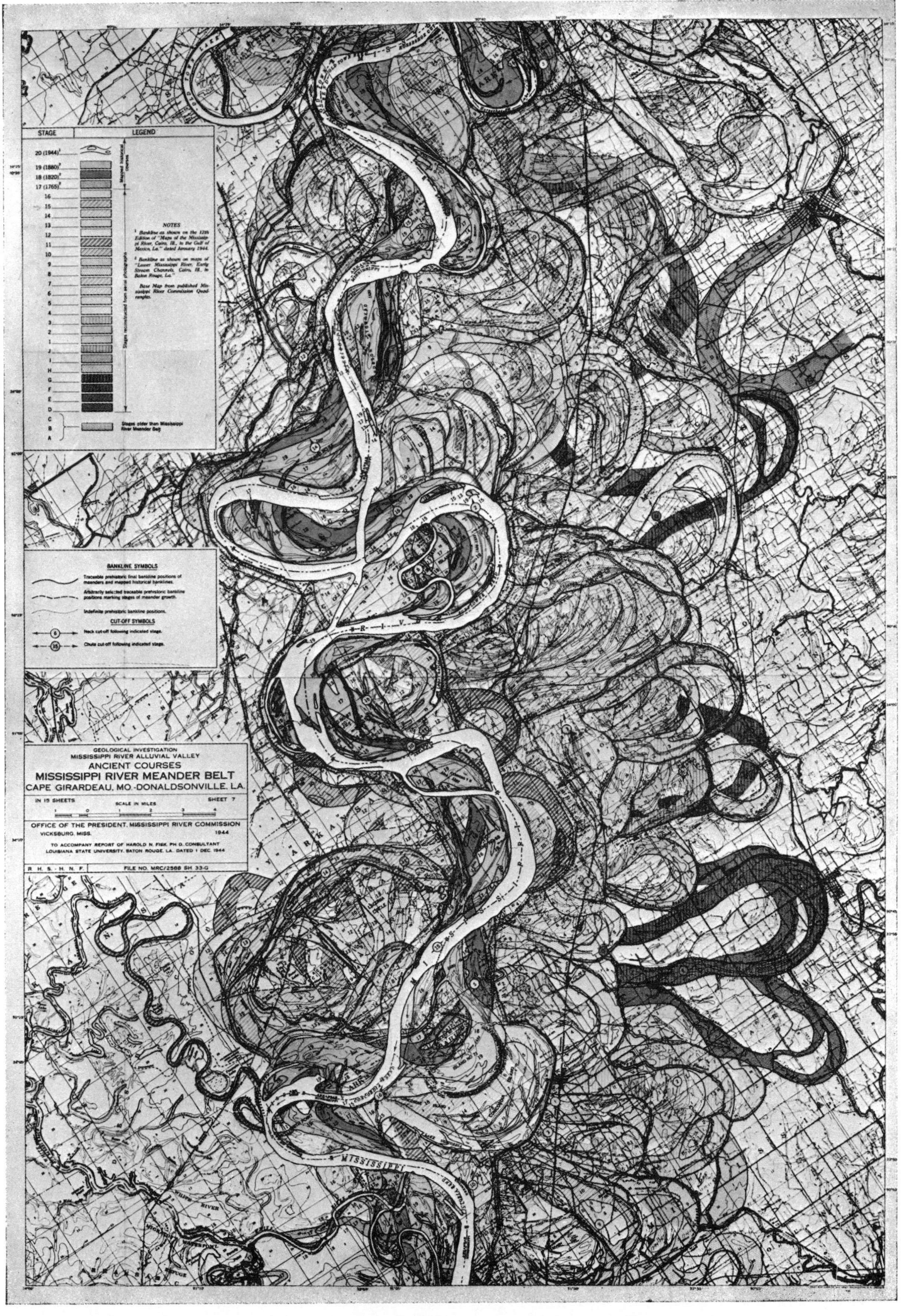

FIG. 56. Reduced photograph of plate 22, sheet 6, in Fisk, 1944, showing reconstructed channels of the present Mississippi River meander belt.

	Present Mississippi		Sunflower		Yazoo-Tallahatchie	
Period	No. of Sites	Per Cent	No. of Sites	Per Cent	No. of Sites	Per Cent
B–A	10	.178	3	.061	0	0
C–B	12	.214	12	.245	2	.047
D–C	11	.196	11	.224	12	.286
E–D	11	.196	4	.081	13	.310
F–E	11	.196	14	.286	11	.262
G–F	1	.018	5	.102	4	.095
	—		—		—	
	56		49		42	

more recent levees of the present stream. On the strength of these figures alone it would be hardly possible to draw any inferences regarding this apparent trend of population distribution. That a trend is discernible, however, is very encouraging, and suggests further application of this method when a larger sample is available.

CORRELATION OF ARCHAEOLOGY WITH THE DRAINAGE HISTORY OF THE PRESENT MISSISSIPPI MEANDER BELT

At the moment, this is the most promising approach. Our sample, though not as large as we would wish, is sufficient for a "trial run" at least. From the mechanical standpoint, conditions are ideal. Fisk's plate 22 gives, on fifteen large sheets at the scale of 1:625000, a complete reconstruction of channel positions of the Mississippi River from Cape Girardeau, Missouri, to Donaldsonville, Louisiana. A sample of this admirable map, shown in figure 56, conveys a very imperfect idea of the original without the use of color. The base map upon which this is overlaid is the same, even to scale, as the quadrangle sheets which we used in the field, enabling the transfer of site locations from one to the other with absolute precision.

Having transferred the site data, the next step is to determine and list the sites that appear to be datable by reference to extinct channel topography. The word "datable" is used here in a special and incomplete sense. The only "date" that can be assigned to any individual site is a minimal date, a "not-earlier-than," expressed in terms of Fisk's channel chronology. Such determinations may be based upon three types of site-channel relationship, which will be referred to hereinafter as: (1) "bankline," (2) "inside-bend," and (3) "mid-channel."

1) "Bankline" position, as the term implies, refers to a site that is not only located directly on the bankline of an extinct channel but is so distributed with reference to the bankline as to render it fairly certain that the site was in being either before the cut-off when the channel was active or not too long thereafter, when it was still a lake. Further implications of this statement will be discussed *passim*. This is the most satisfactory type of site-channel relationship and, fortunately, the most common. Of the 79 sites used in the present trial correlation 73 showed this type of relationship. It must be pointed out, however, that bankline position does not give an iron-clad minimal date. It is conceivable that a meander might sweep up to the edge of a pre-existing site to be arrested there by a cut-off. The chance of this occurring often enough to distort the over-all correlation picture, however, is so slight it can be safely ignored.

2) What we have characterized as an "inside-bend" position refers to the location of a site in a position that has been crossed by the outward sweep of a meander, which we can assume with reasonable certainty would have destroyed any pre-existing sites that lay in its path. Consequently, the site cannot be older than the meander in question. Such locations are usually, though not necessarily, on or within inside bends, hence the name, and may or may not have bankline positions as well. They give practically certain minimal dates in terms of the channel chronology. Seven of

the sites used in the correlation showed this type of position. In figure 57, Site 14–O–2 (Owens) is a good example of an inside-bend position, which is also a bankline position. It should be apparent, however, that any site located within the semi-lunar space between the Stage 13 and 14 stages of the Beaverdam Lake meander whether on the bankline or not would have an equally certain minimal date at Stage 14, since a pre-existing site would have been erased by the river in its progress from its Stage 13 to its Stage 14 position.

3) "Mid-channel" position refers to a site location directly over, that is to say between the banks, of a former channel. This gives the strongest kind of minimal date, since the only way the site can be older than the channel is for it to have been on an island, which, in view of the way islands are usually formed in the Mississippi, is an extremely remote contingency. It might be supposed that this type of minimal dating is even stronger than those already discussed, owing to the time that must be allowed for filling the channel before it could become dry land fit for human habitation. To do so would be to underestimate the levee-building capacities of the Mississippi River. The only situation in which this time element would have to be taken into account would be in the case of a site located in mid-channel of an isolated cut-off out on the margin of the meander belt relatively unaffected by subsequent activities of the river. So far no cases of this kind have been encountered. All sites used in the present study that have mid-channel positions — 9 of our 79 sites — were on or near the banklines of more recent channels. We may therefore assume that filling of the older channels, through the normal process of levee-building, was rapid, and consequently

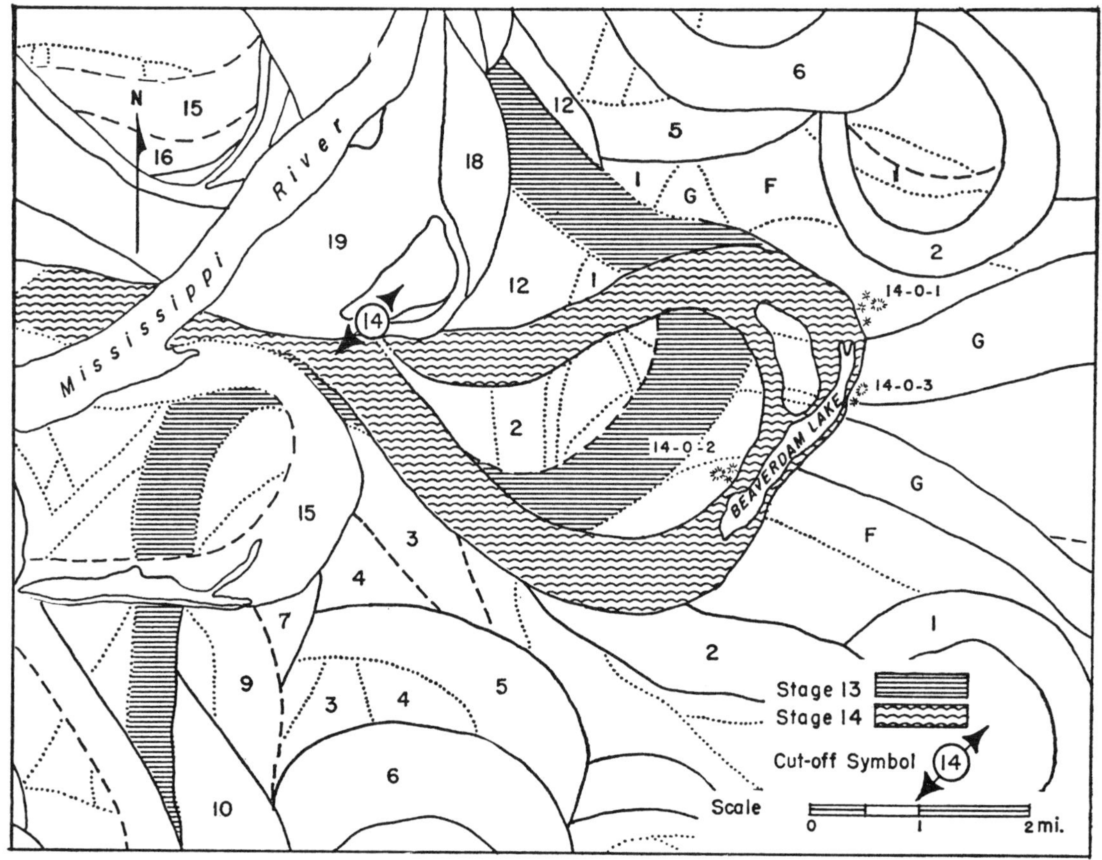

Fig. 57. Site-channel associations on Beaverdam Lake, Tunica County, Mississippi.

no extra significance is given to these mid-channel positions in the present study. An example of mid-channel position, with very "tight" dating may be seen in figure 58 in which 13–O–10 (Hollywood) is located squarely within the banks of a Stage 11 channel and near the bankline of the succeeding Stage 12 cut-off. Clearly, the site could not have been established here until levee-building in Stage 12 had filled the older Stage 11 channel. The fact that it is also an inside-bend position makes the minimum dating still more certain.

So far, we have been discussing the possibilities of correlation in its negative aspect, i.e., in terms of minimal dating. There is a positive aspect, too, which must not be overlooked, though its demonstration is somewhat difficult at our present stage of knowledge. In defining bankline position, above, we have referred to the obvious fact that it does not mean that the site was in being at the time the channel in question was active. In fact, the distribution of sites would *appear* to indicate that this was more likely *not* to have been the case. One has to use the word "appear" because present site distribution tells a partial and possibly misleading story, owing to what may be called a survival factor, which varies greatly according to the position of the site.

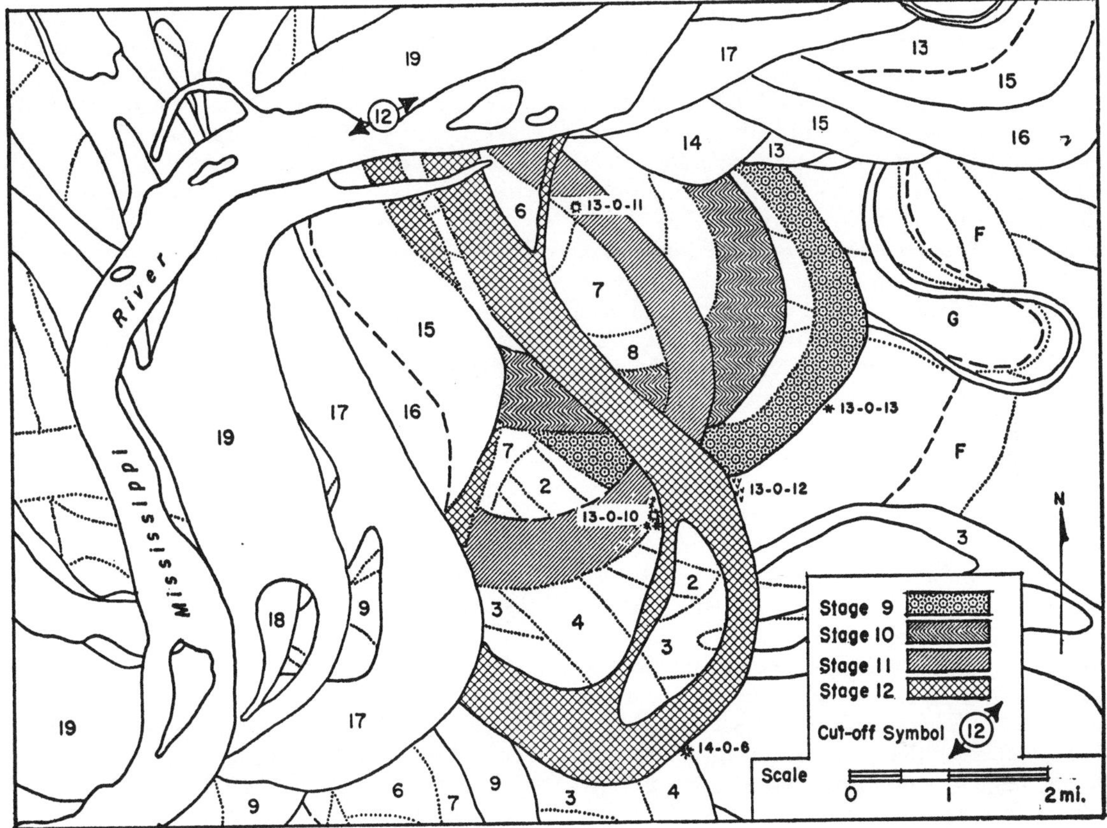

FIG. 58. An example of "tight" dating, Hollywood Site (13–O–10), Tunica County, Mississippi.

Sites on an active meandering stream have little chance of survival. If on the outside of bends, they are doomed; if on the inside, they are safe so far as the "sweep" of that particular meander is concerned, but are apt to be erased by subsequent meanders. Only sites out on the margin of the meander belt, on the last channel or cut-off position of a meander are relatively safe. After the cut-off the indefatigable river starts a new meander, usually but not always, leaving the last channel position as an oxbow lake, which rapidly fills, at the ends first, to become a swamp and finally dry land. Sites on such a cut-off lake, have, therefore, a reasonable chance of survival, so it is not surprising that most of our site-channel associations are of this kind. We must, therefore, be on our guard against reading too much into the evidence of site distribution, because it obviously reflects to a large extent the survival situation. On the other hand, there are factors, independent of mere survival, that favor this kind of association. For a considerable length of time the shores of a cut-off lake continue to be a favorable place on which to live, perhaps more favorable than the banks of the river itself. This is certainly the case so long as the lake remains a body of open water. One has only to recall the large plantation houses that line the shores of such lakes in the area today. It is clearly impossible to put a term of years to this optimum period. It depends, first of all, on the rate of filling, which is a product of extremely variable hydrographic conditions at the cut-off ends, and on the size and shape of the meander itself. Since filling takes place progressively from the ends toward the center, the longer the meander, the longer it takes to fill. Old Town Lake, south of Helena, Arkansas, which still shows a considerable expanse of open water occupies the center portion of an extremely long meander which was cut off in Stage 8. This is an exceptional case, however. Most of the persent cut-off lakes date from Stage 13 and later. An average cut-off date of the 25 principal oxbow lakes between Cape Girardeau, Missouri, and Donaldsonville, Louisiana, falls between Stages 16 and 17. This might appear to suggest that the average duration of optimum conditions for habitation after a cut-off corresponds to the interval between Stages 16 and 17 and the present, say 3 to 4 stages. But, against this must be reckoned the larger number of recent cut-off meanders that have entirely filled and consequently do not show today as lakes. There are scores of such filled meanders with cut-off dates ranging from Stages 12 to 18. Furthermore, it is quite certain that the building of artificial levees has decelerated the rate of filling during the last century or so. There does not seem to be any point in attempting to arrive at a statistical balance between cut-offs that are still lakes and those that have filled, but it would seem conservative to cut the average time for filling down to about 2 stages. This is an important postulation. Translated into archaeological terms, it means that the dating indicated by our correlation chart may be subject to a lag of two stages, or about 200 years. Lest it appear that we are indulging in specious accuracy in this matter, however, let it be emphasized again that there are countless factors working against any such uniformity as might be indicated in the figure just given. Each cut-off meander has its own history, depending on circumstances of local drainage. For example, long after it has ceased to be an open lake a meander might continue to be a desirable place of Indian habitation, owing to the fact that it was occupied by some smaller stream of local importance. We must remember, again, that we are dealing here with the recent period in which the Mississippi has been in a state of "poise," so there is no differential in height of levees that would hasten the abandonment of older natural levees in favor of those of more recent date.

Getting back to the question, then, as to just what we mean by the association of sites with abandoned channels in the present Mississippi meander belt, it is clear that a simple statement will not suffice. Such a site may be contemporary with its channel — we know that in early historic time villages of Mississippi River tribes were often directly on the river bank; it may conceivably, but improbably, be earlier; it is very likely to be later, and there is some *a priori* ground for postulating two stages as a rough working average for the interval, though under certain conditions it may be very much later. In sum, on the negative or minimal side, our dating criteria are unassailable. The validity of the result, as expressed in minimal dates, will be limited only by the reliability of Fisk's reconstruction and the adequacy of our own field and laboratory studies — at the present writing, still a very considerable limitation. On the positive side there is apparent a vast area for interpretation and we have a great deal to learn. The results of the trial correlation presented here will be judged accordingly.

The Trial Correlation

Figure 59 presents in a scatter diagram the time relationships of 79 sites and the extinct channels with which they are topographically associated. The number of sites available for this study is limited by the fact that Fisk's plate 22 covers only the present Mississippi meander belt and by the fact that not all sites found by the Survey within the area of plate 22 are referable to abandoned channels. The number of such cases, however, was not large. Indeed, one of the conditions of happy augury for this method of dating is the very high proportion of sites that are located on or near the banks of former channels. It must be remembered that, when doing the field work, we did not have Fisk's maps. Although dimly aware that the best hunting was along the older meanders, we did not concentrate on them unduly. Yet of 148 sites located within the area covered by Fisk's plate 22, 140 or 94.6 per cent are within, on, or near (within one-half mile of) former Mississippi channels. This is a satisfactory, not to say impressive figure. For various reasons, chiefly inadequacy of field survey methods, the precise channel associations of many of these 140 sites could not be determined, and the sample was further reduced by lack of adequate pottery collections to the final number of 79. It is not maintained that this is an adequate sample for purposes of correlation, nor has any attempt been made to evaluate it statistically, but it is certainly sufficient for an experimental effort to find out something about the possibilities of this kind of dating in the future.

Horizontal position on the diagram represents time in terms of hydrography, Stages 1 to 14 in Fisk's reconstruction; vertical position represents time in terms of the pottery chronology described in the preceding section with Horizons G to A spaced equally as though the intervals between them were of equal length, which is of course problematical. Period assignments are mainly on the basis of the seriation graphs, except in cases of

	14	13	12	11	10	9	8	7	6	5	4	3	2	1
A		13-N-5	12-O-6 13-O-10 13-O-11 14-O-6	10-P-2 10-Q-1 13-P-7 13-P-11		14-O-4 19-L-6	15-N-3	13-P-6		17-M-2				
B	14-O-3		11-P-2 11-P-3 13-O-5 13-O-12	10-P-3 12-O-1 13-N-6 15-N-6	10-P-1	11-P-1 13-O-4 15-O-10 17-M-11	12-O-5 13-N-16 15-N-2	13-P-1	16-M-6					
C				13-N-4 13-N-8 13-N-12 13-N-15	10-P-3 15-N-5	13-N-11 13-N-17 13-O-8 17-M-12 14-O-8 17-M-16	12-O-2 13-N-13 15-N-4		20-M-4	13-O-3 20-L-2			19-L-1	19-L-3
D	14-O-1				17-M-1 17-M-14	10-Q-3 13-N-9 15-O-1			20-M-5					
E	14-O-2					15-N-10 17-M-13		13-P-4 13-P-10	17-K-6 17-M-17	16-N-1 16-N-2 16-N-7 20-L-2	16-N-4 16-N-5 16-N-20	16-M-3		16-N-14
F								13-P-3 13-P-8 13-P-9						
G														

FIG. 59. Trial correlation of archaeological and geological dating on the Lower Mississippi River.

long-occupied or reoccupied sites in which the "average" date represented on the graph came too far from representing the earliest level of the site. It may be repeated here that for purposes of correlation we are interested only in the lowest level or "bottom" date of the site. In such cases an earlier assignment was given on a conservative but purely subjective basis. No effort was made to arrange the sites on the diagram chronologically *within* the rectangles.

Before proceeding to a discussion of this diagram, it will be well to emphasize once more that the "associations" represented here are not positive associations in a normal statistical sense. For example, Site 10–P–11 in the fourth square, second row, does not have a positive Stage 10 date. It is associated with a meander of Stage 10; the nature of the association is such that it presumably cannot be earlier than Stage 10 but it can be, and probably is, later than Stage 10. In short, it represents a minimal date with the upper end left open. It could be the site of a plantation house of 1860, though we hasten to deny that our pottery dating is that far off. Once this essential fact is grasped, interpretation of the diagram becomes relatively simple.

The general distribution of sites indicates a fairly satisfactory correlation. There is a tendency to pile up along a general slope from upper left to lower right. The scattering of sites to the right of this slope need give us no concern whatever. They merely reflect the statement already made that under certain conditions the shores of a cut-off meander may continue to be a favorable location for habitation for a long time after the cut-off. The little groups of sites in the Stages 4 and 5 columns, fifth row, are in fact an illustration of this point. The three sites in period F–G, Stage 4, for example, lie close together on the bankline of an old cut-off channel now occupied by the Little Sunflower River, a situation which would be a favorable one presumably right down to the present time. Three of the four sites in the same period, Stage 5, are likewise on one meander, called Annis Brake, though in this case the reasons for continuing occupation are not as evident. However, the fact that Annis Brake is still a swamp suggests that it remained an open lake for a long time after its cut-off in Stage 5.

The three sites in the extreme left-hand column cannot be so comfortably ignored. All three are located on Beaverdam Lake, Tunica County, Mississippi, a cut-off meander dated by Fisk in Stage 14 (fig. 57). The position of 14–O–1 (Evansville), a site altogether too early for Stage 14, according to our ideas of pottery chronology, might be laid to one of those theoretically possible instances in which a meander sidled up to a pre-existing site and stopped, but 14–O–2 (Owens) which is still earlier in terms of pottery has an inside-bend position and could not conceivably have been there prior to the supposed Stage 14 cut-off. We have to assume for reasons of self-respect that our pottery chronology is not that far off the track. Fisk, when appealed to, very generously conceded that his dating of the Beaverdam Lake meander on which these sites are located may have been in error.[8] If this is the case, the Beaverdam Site (14–O–3) would also be removed from the Stage 14 column, and the appearance of our diagram would be much improved.

Apart from the Beaverdam Lake sites, which we have just unloaded onto Fisk, it should be evident from what has already been said that the most significant site-channel associations in each row are those that lie nearest the left-hand side of the diagram. These give what we shall refer to hereinafter as a *minimal association line*, represented by the solid line on the diagram. By the same token, associations become progressively nonsignificant with increase of distance to the right of this line. For this reason, the application of normal statistical methods appears to be ruled out. For example, regression lines might be supposed to give a more precise expression to the correlation situation than the zigzag line shown here, but they would actually be skewed by the

[8] Letter to Ford, March 23, 1948. "It is entirely possible that there has been a misdating of this meander, since it is a constricted neck cut-off in which more recent river activity has destroyed much of the accretion area. At any rate, the lack of correlation at this point strongly suggests that we have missed the boat and we will do our best to get at the true story."

pull of these nonsignificant associations upward and to the right. The same difficulty would be encountered in the application of any other method involving the use of the theory of means. It is therefore judged preferable to let the diagram stand on its own merits without benefit of statistical elaboration.

Further mechanical adjustments might be in order, however. Attention has been called to the fact that the pottery periods are arbitrarily given equal duration on the diagram. A further step, provided we felt more confidence in our sample, would be to adjust the minimal association line to a constant slope, which would involve lengthening period G–F. To do so now would hardly be warranted, though it would perhaps conform to general archaeological probabilities.

Summary of Trial Correlation

If our methods so far do not conceal some unsuspected error, we may venture to hypothesize a tentative *minimal* site-channel association correlation as follows:

Period	Stage
B–A	13
C–B	12
D–C	11
E–D	10
F–E	9
G–F	7

Let us repeat, this highly tentative schedule does no more than give the latest channel associations so far found for sites in each archaeological period. This is not necessarily equivalent to actual stage dating for each period, as we shall presently show. Its reliability is left to the reader's own judgment. There appear to be no mathematical means for checking it. It is, of course, essentially a question of adequacy of sample. For example, the largest total number of sites we have for any period is 20 sites in period D–C, and the latest channel association shown by any of these is in Stage 11. If we had 40 D–C sites instead of 20 what would be the chance of occurrence of an association later than Stage 11? Our guess, which is no better than the reader's, is that they would not be very great. On the other hand, in period G–F where we have only three sites, and all on the same meander at that, the chances are fairly good that an increase of sample might produce an association later than Stage 7.

Whether these "latest possible" channel *associations* are equivalent to "latest possible" channel *dates* is another question. We have repeatedly stressed the fact that sites may be, in fact generally are, later than the date indicated by their channel associations. The question, then, is how to interpret the diagram in the light of that fact. Again, it is a matter of the evaluation of sample. For example, the number of D–C sites with minimal Stage 11 associations is four (4th cell, 3rd row). To what extent is it possible that none of these four sites actually dates from the time its channel was active or first cut off? In other words, could *all* of these four sites exhibit the lag between *minimal* and *actual* date that has already been discussed as theoretically possible? With the number of sites no greater than four, it is certainly possible. Again, we can expect no help from statistics. We have simply to go on collecting sites with channel associations until common sense tells us that the possibility of this kind of error has been eliminated. In the meantime, on the theory that a hypothesis is better than a vacuum, we may let the present correlation stand, treating it as though it represented the actual stage dating that is our ultimate objective. We are encouraged by the fact that it looks inherently reasonable in relation to general archaeological probabilities in the Southeast. It is hardly necessary to add that considerably more and better field work has got to be done on the problem before it can be regarded as anything more than a working hypothesis.

Absolute Dating

When it comes to absolute chronology, there is little at this stage that can, or should be, said. Fisk at one time indicated his intention of publishing a paper on the dating criteria used in his channel reconstruction, but as yet it has not appeared. We have only his statement that "Stages 1 to 17 cover intervals of approximately 100 years. This interval was determined by comparison with known rates of channel migration since 1765 (end of stage

17)."[9] All numbered stages, therefore, equate approximately with the corresponding centuries in the Christian era. This makes it almost fatally convenient to substitute centuries for stages, but we will endeavor to resist the temptation. Fisk would probably agree that his absolute dating in this geologically insignificant period is not very much better than the estimates of the archaeologists — in other words, not very good. As a system of *relative* dating, however, channel chronology is probably more reliable than anything local archaeology has yet to offer, and we are immensely gratified that our stratigraphic column checks as closely with it as the results in figure 59 appear to indicate.

Comparison with Krieger's Estimates Based on Cross-dating with the Southwest. The possibility of bringing the absolute dating of the Southwest, based on tree-ring studies, to bear on the channel-correlation problem by means of cross-dating through Texas is an intriguing one. Krieger, in his recent study of cultures and chronology in northern Texas, presents a chart which roughly correlates the prehistoric sequences from New Mexico through Texas to the Lower Mississippi Valley. Dating for the upper half of this chart is derived primarily from Southwestern trade sherds from sites as far east as the Texas-Louisiana border.[10] The earlier portion is based on estimates in the usual way. The net

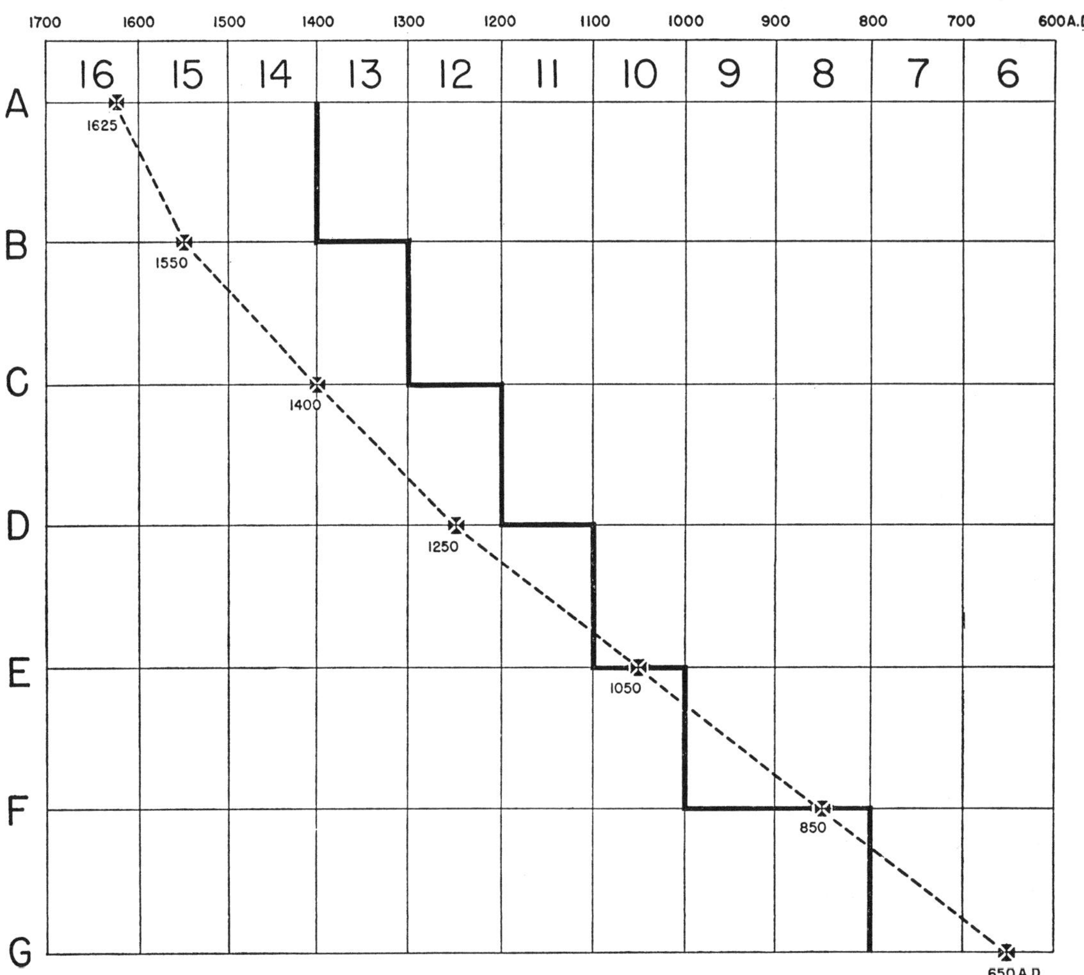

Fig. 60. Comparison of Krieger's estimates based on cross-dating with the Southwest and the site-channel correlation shown in figure 59. (Krieger's dating shown by dotted line.)

[9] Fisk, 1944, p. 45.

[10] Krieger, 1946, pp. 259–72, fig. 26.

effect of this new evidence of Krieger's has been to push back by about 150 years the guess dates of Ford and Willey.[11]

In another section of this report the sequence established by Ford at the mouth of the Red River in Louisiana are compared with the lettered time scale used here. The correlation is roughly as follows:

Survey Area	Red River
B–A	Historic
C–B	Plaquemine
D–C	Coles Creek
E–D	Troyville
F–E	Marksville
G–F	Tchefuncte

This makes it possible to project Krieger's estimates into the Survey Area and compare them with the channel chronology. From the spacing of period names in the Lower Mississippi column of Krieger's chart and the aid of a little arithmetical juggling, we get the following figures:

Survey Area	Krieger's Estimates
A	A.D. 1625
B	1550
C	1400
D	1250
E	1050
F	850
G	650

In figure 60 these dates have been plotted on a simplified version of our site-channel correlation diagram with all due reservations for the tenuous nature of the bridgework they represent. In case the reader suspects that we have forgotten how many hypothetical elements enter into this comparison, they are recapitulated here: (1) dating of sites mainly by means of surface collections in terms of a highly tentative pottery chronology and an imperfect seriation technique; (2) correlation of site and river-channel dating based on an inadequate number of site-channel associations; (3) arbitrary estimates of absolute time entering into the channel chronology; (4) rough equation of Survey Area chronology with the more fully worked-out cultural sequence in the Red River area of Louisiana; (5) equation of the latter with Texas cultures, themselves dated in turn by very slender evidences of trade with the Southwest. Taking all these factors of possible error into account and further considering the fact that Krieger never intended his somewhat generalized diagrammatic scheme to be put to any such use, it is nothing short of astonishing to find the two "date lines" agreeing so well.

It is of possible significance that the agreement is closer in the earlier periods than in the later. There are certain inherent difficulties on our side in these later periods that have not yet been openly confessed. If we are to trust our own findings, there were no sites existing on this part of the Mississippi River later than Stage 13 — only one site in fact later than Stage 12. On the other hand, we know that the area was well peopled at the time of De Soto in 1541 which date would fall, according to Fisk, in or about Stage 15. We have the choice of assuming: (1) that so far we have not found any sites with channel associations of the De Soto period; (2) that *all* of the sites of the De Soto period so far found exhibit the lag between minimal and actual dating so frequently alluded to above; (3) that Fisk's 100-year stage time scale is in error and that 1541 actually falls somewhere around Stages 12 to 13. Choice between these alternatives would be futile at the present time, but it is interesting that the widest discrepancy between Fisk's and Krieger's dating seems to occur just in this least satisfactory portion of our site-channel correlation.

CONCLUSIONS ON THE SITE-CHANNEL CORRELATION APPROACH

The analysis described in the foregoing pages was frankly experimental. The sample was not regarded as adequate from any point of view, the relative dating on our side still in a tentative stage, on the other (Fisk's) accepted on trust. The most we could expect

[11] Ford and Willey, 1941.

was some intimation of the future possibilities of this line of investigation. These expectations were abundantly fulfilled. With a larger sample of sites collected under stricter topographic control and new methods of analysis that will undoubtedly suggest themselves as the work proceeds, we may look forward to the time when we shall be able to discuss the archaeology of the Lower Mississippi Valley in terms of Mississippi River stages with considerable confidence. Once this happy state is reached, conversion to absolute dating via dendrochronology, carbon 14, or some other as yet undiscovered method of dating archaeological materials will be a foregone conclusion.

Section VIII
ANALYSIS OF OCCUPATION SITE PLANS

ANALYSIS OF OCCUPATION SITE PLANS

INTRODUCTION

As ALREADY explained in Section II, the field work done in the Survey Area was intended to be in the nature of a random sampling. We were not trying to locate every spot which had been occupied in prehistoric times but were endeavoring to visit and describe enough sites in all parts of the area to make possible a general reconstruction of its prehistory. We also wanted a proportionate representation of the different classes of sites, refuse mounds, burial mounds, etc. Notwithstanding these good intentions, we are aware that our sample is weighted on the side of sites having mounds. Simple flat village sites without conspicuous surface features have tended to be overlooked. The reason for this selection is clear and seemingly unavoidable in the type of survey work we were doing. Information about sites was obtained by questioning almost every local person we happened to meet in the course of a day's work. Naturally, every one knew where such obvious features as Indian mounds were to be found, but only the exceptionally observant had noticed the bits of refuse and pottery fragments plowed up in the fields that marked the presence of simple village sites. Only on the lower courses of the Yazoo and Sunflower rivers was sufficient information about such sites obtained. In these regions some of the refuse deposits contain quantities of mussel shells; therefore, the low mounds of glistening shell fragments scattered over fields are striking enough to be noticed and remembered by the people of the neighborhood.

Between the different types of mound sites we do not think that we have made much selection. There may have been a tendency to hear of and visit the larger and more striking groups to the neglect of the smaller, yet our inquiries were made frequently over the routes we traveled, and some very small sites in rather inaccessible places were learned of and visited.

A more serious factor affecting the comparisons we are about to make in this section is the rapid destruction taking place on nearly all these sites by cultivation, levee or road construction, use of mounds as sites for houses, barns and other buildings, and treasure-hunting, not to mention the activities of nonprofessional archaeologists and pot-hunters. Larger sites with large mounds are naturally somewhat more resistant to destruction, which again has the effect of weighting the sample in their favor. Another serious effect of these agencies of destruction, from our point of view, is the increasing difficulty of identifying mounds as to type. Again, this applies more to smaller mounds, which lose their identity very rapidly under cultivation. It is, for example, very unusual to find a small rectangular mound that can be still identified as such. The presence of ramps or stairways on rectangular mounds is another case in point. Only on the largest mounds, with sides too steep for cultivation, or on smaller mounds accidentally preserved, can traces of ramps still be seen. Yet it is probable that a majority of the rectangular temple mounds originally had them. A great many other features have doubtless vanished or have been so thoroughly obscured that we were not even likely to suspect their former presence.[1]

At each site visited, notes were taken on all observable surface features, such as the size and shape of mounds, location of refuse concentrations, presence or absence of burned clay daub which, we know from work in other areas, often indicates the intentional burning of buildings, and so forth. If called for by the size and complexity of the features a sketch map was also made. Most of the mapping was done by compass, pacing, and estimating. The more complex sites, however, were mapped with plane table and alidade. The resulting accumulation of notes and maps together form a considerable body of data, which, in spite of shortcomings, seems worthwhile to present in this report.

[1] Comparison of Peabody's description and map of the Oliver Site (16-N-6) in 1904 with its present condition (fig. 28) illustrates the rapidity of destruction through cultivation. Of the fifteen mounds described by Peabody, only two were recorded by the Survey party in 1941.

CLASSIFICATION OF SITES

The large number of sites renders individual description impracticable. It is doubtful whether the reader could be given a very clear picture by that means. Sites have therefore been somewhat arbitrarily classified into seven groups according to what we have been able to deduce as to the principal purpose and plan of each.

1) Village sites without mounds.
2) Sites with one or more conical burial mounds.
3) Small ceremonial centers with rectangular temple mounds.
4) Large ceremonial centers with rectangular temple mounds.
5) Large rectangular village sites with temple mounds (St. Francis-type "towns").
6) Large irregular village sites with rectangular mounds.
7) Unclassified sites (site and/or mounds so badly damaged that it is impossible to determine their original form).

In the following pages we shall attempt a general summary of our observations in respect to each of these categories, after which we shall present a series of maps showing distribution of these types in the various time periods.

Village Sites Without Mounds

There is not much to be said under this heading, except that in our area such sites appear to be very rare. One possible reason has already been given, i.e., our failure to find them, but we suspect that they are comparatively rare anyhow. In almost every instance where a site without mounds is found, some local character appears with a story of a mound that was there when he was a "little old kid of a boy." Mound-building seems to have been as old as pottery-making in this part of the Mississippi Valley, perhaps older, and since we have not yet found a village site or midden without pottery, the general scarcity of sites without mounds is perhaps not surprising.

At the other end of the time scale, we know from ethnographic sources and from finds in neighboring areas that mound-building was in decline if not complete abeyance in the late prehistoric and historic periods. However, we know that most of the Survey Area was unoccupied at this time — we have not yet found a site with historic materials — so the chances of the addition of late sites without mounds to our sample are not very good either. In general, we may conclude that the small number of flat villages without mounds reflects a real scarcity of this type of site at all periods in this part of the Mississippi Valley.

Sites With Conical Burial Mounds

Sixty out of the 383 sites visited by the Survey had mounds that could be identified as conical. These are listed in table 11. This figure may not be accepted as an accurate indication of the original number of this type of site in the Survey Area, since most of the conical mounds were small in size and, not offering sufficient summit area to be of value as places of refuge in time of floods, they have been plowed down or otherwise destroyed by the hundreds. Or, as is often the case, they have been so altered in shape that the field notes have classed them as "indeterminate." Another limiting factor is the circumstance that conical mounds throughout the Mississippi Valley tend to be located on the bluffs, whereas our investigations were strictly confined to the flood plain and older alluvial plains.

There seem to be little or no observable differences in size, number, or arrangement of conical mounds from one period to another. Numbers vary from one lone mound to as many as forty. From two to six seems to be about the average. In most cases where there is more than one mound, they are grouped about without any indication of definite plan. Some groups show the mounds clustered while in others they are widely separated, from 2 to 300 meters apart. In a few sites, they are placed in a line, generally along the top of a low ridge. In most cases, there is very little refuse near the mounds and it has not always been possible to gather an adequate collection for dating purposes.

In the Sunflower and Lower Yazoo areas there is frequently found a concentration of village-site refuse a short distance from the conical mound, or mounds. This association occurs too consistently to be fortuitous and so the collections from such village sites have sometimes been used to date the mounds. In the Yazoo area, particularly, the village refuse contains large amounts of mussel shell, and the sites are sometimes described locally as "shell ridges."

The mounds listed here as conical are not always circular. From the site listing it will be noted that an occasional mound is oval in plan. However, the great majority seem to have been originally small, rounded cones 40 to 100 feet in diameter and 5 to 15 feet high. In most cases, plowing has reduced the original heights, increased the diameters, and rounded over the tops.

Where we have been correct in identifying mounds as conical in shape, there can be little doubt that they were burial mounds, built expressly for that purpose. This we infer from experience in other parts of the Southeast and from the few recorded excavations in them. This inference is strengthened by the frequent occurrence of bone fragments on or near mounds that are being, or have been, destroyed by cultivation.

TABLE 11: SITES WITH CONICAL MOUNDS.[2]

	NO. OF MOUNDS	SIZES	ARRANGEMENT	REMARKS
Period C–B				
Arkansas River Area				
Brandenburg B (16–L–5)	1	50′ x 1½′	...	Plowed up burials
Memphis Area				
Lakeside (13–N–18)	3	110′ x 9′ 60′ x 11′ 50′ x 4′	In straight line	Plowed up burials
Starkley (13–N–16)	1	12′ high, tri. shape	...	Material scanty
St. Francis Area				
Twist Group (11–N–16)	40 or more	Range from 60′ x 10′ to 40′ x 1′	...	Material scanty
Yazoo Area				
Bay Lake (19–N–3)	4	Mutilated too badly to measure	Irregular	Shell midden; rich
Period D–C				
Sunflower Area				
Charleston (16–P–1)	3	150′ x 15′ 60′ x 5′ 90′ x 6′	Irregular	Abundant material, especially flint chips
Marlow Cemetery (18–N–2)	1	60′ x 8′	...	...
Cook (17–N–15)	2	45′ x 3′ 30′ x 1′	Irregular	Plowed up burials

[2] In this, and following tables 12 to 15, sites are listed by period and grouped according to the five areal subdivisions outlined in Section V, p. 226.

TABLE 11: SITES WITH CONICAL MOUNDS (*Continued*)

	NO. OF MOUNDS	SIZES	ARRANGEMENT	REMARKS
Memphis Area				
Rawlinson (13–N–13)	2	60′ x 6′ 80′ x 3′	E–W	...
Collins (13–O–9)	3	50′ x 4′ 50′ x 4′ 60′ x 3′	Irregular	...
Stoddard (13–O–8)	2	60′ x 4½′ 60′ x 6′	E–W	...
Huber (13–O–3)	1	Dome shaped, small	...	...
St. Francis Area				
Williams (11–N–8)	8	90′ x 9′ 55′ x 5′ 45′ x 3′ and smaller	Irregular	...
Cross County Club (11–N–10)	1	60′ x 4′	...	Scanty material
Delta (11–N–11)	6	100′ x 10′ — others, 150′ x 4′	...	Scanty material
Gilliland (11–O–9)	2	40′ x 4′ others? (plowed down)	...	Scanty material
Lansing (12–N–7)	Many	20–30′ diam. 2–4′ high	Linear	Scanty material
Emory (11–O–5)	1	60′ x 4′	...	Scanty material
Prosperity (11–O–11)	1	50′ x 2′	...	Scanty material
Period E–D				
Yazoo Area				
Brooks (18–M–5)	1	Oval 120′ x 75′ x 10′	...	...
Sunflower Area				
Boykin Bayou (17–M–14)	1	50′ x 6′	...	...
May (17–N–5)	1	100′ x 3′ (plowed)	...	Fairly abundant material
Oxbow Bend (16–O–11)	1	90′ x 3′	...	Abundant 100 m. west of mound

TABLE 11: SITES WITH CONICAL MOUNDS (*Continued*)

	NO. OF MOUNDS	SIZES	ARRANGEMENT	REMARKS
Memphis Area				
Hughes (13–M–1)	2	Oval 150′ x 120′ x 10′ 100′ x 1½′	N–S	Material abundant
Broom (14–M–3)	3	100′ x 10′ (?) 36′ x 2′ 45′ x 2′	Irregular	Burials and pots from large mound; moderately abundant material
Canon (14–O–13)	1	100′ x 30′ x 12′	...	Material abundant
St. Francis Area				
Westmorland (12–N–6)	7	80′ x 4′ 50′ x 3′ 25′ x 1′, etc.	Irregular	Scanty material
Pinkston (11–O–6)	1	60′ x 5′	...	Scanty material
Rogers Place (11–N–2)	5	80′ x 5′ 24′ x 3′ 30′ x 2′ 40′ x 2′, etc.	Irregular	Scanty material
Roberts (11–N–3)	4	60′ x 3′ 40′ x 1′ 40′ x 1½′, etc.	Irregular	Material abundant
Period F–E				
Yazoo Area				
Porter Bayou (18–M–1)	3	Oval 70′ x 120′ x 12′ — conicals 60′ x 8′ — 45′ x 3′	Irregular	Scanty near mounds; collection from village site abundant
Arkansas River Area				
Bond (17–K–6)	1	Conical 50′ x 4′	...	Village site east of mound; scanty
Westlake (18–K–2)	2	30′ x 3′ — 40′ x 1′	...	Scanty
Sunflower Area				
Hopson Bayou (16–N–11)	1	40′ x 3′	...	Scanty
Prowell (15–O–7)	3	3′ high spread 2 destroyed conicals	...	Abundant
Ellis (16–N–3)	3	Oval 100′ x 130′ x 12′ 2 destroyed	...	Abundant on "C"

TABLE 11: SITES WITH CONICAL MOUNDS (*Continued*)

	NO. OF MOUNDS	SIZES	ARRANGEMENT	REMARKS
Tidwell (15–O–16)	1	60′ x 5′	...	Abundant
Flower (16–O–16)	1	"Very small mound"	...	Moderately abundant
Acree Place (16–N–1)	2	100′ x 4′ — 16′ x 6′	...	Material scanty; human bones
Ware (15–O–18)	3	45′ x 3′ — 75′ x 6′ — — x – ?	...	...
Joe Smith (17–N–18)	1	Oval 75′ x 25′ x 6′	½ mile mound to village site	Rich midden in village site
Cassidy Bayou (17–O–11)	1	90′ x 9′	...	Village site east of mound rich in material
Barbee (15–O–2)	1	100′ x 8′	...	Scanty material west of mound
Dickerson (15–N–10)	1	90′ x 9′	...	Large rich village site covering 40 acreas
D'Orr (15–O–12)	1	"Small mound"	...	Rich village site
Aderholt (16–N–20)	2	"Small mounds"	...	...
Harris Bayou (16–N–14)	1	80′ x 5′	...	Rich village site ⅓ mile NW of mound
Boyer (17–N–8)	1	100′ x 9′ (?) plowed down	Burials	Village site 300′ NE
Blue Lake (16–P–8)	2	plowed down	...	Abundant
Thomas (15–P–1)	1	45′ x 3′	...	...
Everett (16–O–3)	2	60′ x 5′ — 40′ x 3′	...	...
St. Francis Area				
Burns (12–N–9)	1	Plowed down (small)	...	Scanty
Swan Place (12–N–15)	1	40′ x 5′	...	Scanty
DeRossett's Place (12–N–10)	1	15′ x 100′	...	Scanty; human bones

TABLE 11: SITES WITH CONICAL MOUNDS (*Continued*)

	NO. OF MOUNDS	SIZES	ARRANGEMENT	REMARKS
Period G–F				
Sunflower Area				
Wilnot (17–N–16)	1	60′ x 3′	...	Scanty
Garner (16–O–15)	1	75′ x 5′	...	Village site to east
Boles Lake (17–M–13)	1	60′ x 9′	...	Village site to east
Stover (16–O–14)	1	45′ x 3′	...	Village site 100 yds. to S.
Henderson (16–O–7)	2	30′ x 2′ — 75′ x 5′	...	Scanty
Twin Lakes (16–P–3)		"Several low dome-shaped mounds"	...	...

Small Ceremonial Centers

Seventy-eight of the sites classed as small ceremonial centers are listed in table 12. These sites are fairly evenly distributed through the Survey Area and judging entirely on the basis of surface collections they were being constructed and used from time E up to A. Three sites in the Sunflower area seem to date in period F–E, but, as the association of the surface material with the mound structures is not beyond question (see p. 337), this earlier dating will not be insisted upon.

The availability of surface material varies on these sites of course according to whether the fields are in cultivation or have grown up in grass. However, at most of these mound groups there is no thick and extensive deposit of midden, and sherds are available mainly on the flanks of the mounds where they have been swept down from buildings that stood on the summits, or in a few concentrations that seem to indicate house sites on the level ground. In most cases, these houses are further indicated by low rises and appear to have been arranged about a court or plaza along with the larger and better-defined mounds. A few sites yield almost no sherd material at all. These sites will not appear in the study as the lack of an adequate collection has made it impossible to date them.

The number of mounds at these small ceremonial centers ranges from one to six or eight. An arrangement of two mounds at either end of a plaza area seems to be most common. At each site there is a principal mound which varies in height from 5 to as much as 25 feet. Eight to 15 feet seems to be an average height. This question of original height is sometimes impossible to settle as cultivation has torn down and spread many of the mounds. In some instances, this has also obscured the form. In the fifty-five examples where the original outlines could be determined some variation of form was noted. Analysis does not show either areal or temporal differences in these mound shapes so they are listed below without showing areas and periods.

1. Flat-topped, square in shape — 12
   - With ramp for stairway — 3
2. Flat-topped, rectangular in shape — 43
   - With ramp for stairway — 2
   - With two levels on top of mound — 7
   - With two levels on top of mound and also ramp for stairway — 4

At most of the sites there are several other mounds, or slightly elevated house sites, in addition to the large mounds described above. When the forms of these have been preserved, they are usually seen to be rectangular. However, a few were conical.

At thirty-seven of the seventy-eight small ceremonial centers several mounds were so located that they clearly outlined a plaza area. At fourteen other sites we think that we have been able to determine the position and outline of the plaza by the distribution of refuse material, unusual concentrations of which have been assumed to mark the buildings that were placed about it. Plaza areas at these sites are generally relatively free from refuse accumulations and are roughly oval in shape varying from 200 to 400 feet long and about half as wide. The long axis of the plazas generally runs in an east-west direction, and there is a decided tendency for the largest mound to be placed on the western end so that it looks eastward across the plaza. This is shown by the following tabulation of fifty-one sites at which the orientation was recorded.

Mound faces across the plaza toward:

North	1
Northeast	5
East	22
Southeast	14
South	4
Southwest	2
West	1
Northwest	2

In the case of mounds which have ramps for stairways, these are almost always on the side toward the plaza. The rectangular mounds are usually arranged with the long side facing the plaza.

As stated above, practically all of these sites are in various stages of destruction from cultivation, levee construction, or erosion. Genally, this process has revealed burned clay daub that shows impressions of grass and canes. This may indicate the intentional destruction of wattle-and-daub-type buildings by fire. Analysis does not clearly show any temporal difference in regard to this custom but suggests that it may be more common for the later sites than for the earlier. Superimposed building levels, each covered with a thick layer of burned daub, were exposed by erosion in the larger mounds at several of the later sites.

The sites of this class seem to have served primarily as ceremonial centers rather than actual village sites. This is indicated by the paucity of refuse and the fact that most of the material found has come down from the houses that stood on mound tops or on low elevations around the plaza area. Not enough houses are indicated for the substantial populations which must have constructed and used these centers. Probably the people who used each of these mound groups lived scattered through the surrounding country somewhat after the arrangement of the Natchez Tribe in 1700.

Plans of a number of typical small ceremonial centers are shown in figure 61.

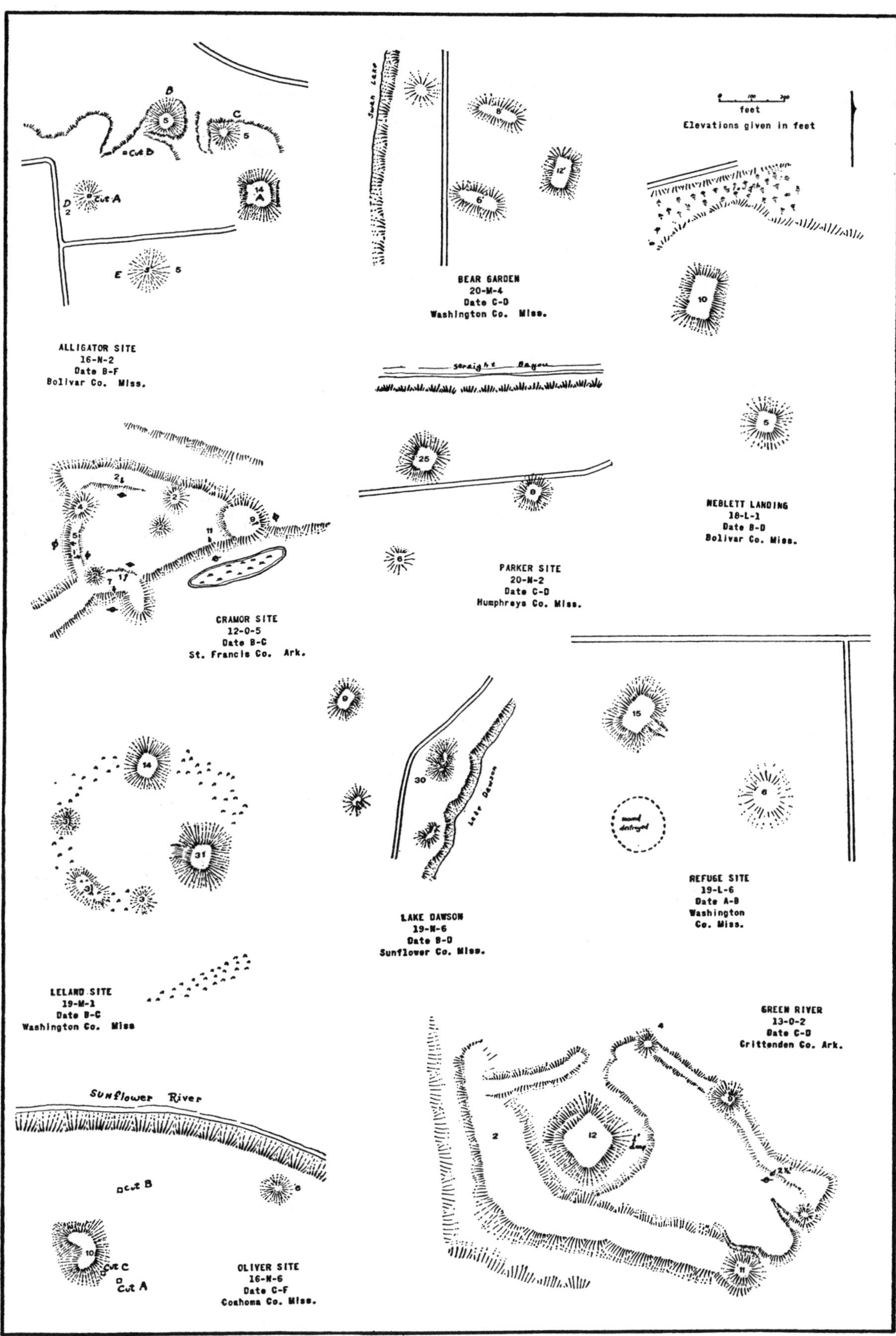

Fig. 61. Plans of typical small ceremonial centers.

TABLE 12: SMALL CEREMONIAL CENTERS.

SITE	TIME RANGE	PLAZA LENGTH	ORIENT.	HEIGHT MOUND A	TYPE A	OTHER MOUNDS*	DAUB	REFUSE	REMARKS
Period B–A									
Yazoo Area									
Refuge (19–L–6)	Short	300′	SE	15′	Sq. w/ Ramp	2 (?)	Some	Scanty	. . .
Stoneville (19–M–3)	Short	150′ (?)	SW	6′	?	. . .	. . .	. . .	. . .
Kinlock (19–N–1)	F–A	225′	N	14′	Rect.	1 (square) 3 (?)	. . .	Moderate	Quantities of shell
Arkansas River Area									
Jones Place (16–K–1)	Short	175′	SE	5′	?	1 (?) (3′ high)	Yes	Moderate	Floor levels in "A"
Ellis (15–N–2)	D–A	?	?	6′	Square	. . .	. . .	Moderate	. . .
Sunflower Area									
Mattson (16–N–9)	Short	?	E (?)	12′	?	None	. . .	. . .	Small amount of sherds in patches E of mound
Myer (16–N–10)	Short	200′ (?)	E (?)	15′	Square	None	Abundant	Very scarce	. . .
Vance (17–N–9)	Short	?	?	?	?	None	. . .	. . .	Small amount of sherds to N & E
Memphis Area									
Johnson Cemetery (14–O–6)	Short	?	?	12′	Square (?)	None	Abundant	Scanty	. . .
Mound Place (12–P–1)	Short	220′	E	10′	?	1 (double conical)	. . .	. . .	. . .
Kent Place (13–N–4)	D–A	?	E	?	?	1 (?)	. . .	Abundant	. . .
Perry (14–O–4)	Short	?	?	10′	Rect.	3 (?)	Abundant	Scanty	. . .

* Question marks (?) in this column indicate that shapes of auxiliary mounds could not be determined. The three dots in this and other columns indicate a regrettable lack of data in our field notes.

TABLE 12: SMALL CEREMONIAL CENTERS (*Continued*)

SITE	TIME RANGE	PLAZA LENGTH	ORIENT.	HEIGHT MOUND A	TYPE A	OTHER MOUNDS	DAUB	REFUSE	REMARKS
Brackenseed Place (12–O–6)	Short	200′	SE	10′	Square	1 (?)	Some	Scanty	. . .
Period C–B									
Yazoo Area									
Panther Burn (20–M–3)	Short	?	?	8′	Rect. (?)	None	. . .	Scanty	. . .
Arcola High School (19–M–6)	D–B	300′	NE	5′	?	1 (?)	. . .	. . .	Daub and sherds on mound to E only
Barlow (18–N–1)	Short	?	?	12′	Rect.	None	On mound only	On mound only	Some burials
Silver City (20–O–5)	Short	?	?	15′	Rect. stepped	None	. . .	. . .	. . .
Deer Creek (19–L–4)	Short	?	SE	12′	Rect.	1 (?)	Some	Scanty	. . .
Sheldon (19–M–2)	Short	?	?	9′	Rect. (?)	1 (?)	. . .	Moderately abundant	. . .
Steiner (18–N–4)	Short	?	SE (?)	?	?	None	Some	Daub and pottery to SE of mound	. . .
Failing (19–N–5)	Short	?	E	?	?	1 (?)	Abundant	Abundant	. . .
Bay Lake (19–N–3)	Short	300′ (?)	E by N	6′	Sq. w/ Ramp	2 (?)	Abundant	Abundant	. . .
Neblett Landing (18–L–1)	D–B	300′	E by S	9′	Rect.	1 (square)	Moderately abundant	Moderately abundant	. . .
Lamkin (20–O–3)	D–B	150′	SE	12′	Rect.	1 (?)	Moderately abundant	Moderately abundant	. . .
Arkansas River Area									
Cooks Mound (17–K–5)	D–B	?	Mound E–W; N–S	25′	Square	None	Scarce	. . .	Possible plaza occupied by levee

TABLE 12: SMALL CEREMONIAL CENTERS (*Continued*)

SITE	RANGE TIME	PLAZA LENGTH	ORIENT.	HEIGHT MOUND A	TYPE A	OTHER MOUNDS	DAUB	REFUSE	REMARKS
Sunflower Area									
Dockery (17–N–11)	Short	150′	E	5′	?	1(?)	Scarce	...	...
Spendthrift (16–O–2)	E–B	?	?	15′	Rect.(?)	None	Very abundant	Moderately abundant	...
Merigold (17–N–1)	Short	300′	SE	18′	Sq. w/ Ramp	6(?)	Abundant	Moderately abundant	...
Powell Bayou (17–O–9)	Short	150′	E	12′	Rect.	3(?)	Abundant on mounds	Abundant	...
Wilford (15–O–10)	Short	?	E by N	10′	Sq. w/ Ramp & Apron	None	Scanty	Very scanty	...
Salomon (15–O–1)	E–B	400′	SE	27′	Rect. w/ Ramp & Apron	4 (rect.) 6 (square)	...	Scanty	...
O'Donnell (17–M–12)	E–B	?	?	8′	Rect.(?)	None	...	Scanty	...
Walford (17–N–2)	Short	400′	E	10′	?	1 (rect.?)	...	...	...
Corn Lake (15–P–4)	D–B	300′	E	...	Rect.	?	Abundant	Moderately abundant	...
White (16–P–4)	F–B	?	S	6′	Rect.	1(6′?)	...	...	...
Dunn (16–O–1)	F–B	310′	NE	15′	Rect. stepped	1(2′?)	Abundant	Scanty	...
Alligator Mounds (16–N–2)	F–B	450′	SE	15′	Stepped w/Ramp	1 (rect. 12′)	Abundant	...	...
Bush (17–M–11)	Short	240′	S	12′	Rect.	1(2′?)	Abundant	Abundant	...

TABLE 12: SMALL CEREMONIAL CENTERS (*Continued*)

SITE	TIME RANGE	PLAZA LENGTH	ORIENT.	HEIGHT MOUND A	TYPE A	OTHER MOUNDS	DAUB	REFUSE	REMARKS
Memphis Area									
Shawnee Village (11–P–1)	Short	...	E by N	8′	Rect.	1 (4′ Rect.)	Abundant	Scanty	...
Commerce (13–O–11)	Short	?	S	18′	Rect. w/Ramp	5 (House mounds)	...	Scanty	...
West Mounds (14–O–10)	Short	200′	E	18′	Rect. w/Ramp	1 (5′ rect.?)	Abundant	Scanty	...
Bradley (11–P–2)	Short	?	?	10′	?	(Wrecked by levee construction)	...	Scanty	...
Nickel (13–N–15)	D–B	?	E	12′	Square	1 (5′?)	Some	Moderately abundant	...
Beaverdam (14–O–3)	Short	?	?	11′	?	...	Abundant	Scanty	...
Pouncey (12–O–2)	E–B	?	S	15′	Rect.	1 (10′ rect.) 1 (6′ conical)	Abundant	Moderately abundant	...
St. Francis Area									
Welshans Place (12–N–5)	Short	...	NE	5′	Rect.	1 (3′?) 1 (2′?)	...	Moderately abundant	...
Period D–C									
Yazoo Area									
McLean (19–O–1)	D–B	120′	...	15′	Rect. (?)	1 (?)	Some	Some	...
Swan Lake (20–M–5)	E–C	250′	SW	24′	Rect. w/ Ramp	9′ (rect.) 9′ (rect.) 2 (?)	...	Moderately abundant	...
Whaley (18–P–2)	Short	150′	SE	5′	Rect.	1 (8′?)	Abundant	Abundant	...
Lessiedell (20–M–4)	Short	400′	W	12′	Rect.	1 (6′?)	...	...	...
Midnight (20–N–1)	Short	...	...	10′	Rect. w/ Ramp	...	...	...	...

TABLE 12: SMALL CEREMONIAL CENTERS (*Continued*)

SITE	TIME RANGE	PLAZA LENGTH	ORIENT.	HEIGHT MOUND A	TYPE A	OTHER MOUNDS	DAUB	REFUSE	REMARKS
Ely (19–L–3)	Short	300′(?)	SE?	3′	?	...	Some	Moderately abundant	...
Belzoni (20–O–2)	Short	...	...	12′	Rect.	...	...	Abundant	...
Hollyknowe (19–M–5)	Short	225′	E	5′?	?	...	...	Scanty	...
Polk (19–M–7)	Short	...	...	5′	?	...	Some	Scanty	...
Arkansas Area									
Tinsley Mound (15–M–1)	E–B	200′	E	4′	?	1 (4′?)	Few	Moderately abundant	...
Wynn (17–L–4)	Short	400′	NE	11′	Square	1 (4′?)	...	...	...
Hogg Lake (18–K–1)	F–C	150′	...	5′	Square	1 (?)	...	Some	...
Sunflower Area									
Bear Ridge (17–M–1)	E–B	200′	NE	10′	?	1 (4?) 1 (4?) 1 (5′?) 1 (1′?) 1 (4′?) 1 (1′?)	Some	Abundant	...
Buford (17–O–1)	Short	...	...	30′	Rect.	2 (conical)	None	Moderately abundant	...
Oliver (16–N–6)	F–C	600′	E	26′	Rect.	1 (?)	Some	Abundant	...
Roosevelt (17–M–18)	Short	300′	E	5′	?	1 (2′?)	...	...	...
Shady Grove (16–P–2)	E–B	180′	E	18′	Rect.	1 (5′ conical)	...	...	...
Whiting (15–O–15)	E–C	...	...	...	...	...	Some	...	...
Memphis Area									
Greer (13–N–17)	D–B	...	...	14′	Rect.	...	...	...	...

Table 12: Small Ceremonial Centers (*Continued*)

SITE	TIME RANGE	PLAZA LENGTH	ORIENT.	HEIGHT MOUND A	TYPE A	OTHER MOUNDS *	DAUB	REFUSE	REMARKS
Murdock Place (13–N–12)	Short	...	...	9′	Rect.	...	...	...	...
Barrett (13–O–1)	D–B	400′	E(?)	9′	Rect.	1 (7′)	Few	Scanty	...
Dundee (14–O–8)	Short	?	?	15′	?	1 (conical, 100 x 12) 1 (conical, 70 x 3)	Abundant	Moderately abundant	...
Green River Plantation (13–O–2)	Short	...	...	12′	Square	1 (11′square) 1 (9′conical)	None	Scanty	...
St. Francis Area									
Block (11–N–6)	Short	250′	SE	15′	?	4 others	Some	Scarce	...
Lewis Place (11–O–7)	Short	200′	SE	7′	...	1 (7′ rect.)	...	Scarce	...
Period E–D									
Yazoo Area									
Choctaw (18–M–6)	Short	...	...	12′	Rect.	None	Some	Abundant on mound	...
Sunflower Area									
Rufus Davis (16–N–4)	F–D	...	...	12′	Rect.	1 (conical)	Some	Moderately abundant	...
Memphis Area									
Thompson Lake (12–O–3)	Short	...	...	...	Rect. stepped	1 (conical)	...	Scanty	...
Evansville (14–O–1)	E–C	300′	NW	12′	Rect. stepped	3 (?)	Quantities	Moderately abundant	...
Owens (14–O–2)	F–D	400′	NW	12′	Rect. stepped	1 (3?)	Quantities	Abundant	...

TABLE 12: SMALL CEREMONIAL CENTERS (*Continued*)

SITE	TIME RANGE	PLAZA LENGTH	ORIENT.	HEIGHT MOUND A	TYPE A	OTHER MOUNDS	DAUB	REFUSE	REMARKS
Period F–E									
Sunflower Area									
Indian Creek (15–P–3)	Short	...	...	12′	Rect. stepped	...	Some	Scanty	...
Posey Mound (15–O–6)	F–D	...	...	15′	Rect.	...	Some	Moderately abundant	...
Nelson (17–M–17)	Short	...	SE	5′	Square	...	...	Moderately abundant	...

Large Ceremonial Centers

The division between "small" and "large" ceremonial centers is entirely arbitrary. Sites in the latter class are distinguished solely by having more and larger mound structures. Twelve sites have been listed in this class (table 13). Collections from these sites date from times D to A, with the majority — all but two — dating between C and A. Closer dating of these sites is difficult because of their size. Separate collections taken from different locations on one of these sites usually show significant chronological differences. The mere size alone of some of the mounds would indicate a fairly long period for their construction. There are good reasons for believing that the majority of these sites were flourishing about time B on our chronological scale.

The central plazas about which these mound groups are arranged differ from those already described only in being larger, from 250 to 450 feet long. The Winterville Site (19–L–1) is atypical, however, in having the great central mound located in the center of a huge oval space, some 1200 feet long surrounded by sixteen lesser mounds, so that in effect there are two plazas (fig. 62). The comparable Lake George Site in Quadrangle 21–N, not covered in this report, has precisely the same arrangement, so it may be culturally significant.

The orientation of the large ceremonial centers is generally similar to that of the small, though the tendency toward an eastward orientation is perhaps not quite so pronounced, as may be seen in the following list.

Principal mound faces across the plaza toward:

North	0
Northeast	2
East	1
Southeast	5
South	2
Southwest	0
West	1
Northwest	1

Most of the sites of this class have several large rectangular platform mounds, though one is always considerably larger than the rest and dominates the group. These dominant mounds, upon which it is reasonable to infer the principal "temple" was located, range from 15 to 54 feet in height. Since they are generally large and steep-sided enough to have escaped cultivation, their original shapes are clearly apparent and may be classified as follows:

1. Flat-topped, square in shape		8
With ramp for stairway	5	
With apron on one side	1	
2. Flat-topped, rectangular in shape		3
With ramp for stairway	1	
Stepped (top in two levels)	1	

Nearly all of these principal mounds have been subjected to some erosion, and in the majority of cases this has exposed both refuse and burned clay daub from building levels in the mounds. The material is scattered down the sides of the mounds and in the fields near by, and this has been one of the principal sources for the pottery collected to date on these sites.

The smaller mounds on these large sites are either rectangular or square, and in a few instances well enough preserved for ramps to be discerned. One is rectangular in shape and has a small conical mound located on one end of its summit platform.

Like the preceding class of small ceremonial centers, these sites seem to have been primarily religious sites. Refuse is very scanty at some of them, and where moderate amounts are found, it usually seems to have been derived from structures that stood on the mound tops. Deep rich midden deposits such as would have been produced by the large population that must have built and used these centers were not found. Equally significant perhaps with the lack of deep refuse deposits is the almost complete absence of burials. There is a consistent record of failure on the part of local pot-hunters to get anything out of these sites in which the archaeologist can take a grim satisfaction.

Plans of several large ceremonial centers are shown in figure 62.

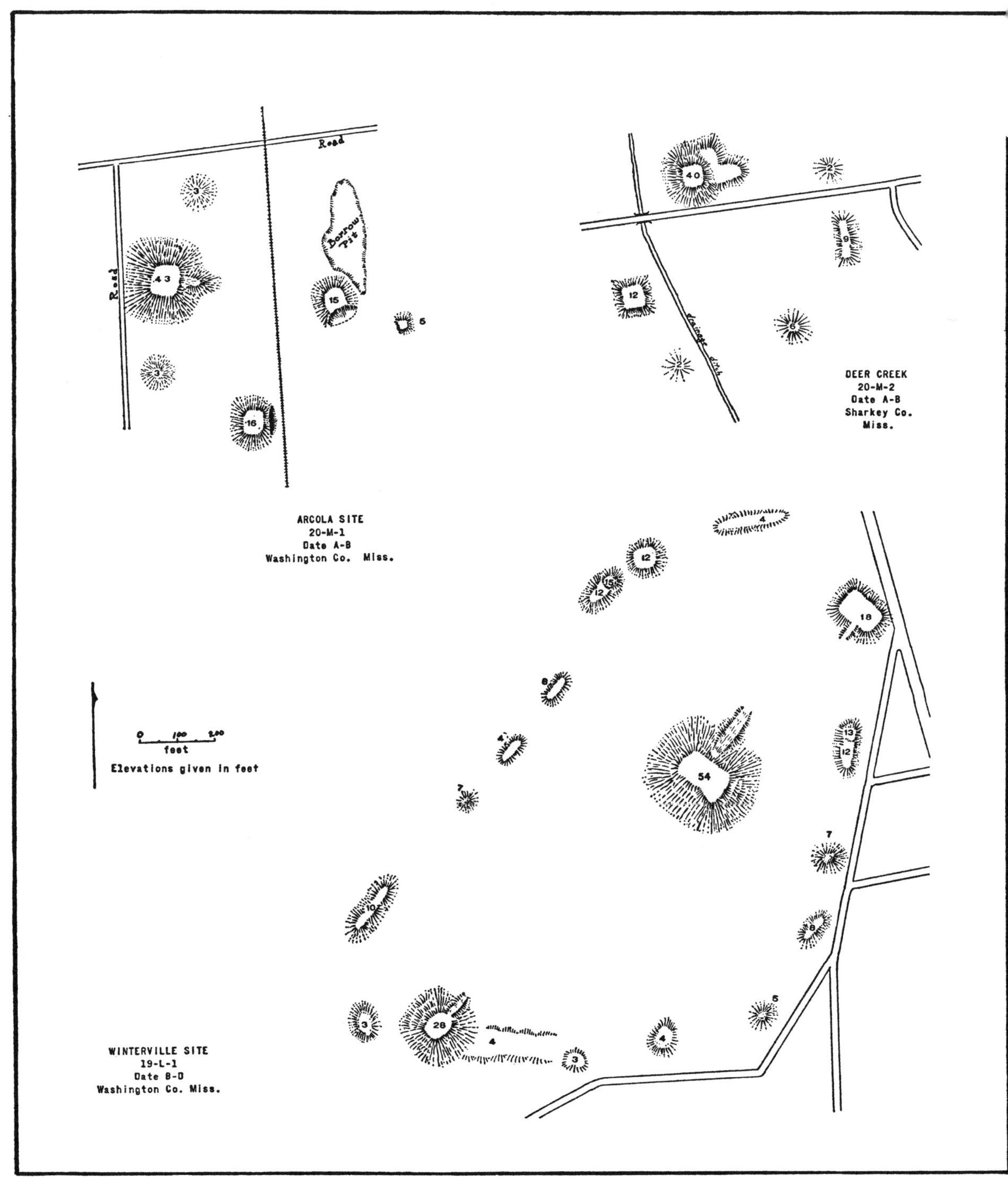

FIG. 62. Plans of typical large ceremonial centers.

TABLE 13: LARGE CEREMONIAL CENTERS.

SITE	TIME RANGE	PLAZA LENGTH	ORIENT.	HEIGHT MOUND A	TYPE A	OTHER MOUNDS	DAUB	REFUSE	REMARKS
Period B–A									
Yazoo Area									
Refuge (19–L–6)	Short	300′	SE	15′	Sq. w/ Ramp	B(6′?) C(?)	Some	Scanty	. . .
Arcola (20–M–1)	Short	250′	E by S	43′	Sq. w/ Ramp 3 more?	B(15′ sq.) C(16′ sq.)	On mound E	Scanty	. . .
Deer Creek (20–M–2)	Short	300′	SE	40′	Sq. w/ Apron	B(12′ sq.) C(6′?) D(9′ rect.)	. . .	Moderately abundant	. . .
Sunflower Area									
Fitzhugh (15–N–1)	C–A	550′	SSE	20′	Rect. stepped	2 (square) 9′(?)	Abundant	Scanty	. . .
Memphis Area									
Hollywood (13–O–10)	Short	450′	S	20′	Sq. w/ Ramp	12 (?) 2 (5′ high)	Abundant	Abundant w/burial	Approaches St. Francis type
Period C–B									
Yazoo Area									
Leland (19–M–1)	Short	300′	W by N	31′	Sq. w/ Ramp	B(14′ sq.) 3 (mounds)	. . .	Moderately abundant	. . .
Winterville (19–L–1)	D–B	350′	NE	54′	Rect. w/ Ramp	B (square w/R 18′) 5 (other mounds)	Abundant on mounds	Moderate	. . .
Lake Dawson (19–N–6)	D–B	250′	NW	30′(?)	?	2 (rect.) 1 (?)		Moderately abundant	. . .
Jaketown (20–O–1)	B–G	250′	E by N	15′	Sq. w/ Ramp	1 (square) 3 (?)	. . .	Moderately abundant	. . .

TABLE 13: LARGE CEREMONIAL CENTERS (*Continued*)

SITE	TIME RANGE	PLAZA LENGTH	ORIENT.	HEIGHT MOUND A	TYPE A	OTHER MOUNDS	DAUB	REFUSE	REMARKS
Sunflower Area									
Cason (17–P–2)	E–B	?	S	18′	Square (?)	3 (?)	Some	Moderately abundant	...
Period C–D									
Yazoo Area									
Summerfield (20–N–2)	Short	250′	ESE	25′	Square	1 (rect.) 1 (?)	Grass daub	Scanty	...
Arkansas River Area									
Baytown (15–L–2)	Short	450′	NE	20′	Rect.	1 (rect. w/con.) 1 (square) 6 (?)	...	Moderately abundant	...

Large Rectangular Village Sites with Temple Mounds

The variety of settlement which we will call the "St. Francis-type" site was evidently a planned village laid out in rectangular form so far as the natural features of the sites permitted. In contrast to the classes of ceremonial centers which have been described in the foregoing section, these are places where fairly large numbers of people lived and the ceremonial center, the plaza with its surrounding mounds, has become the center of a town.

The 21 sites that have been assigned to this class are listed and some of their characteristics are described in table 14. Plans of representative sites are given in figure 63. The St. Francis Basin in Arkansas seems to be the center of the distribution and is the area in which are found the best developed examples of the type; Parkin (11–N–1), Rose Mound (12–N–3), Castile Landing (13–N–21), the Vernon Paul Place (11–N–9), and Fortune Mound (11–N–15).

As one approaches these sites across the level flood plain, the first impression is made by the unusual depth of the refuse that has accumulated. The entire area of Rose Mound (12–N–3) (see fig. 52) stands up about 10 feet above the surrounding plain. Cuts into this "mound" showed 2.5 meters of rich refuse deposit. This impression of the elevation of the entire village area is heightened by the wide ditch which surrounds most of the sites of this type. The concentration of the refuse in a rectangular area surrounded by a ditch indicates almost conclusively that these towns were fortified. A stockade as well as a ditch probably protected as well as defined the village area.

Despite the unusual depth of refuse at these sites, they do not seem to have been occupied for any great length of time. The Rose Mound Site (12–N–3) is the only one from which the surface collection showed a Baytown Period occupation. That mixture of Baytown and Mississippi types was the reason for the strata cut which Phillips put into this site (see p. 287). In general, however, the refuse accumulation seems to be due to a dense concentration of dwelling sites rather than any unusual length of occupation. The rate of midden accumulation may also have been speeded up somewhat by soil brought in from outside the village areas. The dirt from the surrounding ditches has certainly been added to the pile. Mussel shells have not contributed materially to the bulk of these deposits, as in the Tennessee and Yazoo River valleys; the deposits are primarily ordinary living refuse: food bones, ashes, charcoal, burnt clay daub, and pot-sherds by the hundreds of thousands.

The names of many of the St. Francis-type towns are familiar to those acquainted with the literature of Mississippi Valley archaeology, for they have long been famous for the quantities of burial pottery which they have yielded. They are mentioned by Cyrus Thomas and Holmes in their surveys of Eastern sites and antiquities, and most of them were visited by C. B. Moore.[3] Between visits of scientific investigators, local pot-hunters have probed these sites with iron wagon rods and nearly all the larger museums of the U. S. have collections from them, more or less adequately labeled. Even more material appears to have gone onto the collector's market.

The burials in these sites are not in mounds, nor concentrated in "cemeteries." They are scattered about without apparent arrangement in the midden areas and there is a strong possibility that the practice of the inhabitants of the sites was to bury their dead beneath the floors of the houses. This is in contrast to the conditions found at the ceremonial centers described previously, where burials are rare, and when found are accompanied by little or no grave material.

The arrangement of the mounds and dwelling areas on these rectangular St. Francis-type sites is fairly consistent. Low heaped-up piles of refuse show that the houses were grouped around the borders of the area leaving a slightly lower plaza in the center. The general effect is that of a very large rectangular mound somewhat more elevated on the edges than in the center. They are frequently referred to as "mounds" (see Rose Mound), but this is of course a misnomer. Many of them do have mounds of the usual late rec-

[3] Thomas, 1894; Holmes, 1903; Moore, 1910.

tangular platform type, but these are generally not as large as those described for the large ceremonial centers. Six of the twenty-one sites grouped in this class had no mounds at all. Either they had never been built or had been destroyed by the intense cultivation to which all of these sites have been subjected. At the fourteen sites that had mounds the dominant temple mound was uniformly located near the center of the western side of the site. These principal mounds range from 1.2 to 4.5 meters in height. At five sites it could be determined that this principal western mound was an elongated rectangle with a long side facing the east toward the plaza. Four mounds were of the stepped type with an apron to the north or south of the higher portion of the mound, so that a building on either level might have faced eastward across the plaza. Additional mounds numbering from one to eight border the plaza area at most of the sites. About some of these, however, we cannot be too certain. All have been plowed over and it is often impossible to determine whether a low rise on these sites is the remains of a structure or a pile of refuse that was unintentionally accumulated upon a house site.

The orientation of the straight sides of nearly all of these sites was very close to east-west and north-south. The dominant mound, as already noted, stood on the western edge of the site and the plaza, if there was one, lay directly to the east or southeast of it. This corresponds to the most popular mound-plaza orientation in the mound groups of the ceremonial-center types.

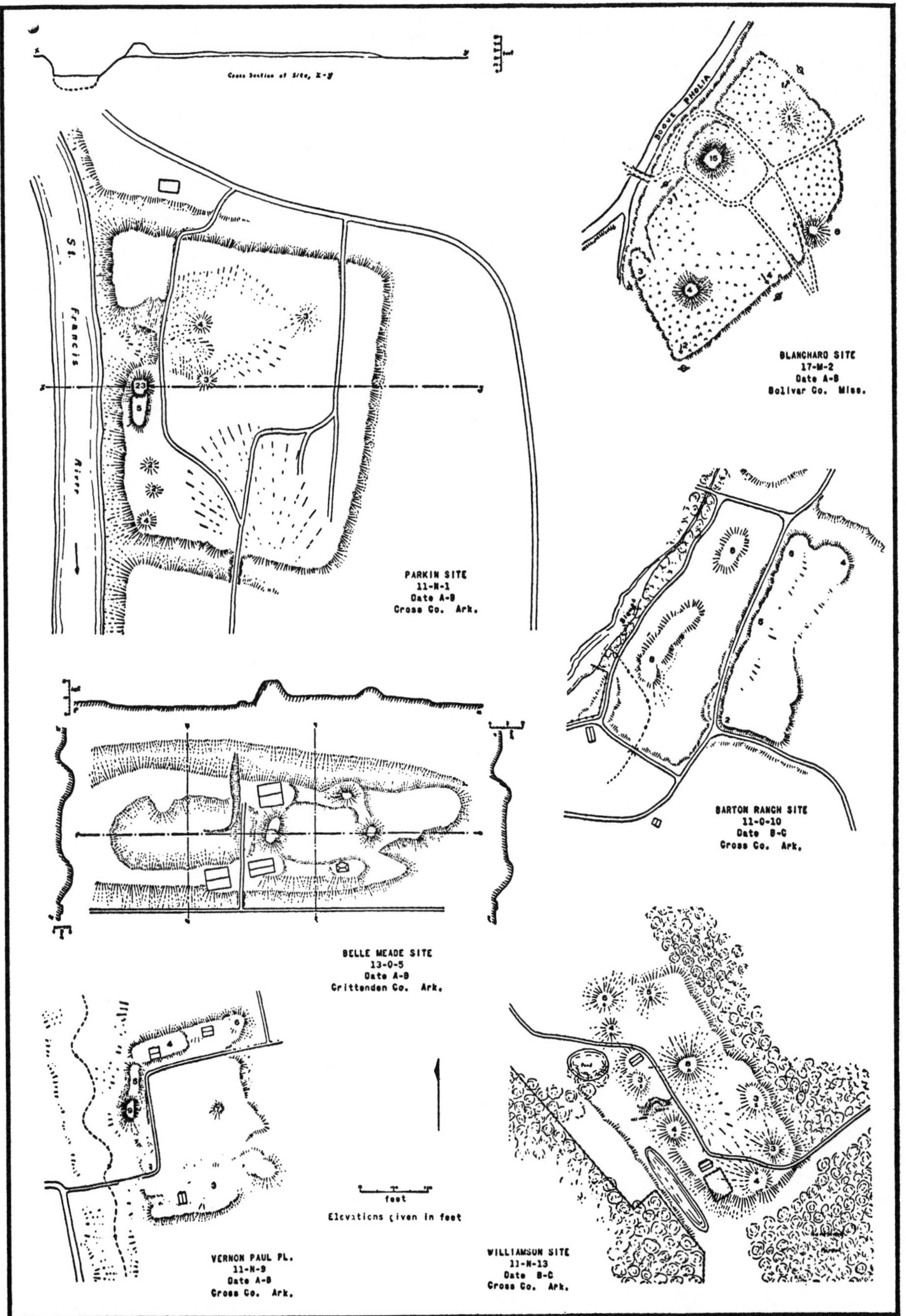

FIG. 63. Typical "St. Francis-type" sites.

TABLE 14: "ST. FRANCIS-TYPE" SITES.

SITE	TIME RANGE	PLAZA LENGTH	ORIENT.	HEIGHT MOUND A	TYPE A	OTHER MOUNDS	DAUB	REFUSE	REMARKS
Period B–A									
Arkansas River Area									
Old Town (15–N–3)	Short	?	SE	1 (12′ sq.)	Stepped	4′	Yes	Abundant	Surrounded by wall
Sunflower Area									
Blanchard (17–M–2)	Short	400′	SE	1 (15′ sq.?)	...	3 (square ?)	?	Abundant (6′ deep)	...
Memphis Area									
Beck (13–O–7)	Short	300′	E by N	1 (10′ sq.)	...	7 (?)	?	Abundant (around edge of plaza)	...
Bell Place (10–P–2)	Short	...	E?	...	...	...	...	Rectangular midden 400′ x 300′ oriented	...
Belle Meade (13–O–5)	Short	275′	E	1 (10′)	Rect. stepped	5 (?)	Yes	Abundant (about edges of plaza)	...
St. Francis Area									
Big Eddy (12–N–4)	Short	350′	E by S	?	...	2 (?)	...	Deep midden w/burials	...
Clay Hill (13–N–7)	Short	...	Midden area; 2 indefinite mounds	...	...	...	...	...	...
Manly (12–N–2)	Short	...	No mounds	...	...	...	...	...	...
Rose Mound (12–N–3)	C–A	...	No mounds E–W	...	...	...	Abundant	...	...

TABLE 14: "ST. FRANCIS-TYPE" SITES (*Continued*)

SITE	TIME RANGE	PLAZA LENGTH	ORIENT.	HEIGHT MOUND A	TYPE A	OTHER MOUNDS	DAUB	REFUSE	REMARKS
Parkin (11–N–1)	Short	600'?	E	23	Rect. stepped	3	Abundant	Deep midden w/burials	...
Cummings (11–O–4)	Short	300'	E	1 (5'?)	...	2 (?)	Abundant	Deep midden w/burials	...
Castile (13–N–21)	Short	275'	E	1 (9')	Rect. stepped	None	Abundant	Deep midden w/burials	...
Vernon Paul (11–N–9)	Short	250'	E	1 (9')	Rect. stepped	1 (rect.) 1 (conical) 2 (?)	Abundant	Deep midden w/burials	...
Fortune Mound (11–N–15)	Short	200'	E	1 (Plowed down?)	...	...	Abundant	Deep midden w/burials	...
Neeley's Ferry (11–N–4)	Short	200'	E	1 (12' rect.)	...	1 (rect.) 1 (?)	Abundant	Deep midden w/burials	...
Period C–B									
Memphis Area									
Cramor Place (12–O–5)	Short	175'	E by S	1 (4'?)	...	1 (rect.) 3 (?)	...	Moderately abundant	...
Carson Lake (10–P–1)	Short	...	E–W	...	Rect. midden area w/ditches	...	...	Abundant	Burials
St. Francis Area									
Barton Ranch (11–O–10)	Short	...	...	...	Rect. midden area w/ditches	...	...	Deep midden w/burials	...
Richard Bridge (11–O–8)	Short	175'	SE	1 (3'?)	Culti-vated	...	Abundant	Deep midden	...

TABLE 14: "ST. FRANCIS-TYPE" SITES (*Continued*)

SITE	TIME RANGE	PLAZA LENGTH	ORIENT.	HEIGHT MOUND A	TYPE A	OTHER MOUNDS	DAUB	REFUSE	REMARKS
Williamson (11–N–13)	Short	300′	SE	1 (8′?)	...	8(?)	Abundant	Deep midden w/burials	...
Turnbow Place (11–N–12)	Short	250′	SE	10	Rect. stepped	2 (rect.) 2(?)	Abundant	Deep midden w/burials	...

TABLE 15: IRREGULAR VILLAGE SITES WITH MOUNDS.

SITE	TIME RANGE	PLAZA LENGTH	ORIENT.	HEIGHT MOUND A	TYPE A	OTHER MOUNDS	DAUB	REFUSE	REMARKS
Period B–A									
Memphis Area									
Walls (13–P–1)	Short	?	?	?	?	...	Abundant	Deep	Many burials
Irby (13–P–10)	F–A	?	?	?	?	...	Abundant	Deep	Mounds badly mutilated
Cheatham (13–P–6)	Short	?	E	6′	Square	4	...	...	...
Woodlyn (13–P–11)	Short	?	?	3′	?	...	Present	Deep	...
Shelby (12–P–2)	Short	300′	S	10′	Rect.	Flat-top round (120′ x 6′)	Present	Abundant	(Site excav. by Univ. of Tennessee)
Upper Nodena (10–Q–1)	Short	?	?	5′	...	...	Present	Shallow	Many burials
Period C–B									
Arkansas River Area									
Dupree (16–L–6)	Short	250′	E	10′	Square w/conical on top	...	Abundant	Abundant	Numerous house mounds
Yazoo Area									
Stokes Bayou (16–M–6)	Short	250′	E	9′	?	4 (shapes uncertain)	Abundant	Abundant	...

Large Irregular Village Sites with Temple Mounds

In the Memphis area, particularly, are found a few places where there are fairly deep and extensive accumulations of refuse material, indicating the locations of true town sites, but the shape of these sites is not clearly defined. Whether they were surrounded by defense walls is a question that will have to be settled by excavation. Each of these town sites has one or more small mounds arranged about a plaza. Where the mounds are not too badly plowed down it can be seen that they were of the pyramidal type but none were very large. Ten feet is the present height of the tallest. The principal mound-plaza orientation can be made out only at half of the sites. Three have the mound on the west side of the plaza looking across the plaza to the east and one faces toward the south across the plaza.

These villages are also extensive cemeteries. Burials probably were made beneath the floors of houses and substantial amounts of pottery were placed in the graves with the dead. Such localities as the Walls Site (13–P–1) described on page 246 may be considered a typical example.[4]

Unclassified Sites

Under this heading all that requires to be said is that there are too many of them. Of the 383 sites catalogued by the Survey, 162 or 42 per cent fall into this unfortunate category. The percentage is going up year by year at an accelerated rate, owing to the increasing use of heavy earth-moving equipment since the late war.

TEMPORAL DISTRIBUTION OF THE SEVERAL CLASSES OF SITES

The plotting of the areal distribution of the various classes of sites which we have described in the foregoing section was the next step in the analysis. First a list of all the dated sites was drawn up which showed the time range during which each site had been occupied. The length of this time range was already estimated as described in a foregoing section.

In assigning dates to such features as mound structures, it obviously could not be assumed that temple mounds had been built during the early periods of some of the long time-range sites. Jaketown (20–O–1), Kinlock (19–N–1), or Alligator (16–N–2) will serve as examples. These sites had probably been occupied for many years before the trait of building rectangular mounds was introduced, and for this reason the mounds at such sites are considered to date toward the end of the occupation span. For the earlier periods such sites are guessed to have been simple villages with conical mounds or no mounds at all. This working assumption would have to be checked by excavation at each of the sites involved to be absolutely certain of each case, but it probably holds true for the average. At least we avoid the error of pushing the comparatively late trait of rectangular mound-building too far back in time.

The maps given in figures 64 to 69 were drawn from the tables already presented. These show, so far as our information makes it possible, the sites occupied during the several arbitrary periods of our time scale and the class to which we have assigned each occupation. These classes are indicated by a simple system of symbols as set forth in the legend accompanying each map.

Again, we must remind the reader of the reservations which have been scattered through the preceding pages in regard to our sampling of sites, and the difficulties of determining the characteristics of many of the half-destroyed sites, not to mention the uncertainties attending the dating of them. Our Survey made no pretense of being complete and can only be considered as a random sampling somewhat loaded in favor of the later, larger, and more impressive sites. Having now made the apologies indicated by the circumstances and scientific custom, we will proceed to a discussion of the occupation types in the various periods.

Period G–F (Figure 64)

The most notable thing about this period is the scarcity of classifiable sites. Out of a total of 383 sites catalogued by the survey only fourteen were datable within this period and

[4] See also Brown, 1926, pp. 122–24.

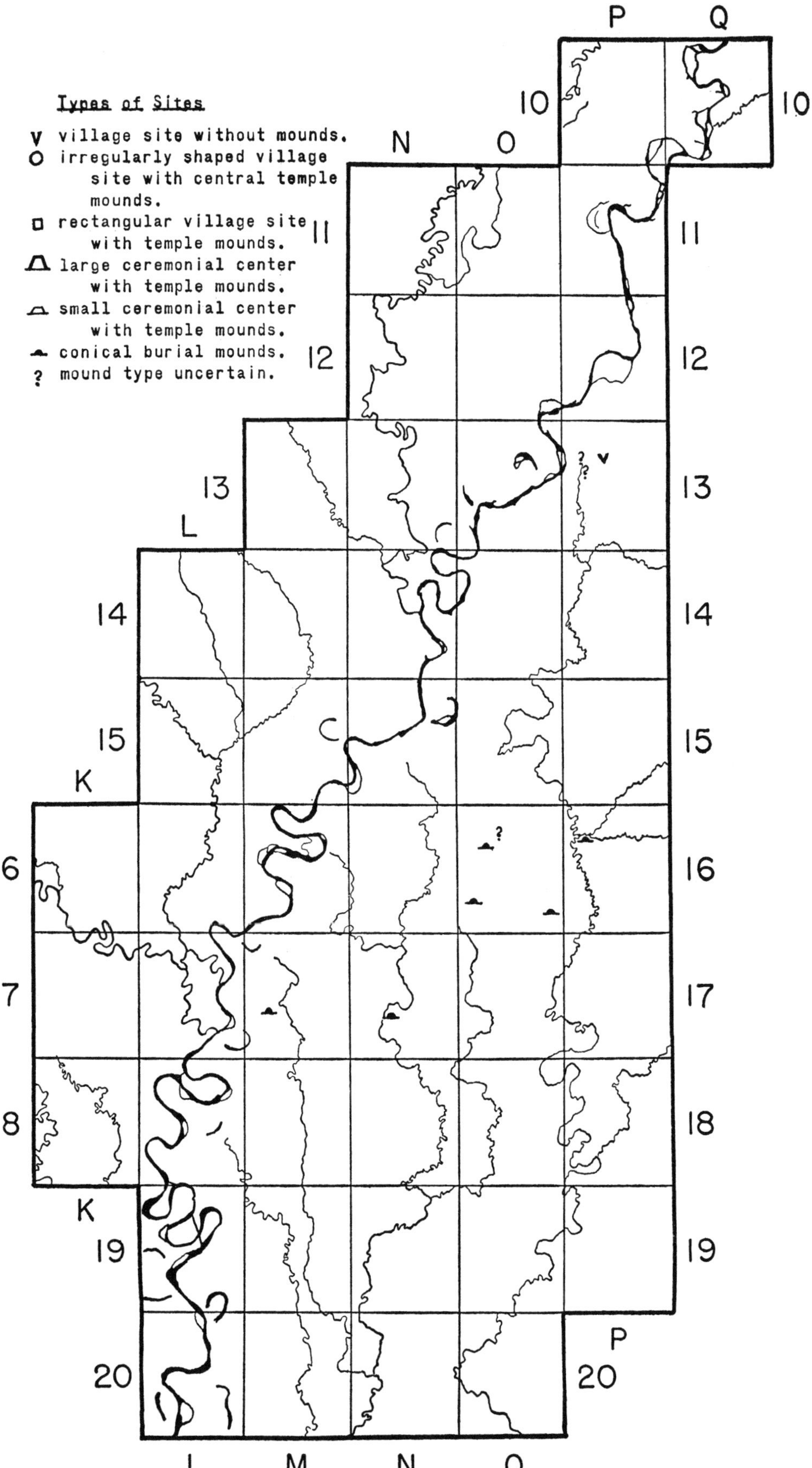

Fig. 64. Distribution of occupation patterns in the Tchula Period (G–F).

of these only seven could be classified as to type. Six of these were marked by one or more conical burial mounds. While it is probably true that the population was relatively scanty in this early period, circumstances unfavorable to the finding of sites have undoubtedly underloaded the picture here. Some of the many conical mounds that we have been unable to date, for lack of sufficient pottery, were almost certainly built at this time. Further excavation in sites of later date would in many cases disclose bottom levels of this period. Such was in fact the case in two of the sites tested by the Survey, Lake Cormorant (13–P–8) and Jaketown (20–O–1). Most important of all perhaps is the likelihood that many early sites have been covered by a thick mantle of alluvium and will forever remain undiscovered.

The distribution of these early sites, however, few as they are, may be significant. None were found west of the Mississippi and most of them are well to the east of it in the drainage of the Yazoo-Tallahatchie and Sunflower rivers. This fact has already been commented on in Section VII (p. 297), where a rough correlation between early sites and earlier Mississippi meander belts was demonstrated. More striking perhaps is the fact that these early sites tend to cluster in that portion of the Yazoo Basin nearest the point where the Tallahatchie comes down out of the "hills." It will be recalled (p. 75) that it was here that the early pottery types, Withers and Twin Lakes Fabric-impressed, and their companions were found in great abundance. If the evidence were stronger numerically, it would be tempting to hypothesize that the earliest mound-building population of which we have present knowledge first came into this part of the area from the east. At the moment we can only suggest it as an interesting possibility.

Period F–E (Figure 65)

We have located more sites that were occupied in the period F–E. As figure 65 shows, the majority of them have conical burial mounds and are located in the same Yazoo-Tallahatchie-Sunflower drainage area as were the few sites of the preceding period. Some, however, are west of the Mississippi flood plain on the Arkansas and St. Francis rivers. It is difficult to believe that the distribution indicated for this period is entirely a function of our accidental selection, or of our having done more intensive work in the Yazoo Basin. It probably reflects, however faintly, the distribution of the population of the Survey Area at this time. The tendency for conical mound sites to cluster in the area near where the Tallahatchie enters the flood plain is even more striking than before.

It will be noted that there are three small ceremonial centers with rectangular mounds indicated as of this date. These are Indian Creek (15–P–3), Posey (15–O–6), and Nelson (17–M–17). This is the dating indicated by the collections of surface material gathered on each of these sites. There is, of course, whenever a site is dated by surface material alone, a reasonable doubt. This is particularly true when village-site material is used to date mounds. Even if the sherds are picked up directly on the mound surface, there is always the possibility that they were transported from the village site with the mound fill. In two of the three above-mentioned sites the dating of the mounds is particularly questionable because there were minor percentages of later sherds in the collections. The Nelson Site, however, showed a pure early Baytown complex of the period we are concerned with here. This makes the site extremely important, since it may attest the introduction of temple mounds in this very early period. Unfortunately, its importance was not appreciated at the time the site was visited, and our information is not as complete as it might have been. The mound is described in the field notes as 8 meters square and 1.5 meters high and the collection was picked up on a village site "south and east of it," distance not given.

There is something inherently suspicious about the size and shape of this mound. Not only is it extremely small for a rectangular platform mound, but it is most unusual to find a mound of this size which has sufficiently retained its shape to be recognizable. On several occasions small rectangular mounds have proved on further investigation to have been built by local white residents as stock refuges, foundation platforms for buildings, or other purposes. We have, therefore, to reckon with the possibility that such was the case here.

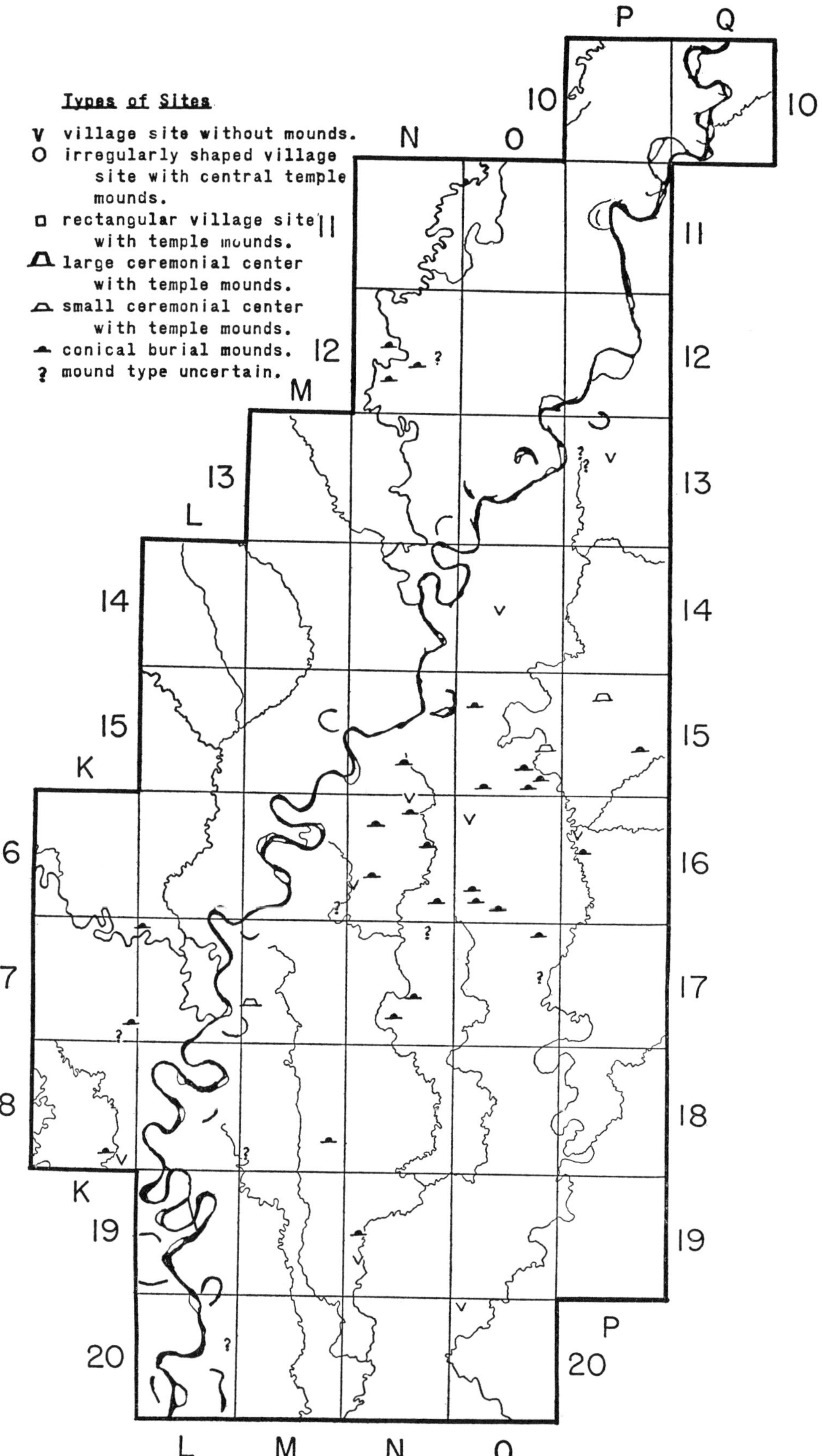

FIG. 65. Distribution of occupation patterns in the early Baytown Period (F–E).

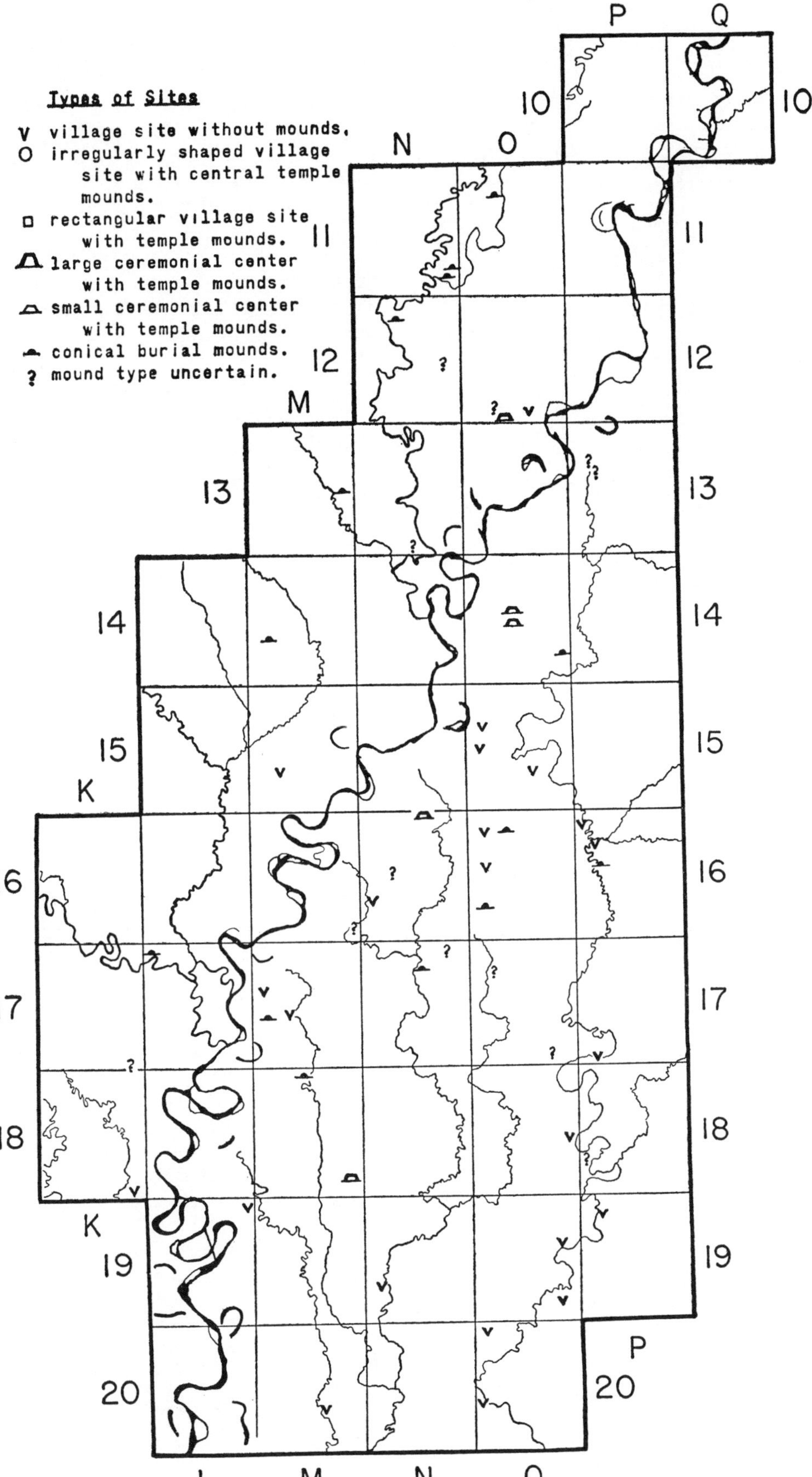

Fig. 66. Distribution of occupation patterns in the middle Baytown Period (E-D).

In view of the serious doubts in regard to all three occurrences, it would be unwise to postulate the appearance of rectangular platform mounds in period F–E, though it must be allowed to stand as a remote possibility. The evidence is rather better for the next period, E–D.

Period E–D (Figure 66)

In this period, if we may trust our information, conical mounds are rapidly disappearing. Their decrease from the preceding period is rather striking. At the same time there is a corresponding increase in the number of village sites without mounds, the reasons for which are not apparent. Possibly it is merely due to the fact that it is easier to find flat village sites of this less remote period. Another possibility is that, for some reason or other, it was not until this time that the primitive inhabitants began to make extensive use of shellfish for food. Most of the village sites without mounds on the Yazoo-Tallahatchie and Lower Sunflower rivers in this period are shell middens. These seem to have been the only streams in the area affording a supply of this type of food. Why they were not utilized much earlier, as in other parts of the Southeast, is an interesting question. Maybe they were, but so far our efforts to find deep deposits containing "archaic" materials have been unsuccessful.

There are five sites with rectangular temple mounds, classified here as small ceremonial centers, that date in period E–D. These are Thompson Lake (12–O–3), Evansville (14–O–1), Owens (14–O–2), Rufus Davis (16–N–4), and Choctaw (18–M–6). The dating of all these sites is subject to the possibilities of error already discussed, but it is hardly reasonable to suppose that *all* of them have been misdated. It seems probable, therefore, that this type of ceremonial center is becoming established in the Survey Area at this time. The distribution of these rectangular mound sites is quite different from that of conical mounds in the two preceding periods. Their tendency to lie nearer the Mississippi suggests the possibility that this trait, whether carried by a migrant population or by simple diffusion, was moving along the central part of the valley, leaving the regions back from the river to people who were still building burial mounds and, in the case of the Yazoo and Sunflower areas, shell middens. Note that we are not yet prepared to say in which direction the trait was moving.

Period D–C (Figure 67)

This period saw a great increase in the number of temple-mound sites, and in addition to the small sites of this class there are now several which we have classified as large ceremonial centers. Their distribution still centers about the Mississippi River as though this were the main distributary for the trait, but they are now found over the full width of the flood plain, and some are a considerable distance back up the principal tributaries.

The locations of burial mound sites in this, the preceding, and succeeding period is worth consideration. The three maps (figs. 66, 67, and 68) suggest that as the temple-mound type of site enters the Survey Area along the Mississippi River and spreads both east and west the burial mound-building trait retreats before it. At this period, D–C, burial mounds were found along the St. Francis River, along the Lower Arkansas River, and, as we know from the surveys of Ford and others, east of the Yazoo River in the hills of Mississippi.

Period C–B (Figure 68)

Sites that date in this period are more numerous than at any of the preceding times. A review of the maps so far discussed gives the reader a fairly correct impression of the rate at which the population of the Survey Area increased during the time span covered.[5] Most of the C–B period sites are ceremonial centers both large and small. A few sites, on the peripheries it will be noted, are burial mounds.

There is an interesting problem (to the archaeologist at least) regarding the people

[5] Phillips injects a sour note at this juncture by pointing out that in the Mississippi flood plain the important factor is survival. All other things being equal, there must be more late sites because the River has had more time to destroy the early ones. The argument for increase of population must therefore rest on the larger size of sites, in the late periods, not on their greater number.

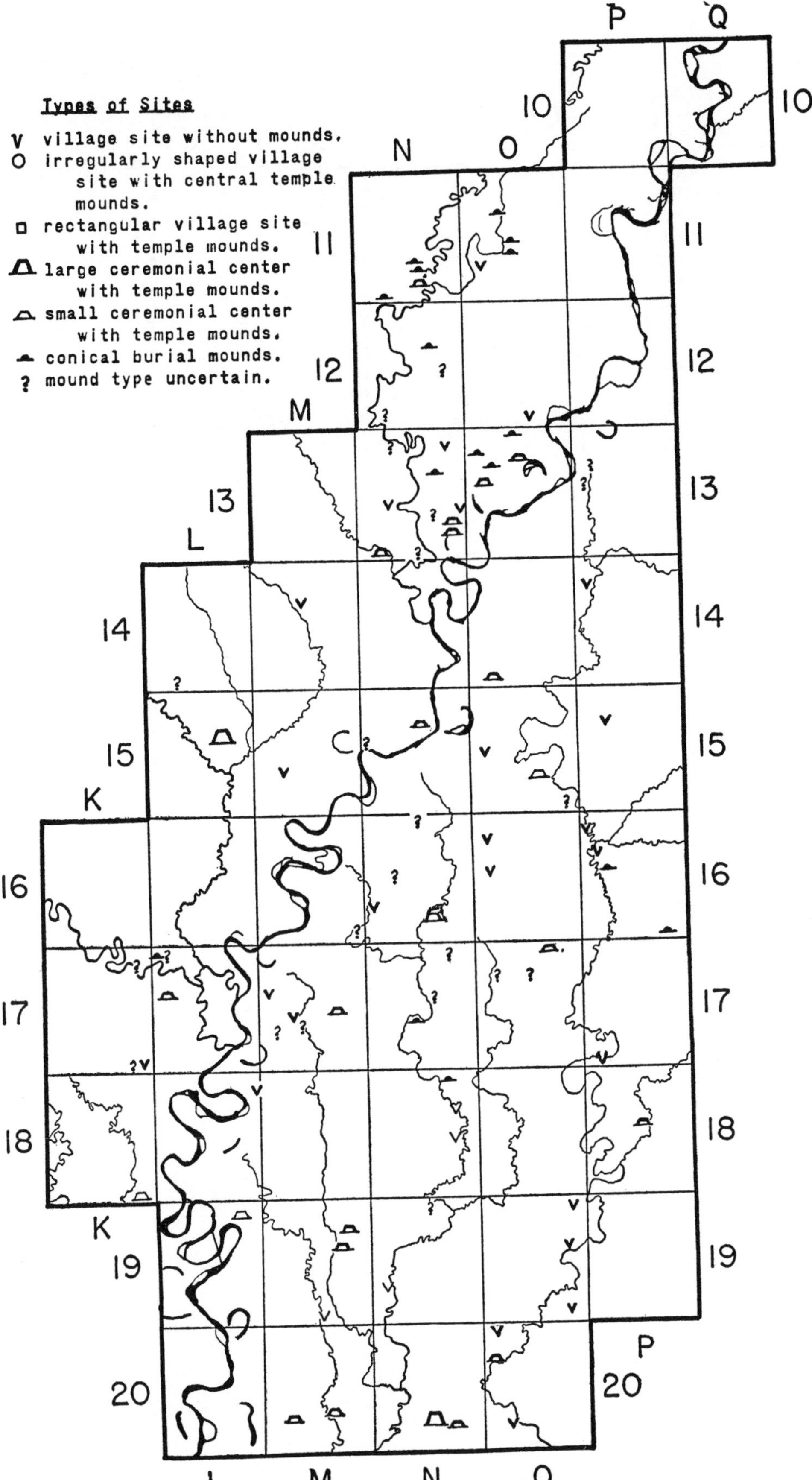

FIG. 67. Distribution of occupation patterns in the late Baytown Period (D–C).

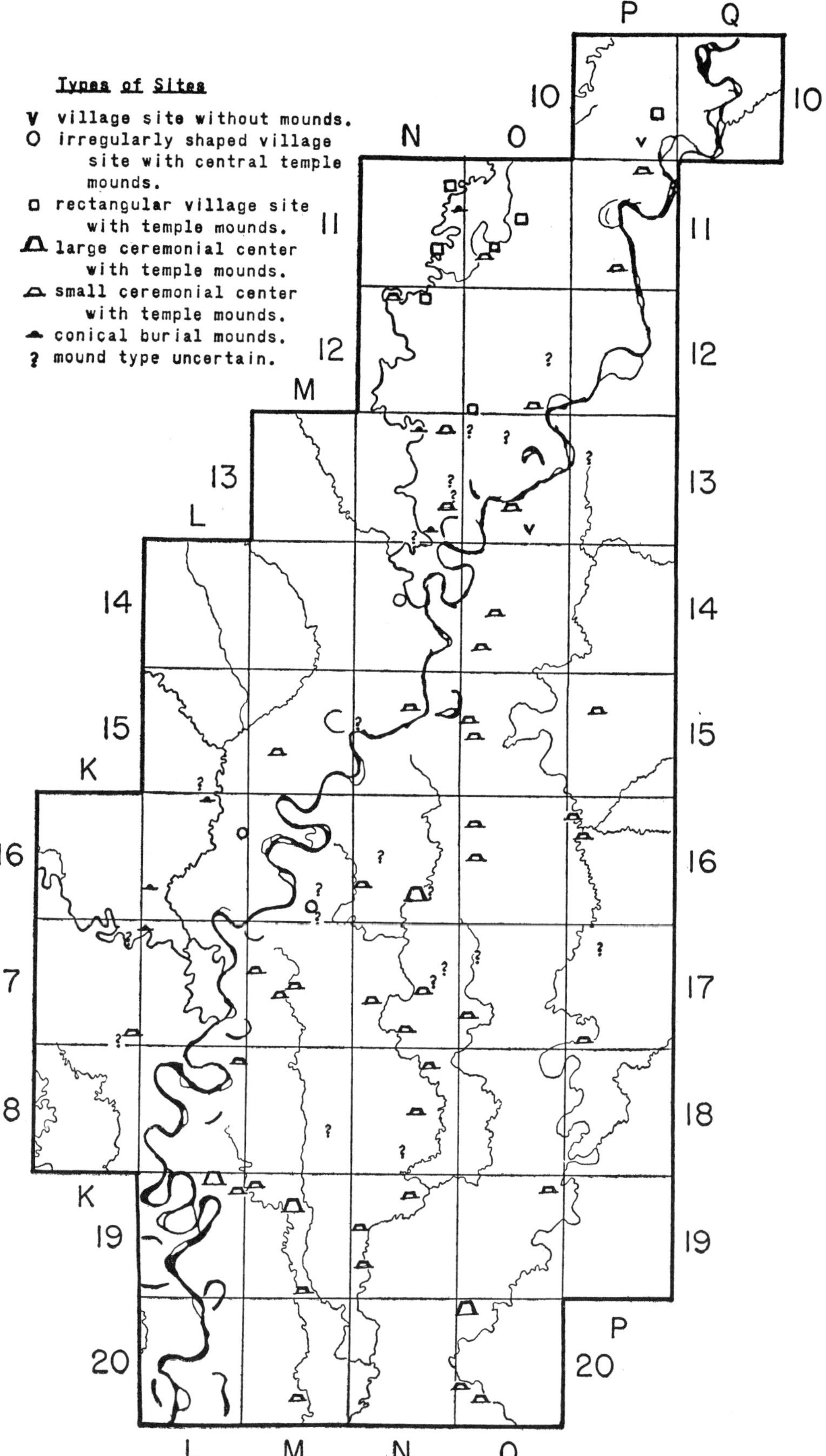

FIG. 68. Distribution of occupation patterns in the early Mississippi Period (C–B).

who built and used the temple-mound ceremonial centers up to this time. What did they do with their dead? Burials in the temple mounds themselves are very rare as we know from the examination of many of these mounds in the process of being destroyed. And there are no cemeteries in the fields surrounding the mounds or in the village sites of these dates. If there were such, it is inevitable that they would have been plowed up and human bones scattered over the fields. Professional diggers have had no better luck than pot-hunters when they have dug in these sites. For example, Clarence B. Moore never had any success at any of the sites which we have dated before this time. The absence of cemeteries with accompanying grave goods accounts for the fact that this occupation is almost unknown to the literature. Some of the popular pottery types such as Baytown Plain, Larto Red Filmed, Mazique Incised have never been illustrated by examples of whole pots.

The temple-mound sites prior to this date appear to have been built primarily as ceremonial centers. Refuse is relatively scanty on the sites and nearly always appears to have come from buildings that were placed on the tops of mounds, or on the level ground about the edge of the plaza area. These centers probably served populations which were scattered over the surrounding countryside in dwellings which were arranged in groups or villages only at particularly favored spots where there was a constant food supply. The shell middens in the Sunflower and Yazoo basins mark places where the population concentrated to exploit the mussel beds of the rivers. In the other areas it may be inferred that the people had primarily an agricultural subsistence and lived near their fields.

In period C–B a new type of occupation pattern appears in the basin of the St. Francis River. These are true village sites where large populations are concentrated. These villages seem to have been laid out according to a preconceived plan, for they are rectangular in outline, are sometimes oriented with the cardinal directions, and many were surrounded by a moat and probably palisades. There is no question as to what the people who occupied these towns did with their dead. They buried them in the great heaps of refuse they were in the process of accumulating, probably beneath the floors of the houses, and placed quantities of pottery and other goods with them.

The distribution of these St. Francis-type "towns" is incomplete because our Survey efforts stopped midway in ascending the St. Francis. We know, however, that this same type of site continues, with only slight modifications up the St. Francis and the Mississippi into southeast Missouri. So far as large compact settlements are concerned, our area appears to be marginal to a larger and more intense development centering about the mouth of the Ohio River.

Period B–A (Figure 69)

Ceremonial centers are still present but by no means as numerous as in the preceding period. Burial mounds are conspicuously absent. A general decrease in population seems to be indicated in this period, particularly on the Yazoo-Tallahatchie and Sunflower rivers. Possibly this is a reflection of the depopulation trend which left this portion of the Mississippi Valley almost uninhabited by 1698 (see p. 410). The two most densely populated regions in this period seem to have been along the St. Francis River and the Mississippi above the mouth of the St. Francis.

We shall present in the following section our reasons for thinking that 1541, the date of De Soto's passage through the Survey Area, falls somewhere about the end of period C–B or the beginning of B–A. If this is correct, then the population distribution that he encountered cannot have been very different from that shown by figure 69.

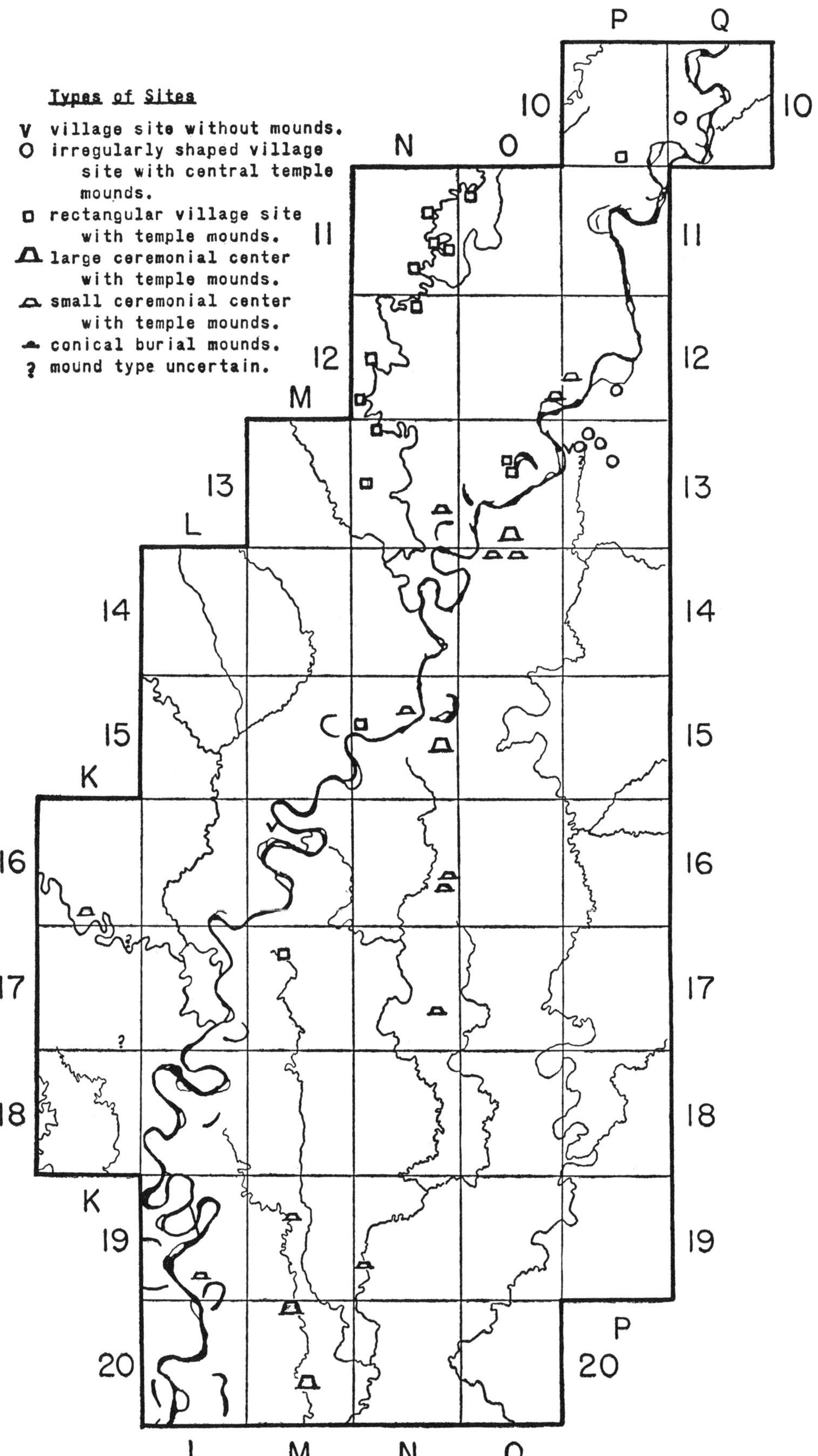

Fig. 69. Distribution of occupation patterns in the late Mississippi Period (B–A).

Section IX
IDENTIFICATION OF SITES FROM DOCUMENTARY SOURCES

IDENTIFICATION OF SITES FROM DOCUMENTARY SOURCES

IN THE original outline of this report the opening section on physiography was to be followed by an equally comprehensive presentation of the ethnography of the Survey Area so far as it is known. At that time we were unaware of the great uncertainty that surrounds much of what is "known in the ethno-historical field." We were likewise unaware of the special difficulties our point of view as archaeologists would get us into. The obvious starting-point for the American archaeologist venturing into the unfamiliar field of ethnography is to attempt to localize the earliest encounters between red and white men in his area. To him, the direct historical approach is not a choice of method but a categorical imperative. Unfortunately, it sounds a great deal simpler than it is. After several months of concentrated effort, we failed to get beyond this starting-point. It was clear that the section on ethnography would have to wait. The most we could hope to do was to expose our ignorance of the exact locality of such encounters and the reasons therefore. Such an exposure, nevertheless, seems worthwhile. It was a salutary experience for us, and it might be for others.

We have referred to the special difficulties inherent in the point of view of the archaeologist. These may perhaps be best expressed in terms of scale. For the ethnographer, concerned with questions of culture and culture-contact, often on a regional or continental scale, approximate locations are generally sufficient. He can easily show that two groups have been in contact sufficiently to have affected their culture without knowing precisely where either was at any given time. The archaeologist, on the other hand, in his capacity of field worker, thinking in terms of site or small groups of closely linked sites, works within the narrowest possible limits of space and time. The ethnographer quite naturally tends to place more reliance on documentary and cartographic sources than we, as archaeologists, are able to do. We, on the other hand, are likely to give more weight to local topographical and archaeological considerations than might be regarded as reasonable by the ethnographer. This is advanced by way of excuse for what may appear to be an unconscionably critical and detailed treatment of certain longstanding ethnographic problems in the pages to follow.

In the Lower Mississippi Valley there are two "contact" periods separated by 132 years of utter blankness so far as the historical record is concerned. Narratives of De Soto's brief *entrada* of 1541–43 afford a vivid but tantalizing picture of Mississippi culture at a time which must have been very close to its peak of development — tantalizing because the long interval of darkness which followed makes it so very difficult to identify the peoples involved — or even to locate them.

Because of this long hiatus in the historical record, the really practicable contact period is that of the early French penetrations and establishments on the Lower Mississippi, beginning with the "discovery" of Jolliet and Marquette and extending roughly over the next half century. Here, we have a real chance to identify late archaeological complexes with living peoples in terms of site, so dear to the archaeological mind. The French of the seventeenth and eighteenth centuries are often credited with a flair for ethnography, which signifies probably less in the nature of a national characteristic than a result of the fact that their explorations were made by — or accompanied by — intelligent and articulate men, generally of the clergy. Whatever the cause, we have a wealth of documentary and cartographic material for this period of Mississippi Valley history. We have learned to our cost, however, that it must be used with circumspection and shall be careful to point out, in the proper place, the reasons why.

English penetrations during this period were negligible so far as documentary results are concerned, with one notable exception, that which resulted in Adair's classic "History of the American Indians," the chief source for the ethnography of the Chickasaw and Choctaw. Overland trade from the English settlements in Carolina was opened up with these tribes as early as 1698, the Chickasaw remaining solidly in the English interest from that time on. These contacts were primarily commercial, however, and it is a rare trader — Adair is the exception that proves the rule — who is also an ethnographer. Otherwise, we may expect little help from the English. The Americans came too late.

Taking into account the nature of these sources, and the rather special approach of the archaeologist described above, there are two obvious points of departure for the study of ethnography in this area, two specific but not altogether unrelated problems of identification: (1) location of the tribes visited by De Soto immediately before and after crossing the Mississippi in 1541; and (2) location of the Quapaw villages described by the French in the last quarter of the seventeenth century. The first is largely a question of tribal location and identification with archaeological complexes — we can hardly hope to identify actual De Soto sites, though it will not be for lack of trying. The second is strictly a question of site identification.

Notwithstanding the generally accepted theory that the Quapaw were recent intruders into the Lower Mississippi area — a theory which has never to the writers' knowledge, been critically examined — it is not impossible that they had been in their historic territory for a long time. It might be expected, then, that site determinations based on French sources could be projected back to the time of De Soto, and it might be thought advisable to examine the sources in that order. However, as archaeologists, we are slaves of chronology. We feel more comfortable looking at events in the order of their occurrence. Furthermore, this is the most effective way to exhibit one of the most interesting things about the early history of the Lower Mississippi, to wit, the remarkable contrast in the ethnography of the two periods. In the 132 years that separated the explorations of De Soto and Jolliet the most sweeping changes seem to have taken place, and they are not changes for the better culturally speaking. Any light that can be thrown on the nature and causes of these changes will be of material benefit to our understanding of the archaeology of the region. We shall, therefore, begin with the earlier of the two problems: the location of the tribes visited by De Soto.

DE SOTO AND THE 1541 DATE LINE

Narrative of the Expedition from Chicaça to Quiguate

Toward the middle of the sixteenth century the Alluvial Valley of the Mississippi River was illuminated for a brief instant, then plunged again into total darkness for almost a century and a half. In the late spring of 1541 De Soto and his small army of thoroughly disillusioned *conquistadores* crossed the Mississippi into what is now Arkansas, made a short thrust northward to visit a powerful tribe called Pacaha, turned south again, and then westward toward further and more bitter disappointment. After seven months of fruitless wandering in the mountains and forests of central and southern Arkansas, they came back again into the Alluvial Valley, where De Soto found his final resting-place. There followed Moscoso's futile attempt to reach Mexico overland through Texas, his return to the Mississippi, and final escape by water. Thus, so far as the Mississippi is concerned, the narrative divides itself into three chapters. It is with the first chapter that we are at present solely concerned, and it may be called "From Chicaça to Quiguate."

The period covered is no more than four months, from the beginning of May to the end of August, 1541,[1] a stay which probably had slight political or social consequences, and was certainly as unfruitful as any other portion of the *entrada* from the standpoint of the expedition's objectives. But for our purposes the chronicles of these four months are tre-

[1] Unless otherwise specified, dates are in the old style. To translate into Gregorian calendar, add thirteen days.

mendously important. If we could by their means identify a single site or group of sites visited by the expedition, we would then have an anchor for our archaeological time scale a century and a half earlier than the period usually regarded as "historic" in this area. We are thereby excused from entering into a tedious amount of detail in order to establish, if possible, this date line. It is worth it, and the by-product will be a closer understanding of Lower Mississippi culture at this period.

We shall begin with a full narrative account of this four-month's period, which takes the weary Spaniards from their winter camp at Chicaça in northern Mississippi to Quiguate, "somewhere" in Arkansas. This is in effect a rather free compilation of all four primary sources, giving preference in the generally accepted order of reliability, as follows: Ranjel, Biedma, Elvas, and Garcilaso.[2] The last-named is commonly regarded as completely unreliable and resorted to only in cases of desperate necessity when one wants very much to prove a point. On the other hand, though not always to be trusted in matters of time, distance, population, and battle statistics, the Inca is far more generous with descriptive detail than the other three chroniclers. Such material, carefully screened for exaggeration and sheer invention, can be very useful in determining what kind of people the Spaniards encountered and how they lived.

From Chicaça to Quizqui

It was a dolorous winter, that of 1540–41, in Chicaça. Food was scarce, clothing insufficient. The severities of the winter and the wretched situation of the army were accentuated by the active inhospitality of their Chickasaw hosts, who founded at this time a reputation for warlike prowess that was preserved right down to the nineteenth century. The whole thing culminated (Friday, March 4th, according to Ranjel) in a dawn attack on the Spanish camp in which De Soto lost a good many horses and some men, together with most of their remaining clothing and equipment. It is likely that if the Chickasaw had possessed the good sense to follow up their success on this sorry Friday, the entire expedition might have been destroyed and the reader spared the rest of this narrative and the comlicated discussion to follow. Whether terrified by the stampeding horses or some other reason best known to themselves — it was certainly not the effectiveness of the army's resistance — the savages drew off, giving the demoralized Spaniards opportunity to reform their lines at another village a short distance off. Here they made haste to set up a forge, with bellows of bearskin, for retempering their arms. They made new saddle frames, new lances and targets, and in a week had made good their losses in material and renewed their strength. It was not until the 15th that the bad judgment of the Indians counseled a new attack, which the recuperated Spaniards easily beat off. This success was said to have been due to the fact that the new camp was in the midst of a plain where the cavalry could manoeuvre. Always those horses! Cunningham-Graham was right; the horse has never been credited sufficiently for its share in the conquest of Spanish America.

Another six weeks was spent in this place in preparation for a further advance into the wilderness. From captives, De Soto informed himself of the region ahead. Would we were similarly informed, for the question of the direction taken from Chicaça is crucial for the whole De Soto problem, as we shall see. On the 26th of April, the army set forth in a northwest direction according to Biedma, arriving at Limamu or Alibamo, a "small town," that night. Here De Soto expected to obtain supplies for the "desert" he knew lay ahead, but apparently he was disappointed, for the next days three parties were dispatched in as many directions to scare up provisions. One of these, under Juan de Añasco, found a "barricade" (Ranjel) or "staked fort" (Elvas) directly athwart the trail the army was to take, manned by a large number of war-painted savages, 300 according to Biedma, 4000 according to

[2] For discussion of De Soto sources, see Swanton, 1932a, pp. 570–71; Swanton, 1939, pp. 4–11. The texts of Ranjel, Biedma, and Elvas used here are those published under the editorship of Edward Gaylord Bourne in the Trail Makers Series (Bourne, 1904, vols. I and II) and for Garcilaso the Spanish text of the 1722 Madrid edition. Quoted passages have been translated by Mrs. James A. Ford.

Garcilaso, a fair example of the latter's journalistic tendencies. Añasco prudently withdrew and sent word to the Governor who came up with the main force and promptly ordered a frontal attack. Too promptly, apparently, for, although the fort was carried by the Spaniards, by neglecting to deploy a force to cut off their retreat, practically all the Indians were able to make their escape.

Biedma makes a very interesting comment on this engagement.

> At this time befell us what is said never to have occurred in the Indias. In the highway over which we had to pass, without there being either women to protect or provisions to secure, and only to try our valour with theirs, the Indians put up a very strong stockade directly across the road, about three hundred of them standing behind it, resolute to die rather than give back.[3]

This is, one must say, contrary to accepted notions of Indian warfare. It suggests — however close the resemblance of the name of the locality to that of the historic Alabama tribe — that these intrepid warriors were Chickasaw who, in 1736 at Ackia, served Bienville in much the same way. We shall return to this point later.

The Limamu encounter took place on April 28th. The next day was spent in further search for supplies, apparently without much success, for the Governor was obliged to resume the march on the 30th, though the army was not ready and the wounded had need of repose. At such times the command was always "forward." They couldn't go back, having eaten everything behind them. All accounts agree on the general nature of the ensuing march, but only Garcilaso gives the direction as north, which probably is to be read northwest. Biedma's original direction of northwest from Chicaça seems to refer to the course only so far as Limamu, where the Governor hoped to recruit supplies, which may in fact have been a detour; it cannot be safely taken as the direction of the wilderness march they are now beginning. The way led through "a deserted country and by a rough way mountainous and swampy" (Ranjel). Swanton has pointed out that "mountainous" is a mistranslation of *montes* which was used more commonly in sixteenth-century Spanish to denote "forests." Elvas describes it in similar terms, "through a wilderness, having many pondy places, with thick forests, fordable, however, on horseback all to (except) some basins or lakes that were swum." It took nine days according to Ranjel; eight according to Biedma; seven according to Elvas; while Garcilaso, who observes a large carelessness in such details makes it three. All accounts are barren of details concerning this march. By this time it was old stuff for De Soto and his ragged companions. Ever since leaving Tampa Bay, there had been passages through uninhabited regions separating the seats of one tribe from those of the next. We may assume that they usually followed well-marked trails guided by Indians pressed into service at the last villages. The interpreter, Juan Ortiz, a survivor of the Narvaez disaster in Florida twelve years before, had long since passed out of the area of his linguistic competence, but through a series of intermediaries picked up along the route was able to communicate after a fashion with the guides, enough at least to apprise them of the unpleasant penalty for error — to be torn to pieces by the Spanish dogs. Garcilaso tells us that by the time the army reached Chicaça it took twelve or fourteen interpreters to put Ortiz in touch with the inhabitants. One can imagine the distortions of fact that took place in the process. Notwithstanding the enormous difficulty of communication, we can assume that the Governor knew at all times where he was going, at least as far ahead as the next group of villages. In the present case he must have known that he was headed toward a great river, though none of the accounts mention the fact. The Chickasaw undoubtedly told of the river — in fact there is evidence that De Soto had already heard of it in the preceding summer of 1540 when he was on or near the Tennessee — and of the rich towns upon its banks, very sensibly exaggerating the latter point for the quicker riddance of their unwelcome visitors. But in two years the Spaniards had been told of so many great rivers and so many rich towns upon them —

[3] Biedma, in Bourne, 1904, vol. II, p. 24.

perhaps it is not strange at all that the Mississippi is not mentioned until they find themselves upon its banks.

We may assume that the army marched long hours each day and as rapidly as the terrain and the condition of the wounded permitted. They always hurried through uninhabited country, for reasons that are sufficiently obvious. Here they had extra cause by reason of the low state of the commissary at the start.

On the 9th day of this march (following Ranjel, who is most reliable in matters of time and distance) about midday, the army came upon the village of Quizqui, or Quizquiz, surprising its inhabitants so completely that many of them were seized as they ran out of their houses. According to one account (Biedma), three hundred women were taken in this fashion, the men being at work in the fields. This is an extremely interesting point, if true, indicating an advanced agricultural economy, such as was later found only in the extreme southern part of the Mississippi Valley, notably among the Choctaw and Tunica. Among these women was the mother of the Cacique which indicates possibly that Quizqui was the chief town of the "province." It was located "near the banks of the Espiritu Santo" (Biedma) or, at most, 2 leagues away (Ranjel). The abruptness with which the Spaniards came upon the first village and its surprised inhabitants is rather puzzling, and at the same time interesting from the point of view of locating these villages. Where, one might ask, were the frontier settlements, the outlying hamlets and fields from which intelligence of the army's approach would have sped to the "capital"? A column of a thousand-odd men and horses, not to mention the vast herd of swine driven along in its wake does not steal silently through the countryside. It was no doubt the advance guard of cavalry that surprised the town, but at midday the main body could not have been far behind. Two explanations are possible. One, that Quizqui may itself have been a frontier settlement, an outlier of the more powerful groups on the other side of the river. In fact, Biedma tells us that this town was, "with many towns about there, tributary to a lord of Pacaha, famed throughout all the land," the first mention of a political power that we are going to hear a great deal about as the story unfolds. The alternative explanation is more interesting in relation to the problem of locating Quizqui and the crossing-place of the Mississippi. Assuming for the moment that the route from Chicaça lay westward across the Yazoo Basin rather than northwestward along the bluffs as some maintain, it follows that the Quizqui villages and fields were strung out along the natural levees of the Mississippi with that linearity of distribution that has been commented on in an earlier section. An approach from the east, across the bottoms, might understandably come upon the main settlements as suddenly as appears in fact to have happened in the present instance. There are, of course, a great many more sides to this question, which will be discussed at length in a later section, but this is not the least important of them.

Events at the first Quizqui village are not very clear. The Governor seems to have used the Cacique's mother and other women as hostages in an attempt to get hold of the Cacique. The latter stipulated that the women should be released first, to which the Governor yielded in view of the weakness of his men and the lack of food. The Cacique did not come, however, but sent his warriors armed for attack. Confronted by the Spanish cavalry drawn up in readiness, they thought better of it and six chiefs came in for a parley, "stating that they had come to find out what people it might be; for that they had knowledge from their ancestors that they were to be subdued by a white race." [4] The embassy returned to the Cacique presumably with propitiary terms from the Governor, but the prudent Cacique "came not, nor sent another message." There was little maize in this place so the army moved on to another village "a league beyond" (Ranjel), "half a league from the Great River" (Elvas), where it was found in sufficiency. That these people still had maize in quantity at this time of year is still another indication of an advanced agricultural economy. Here the

[4] Elvas, in Bourne, 1904, vol. I, pp. 111 and 112. Gladwin will be happy to note that news of Alexander's seafarers reached even here, the remote fastnesses of the Mississippi (see Gladwin, 1947).

army remained about ten days, which must have been a welcome respite for the jaded soldiery. On May 21st (still following Ranjel) they "went along to a plain between the river and a small village, and set up quarters and began to build four barges to cross over to the other side. Many of these conquerors said this river was larger than the Danube." All the maize they could lay hands on in the villages behind was brought together there to supply the army during the boat-building operations. Having cleaned them out, we hear no more about the unfortunate Quizqui. We can only hope that their charming illusions about the wonderful white race remained intact.

Not very much can be gleaned by way of description of the Quizqui villages. We can infer that one of them, presumably the "capital" was not small, as Indian villages go, from the fact that three hundred women were captured in it. This and other circumstances, such as the apparent lack of outlying settlements already referred to, indicate a village type of organizàtion as opposed to the scattered hamlet type found among some tribes in the region. Garcilaso is, unfortunately, the only one to mention the existence of mounds in Quizqui.

> A un lado del Pueblo estava la Casa del Curaca, puesta en un cerillo alto, hecho à mano, que servia de Fortaleça. No podian subir à ella, sino por dos escaleras. A esta Casa se recogieron muchos Indios.[5]

Nothing is said about stockades in connection with any of these villages. Such adjuncts are frequently mentioned in the course of subsequent encounters in the trans-Mississippi region. One would expect such mention here, if a stockade existed, in connection with the assault on the first village. It appears safe to assume, therefore, that the Quizqui villages were not fortified. It seems to go with the fact that the men of this tribe were farmers rather than hunters and perhaps explains why they were in a position of vassalage to the more warlike Pacaha across the river. Perhaps it also explains why this, the only tribe encountered by De Soto on the east bank of the Mississippi, is never heard of again.

The Mississippi Crossing and the Province of Aquixo

In slightly less than a month, four large *piraguas* were completed, each capable of carrying sixty to seventy men and five or six horses (Biedma). A large force of Indians (7000, according to Ranjel) had gathered on the farther shore ostensibly to dispute the passage. Garcilaso, for once on the conservative side, gives the number as 6000. They came over daily to reconnoiter in two hundred large canoes (Elvas) — two hundred and fifty by Biedma's reckoning — but this presumably would not represent the total force. Their overtures seem to have been peaceful, in the beginning at any rate. According to Elvas, the first deputation came ashore stating that they were vassals of a great lord named Aquixo, "who was the suzerain of many towns and people on the other shore" and that next day he would come in person to pay his respects to the Governor. There follows the passage from Elvas, so often quoted, which will bear quoting again, as perhaps the most vivid picture we shall ever have of a Lower Mississippi culture in being.

> The next day the Cacique arrived, with two hundred canoes filled with men, having weapons. They were painted with ochre, wearing great bunches of white and other plumes of many colours, having feathered shields in their hands, with which they sheltered the oarsmen on either side, the warriors standing erect from bow to stern, holding bows and arrows. The barge in which the Cacique came had an awning at the poop, under which he sate; and the like had the barges of the other chiefs: and there, from under the canopy, where the chief man was, the course was directed and orders issued to the rest. All came down together, and arrived within a stone's cast of the ravine, whence the Cacique said to the Governor, who was walking along the river-bank with others who bore him company, that he had come to visit, serve, and obey him; for he had heard that he was the greatest of lords, the most powerful on all the earth, and that he must see what he would have him do. The Governor expressed his pleasure,

[5] Garcilaso, 1722, p. 176. Translation: "On one side of the village was the house of the chief, placed high on a little hill, made by hand, which served as a fortress. It could not be climbed except by two stairways. At this house many Indians had gathered."

and besought him to land, that they might the better confer; but the Chief gave no reply, ordering three barges to draw near, wherein was great quantity of fish, and loaves like bricks, made of the pulp of *ameixas*,[6] which De Soto receiving, gave him thanks and again entreated him to land.

Making the gift had been a pretext, to discover if any harm might be done; but, finding the Governor and his people on their guard, the Cacique began to draw off from the shore, when the crossbow-men who were in readiness, with loud cries shot at the Indians, and struck down five or six of them. They retired with great order, not one leaving the oar, even though the one next to him might have fallen, and covering themselves, they withdrew. Afterwards they came many times and landed; when approached, they would go back to their barges. These were fine-looking men, very large and well formed; and what with the awnings, the plumes, and the shields, the pennons, and the number of people in the fleet, it appeared like a famous armada of galleys.[7]

The identity of these well-trained canoemen and warriors would be a matter of intense interest to us, were there a reasonable hope of establishing it. Elvas has just told us they were men of Aquixo, the province directly across the river. Ranjel, however, who marveled at their shields of cane, "so strong and closely interwoven that a cross-bow [bolt] could hardly pierce them," said that they were men of Pacaha farther up the river. These seemingly contradictory statements can perhaps be reconciled. Biedma has already told us that Quizqui and "many towns about there" were tributary to Pacaha. It is not unlikely that Aquixo was also subject to the same power. The Cacique who parleyed from his canopied flagship with De Soto was undoubtedly Lord of Aquixo, a great man in his own country, but possibly subject to a greater one. In short, we may surmise that the dominant political power on this portion of the Misssissippi, both sides, was this same tribe and chief of Pacaha. With due reservations prompted by an awareness of the Spaniards' lack of understanding of political and social patterns that were not feudal in character, one must say that this does not suggest the sort of tribal federation seen in the Iroquois and Creek Confederacies of a later period, but rather a small-scale empire or hegemony of one tribe over its neighbors. We must be careful, however, not to read more into the evidence than it will safely bear.

With such advance reports on the state of Pacaha, the somewhat tarnished vision of riches no doubt flitted once again through the weary Spaniards' minds. The fable of golden Chisca, which had been dangled before them back on the Tennessee, now revived and spurred the final preparations for crossing the great river, which by now must have looked to them somewhat larger than the Danube.

Warlike demonstrations continued as the barges neared completion. It seems to have been the practice of the Indians massed on the farther shore to come over in their canoes "every day at three o'clock in the afternoon" (Biedma) to shower the Spaniards with arrows and maledictions. The arrows "came raining down so that the air was full of them and their yells were something fearful" (Ranjel). Such ineffectual demonstrations were the extent of their opposition, however, for, on the day of the crossing, when a well-directed thrust by water might have been very troublesome to the Spaniards, the Indians made off entirely, and the four clumsy barges with their men and horses were permitted to gain the opposite shore unmolested. The Indian leaders' poor judgment in failing to attack, dictated no doubt by their *manitous*, was manifest. The spirits surely were on the side of the white men and horses, with whom they may have recognized a certain kinship. Moreover, it appears from Elvas' narrative that the river was in flood, very swift and full of snags. The Spaniards seem to have had all they could do to get themselves and their horses over in safety; a vigorous attack would almost certainly have been too much for them, as both Ranjel and Elvas freely admit.

The crossing took place on Saturday, June 18th [8] in the early morning. Two trips of the four barges were sufficient to ferry the entire army across and the operation was completed two hours after sunrise. The same day, or the next — the authorities fail to agree on this point — the army marched to the first Aquixo village. Elvas gives the distance as 1½ leagues.

[6] Persimmons.

[7] Elvas, in Bourne, 1904, vol. I, pp. 113–14.

[8] Ranjel gives it as the 8th, obviously a slip.

A sufficient force was detailed to work the barges upstream to the village, which was not accomplished without difficulty, owing to the swift current that forced them to hug the shore and the Indian sniping that this course made possible. On arrival the barges were taken to pieces and the ironwork retrieved for further use. Whether or not this was the principal Aquixo village is not indicated in the narratives. We are simply told that upon leaving it the army passed through a number of large "towns" of the same people, beautifully situated but entirely deserted. Apparently, the Spaniards saw very little of the people of Aquixo; at any rate, they have left us no information regarding them, beyond the statement of Elvas that the "famous armada of galleys" was of that nation. From captives, however, they learned that about three days off resided a great cacique named Casqui. The supposition is, though on this point there is a question which will be returned to later, that Casqui lay on the route to Pacaha, toward which place De Soto was making with all possible speed, and that the direction was northward up the river.

The Province of Casqui

Between Aquixo and Casqui lay "the worst tract for swamps and water that they had found in all Florida" (Ranjel). This was crossed on Wednesday, June 22nd, and the next day they "entered the land of Quarqui and passed through several small villages" (Ranjel). Ranjel's is the only reference to this place which is probably, as Swanton points out, only an alternative name (or an error) for Casqui. Elvas is quite enthusiastic about Casqui, "The land is higher, drier, and more level than any other along the river that had been seen until then . . . the greater part of the way lying through fields thickly set with great towns, two or three of them to be seen from one." The Inca, for once, is on the side of conservatism, "toda tierra muy fertil, y poblada, aunque los Pueblos eran pequeños, de à quinçe, viente, treinta, y quarenta cases." [9] However, later on, he states that fifteen or twenty thousand persons gathered to witness the adoration of the cross at the principal Casqui village.

This is interesting. The fact that Ranjel speaks of "small villages," that Elvas, although calling them towns says that two or three were to be seen from one, and the Inca's specific statements regarding the small number of houses in each village, all combine to suggest a hamlet type of organization differing significantly perhaps from the large compact villages already encountered at Quizqui and Aquixo and to be seen at Pacaha and Quiguate. This is merely a faint indication that Casqui was culturally divergent from the prevailing pattern in this part of the Mississippi, but it may prove interesting in future discussion of the location and identity of this group.

The principal Casqui village was reached on Friday, June 24th, St. John's Day. The distance from Aquixo, 1½ leagues above the crossing-place, was therefore somewhere between three and four days' march, depending on the time of day they arrived at Casqui, which is nowhere given. One of these marches, it will be recalled, was through a difficult swamp so the distance covered was presumably short.

The Casqui capital "had very good cabins, and in the principal one, over the door, were many heads of very fierce bulls, just as in Spain, noblemen who are sportsmen mount the heads of wild boars and bears" (Ranjel). To this the other chroniclers add practically nothing by way of description. That there was at least one sizable mound of domiciliary character, however, will presently appear.

Events at Casqui deserve a chapter to themselves. Evidently, the chief whom the Spaniards took to be the "Lord of Casqui" was either very naïve or very ingenious. He came out to meet the Spanish column attended by his chief persons bearing gifts of skins, shawls, and fish. Whether he really believed that De Soto was "Son of the Sun" we shall never know.[10] In any case, he treated the Governor

[9] Garcilaso, 1722, p. 179. Translation: "All this land very fertile and well populated, although the villages were small, of fifteen, twenty, thirty or forty houses."

[10] This suggests affiliation with a Natchez-Taensa type of culture, and is particularly interesting in view of the possible hamlet type of village organization of these people, another Natchez trait.

as such, prostrating himself at his feet and expressing only a desire to serve him and be his vassal. The Governor expressed his satisfaction in an appropriate reply — through how many interpreters, one may ask; Juan Ortiz is farther from his linguistic base than ever. That De Soto had private misgivings, however, regarding the sincerity of old Casqui, is evidenced by his courteous refusal to quarter his troops in the village, saying that they preferred to camp outside in the open fields owing to the excessive heat. In character with his role of humble neophite. Casqui demanded a "sign" to which, after the Spaniards should have departed, he and his people could appeal, particularly for rain, of which the crops then stood in great need. In response, the Governor caused to be made

> . . . a very tall cross . . . made of two pines [probably cypress], . . . as it is the custom of the Caciques to have near their houses a high hill, made by hand, some having the houses placed thereon, we set up the cross on the summit of [such] a mount, and we all went on bended knees, with great humility, to kiss the foot of that cross. The Indians did the same as they saw us do, nor more nor less; then directly they brought a great quantity of cane, making a fence about it; and we returned that night to our camp.[11]

This affecting incident brings to mind a similar one that took place one hundred and forty-one years later. On his way down the Mississippi in 1682, La Salle erected a cross in a Quapaw village that could not have been very far from this older Casqui site, and on his return from the Gulf found that the Indians had surrounded it with a palisade.[12] The parallel is not without interest.

Impatient to reach the imagined splendors of the celebrated Pacaha, De Soto remained with the hospitable Casqui less than two days. Having arrived at the "capital" some time Friday and erected the cross on Saturday, he gave the order to march on Sunday, June 26th. The wily Lord of Casqui, seizing a heaven-sent opportunity of witnessing the discomfiture of his old enemy, Pacaha, accompanied the army with a large force of Indians. Pacaha was said to be but one day's journey "by river upward" (Biedma) separated from the Casqui territory by a "lake, like an estuary, that entered the Rio Grande" (Elvas). The night of Sunday, 26th, was spent at another Casqui village and the next day, after passing two more Casqui villages, the army arrived at the lake "which was half a cross-bow shot over, of great depth and swiftness of current" (Elvas). Curious lake! The Inca's description makes more sense, "a swamp that was very difficult to cross, having deep miry places at the entrance and exit and clear water in the middle, but so deep that for the space of twenty paces it was necessary to swim." [12a] This is an excellent description of a cut-off lake in process of becoming a swamp, but can only be reconciled with Elvas' reference to the swift current by supposing it to have been an abandoned Mississippi channel occupied by a smaller stream. The Casqui allies had just completed a bridge across this lake or stream, of timbers thrown across from tree to tree in some manner that is difficult to imagine unless we suppose that it was only the timbered borders of this questionable body of water that were bridged leaving the deep central portion to be swum, as suggested by Garcilaso's description. This is further indicated by the same author's unenthusiastic reference to this work of engineering in the plural, "unas malas Puentas." In any case, it seems to have been a sufficient bridge for the purpose and the army got across in safety and found themselves at last in the promised land of Pacaha.

The "Empire" of Pacaha

Evidently, this curious lake with its swift current formed the boundary between the Casqui and Pacaha domains, and the principal Pacaha village was not far from it. As to the total distance between the Casqui and Pacaha "capitals," there is a good deal of variance in the narratives. The information of the Casqui informants that Pacaha was but a day's journey

[11] Biedma, in Bourne, 1904, vol. II, pp. 27–28.

[12] "Relation of Father Membré," in LeClercq, 1881, vol. II, p. 169.

[12a] Garcilaso, 1722, p. 181: . . . y al fin del as llegaron à una Cienega muy mala de pasar, que à la entrada, y à la salida tenia grandes atolladeros, y el medio era de agua linpia, mas tan honda, que por elpacio de veinte pasos fe avia de hadar.

may have been colored by their desire to get rid of the Spaniards; perhaps it was based on the Indians' speedier mode of travel. In any case, it took the army two days, if not three. Ranjel says they arrived at Pacaha Wednesday (having left Sunday), but there are indications in Elvas that, after crossing the so-called lake, De Soto paused while messengers were sent ahead to assure the Lord of Pacaha of his peaceful intentions. This may very well have consumed the best part of one day. Biedma simply calls it a two-days' march without entering into particulars. Garcilaso is away off from the others, making it three days to the "swamp," which was crossed on the fourth day, and three more to "Capaha" as he calls it.

We have heard so much about Pacaha it has become a land of promise for us as well as De Soto. Dominant politically over Quizqui, Aquixo, and probably Casqui as well, Pacaha would seem to offer the best possibility of making contact with archaeology, provided — and this is the big "if" — we can succeed in locating the place. Fortunately, our chroniclers were sufficiently impressed to give considerable descriptive information which it will be worth-while to quote *in extenso*. Thus Ranjel:

On Wednesday [June 29th] they came to the village of Pacaha, a village and lord of wide repute and highly thought of in that country.

This town was a very good one, thoroughly well stockaded; and the walls were furnished with towers and a ditch round about, for the most part full of water which flows in by a canal from the river; and this ditch was full of excellent fish of divers kinds. . . . In Aquixo, and Casqui, and Pacaha, they saw the best villages seen up to that time [a pregnant statement — they had seen a good many], better stockaded and fortified, and the people were of finer quality, excepting those of Cofitachequi.[13]

And the concise Biedma:

In the morning, we took up our course for Pacaha, which was by the river upward. We travelled two days, and then discovered the town on a plain, well fenced about, and surrounded by a water-ditch made by hand.[14]

Elvas follows Ranjel very closely:

On Wednesday, the nineteenth day of June [should be 29th], the Governor entered Pacaha, and took quarters in the town where the Cacique was accustomed to reside. It was enclosed and very large. In the towers and the palisade were many loopholes. There was much dry maize, and the new was in great quantity, throughout the fields. At the distance of half a league to a league off were large towns, all of them surrounded with stockades.

Where the Governor stayed was a great lake, near to the enclosure; and the water entered a ditch that well-nigh went round the town. From the River Grande to the lake was a canal, through which the fish came into it, and where the Chief kept them for his eating and pastime. With nets that were found in the place, as many were taken as need required; and however much might be the casting, there was never any lack of them.[15]

There follows the famous description of the fishes of the Mississippi "differing from those of the fresh waters of Spain." Garcilaso's description of "Capaha" (his version of "Pacaha," which for many years led scholars to identify this tribe with the Quapaw) is in some respects the most interesting of all:

Otras dos jornadas caminaron, pasada la Cienega, y al tercero dia bien temprano llegaron à unos cerros altos, de donde dieron vista al Pueblo principal de Capaha, que era frontera, y defensa de toda la Provincia, contra la de Casquin: y por ende lo tenian fortificado de la manera que dirèmos. El Pueblo tenia quinientas casas grandes, y buenas; estava en un sitio algo mas alto, y eminente que los derredores; tenianlo hecho casi Isla, con una cava, ò foso de diez, ò doce braças fondo, y de cinquenta pasos en ancho, y por donde menos, de quarenta, hecho à mano: el qual estava lleno de agua, y la recibia del Rio Grande, que atras hecimos mencion, que pasava tres leguas arriba del Pueblo. Recibiala por una canal abierta, à fuerça de braços, que desde el foso iba hasta el Rio Grande à tomar el agua: la canal era de tres estados de fondo, y tan ancha, que dos Canoas de las grandes bajavan, y subian por ella juntas, sin tocar los remos de la una, con los de la otra. Este foso de agua, tan ancho como hemos dicho, rodeava las tres partes del Pueblo, que aun no estava acabada la obra: la otra quarta parte estava cercada de una muy fuerte paliçada, hecha pared, de gruesos maderos hincados en tierra, pegados unos à otros, y otros atravesados, atados, y embarrados, con barro pisado con paja, como ya lo hemos dicho arriba. Este gran foso, y su canal, tenia tanta

[13] Ranjel, in Bourne, 1904, vol. II, pp. 139–40.
[14] Biedma, in Bourne, 1904, vol. II, p. 28.
[15] Elvas, in Bourne, 1904, vol. I, pp. 123–24.

cantidad de pescado, que todos los Españoles, è Indios que fueron con el Governador, se hartaron dèl, y pareciò que no le avian sacado un pece.[16]

The evident discrepancies in the Inca's account in matters of time and distance should not cause us to overlook the really valuable information it furnishes. Such an item as that the palisade at Pacaha was plastered with clay daub reinforced with straw is an observation that has all the earmarks of veracity, there being no conceivable object in adding it for purposes of embellishment. But what about the "high hills" mentioned earlier in the passage? This is extremely interesting because the only topographical feature west of the Mississippi anywhere near the probable location of Pacaha is Crowley's Ridge. We either have to accept this as a clear reference to Crowley's Ridge or ignore it entirely.

Events at Pacaha, though extremely interesting, not to say amusing, in view of the behavior of that prime opportunist, old Casqui, contribute little to our present concern and may therefore be passed over briefly. We left the army encamped on the frontier of Pacaha awaiting the outcome of De Soto's emissaries. Their assurances of the Governor's peaceable intentions evidently failed to impress the Pacaha chieftain, who retired by canoe with many of his people to an island stronghold on the Mississippi. This evacuation was still in progress when the Spaniards and their Indian allies entered the town. Many people were taken and much booty. Elvas says that the captives were turned over to the Casqui, who were, however, prevented from killing them. Garcilaso, on the other hand, says that these unfortunates to the number of one hundred and fifty were promptly scalped — "les quitaron los cascos de la cabeça" — which is probably nearer the truth. The booty was welcome and gives an interesting side-light on the way the Spaniards clothed themselves, their original outfits having long since gone to pieces.

Many shawls, deer-skins, lion and bear-skins, and many cat-skins were found in the town. Numbers who had been a long time badly covered, there clothed themselves. Of the shawls they made mantles and cassocks; some made gowns and lined them with cat-skins, as they also did the cassocks. Of the deer-skins were made jerkins, shirts, stockings, and shoes; and from the bear-skins they made very good cloaks, such as no water could get through. They found shields of raw cow-hide out of which armour was made for the horses.[17]

It will be recalled that the shields of the warriors who opposed the crossing were said to be of woven cane, a point of possible cultural interest. Finally, as a minor archaeological note, Biedma mentions as part of the loot "some beads made of sea-snails."

One incident of the pillage is interesting for the light it throws on the religious and mortuary practices of the Pacaha. Unfortunately, we have to depend entirely on Garcilaso. This is the kind of information that he is often the only one to supply. Not content, he tells us, with sacking the town and butchering the captives, the Casqui allies made for the temple,

. . . que estava en una Plaça Grande que el Pueblo tenia: el qual era entierro de todos los Señores que

[16] Garcilaso, 1722, pp. 181–82. Translation: "They travelled another two days' journey, past the swamp, and on the third day very early they arrived at some high hills, from which they could see the principal villages of Capaha, that was a frontier and defense of all the province against that of Casquin, and therefore they had fortified it in the manner that we shall tell of. The village had five hundred large and good houses, it was in a location somewhat higher and more prominent than the surroundings; they had made it almost an island with an excavation or ditch of ten or twelve fathoms (*bracas*) deep, and of fifty paces in width, and sometimes less than forty, made by hand; it was full of water that came from the Rio Grande, that we mentioned before, which passed three leagues above the village. The water was received through an open canal, dug by hand (*a fuerca de bracos*), that extended from the ditch to the river: the canal was of three estados (?) of depth; and so wide that two of their large canoes could pass through it together, without the paddles of one touching those of the other. This ditch of water, wide as we have said, surrounded the three parts of the village, which work still was not finished; the other fourth part was walled in by a very strong palisade of strong timbers, driven into the ground, held together by other timbers placed across and tied, the whole plastered with clay, reinforced with straw, as we have already described above. This large ditch, and its canal, held such a quantity of fish, that all the Spaniards, and Indians who were with the Governor, surfeited themselves and it seemed that they had not taken out a single fish."

[17] Elvas, in Bourne, 1904, vol. I, p. 122.

avian sido de aquella Provincia, padres, y abuelos, y antecesores de Capaha. Aquellos Templos, y Entierros, como yà en otras partes se ha dicho, son lo mas estimado, y venerado que entre estos Indios de la Florida se tiene, . . .

Derribaron por el suelo todas las Arcas de madera, que servian de sepulturas, y para satisfaccion, y vengança propria, y afrenta de sus enemigos, echaron por tierra los huesos, y cuerpos muertos, que en las Arcas avia, y no se contentò con los derramar por el suelo, sino que los pisaron, y cocearon con todo vilipendio, y menosprecio. Quitaron muchas cabeças de Indios Casquines, que los de Capaha avian puesto por señal de Triumpho, y Victoria, en puentas de Lanças, à las puertas del Templo, y en lugar dellas pusieron otras cabeças, que ellos aquel dia cortaron de los vecinos del Pueblo: en suma, no dejaron de pensar cosa, que no la hiciesen.[18]

As already stated, Pacaha had established himself on an island refuge from which no overtures of De Soto could dislodge him. In the meantime, the Casqui chief sent back for more men and canoes. This has been used as evidence that the Casqui province was located on or near the Mississippi or a tributary thereof, since it was possible to bring reinforcements up from there to Pacaha by water. We shall have occasion to return to this point later. Upon the arrival of the Casqui reinforcements, the combined Spanish-Indian forces moved up the river by land and water. Arrived at the island occupied by Pacaha there was a battle, but that is about all one can say with certainty. It is impossible to reconcile the accounts of Elvas and Garcilaso, the only two narrators who reported the episode. According to the first, Pacaha was routed almost without a fight; according to the Inca, he put up stiff resistance and the Spaniards were obliged to withdraw. Both agree, however, that the Casqui behaved very badly in the affair, running off with whatever booty they could lay their hands on, leaving the Spaniards to do the fighting. It was probably anger at this defection that prompted De Soto to make peace with Pacaha. According to Elvas, he even turned back with his new ally and over-ran part of the Casqui country. Once more the crafty old Casqui chief showed his talent for diplomacy, presenting himself before the Governor in all humility and, after the tension had been broken by the antics of a clown in his retinue, pouring out his gratitude to the rain-giving cross left by the Spaniards in his capital, a recital couched in such affecting terms as to bring iron tears down the Conqueror's cheeks. The result was that a three-cornered peace was patched up on the spot, Pacaha and Casqui vying with each other to gain De Soto's favor by the presentation of sisters, wives, and daughters, and we have as epilogue (in Elvas) that delightful contest over the point of honor, as to which of the ancient rivals was to have the Governor's right hand when they sat down to dinner.

De Soto remained about a month altogether at Pacaha, during which time small parties were sent out to capture Indians and explore the country. Biedma gives an account of one of the expeditions, in which it appears that he himself took part. His very brief account of this journey is so interesting and culturally significant as to warrant quotation in full.

. . . particularly was one undertaken to the northwest, where we were told there were large settlements, through which we might go. We went in that direction eight days, through a wilderness which had large pondy swamps, where we did not find even trees, and only some wide plains, on which grew a plant so rank and high, that even on horseback we could not break our way through. Finally, we came to some collections of huts, covered with rush sewed together. When the owner of one moves away, he will roll up the entire covering, and carry it, the wife taking the frame of poles over which it is stretched; these they take down and put up so readily, that though they should move anew every hour, they conveniently

[18] Garcilaso, 1722, pp. 182–83. Translation: ". . . which temple was in a large plaza in the midst of the village, and was the sepulchre of the lords of that province, fathers, grandfathers and ancestors of Capaha [Pacaha]. These temples and burial places are most highly venerated by all the Indians of Florida. . . . They [The Casqui] threw down the chests of wood that served as tombs, and, to satisfy their vengeance and affront their enemies, poured the bodies and bones out upon the ground, and, not content with this, trampled and kicked them with all contempt and scorn. They took down many Casqui heads [scalps?] that those of Capaha had placed in triumph on the points of lances at the doors of the temple, and put other heads in their places that they had that day cut off from the inhabitants of the village. In short there was no indignity they could think of that they did not carry out."

enough carry their house on their backs. We learned from this people that there were some hamlets of the sort about the country, the inhabitants of which employed themselves in finding places for their dwellings wherever many deer were accustomed to range, and a swamp where were many fish; and that when they had frightened the game and the fish from one place, so that they took them there not so easily as at first, they would all move off with their dwellings for some other part, where the animals were not yet shy. This Province, called Caluç, had a people who care little to plant, finding support in meat and fish.[19]

This is probably the earliest European description of tall-grass prairie vegetation and certainly the earliest account of a prairie hunting type of culture. The portable houses of rush mats suggest the Illinois, whose permanent dwellings were of woven rushes,[20] and these "nomads" may have been a band of Illinois or similar village people on a summer hunt. Against this is the fact that sedentary prairie tribes ordinarily hunted in winter and cultivated their crops in the summer. Furthermore, the general sound of Biedma's description evokes a truly nonsedentary culture. One is inclined to infer that we have here — only eight-days' journey from an advanced center of Mississippi culture — a people in a nomadic hunting stage that might be described archaeologically as "archaic." The tantalizing part of the story lies in the fact that so few details are given concerning the route that it is next to impossible to locate these nomads, even if we knew where to locate Pacaha, the starting point.

Whether this is the same expedition reported by Garcilaso is not clear, but appears unlikely. According to this writer, who always makes things sound more civilized than they were, certain "merchants" who came to Capaha (Pacaha) with salt, and other wares, told the Governor that in the mountains 40 leagues off was a province rich in salt and that yellow metal the Spaniards seemed so desirous of finding:

Con estas nuevas se regocijaron grandemente los Castellanos, y para las verificar, se ofrecieron dos soldados à ir con los Indios. Estos eran naturales de Galicia, el uno llamado Hernando de Silvera, y el otro Pedro Moreno, Hombres diligentes, y que se les podia fiar qualquiera cosa. Encargoseles, que por donde pasasen, notasen le disposicion de la tierra, y trugesen relacion si era fertil, y bien poblada. Y para contratar, y comprar la Sal, y el Oro, llevaron Perlas, y Gamuças, y otras cosas de legumbres, llamadas Frisoles, que Capaha les mandò dàr, è Indios que los acompañasen, y dos de los Mercaderes, para que los guiasen. Con este acuerdo fueron los Españoles, y al fin de los once dias, que tardaron en su viage, bolvieron con seis cargas de Sal de piedra cristalina, no hecha con artificio, sino criada assi naturalmente. Trugeron mas una carga de Açofar muy fino, y muy resplandeciente, y de la calidad de las tierras que avian visto, digeron, que no era buena, porque era esteril, y mal poblada. De la burla, y engaño del Oro se consolaron los Españoles con la Sal, por la necesidad que della tenian.[21]

Apart from their intrinsic interest, warrant for quoting these passages will be found in the discussion of the De Soto route, since Biedma's prairies and the Inca's salt mine are factors in the location of Pacaha. For the present, it is sufficient to note that these reports of poor and thinly populated country were such as to discourage further penetration up the Mississippi. On July 29th, De Soto gave orders to march southward over the trail by which they had come, this time bound for a province of great abundance named Quiguate. One would suppose the Governor's credulity regarding these fabulous places somewhat diminished by

[19] Biedma, in Bourne, 1904, vol. II, pp. 29–30.

[20] Alvord, 1922, vol. I, p. 42.

[21] Garcilaso, 1722, p. 187. Translation: "With this news the Spaniards greatly rejoiced and in order to verify it, two soldiers offered to go back with the Indians. They were natives of Galicia, one called Hernando de Silvera, and the other Pedro Moreno, diligent men who could be trusted with anything. They were charged that where they might pass they were to note the disposition of the land and bring back a report if it was fertile and well populated. In order to bargain for the salt and gold, they carried pearls and chamois skins (Gamuças) and a kind of vegetable called beans that Capaha directed to be given to them, also Indians to accompany them and two of the 'merchants' to serve as guides. With this arrangement, the Spaniards left, and at the end of eleven days returned with six loads of crystalline salt, not manufactured but taken from a natural deposit. They also brought a load of copper, very fine and resplendant, and of the quality of the lands that they had seen, they said that it was not very good, but was sterile and poorly populated. For the hoax and deceit of the gold they consoled themselves with the salt, because of the great need they had for it."

now, but he had to go somewhere and he would *not go back.*

Two-days' march brought the army again to the chief village of Casqui and on the following day, Sunday, July 31st, they set out for Quiguate. This portion of the route is very difficult to make out. Ranjel says that they spent the first night at a Casqui village and the second day arrived at another

> which is on the river of Casqui, which is a branch of the great river of Pacaha, and this branch is as large as the Guadalquivir. Thither came Casqui and assisted them across the river in canoes, August 2.
>
> On Wednesday, they slept in a burned village. The next day, Thursday, in another near the river, where there were many pumpkins and an abundance of corn, and beans. And the next day, Friday [August 5th], they came to Quiguate, which is the largest village which they saw in that country, situated on the river of Casqui; and it was later known that the banks of this river were thickly populated further down (although they did not find it out there) and along it they took the trail of Coligua which was not peopled in the intervening country.[22]

Biedma agrees that Quiguate was the largest town in Florida but adds nothing further in the way of description beyond the fact that it was situated on "an arm of the Rio Grande." Elvas likewise states that it was the largest town the Spaniards had seen, which is indeed borne out by the further statement that the army was lodged in half the town, the other half being burned lest it afford cover for an attack. He goes on at some length to describe the Governor's efforts, finally successful, to get hold of the Cacique and thereby secure the services of his people, but in the entire account there are no details of archaeological interest. In regard to the province as a whole, he merely states that, like Casqui and Pacaha, it "was level and fertile having rich river margins, on which the Indians made extensive fields."

Garcilaso's account of this portion of the route, from Casqui to Quiguate is so radically divergent from the others that one feels little confidence even in purely descriptive passages, which, however, are given here for what they are worth:

> Al fin del quinto dia llegaron al Pueblo principal llamado Quiguate, de quien toda la Provincia tomava nombre. El qual estava dividido en tres Barrios iguales, en el uno dellos, estava la Casa del Señor, puesta en un cerro alto, hecho à mano: en los dos barrios se alojaron los Españoles, y en el tercero se recogieron los Indios, y huvo bastante alojamiento para todos.[23]

Considering the size and probable importance of Quiguate, and the fact that the Spaniards remained there twenty days (Ranjel), we are given surprisingly little information about the place. The few available facts can be stated in a single short sentence. "Capital" of a rich and fertile province, Quiguate was unusually large, had at least one mound of domiciliary character, and was situated on the river of Casqui, whatever stream that may have been.

At Quiguate information was obtained of a province called Coligua, lying somewhere to the northwest, "in the mountains." The Spaniards had seen enough, more than enough, of the Alluvial Valley. It was apparent that no gold was to be found here — perhaps in the mountains. But, if we may trust Biedma, who is the only one that mentions it, there was another reason for heading west. This author has in fact alluded to it before in connection with Pacaha and the explorations made therefrom "to discover if we could take a path to the northward, whereby to come out on the South Sea." Here, at Quiguate, "we remained . . . eight or nine days, to find guides and interpreters, still with the intention of coming out, if possible, on the other sea; for the Indians told us that eleven days' travel thence was a province where they subsisted on certain cattle, and there we could find interpreters for the whole distance to that sea." [24]

Accordingly, on Friday, August 26th, the army was on the march again bound for Coligua, in a northwest direction presumably, which would have speedily taken them outside the limits of the Survey Area. They will

[22] Ranjel, in Bourne, 1904, vol. II, p. 146.

[23] Garcilaso, 1722, p. 188. Translation: "At the end of the fifth day they arrived at the principal village called Quiguate, from which all the province took its name. It was divided into three equal wards, in the one of them, was the house of the chief placed on a high hill, made by hand; in two of these wards the Spaniards were quartered and in the third the Indians took refuge, yet there was sufficient lodging for all."

[24] Biedma, in Bourne, 1904, vol. II, p. 31.

be back, but it will be in another more southerly (?) part of the Mississippi Valley. So far as this portion of the area is concerned, the curtain rolls down for almost a century and a half. When next we see these tribes and places again, it will be through the eyes of the French and the names will be disconcertingly different.

Discussion of the Route

The Problem in Terms of Archaeology

An enormous and highly controversial literature has gathered about the problem of De Soto's line of march through the Southeast, culminating in the monumental "Final Report of the United States De Soto Expedition Commission." [25] Because of the importance of fixing the place of discovery of the Mississippi River, the report deals very fully with the portion of the route described in the preceding pages. With nothing short of admiration for the vast learning and industry applied to the De Soto problem by Swanton and his associates of the Commission, it is nevertheless our opinion that no part of the route within the limits of the Survey Area has been identified beyond question, a statement that can be made even more emphatic when limited to the portion of the route under consideration here, i.e., Chicaça to Quiguate. Swanton, himself, would probably agree to this statement, in fact he says: "This Final Report of the Fact Finding Committee does not profess finality in the sense that the exact line of march pursued by De Soto and Moscoso has now been established for all time and no future effort need be expended in this direction. No such finality ever will be attained." [26] Swanton is, of course, speaking of the De Soto route as a whole. In the concluding section of the report he lists specific locations along the route in terms of their probable correctness. The first group of nine locations regarded as satisfactorily located are all well east of the Mississippi. The second group of twenty-eight locations regarded as established with "approximate correctness" includes four locations within the portion of the route under consideration here. These are as follows:

The trail west from the Chickasaw country, the Welch trail shown on the Mitchell Map, Mississippi.

The point where De Soto reached and crossed the Mississippi River, near Sunflower Landing, Mississippi.

The site of Aquixo, near Avenue, Arkansas.

The site of Casqui, on Crowley's Ridge near Helena, Arkansas.[27]

Whether the finality disclaimed by Swanton can ever be attained for this part of the route is another question. We are not disposed to take an altogether pessimistic view of the possibilities. It depends very much on archaeology. Swanton and his co-workers have been obliged to work almost without benefit of archaeology. It must be apparent that until we can relate specific sites and materials to the years 1541–43 with a fair degree of accuracy, it is hardly reasonable to expect much more than the approximate location of De Soto place-names that Swanton has given us. Though not yet in this fortunate position, we do have archaeological data that were not available to Swanton, sufficient at least to excuse our brash entry into this very difficult field of inquiry. They permit us to be somewhat more discriminating in the selection of sites for possible identification with De Soto place-names. The usual procedure has been to establish the approximate location of events and places described in the narratives by a combination of dead reckoning and topographical study; then having established such locations, to look for archaeological sites on the ground tallying with them, without regard to the all-important question as to *when* such sites were being occupied. Little attention has been paid to the archaeological character of the sites or the materials found on them. Obviously, it is not sufficient that a given site occurs

[25] The final report was written by Dr. Swanton and will be referred to here for convenience as Swanton, 1939. In so doing, we must not overlook the important contributions made by other members of the Commission. A great deal of the research on the portion of the Route under discussion here was done by the late Colonel Fordyce of Little Rock, Arkansas.

[26] Swanton, 1939, p. 1.

[27] Swanton, 1939, p. 291.

in a *place* that satisfies documentary requirements, it must also have existed at the proper *time*. In a comparatively rich archaeological area such as the Mississippi Alluvial Valley, the mere finding of a site in a desired location contributes very little to the discussion. A complete archaeological map of the area would furnish sites for almost any line of march one might care to hypothesize.

Unfortunately, we are not yet in a position to bring archaeology to bear on the De Soto question with anything approaching precision; in fact, much of our interest in De Soto lies in the hope that we may be able to bring the 1541 date line to bear on archaeology. The best we can do, at the moment, is to set up an hypothetical 1541 period in terms of archaeology — within limits that will at least eliminate a large number of sites from consideration — and test this working hypothesis against the narratives and the De Soto Commission's interpretation of them. This is admittedly a limited and perhaps unduly critical approach. Our only extenuation is that at this stage we are more interested in methods than in final results. This is an attempt to show how archaeology and this phase of history can be brought closer together, not an effort at once to close the gap between them.

The Archaeology of A.D. 1541

Starting with general archaeological considerations, it now appears that previously accepted chronological schemes, which relegated the so-called Temple Mound II or late Mississippi culture to the period between 1541 and 1700, erred on the side of conservatism. Cross-dating between the Mississippi and Southwest through Texas [28] is only one of a number of recent developments in Southeastern archaeology indicating that more time must be allowed for this late prehistoric stage of culture. Our own tentative effort toward chronology by means of correlation with recent channel history (p. 296) also appears to support such a revision, in fact would seem to suggest that even more time is required for the Mississippi stage than is allowed by Krieger.[29] Even a modest revision would remove one source of previous difficulty in applying archaeology to the De Soto problem. It has always been clear that the descriptive material in the narratives, so far as it goes, refers to a fully developed late Mississippi or Temple Mound II stage of culture, yet we have been told that this stage was not reached until after 1541. For example, the following traits, from Ford and Willey's definition of Temple Mound II as manifested in the Mississippi Valley, are encountered in the most casual reading of the De Soto accounts of this portion of the route.

> . . . Concentration of population into large compact villages;
>
> Utilization of temple mounds as adjuncts to the village in contrast to the earlier practice of not placing houses in their vicinity;
>
> Surrounding villages with wooden stockades [to which might be added the very important detail that stockades were plastered with daub and had projecting bastions, cf. Garcilaso's description of "Capaha," p. 356] [30]

General historical probabilities may also be invoked. The culture stage defined as Temple Mound II represents the peak of development, materially speaking, in this portion of the Mississippi Valley. This peak was followed by a marked decline in population and culture, as we shall see when we come to examine the sources for the French contact period. The latter, dating from 1673 on, reveal a remarkable discrepancy between the actual conditions of that time and the Temple Mound II culture as defined or as described by the De Soto documents. This regression is admitted by all interested students but has generally been regarded as catastrophic and therefore relegated to a period of very short duration. There is no question that epidemics of European diseases plus an outbreak of intense tribal warfare, the result of relayed pressures from the East, decimated the peoples of the Mississippi Valley generally. That, however, does not satisfactorily explain the situation in this particular area. Take for example only the St. Francis and Yazoo basins, with which we

[28] Krieger, 1946.

[29] Since the above was written, Krieger has revised his estimates still further, suggesting that some of the characteristic traits of Mississippi culture were already present in Texas as early as A.D. 500.

[30] Ford and Willey, 1941, pp. 353–54.

are archaeologically most familiar. In 1673 the first of these very considerable areas was occupied by only one tribe, the Quapaw; the second was completely deserted except for a number of splinter groups located on its southeastern margin, along the Yazoo River. These Yazoo River groups may have been remnants of tribes formerly more extended and powerful, but the Quapaw are thought to have been recent intruders into the area. Of the populous groups responsible for the immense number of large Temple Mound II sites in the Yazoo and St. Francis basins, there were not even any decimated remnants left to tell the French how powerful their ancestors were. We are not going to speculate here as to the causes of this evident depopulation. The point is that it probably did not happen overnight. With all due allowance for the rapidity of cultural disintegration under the impact of white civilization (in this case indirect), it does not seem possible to allow less than a half century for the period of regression. This would push the end of the fully developed Temple Mound II culture in this area back to about 1625. If we were to adhere to the conservative dating of Ford and Willey, we would have to crowd the entire development of that stage and all the sites that manifest it into the short period between 1575 (their date for the beginning of Temple Mound II) and 1625. This could only be done by postulating an exceptionally large population. A great many large sites would have to be occupied simultaneously in order to crowd them into the time allowed. Chronologically speaking, there is not enough room for all the archaeology we have got to account for. The earlier dating proposed by Krieger and others relieves this crowding and makes us feel more comfortable all around.

Thus, the internal evidence of the De Soto documents finds support in recent archaeological developments, and the two lines of evidence seem to agree with general archaeological and historical probabilities. This sounds as though we have chalked up an important decision and greatly limited the problem of identification of De Soto places and peoples. Unfortunately, our concepts of the local manifestations representing the Temple Mound II stage of culture are still regrettably vague, and we know little as yet about the precise chronological relations between them. In the chronological scheme followed here, the Mississippi stage, lasting from C to A on our ceramic scale, corresponds roughly to the broader concept of Temple Mound II culture. Judging from the temporal distribution of large village sites and ceremonial centers (see pp. 340–43), the earlier part of this stage, period C–B, witnessed the full development of that culture; the later part, period B–A, showing signs of the regression referred to above. The De Soto narratives seem to describe the culture at or near its peak of development. Logically, this would be in the latter part of period C–B or early B–A. A reasonable postulation would be that the 1541 date line is not far from point B on the time scale. Let it be emphasized again that this admirable precision is tainted with specious accuracy. We know next to nothing about the absolute length of the Mississippi Period and have only guessed as to the position of 1541 within it. Nor do we yet have a satisfactory definition, even in terms of pottery, of the various subdivisions of the area at this time. Again it must be pointed out that for most sites that will enter into this discussion we have nothing more than surface collections. The necessarily crude sampling methods of the Survey do not always give a complete and accurate measure of the pottery complex, even on the surface, to say nothing of the deeper levels of a site. It has been emphasized again and again that we are dating pottery collections, not sites, that such dates, however useful in working out the main chronological outlines of the area, tell us very little about the history of this or that particular site. Nevertheless, we shall depend primarily on seriation dates in the ensuing discussion, giving first priority to sites that date somewhere around point B on the time scale but, such being our lack of confidence in the precise accuracy of the seriation technique, not excluding altogether from consideration any sites dating between C and A.

In some cases, however, it will be necessary to assess the pottery collections independently of seriation results. This is particularly required in the case of sites showing a long occupation or reoccupation where the theoretical average date furnished by seriation is inadequate for the purpose in hand. It will be recalled that point C on the seriation time scale marks the transition from clay- to shell-tempered pottery in the area. Regardless of whether it was a gradual or abrupt transition, C is for practical purposes the point where percentage frequencies of the two temper groups are approximately equal. Throughout the succeeding period, C–B, clay-tempering is in decline. B is approximately the point where percentage frequencies of clay-tempered types become so small as to be negligible. A 100-per cent shell-tempered complex is, therefore, theoretically post-1541, though we have given sufficient reasons for not taking this dictum too literally. On the other hand, a complex with anything more than minor percentages of clay-tempered pottery is likely to be too early. The ideal ceramic formula, for a site of the De Soto period, in short, is a predominantly shell-tempered complex with just enough clay-tempered minorities to indicate nearness to point B on the time scale. This is admittedly vague. It is unfortunate that neither our classification nor chronology are sufficiently refined to enable us to specify marker types for the De Soto period. We can name a large number of types that are definitely too early, and a few that we think are too late, but there remains a large group, any one of which so far as we know might have been in use in 1541, and of these we can as yet find no reason for preference.

We trust that the foregoing has made it sufficiently clear that archaeology is not yet in a position for final identification of De Soto sites (assuming that locations can first be approximately established by documentary means). It can at most provide a rough working hypothesis in terms of a tentative ceramic scale that will eliminate some of the uncertainty that has resulted from the indiscriminate use of archaeological data by De Soto scholars in the past.

Location of Chicaça

It is unfortunate for any attempt to trace De Soto's route through our area that we are confronted at the very outset by uncertainty in regard to the location of Chicaça. Briefly, there are two alternatives, the historic Chickasaw location in Lee County, Mississippi, and a supposed earlier location in southern Pontotoc or northern Chickasaw counties. We shall simply designate them here as the Lee and Pontotoc theories. Swanton argues for the more southerly Pontotoc location, because it fits better with his interpretation of subsequent movements, but he shows little real enthusiasm for the evidence. His detailed discussion of the route from Black Warrior River to the Chickasaw towns seems to favor either location about equally.[31] He cites, without approval or disapproval, Lewis' flat statement (based on, but not quite agreeing with, Claiborne) that in De Soto's time the Chickasaw towns were near Redland, Pontotoc County.[32] So much for the arguments in favor of the Pontotoc theory. The only real argument against the Lee County theory is that the potsherds "scattered over the Chickasaw oldfields . . . are almost without exception of modern type, associated with trade objects of the eighteenth and early nineteenth centuries. . . ."[33] Subsequent archaeological investigations by Jesse Jennings have shown this statement to be incorrect. An older horizon was found to be well represented in the Chickasaw Old Fields. This older material is related to the historic Chickasaw, but Jennings is unwilling to state in so many words that the relationship is ancestral, though, upon consideration of his material, it seems a fair assumption. In any case, the presence of earlier material in quantity on the Lee County sites vitiates Swanton's principal argument against their having been visited by De Soto. In summing up, Swanton returns again to what is, after all, his main argument for the Pontotoc theory:

> Upon the whole such evidence as has been brought forward up to this point seems to us unfavorable to the supposition that the Lee County sites were those visited by De Soto, but the most important point is the fact that they are so far to the north that it would be necessary to assume the Spaniards to have returned some distance toward the south when they picked up the trail to the Mississippi. This rests on

[31] Swanton, 1939, pp. 220–21.

[32] Lewis, 1937. The author opens this paper with the statement that ". . . there can scarcely be said to be a single point on the entire line of march which has been established beyond cavil," then proceeds to give the exact location of Chicaça "on the S.½ of the S.W.¼ of section 21, and the N.½ of the N.W.¼ of section 28, town 11, range 3 E in Pontotoc County," without any apparent evidence in its support.

[33] Swanton, 1939, p. 222.

the assumption that the trail passed south of the Yocona and reached the Mississippi near the present Sunflower Landing in Coahoma County.[34]

Jennings, who had the advantage of more recent archaeological findings, his own, refused steadfastly to be drawn to any conclusion on this Lee vs. Pontotoc question, in a masterpiece of scientific caution which we find worthy of emulation.[35] We must point out, however, that the assumed location of Chicaça in Pontotoc County cannot be used legitimately as an argument in favor of the Sunflower Landing crossing, since the latter has already been used to locate the former.

The Route from Chicaça to Quizqui

The location of Alimamu, apparently not more than one day's march from Chicaça is of secondary importance from the point of view of establishing De Soto's route, but the ethnic identification of the place, on account of the close resemblance of the name to that of the historic Alabama, is a matter of considerable interest. Apparently, no effort has been made to locate the place with precision. Swanton suggests the headwaters of the Yocona or Skuna rivers in western Pontotoc or eastern Lafayette or Calhoun counties, and refers to several sites in this area located by Calvin Brown. Only one of these is treated as a real possibility, a small site on the Yocona on what is called the Hartsfield Place. Swanton himself is not impressed by this site and consoles himself in the following terms:

> . . . but it is by no means certain that enough remains would be left on these Alabama sites to identify them since the "Alimamu" town was small and may not have been occupied for a long period and the stockade is, . . . said to have been only a temporary affair where no pottery should be looked for.[36]

This sort of reasoning is a trifle disingenuous. It is true that Elvas refers to the first Alimamu town as "small' and Biedma describes the stockade — a distinct location from the small town, be it noted — as though it might have been a temporary affair. However, as we have already pointed out in the narrative section, there is something inherently improbable in Biedma's relation of this episode. For once, Garcilaso makes more sense than the others. He describes the country between Chicaça and "Alibamo," as he calls it, as "poblada de muchos Pueblos pequeños, de à quince, y de viente Casas."[37] The Governor pitched camp a quarter of a league beyond any of these settlements and sent out parties to reconnoiter the country. These returned with reports of a fort near by manned by 4000 warriors. The Inca's description of this fort will bear quoting at length:

> El qual era quadrado, de quatro Lienços iguales, hecho de maderos hincados, y cada Lienço de pared tenia quatrocientos pasos de largo. Por de dentro en este quadro avia otros dos Lienços de madera, que atravesavan el Fuerte de una pared à otra. El Lienço de la frente, tenia tres puertas pequeñas, y tan bajas, que no podia entrar hombre de acavallo por ellas. La una puerta estava en medio del Lienço, y las otras dos à los lados, junto à las esquinas. En derecho destas tres puertas, avia en cada Lienço otras tres, para que si los Españoles ganasen las primeras, se defendiesen en las del segundo Lienço, y en las del tercero, y quarto. Las puertas del postrer Lienço, salian à un Rio, que pasava por las espaldas del Fuerte. El Rio, aunque era angosto, era muy hondo, y de barrancas muy altas, que con dificultad las podian subir, y bajar à pie, y de ninguna manera acavallo. . . . Sobre el Rio tenian Puentes, hechas de madera, flacas, y ruines, que con dificultad podian pasar por ellas. A los lados del Fuerte no avia puerta alguna.[38]

[34] Swanton, 1939, p. 222.

[35] Jennings, 1941, pp. 218 et seq.

[36] Swanton, 1939, p. 233.

[37] Garcilaso, 1722, p. 172. Translation: ". . . populated with many small villages of fifteen or twenty houses."

[38] Garcilaso, 1722, p. 173. Translation: [The Fort] "was square, of four equal sides, made of posts thrust into the ground and each wall was 400 paces long. Within this square there were two other walls of posts, running across the fort from one wall to the other. The front wall had three small doors, so low that a man could not enter them on horseback. One door was in the middle of the wall, and the other two at the ends, next to the corners. Straight ahead of these three doors there were in each wall three others, in order that if the Spaniards might attain the first, they might defend themselves in those of the second wall, and in those of the third, and fourth. The doors of the last wall opened out to a river, that passed by the back part of the fort. The river although very narrow, was very deep, and had very steep banks, difficult to go up and down on foot and impossible on horseback. . . . Over the river they had bridges, made of wood, frail and ruinous, so that only with difficulty were they able to pass over them. On the sides of the fort there was not one door."

Allowing a possible hundred per cent for exaggeration, this is still no small fort, nor is it possible to regard it as a temporary structure thrown up hastily to dispute the Spanish army's passage. Biedma was perhaps misled by the fact that it was a fort pure and simple rather than a stockaded town, the only type of defensive works the Spaniards had previously encountered. This time it is the Inca who is supported by archaeology. His combination of small scattered villages or hamlets with a square stockade hard by for refuge in time of trouble accords very closely with historic Chickasaw archaeology as described by Jennings.

In view of this interesting correspondence, we are inclined to wonder if the coincidence of the name "Alimamu" or "Alibamo" with the historic Alabama has not obscured the real nature of this settlement. Considering how close it was to the main Chickasaw villages where the army wintered, and that the intervening country was settled in what was later typical Chickasaw fashion, it seems reasonable to suppose that those Alimamu were simply a branch of the Chickasaw or a group which had been united with them. Except that Biedma calls Alibamo a province, there is no indication in the narratives that the Spaniards regarded the inhabitants as distinct from the Chickasaw people. Ranjel merely states in offhand fashion that they "set out from the plain of Chicaça and arrived at Limamu for the night." Elvas likewise: "On the 25th day of April he left Chicaça and went to sleep at a small town called Alimamu." Garcilaso, as we have seen, calls the fort "Alibamo," but mans it with the same people who had already inflicted so much injury on the Spaniards — the Chickasaw. Later, he refers to Alibamo as the "last camp in the province of Chicaça." [39]

In short, the location of Limamu seems to be more closely tied up with the Chickasaw problem than has been indicated by Swanton. The same sort of sites should be looked for in both cases, and these will perhaps not differ markedly from the historic Chickasaw sites described by Jennings. We must conclude, then, that the locations of De Soto's Chicaça and Limamu are still open questions, and that, in consequence, an assumed location of either of these places cannot be used in support of further locations along the route.

We now come to one of the most controversial questions in all the voluminous De Soto literature, the direction and line of march from Chicaça-Limamu to the Mississippi. First, as to the direction; the narratives are very careless on this point, Ranjel and Elvas being completely silent, Biedma stating merely that the direction from Chicaça to Limamu was northwest. We have already pointed out that it is unsafe to assume that Limamu was on the direct route from Chicaça to the Mississippi. This leaves only Garcilaso who gives the direction from "Alibamo" to the Mississippi as north.

> Del alojamiento de Alibamo, que fue el postrero de la Provincia de Chacaça, saliò el Exercito, pasados los quatro dias, que por necesidad de los heridos alli estuvo; y al fin de otros tres, que caminò por un despoblado, llevando siempre la via al Norte, por huir de la Mar, llegò à dar vista à un Pueblo, llamado Chisca, el qual estava cerca de un Rio grande, que por ser el mayor de todos los que nuestros Españoles en la Florida vieron, le llamaron el Rio Grande, sin otro renombre.[40]

It is, of course, upon this statement that the claim of Memphis as the place of De Soto's "discovery" of the Mississippi is based.

Perhaps it is time to point out that the three principal claimants to this honor are, in Swanton's order of preference: Sunflower Landing, Coahoma County, Mississippi; Commerce Landing, Tunica County, Mississippi; and the Fourth Chickasaw Bluffs at Memphis, Tennessee. From either of the supposed locations of Chicaça-Limamu the direction to Memphis is northwest; to Commerce Landing, slightly north of west, to Sunflower Landing, about due west. In order to bring the Spaniards to Sunflower Landing, Swanton is

[39] "Del alojamiento de Alibamo, que fue el postrero de la Provincia e Chicaça."

[40] Garcilaso, 1722, p. 176. Translation: "The army departed from Alibamo, the last village of the Province of Chicaça, after four days spent there in care of the wounded, and in three more, in which the way led through an unpopulated area, bearing always to the north in order to go away from the sea, they reached a village called Chisca [Quizqui] situated near a great river, larger than any our Spaniards had seen in all Florida and they called it the Rio Grande, without any other name."

obliged to brush off Garcilaso completely, "an uncertain guide at best." Now this may be entirely permissable when the Inca is in conflict with more trustworthy sources, but in this particular case he is our sole informant. Against this "uncertain" direction of the Inca, Swanton quotes from Elvas' brief résumé of the expedition in his final chapter, which, in order to show clearly its summary character, is quoted here in full:

> From the port of Espiritu Santo to Apalache they marched west and northeast; from Cutifachiqui to Xuala, north; to Coça, westwardly; and thence to Tascaluça and the River Grande, as far as the Provinces of Quizquiz and Aquixo, to the westward; from thence to Pacaha northwardly, to Tula westwardly, to Autiamque southwardly, as far as the Province of Guachoya and Daycao.[41]

This is a very broad and careless summary of three years' wandering in the South, as comparison with Swanton's map of the expedition will readily show. The very considerable dip to the south from Coça to Mabila, for example, is completely ignored. One might as well argue from this that Mabila was west of Coça as that Quizqui was west of Chicaça-Alimamu. As a matter of fact, Swanton makes ingenious use of this very omission, arguing that since this portion of the route obviously wasn't westward, nor the next part from Mabila to Chicaça, the part from Chicaça to the Mississippi must have been in order to make good Elvas' statement. A loyal Memphian might argue that a northwest leg from Chicaça as compensation for the omitted southwest Coça-Mabila leg would make the statement still better. Swanton clinches the argument by stating that "as an authority Elvas outranks Garcilaso incomparably." True, all things being equal, but in this case Garcilaso makes a direct statement, whereas Elvas makes one that is incomparably vague and certainly not intended to be applied to any detailed portion of the route. It would seem fair enough, in this case, to cancel out Elvas' vagueness against Garcilaso's general unreliability and proceed as though nothing whatever had been said about the direction from Limamu to the Mississippi.[42]

From Limamu to Quizqui, the reader will recall, the way led through an uninhabited "wilderness" for nine days and that is about all that can be said about it, since practically no topographical details are given. Nevertheless, a great deal of ink has been spilled about this march. As previously noted, a mistranslation of the word *monte* as referring to mountains rather than forests gave the Memphians an opportunity to discount the possibility that the Spaniards crossed the Yazoo Basin, in which there are certainly no mountains to be found. On the other hand, Elvas' reference to "lakes and pondy places" has been used to prove that the army must have crossed the Yazoo Basin. Swanton rightly points out that a great deal depends on what sort of season they were having at the time. There were, no doubt, fewer swamps and "pondy places" on the route along the bluffs to Memphis, particularly if the season was a dry one. Swanton follows up ingeniously by recalling that later in the Casqui country the ceremony of the cross was for the purpose of bringing rain, from which "severe drought" he argues that it must have been a dry spring. One may properly question to what extent a dry spell in Arkansas in late June precludes its having been wet in the Mississippi hills in early May. However, with all due allowances for somewhat closer reasoning than the facts will bear — on both sides — it does appear that Elvas' description better fits the normal conditions in the Yazoo Basin than those of the hills.[43] The other meager descriptions of this wilderness journey fit one theory about as well as the other.

The objection frequently urged against the Sunflower and Commerce Landing theories, that the Yazoo Basin bottoms and backswamps

[41] Elvas, in Bourne, 1904, vol. I, p. 221.

[42] The only other evidence on this point is the De Soto map which places Quizqui northwest of Limamu, but as Swanton points out, this map is frequently misleading.

[43] A great deal depends on the translation of such passages. For example, compare Robertson's rendering: "He marched seven days through an unpopulated region of many swamps and thick woods, but all passable on horseback except several marshes or swamps which were crossed by swimming" (Robertson, 1933, vol. 2, p. 156). If we hailed from Memphis, we would prefer this version.

were impenetrable before the days of modern levee-building, is dealt with at length by Swanton, successfully in our opinion, by showing that a number of trails across the basin actually existed in the seventeenth and early eighteenth centuries. While none of them, of course, can be identified as the trail followed by De Soto, their mere existence is a sufficient proof that such a trail was a possibility in 1541. Again, it is a question of season. Any trail across the bottoms would have been extremely difficult, if not impassible, for several months after the annual "rise" which normally occurred in June. The time in question was early May, presumably well ahead of the rising waters.

An entirely different objection might be urged to this wilderness march across the Yazoo Basin. A glance at the site map (fig. 2) shows this entire region to be a rich archaeological area, with sites distributed pretty evenly over its entire extent wherever natural levees have afforded habitable locations. At first blush, this does not square with the uninhabited wilderness described with singular unanimity by all accounts. However, careful checking of sites along Swanton's proposed route failed to show any that satisfy the hypothetical requirements laid down at the beginning of this section, until the Sunflower River is reached. Here we come upon a number of sites lying directly athwart the supposed route to Sunflower bend, that will have to be explained. But this properly belongs in the following section.

The Location of Quizqui

There are a considerable number of sites in the general vicinity of Sunflower Landing that qualify archaeologically, in terms of our working hypothesis, as Quizqui villages. Before examining them it may be well to review the documentary conditions. It is clear that we have to look for a group of closely related villages; Ranjel mentions three and a possible fourth; Elvas, two; Biedma and Garcilaso, one. All accounts seem to agree that the first village encountered was the "capital." It was apparently fairly large, and, if we may trust the memory of Garcilaso's informants, had at least one large platform mound.

As to the geographical relationships of these villages to each other, and to the Mississippi, there is considerable lack of agreement. Biedma says the "capital" was "near the banks of the River Espiritu Santo." Likewise, Garcilaso. From Ranjel, on the other hand, one infers that it was some distance inland. "A league beyond this village they came upon another . . . and soon again, after another league, another. . . . There they saw the great river." It was Elvas' second town that was near (half a league) the river. A composite account, making due allowance for these discrepancies, would run somewhat as follows: several villages strung along at intervals of 2 or 3 miles, one from the other, none of them far from the Mississippi, at least one of them in fact very near it.

The changes in channel position in the neighborhood of Sunflower Bend, from the mid-sixteenth century [44] to the present, have not been great. The Bend was about the same shape as at present but situated about 3 miles farther upstream, a change hardly sufficient to be taken into account in an inquiry of this kind.

The sites we shall have to consider may be discussed for greater convenience in four groups, see map, figure 70. The first group, situated on or near the Sunflower River, has already been mentioned. Of these, Mattson (16-N-9), Myer (16-N-10), and Spendthrift (16-O-2) are dated by seriation (see fig. 19) very close to point B, our hypothetical 1541 date line. Crawford Lake (16-N-19) is dated somewhat earlier, middle of period C-B, and the pottery differs in some important respects, such as lack of Bell Plain, but not sufficiently to preclude relationship with the first-mentioned sites. Dating of the Oliver Site (16-N-6) is somewhat uncertain inasmuch as the results of seriation and stratigraphy do not agree. Without getting involved again in the argument as to whether or not this was a stratified, i.e., reoccupied, site, we can simply

[44] Fisk, 1944, pl. 22, sheet 7. For purposes of this discussion, we are assuming that Fisk's Stage 15 approximately represents channel conditions in 1541, notwithstanding the fact that our tentative correlation (p. 297) indicates that this date may actually have fallen within an earlier stage.

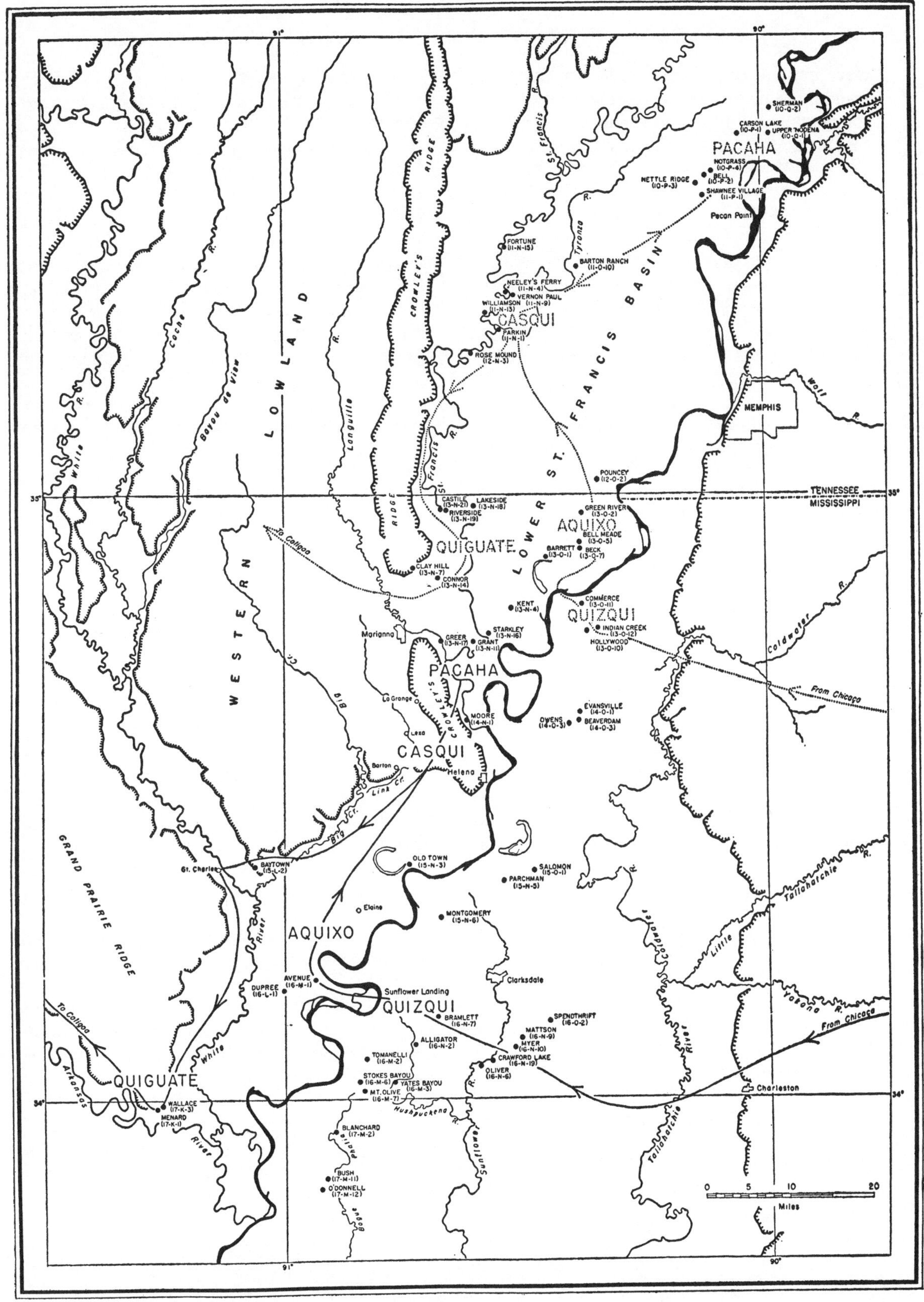

FIG. 70. Map showing hypothetical routes of De Soto's line of march through the Survey Area. (Sunflower Landing theory shown in solid line, Commerce Landing theory, dotted.)

state that the main occupation was probably too early for 1541, but the site may have been still occupied at that date and even later.[45]

Four of these sites, Oliver, Mattson, Myer, and Spendthrift have single large platform mounds, the fifth, Crawford Lake, has vestiges of what may have been the same. In short, here is a group of apparently related sites that fit the description of the Quizqui villages except that they are definitely too far from the Mississippi. Their importance to the present discussion is that they lie directly athwart the approaches to Sunflower Bend from the east. Yet all narratives of the expedition agree that no settlements were met with between Limamu and Quizqui itself, and it seems reasonable to suppose that if the Quizqui had possessed inland settlements in this area the "capital" would have been forewarned of the Spaniards' approach. This is the first indication that something is wrong, either with our dating criteria or with the Sunflower Landing theory.

The second group of sites on the Hushpuckena River or affluents thereof is better situated with respect to Sunflower Bend. These are Alligator (16-N-2), Bramlett (16-N-7), Tomanelli (16-M-2), Yates Site (16-M-3), Stokes Bayou (16-M-6), and Mount Olive (16-M-5). If the crossing was made somewhere near Sunflower Landing, or its earlier counterpart a few miles upstream, one or more of these sites would almost certainly have to be identified with the Indians of Quizqui. One of them was in fact suggested by Swanton as a possible location of the Quizqui capital.

> Garcilaso states that the chief of this tribe . . . had his house on an artificial mound, represented as a high one, and it seems to have been in the village they first entered. . . . There is a group known as the Alligator mounds near the station of that name which are not far from Sunflower landing, but residents of the section remember that as late as 1889 there were three mounds near the landing itself, one of them of considerable height.[46]

No information was obtained by the Survey respecting Swanton's three mounds near the landing, but the Alligator Site was visited and carefully investigated with the De Soto question in mind. Unfortunately, this is another site like Oliver whose dating is open to more than one interpretation. Seriation of the very large surface and stratigraphic collections (fig. 19) indicated a long-continued occupation from E to B on the time scale. Stratigraphic analysis, on the other hand, seemed to indicate a reoccupation of the site with the date of the upper component somewhat uncertain (p. 264). According to the first interpretation, the site was almost certainly occupied in 1541; according to the second, that date might have fallen within the uncertain interval between the two occupations.

The general character of the site accords very well with what the meager descriptions of the Quizqui "capital" might lead us to expect (see fig. 33). There are two large rectangular platform mounds, 3.6 and 4.5 meters high, and a number of smaller mounds of uncertain character completing a well-defined plaza arrangement.

The Alligator Site is situated on the south bank or natural levee of an old meander now occupied in part by Alligator Bayou about a mile above the confluence of that stream and Hushpuckena River. Four miles to the northeast on the same meander is the Bramlett Site (16-N-7). This appears to be the site described by Brown as "three small mounds west of Bobo"[47] and may be the same as the three mounds near Sunflower Landing cited by Swanton. Today it is little more than the ruin of a site. There is no way to tell what the mounds originally looked like, though one of them seems to have been fairly large. The pottery agrees very closely with that of the Alligator Site, and the seriation date falls in period C-B not too far from our hypothetical 1541 date line. The two sites would make an ideal setup if they were a little later, a little nearer the Mississippi, and if the meander they are situated upon, now called Annis Brake and occupied in part by Alligator Bayou, were of the right age. Unfortunately, it belongs to Stage 5 in Fisk's reconstruction, a thousand years earlier than De Soto's visit. These sites,

[45] Griffin would like to be placed on record at this point as believing that the Mississippi Period occupation represented by the upper levels at the Oliver Site was definitely post-1541. See p. 256.

[46] Swanton, 1939, p. 248.

[47] Brown, 1926, p. 106.

if they existed in 1541, were no nearer the Mississippi than they are today, a distance of about 6 or 8 miles. To be sure the first Quizqui village entered by the Spaniards may have been that far from the river, but the others were quite certainly nearer.

Farther to the south and southwest are a number of sites which, though farther away from Sunflower Bend, are as close or closer to the Mississippi than the Alligator and Bramlett sites just considered. About 6 miles east and a little south of Alligator is the Tomanelli Site (16–M–2). This site has three moderately large mounds, the largest being about 30 meters in diameter and 3.3 meters high, and a number of low house mounds. The large mounds are described on the field card as conical, but the late pottery complex suggests the possibility of an original rectangular form for some of them. It is dated by seriation in the middle of period C–B but, with only 2 per cent of clay-tempered showing, may very well have been later.

The Yates Site (16–M–3), about 5 miles down the Hushpuckena River from Alligator, may have been occupied in 1541. A large site with several sizable mounds one or two of which were almost certainly rectangular at one time, it exhibited a pottery situation difficult to interpret. The collection as a whole is dated in the middle of period D–C, too early for consideration here, but according to the field notes there were areas that yielded later material. Like the Tomanelli Site, it would repay further investigation. Three miles south of Tomanelli and about a mile east of the present artificial levee is the Stokes Bayou Site (16–M–6), named after a small stream which occupies an abandoned Mississippi meander of earlier date (Stage 4). It is an excellent example of the type of site we are looking for, with one dominant rectangular mound and a number of smaller mounds of uncertain form in a plaza arrangement, and the seriation date is just about right. The near-by small site of Mount Olive (16–M–5) is dated slightly earlier but not too early for consideration here.

This completes what we have called the Hushpuckena group of sites. In summary, it can be said that here is ample material for identification with the Quizqui villages. To attempt to indicate the order of eligibility would imply a closer control of pottery-dating than we actually possess. As far as we can tell, any or all of these sites could have been occupied in 1541. They lend a certain amount of credibility to the Sunflower Landing theory, but actually prove nothing. All one can say is that, if the Sunflower Landing hypothesis is ever established, these sites and others in the vicinity that we may have missed would require close investigation.

Up to this point we have been examining sites in the immediate vicinity of the proposed route to Sunflower Landing which obviously warrant first consideration. However, it is not the Commission's contention that the crossing was made exactly at Sunflower Bend, but rather somewhere near it. Sites within a reasonable distance of the bend, say 20 miles either way, should not be overlooked. Two groups, one to the south and one to the north, are shown on our map. The southern group, located on the headwaters of Bogue Phalia, is perhaps the better possibility, since it is evident that the Quizqui villages lay below the crossing place. Garcilaso, the only one to give the distance, says 13 leagues below, but this is plainly an exaggeration. These sites are Blanchard (17–M–2), Bush (17–M–11), and O'Donnell (17–M–12). All three are typical Temple-mound sites with smaller house mounds and plaza arrangement. Pottery complexes of the first two have been dated by seriation in period B–A, theoretically a little too late for 1541; that of the third, well down in period C–B may be a little too early. Until the matter of De Soto's route is finally settled, however, these sites should remain on the list of possibilities.

The group north of Sunflower Bend, occupying the general area of the headwaters of the Sunflower and Little Sunflower rivers, consists of Montgomery (15–N–6), Parchman Place (15–N–5), and Salomon (15–O–1). All three deserve to rank among the major sites of the Yazoo Basin. It is a reasonable probability that at least two of them were in occupation in De Soto's time, so they constitute important evidence in this discussion. If they weren't Quizqui villages, what were they?

The site catalogued by the Survey as Montgomery (15–N–6) is part of a vast congeries of mounds and village-site remains long known in archaeological literature as the Carson Group. A plan of this group, made by W. H. Holmes, at a time when the mounds were in far better shape than at present, is to be found in the Bureau of American Ethnology's 12th Annual Report[48] and is reprinted in Brown's "Archaeology of Mississippi." The group extends for over a mile along the south and east banks of Ritchie's Bayou, a small stream occupying successively two abandoned Mississippi meander channels of Stages 5 and 11, respectively. Horseshoe Lake, about a mile to the north, is a recent Mississippi cut-off, and the sixteenth-century main channel was only about 2 miles to the west. According to Fisk's chronology, no part of the site could have been directly on the river in 1541, but it was close enough to satisfy the documentary requirements for the Quizqui "capital."

With none but the larger mounds now remaining, the group no longer appears as a unit. It was catalogued under the names of Montgomery (15–N–6), Stovall (15–N–7), and Carson (15–N–8), a procedure justified, so we thought, by the fact that the three portions of the group do not appear to date from the same period. The eastern portion, for which we retained the name Carson, originally comprised more than thirty mounds, of which only the three largest are visible today. The largest, a pyramidal mound about 60 meters square and 4 meters high now supports a large dwelling house. A few traces of daub were seen about the mound, but no pottery. A short distance to the west is what remains of a large mound, now reduced to a shapeless mass about 2 meters high. This is apparently Holmes' Mound C, described as oval in shape, 66 by 45 meters by 4.8 meters high — a distressing example of what intense cultivation can do to a mound during the course of half a century. On the other side, to the east of the large pyramidal mound, is a large double conical mound about 4 meters high. Unfortunately, at the time of the Survey's visit, the mounds and surrounding fields were in grass and no collections were obtainable. Judging from the characteristics of the mounds alone, there would appear to be a fair probability that this portion of the Carson Group was in occupation in 1541.

[48] Thomas, 1894, pl. XI.

Of the central portion of the group, catalogued as Stovall (15–N–7), there remains only a very large double conical mound now about 6 meters high, Holmes' Mound B, estimated at 10.2 meters high! Pottery obtained in the vicinity of this mound included a mixture of early and late types, difficult to interpret on account of the small size of the sample.

It is the western portion of the group catalogued as Montgomery (15–N–6) in which we are chiefly interested at the moment. Holmes' map shows a well-developed temple mound-plaza assemblage — the dominant mound of which is now reduced to 3 meters in height — surrounded by a rectangular enclosing wall which is no longer visible. The large pottery collection from this site was not seriated, owing to a suspicion that a significant number of Baytown Plain sherds were lost subsequent to a preliminary field sorting in 1940. However, with or without these missing sherds, the date would fall close to point B on the time scale, so there is an excellent chance that the site was occupied in 1541, and it is quite likely that the near-by Carson Mound, from which we got no collection, dates from the same period.

A great deal more might be said about this site or series of sites. It plainly deserves a more thorough investigation than was made by the Survey. Since it lies only 7 miles above the mid-sixteenth-century location of Sunflower Bend, it also deserves a great deal more consideration as a possible Quizqui site than we have been able to give it.

Closely related ceramically to Montgomery is the Parchman Site (15–N–5) about 8 miles to the northeast on a small bayou called Mill Creek, occupying a Mississippi channel of Stage 10. More imposing than the Montgomery Site, this site also exhibits a well-defined plaza arrangement dominated by a large platform mound of uncertain shape, about 60 meters in diameter at the base and 6 or 7 meters high. There is, however, no trace of a stockade, though the Montgomery Site has taught us that an enclosure well-marked fifty years ago may be invisible today. The pottery complex is dated by seriation as late in period B–A. This is theoretically too late for 1541 but does not exclude the possibility that the site was already occupied at that time.

About 1 mile north of the Parchman Site, Mill Creek turns sharply to the east into Hull Brake of Stage 9. The town of Coahoma is on the south bank of Hull Brake about 2 miles from the Parchman Site. About 2 miles farther east, on the same side of the brake is the imposing Salomon Site (15–O–1), consisting of a very large rectangular mound now about 8 meters high, flanked by lower mounds, and facing, across what was undoubtedly a plaza, another large rectangular mound about 5 meters high. Vestiges of a ramp on the plaza side of the big mound are plainly visible. The site was not enclosed so far as can be seen at the present time. A large pottery sample indicates close relationships with Montgomery and Parchman but a somewhat earlier mean date, in the middle of period C–B. The site shows evidence of long occupation, hence it appears highly probable that 1541 was included in the span.

It certainly looks as though these three important sites Montgomery, Parchman, and Salomon have to be reckoned with in any final solution of the De Soto problem in this area. In the meantime, they do more harm than good to the Sunflower Landing theory. Two of them, Parchman and Salomon, are too far above the Landing. A crossing-place this far up the river would not square with the Commission's interpretation of subsequent trans-Mississippi movements. On the other hand, if they were not Quizqui towns, one is entitled to wonder why there is no allusion to them in the documents. The army was held up almost a month preparing for the crossing. It is hardly conceivable that settlements of the importance and magnitude indicated by these remains less than 20 miles away would have gone unvisited and unrecorded.

Conclusions on the Identification of Quizqui

If we seem to have taken the reader through a harrowing amount of detail without commensurate results, it has at least not been done without a purpose. The purpose was simply to show how intricate a problem like this can become, even with the incomplete archaeological data at our disposal. When it is recalled that the aim of the Survey was not a complete listing of all sites in the area, but only a fair sampling thereof, one appreciates how naïve, from the standpoint of archaeology, sometimes has been the treatment of this sort of problem in the past. Our final impression, so far as Quizqui is concerned, is that of an embarrassment of riches. There are too many eligible sites. The general effect is uncomfortable, both for our hypothesis of dating and for the Sunflower Landing theory. On the one hand, it is not quite consistent with what we infer about the density of population in the Mississippi Valley to suppose that all these sites were flourishing at the same time; on the other hand, it suggests a more dense and politically significant occupation of the district than is indicated in the De Soto narratives. From these we get a distinct impression of Quizqui as a relatively weak group, politically subject to more powerful tribes across the river. With these uncertainties in mind, it would be injudicious at this stage to use these findings either for or against the Sunflower Landing theory. That theory will stand or fall, as Swanton was fully aware, on the interpretation of events on the other side of the Mississippi River.

From Quizqui to Aquixo: The Mississippi Crossing and the Sunflower Landing Theory

Having brought De Soto and his tatterdemalions to the banks of the Mississippi, it may be well to pause for a moment for a restatement of the problem that lies behind this complicated discussion. We are trying to check what may be called the official version of the De Soto line of march through the Survey Area against the available site information in terms of a hypothetical pottery date line for the period involved. The results so far have not been particularly encouraging either to the official theory or to our hypothetical dating criteria. We seem to be no nearer making contact between archaeology and history in 1541, but can take comfort in the belief that we have narrowed the problem somewhat and indicated some points at which further research should be directed.

It may also be well, during this pause while De Soto's shipwrights are putting together their clumsy barges, to say something about the Sunflower Landing theory. Why Sunflower Landing? Why just here? The discussion thus far has brought out only what may be called permissive factors. Assuming that De Soto set out in the right direction from the Chickasaw country, and it wasn't too wet, he could have crossed the Yazoo Basin and reached the Mississippi at or near Sunflower Landing, where there are a sufficient number of sites that could have been the Quizqui villages. He could have, but did he? What are the positive arguments, those that point to Sunflower Landing and to no other place of crossing?

Fortunately, there are only three. Swanton's most closely reasoned argument in the whole discussion, which may for convenience be called the three-rivers argument,[49] we need not go into here, for its only purpose is to demonstrate that the crossing must have been made somewhere between the mouths of the Arkansas and St. Francis rivers. The three arguments that bear directly upon Sunflower Landing are: (1) the de l'Isle map, (2) the topography at Sunflower Bend, and (3) the sequence and location of events on the other side of the river.

From the de l'Isle map of 1718 on, a number of cartographers give "Point d'Oziers" (Willow Point) as the place of De Soto's discovery of the Mississippi River, which place Swanton identifies with Sunflower Landing without saying exactly why. Assuming this identification to be correct, there is still no evidence, or at least Swanton has not been able to produce any, that de l'Isle was in possession of any information unknown to us. It appears, from Swanton's own discussion of this map, and a possible work sheet used in its preparation, that de l'Isle's depiction of the De Soto route is no more than an interpretation of the Elvas narrative in the light of the imperfect geographical knowledge of the time.[50] So this can hardly be regarded as an argument for a Sunflower Landing crossing-place, but rather as an interesting anticipation of the Commission's final opinion on the subject. As an aside, we might add that Lewis and Rowland use the self-same map to prove that the crossing was made at or near Commerce Landing some 60 miles (airline) above Sunflower Landing.

The second line of argument has to do with the topography at Sunflower Bend. Elsewhere, Swanton is inclined to stress the changes in local topography incident to the instability of the Mississippi and its flood-plain tributaries. Here he is inclined to minimize such changes.

> The exact place where all this happened [the crossing of the river] we shall probably never know owing to the constant changes in the river [good, so far], although the banks at Sunflower Landing are made up largely of stiff bluish mud which is very tenacious and not easily eroded. At least this bend is recognizable as far back as the Ross map compiled from data collected in 1765, and we have more assurance of permanency than in most places along the Father of Waters.[51]

We have examined the "stiff bluish mud" at Sunflower Bend and it seems to be a superficial deposit perhaps related to the similar phenomena described by Russell in Louisiana.[52] Whatever its origin, it cannot be said to have had any local stabilizing effect on the Mississippi. Fisk's great map of the former courses of the present meander belt shows about the same degree of change for all stages in the immediate vicinity of Sunflower Bend as in other portions of the flood plain. This fact reduces the value of the local topographical argument to a point where it becomes unnecessary to discuss it.

The third argument, however, having to do with the movements of the Spaniards immediately after crossing the river, is the really important one. Reduced to the simplest terms, it amounts to this: After leaving the Aquixo villages, across the river from Quizqui, the army crossed the "worst" swamp in all Florida and came upon higher ground upon which were located the villages of Casqui. According to Swanton, this high ground could only have been at the southern end of Crowley's Ridge. Working back from there by dead reckoning — the itinerary is well documented for this portion of the route — the crossing-place can only have been at or near Sunflower

[49] Swanton, 1939.
[50] Swanton, 1939, pp. 12–14.
[51] Swanton, 1939, p. 248.
[52] Russell, 1936, pp. 78 et seq.

Landing. Thus, the ensuing movements from Aquixo to Casqui are crucial to the whole question. To anticipate even further, it appears that the assumed location of Casqui at the southern end of Crowley's Ridge is the sole anchor for the entire line of march so far as it involves the Survey Area. We shall be obliged, therefore, to examine the evidence from here on with some care.

The Location of Aquixo

It will be recalled that the Aquixo villages were located presumably on or very near the Mississippi not very far above the crossing-place. Elvas brings the army — barges included — to the first Aquixo village the same day, giving the distance as 1½ leagues. Ranjel, usually more reliable in matters of time and distance, makes it early the following day. The other Aquixo villages lay farther upstream. These are variously referred to as "good towns," "large towns," etc., but their number is nowhere given. Some, if not all of them, seem to have been palisaded, for on a later occasion Ranjel comments: "In Aquixo and Casqui, and Pacaha, they saw the best villages seen up to that time, better stockaded and fortified and the people were of finer quality excepting those of Cofitachequi."

We have to look, therefore, for a group of related sites of fairly large size, some of which should show traces of former palisades, near the Stage 15 channel of the river and within 10 or 15 miles above the contemporary location of Sunflower Bend. The choice is not very wide, as may be seen by reference to figure 70. This is not due to lack of searching by the Survey. The eligible sites among the few that we were able to find in this district may be discussed very briefly. These are: Avenue (16–M–1), Dupree (16–L–6), and Old Town (15–N–3). None of them answer to the requirements outlined above in very satisfactory fashion.

Swanton mentions only one site specifically as a possible Aquixo village: "On the west side [of the Mississippi River] are indications of considerable towns and here at the Avenue site the archeologist Clarence B. Moore recovered some very beautiful specimens of pottery." [53] This site was visited by the writers in the spring of 1940 and catalogued as 16–M–1. Identification in this instance was pretty certain, as we were lucky enough to find a negro who was present at Moore's excavations. Neither Moore's description nor our findings indicate an important site, but the main circumstance that adversely affects its eligibility from the standpoint of the Sunflower Landing theory is that it is below rather than above the contemporary location of Sunflower Bend. The pottery illustrated by Moore, which included examples of the late "teapot" shape (see p. 196) and our own seriation date, late in period B–A, indicate a post-1541 date for the site.

The Dupree Site (16–L–6) has more of the character of the kind of site we are looking for, but is not only located below the mid-sixteenth-century counterpart of Sunflower Bend, but is also too far from the active channel of that period. It may conceivably have been an inland village of the Aquixo *not* visited by De Soto, but, as on the Avenue Site, the pottery complex indicates a post-1541 date.

Several sites, or vestiges of sites, were found in the vicinity of Elaine, Arkansas, apparently battered remains of small conical mounds, which afforded pitiful pottery collections insufficient for dating purposes. Their location is not altogether satisfactory either, though it might appear so on the map. Actually, they are strung out along the bank of the old channel now occupied by Swan Lake, assigned by Fisk to Stage 12, so the chances are they were not on the Mississippi in 1541.

This leaves only the Old Town-Buie sites, catalogued as 15–N–3 and 15–N–4, respectively, as a possible location of one of the Aquixo towns. These sites probably represent discontinuous portions of the same site. The "Old Town Works," a famous landmark and resort of pot-hunters, was briefly described in the Bureau report and illustrated by a map.[54] The topography of the region has been so altered by levee-building operations that it is impossible to reconcile our Survey sketches

[53] Swanton, 1939, p. 237. The pottery is described and figured in Moore, 1911, pp. 401–05.

[54] Thomas, 1894, pp. 234–35.

with Thomas' map. About all that can be said is that it seems to be the same site. Being outside the present levee, the sites have been covered by several feet of recent alluvium, and as a result we were only able to make collections along exposed profiles of the levee borrow-pits. These collections, hardly adequate for dating so large a site, gave a seriation date late in period B–A, which indicates that the portion of the site catalogued as "Old Town" may have been too late for the De Soto period; the Buie portion, however, showed some earlier material and was dated in period C–B. Unfortunately, we cannot tie either of these locations into the Thomas map. The latter shows two earthwork enclosures, the only evidence we have of palisaded villages in the area concerned with the present discussion. The location of Old Town, about 12 miles airline north of the older counterpart of Sunflower Bend, does not place the site out of question. The obvious thing to say is that it would repay further investigation, but its present mutilated condition does not offer much hope of a final determination.

This exhausts the rather unsatisfactory archaeological information that we are able to bring to bear on the location of Aquixo in terms of the Sunflower Landing hypothesis. With all due regard to the possibility that the old Aquixo sites, being near the river, have been destroyed by its uneasy shifting, it still remains a matter for surprise that the archaeological remains in this district are so slight. By all accounts, this was a populous and important tribe whose "towns" favorably impressed even the most conservative of the Spanish chroniclers. If Elvas was correct in attributing the "famous armada of galleys" to the Aquixo, an exceptionally large population is indicated. In conclusion, it must be conceded that the essentially negative evidence is damaging to the Sunflower Landing hypothesis.

The Route from Aquixo to Casqui: The Great Swamp

According to Ranjel, it was Tuesday, June 21st, when the Spaniards left the first town and passed through others comprising "the settlement of Aquixo, which is very beautiful, or beautifully situated." We may infer from this comment alone that the way ran along the natural levee through cultivated fields no doubt. The next day, Wednesday,

> . . . they passed through the worst tract for swamps and water that they had found in all Florida, and on that day the toil of the soldiers was very heavy.
>
> The next day following, Thursday, they entered the land of Quarqui, [sic!] and passed through small villages; and the next day, Friday, St. John's day, they came to the village of the Lord of Casqui, . . .[55]

Elvas' account is closely parallel but furnishes a few additional details:

> . . . the day following he went in quest of a province called Pacaha, . . . He passed through large towns in Aquixo, which the people had left for fear of the Christians. From some Indians that were taken, he heard that three days' journey thence resided a great Cacique, called Casqui. He came to a small river, over which a bridge was made, whereby he crossed. All that day, until sunset, he marched through water, in places coming to the knees; in others, as high as the waist. They were greatly rejoiced on reaching the dry land; because it had appeared to them that they should travel about, lost, all night in the water. At mid-day [next day, presumably] they came to the first town of Casqui, where they found the Indians off their guard, never having heard of them. Many men and women were taken, much clothing, blankets, and skins; such they likewise took in another town in sight of the first, half a league off in the field, whither the horsemen had run.
>
> This land is higher, drier, and more level than any other along the river that had been seen until then.[56]

Biedma is terse as usual:

> We found some good towns on the other side [Aquixo]; and once more following up the stream, on the way to that Province of Pacaha, we came first to the province of another lord, called Icasqui, against whom he [Pacaha] waged severe war.[57]

Garcilaso is somewhat hazy on this portion of the route, stating simply that after crossing the Mississippi, the army marched four days through an unpopulated country and on the fifth:

[55] Ranjel, in Bourne, 1904, vol. II, p. 138.

[56] Elvas, in Bourne, 1904, vol. I, p. 117.

[57] Biedma, in Bourne, 1904, vol. II, p. 26.

. . . asomaron por unos cerros altos, y descubrieron un Pueblo de quatrocientas casas, asentado à la ribera de un Rio, mayor que Guadalquivir por Cordova.[58]

Let us see what Swanton makes of this. A good deal, it appears, since it is upon the interpretation of these passages, particularly Elvas, that the entire Sunflower Landing theory really depends.

We are to look for a well-populated district [Aquixo], evidently along the natural levee close to the Mississippi, a bad swamp, and a distinctly higher yet level stretch beyond [Casqui], followed again by a low, swampy province (Pacaha) close to the river. These succeeded one another from south to north along the river for Aquixo and Pacaha were directly upon it, while Casqui must have bordered it because it dispatched canoes to De Soto's aid when he wished to attack the Pacaha Indians in a town where they had taken refuge. . . . South of Crowley's Ridge . . . we have the exact succession of terrain called for if we suppose they crossed the river near Sunflower Landing. On the west side are indications of considerable towns [we found very few of them it seems] and here at the Avenue site the archeologist Clarence B. Moore recovered some very beautiful specimens of pottery. Just beyond this, to the north and west of Oldtown Lake is a swamp which, before the days of the levees, must have been sufficiently bad to elicit the chroniclers' criticisms, and north of this one begins to rise into the higher ground about Crowley's Ridge. The Ridge itself, it should be noted, while "high and dry," is irregular and in no respect "level," but the land upon its southern flank is of just that description, and this feature strikes the traveler at once when coming from the swamps or from the ridge.

The character of the country falls so markedly in line with what we would expect if the Sunflower Landing hypothesis were correct, that we consider it conclusive.[59]

There is one point here which cannot be passed over without comment. The actual location of Casqui, which in turn is tied up with the location of Pacaha will be discussed later. Here we are primarily concerned with the route from the first Aquixo village to Casqui, and in particular the location of that dreadful swamp. The reasoning, here, is faultless, so far as we can see, provided that Casqui is located as on Swanton's map. This is not so much the "southern flank" of Crowley's Ridge, but more to the west of the southern end of the Ridge, on the older alluvial plain north of the Big Creek-Lick Creek escarpment (see fig. 1). This more westerly location is necessary to take the Spaniards across the backswamp "north and west of Old Town Lake." If Casqui were located on the southern flank of Crowley's Ridge, as suggested in Swanton's text, the best route from the landing-place opposite Sunflower Bend would have followed then, as it does now, the higher natural levees along the river. It appears, therefore, that the afore-said swamp has had not a little to do with Swanton's location of Casqui; though there are, unfortunately, a number of other troublesome considerations that must be examined in connection with that question.

The Location of Casqui

We have examined the evidence that would bring De Soto from Sunflower Bend to the southern and western flanks of Crowley's Ridge and found it somewhat unsatisfactory; first, on account of the lack of archaeological confirmation for the location of the Aquixo villages; second, because it seemed to involve the Spaniards in a formidable swamp they might better have avoided. We now come to the location of Casqui itself.

Swanton's discussion of this problem, so vital to the whole theory, is too long to be quoted in full, and too complex to be abstracted without danger of injustice to the argument. It is a magnificent attempt to rationalize the confused and conflicting accounts into a theory consistent with present and past geographical conditions of the region. It is not, in our opinion, entirely successful. A certain number of important elements in the reasoning refuse to be harmonized. A sample of these will suffice.

To begin with, Swanton lays great stress on Elvas' characterization of the Casqui country as "higher, drier and more level than any other along the river they had seen until then." To him, it can indicate only the higher land about Crowley's Ridge. We have already quoted the passage in which he points out that

[58] Garcilaso, 1722, p. 179. Translation: "They saw from some high hills a town of 400 houses located on the bank of a river larger than the Guadalquiver at Cordova."

[59] Swanton, 1939, pp. 237–38.

it cannot be the Ridge itself that is described, it being "in no respect 'level,'" but the older alluvial land at its base. In our opinion Elvas' words could apply as well to any well-developed Mississippi meander-belt ridge, particularly if it had been cleared and cultivated as appears to have been the case in this instance. This interpretation is confirmed by a later statement of Elvas made in connection with his account of Quiguate. "The country of Aquiguate, *like that of Casqui and Pacaha* [italics are ours], was level and fertile, having rich river margins, on which the Indians made extensive fields." The association of Casqui and Pacaha in the Fidalgo's mind is interesting in view of the contrast between the two places envisaged by Swanton — "a distinctly higher, yet level stretch (Casqui), followed again by a low swampy province (Pacaha)" — in the passage already cited.

Greater difficulties, perhaps, are posed by the rivers in this portion of the narratives. The "River of Casqui," for example, presents insuperable difficulties against which Swanton battles valiantly, but in our opinion unsuccessfully. One should say the "Rivers of Casqui," for Swanton holds that the rivers so designated by Garcilaso and Ranjel were not the same, notwithstanding the fact that both writers liken their rivers to the Guadalquivir back home in Spain. The first "River of Casqui" upon which the Inca places the two principal Casqui villages, Swanton suggests, was the l'Anguille, "for evidences of old channels and lakes show that it once flowed down close to Crowley's Ridge" thus rendering any such position of the l'Anguille entirely out of the question. Ranjel's "River of Casqui," Swanton thinks, was the White. We shall have occasion to return to this question later. The point here is simply that the impossibility of harmonizing two references to what would seem on *a priori* grounds to have been the same river considerably weakens the official theory.

A further difficulty lies in the fact that, in Swanton's view, the Casqui must have been a Mississippi River tribe as well, because the Casqui chief was able to bring reinforcements by canoe up to Pacaha, which was unquestionably on or near the river. This obliges him to extend the territory of the Casqui from White River to the Mississippi, which is by no means impossible, of course, but is not consistent with what we know about tribal distributions in this area.

Finally, there is the question of the problematical body of water that marked the boundary between Casqui and Pacaha. This bothered Swanton as much as it does ourselves.

> Remembering the direction in which the Spaniards were moving and the topography of the country as a whole, there would seem to be every reason to suppose that the stream or swamp between the provinces was the St. Francis or rather one of its branches, *probably the l'Anguille* [italics are ours], for when we try to square the descriptions of this body of water with the St. Francis itself we are met with difficulties.[60]

The difficulties lie in the fact that the descriptions do not seem to refer to a stream of the magnitude of the present St. Francis. Swanton gets around the difficulty by means of evidence drawn mainly from Fuller[61] that prior to the New Madrid earthquakes of 1811–12 the mouth of the St. Francis was considerably higher up the Mississippi, in the vicinity of Memphis. This argument finds some support in Fisk's reconstruction, though according to this authority, the old mouth of the St. Francis was not so far up-river as Swanton would have it, and the change to the present course occurred sometime between Stages 12 and 15. Whether removal of the St. Francis, if it can be demonstrated, would leave the l'Anguille tranquilly flowing in its place to be bridged by the Casqui and crossed by the Spaniards is another matter, but it seems very likely. If, on the other hand, removal of the St. Francis before 1541 cannot be demonstrated, the damage to Swanton's reasoning would be considerable.

The above is a very inadequate — perhaps unfair — *precis* of Swanton's argument in respect to the location of Casqui. It holds that the territory claimed by this tribe extended from the Mississippi River, about the present mouth of the St. Francis, across and around the southern end of Crowley's Ridge, thence southwestward across the older alluvial plain north of the Big Creek escarpment to White River. This wide area they claimed, but their

[60] Swanton, 1939, pp. 250–51.

[61] Fuller, 1912.

settlements — in order to fit Elvas' reference to "high, level ground" and Garcilaso's river "larger than the Guadalquivir," are to be looked for on the lower southwestern slopes of the Ridge along the banks of Lick and Big creeks. The search, therefore, is fairly narrow.

> The second town of Garcilaso, the "capital" of Casqui, might be identified by means of the artificial mound mentioned by Ranjel and Biedma as well as Garcilaso. There are, or were, such mounds southwest of Barton, and between Lexa and La Grange.[62]

At this point, archaeology comes into play — or should. Unfortunately for Swanton's hypothesis, it was precisely in this area that the Survey was unable to locate any sites whatever, despite the fact that, on Swanton's own request, a diligent search was made. Whatever reservations we have been compelled to make in the foregoing pages, because of the negative character of the evidence, do not apply here. This is part of the older alluvial plain called the Western Lowland, out of reach of the Mississippi and its depradations. If there were sizable village sites with mounds here in 1541, it is inconceivable that some remains of them would not have been found here by the Survey.

At the extreme southern tip of Crowley's Ridge, in a situation that would not suit Swanton's reasoning at all, we found some sites, but there were no evidences of rectangular mounds and the pottery was, according to our hypothesis, altogether too early. To be sure, a handful of later sherds was picked up on one of these, the Helena Site (14–N–6), but the bulk of the material was early and the mounds, so far as we could tell, were originally conical in form. Twelve miles west of Barton is the Broom Site (14–M–3), with a 99-per cent clay-tempered complex dated in period E–D, certainly too early for 1541. This exhausts the archaeological data we are able to bring to bear on the assumed location of Casqui.

It is impossible to escape the conclusion that neither documentary nor archaeological evidence supports Swanton's hypothetical location of Casqui. We have already pointed out the importance of this location to the Sunflower Landing theory, and we are going to see how crucial it is to further interpretation of the route. It is not too much to say that failure at this point makes an open question of every determination between Chicaça and Quiguate and beyond.

Pacaha

For us, as well as De Soto, Pacaha the golden is a land of disenchantment. It was the seat of the dominant political power on this portion of the Mississippi in 1541, and from all indications, of the highest culture as well. Here it was, we fondly hoped to make contact with archaeology. So far as the official theory is concerned, any such hope has gone glimmering. Since we have arrived at the point of complete uncertainty in respect to the location of Casqui, it has become superfluous to discuss in detail the route from thence to Pacaha or the location of the latter place. Swanton's brief concluding statement is sufficient.

> At any rate it is safe to assert that the so-called Province of Pacaha was in the lowlands near the present mouth of the St. Francis River [the same being safely out of the way — cf. p. 378]. . . . There are now several small connecting channels between the Mississippi and the St. Francis which look like canals and it is probably on one of these that Pacaha was located. The region is full of mounds of considerable magnitude.[63]

Considering the normal changes that have taken place in the local drainage since 1541, not to mention the more sweeping changes invoked by Swanton himself, owing to the necessity of getting rid of the St. Francis, it seems useless to look for channels that may have been the "canal" of Pacaha. As to the statement that the region is full of mounds of considerable magnitude, it depends on what is meant by region. With the exception of the Moore Site (14–N–1) with one small mound and a pottery complex that might not be too late for 1541, we were unable to locate any sites in the immediate vicinity of the present mouth of the St. Francis (see fig. 70). About 10 miles to the north are two sites, each with

[62] Swanton, 1939, p. 249.

[63] Swanton, 1939, pp. 251–52.

remains of a single large mound, that might qualify as to date, and are near enough to the Mississippi, but lack the size and importance we would expect to find in Pacaha sites. These are Grant (13-N-11) and Starkley (13-N-16). West of these, near the junction of the l'Anguille with the St. Francis, is the Greer Site (13-N-17) with a large rectangular mound, tentatively dated by our insufficient pottery sample in period D-C. This may have been a major site but its location is too far from the Mississippi to meet the requirements for Pacaha. About 5 miles north of the Starkley Site are two sites, Kent (13-N-4) and Murdock (13-N-12), that might be worth considering, if we still had any enthusiasm left for the official theory. These two sites, catalogued separately, are practically contiguous. One or both of them was the Kent Site excavated by C. B. Moore.[64] Moore found a very small amount of trade material with a few of the burials in this place, and our collections indicate a date extending from D to A on the time scale which almost certainly includes the year 1541. There were large platform mounds and some evidence of a former palisade on the site. These sites are not too far from the contemporary channel of the Mississippi nor too far north of the supposed location of Casqui — assuming that the St. Francis can be got rid of — to qualify as a possible location of one of the Pacaha villages. North of Kent and Murdock, the archaeological picture improves markedly. There are a great many sites that fit our hypothetical conditions, but it is useless to consider them further since they lie too far from the theoretical site of Casqui.

An important angle in the problem of Pacaha is the location of that strange and fascinating country of Caluça, the land of the nomad hunters. Biedma's brief description of this exploration, quoted on page 359, bears the stamp of authenticity. Certain details could not have been invented by a European of that period. Unfortunately, there is a certain amount of confusion in regard to the name Caluça, which may have been the objective of an earlier exploratory expedition from Chicaça. Thus Ranjel:

On Monday, January 3, 1541, the Chief of Chicaça came proffering peace, and promptly gave the Christians guides and interpreters to go to Caluça, a place of much repute among the Indians. Caluça is a province of more than ninety villages not subject to any one, with a savage population, very warlike and much dreaded, and the soil is fertile in that section.[65]

There is no indication, however, that De Soto took up the Cacique's offer, which was doubtless designed only to get rid of unwelcome visitors anyhow. The most plausible supposition is that these Caluças were two distinct places, that only the names are confused — though it is perfectly possible they were both named Caluça — and that Biedma's party did actually visit the second one. Eight days northwest from any point on the Mississippi from the Arkansas River to New Madrid would have taken them across one or more of the prairies of the Western Lowland, not very large to be sure, but sufficiently impressive perhaps to those who had never seen or heard of tall-grass prairies. It is rather surprising to find the culture so radically different from that of the tribes on the river, and we must admit the possibility that our informant has exaggerated its nomadic aspects. The name Caluça is interesting. "Okalusa" in Muskogean is Black Water, which may have been an earlier name for the Black River. In any case, this would seem to be a strong indication, not that the nomadic people encountered were Muskogean-speakers, but that the Pacaha were.

Swanton treats this and the expedition described by Garcilaso (see p. 359) as the same, which seems to us not to have been the case. The latter was more in the nature of a small trading expedition with salt as the main object perhaps, but with the further purpose of running down certain rumors of gold and pearls. One feels that by this time, the Spaniards were no longer very hopeful in these matters, still it would be foolish not to investigate. . . . The party returned in eleven days with a small cargo of rock salt and copper and nothing good to say about the country traversed. No more than the Biedma exploration, does this help to locate Pacaha, though the Commission Report points out that "There

[64] Moore, 1911, pp. 406-10.

[65] Ranjel, in Bourne, 1904, vol. II, p. 132.

is an old salt mine near Bald Knob and back in the hills there are traces of copper." [66]

One further comment on these explorations and we shall have done with Pacaha, for the present at least. Although one of these expeditions was specifically to the northwest and the other may have been in the same general direction, it can be safely assumed that, in the course of the month's stay at Pacaha, information on the country up the river to the north was likewise sought and obtained. Evidently, all reports agreed in describing a poor and thinly populated country. Now this is very difficult to reconcile with the archaeological situation, since it is precisely to the north of the supposed location of Pacaha — on the St. Francis from Parkin to Marked Tree and on the Mississippi above Memphis — that the greatest number of large sites of the period are to be found.

In sum, while the archaeological evidence is sufficient to indicate a possibility that Pacaha was located in the vicinity or slightly to the north of the present mouth of the St. Francis, it is not such as to lend any great support to the Sunflower Landing theory. Almost any point farther up the Mississippi for a hundred miles or more would offer better evidence. We are obliged to conclude that, like every other De Soto place so far considered, the location of Pacaha depends on the location of Casqui. To the extent that the latter is uncertain, so are all the rest. A very disappointing conclusion. . . .

Return to Casqui: Casqui to Quiguate

With De Soto, we are obliged to turn back empty-handed from Pacaha, to a very doubtfully located Casqui and from there on south to Quiguate, the "largest town in all Florida" and one that we would give a great deal to be able to locate. Unfortunately, like everything else, its location depends on that of Casqui so we start off with three strikes against us. We can therefore examine this portion of the Commission's theory somewhat more briefly, taking care, however, to note any additional evidence bearing on the problem of Casqui.

The return from Pacaha to Casqui was made in two days over the same route used in going up and making use of the same famous bridge — repaired in the meantime — and camp was made near the "capital" as before. No new details can be adduced either for or against the location of Casqui, though some might think it strange that Crowley's Ridge, a remarkably conspicuous feature when seen from the lowlands about the mouth of the St. Francis, was not mentioned by any of the narrators.

Sunday, July 31st, the Army set out for Quiguate. That night was spent at a Casqui village, and the next at another, which was on the "River of Casqui." Next morning, the river was crossed with the aid of canoes furnished by the Casqui chief. It will be recalled that the official theory requires that this "River of Casqui" be White River and the crossing is thought to have been made somewhere in the vicinity of St. Charles. "The numerous remains at Indian Bay would supply the village site mentioned." [67] Unfortunately, this great site catalogued by us as Baytown (15–L–2), which has given its name to one of our principal time divisions, is too early, according to our interpretation, to have been visited by De Soto. No further progress seems to have been made on the day of crossing. The next day, Wednesday, the Army camped at a burned village of unstated affiliation and the next night, Thursday, at a live village well stocked with food. This last was evidently a village of the Quiguate tribe, for on Friday they reached the "capital." The distance from the place of crossing, therefore, was at least two whole days' march and as much of the third as it took them to reach the capital, say about 25 to 35 miles altogether. There can be no question that the direction was downstream, for both Thursday's village and Quiguate were on the River of Casqui. For this Ranjel's statement — puzzling enough in another connection — is sufficient. "It was later known that the banks of this stream were thickly populated *farther down*" (italics are ours).

[66] Swanton, 1939, p. 252.

[67] Swanton, 1939, p. 252.

The Location of Quiguate

Forty miles down White River from the neighborhood of St. Charles would have brought the Spaniards close to its confluence with the Arkansas. The Menard Site (17–K–1), regarded by the Commission as the most likely location of Quiguate, admirably fulfills their requirements of the route. Archaeologically, its position is not too clear, however. It and the adjacent Wallace Site (17–K–3) together might constitute a village that could be described as the "largest town in all Florida," but, if our interpretation is correct, most of the material from these sites, particularly the latter, is of post-De Soto date.[68] There is earlier material present, but not in sufficient quantity to suggest an unusually large village in 1541. Discussion of the location archaeologically, however, becomes academic in view of the more serious geographical difficulties involved.

To begin with, the lower White River flows through a very watery region to its junction with the Arkansas. The only practicable route downstream from St. Charles today — and probably in 1541 also — is to follow the eastern edge of Grand Prairie Ridge, though even this involves the crossing of numerous swamps and bayous fingering up from the White River Lowland. A better route would be still farther west. This makes it difficult to credit Ranjel's statement that the village where the Army camped Thursday night was "near the river." This perhaps is a minor difficulty hardly worth mentioning. More serious is the same writer's statement — already cited in another connection — that the river was thickly populated lower down, "although they did not find it out there, and along it they took the trail of Coligua which was not peopled in the intervening country." It is absolutely hopeless to reconcile this statement by the most reliable of the four authorities with the geography of the lower White River. Ranjel certainly knew that his river of Casqui was a tributary of the Mississippi, a "branch of the great river of Pacaha," to use his own words, so he cannot be supposed to have mistaken settlements down on the Mississippi for White River settlements. As for his completely puzzling statement about the route to Coligua, there is no way to get around it except by some desperate rationalization such as that proposed by the Commission Report:

> Readers of Bourne's translation of the Ranjel narrative have been confused at this point by an earlier sentence in which he is made to say, when speaking of the River of Casqui, "along it they took the trail of Coligua." But this actually refers to something that had just gone before and the whole section properly reads: "And it was learned afterwards that the banks of that river below were very well peopled (although there they did not happen to find it out), and for that reason they took the road to Coligua through an unpopulated country."[69]

Having brought De Soto to a point within the angle formed by the confluence of the White and Arkansas rivers, it is obvious that no further travel down the former is possible, so the only way you can interpret Ranjel's statement is to suppose that he meant something entirely different from what he said. To the reader unhampered by a theory the statement is not so deeply mysterious and may be paraphrased as follows: The River of Casqui below Quiguate was unpopulated for a stretch, but there were settlements lower down, although they didn't find this out until later. Part of the way to Coligua also lay down river through this unpopulated country. The inference seems to be that if they had known about the settlements farther down they would not have turned off toward Coligua. According to Elvas, however, they did know about the down-river settlements and chose Coligua anyway. The Cacique of Quiguate, being asked what part of the neighboring country was most inhabited, replied:

> . . . that to the south, or down the river, there were large towns, and the Caciques governed wide territories, with numerous people; and that to the northwest was a province, near some mountains, called Coligoa. He [De Soto], with the others, deemed it well to go thither first; saying that the mountains, perhaps, would make a difference in the soil, and that silver and gold might afterward follow.[70]

[68] See p. 414, for discussion of Menard and Wallace sites as a possible location of one of the Quapaw settlements in the late seventeenth century.

[69] Swanton, 1939, p. 253.

[70] Elvas, in Bourne, 1904, vol. I, p. 132.

This, of course, is impossible to reconcile with Ranjel's account, particularly in respect to the direction of Coligua. In this case, the Commission naturally prefers the Elvas version without calling attention to the fact that Ranjel is backed up to a certain extent by Garcilaso.

> Seis dias estuvieron los Españoles en el Pueblo, llamado Quiguate, y el seteno salieron de èl, y en cinco jornadas, que caminaron siempre por la ribera del Rio de Casquin abajo, llegaron al Pueblo principal de otra Provincia, llamada Colima, . . .[71]

Biedma is no help at all at this juncture. Even preferring Elvas as to the direction of Coligua, as does the Commission, we still have those troublesome settlements down the river to explain. The only way you can make this fit White River at all is to suppose that Quiguate was much higher up the river, in which case its geographical relations with Casqui and Pacaha — we must cling to the one apparent certainty that Pacaha was on the Mississippi — become utterly impossible.

An even greater difficulty is posed by the failure of all four narratives to mention any river that could have been the Arkansas. We must bear in mind the fact that the army remained at Quiguate for three weeks (according to Ranjel), during which time we may be sure the surrounding country was thoroughly ransacked. Swanton is fully aware of this anomaly and invokes a hydrographic change to account for it.

> It is strange that no mention seems to be made of the Arkansas River which now runs only a few miles to the south [of the Menard Site — the distance is actually about a mile]. . . . It is known that the Arkansas River once flowed into the present Bayou Bartholomew and also into Bayou Boeuf and Bayou Macon, and the deflection of the stream into its present course at Pine Bluff is believed to have been so recent that Mississippi flood-plain experts are sympathetic with the idea that this may have happened since the time of De Soto.[72]

According to Fisk's reconstruction, this change took place between Stages 11 and 12, several centuries too early to help the Commission out of this particular dilemma.

General Conclusions on the De Soto Commission Hypothesis

Soon after leaving Quiguate, we may assume, the Spaniards passed out of the Survey Area where we do not propose to follow them. Their return later on, to the southern portion of our area, forms another chapter that will have to be dealt with when the archaeological materials for that area are in hand. The location of Coligua and subsequent points are not without concern, as they reflect back in a general way on the problems already discussed, but our present object is to check only that portion of the route upon which we can bring some first-hand archaeological knowledge to bear. It is acknowledged that subsequent determinations, such as the location of Coligua at Little Rock and the identification of the River of Coligua as the Arkansas, may be so certain as to reflect back some credit on the Commission's findings in the Survey Area. On the other hand, it is our opinion that, in all attempts to locate the De Soto line of march, too much use of this method of reasoning forward and backward along the route has been made. It is unsafe to regard any point as established unless it can stand on its own merits by close agreement with existing topographical and archaeological conditions. Only such points can be used as anchors for a certain distance forward and backward along the route. Unfortunately, for the portion of the route discussed above, we have not one such anchor. We have shown how crucial for the Commission's reconstruction is the location of Casqui. The crossing of the Mississippi at Sunflower Landing, the location of Pacaha near the mouth of the St. Francis, the identification of the River of Casqui as the White, and the location of Quiguate at the confluence of the White and Arkansas rivers, all depend on reasoning forward and

[71] Garcilaso, 1722, p. 188. Translation: "Six days the Spaniards remained in the town called Quiguate and on the seventh departed. In five days, always following the River of Casqui downstream, they reached the capital of the other province, named Colima."

[72] Swanton, 1939, pp. 252–53.

backward, from an assumed location of Casqui at the southern end of Crowley's Ridge. We have criticized pretty freely the interpretations and reasoning upon which this all-important identification was based. This is anybody's territory and we freely admit that our destructive reasoning may be as wide of the mark as we believe the Commission's theoretical construction to be. Archaeology is another matter. We hold that, given the Commission's location of Casqui in a district entirely secure from the destructive activities of the Mississippi, village remains attributable to the Casqui ought to have been found. The final conclusion, therefore, is that Casqui has not been correctly located and that, in consequence, no other identification proposed by the Commission within this portion of the Survey Area can be safely regarded as established.

Alternative Theories

So much space has been devoted to the foregoing discussion of what we have termed for convenience the official De Soto theory, that we shall have to deal with alternative theories more briefly than they deserve. For a full account of the numerous attempts at reconstruction of the De Soto route in whole or part, the reader is referred to the Commission Report,[73] from which it will be seen that there are almost as many theories regarding the Mississippi crossing-place as commentators. For present purposes, however, it is unnecessary to examine critically those earlier theories whose authors had not seen, or at any rate not recognized the value of, the Ranjel narrative. Since its rediscovery and publication in English in part by Lewis in 1904 and in full by Bourne in the same year, the theories have tended to reduce themselves to three, the Sunflower Landing theory already discussed and the Commerce Landing and Memphis theories, which will now be dealt with as briefly as possible.

The Commerce Landing Theory

This hypothesis, sometimes also designated as the Tunica theory, is principally associated with the name of T. H. Lewis.[74] It has been warmly advocated by Dunbar Rowland, Mississippi State Archivist, who, however, has not to our knowledge added any new evidence or interpretations to those of Lewis.[75] Charles A. Barton has written an excellent study of the crossing-place and location of the various Quizqui villages, which deserves more consideration than we shall have space to give it. In the main, however, Lewis deserves the chief credit, not only as originator, but as the only proponent of the theory who has attempted to work it out in some detail backwards and forwards on *both* sides of the river.

Starting from the fort at Alimamu, which he seems to have been able to locate with remarkable precision, near New Albany, Union County, Mississippi, Lewis brings the Spaniards across the northern part of the Yazoo Basin to the Mississippi, which was crossed "either at Council Bend or Walnut Bend" in the vicinity of Commerce Landing, Tunica County, Mississippi. From Aquixo, which he does not attempt to locate specifically, De Soto headed inland in a generally northwesterly direction, crossing Fifteen-Mile Bayou and a swamp, to Casqui, on the St. Francis River near the mouth of the Tyronza. From Casqui to Pacaha, they were obliged to cross the Tyronza (by means of the famous bridge), the latter "capital" being "probably located in the vicinity of Osceola, in Mississippi county, but not further northward." Returning by way of the principal Casqui village, they proceeded to another Casqui village on the St. Francis which they crossed and followed downstream to Quiguate, on the west side of the river, in the northern part of Lee County or the southern part of St. Francis County. From Quiguate, they marched northwest to the River of Coligua, which Lewis identifies with the White. Subsequent movements on the White River need not detain us here. It is sufficient for our purposes to note

[73] Swanton, 1939, Section II, pp. 12–46.

[74] Lewis, 1902; reprinted in Rowland, 1927.

[75] Rowland, 1927.

that the theory requires that the River of Cayas, Utianque, or Anilco, as it is variously called, be the Arkansas, from whose mouth the remnants of the expedition floated down the Mississippi bound for New Spain.

Lewis was a Mississippi patriot. The Sunflower Landing theory had not yet been invented; Memphis was the serious contender. One must deplore his disingenuous treatment of the evidence in an effort to show that the Spaniards in setting out from Limamu could not possibly have taken the road to Memphis. Aside from this, it must be admitted that his reconstruction makes a good deal of sense both topographically and archaeologically. Lewis does not attempt to furnish archaeological sites for identification with the various "provinces," but he could easily have done so. For Quizqui there is an abundance of eligible sites, rather too many considering the impression the documents give of a relatively unimportant community. Not too far south of Commerce Landing are three sites located on a Mississippi meander of Stage 14 now occupied by Beaverdam Lake. These sites were catalogued as Evansville (14–O–1), Owens (14–O–2), and Beaverdam (14–O–3). The dating of these sites has already been discussed in another connection (p. 302). Seriation dates of all three are definitely too early for 1541, but they all have rectangular mounds, or remains of same, and some shell-tempered pottery, so the possibility of their having lasted up to De Soto's time cannot be ruled out. North of these sites, and immediately below Commerce Landing are two large sites, Hollywood (13–O–10) and Indian Creek (13–O–12) that seem to have been occupied about the right time. These sites are admirably situated on McKinney Bayou, about 2 miles from what was probably the main channel of the Mississippi in 1541 (Stage 15). McKinney Bayou and its continuation, Indian Creek, occupy old Mississippi channels of Stage 12. Their 1541 counterpart could have been the small river mentioned in connection with the first Quizqui village. Hollywood is a very imposing mound site of period B–A, with a dominant pyramidal mound 20 feet high and many smaller mounds arranged about a plaza and traces of a rectangular earthwork enclosure.[76] Indian Creek is a large but less imposing site of slightly earlier date in period C–B. Directly at Commerce Landing, also on a meander of Stage 12, is the well-known Commerce Landing Site (13–O–11), similar to Hollywood in scale and impressive size of mounds with a closely related pottery complex. In sum, the archaeological evidence for the location of Quizqui at or below Commerce Landing is as good if not better than that in the neighborhood of Sunflower Landing.[77]

When we cross the river to the Arkansas side and the problem of Aquixo, the eligible sites are still more abundant. We shall discuss only the outstanding ones. A short distance down the river — we must bear in mind that Commerce Landing is only taken as an approximation; Lewis allows himself considerable leeway — is the Kent-Murdock group (13–N–4, 13–N–12) already discussed as a possible location of Pacaha. If these sites could have been Pacaha towns in terms of the Sunflower Landing theory, they could as readily have been Aquixo towns in terms of the Commerce Landing theory. Both provinces were directly on the Mississippi. Better situated, however, in fact exactly where Lewis would have wanted it, is the Barrett Site (13–O–1) located on what was formerly Council Bend. This site has remains of large pyramidal mounds and the pottery, though "mean-dated" by seriation in

[76] Described by Brown as the Bowdre Site, 1926, pp. 120–21. Brown's description suggests the bastioned type of fort found at the Angel Site in southern Indiana.

[77] For a more detailed study of sites in this district, see Barton, 1927. This writer, a close student of local topography and Indian settlements, believed that the river mentioned in connection with the first Quizqui village was Indian Creek and its continuation in McKinney Bayou. In addition to the big sites mentioned above, he was able to show that the banks, particularly on the east, of the old Mississippi channels now occupied by these small streams were lined with almost continuous signs of occupation. "Our only embarrassment in this region is a wealth of villages and rivers. If Mr. Malone (his Memphis opponent) could only have borrowed a few to scatter about the old Bethel place and Brown's Hill." Barton thinks that Hollywood, which he calls DeBeVoise Mound, was the Quizqui "capital" and Commerce, which he calls the Abbey Mound, the village near which the barges were built for the crossing.

period D–C, indicates a fairly long span which probably came down to 1541 or even later. About 6 miles northeast of the Barrett Site, on the south side of Fifteen-Mile Bayou, is the Green River Site (13–O–2), similar in general character but with an earlier pottery complex. This was one of the few sites encountered by the Survey which combined pyramidal mounds and a pure Baytown Period pottery complex. However, owing to the fact that the site was covered by plantation buildings, conditions for collecting were unfavorable and our sample though adequate came from a very small portion of the site. The Nickey Mound (13–O–4), a quarter of a mile to the northwest, could have been catalogued as part of the Green River Site. This is the remnant of a large mound of indeterminate shape, probably originally rectangular, having a pottery complex dating very close to our hypothetical 1541 "ceramic formula." Likewise admirably situated from the point of view of Lewis' interpretation of the Aquixo problem are two sites so closely related that they could almost have been catalogued as one, Belle Meade (13–O–5) and Beck (13–O–7). Belle Meade is one of the few sites in this district that shows some evidence of having been palisaded, as we know the Aquixo villages to have been. It will be recalled that evidence of former palisades does not always take the form of a wall formed by the earth banked up against the palisade. You have also the "St. Francis" type of site (see p. 329) in which the whole village area is in effect a mound, usually with a definite rectangular shape, indicating that the accumulation of débris took place within a palisaded wall. Belle Meade, the first site of this type encountered in the present discussion, shows an accumulation of about 2 meters indicating a considerable period of occupation. It would answer very well to the expression "fenced village" used so frequently in the narratives covering this portion of the route. Seriation dates of both of these sites are in the B–A period, theoretically post-De Soto, Belle Meade being considerably closer to point B, our hypothetical 1541 date line, than Beck. However, the accuracy of our dating is not such as to permit us to say that either of these sites could not have been visited by the expedition.

The tally of sites that could be referred to the Aquixo — if the crossing-place were in the neighborhood of Commerce Landing — is not complete. About 12 miles above the Landing and 2 miles west of the Mississippi at Cow Island Bend is an important site catalogued as Pouncey (12–O–2) with two large pyramidal mounds and smaller house mounds arranged in a typical plaza assemblage. The pottery complex is dated by seriation fairly early in period C–B, but the large percentage of Bell Plain (23 per cent) indicates a terminal date in B–A, so it is reasonable to assume that the occupation span included the year 1541 in terms of our present hypothesis.

These are not the only sites that could be adduced as possible candidates for the designation of Aquixo, but should be sufficient to indicate a well-populated region with "good towns" corresponding to the uniformly favorable descriptions of the place. Comparison with the discussion of Aquixo in terms of the Sunflower Landing theory (p. 375) will serve to emphasize the point.

Attention has already been called to the apparent circumstance that it was not until after De Soto left the first Aquixo village, bound upriver for Pacaha, that he first heard of Casqui, and it was suggested that he may have changed the direction of his march in order to visit it. The same thing, evidently, was in Lewis' mind when he located Casqui on the St. Francis River near the mouth of the Tyronza. The distance from Aquixo to Casqui, based on an average day's march of 12 miles, would have been somewhere in the neighborhood of 30 to 40 miles. The airline distance from Council Bend to the mouth of Tyronza River is 25 miles, so it is entirely possible for the Spaniards to have reached that general vicinity. Any route between the two localities would have involved the Spaniards in the backswamp lying between the present Mississippi meander belt and the older St. Francis segment of the Mississippi meander belt. To attempt to identify the "worst swamp" which made the land about Casqui look high and dry by comparison would be entirely futile at this stage of inquiry. There is an embarrassment of riches in this regard. Equally futile, perhaps, it would be to suggest sites for identification with the Casqui villages. The confluence of the Tyronza and St. Francis rivers is the approximate center of an immensely rich archaeological development which reached its peak about, or shortly after, the time of De Soto. A few of the outstanding sites are shown in figure 70, but there are many more. These are all large fortified village sites of the type designated in Section VIII as the "St. Francis type," and most of them have remains of large pyramidal mounds. If a large site is needed for the Casqui "capital" and a large mound on it for the erection of the famous cross, such a site as Parkin (11–N–1) or Neeley's Ferry (11–N–4) would perfectly fill the bill. As in the case of Quizqui, there are more sites than we need, and they are perhaps too large, particularly if we give credence to Garcilaso's description of Casqui as a province with one or two large towns and a large number of small scattered villages. However, between too many sites and none at all, there cannot be any question of choice. So far as Casqui is concerned, the Commerce Landing theory has in abundance the archaeology that the Sunflower Landing theory so conspicuously appears to lack.

In placing Pacaha in the neighborhood of Osceola, Lewis has, in our opinion, over-estimated the distance between the two places. It will be recalled that the Spaniards, on their return to Casqui, covered the distance in two days, say about 25 to 35 miles. It would seem more reasonable to look for Pacaha in the vicinity of Pecan Point, an important cultural center in the period we are discussing. The famous old Pecan Point Site has gone into the Mississippi River, but there are other sites near by of the same period. This district was visited by one of the members of the Lower Mississippi Archaeological Survey in 1940 and marked down for further investigation but unfortunately it has not yet been done. Consequently, with the exception of a small site at Shawnee Village (11–P–1) which appears to be of the right period, it is not possible to describe any sites that might be identified with Pacaha. A few miles farther north, however, are the sites around Nodena, from which Dr. Hampson has made very important collections, which he has kindly placed at our disposal. These sites were catalogued as Carson Lake (10–P–1), Bell (10–P–2), Nettle Ridge (10–P–3), Notgrass (10–P–4), Upper Nodena (10–Q–1), and Sherman (10–Q–2). None of them are on or very near the Stage 15 channel of the Mississippi, so would not do as the theoretical site of the Pacaha village described in the narratives, but they indicate clearly that the region was heavily occupied by an advanced culture very closely related to that of Pecan Point at a time we assume to have been close to 1541.

So far, Lewis' theory, if we pull his Pacaha down from Osceola to the vicinity of Nodena or Pecan Point, agrees remarkably with the geographical and archaeological conditions. The rest of it from Casqui to Quiguate is subject to difficulties which we shall make no attempt to minimize here. Assuming the Casqui capital to have been on the St. Francis River at or near Parkin, we have to allow 20 to 30 miles downstream to the point where the River of Casqui was crossed and another 25 to 35 miles from there to Quiguate. Any way you figure it, this brings them pretty far down the St. Francis. Lewis' location of Quiguate somewhere near the St. Francis-Lee County line appears to be too far upstream. Yet this point is only about 20 miles airline above the present mouth of the river. Then what about the settlements farther down the river that Ranjel says De Soto did not find out about until later and Elvas says he knew about but decided to go to Coligua anyhow?

The problem is complicated further by the fact that we do not know for certain where the mouth of the St. Francis was in 1541. According to Fisk, the St. Francis flowed into the Mississippi not far below Memphis through what is known as the Fifteen-Mile Bayou By-Pass Channel until Stage 15, just about the time of De Soto. Either course is awkward for Lewis' location of Quiguate. If it was still following Fifteen-Mile Bayou, then those troublesome downstream villages would have been in the same place where he has already located Aquixo. If the St. Francis had already changed to its present course, those settlements would have to be found in an area that we found to be singularly barren of archaeology when looking for Swanton's Pacaha. The only way out of the difficulty that we can see is to disparage the information, which after all was not verified, and may actually have been intended to mislead. The fact that the Commission theory runs into the same difficulty, only more so, might have comforted Lewis, but does not help his argument. In a more general sense, the location of Quiguate is the essential weakness in Lewis' whole theory. It does not seem credible that the Spaniards could have got back, at Quiguate, to a point so near Aquixo where they had already been without being aware of the fact.

The archaeological evidence for Lewis' Quiguate is not particularly decisive one way or another. There are several sites of the right period in the area where he would like to have them, such as Lakeside (13-N-18), Riverside (13-N-19), Castile Landing (13-N-21), Clay Hill (13-N-7), and Connor (13-N-14), but none of them are on a scale commensurate with the description of Quiguate as the "largest town in all Florida." It is hardly necessary to add, however, that in an area subject to floods, the remains we find today may represent only a small portion of an original site.

When it comes to the route from Quiguate to Coligua, it appears to us, provided the identification of the River of Coligua with the White can be made to harmonize with subsequent movements of the army in Arkansas,[78] that Lewis comes off better than the Commission. From his assumed location of Quiguate, the army could have started down the St. Francis, as Ranjel says, and then turned west or northwest through Marianna Gap and across the Western Lowland to the White River. The four swamps crossed in as many days before reaching the River of Coligua described by the same reliable authority would have been the l'Anguille, Big Creek, Bayou de View, and the Cache River. These streams and their low bottom lands are subject to backwater flooding at which times they are more like swamps than rivers.

It seems the more thoroughly a problem of this sort is studied the more the difficulties are multiplied and consequently the more vulnerable to destructive criticism the resulting theoretical reconstruction becomes. We must bear this in mind in comparing the Sunflower Landing and Commerce Landing theories. The latter has not been worked out with the same painstaking attention to detail as the former. That is undoubtedly one reason why we have found less to criticize in it. On the other hand, there are certain basic archaeological consideraitons, which do not depend on detailed analysis, that seem to be accounted for in the Commerce Landing theory and not in the Sunflower Landing theory. Reduced to the simplest terms, the political situation on this portion of the Mississippi seems to have been as follows: a Pacaha-Aquixo "axis" on the west side of the river, with Quizqui as a dependency on the east side, and a rival power, Casqui, not on the Mississippi but not far from it on a tributary stream. Now it is of course true that political and cultural situations do not invariably coincide, but when they do, the fact is likely to be significant. In precisely the areas on the Mississippi where Lewis would locate Quizqui, Aquixo, and Pacaha, we find a very close cultural distribution of the required period. This we have tentatively referred to as the Walls-Pecan Point facies of the Memphis area. On the St. Francis, where he would locate Casqui, we find a related but sufficiently distinct culture in the same general period. If we were to envisage a classificatory terminology, purely for the sake of clarifying this discussion, we would find that the Quizqui and Aquixo foci were practically indistinguishable, and both more closely related to the Pacaha Focus than to the Casqui Focus; in other words, a precise reflection of the political situation clearly described in the De Soto narratives. The same thing cannot be done in terms of the Sunflower Landing theory. The closest relations between what we would then be calling the Aquixo Focus would not be with Quizqui or Pacaha, but with a Quiguate Focus on the Lower Arkansas River. There would not be any Casqui Focus, because there were no sites, and the Pacaha Focus would be insufficiently documented for purposes of comparison. It is not maintained here that this argument is conclusive. We must not lose sight of the fact that our dating criteria are still in a hypothetical stage. We must also remind ourselves and the reader of the self-imposed

[78] Regarded as an impossibility by the Commission for whom the River of Coligua must be the Arkansas. See Swanton, 1939, p. 239.

limitations of the argument. To stand up, either theory has to be reconcilable with subsequent problems of identification outside the scope of this report. To be more explicit, the proponent of the Commerce Landing theory has to be able to show that the River of Coligua *could* be the White River. Lewis did so to his own satisfaction, but the Commission ruled that it had to be the Arkansas. We cannot now even venture an opinion on this crucial question. All we can say in conclusion, therefore, is that within the limitations of our present inquiry, the Commerce Landing theory accords remarkably well with the geographical and archaeological conditions of the Survey Area.

The Memphis Theory

The hypothesis that De Soto discovered and crossed the Mississippi River somewhere in the neighborhood of the Fourth Chickasaw Bluff, the present location of Memphis, is a venerable one, going back at least to Thomas Nuttall in 1821. It was strongly held throughout the nineteenth century, but with the loss of confidence in Garcilaso as an authority which followed upon the rediscovery and translation of the Ranjel text, it has suffered at the hands of disinterested scholars in the twentieth. Another reason, no doubt, is the fact that advocates of a Memphis crossing have been content to bring De Soto to the Mississippi at Memphis without paying much attention to what happened on the other side. Thus, we can hardly speak of their arguments as a comprehensive theory comparable to those already discussed. These arguments have generally fallen under two heads, one positive and one negative: first, that the direction from Alimamu, given by Garcilaso as "always north," rules out a westward course across the Yazoo Basin; second, that such a course was impossible anyhow because of the impossibility of crossing the backswamps of the Tallahatchie Basin. These arguments are by no means as contemptible as their opponents often maintain. We have already dealt with them, elsewhere, and our findings may be briefly summarized here. In regard to the direction from Alimamu, it is true enough that Garcilaso is an uncertain guide, but since his is the only direct statement on this point, it cannot be ignored. In regard to the alleged difficulty of crossing the Yazoo Basin, Swanton and others have shown that many trails did cross the basin at many points, proving at least that it could be done. These trails were undoubtedly seasonal — and a great deal of ink has been used trying to show what sort of weather the Spaniards were having that spring. When everything has been said on both sides, and the meager texts have been tortured to favor one or the other, the feeling still remains that as between the upland route to Memphis and the Yazoo Basin route to Sunflower Landing, the former has the advantage. As between Memphis and Commerce Landing, the argument is an academic one, as a glance at the map will readily show. Only the last 10 to 15 miles to Commerce Landing would have been across the basin and at this point the backswamp is not extensive.[79]

Our conclusion, therefore, is that all the arguments for and against Memphis have proved nothing one way or the other. Archaeology is left with a wide open field. Unfortunately, it takes us beyond the limits of our Survey. The immediate vicinity of Memphis was not investigated, though one site was visited, Shelby (12–P–2), that would qualify excellently as one of the Quizqui villages. Assuming the crossing to have taken place at or near Memphis, the Aquixo villages are to be looked for in the vicinity of the Bradley Site (11–P–2). Following the same reasoning as was used in connection with the Commerce Landing theory, Casqui would be sought somewhere on the Tyronza or Left Hand Chute of Little River, preferably the latter, say in the general vicinity of Lepanto or above it. The Tyronza could be postulated as the "swamp" that was crossed before reaching the first Casqui villages. Pacaha would then be on the Mississippi above Osceola, the Tyronza again being crossed, this time by means of the famous bridge. Such a theory would identify the Left Hand Chute of Little River and the St. Francis as the River of Casqui. On the way to Quiguate, the latter would have to be crossed at or below Marked

[79] See Barton, 1927, p. 76.

Tree, where there is a large site, not visited by the Survey, and Quiguate would then be somewhere in the neighborhood of Parkin. Such a theory, which, let us hasten to add, is not proposed here, because we have not the archaeology for testing it, avoids one major difficulty run into by the other two theories, i.e., the settlements reported but unvisited downstream from Quiguate. It has another great advantage. The sites around Parkin are the largest and most compact village sites in the entire area covered by the Survey. These are the only sites that correspond to the enthusiastic narrators' comments about Quiguate, "the largest town in all Florida."

This brief sketch, advanced as no more than a suggestion for further research, shows at least that the Memphis theory is not to be lightly dismissed simply because it has rested in the past almost exclusively upon negative arguments. A more positive approach is indicated.

Ethnic Identification of De Soto "Provinces"

Until further progress has been made toward solution of the problem in archaeological terms, there is little to add to what Swanton has already said about the tribal or linguistic affiliations of the various groups encountered by De Soto.[80] This may be summarized briefly here for the sake of discussion later on in connection with the ethnic situation in the French contact period at the close of the following century. No linguistic affiliation is claimed by Swanton for the Quizqui and Aquixo, although he suggests they may have been Tunica because of the evidence that they were dominated by the Pacaha. The latter, he is "inclined to think" were Tunica because "Macanoche, the name of one of the Pacaha chief's sisters, seems to contain the Tunica word *nuhtci* 'woman.' "[81] In an earlier statement he calls attention to the fact that a site in northwestern Mississippi called Tunica Oldfields "is almost opposite the sites occupied by these Pacaha in 1541."[82] Obviously, he does not insist upon the point, but he is very emphatic in his belief, stated as early as 1912,[83] that the earlier idea that Pacaha, or Capaha as Garcilaso renders it, was equivalent to Quapaw has no more foundation than a confusion of names. The main reason is that the glimpses we get of Pacaha culture, "such as the presence of a temple, seem to ally them with the Lower Mississippi tribes." It is interesting that these glimpses are mainly afforded by Garcilaso, the same author who is responsible for the confusion of names. Temple mounds and temples upon them are by no means exclusive Lower Mississippi traits. Other traits glimpsed in Garcilaso, such as the bastioned palisade daubed with clay, relate Pacaha to sites up the river, to the lower Ohio specifically, whence the Quapaw are supposed to have come. So far as any real evidence is concerned, Pacaha could have been Quapaw as well as Tunica. It may very well have been neither. We shall return to this point when we have found out something about the location of Quapaw sites in the seventeenth century.

About the identity of the Casqui, Swanton seems to have no doubt whatever. "They appear in later history as the Casquinampo and are known to have lived at different times on the Cumberland and Tennessee rivers."[84] If there is any evidence for this statement beyond the similarity of names, the present writers have not seen it.

Of the Indians of Quiguate, the "largest town in Florida," Swanton can only say that the name sounds Natchesan, which would imply a very extensive spread of that people in 1541, for, according to the same authority, the Quigualtam or Quigualtanqui of De Soto, who *were* Natchez, were located about where the Natchez were later found by the French. To be sure, the correspondence of the name Quiguate with Quigualtam is certainly very

[80] Swanton, 1939, pp. 51–54.
[81] Swanton, 1939, p. 52.
[82] Swanton, 1932b, pp. 62–63.
[83] Swanton, 1912, p. 150.
[84] Swanton, 1939, p. 52. See also Swanton, 1946, p. 143. "Kaskinampo — a tribe which appears first in history in 1541 in the De Soto narratives under the name of Casqui or Casquin. They were found near the present Helena, Arkansas."

striking. On the other hand, later Natchez archaeology is well known. Except for a few trade sherds and vessels of post-1541 date, found at or near Menard (17–K–1), there is nothing here nor at any other site discussed above as possible locations of Quiguate that would suggest a culture ancestral to the Natchez.

This is plainly not very much to go on. The palaeontologist with half a tooth has a better change of reconstructing his animal. But some of these "leads" may prove to be not without interest when compared with the somewhat more satisfactory ethno-historical information available in the documents of the later French period.

Conclusions on the De Soto Problem

Notwithstanding the self-imposed limitations on the foregoing discussion, it is disappointing not to be able to wind up with at least some tentative conclusions. All we can say with conviction is that no theory yet advanced fully satisfies the topographical and archaeological conditions; that as a result it is idle to speak of positive identification of any single site as having been visited by De Soto. General archaeological probabilities at the present time are, in our opinion, best satisfied by the Commerce Landing or Tunica theory, though certain conditions favor still more the Memphis theory, as yet unchecked by first-hand archaeological data. Actually, these two theories are closely parallel. But for the state line between them, one might wonder why there has been such furious debate on the part of their respective — and respectable — proponents. The real conflict is between these and the supporters of the Sunflower Landing theory. Fundamental differences of interpretation are involved. Once again we must candidly admit that these are not all archaeological. If they were, we would not hesitate to declare in favor of the more northerly location of the Mississippi crossing-place. Our position is weakened by the fact that we have failed, for reasons already stated, to deal with one of the Commission's strongest arguments — the argument of the rivers (see p. 374). We are obliged, therefore, to qualify what might otherwise have been a strong terminating statement somewhat as follows: Present archaeological evidence, so far as it goes, favors a route that would bring De Soto across the Mississippi River somewhere between Memphis and the present mouth of the St. Francis River. In that case, the politically related groups, Quizqui, Aquixo, and Pacaha would be represented archaeologically by Mississippi period sites along the present Mississippi meander belt, from Osceola, to Commerce, or slightly below. These sites present a homogeneous culture which we have elsewhere referred to as the "Walls-Pecan Point" complex. Casqui and Quiguate would be represented by sites on the older St. Francis segment of the Mississippi meander belt now occupied by the St. Francis and its tributaries, the Tyronza and Little rivers. Logical interpretation of the documentary evidence unsupported by archaeology has been used by the De Soto Commission to show that the crossing must have taken place below the mouth of the St. Francis River. We have examined that reasoning insofar as it applies to locations within the Survey Area and checked it against available archaeological data with negative results. That portion of the reasoning that depends on determinations outside the Survey Area we are unable to dispute. The doubts encountered in the one part, however, are sufficient to raise doubts about the other, and to suggest that the Commission's reconstruction of the trans-Mississippi portion of the De Soto route, at least as far as the Province of Anilco, must be regarded as an unproved hypothesis. On the positive side we have indicated an alternative hypothesis that deserves at least as much consideration. Finally, we hope that we have sufficiently indicated the difficulties inherent in this kind of study to forestall criticism in respect to the lack of positive results.

THE IDENTIFICATION OF QUAPAW SITES OF THE PERIOD 1673–1690

The Use of Documentary Sources in Archaeological Studies

The preceding discussion of the De Soto problem has at least made it sufficiently clear that the really practicable contact period for the Mississippi Alluvial Valley is that of the early French penetrations into the area, beginning with the "discovery" of Jolliet-Marquette in 1673 and extending roughly over the next quarter century. The most important expeditions during this period were as follows:

1673 — Voyage of Jolliet and Marquette.
1682 — Expedition of La Salle down the Mississippi to the Gulf and return.
1686 — Voyage of Tonti down the Mississippi to the Gulf to look for La Salle after the disastrous expedition from France by sea. On the return journey he founded a small post at the Arkansas which remained a more or less permanent establishment throughout the French Period.
1687 — Survivors of the La Salle expedition (Jean Cavelier, Joutel, and others) return to Canada by way of the "Caddo" country and the Arkansas Post.
1690 — Tonti's second relief expedition to make contact with other survivors of the La Salle expedition left in Texas. Goes down the Mississippi to the Taensa and from thence overland to Natchitoches and beyond, returning by approximately the same route.
1698–99 — Tonti accompanies the missionaries, de Montigny, St. Cosme, and Davion down the Mississippi to the Arkansas. The first mission establishments in the Lower Mississippi Valley.
1700 — Father Gravier's voyage down the Mississippi.
1700 — Tonti's last voyage down the Mississippi to the new French establishments on the Gulf.
1700 — Le Sueur's voyage up the Mississippi.
1700 — Voyage of Father Du Rhu up the Mississippi.

Thanks to the recent critical researches of the late Father Jean Delanglez, we are enabled to handle the source materials for most of these expeditions with far more confidence than was ever possible before. The extent of our indebtedness to this scholar will be sufficiently apparent in the constant repetition of his name in the pages to follow. Most important, however, has been the salutary effect of his remorseless criticism of sources, which in our somewhat naïve view as archaeologists have tended to assume a sacred character. This is particularly true on the cartographic side. The interpretation of early maps is often undertaken by the archaeologist and ethnographer with a light-hearted innocence that must sometimes strike the historiographer as pathetic. It is not difficult to imagine our attitude if a mere historian were to attempt to interpret technical archaeological data without previous training in archaeology. The interpretation of early maps is apparently just as complex and difficult as the interpretation of stratigraphy, if not more so. To begin with, we seldom realize how many such maps there are. The few published collections and atlases available to the non-specialist afford a mere sampling, in which it is always important to know what were the bases of selection — which may be wholly inappropriate for the particular problem. For it is an unfortunate fact that a map may be "good" in one portion and wholly worthless in another. For example, Delanglez in his "El Rio del Espiritu Santo" studied hundreds of maps of the sixteenth and seventeenth centuries, which gave an excellent idea of the progress of cartographic knowledge of the Gulf Coast, but showed no increase of knowledge whatever so far as the Mississippi River was concerned.[85] So it is not enough to know that a map is good; you have to know what portions of it may be relied upon, and which are merely added to fill in space. In this connection it is well to remember that map-making was formerly an art as well as a science. Most important — and this places the whole subject outside the competence of the archaeologist — is to know the sources of the map-maker's information, genetic and otherwise. Most maps are based on earlier maps with new information added. The latter may be the result of new explorations and discoveries, it may be a reinterpretation of old information, or it may be wholly imaginary. Needless to say, it is important to know which. Worse — and this applies particularly to the French maps of the Mississippi Valley in the seventeenth and early eighteenth century — maps may be changed and new information

[85] Delanglez, 1943–44.

added for political and other considerations having nothing to do with the science of cartography. It is disquieting to find that maps created for the sole purpose of deceiving certain persons at the court of France in the seventeenth century are still capable of deceiving unwary students today. Finally, there is a commercial aspect to the business which it is well to know something about, in case there are any lingering illusions in the student's mind. Delanglez, in the work cited above, gives an excellent picture of the more rackety aspects of the cartographic business in the sixteenth and seventeenth centuries.

> . . . maps of the New World, and especially maps of the interior, were seldom made from accounts of discovery and exploration. The majority of mapmakers were satisfied with reproducing the work of their predecessors. True geographers were few and far between, and many who are today accepted as cartographers were simply draughtsmen, engravers, or map publishers, whose main concern was to issue "new" maps. The only change often consisted in scratching the date of publication off the plate and replacing it by a more recent date, notwithstanding the emblazoned assertion that the map embodied the latest information derived from memoirs of travelers recently returned from the faraway countries represented on the map. Sometimes the map publisher did not even bother to alter the plate. He merely erased the last two digits on the unsold maps in stock, inserted the more recent date with pen and ink, and advertised the map as a new edition. This was not all. Map publishers indiscriminately compiled atlases of dated and undated maps by various authors, with the result that today we find these maps listed under the date of publication of the atlas, which in some cases varies as much as fifty years from the true date of an individual map. It is therefore very difficult, unless one has independent knowledge of the maps in these atlases, to study the cartographical development of a particular area of the New World, such as the Mississippi Valley and the adjacent states with which we are here concerned. Another convenient way of making a new map, quite different from those already on the market, and hence likely to interest the publisher's clients, was as follows. The cartographer or the draughtsman would insert, more or less indiscriminately, various place-names, rivers, and other geographical features to be found on whatever previously printed or manuscript maps he happened to have at hand. The cartographic freaks produced by this desire for completeness and novelty can easily be imagined.[86]

Having these considerations in mind, we must be on guard against any argument in favor of a site or group identification that depends on cartographic evidence alone. This is not to say that contemporary maps are useless but, generally speaking, their use requires more critical analysis than we archaeologists have time or competence to give. These remarks may be taken in explanation for the rather slender use of maps in the present study.

Getting back to the subject in hand, it seems advisable to describe each one of the expeditions listed above in turn, so far as they relate to the Quapaw, drawing heavily on the documents so that this section may serve as a source book for other students interested in this particular problem. So far as the present writers are aware, there is no single publication to which the interested student may turn for this material. Swanton's definitive "Indian Tribes of the Lower Mississippi Valley" (1911) stops short of the Quapaw. Although he has written extensively about them, in one place or another, nowhere has he brought together the source material with the admirable thoroughness he has devoted to the other major tribes of the Southeast. That done, we shall attempt to worry out of this material some reasonable guesses as to the probable location of the various Quapaw villages at this time, with a side glance at the problem of identifying these villages with archaeological sites discovered by the Lower Mississippi Archaeological Survey. Readers looking for certainties in this regard are advised to stop right here. As we have already discovered in looking for De Soto sites, the identification of historic sites in the unstable topography of the Mississippi Alluvial Valley is an undertaking just short of hopeless. Finally, let it be noted that we are not attempting to write an ethnography of the Quapaw. Aspects of their culture will be considered only so far as they contribute to the archaeological problem.

Nomenclature of the Quapaw Villages

It is unfailingly the case in early documents relating to the American Indians that each tribal or place name has as many versions as the writers who mention it. Consequently, it

[86] Delanglez, 1943–44, pp. 189–90.

may be well at this point to say something about the nomenclature used in the pages to follow. To begin with, there is the question as to whether the villages concerned ought to be called Quapaw or Arkansas. Even so simple a question we are not prepared to answer categorically, because it involves the more complicated question as to just what sort of group they were, a tribe or a confederacy. The name Arkansas, which got fastened upon them quite by accident — not even a Siouan word it would seem — is invariably used by early writers as a generic term for a group of villages (tribes?) of which Kappa (Quapaw) was only one. However, it was the identity of this one village that survived the longest, and by the time the pioneer ethnographers (Mooney, Dorsey, Thomas) got to work on what was left of the Siouan tribes, the term Quapaw had supplanted Arkansas altogether. We shall therefore use Quapaw in the same generic sense.

As we shall soon see, there were, in the last quarter of the seventeenth century, at least four Quapaw villages, of which two were on the Mississippi River, or what was regarded as the Mississippi River, a third was at or near what was thought of as the mouth of the Arkansas River, and a fourth was on the Arkansas River. The reason for stating these geographic relations in such a curiously indefinite fashion will become painfully evident as the argument unfolds. Not only do we have to consider the possibility that seventeenth-century notions of geography in this area were different from our own, but the geography itself may have been different. Thomas, in the "Handbook of the American Indians," [87] lists these villages, in the order described above as follows: Ukakhpakhti, Tongigua, Tourima, and Uzutiuhi. The first and last names are no doubt intended to be linguistically correct as derived from living Quapaw informants, the others are apparently taken from documentary sources. Since we have no correct versions of Tongigua and Tourima, it hardly seems worthwhile to afflict the reader with Ukakhpakhti and Uzutiuhi. We shall therefore hereinafter designate the four villages as Kapa, Tongigua, Tourima, and Osotouy, respectively, these being the versions most frequently encountered in the sources.

The Jolliet-Marquette Expedition of 1673

Sources

Owing to Jolliet's mishap in the rapids above Montreal, in which all his papers were lost, and the unaccountable loss of Marquette's journal, the available documents covering the memorable voyage of 1673 are extremely meager, as may be seen by the brief list that follows:

1) Marquette's map of 1673–74. Reproduced in many publications, one of the latest being Tucker, 1942, pl. V. The only autograph document of the Jolliet expedition and a remarkably careful and accurate piece of work. (See Delanglez, 1945a, p. 30.)

2) Dablon's Relation of 1674. Printed for the first time in Delanglez, 1944b, pp. 317–24. The verbal report of Jolliet committed to writing by Dablon. Brief and deficient in detail required for our present purposes.

3) Jolliet's map of 1674 and the dedicatory epistle to Frontenac inscribed thereon. The original of this map, drawn from memory by Jolliet after the loss of his papers in the rapids above Montreal, has itself been lost, but a number of copies (five) have come down to us. For a critical discussion of these copies and an attempt at reconstruction of the lost original, see Delanglez, 1946b.

Two of these copies, the Joliet (sic) map of 1674 and the Randin map of 1674–81, are reproduced in Tucker, 1942, pls. IV and VI.

4) Dablon's *Rècit.* Until recently thought to have been the work of Marquette. Included by Dablon in the Relation of 1677–78 and now known to have been written by him. Several copies of this relation are extant. The Montreal copy, printed in text and translation in Shea, 1903, will be used in the present study.

Unfortunately, it is only the last named, not really a primary source at all, that gives a narrative of the expedition in any sort of detail. In using it, in the account that follows, we must be careful to bear in mind its shortcomings. According to Delanglez, Dablon did not have Marquette's lost journal when he

[87] Hodge, 1907, p. 336.

wrote the *Rècit*, but he had Marquette's map and Jolliet's map, including the dedicatory letter to Frontenac, and he had almost certainly talked with Jolliet and some of the other men who had taken part in the expedition.[88] So it seems possible that many, if not most, of the events described actually took place, but it would not be surprising if the good father had scrambled them somewhat as to time and place.

Narrative of the Expedition

In the late spring of 1673, Louis Jolliet, Father James Marquette, S.J., and five anonymous compatriots floated down the Wisconsin River and out upon the broad waters of the Mississippi to discover it for another time. Objection to the term "discovery" in this connection has been voiced, in view of the previous discoveries of De Soto, Cabeza de Vaca, and others, but it may be argued that, so far as the world's knowledge of geography is concerned, this was the effective discovery. This time the Mississippi River stayed discovered.

The contrast with the expedition of De Soto one hundred and thirty-two years before is implicit in their different aims. That of De Soto was conquest — that it bore the character of an exploration was due simply to the fact that De Soto had first to find something worth conquering. This, on the other hand, was a voyage of discovery pure and simple, to discover the great river of Indian report and find out if it emptied into the Vermillion Sea (Gulf of California) or the Gulf of Mexico, and secondarily, but perhaps not less importantly, to discover new souls to be won for the greater glory of God. Between them lay also more than a century's slow accumulation of knowledge of the New World and its peoples. For the French, these had been years of accommodation to the ways of life and travel on the lakes and rivers of the eastern woodlands. The result is that Dablon's *Rècit* reads like a summer's idyll after the dark and bloody chronicle of De Soto.

With the Illinois tribes encountered above the mouth of the Ohio, we are not concerned, though it is important that these first encounters were of a friendly nature, and that as a result, Jolliet went on down the river armed with the precious calumet of peace "ce quil est comme un Passeport et une sauuegarde [sic] pour aller en assurance (parmi toutes Les Nations)." [89] Not far below the Ohio came the first opportunity to use this indispensable passport.

While thus borne on at the will of the current, we perceived on the shore Indians armed with guns, with which they awaited us. I first presented my feathered calumet, while my comrades stood to arms, ready to fire on the first volley of the Indians. I hailed them in Huron, but they answered me by a word, which seemed to us a declaration of war. They were, however, as much frightened as ourselves, and what we took for a signal of war, was an invitation to come near, that they might give us food; we accordingly landed and entered their cabins, where they presented us wild-beef and bear's oil, with white plums, which are excellent. They have guns, axes, hoes, knives, beads, and double glass bottles in which they keep the powder. They wear their hair long and mark their bodies in the Iroquois fashion; the head-dress and clothing of their women were like those of the Huron squaws.

They assured us that it was not more than ten days' journey to the sea; that they bought stuffs and other articles of Europeans on the eastern side; that these Europeans had rosaries and pictures; that they played on instruments; that some were like me, who received them well. I did not, however, see any one who seemed to have received any instruction in the faith; such as I could, I gave them with some medals.[90]

One wonders how Dablon, who is putting these words into Marquette's mouth, thought that Marquette was able to communicate with these people. By what language? His Huron apparently was not understood. A great deal of ink has been spilled over the identity of these people with guns, not named in the *Rècit* but almost certainly represented by the name *Monsoupelea* on Marquette's map. The most recent summary of the little that is known and the lot that is conjectured about this enigmatic group is in Griffin's "Fort Ancient Aspect." [91]

[88] Delanglez, 1945a, p. 45. For a full discussion of the authorship of the *Rècit* and the sources upon which it is based, see Delanglez, 1946c.

[89] Dablon, in Delanglez, 1944b, p. 318. Translation: ". . . like a passport or safeguard by means of which one may go in safety among all the tribes."

[90] Shea, 1903, pp. 46–47.

[91] Griffin, 1943b, pp. 12 et seq.

Fortunately, although of considerable interest to us as a possible tribe to put into that ethnographic vacuum that constitutes the northern part of the Survey Area, Marquette's *Monsoupelea* do not seem to have any bearing on the Quapaw problem, so we can sidestep this controversial subject — for the time being. The narrative continues:

> This news roused our courage and made us take up our paddles with renewed ardor. . . . We had now descended to near 33° north, having almost always gone south, when on the water's edge we perceived a village called Mitchigamea. We had recourse to our patroness and guide, the Blessed Virgin Immaculate; and, indeed, we needed her aid, for we heard from afar the Indians exciting one another to the combat by continual yells. They were armed with bows, arrows, axes, war-clubs, and bucklers, and prepared to attack us by land and water; some embarked in large wooden canoes, a part to ascend the rest to descend the river, so as to cut off our way, and surround us completely. Those on shore kept going and coming, as if about to begin the attack. In fact, some young men sprang into the water to come and seize my canoe, but the current having compelled them to return to the shore, one of them threw his war-club at us, but it passed over our heads without doing us any harm. In vain I showed the calumet, and made gestures to explain that we had not come as enemies. The alarm continued, and they were about to pierce us from all sides with their arrows, when God suddenly touched the hearts of the old men on the waterside, doubtless at the sight of our calumet, which at a distance they had not distinctly recognized; but as I showed it continually, they were touched, restrained the ardor of their youth, and two of the chiefs having thrown their bows and quivers into our canoe, and as it were at our feet, entered and brought us to the shore, where we disembarked, not without fear on our part. We had at first to speak by signs, for not one understood a word of the six languages I knew; at last an old man was found who spoke a little Ilinois.[92]

At this point, we must pause to bring up a question that will be discussed at length a little later. We shall have to anticipate that discussion by stating here that it is Delanglez' opinion that the village here called Mitchigamea was actually Kappa, northernmost Quapaw village. Part of the evidence for this belief lies in the last sentence of the passage just quoted. If this had really been a village of the Mitchigamea, an Illinois-speaking tribe, the statement that at last an old man was found who spoke a little Illinois would be completely senseless. Granting that the dialect spoken by the Mitchigamea may have been considerably divergent from that known to Marquette, it is nevertheless unlikely that they would have had to resort to signs until this providential old man turned up. On the contrary, it seems more probable that, as Delanglez believes, this was a Quapaw village, that the old man knew a little Mitchigamea and that somewhere along the line the identities of the village and of the language used became confounded. This is not the only evidence on this point, however, as we shall see.

Possibly due to the inadequacy of this old interpreter, Jolliet and Marquette seem to have got little information at Mitchigamea or Kappa, if indeed the two were the same.

> We showed them by our presents, that we were going to the sea; they perfectly understood our meaning, but I know not whether they understood what I told them of God, and the things which concerned their salvation. It is a seed cast in the earth which will bear its fruit in season. We got no answer, except that we would learn all we desired at another great village called Akamsea, only eight or ten leagues farther down the river. They presented us with sagamity and fish, and we spent the night among them, not, however, without some uneasiness.[93]

At the risk of appearing to make too much of this useless old interpreter, we pause again to point out that it must have been from him that they got the name Akansea, said to be another Algonquian word. It may be that the old man was a Mitchigamea, from long captivity perhaps a bit rusty in his native tongue. It is difficult otherwise to account for his giving two Algonquian names to a Siouan group.

The rest of the narrative has to do with the village of Akansea:

> We embarked next morning with our interpreter, preceded by ten Indians in a canoe. Having arrived about half a league from Akamsea (Arkansas), we saw two canoes coming toward us. The commander was standing up holding in his hand the calumet, with which he made signs according to the custom of the country; he approached us, singing quite agreeably, and invited us to smoke, after which he presented us

[92] Shea, 1903, pp. 47–49.

[93] Shea, 1903, p. 49.

some sagamity and bread made of Indian corn, of which we ate a little. He now took the lead, making us signs to follow slowly. Meanwhile they had prepared us a place under the war-chiefs' scaffold; it was neat and carpeted with fine rush mats, on which they made us sit down, having around us immediately the sachems, then the braves, and last of all, the people in crowds. We fortunately found among them a young man who understood Ilinois much better than the interpreter whom we had brought from Mitchigamea.[94]

There follows an interesting account — our first — of Quapaw culture, which we may have occasion to refer to later. Notwithstanding its obvious shortcomings as first-hand information, it agrees fairly well with what we know of the Quapaw from later and better sources.

Having achieved the main object of the expedition, ascertainment of the fact that the Mississippi flowed into the Gulf of Mexico, and being perhaps more apprehensive of the dangers that might lie in that direction than Dablon thought it necessary to state, Jolliet and Marquette turned their canoes back up the river again, leaving behind them two very tantalizing questions of ethnic identity, the Monsoupelea and the Mitchigamea. It is with the latter only that we are concerned.

The Mitchigamea Problem

Reference has already been made to Delanglez' theory that Mitchigamea, as described in the *Rècit*, was in reality the northernmost Quapaw village. That theory is set forth in a recent publication, "Marquette's Autograph Map of the Mississippi River." [95] It is not our intention to follow his very interesting argument in detail, since a large portion of it hinges on later evidence which we have not yet considered. In short, we are not concerned at the moment with the location of the village in question — that will come later — but solely with its ethnic identification. Delanglez' ideas on this specific problem can be reduced to two alternatives. Either Marquette misinterpreted information obtained from "the old man who spoke a little Ilinois," or Dablon misinterpreted Marquette's map in writing the *Rècit*. A glance at this map, reproduced in figure 71, will make this clear. It depends on which of the two pairs of huts (used as symbols for villages) was intended by Marquette to go with the name Mitchigamea, the one about 50 miles west of the Mississippi that stands directly over the name, or the one directly on the river just after the name. As Delanglez points out, all the village symbols west of the Mississippi on Marquette's map are placed over their respective names, so one must conclude that the inland symbol was certainly intended to represent a Mitchigamea village. In which case the symbol on the river may have been intended to go with Akansea. The latter version would absolve Marquette of any misinterpretation and put the onus on Dablon. In other words, "Marquette inscribed Metchigamea on his map because . . . an Illinois-speaking Indian told him that there was a village inland which was called Metchigamea." [96] This explanation is supported by the passage in the *Rècit* concerning trade goods

. . . that the hatchets, knives, and beads, which we saw, were sold them, partly by the nations to the east, and partly by an Ilinois town four days' journey to the west;[97]

the source of which, Delanglez believes, is the passage in Jolliet's dedicatory letter to Frontenac:

"I saw a village which was only five days' journey from a nation that trades with those of California; if I had arrived two days earlier, I would have been able to speak with those who had come from there and had brought a present of four hatchets." [98]

All this certainly leads one to believe that Marquette understood this inland village to be Mitchigamea and not the village on the river. On the other hand, Dablon, as already noted, relying heavily on Marquette's map, so framed the *Rècit* as to have Mitchigamea in both places. Delanglez goes even farther in denigration of the *Rècit* by suggesting that Mitchigamea, alias Kappa, was actually the terminus of the expedition, that Marquette laid down Akansea and the western tributary opposite

[94] Shea, 1903, pp. 49–50.
[95] Delanglez, 1945a, pp. 41–48.
[96] Delanglez, 1945a, p. 47.
[97] Shea, 1903, p. 50.
[98] Delanglez, 1945a, p. 47.

from heresay; consequently, all that portion of the *Rècit* covering the visit to Akansea was more of Dablon's "interpretation." Again, we cannot go into the details of this charge, because it involves material not yet considered, but on the whole it does not appear to us that Delanglez has proved the point.

In short, after weighing a good deal of evidence that we have not been able to set down here, we have come to the conclusion that Delanglez is right so far as the identity of the Mitchigamea of the *Rècit* is concerned. It probably *was* a Quapaw village. Whether it can be identified with Kappa, the northernmost Quapaw village visited by La Salle and his followers at various times from 1682 to 1690, and the "Old Kappa" of the missionaries of 1698–1700, can be discussed to more purpose after we have considered the evidence of these later travelers.

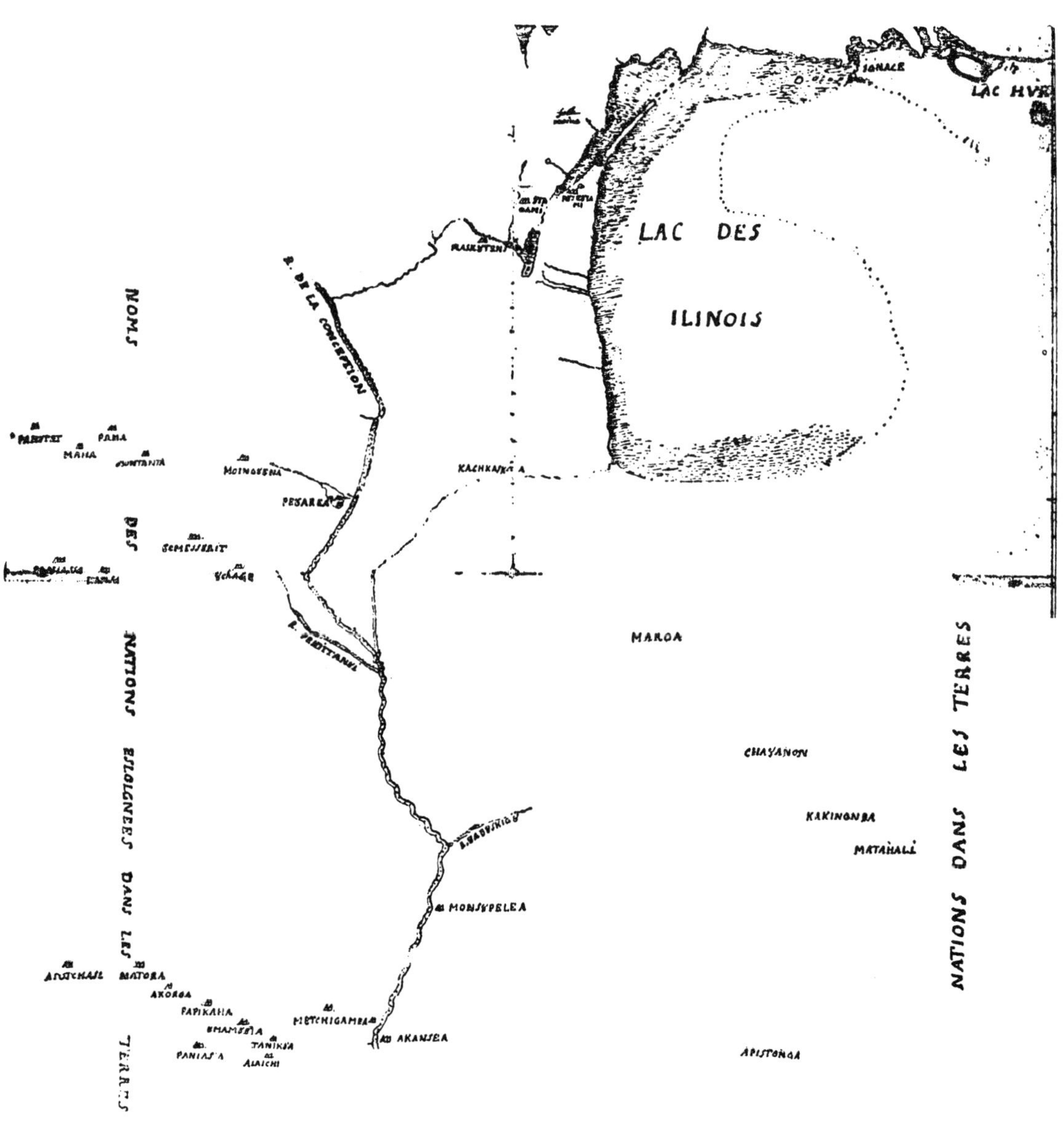

FIG. 71. Portion of Marquette's map of 1673–74. (Reproduced from Tucker, 1942, pl. V.)

The La Salle Expedition of 1682

Sources

The sources for La Salle's first and only voyage on the Mississippi[99] are extremely numerous. Fortunately, for the portion of the expedition with which we are here concerned, they are remarkably consistent, so it will perhaps be sufficient to merely list them without very much in the way of critical comment.

1) Detached fragment in La Salle's hand, undated. In Margry II, 196–203. Contains some interesting general statements about the Lower Mississippi but no ethnographic details.

2) La Salle's letter to an unnamed friend dated Michilimackinac, October, 1682. In Margry II, 288–301. Refers to the expedition just completed but gives no specific details.

3) La Métairie's first procès-verbal, dated Akansas, March 13–14, 1682. In Margry II, 181–85. Notarized description of the ceremony of taking possession at Kappa, the first Arkansas village.

4) La Métairie's second procès-verbal, dated at the mouth of the Mississippi, April 9, 1682. In Margry II, 186–93. Similar to the above in describing the second ceremony of taking possession, but gives more details of the expedition and some ethnographic data.

5) Father Membré's letter, dated *La Rivière de Mississippi*, June 3, 1682. In Margry II, 206–12. Translation of Margry's text in Habig, 1934, 207–14. This document has come down in the form of a copy "made by nobody knows whom" (Delanglez). It nevertheless seems to bear the marks of authenticity.

6) Tonti's letter dated Michilimackinac, July 23, 1682. Text and translation in Habig, 1934, 215–29. Has also come down in form of a copy.

7) Official Relation of 1683. Not printed in Margry. First published by Thomassey, in "De La Salle et ses Relations Inédites," 1869, and later by Gravier in "Decouvertes et Establissements de Cavelier de la Salle," 1870. Translation in Habig, 1934, 244–56. This relation has been ascribed to La Salle (Thomassey and Gravier) and to Father Membré (Habig), but Delanglez thinks it was written by Bernou who embodied in it both Membré's letter of June 3, 1682, and Tonti's letter of July 23, 1682 (nos. 5 and 6, above), particularly the latter (Delanglez, 1940a, p. 7).

8) Relation of Henri de Tonti. Memoir dated Quebec, November 14, 1684. In Margry I, 573–616. Margry's text reprinted with translation in Anderson, 1898b. This is one of the two basic documents. It is referred to by Delanglez as I Tonti, Margry. Since we shall use Anderson's translation, it will be hereinafter referred to as I Tonti, Anderson.

9) Tonti's memoir of 1693. Describes his travels of 1678 to 1690. First publication was in English, by Thomas Falconer in "On the discovery of the Mississippi," London, 1844. Reprinted in B. F. French, "Historical Collections of Louisiana," Part I, 52–78, New York, 1846. Published for the first time in French by Margry, in "Relation et memoires inédites," Paris, 1867, 5–36. The Falconer translation was again reissued — through the French reprint — in the "Collections of the Illinois State Library," I, 1903, 128–64, and again by I. J. Cox in "The journeys of René Robert Sieur de la Salle," New York, 1905, I, 1–58. Finally L. P. Kellogg reprinted the memoir "with many textual corrections" from the "Collections of the Illinois State Historical Library," in "Early Narratives of the Northwest, 1634–99," New York, 1917, 283–322 (Delanglez, 1944b.)

This, the second basic document, will be herein referred to, following Delanglez, as II Tonti, Kellogg.

It was this memoir that was used by a "literary jobber" as a basis for the "dernieres Decouvertes dans l'Amerique Septentrionale de M. de la Salle; Mises au jour par M. le Chevalier de Tonti, gouverneur du Fort Saint Loüis aux Islinois," Paris, 1697, a work that is to be shunned like the plague.

10) Narrative of Nicolas de la Salle (the "Little La Salle"). In Margry I, 547–70. Margry's text and translation in Anderson, 1898a. This is the most detailed account of all, but the author unfortunately shows here and there "a complete detachment from chronology." (Delanglez, 1940b, p. 301).

11) LeClercq's "Premier Etablissement de la Foy dans la Nouvelle France," Paris, 1691. Translation by J. G. Shea, New York, 1881. For the La Salle Expedition of 1682 this is not a primary source at all (Delanglez, 1944a, p. 262).

12) Hennepin's "Nouvelle Decouverte d'un tres grand Pays, situé dans l'Amerique," Utrecht, 1697. Contemporary English translation reprinted as Volume I of Thwaites' "A New Discovery," Chicago, 1903. Contains a wholly spurious account of a voyage down the Mississippi in 1680, which Hennepin never made. Lifted bodily out of LeClercq.

Narrative of the Expedition

La Salle and his not inconsiderable party of canoe-borne Frenchmen and Indians[100]

[99] For a critical discussion of the claims made for, but apparently never by, La Salle to the discovery of the Upper Mississippi prior to the voyage of Jolliet and Marquette, see Delanglez, 1938b.

[100] Tonti lists 23 Frenchmen, including La Salle, himself, and Father Membré, and 27 Indians of which 10 were women and 3, children. I Tonti, Anderson, 1898b, pp. 60–63.

reached the Mississippi, by way of the Illinois River, on February 6, 1682. They were at the Tamoroa village across the river from St. Louis on the 14th, and reached the Ohio River a day or two later. From the Ohio on south there seem to have been no incidents worth recording — Tonti speaks of inundated country with lodges here and there upon the bank — until camp was made some 40 leagues below on the east side of the river for the purpose of hunting. This location on a "hill" not being suitable, they descended to some other hills 3 leagues farther down on the same side. The "hills" in question were the Chickasaw Bluffs, but just which ones, is not necessary for us to determine.

Here the armorer of the expedition, Prudhomme by name, got lost while hunting and the whole party was delayed ten days looking for him. A small fort was thrown up, in the naming of which La Salle showed the more amiable side of his nature — Fort Prudhomme. During the search for this man, contact was made with some Chickasaw, and at one point La Salle started off for the Chickasaw villages, but turned back when he found that his guides had deceived him in respect to the distance. Prudhomme finally turned up, considerably the worse for wear and cured, we may suppose, of solitary hunting, and on March 3rd (I Tonti, Anderson gives the 5th) the voyage down the river was resumed. From this point we will follow the narratives of the expedition with some care.

On the 12th, having travelled by boat for fifty leagues [from a point three leagues below Fort Prudhomme?] and found little game, the banks of the river being covered so thickly with cane that it is almost impossible to enter the woods, we had consumed the last of our provisions when, the weather being foggy, we heard from the right bank war-cries, in the manner of the Savages, and the beating of a drum. M. de la Salle did not doubt that this was a village.[101]

This was Kappa, the northernmost Quapaw village. All accounts are in agreement that its inhabitants were the first Indians encountered below Fort Prudhomme. Only Métairie's second procès-verbal mentions another village — "On passa la rivière des Chépontia et le village des Matsigamea" [102] — but gives no indication that the expedition did more than pass it. It seems very likely that they actually did not even do this. Delanglez has proved pretty conclusively that La Salle had with him on this expedition a copy of Jolliet's map,[103] which, we can assume from the copies that have come down to us, laid down this name on the west side of the river above the Quapaw villages. The manner in which it got into the Jolliet-Marquette documents has already been discussed. The passage quoted above, therefore, probably means no more than, "We must have passed Matsigamea, it's here on the map." [104]

Events at Kappa bore out the good opinion Father Marquette had formed of the Arkansas nine years before. On hearing cries and drumbeats out of the fog, La Salle immediately crossed over to the other side of the river — Métairie's first procès-verbal says to an island — and dug in. Two Indians presently came within bowshot in a canoe and let fly an exploratory arrow, which not drawing any return fire, they landed and accepted the proffered calumet. They returned to their village with the good news and a Frenchman and two of La Salle's Indians as hostages. Soon the chief and some of his principal men came back bearing a calumet and an invitation to come to the village, which was gladly accepted. Arrived there, the French were received with all possible demonstrations of joy and affection. The good Father Membré can scarcely contain his enthusiasm for these people:

Mais, mon Révérend Père, ce que je vous dis là n'est rien en regard des bonnes qualitez de l'esprit de ces Sauvages, qui sont joyeux, honnestes et libéraux,

[101] I Tonti, Anderson, 1898b, pp. 71–73.

[102] Margry II, p. 189. Translation: "We passed the river of Chépontia and the village of the Matsigamea."

[103] Delanglez, 1946a, p. 9, footnote 16.

[104] This is the first mention, so far as we know, of the name Chépontia, which appears on maps from this time on, usually as Chepoussa, designating a western tributary of the Mississippi in various locations between the Missouri and Arkansas rivers. In this case, it would seem to have designated the St. Francis River. The association of the name Matsigamea with what may have been an early name for the St. Francis River is interesting as a possible origin of the practice of locating the Mitchigamea at the mouth of the St. Francis River followed by all cartographers in the first half of the eighteenth century. So far as we know, there is no evidence that anybody ever visited the Mitchigamea at that place.

La jeunesse, la plus leste que nous ayons veue, est n'eantmoins si modeste et si retenue que pas un ne s'émancipa d'entrer dans nostre cabane, se tenant tous à la porte sans bruit. Ils sont tous si bien faits et proportionnez que nous admirions leur beauté . . . perdismes pas un espingle chez neux.[105]

Unfortunately, it must be recalled that Father Membré was equally enthusiastic about the Illinois on first acquaintance. Later, after wrestling vainly for their salvation, he said some very hard things about them.

La Salle remained at Kappa several days,[106] two of which were given over to an elaborate ceremony in which possession of the Arkansas country was duly taken in the name of *Louis le Grand*, the docile savages looking on in uncomprehending delight. The column bearing the arms of France, erected for the purpose, seems to have been the object of their most touching regard.

Nous vismes après la fin de la cérémonie, qui dura toute la nuit et le 14e, les Akansas presser leurs mains sur cette colonne and puis s'en refrotter par tout le corps, pour tesmoigner la joye et la confiance qu'ils prenoient de la voir dressée dans leur village.[107]

On the return journey it was found that they had erected a stockade around this venerated post. The similar treatment accorded to the cross erected by De Soto at Casqui has already been noted (p. 355). The parallelism is rather striking.

At Kappa, two guides were provided to conduct La Salle to the Taensa, who seem to have been closely allied with the Quapaw at this time. Father Membré calls them "interpreters" as well, seeing that they spoke a little Illinois and understood a little Taensa.[108] On the way thither La Salle visited several more Arkansas villages — the accounts are not in agreement as to the number — but nothing of particular interest was recorded in connection with these brief visits. With events at the Taensa and farther down the river we are not at present concerned.

Notwithstanding the warm enthusiasm of the French for their new allies, the Arkansas, they tell us really very little about them, so little in fact that it is possible to quote them fully without unduly prolonging this section of the report. Italics are freely scattered throughout these passages in order to emphasize information bearing on questions of location.

It may be affirmed that these are the best-formed Savages that we have seen. They clothe themselves with Buffalo skins. They thatch their lodges with the bark of tree like the cedar, which reaches the height of a hundred feet without a branch [cypress], and of which they construct pirogues that run as well as bark canoes. They have peaches in abundance, cocks and hens, and many fruits unknown to us. We ascertained the civility of these people by the good reception they gave to the Chickasaw who was with us, although they are always at war with his nation. They gave us two interpreters to conduct us to the Taensas, and *on the way we passed two villages of the Enansa* (*Akansa*) *nation.* After passing the last village, our Savages killed the first alligator. Here ends all trapping of beavers and otters, which are devoured by those animals. As to the buffalo, it is found all the way to the sea.[109] (Italics are ours.)

They regaled us for five days with the best they had, and after having danced the calumet to M. de La Salle, they conducted us to the *village of Tongengan*, of their nation, *eight leagues from Capa.* These received us in the same manner, and from thence they went with us *to Toriman, two leagues further on*, where we met with the same reception.

It should be remarked that these villages, with *another called Osotouy, which is six leagues to the right descending the river*, are commonly called Arkansas. *The first three villages are situated on the Great River. . . .* They have cabins made with the

[105] Margry II, p. 208. Translation: "But, Reverend Father, one cannot say enough about the good qualities of these savages, who are joyous, honest and generous. The young people, the most nimble we have seen, are nevertheless so modest and retiring that not one of them tried to force himself into our cabin, but remained outside the door in silence. They are all so well-made and well-proportioned that we admire their beauty as well as their modesty. In a word, we didn't lose a single blunderbuss while we were with them."

[106] The time is variously given as three to five days.

[107] La Métairie's first procès-verbal. Margry II, p. 185. Translation: "After the ceremony, which lasted all that night and the next day, we saw the Arkansas rubbing their hands on this column and then over their bodies, to express the joy and confidence they felt in seeing it standing in their village."

[108] Letter from the Mississippi River, in Habig, 1934, p. 211.

[109] I Tonti, Anderson, 1898b, p. 75.

bark of cedar; they have no worship, adoring all sorts of animals. Their country is very beautiful, having abundance of peach, plum, and apple trees. Vines flourish there. Buffaloes, deer, stags, bears, turkeys, are very numerous. They even have domestic fowls. . . . [110]

On arriva le 12ᵉ Mars aux Kapaha,[111] village des Akansas, où, la paix faite et la possession prise, le quinziesme on passa *un autre de leurs villages, situé sur le bord de leur rivière, et deux autres plus esloignez dans la profondeur des bois,* et on arriva à *celuy d'Imaha, le plus grand de ceux de cette nation. . . .* [112]

There are also *three other villages of the same nation,* but we did not see them, except one which was on our way and where we were received in the same manner . . . . we took our leave from that place on the following day, the seventeenth of March.[113]

We saw a quantity of fowl there, and the peaches had been formed on the trees. They gave us some guides to go to the Taensas, their allies, 80 leagues farther down; and we arrived there on the 22nd, after having entered *two other villages of the Akansas, 6 and 3 leagues distant from the first.*[114]

The Akansas said that they had four villages, and showed by signs where they were. He found among them an Illinois slave, who served as interpreter. He told us they were called Akansa.[115]

The fourth day we departed. The Akansas escorted us to the water's edge, passing their hands over our bodies. This is their caress, . . . *We made about eight leagues and saw an Akansa village on the left. . . . We made six leagues more and reached the river named Akansa. Here is another Akansa village, where we encamped.* They gave the Frenchmen a good reception, begging them to remain to dance the calumet; but we thanked them and set forth early the next morning.[116]

Quapaw Villages in 1682: Summary

Leaving aside for the moment the problem of actually locating the Quapaw villages and the complicated hydrographic questions incident thereto, we can summarize the above testimony rather better than might be expected. There seem to have been at least three villages at this time and a probable fourth. At any rate, only three villages were visited by the expedition. The first two of these were on the Mississippi or on what La Salle and his people regarded as the Mississippi. The third was at or near what they regarded as the mouth of the Arkansas River. The first, or northernmost village, Kappa, was in all probability the Mitchigamea, visited by Jolliet and Marquette nine years before. It was located on the west side of the Mississippi, not far from the actual river bank. The second village, Tongigua, was 6 to 8 leagues below Kappa. Only Nicolas de la Salle tells us which side of the river it was on — the east. Not far below this, if we prefer Tonti's 2 or 3 leagues to Nicolas de la Salle's 6, was Tourimas, or Imaha, as it is called by La Métairie, who declares it to have been the largest village of the three. La Métairie is also sole authority for the statement that between Tongigua and Tourima, not right on the river, but back in the bush, were two more unnamed villages. However probable it may be that there were

[110] II Tonti, Kellogg, 1917, p. 298.

[111] La Métairie uses this name consistently, even indicating that the chief of the village was also named Capaha. The identity of this name with Garcilaso's version of Pacaha does not seem to have been noted by any of the narrators of the expedition. In the case of La Salle, the omission may have been deliberate. In the autograph fragment he attempts to show that his Mississippi River could not have been the same as De Soto's Chucagoa, and in the list of tribal names on the Mississippi which "were not known to the people of De Soto," he carefully omits the Capaha, by that or any other name.

[112] La Métairie's second procès-verbal, Margry II, p. 189. Translation: "We arrived on the 12th of March at Kapaha, one of the Arkansa villages. Having made peace and taken possession, we went on, passing another of their villages, on the river, and two others farther inland in the woods, and arrived at Imaha, the largest village of this tribe."

[113] Father Membré's letter from the Mississippi, Habig, 1934, p. 210.

[114] Tonti's letter from Michilimackinac, Habig, 1934, p. 219.

[115] This perhaps explains the circumstance that Akansa is an Algonquin word. Jolliet and Marquette apparently got the name, too, through the mouth of an Illinois-speaking Indian, possibly the same individual. Narrative of Nicolas de la Salle, Anderson, 1898a, p. 21.

[116] Narrative of Nicolas de la Salle, Anderson, 1898a, pp. 23, 25.

additional Quapaw villages at this time, it seems best to disregard this unsupported statement altogether. No one but Nicolas de la Salle tells us that Tourima was at or near the mouth of the Arkansas River, but in this he is backed up by later and better authority (Joutel). Actually, it was on the Arkansas, but within a few hundred yards of the Mississippi. "Six leagues to the right descending the river," which can only be interpreted to mean 6 leagues to the right of the Mississippi up the Arkansas River, was the fourth village, Osotouy. This is only mentioned by Tonti in his Memoir of 1693, and it is not unlikely that he is here interpolating information obtained on a later expedition. So far as the expedition of 1682 is concerned, then, we must disregard this village on the Arkansas, as we have no real proof of its existence at that time. Translation of these relative locations into terms of present-day geography will be deferred until evidence from subsequent voyages has been examined.

Tonti's Expedition of 1686: First Establishment at the Arkansas

Whether it be accurate to describe this, Tonti's second descent of the Mississippi — he was to make at least two more — as a relief expedition is a question we do not have to go into. We shall take Tonti's own word for it, that the news of La Salle's disaster on the Gulf in 1685 prompted the undertaking. However, it is no less certain that the faithful lieutenant also used it as an opportunity of furthering his own affairs by the establishment of a fur-trading post on the Arkansas, a strictly commercial venture. The sources for this second Mississippi voyage of Tonti are fewer and more barren of the kind of detail we are looking for than those of the La Salle expedition of 1682. Tonti is credited with being the sort of man who could perform prodigious journeys without seeming to be aware that they were worth talking about.[117] We may wish he had been a journalist as well, but console ourselves with the thought that the little he did write — when not tampered with by others — can be relied upon. Again we are indebted to Father Delanglez whose calendar of Tonti voyages lists all his writings in full.[118] Those in which the expedition of 1686 and the establishment at Arkansas Post are referred to are as follows:

1) Procès-verbal drawn up at the mouth of the Mississippi and signed by Tonti and as many of his party as could do so, April 13, 1686. In Margry III, pp. 554–58.

2) Tonti's letter to Seignelay, dated Montreal, August 24, 1686. Margry III, pp. 553–54.

3) Tonti's letter to Villermont, dated Montreal, August 25, 1686. In Margry III, pp. 559–62.

4) Autograph document granting to the Jesuits certain tracts of land near Tonti's establishment on the Arkansas, dated November 26, 1689.

5) Tonti's Memoir of 1693. Already cited as II Tonti, Kellogg (see p. 399).

6) Letter from Tonti to his brother in France, dated March 4, 1700. Printed for the first time in translation, in Delanglez, 1939, pp. 220–25.

Only the first of these documents described the expedition in any sort of detail, and will be drawn upon principally in the account that follows. However, a slight acquaintance with developments in La Salle's career subsequent to 1682 is a necessary prerequisite. After their return from the Gulf in the fall of 1682, La Salle and his lieutenant were very busy building Fort St. Louis on the Illinois and gathering about it the western allies of the French consisting of the Illinois, Miami, Shawnee, and other scattered fragments left in the wake of the Iroquois expansion. This was to be the western bastion against that relentless foe and at the same time the depot for a new commercial enterprise. For the outlines of La Salle's grand scheme had now taken shape in his mind. The western fur trade, constantly threatened by the Iroquois, who controlled the more practicable routes to Canada, would find a new outlet through the Mississippi at whose mouth he would establish a colony that would be the key to the trade of the vast interior of a continent. The new establishment was to be made and supplied direct from France by sea. To push this grandiose scheme at court, La Salle left the Illinois in the fall of 1683 bound for France. It was a propitious time. France was again at war with Spain, consequently any proposal for strengthening her position in the

[117] Delanglez estimates that Tonti traveled some 35,000 miles *on foot or by canoe* in what is now the United States and Canada (1944a, p. 256).

[118] Delanglez, 1944a, pp. 258–63.

Gulf of Mexico was bound to be received with favor. In fact, the minister Seignelay was already toying with plans for a movement against Spain in that quarter. La Salle, doubtless on the advice of his backers at court, quickly amended his grand design, up to now a perfectly reasonable one, to include a reckless scheme for the invasion of New Biscay. This attack was to be made overland from the Mississippi by a mixed force of French, Indians, and buccaneers from Santo Domingo. With all due allowance for the faulty geographical knowledge of the day, which placed the Mississippi a great deal too near the settlements of New Biscay and New Mexico,[119] even so great an apologist as Parkman is obliged to condemn this scheme as completely mad. The excuse that La Salle was gambling on quick peace to save him from having to carry it out only puts him in a still less creditable light. Be that as it may, the proposal found favor at court and La Salle was granted four vessels instead of the two he asked for. With these and nearly four hundred men and a few women he sailed from New Rochelle, July 18, 1684. The expedition, doomed by a divided command from the very start, was a lamentable failure. One ship containing vital stores was lost to Spanish pirates off Santo Domingo. The others (by accident or design) missed the mouth of the Mississippi completely by making their landfall too far west, on the Texas coast.[120] Here a second vessel was lost in the shallow entrance of Matagorda Bay. The naval commander of the expedition sailed back to France in a third. The fourth was lost under circumstances not wholly clear. La Salle was left with a pitiful remnant of his "colony," stranded on a miserably inhospitable shore, beset by hostile Indians, and without the least idea where he or his "fatal river" were.

Tonti, at Fort St. Louis on the Illinois, got the news of his patron's difficulties late in 1685, though he could scarcely have heard by then how serious they really were. His first move was to send a party of Indians to the Mississippi in search of news, but they returned in February without any. He then determined to go down the river himself. With twenty-five [121] French and four Shawnee, and as many provisions for La Salle as the bark canoes would hold, he left the fort on February 13, 1686. The first encounter with Indians after leaving the Illinois villages was some 70 leagues below, where they ran head-on into a war party of Quapaw.

> . . . les quels se mirent en défense, nous voyant; mais leur ayant fait connoistre qui nous estions, nous nous montrasmes le calumet les uns aux autres. — Je desbarquay où ils estoient, et leur dis le sujet de mon voyage. — Nous naviguasmes ensemble et arrivasmes à leur village le 19 Mars. Ils me dansèrent le calumet pour affermir la paix entre nous. Le village appelé . . . (sic), qui est à sept lieues au dessous, l'imita, et le village des Omma, à trois lieues au dessous, en fit en mesme.[122]

For the missing name of the second Arkansas village that honored Tonti with the calumet ceremony — the copyist was no doubt defeated at this point by Tonti's notoriously crabbed hand — Tongingua or Tongengan, as Tonti elsewhere renders it,[123] can be safely supplied. Omma, 3 leagues below, is Tourima already encountered under similar names such as Imma or Imaha. The fourth Arkansas village, Osotouy, is not mentioned, quite understandably, since it was not on the route down the Mississippi. It played an important part on the return journey, however.

The remainder of the voyage can be passed over very briefly. After various encounters farther down the river, with Taensa, Natchez, the mysterious Pischenoas, and the Quinipissa,

[119] A notion deliberately promoted by certain geographers and friends of La Salle to further his scheme. See Delanglez, 1938b, pp. 65–69.

[120] Whether La Salle designedly overshot the Mississippi as Delanglez maintains (Delanglez, 1938b, pp. 65–69) is one of those fine points of historical interpretation, on which we as archaeologists fortunately are not obliged to make up our minds.

[121] II Tonti, Kellogg, 1917, gives the number of French as thirty (p. 307).

[122] Margry III, p. 556. Translation: ". . . who on seeing us put themselves in a state of defence, but having made known to them who we were, we presented the calumet and they did likewise. I went ashore to them and told them the object of my voyage. We travelled together and arrived at their village on the 19th of March (1686). They performed the calumet ceremony to confirm the peace between us. The village called . . . seven leagues below did the same, and the village of Omma, three leagues below that, did the same."

[123] II Tonti, Kellogg, 1917, p. 298.

Tonti reached the Gulf where he looked in vain for traces of La Salle. On his return he stopped at the Yazoo, from whom he got a vague report that La Salle's ships had been seen taking on fresh water in Mobile River (which could not possibly have been true) but did not follow it up.[124]

At the Arkansas occurred an event of great interest in the history of the state of Arkansas, as well as of considerable importance to us in the present connection, since it bears on the location of Osotouy on the Lower Arkansas River. It is referred to very briefly in Tonti's Memoir of 1693.

> When we were at Akansas, ten of the Frenchmen who accompanied me asked for settlements on the River Akansas, on a seigniory that M. de La Salle had given me on our first voyage. I granted the request to some of them. They remained there and built a house surrounded with stakes.[125]

This Arkansas River grant is not mentioned in any of the documents of the 1682 expedition, nor in those of Tonti's relief expedition of 1686. Possibly Tonti was not sure at this time of the legality of his claim. He states it very clearly, however, in the document of 1689, in which a portion of this grant is offered to the Jesuits for purposes of establishing a mission upon it, and adds some details of great interest, which, however, need not detain us at the moment. Of the six traders established by Tonti at this post, the names of only two have come down to us, Jean Couture and Jacques Cardinal (called Launay),[126] the former apparently being the man in charge. We shall have occasion to refer to Jean Couture's Arkansas Post frequently in the pages to follow, since its precise location is a matter of crucial importance in the identification of the site of the fourth Quapaw village of Osotouy.

Our immediate interest is the fact that the evidence of the 1686 expedition confirms that of 1682. To be sure this is partly because the best account of the expedition of 1682, Tonti's, was written after 1686, but the correspondence with the contemporary accounts is sufficiently close. We are therefore justified in assuming that the locations of the four villages had not changed in the interim and that these locations were in 1686 substantially as given on page 402. We shall now see whether this assumption holds good for the following year, 1687, when the survivors of the La Salle disaster passed through the Quapaw country on their way to Canada.

The Return from Texas in 1687

While Tonti was looking for La Salle at the mouth of the Mississippi, La Salle was looking for the Mississippi, and not finding it. After each unsuccessful effort the plight of the Texas "colony" became more desperate until, at the end of the year 1686, La Salle determined to attempt with a small party the long overland journey to Canada via the Illinois. With the details of that tragic expedition we are not concerned, nor with the events that took place in the Cenis villages after the murder of La Salle in the following March (1687). It is sufficient for our purposes to note that seven members of the party, faithful to La Salle, finally succeeded in breaking away from the murderers and resumed the long march through east Texas to the Arkansas and on to Canada. These were the two Caveliers, the Abbé Jean, elder brother of La Salle, and the "young Cavelier," a nephew, hardly more than a schoolboy; Father Anastasius Douay, Recollect; Henri Joutel, the real leader of the party; De Marle, who was drowned before reaching the Arkansas; one Teissier and a young Parisian, named Barthelemy.

Three of this number left accounts, or at any rate such are attributed to them. That of Jean Cavelier, of which a second version only, printed for the first time by Delanglez,[127] covers the Arkansas portion of the journey, was written long after the event and "for purpose of procuring pecuniary aid from the French minister Seignelay." It contains statements flagrantly at variance with those of the first version as well as statements which, when

[124] In his letter to Villermont he says it was the Quinipissa who gave him this news (Margry III, p. 561).

[125] II Tonti, Kellogg, 1917, p. 308. This, if we except the Spanish settlements in California and the Southwest, was the first European settlement west of the Mississippi.

[126] Faye, 1943, p. 633.

[127] Delanglez, 1938a.

checked against independent trustworthy evidence are shown to be "inaccurate, misleading, or wholly false." [128] The account published in LeClercq's "First Establishment of the Faith in New France" [129] is attributed to Father Douay but actually follows Cavelier, so may be assumed to be equally untrustworthy. Joutel's account, on the other hand, fortunately the longest and most detailed, is universally regarded as one of the most reliable sources in the entire history of French explorations in the Mississippi Valley. We may proceed at once therefore to repeat what he has to say about the Quapaw villages as he saw them in the summer of 1687. The most complete text is that of Margry.[130] The only available translations, so far as we are aware, are simply reprints of the first English translation of 1714, which is based on Michel's French edition of 1713, which is itself a mere abridgment of the original journal.[131]

Coming from the country of the Cahinnio on the Ouachita River, Joutel and his oddly assorted companions, struck the south bank of the Arkansas at a point within view of the Quapaw village of Osotouy on the opposite shore. The first thing they saw was the tall cross before the door of Jean Couture's house hard by the village, and their satisfaction at seeing this evidence of civilization after two and a half years in the wilderness can readily be imagined. We will pass over the joyful events of the meeting with their compatriots and get down to those passages that concern the present inquiry.

> . . . nous apprisemes aussi que quatre villages composoient cette nation des Akansas et portoient différents noms. Deux de ces villages sont situez sur le bord du fleuve Colbert, et deux autres sur la rivière Akansas.
>
> Celuy dans lequel nous estions estoit sur une petite hauteur, où ladite rivière ne desborde point. La maison [of Jean Couture] est postée, à une demi portée de pistolet du village, sur un lieu un peu élevé; . . .[132]

Joutel goes on to describe the village and by inference all Quapaw villages, as markedly different from those already encountered amongst the "Caddo" tribes in that the houses are long arbor-like structures accommodating several families, each with its own fire. There follows a rather favorable description of the people and a very enthusiastic one of the country which must be read in relation to the poor country traversed in getting there. Then another enumeration of villages, somewhat repetitious but worth quoting.

> Les villages de la nation s'appeloient: le premier *Otsoté* [italics his], le second Thoriman, le troisiesme Tonguinga, et le quatrième Cappa, ... Quoyque cette nation s'appelast Akansa en général, il n'y a pas un desdits villages qui en porte le nom. Les deux premiers sont situez sur la rivière dite des Akansas, et les deux autries sur la fleuve Colbert, l'un d'un bord et l'autre de l'autre.[133]

Joutel did well to wonder that none of these villages bore the tribal name Akansa. He was quite naturally ignorant of the fact that the name is Algonquian and was given to Jolliet and later to La Salle by Illinois-speaking Indians.[134] What they called themselves at this time — later they knew themselves as Quapaw — is not known, a circumstance that has led some observers to characterize them as a confederacy rather than a single tribe. However, it must be admitted that the impression derived from Joutel, the only early informant who visited all four villages, is one of a closely integrated group. However, at the moment, we are not so much concerned as to *what* they were, but *where* they were, these Arkansas villages.

[128] Delanglez, 1938a, p. 8.

[129] LeClercq, 1881.

[130] Margry III, pp. 91–534.

[131] Joutel, 1896; Stiles, 1906. See References.

[132] Margry III, p. 442. Translation: "We also learned that this nation of Arkansas is composed of four villages, each having its own name. Two of these villages are situated on the Mississippi River and two on the Arkansas.

"That in which we were occupies a slight elevation that is never overflowed by the river. The house (of Jean Couture) is located about a half pistol-shot from the village, also on a slightly elevated spot."

[133] Margry III, p. 444. Translation: "The villages of this nation are named as follows: the first, Otsoté; the second, Thoriman; the third, Tonguinga; and the fourth, Cappa. Although the general term for the nation is Akansa, none of the said villages carries that name. The first two are situated on the river called Akansa, and the other two are on the Colbert (Mississippi) on each side."

[134] See footnote 115, p. 402.

Joutel's party arrived at Osotouy on the 24th of July. The news quickly spread to the other villages from which came chiefs and deputations, and the next few days were spent in negotiations for guides, a canoe, and supplies for the continuance of the journey, not to mention the equally exhausting entertainments of a purely social nature including the inevitable calumet ceremony. By the 27th all was arranged and at ten o'clock in the morning the party, augmented by their Indian conductors and Jean Couture — without whose services as interpreter none of this would have been possible — moved off down the river headed for the village of Tourima.

Nous arrivasmes sur les six heures du soir au premier village, ou plutost au second, nommé Thoriman, lequel estoit distant du premier d'environ cinq à six lieues.[135]

Here they were given the same rousing welcome as at Osotouy, and, although the Thoriman chief had already agreed at that village to send one of his people along with them, the thing had to be deliberated in council all over again. This and another round of feasts — Joutel says what they needed was several stomachs — occupied the following day, though Joutel found time to reconnoiter.

Je fus voir le fleuve Colbert, lequel n'estoit esloigné du dit lieu que d'environ une portée de fusil ou deux, lequel se trouve fort large et bien rapide. J'appris du dit Couture que ce village estoit dans une espèce d'isle, sur laquelle nous estions descendus par une fourche que fait la dite rivière, environ une lieue au-dessus, quoyqu'elle soit encore belle devant le dit village. Le dit Couture me dit aussi qu'un autre bras passoit derrière le premier village, mais qu'il estoit plus petit.[136]

The precise interpretation of this difficult passage will be attempted later. Among other things, it yields the important information that Touriman, while definitely on the Arkansas, or what Joutel thought was the Arkansas, was within a few hundred yards of the Mississippi, and here we are not obliged to add "or what he thought was the Mississippi." His use of the term *fleuve* and the characterization *fort large et bien rapide* could not conceivably refer to any other.

On the 29th they left Tourima accompanied by the chief and twenty of his stalwarts.

. . . et nous entrasmes dans le fleuve *Colbert ou Mississippi, que nous avions tant désiré* [italics his]. Nous le traversasmes de l'autre bord, où j'admiray la beauté du fleuve, qui a approchant un quart de lieue de large et un courant fort rapide. . . . Nous arrivasmes sur les onze heures du matin à l'autre village [Tonguinga], qui n'est esloigné environ que de deux lieues de celuy d'où nous estions partis; nous fusmes recues comme au précédent. . . .

Celui-cy estoit construit de la mesme façon que les autres, à la réserve qu'il n'estoit pas tout à fait si grand, ce qui fait qu'il porte le nom de Tongigua, qui signifie petit village, suivant que le nommé Couture nous le dit. Il est situé sur le bord du fleuve Colbert, à la droite en remontant. Le fleuve est fort large à l'endroit du dit village, quoyqu'il ne le soit pas partout.[137]

The importance of this passage cannot be sufficiently emphasized without touching upon certain geographic or hydrographic problems which will be discussed at length in the con-

[135] Margry III, p. 452. Translation: "We arrived at six o'clock in the evening at the first, or rather second, village, named Thoriman, about five to six leagues distant from the first."

[136] Margry III, p. 454. Translation: "I went to see the Colbert River [too bad we do not have a word that renders the importance of "fleuve"] only about one or two musket shots away [from the village], very wide and rapid. I learned from Couture that this village is on a sort of island to which we had come by way of one fork which the said river [Arkansas] makes about a league above, although still beautiful in front of the village. Couture also told me that another branch passes behind the first village, though somewhat smaller."

[137] Margry III, p. 457. Translation: ". . . and we entered into the river *Colbert or Mississippi which we had so much desired.* We crossed to the other side, where I admired the beauty of the river which is here close to a quarter of a league in width and has a very strong current. . . . At eleven o'clock in the morning we arrived at the other village [Tonguinga or Tongigua — Joutel is not consistent in his spelling of these names] which is about two leagues distant from the one we had just left. There we were received in like manner. . . .

"This village is built in the same fashion as the others except that it is not nearly so large, from which according to Couture, it bears the name Tongigua meaning little village. It is situated on the bank of the river Colbert on the right hand going up. The river is quite wide in the vicinity of this village, although this is not the case everywhere."

cluding pages of this section. We refer to the difficulty of reconciling contemporary accounts with present-day geography. It seems that either contemporary notions of geography of the region about Big Island were different than ours or the geography itself was different. For example Tourima was certainly at or very near what La Salle and his followers regarded as the mouth of the Arkansas River. Nicolas de la Salle was the first to give this location, and now Joutel confirms it in no uncertain terms. For reasons that will also later become apparent, we are equally sure that Tourima could not have been anywhere near the *present* mouth of the Arkansas River. There are only two ways of getting around this difficulty: either La Salle and his people had a different conception of the hydrography of this part of the Mississippi Valley, or the mouth of the Arkansas River was not in the same place where it is now. Delanglez, in considering this same question of the location of the Quapaw villages, adopts the first alternative. The map (fig. 72) will be useful in following what he says.

These and other descriptions of this section of the Mississippi by seventeenth century travelers will be quite clear if we remember that they conceived the confluence of the White River and Arkansas River quite differently from ourselves. We distinguish the mouth of the White River from that of the Arkansas, ten miles farther south; we call the channel west and south of Big Island the lower course of the Arkansas, and we call the river east of Big Island, the Mississippi. In the seventeenth century the junction of the branch of the White River [White River Cut-off] with the Arkansas was considered the mouth of the Arkansas River. Hence the lower course of the Arkansas was regarded as the western branch of the Mississippi, and our Mississippi was the eastern branch of the river.[138]

Delanglez does not give textual evidence for this assumption. It is very likely based on Faye (1943), but Faye does not give any evidence for it either.[139] That La Salle and Tonti did regard the Mississippi as having two branches separated by an island, and that in descending they chose the "west branch" is quite evident, but this real or imaginary fork was above the Quapaw villages and the island, "60 or 80 leagues" long cannot possibly have been Big Island.[140]

It requires a certain amount of brashness on our part to take issue with historiographers of the caliber of Delanglez and Faye on their own ground. However, we cannot avoid the conclusion that their theory of a west branch of the Mississippi around Big Island is no more than a working hypothesis resulting from an effort to interpret the documentary evidence within the framework of existing geography. Both writers, apparently, have failed to note that it falls down completely when applied to the most detailed and reliable testimony of all, that of Joutel.

The passage from Joutel last quoted simply cannot be reconciled with this particular west branch theory. Tourima would have to be placed in one of the angles formed by the junction of the Arkansas River and the White River Cut-off, or to be precise, at the junction of their counterparts of 1687. Let us assume for the moment that such was the case, and

[138] Delanglez, 1945a, p. 43.

[139] Faye, 1943, pp. 642–43.

[140] See La Salle autograph fragment in Margry II, p. 200.

"J'ay faict sans y penser cette digression au sujet de cette rivière, quoyque plusieurs autres m'ayent dit que Chucagoa tombe dans Mississippi, ce qui seroit possible, quoyque nous n'en ayons pas veu le confluent, parceque, au dessus du village des Acansas, il y a une grande isle ou plustost plusieurs qui ont soixante ou quatre-vingts lieues d'estendue. Nous prismes le canal occidental en descendant, et, comme nous avions laissé aux Acansas tout nostre équipage, il fallut reprendre le mesme canal en remontant . . ."

Translation: "I have unintentionally digressed on the subject of this river, although several have reported to me that the Chucagoa [De Soto's river] falls into the Mississippi, which may be possible, although we did not see the confluence because, above the village of the Acansas, there is a large island, or rather several islands, sixty to eighty leagues in extent. In descending, we took the western channel and, as we had left all of our gear at the Acansas, were obliged to take the same passage on the return voyage. . . ."

In an earlier publication than the one cited above, Faye deals exhaustively with this "west branch" and the special reasons La Salle had for preferring it. He places the fork at Buck Island (Island 53) about 40 miles below Memphis and says that the "east branch" followed the now forgotten pass called Buck Island Bayou to the Coldwater, thence by way of the Tallahatchie and Yazoo to the Mississippi at Vicksburg (Faye, 1942, pp. 924–27).

attempt to rationalize the passage with a hydrographic situation approximately that of today. The reader is urged to follow this carefully with the map (fig. 72). On leaving Tourima, our travelers would have entered at once into the Cut-off, and crossed to the other side. Note that it was right here that Joutel admired the beauty of the river that they had so long desired to see, saying that it was a quarter of a league wide (over a half mile) and had a rapid current, *fort rapide*, in fact. The present White River Cut-off is less than one-eighth of a mile wide and has a current so notoriously sluggish that it doesn't even flow consistently in one direction.[141] But this is not the worst difficulty — it might be argued that the stream carried more water in 1687. Tongigua, 2 leagues above Tourima, would be approximately at the junction of the Cut-off and White River. Just before arriving there, or just after leaving there next day (we have to anticipate a bit here), they would have noticed something peculiar. They would be going *downstream*, down the White River, instead of up, and before reaching Kappa they would have left the White and entered the Mississippi and found themselves going upstream again. Joutel's account leaves no room for uncertainty on this point. Between Tourima and Tongigua and between Tongigua and Kappa they bucked the current all the way. No one ascending the Mississippi in a pirogue is likely to have any doubts as to the direction of the current, much less Joutel who was never a careless observer. In sum, with no direct evidence to support the west-branch theory, and with Joutel's account so clearly at odds with it, there seems to be no alternative but to reject the theory.

We have left Joutel and his people rather long at Tongigua. Actually, they only spent the night of the 29th there, pushing on for Kappa in the morning.

> Le 30, nous partismes du dit village pour aller à celuy des Kappa, lequel estoit le dernier de cette nation et que l'on nous dit estre distant d'environ huit lieues. Comme le dit fleuve a son cours fort rapide, nous estions obligez de le traverser souvent pour éviter les grands courans, . . .[142]

On the way they met twenty canoes of Tongiguans, returning from some doings at Kappa. This and stormy weather slowed their pace, so that they arrived late that night at Kappa which Joutel describes in the following terms.

> Ce village est situé sur la gauche du fleuve, en remontant, sur une escore ou hauteur, qui a bien trente pieds de haut. Le dit village est plus grand que les autres. . . . Suivant ce que j'ay pu apprendre, il sortiroit quatre cents guerriers de ce village et bien trois cents des autres. . . .[143]

Events at Kappa, where Joutel and his companions remained for several days, however interesting in their own right, need not detain us, as they contribute nothing further to the problem of this study.

Before leaving Joutel, however, we cannot refrain from commenting again on the sober accuracy of this simple unlearned man. His information on the four villages tallies so closely with the data already derived from the La Salle and Tonti documents of 1682 and 1686 as to give us a fairly comfortable feeling of stability of Quapaw occupation, for this short period at least. Besides, it gives us an extra confidence in the additional topographic details for which we are dependent on Joutel alone, notwithstanding the fact that these details oblige us to reject certain assumptions that might have carried us along all right thus far and force us to look for new geographic explanations. Before doing so, however, we have the evidence of several later Mississippi voyages to examine.

[141] The White River Cut-off is in effect a distributary for both the White and Arkansas rivers. When the White is high and the Arkansas low, it flows south, with reverse conditions, its flow is likewise reversed.

[142] Margry III, p. 458. Translation: "On the 30th we left this village to go to Kappa, the last village of this nation, which we were told was about eight leagues [from Tongigua]. As the river here maintains a very rapid course, we were often obliged to cross from one side to the other to avoid the swift currents."

[143] Margry III, p. 462. Translation: "This village is situated on the left side of the river going up, on a bluff a good thirty feet high. It is larger than the others. According to what I was able to find out, it can put 400 warriors into the field, and about 300 others."

Tonti's Voyage of 1690

What might be called Tonti's second relief expedition, since one of its purposes was to contact other survivors of La Salle's Texas colony, may be dealt with very briefly. The only source is Tonti's Memoir of 1693 (II Tonti, Kellogg) and the only useful information it contains is an enumeration of the four villages — this time Tonti visited all of them — to wit, Kapa, Tongenga, Torimans, and Ossotoué "where my commercial house is." There is nothing in this brief account to indicate any changes in location, since Joutel's passage through the same four villages in reverse order three years before. This time Tonti went up the Arkansas River to his post at Osotouy whose inhabitants saw their patron apparently for the first time, then back down to the Taensa, thence overland to the "Caddo" country of east Texas. Failing to accomplish any of the objects of the expedition, he returned north by way of the Koroa and the Arkansas villages where he was laid up by illness for a couple of weeks. Unfortunately, he gives no details whatever of this stay.

The evidence of this voyage, negative though it be, is nonetheless important, for the next accounts we have, those of the missionaries whom Tonti accompanied to the Arkansas in 1698–99 indicate sweeping changes. The date 1690, therefore, marks the last picture we have of what might be called the unacculturated phase of Quapaw occupation. Between 1690 and 1698 English trade and the smallpox had reached them and they were never the same again. This would be the fitting point to bring this discussion to a close, since we are interested primarily in locating "unacculturated" sites. However, the later accounts, even in describing the changed conditions, reflect back on the earlier situation, and therefore cannot be overlooked.

Missionary Voyages, 1698–1700

Late in 1698 the indefatigable Tonti visited the Arkansas country again, this time as escort to a group of priests of the Foreign Missions bound for their pioneer mission posts on the Lower Mississippi. The party, besides Tonti, consisting of M. de Montigny, St. Cosme, and Davion, left Michilimackinac in September, 1698, and arrived at Kappa, now deserted and henceforth to be called "Old Kappa," in December of that year. From here we can let St. Cosme speak for himself.

> On St. John's day (December 27th), after travelling about five leagues [from Old Kappa], we observed some wooden canoes and a savage at the water's edge. As we were near and feared that he would take to flight, on seeing us, one of our men took the calumet and sang. He was heard in the village, which was close by. Some fled, while the others brought the calumet and came to receive us at the water's edge. On approaching us they rubbed us and then rubbed themselves, which is a mark of attention among savages. They took us on their shoulders and carried us into the cabin of a chief. A hill of heavy soil [mound?] had to be ascended, and as he who carried me was sinking under the burden, I feared that he would let me fall, so I got down in spite of him and walked up the hill. But as soon as I reached the top I was compelled to get on his back to be carried to the cabin.[144]

There follows the now familiar calumet ceremony, which lasted all that night. The account proceeds:

> We were greatly consoled at seeing ourselves at the seat of our missions, but we were deeply afflicted at finding this nation of the Acansças, formerly so numerous, entirely destroyed by war and by disease. Not a month had elapsed since they had rid themselves of smallpox, which had carried off most of them. In the village are now nothing but graves, in which they were buried two together, and we estimated that not a hundred men were left. All the children had died, and a great many women . . . though they are in a country teeming with game, we found none [no meat] in their villages, owing to the fact that they were weakened by disease and in continual dread of their enemies. . . .
>
> We remained two days and a half in this village, and after planting a Cross in it, which we told the savages was to be the sign of our union, we left on the 30th of November (December) for their other village, about nine leagues distant from this one.[145]

At this point, to the missionaries' grief, Tonti was obliged to leave them on account of pressing affairs at the Illinois.

> We slept at the mouth of the river of the Acansças, which is a fine one and distant two hundred and fifty

[144] Kellogg, 1917, pp. 358–59.

[145] Kellogg, 1917, pp. 359–60.

or three hundred leagues from that of the Illinois. On the following day we reached the village at an early hour. Six savages came to meet us with the calumet, and led us to the village with the same ceremonies as those observed at the first one. We passed two days there. This village seemed to be more populous than the first; there were more children in it. . . . We started on the 2nd of January (1699) and camped [again] at the mouth of the river, where the French who were returning would allow us but one day for writing.[146]

It may appear strange that after expressing joy at having reached the "seat of our missions" the good fathers moved on down the river without leaving one of themselves with the Arkansas. The reason is sufficiently apparent in passages not quoted above. Evidently, they promised the chiefs of the two villages that if they would bring their people together in one village they would be given a missionary, and it appears from other sources that de Montigny was chosen for that post.

Next year, 1700, the Arkansas villages were visited by the Jesuit, Father Gravier, on his way down to Bienville's Fort Mississippi. On October 30th he reached Old Kappa, "now recognized only by its old outworks (palisades?), for not a cabin remains." He camped a half league from the old town, probably above it, though the indication is not entirely clear, and the next day, the 31st,

We arrived, about 9 o'clock in the morning, at the Village of Kappa Akansea, who are on the 24th degree, according to Father Marquette's calculation.[147] The Village is half a league from the water's edge. Monsieur de Montigny had erected a Cross on the Hill, which is very steep and 40 feet high. After saluting the Cross and chanting the *Vexilla Regis* with the French [Father Gravier was escorted by five canoes manned by Frenchmen], we gave notice to the Akansea by 3 Gunshots; and in less than ten minutes, at the most, two Young men appeared with Swords in their hands,—closely followed by the Chief of the Kappa and that of the Tourima, and 20 or 30 well-formed young men with their Bows and arrows. Some had swords and 2 or 3 English guns. . . . The Chiefs invited me to go to their village, which consists of 40 cabins.[148]

There follows several pages of extremely interesting comment on the manner in which he was entertained at this village, and how he was urged to remain at least one night to receive the "Chief's Calumet," but Gravier was in a hurry to get on—and we likewise. He doesn't say where they camped that night, but the next day,

On the 1st of November . . . we continued our voyage and discovered the River of the Akansea, 8 leagues from the Village of the Kappa. The Sittèoui Akansea [Osotouy] are 5 leagues above Its Mouth, and are much more numerous than the Kappa and the Tourima; these are the 3 villages of the Akansea. That River [the Arkansas], which is to the North of the Mississippi, is very fine; it divides into 3 branches at a League from the Village of the Ousitteoui; it runs to the Northwest, and, by ascending it, one reaches the River of the Missouris, by making a portage.[149]

The last statement is interesting as an indication that at this time (1700) the White River was regarded as a branch of the Arkansas. However, Gravier did not ascend to Osotouy so the information on these three branches of the Arkansas a league below that village is not first-hand. Instead, he hurried on down the river to the Tunica, where we will not follow him.

This completes the list of sources that will be used in the present inquiry. The voyage of Le Sueur up the Mississippi in 1700 would perhaps be an important contribution, but unfortunately his journal is not yet available in print. Before undertaking a general discussion of the location of the original four villages, it may be well to attempt a synthesis of the not altogether congruent testimonies of St. Cosme and Gravier. As a matter of fact, there is more agreement than you would expect from a Recollect and a Jesuit. The only real difficulty is the number of villages existant at this time. St. Cosme implies only two—"we left on the 30th for their other villages"—one on the Mississippi and one on the Arkansas. Gravier speaks of the "3 villages of the Arkansas" but appears to be using the word in an ethnic sense

[146] Kellogg, 1917, pp. 360–61.
[147] As Delanglez points out (1945a, p. 44), this is an error of transcription for 34°.
[148] Jesuit Relations, 1900, vol. 65, pp. 117, 119.
[149] Jesuit Relations, 1900, vol. 65, p. 125.

not inconsistent with the possibility that two of the groups, Kappa and Tourima, were united in one village.[150] This assumption is supported by the fact that he was greeted on the river bank at "Kappa Akansea" by the Kappa and Tourima chiefs who escorted him to "their village." It would be in the interest of simplicity if we could show that the Kappa, on abandoning their village, joined with the Tourima, but it is plain from both accounts that the new village was not at the location of the Tourima of 1682–87. Thus is added a fifth possibility for site identification. As such, it may not be amiss to devote a little space to this village.

New Kappa, as we may call it for convenience, was on the Mississippi about 5 leagues below the site of Old Kappa, according to St. Cosme's estimate. Gravier merely says he camped within a half league of the old town and arrived at New Kappa at nine o'clock next morning, so it could hardly be more than 5 leagues — was probably less. The distance from New Kappa to the Arkansas River is given by Gravier as 8 leagues, but may have been less because St. Cosme gives the entire distance from New Kappa to Osotouy as only 9 leagues and Gravier states that Osotouy was 5 leagues above the mouth of the Arkansas. Neither tells us which side of the Mississippi New Kappa was on. Both agree that it was a small village and give the same reason — smallpox. Both accounts mention a hill, which must almost certainly have been an artificial mound, as St. Cosme says the chief's house was upon it, and Gravier says that it was 40 feet high and very steep. There is no possibility of a natural elevation of this magnitude within a good many miles of the spot. It is curious that this should be the first evidence we have encountered that the Quapaw were mound builders, and in a weak village, too, that has every indication of recent establishment.

The possibility that New Kappa may have been the older site of Tongigua must not be overlooked. It may be that all three villages, Kappa, Tongigua, and Tourima, hard hit by the smallpox, united at the site of Tongigua, the "small." The name Tongigua, however, is not mentioned in either of the missionary accounts.

There remains the question of Osotouy. Was it still in the same location as in 1682–87? Gravier did not visit it, so we may perhaps not rely too strongly on his statement that it was 5 leagues up the Arkansas. St. Cosme did, though not mentioning the place by name — to him it was just the "other village" — but doesn't give the distance, only that it was 9 leagues all told from New Kappa. There are too many discrepancies here. If we accept Gravier's 8 leagues from New Kappa to the Arkansas River, St. Cosme's "other village" could hardly be the Osotouy of 1682–87. Furthermore, St. Cosme's party camped at the mouth of the Arkansas and reached the village "at an early hour" next day. (Shea renders it "early next morning.") Two possibilities present themselves: St. Cosme may not have visited Osotouy, his village may have been Tourima which was on the Arkansas in 1687, though practically at its mouth, or Osotouy may have been moved down the river since 1687. As stated above, Gravier's 5 leagues need not obviate this possibility, since he didn't go up the Arkansas himself and may simply have been quoting an earlier authority such as Joutel. We shall have to leave this question in the air it seems. The important thing to note is that, while throwing some additional light on the location and nature (palisades?) of Old Kappa, and giving us a possible new village site to look for — with a 40-foot mound to help us find it — these accounts of 1698–1700 are no help at all in regard to the location of Tongigua, Tourima, or Osotouy. We cannot say with certainty, therefore, that any of the four Quapaw villages of the period 1682–90 were in the same locations in 1700.

[150] Shea's translation of St. Cosme (1861, p. 72) helps out at this point. Where Kellogg renders, "In the village are now nothing but graves, in which they were buried two together, and we estimated that not a hundred men were left," Shea has, "There was nothing to be seen in the village but graves. There were two (tribes) together there and we estimated that there were not a hundred men; . . ."

Summary of Documentary Evidence

Table 16, summarizing the evidence so far as it relates to Quapaw village locations, requires little comment. Double lines, separating the Jolliet-Marquette and the Missionary documents from those of the La Salle period, serve to emphasize breaks in the continuity, possible or actual. Thus, the Quapaw occupation of the short period 1673–1700 is really divided into three phases.

As to the first, there is nothing in the testimony of Marquette or Dablon that cannot be reconciled with the theory that Mitchigamea was Kappa and Akansea was Tongigua; neither is there any positive evidence in favor of these identifications. They must be regarded as unproved hypotheses.

The documents of the La Salle period are remarkably congruent. There is not one discrepancy of a nature serious enough to require explaining away. It can be stated with approximate certainty that the locations of the three villages, Kappa, Tongigua, and Tourima remained unchanged from 1682 to 1690, and the fourth, Osotouy, from 1686 to 1690. These locations, in terms of contemporary geography — what they may be in terms of present-day geography is another story — are as follows:

Kappa — West bank of Mississippi River, 6 to 8 leagues above Tongigua.

Tongigua — East bank of Mississippi River, 2 to 3 leagues above the mouth of the Arkansas River.[151]

Tourima — On the Arkansas River a few hundred yards from its mouth.

Osotouy — North bank of the Arkansas River, 5 to 6 leagues above its mouth.

In the third phase, which began sometime between 1690 and 1700, the following changes have taken place. Kappa and Tourima have been abandoned, their people, or what was left of them after a smallpox epidemic, combined in a new village, "Kappa Akansea," or as we have called it here, "New Kappa." Tongigua seems to have dropped out of sight altogether, its small population possibly submerged in the New Kappa village. The location of Osotouy seems to have been moved down the Arkansas to a point nearer what was then regarded as its mouth, but the evidence is far from satisfactory. New Kappa cannot be located on the evidence so far examined. It may have been the site of Tongigua — that it was a preexistent site is evidenced by the 40-foot mound mentioned by Gravier — on the other hand, it appears to have been higher up the Mississippi than the Tongigua of 1682–87. New Kappa is an interesting problem for future research. Our main concern here is to locate the four villages of the La Salle period.

Location of Quapaw Villages in Terms of Present-Day Geography

The Hydrographic Problem

Having said a great deal about Quapaw village locations of 1682–90 in terms of contemporary geography, we must now try to locate them in terms of our own. We have made it sufficiently clear that the two geographies are not the same. Either their notions of the hydrography of the region about Big Island were different from ours or the hydrography itself was. Delanglez' choice of the first alternative by assuming that La Salle and his followers regarded the Lower White River, the White River Cut-off, and the Lower Arkansas River, in other words the passage around Big Island, as a "West Branch" of the Mississippi we have rejected on internal evidence, specifically that of Joutel. Before suggesting alternative theories, it will be necessary to review the available information about recent hydrographic changes in this area. Understanding of this rather involved discussion will be facilitated by following it on the map (fig. 72).

Unfortunately, Fisk's plate 22, our usual reliance in such matters, does not give Lower Arkansas and White River channel positions previous to Stage 17 (1765), at which time in the area around Big Island they were substan-

[151] Nicolas de la Salle's estimate of 6 leagues may be disregarded, in view of the close agreement of the more reliable authorities, Tonti and Joutel.

tially the same as at the present time. In another context, however, he states that in Stages 12 through 15 the mouth of the Arkansas was "west of Rosedale, Miss." and the White River was tributary to the Arkansas at a point "five miles east of Yancopin."[152] This would put the mouth of the Arkansas in the vicinity of the present junction of Moore Lake and Knowlton Bayou. The mouth of the White would be about where the Cut-off joins the Arkansas today. According to Fiske's chronology, this would be the situation up to about 1600. Some time in Stage 16 between 1600 and 1700 the Arkansas found a new outlet to the Mississippi near Caulk Neck a few miles below its present mouth, and in the same period, but not necessarily at the same time, the White River was diverted around Big Island to its present junction with the Mississippi at what is now Montgomery Island, its old channel to the Arkansas becoming the Cut-off that we see today.[153] Whether these changes occurred before or after the La Salle period, we do not know; therefore, until we can reconstruct the channel situation about Big Island specifically for the years 1682–90, we must consider the location of the Quapaw villages in terms of two hydrographic possibilities. The earlier Stage 16 situation, i.e., with the mouth of the combined Arkansas and White rivers at Moore Lake, seems to fit the documentary requirements better, but not so conclusively as to permit us to rule out the later possibility, however desirable that would be in the interests of simplicity. It is not entirely impossible to rationalize the documentary evidence in terms of these later Stage 17 (substantially the same as present) conditions by assuming that La Salle and his people conceived of the Cut-off and Lower White River as a northern branch of the Arkansas, and that in consequence the new mouth of the White River at Montgomery Island was to them the mouth, or a mouth, of the Arkansas. We will consider this possibility in greater detail.

Location of Osotouy

Though we have the least documentary information about it, the village of Osotouy is the easiest to locate. Thanks to Joutel, we know that it was on the north bank of the Arkansas River on land that was never overflowed. Going up the Arkansas from its mouth (wherever it was), the first location that answers to this description is the southern extremity of Grand Prairie Ridge. The river now flows about a mile south of the ridge at this point, but there are abundant indications that it was formerly closer, and we may assume that such was the case in 1687. The edge of the ridge from its southern extremity, occupied by the famous Menard Site (17–K–1), for several miles northeastward along the bank of what is now Menard Bayou is practically a continuous village site, though catalogued by the Lower Mississippi Archaeological Survey as Wallace (17–K–3), Poor (17–L–3), Massey (17–L–1), and Ellerton (17–L–2). One of these sites is almost certainly the ancient village of Osotouy. Faye, partly by means of archival material which we have not seen, has located Jean Couture's post hard by the village with greater precision than one would think possible considering the documentary sources alone.

> The site identified is in Arkansas County, Survey 2351, Section 20, T8S, R2W, 33° 58′ 55″, 91° 15′ 22″ west of Greenwich. . . . Only this point on the upland conforms to the topography of Tonti — 1689 in *Mid-America*, XXI (1939), 236–237, and to the emphasized topography of Joutel as cited.[154]

The reference is to a Tonti letter already cited (p. 403), in which he offers certain portions of his Arkansas River grant to the Jesuits for the establishment of a mission. The relevant passage is as follows:

> Nous accordons . . . deux arpent de front et quattre de profondeur pour une chapelle et maison que nous Luy feront battir a ving arpent de nostre fort a L'est . . . en outre nous luy accordons quarent et deux arpent de front et quattre ving en profondeur alautre bord de la dit Riuier au Sus auec droit de Chasse et de pesche la ditte (verso) Ladit Concession Commensant a quinze arpent du village des Akanzea prenant de L'est a L'oest a L'est du dit village pour la plus grande Commodité du missionnair ou nous

[152] Fisk, 1944, table 5. "Stages in the Development of the Arkansas River."

[153] Letter of H. N. Fisk, December 16, 1948.

[154] Faye, 1943, p. 634, note 1.

luy feront pariellement battir une Chappelle et maison. . . .[155]

This passage, it must be confessed, is not crystal clear. If this were all we had to go on, it might be difficult even to say on which side of the river the village was located. Fortunately, Joutel's description of the post and village, as he first saw them from the south bank of the Arkansas River, leaves no doubt on this point.

Nous aperceusmes de l'autre costé, sur le bord de la dite rivière, une grande croix plantée comme sont celles que font planter les missionaires en France et ailleurs où ils vont. A l'endroit de la dite croix estoit une maison à la manière de France, et au dessous se trouvoit le village des Sauvages.[156]

With that uncertainty removed, Tonti's letter becomes a very useful document. It tells us exactly where the village was, in reference to Jean Couture's post, which Tonti rather grandly calls a fort. If the Jesuit grant was to be 20 arpents east of the post and 15 east of the village, then by simple arithmetic the village must have been 5 arpents east of the post. In fine, if Faye is correct in his location of Jean Couture's post, which unfortunately we cannot check, Osotouy, 300 yards[157] east of that point, coincides exactly with our Wallace Site (17–K–3). The archaeological aspects of this identification are discussed elsewhere (p. 418.

Location of Tourima

The location of Osotouy, at the Wallace Site or very near it, does not help very much toward a solution of the geographic problem and the location of Tourima, at the mouth of what was then regarded as the Arkansas River. Joutel reckoned the distance from Osotouy to Tourima at 5 to 6 leagues, which corresponds closely to Tonti's and Gravier's estimates of 6 and 5 leagues, respectively, in other words, some 14 to 16½ miles.[158] The distance from the Wallace Site to the old mouth of White River at Montgomery Island, following Stage 18 meanders on the Arkansas and Stage 17 meanders on the Cut-off and White River is about 25 miles, and to our postulated mouth of the Arkansas River at Moore Lake about 22 miles. The excess of actual distance over documentary estimates is not serious in view of the fact that we are not able to measure it along contemporary stage meanders, nor is the difference between the two measurements enough to weigh more than slightly in favor of the earlier Stage 16 solution.

What does appear to favor that solution, however, is Joutel's description of the day's voyage from Osotouy to Tourima, which is very difficult if not impossible to interpret in terms of Stage 17 hydrography. After leaving Osotouy, says Joutel,

Je remarquay qu'il y avoit un b[r]as de la dite rivière que nous rejoignismes, ce qui fairoit juger que le village, que nous venions de quitter, devoit estre dans une isle.[159]

This has to be considered along with another equally puzzling passage, already quoted (p. 414).

I learned from Couture that this village (Tourima) is on a sort of island, to which we had come by way of one fork which the said river (Arkansas) makes

[155] Tonti letters, 1689, p. 236. Translation: "We grant . . . two arpents of [river] frontage and four in depth for a chapel and house, which we will have built for him [the missionary] 20 arpents to the east from our fort . . . and in addition we grant 42 arpents of frontage and 80 in depth on the other side of the river to the south with hunting and fishing rights. The said concession begins 15 arpents from the village of the Akanzea going from east to west, i.e., to the east of the said village, for the greater convenience of the missionary, where we will in like manner [?] build a chapel and house."

[156] Margry III, p. 436. Translation: "We saw on the other side, on the bank of the said river, a large cross like those erected by missionaries in France or wherever they are. At the side of this cross was a house built in the French manner, and below it was the village of the Indians."

[157] Figuring an arpent at 11.5 rods (Webster's International, 2nd edition).

[158] Reckoning the league at 2.75 miles. Since writing the above, we have encountered the statement that the league in which distances were recorded by La Salle was the common French post league of the period, a unit of 2.4 English miles. (Butler, 1934, p. 4, footnote.) If this is correct, our estimates should be revised slightly but not sufficiently to affect our tentative conclusions.

[159] Margry III, p. 451. Translation: "I noted that there was a branch of the same river which we rejoined, from which it appears that the village we had just left (Osotouy) was on an island."

about a league above, although still beautiful in front of the village. Couture also told me that another branch passes behind the first village, though somewhat smaller.[160]

In terms of Stage 17 hydrography, these references to forks and branches would have to be interpreted as follows. The fork 1 league above Tourima would be the junction of the contemporary White River Cut-off and the Arkansas River. Note that this junction is a great deal more than 1 league above the contemporary mouth of the White River, which we are assuming for the moment Joutel thought was the mouth of the Arkansas. However, this is not the greatest difficulty. The "other branch," somewhat smaller than the Arkansas, passing behind Osotouy, can only be interpreted as the White River. Now it is perfectly clear in the passages quoted that this other branch was above the fork already discussed, just the reverse of the actual conditions in Stage 17. Remember that this solution requires that Joutel regarded the White River Cut-off and Lower White River as a continuation of the Arkansas. In going down, therefore, from Osotouy, the fork, i.e., the junction of the Cut-off with the Arkansas, would be encountered first, then the White River. There does not seem to be any way to get around this difficulty except to do away with the White River altogether, i.e., by supposing that the "other branch" was some smaller tributary or ancient cut-off like Menard Bayou and that Joutel passed the White River without referring to it.

We can get around these difficulties very neatly if we are permitted to assume that, at the time of Joutel's voyage, the old mouth of the Arkansas at Moore Lake was still open, but the new outlet comparable to the present Lower Arkansas had already been found. This would satisfy Joutel's reference to the "fork which the Arkansas makes," and its location would not be far from the league above Tourima that Joutel specifies. The branch that went behind Osotouy would be White River coming in "five miles east of Yancopin," most important of all, branch and fork would have been encountered in the order named. This is a pure postulation on our part, designed to fit the evidence given by our most reliable informant, Joutel. It is not backed up by the authority of Fisk who, as stated earlier, does not give the channel conditions around Big Island earlier than Stage 17, either in his plate 22 or in the letter already quoted. These are the conditions we have in mind in referring to the "Stage 16 solution," and it must be thoroughly understood that they constitute no more than a working hypothesis.

If the reasonableness of this postulation be granted, the first place to look for Tourima would be in the vicinity of Moore Lake and Knowlton Bayou, specifically along the outside bend of the prominent Stage 16 Mississippi meander at this point. We may infer that the mouth of Joutel's Arkansas was on an outside bend, because on entering the Mississippi the Indian canoemen immediately crossed over to catch the slack water on the other side. According to Fisk's plate 22, a considerable portion of the Stage 16 bankline in this vicinity can be traced, so there is a reasonable chance that the site still exists. When we talk about looking for it, however, we might as well admit to using the words in a figurative sense. Big Island is not the sort of place where archaeological sites are found, unless by accident. Second choice, based on the later Stage 17 conditions, would also be on Big Island, in the bight of land between White River and Montgomery Island, not quite so hopeless perhaps, since there are a few, probably ephemeral, clearings shown on the Mississippi River Commission quadrangle in the vicinity. After bringing the reader through all this tiresome and possible unintelligible argument, we have to conclude sorrowfully that the chances of actually finding the site of Tourima are so remote as to be practically nonexistent.

Location of Tongigua and Kappa

It is unfortunate that the only possibility of locating the two Quapaw villages that were on the Mississippi is by means of dead reckoning from a very uncertain Tourima with two alternative locations at the mouth of what was, or was thought to be, the Arkansas River. Nor are the prospects improved by the fact

[160] Margry III, p. 454. Translation is ours.

that we do not know whether to reckon along the reconstructed Stage 16 or Stage 17 channel of the river, and the two give very different results, owing to the big Stage 16 loop now occupied in part by Lake Concordia. These two sets of alternatives can be paired off, however, without doing violence to the probabilities of the situation, that is to say, from the preferred position of Tourima, at what we assume to have been the mouth of the Arkansas in Stage 16, we can reckon along the reconstructed Stage 16 channel, whereas from the "second-choice" location of Tourima, based on what we know to have been the Stage 17 situation, we can by the same reasoning reckon along the Stage 17 channel. We have already given our reasons for preferring the Stage 16 solution in discussing the location of Tourima. There are no additional details in the narratives about Tongigua or Kappa that would tend to affect this preference one way or the other.

Preferred locations of the last-named villages are shown on the map (fig. 72) in bold letters. That of Tongigua, on or near the present Montgomery Island, looks extremely unfavorable from the point of view of finding the site on the ground, owing to the very small amount of Stage 16 east bankline in this vicinity that has escaped erasure by subsequent meandering. However, not too far from this small remnant of Stage 16 bankline, we found a very interesting group of mounds, catalogued as Waxhaw (17–L–5). The site is, or was, outside the levee directly on the present river bank on an outside bend, consequently threatened with immediate destruction. It was covered by a heavy mantle of silt and no pottery collections could be made. At the time of our visit we had no idea we were so near a historic location or we surely would have put down some test pits. The site, if it still exists, would repay further investigation.

The preferred location of Kappa is somewhat more hopeful perhaps. Reckoning 10 leagues (Tonti's and Joutel's estimates) above Tourima along the reconstructed Stage 16 channel brings us to a point just below the southern extremity of Laconia Circle. Here again there is practically nothing left of the contemporary bankline on the west side of the river, the side on which Kappa was located. About 2 miles farther upstream, however, at Henrico, a short section of the west bankline at this stage can be traced within the levee protecting Laconia Circle. Our calculations could easily be that far off so there is a very slight possibility that Kappa is still there. The Lower Mississippi Archaeological Survey, in one day's visit, failed to verify reports by local informants of sites in Laconia Circle, but our search was hampered by bad weather and was by no means exhaustive.

Second-choice locations, indicated on the map by names in parentheses, are hardly more favorable from the standpoint of survival and ultimate identification. Tongigua would be near the preferred choice for Kappa, discussed above, but on the east side of the river, and in this vicinity there are but few scraps of Stage 17 east bankline left and these are outside the levees where survey conditions are extremely difficult not to say impossible. Kappa, on the other hand, just below Knowlton, Arkansas, might be found, if it should turn out that the Stage 17 solution is the correct one, which we doubt. The Stage 17 west bank here runs along for several miles just outside the levee and close enough to it so that a site near the river bank at this time, or part of it, might now be within the levee. Oddly enough, this is approximately the same location for Kappa proposed by Delanglez, who reckoned from what he thought La Salle thought was the mouth of the Arkansas, namely its present junction with the White River Cutoff. The extra distance he evidently made up by measuring along the Mississippi by some course other than that used by us.

Conclusions on the Location of Quapaw Villages of 1682–90

The rather meager conclusions of this long inquiry can be set down briefly as follows:

1) Osotouy is the Wallace Site (17–K–3) or very near it.

2) Tourima is on Big Island either in the vicinity of Moore Lake or in the northeastern corner of the island. In either case, the chances of finding it, if it still exists, are remote.

3) Tongigua is either on or near Montgomery Island or in the vicinity of Henrico, Arkansas, but in either case its chances of having survived are extremely slight.

4) Kappa is either near Desha, Arkansas, or a few miles below Knowlton, Arkansas. In either case, there is a possibility that the site exists and may yet be found.

5) All of these tentative locations, except that of Osotouy are the result of so many variables that it would be worth-while to search every scrap of Stage 16 and Stage 17 bankline left between Moore Lake and Knowlton, Arkansas. This has been put down on the program for future work by the Lower Mississippi Archaeological Survey, but we will be most happy if someone else will undertake it.

Aside from Osotouy, whose location we owe largely to the work of others,[161] our search has been so unrewarding as to lead to the very natural question, "why bother to print it?" One answer to such a question is that it is time the difficulties of village-site identification in the Lower Mississippi Valley were understood and appreciated. There have been many published statements about the location of Quapaw villages — those of Faye and Delanglez cited here are among the best — but none have shown an awareness of the extreme complexity of this problem. Indeed, it was not until the publication of Fisk's monumental report that such an awareness was possible. So that is one answer. The waste of a little ink now may save a great deal of ink later on. Another answer is that science proceeds by successive approximations. Although we have not successfully located any of the Mississippi River sites of the Quapaw, we have greatly narrowed the search. By holding strictly to the limitations imposed by the contemporary hydrographic situation, even when the same cannot be accurately determined, we have discovered what a large proportion of the adjacent flood plain can be eliminated from consideration. The next archaeological attack on this problem, whether by ourselves or others, will benefit by the experience.

The Archaeological Problem

So far as the present writers are aware, no attempt has ever been made to identify Quapaw culture in terms of archaeology. Speculations have been numerous. At one time or another the Quapaw have been credited with responsibility for most of the prominent mound sites in the area, but it has never been proved even that they were mound-building Indians. In the literature examined in connection with the present study, only two doubtful references to mounds have been encountered. These are Cosme's account of being carried up a "hill" on the back of an Indian, at the New Kappa village, and Gravier's reference to a "hill," 40 feet high and very steep, at the same place. Unless they are both referring to the steep river bank, which does not seem likely, this "hill" must have been an artificial mound. There is no possibility of the existence of a natural elevation 40, or even 10, feet high within a good many miles of New Kappa. However, it scarcely needs to be pointed out that the presence of a large mound on a Quapaw site does not prove that the Quapaw built it. In the present instance the probabilities are against it, as we have already pointed out (p. 412). Until better evidence is brought forward that the Quapaw built mounds, the safer guess is that this particular group had reoccupied an older site containing a mound or mounds built by some other people.

The possibility that the Wallace Site (17-K-3) may have been the village of Osotouy is the first definite lead toward the identification of Quapaw archaeology. In advance of any excavation of the site, it would be rather foolish to take it very seriously, but there are one or two interesting circumstances in this connection. As the name implies, it was on this site that we first picked up the pottery type Wallace Incised, which we now know to be a rather distinctive type with a limited distribution, which corresponds closely to the general area known to have been occupied by the Quapaw. Its chronological position is also suitable. Wherever found, it seems to be the latest pottery on the site. On the other hand, it must be admitted that we know altogether too little about the type. Our Survey efforts in the Arkansas River Lowland and Lower White River Basin at the start of the first field season (1940) were somewhat sketchy, nor did we have the Quapaw problem in mind at the time. We have long planned

[161] Faye, 1943.

to go back, but aside from a week devoted to stratigraphic testing at the Menard (17–K–1) and Massey (17–L–1) sites in 1941, we have not yet done so. So there is a chance that the coterminous distribution of the Quapaw and Wallace Incised is partly the result of our incomplete knowledge of the latter. In particular, we do not know how far up the Arkansas River it is to be found. Another disturbing fact is that we did not find any evidence of European contact on the Wallace Site, nor in the levels containing Wallace Incised on the Menard Site near by.[162]

Typologically, Wallace Incised looks like the sort of pottery that a Siouan group would bring into the lower Mississippi Valley. It has a vague resemblance to certain Oneota types, but this may be wishful thinking. Again, it must be confessed that we do not know enough about the type nor its range of variation. Any further remarks might appear to over-work the slender evidence. We may conclude by saying that the Quapaw authorship of Wallace Incised is at least an interesting possibility, at most a working hypothesis demanding further investigation.

1541 TO 1673: CULTURAL AND POLITICAL DISCONTINUITIES AND THEIR POSSIBLE CAUSES

The changes revealed by a comparison of the Spanish and French sources for this portion of the Lower Mississippi Valley are almost revolutionary in their nature and extent. They are not only in excess of the normal developmental changes that might take place in a period of a century and a half, but they are in the wrong direction, regressive rather than developmental. Therefore, they demand explanation.

Most striking of all these changes, perhaps, is the diminution of population. In the area which De Soto found occupied by the Quizqui, Aquixo, Casqui, Pacaha, and Quiguate, the French found only the Quapaw. Any one of these groups, except perhaps the Quizqui, appears to have had more and larger villages than the Quapaw. A far greater density of population also is indicated by the frequent reference, in the De Soto accounts, of the fact that from one village several others could be seen. Compare this with the known distribution of the four Quapaw villages strung out along the river with as much as 20 miles from one to another. Again, with all due allowance for exaggeration, the Spanish estimates of the Indian forces that opposed them are far in excess of the number of warriors the Quapaw could have put into the field. An estimate of the average population of the five tribes encountered by De Soto as equal to that of the Quapaw in the late seventeenth century — before the smallpox — would be on the conservative side. In other words, there was a decrease in population in this area amounting to at least eighty per cent.

On the cultural side the changes are no less interesting. It looks as though De Soto arrived on the scene at the climax of "Mississippi" development, using the word in its archaeological sense. There are frequent references to large platform mounds with chiefs' houses and temples upon them. Villages were stockaded and, in at least one instance, the walls were plastered with clay and provided with "towers," probably projecting bastions of the well-known Angel Site type. Such mounds and outworks were outside the range of Quapaw culture in the late seventeenth century. In all the descriptive material of the French period — which adds up to a fairly complete picture — there are no certain references to mounds and only one rather doubtful reference to a stockade. More specifically, there is Garcilaso's reference to what must have been a mortuary temple at Pacaha, with the ancestors' bones stored in boxes according to the custom of tribes to the south such as the Natchez and Taensa, which finds no parallel in the accounts of Quapaw culture.

[162] Moore found a few trade articles in graves near the Menard Mound, possibly on the Wallace Site itself, but the pottery associations are not given (1908a, p. 490).

Changes on the political side are equally significant. The seventeenth-century Quapaw were either a single tribe or a close-knit confederacy of small tribal units — the difference is purely a question of definition. The important thing is that the villages or tribes were associated together on terms of comparative equality, at least there is no evidence to the contrary. In the sixteenth century the pattern seems to have been entirely different. At least three and possibly four of the tribes encountered by De Soto were united under the hegemony of Pacaha. It seems quite definitely not to have been a confederacy of equals, but rather something in the nature of a small-scale and perhaps ephemeral empire. In short, in the period between De Soto and the French, political decentralization seems to have gone hand in hand with cultural disintegration.

This brings us back to a long-standing question already touched upon (p. 356), the possible identification of Pacaha (or Capaha) with the Quapaw. It looks as though we were piling up evidence against any such possibility. On the other hand, in looking for the possible agents of disintegration, we must not overlook the Quapaw themselves. There is a reasonable chance that the traditional explanation is correct, that the Quapaw actually did move down the Mississippi from a former home on the Ohio. If they had but lately moved into the vicinity of the Arkansas in 1673 it is not unreasonable to suppose that they may have been in the vicinity of the St. Francis or Pecan Point (depending on the De Soto theory favored) in 1541. If they came from the Lower Ohio they could have brought with them an advanced Mississippi type of culture. Specifically, they could have brought rectangular temple mounds and the bastioned stockade such as Garcilaso described at Pacaha. Granting too, that they may have been a numerically strong and warlike group at this time, is it inconceivable that De Soto found them just at the height of their power when they had brought their softer neighbors to the south under an uneasy and probably short-lived rule? Yes, it is inconceivable somehow. Whether it be the different style of the Spanish chroniclers, the distortion due to their use of the terminology of European feudalism, or whatever, one still feels that the Pacaha were not Quapaw nor ever could have been. The only way this question can be settled is by a careful check of the De Soto documents against a reconstruction of Quapaw culture from all sources, a task far beyond the limits of the present study.

If it was not the Quapaw who were responsible for the depopulation and cultural breakdown in this area, was it the Chickasaw? Here we are on firmer ground. Early references to the various small groups found by the French on the Yazoo and on the Mississippi below Vicksburg almost invariably end with the observation that they were brought to their low condition by the depradations of the Chickasaw. Of course we must bear in mind that to the French the Chickasaw were the "Iroquois of the South," the villains responsible for every calamity. However, the ethnic situation on the Yazoo alone is sufficiently revealing. Here at the end of the seventeenth century in a stretch of some hundred-odd miles of river valley the following splinter groups were found: Tunica, Koroa, Yazoo, Ofo, Tioux, Ibitoupa, Choula, Chakchiuma, and Taposa. The known history of all these groups is generally the same. Without exception, they appear to have been surviving remnants of larger aggregates, and in almost every instance the Chickasaw are mentioned as the cause of downfall. Most significant is the fact that they are divided among three linguistic stocks, Muskogean, Tunica, and Siouan, a pretty certain indication that they were thrown together by circumstance. In other words, the Yazoo River, in the late seventeenth century, appears as a refuge area crowded with remnants of larger groups dispersed and driven out of their former homes. What more reasonable than to suppose that some of their homes were in the ethnographic blank spaces of the Yazoo and St. Francis basins? There is not a little evidence in the case of some of them, notably the Tunica, Yazoo, and Ofo, that this was actually the case.[163]

The outlines of an hypothesis are beginning to emerge. In the century or two before De

[163] See Swanton, 1946, pp. 81 et seq. "Sketches of the Southeastern Tribes and Their Population," under appropriate tribal headings.

Soto, Mississippi culture in the northern Alluvial Valley reached its peak of development, as attested by the scores of imposing mound sites of this period. This generalization is based on the work described in this report, but can be extended on the strength of general information farther north to the mouth of the Ohio River and beyond. De Soto came onto the scene during this climactic period, but there is no evidence that his coming had anything to do with bringing about its end. Either shortly before or after De Soto, it is not yet clear which, the Quapaw came down the Mississippi and displaced some of the older inhabitants, thus beginning the process of decline, or hastening it, if already begun. This portion of our hypothesis is pure speculation and cannot be otherwise until the Pacaha-Quapaw question has been finally settled. At the same time a new power was arising in the hills of northern Mississippi and western Tennessee, the Chickasaw. Their warlike propensities were already established by 1540 as De Soto found to his cost. That they were subsequently responsible for the depopulation of all but the extreme southern and southeastern portions of the Yazoo Basin is practically certain and they may have cleared out parts of the St. Francis Basin as well. Only the Quapaw appear to have been able to stand up to them, though signs are not wanting that they too were weakening at the close of the seventeenth century. With tribal disintegration and depopulation came a falling off from what appears archaeologically at least a more advanced pattern of culture. Platform mounds continued to be built but on a smaller scale, in fact, it is doubtful if any of the important mound sites in the Yazoo and St. Francis basins were established after 1541. By the time of the coming of the French a radically different picture of tribal distribution is presented, the most conspicuous feature of which is the large number of small shattered groups living on the southern periphery of the area each having its rather pathetic tradition of former greatness.

The temptation is strong to relate this series of events to one of the familiar recurrent patterns of history, to see in them another, perhaps attenuated, example of "the steppe and the sown." That the older and more populous tribes were more dependent on agriculture than their destroyers is a reasonable inference. There is even some positive evidence to this effect. The fact that when the Spaniards assaulted Quizqui the men were all away in the fields has already been emphasized in this connection, and we know that among the seventeenth-century Tunica, the men did the farming. These facts alone indicate a more advanced state of agriculture, and a corresponding decrease in hunting on the part of the older river-bottom tribes. That such a development was attended by a falling off in military prowess is another reasonable inference. That no such falling off was exhibited by the Chickasaw in the clay hills is an historic fact, nor by the Quapaw for that matter, whose proximity to the prairies of the Western Lowland and Grand Prairie Ridge prevented theirs from becoming a pure flood-plain type of culture. Without trying to wring out more meaning than the facts will bear, it does appear that environment has played its traditional role in these events. Here again is demonstrated, in microcosmic fashion, the lesson that history never tires of vainly repeating, that the land can be too good to the people who dwell upon it, that a reasonable amount of adversity may be a condition to survival.

SECTION X
SUMMARY AND CONCLUSIONS

SUMMARY AND CONCLUSIONS

THE results of the first phase of a continuing survey program in the northern part of the Lower Mississippi Valley have been presented in the foregoing pages under various headings written by various hands not always animated by identical points of view. The effect has been perhaps to create the impression that we have settled many questions, whereas we have all too often only settled the same questions in several different ways. This cannot fail to have left the reader, provided he has not already left the report, in considerable confusion, and it now becomes our duty to straighten him — and ourselves — out. What is required at this point is a general summary of what the three authors can agree on, or failing that, at least to bring together their conflicting interpretations so the reader may compare and judge between them. Up to now, we have attempted to keep such disagreements in the background by writing more or less consistently in the first person plural, giving an effect of praiseworthy unanimity. We have bribed each other's silence by promises of an opportunity to express dissenting opinions and prejudices in the concluding section. A change of style is therefore indicated if we are to give scope to these individual interpretations. From here on, the third person singular will frequently appear in order to make clear which author's point of view is being expressed.

The plan of this concluding section is as follows. We shall first review briefly what we have done and what we, each and severally, think of it. Following this, we shall present a summary of the archaeology of the area period by period, a sort of culture-historical reconstruction, in which we shall use any information that is available whether obtained by us or others. Finally, we shall conclude by attempting to fit our findings into the general picture of Eastern archaeology with a few observations in regard to their bearing on the over-all chronological problem.

AUTHORS' REVIEW

It may not be good form to forestall adverse criticism by offering a review of one's own work, but in the case of a report that makes no pretense of finality it is excusable. Nothing is more exasperating than being criticized for failure to succeed in something one has not tried to do. That is sure to happen to the Lower Mississippi Archaeological Survey. We have merely presented a progress report and are as dissatisfied with it as the most carping critic could possibly be. This is our opportunity for expressing that dissatisfaction, but, since there are three of us, it takes different forms and applies unequally to different sections of the work. A rather detailed review is required for which we beg, once more, the reader's indulgence.

In the long opening section, dealing with the geographical conditions of the Survey Area, a great deal of emphasis was placed on the physical differences between the various areal subdivisions and it was confidently predicted that these differences would be reflected in the archaeology. We now have to explain why this expectation has not been fulfilled, or at least why very little more was said about it. At the time when Phillips was writing this section, inspired by the enlightened environmentalism of Kroeber, Ford was carrying out the seriation analysis described in Section V, in which Mississippi River Commission quadrangles were used as convenient units of area and grouped into five subdivisions on a purely empirical basis. In other words, while Phillips was saying all those fine things about natural conditions and their effect on culture and the shape of cultural distributions, Ford was working out a grouping quite independent of natural subdivisions, in many cases crosscutting them, which nevertheless seemed to give satisfactory results, and eventually became the framework for most of our archaeological generalizations about the area. Phillips is, not unnaturally, unhappy over this and harbors a suspicion that an analysis that took these natural subdivisions more into account might have produced better results. However, it may be pointed out here that the work of the Survey has so far been confined almost entirely to the St. Francis and Yazoo basins which are both comprised in one major type of area, to wit, flood plain of Mississippi-Ohio derivation (see classification, p. 20). Very little work was done in flood-plain areas of "other than Ohio-Mississippi" derivation. A few sites were located in the lower part of the Arkansas River Lowland, but the Survey was not carried into the White-Black River Lowland nor the Boeuf Basin. Thus, no opportunity is yet afforded to make cultural comparisons between these two major categories of flood plain. From general information, however, it can be fairly confidently predicted that the flood-plain areas of other than Mississippi-Ohio derivation are not going to show as dense an occupation, particularly in the Mississippi Period, as the more fertile portions of the flood plain covered by the Survey. As for the older alluvial plains and upland remnants, we have produced no new comparative information at all. Thus, it cannot be said that the moderate environmentalist point of view in Section I has been refuted. It has remained unfulfilled simply in the sense that it has not been tested.

The pottery classification described in Section III is a joint responsibility. We all had a hand in it and are all equally dissatisfied with it. This is normal. The archaeologist who thinks he has achieved a final classification of anything is a rare and probably untrustworthy individual. Most of the shortcomings of our classification have been fully exposed in the type descriptions. Our guess is that very few of our types will stand up when more and better material is available. Many of them will break down into more specialized groups, a few (we may hope) will be combined into more general groups. It is not likely that the total number of types will be reduced. The outlook for the Southeast as a whole, so long as present typological methods remain in favor, is not pleasant to contemplate. Where we are now counting types in tens, they will be counted in hundreds. However, the proof of the typing is in the using. Our classification cannot be too bad or it would not have produced the consistent patterning of types through time that is shown in the seriation and stratigraphic analyses of Sections V and VI. It seems to have been equal to the purposes for which it was devised, which is all that should be asked of any classification.

Section IV presents a series of distributional studies of certain characteristic pottery forms and designs that have a special interest from the wider point of view of relationships with Mesoamerica and the Southwest. These have been entirely the work of Griffin and have led him to several important conclusions, to wit, that in the Mississippi Period there were more or less direct contacts between the northern part of our area and the Southwest, that these contacts may have begun fairly early, as early as Developmental Pueblo, that the exchange of traits may not have been entirely in one direction, and that the route was not through Texas. It is Griffin's belief that in the recent emphasis of Southeastern students on connections between the Southeast and Mesoamerica, these important evidences of Southwestern connections have been overlooked. His co-authors heartily endorse this opinion. There are in fact many other ceramic traits not covered by Griffin, coming under the heading of miscellaneous small pottery objects, such as disks, ladles, trowels, etc., that point the same way. But to agree that this is a neglected phase of research is not to regard it as *the* answer to a long-standing problem. Griffin's findings in this section present one more evidence of the complexity of processes that underlies any focalization of traits that we refer to as "culture." There is enough of this kind of evidence already to make an expression such as "the origin of Mississippi culture" look faintly ridiculous.

The seriation analysis described in Section V is at once the most fruitful source of results in the report and conflict among the authors. Results, because the chronological framework upon which our findings are hung derives from it; conflict, because, although we all profess belief in the general validity of the method, no two of us have the same degree of confidence in its results. Before commenting further on the nature of our disagreement, it may be well to point out wherein the seriation technique differs from other methods of analysis. The usual method of organizing archaeological data over a large area is to isolate culture groupings, "phases,"[1] "foci," or whatever one chooses to call them, by combining units, usually sites or levels within sites, and to rationalize on the basis of fairly complete trait inventories the inter-relations of these groupings in terms of space and time. This is an inadequate statement of a complicated procedure but the essential features are that it is a process of combination, of "building-up" from smaller to larger units, and that a good deal of detailed information is needed even to begin it. We have not yet made an attempt to organize our findings in this way; in fact, it may be doubted whether it is possible at the present time. If we have occasionally referred to groups of sites or localities by some convenient designation outside of the seriation framework, no classificatory significance has been implied. The grouping in question is valid only for the particular matter in hand.

The seriation method, on the other hand, makes an effort to grasp the main outlines of the prehistory before the details are known, by means of graphic delineation of the behavior of one trait complex, in this case pottery, through time. Having established the over-all pattern, the stream of time represented is cut into units at points where shifts in patterning occur. Thus, in a sense, the seriation method works from the general to the particular, the reverse of the conventional method, and is therefore well suited to an initial attack on an area. The contrast must not be over-stressed, however. The results are not as different as the methods. The "periods" derived from seriation are not as different conceptually from "foci" as one might think. They have typological as well as temporal implications, since the cuts are made at points where typological shifts affect the general pattern. Ford stands on the unshakable philosophical ground that none of these concepts have any cultural "reality" anyhow, all being arbitrary constructs of the archaeologist. If there are differences they are differences of degree not of kind. This is consistent with his view that the predominating characteristic of culture is continuity both in space and time. To the extent that such a view is correct, any divisions spatial or temporal, however derived, must of course be wholly arbitrary.

As applied specifically to pottery, the only thing we are in a position to generalize about, Ford's idea is that it was developing in a continuum throughout its entire history in the Mississippi Valley, that whether new types evolve by modification of older ones or come in as new ideas from outside, they take their place in an uninterrupted cultural flow. The logical consequence of such a view is that, in most cases a "mixed" pottery complex represents a single brief span of time on that continuum, an "instant" for all practical purposes, when both elements of the mixture were being made and used side by side. The importance of this postulation for the seriation method can hardly be exaggerated. Ford does not deny that mixed complexes sometimes do result from reoccupation of sites. Such collections he frankly banishes from his graphs and says so (p. 233).

Griffin and Phillips, on the other hand, while not rejecting the general theory of continuity, are inclined to feel (with emphasis in order named) that there are more instances of mixture through reoccupation of sites than Ford has recognized. In particular, as pointed out in the individual sections written by them, they have tended to see indications of at least one significant break in the otherwise placid stream of pottery continuity at the point where the tempering material shifts from clay to shell, in other words between the Baytown and Mississippi periods. They feel that, by including mixed collections on the graphs, Ford has effected a spurious transition that seems to prove his continuity hypothesis, but in reality leaves the question open. Another way of putting it would be that the seriation technique, being based on the assumption of continuity, is unable to cope with a "break"

[1] In the sense in which this term is used in Mesoamerica and the Southwest.

of the nature described above, consequently, to establish whether such a break is really there or not, some other method of analysis is required. The upshot is that this compact majority of two, while perfectly willing to endorse and even use the results of the seriation analysis, do not regard the evidence it shows of such continuity as final.

Griffin would like to have it stated that he started with the opinion that there was a break between the earlier horizon and the Mississippi Period. Phillips only came to it gradually as a result of his independent analysis of stratigraphic collections in Section VI, where the reader may follow his painful lucubrations on the subject. One might have thought that stratigraphy would have settled the Baytown-Mississippi continuity question one way or the other. It did not. The only conclusion we are able to agree on is that the subjective element enters into the stratigraphic method just as surely as into the seriation method. That more stratigraphic cuts gave evidence of discontinuity than the reverse Ford attributes to a bias on the part of Phillips in favor of that solution. Phillips naturally protests his innocence, but the reader will have to decide between them. We have perhaps made too much of this issue, which, after all, involves only one point on the time scale. In general, the results of seriation and stratigraphy were in satisfactory agreement.

The experimental correlation of archaeological and geological time scales presented in Section VII is so tentative, and the various possibilities of error are so thoroughly exposed in that section, that nothing further need be said about it here. We are all agreed that the results are sufficiently promising to justify further work along these lines. We cannot predict that this is going to result in a new archaeological technique that will supersede those now in use in the area. What is more likely is that by using the channel sequence as a control in seriation and stratigraphic studies some of the present difficulties of interpretation that have been so fully confessed above will be eliminated.

More important from a long-range point of view is the possibility that correlation of archaeology and hydrography plus C^{14} dating will result in an accurate absolute time scale for the entire Mississippi Alluvial Valley, which would be as welcome to the hydrographer as to the archaeologist.

The study of spatial and temporal distributions of sites as to type in Section VIII is another promising approach. In its present form it can be no better than the dating on which it is based. The difficulty of dating sites from surface collections whether by seriation or any other method has been repeatedly emphasized and the lack of agreement among the three authors as to the dating of individual sites freely exposed. The period date for the first appearance of new types of mounds and site plans, as set forth in Section VIII, cannot be regarded as final. Phillips and Griffin, for example, hold reservations concerning the appearance of small ceremonial centers with rectangular platform mounds as early as the middle Baytown Period (E–D). On the other hand, there can hardly be any question about the relative order of appearance of the various types of sites, and the population distributions during the several periods indicated by the maps (figs. 64 to 69) is probably in the main correct. With more and better data of the same sort, some very interesting demographic questions might be indicated.

The long Section IX dealing with the problems — but containing no solutions — of the identification of sites from documentary sources might, in its author's (Phillips) opinion, better have been published separately, if at all. It is principally due to Griffin that it has been included here. He feels that, notwithstanding the meager results, it is a valuable contribution as an object lesson for archaeologists who brashly enter the field of history. It also contains leads for further research. The search for Quapaw sites of the contact period was shown to be difficult but not quite hopeless. The Lower Mississippi Survey has not been back in the Lower Arkansas region since this study was made. In particular, further investigation of the Wallace Site (17–K–3) is indicated, but the entire area should be thoroughly searched as well. The importance of establishing the latest pottery typology in this area is sufficiently apparent in the uncertainties and disagreements that crop up whenever the late Mississippi Period falls under discussion. In some respects this most recent period, which ought to be the best known, has been the hardest to deal with chronologically. This will continue to be the case until we can fix its terminus by means of a few good contact sites.

SUMMARY BY PERIODS

We have little that is really new to contribute to the prehistory of the Lower Mississippi Valley other than an outline of ceramic chronology and the information derived from observing and mapping a large number of sites. Nevertheless, it seems worth-while to present a summary of the local archaeology by periods, for which we shall draw on whatever information is available. Local evidence for the earlier periods is almost entirely lacking. These *lacunae* we shall attempt to fill by guesswork based on evidence from neighboring regions. These guesses may or may not be proven correct by further investigations, but we do not expect they will be far from the truth. At the moment, they will serve as a step in the gradual approximation to the correct picture of the prehistory of the region.

The Pre-ceramic Period (Before Time G)

While there is so far little indication of a pre-ceramic period in the Survey Area, such sites are presumed to exist, and, indeed, a few sites, without pottery but with large projectile points, were noted, and meager collections made therefrom. It is also likely that such stone implements as are found on the early ceramic sites will in large measure be carry-overs from pre-ceramic occupations. We found actual evidence of such an occupation at only one site, Jaketown (20–O–1). This has been described in Section VI and it may be recalled that the evidence, while convincing, is rather slight. It consists of deep deposits containing numbers of the baked-clay artifacts known as "Poverty Point Objects" underlying strata that yielded our earliest ceramic complex, the Tchula. There cannot be much doubt that more pre-ceramic remains will be found when they are searched for carefully. Such evidences have been described by Webb and his associates in the not too distant Pickwick Basin on the Tennessee River to the northeast;[2] by Collins and later Ford and his fellow workers to the southward near the mouth of the Mississippi River;[3] by C. H. Webb in northern Louisiana[4] and by Harrington[5] and later Dellinger[6] in the bluff sites in the Ozarks to the northwest. One promising area for such work is the Lower Yazoo River where shell middens dating as early as middle Baytown are found. These collecting stations which proved so attractive at that time were probably utilized in earlier times as well, exactly as in the Tennessee Valley. A further reason favoring the Yazoo is the greater age of the meander belt which is now occupied by that river. According to Fisk, the Yazoo meander belt was somewhat higher 2000 years ago in relation to the then young, present Mississippi meander belt. The Mississippi floods would not then have risen as high in the Yazoo area as in more recent times and for this reason we may suppose the area to have been more attractive for habitation in this early period. So far only one of these shell middens has been tested stratigraphically, Shell Bluff (19–O–2).

This is the regrettable state of knowledge on the subject of the Archaic in the Survey Area. However, we shall not let our attempted reconstruction be stopped by the lack of local information. As Haag[7] has pointed out, the culture which immediately precedes the appearance of pottery in the Southeast has a relative degree of uniformity. We may infer that resemblances on this time level between the cultures found in Tennessee, Kentucky,

[2] Webb and DeJarnette, 1942.

[3] Ford and Quimby, 1945. The ceramic-bearing Tchefuncte culture which they describe shows close relationships with the non-ceramic "Archaic Horizon" recently summarized by Haag (1942b). The Copell Site excavated by Collins (1941) and included by Ford and Quimby as a site of the Tchefuncte culture may be a pre-ceramic site.

[4] Webb, 1948.

[5] Harrington, 1924.

[6] Dellinger and Dickinson, 1942.

[7] Haag, 1942b, pp. 211–14.

Georgia, and Louisiana are greater than at later periods. Thus, it seems fairly safe to do some interpolation from the known materials and predict what the archaeologist will find when pre-ceramic sites are discovered here.

In an attempt to provide a probable complex for the pre-ceramic level, we can examine the evidence recently gathered from the Archaic sites immediately to the west, south, and east. The closest is that known as the Poverty Point Site described by Clarence H. Webb,[8] located in West Carroll Parish, Louisiana, on the west side of Bayou Macon. Its geographical proximity to the Survey Area, plus the appearance of the diagnostic Poverty Point baked-clay objects in the bottom levels of Jaketown (20–O–1), indicates that for the southern part of the Survey Area this is the pre-Tchula culture. An outstanding feature of the Poverty Point Site which covers some 200 acres is the considerable evidence of stone vessels, at least two to three hundred different vessels being counted by C. H. Webb alone. The steatite and sandstone was almost certainly derived from the southern Appalachians, and a close connection with the northern Alabama "Archaic (3)" is evident.[9] The flint projectile points are large-stemmed and corner-notched forms with narrow, medium, and wide blades. They resemble dominant forms found in "Archaic (3)" and "Pottery (1)" levels of northern Alabama. They also resemble some of the Tchefuncte types. There is, however, more variety of flint drills, flint gravers, large leaf-shaped, trianguloid scrapers, two-holed gorgets, stone beads or red jasper made in tubular, barrel-shaped, rectangular, and bird effigy forms, crinoid stem beads, hematite plummets of both grooved and perforated styles, pebble pendants, stone and clay tubular pipes, crude clay human figurines, and the full grooved axe.

Noticeably absent from this list is any mention of bone or shell artifacts which are quite common in the shell middens throughout the Southeast. Perhaps this will be changed with excavation at Poverty Point.

The Poverty Point Site is oriented to the northern Alabama area not only by its typology, but also because of its emphasis on stone raw materials. The Poverty Point baked-clay objects and their homologous relatives in the Sacramento Delta of California are probably the result of similar reaction to a stoneless environment on the part of groups accustomed to stone-boiling, or as some archaeologists have called it, "hot-rock cooking." [10]

C. H. Webb has also commented on the presence of a similar complex but on small sites in northwestern Louisiana. He has evidence of the presence of Folsomoid and Scottsbluff-like points in northwestern Louisiana, but so far there is no record of such points having come from the Lower Alluvial Valley of the Mississippi River, let alone the more limited Survey Area.

South of the Survey Area on the Gulf Coast the Copell pre-ceramic material includes chipped knives, large stemmed points, retouched flake scrapers, elliptical bar weights, crude boatstones, deer bone awls, socketed bone and antler projectile points, antler atlatl hooks, perforated mammal penis bones, raccoon penis awls, tubular shell beads, use of asphaltum, Busycon shell vessels, and inner whorls of conch shells.

To the east in northern Alabama, Webb and DeJarnette's recently named "Archaic (3)" begins, according to these authorities, with the introduction of sandstone and steatite vessels. Projectile points are mainly large, stemmed forms with straight bases and narrow to broad blades. They were used with antler atlatl hooks and various stone atlatl weights. Antler spear points, disk shell beads, shell pendants, stone cylindrical and barrel-shaped beads, stone gorgets, steatite and sandstone bowls are other artifacts of the period. Burials are flexed or partially flexed, placed in circular graves, often in a sitting position. Some burials were headless or otherwise dismembered. Presumably, it is possible to add to this list the following traits which appear in this horizon: grooved axes, ground stone celts, conical tubular pipes, bell pestles, grooved weights or sinkers, flaked celts, "hoes" and "side-notched hoes" or choppers (which seem to have preceded the grooved axe), antler-tine flakers and drifts, bone fish

[8] Webb, 1948.

[9] Webb and DeJarnette, 1948a.

[10] Webb and DeJarnette, 1948b, p. 18.

hooks, and many types of bone awls including the split bone awl. Boatstones are very rare while bannerstones are somewhat more common. The former is more common to the south and the latter is more typical toward the north.

The subsistence pattern in this early period was undoubtedly hunting and gathering. Although a small amount of agriculture may have been practised,[11] it is certain that the primary dependence was not upon it. Corn probably was not known. The population was small, scattered, and anything resembling a permanent settlement is to be expected only at places where there was a constant supply of natural foods, such as the mussel beds mentioned above. Pottery was unknown but soapstone vessels were probably used. Stone-boiling was the primary method of food preparation and in the flood-plain areas where stones were not available small lumps of clay were shaped in the hands and, after being thoroughly fired, used for the same purpose. At least this seems to be the most probable interpretation of the so-called "Poverty Point Objects."

The bow was probably unknown and the principal weapon was the atlatl which sometimes had a bone hook and weights, frequently made of stone, which are supposed to have given the weapon better balance. In this region the majority of the weights were probably "boatstones" although a few of the "bannerstone" type may have been employed. Bone implements, which included points, awls, and the small double-pointed bone "splinter points" were cut from the green bone by a sawing technique using small thin slabs of sandstone. Fishhooks were made of bone, and antler sections were used as flint flakers and as handles for small cutting tools. There probably was some use of marine conch shells as containers, and fragments of them were worked into simple ornaments.

The flint points and blades at these undiscovered sites will almost certainly be a percussion industry utilizing small pebbles found in the gravel deposits in the hills to the east and west of the valley. A relatively long, narrow, thick point with a wide stem separated from the blade by a slight shoulder will be the most common form. In addition, we may expect a few wider blades that are also stemmed, small flint "drills," and turtle-back scrapers.

The trait of smoking may have appeared in this area prior to the introduction of pottery and if so the tubular pipe, probably with a flattened bit, is the type to be expected.

It is practically certain that the future archaeologist will experience some difficulty determining the house types of the inhabitants in this period. He will find numerous hearth areas in the midden deposits but the only indications of structures will be small scattered post molds which may indicate simple brush shelters — or may not.[12]

The burials will mostly be tightly flexed in simple round holes dug into the midden areas and there will be very little grave goods. Burial in the flesh will be the most common practice.

The social organization that may be inferred for this culture is a simple one, probably comparable to the band organizations described in the Great Basin area by Steward;[13] small groups held together and controlled through kinship. But it is probable that in this region the necessity for obtaining food did not cause such constant movement as in the less hospitable western country. The band-hunting territories were probably smaller and the country may have supported a larger population than the regions Steward describes.

The Tchula Period (Time G–F)

The Tchula Period is roughly coeval with the Tchefuncte culture near the mouth of the Mississippi River, with the early fiber-, sand-, and limestone-tempered pottery horizons of the Tennessee River Valley, with the Baumer and Red Ocher cultures of southern and central Illinois, and the Adena of the central Ohio Valley.

Although it might be supposed that the first ceramic period in the Survey Area would produce a relatively simple pottery complex with clear indications of the direction from which it came, such does not seem to be the

[11] Griffin thinks this unlikely.

[12] Webb and DeJarnette, 1942, p. 318; Ford and Quimby, 1945, p. 88.

[13] Steward, 1938.

case. For one thing, the area is large enough to produce significantly different type groupings in its different parts. At this time it would be going ahead of the evidence to be dogmatic as to which type grouping has priority.

In the northern and eastern parts of the Survey Area the earliest sites have a pottery complex with the closest connections to the east. These sites show high proportions of Withers Fabric-impressed, Baytown Plain, and Mulberry Creek Cord-marked. Four of the sites, Withers (13–P–9), Norman (16–O–8), Garner (16–O–15), and Wilnot (17–N–16) had a very small amount of fiber-tempered ware. The decorated types are Crowder and Twin Lakes Punctated, Cormorant Cord-impressed, Jaketown Simple Stamped, Tammany Pinched, Indian Bay Stamped, and Larto Red Filmed. It is in this region that the heavy proportions of sand-tempered types (combined with clay-tempered in the seriation charts) Twin Lakes Fabric-impressed, Blue Lake Cord-marked, and Thomas Plain were picked up. In this area of the Survey, the earliest and strongest pottery connections are to the east. These types were comparable to but not identical with sand-tempered wares described by Jennings in northeastern Mississippi. Ford and Phillips interpret this preponderance of sand-tempering as a local specialization without chronological significance, while Griffin sees in it a reflection of the priority of sand- over clay-tempering that obtains in northern Alabama. This is one of the minor unsolved problems of the Survey.

In the main this northern Tchula Period complex can be regarded as an early expression of the coarse, thick, granular-tempered, paddled Woodland pottery with simple bowl and jar shapes, flat, rounded, or conoidal bases,[14] that is the dominant ware throughout the eastern United States for a considerable but as yet unknown span of time. The fabric-impressed surface which is so common in this period is concentrated in an area from Hannibal, Missouri, south to about Greenville, Mississippi, and east to the Appalachians. It is usually associated with smaller proportions of cord-marked and plain surface types and has a minimum of decoration. The pottery appears in the area outlined above associated with many late Archaic traits which have come down with very little change.

To the north and in the central Ohio Valley the earliest pottery is plain and cord-marked with only small proportions of fabric-impressed types. In general character, however, this northern Woodland pottery shows its connection to that of the Middle South. It is marked by association with burial mounds In Illinois, the central Ohio Valley, and the Lake Huron region.

In the Survey Area it is assumed without proof that the small mounds at such sites as Wilnot (17–N–16), Garner (16–O–15), Stover (16–O–14), and Henderson (16–O–7) belong to this Tchula Period. Test excavations at Twin Lakes (16–P–3), a site with a mixed Tchula and early Baytown complex (which had to be abandoned on account of high water), penetrated a small burial mound and produced a small copper bead and a copper-covered wooden artifact so disintegrated that it was not identified. This uncertainty of temporal allocation of the earliest burial mounds in the Survey Area also obtains in eastern Mississippi where the Miller I complex is as yet poorly known. The fact that most of the burial mounds assigned to period G–F are in the Sunflower area and clustered close to the Little Tallahatchie and Yocona flowing in from the east may be significant as to the direction from which the concept of mound burial in the Lower Mississippi was derived.

In the southern part of the Survey Area, the earliest pottery complex differs from that described above. Here there is an absence of fabric- and cord-impressed surfaces. The decorative types which most clearly indicate connection with the early pottery of northern Alabama are also very rare. On the other hand, certain decorated types, Tchefuncte Stamped, Jaketown Simple Stamped, Tammany Pinched, and Lake Borgne Incised represent relationships farther down the Mississippi south of the mouth of Red River. At the Jaketown Site (20–O–1), in the deepest levels, some of

[14] However, no basal sherds indicative of conical or conoidal bottoms appeared in the Survey collections. The distribution of essentially "Woodland" pottery seems to have outrun that of its most characteristic basal feature.

the plain sherds which exhibited the most "primitive" condition were called Tchefuncte Plain, but the separation of them from those called Baytown Plain was most arbitrary, as is usually the case when "borderlines" between closely related types are approached.

It is presumed that as additional early sites are located and excavated farther south in the Survey Area the early ceramic complexes will continue to reflect known pottery types of the Tchefuncte Period. The strong emphasis here upon plain surface granular-tempered pottery connects the southernmost Mississippi Valley area to the east along the Gulf Coast of Florida, and to the west into the Louisiana, eastern Texas, eastern Oklahoma, and southern Arkansas areas. In all these southern areas paddle-surfaced pottery barely makes its appearance and a significant division is thereby recognized. It has been suggested by Griffin that the Tchefuncte complex is best explained as the result of influences moving in from the east and northeast and merging to produce a distinctive entity.[15] The early Texas sites do not offer prototypes which would indicate a movement from the west, nor are early ancestors visible on the Mesoamerican scene.

We have already mentioned one of the major Tchula Period pottery types in all parts of the Survey Area, Withers Fabric-impressed with its sand-tempered equivalent, Twin Lakes Fabric-impressed. It is clear that these types are closely connected to Saltillo Fabric-impressed of northeast Mississippi, which along with small amounts of the Wheeler and Alexander Series immediately precedes the Hopewellian Period in that area.

Through northeast Mississippi we make contact in the Tchula Period with the northern Alabama shell heaps, specifically with the period now called "Pottery (2)" by Webb and DeJarnette. Following the "Archaic (3)" Period, these authors have proposed three pottery periods.[16] "Pottery (1)" is defined as "Beginning with the introduction of fiber-tempered pottery to Pottery (2) times"; and "Pottery (2) beginning with the introduction of grit-tempered pottery to Pottery (3) times." The last period called "Pottery (3)" is the shell-tempered pottery occupation up to the historic contact period.

This method of naming and defining periods seems straightforward and has the virtue of simplicity. The definition of "Pottery (1)" which is contemporary with part of the Tchula Period, includes, in addition to fiber-tempering, sand-tempered sherds "in small quantity"; flint types 7, 13, 18, 27; long cylindrical shell beads; antler projectile points; burials partially flexed; burials sometimes headless or dismembered; "cremation but rarely."[17] The new flint types are somewhat shorter and broader, and the blade is generally triangular in shape. The stems have a straight or slightly convex base. Very similar forms also appear in Kentucky Adena and in Tchefuncte. At the same time, many of the older archaic forms continue into the "Pottery (1)" levels.[18]

It must be admitted that "Pottery (1)" cannot be recognized as a culture complex with any certainty though such a "period" may have existed. Any clear recognition of it for comparative purposes is perhaps unnecessary here, since it is unlikely either that a pure fiber-tempered site will be found in the Alluvial Valley or even if one is, that the Wheeler Basin "Pottery (1)" complex will be strongly represented.

It is "Pottery (2)" with which we are here concerned. This includes all "grit-tempered pottery" which makes the "period" excessively comprehensive and not at all comparable to that immediately preceding. It would presumably include most of the sand-tempered, all of the limestone-, and all of the clay- and crushed rock-tempered types in northern Alabama. If our knowledge of other areas has any bearing on the interpretation of northern Alabama, this means from Adena to Mississippi — a fair time span. It should be possible

[15] Griffin, 1945.

[16] Webb and DeJarnette, 1948a.

[17] Webb and DeJarnette, 1948a, p. 20.

[18] Long cylindrical shell beads are quite rare and, from the burial associations (Webb and DeJarnette, 1948a, p. 66) or other evidence, it is difficult to say why this trait was specifically assigned to this level. Antler projectile points are hardly a new trait at the "Pottery (1)" zone, nor are they particularly characteristic of it. The last three traits, "burials partially flexed," "burials sometimes headless or dismembered," and "cremation but rarely," are not satisfactory to distinguish "Pottery (1)," although they may be present.

to indicate subdivisions within "Pottery (2)" which would be more useful for comparative purposes in the general eastern United States pattern. At Flint River (Ma°48) which was the first site report to divide the occupation according to this sixfold time scheme, the following items are listed for "Pottery (2)":

Grit-tempered potsherds in midden
Wide range of vessel forms and surface finish
Flint types 6, 8, 16, 22, 44, maximum
Antler spearpoints, antler drifts
Stone gorgets
Limestone celts and hoes
Burials partially flexed
Increase in the number of burials with artifacts but no pottery used as burial offering
Slight evidence of possession of copper
Cylindrical shell columella beads, oblique end perforated
Shell gorgets and pendants.[19]

One of the most important sites in the Tennessee Valley from the point of view of ceramic studies is the Whitesburg Bridge Site (Ma^{v}10) for, as Webb and DeJarnette point out,

> The presence of a large concentration of limestone pottery in Zones A and B, while many of the artifacts in these zones are quite similar to those in the non-pottery zones, D and E, would seem to suggest continuous occupancy by a single people in Pottery 2 period who took on the manufacture of grit tempered pottery and continued to use many of the same types of artifacts in bone and stone as in the Archaic 3 period. After the Pottery 2 period, occupancy seems to have completely ceased. This site is remarkable in the fact that so little shell-tempered pottery was found there. Only two sherds with shell tempering were found in the whole excavation, and not a single burial which could be assigned to the Pottery 3 period.[20]

The pottery study by Dunlevy assigns 60 sherds or 1.33 per cent to the Wheeler fiber-tempered complex, 249 sherds or 5.44 per cent to the Alexander Series sand-tempered complex, 4187 sherds or 93.06 per cent to the limestone-tempered complex. It is here highly significant that Long Branch Fabric-marked is 86.34 per cent of the total pottery at the site, Mulberry Creek Plain is only 5.29 per cent, and Wright Check Stamped at 1.02 per cent is the only other type to be above one per cent. There were very few specimens of simple, complicated, cord-marked, or brushed surfaces and only one incised specimen. In the Alexander complex after the plain sand-tempered type, Benson Fabric-marked is next highest, being about 20 per cent of the total Alexander group. It may be regarded as likely that at Whitesburg Bridge the Alexander Series is partly contemporary with the fabric-impressed, limestone-tempered pottery.

This complex contrasted with that at Flint River, which is a short distance upstream on the same side of the Tennessee, indicates a time differential in "Pottery (2)" occupations and it can be rather confidently asserted that Whitesburg Bridge "Pottery (2)" occupation is earlier. It is difficult to find out exactly how the rest of the artifact complex or other features differentiate the two sites to fit with the suggestion of time difference in the pottery complex. Perhaps the sheet copper armband, spatula, and "spangle," the gorgets, cylindrical columella beads at Flint River are part of the differentiating criteria. Perhaps further analytical study of the published reports will provide interesting leads which will then need to be checked against the basic data in order to provide the traits which are added at these various levels.

To the east and south of the Survey Area in Clarke County, Alabama, the McQuorquodale Mound[21] seems to equate roughly with the Tchula Period because of the presence of the fiber and early sand-tempered pottery. It was also marked by tetrapodal feet on various vessels, steatite vessel fragments, mica sheets, crude greenstone celt, faceted and grooved galena nodules, conical siltstone cup, two-hole gorgets, copper ear spools and a copper bead, stemmed and side-notched projectile points, extended, bundle and disarticulated skull burials. Wimberly and Tourtelot in 1941 inclined to the view that this site was in the Hopewell Period with strong Woodland affiliations. Griffin allocated the site to the general Adena-Tchefuncte level.[22] The subsequent location by Wimberly of a series of sites including two

[19] Webb and DeJarnette, 1948a, p. 20.
[20] Webb and DeJarnette, 1948b, pp. 43–44.
[21] Wimberly and Tourtelot, 1941.
[22] Griffin, 1946, figs. 2, 4, and p. 51.

sequent Marksville-Santa Rosa sites rather clearly indicates that the McQuorquodale Site is on a pre-"southern Hopewell" level.

In the United States National Museum there is a group of site collections from Oktibbeha County, Mississippi, that were made by Lewis E. Long of Mississippi State College at Starkville. One of these sites (Site B, Cat. No. 369336–47) on the basis of the pottery represented can be equated with the early part of the Tchula Period. Near the Arch Reynolds Place some 3¾ miles northwest of Starkville, Long collected a high proportion of the Wheeler fiber-tempered series including Bluff Creek Punctate, Wheeler Dentate Stamped; sherds of the Alexander group including Alexander Incised, and sand-tempered cord-marked and fabric-impressed sherds. Some of the sand-tempered plain sherds indicate the presence of tetrapodal feet.

Jenning's postulated Miller I horizon of northeastern Mississippi included high proportions of fabric-impressed, sand-tempered pottery, some cord-marked, and representatives of the Alexander and Wheeler series. It is thus a pre-Hopewell complex which fits in well with the Tchula material. It is to be hoped that it will soon be possible to elaborate on the culture of early sites in the eastern part of the state of Mississippi.

These eastern sites and materials afford comparative data for the Tchula Period, but do not answer the important question as to the antecedents of this, the earliest pottery in the Survey Area. There are three general theories concerning the origin of pottery in the Lower Mississippi Valley: (1) It is possible that somewhere in the eastern or southeastern parts of the United States pottery was invented and followed the simple vessel shapes of the earlier stone bowls. If such was the case, the most logical area for this development would be the southern Appalachians where the stone bowls and fiber-tempered ware are found in conjunction, with the former preceding the latter. The plain and simple stamp surfaces of the fiber-tempered ware resemble the smoothed and striated or gouged surface of the steatite and sandstone bowls. (2) An alternative theory widely held is that early Woodland pottery was brought over from northeast Asia by migrating groups and that this pottery is the earliest in the eastern United States and the probable ancestor of the succeeding forms.[23] According to this theory, stimulus diffusion would be responsible for the fiber-tempered pottery in the Southeast. (3) A third, or "double-barreled" theory considers that the Woodland paddle-stamped wares probably came from Asia as outlined above, but that the predominantly smoothed wares that eventually develop into the Mississippian ceramics come from an old pottery base that was shared with Mesoamerica. Tchefuncte ceramics are supposed to represent an early form of this southern tradition.[24] Griffin leans toward the second alternative, while Ford and Phillips favor the third. Griffin's rejection of the latter is based on the fact that no evidence of the postulated "old pottery base" has yet been found in Mesoamerica. It must be conceded, however, that the evidence is not very satisfactory for any of these theories at the present time.

The only evidence we have on a comparable time level in the little-known region bordering the Survey Area on the northwest is afforded by three sites excavated by Clarence B. Moore on the Black River in northern Arkansas, Perkins Field, Little Turkey Hill, and Harter Knoll. According to Moore, the "mounds" on these sites were not intentional structures but small accumulations of dwelling site refuse.[25] At Little Turkey Hill and Harter Knoll he specifically mentions the scarcity of potsherds met with in digging. At these three sites Moore found a total of seventy burials. The majority were closely flexed and had no accompanying grave goods. His scanty collection from here includes:

Tubular pipes of claystone (one he describes as a large bead)
"Coarsely chipped" knives and arrowpoints of flint
Hammerstones
Double-pointed "piercing implement" of bone
Tortoise carapace

[23] McKern, 1937; Griffin, 1946, pp. 44–45.
[24] Ford and Quimby, 1945, p. 95; Ford and Willey, 1941, pp. 340–41.
[25] Moore, 1910, pp. 354–58.

Discoidal beads made from the axis of a marine shell
Barrel-shaped beads of claystone and red jasper
Prism-shaped bannerstone, and
An engraved conch shell made into a drinking cup which Moore indicates accompanied some burials that differ from the others found (at Little Turkey Hill) and which may be intrusive.

As neither Moore, nor any other investigator so far as we know, has excavated any of the burial mounds in the Survey Area which we have tentatively dated in the Tchula Period, it is not now possible to describe the mound burials of the period with any confidence. Judging from evidence from the comparable Tchefuncte Period in Louisiana,[26] these mounds probably contain a proportion of flexed and/or secondary burials with very little grave goods accompanying the dead. There may be some cremations.

On the basis of the evidence now available, we expect that the Tchula Period will prove to be the time at which the trait of secondary burial in small conical mounds first appears in this portion of the Mississippi Valley. This ceremonial complex makes a strong imprint on the succeeding developments in the region, but as to the direction from which it moved into our area, or its ultimate origin, we are not prepared to agree. Ford is inclined to think that the movement was from the south and that secondary burial was a part of the complex. On the other hand, we have already presented considerable evidence in favor of an eastern origin for much of the Tchula pottery complex, and it may be that the trait of mound-building came with it. In any case, we can deduce that this trait complex represents something new in religio-social control of the population at this time; that the use of these small mounds for burial reflects a more complex and centralized social structure than is indicated by the remains of the preceding non-ceramic period.

In the preceding pages we have given reasons why the number of sites we have located in each period will not necessarily be an accurate measure of population. At best, the proportions are to be taken as approximations. With these reservations, our evidence indicates a rather sparse population in the Tchula as compared with later periods.

[26] Ford and Quimby, 1945.
[27] Ford and Willey, 1941.

The Early Baytown Period (Time F–E)

Again, we have little more factual data to contribute than the ceramic picture and superficial site-data already given. We will, therefore, try to sketch in something of the cultural assemblages by drawing on information obtained by other investigators.

This period corresponds culturally to what is known as the "Hopewellian" horizon. Ford and Willey have called it "Burial Mound II,"[27] and Griffin has designated it as the time of "Hopewell and Middle Woodland Groups."[28] Judging from our ceramic evidence, early Baytown was roughly coeval with Marksville as it has been described near the mouth of the Red River in Louisiana.

The ceramic complex of the early Baytown Period is dominated by plain clay-tempered pottery which we have classified as Baytown Plain. The cord-marked type Mulberry Creek increases through this period in all the subareas, but with a markedly differentiated popularity as has been shown (map, fig. 7). The pottery which serves best to mark the period are types of relatively low percentage frequency: Marksville Stamped and Marksville Incised. These show a higher percentage in the southern part of the area we have covered. The distribution of sites showing these types is interesting for out of forty-two sites graphed in the seriation charts, twenty-five or well over half are located in the Sunflower area. Two sites are listed for the Memphis, four for the St. Francis, five for the Lower Arkansas, and six for the Lower Yazoo. These Marksville types are almost completely absent north of the Arkansas River and west of the Mississippi. They have not been reported from western Tennessee and Kentucky or from southeastern Missouri.

Indian Bay Stamped shortly precedes this period and lasts sporadically on sites which have their placement in the next period. It

[28] Griffin, 1946, fig. 5.

occurs in greatest numbers in sites placed early in the period such as Porter Bayou (18–M–1), Harris Bayou (16–N–14), and Aderholt (16–N–20), where it outnumbers the combined Marksville Stamped and Incised types. Churupa Punctated is not a good marker in the Survey Area, as has been pointed out in the type description. For a different reason Evansville Punctated is not a significant marker, for it is so generalized in character that it covers most of the clay-tempered pottery period. While Mazique Incised is present on the seriation charts, this is largely because a type originally called Oxbow Incised was combined with Mazique on the charts. It appears that Mazique does not occur significantly in this period and belongs primarily to middle and late Baytown. The same thing may be said of the presence of Coles Creek Incised at sites assigned to this period, particularly in the Sunflower area.

Types that are dropping out at this time include Crowder, Twin Lakes, and Orleans Punctated, Cormorant Cord-impressed, and Withers Fabric-impressed, which is maintained longest in the Memphis and Sunflower areas. A few specimens of Wheeler Check Stamped appear on the graphs in the Sunflower and Memphis area in this period, but we are not able to agree on the significance of this record. Griffin thinks it conforms with the appearance of check stamped in small proportions in eastern and southern Hopewell and middle Woodland sites, although this type of paddling does not reach the area around the mouth of the Red River and farther south until about Coles Creek times. He feels that the type came into the Survey Area both early and late from northern Alabama but the early movement may have been up the Tombigbee drainage from the vicinity of Clarke County, Alabama, where it precedes the appearance of Hopewellian sites. Ford, on the other hand, attributes these apparent early appearances on the seriation graphs to mixed collections. He does not think that the type was in the Survey Area in early Baytown times.

The dominant types numerically in this period are Baytown Plain and Mulberry Creek Cord-marked. Their relationship to each other depends upon the geographical location of the sites. In the Yazoo area Mulberry ranges from 2 to 15 per cent on the four sites of this period while Baytown ranges from 77 to 95 per cent. In this area the proportion one could expect would be 85 per cent Baytown and 9 per cent Mulberry Creek. This is approximately the proportion in the Lower Arkansas area. It is expected that the amount of Mulberry Creek Cord-marked on sites of this period will become progressively less as the Survey moves southward. In the St. Francis area the proportions are not consistently represented and the sites of this period are few in number. An approximation would be that Mulberry would run around 20 per cent and Baytown around 70. The Memphis area is also poorly represented in this period, and the data are not available for the correct presentation but the proportion of Mulberry approaches 40 per cent and Baytown is slightly less than 50 per cent. In the Sunflower area, where over half of the sites of this period are located, Mulberry Creek is clearly the most common type, ranging from 10 to 94 per cent with an average of close to two-thirds. Baytown Plain, while it has a corresponding wide range from 4 per cent to 88 per cent, will average out somewhat below one-third.

Larto Red Filmed appears in significant quantity for the first time in this early Baytown Period. Its occurrence in the Yazoo-Sunflower portions of the Survey Area is proportionately greater than in the area about the mouth of Red River where it was first described. Larto, in the Survey Area, is related not only to Tchefuncte Red Filmed but also to the red filmed pottery of the Florida Gulf Coast. The absence of red filming to the west in the "Caddo" area in the early ceramic levels does not indicate a derivation of Larto from that direction.

In the Yocona drainage about 50 miles east of the Yazoo Basin the Slaughter mound group of four mounds [29] almost certainly belongs in the early Baytown period. This site is located in LaFayette County, Mississippi, some 8 to 10 miles southeast of Oxford. The collection in the U. S. National Museum (Cat. No. 386125) is composed of the following types.

[29] Swanton, 1939, p. 233.

Mulberry Creek Cord-marked	25
Baytown Plain	5
Tishomingo Cord-marked	1
Saltillo Fabric-impressed	1
Marksville Stamped (rocked dentate)	1
Marksville Incised	1
	34

Another site, presumably of this period, is located in Oktibbeha County, Mississippi, on the Pearson Place 3¼ miles north and 2¼ miles west of Starkville.[30]

Tishomingo Cord-marked	21
Tishomingo Plain	46
Saltillo Fabric-impressed	2
Alligator Bayou Stamped	4
Basin Bayou Incised	2
	75

The last two types in the above list are sand-tempered equivalents of Marksville Stamped and Marksville Incised. These names are used by Gordon Willey in his analysis of the Florida Gulf Coast area and probably also by Wimberly in his forthcoming report on a series of early Woodland sites in Clarke County, Alabama, which demonstrated among other things an excellent sequence within the Hopewellian Period.

Farther south in eastern Mississippi is a Hopewellian site on which a brief report has been made by Collins:

> Following the excavation of the Crandall mounds, work was begun on a much larger mound of a different type on the property of Dr. B. J. and Mr. R. L. McRae, near the town of Increase. Approximately one third of the mound was excavated by trenching, and while no skeletal material and only a few artifacts were found, the peculiar stratification seemed to warrant as thorough an examination as was made. . . . This stratification consisted of a series of brilliantly colored sand layers, yellow, brown, orange, blue-gray, and pure white, from which, at the center of the mound, there suddenly arose a dome-shaped structure of compact yellow clay. This clay dome and the succession of colored sand strata probably had a ceremonial significance, having been placed on the floor of what had very likely been a temple, the site of which was later covered over with a mound of earth, on top of which, still later, there probably stood a temple or council house. Colored sand strata in much the same arrangement have also been found in the effigy mounds of Wisconsin.
>
> Within this small inner mound or clay dome was found a rectangular ornament of sheet copper and silver enclosing a core of wood, shown *in situ* in figure 93. Both copper and silver are shown by analysis to be native American, probably from the Lake Superior region. Silver and copper ornaments practically identical to this have been found in small numbers in Florida, Tennessee, Ohio, and Michigan.
>
> Thin, flaked, knives, struck with a single blow from flint cores, were found both in the mound and in the adjoining field. These are identical in every respect with the flaked knives from Flint Ridge in Ohio which, while abundant in the Ohio mounds, are rarely found in other localities.
>
> With the most significant features of the McRae mound so strongly suggesting northern influence, we must conclude that the builders of this Mississippi mound maintained at least a close trade relationship with the northern tribes. While undoubtedly the many mounds and various other earthworks of North America were built by Indian tribes of diverse stocks, there are certain resemblances between even the most distant of them which suggest a contact something more than sporadic.[31]

Collins' reference to the Hopewell flake knife in this area is now further substantiated by the appearance of flake knives possibly of Flint Ridge, Ohio, flint at the Bynum Site in Lee County, Mississippi. This type of implement is as much a marker of the Hopewell culture as is the ornate decorated pottery, platform pipes, conjoined tubes, or obsidian. The pottery complex from the site was not discussed in this preliminary report, but the following sherds (classified as to sand- and clay-temper) are in the U. S. National Museum (Cat. No. 231027).

	Sand	Clay	Total
Plain surface	15	4	19
Simple stamp	10	2	12
Curvilinear complicated stamp	4	..	4
Check Stamp	..	1	1
Fabric-impressed	6	2	8
Cord-marked	16	2	18
Flint River Cord-marked (limestone-tempered	..	..	4
Miscellaneous punctated — some like Bluff Creek	9	..	9

[30] U. S. National Museum, Cat. No. 369367–75; collected by Lewis E. Long.

[31] Collins, 1926, pp. 91–92.

	SAND	CLAY	TOTAL
Plain rocker stamp-like Indian Bay	1	..	1
Rocked dentate stamp	1	..	1
Zoned punctate	1	1	2
Hopewell-Marksville rim	2	4	6
Marksville Stamped	..	7	7
Marksville Incised	..	2	2
	—	—	—
	65	25	94

Among the plain sand-tempered sherds from the McRae Site were three tetrapod fragments and two flat circular bases.

Farther to the south in Clarke County, Alabama, the complex in this period corresponding to early Baytown takes on even more of the cast of the Gulf Coast. First of all, there is Moore's report of mounds near Jackson where he excavated a copper conjoined tube. He does not mention any pottery but refers to crude quartzite projectile points, bundle burials, and isolated skull burials in a mound 2 feet high and 43 feet in diameter. The Hopewellian Period sites in the Clarke County area will be given a competent analysis by Wimberly.

At the mouth of the Tensas and Appalachee rivers, in the northeast corner of Mobile Bay, Moore secured another copper conjoined tube at the Blakely Site, a small shell heap several acres in extent. Moore sunk test pits at various points uncovering some burials which were primarily flexed, and some cremations. One extended burial had an excellent sherd of Alligator Bayou Stamped. There were also fragments of tetrapodal vessels.

The early Baytown Period shows an increase in number of sites over the preceding period and except for three sites, whose dating may be questioned, all of the mounds are of the conical type. The rectangular mounds which our surface collections seem to date as of this early period are all in the Sunflower area and are at sites Indian Creek (15-P-3), Posey Mound (15-O-6), and Nelson (17-M-17). We have already discussed the dating of these three sites (see p. 337). The question as to whether some rectangular mounds were constructed as early as our period F-E will have to wait upon excavation of these or similar sites.

The conical mounds found together at a site range in number from one to four, and there is no discernible plan of arrangement. While most of the mounds seem originally to have been round at the base, a few are oval. Sizes range from bare rises in the ground about 30 feet in diameter and 2 feet high to well-formed cones 100 feet in diameter and 9 feet high. Most of these mounds are being cultivated and in several it was noted that human bones had recently been plowed up.

At about half of the mound sites of this period, there is a midden area, usually not around the mounds but situated to one side at various distances from 100 yards to a half mile. In the Lower Yazoo and Sunflower River areas, these middens generally have a high content of mussel shells, indicating that considerable dependence was placed upon this source of food.

We did not excavate any of the burial mounds that have been dated in this period, and, unfortunately, for one reason or another, we have not succeeded in dating by our techniques any of the sites that are reported by Clarence B. Moore that show features that presumably relate to this "Marksville-Hopewellian" time level. One such site is at Anderson Landing in Sharkey County, Mississippi.[32] This is located near the mouth of the Sunflower River about 30 miles south of the southern border of our Yazoo sub-area. Here Moore dug in a conical mound 62 feet in diameter at the base and 6 feet 7 inches high. He records traces of burials at three points ranging from the top of the mound to the base, but apparently was not able to determine the methods of burial. Four pottery vessels were found: two plain, one of these a bowl; one Marksville Incised, showing a "serpent" design and with a cross-hatched rim; and the fourth a Marksville Stamped vessel with a cross-hatched rim. The two decorated vessels are illustrated in Moore's report.[33]

[32] Moore, 1908b, pp. 586-87.

[33] Moore, 1908b, figs. 3, 4.

Other sites which have been excavated and reported on, that seem to be approximately equivalent in age to our early Baytown Period, are: the Miller II sites in Pontotoc County, Mississippi (Jennings, 1941); the Crooks Site, in La Salle Parish, Louisiana, north of the mouth of the Red River (Ford and Willey, 1940); and the older level in the Kirkham Site, Clark County, Arkansas (Dickinson and Lemley, 1939).

Our early Baytown Period undoubtedly is the time when the complex of Hopewellian-Marksville-like cultural traits reach their peak in the Survey Area. Emphasis on mound burial, probably in most cases secondary interment, undoubtedly marks the period. There seems to have been population increase, as suggested by our finding more sites, and it is possible that this may reflect a shift toward more dependence on agriculture for subsistence although direct evidence of its presence is lacking.

The strong surge of cord-marked pottery that is coming into the Survey Area at this time, apparently from the east by way of the hill country in northern Mississippi, offers interesting possibilities for interpretation. The paddle-surface pottery tradition as the dominant type of ware is represented by Withers Fabric-marked from the earliest times in the Sunflower and Memphis chronological columns. At time F, the beginning of our early Baytown, fabric-marking is being replaced by a paddle wrapped with cords, resulting in the type Mulberry Creek Cord-marked. Mulberry Creek reaches its peak of popularity at the close of early Baytown, time E. This tradition is in marked contrast with the predominantly smoothed wares that dominate these early periods lower down the Mississippi Valley.[34] This may be solely a movement of cultural ideas. On the other hand, these two traditions may have been carried by different ethnic groups. Whichever may prove to be the case, we seem to have a merging here of the widespread "Woodland" ceramic pattern with pottery which has not been paddled and may be of another tradition (see discussion p. 435).

The Middle Baytown Period (Time E–D)

As we have defined it from the ceramic chronology, the middle Baytown Period is the stretch of years that lie between the disappearance of the decorated Marksville types of early Baytown and the first showing of shell-tempered pottery. Ceramically, it is a poorly characterized period. Mulberry Creek Cord-marked, which appears to have reached its peak about time E, declines slowly in popularity throughout the period while Baytown Plain shows a corresponding increase. Larto Red Filmed and Mazique Incised, both types with long time ranges, seem to reach their popularity peaks, and they show in larger proportions in the southern part of the Survey Area. Other decorated types were in very small proportions; either as relicts of the preceding period, or, as new decoration ideas just beginning a life cycle which will reach a peak in succeeding times.

The period was particularly ill defined in the St. Francis area. The types listed include only two Mazique Incised and three Wheeler Check Stamped sherds. This was apparently neither a north-south or east-west thoroughfare during this period. In the Memphis area there are very minor amounts of Evansville Punctated, Oxbow-Mazique, and Coles Creek Incised. Larto Red Filmed is consistently present in minor proportion and Wheeler Check Stamped is beginning to increase although still averaging less than 2 per cent. In the Sunflower area the decorated types include one specimen each of Indian Bay Stamped and Withers Fabric-impressed (an obvious anachronism), Oxbow-Mazique Incised, Larto Red Filmed (about 1 per cent) and one specimen of Yates Net-impressed. In the Lower Yazoo there is more variety in the companion types, particularly in the closing part of the period when the cross currents from the Florida Gulf Coast and from east Texas were meeting near the mouth of the Red River. The earlier sites still have Indian Bay Stamped and Marksville types, while the later sites include Churupa Punctated, French Fork Incised, Woodville Red Filmed, Chevalier Stamped, Coles Creek, and Mazique Incised, while Larto is consistently present around 2 to 4 per cent. On some of these sites Mississippi types are present, but nobody believes they belong in this period even though they have higher proportions than some of the types that do belong. Such out-of-place occurrences are to be expected in the seriation of surface collections.

Most of the mounds that we have dated as belonging to this period are conical and prob-

[34] Ford and Willey, 1940; Ford and Quimby, 1945.

ably indicate a continuation of some of the burial practices of the early Baytown. In addition there are five sites which have rectangular temple mounds.[35] Two of these sites have more than one mound and a plaza arrangement is discernible. At both, the plaza lies to the northwest of the principal mound. None of these mound sites seem to be the locations of true villages. The refuse that is found scattered around in the fields seems to have come from buildings that were placed upon the tops of mounds, or from a few satellite buildings that stood on level ground about the plaza area. At none of the sites is there sufficient refuse to mark the place as having been occupied by enough people to have erected the mounds. These seem to be ceremonial centers, probably for a population scattered or living in small hamlets in the surrounding countryside.

This pyramidal mound ceremonial center is a new idea for this part of the Mississippi Valley and has obvious Mesoamerican connections. Its appearance here undoubtedly marks a change in the religio-social structure of the communities. The "Hopewellian"-like burial mound complex of the preceding periods seems to indicate a group of religious ideas primarily concerned with care for the bones of the dead. That mortuary complex probably had a fairly simple pantheon of nature spirits and ghosts that could be controlled by shamanism not dissimilar to that of historic tribes in the northern Woodland area. The political organization was very likely based on real or theoretical kinship; the dead were cared for and burial mounds built by relatives; and the presence of any marked social stratification is rather doubtful. In marked contrast, the temple mounds in plaza arrangement that are found for the first time in middle Baytown suggest the introduction of (1) a true demanding "God" — probably the sun; (2) a priesthood, and accompanying religio-social stratification; and (3) sufficient control over enough people to build and serve these ceremonial centers — quite a different thing from what we are here interpreting as the motivation in early Baytown. These basic forms, which made possible a conquest warfare pattern and the establishment of small "kingdoms" were present in this region when De Soto came through in 1541, and the remnants of such a system are clearly described by the French explorers for the Natchez and Taensa around 1700. If these germs of theocratic control may be deduced from this appearance of temple mounds in middle Baytown, we have a possible explanation of the machinery by which the later middle Mississippi cultures were extended so widely over the eastern United States.[36] These, however, are only postulated techniques of social control. One of the factors which allowed them to operate effectively must have been an increase in population in the area where the Mississippian culture was in process of developing, which in turn resulted from a larger and more dependable food supply. Improvement of, and more emphasis on, agriculture is suggested.

Our evidence can be brought to bear somewhat on the two latter questions. An increase in population about this time is indicated in the site distribution maps in Section VIII (figs. 64 to 69). There is no direct evidence in regard to the increasing importance of agriculture or information bearing on the question of corn cultivation. All we have is the suggestion given by the locations of the sites on natural levees where light arable soils are found.

We have not been able to date any of the sites C. B. Moore excavated in our area as of this period, and there seems to be a good reason why a careful reading of his reports leaves us in the dark as to burial traits. In this as well as the succeeding period there seem to have been very few burials made and these practically never have any offerings with them. We have assigned sites with burial mounds to this period, but so far as we know none have been excavated and reported on or the material preserved in collections. The early temple-mound sites are notorious among pothunters for the absence of burials. Nor in the course of our collecting did we see many human bone fragments in the fields about these

[35] Griffin questions the dating of the pyramidal mounds on these sites believing that they belong to the next period. The uncertainty of dating mounds by surface pottery upon and around them is discussed elsewhere (p. 337).

[36] Ford and Willey, 1941; Griffin, 1946, pp. 75 ff.

sites such as are so common for the late Mississippi villages where burials are constantly being plowed up.

Comparison of middle Baytown with the cultures that have been described in neighboring areas is rendered a little difficult by the fact that there is not even a hint of a burial complex which can be used. The ceramics from refuse deposits are the sole basis, and, as we have indicated, the period in our region is marked more by the absence of types that characterize the preceding and succeeding periods, rather than by any types peculiar to it. Middle Baytown corresponds to the early part of what Ford roughed out as the "Deasonville" Period in the Lower Yazoo Basin, just south of our Yazoo sub-area.[37] It seems to be generally coeval with the yet undescribed "Troyville Period" culture about the mouth of Red River in Louisiana. It is early during the middle Baytown Period that cord-marked pottery reaches its maximum popularity and distribution in the Lower Mississippi. As we have indicated, it seems to have come from the northeast by way of the region of the mouths of the Tallahatchie and Coldwater rivers in northern Mississippi, and a possible interpretation of this strong influx, particularly into the Yazoo and Sunflower basins, might have been a movement of people. It is possible that, as a result of the increasing importance of agriculture in the cultural scene, people living in the north Mississippi hills with a Woodland type of hunting and gathering culture may have been attracted to the rich bottom lands of the Mississippi flood plain where planting was easier and more rewarding. Whatever the explanation may be for this intrusion, the cord-marked ware passes its peak of popularity during this period and in the succeding late Baytown it is submerged in all the sub-areas by smooth-surfaced ware.

One of the authors (Ford) thinks that we have presented evidence to show that during the middle and late Baytown periods there was a movement northward through the Survey Area of certain ceramic features. These traits are red filming, the line-filled triangle decoration, and the slightly later traits of polishing, the carinated bowl form, and incised lines parallel to the rim. It seems likely that the rectangular temple mounds in plaza arrangement were also drifting northward beginning in middle Baytown and, like the ceramic features just cited, derive from the Troyville and later Coles Creek culture periods about the mouth of Red River where they characterize the periods.

Whether or not this is the correct interpretation, it seems reasonable that these elements form a partial foundation for the later Mississippian culture of the Survey Area. Some of these features can apparently be traced from the preceding Marksville Period. Others, however, such as rectangular mounds in plaza arrangement, polished pottery, and the carinated bowl with straight vertical sides, while they have come to the Survey Area from toward the mouth of Red River, are just as new and rootless there as here. These are very few traits upon which to base deductions as to cultural connections. However, the single trait of rectangular temple mounds arranged about a plaza is a complex within itself and the important effects of the arrival of this trait with the marked changes in religio-political organization which it implies demands all the consideration we can give its history.

Ten years ago most Eastern archaeologists assumed that rectangular mounds were a firmly welded part of the Mississippi Basic Culture that had been outlined by Deuel.[38] This sweeping generalization has been modified considerably, and it is now a well-known fact that this trait appeared in the Lower Mississippi Valley area considerably before the other features that were supposed to define Mississippian cultures, such as shell-tempered pottery with handles, the bottle form, triangular projectile points, extended burials with grave goods, rectangular houses with wall trenches, etc. Our interest centers on the fact that temple mounds may have been here in the Lower Mississippi Valley on the middle Baytown-Troyville time horizon, considerably before the crystallization of classic Mississippian culture.[39]

[37] Ford, 1936.

[38] Cole and Deuel, 1937, pp. 207–19.

[39] Again, we call attention to disagreement among the authors. Ford thinks temple mounds were already present in middle Baytown. Griffin and Phillips think they may have been, but would prefer to have more evidence.

It has been assumed for a long time that this mound-building complex was derived from Mesoamerica where it reached its highest development, but the time and the routes by which it arrived in the eastern United States have been obscure. As Eastern archaeologists have acquired more control over the general outline of cultural relations and at the same time have developed and improved relative chronologies and time correlations between them, it has become possible to outline the histories of single trait complexes with more and more confidence. By these means we are gradually solving the mystery of the temple-mound complex. The recent work of Alex Krieger and his associates in outlining the prehistory of Texas has been an essential contribution to the solution.

The Late Baytown Period (Time D–C)

Late Baytown is the time span during which the trait of shell-tempering begins to become prominent in the ceramic complex. In all the sub-areas our plain type, Neeley's Ferry Plain, begins to increase in popularity, primarily at the expense of Baytown Plain. Mulberry Creek Cord-marked is declining in popularity and in all sub-areas except the Sunflower it disappears about the end of the period; there it lasts a little longer. The red-slipped, incised, and punctated clay-tempered types begin to be replaced by correspondingly decorated shell-tempered types in the sub-areas that lie along the Mississippi River. However, one paddled clay-tempered type, Wheeler Check Stamped, which appeared near the end of middle Baytown, hangs on, and even reaches its peak in late Baytown, particularly in the Memphis sub-area, where it seems to be a marker type for the period. Like the earlier paddle-stamped types, Withers Fabric-impressed and Mulberry Creek Cord-marked, this type apparently came from the east.

For the Survey Area as a whole, the most common decorated type is still Larto Red Filmed, but there is a considerable decrease from the preceding period. Its maximum frequency at the beginning of the period is about 2 to 3 per cent and lies in the southern part of the area east of the Mississippi diminishing steadily to the north and westward. By the end of the period it has practically disappeared.

Other decorated clay-tempered types which reached their maximum in the preceding period still maintain small but significant percentages but decline throughout the period. These are in order of numerical importance Mazique (and the closely related provisional type Oxbow) Incised, Evansville Punctated, and Coles Creek Incised. The latter type is limited to the southern part of the area (see p. 96). Along with this decrease in decorated clay-tempered types is a corresponding increase in decorated shell-tempered types which reach their maximum in the following periods. In other words, late Baytown is the period in which the shift from clay- to shell-tempering took place and the end of the period, time C, is the point at which the two contrasting temper groups are approximately equal.

Of the sites which we have dated in period D–C, twenty-six have rectangular temple mounds and sixteen have conical mounds which very likely contain burials. The balance had no mounds or the mounds were so badly mutilated that the original shape was not apparent. The temple-mound sites have from one to five mounds and in at least four cases one or more conical mounds accompanied the prominent pyramid, apparently also arranged about a plaza. Orientation varies, but the majority of sites tends to have the principal mound on the west or northwest of the plaza. Burned daub found on some of the sites suggests that the intentional destruction of buildings by fire, so common in the later Mississippian Period, was practised.

The sites with only conical mounds have from one to eight mounds, irregularly arranged, and most of these sites have little surface material on them. They are evidently not village sites in most cases. The mounds range in size from 150 feet in diameter, 15 feet high, to low rises that are 3 feet high and 40 feet in diameter. On only one did we note that burials had been plowed up.

Apparently, during this period there were few if any burials accompanied by grave goods. The same condition is true as for the preceding middle Baytown and for the beginning of the following early Mississippi periods; the sites are usually in cultivation, but human bones are rarely plowed up, and local collectors have no pottery that belongs to this period. It seems worth-while to emphasize this fact for it explains why these cultural periods were so completely overlooked in past years when archaeologists gave their attention almost completely to burial collections.

The Chandler Landing Site, on White River in Arkansas, about 40 miles west of our St. Francis area, appears to date somewhere near the close of the Baytown Period and very well may have been occupied at this time.[40] Here, Moore excavated two conical mounds, one 7½ feet by 65, and the other 4½ by 40 feet. The burials scattered through these mounds were in very poor condition, but it was determined that a few were extended. Bunched burial was found at one place. The very scanty grave goods from these two mounds included one pot which seems to be of our type Baytown Plain.[41] In addition, he discovered a "finely wrought" leaf-shaped flint blade 9.75 inches long and 2.3 inches wide; two nicely made long celts; fragments of wood stained with copper; a shell bead and perforated pearls; well-made boatstones without grooves; three stone pipes of a modified "platform" shape; and a clay elbow pipe, which like the stone pipes has a long stem made in one piece with the bowl.

The traits from Chandler Landing made a short list, but as a whole, and the pipes in particular, this list suggests relationships to what Krieger[42] has set up as the Haley, Gahagan, and Spiro foci of the Gibson Aspect. Comparison is with such sites as Moore's Haley Place,[43] the excavation of the Eufaula Mound described by Orr,[44] and the excavations of the Gahagan Site reported by Moore[45] and Clarence Webb.[46]

It is interesting that a site which shows some of the features of the early "Caddo" cultures should have been found so near the borders of the area we have surveyed, for it is just after the late Baytown Period that new traits seem to have been added to the local culture to form Mississippi, and it seems likely that the cultures that flourished at that time in the adjacent parts of Texas, Oklahoma, Arkansas, and Louisiana provided some of these traits.

Late Baytown is approximately coeval with the Coles Creek Period culture found in Louisiana as is shown by the presence of an appreciable percentage of the type Coles Creek Incised in the southern sub-areas. Detailed descriptions of excavations which have been made at sites in Louisiana covering this culture have not been published, but it seems to be of considerable significance that burials are rather rare and are not accompanied by grave goods.[47]

This also seems to be the time of the clay-tempered pottery horizon found by Webb and his associates in Wheeler and Pickwick basins in the Tennessee River Valley.[48] This horizon is perhaps best exemplified at the McKelvey Site in Pickwick Basin from which the dominant pottery type of the complex, McKelvey Plain, takes its name.[49] Despite the fact that the major occupation at this site was during the time when clay-tempered pottery was being made, only two burials were found which could be assigned to this occupation. This assignment was based on stratigraphy, for these skeletons had nothing with them. Also, at a number of other sites in these Tennessee River basins, there are traces of occupation at the time when clay-tempered pottery was in vogue. In spite of extensive excavations, no burials accompanied by clay-tempered wares have been discovered.

Late Baytown also correlates in time with the earlier part of the Weeden Island II Period found along the northwest coast of Florida.[50] In that region burials were still being made in small conical mounds, a retention of the earlier Hopewellian burial complex, and while the abundant accompanying ceramics have developed a strong regional character, there are some traits that may be ancestral to pottery features that are found in our next period, the Mississippi.[51] These will be discussed later.

[40] Moore, 1910, pp. 341–48.

[41] This classification is based on the illustration of this vessel in Moore, 1910, fig. 64.

[42] Krieger, 1946, fig. 26.

[43] Moore, 1912, pp. 527 ff.

[44] Orr, 1941.

[45] Moore, 1912, pp. 511–22.

[46] Webb and Dodd, 1939.

[47] For a typical example, see Walker, 1936.

[48] Griffin, 1946, fig. 7.

[49] Webb and DeJarnette, 1942, pp. 9–25.

[50] Willey and Woodbury, 1942, fig. 25.

[51] Willey, 1945, p. 245; Griffin, 1946, p. 77.

Just what the cultural situation was to the north of our Survey Area, about the mouth of the Ohio River, is not too clear. Presumably the Lewis culture briefly described by Bennett,[52] and Martin, Quimby, and Collier,[53] was in part contemporaneous with late Baytown. This seems to be a typical "Woodland" type of culture marked by cord-marked pottery but which had rectangular houses. If any burials of the Lewis Focus have been found, they have not been described.[54]

The situation found at this time in regard to burial custom has been briefly reviewed, for it is shortly after late Baytown, apparently toward the end of the next period, the early Mississippi, that extended single and multiple burials in the flesh, accompanied by quantities of pottery and other grave goods, become a prominent part of the archaeological picture. It is plain that this trait, which characterizes "Middle Mississippi culture" in all parts of the East to which it spread, could not have been derived from the preceding Baytown periods in this part of the Mississippi Valley, a matter which we will discuss later after the local Mississippian burial customs have been described.

Early Mississippi Period (Time C–B)

Our "early" Mississippi Period does not correspond to any preconceived ideas derived from a general view of the entire Mississippi Valley. Although it does conform in relative time and certain characteristics with what Ford and Willey refer to as the "early Middle Mississippi" of this area,[55] it has been set up in each of the sub-areas strictly on the basis of local characteristics. It is the early part of the period during which shell-tempered pottery was dominant in the surveyed region and while there are some general similarities, the quantitative picture of the ceramic complex differs from one sub-area to another. This local variation should not be surprising for it has obtained in each of the periods we have examined up to this time, but in the later periods is more readily recognized. Our ceramic picture for the Tchula and early part of the Baytown periods is somewhat more uniform in the different sub-areas than in the latter half of the Baytown and in the Mississippi periods.

In the St. Francis sub-area, period C–B seems to have been predominantly a time of plain undecorated pottery. This may be deduced from the few surface collections which have dated in the early Mississippi but show most plainly in the strata cut which Phillips made in the Rose Mound (12–N–3) (see fig. 53 and discussion on p. 288). At this time in the St. Francis, Barton Incised is the only decoration showing any degree of popularity and minute percentages of Fortune Noded, Ranch Incised, Parkin Punctated, and Bell Polished Plain are also found. Parkin in particular begins to gain in popularity toward the end of the period and some of the occurrences in the early part of this period may be accidental. The predominantly plain ware of the earliest Mississippi conforms quite well to the situation of the latter part of the Baytown. It, too, features mainly plain undecorated pottery in the St. Francis.

The Memphis sub-area lying along the Mississippi River presents a marked contrast. Decorated types, Barton Incised and Parkin Punctated, are comparatively abundant and minor types include Old Town Red Filmed, Avenue Painted, Kent Incised, Ranch Incised, and several others that are really popular only in the next period. The actual presence of these minority types as indicated on the seriation graph is debatable. The polished ware, Bell Polished Plain, is present in substantial quantities and becomes the dominant type in the next period.

Farther to the southward down the Mississippi River there is a similar number of decorated types in the early Mississippi Period, but the proportions of the types change slightly. There is progressively less Parkin

[52] Bennett, 1944, pp. 12–22.

[53] Martin, Quimby, and Collier, 1947, p. 294.

[54] It is also suggested that the Old Village Level at Cahokia should logically overlap some of late Baytown as well as our early Mississippi. The Lewis culture came in at the close of Hopewell but clearly precedes early Kincaid in which there are Old Village trade pieces. Old Village must also be equal to our early Mississippi if we are to subscribe to the theory that shell-tempering moved into the Survey Area from the north.

[55] Ford and Willey, 1941, fig. 2, pp. 348–49; Griffin, 1946, pp. 75–80.

Punctated, Barton Incised, and Old Town Red Filmed. The curvilinear incised design, Leland Incised, is an important element beginning to appear in the southernmost area, the Yazoo.

The Lower Arkansas River sub-area resembles the St. Francis in that there is very little decorated material in the early part of the C–B time period. Decorated types come in the latter half of the period and persist to the end of the history. Again this situation is consistent with the ceramic complex that prevailed toward the end of the Baytown Period which, like late Baytown in the St. Francis, has only small quantities of decorated material.

An interesting question to consider at this point is the derivation of the few decorated pottery types which are featured in period C–B, the early Mississippi. These are the shell-tempered types which appeal to Ford as most easily derived from corresponding clay-tempered types of the preceding Baytown Period. According to his view, the possible developmental sequences are: Mazique Incised to Barton Incised; Larto Red Filmed to Old Town Red Filmed; Coles Creek Incised to the comparatively scarce Mound Place Incised; and a polished variety of Baytown Plain, analogous to Coles Creek Polished Plain farther south, to Bell Plain. The curvilinear incised variety of Leland Incised, prominent in the Yazoo area may have derived from the clay-tempered types French Fork and Yokena Incised which have frequency centers farther to the south near the mouth of Red River. It obviously is related in some way to the stream of decoration ideas which terminate in A.D. 1700 in Fatherland Incised, Bayougoula Incised, and Chicachae Combed, the marker types for the ceramics of the Natchez, Bayougoula, and Choctaw Indians, respectively. The fine cross-hatching between trailed lines which has been included as a variation in this type has obvious relations to Walls Engraved to the north, and to certain "Caddo" types of the Ouachita and Red River valleys. Relations to Moundville Engraved can also be seen. The earliest similar use of cross-hatched areas is again found in one of the variations of French Fork Incised.

While recognizing the inherent probabilities of these sequences which Ford envisages, Griffin and Phillips are not yet able to see the means by which these transitions were effected nor the specific areas where they took place. In particular, they are doubtful about the transition from Coles Creek to Mound Place Incised and from Yokena-French Fork to Leland Incised. They are more impressed with the number of features of shape, etc., connected with these types that do not appear to have crossed over with the decorative techniques.

The acquisition of a more complete knowledge of the ceramics of period C–B is hampered by the fact that no burials have been reported which can with certainty be dated in the early part of this time span. The large sites that date during this time are notably lacking in productive cemeteries. Phillips' stratigraphic excavation into the Rose Mound (12–N–3) seems to confirm what we had suspected from Moore's reports, that the rich cemeteries of the St. Francis area date toward the end of the occupation of the older of these sites, around time B and later.

We deduce that, although it is obvious that some new ceramic ideas, such as shell-tempering, handles, and the bottle form, came into the Survey Area at the beginning of the Mississippi Period (time C), the majority of the traits that suggest connections with Mesoamerica and the Southwest, as will be discussed later, do not appear in full force until the end of our early Mississippi, about time B.

For information on burial traits of the early part of the Mississippi Period, we have to go outside the area covered by our Survey. Six sites which appear to date about this time have been excavated and partially reported by Ford and Chambers in the valley of the Big Black River, some 30 to 40 miles south of the southern limits of the area covered by our Survey.[56] The burials recovered in these sites were inclusive in small conical mounds and only one site, Pocahontas, had an accompanying rectangular mound. This is interesting, for it throws further light on the question of the retention of the construction of mounds

[56] Ford, 1936, pp. 115–28. Griffin thinks these sites are later than time B, more closely related to Moundville than to our early Mississippi Period.

for burial purposes to a fairly late date on the borders of the Mississippi River flood plain, a matter already discussed in the section devoted to site plans. Attention should also be called to the fact that both the Choctaw and the Natchez Indians continued to make secondary as well as primary burials in conical mounds until the Historic Period. These groups, located in southern Mississippi, contrast markedly in burial practice to the "Caddo" people west of the Mississippi and the late Mississippian culture farther up the Mississippi Valley. The traits which characterize this Big Black River group of sites are summarized by Ford and need not be repeated here.[57]

We have found more sites that were inhabited during the early Mississippi Period than we were able to date for any of the earlier or later times. Eighty-three sites were shown on our map for the period (fig. 68). Rectangular temple mounds in plaza arrangement are typical, and some of the largest sites found, such as the Winterville Site (19–L–1), were occupied at this time. Both the large and small temple-mound sites seem to have been primarily ceremonial centers and apparently were not true villages, at least during the early phases of the period. The majority of sites where the relation of the principal mound to the plaza can be determined show that this mound was placed on the west or northwest side of the plaza and the view across the plaza from it was toward the east or southeast, the general direction of the rising sun.

During period C–B there appears a new feature in the occupation pattern. The population started clustering into larger groups and true towns were established. These seem to have been of two kinds, towns in which the houses were arranged within a rectangular area and probably surrounded by defensive works, and unplanned towns which have no regular shape. The first type was most common along the St. Francis River where such large rectangular middens as at Richard Bridge (11–O–8), Barton Ranch (11–O–10), Turnbow (11–N–12), and Williamson (11–N–13) sites seem to have been established at this time. It appears that the populations have moved in and formed a town about the ceremonial center. In these rectangular sites there is usually a central plaza area, indicated by a relative scarcity or thinness of refuse, and one or more rectangular mounds border the plaza, with orientation similar to that described.

The unplanned towns established at this time are few in number and are more widely scattered throughout the Survey Area. This is not a very certain classification, and it is possible that these may have also been planned villages that were also protected by fortifications. However, in these cases our surface examination has revealed nothing more than rather thick accumulations of refuse scattered over a poorly defined area. No particular plan can be seen.

A limited clustering of population is not entirely a new thing for the Mississippi Valley as small villages have been a feature of the Baytown Period. We have also described the fairly extensive shell-midden sites in the Sunflower and Yazoo basins which date from these earlier periods. However, there has not been anything which looked like a tendency toward urbanization — however modest our present example may be. The Baytown Period sites probably represent small bands of related people; the concentrations at certain places in the Yazoo and Sunflower areas were almost certainly motivated by a localized dependable food supply. Here in the early Mississippi Period, principally in the St. Francis Basin, there are suggestions that the towns were planned and controlled by central authority to a much greater degree than had been the case before.

The increase in central control, as well as the clustering of population, may have been reciprocal functions of a more effective organized warfare pattern. With the appearance of all these features, the scene is set for the subjugation of neighboring people and the creation of small empires which, given time, potentially might become big ones just as has happened so frequently in other parts of the world.

This interpretation of the significance of the occupation pattern is not entirely based upon parallel histories of peoples at about this same stage of cultural development elsewhere. If our dating is about right, De Soto passed through this region sometime after the de-

[57] Ford, 1936, pp. 126–28.

velopment of this pattern. Although the reports of the chroniclers were undoubtedly colored by their own European background, it is quite clear that at that date the country was divided into "provinces," each rather effectively controlled by rulers; the population was mainly concentrated in fortified towns, and there was a conquest warfare pattern — in which the Spaniards did not miss the opportunity to take part.

It might be worth-while to speculate briefly on the origin of this complex. There is a possibility that after the introduction of the plaza-temple-mound complex with attendant priesthood in middle Baytown times, there was a gradual growth of these centers as instruments of social control which kept pace with the increasing population. Now in early Mississippi centers, the originally religious functionaries had so far shifted emphasis to political control that the organized groups of people began to come into conflict with one another as units. This was a much more serious affair than the pattern of privately organized war parties of the historic Eastern tribes, a pattern which probably prevailed in the Mississippi Valley region during the earlier Baytown Period. For protection against organized warfare, populations at this stage of cultural development have to concentrate into towns which can be defended, and effective resistance demands that they themselves also accept a degree of centralized control. Once this is done, they are also in a position to initiate aggression against their neighbors.

Whether this process is an inevitable end result of the typical American ceremonial-center complex that is found in Peru, Mesoamerica, and the Mississippi Valley or whether the events in the Mississippi Valley at this time were touched off by further diffusion of ideas from central Mexico where this pattern was already established and the Aztecs were well along with their program of conquest, is a question which may be answered by future research.

Late Mississippi Period (Time B–A)

This period marks the culmination of the development and decline of Mississippian cultures. This climax was produced by a combination of features some of which are late introductions and others which were in the region at least as early as late Baytown. Still others, though changed in form, have roots that reach back into even earlier stages of the local history. There are no observable major modifications in the cultural complex that would require a migratory movement as an explanation.

The changes in the ceramic complex from the preceding period involve few novel and startling types or features, but are expressed mainly in shifts in percentage relationships among types already discussed. There is evident a definite increase in the quantity of decorated pottery, as well as greater variety in design and shape. A marked increase in the use of polishing is evidenced by the strong upsurge of Bell Plain in the north, particularly in the Memphis area, and by a corresponding increase in slightly different polished plain ware in the south which we have been obliged by sorting difficulties to call by the same name. Along with this rise in polishing, there is an increase in the use of engraving — the two are probably not unconnected — the types in question being Walls and Hull Engraved. There is also a sharp increase in the practice of polishing over incision in curvilinear style as in Leland Incised and the provisional type Blanchard Incised. Painted types, Carson Red on Buff, Nodena Red and White reached their maximum about time B or shortly thereafter, and became popular as burial furniture, while Avenue Polychrome seems to have reached its peak later toward the close of the period. We infer that the few vessels of negative painting in burial collections, one of which is illustrated in figure 111, *j*, would fall about this same time, but only one sherd of the type was found in the Survey Area (see p. 199).

It was also in this period that a group of closely related types, Kent, Ranch, and Rhodes Incised, decorated companion types to Bell Plain, become relatively common in the Memphis area. Parkin Punctated, which is not confined to any one area, also increases, whereas Barton Incised shows a decline.

Few, if any, of the types so far mentioned appear to have lasted into the Historic Period.

using the term in reference to the French penetrations in the late seventeenth century. In the Lower Arkansas area, however, there are several variants, as yet undifferentiated typologically, and at least one defined type, Wallace Incised, that Griffin and Phillips believe to be historic Quapaw. Ford is not convinced that the evidence on this point is conclusive. It cannot well be until a historic Quapaw site has been identified (see discussion p. 418).

Up to now, we have not said very much about vessel shapes but in this period there is such a proliferation of forms that the subject cannot be ignored. Many of the most interesting and provocative shapes have been discussed in detail in Section IV. Here, we wish merely to recapitulate the general trends for as much of the history as we have information. For the Tchula Period we have no specific shape information except by inference from Tchefuncte shapes to the south and in the Baumer Focus to the north, in both of which simple bowl or jar shapes are dominant. Baytown Period shapes have to be deduced mainly from sherds, which is a difficult business. They are, on the whole, extremely simple. Simple bowls with rounded, flattened, and occasionally flat bottoms are in the majority throughout the period. Jars tend to be deep cauldrons with slightly recurved rims, vague shoulders, and rounded or flat bottoms, either round or square. There are some barrel-shaped and beaker forms probably late in the period. Handles are absent or very rare, lugs are triangular, but rare and probably late. Bottles, effigy, and eccentric forms are conspicuously absent throughout the period.

In the Mississippi Period jars become dominant numerically over bowls. The characteristic jar form is sub-globular with straight or slightly outcurved rim and rounded or slightly flattened but not flat bottom. Mississippi jars are normally provided with handles and/or lugs and the former are almost invariably of the strap variety. A few loop handles occur and there is some stratigraphic evidence that they belong in the earlier part of the period. Bowls occur in a wide variety of forms but a simple form with rounded base and curved sides is by far the most common. Rim effigy bowls become a popular form, particularly for burial purposes, about the middle of the period. About the same time, a large assortment of new forms appeared, the most common being the bottle, in a wide variety of shapes, with occasional annular and tripod supports, human effigy and head vases, a wide variety of animal and vegetable forms, compound vessels, spouted and eccentric forms. Some of the most significant of these shapes have been discussed in detail in Section IV. This is also the time when a host of new design elements make their appearance, some of which are associated with the well-known "Southern Cult." The latter are most often executed by engraving of the type here defined as Walls and Hull Engraved, and (very rarely) in direct and negative painting.

These are the features that are usually thought of as characterizing the Mississippi culture in this part of the valley for they are well represented in the large collections from the rich cemeteries of the period. They are at the same time the features that do not seem to have their roots in the earlier cultures of the area, and consequently some other explanation for their existence must be sought.

Characteristic of late Mississippi culture in this area are a large number of traits that come under the heading of miscellaneous small pottery objects. The list includes: miniature vessels; ladles (fig. 93, *o*,); disks made from potsherds, both plain and perforated (the latter sometimes called "spindle whorls"); discoidals; rattles (heads on rim effigy bowls are also occasionally hollow and furnished with rattles); figurines (rare); ear plugs of a small mushroom type; small cylindrical pot supports: "standards," rounded cones of poorly fired clay with holes in the top or sides remarkably similar to the "pot supports" at Snaketown;[58] and pipes. The latter are commonly of the large blocky elbow type with massive base and enlarged stem hole.

In regard to sites of the late Mississippi Period, the most important single characteristic is the trend toward larger and more concentrated villages, a continuation of the tendency already noted in the preceding period. This

[58] Haury, 1937, p. 244.

is particularly the case in the St. Francis area where large rectangular accumulations of refuse mark the sites of what were probably walled villages, such as are described in the narratives of the De Soto expedition. This type of village has been designated as the "St. Francis type" and discussed at length in Section VIII. On the east side of the Mississippi such compact sites are less well defined and they become less frequent to the south. It is in the village refuse on these sites in and among the houses and even under them that enormous number of burials have been found, and the sites are locally known as "cemeteries."

In the northern part of the area burials are primarily extended in the flesh and accompanied by large amounts of grave goods, chiefly pottery, and it is on the basis of this pottery that Holmes originally formulated the concept of a "Middle Mississippi Province." Below the mouth of the St. Francis River the emphasis shifts to secondary burial. In the southern part of the Survey Area, however, these compact sites or "cemeteries" are absent. Here, the sites of comparable size and importance are almost without exception groups of rectangular mounds, often quite large, of the ceremonial-center type described for the preceding period, and burials are still conspicuous by their absence.

Up to this point, we have been able to say nothing about house types though Griffin stubbornly maintains that these Indians must have had some kind of shelter. The early excavations reported by Thomas afford some evidence indicating a rectangular house of wattle-and-daub construction. Our own stratigraphic pits have uncovered short segments of post-hole patterns, and in several instances these occurred in wall trenches. From the type of daub found in this period the use of cane mats as an outside covering for the plastered walls is inferred.

Considerable material derived from burials could be brought together to illustrate the non-ceramic aspects of the culture, but due to the fact that we lack comparable material from earlier horizons in the Survey Area, it does not seem advisable to deal with it in more than summary fashion in this report. The following characteristic traits may be listed briefly:

Dominant type of projectile point is a small thin willow leaf (or half willow leaf with flat base) made from very flat flakes often retouched only on one side. Small triangular points are second in importance.

Small chipped flint celts or "chisels" made from pebbles or occasionally petrified wood, with bits ground to a fine edge and polished.

Flint agricultural tools, "hoes" and "spades," are part of this complex but are not as varied or numerous as in Mississippi Period cultures to the north in the Cahokia area.

Discoidals are fairly common, particularly the smaller sizes. Large bi-concave type occasional.

Large circular stone Moundville-type palettes present but rare.

Stone effigy pipes of the crouching human or animal type rare.

Seated stone figures of the Cumberland type occasionally found.

Bone artifacts fairly well represented in the northern portion of the area from which we have the best information. Included are: antler arrowpoints, small cylindrical sections of antler designated as "flakers," use of scapulae of larger mammals for various implements, deer-jaw graters, tubular bone beads, long bone hairpins with decorated heads and occasional combs, deer, elk, and bison astragali cut into cubes.

Articles of shell include *unio* "spoons," disk and tubular beads, ear pins of the disk and mushroom types, small conch-shell pendants perforated at the beak. Circular shell gorgets are present but extremely rare. This area seems to be marginal in this respect to the Nashville-eastern Tennessee area. This is also true of mask-type gorgets. Decorated elements found on shell gorgets in other areas seem to be confined here to pottery.

Evidences of copper are very rare, confined to rolled tubular beads and similar small ornaments. The large showy lance head found by Moore at the Rose Site is exceptional, and there is one excellent example of repoussé copper from the Shugtown Site in northeastern Arkansas.[59]

[59] In the University of Arkansas Museum. Mistakenly attributed to Spiro in Phillips, 1940, pp. 356–58.

This late Mississippi Period culture which we have just described brings us to the threshold of the Historic Period and by that term we mean the time of the first French penetrations in the last quarter of the seventeenth century. Unfortunately, we cannot establish this date as the terminus of the late Mississippi Period because of an apparent gap of uncertain length between the end of our archaeological record and the beginning of the documentary record of the French. On certain sites with a fully developed late Mississippi culture Moore found small amounts of European trade materials, but the precise associations of these objects with specific Indian material is in all cases uncertain, and in addition the exact date of the European material has never been established. The possibility of the introduction of European articles in this region ranges as far back in time as 1541, the date of De Soto's *entrada.* The contrast between the population distribution in 1541 and the later French period has been discussed (p. 419). Both the population distribution and plans of the towns of our late Mississippi Period, as well as deductions from possible De Soto contacts in other areas have suggested to us that De Soto and his party passed through the northern part of the Survey Area in time B–A, though we are not in perfect agreement as to the exact position of the event. Ford and Griffin would place it well on in the period; Phillips, at the beginning, near time B. In any case, it is probably safe to say that De Soto saw the Mississippi culture in full bloom. The population indicated in the narratives, with due allowance for exaggeration, would seem to be sufficient to account for the large number of sites we have dated here.

The demographic situation described by the French chroniclers after 1672 is in marked contrast. After this time the St. Francis, Memphis, and to a large degree the Sunflower and Yazoo sub-areas were devoid of people. The Quapaw villages about the mouth of the Arkansas and the splinter groups on the Yazoo were the only tribes left in the area at this time.

The sites with European material referred to above are in the majority of cases in areas deserted at this later time. Therefore, they seem to date earlier although not necessarily as early as 1541.

This marked disappearance of population in the Survey Area from time B to the Historic Period requires an explanation. Several have been advanced. Either warfare or epidemics of European diseases seem to be the most popular theories at present.[60]

THE ORIGINS OF MISSISSIPPI CULTURE IN THE SURVEY AREA

As indicated in the Introduction, this was a major problem from the outset of the Survey. As the work proceeded, the problem has become more complex and we can no longer recognize it in terms of a single origin for Mississippi culture. We are even more certain that *the* center for its development is not in the Survey Area at all. In fact, we are becoming increasingly doubtful that a single center for this development exists anywhere. We envisage rather a number of centers in which this culture was developing more or less simultaneously along parallel lines with continuing interaction between them. We are confining our observation to the center localized in the Survey Area.

Here the problem is clearly one of multiple origins of which five major elements can be discerned. These are:

1) Continuity from the pre-existing Baytown Period.
2) Influences coming from the northward.
3) Indirect influences transmitted from Mesoamerica.
4) More direct influences from the Southwest.
5) The X-factor.

1) Although there has been revealed in these pages a considerable amount of disagree-

[60] A minor difference of opinion between the authors should be acknowledged at this point. Ford feels that, in the hypothetical explanation offered at the end of Section IX, Phillips has slighted the role played by epidemics of European diseases in the depopulation of the area. There is no question that the well-documented epidemics of 1698–1700 all but wiped out the remaining population. Whether these had their predecessors we can only surmise.

ment on the question of continuity from Baytown to the Mississippi Period, this has been concerned with specific and for the most part technical matters. As to the general proposition that there was a significant degree of continuity in both population and culture, there has never been any argument. It is the extent of this continuity that has been in question. We can all recognize in the area certain traits such as pyramidal mounds, plaza arrangement, the trend toward increasing population and larger towns, lack of burial concentrations, red-filmed pottery and the strength of bowl forms, use of certain decorative techniques such as, all-over punctation, line-filled triangles on the rim and other simple decorative devices and forms, that were carried over from the Baytown Period into the Mississippi culture.

2) Undoubtedly, some elements that enter into the make-up of Mississippi culture came from the north. The area is marginal for a number of important traits such as shell-tempering, round-bottomed jars, loop and strap handles, small, short-necked, wide-mouthed bottles, agricultural tools, and triangular projectile points. The center or centers of origin for these traits is problematical, but it is fairly certain that it is *not* in the Survey Area. Possibly, there should be added to this group, the practice of fortifying villages, single primary extended burials with grave goods, the effigy complex, and negative painting; but the evidence on these points is far from conclusive. The center of distribution and popularity center of these traits lies somewhere between southeast Missouri and the middle Cumberland region of Tennessee. While the northern part of the Survey Area is a southern extension of this distribution, the lower portion is definitely marginal. The mechanism by which this northern influence reached the area, whether by migration or simple diffusion, cannot yet be shown.

3) When we speak of Middle American influences it should be made clear that these are indirect and in part had already been incorporated in the culture of the late Baytown Period. We have mentioned the pyramidal mound complex as a carry-over from the earlier period, which, Ford thinks, on the evidence now available, was probably introduced from east Texas as early as middle Baytown times. Griffin and Phillips would prefer to place this event slightly later, about the beginning of the late Baytown Period. In either case, introduction into the southern part of the area, followed by a northward movement of the complex through it, is indicated. If Ford is correct and pyramidal mounds did arrive this early in our area, they must have slightly preceded the introduction of certain ceramic traits that also appear to have an ultimate Mesoamerican origin, such as polished pottery and the carinated bowl form. An alternative explanation suggested by Griffin is that these ceramic traits arrived in our area already welded into the Mississippi culture which was moving southward from the Cahokia area, which in turn had received a strong stimulus from the early Gibson Aspect in east Texas by a direct overland route by-passing the Alluvial Valley. Another Mesoamerican feature which was added late in the Mississippi Period is engraving on polished pottery. We are agreed that this technique reached the Mississippi via the "Caddo" area.

On the hotly debated question of the origins of the so-called "Southern Cult" we have very little to contribute at this time. The appearance of cult elements in our area is practically confined to engraved and painted decoration on pottery. The time of this pottery is apparently late, in the latter part of the Mississippi Period. This, however, is not particularly significant for the "Cult" as a whole, because it is clear on the present showing that our area is not an important center for this material. The stylistic relationships of the cult material in our area are closest to the Moundville center, as Griffin has pointed out in a previous section (p. 214), and it is possible that these ideas reached the Mississippi from this quarter.

Other ceramic traits that have been so often discussed from the point of view of Mesoamerican connections may be briefly dismissed here. Some of them, stirrup-neck bottles, tripods, tetrapods, spouted forms, and negative painting, have been covered in the distributional studies in Section IV. On the problem as a whole the only thing we should like to emphasize is their time position in the late Mississippi Period. As indicated in Section IV each of such traits presents its own special problems. The kind of generalizations that have sometimes been made in the past dealing with them as a closely-knit complex no longer appear to be tenable. Each has its own separate history and each its contribution to the manifold problem of the origins of Mississippi culture.

While the sum total of traits that may have had a Mesoamerican origin is not great, they undoubtedly were of great importance in the formation of Mississippi culture. The temple-mound complex with the profound changes in religious orientation implied seems to have paved the way for many additional culture traits of a minor artifactual nature.

4) Certain connections with the Southwest have been intimated in some of the pottery-type descriptions and in the discussion of the distribution of Mississippi Period shapes and other features in Section IV. These, plus other indications, may be taken as opening a relatively new field for investigation. Some of the forms appear fairly early in the Southwestern area, such as the bottle form (as called in the Southeast) which begins in Basket Maker III and is common in Pueblo I. The "bird" or "duck" pot begins in Basket Maker III and is common in Pueblo I and II. A similar form appears in the Mississippi Period particularly in southeast Missouri and less commonly in the northern part of the Survey Area. The basket-handle bowl is in Pueblo I, Sedentary Hohokam, Casas Grandes, and in southeast Missouri in a context closely related to our Mississippi Period culture in the Survey Area. One specimen has been reported in the Survey Area. Compound vessels of the horizontal type are in the Anasazi area in Pueblo II and III and later at Casas Grandes. Human effigy figures of the Survey Area have rather strong morphological and decorative connections with Casas Grandes, but some really striking connections with the Anasazi area in Pueblo II and III are also present. The man-bowl ("Chacmool" effigy) is found in Casas Grandes, southeast Missouri, central Tennessee, and the Survey Area. Handles on jars appear suddenly without visible antecedents in the eastern United States. The nearest area where they were common is the Southwest and here they appear as early as Basket Maker III. Various other decorative features such as punctated pottery, incised line decoration of line-filled triangles, other simple patterns, and noded vessels are found in both areas. The great center of painted pottery of the Mississippi culture, the northern part of our Survey Area, is geographically closer to the Southwest than other Mississippi units, and it is in this area that the stepped design is most frequently used. Other minor traits that might be mentioned are pot supports ("Pueblo corn goddess symbols"), labrets, pottery trowels or "plastering tools," ladles, pottery disks, pottery elbow pipes. These are merely some of the many traits that can be cited in support of some kind of contact between the Southwest and Mississippi Valley and most if not all of them are in the Mississippi Period culture of the Survey Area. The thing that intrigues Griffin and horrifies his co-authors is the fact that this evidence appears to align Mississippi culture in its early stages with Developmental Pueblo. At first glance, it would appear that the direction of diffusion must have been from west to east, but it is a curious fact that most of these traits appear to be better established in the Mississippi than in the Southwest. The whole effigy complex, both human and animal is a case in point. Any further conclusions would be premature. Griffin is planning a separate paper which will discuss the whole problem as he sees it, unimpeded by the conservative thinking of his collaborators.

5) At certain points in the histories of various culture areas there have been sudden florescences which never fail to impress students of history. These Kroeber has called "cultural climaxes." The latter part of the Mississippi Period was such a climax.

There has been much discussion among historians as to the factors which make for such a florescence and although details differ from example to example, certain conditions may be consistently present. A résumé of the factors which appear to account for the Mississippi climax may add to the understanding of this problem. These are:

a) Introduction of a new and improved variety of corn and improved agricultural methods. More dependence appears to have been placed on agriculture.

b) Population increase. This may be assumed to have resulted from the more abundant food supply.

c) Introduction of improved systems of social and political control as suggested by the arrival of the Mesoamerican temple-mound complex.

d) Widespread contacts with peoples with different cultures of similar or slightly superior technological level who could offer ideas useful to the developing Mississippi culture but which were not sufficiently different or superior to it to be damaging.

e) Parallel growth in contiguous but different parts of the central valley of the Mississippi River. These slightly different centers stimulated one another and undoubtedly speeded the process of cultural change.

The interplay of all these factors resulted in the comparatively rapid crystallization of the extensive culture we call Mississippi. Introduced and local cultural traits were quickly welded together to produce traits that appear unlike the items from which they were derived and thus it is difficult for the archaeologist to trace them. This is what we have designated as the X-factor, the contributions made by the culture to its own development. In the case of the Survey Area these are, so far as we know now, mainly in the field of ceramics, in the proliferation of new shapes and modeled elements and in painting and engraving. We may look for prototypes over wide distances, as in many cases we have done, but the special style and flavor are their own.

CHRONOLOGICAL ALIGNMENTS, CULTURAL AND CALENDRICAL

There has been available for some years a sequential arrangement of culture complexes based on the work of Ford and his associates in the lower portion of the Mississippi Alluvial Valley. Up to this point, our discussion of chronology has been limited to the findings in the Survey Area alone not uninfluenced, however, by our ideas as to the way they relate to this lower valley chronology, but as yet we have not attempted a correlation between the two areas. Such a correlation is offered in figure 73. Along with this correlation we have placed in the right-hand column our interpretation of the chronological relations between the Mississippi Valley and Krieger's east Texas sequence. This has been included because of our concern with cultural influences that may have entered our area from this direction.

TABLE 17: VARIOUS ESTIMATES OF LOWER MISSISSIPPI VALLEY CHRONOLOGY.

	JENNINGS, 1944	VAILLANT, 1939 FORD AND WILLEY, 1941 GRIFFIN, 1946	KRIEGER, 1946	CORRELATION WITH EXTINCT CHANNEL CHRONOLOGY; FISK, 1944	ALTERNATIVE SUGGESTED IN THIS REPORT
	1700	1700	1700	1450	1700
Natchez					
	1650	1600	1600	1350	1500
Plaquemine					
		1550	1500	1250	1200
Coles Creek					
	1550	1400	1250	1100	850
Troyville					
	1400	1150	1050	1000	700
Marksville					
	1300	950	850	800	500
Tchefuncte					
	1200	850		700	0

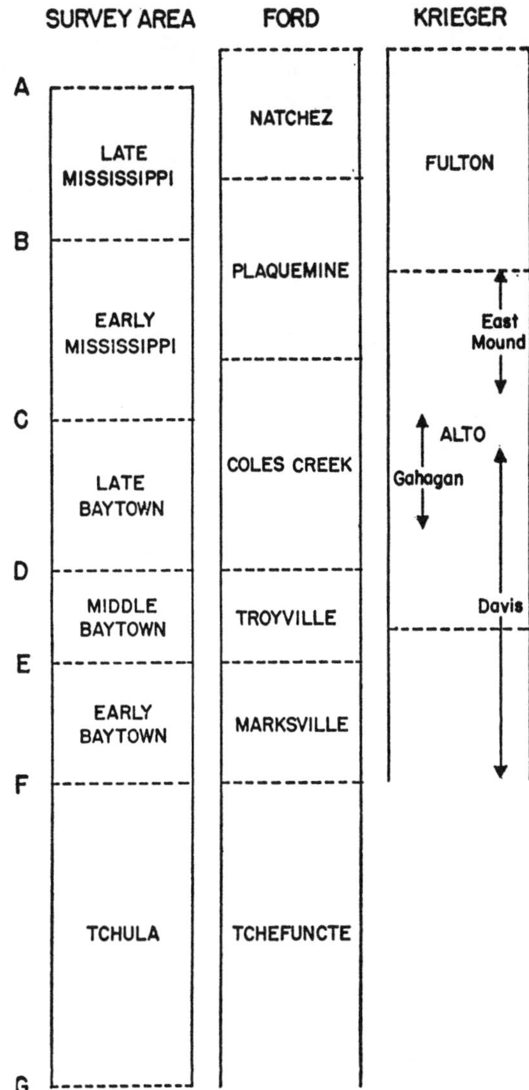

Fig. 73. Correlation of Survey Area dating with Lower Mississippi and east Texas chronologies.[61]

As a result of the radical shortening of the Southwestern time scale brought about by dendrochronology in the late twenties, Eastern archaeologists started pulling up their dates in a panic. They were also influenced by the location of the De Soto date line in the Coles Creek Period, based on the identification of the Troyville Site at Jonesville, Louisiana, with the town of Anilco where the expedition wintered in 1541–42.[62] A similar misconception placed Moundville, and the "Southern Cult" so abundantly manifested there, in the post-De Soto period. Since the early 1940's this trend has been reversed. A notable expression of this reversal was the simultaneous publication of papers by Krieger and Wedel pushing back the dating in Texas and the Central Plains respectively by means of correlations with events in the Southwest.[63]

We stand before the threat of the atom in the form of C^{14} dating. This may be our last opportunity for old-fashioned uncontrolled guessing. We therefore present for comparison in table 17 a series of time estimates. The first two columns represent examples of the conservative thinking that prevailed until recently. The third column, as indicated, represents Krieger's position in 1946 which he has subsequently modified in the direction of still earlier dating (1949). The last column is the alignment proposed by Griffin and endorsed by Phillips and Ford with some minor misgivings. In this scheme a great deal hinges on the significance of the apparent connections between the Mississippi Valley and the Southwest, although this is not the only basis for Griffin's estimates. We agree (and this includes Griffin) that this early Southwest-Mississippi connection is an interesting but unproved hypothesis.

THE PATTERN OF EASTERN PREHISTORY

The trend toward earlier dating discussed above calls for a re-examination of long-accepted ideas about the general development of culture in North America. Events formerly crowded together into a comparatively brief span of time are now being pulled apart so that it is possible to speak of intervals between them. This enables us to see differences in cultural intensification previously blurred by excessive foreshortening. With additional depth the picture has acquired shading, and a great deal of interest as well.

In his classification of ethnographic areas in North America, Kroeber found great diffi-

[61] Griffin and Phillips would now place the Davis Site within the Coles Creek Period of Ford. Ford, on the other hand, believes that the Plaquemine should be aligned C–B and that the entire Krieger (east Texas) chronology dates after time C.

[62] Walker, 1936, p. 57; Swanton, 1939, p. 260.

[63] Krieger, 1947; Wedel, 1947.

culty in dealing with the vast continental area, from the Rockies to the Atlantic, on account of its relative "lightness of cultural contour," and was obliged to include it all in a generalized "Eastern Area." Looking at the prehistory of this eastern area with the same breadth of view, and the deeper perspective now afforded, no corresponding lightness of contour is revealed. We no longer see a single straight line of development leading up to such modest heights as were attained. On the contrary, there seem to have been at least two cultural climaxes, separated in time and, quite as definitely, in place. The curve of eastern development has two peaks, or perhaps it would be more correct to say there are two curves of development, not , and the main events of Eastern prehistory can be interpreted in terms of the interplay between them. However, it is with the peaks that we are at present concerned. The first, Hopewell, localized in the central Ohio Valley, is the culmination of a major "period" (or "pattern" — these terms are never wholly typological nor wholly temporal) for which the term Woodland is perhaps as good as any. It corresponds roughly to Ford and Willey's Burial Mound Stage if you prefer the term. The second, for which no convenient local designation is at hand, is the culmination of the later Mississippi or Temple Mound Stage. By the estimates proposed here there is at least half a millennium between them.

The Mississippi climax is at present very much more difficult to localize. It seems to have taken place over a remarkably wide front, a circumstance that has resulted in various explanatory concepts, the most widely accepted being that of the well-known "Southern Cult." We would like to have been able to report that this climax was centered in the Lower Mississippi Valley — having in mind the spectacular historic Natchez-Taensa culture, it would be a reasonable expectation — but we simply do not as yet have the evidence. There are enough indications to justify the suspicion that it lay somewhat farther up the river. Some day, we may be able to speak of a "Cahokia climax." However, in spite of the present difficulty in "centering" it, the concept of a Mississippi climax, in a temporal sense, appears to be a valid one. We are concerned here not with precise definitions but with an over-all pattern of history. The point is that these two moments of particular intensity, for which the terms Hopewell and Mississippi will have to serve in lieu of better, are distinct and separable; not merely two proximate stages in a continuum. While there was undoubtedly considerable carry-over from one to the other, the second or Mississippi climax was essentially the result of new forces that appeared in the Southeast for the first time.

This is no departure from accepted theory. Whatever dates are favored, there is general agreement that many of the elements of Mississippi culture "came in" from outside and almost everybody seems to think they came from Middle America. In this report we have given reasons for not overlooking the Southwest in this connection. New ideas about dating can have some interesting effects on these facets of the Mississippi problem, as we shall point out, but it is the relationship of Mississippi to the earlier Hopewell climax that now looks so very different. We have now got them far enough apart in time to suggest that a period of Hopewell stagnation or decline intervened. Equally significant is the interval of space, about which we have as yet said nothing.

The enlargement of the concept Hopewell and its areal extension to cover practically the entire eastern United States has tended to reduce the original importance of the central Ohio Valley. A very proper concern for the humbler village aspects of the culture has followed the earlier preoccupation with the great earthworks and complicated burial structures, but the importance of these as indications of cultural climax cannot be denied. Nothing comparable has turned up in any other area on the Hopewell time level, and we can say now that none is likely to. Please note that we are not saying anything about Hopewell origins — the three authors would have to write that chapter separately. Regardless of where the first culture that can be called Hopewellian appeared, however, we can agree that the central Ohio Valley saw its culmination. On the other hand, it is equally certain that neither the first nor the culminating Mississippi culture occurred in the central Ohio Valley. This definite separation in both time and space enables us to visualize the standard culture-historical situation, in which climax and decay in one area are paralleled by inception and rise in another. While the post-climactic stagnation and decline of Hopewell was taking place in the north, the new forces of Mississippi were gathering in the south. We might suggest that the unexciting character of our middle Baytown Period (E–D) reflects this interval when Hopewell had lost its momentum and Mississippi had not yet begun to "roll."

Without straining too hard for historical uniformities, it is possible to see a corresponding post-climactic Mississippi decline. In the Survey Area, owing to the lack of certain identification of historic pottery complexes, the evidence is largely documentary rather than archaeological, and is summarized at the end of Section IX (pp. 419–21). That a wholesale disintegration of culture took place in the 140-year interval between De Soto and the French is indisputable, and it cannot all be laid to the white man and his diseases. There are also indications that the climactic Mississippi culture, represented by the Natchez and Taensa in the late seventeenth century, had been slowly shrinking downstream from earlier and more vigorous centers farther north. This contraction can hardly have begun so late as the introduction of smallpox and measles. These indications are paralleled by abundant evidence throughout the Southeast. In most areas where the archaeology is sufficiently known, a period of regression of uncertain length intervenes between the peak of Mississippi culture and the Historic Period. It might be suggested that the "lightness of cultural contour" deplored by Kroeber is partly due to this protohistoric regression. The profile of Eastern culture at the time of De Soto, or better perhaps, a thousand years earlier, might show considerable ups and downs from one region to another.

In offering these generalizations we cannot claim to have presented anything new or revolutionary. The tendency to dichotomize Eastern prehistory goes back to the day of "Mound Builders" and "Indians." More recently it has taken the form of a possible twofold origin of Eastern culture, a northern (i.e., Asiatic) origin for Woodland and a southern (i.e., Mesoamerican) origin for Mississippi. This is undoubtedly a terrific over-simplification, but it must be admitted that the farther Hopewell is pushed back into the past the more independent it and its parent Woodland become of the Mesoamerican cultural "hearth." Mississippi, by the same token, is pushed back far enough to share in the general expansion of Mesoamerican culture in the post-classic Expansionistic Period, albeit on the very periphery of its influence. Relations with the Southwest are likewise affected. According to the dating suggested here, Hopewell is on a Basket Maker level and the rise of Mississippi corresponds roughly in time to the Pueblo development. These comparisons greatly reinforce the general theory of Mesoamerican origin, direct and/or via the Southwest, for Mississippi culture, about which there never has been very much doubt, and at the same time cause us to look elsewhere for the springs of Hopewell. For it seems a logical proposition that if the roots of both Hopewell and Mississippi lay in Mesoamerica, the contrast between them would not be so evident. The place to look, obviously, is at home, right here in the eastern United States. Whatever the ultimate origins of Woodland may be, the elements that combine to produce the special character of its Hopewell climax cannot be derived from anywhere outside the eastern United States *at the time* postulated here. In short, the new dating, unless it be accompanied by a similar lengthening of dates in other New World areas, strikes a blow for the independence of Eastern culture, at least in the period of its first significant efflorescence.

We may, therefore, bring this joint effort to an amicable close with the complacent reflection that the archaeology of the Lower Mississippi Valley, and eastern North America generally, is even more interesting, and perhaps more important, than we thought.

REFERENCES

REFERENCES

Abell, Walter
1946. Stone disks as treaty "suns." *American Antiquity*, vol. 12, no. 1, pp. 1–9.

Adams, Robert M. and Walker, Winslow M.
1942. Archaeological surface survey of New Madrid County, Missouri. *Missouri Archaeologist*, vol. 8, no. 2.

Alvord, Clarence W.
1922. The Illinois country, 1673–1818. Centennial History of Illinois, vol. I. Chicago.

Anderson, Melville B. (Translator)
1898a. Relation of the discovery of the Mississippi River — written from the narratives of Nicolas de La Salle, otherwise known as "the little M. de La Salle." Caxton Club. Chicago.
1898b. Relation of Henri de Tonty concerning the explorations of La Salle from 1678 to 1683. Caxton Club. Chicago.

Arrow Points
1931. Effigy bottles. Vol. 19, no. 2, p. 2.
1936. Notes on ceremonies and stone objects. (A report by R. P. Burke and H. H. Paulin of a site on the Tallapoosa River.) Vol. 21, nos. 3 and 4, p. 33a.

Ashley, Margaret E.
1932. A study of the ceramic art of the Etowans. In: Moorehead, 1932, pp. 106–35.

Atwater, Caleb
1820. Description of the antiquities discovered in the state of Ohio and other western states. *American Antiquarian Society, Transactions and Collections*, vol. 1, pp. 105–267.

Barrett, S. A.
1933. Ancient Aztalan. *Public Museum of the City of Milwaukee, Bulletin*, vol. 13.

Barton, Charles A.
1927. Where did De Soto discover the Mississippi River? In: Rowland, 1927, pp. 52–96.

Bauxar, Joseph ..
1940. The Norman Site excavations near Wagoner, Oklahoma. *Oklahoma Prehistorian*, vol. 3, no. 3, pp. 2–15.

Beals, Ralph L.; Brainerd, George W.; and Smith, Watson
1945. Archaeological studies in northeast Arizona. *University of California, Publications in American Archaeology and Ethnology*, vol. 44, no. 1.

Bennett, John W.
1944. Archaeological horizons in the southern Illinois region. *American Antiquity*, vol. 10, no. 1, pp. 12–22.

Black, Glenn A.
1944. Angel Site, Vanderburgh County, Indiana. *Indiana Historical Society, Prehistory Research Series*, vol. 2, no. 5, pp. 451–521.

Boston, B.
1941. The De Soto map. *Mid-America*, vol. 23, no. 3 (July), pp. 236–50.

Bourne, Edward G. (Editor)
1904. Narratives of the career of Hernando De Soto. Trail Maker's Series. 2 vols. New York.

Bowman, Isaiah
1911. Forest physiography: physiography of the U. S. and principles of soils in relation to forestry. New York and London.

Bradfield, Wesley
1931. Cameron Creek Village: a site in the Mimbres area in Grant County, New Mexico. *Archaeological Institute of America, School of American Research, Monograph*, no. 1. Santa Fe.

Brainerd, George W.
1949a. A stirrup pot from Lower California. *Masterkey*, vol. 23, no. 1, pp. 5–8.
1949b. Human effigy vessels of Pueblo culture. *Masterkey*, vol. 23, no. 4, pp. 121–24.

Brew, John Otis
1946. Archaeology of Alkali Ridge, southeastern Utah, with a review of the prehistory of the Mesa Verde Division of the San Juan and some observations on archaeological systematics. *Peabody Museum, Harvard University, Papers*, vol. 21.

Brown, Calvin S.
1926. Archeology of Mississippi. *Mississippi Geological Survey*. University.

Burnett, E. K.
1945. The Spiro Mound collection in the Museum. *Museum of the American Indian, Heye Foundation, Contributions*, vol. 14.

Bushnell, David I., Jr.
1922. Villages of the Algonquian, Siouan, and Caddoan tribes west of the Mississippi. *Bureau of American Ethnology, Bulletin* 77.

Butler, Ruth L. (Editor)
1934. Journal of Paul du Ru. Caxton Club. Chicago.

Carey, Henry A.
1931. An analysis of the northwestern Chihuahua culture. *American Anthropologist*, n.s., vol. 33, pp. 325–74.

Chawner, W. D.
1936. Geology of Catahoula and Concordia parishes, Louisiana. *Department of Conservation, Louisiana Geological Survey, Bulletin*, no. 9.

Claflin, William H., Jr.
1931. The Stalling's Island Mound, Columbia County, Georgia. *Peabody Museum, Harvard University, Papers*, vol. 14, no. 1.

Colby, Charles C.
1921. Source book for the economic geography of North America. Chicago.

Cole, Fay-Cooper and Deuel, Thorne
1937. Rediscovering Illinois; archaeological exploration in and around Fulton County. Chicago.

Collins, Henry B., Jr.
1926. Archeological and anthropometric work in Mississippi. *Smithsonian Miscellaneous Collections*, vol. 78, no. 1, pp. 89–95.
1932. Excavations at a prehistoric Indian village site in Mississippi. *U. S. National Museum, Proceedings*, vol. 79, art. 32, pp. 1–22.
1941. Relationships of an early Indian cranial series from Louisiana. *Washington Academy of Science, Journal*, vol. 31, no. 4, pp. 145–55.

Collot, Georges H. V.
1924. A journey in North America. . . . 2 vols. Firenze.

Conant, Alban Jasper
1879. Foot-prints of vanished races in the Mississippi Valley; being an account of some of the monuments and relics of pre-historic races scattered over its surface, with suggestions as to their origin and uses. St. Louis.

Cosgrove, H. S., and C. B.
1932. The Swarts Ruin: A typical Mimbres site in southwestern New Mexico. *Peabody Museum, Harvard University, Papers*, vol. 15.

Covarrubias, Miguel
1943. Tlatilco, archaic Mexican art and culture. *Dyn, The Review of Modern Art*, vol. 4, no. 5, pp. 40–46.

Coxe, Daniel
1741. A description of the English province of Carolana. By the Spaniards call'd Florida, and by the French, La Louisiane. London.

Croswell, C.
1878. Mound explorations in southeastern Missouri. *St. Louis Academy of Science, Transactions*, pp. 531–38.

Delanglez, Jean
1935. The French Jesuits in Lower Louisiana, 1700–1763. New Orleans.
1938a. The journal of Jean Cavelier. Institute of Jesuit History. Chicago.
1938b. Some La Salle journeys. Institute of Jesuit History. Chicago.
1940a. La Salle's expedition of 1682. *Mid-America*, vol. 22, no. 1, pp. 3–37.
1940b. A calendar of La Salle's travels, 1643–1683. *Mid-America*, vol. 22, no. 4, pp. 278–305.
1941. Hennepin's "description of Louisiana": critical essay. Institute of Jesuit History. Chicago.
1943–1944. El Rio del Espíritu Santo. *Mid-America*, vol. 25, no. 3, pp. 189–219, no. 4, pp. 231–49; vol. 26, no. 1, pp. 62–84.
1944a. The voyages of Tonti in North America, 1678–1704. *Mid-America*, vol. 26, no. 4, pp. 255–300.
1944b. The 1674 account of the discovery of the Mississippi. Jolliet's account as given by Dablon in the relation of that year. *Mid-America*, vol. 26, no. 4, pp. 301–24.
1945a. Marquette's autograph map of the Mississippi River. *Mid-America*, vol. 27, no. 1, pp. 30–53.
1945b. The discovery of the Mississippi — Primary sources. *Mid-America*, vol. 27, no. 4, pp. 219–31.
1946a. The discovery of the Mississippi — Secondary sources. *Mid-America*, vol. 28, no. 1, pp. 3–22.
1946b. The Jolliet lost map of the Mississippi. *Mid-America*, vol. 28, no. 2, pp. 67–144.
1946c. The "Rècit des voyages et des decouvertes Pere Jacques Marquette." *Mid-America*, vol. 28, no. 3, pp. 173–94; no. 4, pp. 211–58.

Dellinger, Samuel C. and Dickinson, S. D.
1940. Possible antecedents of the middle Mississippian ceramic complex in northeastern Arkansas. *American Antiquity*, vol. 6, pp. 133–47.
1942. Pottery from the Ozark Bluff shelters. *American Antiquity*, vol. 7, no. 3, pp. 276–89.

Dickinson, S. D.
1936. Ceramic relationships of the pre-Caddo pottery from the Crenshaw Site. *Texas Archeological and Paleontological Society, Bulletin*, vol. 8, pp. 56–68.

Dickinson, Samuel D. and Dellinger, Samuel C.
1940. A survey of the historic earthernware of the Lower Arkansas Valley. *Texas Archeological and Paleontological Society, Bulletin*, vol. 12, pp. 76–96.

DICKINSON, S. D. AND LEMLEY, HARRY J.
1939. Evidences of the Marksville and Coles Creek complexes at the Kirkham Place, Clark County, Arkansas. *Texas Archeological and Paleontological Society, Bulletin*, vol. 11.

DOUGLAS, FREDERIC H. AND D'HARNONCOURT, RENE
1941. Indian art of the United States. The Museum of Modern Art. New York.

DRUCKER, PHILIP
1947. Some implications of the ceramic complex of La Venta. *Smithsonian Miscellaneous Collections*, vol. 107, no. 8.

DUNSTON, C. E.
1910. Preliminary examination of the forest conditions of Mississippi. *Mississippi State Geological Survey, Bulletin*, no. 7.

DU SOLIER, WILFRIDO; KRIEGER, ALEX D.; AND GRIFFIN, JAMES B.
1947. The archaeological zone of Buena Vista, Huaxcama, San Luis Potosí, Mexico. *American Antiquity*, vol. 13, no. 1, pp. 15–32.

EKHOLM, GORDON F.
1944. Excavations at Tampico and Panuco in the Huasteca, Mexico. *American Museum of Natural History, Anthropological Papers*, vol. 38, part V.

ELLIOTT, D. O.
1932. The improvement of the Lower Mississippi River for flood control and navigation. War Department, Corps of Engineers, U. S. Army, U. S. Waterways Experiment Station, 3 vols. Vicksburg.

EVANS, ESTWICK
1819. A pedestrious tour of four thousand miles, through the western states and territories, during the winter and spring of 1818. Concord, N. H.

EVERS, EDWARD
1880. The ancient pottery of southeastern Missouri. Contributions to the Archaeology of Missouri by the Archaeological Section of the St. Louis Academy of Science, Part I: Pottery, pp. 21–30.

FAIRBANKS, CHARLES H.
1946. The Kolomoki Mound group, Early County, Georgia. *American Antiquity*, vol. 11, no. 4, pp. 258–60.

FAYE, STANLEY
1942. The Forked River. *Louisiana Historical Quarterly*, vol. 25, no. 4, pp. 921–42.
1943. The Arkansas post of Louisiana: French Dominion. *Louisiana Historical Quarterly*, vol. 26, no. 3, pp. 633–721.
1944. The Arkansas post of Louisiana: French Dominion. *Louisiana Historical Quarterly*, vol. 27, no. 3, pp. 629–716.

FENNEMAN, NEVIN M.
1938. Physiography of eastern United States. (1st ed.) New York.

FEWKES, JESSE W.
1898. An ancient human effigy vase from Arizona. *American Anthropologist*, vol. 11, no. 6, pp. 165–70.
1904. Two summers' work in Pueblo ruins. Washington.
1914. Archeology of the Lower Mimbres Valley, New Mexico. *Smithsonian Miscellaneous Collections*, vol. 63, no. 10.

FINCH, VERNOR C. AND TREWARTHA, GLENN T.
1936. Elements of geography. (1st ed.) New York and London.

FISK, HAROLD N.
1938. Geology of Grant and LaSalle parishes, Louisiana. *Louisiana Department of Conservation, Geological Bulletin*, no. 10, pp. 149–74.
1944. Geological investigation of the alluvial valley of the Lower Mississippi River. *War Department, Corps of Engineers, U. S. Army, Mississippi River Commission Publication*, no. 52.

FLINT, TIMOTHY
1826. Recollections of the last ten years, . . . Boston. (New York, 1932.)
1828. A condensed geography and history of the western states, of the Mississippi Valley. 2 vols. Cincinnati.
1832. The history and geography of the Mississippi Valley. (2nd ed.) 2 vols. Cincinnati.

FORD, JAMES A.
1935. Ceramic decoration sequence at an old Indian village site near Sicily Island, Louisiana. *Department of Conservation, Louisiana Geological Survey, Anthropological Study*, no. 1.
1936. Analysis of Indian village site collections from Louisiana and Mississippi. *Department of Conservation, Louisiana Geological Survey, Anthropological Study*, no. 2.

FORD, JAMES A. AND QUIMBY, GEORGE I., JR.
1945. The Tchefuncte culture, an early occupation of the Lower Mississippi Valley. *Society for American Archaeology, Memoirs*, no. 2.

FORD, JAMES A. AND WILLEY, GORDON R.
1940. Crooks Site, a Marksville period burial mound in La Salle Parish, Louisiana. Department of Conservation, Louisiana Geological Survey, *Anthropological Study*, no. 3.

1941. An interpretation of the prehistory of the eastern United States. *American Anthropologists*, n.s., vol. 43, no. 3, pp. 325–63.

FOSTER, J. H.
1912. Forest conditions in Louisiana. *U. S. Department of Agriculture, Forest Service Bulletin*, no. 114.

FRENCH, B. F.
1846–1853. Historical collections of Louisiana, embracing many rare and valuable documents relating to the natural, civil, and political history of that state. 7 vols. New York.

FULLER, MYRON L.
1912. The New Madrid earthquake. *U. S. Geological Survey, Bulletin*, no. 494.

FUNKHOUSER, WILLIAM D. AND WEBB, WILLIAM S.
1931. The Duncan Site; on the Kentucky-Tennessee line. *University of Kentucky, Department of Anthropology and Archaeology, Reports in Archaeology and Anthropology*, vol. 1, no. 6, pp. 418–87.

GANNETT, HENRY
1909. Distribution of rainfall. *U. S. Geological Survey, Water-Supply Paper*, no. 234.

GARCILASO DE LA VEGA
1722. La Florida del Inca. Madrid.

GILLIN, JOHN
1941. Archaeological investigations in central Utah. *Peabody Museum, Harvard University, Papers*, vol. 17, no. 2.

GLADWIN, HAROLD S.
1947. Men out of Asia. New York.

GLADWIN, HAROLD S.; HAURY, EMIL W.; SAYLES, E. B.; AND GLADWIN, NORA
1937. Excavations at Snaketown, I. *Medallion Papers*, no. 25.

GLADWIN, WINIFRED AND HAROLD S.
1930. Some Southwestern pottery types — Series I. *Medallion Papers*, no. 8, pp. 3–15.
1931. Some Southwestern pottery types — Series II. *Medallion Papers*, no. 10, pp. 17–49.
1933. Some Southwestern pottery types — Series III. *Medallion Papers*, no. 13, pp. 3–29.

GRIFFIN, JAMES B.
1937a. The archaeological remains of the Chiwere Sioux. *American Antiquity*, vol. 2, no. 3, pp. 180–81.
1937b. The chronological position and ethnological relationships of the Fort Ancient aspect. *American Antiquity*, vol. 2, no. 4, pp. 273–76.
1938. The ceramic remains from Norris Basin, Tennessee. In: Webb, 1938, pp. 253–58.
1939. Report on the ceramics of Wheeler Basin. In: Webb, 1939, pp. 127–65.
1941. Additional Hopewell material from Illinois. *Indiana Historical Society, Prehistory Research Series*, vol. 2, no. 3, pp. 163–223.
1943a. An analysis and interpretation of the ceramic remains from two sites near Beaufort, South Carolina. *Bureau of American Ethnology, Bulletin* 133, pp. 155–68.
1943b. The Fort Ancient aspect: its cultural and chronological position in Mississippi Valley archaeology. Ann Arbor.
1945. The ceramic affiliations of the Ohio Valley, Adena Culture. In: Webb and Snow, 1945, pp. 220–46.
1946. Cultural change and continuity in eastern United States archaeology. *R. S. Peabody Foundation for Archaeology, Papers*, vol. 3, pp. 37–95; 307–48.

GRIFFIN, JAMES B. AND MORGAN, RICHARD, G. (EDITORS)
1941. Contributions to the archaeology of the Illinois River Valley. *American Philosophical Society, Transactions*, n.s., vol. 32, part 1, pp. 1–209.

HAAG, WILLIAM G.
1939a. Description of pottery types. *News Letter of the Southeastern Archaeological Conference*, vol. 1, no. 1 (mimeographed).
1939b. *See* 1939a, vol. 1, no. 2.
1939c. *See* 1939a, vol. 1, no. 3.
1939d. *See* 1939a, vol. 1, no. 4.
1939e. *See* 1939a, vol. 1, no. 5.
1939f. *See* 1939a, vol. 1, no. 6.
1942a. A description and analysis of the Pickwick pottery. In: Webb, 1942, pp. 509–26.
1942b. Early horizons in the southeast. *American Antiquity*, vol. 7, no. 3, pp. 209–22; 311–18.

HABIG, MARION A.
1934. The Franciscan Père Marquette. A critical biography of Father Zénobe Membré, O.F.M., La Salle's chaplain and missionary companion, 1645(ca.)–1689. *Franciscan Studies*, no. 13. New York.

HALL, R. CLIFFORD
1910. Preliminary study of forest conditions in Tennessee. *Tennessee State Geological Survey, Bulletin*, no. 10, extract A.

HARRINGTON, M. R.
1920. Certain Caddo sites in Arkansas. *Museum of the American Indian, Heye Foundation, Indian Notes and Monographs, Miscellaneous Series*, no. 10.
1922. Cherokee and earlier remains on Upper Tennessee River. *Museum of the American In-*

dian, Heye Foundation, Indian Notes and Monographs, Miscellaneous Series, no. 24.

1924. Explorations in the Ozark region. *Museum of the American Indian, Heye Foundation, Indian Notes*, vol. 1, no. 1, pp. 3–7.

1930. Archeological explorations in southern Nevada. *Southwest Museum Papers*, no. 4, pp. 1–25.

HARSHBERGER, JOHN W.

1911. Phytogeographic survey of North America. A consideration of the phytogeography of the North American continent, including Mexico, Central America, and the West Indies, together with the evolution of North American plant distribution. Die Vegetation der Erde XIII (hrsg. by A. Engler and O. Drude). New York and Leipzig.

HAURY, EMIL W.

1936. The Mogollon culture of southwestern New Mexico. *Medallion Papers*, no. 20.

1937. Figurines and miscellaneous clay objects. In: Gladwin, Haury, Sayles, and Gladwin, 1937, pp. 233–45.

1941. Excavations in the Forestdale Valley, east-central Arizona. *University of Arizona, Bulletin*, vol. 11, no. 4.

1945. The excavation of Los Muertos and neighboring ruins in the Salt River Valley, southern Arizona. *Peabody Museum, Harvard University, Papers*, vol. 24, no. 1.

HEWETT, EDGAR L.

1908. Les Communautés Anciennes dans le Désert Américain. Genève.

HEYE, GEORGE G.; HODGE, F. W.; AND PEPPER, GEORGE H.

1918. The Nacoochee Mound in Georgia. *Museum of the American Indian, Heye Foundation, Contributions*, vol. 4, no. 3.

HILGARD, EUGENE W.

1860. Report on the geology and agriculture of the State of Mississippi. Jackson.

HODGE, FREDERICK W.

1907. Handbook of the American Indians north of Mexico. *Bureau of American Ethnology, Bulletin* 30, 2 vols.

1923. Circular kivas near Hawikuh, New Mexico. *Museum of the American Indian, Heye Foundation, Contributions*, vol. 7, no. 1, pp. 1–37.

HODGES, T. L.

1945. Suggestion for identification of certain Mid-Ouachita pottery as Cahinnio Caddo. *Texas Archeological and Paleontological Society, Bulletin*, vol. 16, pp. 98–116.

HOLMES, WILLIAM H.

1884. Illustrated catalogue of a portion of the ethnologic and archaeologic collections made by the Bureau of Ethnology during the year 1881. *Bureau of Ethnology, 3rd Annual Report for 1881–82*, pp. 433–506.

1886. Ancient pottery of the Mississippi Valley. *Bureau of Ethnology, 4th Annual Report for 1882–83*, pp. 367–436.

1903. Aboriginal pottery of the eastern United States. *Bureau of American Ethnology, 20th Annual Report for 1898–99*, pp. 1–237.

HOOTON, EARNEST A.

1920. Indian village site and cemetery near Madisonville, Ohio. *Peabody Museum, Harvard University, Papers*, vol. 8, no. 1.

HOUGH, WALTER

1903. Archeological field work in northeastern Arizona. The Museum-Gates Expedition of 1901. *U. S. National Museum, Annual Report for 1901*, pp. 279–358.

JAMES, EDWIN (COMPILOR)

1905. Account of an expedition from Pittsburg to the Rocky Mountains. In: "Early Western Travels, 1748–1846" (Reuben Gold Thwaites, ed.), vol. 17, part 4 — James' account of S. H. Long's Expedition, 1819–20. Cleveland.

JEANÇON, JEAN A.

1929. Archaeological investigations in the Taos Valley, New Mexico, during 1920. *Smithsonian Miscellaneous Collections*, vol. 81, no. 12.

JEFFERSON, MARK S. W.

1902. Limiting width of meander belts. *National Geographic Magazine*, vol. 13, pp. 373–85.

JENNINGS, JESSE D.

1941. Chickasaw and earlier Indian cultures of northeast Mississippi. *Journal of Mississippi History*, vol. 3, no. 3 (July), pp. 155–226.

JESUIT RELATIONS

1900. Travels and explorations of the Jesuit Missionaries in New France, 1610–1791 (Reuben Gold Thwaites, ed.), vol. 65 — Lower Canada, Mississippi Valley, 1696–1702. Cleveland.

JONES, JOSEPH

1876. Explorations of the aboriginal remains of Tennessee. *Smithsonian Contributions to Knowledge*, no. 259.

1880. Explorations of the aboriginal remains of Tennessee. *Smithsonian Institution, Contributions to Knowledge*, vol. 22, pp. 1–171.

JONES, WALTER B. AND DEJARNETTE, DAVID L.

1936. Moundville culture and burial. *Geological Survey of Alabama, Museum Papers*, no. 13.

JOUTEL, HENRI
1896. Joutel's journal of La Salle's last voyage. (A reprint of the first English translation, London, 1714; with the map of the original French edition, Paris, 1713, in facsimile.) Melville B. Anderson, editor. Caxton Club. Chicago.

JUDD, NEIL M.
1926. Archeological observations north of the Rio Colorado. *Bureau of American Ethnology, Bulletin* 82.

KELEMAN, PÁL
1943. Medieval American art. 2 vols. New York.

KELLOGG, LOUISE PHELPS (EDITOR)
1917. Early narratives of the Northwest, 1634–1699. New York.

KELLY, A. R.
1938. A preliminary report on archeological explorations at Macon, Ga. *Bureau of American Ethnology, Bulletin* 119.

KIDDER, ALFRED V.
1915. Pottery of the Pajarito Plateau and of some adjacent regions in New Mexico. *American Anthropological Association, Memoirs*, vol. 2, part 6, pp. 407–61.
1916. The pottery of the Casas Grandes district, Chihuahua. "Holmes Anniversary Volume," pp. 253–68. Washington.
1931. The pottery of Pecos, vol. I. *Department of Archaeology, Papers of the Southwestern Expedition*, no. 5. New Haven.
1936. The pottery of Pecos, vol. II. *Department of Archaeology, Papers of the Southwestern Expedition*, no. 7. New Haven.

KLAGES, KARL H. W.
1942. Ecological crop geography. New York.

KLIMM, LESTER E.; STARKEY, OTIS P.; AND HALL, NORMAN F.
1940. Introductory economic geography. (2nd ed.) New York.

KNEBERG, MADELINE D. AND LEWIS, THOMAS M. N.
1947. The archaic horizon in western Tennessee. *Tennessee University, Record Extension Series*, vol. 23, no. 4.

KNIFFEN, FRED B.
1936. A preliminary report of the mounds and middens of Plaquemines and St. Bernard parishes, Lower Mississippi River Delta. *Louisiana Department of Conservation, Geological Bulletin*, no. 8, pp. 407–22.

KRIEGER, ALEX D.
1944. The typological concept. *American Antiquity*, vol. 9, no. 3 (January), pp. 271–88.
1946. Culture complexes and chronology in northern Texas, with extension of Puebloan datings to the Mississippi Valley. *University of Texas, Publication* no. 4640.
1947. The eastward extension of Puebloan datings toward cultures of the Mississippi Valley. *American Antiquity*, vol. 12, no. 3, pp. 141–48.
1949. *See* under Newell and Krieger, 1949.

KROEBER, ALFRED L.
1939. Cultural and natural areas of native North America. *California University, Publications in American Archaeology and Ethnology*, vol. 38.

LECLERCQ, CHRÉTIEN, FATHER
1881. First establishment of the faith in New France. Translated and edited by John Gilmary Shea. 2 vols. New York.
1903. Account of La Salle's attempt to reach the Mississippi by sea, and of the establishment of a French colony in St. Louis Bay. In: Shea, 1903, pp. 189–200.

LEMLEY, HARRY J.
1936. Discoveries indicating a pre-Caddo culture on Red River in Arkansas. *Texas Archeological and Paleontological Society, Bulletin*, vol. 8, pp. 25–55.

LEMLEY, HARRY J. AND DICKINSON, S. D.
1937. Archaeological investigations on Bayou Macon in Arkansas. *Texas Archeological and Paleontological Society, Bulletin*, vol. 9, pp. 11–47.

LEWIS, THEODORE H.
1902. Route of De Soto's expedition from Taliepacana to Huhasene. *Mississippi Historical Society, Publication*, vol. 6, pp. 449–67. Oxford. (Reprinted in: Rowland, 1927, pp. 12–30.)
1937. De Soto's camps in the Chickasaw country in 1540–1541. (Reprinted from: *National Magazine*, November, 1891.) *Minnesota Archeologist*, vol. 3, pp. 29–32.

LEWIS, THOMAS M. N. AND KNEBERG, MADELINE D.
1941. The prehistory of the Chickamauga Basin in Tennessee. *University of Tennessee, Division of Anthropology, Tennessee Anthropological Papers*, no. 1.
1946. Hiwassee Island: an archaeological account of four Tennessee Indian peoples. Knoxville.

LILLY, ELI
1937. Prehistoric antiquities of Indiana. Indianapolis.

LINTON, RALPH
1940. Crops, soils, and culture in America. In: "The Maya and Their Neighbors," p. 32–40. New York.

LISTER, ROBERT H.
1947. Archaeology of the Middle Río Belsas Basin, Mexico. *American Antiquity*, vol. 13, no. 1, pp. 67–78.

LIVINGSTON, BURTON E. AND SHREVE, FORREST
1921. The distribution of vegetation in the United States, as related to climatic conditions. *Carnegie Institution, Publication* no. 284.

LUMHOLTZ, CARL
1902. Unknown Mexico. 2 vols. New York.

MCKERN, WILLIAM C.
1937. An hypothesis for the Asiatic origin of the Woodland culture pattern. *American Antiquity*, vol. 3, no. 2, pp. 138–43.

MARBUT, CURTIS FLETCHER
1935. Soils of the United States. In: Atlas of American Agriculture, part III. Washington.

MARGRY, PIERRE
1879. Mémoires et documents pour servir à l'histoire des origines françaises des pay d'outremer. 3 vols. Paris.

MARTIN, PAUL S.
1939. Modified Basket Maker sites, Ackmen-Lowry area, southwestern Colorado, 1938. *Field Museum of Natural History, Anthropological Series*, vol. 23, no. 3.

MARTIN, PAUL S.; QUIMBY, GEORGE I., JR.; AND COLLIER, DONALD
1947. Indians before Columbus: twenty thousand years of North American history revealed by archeology. Chicago.

MARTIN, PAUL S. AND RINALDO, JOHN B.
1947. The Su Site; excavations at a Mogollon village, western New Mexico, third season, 1946. *Field Museum of Natural History, Anthropological Series*, vol. 32, no. 3.

MARTIN, PAUL S. AND WILLIS, ELIZABETH S.
1940. Anasazi painted pottery in Field Museum of Natural History. *Field Museum of Natural History, Anthropological Memoirs*, vol. 5.

MATTHES, GERARD H.
1941. Basic aspects of stream-meanders. *National Research Council, American Geophysical Union, Transactions*, part III, pp. 632–36.

MATTOON, WILBUR R.
1915. The southern cypress. *U. S. Department of Agriculture, Bulletin*, no. 272.

MAYER, BRANTZ
1846. Mexico: as it was and as it is. (3rd edition.) Baltimore.

MERA, H. P.
1932. Wares ancestral to Tewa Polychrome. *Laboratory of Anthropology, Technical Series, Bulletin*, no. 4.
1945. Negative painting in Southwest pottery. *Southwestern Journal of Anthropology*, vol. 1, pp. 161–65.

MERRIAM, C. H.
1898. Life zones and crop zones of the United States. *U. S. Department of Agriculture, Biological Survey, Bulletin*, no. 10.

MOEDANO, HUGO
1941. Estudio preliminar de la ceramica de Tzintzuntzan; temperada III. *Revista Mexicana de Estudio Antropologicos*, vol. 5, no. 1, pp. 21–42.

MOORE, CLARENCE B.
1897. Certain aboriginal mounds of the Georgia coast. *Academy of Natural Sciences of Philadelphia, Journal*, vol. 11, pp. 1–138.
1898. Recent acquisitions. *Academy of Natural Sciences of Philadelphia, Journal*, vol. 11, pp. 185–88.
1899. Certain aboriginal remains of Alabama River. *Academy of Natural Sciences of Philadelphia, Journal*, vol. 11, pp. 351–94.
1901. Certain aboriginal remains of the northwest Florida coast. Part I. *Academy of Natural Sciences of Philadelphia, Journal*, vol. 11, pp. 423–516.
1902. Certain aboriginal remains of the northwest Florida coast. Part II. *Academy of Natural Sciences of Philadelphia, Journal*, vol. 12, pp. 127–355.
1903a. Certain aboriginal mounds of the central Florida west-coast. *Academy of Natural Sciences of Philadelphia, Journal*, vol. 12, pp. 359–438.
1903b. Certain aboriginal mounds of the Apalachicola River. *Academy of Natural Sciences of Philadelphia, Journal*, vol. 12, pp. 439–94.
1905. Certain aboriginal remains of the Black Warrior River. *Academy of Natural Sciences of Philadelphia, Journal*, vol. 13, pp. 125–244.
1907. Moundville revisited. *Academy of Natural Sciences of Philadelphia, Journal*, vol. 13, pp. 337–405.
1908a. Certain mounds of Arkansas and of Mississippi — Part I: mounds and cemeteries of the Lower Arkansas River. *Academy of Natural Sciences of Philadelphia, Journal*, vol. 13, pp. 480–557.
1908b. Certain mounds of Arkansas and of Mississippi — Part II: mounds of the Lower Yazoo and Lower Sunflower rivers, Mississippi. *Academy of Natural Sciences of Philadelphia, Journal*, vol. 13, pp. 564–92.
1908c. Certain mounds of Arkansas and of Mississippi — Part III: the Blum Mounds, Mississippi. *Academy of Natural Sciences of Philadelphia, Journal*, vol. 13, pp. 594–600.

1909. Antiquities of the Ouachita Valley. *Academy of Natural Sciences of Philadelphia, Journal*, vol. 14, pp. 7–170.

1910. Antiquities of the St. Francis, White, and Black rivers, Arkansas. *Academy of Natural Sciences of Philadelphia, Journal*, vol. 14, pp. 254–364.

1911. Some aboriginal sites on Mississippi River. *Academy of Natural Sciences of Philadelphia, Journal*, vol. 14, pp. 367–480.

1912. Some aboriginal sites on Red River. *Academy of Natural Sciences of Philadelphia, Journal*, vol. 14, pp. 482–644.

1913. Some aboriginal sites in Louisiana and Arkansas. *Academy of Natural Sciences of Philadelphia, Journal*, vol. 16, pp. 7–99.

1915. Aboriginal sites on Tennessee River. *Academy of Natural Sciences of Philadelphia, Journal*, vol. 16, pp. 171–428.

1916. Additional investigations on Mississippi River. *Academy of Natural Sciences of Phildelphia, Journal*, vol. 16, pp. 492–508.

1918. The northwestern Florida coast revisited. *Academy of Natural Sciences of Philadelphia, Journal*, vol. 16, pp. 515–79.

Moorehead, Warren K.

1906. A narrative of explorations in New Mexico, Arizona, Indiana, etc. *Phillips Academy, Department of Archaeology, Bulletin*, no. 3.

1910. The Stone Age in North America. 2 vols. Boston and New York.

1929. The Cahokia Mounds. Part I. *University of Illinois, Bulletin*, vol. 26, no. 4, pp. 1–106. Chicago.

1932. Etowah Papers I: Exploration of the Etowah Site in Georgia. *Phillips Academy, Department of Archaeology, Publications*, vol. 3.

Morris, Earl H.

1919. The Aztec Ruin. *American Museum of Natural History, Anthropological Papers*, vol. 26, part I.

1939. Archaeological studies in the La Plata district, southwestern Colorado and northwestern New Mexico. *Carnegie Institution, Publication* no. 519.

Myer, William E.

1917. The remains of primitive man in Cumberland Valley, Tennessee. *19th International Congress of Americanists, Proceedings*, pp. 96–102.

1928. Two prehistoric villages in Middle Tennessee. *Bureau of American Ethnology, 41st Annual Report for 1919–1924*, pp. 485–614.

Newell, H. Perry and Krieger, Alex D.

1949. The George C. Davis Site, Cherokee County, Texas. *Society for American Archaeology, Memoirs*, no. 5. (*American Antiquity*, vol. 14, no. 4, part 2.)

Newkumet, Phil J.

1940. Preliminary report on excavation of the Williams mound, Le Flore County, Oklahoma. *Oklahoma Prehistorian*, vol. 3, no. 2.

Nuttall, Thomas

1905. A journal of travels into the Arkansas Territory during the year 1819. In: "Early Western travels, 1748–1846" (Reuben Gold Thwaites, ed.), vol. 13.

Orr, Kenneth G.

1941. The Eufaula Mound. *Oklahoma Prehistorian*, vol. 4, no. 1.

1946. The archaeological situation at Spiro, Oklahoma; a preliminary report. *American Antiquity*, vol. 11, no. 4, pp. 228–56.

Palmer, (?)

1917. Article in: *Arkansas Historical Society, Publications*, vol. 4, pp. 431–32; 445–47.

Peabody, Charles

1904. Exploration of mounds, Coahoma County, Mississippi. *Peabody Museum, Harvard University, Papers*, vol. 3, no. 2.

Pepper, George H.

1906. Human effigy vases from Chaco Cañon, New Mexico. "Boas Anniversary Volume," pp. 320–334.

Phillips, Philip

1939. Introduction to the archaeology of the Mississippi Valley. Ph.D. thesis, Department of Anthropology, Peabody Museum, Harvard University.

1940. Middle American influences on the archaeology of the southeastern United States. In: "The Maya and Their Neighbors," pp. 349–67. New York.

Potter, W. B.

1880. Archaeological remains in southeastern Missouri — Earthworks of Missouri, Part I: Pottery. *Archaeological Section of the St. Louis Academy of Science, Contributions to the Archaeology of Missouri*, part I, pp. 5–19.

Putnam, F. W.

1878. Archaeological explorations in Tennessee. *Peabody Museum, Harvard University, 11th Annual Report* (vol. 2), pp. 305–60.

Quimby, George I., Jr.

1942. The Natchezan culture type. *American Antiquity*, vol. 7, no. 3, pp. 255–75; 311–18.

Richardson, William

1940. Journey from Boston to the western country and down the Ohio and Mississippi rivers to New Orleans, 1815–1816. Privately printed for the Valve Pilot Corp. New York.

RIDGWAY, R.
1912. Color standards and color nomenclature. Washington.

ROBERTS, FRANK H. H., JR.
1932. The village of the Great Kivas on the Zuñi Reservation, New Mexico. *Bureau of American Ethnology, Bulletin* 111.

ROBERTSON, JAMES A. (TRANSLATOR AND EDITOR)
1933. True relation of the hardships suffered by Governor Fernando De Soto and certain Portugese gentlemen during the discovery of the province of Florida. Now newly set forth by a gentleman of Elvas. *Florida State Historical Society, Publication* no. 11, vols. 1 and 2.

ROWLAND, DUNBAR
1927. A symposium on the place of discovery of the Mississippi by Hernando De Soto. *Mississippi Historical Society, Special Bulletin,* no. 1.

RUSSELL, RICHARD J.
1936. Physiography of Lower Mississippi River Delta. *Louisiana Department of Conservation, Geological Survey Bulletin,* no. 8, pp. 3–199.
1944. Lower Mississippi Valley loess. *Geological Society of America, Bulletin,* vol. 55, no. 1, pp. 1–40.

SAYLES, EDWARD B.
1936. Some southwestern pottery types, Series V. *Medallion Papers,* no. 21.

SCHULTZ, CHRISTIAN, JR.
1810. Travels on an inland voyage through the states of New York, Pennsylvania, Virginia, Ohio, Kentucky, and Tennessee, and through the territories of Indiana, Louisiana, Mississippi, and New Orleans. Performed in the years 1807 and 1808. 2 vols. New York.

SETZLER, FRANK M.
1933. Pottery of the Hopewell type from Louisiana. *U. S. National Museum, Proceedings,* vol. 82, art. 22, pp. 1–21.

SETZLER, FRANK M. AND JENNINGS, JESSE D.
1941. Peachtree Mound and village site, Cherokee County, North Carolina. *Bureau of American Ethnology, Bulletin* 131.

SHANTZ, H. L. AND ZON, RAPHAEL
1924. Atlas of American Agriculture. Part I: the physical basis of agriculture; Section E: natural vegetation. *U. S. Department of Agriculture, Bureau of Agricultural Economics, Advance Sheets,* no. 6.

SHEA, JOHN D. G. (EDITOR)
1861. Early voyages up and down the Mississippi, by Cavelier, St. Cosme, Le Sueur, Gravier, and Guignas. Albany.
1903. Discovery and exploration of the Mississippi Valley, with the original narratives of Marquette, Allouez, Membré, Hennepin, and Anastase Douay. (2nd ed.) Albany.

SHELFORD, VICTOR E.
1926. Naturalist's guide to the Americas. Ecological Society of America, Committee on the Preservation of Natural Conditions.

SHEPARD, ANNA O.
1936. The technology of Pecos pottery. In: Kidder, 1936, pp. 389–587.

SHETRONE, HENRY C. AND GREENMAN, EMERSON F.
1931. Explorations of the Seip group of prehistoric earthworks. *Ohio Archaeological and Historical Quarterly,* vol. 40, no. 3, pp. 349–509.

SHIMEK, B.
1911. The prairies. *Iowa State University, Laboratory of Natural History, Bulletin,* vol. 6, no. 2, pp. 169–240.

SHIPP, BARNARD
1881. The history of Hernando de Soto and Florida. Or, record of events of fifty-six years, from 1512 to 1568. Philadelphia.

SMITH, HALE G.
1951. The Crable Site, Fulton County, Illinois; a late prehistoric site in the Central Illinois Valley. *Museum of Anthropology, University of Michigan, Anthropological Papers,* no. 7.

SNYDER, J. F.
1908. Prehistoric Illinois: the Brown County ossuary. *Illinois State Historical Society, Journal,* vol. 1, nos. 2 and 3, pp. 33–43.

SPIER, LESLIE
1917. An outline for a chronology of Zuñi Ruins. *American Museum of Natural History, Anthropological Papers,* vol. 18, pt. 3, pp. 207–331.

STEVENSON, JAMES
1883. Illustrated catalogue of the collections obtained from the Indians of New Mexico and Arizona in 1879. *Bureau of American Ethnology, 2nd Annual Report,* pp. 307–22.

STEWARD, JULIAN H.
1936. Pueblo material culture in western Utah. (Early inhabitants of western Utah, part 2.) *University of New Mexico, Bulletin,* no. 287. (*Anthropological Series,* vol. 1, no. 3.)
1937. Ancient caves of the great Salt Lake region. *Bureau of American Ethnology, Bulletin* 116.
1938. Basin-plateau aboriginal sociopolitical groups. *Bureau of American Ethnology, Bulletin* 120.

STILES, HENRY REED (EDITOR)
1906. Joutel's journal of La Salle's last voyage, 1684–1687, with a frontispiece of Gudebrod's

statue of La Salle and the map of the original French edition, Paris, 1713, in facsimile.

STODDARD, H. L.
1904. The abstruse significance of the numbers thirty-six and twelve. *American Antiquarian and Oriental Journal*, vol. 26, no. 1, pp. 153–64.

STREBEL, HERMANN
1889. Alt-Mexico. Archäologische Beiträge zur Kulturgeschichte seiner Bewohner. Vol. 2. Hamburg and Leipzig.

STRONG, W. D.; KIDDER, ALFRED II; AND PAUL, A. J. DREXEL, JR.
1938. Preliminary report on the Smithsonian Institution–Harvard University archaeological expedition to northwestern Honduras, 1936. *Smithsonian Miscellaneous Collections*, vol. 97, no. 1.

SWALLOW, GEORGE C.
1858. Indian mounds in New Madrid County, Missouri. *Academy of Science of St. Louis, Transactions*, vol. 1, p. 36.
1875. Inventory of objects from mounds in New Madrid County and a brief description of excavations (improvised title). *Peabody Museum, Harvard University, 8th Annual Report*, pp. 16–46.

SWANTON, JOHN R.
1911. Indian tribes of the Lower Mississippi Valley and adjacent coast of the Gulf of Mexico. *Bureau of American Ethnology, Bulletin* 43.
1912. De Soto's line of march from the viewpoint of an ethnologist. *Mississippi Valley Historical Association, Proceedings*, vol. 5, pp. 147–57.
1923. New light on the early history of the Siouan peoples. *Washington Academy of Science, Journal*, vol. 13, pp. 33–43.
1931. Source material for the social and ceremonial life of the Choctaw Indians. *Bureau of American Ethnology, Bulletin* 103.
1932a. The ethnological value of the De Soto narratives. *American Anthropologist*, n.s., vol. 34, no. 4, pp. 570–90.
1932b. The relation of the southeast to general culture problems of American pre-history. National Research Council, Division of Anthropology and Psychology, Committee on State Archaeological Surveys, Conference on Southern Prehistory.
1939. Final report of the United States De Soto Expedition Commission. *76th Congress, 1st Session, House Document*, no. 71.
1942. Source material on the history and ethnology of the Caddo Indians. *Bureau of American Ethnology, Bulletin* 132.
1946. The Indians of the southeastern United States. *Bureau of American Ethnology, Bulletin* 137.

TAYLOR, WALTER W.
1948. A study of archeology. *American Anthropologist*, n.s., vol. 50, no. 3, part 2. (*American Anthropological Association, Memoirs*, no. 69.)

TELLO, JULIO C.
1943. Discovery of the Chavín culture in Peru. *American Antiquity*, vol. 9, no. 1, pp. 135–60.

THOMAS, CYRUS
1894. Report on the mound explorations of the Bureau of Ethnology. *Bureau of Ethnology, 12th Annual Report.*

THOMPSON, J. ERIC
1936. Archaeology of South America. *Field Museum of Natural History, Leaflet*, no. 33.

THORNTHWAITE, C. WARREN
1931. The climates of North America, according to a new classification. *Geographical Review*, vol. 21, pp. 633–55.
1933. The climates of the earth. *Geographical Review*, vol. 23, pp. 433–40.

THRUSTON, GATES P.
1890. Antiquities of Tennessee, and adjacent states. (1st ed.) Cincinnati.
1897. Antiquities of Tennessee, and the adjacent states. (2nd ed.) Cincinnati.

THWAITES, REUBEN GOLD (EDITOR)
1903. A new discovery of a vast country in America; by Father Louis Hennepin. 2 vols. Chicago.

TONTI, H.
1898. *See* under Anderson, 1898b.

TONTI LETTERS
1689. *Mid-America*, vol. 21, no. 3, pp. 209–38 (1939).

TOSCANO, SALVADOR; KIRCHOFF, PAUL; AND DE LA BORBOLLA, DANIEL F. RUBIN
1946. Arte pre colombino del Occidente de Mexico. Mexico.

TUCKER, SARA JONES
1941. Archival materials for the anthropologist in the national archives, Washington, D. C. *American Anthropologist*, n.s., vol. 43, no. 4, pp. 617–44.
1942. Indian villages of the Illinois country. Part I: Atlas. *Illinois State Museum, Scientific Papers*, vol. 2.

VAILLANT, GEORGE C.
1927. The chronological significance of Maya ceramics. Ph.D. thesis, Department of Anthropology, Peabody Museum, Harvard University.

1932. Some resemblance in the ceramics of Central and North America. *Medallion Papers*, no. 12.

1939. Indian arts in North America. New York, London.

Voegelin, Erminie W.

1939. Some possible sixteenth and seventeenth century locations of the Shawnee. *Indiana Academy of Science, Proceedings*, vol. 48, pp. 13–18.

1941. The place of agriculture in the subsistence economy of the Shawnee. *Michigan Academy of Science, Arts, and Letters, Papers*, vol. 26, pp. 513–20.

1944. Mortuary customs of the Shawnee and other eastern tribes. *Indiana Historical Society, Prehistory Research Series*, vol. 2, no. 4, pp. 225–444.

Walker, Winslow M.

1936. The Troyville Mounds, Catahoula Parish, Louisiana. *Bureau of American Ethnology, Bulletin* 113.

Webb, Clarence H.

1944. Stone vessels from a northeast Louisiana site. *American Antiquity*, vol. 9, no. 4, pp. 386–94.

1945. A second historic Caddo site at Natchitoches, Louisiana. *Texas Archeological and Paleontological Society, Bulletin*, vol. 16, pp. 52–83.

1948. Caddoan prehistory: the Bossier Focus. *Texas Archeological and Paleontological Society, Bulletin*, vol. 19, pp. 100–47.

Webb, Clarence H. and Dodd, Monroe, Jr.

1939. Further excavations of the Gahagan Mound; connections with a Florida culture. *Texas Archeological and Paleontological Society, Bulletin*, vol. 11, pp. 92–126.

1941. Pottery types from the Belcher Mound Site. *Texas Archeological and Paleontological Society, Bulletin*, vol. 13, pp. 88–116.

Webb, William S.

1938. An archaeological survey of the Norris Basin in eastern Tennessee. *Bureau of American Ethnology, Bulletin* 118.

1939. An archaeological survey of Wheeler Basin on the Tennessee River in northern Alabama. *Bureau of American Ethnology, Bulletin* 122.

Webb, William S. and DeJarnette, David L.

1942. An archeological survey of Pickwick Basin in the adjacent portions of the states of Alabama, Mississippi, and Tennessee. *Bureau of American Ethnology, Bulletin* 129.

1948a. The Flint River Site, Ma^{o}48. *Alabama Museum of Natural History, Museum Papers*, no. 23.

1948b. The Whitesburg Bridge Site, Ma^{v}10. *Alabama Museum of Natural History, Museum Papers*, no. 24.

Webb, William S. and Funkhouser, William D.

1929. The Williams Site; in Christian County, Kentucky. *University of Kentucky, Reports in Archaeology and Anthropology*, vol. 1, no. 1.

Webb, William S. and Snow, Charles E.

1945. The Adena people. *University of Kentucky, Reports in Anthropology and Archaeology*, vol. 6.

Wedel, Waldo R.

1943. Archeological investigations in Platte and Clay Counties, Missouri. *Smithsonian Institute, U. S. National Museum, Bulletin* 183.

1947. Culture chronology in the central Great Plains. *American Antiquity*, vol. 12, no. 3, pp. 148–56.

Willey, Gordon R.

1945. The Weeden Island culture: a preliminary definition. *American Antiquity*, vol. 10, no. 3, pp. 225–54.

1948. The cultural context of the Crystal River negative-painted style. *American Antiquity*, vol. 13, no. 4, pp. 325–28.

1949. Archeology of the Florida Gulf Coast. *Smithsonian Miscellaneous Collections*, vol. 113.

Willey, Gordon R. and Phillips, Philip

1944. Negative-painted pottery from Crystal River, Florida. *American Antiquity*, vol. 10, no. 1, pp. 173–85.

Willey, Gordon R. and Woodbury, Richard B.

1942. A chronological outline for the northwest Florida coast. *American Antiquity*, vol. 7, no. 3, pp. 232–54.

Williams, F. E.

1928. The geography of the Mississippi Valley. *American Academy of Political and Social Science, Annals*, vol. 135, no. 224, pp. 7–14.

Williams, Samuel C.

1928. Early travels in the Tennessee country, 1540–1800. Johnson City.

Willoughby, Charles C.

1897. An analysis of the decorations upon pottery from the Mississippi Valley. *Journal of American Folk-lore*, vol. 10, no. 36, pp. 9–20.

1922. The Turner group of earthworks, Hamilton County, Ohio. *Peabody Museum, Harvard University, Papers*, vol. 8, no. 3.

Wimberly, Steve B. and Tourtelot, Harry A.

1941. The McQuorquodale Mound; a manifestation of the Hopewellian phase in south Alabama. *Geological Survey of Alabama, Museum Papers*, no. 19.

Woodward, Arthur

1931. The Grewe Site, Gila Valley, Arizona. *Los Angeles Museum of History, Science, and Art, Occasional Papers*, no. 1.

WRAY, DONALD E. AND SMITH, HALE G.

1943. The Illinois confederacy and Middle Mississippian culture in Illinois. *Illinois State Academy of Science, Transactions*, vol. 36, no. 2, pp. 82–86.

1944. An hypothesis for the identification of the Illinois confederacy with the Middle Mississippian culture in Illinois. *American Antiquity*, vol. 10, no. 1, pp. 23–27.

YOUNG, BENNETT H.

1910. The prehistoric men of Kentucky. *Filson Club, Publication* no. 25.

COLLOTYPE FIGURES 74–113

a

b

c

a, Edgefield Site (13-P-2), Mound A, from the east (a typical conical burial mound of the early Baytown Period. *b*, Winterville Site (19-L-1), Mound A, from the east (the dominant rectangular temple mound of a large ceremonial center of the Mississippi Period – note ramp at right of truck). *c*, Rose Mound (12-N-3), from the southwest (a typical "St. Francis-type" village site).

SERIES OF PROGRESS VIEWS OF STRATIGRAPHIC EXCAVATION ON CUT A, ROSE SITE (12-N-3), April, 1947. *a,* Laying out the cut; *b,* Starting Level 2; *c,* Checking depth at bottom of Level 6; *d,* Post-holes in bottom of Level 10 at –130 cm.; *e,* Level 12; *f,* Level 15; *g,* Level 19; *h,* Checking depth at bottom of Level 22, –250 cm.; *i,* Undisturbed bottom of Level 25, –280 cm.

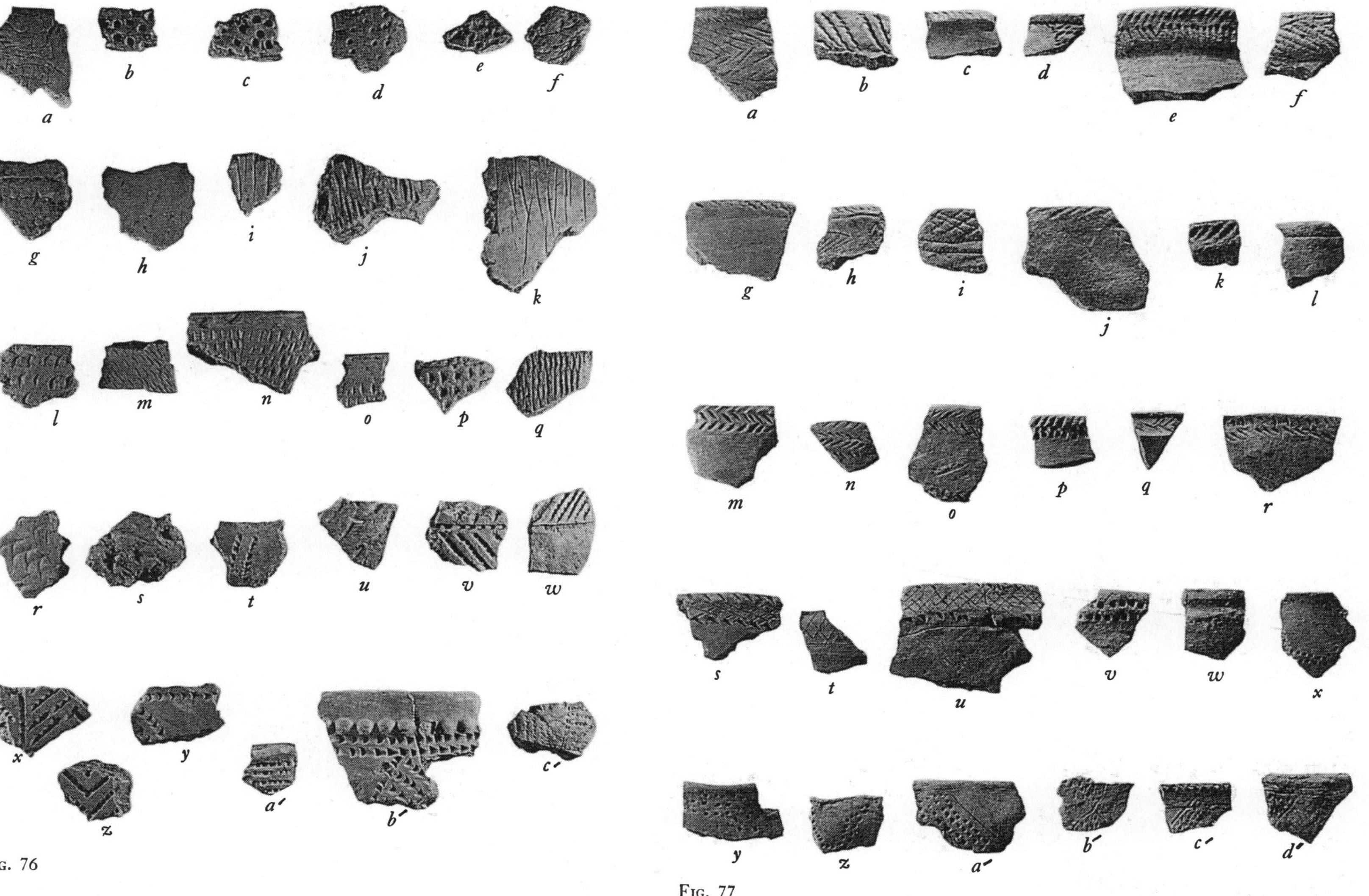

FIG. 76

FIG. 77

FIG. 76: *a–f*, Bluff Creek Punctated; *g, h*, Tchefuncte Plain; *i–k*, Jaketown Simple Stamped; *l–q*, Tammany Pinched; *r–u*, Tchefuncte Stamped; *v–c′*, Lake Borgne Incised. FIG. 77: *a–l*, Cormorant Cord-impressed; *m–r*, Twin Lakes Punctated; *s–u*, Cross-hatched rims; *v–z*, Crowder Punctated; *a′–d′*, Orleans Punctated.

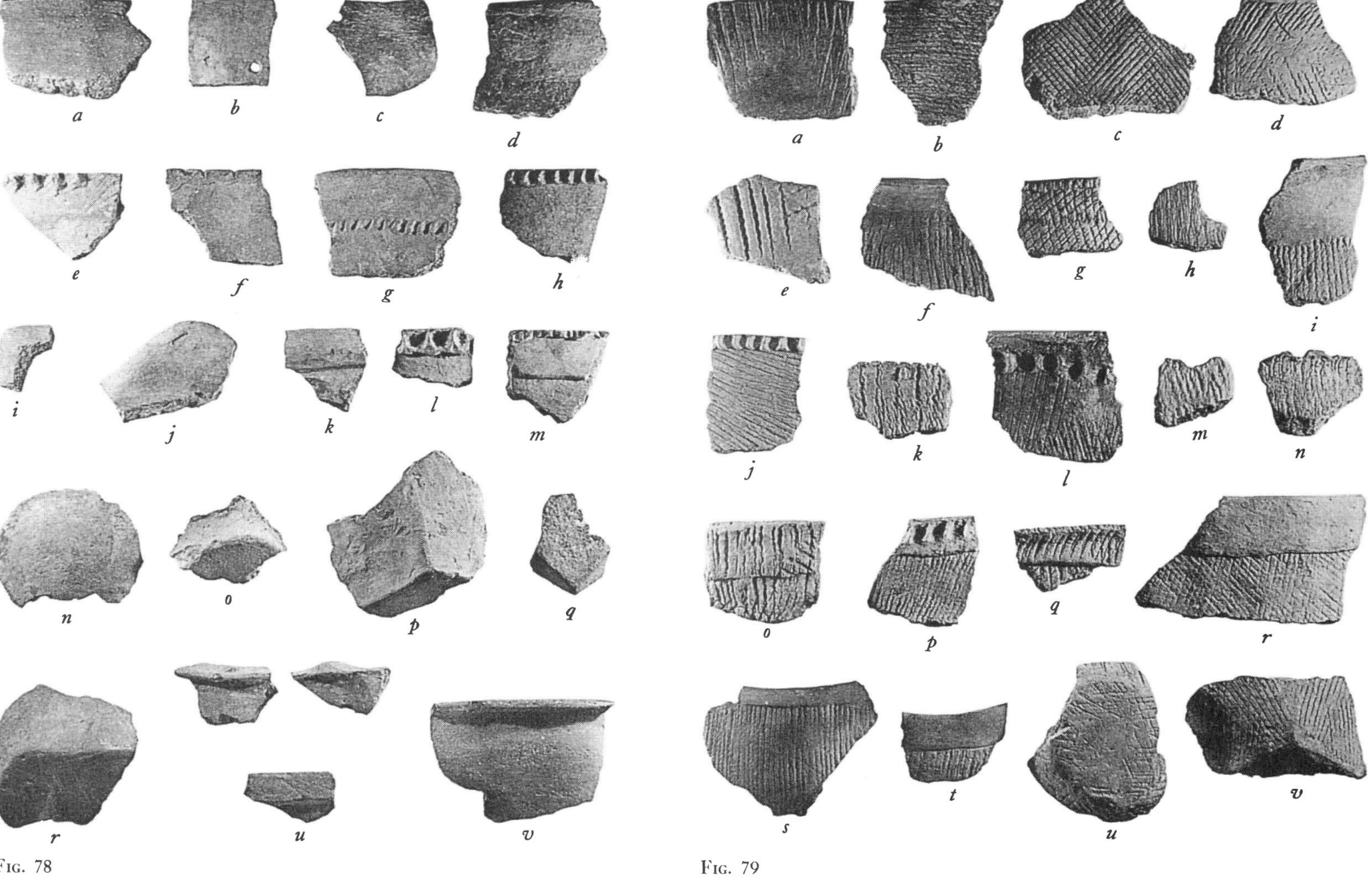

FIG. 78 Baytown Plain.

FIG. 79 Mulberry Creek Cord-marked.

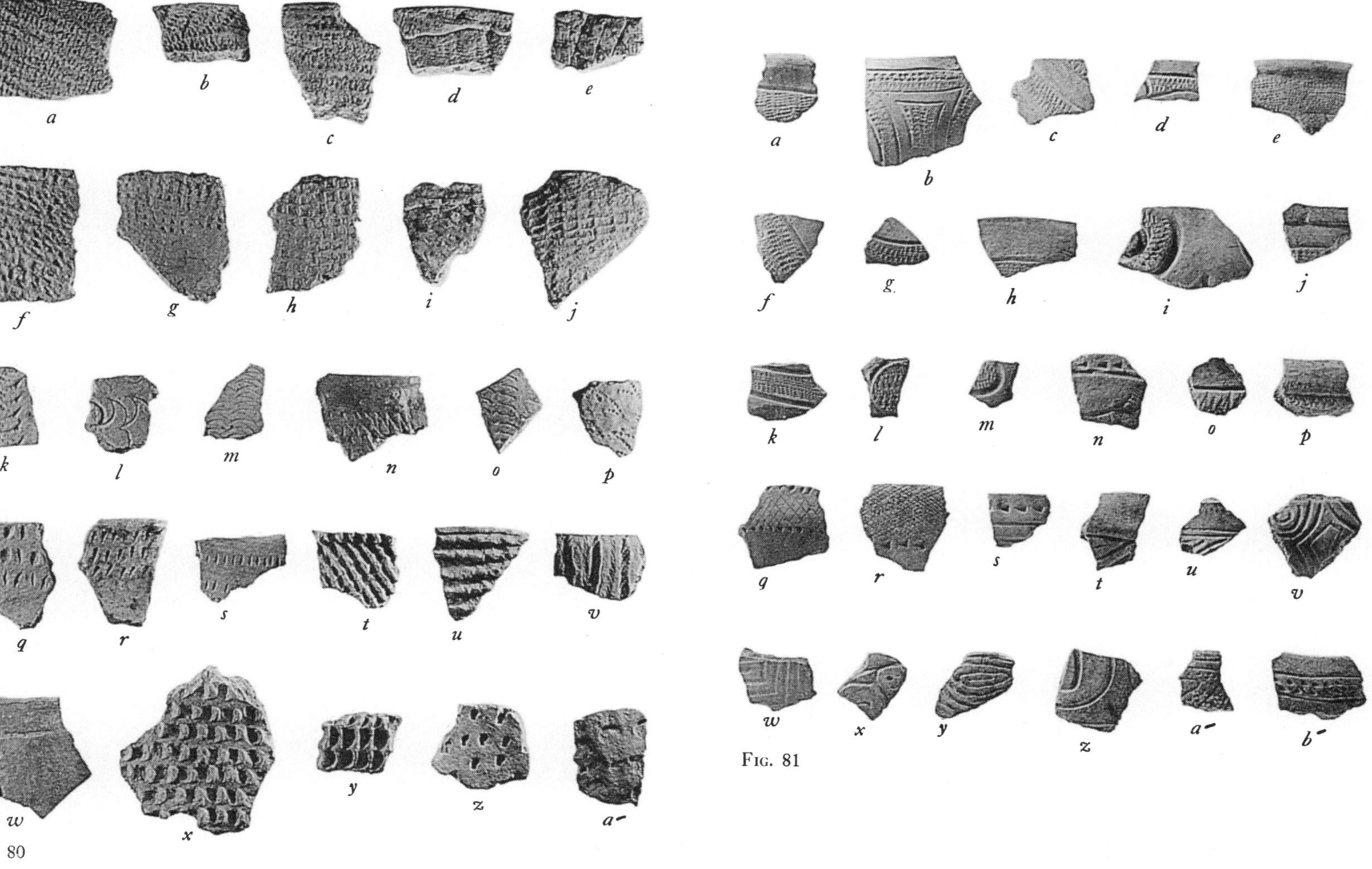

FIG. 80: *a–d*, Withers Fabric-impressed; *e*, Yates Net-impressed; *f–j*, Wheeler Check Stamped; *k–p*, Indian Bay Stamped; *q–a′*, Evansville Punctated. FIG. 81: *a–p*, Marksville Stamped; *q*, *r*, Marksville Cross-hatched rim; *s–z*, Marksville Incised; *a′*, *b′*, Churupa Punctated.

FIG. 82

FIG. 83

Fig. 82: *a–e*, Coles Creek Incised; *f–m*, Mazique Incised; *n–p*, Oxbow Incised; *q*, *r*, Chevalier Stamped; *s–w*, French Fork Incised. Fig 83: *a–k*, Woodville Red Filmed; *l–u*, Larto Red Filmed.

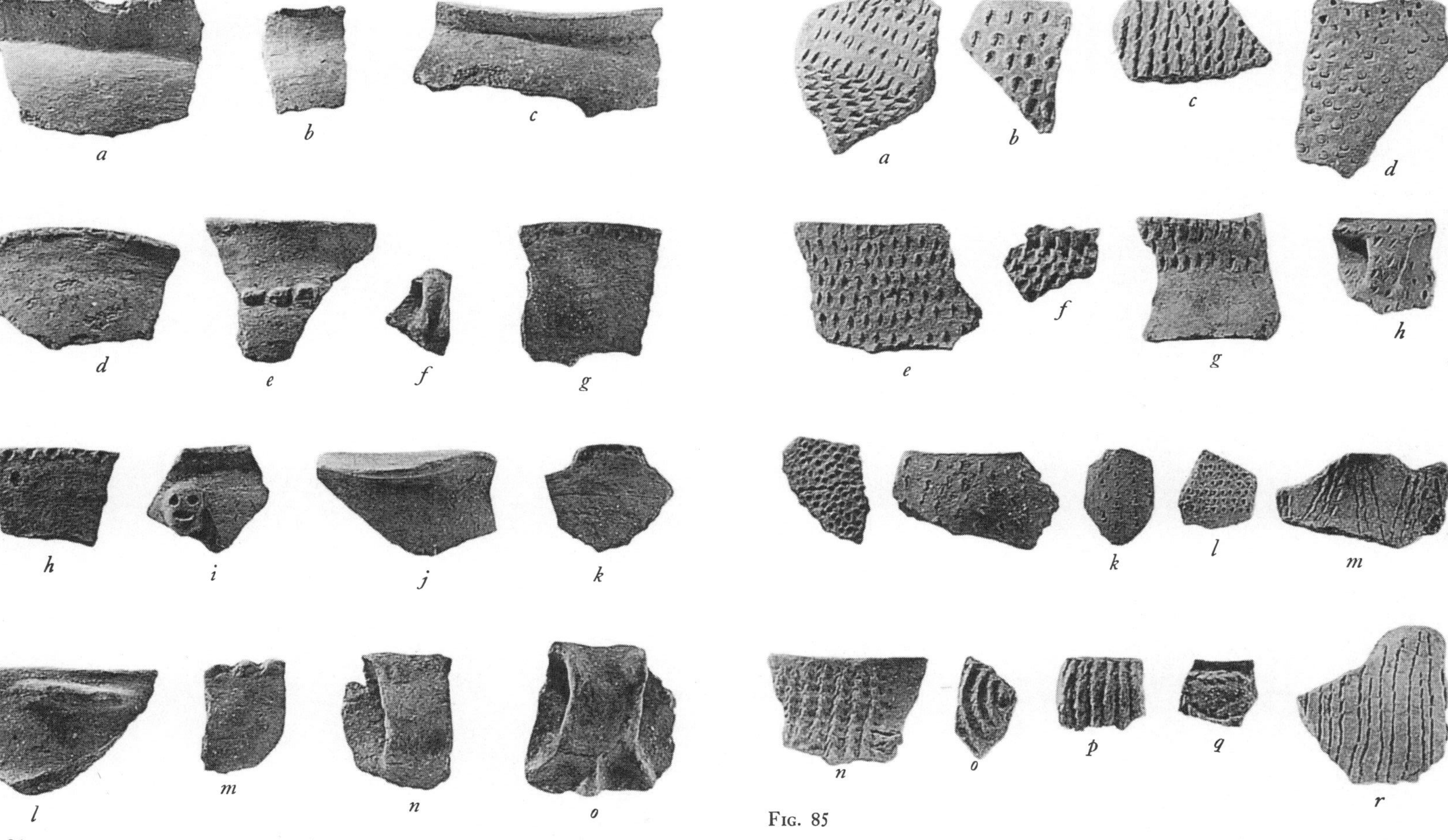

Fig. 84

Neeley's Ferry Plain.

Fig. 85

Parkin Punctated.

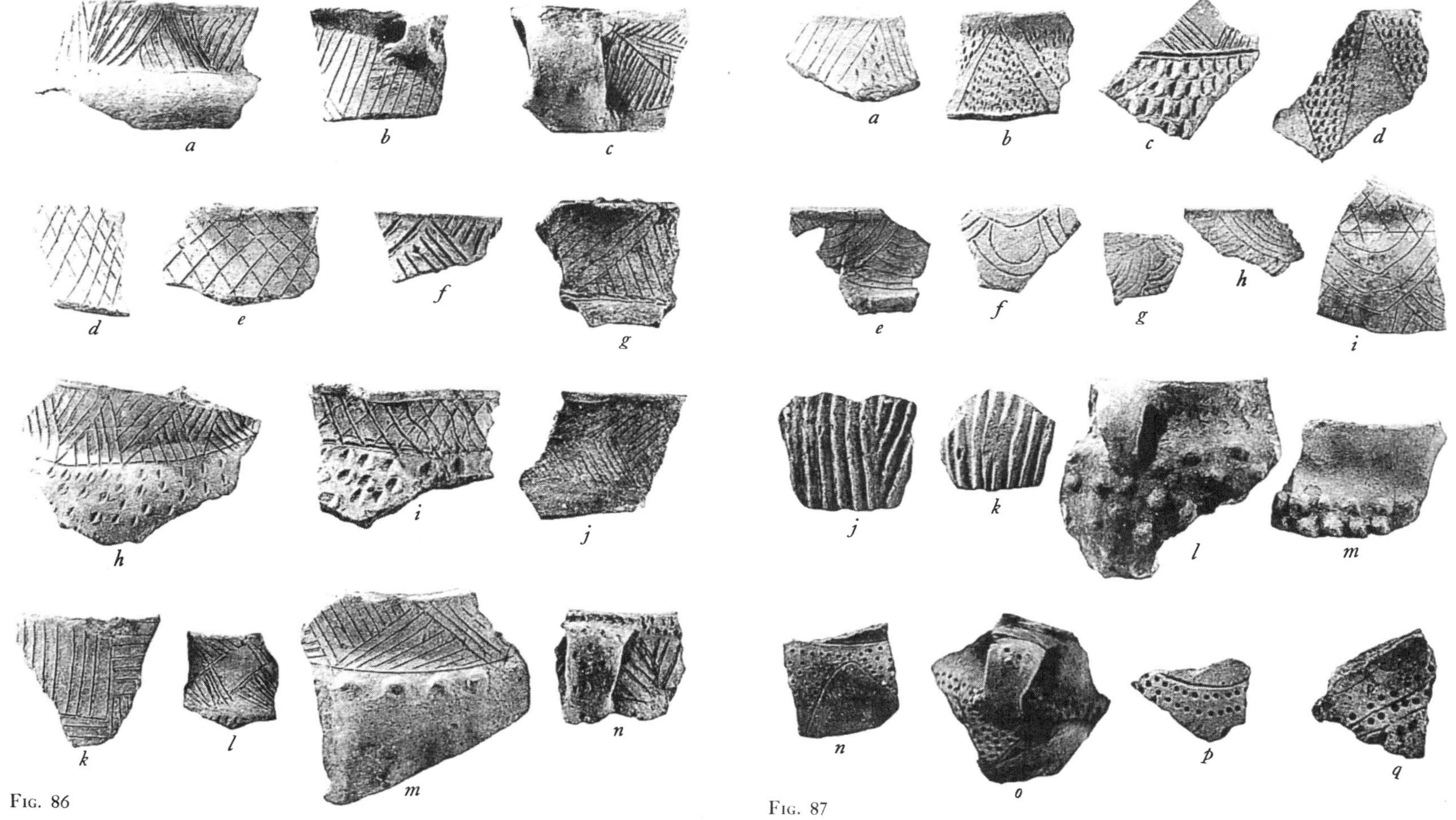

FIG. 86

FIG. 87

FIG. 86: Barton Incised. FIG. 87: *a–d*, Barton Incised; *e–i*, Ranch Incised; *j, k*, Vernon Paul Appliqué; *l, m*, Fortune Noded; *n–q*, Manly Punctated.

FIG. 88: Bell Plain. FIG. 89: *a–d*, Kent Incised; *e–i*, Rhodes Incised; *j–n*, Walls Engraved; *o*, *t–w*, Mound Place Incised; *p–s*, Hull Engraved.

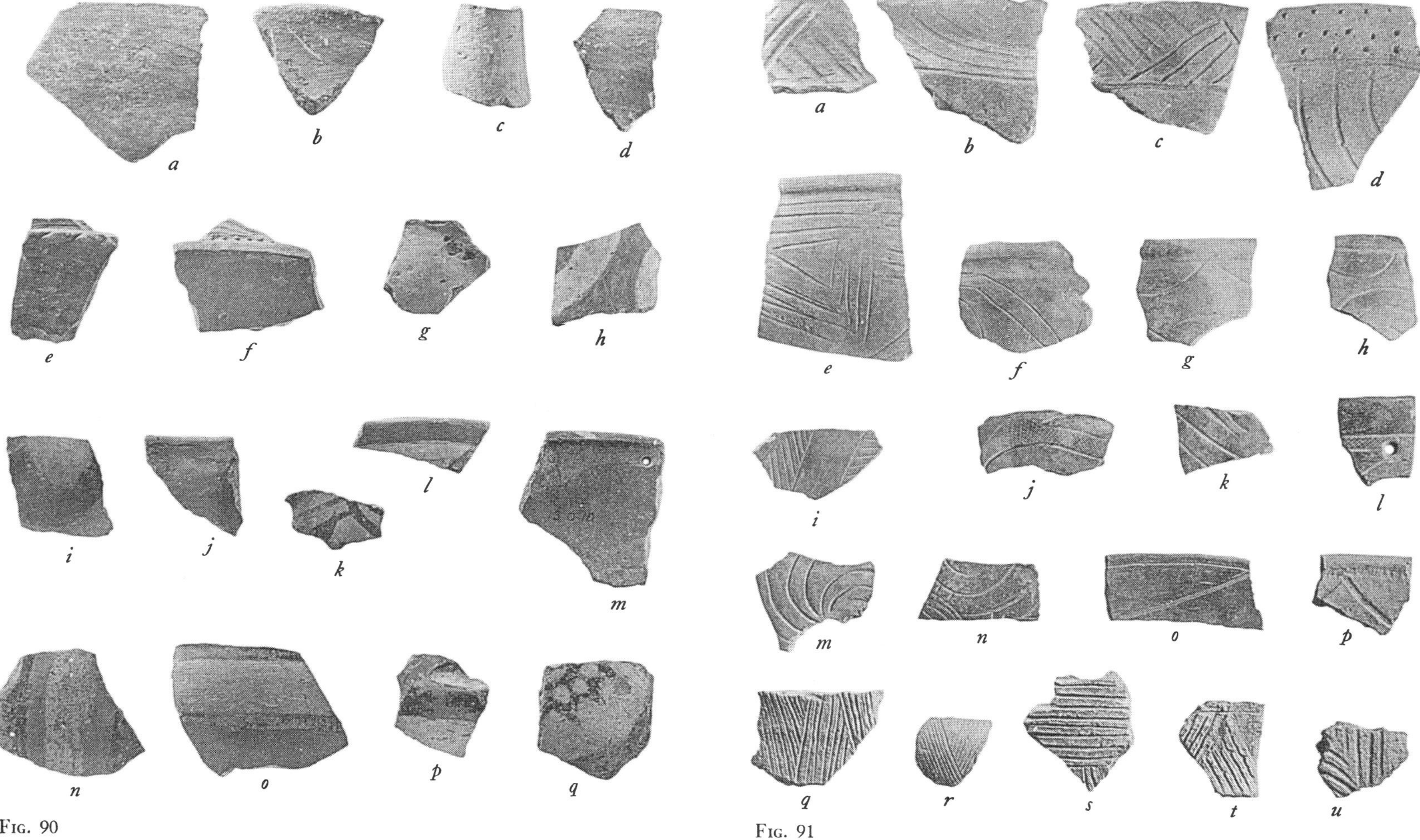

FIG. 90 FIG. 91

Fig. 90: *a–f*, Old Town Red; *g*, Hollywood White Filmed; *h*, *k–m*, Nodena Red and White; *i*, *j*, Carson Red on Buff; *n–p*, Avenue Polychrome; *q*, Negative Painted. Fig. 91: *a–d*, Wallace Incised; *e–n*, Leland Incised; *o*, *p*, Blanchard Incised; *q–u*, Arcola Incised.

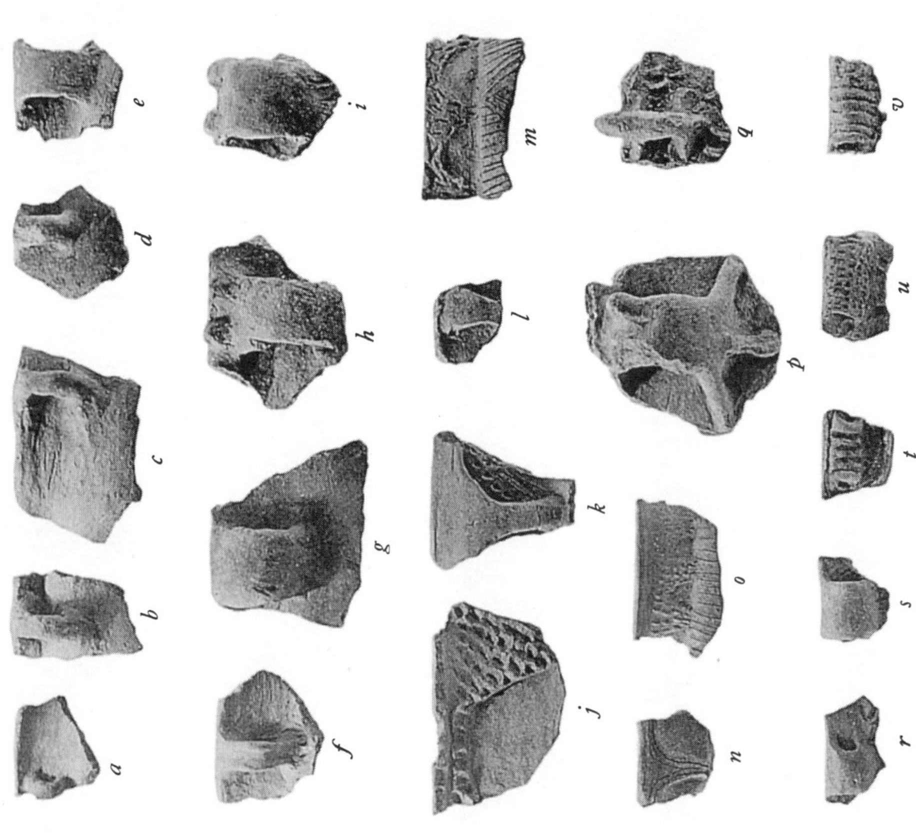

HANDLES (Neeley's Ferry Plain and related types): *a–d*, loop handles; *e–i*, strap handles; *j–o*, decorative handles; *p*, *q*, zoomorphic handles; *r–v*, "ribbon" handles.

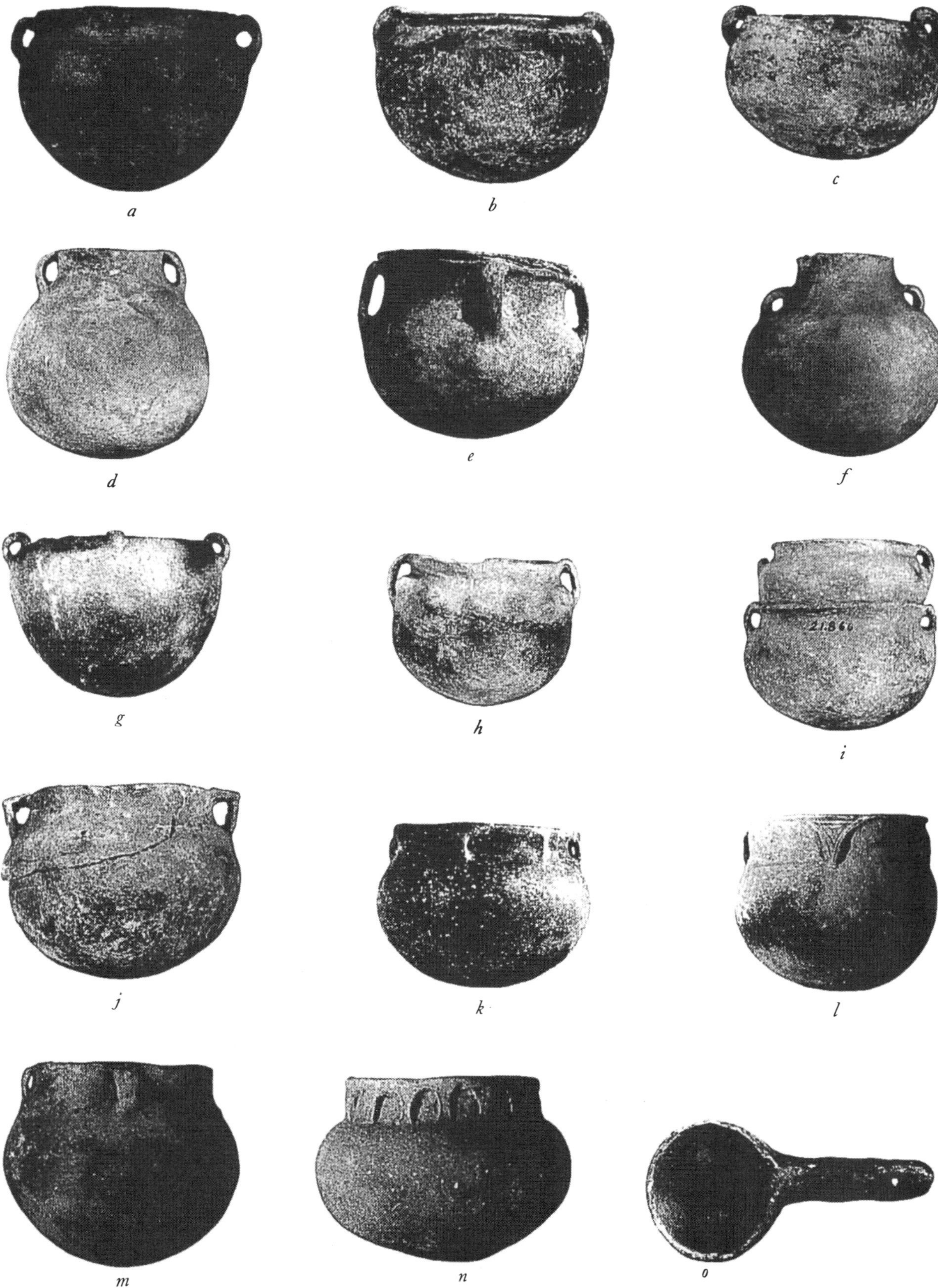

a b c d e f g h i j k l m n o

FIGURE 93

NEELEY'S FERRY PLAIN JARS

a, Two-handled jar with short, slightly flared rim. (Height, 6¼ inches; diameter, 8¼ inches.) Rose Mound, Cross County, Arkansas (12–N–3). Peabody Museum, Harvard University, Cat. No. 218. Phillips, Neg. 1602.

b, Two-handled jar with very small lugs (not visible in photograph), outrolled lip. (Diameter, 7½ inches.) Rose Mound, Cross County, Arkansas (12–N–3). Peabody Museum, Harvard University, Cat. No. 21840. Phillips, Neg. 1230.

c, Two-handled jar, handles project above lip, bifurcated lugs barely visible in photograph. (Height, 3½ inches; diameter, 5¾ inches; oral diameter, 4½ inches.) Rose Mound, Cross County, Arkansas (12–N–3). Peabody Museum, Harvard University, Cat. No. 21997. Phillips, Neg. 1418.

d, Two-handled bottle, globular body, short, relatively narrow rim. (Height, 6 inches; diameter, 5¾ inches; oral diameter, 3 inches.) Neeley's Ferry, Cross County, Arkansas (11–N–4). Peabody Museum, Harvard University, Cat. No. 21754. Phillips, Neg. 1441.

e, Jar with four strap handles, appliqué strip on rim which is a very late feature throughout eastern United States. (Diameter, 4¾ inches.) Mound above Turkey Island, Cross County, Arkansas. Museum of the American Indian, Cat. No. 17/1404. Phillips, Neg. 2247.

f, Globular bottle with two handles at base of rim, short neck, round bottom. (Height, 8¼ inches.) Rose Mound, Cross County, Arkansas (12–N–3). Peabody Museum, Harvard University, Cat. No. 22011. Phillips, Neg. 1252.

g, Two-handled jar with lugs, lugs and handles project above lip, round bottom. (Diameter, 7½ inches.) Rose Mound, Cross County, Arkansas (12–N–3). Peabody Museum, Harvard University, Cat. No. 21954. Phillips, Neg. 1233.

h, Two-handled jar, short neck, horizontal row of nodes at shoulder line, round bottom. Rose Mound, Cross County, Arkansas (12–N–3). (Diameter, 5¼ inches; height, 4 inches.) Peabody Museum, Harvard University, Cat. No. 21989. Phillips, Neg. 1314.

i, Composite jar with two jars superimposed, two strap handles, round bottom. Rose Mound, Cross County, Arkansas (12–N–3). (Height, 5½ inches.) Peabody Museum, Harvard University, Cat. No. 21866. Phillips, Neg. 1269.

j, Jar, two strap handles, with lugs, round bottom. (Height, 5½ inches; diameter, 7½ inches.) Rose Mound, Cross County, Arkansas (12–N–3). Peabody Museum, Harvard University, Cat. No. 21870. Phillips, Neg. 1599.

k, Jar with four strap handles, between which are vertical fillets, round bottom. (Diameter, 4¾ inches.) Blytheville, Mississippi County, Arkansas. Museum of the American Indian, Cat. No. 5/2995. Phillips, Neg. 2586.

l, Jar with four strap handles which are luted on, incising on handles follows the outlines of the handle, round bottom. (Diameter, 9½ inches.) Beck Place, Crittenden County, Arkansas (13–O–7). University of Arkansas, Cat. No. Beck Place. Phillips, Neg. 3027.

m, Jar with four strap handles, node on each handle, round bottom. (Diameter, 7 inches.) Golightly Place, Crittenden County, Arkansas (11–P–3). University of Arkansas, Cat. No. Go. 9a. Phillips, Neg. 3229.

n, Jar with arcaded rim, short wide neck, flattened body, round bottom. (Diameter, 5¼ inches.) Upper Nodena, Mississippi County, Arkansas (10–Q–1). University of Arkansas, Cat. No. U.N. 7a. Phillips, Neg. 3481.

o, Ladle with long handle, perforation at end of handle. Upper Nodena, Mississippi County, Arkansas (10–Q–1). (Length, 3½ inches.) Museum of the American Indian, Cat. No. 17/4734. Neg. 2417.

FIGURE 94

VARIANTS OF PARKIN PUNCTUATED

a, Two-handled jar with punctates on both body and rim. (Diameter, 4¾ inches; height, 3¼ inches.) Rose Mound, Cross County, Arkansas (12–N–3). Peabody Museum, Harvard University, Cat. No. 22089. Phillips, Neg. 1317.

b, Jar with four strap handles, punctate on both body and rim (note appliqué fillet on rim). (Diameter, 5¾ inches.) Halcomb Mounds, Cross County, Arkansas. Peabody Museum, Harvard University, Cat. No. 21612. Phillips, Neg. 1160.

c, Two-handled jar, nodes on upper shoulder area, punctate in parallel horizontal rows on body, plain rim. (Diameter, 4¾ inches; height, 3¾ inches.) Halcomb Mounds, Cross County, Arkansas. Peabody Museum, Harvard University, Cat. No. 21574. Phillips, Neg. 982.

d, Two-handled jar, punctate on body, rude chevron pattern incised on rim just below lip. (Diameter, 6¼ inches; height, 5 inches.) Rose Mound, Cross County, Arkansas (12–N–3). Peabody Museum, Harvard University, Cat. No. 21963. Phillips, Neg. 1270.

e, Two-handled jar with lugs, punctate on body and rim. (Diameter, 5¼ inches; height, 4 inches.) Halcomb Mounds, Cross County, Arkansas. Peabody Museum, Harvard University, Cat. No. 21588. Phillips, Neg. 1615.

f, Jar with four strap handles, punctate on body and handles, undecorated rim. (Diameter, 6 inches.) No site. University of Arkansas, Cat. No. 219. Phillips, Neg. 3017.

g, Jar with four strap handles with contracting sides, punctate on body and lip, notched outer lip edge, four nodes on each handle. (Diameter, 6½ inches.) Upper Nodena, Mississippi County, Arkansas (10–Q–1). University of Arkansas, Cat. No. U.N. 15a. Phillips, Neg. 3479.

h, Jar with multiple strap handles with contracting sides, punctate on body and lip, undecorated rim and handles, notched outer lip edge. (Diameter, 5 inches.) Upper Nodena, Mississippi County, Arkansas (10–Q–1). University of Arkansas, Cat. No. U.N. 92b. Phillips, Neg. 3484.

i, Arcaded handle jar, punctate on body and rim, nodes on outer lip edge, faces in every lunette, eyes and mouth incised, nose applied. (Diameter, 6¼ inches.) Beck Place, Crittenden County, Arkansas (13–O–7). University of Arkansas, Cat. No. Beck Place. Phillips, Neg. 3501.

j, Jar with two strap handles, punctate on body, parallel vertical incising on outer lip edge, undecorated rim, hole and two nodes on each of the handles. Nodena Place, Mississippi County, Arkansas (10–Q–1). Alabama Museum of Natural History, Neg. 1850.

k, Jar with four strap handles with contracting sides, punctate on body and outer lip edge, undecorated rim. (Height, 5 inches.) Bell Place, Mississippi County, Arkansas (10–P–2). Lemley Collection, Cat. No. V–735, Hope, Arkansas.

l, Bell-shaped bowl, punctate in vertical rows on lower body, indented vertical rim fillets.* (Diameter, 8¼ inches.) Nodena Place, Mississippi County, Arkansas (10–Q–1). University of Arkansas, Cat. No. Nod. 33a. Phillips, Neg. 3318.

m, Jar, punctate on body and outer lip edge, indented parallel vertical fillets on rim.* (Diameter, 7 inches.) Bradley Place, Crittenden County, Arkansas (11–P–2). University of Arkansas, Cat. No. Br. 96a. Phillips, Neg. 3504.

n, Multiple free-standing handle jar, linear punctate on upper body, punctate on handles, lower body and lunettes undecorated.* (Diameter, 4¾ inches.) Cross County, Arkansas. Museum of the American Indian, Cat. No. 16/7829. Phillips, Neg. 2321.

o, Jar with two lugs, undecorated lower body, parallel horizontal punctate within incised lines.† Dupree, Hinds County, Mississippi. Miss. 31.

* This style of punctate was originally called Castile Linear Punctate.
† Vessel from west central Mississippi derived from Parkin Punctated.

Variants of Parkin Punctated

VARIANTS OF BARTON INCISED

FIGURE 95

VARIANTS OF BARTON INCISED

a, Two-handled jar with lugs, incised rim with horizontal row of nodes on upper shoulder area, undecorated body. (Diameter, 5¼ inches.) Twist Plantation, Cross County, Arkansas (11–N–14). Museum of the American Indian, Cat. No. 12/6485. Phillips, Neg. 2506.

b, Small jar, four small lugs, diagonal incising on rim, undecorated body. (Diameter, 5¼ inches; height, 4 inches.) Neeley's Ferry, Cross County, Arkansas (11–N–4). Peabody Museum, Harvard University, Cat. No. 21157. Phillips, Neg. 1611.

c, Two-handled jar, diagonal incising on rim with horizontal row of nodes on upper shoulder area, undecorated body. (Diameter, 4¾ inches; height, 3¾ inches.) Neeley's Ferry, Cross County, Arkansas (11–N–4). Peabody Museum, Harvard University, Cat. No. 21023. Phillips, Neg. 1612.

d, Four-handled jar, single row of nodes on lip, incising on body. (Diameter, 5 inches; height, 3¼ inches.) Rose Mound, Cross County, Arkansas (12–N–3). Peabody Museum, Harvard University, Cat. No. 22029. Phillips, Neg. 1316.

e, Small jar with four small lugs, rim incised with diagonal lines forming upright and inverted triangles, undecorated body. (Diameter, 4¾ inches; height, 3¼ inches.) Rose Mound, Cross County, Arkansas (12–N–3). Peabody Museum, Harvard University, Cat. No. 22285. Phillips, Neg. 1629.

f, Deep bowl, crude diagonal incising on rim, undecorated body. (Diameter, 5 inches; height 3½ inches.) Stanley Mounds, Cross County, Arkansas. Peabody Museum, Harvard University, Cat. No. 20165. Phillips, Neg. 1673.

g, Two-handled jar with human effigy bottle inside vessel, incising on rim forms upright and inverted triangles, Parkin Punctate on body. Turkey Island, Cross County, Arkansas. Reproduced from Moore, 1910, p. 322, fig. 46.

h, Bowl with incised diamond design, rudimentary handles. (Diameter, 4½ inches; depth, 3 inches.) Walnut, Mississippi County, Arkansas. Alabama Museum of Natural History, Cat. No. Wal. 19; Neg. No. 1903.

i, Large jar with four lugs, diagonal incising on rim forming upright and inverted triangles, Parkin Punctate in parallel horizontal rows on upper shoulder area. (Diameter, 9½ inches; height, 6¾ inches.) Castile Place, St. Francis County, Arkansas (13–N–21). Andover, Cat. No. 39897. Phillips, Neg. 1459.

j, Four-handled jar, diagonal incising on rim, parallel horizontal rows of punctate on upper body, punctate on handles, and single row on lip. (Diameter, 6½ inches; depth, 5 inches.) Walnut, Mississippi County, Arkansas. Alabama Museum of Natural History, Cat. No. Wal. 90; Neg. No. 1293.

k, Four-handled jar, diagonal incising on rim, punctate on handles and body. (Diameter, 6¼ inches; height, 5 inches.) Cummings Place, Poinsett County, Arkansas (11–O–4). Museum of the American Indian, Cat. No. 17/3324. Phillips, Neg. 2260.

l, Two-handled jar, diagonal incising on rim forming upright and inverted triangles, punctate on body. (Height, 4½ inches.) Turkey Island, Cross County, Arkansas. Museum of the American Indian, Cat. No. 17/4747. Phillips, Neg. 2245.

m, Small jar with two perforated lugs, vertical and diagonal incising on rim, punctate on body. (Diameter, 5½ inches.) Cummings Place, Poinsett County, Arkansas (11–O–4). Museum of the American Indian, Cat. No. 17/4798. Phillips, Neg. 2238.

n, Two-handled jar, diagonal incising on rim forming upright and inverted triangles, punctate on body. (Diameter, 6½ inches.) Barton Ranch, Crittenden County, Arkansas (11–O–10). University of Arkansas, Cat. No. Bar. 79b. Phillips, Neg. 3478.

o, Small jar, diagonal incising on rim forming upright and inverted triangles. (Diameter, 3¾ inches.) North of Helena Crossing, mouth of St. Francis, Phillips County, Arkansas (14–N–6). Museum of the American Indian, Cat. No. 11/9246. Phillips, Neg. 2499.

Figure 96

VARIANTS OF KENT INCISED

a, Jar with four strap handles with contracting sides, punctate on rim, incised parallel lines below handles and above base, between these lines are parallel vertical lines in groups of two. (Diameter, 6 inches.) Upper Nodena, Mississippi County, Arkansas (10–Q–1). University of Arkansas, Cat. No. U.N. 266b. Phillips, Neg. 3477.

b, Jar with two strap handles, vertical incised lines on body which extend onto the handles, undecorated rim, incising on the outer rim edge. (Diameter, 7¼ inches.) Bell Place, Mississippi County, Arkansas (10–P–2). University of Arkansas, Cat. No. Bell 143. Phillips, Neg. 3102.

c, Jar with two strap handles with contracting sides, punctate on handles, body incised with parallel vertical lines, lip is sharply beveled with piecrust notching. (Diameter, 5½ inches.) Golightly Place, Crittenden County, Arkansas (11–P–3). University of Arkansas, Cat. No. Go. 12a. Phillips, Neg. 3233.

d, Arcaded handle jar, parallel vertical lines on body, undecorated lunettes and handles, notched lip edge. Probably Nodena, Mississippi County, Arkansas (10–Q–1). (Diameter, 4¾ inches.) University of Arkansas, Cat. No. Nd. 118. Phillips, Neg. 3270.

e, Kent Incised jar with four small horizontal lugs, parallel vertical incised lines on body, groups of four parallel diagonal lines on rim alternating right and left. Kent Place, Lee County, Arkansas (13–N–4). Museum of Anthropology, University of Michigan, Neg. 4239.

f, Jar with horizontal rows of short vertical appliqué strips obliquely notched on rim, parallel vertical incised lines on body, and a horizontal row of short vertical incisions on upper rim. (Diameter, 5½ inches.) Walnut, Mississippi County, Arkansas. Alabama Museum of Natural History, Cat. No. Walnut; Neg. No. 1913.

g, Jar with four effigy strap handles, parallel vertical lines on body, rim is decorated with incised lines forming upright and inverted triangles of style of Parkin Incised. (Diameter, 8 inches.) Beck Place, Crittenden County, Arkansas (13–O–7). University of Arkansas. Phillips, Neg. 3463.

h, Arcaded handle jar, handles punctated, incised parallel lines on body, punctate on outer lip edge. (Height, 4⅞ inches.) A. S. Catching Place, Mississippi County, Arkansas. Lemley Collection, Cat. No. V–635, Hope, Arkansas.

i, Jar with vertical appliqué strips, body decorated with parallel diagonal incised lines, enclosed by parallel vertical lines. (Diameter, 5 inches.) Bradley Place, Crittenden County, Arkansas (11–P–2). University of Arkansas, Cat. No. Br. 11a. Phillips, Neg. 3203.

j, Large jar with vertical appliqué strips on rim, parallel diagonal incised lines on body enclosed by parallel vertical lines, notched outer lip edge. (Diameter, 8 inches.) Bell Place, Mississippi County, Arkansas (10–P–2). University of Arkansas. Phillips, Neg. 3136.

k, Arcaded handle jar, punctate on handles, parallel diagonal incised lines on body, enclosed by parallel vertical lines, nodes on upper outer rim (note beveled inner rim). (Diameter, 5⅞ inches; height, 4⅜ inches.) Walls area, Mississippi (13–P–1). University of Mississippi, Cat. No. 3532. Phillips, Neg. 4483.

l, Large jar, body is decorated with incised lines forming upright and inverted triangles, punctate on rim within incised inverted triangles, which resemble arcaded handles, punctate on outer rim edge. (Diameter, 10 inches; height, 6¾ inches.) Rose Mound, Cross County, Arkansas (12–N–3). Peabody Museum, Harvard University, Cat. No. 22264. Phillips, Neg. 1751.

m, Arcaded handle jar, deeply notched rim, body is incised with parallel lines forming upright and inverted triangles; below these is a curvilinear design of Ranch Incised. (Diameter, 8½ inches.) Upper Nodena, Mississippi County, Arkansas (10–Q–1). University of Arkansas, Cat. No. U.N. 132c. Phillips, Neg. 3485.

n, Arcaded handle jar, body is incised with parallel lines forming upright and inverted triangles. Rose Mound, Cross County, Arkansas (12–N–3). Museum of the American Indian, Cat. No. 17/3428. Phillips, Neg. 2267.

o, Jar with incised arcades, nodes on rim, body is incised with parallel lines forming upright and inverted triangles. Beck Place, Crittenden County, Arkansas (13–O–7). University of Arkansas, Cat. No. Beck Place. Phillips, Neg. 3505.

p, Jar with notched vertical fillets on rim, diagonal incisions on outer rim edge, body is incised with parallel lines forming upright and inverted triangles. (Diameter, 5½ inches.) Pecan Point, Mississippi County, Arkansas. Museum of the American Indian, Cat. No. 17/4780. Phillips, Neg. 2237.

q, Effigy jar, parallel vertical incising on body, plain rim, incising on outer rim edge. (Length, 9½ inches.) Beck Place, Crittenden County, Arkansas (13–O–7). University of Arkansas. Phillips, Neg. 3433.

r, Jar with punctated vertical appliqué, body is incised with parallel lines forming upright and inverted triangles. Walls area, Mississippi (13–P–1). (Height, 5½ inches.) University of Mississippi, Cat. No. 3560. Phillips, Neg. 4526.

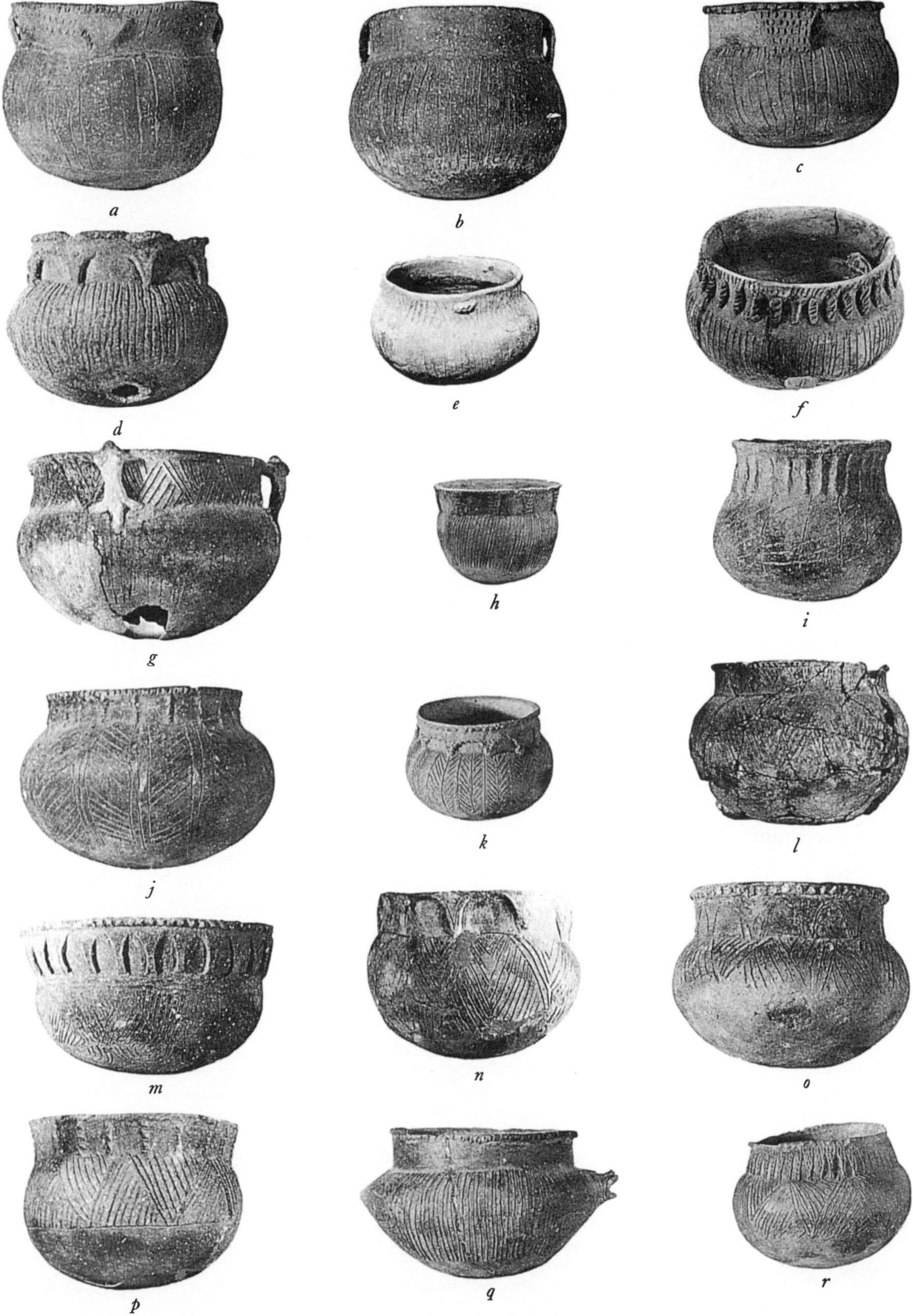

Variants of Kent Incised

a b c d e f g h i j k l m n o p q

Mississippi Types of Minor Importance

Figure 97

MISSISSIPPI TYPES OF MINOR IMPORTANCE

a, Vernon Paul Appliqué jar with four strap handles with contracting sides, undecorated rim. (Diameter, 5 inches.) Vernon Paul, Cross County, Arkansas (11–N–9). University of Arkansas, Cat. No. V.P. 93d. Phillips, Neg. 3511.

b, Vernon Paul Appliqué two-handled bowl with lugs, vertical appliqué on body made by applied fillets, bottom third covered with oblique punctate impressions. (Diameter, 4½ inches; height, 3 inches.) Halcomb Mounds, Cross County, Arkansas. Peabody Museum, Harvard University, Cat. No. 21652. Phillips, Neg. 1187.

c, Vernon Paul Appliqué bowl with rudimentary handles, appliqué on rim, two horizontal rows of punctates on upper shoulder area. (Diameter, 6 inches; depth, 5 inches.) Walnut Site, Mississippi County, Arkansas. Alabama Museum of Natural History, Cat. No. Wal. 48; Neg. No. 1906.

d, Wallace Incised bowl with high flaring rim. (Diameter, 7½ inches.) Greer, Jefferson County, Arkansas (13–N–17). Museum of the American Indian, Cat. No. 17/4262. Phillips, Neg. 2253.

e, Jar with flared rim, Wallace Incised on body, incised design and short, irregular punctate on rim. (Diameter, 6¼ inches; height, 3¾ inches.) Greer, Jefferson County, Arkansas (13–N–17). Museum of the American Indian, Cat. No. 17/4263. Phillips, Neg. 2262.

f, Wallace Incised bowl with flaring rim. (Diameter, 6½ inches; height, 3½ inches.) Greer, Jefferson County, Arkansas (13–N–17). Museum of the American Indian, Cat. No. 17/4252. Phillips, Neg. 2277.

g, Jar with Owens Punctated within incised design on both body and rim. (Diameter, 7¼ inches.) Beck Place, Crittenden County, Arkansas (13–O–7). University of Arkansas, Cat. No. Beck 246. Phillips, Neg. 3022.

h, Jar with two effigy handles, undecorated body, decoration of rim consists of punctate within incised lines. (Height, 4.7 inches.) Glass, Warren County, Mississippi. Reproduced from Moore, 1911, p. 387, fig. 12.

i, Jar, decorated with Owens Punctate within incised curvilinear pattern on both body and rim. (Height, 6¼ inches.) Menard Mound, Arkansas County, Arkansas (17–K–1). Museum of the American Indian, Cat. No. 17/3308. Phillips, Neg. 2269.

j, Fortune Noded small two-handled jar, nodes on body, undecorated rim. (Diameter, 5 inches.) Cross County, Arkansas. Museum of the American Indian, Cat. No. 12/6484. Phillips, Neg. 2457.

k, Fortune Noded small jar, with two strap handles and two lugs, small nodes on body, undecorated rim, incised line separates body and rim. (Rim diameter, 4½ inches; bowl diameter, 6 inches; height, 4½ inches; rim height, ⅞ inch.) Nodena, Mississippi County, Arkansas (10–Q–1). Alabama Museum of Natural History, Cat. No. Nodena 719; Neg. No. 1880.

l, Fortune Noded jar with four strap handles, nodes on body, handles, and a single row of nodes on rim. Pecan Point, Mississippi County, Arkansas. Lemley Collection, Cat. No. V–934, Hope, Arkansas.

m, Fortune Noded small jar, rim and body covered with small nodes, arcaded handles. (Height, 3.7 inches.) Bradley Place, Crittenden County, Arkansas (11–P–2). Reproduced from Moore, 1911, p. 446, fig. 59.

n, Fortune Noded small two-handled jar, large nodes on body, undecorated rim. (Height, 4 inches.) Williamson Site, Cross County, Arkansas (11–N–13). Museum of Anthropology, University of Michigan, Neg. 4207.

o, Fortune Noded small bowl, large nodes on body, undecorated rim. (Diameter, 3¾ inches; height, 2¾ inches.) Rose Mound, Cross County, Arkansas (12–N–3). Peabody Museum, Harvard University, Cat. No. 22031. Phillips, Neg. 1237.

p, Fortune Noded small bowl, large nodes on body and rim. (Diameter, 3¼ inches.) Rose Mound, Cross County, Arkansas (12–N–3). Museum of the American Indian, Cat. No. 17/4240. Phillips, Neg. 2405.

q, Fortune Noded small jar, large nodes on body, short rim with vertical appliqué strips which which are horizontally notched. (Diameter, 4¼ inches; height, 2¾ inches.) Rose Mound, Cross County, Arkansas (12–N–3). Museum of the American Indian, Cat. No. 17/3276. Phillips, Neg. 2292.

Figure 98

RHODES INCISED ON BELL PLAIN AND NEELEY'S FERRY PASTE *

a, Wide-mouthed bottle, body incised with swastika design, undecorated rim, everted lip, indented disk base. (Height, 5¼ inches.) Beck Place, Crittenden County, Arkansas (13–O–7). University of Arkansas, Cat. No. Beck 228. Phillips, Neg. 3046.

b, Vessel with strongly angled shoulder, short wide neck, high base resembling common Natchezan style, swastika spiral on body. (Diameter, 7 inches; height, 4½ inches.) Beck Place, Crittenden County, Arkansas (13–O–7). University of Arkansas, Cat. No. Beck 247. Phillips, Neg. 3021.

c, Wide-mouthed bottle with globular body, wide plain rim, swastika spiral on body. (Diameter 5½ inches; height, 4⅛ inches.) Walls area, Mississippi (13–P–1). University of Mississippi, Cat. No. 3544. Museum of Anthropology, University of Michigan, Neg. 4363.

d, Wide-mouthed bottle, body incised with swastika spiral, flared neck. (Height, 8.6 inches.) Rose Mound, Cross County, Arkansas (12–N–3). Reproduced from Moore, 1910, p. 298, fig. 26.

e, Jar with arcaded handles, arcades and lip are punctated, body incised with swastika spiral. (Diameter, 3⅞ inches; body diameter, 6¼ inches; height, 3⅞ inches.) Walls area, Mississippi (13–P–1). University of Mississippi, Cat. No. 3543. Museum of Anthropology, University of Michigan, Neg. 4362.

f, Bowl incised with swastika spiral, horizontal flange rim. (Diameter, 7⅞ inches; height, 4¾ inches.) Walls area, Mississippi (13–P–1). University of Mississippi, Cat. No. 3367. Museum of Anthropology, University of Michigan, Neg. 4365.

g, Jar with arcaded handles, swastika spiral on body, short wide rim, single row of nodes on outer rim edge. (Diameter at lobes, 7⅛ inches; height, 3⅞ inches.) Walls area, Mississippi (13–P–1). University of Mississippi, Cat. No. 3542. Museum of Anthropology, University of Michigan, Neg. 4361.

h, Jar with eight appliqué handles, beaded rim, swastika spiral on body, short wide rim (note beveled inner rim). (Rim diameter, 3¾ inches; bowl diameter, 5⅜ inches; rim height, 1 inch; bowl height, 3½ inches.) Nodena, Mississippi County, Arkansas (10–Q–1). Alabama Museum of Natural History, Cat. No. Nod. 524; Neg. No. 1857.

i, Jar with arcaded handles, swastika spiral on body, beaded rim, nodes (human heads—Moore) on upper shoulder area between swastikas. (Diameter, 8.7 inches.) Rhodes Place, Crittenden County, Arkansas. Reproduced from Moore, 1911, p. 424, fig. 38.

j, Jar with six appliqué handles, swastika spiral incised on body, row of nodes on lip, short wide rim, punctate on handles. (Diameter, 4¼ inches.) Bradley Place, Crittenden County, Arkansas (11–P–2). University of Arkansas, Cat. No. Br. 32d. Phillips, Neg. 3188.

k, Jar with arcaded handles, swastika spiral on body, short wide rim, row of nodes on outer lip edge. (Diameter, 8¾ inches.) Golightly Place, Crittenden County, Arkansas (11–P–2). University of Arkansas, Cat. No. Go. 29a. Phillips, Neg. 3509.

l, Jar with arcaded handles, curvilinear festoons punctated on body, incising on handles, short wide rim. (Diameter, 7¼ inches.) Probably Bradley Place, Crittenden County, Arkansas (11–P–2). (University of Arkansas, Cat. No. Beck Place. Phillips, Neg. 3167.

m, Jar with punctated arcaded handles, swastika spiral incised on upper body, single row of nodes on lip, short wide rim. Probably Beck Place, Crittenden County, Arkansas (13–O–7). (Diameter, 9 inches.) Phillips, Neg. 3058.

* Bell Plain Paste (*a–d*, *f*); Neeley's Ferry (others).

Rhodes Incised on Bell Plain and Neeley's Ferry Paste

Miscellaneous Incised Types

Figure 99

MISCELLANEOUS INCISED TYPES

a, Ranch Incised jar with arcaded handles, notched upper rim edge. Nodena Place, Mississippi County, Arkansas (10–Q–1). University of Arkansas, Cat. No. Nod. Phillips, Neg. 3321.

b, Ranch Incised jar with arcaded handles, nodes on handles, and single row on outer lip edge. (Height, 8 inches.) Pecan Point, Mississippi County, Arkansas. Lemley Collection, Cat. No. V–993, Hope, Arkansas.

c, Jar with arcaded handles, punctate on rim and handles, body incised with curvilinear design of whirling swastika which might have been classified as Rhodes Incised if only body fragments had been found. (Diameter, 6½ inches.) Bell Place, Mississippi County, Arkansas (10–P–2). University of Arkansas, Cat. No. Bell Place. Phillips, Neg. 3475.

d, Ranch Incised jar with arcaded handles, punctate on handles, and outer lip edge. Diameter, 7½ inches; height, 6 inches.) Bradley Place, Crittenden County, Arkansas (11–P–2). Museum of the American Indian, Cat. No. 17/4152. Phillips, Neg. 2268.

e, Jar with four small handles with Barton Incised rim and Ranch Incised body. (Diameter, 5½ inches; height, 4¼ inches.) Rose Mound, Cross County, Arkansas (12–N–3). Peabody Museum, Harvard University, Cat. No. 22171. Phillips, Neg. 1142.

f, Ranch Incised frog effigy jar, single row of nodes on outer rim. (Diameter, 6¾ inches; length, 7¼ inches.) Bell Place, Mississippi County, Arkansas (10–P–2). University of Arkansas, Cat. No. Bell Place. Phillips, Neg. 3472.

g, Ranch Incised jar with punctated vertical appliqué, nicked outer lip edge. (Diameter, 8 inches.) Beck Place, Crittenden County, Arkansas (13–O–7). University of Arkansas, Cat. No. Beck. Phillips, Neg. 3499.

h, Jar with Ranch Incised on shoulder area only, incised triangles on rim, simulating arcaded handles, notched outer rim just below lip, and beveled inner rim. (Diameter, 7⅞ inches; height, 8¼ inches.) Walls area, Mississippi (13–P–1). University of Mississippi, Cat. No. 3550. Museum of Anthropology, University of Michigan, Neg. 4360.

i, Leland Incised jar with elongated body, short wide neck and high base. (Diameter, 7½ inches; height, 4¼ inches.) Menard Mound, Arkansas County, Arkansas (17–K–1). Museum of the American Indian, Cat. No. 17/4760. Phillips, Neg. 1952.

j, Leland Incised jar with short neck. Mississippi. (Height, 4 inches.) Reproduced from Holmes, 1903, p. 104, pl. LII, *b*.

k, Leland Incised bottle with wide neck, slightly flared toward lip. (Height, 6 inches.) Mississippi. Reproduced from Holmes, 1903, pl. LII, *d*, p. 104.

l, Fatherland Incised jar, with short flared rim. (Height, 4¾ inches.) Mississippi. Reproduced from Holmes, 1903, pl. LII, *e*, p. 104.

m, Leland Incised bowl with swastika design on body below a single incised line on rim. (Height, 3.3 inches.) Neblett Landing, Bolivar County, Mississippi (18–L–1). Reproduced from Moore, 1911, p. 398, fig. 21.

n, Leland Incised bowl with design on body below a single incised line on rim. (Height, 6 inches.) Mississippi. Reproduced from Holmes, 1903, pl. LII, *c*, p. 104.

o, Straight-sided jar of Bayogoula Incised, lines incised on rim. (Height, 4 inches.) Neblett Landing, Bolivar County, Mississippi (18–L–1). Reproduced from Moore, 1911, p. 396, fig. 18.

p, Blanchard Incised bowl with scalloped rim, incised festoon on inner rim. (Diameter, 6 inches.) Neblett Landing, Bolivar County, Mississippi (18–L–1). Reproduced from Moore, 1911, p. 397, fig. 20.

q, Effigy bowl of mythological beast, body and legs indicated on body of vessel by incised lines, horizontal row of notches on outer lip. (Height, 2.5 inches.) Rose Mound, Cross County, Arkansas (12–N–3). Reproduced from Moore, 1910, p. 289, pl. XI.

r, Shouldered jar, plain body, high wide rim, incised design suggestive of L'eau Noir Incised, but with design similar to certain southern-cult designs. (Height, 4 inches.) Beck Place, Crittenden County, Arkansas (13–O–7). University of Arkansas, Cat. No. Beck 232. Phillips, Neg. 3055.

Figure 100: BOWLS OF NEELEY'S FERRY PLAIN, AND OLD TOWN RED

a, Neeley's Ferry Plain deep bowl with two lugs, appliqué horizontal strip around body, very typical of St. Francis sites, round bottom. (Diameter, 8 inches; height, 5 inches.) Neeley's Ferry, Cross County, Arkansas (11–N–4). Peabody Museum, Harvard University, Cat. No. 21045. Phillips, Neg. 1354.

b, Neeley's Ferry Plain deep bowl with two modeled lugs, very typical shape for St. Francis sites. (Diameter, 9 inches; height, 5½ inches.) Halcomb Mounds, Cross County, Arkansas. Peabody Museum, Harvard University, Cat. No. 21597. Phillips, Neg. 1118.

(Continued on following page)

Figure 100 (*Continued*)

BOWLS OF NEELEY'S FERRY, BELL PLAIN, AND OLD TOWN RED

c, Neeley's Ferry Plain bowl with appliquéd vertically nicked horizontal strip below rim. (Diameter, 8¾ inches, height, 3½ inches.) Halcomb Mounds, Cross County, Arkansas. Peabody Museum, Harvard University, Cat. No. 21657. Phillips, Neg. 1711.

d, Neeley's Ferry Plain bowl with notched rim. (Diameter, 4½ inches; height, 2 inches.) Halcomb Mounds, Cross County, Arkansas. Peabody Museum, Harvard University, Cat. No. 21571. Phillips, Neg. 1185.

e, Neeley's Ferry Plain bowl with four nicked lugs. (Diameter, 7½ inches; height, 3 inches.) Halcomb Mounds, Cross County, Arkansas. Peabody Museum, Harvard University, Cat. No. 21547. Phillips, Neg. 1700.

f, Neeley's Ferry Plain simple bowl, round bottom. (Diameter, 9½ inches; height, 3½ inches.) Stanley Mounds, Cross County, Arkansas. Peabody Museum, Harvard University, Cat. No. 20202. Phillips, Neg. 1320.

g, Neeley's Ferry Plain simple bowl, round bottom, traces of red film. (Diameter, 5¾ inches; height, 1¾ inches.) Fortune Mound, Cross County, Arkansas (11–N–15). Peabody Museum, Harvard University, Cat. No. 21466. Phillips, Neg. 1670.

h, Old Town Red bowl with appliquéd notched strip below rim. (Diameter, 6 inches; height, 3 inches.) Rose Mound, Cross County, Arkansas (12–N–3). Peabody Museum, Harvard University, Cat. No. 22062. Phillips, Neg. 1760.

i, Neeley's Ferry Plain bowl with two horizontal, unusually narrow notched lugs, perforated at each end. (Diameter, 6¾ by 6 inches.) Rose Mound, Cross County, Arkansas (12–N–3). Museum of the American Indian, Cat. No. 17/1392. Phillips, Neg. 2306.

j, Neeley's Ferry Plain beanpot with handle missing, suggestive of Trappist and Spoon River foci of Illinois. (Diameter, 5½ inches; height, 4 inches.) Rose Mound, Cross County, Arkansas (12–N–3). Peabody Museum, Harvard University, Cat. No. 21849. Phillips, Neg. 1294.

k, Neeley's Ferry Plain bowl, parallel vertical incising on outer lip edge, below is a horizontal row of nodes on upper rim. (Diameter, 5¼ inches.) St. Francis River, Arkansas. Museum of the American Indian, Cat. No. 8/7225. Phillips, Neg. 2590.

l, Neeley's Ferry Plain flat-bottomed bowl, outslanting sides, appliquéd indented strip below. (Diameter, 7 inches.) St. Francis River, Arkansas. Museum of the American Indian, Cat. No. 8/7219. Phillips, Neg. 2593.

m, Neeley's Ferry Plain bowl with double lugs which are perforated. (Diameter, 5½ inches.) St. Francis River, Arkansas. Museum of the American Indian, Cat. No. 8/7218. Phillips, Neg. 2512.

n, Bell Plain bowl with parallel vertical incising on outer lip edge. (Diameter, 10 inches.) Golightly Place, Crittenden County, Arkansas (11–P–3). University of Arkansas, Cat. No. Go. 7a. Phillips, Neg. 3245.

o, Bell Plain bowl with row of notches on outer lip edge. (Diameter, 10 inches.) Bell Place, Mississippi County, Arkansas (10–P–2). University of Arkansas. Phillips, Neg. 3092.

p, Bell Plain rectanguloid bowl, notched appliqué rim strip. Pecan Point, Mississippi County, Arkansas. Lemley Collection, Cat. No. V–677, Hope, Arkansas.

q, Bell Plain bowl with notched outer lip edge. (Diameter, 9¼ inches.) Bell Place, Mississippi County, Arkansas (10–P–2). University of Arkansas, Cat. No. Bell Place. Phillips, Neg. 3091.

r, Bell Plain bowl with four wide lugs, vertical ridges from lugs to base. (Width, 5½ by 4½ inches; depth, 3¼ inches.) Nodena, Mississippi County, Arkansas (10–Q–1). Alabama Museum of Natural History, Cat. No. Nod. 561; Neg. No. 1864.

s, Bell Plain bowl with two notched vertical perforated lugs. (Diameter, including lugs, 8¾ inches; bowl diameter, 6½ by 7 inches; depth, 3¾ inches.) Nodena, Mississippi County, Arkansas (10–Q–1). Alabama Museum of Natural History, Cat. No. Nod. 689; Neg. No. 1879.

t, Bell Plain bowl with four scallops on rim, each with two shallow scallops, and remainder of rim has vertical notches on outer lip edge. (Diameter, 10¼ inches; depth, 3½ inches; scallops, ⅝ by 2 inches.) Nodena, Mississippi County, Arkansas (10–Q–1). Alabama Museum of Natural History, Cat. No. Nod. 796; Neg. No. 1892.

u, Bell Plain bowl with double lugs; each lug is perforated. (Diameter, 5½ inches; height, 3 inches; depth, 1⅛ inches.) Walnut, Mississippi County, Arkansas. Alabama Museum of Natural History, Cat. No. Wal. 257; Neg. No. 1915.

v, Bell Plain bowl with parallel vertical incising on outer lip edge. (Diameter, 7¾ inches.) Beck Place, Crittenden County, Arkansas (13–O–7). University of Arkansas, Cat. No. Beck Place. Phillips, Neg. 3032.

BOWLS OF NEELEY'S FERRY, BELL PLAIN, AND OLD TOWN RED

Effigy Bowls of Birds and Beasts

Figure 101

EFFIGY BOWLS OF BIRDS AND BEASTS

a, Neeley's Ferry Plain bird effigy bowl, simple lug tail, effigy on rim. (Height, 4¼ inches; diameter, 7½ inches.) Neeley's Ferry, Cross County, Arkansas (11-N-4). Peabody Museum, Harvard University, Cat. No. 21053. Phillips, Neg. 1589.

b, Neeley's Ferry Plain bird effigy bowl, simple lug tail, very thin head, effigy on rim. (Diameter, 7½ inches.) Halcomb Mounds, Cross County, Arkansas. Peabody Museum, Harvard University, Cat. No. 21688. Phillips, Neg. 1151.

c, Bell Plain bird effigy jar, appliqué wings, short wide neck, simple lug tail; effigy is part of body rather than rim. (Length, 6 inches.) Rhodes Plantation, Golden Lake, Mississippi County, Arkansas. University of Arkansas. Phillips, Neg. 3430.

d, Neeley's Ferry Plain conventionalized effigy bowl, effigy on flat rim, vertical tail has four feathers and perforation. (Diameter, 6¼ by 9¼ inches; height, 2¾ inches.) Neeley's Ferry, Cross County, Arkansas (11-N-4). Peabody Museum, Harvard University, Cat. No. 21147. Phillips, Neg. 1334.

e, Neeley's Ferry Plain effigy bowl with Mound Incised decoration, effigy on rim, broad incised lug tail, round bottom. (Diameter, 6½ inches.) Turkey Island, Cross County, Arkansas. Museum of the American Indian, Cat. No. 17/3265. Phillips, Neg. 2137.

f, Neeley's Ferry serpent effigy bowl, effigy on rim, tail curved on itself. (Diameter, 6¾ inches.) Poinsett County, Arkansas. Museum of the American Indian, Cat. No. 4/7125. Phillips, Neg. 2561.

g, Neeley's Ferry Plain serpent effigy bowl, serpent has ears, incised face, effigy starts on body, simple lug tail. (Diameter, 7 by 7¾ inches.) Cummings Place, Poinsett County, Arkansas (11-O-4). Museum of the American Indian, Cat. No. 17/3323. Phillips, Neg. 2127.

h, Neeley's Ferry serpent effigy bowl, head and tail start on body, tail turned on itself, head and tail on short axis. (Height, 4½ inches; diameter, 8 by 7¼ inches.) Halcomb Mounds, Cross County, Arkansas. Peabody Museum, Harvard University, Cat. No. 21621. Phillips, Neg. 1370.

i, Bell Plain effigy bowl, entwined snakes arising from rim on one side, on opposite side is animal effigy which is facing backwards, flat rim, effigy on lug tail. (Bowl height, 3½ inches; serpent effigy height, 4½ inches; animal effigy length, 3¼ inches; height, 2¼ inches.) Marked Tree, Poinsett County, Arkansas. Titterington Collection, Cat. No. 956.

j, Neeley's Ferry serpent effigy bowl, effigy starts on body, figure seated on tail. (Diameter, 9 by 7½ inches.) Poinsett County, Arkansas. Museum of the American Indian, Cat. No. 4/1563. Phillips, Neg. 2603.

k, Neeley's Ferry Plain serpent effigy bowl with Mound Incised rim decoration, effigy on rim, tail incised to represent its turning on itself. (Diameter, 8 by 7¼ inches; height, 6 inches.) Rose Mound, Cross County, Arkansas (12-N-3). Peabody Museum, Harvard University, Cat. No. 22015. Phillips, Neg. 1301.

l, Neeley's Ferry Plain animal effigy bowl, quadrangular effigy on lug tail, eyes, nose, mouth incised, tail is modeled. (Height, 6½ inches.) Warner Place, near Joiner, Mississippi County, Arkansas. Lemley Collection, Cat. No. V-1276, Hope, Arkansas.

m, Neeley's Ferry Plain duck effigy with perforation through bird cone and seated human effigy on lug tail. (Height, 6¾ inches.) M. W. Hazel Place, Little River, near Marked Tree, Poinsett County, Arkansas. Lemley Collection, Cat. No. V-1610, Hope, Arkansas.

n, Neeley's Ferry or Bell Plain effigy bowl, effigies on lug tails, arms on rim, bodies curved outward. (Cummings Place, St. Francis River, Poinsett County, Arkansas (11-O-4). Lemley Collection, Cat. No. V-1625, Hope, Arkansas.

o, Neeley's Ferry or Bell Plain effigy bowl, human effigy on rim with pyramidal cap suggestive of Cumberland area, nodes on cap, projection on back of head, broad lug tail. (Height, 6¾ inches.) George C. Brown Place, near Hughes, St. Francis County, Arkansas. Lemley Collection, Cat. No. V-1190, Hope, Arkansas.

p, Neeley's Ferry Plain animal effigy bowl, effigy on rim, lug tail. (Diameter, 7¾ inches; height, 4¼ inches.) Neeley's Ferry, Cross County, Arkansas (11-N-4). Peabody Museum, Harvard University, Cat. No. 21266. Phillips, Neg. 1336.

q, q', Neeley's Ferry Plain animal effigy bowl, effigy on rim, animal on lug tail. (Length, 10½ inches.) Vernon Paul, Cross County, Arkansas (11-N-9). University of Arkansas, Cat. No. V.P. 82b. Phillips, Neg. 3434.

FIGURE 102

EFFIGY HEAD BOWLS OF BIRDS, BEASTS, AND MAN

a, Bell Plain bird effigy bowl, simple lug tail, effigy starts on body, effigy facing inward. (Height, 7 inches.) A. S. Catching Place, Mississippi County, Arkansas. Lemley Collection, Cat. No. V–749, Hope, Arkansas.

b, Neeley's Ferry or Bell Plain bird effigy bowl, simple lug tail, effigy starts on body, effigy facing inward. (Diameter, 8¼ inches.) Blytheville, Mississippi County, Arkansas. Museum of the American Indian, Cat. No. 5/2987. Phillips, Neg. 2602.

c, Neeley's Ferry or Bell Plain bird effigy bowl, simple lug tail, effigy starts on body, body and tail are incised to represent feathers and wings. (Diameter, 4¼ inches.) Mississippi County, Arkansas. Museum of the American Indian, Cat. No. 3/5559. Phillips, Neg. 2519.

d, Bell Plain bird effigy bowl, effigy starts on body, tail reconstructed, row of nodes on outer rim, appliqué representing wings on body, effigy facing inward. (Diameter, 6 inches; depth, 3 inches.) Nodena, Mississippi County, Arkansas (10–Q–1). Alabama Museum of Natural History, Cat. No. Nod. 232; Neg. No. 1826.

e, Bell Plain turkey buzzard effigy bowl, effigy starts on body, simple lug tail, head is incised. (Length tail to head, 10 inches.) Nodena, Mississippi County, Arkansas (10–Q–1). Alabama Museum of Natural History, Cat. No. Nod. 851; Neg. No. 1898.

f, Bell Plain effigy bowl, effigy starts on rim, tail is incised to represent its turning on itself, small hole through head and through tail. Bell Place, Mississippi County, Arkansas (10–P–2). Lemley Collection, Cat. No. V–806, Hope, Arkansas.

g, Bell Plain effigy bowl, effigy starts on body, simple lug tail, head represents mythical being with weeping eye. Nodena, Mississippi County, Arkansas (10–Q–1). Alabama Museum of Natural History, Cat. No. Nod. 315; Neg. No. 1835.

h, Bell Plain bat effigy bowl, head faces inward, simple lug tail, appliquéd inverted triangles on body representing wings. Nodena, Mississippi County, Arkansas (10–Q–1). Alabama Museum of Natural History, Cat. No. Nod. 376; Neg. No. 1839.

i, Bell Plain human effigy bowl, effigy starts on body, tail is incised to represent its turning on itself, effigy faces inward. A. S. Catching Place, Mississippi County, Arkansas. Lemley Collection, Cat. No. V–795, Hope, Arkansas.

j, Bell Plain human effigy bowl with Mound Incised design, effigy starts on rim and faces inward, rattle in head, simple lug tail. (Length, 9½ inches.) Blytheville, Mississippi County, Arkansas. University of Arkansas, Cat. No. Chickasawba Mound. Phillips, Neg. 3439.

k, Bell Plain human effigy bowl with Mound Incised rim decoration, effigy starts on body, simple lug tail, face is modeled and incised and suggests the face of a Caucasoid, curled pigtail descends from back of head to outer rim forming a rough handle, lug tail has incised outlining parallel lines. (Flattened base, 3½ by 3⅛ inches; height, 3 7/16 inches; head height, 5 7/16 inches; tip to tip, 8¾ inches.) Walls Site, Davies Collection, Mississippi (13–P–1). University of Mississippi, Cat. No. 3302. Museum of Anthropology, University of Michigan, Neg. 4348.

l, Bell Plain human effigy head bowl with Mound Incised decoration on rim; effigy starts on body, simple lug tail, well-modeled face, incised headdress. Flattened base, 2 9/16 inches; height, 3 9/16 inches; total, 5⅝ inches; head height, 3 inches; tip to tip, 8⅞ inches.) Walls Site, Davies Collection, Mississippi (13–P–1). University of Mississippi, Cat. No. 3298. Museum of Anthropology, University of Michigan, Neg. 4343.

m, Bell Plain human effigy head bowl; effigy starts on body, head is modeled, facial characteristics suggest Negroid features, tail has a circular disk vertically placed on the end of a projecting rod, the outer edge of both sides of the disk are decorated with a continuous row of small, circular punctates. Height, 3 inches; head height, 5½ inches; tip to tip, 10 5/16 inches.) Walls Site, Davies Collection, Mississippi (13–P–1). University of Mississippi, Cat. No. 3303. Museum of Anthropology, University of Michigan, Neg. 4350.

n, Bell Plain human effigy head bowl, effigy starts on rim, head is modeled, two projections on back of head, simple lug tail on which three chevrons are incised. (Height, 6¾ inches.) Bell Place, Mississippi County, Arkansas (10–P–2). Lemley Collection, Cat. No. V–808, Hope, Arkansas.

o, Bell Plain human effigy head bowl, effigy starts on body, and faces outward, conical hat, simple lug tail. (Height, 7⅛ inches.) Bell Place, Mississippi County, Arkansas (10–P–2). Bell Place, Mississippi County, Arkansas (10–P–2). Lemley Collection, Cat. No. V–576, Hope, Arkansas.

p, Bell Plain human effigy head bowl, two effigies face each other, effigies start on body, row of nodes on outer lip. (Height, 7¼ inches.) Pecan Point, Mississippi County, Arkansas. Lemley Collection, Cat. No. V–627, Hope, Arkansas.

a *b* *c*

d *e* *f*

g *h* *i*

j *k* *l*

m *n* *o* *p*

EFFIGY HEAD BOWLS OF BIRDS, BEASTS, AND MAN

a *b* *c* *d*

e *f* *g* *h*

i *j* *k* *l*

m *n* *o* *p*

q *r* *s* *t*

Bottle Forms

Figure 103

BOTTLE FORMS

a, Neeley's Ferry Plain bottle, short wide neck, globular body, engraved design on body, low annular base. One of the rare St. Francis shapes with engraving. (Diameter, 6¾ inches; height, 7½ inches; oral diameter, 3½ inches; basal diameter, 3¾ inches.) Fortune Mound, Cross County, Arkansas (11–N–15). Peabody Museum, Harvard University, Cat. No. 21477. Phillips, Neg. 1368.

b, Neeley's Ferry Plain bottle, high narrow neck, globular body, low punctated annular base. (Height, 9¼ inches.) Arkansas County, Arkansas. Buffalo Museum of Natural Science, Cat. No. 453. Phillips, Neg. 56.

c, Bell Plain bottle, high narrow cylindrical neck, globular body, low annular base. (Height, 9¼ inches.) Turkey Island, Cross County, Arkansas. Museum of the American Indian, Cat. No. 17/4547. Phillips, Neg. 2130.

d, Neeley's Ferry or Bell Plain bottle with narrow cylindrical neck of medium height, fillet at base of neck, low flaring annular base, three appliqué faces on shoulder not visible in photograph. (Height, 10 inches.) Cross County, Arkansas. Museum of the American Indian, Cat. No. 12/6517. Phillips, Neg. 2461.

e, Neeley's Ferry or Bell Plain bottle with narrow cylindrical neck, globular body, low annular base. (Diameter, 7¼ inches; height, 10¼ inches; oral diameter, 2¼ inches; basal diameter, 3¾ inches.) Halcomb Mounds, Cross County, Arkansas. Peabody Museum, Harvard University, Cat. No. 21711. Phillips, Neg. 1412.

f, Neeley's Ferry or Bell Plain bottle, narrow cylindrical neck, fillet at base of neck, carinated body, perforated annular base. (Height, 11½ inches.) St. Francis River, near Monette, Arkansas. Museum of the American Indian Cat. No. 5/5569. Phillips, Neg. 2528.

g, Neeley's Ferry or Bell Plain bottle, high wide back, carinated shoulder and horizontal should area, annular base. (Diameter, 7¾ inches; height, 7 inches.) Stanley Mounds, Cross County, Arkansas. Peabody Museum, Harvard University, Cat. No. 20192. Phillips, Neg. 1405.

h, Neeley's Ferry Plain jar with basal fillet, flaring rim, annular base. (Diameter, 4¾ inches; height, 4 inches; basal diameter, 3 inches.) Neeley's Ferry, Cross County, Arkansas (11–N–4). Peabdoy Museum, Harvard University, Cat. No. 21088. Phillips, Neg. 1544.

i, Neeley's Ferry or Bell Plain bottle, flattened globular body, narrow neck, high perforated base. (Height, 8 inches.) Neeley's Ferry, Cross County, Arkansas (11–N–4). Peabody Museum, Harvard University, Cat. No. 21299. Phillips, Neg. 1505.

j, Neeley's Ferry or Bell Plain bottle, globular body, narrow neck, perforated annular base. (Height, 8¾ inches.) Neeley's Ferry, Cross County, Arkansas (11–N–4). Museum of the American Indian, Cat. No. 17/4738. Phillips, Neg. 2129.

k, Neeley's Ferry Plain bottle, globular body, wide straight neck, punctated annular base. (Diameter, 7 inches; height, 9 inches.) Neeley's Ferry, Cross Countря, Arkansas (11–N–4). Peabody Museum, Harvard University, Cat. No. 21319. Phillips, Neg. 1747.

l, Bell Plain bottle, globular body, wide neck, fillet at base of neck, punctated annular base. (Diameter, 7½ inches; height, 8½ inches.) Neeley's Ferry, Cross County, Arkansas (11–N–4). Peabody's Museum, Harvard University, Cat. No. 21213. Phillips, Neg. 1506.

m, Bell Plain squat bottle, straight wide neck, disk base indented wtih short vertical notches. (Height, 5¾ inches.) Bell Place, Mississippi County, Arkansas (10–P–2). University of Arkansas, Cat. No. Bell 184. Phillips, Neg. 3110.

n, Bell Plain bottle, flattened globular body, wide neck, slightly flaring rim, low annular base. (Height, 7½ inches.) Bell Place, Mississippi County, Arkansas (10–P–2). University of Arkansas, Cat. No. Bell 179. Phillips, Neg. 3096.

o, Bell Plain bottle, flattened globular body, high wide neck with slightly flaring rims, beveled inner rim, perforated annular base. (Height, 10 inches; oral diameter, 3¾ inches.). Bradley Place, Crittenden County, Arkansas (11–P–2). Museum of the American Indian, Cat. No. 17/4612. Phillips, Neg. 1974.

(*Continued on following page*)

Figure 103 (*Continued*)

BOTTLE FORMS

p, Bell Plain bottle, flattened globular body, short wide neck, slight recurve near base with punctate suggestive of Parkin Punctate, four appliqué handles, low annular base. (Height, 5¼ inches.) Pecan Point, Mississippi County, Arkansas. Museum of the American Indian, Cat. No. 17/4100. Phillips, Neg. 2010.

q, Nodena Red and White bottle, globular body, high neck, annular base, swastika whorl on body, horizontal lines on neck. (Height, 9 inches.) Vernon Paul, Cross County, Arkansas (11–N–9). University of Arkansas, Cat. No. V.P. 21a. Phillips, Neg. 3390.

r, Nodena Red and White bottle, globular body, high neck, flared at rim, low annular base, swastika whorl on body extending onto base, horizontal lines on rim. (Height, 8 inches.) Hazel Place, Little River, near Marked Tree, Poinsett County, Arkansas. Lemley Collection, Cat. No. V–1605, Hope, Arkansas.

s, Nodena Red and White bottle, flattened body, straight narrow neck, annular base, swastika whorl on body extending onto base, five stepped designs in red around the neck, three are upright and two are inverted — three contain a red dot in the center; single red horizontal line at lip. (Height, 9 inches.) Marked Tree, Poinsett County, Arkansas, Titterington Collection, Cat. No. 957.

t, Nodena Red and White bottle, globular body, carafe neck, low annular base, swastika whorl on body, horizontal painted lines on neck. (Height, 15 inches; rim height, 3½ inches; bowl height, 8¾ inches; basal height, ¾ inches; rim diameter, 2¼ inches; bowl diameter, 7 inches; basal diameter, 3½ inches.) Nodena, Mississippi County, Arkansas (10–Q–1). Alabama Museum of Natural History, Cat. No. Nod. 248; Neg. No. 1861.

Figure 104

BOTTLES INCLUDING VERTICAL COMPOUND FORMS

a, Neeley's Ferry Plain bottle, globular body, wide neck. (Diameter, 7¾ inches; height, 7½ inches; oral diameter, 3¼ inches.) Neeley's Ferry, Cross County, Arkansas (11–N–4). Peabody Museum, Harvard University, Cat. No. 21120. Phillips, Neg. 1524.

b, Neeley's Ferry Plain bottle, flattened globular body, low wide neck. (Diameter, 9 inches; height, 7¾ inches.) Neeley's Ferry, Cross County, Arkansas (11–N–4). Peabody Museum, Harvard University, Cat. No. 21187. Phillips, Neg. 1512.

c, Neeley's Ferry Plain pear-shaped bottle; short straight wide neck, ring base. (Height, 6¼ inches.) Cross County, Arkansas. Museum of the American Indian, Cat. No. 12/6503. Phillips, Neg. 2449.

d, Bell Plain bottle, flattened body, low neck. (Height, 7 inches.) Rose Mound, Cross County, Arkansas (12–N–3). Peabody Museum, Harvard University, Cat. No. 22053. Phillips, Neg. 1204.

e, Neeley's Ferry Plain bottle, globular body, high straight neck. Barton Ranch, Crittenden County, Arkansas (11–O–10). (Height, 7¼ inches.) University of Arkansas Cat. No. B.A.R. 76b. Phillips, Neg. 2992.

f, Bell Plain bottle, flattened body, low neck. (Height, 7½ inches.) Bell Place, Mississippi County, Arkansas (10–P–2). University of Arkansas, Cat. No. Bell 172. Phillips, Neg. 3087.

g, Bell Plain bottle, flattened body, three dimples in body, low wide neck, disk base. (Height, 5½ inches.) Bell Place, Mississippi County, Arkansas (10–P–2). University of Arkansas, Cat. No. Bell 163. Phillips, Neg. 3098.

h, Neeley's Ferry or Bell Plain bottle, narrow contracting neck, Caddoan form. (Height, 9¾ inches.) Menard Mound, Arkansas County, Arkansas (17–K–1). Museum of the American Indian, Cat. No. 17/4765. Phillips, Neg. 2119.

i, Neeley's Ferry Plain bottle, globular body, short narrow neck. (Height, 9½ inches.) Carden Bottom, Yell County, Arkansas (L. F. Branson Collection). Museum of the American Indian, Cat. No. 5/6447. Phillips, Neg. 2533.

j, Neeley's Ferry compound vessel, jar over bottle, jar has strap handles, globular body. (Height, 7¾ inches.) St. Francis River, near Monette, Arkansas. Museum of the American Indian, Cat. No. 8/7248. Phillips, Neg. 2573.

k, Neeley's Ferry compound vessel, bottle over jar, jar has globular body, short wide neck, four strap handles on rim, bottle has high neck, flared rim. St. Francis River, near Monette, Arkansas. Museum of the American Indian, Cat. No. 5/5568. Phillips, Neg. 2566.

l, Neeley's Ferry compound vessel, bottle over jar, jar has four loop handles, bottle has straight high neck. (Height, 11½ inches.) St. Francis River, near Monette, Arkansas. Museum of the American Indian, Cat. No. 5/5567. Phillips, Neg. 2565.

m, Neeley's Ferry compound bottle, globular body, the two vessels joined at mid section, short narrow neck. (Diameter, 8 inches; height, 7¾ inches.) Stanley Mounds, Cross County, Arkansas. Peabody Museum, Harvard University, Cat. No. 20262. Phillips, Neg. 1308.

n, Neeley's Ferry compound vessel, bottle over jar, jar has globular body, bottle has high straight neck. (Height, 8½ inches.) Old Town Ridge, 6 miles north of Monette, Craighead County, Arkansas. Lemley Collection, Cat. No. V–96, Hope, Arkansas.

o, Kent Incised jar on bottle base. (Height, 6 inches.) Wapanoca, Crittenden County, Arkansas. University of Arkansas, Cat. No. Wa. 11b. Phillips, Neg. 3379.

p, Neeley's Ferry or Bell Plain bottle, flattened body, short wide neck, punctate suggestive of Parkin Punctated on lower rim, diagonal incised lines on lip. (Height, 4½ inches.) Neeley's Ferry, Cross County, Arkansas (10–Q–1). Museum of the American Indian, Cat. No. 17/3433. Phillips, Neg. 2217.

q, Bell Plain bottle, flattened body, indented median flange, short wide neck, beveled inner rim. (Height, 5½ inches.) Pecan Point, Mississippi County, Arkansas. Museum of the American Indian, Cat. No. 17/4789. Phillips, Neg. 2012.

r, Bell Plain bottle, globular body, short neck of jar form suggestive of Rhodes Incised, rope relief around base, middle of bowl, base of rim, with six transverse connections from base to middle and six from middle to top at off-sets. (Diameter, 8 inches; height, 6 inches.) Nodena, Mississippi County, Arkansas (10–Q–1). Alabama Museum of Natural History, Cat. No. Nod. 464; Neg. No. 1848.

s, Bell Plain bottle, flattened body, short wide neck, flared rim, band of punctate on lower rim similar to Parkin Punctated jars. (Diameter, 6¼ inches; height, 6 inches.) Fortune Mound, Cross County, Arkansas (11–N–15). Peabody Museum, Harvard University, Cat. No. 21458. Phillips, Neg. 1374.

t, Bell Plain compound vessel, bottle over jar, jar has four handles, notched lip, bottle has high neck, fillet effigy at base of neck representing a quadruped. (Height, 11 inches.) Davenport Public Museum, Cat. No. 8210. Phillips, Neg. 704.

a b c d

e f g h

i j k l

m n o

q r s t

BOTTLES INCLUDING VERTICAL COMPOUND FORMS

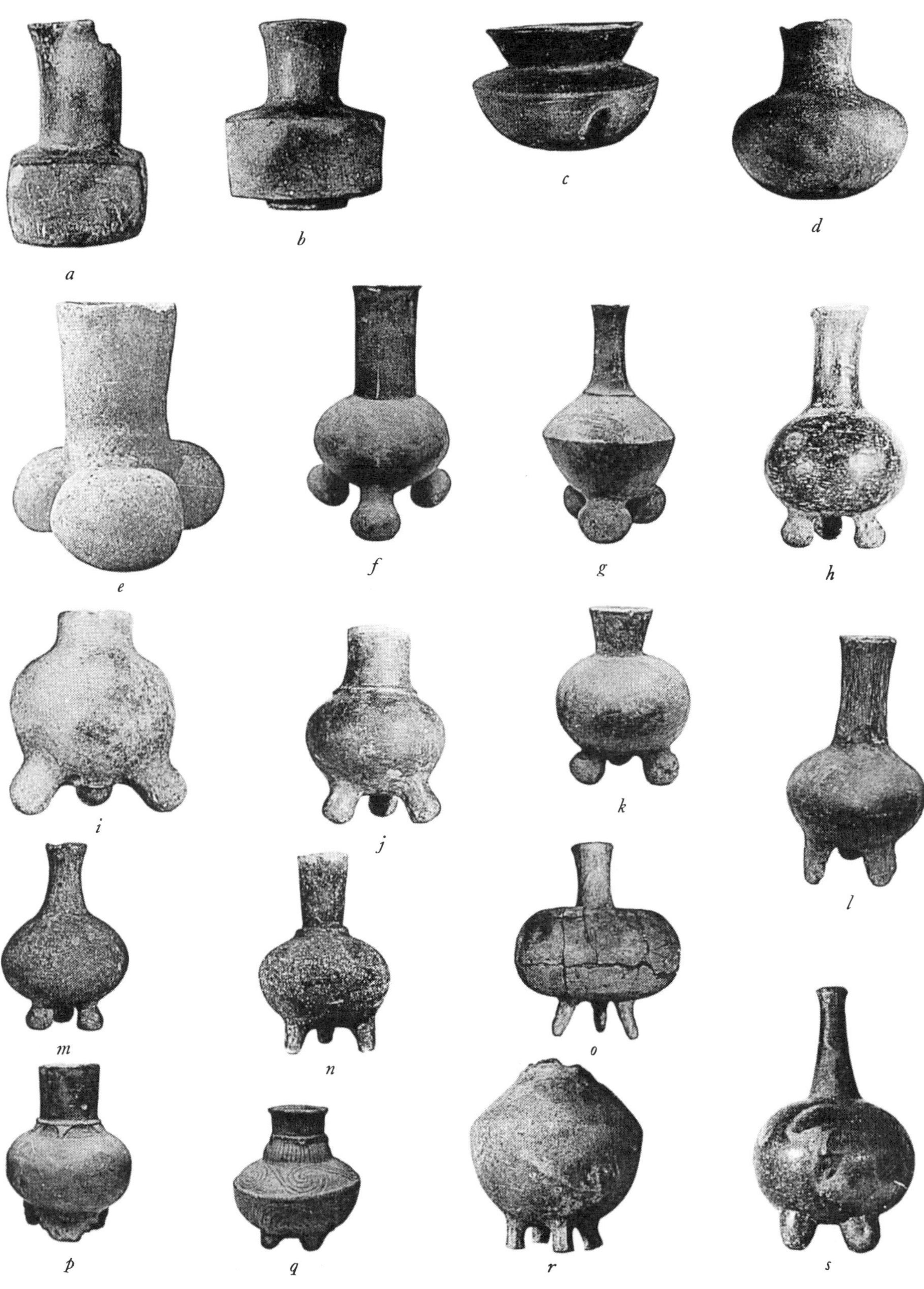

Bottles, Tripods, and Tetrapods

Figure 105

BOTTLES, TRIPODS, AND TETRAPODS

a, Bell Plain bottle with rectangular body, high wide flaring neck. (Height, 5½ inches.) Beck Place, Crittenden County, Arkansas (13–O–7). University of Arkansas, Cat. No. Beck 238. Phillips, Neg. 3063.

b, Bell Plain bottle with rectangular body, high wide flaring neck, annular base. (Height, 6½ inches.) Chickasawba Mound, near Blytheville, Mississippi County, Arkansas. University of Arkansas. Phillips, Neg. 3253.

c, Bell Plain bowl with angled, sharply insloping shoulder and outslanting rim attached at 45-degree angle. (Diameter, 6¼ inches; height, 3¾ inches.) Rose Mound, Cross County, Arkansas (12–N–3). Museum of the American Indian, Cat. No. 17/4230. Phillips, Neg. 1977.

d, Neeley's Ferry Plain bottle with globular body, half of mouth is blocked by horizontal projecting clay ledge on inner rim just below lip. (Height, 8¼ inches.) St. Francis River, near Monette, Arkansas. Museum of the American Indian, Cat. No. 5/5571. Phillips, Neg. 2540.

e, Neeley's Ferry Plain eccentric tripod. (Height, 6¼ inches.) Vernon Paul, Cross County, Arkansas (11–N–9). Reproduced from Moore, 1910, p. 309, fig. 34.

f, Bell Plain bottle with bulbous tripods, globular body, high straight neck, beveled inner lip. (Height, 11¼ inches.) Pecan Point, Mississippi County, Arkansas. Lemley Collection, Cat. No. V–956, Hope, Arkansas.

g, Bell Plain bottle with carafe neck, carinated shoulder and three ball tripods. (Height, 10½ inches). George Looney Place, Mississippi County, Arkansas. Lemley Collection, Cat. No. V–913, Hope, Arkansas.

h, Bell Plain bulbous-leg tripod bottle, globular body, high neck, flared at rim area. (Diameter, 5¼ inches; height, 8¼ inches; oral diameter, 2¼ inches.) Halcomb Mounds, Cross County, Arkansas. Peabody Museum, Harvard University, Cat. No. 21561. Phillips, Neg. 1399.

i, Neeley's Ferry Plain bottle, globular body, short straight neck, cylindrical tripod. (Height, 8¾ inches.) Halcomb Mounds, Cross County, Arkansas. Peabody Museum, Harvard University, Cat. No. 21717. Phillips, Neg. 1109.

j, Neeley's Ferry or Bell Plain bottle, short wide flared neck, fillet around base of neck, cylindrical tripod. (Height, 8¼ inches.) Neeley's Ferry, Cross County, Arkansas (11–N–4). Peabody Museum, Harvard University, Cat. No. 21320. Phillips, Neg. 1497.

k, Neeley's Ferry Plain bottle, globular body, short flared neck, small bulbous tripods. Bell Place, Mississippi County, Arkansas (10–P–2). Lemley Collection, Cat. No. V–776, Hope, Arkansas.

l, Neeley's Ferry Plain tripod bottle, stepped slab legs, globular body, high carafe neck. (Height, 12¼ inches.) Pecan Point, Mississippi County, Arkansas. Lemley Collection, Cat. No. V–535.

m, Neeley's Ferry Plain tripod bottle, globular body, carafe neck, small bulbous tripods. (Diameter, 5¼ inches; height, 7¼ inches; oral diameter, 1½ inches.) Neeley's Ferry, Cross County, Arkansas (11–N–4). Peabody Museum, Harvard University, Cat. No. 21071. Phillips, Neg. 1348.

n, Neeley's Ferry Plain bottle, globular body, high neck, fillet around base of neck, short cylindrical tripods. (Height, 9 inches.) Neeley's Ferry, Cross County, Arkansas (11–N–4). Museum of the American Indian, Cat. No. 17/4208. Phillips, Neg. 1991.

o, Neeley's Ferry Plain bottle, flattened body, carafe neck, narrow cylindrical tripods. (Diameter, 8¼ inches; height, 9 inches; oral diameter, 2 inches.) Neeley's Ferry, Cross County, Arkansas (11–N–4). Peabody Museum, Harvard University, Cat. No. 21302. Phillips, Neg. 1513.

p, Bell Plain tripod bottle, stepped-slab legs, globular body, straight wide neck, fillet at base of neck, arcaded handles below fillet. (Height, 7¼ inches.) Banks and Danner Place (Old Bradley Place), Crittenden County, Arkansas (11–P–2). Lemley Collection, Cat. No. V–951, Hope, Arkansas.

q, Tripod bottle, stepped slab legs, shouldered body, short wide neck, expanded near base, in expanded area is small Kent Incised design, Rhodes Incised on shoulder and lower body. Banks and Danner Place (Old Bradley Place), Crittenden County, Arkansas (11–P–2). Lemley Collection, Cat. No. V–950, Hope, Arkansas.

r, Bell Plain tetrapod bottle, carinated body, neck missing, a most unusual cylindrical-leg tetrapod. (Height, 7 inches.) Wapanoca, Crittenden County, Arkansas. University of Arkansas, Cat. No. Wa. 22a. Phillips, Neg. 3364.

s, Bell Plain tetrapod bottle, globular body, carafe neck. (Height, 13 inches.) Beck Place, Crittenden County, Arkansas (13–O–7). University of Arkansas, Cat. No. Beck Place. Phillips, Neg. 3508.

Figure 106

STIRRUP NECKS, COMPOUND AND MISCELLANEOUS FORMS

a, Neeley's Ferry or Bell Plain stirrup-necked bottle, globular body. (Bowl diameter, 6 inches; vessel height, 6¾ inches.) Nodena, Mississippi County, Arkansas (10–Q–1). Alabama Museum of Natural History, Cat. No. Nod. 72; Neg. No. 1811.

b, Neeley's Ferry stirrup-necked bottle, globular body. (Height, 6.4 inches.) Neeley's Ferry, Cross County, Arkansas (11–N–4). Reproduced from Moore, 1910, p. 316, fig. 43.

c, Bell Plain stirrup-necked bottle, shouldered body. (Height, 8¼ inches.) Pecan Point, Mississippi County, Arkansas. Lemley Collection, Cat. No. V–691, Hope, Arkansas.

d, Neeley's Ferry or Bell Plain modified stirrup-necked bottle with two human faces. (Diameter, 3 inches; depth, 3¾ inches; length, 1½ inches.) Walnut, Mississippi County, Arkansas. Alabama Museum of Natural History, Cat. No. Wal. 74; Neg. No. 1909.

e, Neeley's Ferry or Bell Plain modified stirrup-necked bottle, globular body, disk base. Bell Place, Mississippi County, Arkansas (10–P–2). Lemley Collection, Cat. No. V–563, Hope, Arkansas.

f, Neeley's Ferry modified stirrup-necked bottle, flattened globular body. (Diameter, 5½ inches; height, 6¼ inches.) Stanley Mounds, Cross County, Arkansas. Peabody Museum, Harvard University, Cat. No. 20170. Phillips, Neg. 1276.

g, Neeley's Ferry Plain modified stirrup-necked or double bottle. (Height, 5½ inches.) Upper Nodena, Mississippi County, Arkansas (10–Q–1). University of Arkansas, Cat. No. U.N. 214a. Phillips, Neg. 3340.

h, Bell Plain double bottle, bodies open into each other, necks are straight and joined by a vertical bridge, suggestive of Peruvian whistling jars. (Length, 6¾ inches.) Lee County, Mound. University of Arkansas. Phillips, Neg. 3516.

i, Bell Plain modified stirrup-necked bottle, bodies open into each other, globular rim at juncture, disk bases. Bradley Place, Crittenden County, Arkansas (11–P–2). Memphis Public Museum; Mason Collection, No. 1–A–34.

j, Bell Plain double bottles, bodies open into each other, rims are straight and short and are joined by a horizontal rod, disk bases. (Over-all length, 9¼ inches.) Nodena, Mississippi County, Arkansas (10–Q–1). Alabama Museum of Natural History, Cat. No. Nod. 555; Neg. No. 1862.

k, Bell Plain double fish effigy bottle, bodies open into each other, rims are straight and are joined by a horizontal strap handle. (Over-all diameter, 9½ inches.) Nodena, Mississippi County, Arkansas (10–Q–1). Alabama Museum of Natural History, Cat. No. Nod. 675; Neg. No. 1878.

l, Bell Plain double bottle, bodies open into each other, necks are straight and short, and are joined by a horizontal strap handle bridge. (Height, 4½ inches.) L. W. Gosnell Place, edge of city of Blytheville, Mississippi County, Arkansas. Lemley Collection, Cat. No. V–154, Hope, Arkansas.

m, Triple jar, bodies open into each other, necks are not joined. (Diameter, 6 inches.) Matlock Plantation, Shawnee Village, Mississippi County, Arkansas. University of Arkansas. Phillips, Neg. 3515.

n, Neeley's Ferry Plain horned bottle, high wide neck, everted rim, disk base. (Height, 3¾ inches.) Rose Mound, Cross County, Arkansas (12–N–3). Museum of the American Indian, Cat. No. 17/4244. Phillips, Neg. 2407.

o, Bell Plain horned bottle, neck broken off, disk base. (Length, 7¾ inches.) Bradley Place, Crittenden County, Arkansas (11–P–2). University of Arkansas, Cat. No. Br. 47a. Phillips, Neg. 3455.

p, Bell Plain horned bottle, high thin slightly flared neck, annular base. (Height, 8½ inches.) Allcorn Place, near Marked Tree, St. Francis River, Poinsett County, Arkansas. Lemley Collection, Cat. No. V–1600, Hope, Arkansas.

q, Bell Plain horned bottle, high thin neck. Twist Place, St. Francis River, Cross County, Arkansas (11–N–14). Lemley Collection, Cat. No. V–1553, Hope, Arkansas.

r, Neeley's Ferry Plain pedestal base bowl, there are traces of red pigment over the lightly polished interior surface. (Diameter, 3½ inches.) Rose Mound, Cross County, Arkansas (12–N–3). Museum of the American Indian, Cat. No. 17/1387. Phillips, Neg. 2409.

s, Neeley's Ferry or Bell Plain shell effigy bowl. (Length, 5 inches; width, 4 inches.) Rose Mound, Cross County, Arkansas (12–N–3). Museum of the American Indian, Cat. No. 17/4222. Phillips, Neg. 2418.

t, Neeley's Ferry or Bell Plain foot effigy, two spouts—spout in center of jar is short, that which represents leg is high, thin, and bulges near the base. (Length, 5½ inches.) Beck Place, Crittenden County, Arkansas (13–O–7). University of Arkansas, Cat. No. Beck Place. Phillips, Neg. 3413.

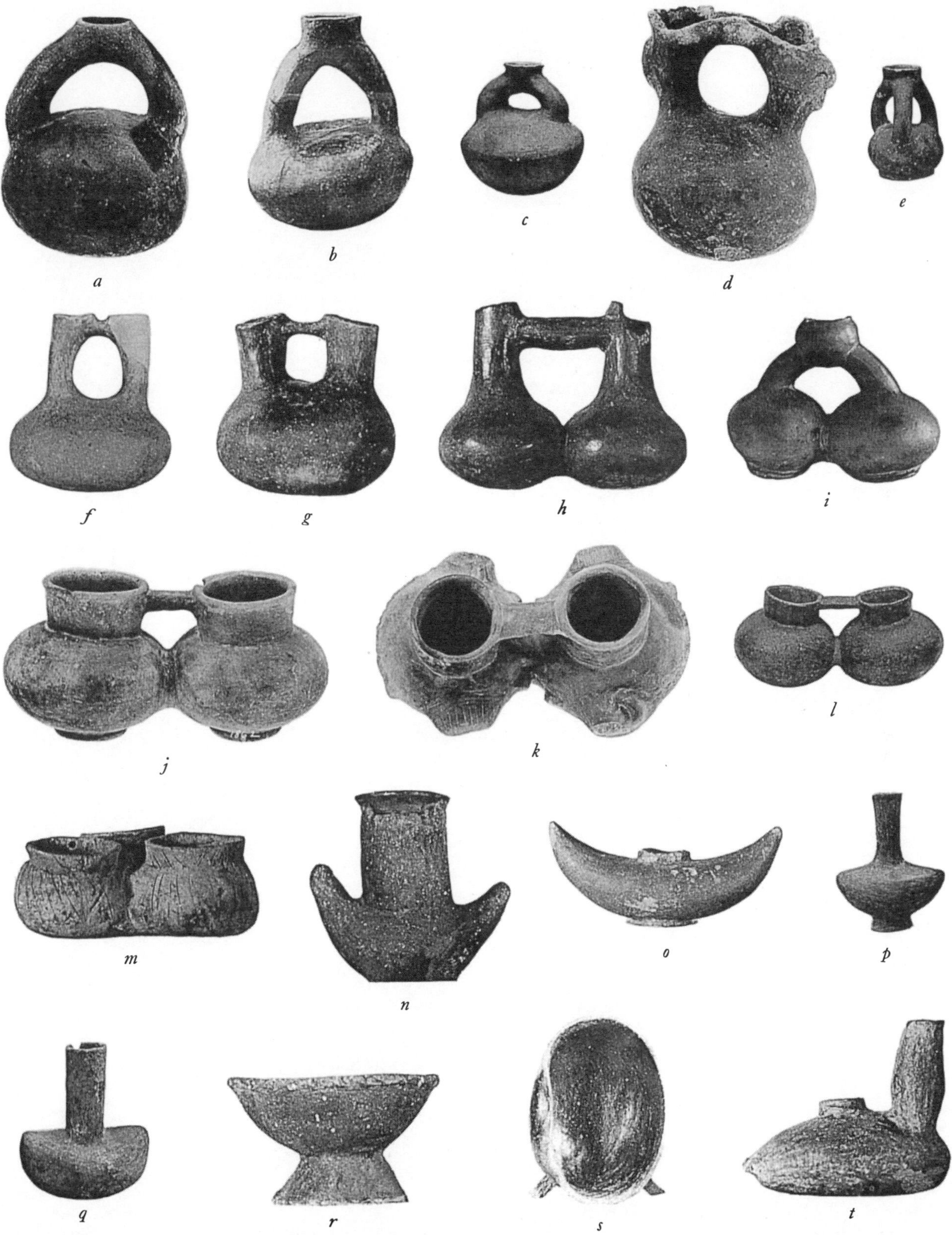

Stirrup Necks, Compound, and Miscellaneous Forms

Human Effigy Vessels

Figure 107

HUMAN EFFIGY VESSELS

a, a′, Bell Plain human effigy vessel, kneeling hunchback with hands on knees, incising on face resembles head vases, single perforation in ear, incised scroll swastika on back, vessel opening in back of head of hooded bottle type. (Height, 7½ inches.) Upper Nodena, Mississippi County, Arkansas (10–Q–1). University of Arkansas, Cat. No. U.N. 12a. Phillips, Neg. 3437.

b, b′, Bell Plain human effigy vessel, kneeling figure with hands on knees, incising on face, three projections on back of body suggestive of back bone, vessel opening in back of head of hooded bottle type. (Height, 7¼ inches.) Upper Nodena, Mississippi County, Arkansas (10–Q–1). University of Arkansas, Cat. No. U.N. 177a. Phillips, Neg. 3416.

c, Bell Plain human effigy vessel, sitting figure with arms crossed and resting on knees which are uplifted, facial decoration, ear treatment, and perforated projection on forehead are very close to head vases of this area, vessel opening in back of head of hooded bottle type. Walnut, Mississippi County, Arkansas. Alabama Museum of Natural History, Cat. No. Wal. 712; Neg. No. 1924.

d, Probably Old Town Red human effigy vessel, kneeling figure, hands resting on knees which are doubled under body, face is modeled, no incising, vessel opening in back of head of hooded bottle type. L. W. Gosnell Place, Blytheville, Mississippi County, Arkansas. Lemley Collection, Cat. No. V–480, Hope, Arkansas.

e, Neeley's Ferry human effigy vessel, sitting figure with outstretched legs, eyes, nose, and mouth applied, projection on back, vessel opening in top of head. Parkin, Cross County, Arkansas (11–N–1). Lemley Collection, Cat. No. V–475, Hope, Arkansas.

f, Bell Plain effigy bottle, three human faces modeled on sides which are most closely comparable with Charleston, Missouri, style of face, each face forms a lobe, short, wide-neck, slightly flared rim. Nodena, Mississippi County, Arkansas (10–Q–1). Alabama Museum of Natural History, Cat. No. Nod. 435; Neg. No. 1844.

g, g′, Neeley's Ferry human effigy vessel, kneeling hunchback, modeled head on projection from neck, flared rim. (Height, 7½ inches.) Earle, Tyronza River, Arkansas. University of Arkansas. Phillips, Neg. 3441.

h, Bell Plain human effigy bottle, flattened globular body, notched edge disk base and notched ridge around shelter area just below neck, neck is in the form of a human head, conical in outline, face is modeled, notched vertical ridge on both sides of the face, vessel opening in back of head of hooded bottle type. (Diameter, 6½ inches.) Walnut, Mississippi County, Arkansas. Alabama Museum of Natural History, Cat. No. Wal. 12; Neg. No. 1291.

i, Bell Plain gourd effigy with vertical opening, decorating suggestive of pyramidal human caps, circular opening of vessel takes form of mouth. (Height, 8½ inches.) Beck, near Hughes, Crittenden County, Arkansas (13–O–7). University of Arkansas. Phillips, Neg. 3056.

j, Bell Plain gourd effigy bottle with representation of human face and pyramidal cap, globular body, round bottom, notched ridge on shoulder area on back and sides only, circular opening of vessel takes form of mouth. (Height, 8.3 inches.) Bradley Place, Crittenden County, Arkansas (11–P–2). Reproduced from Moore, 1911, p. 436, fig. 46.

k, Bell Plain gourd effigy bottle with suggested human facial features, and arms and legs of seated types, circular opening of vessel takes form of mouth. (Height, 7 inches.) Rose Mound, Cross County, Arkansas (12–N–3). Museum of the American Indian, Cat. No. 17/1395. Phillips, Neg. 1955.

Figure 108

EFFIGY VESSELS OF FROG, OPOSSUM, AND OTHER BEASTS

a, Unusual form of Bell Plain — animal-head effigy jar, neck projects from top of back of head, eyes and ears applied, nose indented, mouth and teeth incised. (Height, 7¼ inches.) L. W. Gosnell Place, Blytheville, Mississippi County, Arkansas. Lemley Collection, Cat. No. V–419, Hope, Arkansas.

b, Unusual form of Bell Plain — animal head effigy jar, neck projects from top of back of head, flared rim, eyes, ears, teeth, and legs applied. Kent Place, Lee County, Arkansas (13–N–4). Formerly in W. P. Murdock Collection.

c, Bell Plain animal-head effigy jar, neck projects from top of head, flared rim, ears and eyes applied, mouth incised, disk base. (Height, 5¾ inches; diameter, 5⅞ inches.) Walls area, Mississippi (13–P–1). University of Mississippi, Cat. No. 3382. Phillips, Neg. 4352.

d, Bell Plain frog effigy jar, legs form tetrapodal base, eyes applied, vessel opening on back. (Length, 7 inches.) Nodena, Mississippi County, Arkansas (10–Q–1). Alabama Museum of Natural History, Cat. No. Nod. 732; Neg. No. 1883.

e, Bell Plain frog effigy jar, head projects from side of body, legs are applied on body, eyes applied, vessel opening on back. (Diameter, 5 inches.) Rhodes Place, Crittenden County, Arkansas. Museum of the American Indian, Cat. No. 17/4805. Phillips, Neg. 2157.

f, Bell Plain frog effigy jar, head projects from side of body, legs are applied on body, eyes are applied, mouth incised, vessel opening on back. (Height, 5⅜ inches.) Pecan Point, Mississippi County, Arkansas. Lemley Collection, Cat. No. V–675.

g, *g'*, Bell Plain frog effigy jar, head projects from side of body, legs applied on body, claws incised, low wide rim, row of short parallel vertical incised lines on upper rim, two strap handles. (Height, 5½ inches.) Bradley Place, Crittenden County, Arkansas (11–P–2). Museum of the American Indian, Cat. No. 17/3263. Phillips, Neg. 1959.

h, *h'*, Neeley's Ferry or Bell Plain bottle with four applied frog heads, eyes are applied, incised lines radiating from heads, low wide neck, row of punctate on outer rim, disk base. (Height, 4½ inches.) Beck Place, Crittenden County, Arkansas (13–O–7). University of Arkansas. Phillips, Neg. 3429.

i, Bell Plain frog effigy bottle, neck projecting from center of back, legs and eyes applied, mouth incised (note beveled inner rim). (Length, 8 inches.) Nodena, Mississippi County, Arkansas (10–Q–1). Alabama Museum of Natural History, Cat. No. Nod. 636; Neg. No. 1875.

j, Neeley's Ferry or Bell Plain spouted effigy bottle, head incised, legs form tetrapodal base, bottle neck missing. (Length, 7 inches.) Beck Place, Crittenden County, Arkansas (13–O–7). University of Arkansas, Cat. No. Beck Place. Phillips, Neg. 3469.

k, Bell Plain effigy jar, head projecting from side of body, joined to lip by filleted bridge, head is modeled and incised, short wide neck, row of beaded appliqué on outer rim (note beveled inner rim). (Height, 4⅛ inches.) Pecan Point, Mississippi County, Arkansas. Lemley Collection, Cat. No. V–714, Hope, Arkansas.

a *b* *c*

d *e* *f*

g *g′* *h* *h′*

i *j* *k*

EFFIGY VESSELS OF FROG, OPOSSUM, AND OTHER BEASTS

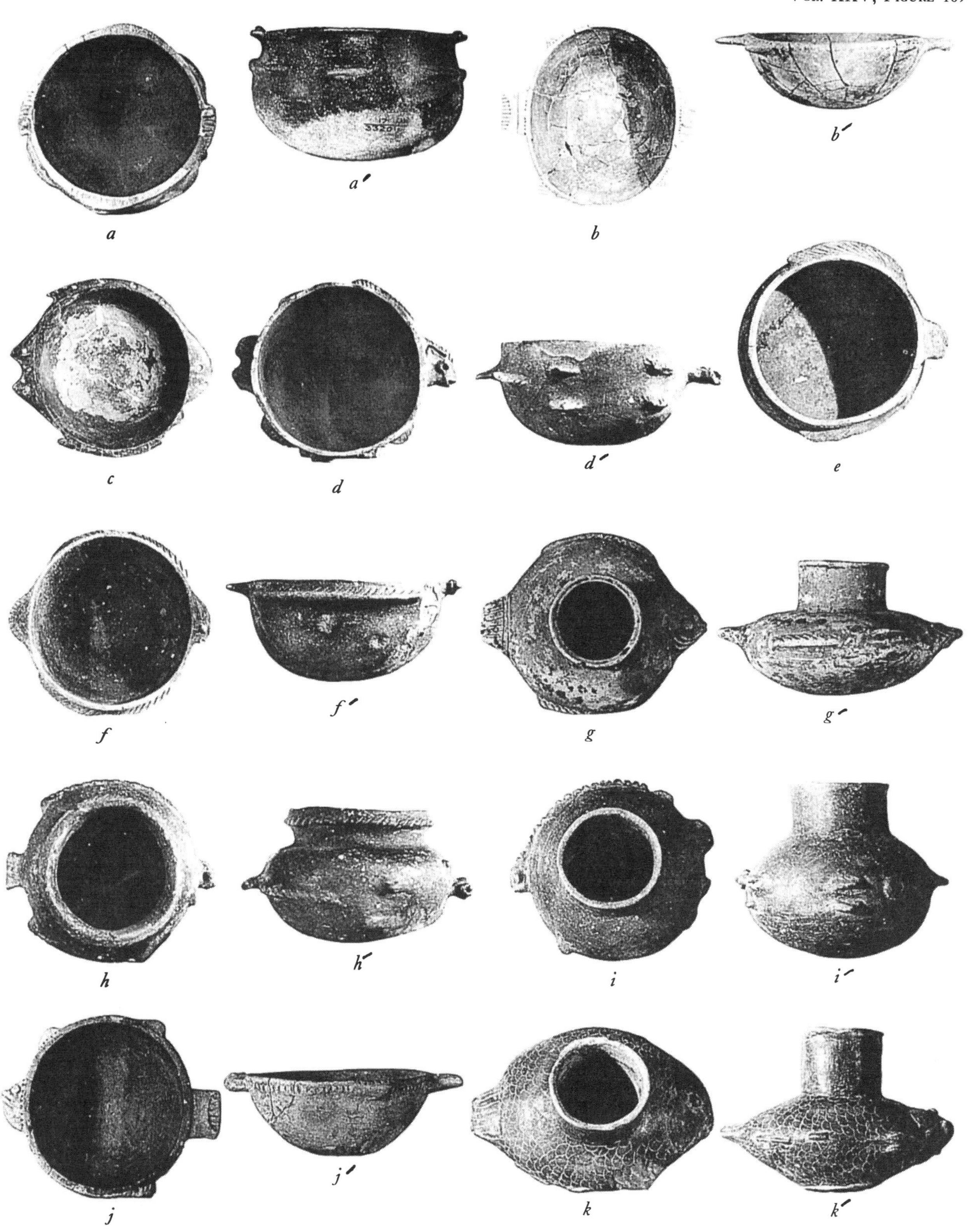

Fish Effigy Bowls and Bottles

Figure 109

FISH EFFIGY BOWLS AND BOTTLES

a, a', Neeley's Ferry fish effigy bowl, two fish heads on opposite sides of vessel at lip level, four lugs in shape of fins, projections on body in shape of fins. (Diameter, 9 inches; height, 5½ inches.) Miller Place, Poinsett County, Arkansas. Museum of the American Indian, Cat. No. 17/3320. Phillips, Neg. 2150.

b, b', Neeley's Ferry Plain upstream fish effigy bowl, head, tail, and three fins form lugs, incising and punctate on each lug, row of nodes on outer lip edge (note similarity to *j, j'*). (Diameter, 11 by 9¼ inches; height, 3½ inches; length, 12¼ inches. Fortune Mound, Cross County, Arkansas (11–N–15). Peabody Museum, Harvard University, Cat. No. 21459. Phillips, Neg. 1393.

c, Old Town Red upstream fish effigy bowl, head, tail, and two fins form lugs; single perforation in head, two in tail, and four perforations in each fin. (Diameter, 11⅛ inches; height, 4¼ inches.) Marked Tree, Poinsett County, Arkansas. Titterington Collection, Cat. No. 961.

d, d' Neeley's Ferry upstream fish effigy bowl, parallel incised lines on head, tail, and fins, which start on body rather than rim. (Diameter, 7 inches.) Twist Plantation, Cross County, Arkansas (11–N–14). Museum of the American Indian, Cat. No. 12/6512. Phillips, Neg. 2501.

e, Neeley's Ferry Plain fish effigy bowl, head and fins on body, fins are incised with parallel lines. (Diameter, 9½ inches.) Cross County, Arkansas. Peabody Museum, Harvard University, Cat. No. 56984. Phillips, Neg. 1091.

f, f', Neeley's Ferry Plain fish effigy bowl, head and tail on rim, fins on outer rim, node on head, fins and tail incised with parallel lines. (Diameter, 8½ inches.) Cross County, Arkansas. Museum of the American Indian, Cat. No. 4/7141. Phillips, Neg. 2530.

g, g', Old Town Red fish effigy bottle, flattened body, head, tail, and fins are part of the body, node on head, tails and fins are incised, straight wide neck. (Height, 9 inches.) Little Warren Place, Mississippi County, Arkansas. University of Arkansas. Phillips, Neg. 3447.

h, h' Neeley's Ferry Plain miniature fish effigy jar, head, tail, and fins are part of body, reinforced indented rim. (Height, 2½ inches; length, 4¾ inches.) Blytheville, Mississippi County, Arkansas. Museum of the American Indian, Cat. No. 5/3000. Phillips, Neg. 2646.

i, i', Neeley's Ferry or Bell Plain downstream fish effigy bottle, head, tail, and fins are part of the body, head and fins are notched, wide neck. (Height, 6 inches.) Bell Place, Mississippi County, Arkansas (10–P–2). University of Arkansas. Phillips, Neg. 3426.

j, j', Old Town Red downstream fish effigy bowl, red interior, incised and punctated head, tail, and fins on rim, parallel vertical incising on outer rim (note similarity to *b, b'*). Length, 7 inches.) Bradley Place, Crittenden County, Arkansas (11–P–2). University of Arkansas, Br. 20a. Phillips, Neg. 3473.

k, k' Bell Plain fish effigy bottle, head, tail, and fins are part of the body, body is engraved to represent scales, high straight neck, disk base. (Length, 9¾ inches.) Upper Nodena, Mississippi County, Arkansas (10–Q–1). University of Arkansas, Cat. No. Upper Nodena. Phillips, Neg. 3432.

Figure 110

VARIANTS OF WALLS ENGRAVED

a, Wide-mouthed bottle with globular body, slightly flattened, engraved swastika whorl—Moundville style. Beck Place, near Hughes, Crittenden County, Arkansas (13–O–7). University of Arkansas, Cat. No. Beck 217. Phillips, Neg. 3076.

b, Wide-mouthed bottle with globular body, engraved with swastika whorl—Moundville style. (Diameter, 5⅛ inches; height, 5⅛ inches.) Walls area, Mississippi (13–P–1). University of Mississippi, Cat. No. 3361. Museum of Anthropology, University of Michigan, Neg. 4415.

c, Wide-mouthed bottle with contracting neck, body engraved with swastika whorl—Moundville style. (Diameter, 6¾ inches; height, 6½ inches.) Walls area, Mississippi (13–P–1). University of Mississippi, Cat. No. 3360. Museum of Anthropology, University of Michigan, Neg. 4355.

d, Wide-mouthed bottle with flattened globular body, engraved feathered spiral and wave swastika on body—Moundville style. (Height, 7½ inches.) Beck Place, Crittenden County, Arkansas (13–O–7). University of Arkansas. Phillips, Neg. 3507.

e, Wide-mouthed bottle with flattened globular body, cross hatching within engraved design. (Height, 6 inches.) Glass, Warren County, Arkansas. Reproduced from Moore, 1911, p. 383, fig. 6.

f, Wide-mouthed jar, shouldered, engraved decoration on body based on swastika and perhaps, in part, derived from the crested serpent—Moundville style. (Height, 4.5 inches.) Rhodes Place, Crittenden County, Arkansas. Reproduced from Moore, 1911, p. 426, fig. 40.

g, Short narrow-necked bottle with flaring rim of Lower Arkansas style, engraved design on body, red paint in lines. (Height, 9 inches.) Greer, Jefferson County, Arkansas. Museum of the American Indian, Cat. No. 17/3449. Phillips, Neg. 2191.

h, Shouldered jar, wide short neck, swastika design engraved on body, engraved upright and inverted triangles on rim (note beveled inner rim). (Height, 5⅞ inches.) Nickels Place, near Hughes, St. Francis County, Arkansas (13–N–15). Lemley Collection, Cat. No. V–1088, Hope, Arkansas.

i, High, wide-necked bottle with globular body, engraved swastika on body, flaring ring base. (Height, 8.6 inches.) Bradley Place, Crittenden, County, Arkansas (11–P–2). Reproduced from Moore, 1911, p. 440, fig. 50.

j, Wide-mouthed bottle, engraved swastika scroll on body, disk base. (Height, 6¼ inches.) Rose Mound, Cross County, Arkansas (12–N–3). Museum of the American Indian, Cat. No. 17/4233. Phillips, Neg. 2198.

k, Shouldered jar with engraved design over whole vessel, wide short rim. (Diameter, 5¼ inches; height, 3¾ inches; oral diameter, 3¾ inches.) Neeley's Ferry, Cross County, Arkansas (11–N–4). Peabody Museum, Harvard University, Cat. No. 21165. Phillips, Neg. 1349.

l, Wide-mouthed jar with contracting neck, engraved swastika, and feathered spiral on body and lower rim. (Height, 6⅛ inches.) Pecan Point, Mississippi County, Arkansas. Lemley Collection, Cat. No. V–722, Hope, Arkansas.

m, Bottle, engraved design on body based on the swastika. (Height, 7.25 inches.) Rose Mound, Cross County, Arkansas (12–N–3). Reproduced from Moore, 1910, p. 291, fig. 19.

Variants of Walls Engraved

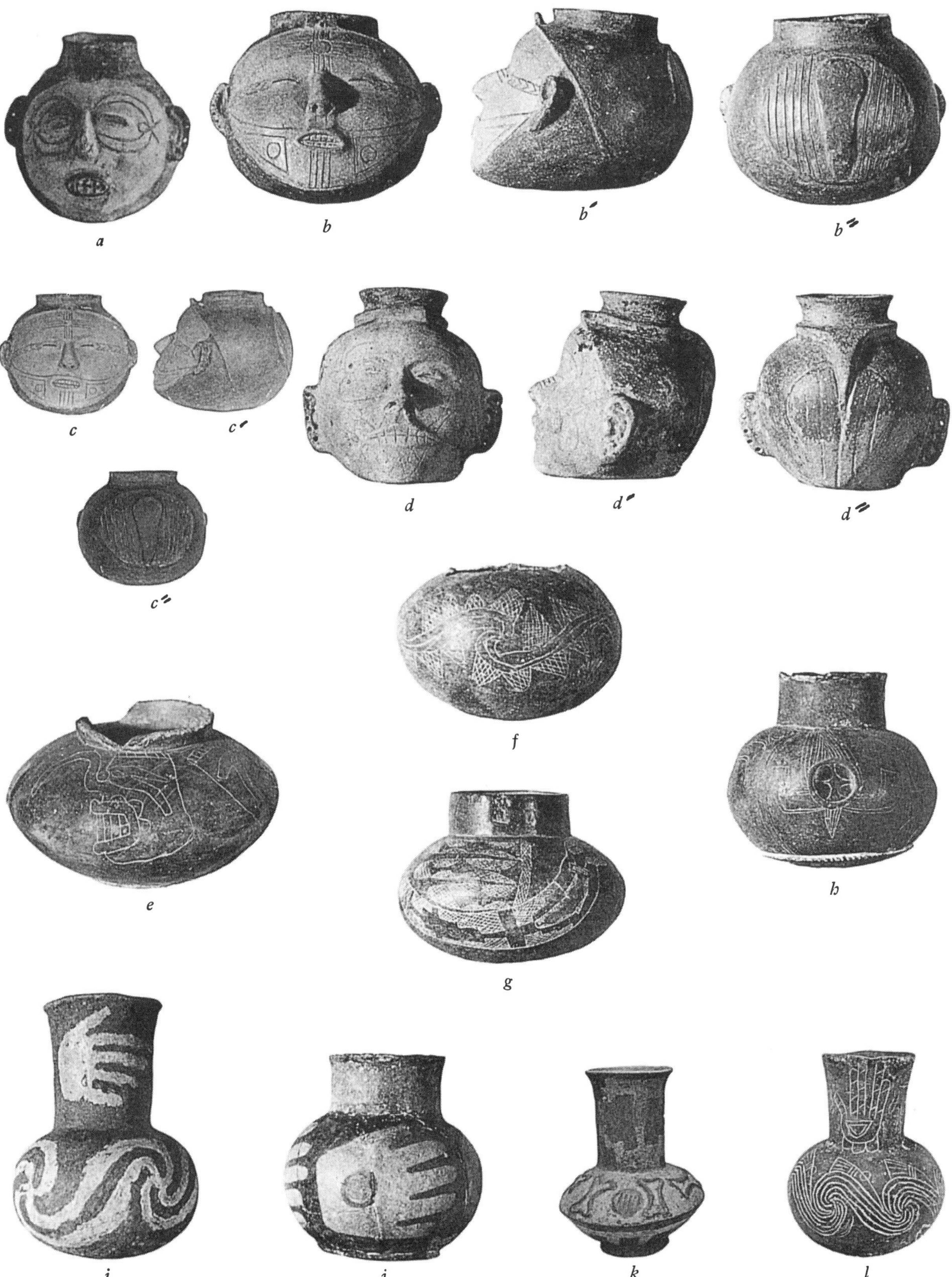

HEAD VASES, ENGRAVED DESIGNS, AND PAINTED HANDS

FIGURE 111

HEAD VASES, ENGRAVED DESIGNS, AND PAINTED HANDS

a, Nodena Red and White head effigy vessel, teeth and eyes incised, other features modeled, two circular lines around eyes, four perforations in ear following lobe, face is white, remainder of vessel is red, vessel opening in top of head. Bradley Place, Crittenden County, Arkansas (11–P–2). Mason Collection, Cat. No. 1114, Memphis, Tennessee.

b–b", Nodena Red and White head effigy vessel, teeth and eyes incised, other features modeled, pattern of incised lines, circles, triangles, vertical lines and chevrons enclosed by double lines on face, four perforations in ear following lobe, face is white, remainder of vessel is red, rectangular lug with single perforation, projections from forehead, vessel opening in top of head, short, wide neck, raised ovoid disk on back of head in center of which is raised section, on either side of which are six vertical incised lines. (Height, 5¾ inches.) Bradley Place, Crittenden County, Arkansas (11–P–2). University of Arkansas. Phillips, Neg. 3420.

c–c", Effigy head vessel with extraordinary similarity to *b–b"*. (Height, 5½ inches.) Cross County, Arkansas. Chicago Natural History Museum, Cat. No. 50292.

d–d", Nodena Red and White head effigy vessel with features very similar to preceding two vessels, except for headdress pattern. (Height, 6¼ inches.) Mattock Place, Mississippi County, Arkansas, University of Arkansas. Phillips, Neg. 3418.

e, Flattened jar, Walls Engraved design of "long nose" god. Walls area, Mississippi (13–P–1). University of Mississippi, Cat. No. 3364. Museum of Anthropology, University of Michigan, Neg. 4356.

f, Flattened globular bottle, neck is missing, Walls Engraved design on body of feathered serpent, strongly resembling Moundville type. (Height, 5¾ inches.) Bell Place, Mississippi County, Arkansas (10–P–2). University of Arkansas, Cat. No. Bell 118. Phillips, Neg. 3070.

g, Short, wide-neck bottle with Walls Engraved design of feathered serpent strongly resembling Moundville type. (Height, 5¾ inches.) Beck Place, Crittenden County, Arkansas (13–O–7). University of Arkansas. Phillips, Neg. 3423.

h, Slightly flattened globular bottle, notched disk base, short wide neck, beveled inner rim, Walls Engraved design similar to hearts at Moundville. (Height, 7 inches.) Rhodes Plantation, Golden Lake, Mississippi County, Arkansas. University of Arkansas. Phillips, Neg. 3141.

i, Nodena Red and White bottle, flattened body, high wide neck, slightly flared rim, white swastika spiral on body, outline of hand on neck, in white pigment. (Height, 9 inches.) Rhodes Plantation, Mississippi County, Arkansas. University of Arkansas. Phillips, Neg. 3401.

j, Negative Painted bottle, flattened body, short wide neck, slightly flared rim, disk base, four outlined hands on body, in palm of each is red spot within a black circle. (Height, 5¾ inches.) Barton Ranch, Crittenden County, Arkansas (11–O–10). University of Arkansas, Cat. No. B. R. 14a. Phillips, Neg. 3399.

k, Nodena Red and White bottle, carinated body, red line encircles greatest diameter, low annular base is red with rectangular sections projecting onto body, upper half of body has appliquéd outlines of bones separated by raised disks on which are incised vertical lines representing hand, neck is high, wide flared rim, on neck are stepped designs in red and white. Bell Place, Mississippi County, Arkansas (10–P–2). Lemley Collection, Cat. No. V–570, Hope, Arkansas.

l, Gray bottle, globular body, high wide neck, engraved spirals of five parallel lines on body, outline of hand on neck, double triangle on palm, engraved hand with Moundville hand-and-eye design. (Height, 8 inches.) Twist Place, Togo, St. Francis River, Cross County, Arkansas (11–N–14). Lemley Collection, Cat. No. V–1551, Hope, Arkansas.

Figure 112

PAINTED VESSELS INCLUDING SOME BIZARRE FORMS

a, Nodena Red and White bottle, stepped-slab tripod base, flattened globular body, high neck, swastika spiral on body, step design on neck. (Height, 10¼ inches.) Halcomb Mounds, Cross County, Arkansas. Peabody Museum, Harvard University, Cat. No. 21635. Phillips, Neg. 1132.

b, Nodena Red and White tripod bottle, stepped slab tripod base, globular body, high wide neck, whorl on body, step design on neck. (Height, 9⅜ inches.) Vernon Paul, Cross County, Arkansas (11–N–9). Lemley Collection, Cat. No. V–1596, Hope, Arkansas.

c, Carson Red on Buff jar, globular body, short wide neck, whorl on body. (Height, 6 inches; neck has been sawed off.) Neeley's Ferry, Cross County, Arkansas (11–N–4). Museum of the American Indian, Cat. No. 17/1411. Phillips, Neg. 2024.

d, Nodena Red and White bottle, globular body, short wide neck, two white vertical stripes alternating with single red stripe on body, single horizontal white stripe between two red ones on neck. (Height, 6¾ inches.) Castile Mound, St. Francis River, St. Francis County, Arkansas (13–N–21). Lemley Collection, Cat. No. V–212, Hope, Arkansas.

e, Nodena Red and White bottle, globular body, Lower Arkansas neck, red and white whorls on body. This may have been a polychrome piece. (Height, 9 inches.) Jones Place (Old River Landing), Arkansas County, Arkansas (16–K–1). Museum of the American Indian, Cat. No. 17/4191. Phillips, Neg. 2042.

f, Carson Red on Buff bottle, flattened globular body, short wide neck, rows of punctate on rim resembling Parkin Punctate, swastika whorl on body. (Height, 6¼ inches.) St. Francis River, Arkansas. Museum of the American Indian, Cat. No. 8/7235. Phillips, Neg. 2162.

g, Nodena Red and White horizontal compound bottle, bodies open into each other, necks are joined by a horizontal bridge, rims are flared, flattened globular bodies, swastikas on the body, inverted and upright stepped pyramids on the rims, circles inside pyramids. (Height, 5½ inches.) L. W. Gosnell Place, Blytheville, Mississippi County, Arkansas. Lemley Collection, Cat. No. V–341, Hope, Arkansas.

h, Nodena, Red and White bottle, flattened globular body, short wide neck, vertical bands on body suggestive of copper gorgets at Moundville. (Height, 6¾ inches.) James Place, near Wilson, Mississippi County, Arkansas. Lemley Collection, Cat. No. V–945, Hope, Arkansas.

i, Nodena Red and White shell effigy bowl, inverted triangles on body, painted interior. (Height, 4½ inches.) Vernon Paul, Cross County, Arkansas (11–N–9). Lemley Collection, Cat. No. V–1588, Hope, Arkansas.

j, Nodena Red and White "duck" effigy tetrapod bottle with legs broken, red and white horizontal stripes on sides of vessel, red circles on front, single row of circles on neck. (Height, 8 inches.) Halcomb Mounds, Cross County, Arkansas. Peabody Museum, Harvard University, Cat. No. 21639. Phillips, Neg. 1126.

k, Nodena Red and White hooded owl effigy bottle, feet and tail form tripod base, curvilinear lines on back and tail, white circles on front, head and neck are white. (Height, 9 inches.) Nodena, Mississippi County, Arkansas (10–Q–1). Alabama Museum of Natural History, Cat. No. Nod. 844; Neg. No. 1896.

l, Nodena Red and White conventionalized duck or turtle effigy, tetrapodal base, the tetrapods are stepped and the lower half is painted red, parallel red stripes on back, stripe at base of neck, red circles on neck. (Height, 10½ inches.) Marked Tree, Poinsett County, Arkansas. Titterington Collection, Cat. No. 965.

m, Nodena Red and White human effigy bottle, white, roughly horizontal lines on body. Mound on Fuller Conner Place, St. Francis River, Cross County, Arkansas. Lemley Collection, Cat. No. V–1595.

n, Nodena Red and White hooded bird effigy bottle, legs and tail form tripods, globular body, vessel opening in back of head. (Height, 7⅜ inches.) Mississippi County, Arkansas. Lemley Collection, Cat. No. V–1267, Hope, Arkansas.

o, Carson Red and Buff bottle, flattened globular body, short wide neck with beveled inner rim, two horizontal rows of circles on body. (Height, 7 inches.) Mound near the limits of the city of Helena, Phillips County, Arkansas (14–N–6). Lemley Collection, Cat. No. V–1083, Hope, Arkansas.

PAINTED VESSELS INCLUDING SOME BIZARRE FORMS

a b c

d e f

g h

i

j

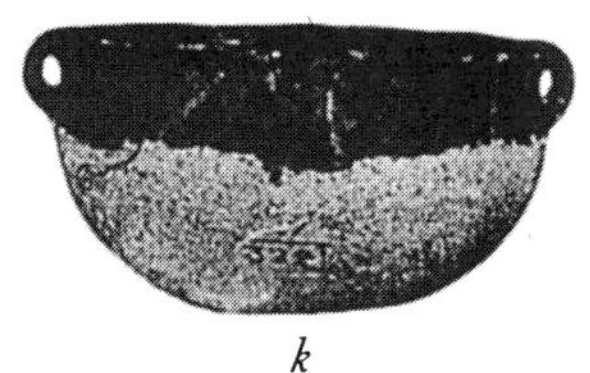
k

Teapots and Lower Arkansas Late Painted Vessels

Figure 113

TEAPOTS AND LOWER ARKANSAS LATE PAINTED VESSELS

a, Old Town Red teapot vessel, contracting spout projecting from side of vessel, small lug handle opposite spout, Lower Arkansas neck. (Height, 7¼ inches.) Menard Mound, Arkansas County, Arkansas (17–K–1). Museum of the American Indian, Cat. No. 17/3307. Phillips, Neg. 2081.

b, Old Town Red teapot vessel, contracting spout projecting from side of vessel, small lug handle opposite spout, Lower Arkansas neck. (Height, 5½ inches.) Near Menard Landing, Arkansas County, Arkansas (17–K–1). Museum of the American Indian, Cat. No. 17/4171. Phillips, Neg. 2085.

c, Bell Plain teapot vessel, contracting spout projecting from upper body of vessel, small lug handle, short narrow neck, wide neck fillet, outrolled lip, flattened body. (Height, 7¼ inches.) Beck Place, Crittenden County, Arkansas (13–O–7). University of Arkansas. Phillips, Neg. 3468.

d, Old Town Red teapot vessel, contracting spout projecting from upper body, small lug, short neck, flared rim, flattened body. (Height, 7¼ inches.) Kent Place, Lee County, Arkansas (13–N–4). Museum of the American Indian, Cat. No. 17/4291. Phillips, Neg. 2079.

e, Bell Plain teapot vessel, contracting spout projecting from upper body, small lug handle, short neck. (Diameter, 6½ inches.) Bradley Place, Crittenden County, Arkansas (11–P–2). University of Arkansas, Cat. No. Br. 49a. Phillips, Neg. 3510.

f, Avenue Polychrome teapot vessel, spout projecting from side of vessel, small lug handle, short neck, vessel is buff with red, pinkish white, and black spiral design on body and spout. (Height, 6¼ inches.) Jones Place (Old River Landing), Arkansas County, Arkansas (16–K–1). Museum of the American Indian, Cat. No. 17/4190. Phillips, Neg. 2084.

g, Bell Plain teapot vessel, contracting spout projecting from side of vessel, small lug handle, neck is small frog effigy jar. (Height, 5.9 inches.) Neblett Landing, Bolivar County, Mississippi (18–L–1). Reproduced from Moore, 1911, p. 396, fig. 17.

h, Unusual Neeley's Ferry Plain teapot vessel, contracting spout projecting from upper body, spout has outrolled lip, handle is in the shape of an animal head facing inward, short straight rim. (Diameter, 8.8. inches.) Rose Mound, Cross County, Arkansas (12–N–3). Reproduced from Moore, 1910, p. 302, fig. 31.

i, Jar with modeled frog effigy applied to side, legs are appliquéd on body of vessel, upper body, rim and frog heads are red, lower vessel is buff, Lower Arkansas bottle neck, formerly had spout. (Height, about 4¼ inches.) Near Old River Landing (Jones Place), Arkansas County, Arkansas (16–K–1). Museum of the American Indian, Cat. No. 17/4770. Phillips, Neg. 2092.

j, Bowl, effigy head and tail modeled on sides of vessel, upper body is red, lower body is buff. (Diameter, 7½ by 6½ inches.) Jones Place (Old River Landing), Arkansas County, Arkansas. Museum of the American Indian, Cat. No. 17/1409. Phillips, Neg. 2053.

k, Jar with four strap handles, upper body and handles have red film, body is buff. (Height, 3¼ inches; diameter, 5¾ inches.) Jones Place (Old River Landing), Arkansas County, Arkansas (16–K–1). Museum of the American Indian, Cat. No. 17/3291. Phillips, Neg. 2075.

ABOUT THE INDEXES

Stephen Williams

Most "Peabody Papers" do not have an index; neither the Phillips's 1970 two-volume treatise nor the Lake George monograph (Williams and Brain, 1983.) However, my other Peabody volume, "The Waring Papers" (Williams, 1968), did, because it was a collection of very different topics. This volume is by nature the result of a rather complex piece of research, which was both carried out in the field by the three archaeologists and their assistants and also written by the three authors. Only *some* of the problems that arose from this joint effort are described in the preface. Indeed the scope of their efforts needs to be emphasized here in a way not mentioned above. For example, the very amount of "space" covered in this research was more than 12,000 square miles, and the time frame, as we now know it, spans at least 3,000 years. The number of sites recorded (382) were quite large, and the number of potsherds was enormous: 350,000!

Well, what has this to do directly with the Index? The amount of data accumulated was massive. Because the projectile points and other stone artifacts were collected but not analyzed, some of the data were not even studied. They remain at the Peabody Museum, catalogued but still awaiting analysis. The problem herein is how to best allow the scholar to access this mass of data in a forthright manner. The volume is filled by lists of sites, maps of the region researched, analysis of the sherds recovered, and various attempts at putting these pottery remains in temporal order. There are separate chapters on everything from site plans to vessel forms, and there is a data-filled chapter on Spanish involvement in the valley from the sixteenth century forward. The final chapter melds together the views of all three authors of the prehistoric events in this part of the Lower Mississippi Valley over a lengthy time span.

Indexing these numerous data bits proved to be a difficult, labor-intensive task that required extensive research. The indexer is Susan Nielsen Hammond, with only modest intrusions by myself. For me, watching the index unfold has been an enlightening experience. How do you keep track of more than 300 sites, numerous pottery types, and the complex early historic time period, with mixed data from many sources? The index revealed two "Moore" sites; not the ones visited by the well-known C. B. Moore but ones named for two *different* owners with the same surname in Arkansas and Mississippi. Moreover, two "Mound City" sites exist, which are not the familiar "Mound City" in Missouri (St. Louis' 'old name' in the nineteenth century). Instead, one is in Arkansas, and the other is in Mississippi. Fortunately, our LMS *site numbers* clearly differentiate these four sites; however a number of other sites have multiple names: for example, the Murdock Place (13-N-12) is also known as either Moore's "Kent Place" or "Walnut Bend" (p. 49). As I ploughed through the text of the indexes, I found *nine* sets of sites with exactly the same name. Of course, all 18 sites have different LMS numbers, but it does give pause to think how easily one could get them confused in this volume. They are, in alphabetical order: Boyer site, Deer Creek site, Dupree site, Ellis site, Indian Creek site, Mitchell site, Moore site, Mound City site, and Shelby site. These are cross-referenced in the index to avoid confusion.

Of course, one must also realize that there has been another major change. With the advent of a national format for site numbers that covers every state, all the sites herein have new numbers in the state records. Therefore, the LMS numbers used here are obsolete. One other modest problem is that some of the site *numbers* in Figure 70 (see pp. 368–369), DeSoto's route, are incorrect, but the site names are correct.

The pottery descriptor index is an extensive and detailed listing of pottery dimensions and traits. Ceramic buffs and seekers for special ceramic markers should have an untold source of new information. The search has been done for you, which is solely the work of Susan Hammond.

MAIN INDEX

Figures and tables without corresponding page numbers are foldouts.

SITE DESCRIPTOR INDEX

POTTERY DESCRIPTOR INDEX

OTHER ARTIFACTS INDEX